UNIVERSITY CASEBOOK SERIES®

FEDERAL INCOME TAXATION OF CORPORATE ENTERPRISE

SIXTH EDITION

by

BERNARD WOLFMAN
Late Fessenden Professor of Law Emeritus
Harvard University

DIANE M. RING
Professor of Law
Boston College Law School

FOUNDATION PRESS
2012

THOMSON REUTERS™

University Casebook Series is a trademark registered in the U.S. Patent and Trademark Office.

© 2005, 2008 BERNARD WOLFMAN
© 2012 by Bernard Wolfman
    FOUNDATION PRESS
    1 New York Plaza, 34th Floor
    New York, NY 10004
    Phone Toll Free (877) 888-1330
    Fax (646) 424-5201
    foundation-press.com
Printed in the United States of America

ISBN: 978-1-59941-888-9

Mat #41060417

In Memory of my co-author, colleague, and teacher,

Bernard Wolfman

D. M. R.

PREFACE

As the Sixth Edition comes to press, I would like to remember my co-author, colleague and teacher Bernard Wolfman who first published a version of this casebook on corporate taxation in 1971. The work still bears the powerful imprint of his vision, experience and theoretical perspective on corporate tax law, combined with his attention to changing legal and commercial times. The structure of the casebook itself, and the decision to begin with *how* corporations are taxed (as opposed to *incorporation* itself) reflected his thoughtful assessment that providing a picture of the core of the corporate tax system (double taxation) was an invaluable way to commence a corporate tax course. That said, Professor Wolfman also appreciated the diversity of views on the pedagogy of corporate tax. Thus, Chapter 3 "Incorporation of Assets" stands as a separate chapter for those instructors who prefer a life-cycle approach to the course and would like to start with incorporation. It was a great professional and personal experience to work with Professor Wolfman on the last two editions of the casebook, and I will greatly miss his wisdom, contributions and participation.

As with prior editions, the focus of this edition is almost entirely on the issues that arise under Subchapter C of the Internal Revenue Code, the statutory source for most of the federal income tax law that is applicable to all widely held and publicly traded U.S. corporations and to thousands of closely held corporations as well. The book does not cover Subchapter S corporations, a subject that may be best studied in a course on the taxation of partnerships. Like the earlier ones, this edition is for students who have completed a basic source in federal income taxation, one that covers the general and pervasive income tax concepts that affect participants in both corporate and noncorporate transactions.

This is a *casebook*. It illuminates the statute through the medium of the cases and rulings that have sought to apply it. Together with excerpts from legislative history, the cases and rulings provide subject matter cohesion while exposing the difficulties of interpretation and the policy tensions that inhere in it. In addition to helping students understand the underlying statutory material and the administrative and judicial overlays, the book encourages them to evaluate the law and the various proposals for changing it.

The predicate of Subchapter C is a classical double tax system, with the corporation taxed on *its* income, and the shareholders taxed on *their* income. Typically, shareholders' income will include the dividends they receive as well as the gain they realize when they sell their stock. The first thing to study, then, is what constitutes the gross and net income of the fictitious entity we call a corporation, and so Chapter 1 is devoted to that subject.

Picking up on the Code's double tax theme, Chapter 2 explores the income tax issues that attend the shareholders' receipt of a corporate dividend. It also focuses on the income tax consequences of the shareholder sale or redemption of stock, whether in liquidation or not and whether at gain or loss.

After studying the special attributes of corporate and shareholder income, the student is at the point where it is sensible to address the question whether to incorporate and to study the income tax consequences to both shareholder and corporation of the incorporation transaction itself. Chapter 3 focuses on the tax free (and taxable) incorporation of assets. It analyzes the concept and consequences of *nonrecognition*. As noted above, despite the decision to introduce incorporation in Chapter 3 after the student has learned about the corporate tax base and the impact of distributions to shareholders, it is quite reasonable for a professor to begin a corporate tax course with Chapter 3, with the birth of a corporation, and many professors choose to do so.

Chapter 4, covering the "reorganization" of corporations—e.g., recapitalizations, mergers, stock-for-stock swaps, and spinoffs—goes further into the subject of nonrecognition and related concepts, and it will occupy a substantial part of the course. Chapter 4 will help the student understand and weigh the considerations involved in so-called taxfree acquisitions, and the student will learn when to choose, and when not to choose, the taxfree over the taxable transaction. In both settings students will come to appreciate the financial world's focus on leverage buyouts and other forms of corporate restructuring, and they will learn about the role net operating loss carryovers play in some of those transactions.

Throughout the course it is important to consider the tax rates, as they are now, as they were until 2003, and as they may become. Since the enactment of legislation in 2003, the top rate for individuals on dividends and on long term capital gains has been 15%, unusual in that the rate for both is the same and so extremely low by historical standards. Capital gains taxation provides, of course, for taxfree recovery of basis, while dividend taxation does not provide for recovery of basis. At 35% the top rate on ordinary income, such as salaries, remains relatively high. Although the legislation providing the reduced tax rate for dividends remains an expiring provision that must be renewed regularly, the fact that it has been renewed through 2012 suggests a degree of permanence which the current edition explores.

Historically, individuals paid tax on dividends at the same rate as they did on their salaries. But long term capital gains typically have faced a much lower "preferential" rate. An important question to ponder throughout is whether the top dividend and capital gain rates should be equal— and so much lower than the top rate on salaries and other ordinary income such as interest and rent.

This current edition has benefitted from the comments of those who have taught and studied from the earlier editions. As in the past, I would be delighted to receive comments and questions from those who use this book.

DIANE M. RING

September 2012

SUMMARY OF CONTENTS

TABLE OF CONTENTS

Chapter 2. Taxation of the Shareholder: Corporate Distributions and Disposition of Investor Interests (Not in Reorganization) 98

TABLE OF CASES

The principal cases are in bold type.

TABLE OF OTHER AUTHORITIES

TABLE OF RULINGS

TABLE OF REVENUE PROCEDURES

UNIVERSITY CASEBOOK SERIES ®

FEDERAL INCOME TAXATION OF CORPORATE ENTERPRISE

SIXTH EDITION

CHAPTER 1

THE CORPORATION INCOME TAX

I. HISTORY AND DESCRIPTION

The modern federal corporate income tax first appeared in 1909 (an earlier federal income tax on corporate income was held an unconstitutional direct tax, along with the individual income tax, in Pollock v. Farmers' Loan & Trust Co., 158 U.S. 601 (1895)). The Supreme Court sustained the constitutionality of the 1909 corporate income tax on the ground that it constituted an "indirect" or "excise" tax on the privilege of engaging in business as a corporation. As such, the tax did not require apportionment under the Constitution. The hallmark of the modern corporate income tax is the treatment of the corporation itself as a taxpayer. The corporation calculates its taxable income and files its own tax return. Generally, the corporation cannot deduct any dividends it pays. Shareholders of a corporation are taxed only upon receipt of a dividend distribution from the corporation or upon disposition of their stock. (A briefly enacted Civil War era income tax treated income earned through corporations as the income of the shareholders and required the shareholders to report their share of that corporate income on their individual income tax returns). In contrast to the tax treatment of corporations, partnerships are not themselves taxable entities. Income generated by a partnership is the income of the partners and immediately taxable to them on their returns.

The effect of the corporate income tax is to subject income earned in corporate solution to a "double tax." The income is taxed once when earned and reported by the corporation, and a second time when distributed to the shareholder and reported as income on the shareholder return. However, to prevent income from being taxed three times rather than two (for example, where a corporation owns stock in another corporation and receives a dividend), § 243 provides that corporate shareholders are usually entitled to a "dividends received" deduction. Individual shareholders, though, are not entitled to a dividends received deduction or exclusion, thus preserving the two levels of tax in our "classical" corporate tax. In some other countries, the tax systems seek to integrate the corporate level tax and the shareholder level tax in order to impose only a single level of tax on income earned in corporate form. This integration can be achieved either at the corporate level by allowing corporations to deduct dividends from their income, or at the shareholder level by exempting dividend income in the hands of the shareholder or granting the shareholder a credit for the tax paid by the corporation. Most countries that pursue integration do not fully implement the ideal of a single level; only partial deductions, exemptions or credits are available. Almost a decade ago the United States made a modest move in the direction of reducing the burden of two levels of tax on corporate income. In 2003, Congress reduced the rate of tax for individual shareholders receiving qualifying dividends.[1] This rate reduction has proved to be more enduring than many observers anticipated.

Even with this reduction in the total tax burden on corporate income, however, Congress left firmly in place the basic structure of the corporate income tax and all it entails. Despite the increasing variety of forms in which to conduct business (including those, such as limited liability companies (LLCs) which combine the legal liability protections of corporate status under state law and the single level of federal income tax of partnership treatment), a vast quantity of commercial activity is conducted in the United States through businesses taxable as a corporation. In 2011, a total of 2,313,000 corporate tax returns were filed. More than twice that number were filed by partnerships and other pass-through entities.[2]

The tax rates faced by corporations on their income have fluctuated widely since Congress imposed a one percent tax on corporate income in excess of $5,000 in 1909. As recently as 1963 the corporate rate on income over $25,000 was 52 percent, and the rate applicable to income up to $25,000 was 30 percent. During wartime Congress often imposed corporate excess profits taxes that exacted levies at extraordinarily high rates on the income remaining after imposition of the ordinary corporate tax to the extent that it exceeded the income of a specified prewar period or exceeded a "normal" return on invested capital.

The tax on corporate income is imposed by § 11 of the Internal Revenue Code of 1986. Today it consists of a four-level series of rates rising from 15 percent on the first $50,000 of taxable income, to 25 percent on the next $25,000, to 34 percent on income above $75,000 up to $10,000,000, and to 35 percent on income above $10,000,000. Taxable income between $100,000 and $335,000 is subject to a surcharge of 5 percent, the result of which is to phase out the graduated rates otherwise applicable to the first $75,000 of income. Taxable income between $15,000,000 and $18,333,333 is subject to an additional surcharge of 3 percent, the result of which is to raise the tax rate on the first $10,000,000 up to 35 percent from 34 percent. In effect, corporations with taxable income in excess of $18,333,333 are subject to a flat rate of 35 percent. The Code also provides a corporate "alternative minimum tax" of 20 percent on items of "tax preference." See §§ 55–59. In 2011, the corporate income tax produced 10.1 percent of the federal revenues, and the individual tax produced 55.1 percent.[3]

For many years, the top rate of tax on dividends was equal to the top rate on ordinary income, for example income from wages and fees (up to 91%). This imposed a very substantial aggregate tax on corporate stock ownership. Since legislation was enacted in 2003, however, this impact has

---

[1] Section 1(h)(11), added by the Jobs and Growth Tax Relief Reconciliation Act of 2003.

[2] IRS 2011 Data Book, Table 2 at 4.

[3] IRS 2011 Data Book, Table 1 at 3. The changes in the rate structure made by the Tax Reform Act of 1986 were designed to shift a substantial amount of the total income tax burden from the individual sector to the corporate sector.

been substantially reduced because the top rate on dividends is the same as the rate on long term capital gains. See § 1(h)(11).

There are a number of special types of corporations that the Code treats discretely, some tax-exempt, like universities, others, like insurance companies, taxable under special formulae. This book is concerned with the ordinary business corporation whose taxable income is subject to tax under § 11.

II. THE CORPORATION'S INCOME—ITS SPECIAL ASPECTS

What does it mean to be taxable as a corporation? What special rules govern taxation of corporations? The answers to these questions are the subject of this chapter.[4] As a starting point, however, the similarities among corporations and other taxpayers should be noted. Just like other taxpayers, corporations are taxed on their "taxable" income, i.e. gross income minus allowable deductions. For the most part, "taxable income" is computed for the corporation as it is for the individual proprietor. The rules defining gross income and allowable business deductions are substantially the same for corporations and individuals. For example, corporations, like individual proprietors, are generally permitted by § 163 to deduct the interest that they pay. The charitable deduction is available to corporations, but with limitations and conditions that are inapplicable to individuals. Not surprisingly, the so-called personal deductions, dependency exemptions, and the standard deduction (all of which are unique to human taxpayers) are not allowed to corporations.

Despite this basic similarity between corporations and other taxpayers, there are distinctive features of the corporate business form that generate special problems in defining gross income earned by a corporation. Other aspects of the corporations' activities pose unique questions about allowable deductions. In both cases, the transactions that raise these issues usually involve transactions and dealings between a corporation and its present or prospective investors. This chapter explores the unique dimensions of defining gross income and deductions for the corporate taxpayer.

A. GROSS INCOME OF THE CORPORATION: SPECIAL RULES

1. RECEIPT OF CAPITAL

Corporations, which are legal constructs, must receive investment funds from the outside in one of two ways: equity investment or debt investment. The former is made by investors known as shareholders, the latter is made by investors known as lenders or bond holders. The legal relationship between a corporation and its shareholders differs from that with its lenders, and these differences have important tax consequences for the corporation. At this stage, the primary question is whether the receipt of

---

[4]After establishing how corporations are taxed during their years of operation, the later chapters consider the more transitory issues of creating, combining, and dissolving corporations as well as special taxation of shareholders.

investment funds (i.e. capital) from shareholders or lenders should be considered income to the corporation.

a. Equity—§§ 118, 1032

Section 118(a) provides that "[i]n the case of a corporation, gross income does not include any contribution to the capital of the taxpayer." Contributions to the capital of a corporation have never been treated as income to the corporation when made by shareholders. On the other hand, contributions made by nonshareholders have presented more difficult problems. See, e.g., United States v. Chicago B. & Q. R.R., 412 U.S. 401 (1973). As amended by the 1986 Act, § 118(b) modifies and simplifies the law by narrowly circumscribing the exclusion for a contribution to the capital of a corporation, making clear that a "contribution in aid of construction or any other contribution [made by] a customer or potential customer" is not within the exclusion. Essentially, the investor must be making the contribution in its capacity as investor in the corporation and not as a current or future customer. (Payments to a corporation from a customer must be income.) Although the law had been moving in this direction for some years prior to 1986, uncertainty and controversy remained. *Compare* Edwards v. Cuba Railroad, 268 U.S. 628 (1925), *with* Teleservice Co. of Wyoming Valley v. Commissioner, 254 F.2d 105 (3d Cir. 1958), *cert. denied*, 357 U.S. 919 (1958). Perhaps the simplest example involves shareholders who agree to provide some additional capital to the corporation. Consider the following example:

> Ike, Mike, and Sally own 40%, 40% and 20% respectively of X Co. The corporation needs more capital investment (about $100,000) so the shareholders all agree to contribute a pro rata amount. Thus, Ike contributes property worth $40,000 (basis $10,000); Mike contributes property worth $40,000 (basis $20,000) and Sally contributes property worth $20,000 (basis $10,000). Because their contributions are proportionate to their ownership it does not matter whether the corporation actually gives stock in return for the newly contributed assets. Either way, Ike will possess 40% of the X Co., Mike 40% and Sally 20%. The only difference that giving out the additional shares would make is that their respective interests in X Co. would be represented by more pieces of paper.

> Under section 118, X Co. is not taxed on contributions. Treas. Reg. 1.118–1 takes the position that as to the shareholders, these contributions represent "additional payments" for the stock they already possess, and thus the contribution is not a taxable event for the shareholder, and the basis of the property they contribute is added to their current basis in the X Co. stock that they hold. Thus, in this case, Ike's basis in X Co. stock increases by $10,000, Mike's basis in X Co. stock increases by $20,000 and Sally's basis in X Co. stock increases by $10,000. [Note it may be useful to review this example after having studied formation of a corporation, and sections 351 and 358].

What is X Co.'s basis in the assets received? The basis in the hands of
the shareholder-contributors. Thus, X Co. takes a $10,000 basis in
Ike's asset; a $20,000 basis in Mike's asset; and a $10,000 basis in Sal-
ly's asset.

When would a non-shareholder, who is also NOT a customer/potential customer, make a "contribution to capital"? Consider for example the possibility of a local civic organization that gives large new flower planters and
shrubs to businesses on Main Street to improve the overall look of the
community center. Could these businesses exclude the value of the planters
and shrubbery under § 118?

A safe harbor under section 118(a) exists for grants received by some
corporate taxpayers for capital projects under several DOT programs and
for some awards made by the Energy Department's National Energy Technology Laboratory to corporate taxpayers for clean coal technology.   Rev.
Proc. 2010-46; Rev. Proc. 2011-30).

Section 118 still leaves some questions regarding "contributions in aid
of construction" made to corporations. Such contributions are clearly not
excluded from income under § 118, however their precise treatment is un-
specified. Should they be included in the income of the corporation (as a
prepayment for services would be)? Or should they be treated as the capital
contribution of another party (the contributor-customer) to a joint venture
with the corporation, with the "contributor-customer" sharing in the overall
income of the venture by enjoying lower charges for service as a result of
the contribution?

What about payments to a corporation in exchange for shares of the
corporation's stock? Such transactions, which are outside the scope of § 118,
are covered by § 1032, added to the Internal Revenue Code in 1954. Section
1032, with a decidedly broad sweep, provides that a corporation does not
have income upon the receipt of payment for its own stock, whether the
stock is newly issued or treasury stock. Prior to 1954, the following type of
case presented a problem: Corporation M buys on the open market 1000
shares of its own common stock at $100 per share. The acquired shares are
held as treasury stock. Subsequently, when the market in M stock goes up,
Corporation M sells in the open market 2,000 shares of its own stock at
$125 per share. Of the shares it sells, 1,000 were newly issued and 1,000
represented the shares it had purchased at $100 per share. The Commis-
sioner sometimes contended that as to the treasury shares the corporation
had recognized gain of $25 per share. In doing so, he relied on Treas. Reg.
118, § 39.22(a)–15(b) (1939 Code), which provided that, although a corporation had no recognized gain or loss on receipt of payment for newly issued
shares, "if a corporation deals in its own shares as it might in the shares of
another corporation, the resulting gain or loss is to be computed in the
same manner as though the corporation were dealing in the shares of
another." See, e.g., Penn–Texas Corp. v. United States, 308 F.2d 575 (Ct.
Cl. 1962).

By enacting § 1032, Congress explicitly chose to eliminate the pre–1954 Code distinction between payments received for treasury shares and payments received for newly issued shares. Does § 1032 represent wise legislative policy? In answering this question, consider what the increase in the price of Corporation M's stock in the above scenario might reflect (perhaps the fact that the corporation has been doing well, generating lots of income). Is there a danger that, without § 1032, more than one corporate level tax could be imposed on the same earnings?

Where a shareholder pays for stock in cash, the tax analysis is fairly straightforward for the corporation under § 1032. However, in some cases, shareholders offer property to the corporation in exchange for stock. Section 1032 then addresses the preliminary question of whether this exchange creates taxable income for the corporation (no). But what about the next question—what is the basis of property received by a corporation in exchange for its stock? Even this question has several versions based on the set of cases in which a corporation can receive property under §§ 118 and 1032 without creating income: What is the basis to the corporation where the transferor (the party transferring the property to the corporation) is in "control" of the corporation within the meaning of §§ 351 and 368(c)? (As to § 351 generally, see Chapter 3). What is the basis if that controlling transferor simply contributes the property to the corporation under § 118 and receives no shares in return? What is the result when the contributing shareholder in each of these cases is not in "control"? What is the basis when a contribution to capital is made by a nonshareholder (who receives no stock in exchange)? If instead the nonshareholder contributes cash that is excluded from the corporation's income under § 118, what is the basis of property purchased by a corporation with that money? See § 362(a) and (c), and Treas. Reg. §§ 1.362–1, 1.362–2, and 1.1032–1(d).

b. Debt

Corporations need not rely exclusively on equity investment by shareholders to raise capital. A corporation can issue debt instruments (e.g., notes, bonds, debentures) for cash or property. Once again the same gross income question arises—does the receipt of capital from a debt investor create corporate level income? Not surprisingly, money or other property received in exchange for a corporation's debt instrument is not income. Just as "borrowed money" is not treated as income in the case of an individual, so to borrowed money is not regarded as income in the case of a corporation. What if a corporation buys its own bonds on the open market and then resells them for a higher price? Unlike the case of resale of stock, no tax issue has arisen in connection with the "resale" of bonds. Why not? (Hint: What conceptually happens to a taxpayer's debt when the taxpayer reacquires it?)

2. REDUCTION OF OUTSTANDING CAPITAL

As considered above, in most cases the receipt of capital investment (equity or debt) does not generate taxable income to the corporation. What happens when the corporation tries to unwind the capital investment and reduce the outstanding capital either by repurchasing and retiring its debt instrument or by repurchasing and canceling some stock shares? This question has been prominent for debt, but not for equity, as demonstrated by the following cases.

a. Debt—§§ 108, 1017

United States v. Kirby Lumber Co.
284 U.S. 1 (1931).

■ MR. JUSTICE HOLMES delivered the opinion of the Court.

In July, 1923, the plaintiff, the Kirby Lumber Company, issued its own bonds for $12,126,800 for which it received their par value. Later in the same year it purchased in the open market some of the same bonds at less than par, the difference of price being $137,521.30. The question is whether this difference is a taxable gain or income of the plaintiff for the year 1923. By [§ 61] gross income includes "gains or profits and income derived from any source whatever," and by the Treasury Regulations . . . that have been in force through repeated reenactments, "If the corporation purchases and retires any of such bonds at a price less than the issuing price or face value, the excess of the issuing price or face value over the purchase price is gain or income for the taxable year." . . . We see no reason why the Regulations should not be accepted as a correct statement of the law.

In Bowers v. Kerbaugh–Empire Co., 271 U.S. 170, the defendant in error owned the stock of another company that had borrowed money repayable in marks or their equivalent for an enterprise that failed. At the time of payment the marks had fallen in value, which so far as it went was a gain for the defendant in error, and it was contended by the plaintiff in error that the gain was taxable income. But the transaction as a whole was a loss, and the contention was denied. Here there was no shrinkage of assets and the taxpayer made a clear gain. As a result of its dealings it made available $137,521.30 assets previously offset by the obligation of bonds now extinct. We see nothing to be gained by the discussion of judicial definitions. The defendant in error has realized within the year an accession to income, if we take words in their plain popular meaning, as they should be taken here. Burnet v. Sanford & Brooks Co., 282 U.S. 359, 364.

Judgment reversed.

NOTES

1. If Kirby Lumber Co.'s wholly owned subsidiary had purchased the parent's outstanding bonds, would the result in the case have been avoided? See § 108(e)(4), adopted as part of the Bankruptcy Tax Act of 1980.

2. Suppose that an insolvent corporation with total assets, all depreciable, worth $1,000 and liabilities of $5,000 was released from $4,500 of its debt by agreement with its creditors. Suppose, too, that the corporation had a net oper-

ating loss carryover of $2,000 and that the adjusted basis of its assets was $1,000. What do §§ 108(a) and (b) and 1017(a) provide in such a case? See McMahon & Simmons, A Field Guide to Cancellation of Debt Income, 63 Tax Law. 415 (2010).

3. What if the corporation's creditors are also its shareholders—does the corporation have income when these creditors reduce or cancel debt? Cf. *Fender Sales*, page 411 infra. Does it matter whether the shareholders held the corporate debt in proportion to their stockholdings and whether they all agreed to a proportionate debt reduction or cancellation? See § 108(e)(6), added to the Code by the Bankruptcy Tax Act of 1980, and Rev. Rul. 76–316, 1976–2 C.B. 22 (forgiveness of principal by shareholder is contribution to capital, but forgiveness of interest already deducted by accrual basis corporation is taxable income to the corporation on tax benefit principles). Prior to the Bankruptcy Tax Act of 1980, several cases relying on § 118 held that the forgiveness by a shareholder of interest already deducted by a corporation was not taxable income to the corporation. See, e.g., Putoma Corp. v. Commissioner, 601 F.2d 734 (5th Cir. 1979); Hartland Associates, 54 T.C. 1580 (1970).

4. What if a corporation acquires its outstanding bonds for less than their issue price, through a third party. In Rev. Rul. 91–47, Corporation D had issued bonds for $500x but the bonds currently had a FMV of $350x. An unrelated party, X became aware that Corp. D sought to reacquire its bonds. After discussion with Corp. D, X formed Newco, and had Newco purchase some of the outstanding Corp. D bonds for $70x which had an issue price of $100x. Shortly after the bond acquisitions by Newco, Corp. D purchased 100% of Newco from X for $70x. Given that X formed Newco to enable D to acquire its bonds and avoid discharge of indebtedness income, the formation of Newco was considered to have no important business purpose. The Service concluded that the substance of the transaction should control and that Corp. D realized $30x in discharge of indebtedness income (the difference between the issue price of the debt ($100x) and the price that Corp. D paid for the Newco Stock ($70x)).

5. In the past, a corporation could avoid recognition of cancellation of indebtedness income by issuing stock in exchange for its debt. See Commissioner v. Motor Mart Trust, 156 F.2d 122 (1st Cir. 1946). Now § 108(e)(8) treats the corporation as satisfying its debt with an amount of money equal to the fair market value of the stock.

6. In response to economic distress, Section 108(i) was enacted through the American Recovery & Reinvestment Act of 2009. It allows a taxpayer that realizes COD income from the reacquisition of certain debt in 2009 and 2010 to include the COD income in gross income over a five year period beginning generally in 2014. Taxpayers are required to increase their earnings and profits during the year of the election of section 108(i).

b. *Equity*

Corporation M issues its $100 par value preferred stock for $100 per share. Years later, the stock is selling at $85 per share in the open market. Sensing a bargain, Corporation M, acting at the direction of its Board, which is controlled by a shareholder who owns 40 percent of the outstanding stock, offers to buy at $90 per share all of its stock that is tendered. Twenty percent of the outstanding stock is tendered, for which Corporation M pays the offered price. Upon delivery of the shares the acquired stock is cancelled, and Corporation M reduces its authorized and outstanding capital by the par value of the shares. Corporation M does not realize income in the transaction. Why not? Cf. J. A. Maurer, Inc., 30 T.C. 1273 (1958). If a reduction in equity capital does not result in corporation income, why should *Kirby Lumber* hold to the contrary in the case of debt capital?

3. RECEIPT OF A DIVIDEND

The next special gross income question for corporations concerns receipt of a dividend. What happens when a corporation is a shareholder in another corporation and receives dividends? As stated in the introduction, special rules are necessary to deal with this very common case of chains of corporate ownership.

Section 301(c)(1) provides the general treatment for taxpayers receiving a dividend: "the portion of [a corporate] distribution which is a dividend (as defined in section 316)" must be "included in gross income." The "portion of a distribution" that is not a dividend is first applied against the basis of the shareholder's stock, and after the basis is exhausted, the excess of the distribution is treated as "gain from the sale or exchange" of the stock. See § 301(c)(2) and (3).

Section 301(b)(1) provides that the "amount of any distribution" shall be the amount of cash plus the fair market value of other property received. But note the important exceptions of § 243. It is a three-tiered provision that permits corporate shareholders to deduct a percentage of the dividends they receive. A corporation that owns at least 80 percent of the voting power and value of the payor corporation may deduct 100 percent of the dividends received if it makes an election under § 243. If a corporation owns 20 percent or more of the payor corporation (by vote and value), the corporation may deduct 80 percent. Finally, a corporation owning less than 20 percent of the payor corporation's stock may deduct only 70 percent of the dividends received. §§ 243(a) and (c). (This dividends received deduction regime applies only in the case of dividends from a domestic corporation. A different mechanism applies to eliminate multiple levels of corporate tax on dividends from a foreign corporation. See §§ 901, 902).

Should there be a dividends received deduction at all? If so, why (and when) should it be less than 100 percent? See American Law Institute—Federal Income Tax Project—Subchapter C (Supplemental Study), Reporter's Draft Study at 97–101 (June 1, 1989). See also, Yale, Corporate Distributions Tax Reform: Exploring the Alternatives, 29 Va. Tax Rev. 329 (2009).

Consider the following hypothetical: Corporation S, a Pennsylvania corporation, distributes to its parent, Corporation P, a dividend consisting of 1,000 shares of General Motors common stock. The shares had an adjusted basis of $50 per share in Corporation S's hands and are worth $85 per share at the time of the distribution. What are the tax consequences of the distribution to Corporation P? Why? For the tax consequences to Corporation S on the distribution of the appreciated General Motors shares, see page 20 et seq. If Corporation P sells the General Motors shares for $90 per share a year after receiving them in the dividend distribution, what will the tax consequences be? Why? See § 301(d). How would the tax consequences of this entire scenario (dividend followed by later sale) change if the General Motors stock had been subject to a liability of $30 per share, which Corporation P assumed upon the dividend distribution from Corporation S? See § 301(b)(2).[5]

Taxpayers have explored additional arbitrage opportunities utilizing the effective exclusion of income under § 243. What if Corporation A purchased some stock in Corporation B shortly before Corp. B paid a dividend? The purchase price that Corp. A paid for the stock would likely have reflected the upcoming dividend. Thus, when the dividend was paid, the value of the Corp. B shares would drop. If Corp. A sold the shares after the dividend distribution, Corp. A would, absent any intervening rule, anticipate taking a loss on the stock. Why would it be undesirable to allow that loss? For constraints on Corp. A's strategy, see § 1059. This provision, expanded as recently as 1997, is an unduly elaborate mechanism dealing with "extraordinary dividends." You can gain an understanding of its general purpose by reading sections (a) through (c). What does subsection (a)(2) do to subsection (a)(1)? Why were they written that way?

TSN Liquidating Corp., Inc. v. United States

624 F.2d 1328 (5th Cir. 1980).

■ Before FAY, KRAVITCH, and RANDALL, CIRCUIT JUDGES.

■ RANDALL, CIRCUIT JUDGE. This case presents the question whether assets distributed to a corporation by its subsidiary, immediately prior to the sale by such corporation of all the capital stock of such subsidiary, should be treated, for federal income tax purposes, as a dividend or, as the district court held, as part of the consideration received from the sale of such capital stock. We hold that on the facts of this case, the assets so distributed constituted a dividend and we reverse the judgment of the district court.

In 1969, TSN Liquidating Corporation, Inc. ("TSN"), which was then named "Texas State Network, Inc.," owned over 90% of the capital stock of Community Life Insurance Company ("CLIC"), an insurance company chartered under the laws of the State of Maine. In early 1969, negotiations began for the purchase of CLIC by Union Mutual Life Insurance Company ("Union Mutual"). On May 5, 1969, TSN and the other CLIC stockholders entered into an Agreement of Stock Purchase (the "Stock Purchase Agreement") with Union Mutual for the sale of the capital stock of CLIC to Union

---

[5]Read § 246A. Why does it have a special limitation in the case of "debt-financed portfolio stock"? What type of arbitrage opportunity does it target? By way of analogy consider other cases of borrowing to acquire assets that generate tax-exempt income, §§ 103(a), 163(a) and 265(a)(2).

Mutual. The Stock Purchase Agreement provided that there would be no material adverse change in the business or assets of CLIC prior to the closing "except that as of closing certain shares and capital notes as provided in Section 4.(i) above will not be a part of the assets of [CLIC]." Since the purchase price of the capital stock of CLIC under the Stock Purchase Agreement was based primarily on the book value (or, in some instances, market value) of those assets owned by CLIC on the closing date, the purchase price would be automatically reduced by the elimination of such shares and notes from the assets of CLIC. On May 14, 1969, as contemplated by the Stock Purchase Agreement, the Board of Directors of CLIC declared a dividend in kind, payable to stockholders of record as of May 19, 1969, consisting primarily of capital stock in small, public companies traded infrequently and in small quantities in the over-the-counter market. On May 20, 1969, the closing was held and Union Mutual purchased substantially all the outstanding capital stock of CLIC, including the shares held by TSN. The final purchase price paid by Union Mutual to the selling stockholders of CLIC was $823,822, of which TSN's share was $747,436. Union Mutual thereupon contributed to the capital of CLIC $1,120,000 in municipal bonds and purchased from CLIC additional capital stock of CLIC for $824,598 in cash paid to CLIC.

In its income tax return for the fiscal year ended July 31, 1969, TSN reported its receipt of assets from CLIC as a dividend and claimed the 85% dividends received deduction available to corporate stockholders pursuant to § 243(a)(1) of the Internal Revenue Code of 1954. TSN also reported its gain on the sale of the capital stock of CLIC on the installment method pursuant to § 453 of the Code. On audit, the Internal Revenue Service treated the distribution of the assets from CLIC to TSN as having been an integral part of the sale by TSN of capital stock of CLIC to Union Mutual, added its estimate ($1,677,082) of the fair market value of the assets received by TSN to the cash ($747,436) received by TSN on the sale, and disallowed the use by TSN of the installment method for reporting the gain on the sale of the capital stock of CLIC since aggregating the fair market value of the distributed assets and the cash resulted in more than 30% of the proceeds from the sale being received in the year of sale. TSN paid the additional tax due as a result of such treatment by the Internal Revenue Service, filed a claim for a refund and subsequently instituted this action against the Internal Revenue Service.

The district court made the following findings of fact in part II of its opinion:

> With regard to the negotiations between CLIC and Union Mutual in early 1969, the Court finds that Union Mutual was interested in purchasing CLIC and proposed a formula for valuing the assets, liabilities, and insurance in force, which, together with an additional amount, would be the price paid for the CLIC stock.

> The investment portfolio of CLIC was heavily oriented toward equity investments in closely held over-the-counter securities. At least in the mind of CLIC's officers, the makeup of CLIC's investment portfolio

was affecting its ability to obtain licenses in various states. As early as the Spring of 1968, the management and principal stockholders of CLIC had begun to seek a solution to the investment portfolio problem. The Court finds, however, that CLIC had never formulated a definite plan on how to solve its investment portfolio problem.

Union Mutual did not like CLIC's investment portfolio but considered bonds to be more in keeping with insurance industry responsibilities. The management of CLIC regarded the Union Mutual offer as a good one, and tried without success to get Union Mutual to take the entire investment portfolio.

Accordingly, the [Stock Purchase Agreement] required CLIC to dispose some of the investment portfolio assets. Thus, the price that would be paid for the CLIC stock was based upon a formula which valued the assets after excluding certain stocks. . .

Plaintiff's disposition of the undesirable over-the-counter stock was necessitated by its sale arrangements with Union Mutual. Plaintiff had no definite plans prior to its negotiations with Union Mutual as to how to get rid of the undesirable stock, when it was to get rid of the undesirable stock, or even that it would definitely get rid of the undesirable stock. Accordingly, the Court finds that the dividend in kind of 14 May 1969 was part and parcel of the purchase agreement with Union Mutual. . .

In part III of its opinion, the district court made the following additional findings:

Union Mutual was interested in purchasing the stock of an approximately $2 million corporation in order that that corporation might be licensed to do business in other states. Tr. 92. As of 30 April 1969, CLIC had assets of $2,115,138. DX 2. On 14 May 1969, CLIC declared a dividend valued at approximately $1.8 million. As a result of this dividend, CLIC was left with assets totaling approximately $300,000. The final purchase price paid by Union Mutual to the selling shareholders of CLIC was $823,822. In addition, Union Mutual contributed $1,120,000 of municipal bonds to the capital of CLIC and purchased additional shares of stock of CLIC for $824,598. DX 3. Thus, subsequent to closing on 20 May 1969, CLIC was worth $2,400,000. DX 3. Thus, CLIC was worth $2 million when the [Stock Purchase Agreement] was signed on 5 May 1969 and worth over $2 million immediately after closing.

There was no business purpose served in this case by the dividend declared by CLIC prior to the sale of all its stock to Union Mutual. It is evident that the dividend benefitted the shareholders of CLIC and not CLIC itself. There was no benefit or business purpose in CLIC's declaration of the dividend separate and apart from the sale. The Court finds that the dividend would not, and could not, have been made without the sale. . .

What actually happened in the period 5 through 20 May 1969 was that the stockholders received $1.8 million in virtually tax-free stocks, as well as over $800,000 in cash, for a total of approximately $2.6 million. This was certainly a fair price for a corporation valued at the time of sale at $2,115,138, and reflects a premium paid for good will and policies in force, as well as the fact that CLIC was an existing business with licenses in eight or nine states. Hence, a $2 million corporation was sold for $2.6 million including the dividend and the cash. . .

After noting the time-honored principle that the incidence of taxation is to be determined by the substance of the transaction rather than by its form and the related principle that the transaction is generally to be viewed as a whole and not to be separated into its component parts, the district court held:

> The distribution of assets to [TSN] from its subsidiary, CLIC, immediately prior to [TSN's] disposition of its entire stock interest in CLIC should be treated as a part of the gain from the sale of the stock. Thus, the Court concludes that the in-kind distribution of 14 May 1969 to the stockholders of CLIC is taxable to [TSN] as gain from the sale of its stock. The alleged dividend was merely intented (sic) to be part of the purchase price paid by Union Mutual to CLIC for its stock. . .

The district court relied for its holding primarily on the cases of Waterman Steamship Corp. v. Commissioner, 430 F.2d 1185 (5th Cir. 1970), *cert. denied*, 401 U.S. 939, 91 S. Ct. 936, 28 L. Ed. 2d 219 (1971), and Basic, Inc. v. United States, 212 Ct. Cl. 399, 549 F.2d 740 (Ct.Cl.1977), all discussed infra.

On appeal, TSN argues that the cases relied upon by the district court are exceptions to what TSN characterizes as the established rule, namely, that assets removed from a corporation by a dividend made in contemplation of a sale of the stock of that corporation, when those assets are in good faith to be retained by the selling stockholders and not thereafter transferred to the buyer, are taxable as a dividend and not as a part of the price paid for the stock for the reason that, in economic reality and in substance, the selling stockholders did not sell and the buyer did not purchase or pay for the excluded assets. The principal cases cited by TSN for its position are Gilmore v. Commissioner, 25 T.C. 1321 (1956), Coffey v. Commissioner, 14 T.C. 1410 (1950), and Rosenbloom Finance Corp. v. Commissioner, 24 B.T.A. 763 (1931). According to TSN, the controlling distinction between the *Coffey* line of cases relied upon by TSN and the *Waterman* line of cases relied upon by the district court is whether the buyer negotiated to acquire and pay for the stock, exclusive of the assets distributed out as a dividend, on the one hand, or whether the buyer negotiated to acquire and pay for the stock, including the assets which were then the subject of a sham distribution designed to evade taxes, on the other hand. In the former case, according to TSN, there is a taxable dividend; in the latter case there is not.

We begin by noting that the district court was certainly correct in its position that the substance of the transaction controls over the form and

that the transaction should be viewed as a whole, rather than being separated into its parts. Further, having reviewed the record, we are of the view
that the operative facts found so carefully by the district court are entirely
accurate (except for the valuation of the distributed assets, as to which we
express no opinion). We differ with the district court only in the legal characterization of those facts and in the conclusion to be drawn therefrom. We
agree with TSN that this case is controlled by the *Coffey*, *Gilmore* and *Rosenbloom* cases rather than by the *Waterman* and *Basic* cases relied upon
by the district court.

In *Coffey*, the principal case relied upon by TSN, the taxpayers owned
the stock of Smith Brothers Refinery Co., Inc. and were negotiating for the
sale of such stock. Representatives of the purchasers and representatives of
the sellers examined and discussed the various assets owned by Smith
Brothers Refinery Co., Inc., and the liabilities of the company, with a view
to reaching an agreement upon the fair market value of the stock. During
these negotiations, the representatives of the purchasers and of the sellers
could not agree upon the value of certain assets (including a contingent receivable referred to as the Cabot payment). The representatives of the purchasers informed the representatives of the sellers that the sellers could
withdraw those assets from the assets of the company and that they would
buy the stock without those assets being a part of the sale, thereby eliminating the necessity for arriving at a valuation of those assets in determining the value of the stock on a net worth basis. The contract of sale provided that the unwanted assets would be distributed by the corporation as
a dividend prior to the sale of the stock. The selling stockholders contended
before the tax court, as the Internal Revenue Service does in the case before
this court, that the Cabot payment distributed to them as a dividend in
kind was "part of the consideration for stock sold and that any profit resulting from its receipt by them is taxable as a capital gain." The tax court rejected that contention because it was contrary to the substance of the
transaction. . . [It] held the distribution to be a dividend.

In *Gilmore*, the purchasers of corporate stock did not wish to pay for
quick assets owned by the corporation, namely cash on hand and United
States bonds, and the parties provided for a presale dividend to exclude
them from the assets to be transferred to the purchaser by means of the
sale of the corporate stock. The tax court held that the assets distributed to
the stockholders by means of a dividend were taxable as a dividend and not
as a part of the sales proceeds for the corporate stock. . .

In *Rosenbloom*, the sole stockholder of Joseph S. Finch Company was
Rosenbloom Finance Corporation. Rosenbloom entered into a contract for
the sale of all the capital stock of Joseph S. Finch Company to Shenley
Products Company. With respect to the unwanted assets, the contract provided:

> All other assets of every character whatsoever owned by the Finch
> Company at the time of the transfer of said shares of stock, as herein
> provided, shall be transferred to the party of the first part (petitioner)

by dividend distribution, prior to the consummation of the sale of said shares of stock herein provided for. . .

The board of tax appeals held that the assets distributed to Rosenbloom Finance Corporation by Joseph S. Finch Company should be treated as an ordinary dividend and not as an amount distributed in partial liquidation. . .

The Internal Revenue Service states that it does not disagree with the holdings in *Coffey*, *Gilmore* and *Rosenbloom*, but it takes the position that they do not apply in the circumstances of this case. The Internal Revenue Service focuses on the receipt by the selling stockholders of CLIC of investment assets, followed immediately by an infusion by Union Mutual of a like amount of investment assets into CLIC, and says that the reinfusion of assets brings the case before the court within the "conduit rationale" of *Waterman*. In *Waterman*, Waterman Steamship Corporation ("Waterman") was the owner of all the outstanding capital stock of Pan–Atlantic Steamship Corporation ("Pan–Atlantic") and Gulf Florida Terminal Company, Incorporated ("Gulf Florida"). Malcolm P. McLean made an offer to Waterman to purchase all the outstanding capital stock of Pan–Atlantic and Gulf Florida for $3,500,000. Since Waterman's tax basis for the stock of the subsidiaries totaled $700,000, a sale of the capital stock of the subsidiaries for $3,500,000 would have produced a taxable gain of approximately $2,800,000. Because the treasury regulations on consolidated returns provided that the dividends received from an affiliated corporation are exempt from tax, a sale of capital stock of the subsidiaries for $700,000, after a dividend payment to Waterman by the subsidiaries of $2,800,000, would, at least in theory, have produced no taxable gain. The Board of Directors of Waterman rejected McLean's offer, but authorized Waterman's president to submit a counter proposal providing for the sale of all the capital stock in the subsidiaries for $700,000, but only after the subsidiaries paid dividends to Waterman in the aggregate amount of $2,800,000. As finally consummated, the dividends and the sale of the capital stock of the subsidiaries took the following form:

(1) Pan–Atlantic gave a promissory note to Waterman for $2,800,000 payable in 30 days as a "dividend."

(2) One hour later, Waterman agreed to sell all of the capital stock of Pan–Atlantic and Gulf Florida for $700,000.

(3) Thirty minutes later, after the closing of the sale of the capital stock of the subsidiaries had occurred, Pan–Atlantic held a special meeting of its new Board of Directors, and the Board authorized Pan–Atlantic to borrow $2,800,000 from McLean and a corporation controlled by McLean. Those funds were used by Pan–Atlantic promptly to pay off the $2,800,000 note to Waterman (which was not yet due).

In its tax return for the fiscal year involved, Waterman eliminated from income the $2,800,000 received as a dividend from Pan–Atlantic and reported $700,000 as the sales price of the capital stock of the two subsidiaries. Since Waterman's tax basis for the stock was the same as the sales price therefor, no taxable gain was realized on the sale. On audit, the Internal Revenue Service took the position that Waterman had realized a long-term capital gain of $2,800,000 on the sale of the capital stock of the subsidiaries and increased its taxable income accordingly. On appeal from a judgment by the tax court in favor of the taxpayer, the Internal Revenue Service contended that the rules applicable to situations where a regular dividend has been declared are not applicable when the parties contemplate that a purported dividend is to be inextricably tied to the purchase price and where, as was the case before the court, the amount of the dividend is not a true distribution of corporate profits. The Internal Revenue Service argued that the funds were supplied by the buyer of the stock, with the corporation acting as a mere conduit for passing the payment through to the seller. This court agreed with the Internal Revenue Service:

> The so-called dividend and sale were one transaction. The note was but one transitory step in a total, pre-arranged plan to sell the stock. We hold that in substance Pan–Atlantic neither declared nor paid a dividend to Waterman, but rather acted as a mere conduit for the payment of the purchase price to Waterman.

Waterman, 430 F.2d at 1192. The opinion of this court began with this sentence:

> This case involves another attempt by a taxpayer to ward off tax blows with paper armor.

Id. at 1185. The opinion stressed the sham, tax motivated aspects of the transaction:

> Here, McLean originally offered Waterman $3,500,000 for the stock of Pan–Atlantic and Gulf Florida. Waterman recognized that since its basis for tax purposes in the stock was $700,180, a taxable gain of approximately $2,800,000 would result from the sale. It declined the original offer and proposed to cast the sale of the stock in a two step transaction. Waterman proposed to McLean that it would sell the stock of the two subsidiaries for $700,180 after it had extracted $2,800,000 of the subsidiaries' earnings and profits. It is undisputed that Waterman intended to sell the two subsidiaries for the original offering price—with $2,800,000 of the amount disguised as a dividend which would be eliminated from income under Section 1502. Waterman also intended that none of the assets owned by the subsidiaries would be removed prior to the sale. Although the distribution was cast in the form of a dividend, the distribution was to be financed by McLean with payment being made to Waterman through Pan–Atlantic. To inject substance into the form of the transaction, Pan–Atlantic issued its note to Waterman before the closing agreement was signed. The creation of a valid indebtedness however, cannot change the true nature of the transaction. . . The form of the transaction used by the parties is relatively unimportant, for the true substance and effect of their agreement was that McLean would pay $3,500,000 for all

of the assets, rights and liabilities represented by the stock of Pan–Atlantic and Gulf Florida.

Id. at 1194–95. This court concluded its opinion in *Waterman* by cautioning against "giving force to 'a purported [dividend] which gives off an unmistakeably hollow sound when it is tapped.' " Id. at 1196 (quoting United States v. General Geophysical Co., 296 F.2d 86, 89 (5th Cir. 1961), *cert. denied*, 369 U.S. 849, 82 S. Ct. 932, 8 L. Ed. 2d 8 (1962)) [page 32 infra]. A final footnote to the opinion stated that the decision should not be interpreted as standing for the proposition that a corporation which is contemplating a sale of its subsidiary's stock could not under any circumstances distribute its subsidiaries' profits prior to the sale without having such distribution deemed part of the purchase price. Id. at 1196 n. 21.

In summary, in *Waterman*, the substance of the transaction, and the way in which it was originally negotiated, was that the purchaser would pay $3,500,000 of its money to the seller in exchange for all the stock of the two subsidiaries and none of the assets of those subsidiaries was to be removed and retained by the sellers. In the case before the court, the district court found that Union Mutual did not want and would not pay for the assets of CLIC which were distributed to TSN and the other stockholders of CLIC. Those assets were retained by the selling stockholders. The fact that bonds and cash were reinfused into CLIC after the closing, in lieu of the unwanted capital stock of small, publicly held corporations, does not convert this case from a *Coffey* situation, in which admittedly unwanted assets were distributed by the corporation to its stockholders and retained by them, into a *Waterman* situation, in which the distribution of assets was clearly a sham, designed solely to achieve a tax free distribution of assets ultimately funded by the purchaser. Indeed, the Internal Revenue Service does not argue, in the case before the court, that the transaction was in any respect a sham. Instead, the Service would have us hold that the mere infusion of assets into the acquired company after the closing, assets which are markedly different in kind from the assets that were distributed prior to the closing, should result in the disallowance of dividend treatment for the distribution of the unwanted assets, and the Service cites *Waterman* as authority for that proposition. We view the sham aspect—the hollow sound—of the transaction described in *Waterman* as one of the critical aspects of that decision, and we decline to extend the *Waterman* rule to a case which admittedly does not involve a sham and which, in other important respects, is factually different from *Waterman*.

The Internal Revenue Service also cites *Basic* as authority for the disallowance of dividend treatment for the distribution of the unwanted assets in this case. Basic Incorporated ("Basic") owned all the capital stock of Falls Industries Incorporated ("Falls"), which in turn owned all the stock of Basic Carbon Corporation ("Carbon"). Carborundum Company ("Carborundum") made an initial offer to acquire all the assets of Falls and Carbon. This offer failed to gel when Basic demanded that Carborundum agree to indemnify Basic for any tax assessments that might become payable on the transaction in excess of those which Basic could anticipate and compute in advance, a proposal that was unacceptable to Carborundum. Carborundum then made a second proposal to acquire directly from Basic the capital stock of Falls and the capital stock of Carbon and requested that Basic transfer the ownership of the capital stock of Carbon from Falls to Basic prior to the transaction. In order to achieve that, Falls distributed the capital stock of Carbon to Basic as a dividend, which put Basic in the position of owning the capital stock of both Falls and Carbon. The sale of such capital stock to Carborundum was then consummated. In its federal income tax return for the year involved, Basic reported dividend income from Falls in the amount of $500,000 as a result of its receipt of the capital stock of Carbon. It thereupon claimed a dividends received deduction in the amount of 85% of the dividend pursuant to § 243(a)(1) of the Code. Finally, it reported a long-term capital gain of $2,300,000 from the sale to Carborundum of the shares of Falls and Carbon. On audit, the Internal Revenue Service determined that the gain from the sale of the shares of capital stock of Falls and Carbon should be increased by the amount of the purported dividend. On those facts, the court of claims held that the distribution of the capital stock of Carbon by Falls to Basic was not a true dividend but was part of the total transaction by which Basic, in substance, sold the capital stock of Falls and Carbon to Carborundum:

> Under the facts and circumstances presented here, plaintiff has not shown that there was a reason for the transfer of the Carbon stock from Falls to Basic aside from the tax consequences attributable to that move. Accordingly, for purposes of taxation, the transfer was not a dividend within the meaning of Section 316(a)(1). Instead, it should be regarded as a transfer that avoided part of the gain to be expected from the sale of the business to Carborundum, and should, therefore, be now taxed accordingly.

Basic, 549 F.2d at 749. Basic was a conduit through which an asset, the capital stock of Carbon, was passed to the buyer. The substance of the transaction was a brief removal of the "dividend" asset (the Carbon stock) on the way to the hands of the waiting buyer. In the case before the court, unlike the situation that obtained in Basic, the distributed assets were retained by the stockholders to whom they were distributed, rather than being immediately transferred to the purchaser.

As additional support for its position, the court in *Basic* focused on the absence of a business purpose, viewed from the standpoint of Falls, for the payment of a dividend of a valuable corporate asset, i.e., the capital stock of Carbon, by Falls to Basic. The district court, in the case before this court, applied the same test to the payment of the dividend of the unwanted assets by CLIC to TSN, the controlling stockholder of CLIC, and found that, strictly from the standpoint of CLIC, the dividend was lacking in business purpose and, indeed, could not have taken place apart from the sale and the subsequent infusion of investment assets into CLIC by Union Mutual. However, it seems to us to be inconsistent to take the position that substance must control over form and that a transaction must be viewed as a whole, rather than in parts, and at the same time to state that the business purpose of one participant in a multi-party transaction (particularly where the participant is a corporation controlled by the taxpayer and is not itself a party to the sale transaction) is to be viewed in isolation from the over-all business purpose for the entire transaction. We agree that the transaction must be viewed as a whole and we accept the district court's finding of fact that the dividend of the unwanted assets was "part and parcel of the purchase arrangement with Union Mutual," motivated specifically by Union Mutual's unwillingness to take and pay for such assets. That being the case, we decline to focus on the business purpose of one participant in the transaction—a corporation controlled by the taxpayer—and instead find that the business purpose for the transaction as a whole, viewed from the standpoint of the taxpayer, controls. The facts found by the district court clearly demonstrate a business purpose for the presale dividend of the unwanted assets which fully explains that dividend. We note that there is no suggestion in the district court's opinion of any tax avoidance motivation on the part of the taxpayer TSN. The fact that the dividend may have had incidental tax benefit to the taxpayer, without more, does not necessitate the disallowance of dividend treatment.

Having concluded that the pre-sale distribution by CLIC to its stockholders (including TSN) of assets which Union Mutual did not want, would not pay for and did not ultimately receive is a dividend for tax purposes, and not part of the purchase price of the capital stock of CLIC, we reverse the judgment of the district court and remand for proceedings consistent with this opinion.

Reversed and remanded.

NOTES

1. When the shareholder is an individual, not a corporation, she is not entitled to a dividends received deduction under § 243(a). If she were, of course, there would not be a double tax on corporate income. As a result, such a shareholder historically has preferred that any pre-sale distribution be characterized as part of the proceeds she receives from the sale of her stock and thus taxable as capital gain rather than ordinary income. In Casner v. Commissioner, 450 F.2d 379 (5th Cir. 1971), a case not mentioned in *TSN Liquidating Corp.*, the Fifth Circuit held that a pre-sale cash distribution to an individual was part of the proceeds of sale. In Rev. Rul. 75–493, 1975–2 C.B. 109, the Service announced its refusal to follow *Casner* and, distinguishing *Waterman Steamship Corp.*, discussed in *TSN Liquidating Corp.*, ruled that a pre-sale cash distribution to an individual was a dividend, not to be treated as part of the proceeds of sale.

Do individual taxpayers still have the same incentive in characterizing distributions now that Congress has permitted certain dividends to be taxed like net capital gains? See § 1(h)(11) enacted in 2003.

2. In Litton Industries, Inc. v. Commissioner, 89 T.C. 1086 (1987), the Tax Court held that the distribution of a promissory note by a subsidiary to its parent was a dividend and not a part of the subsequent sale price of the subsidiary. In so holding, the court distinguished *Waterman Steamship Corp.* on the

ground that the dividend was complete even before Litton attempted to sell its subsidiary. As in *TSN Liquidating Corporation, Inc.*, the transaction was not considered a sham. See also Uniroyal, Inc. v. Commissioner, 65 T.C.M. (CCH) 2690, 1993–214 (following *Litton*).

3. Although stock exchange rules set the ex-dividend date after the record date, the owner of the stock on the record date is the recipient of the dividend income for federal income tax purposes. Accordingly, a corporation that receives dividends on stock that it purchased before the ex-dividend date but after the record date should not include the dividends in its gross income, and is not entitled to the dividends received deduction under § 243. See Rev. Rul. 82–11, 1982–1 C.B. 51.

4. GAIN OR LOSS ON THE DISPOSITION OF PROPERTY—THE RISE AND DEMISE OF *GENERAL UTILITIES*

The final special gross income question for corporations concerns distribution of appreciated (or depreciated) property to its shareholders. Assume an item of property has appreciated (or depreciated) during the time it has been held by a corporation. No gain (or loss) has yet been taken by the corporation with respect to the property. The corporation then distributes the property to its shareholders. Does this distribution constitute a realization event for the corporation, triggering gain (or loss) on the distributed asset?

a. The Evolution of the General Utilities Doctrine

Section 336 now provides that a corporation generally recognizes gain or loss upon the distribution of appreciated or depreciated property to its shareholders in complete liquidation. Under § 311, a corporation recognizes gain, but not loss, upon the disposition of property in a nonliquidating distribution of property that is not in complete liquidation.

One might expect these rules to flow ineluctably from the principle of double taxation of corporate profits. If a corporation were able to avoid tax on the distribution of appreciated property to its shareholders, a substantial amount of income would go untaxed at the corporate level. Yet for more than 50 years the law sanctioned such a result. Under the *General Utilities* doctrine, a corporation could distribute appreciated assets to its shareholders without recognizing any gain. Moreover, after the passage of the 1954 Code, a corporation that sold appreciated property pursuant to a plan of complete liquidation was not taxed on the gain. The following materials trace the development and consequences of the *General Utilities* doctrine.

General Utilities & Operating Co. v. Helvering
296 U.S. 200 (1935).

■ MR. JUSTICE MCREYNOLDS delivered the opinion of the Court.

January 1st, 1927, petitioner—General Utilities, a Delaware corporation—acquired 20,000 shares (one-half of total outstanding) common stock

Islands Edison Company, for which it paid $2,000. Gillet & Company owned the remainder.

During January, 1928, Whetstone, President of Southern Cities Utilities Company, contemplated acquisition by his company of all Islands Edison common stock. He discussed the matter with Lucas, petitioner's president, also with Gillet & Company. The latter concern agreed to sell its holdings upon terms acceptable to all. But Lucas pointed out that the shares which his company held could only be purchased after distribution of them among stockholders, since a sale by it would subject the realized profit to taxation, and when the proceeds passed to the stockholders there would be further exaction. Lucas had no power to sell, but he, Gillet and Whetstone were in accord concerning the terms and conditions under which purchase of all the stock might become possible—"it being understood and agreed between them that petitioner would make distribution of the stock of the Islands Edison Company to its stockholders and that counsel would prepare a written agreement embodying the terms and conditions of the said sale, agreement to be submitted for approval to the stockholders of the Islands Edison Company after the distribution of said stock by the petitioner."

Petitioner's directors, March 22, 1928, considered the disposition of the Islands Edison shares. Officers reported they were worth $1,122,500, and recommended an appreciation on the books to that figure. Thereupon a resolution directed this change; also "that a dividend in the amount of $1,071,426.25 be and it is hereby declared on the Common Stock of this Company payable in Common Stock of The Islands Edison Company at a valuation of $56.12 1/2 a share, out of the surplus of the Company arising from the appreciation in the value of the Common Stock of The Islands Edison Company held by this Company, viz, $1,120,500.00, the payment of the dividend to be made by the delivery to the stockholders of this Company, pro rata, of certificates for the Common Stock of The Islands Edison Company held by this Company at the rate of two shares of such stock for each share of Company Stock of this Corporation."

Accordingly, 19,090 shares were distributed amongst petitioner's thirty-three stockholders and proper transfers to them were made upon the issuing corporation's books. It retained 910 shares.

After this transfer, all holders of Islands Edison stock, sold to Southern Cities Utilities Company at $56.12½ per share. Petitioner realized $46,346.30 net profit on 910 shares and this was duly returned for taxation. There was no report of gain upon the 19,090 shares distributed to stockholders.

The Commissioner of Internal Revenue declared a taxable gain upon distribution of the stock in payment of the dividend declared March 22nd, and made the questioned deficiency assessment. Seeking redetermination by the Board of Tax Appeals, petitioner alleged, "The Commissioner of Internal Revenue has erroneously held that the petitioner corporation made a profit of $1,069,517.25 by distributing to its own stockholders certain capital stock of another corporation which it had theretofore owned." And it asked a ruling that no taxable gain resulted from the appreciation upon its books and subsequent distribution of the shares. Answering, the Commissioner denied that his action was erroneous, but advanced no new basis of support. A stipulation concerning the facts followed; and upon this and the pleadings, the Board heard the cause. It found "The respondent has determined a deficiency in income tax in the amount of $128,342.07 for the calendar year 1928. The only question presented in this proceeding for redetermination is whether petitioner realized taxable gain in declaring a dividend and paying it in the stock of another company at an agreed value per share, which value was in excess of the cost of the stock to petitioner." Also, "On March 26, 1928, the stockholders of the Islands Edison Company (one of which was petitioner, owning 910 shares) and the Southern Cities Utilities Company, entered into a written contract of sale of the Islands Edison Company stock. At no time did petitioner agree with Whetstone or the Southern Cities Utilities Company, verbally or in writing, to make sale to him or to the Southern Cities Utilities Company of any of said stock except the aforesaid 910 shares of the Islands Edison Company."

The opinion recites—The Commissioner's "theory is that upon the declaration of the dividend on March 22, 1928, petitioner became indebted to its stockholders in the amount of $1,071,426.25, and that the discharge of that liability by the delivery of property costing less than the amount of the debt constituted income, citing United States v. Kirby Lumber Co., 284 U.S. 1." "The intent of the directors of petitioner was to declare a dividend payable in Islands Edison stock; their intent was expressed in that way in the resolution formally adopted; and the dividend was paid in the way intended and declared. We so construe the transaction, and on authority of First Utah Savings Bank, supra [17 B. T. A. 804; *aff'd*, 60 App. D.C. 307; 53 F.(2d) 919 (1931)], we hold that the declaration and payment of the dividend resulted in no taxable income."

The Commissioner asked the Circuit Court of Appeals, 4th Circuit, to review the Board's determination. He alleged, "The only question to be decided is whether the petitioner [taxpayer] realized taxable income in declaring a dividend and paying it in stock of another company at an agreed value per share, which value was in excess of the cost of the stock."

The court stated: "There are two grounds upon which the petitioner urges that the action of the Board of Tax Appeals was wrong: First, that the dividend declared was in effect a cash dividend and that the respondent realized a taxable income by the distribution of the Islands Edison Company stock to its stockholders equal to the difference between the amount of the dividend declared and the cost of the stock; second, that the sale made of the Islands Edison Company stock was in reality a sale by the respondent (with all the terms agreed upon before the declaration of the dividend), through its stockholders who were virtually acting as agents of the respondent, the real vendor."

Upon the first ground, it sustained the Board. Concerning the second, it held that, although not raised before the Board, the point should be ruled upon. "When we come to consider the sale of the stock of the Islands Edison

Company, we cannot escape the conclusion that the transaction was deliberately planned and carried out for the sole purpose of escaping taxation.
The purchaser was found by the officers of the respondent; the exact terms
of the sale as finally consummated were agreed to by the same officers; the
purchaser of the stock stated that the delivery of all the stock was essential
and that the delivery of a part thereof would not suffice; the details were
worked out for the express and admitted purpose of avoiding the payment
of the tax and for the reason that the attorneys for the respondent had advised that, unless some such plan was adopted, the tax would have to be
paid; and a written agreement was to be prepared by counsel for the respondent which was to be submitted to the stockholders—all this without
the stockholders, or any of them, who were ostensibly making the sale, being informed, advised, or consulted. Such admitted facts plainly constituted
a plan, not to use the harsher terms of scheme, artifice or conspiracy, to
evade the payment of the tax. For the purposes of this decision, it is not
necessary to consider whether such a course as is here shown constituted a
fraud, it is sufficient if we conclude that the object was to evade the payment of a tax justly due the government.

"The sale of the stock in question was, in substance, made by the respondent company, through the stockholders as agents or conduits through
whom the transfer of the title was effected. The stockholders, even in their
character as agents, had little or no option in the matter and in no sense
exercised any independent judgment. They automatically ratified the
agreement prepared and submitted to them."

A judgment of reversal followed.

Both tribunals below rightly decided that petitioner derived no taxable
gain from the distribution among its stockholders of the Islands Edison
shares as a dividend. This was no sale; assets were not used to discharge
indebtedness.

The second ground of objection, although sustained by the court, was
not presented to or ruled upon by the Board. The petition for review relied
wholly upon the first point; and, in the circumstances, we think the court
should have considered no other. Always a taxpayer is entitled to know
with fair certainty the basis of the claim against him. Stipulations concerning facts and any other evidence properly are accommodated to issues adequately raised.

Recently (April, 1935) this court pointed out: "The Court of Appeals is
without power on review of proceedings of the Board of Tax Appeals to
make any findings of fact." "The function of the court is to decide whether
the correct rule of law was applied to the facts found; and whether there
was substantial evidence before the Board to support the findings made."
"If the Board has failed to make an essential finding and the record on review is insufficient to provide the basis for a final determination, the proper
procedure is to remand the case for further proceedings before the Board."
"And the same procedure is appropriate even when the findings omitted by

the Board might be supplied from examination of the records." Helvering v. Rankin, 295 U.S. 123, 131, 132.

Here the court undertook to decide a question not properly raised. Also it made an inference of fact directly in conflict with the stipulation of the parties and the findings, for which we think the record affords no support whatever. To remand the cause for further findings would be futile. The Board could not properly find anything which would assist the Commissioner's cause.

The judgment of the court below must be reversed. The action of the Board of Tax Appeals is approved.

Reversed.

NOTES

1. The Supreme Court rejected on procedural grounds the Government's argument that the shareholder's sale of the stock should be attributed to the corporation. Implicit in this Government contention was the twofold proposition that a sale by a corporation triggers realization of gain, but that absent a sale (and an "amount realized") by the corporation there is no realization. See § 1001(a). Ten years later the Government succeeded in an "attribution of sale" approach in Commissioner v. Court Holding Co., page 25 infra.

The Supreme Court rejected on its merits the Government's contention that distribution of the stock was the equivalent of a sale in that it satisfied a corporate debt that the corporation owed to its shareholders as a result of the dividend declaration. The Board of Tax Appeals and the Court of Appeals had also rejected this contention. The Supreme Court (page 23 supra) said "[t]his was no sale; assets were not used to discharge indebtedness." Why is "sale" so crucial? Was there no "indebtedness," or was it that assets were not used to "discharge" it?

The Supreme Court's opinion ignored a third contention advanced by the Government. The Government argued that "in making it available to its own stockholders the corporation is realizing the appreciation, and nothing more is necessary. It . . . is incomprehensible how a corporation can distribute to its stockholders something which it has not itself received." Brief for Commissioner at 18–19. In essence, the Government contended that the distribution of the stock, if not a "sale," was nevertheless a "disposition," and that in distributing the appreciation to its shareholder the "amount" was "realized." § 1001(a). The Court's failure to deal with this contention is not explained. The Government's failure to raise the argument in either of the lower courts may be the reason. Nevertheless, the *General Utilities* decision was widely regarded as standing for the proposition that a corporation realized no income (or loss) on the distribution of appreciated (or depreciated) assets to its shareholders. For many years prior to *General Utilities* the Regulations had stated that a liquidating distribution of appreciated (or depreciated) property did not trigger a realization of gain (or loss) (Treas. Reg. 118, § 39.22(a)–20 (1939 Code)), and *General*

Utilities seemed to many to confirm that "rule" in the case of nonliquidating distributions by operating corporations.[6]

How important to your evaluation of the Court's decision in *General Utilities* is the fact that the distributed property was immediately sold by the shareholders, and that the purpose of the distribution before sale was to avoid taxation of gain to the corporation?

2. Why had the Commissioner conceded in the Regulations that no corporate gain or loss was to be recognized in liquidating distributions? On what basis might the tax treatment of interim distributions by an ongoing corporation be differentiated? Should they be differentiated? Might the Commissioner have fared better in *General Utilities* if he had first revoked the provisions of the Regulations as to liquidating distributions and then had promulgated one that asserted that any distribution of an asset to its shareholders would result in corporate realization of gain or loss to the same extent as in a sale? Should he have done so after *General Utilities*? Would such a provision have been valid after that decision? Bear in mind that, despite the *General Utilities* doctrine as it came to be, the Supreme Court ignored the Government's third argument.

Commissioner v. Court Holding Co.
324 U.S. 331 (1945).

■ MR. JUSTICE BLACK delivered the opinion of the Court. An apartment house, which was the sole asset of the respondent corporation, was transferred in the form of a liquidating dividend to the corporation's two shareholders. They in turn formally conveyed it to a purchaser who had originally negotiated for the purchase from the corporation. The question is whether the Circuit Court of Appeals properly reversed the Tax Court's conclusion that the corporation was taxable under § [61] of the Internal Revenue Code[3] for the gain which accrued from the sale. The answer depends upon whether the findings of the Tax Court that the whole transaction showed a sale by the corporation rather than by the stockholders were final and binding upon the Circuit Court of Appeals.

It is unnecessary to set out in detail the evidence introduced before the Tax Court or its findings. Despite conflicting evidence, the following findings of the Tax Court are supported by the record:

The respondent corporation was organized in 1934 solely to buy and hold the apartment building which was the only property ever owned by it. All of its outstanding stock was owned by Minnie Miller and her husband. Between October 1, 1939 and February, 1940, while the corporation still had legal title to the property, negotiations for its sale took place. These

---

[6]In tax parlance a corporation is "liquidating" when it distributes its assets to its shareholders in retirement of their stock. Liquidation does not connote the mere conversion of non-cash assets into cash.

[3]Profits from the sale of property are taxable as income under § [61] of the Internal Revenue Code.... The Treasury Regulations have long provided that gains accruing from the sales of a corporation's assets, in whole or in part, constitute income to it, but that a corporation realizes no taxable gain by a mere distribution of its assets in kind, in partial or in complete liquidation, however much they may have appreciated in value since acquisition. §§ 19.22(a)–19, 19.22(a)–21, Treasury Regulations 103. [1939 Code.]

negotiations were between the corporation and the lessees of the property, together with a sister and brother-in-law. An oral agreement was reached as to the terms and conditions of sale, and on February 22, 1940, the parties met to reduce the agreement to writing. The purchaser was then advised by the corporation's attorney that the sale could not be consummated because it would result in the imposition of a large income tax on the corporation. The next day, the corporation declared a "liquidating dividend," which involved complete liquidation of its assets, and surrender of all outstanding stock. Mrs. Miller and her husband surrendered their stock, and the building was deeded to them. A sale contract was then drawn, naming the Millers individually as vendors, and the lessees' sister as vendee, which embodied substantially the same terms and conditions previously agreed upon. One thousand dollars, which a month and a half earlier had been paid to the corporation by the lessees, was applied in part payment of the purchase price. Three days later, the property was conveyed to the lessees' sister.

The Tax Court concluded from these facts that, despite the declaration of a "liquidating dividend" followed by the transfers of legal title, the corporation had not abandoned the sales negotiations; that these were mere formalities designed "to make the transaction appear to be other than what it was" in order to avoid tax liability. The Circuit Court of Appeals drawing different inferences from the record, held that the corporation had "called off" the sale, and treated the stockholders' sale as unrelated to the prior negotiations.

There was evidence to support the findings of the Tax Court, and its findings must therefore be accepted by the courts. Dobson v. Commissioner, 320 U.S. 489. . . On the basis of these findings, the Tax Court was justified in attributing the gain from the sale to respondent corporation. The incidence of taxation depends upon the substance of a transaction. The tax consequences which arise from gains from a sale of property are not finally to be determined solely by the means employed to transfer legal title. Rather, the transaction must be viewed as a whole, and each step, from the commencement of negotiations to the consummation of the sale, is relevant. A sale by one person cannot be transformed for tax purposes into a sale by another by using the latter as a conduit through which to pass title. To permit the true nature of a transaction to be disguised by mere formalisms, which exist solely to alter tax liabilities, would seriously impair the effective administration of the tax policies of Congress.

It is urged that respondent corporation never executed a written agreement, and that an oral agreement to sell land cannot be enforced in Florida because of the Statute of Frauds, Comp. Gen. Laws of Florida, 1927, vol. 3, § 5779. But the fact that respondent corporation itself never executed a written contract is unimportant, since the Tax Court found from the facts of the entire transaction that the executed sale was in substance the sale of the corporation. The decision of the Circuit Court of Appeals is reversed, and that of the Tax Court affirmed.

It is so ordered.

United States v. Cumberland Public Service Co.

338 U.S. 451 (1950).

■ MR. JUSTICE BLACK delivered the opinion of the Court. A corporation selling its physical properties is taxed on capital gains resulting from the sale. There is no corporate tax, however, on distribution of assets in kind to shareholders as part of a genuine liquidation.[2] The respondent corporation transferred property to its shareholders as a liquidating dividend in kind. The shareholders transferred it to a purchaser. The question is whether, despite contrary findings by the Court of Claims, this record requires a holding that the transaction was in fact a sale by the corporation subjecting the corporation to a capital gains tax.

Details of the transaction are as follows. The respondent, a closely held corporation, was long engaged in the business of generating and distributing electric power in three Kentucky counties. In 1936 a local cooperative began to distribute Tennessee Valley Authority power in the area served by respondent. It soon became obvious that respondent's Diesel-generated power could not compete with TVA power, which respondent had been unable to obtain. Respondent's shareholders, realizing that the corporation must get out of the power business unless it obtained TVA power, accordingly offered to sell all the corporate stock to the cooperative, which was receiving such power. The cooperative refused to buy the stock, but countered with an offer to buy from the corporation its transmission and distribution equipment. The corporation rejected the offer because it would have been compelled to pay a heavy capital gains tax. At the same time the shareholders, desiring to save payment of the corporate capital gains tax, offered to acquire the transmission and distribution equipment and then sell to the cooperative. The cooperative accepted. The corporation transferred the transmission and distribution systems to its shareholders in partial liquidation. The remaining assets were sold and the corporation dissolved. The shareholders then executed the previously contemplated sale to the cooperative.

Upon this sale by the shareholders, the Commissioner assessed and collected a $17,000 tax from the corporation on the theory that the shareholders had been used as a mere conduit for effectuating what was really a corporate sale. Respondent corporation brought this action to recover the amount of the tax. The Court of Claims found that the method by which the stockholders disposed of the properties was avowedly chosen in order to reduce taxes, but that the liquidation and dissolution genuinely ended the corporation's activities and existence. The court also found that at no time did the corporation plan to make the sale itself. Accordingly it found as a fact that the sale was made by the shareholders rather than the corporation, and entered judgment for respondent. One judge dissented, believing that our opinion in Commissioner v. Court Holding Co., 324 U.S. 331, required a finding that the sale had been made by the corporation. Certiorari

---

[2] "... No gain or loss is realized by a corporation from the mere distribution of its assets in kind in partial or complete liquidation, however they may have appreciated or depreciated in value since their acquisition...." Treas. Reg. 103, § 19.22(a)–21. [1939 Code].

was granted, 338 U.S. 846, to clear up doubts arising out of the *Court Holding Co.* case.

Our *Court Holding Co.* decision rested on findings of fact by the Tax Court that a sale had been made and gains realized by the taxpayer corporation. There the corporation had negotiated for sale of its assets and had reached an oral agreement of sale. When the tax consequences of the corporate sale were belatedly recognized, the corporation purported to "call off" the sale at the last minute and distributed the physical properties in kind to the stockholders. They promptly conveyed these properties to the same persons who had negotiated with the corporation. The terms of purchase were substantially those of the previous oral agreement. One thousand dollars already paid to the corporation was applied as part payment of the purchase price. The Tax Court found that the corporation never really abandoned its sales negotiations, that it never did dissolve, and that the sole purpose of the so-called liquidation was to disguise a corporate sale through use of mere formalisms in order to avoid tax liability. The Circuit Court of Appeals took a different view of the evidence. In this Court the Government contended that whether a liquidation distribution was genuine or merely a sham was traditionally a question of fact. We agreed with this contention, and reinstated the Tax Court's findings and judgment. Discussing the evidence which supported the findings of fact, we went on to say that "the incidence of taxation depends upon the substance of a transaction" regardless of "mere formalisms," and that taxes on a corporate sale cannot be avoided by using the shareholders as a "conduit through which to pass title."

This language does not mean that a corporation can be taxed even when the sale has been made by its stockholders following a genuine liquidation and dissolution.[3] While the distinction between sales by a corporation as compared with distribution in kind followed by shareholder sales may be particularly shadowy and artificial when the corporation is closely held, Congress has chosen to recognize such a distinction for tax purposes. The corporate tax is thus aimed primarily at the profits of a going concern. This is true despite the fact that gains realized from corporate sales are taxed, perhaps to prevent tax evasions, even where the cash proceeds are at once distributed in liquidation. But Congress has imposed no tax on liquidating distributions in kind or on dissolution, whatever may be the motive for such liquidation. Consequently, a corporation may liquidate or dissolve without subjecting itself to the corporate gains tax, even though a primary motive is to avoid the burden of corporate taxation.

Here, on the basis of adequate subsidiary findings, the Court of Claims has found that the sale in question was made by the stockholders rather than the corporation. The Government's argument that the shareholders

---

[3] What we said in the *Court Holding Co.* case was an approval of the action of the Tax Court in looking beyond the papers executed by the corporation and shareholders in order to determine whether the sale there had actually been made by the corporation. We were but emphasizing the established principle that in resolving such questions as who made a sale, fact-finding tribunals in tax cases can consider motives, intent, and conduct in addition to what appears in written instruments used by parties to control rights as among themselves....

acted as a mere "conduit" for a sale by respondent corporation must fall before this finding. The subsidiary finding that a major motive of the shareholders was to reduce taxes does not bar this conclusion. Whatever the motive and however relevant it may be in determining whether the transaction was real or a sham, sales of physical properties by shareholders following a genuine liquidation distribution cannot be attributed to the corporation for tax purposes.

The oddities in tax consequences that emerge from the tax provisions here controlling appear to be inherent in the present tax pattern. For a corporation is taxed if it sells all its physical properties and distributes the cash proceeds as liquidating dividends, yet is not taxed if that property is distributed in kind and is then sold by the shareholders. In both instances the interest of the shareholders in the business has been transferred to the purchaser. Again, if these stockholders had succeeded in their original effort to sell all their stock, their interest would have been transferred to the purchasers just as effectively. Yet on such a transaction the corporation would have realized no taxable gain.

Congress having determined that different tax consequences shall flow from different methods by which the shareholders of a closely held corporation may dispose of corporate property, we accept its mandate. It is for the trial court, upon consideration of an entire transaction, to determine the factual category in which a particular transaction belongs. Here as in the *Court Holding Co.* case we accept the ultimate findings of fact of the trial tribunal. Accordingly the judgment of the Court of Claims is affirmed.

■ MR. JUSTICE DOUGLAS took no part in the consideration or decision of this case.

NOTES

1. Would you have expected the Tax Court to draw the same conclusions from the evidence in *Cumberland* as the Court of Claims did? Why? What evidence in *Cumberland* led the Court of Claims to reach a conclusion different from the one the Tax Court reached in *Court Holding Co.*? In the context of the two cases, in what sense is the inquiry as to who made the sale a factual one? What guidance did the Supreme Court provide for the trial courts charged with determining "the factual category in which a particular transaction belongs?"

2. If *General Utilities* had been decided for the Government (on which theory?), might *Court Holding Co.* and *Cumberland* have arisen anyhow? The Supreme Court did not cite *General Utilities* in either case. Why not? In *Cumberland* the Court said that the "corporate tax is. . . aimed primarily at the profits of a going concern," page 28 supra. *Court Holding Co.* did not involve a "going concern"; *General Utilities* did. In *Court Holding Co.* the corporate tax was imposed; in *General Utilities* it was not.

b. Codification and Narrowing of the General Utilities Doctrine—1954 to 1986

In 1954, the *General Utilities* doctrine was codified in § 311(a) to provide that as to nonliquidating distributions, a distributing corporation would not recognize gain or loss on a distribution "with respect to its stock." Section 336(a) provided similar treatment for distributions in complete or partial liquidations. But there were exceptions. Section 311(a) excepted the distribution of installment obligations from corporate tax immunity, and § 311(b) and (c) provided exceptions to the general nonrecognition rule in the case of distributions of LIFO inventory and property subject to liabilities in excess of basis. Section 336 had an exception for the distribution of installment obligations.

Congress also resolved the imputation problem posed by the *Court Holding* case, at least in the context of a complete liquidation. In old § 337 (pre–1986 Code), Congress provided generally that a corporation would not recognize gain or loss on the sale of property pursuant to a complete liquidation.

The period from 1954 to 1986 saw a gradual narrowing of the *General Utilities* doctrine. In 1969 Congress added § 311(d), which provided that distributions of appreciated property in redemption of the distributing corporation's stock would result in recognition of the gain to the distributing corporation, except in certain specified situations. In 1982, Congress narrowed the exceptions to § 311(d). The 1984 Act further narrowed the exceptions to § 311(d), so much so that, with few exceptions, distributions of appreciated property, whether by way of dividend or redemption, were made subject to the corporate income tax. Under § 336, however, distributions in complete liquidation remained generally immune from the corporate tax.

c. Repeal of General Utilities—The Tax Reform Act of 1986

The 1986 Act repealed what was left of the *General Utilities* doctrine, although some anti-abuse exceptions prevent the recognition of loss in certain cases. Specifically, in a nonliquidating distribution the corporation recognizes gain, but not loss. See § 311. In a complete liquidation, gain on the disposition of property to shareholders is generally recognized without limitation, but losses must run the gauntlet of § 336(d) in order to be recognized. See § 336(a) and (d). Congress repealed old § 337; therefore gain or loss on the sale of property pursuant to a complete liquidation must be recognized. There is no exception for either goodwill or land, although some proponents of *General Utilities* repeal had recommended it. How might such an exception be justified? See generally Wolfman, Subchapter C and the 100th Congress, Tax Notes, Nov. 17, 1986, p. 669.

Section 336(b) provides that if distributed property is subject to liabilities the fair market value is treated as though it were at least equal to the liabilities. This follows the principle set out in Crane v. Commissioner, 331 U.S. 1 (1947), and the holding in Commissioner v. Tufts, 461 U.S. 300

(1983), which resolved the question of how much gain must be recognized by a taxpayer who transfers property in exchange for the assumption of liabilities that exceed the fair market value of the property.

New § 337 provides a special rule for a subsidiary liquidating into its parent. Section 337 defers the recognition of gain on property distributed in a complete liquidation if the property is distributed to an "80–percent distributee." Why is it appropriate to grant nonrecognition treatment in this context? Consider the practical relationship between the business decision to liquidate a subsidiary, and the decision to engage in a corporate reorganization (which can receive tax-free treatment) discussed in Chapter 4, infra, page 441.

Although the *General Utilities* doctrine has been repealed (§§ 311 and 336), the *Court Holding* and *Cumberland* opinions have continued significance. They are frequently cited for their treatment of the pervasive "substance-over-form" problem, one that occurs often. A court will sometimes ignore the form of a transaction and delve into its underlying "substance" when determining its tax consequences. See, e.g., Altria Group Inc. v. U.S., 658 F.3d 276 (2d Cir. 2011)(quoting *Court Holding* "To permit the true nature of a transaction to be disguised by mere formalisms which exist solely to alter tax liabilities would seriously impair the effective administration of the tax policies of Congress"); Framatome Connectors U.S., Inc. v. Commissioner, 118 T.C. 32 (2002) (citing *Court Holding* for its substance-over-form doctrine). In some cases, the reliance on *Court Holding* has more closely tracked the original facts of an attribution of sale. See, e.g., Stewart v. Commissioner, 714 F.2d 977 (9th Cir. 1983) (holding that a corporation's sale of its assets to a third party immediately after the sole shareholder had transferred them to the corporation was, in reality a sale by the shareholder and not by the corporation—essentially flipping *Court Holding*!).

d. Current Law—Illustrative Problems

The following problems illustrate the intricacies and application of §§ 311, 336, and 337.

1. In a nonliquidating distribution, X Corporation distributes to its sole shareholder, A, property with a basis of $100 and a fair market value of $200. What are the tax consequences to X Corporation? Suppose instead that the fair market value of the distributed property is $50. What consequences to X Corporation? Why did Congress choose to disallow recognition of loss upon the distribution of property in a nonliquidating distribution?

2. Pursuant to a plan of complete liquidation, Y Corporation distributes property with a basis of $100 and a fair market value of $90. The property is subject to liabilities of $150. What are the tax consequences to Y Corporation? For the consequences of the transaction to the shareholders, see Chapter 2, infra, page 130 et seq.

3. Eighty percent of T Corporation's stock is owned by P Corporation; the remaining 20 percent is owned by an individual, B. In a complete liqui-

dation, T Corporation makes a pro rata distribution to its shareholders of property with a basis of $100 and a fair market value of $200. What are the tax consequences to T Corporation? Suppose instead that the distributed property has a fair market value of $50. Does T Corporation recognize loss on the distribution?

4. C, an individual who is the sole shareholder of Z Corporation, contributes property to Z Corporation that has a basis of $100 and a fair market value of $50. As you will learn in Chapter 3, the basis of the property in Z Corporation's hands will be $100. See § 362(a). Six months later, when the property has a value of $10, Z Corporation distributes the property to C in complete liquidation. Does Z Corporation recognize loss on the distribution?

e. Computation of Gain—Question of Basis—§§ 1012, 334, and 338

Where the distribution of property by a corporation to its shareholders involves appreciated or depreciated property (as opposed to cash), the question of basis is a necessary prerequisite to any computation of gain and income. As a general matter taxpayers prefer to have a high basis in their assets. The following cases explore the rules governing basis in cases of distributions. The first case considers the incentives in the *General Utilities* era to use a distribution strategy to bump up the basis in assets for purposes of depreciation. The second case considers a corporation seeking to acquire the underlying assets of another corporation. The acquirer purchases the stock of the target and then directs the new subsidiary to make a liquidating distribution of the assets, raising the question of what the basis in these assets should now be in the hands of the acquirer that just paid full value for the stock. Both of these cases illustrate an important corporate tax reality—there is often more than one way to structure a corporate transaction. The final choice can be driven by business needs and tax effects. How should the tax system treat alternative transactions? What factors should be relevant in the decision?

United States v. General Geophysical Co.
296 F.2d 86 (5th Cir. 1961), *cert. denied*, 369 U.S. 849 (1962).

■ Before RIVES and WISDOM, CIRCUIT JUDGES, and DAWKINS, JR., DISTRICT JUDGE.

■ WISDOM, CIRCUIT JUDGE. February 25, 1954 General Geophysical Company, the taxpayer, transferred certain depreciable assets having a tax basis of $169,290 and a market value of $746,525 to two of its major stockholders in the redemption of their stock. Later that day the taxpayer reacquired the same assets from the former stockholders in exchange for corporate notes in the amount of $746,525. In its 1954 income tax return the corporation claimed depreciation deductions using as the cost basis the market value of the assets at the time of the transaction. The sole question this litigation presents is whether the corporation's reacquisition of the assets stepped up the basis. We hold that it did not and reverse and decision below.

Earl W. Johnson founded General Geophysical Company in 1933 to engage in oil exploration, and managed its operations until his sudden death in 1953. At his death his estate, his wife, his mother, and a friend Paul L. Davis owned 77% of the corporation's total stock and 94% of its voting shares. The major portion of the remaining shares was owned by Chester Sappington, T. O. Hall, and Albert B. Gruff, who were also officers in the corporation. The Johnson stock was community property: half belonged to the widow and the other half was held by the Second National Bank of Houston as executor and trustee for Johnson's estate. The testimony shows that the bank and Mrs. Johnson soon realized that neither of them could contribute anything of value to running the corporate business, and that they should not attempt it. They realized also that if the corporation were liquidated and its properties sold, they would receive less than the value of their stock in a going concern. Sappington, Hall, and Grubb [sic] believed that they could run the corporation successfully and if so, they should receive its future profits. Accordingly, the corporation agreed to retire the stock held by the bank, the two Mrs. Johnsons, and Davis. After long negotiations the parties settled on a valuation of the stock at $245 a share, payable partly in cash and partly in notes. The attorney for the retiring stockholders advised against this proposal for fear that it would leave the stockholders without sufficient protection in case the corporation should be forced into bankruptcy. He based this legitimate business fear on Robinson v. Wangemann, 5 Cir., 1935, 75 F.2d 756, 758, which holds that when a former shareholder owns notes of a bankrupt corporation, received in the redemption of his stock, he "cannot be permitted to share with the other unsecured creditors in the distribution of the assets of the bankrupt estate." To avoid exposure to this risk, the stockholders proposed that the Johnson stock be retired in exchange for cash and corporate property having a market value equal to that of the stock. The redemption was carried out in accordance with this proposal. A few hours later, the corporation repurchased the property for corporate notes, giving the former stockholders a mortgage on certain of its properties.

Witnesses for the taxpayer insisted that there was no agreement between the corporation and the stockholders to re-exchange the corporate properties transferred to the stockholders in the redemption of their shares. The trial judge so found, and it seems clear that there was no legally binding agreement to that effect. The attorney for the stockholders did testify, however, that he had discussed the possibility of such a resale and before February 25, 1954 had prepared the documents for a resale in case that was decided upon after the initial transfer.

Under Section 1012 of the Internal Revenue Code of 1954, 26 U.S.C.A. 1012, "the basis of property shall be the cost of such property." This requires a determination of when the taxpayer acquired the property and the price he paid for it. Our decision depends on whether or not the transactions in question created an interruption in the ownership of the property, producing a new basis on its reacquisition. The Government asserts that we should disregard the form of the transfer and recognize that the substance of the transactions was a redemption of the corporate stock for cash

and notes, leaving the ownership and basis of the depreciable assets undisturbed. The taxpayer answers that there was no fraud or subterfuge in
these transactions, that the stockholders acquired complete and unfettered
ownership of the properties, and that the trial judge's finding of two separate and independent transactions cannot be overturned on appeal.

The solution of hard tax cases requires something more than the easy
generalization that the substance rather than the form of a transaction is
determinative of its tax effect, since in numerous situations the form by
which a transaction is effected does influence or control its tax consequences. This generalization does, however, reflect the truth that courts
will, on occasion, look beyond the superficial formalities of a transaction to
determine the proper tax treatment.

In the landmark case of Gregory v. Helvering, 1935, 293 U.S. 465 . . .,
the Supreme Court refused to give effect to corporate transactions which
complied precisely with the formal requirements for nontaxable corporate
reorganizations, on the ground that the transactions had served no function
other than that of a contrivance to bail out corporate earnings to the sole
shareholder at capital gains tax rates. In Commissioner v. Court Holding
Co. [page 25 supra] the Supreme Court taxed a corporation on the gain
from the sale of an apartment house notwithstanding a transfer of the
house to the corporation's two shareholders before the sale, since it found
that the transfer was made solely to set in a more favorable tax form a sale
which in reality was made by the corporation. Similarly, in Helvering v.
Clifford, 1940, 309 U.S. 331 . . ., the Supreme Court taxed a trust grantor
on the income of the trust property since the formal transfer of the property
by the grantor was lacking in substance. The Court found that the dilution
in his control seemed insignificant and immaterial and that "since the husband retains control over the investment, he had rather complete assurance that the trust will not effect any substantial change in his economic
position." 309 U.S. at pages 335–336. . . Each case must be decided on its
own merits by examining the form and substance of the transactions and
the purpose of the relevant tax provisions to determine whether recognition
of the form of the transaction would defeat the statutory purpose.

The case at bar presents an unusual tax question created by the conjunction of two parts of the tax code not frequently brought together by a
single transaction: the provisions governing basis and capital gains, and
the rule that no gain is recognized by a corporation when it distributes
property with respect to its stock. The basis of property is determined by its
cost; when the property is sold the owner realizes a taxable gain equal to
the difference between the basis and the proceeds received in the sale.
There is no danger that a taxpayer could effect an artificial sale and repurchase to raise the basis of appreciated property, since such a transaction
would subject him to a tax on the step-up in the basis. There are, therefore,
no provisions to prevent tax avoidance by such a device, and the question
whether a transfer and reacquisition should be recognized as independent
transactions creating tax consequences would generally affect only the *timing* of the imposition of a tax rather than its *amount*. The twist here comes

from the fact that the corporation did not incur a tax on the difference between basis and current market value when it transferred the assets to its shareholders in redemption of their stock. Section 311(a) . . . provides that "no gain or loss shall be recognized to a corporation on the distribution, with respect to its stock, of . . . property." This provision is expressly made applicable to stock redemption distributions by the Treasury Regulations.[2] The rule may be easily justified by the fact that when a corporation transfers appreciated property to its shareholders, as a dividend or in exchange for their shares, the gain created by the appreciation has not accrued to the corporation and should not be taxed to it.[3]

A new horizon of tax avoidance opportunities would be opened by allowing a stepped-up basis to result from the transaction here effected. Corporations would be enabled without difficulty to raise the basis of their assets whenever it fell below the market value by transferring the assets to shareholders by a dividend or stock redemption and then buying back the same assets for the cash that they otherwise would have distributed directly. Since market values are often pushed up by inflation and the basis is frequently reduced under the liberal depreciation rules far faster than the assets actually depreciate, this possibility would have enormous practical significance. These tax avoidance implications do not constitute a license to courts to distort the laws or to write in new provisions; they do mean that we should guard against giving force to a purported transfer which gives off an unmistakably hollow sound when it is tapped. It is a hollow sound for tax purposes; here, we are not concerned with business purposes or the legal effectiveness of the transaction under the law of Texas. Under the tax law, it is of course open to a corporation making a dividend distribution or a stock redemption to distribute appreciated assets rather than cash and to use its cash to purchase similar assets for replacement at a stepped-up basis. Such transactions are however limited by their costs. Moreover, in such a case it would be clear that the corporation had disposed of its former assets and acquired new ones. When, however, a corporation contends that it stepped up the basis by transferring assets to its shareholders and then re-acquiring them, we must scrutinize the transactions to make sure that the alleged divestiture did occur. The transactions should be recognized as creating an interruption in the ownership of the assets sufficient to produce a new basis only when the corporation has made a clear and distinct severance of its ownership prior to the reacquisition.

The facts of these transactions will not support a holding that the corporation had terminated its ownership for these purposes. It parted with bare legal title to the property for a few short hours. It made no physical

---

[2] Treas. Reg. 1.311–1(a) (1955).

[3] If the corporation in effect does realize the gain by handling the sale of the property after its distribution to the shareholders, the gain probably would be attributed to the corporation. See United States v. Lynch, 9 Cir., 1951, 192 F.2d 718, certiorari denied 1952, 343 U.S. 934 ...; Commissioner v. Transport Trading & Terminal Corp., 2 Cir., 1949, 176 F.2d 570, certiorari denied 1950, 338 U.S. 955, 70 S.Ct. 493. These cases were decided before enactment of Section 311, but since that section is largely a codification of the rule laid down by General Utilities & Operating Co. v. Helvering, 1935, 296 U.S. 200 ..., which did precede these cases their validity is probably not undercut by the statute. Mintz and Plumb, Dividends in Kind— The Thunderbolts and the New Look, 10 Tax L. Rev. 41, 45–48 (1954)....

delivery of any of the assets. Its control and use of the property were never interrupted. Even the surrender of its legal title was made under circumstances creating a strong expectation that it would be returned shortly. True, the stockholders may have had complete legal freedom to refuse to resell the assets to the corporation, but there was almost no likelihood that they would do so. It was a foregone conclusion that they would resell the assets to someone, since the very reason for the original redemption was that the stockholders did not wish to continue ownership of the assets and management of the business. And since the assets were already integrated into the operations of the taxpayer and represented 47% of its assets,[4] the taxpayer was the logical, and as a practical matter, the only possible purchaser. That the stockholders had already drawn up papers for the resale, in case they decided to make one, undoubtedly strengthened the confidence with which the taxpayer could look forward to the reacquisition of the properties. There was never the whisper of a suggestion that the company was to cut down on its operations, as would be inevitable if it permanently, parted with 47% of its assets, including three rigs. The most that can be said is that the taxpayer gave to the bank and Mrs. Johnson the power to divest of its ownership of certain properties; they held that power for a few hours and then returned it. The transactions, from the corporation's standpoint, were more like an option than a sale, and the option expired quickly without having been exercised.

The taxpayer asserts that the transactions were prompted by a valid business purpose and were effected without a motive of tax avoidance. We accept these assertions, which are supported by the trial judge's findings, as true. They lend support to the taxpayer's case, but they do not control the disposition of the case. Intent often is relevant in questions of taxation, particularly where the bona fides of a transaction is called into question, but in most cases tax treatment depends on what was done, not why it was done. And our decision in this case rests not on the motivation of the transactions in question but rather on our conclusion that the admitted facts of the two transfers preclude a finding of a sufficient hiatus in the corporate ownership of the assets to justify bestowal of a new basis on them after the reacquisition.[5]

To determine the basis of the assets we look backward to ascertain when the corporation acquired them. We note the transactions here in question, but we can scarcely say that the corporation's ownership dates from that occasion. These transactions, whatever their effect on other legal questions, did not create an interruption in the ownership sufficient to produce a new basis. The basis must be found from the original purchase price and the adjustments made to it. The district court's findings may be correct; his conclusions are in error.

---

[4] The assets transferred were valued by the parties at $746,525. At the rate of $245 per share, that total would represent 3047 shares, or slightly over 47% of the 6461 shares then outstanding.

[5] If these transactions could not have been explained by valid nontax reasons, they obviously would have been only a subterfuge which could not have been effective to change the basis of the assets....

The judgment is reversed.

On Petition For Rehearing

PER CURIAM. The petition for rehearing in this case expresses strongly the petitioner's conviction that this Court failed to recognize the bona fides of the transaction. In denying this petition we wish, again, to make clear that we did not base the decision on a lack of good faith in the parties to the transaction. It is true that we said, "we should guard against giving force to a purported transfer which gives off an unmistakably hollow sound when it is tapped". But this statement was set off (in the same sentence) against the other extreme: "These tax avoidance implications do not constitute a license to courts to distort the laws or to write in new provisions." Throughout the opinion we were careful to say that our decision was not based on any lack of good faith in the parties to the transaction, and that we did not pass on the legal effect of the transaction outside of the tax frame of reference. We do not question the integrity of the parties or suggest that there was any flim-flam. We do not doubt the business purposes of the transaction. The decision does not purport to question the effectiveness of the transaction in protecting the stockholders against the holding in Robinson v. Wangemann, 75 F.2d 756, 5 Cir., 1935. But we hold and reaffirm that *for tax purposes* there was not a sufficient severance of the corporation's ownership over the assets for the transaction to create the tax consequence that when the corporation reacquired the assets it took them with a stepped-up basis. The transaction is analogous to a *Clifford* trust, valid under state law but ineffective for tax purposes to remove the trust income from the settlor's taxable income. Helvering v. Clifford, 1940, 309 U.S. 331... It is ordered that the petition for rehearing filed in the above styled and numbered cause be, and the same is hereby denied.

NOTES

1. If the court in *General Geophysical* had allowed the corporation the higher basis, would taxpayers be engaging in the same planning technique today? Why not? See § 311(b). Note the court's observation: "The twist here comes from the fact that the corporation did not incur a tax on the difference between basis and current market value when it transferred the assets to its shareholders in redemption of their stock."

2. The analysis in *General Geophysical* reflects the tension between substance and form that pervades corporate tax analysis right through to the current day. To what extent should or must taxpayers be permitted to receive the tax treatment of their independent steps (here the distribution, then contribution) despite the net effect of the steps that returns the parties to the original position? The question of the applicability of the "step transaction doctrine" (the grouping of separate steps together as one to tax on the basis of the net result) underlies the following liquidation case.

Kimbell–Diamond Milling Co. v. Commissioner

14 T.C. 74 (1950), *aff'd per curiam*, 187 F.2d 718 (5th Cir. 1951), *cert. denied*,
342 U.S. 827 (1951).

■ BLACK, JUDGE. This proceeding involves deficiencies in income, declared value excess profits, and excess profits taxes for the fiscal years ended May 31, 1945 and 1946... The deficiencies are primarily due to respondent's reduction of petitioner's basis in assets acquired by it in December, 1942, through the liquidation of another corporation known as Whaley Mill & Elevator Co. (sometimes hereinafter referred to as Whaley). By reason of this reduction respondent has adjusted petitioner's allowable depreciation... By appropriate assignments of error petitioner contests these adjustments...

This leaves for our consideration the determination of petitioner's basis in the assets acquired from Whaley.

The facts have been stipulated and are adopted as our findings of fact. They may be summarized as follows:

Petitioner is a Texas corporation, engaged primarily in the business of milling, processing, and selling grain products, and has its principal office in Fort Worth, Texas. Petitioner maintained its books and records and filed its corporation tax returns on an accrual basis for fiscal years ended May 31 of each year...

On or about August 13, 1942, petitioner sustained a fire casualty at its Wolfe City, Texas, plant which resulted in the destruction of its mill property at that location. The assets so destroyed [had an aggregate adjusted basis of $18,921.90]... This property was covered by insurance, and on or about November 14, 1942, petitioner collected insurance in the amount of $124,551.10 ($118,200.16 as a reimbursement for the loss sustained by the fire and $6,350.94 as a premium refund). On December 26, 1942, petitioner's directors approved the transaction set forth in the minutes below:

> THAT, WHEREAS, on or about August 1, 1942, the flour mill and milling plant of Kimbell Diamond Milling Company located at Wolfe City, Texas was destroyed by fire; and
>
> WHEREAS, Kimbell–Diamond Milling Company collected from the insurance companies carrying the insurance on the said destroyed properties the sum of $125,000.00 as indemnification for the loss sustained, which said insurance proceeds were by the proper officers of this corporation promptly deposited in a special account in the Fort Worth National Bank of Fort Worth, Texas, where they have since been kept intact in order to have the same available for replacing, as nearly as might be, the destroyed properties; and
>
> WHEREAS, it has at all times been the intention and desire of Kimbell–Diamond Milling Company to replace its burned mill either

by constructing a new mill or by purchasing facilities of substantially similar kind and use; and

WHEREAS, due to existing building restrictions and other causes, it has been found impractical and impossible to replace the destroyed facilities by new construction, but it has come to the attention of the officers of this corporation that the stock of Whaley Mill & Elevator Company, a Texas corporation, which, among its other assets, owns physical properties substantially comparable to the destroyed Wolfe City Milling plant, can be purchased;

NOW, THEREFORE, BE IT RESOLVED:

1. That the proper officers of Kimbell–Diamond Milling Company be, and they are hereby, authorized, empowered and directed to purchase the entire authorized, issued and outstanding capital stock of Whaley Mill & Elevator Company, a Texas corporation, consisting of 4,000 shares of the face or par value of $100.00 per share, for a sum not in excess of $210,000.00; that payment for the said stock of Whaley Mill & Elevator Company be made, to the extent possible, from the insurance proceeds deposited in a special account in the Fort Worth National Bank, and that the balance of the agreed consideration for the stock of Whaley Mill & Elevator Company be paid out of the general funds of Kimbell–Diamond Milling Company.

2. That as soon as practicable after the purchase of the Whaley Mill & Elevator Company stock hereby authorized has been consummated, all necessary steps be taken to completely liquidate the said corporation by transferring its entire assets, particularly its mill and milling equipment, to Kimbell–Diamond Milling Company in cancellation and redemption of the entire issued and outstanding capital stock of Whaley Mill & Elevator Company, and that the charter of said corporation be forthwith surrendered and cancelled.

On December 26, 1942, petitioner acquired 100 per cent of the stock of Whaley Mill & Elevator Co. of Gainesville, Texas, paying therefor $210,000 in cash which payment, to the extent of $118,200.16, was made with the insurance proceeds received by petitioner as a result of the fire on or about August 13, 1942.

On December 29, 1942, the stockholders of Whaley assented to the dissolution and distribution of assets thereof. On the same date an "Agreement and Program of Complete Liquidation" was entered into between petitioner and Whaley, which provided, inter alia:

THAT, WHEREAS, KIMBELL–DIAMOND owns the entire authorized issued and outstanding capital stock of WHALEY, consisting of 4000 shares of a par value of $100.00 per share, which said stock was acquired by KIMBELL–DIAMOND primarily for the purpose of enabling it to secure possession and ownership of the flour mill and milling plant owned by WHALEY, the parties herewith agree that the said mill and milling plant shall forthwith be conveyed to KIMBELL–DIAMOND by WHALEY under the following program for the complete liquidation of WHALEY viz:

(1) KIMBELL–DIAMOND shall cause the 4000 shares of the capital stock of WHALEY owned by it to be surrendered to WHALEY for cancellation and retirement, whereupon WHALEY shall forthwith convey, transfer and assign unto KIMBELL–DIAMOND all property of every kind and character owned or claimed by it, particularly its flour mill and milling plant, located at Gainesville, Texas, and all machinery and equipment appurtenant thereto, or used in connection therewith, in full and complete liquidation of all of the outstanding stock of WHALEY. The aforesaid distribution in complete liquidation shall be fully consummated by not later than midnight, December 31, 1942.

(2) When the entire assets of every kind and character, owned by WHALEY, have been transferred to Kimbell–Diamond in full and complete liquidation of the capital stock of WHALEY, owned by Kimbell–Diamond, WHALEY shall forthwith make application to the Secretary of State of the State of Texas for its dissolution as a corporation and surrender its corporate charter.

On December 31, 1942, the Secretary of State of the State of Texas certified that the Whaley Mill & Elevator Co. was dissolved as of that date. . .

There is no dispute that the petitioner's adjusted basis in its depreciable assets which were destroyed by fire was $18,921.90; nor that the depreciable assets which it received from Whaley had an adjusted basis in the hands of Whaley of $139,521.62. Petitioner, in the years herein involved, proceeded under the theory that it was entitled to Whaley's basis. Respondent takes the position that petitioner's cost is its basis in the assets acquired from Whaley. . . The petitioner does not controvert the allocation of cost made by respondent to the various assets acquired from Whaley, both depreciable and nondepreciable property. As to the depreciable assets purchased to replace those involuntarily converted, respondent contends that petitioner's basis is limited by [§ 1033(b)] of the Internal Revenue Code. . . Petitioner argues that the acquisition of Whaley's assets and the subsequent liquidation of Whaley brings petitioner within the provisions of [§ 332] and, therefore, by reason of [§ 334(b)(1)*] petitioner's basis in these assets is the same as the basis in Whaley's hands. In so contending, petitioner asks that we treat the acquisition of Whaley's stock and the subsequent liquidation of Whaley as separate transactions. It is well settled that the incidence of taxation depends upon the substance of a transaction. Commissioner v. Court Holding Co., 324 U.S. 331. It is inescapable from petitioner's minutes set out above and from the "Agreement and Program of Complete Liquidation" entered into between petitioner and Whaley, that the only intention petitioner ever had was to acquire Whaley's assets.

---

*There was no counterpart to § 334(b)(2) in the 1939 Code.—ED.

We think that this proceeding is governed by the principles of Commissioner v. Ashland Oil & Refining Co., 99 Fed. (2d) 588, certiorari denied, 306 U.S. 661. In that case the stock was retained for almost a year before liquidation. Ruling on the question of whether the stock or the assets of the corporation were purchased, the court stated:

> The question remains, however, whether if the entire transaction, whatever its form, was essentially in intent, purpose and result, a purchase by Swiss of property, its several steps may be treated separately and each be given an effect for tax purposes as though each constituted a distinct transaction... And without regard to whether the result is imposition or relief from taxation, the courts have recognized that where the essential nature of a transaction is the acquisition of property, it will be viewed as a whole, and closely related steps will not be separated either at the instance of the taxpayer or the taxing authority.

See also Koppers Coal Co., 6 T. C. 1209 and cases there cited.

We hold that the purchase of Whaley's stock and its subsequent liquidation must be considered as one transaction, namely, the purchase of Whaley's assets which was petitioner's sole intention. This was not a reorganization within [§ 332], and petitioner's basis in these assets, both depreciable and nondepreciable, is, therefore, its cost, or $110,721.74 ($18,921.90, the basis of petitioner's assets destroyed by fire, plus $91,799.84, the amount expended over the insurance proceeds). Since petitioner does not controvert respondent's allocation of cost to the individual assets acquired from Whaley, both depreciable and nondepreciable, respondent's allocation is sustained...

Decision will be entered for the respondent.

... Reviewed by the Court.

NOTE

Kimbell–Diamond led to great uncertainty. It was impossible to be sure when a taxpayer would succeed in bringing its apparent purchase of stock within the doctrine. Where a taxpayer wished to avoid application of the doctrine, however, it could readily do so by delaying the liquidation until a considerable period after the purchase of its stock had lapsed. To bring certainty to this area, Congress codified and expanded the *Kimbell–Diamond* rule. Its most recent incarnation is found in § 338, enacted as part of the Tax Equity and Fiscal Responsibility Act of 1982 (TEFRA), prior to the repeal of the *General Utilities* doctrine. A "general explanation" of § 338 follows.

Staff of the Joint Committee on Taxation, General Explanation of the Revenue Provisions of the Tax Equity and Fiscal Responsibility Act of 1982

131–139 (Dec. 31, 1982).

PRIOR LAW

Upon the complete liquidation of a subsidiary corporation, 80 percent of the voting power and 80 percent of the total number of shares of all other classes of stock (other than nonvoting preferred stock) of which is owned by the parent corporation, gain or loss is generally not recognized and the basis of the subsidiary's assets and its other tax attributes are carried over (secs. 332, 334(b)(1), and 381(a)).

Under prior law, however, if the controlling stock interest was acquired by purchase within a 12–month period and the subsidiary was liquidated pursuant to a plan of liquidation adopted within 2 years after the qualifying stock purchase was completed, the transaction was treated as in substance a purchase of the subsidiary's assets (sec. 334(b)(2)). The acquiring corporation's basis in the "purchased" assets was the cost of the stock purchased as adjusted for items such as liabilities assumed, certain cash or dividend distributions to the acquiring corporation, and postacquisition earnings and profits of the subsidiary. The liquidating distributions could be made over a 3–year period beginning with the close of the taxable year during which the first of a series of distributions occurs (sec. 332(b)(3)). Thus, this treatment applied even though the liquidation could extend over a 5–year period after control had been acquired.

In these cases, when the assets were treated as purchased by the acquiring corporation, recapture income was taxed to the liquidating corporation, the investment tax credit recapture provisions were applicable, and tax attributes, including carryovers, of the liquidated corporation were terminated.

Cases interpreting the law applicable before the rules in section 334(b)(2) were adopted, treated the purchase of stock and prompt liquidation in some cases as a purchase of assets (Kimbell–Diamond Milling Co. v. Commissioner 14 T.C. 74, aff'd per curiam, 187 F.2d 718 (5th Cir.), cert. denied, 342 US 827 (1951)). It is not clear whether such treatment still applied after the enactment of section 334(b)(2) in cases where the requirements of that provision were not met.

A stock purchase and liquidation was treated as a purchase of all the assets of the acquired corporation under prior law if section 334(b)(2) applied. Revision of the special treatment of partial liquidations under the Act restricts the options of a corporate purchaser seeking to treat a purchase of a corporation as a purchase of assets in part combined with a continuation of the tax attributes of the acquired entity. Neither prior law nor the Act's revision of the treatment of partial liquidations restrict a corporate purchaser from achieving such selectivity by purchasing assets directly from a corporation while concurrently purchasing the corporation's stock. Selectivity could also be achieved if an acquired corporation, prior to the acquisition, dispersed its assets in tax-free transactions among several corporations which could be separately purchased. The corporate purchaser then through selective qualifying liquidations could obtain asset purchase treatment for one or more acquired corporations while preserving the tax attributes of one or more other corporations. . .

EXPLANATION OF PROVISIONS

GENERAL TREATMENT OF STOCK PURCHASE AS ASSET PURCHASE

The Act repeals the provision of prior law (sec. 334(b)(2)) that treated a purchase and liquidation of a subsidiary as an asset purchase. The amendments made by the Act were also intended to replace any nonstatutory treatment of a stock purchase as an asset purchase under the Kimbell–Diamond doctrine. Instead, an acquiring corporation, within 75 days after a qualified stock purchase, except as regulations may provide for a later election, may elect to treat an acquired subsidiary (target corporation) as if it sold all its assets pursuant to a plan of complete liquidation at the close of the stock acquisition date. The target corporation will be treated as a new corporation that purchased the assets on the day following such date. Gain or loss will not be recognized to the target corporation, except for gain or loss attributable to stock held by minority shareholders as described below, to the same extent gain or loss is not recognized (sec. 337) when a corporation sells all its assets in the course of a complete liquidation. This provision was intended to provide nonrecognition of gain or loss to the same extent that gain or loss would not be recognized under section 336 if there were an actual liquidation of the target corporation on the acquisition date to which prior law section 334(b)(2) applied.

If, because of the application of other provisions of the Internal Revenue Code, the rules of section 337 providing for nonrecognition of gain or loss on the disposition of assets are made inapplicable, gain or loss is recognized under section 338. For example, section 337 does not apply to a sale or exchange of a United States real property interest by a foreign corporation (sec. 897(d)(2)). Thus, if the target corporation is a foreign corporation holding an interest in U.S. real property, gain or loss allocable to such interest is recognized if the acquiring corporation makes an election to which section 338(a) applies. . .

A qualified stock purchase occurs if 80 percent or more of the voting power and 80 percent of the total number of shares of other classes of stock (except nonvoting, preferred stock) is acquired by purchase during a 12–month period (the acquisition period). The acquisition date is the date within such acquisition period on which the 80–percent purchase requirement (the qualified stock purchase) is satisfied. Generally, the 80–percent purchase requirement may be satisfied through the combination of stock purchases and redemptions. However, it is expected that the regulations will provide rules to prevent selective asset distributions.

The election is to be made in the manner prescribed by regulations and, once made, will be irrevocable.

TREATMENT OF TARGET CORPORATION AS NEW CORPORATION

The assets of the target corporation will be treated as sold (and purchased) for an amount equal to the grossed up basis of the acquiring corporation in the stock of the target corporation on the acquisition date. The amount is to be adjusted under regulations for liabilities of the target corporation and other relevant items. It was anticipated that recapture tax liability of the target corporation attributable to the deemed sale of its assets is an item which may result in an adjustment under the regulations.

Under the gross-up formula, if the acquiring corporation owns less than 100 percent by value of the target corporation's stock on the acquisition date, the deemed purchase price is grossed up [as provided in § 338(b)—ED.]. It was not intended that minority shareholders in the target corporation be treated as having exchanged their shares for stock in the new corporation. However, nonrecognition of gain or loss to the target corporation is limited, unless the target corporation is liquidated within one year after the acquisition date, to the highest actual percentage by value of target corporation stock held by the acquiring corporation during the one-year period beginning on the acquisition date. . .

The Act provides that the deemed sale (and purchase) of all its assets by the target corporation applies for purposes of subtitle A of the Internal Revenue Code and is deemed to occur at the close of the acquisition date in a single transaction. Under these rules, the provisions of subtitle F of the Code relating to assessment, collection, refunds, statutes of limitations, and other procedural matters apply without regard to the status of the target corporation as a new corporation. The target corporation thus remains liable for any tax liabilities incurred by it for any period prior to the election. The target corporation is required to file an income tax return for its taxable year ending as of the close of the acquisition date. . .

DEFINITION OF PURCHASE

The term "purchase" is defined as it was under prior law (sec. 334(b)(3)) to exclude acquisitions of stock with a carryover basis or from a decedent, acquisitions in an exchange to which section 351 applies, and acquisitions from a person whose ownership is attributed to the acquiring person under section 318(a). Attribution under section 318(a)(4) relating to options will be disregarded for this purpose. However, if, as a result of a stock purchase, the purchasing corporation is treated under section 318(a) as owning stock in a third corporation, the purchasing corporation will be treated as having purchased stock in such third corporation but not until the first day on which ownership of such stock is considered as owned by the purchasing corporation under section 318(a). This rule may be illustrated by the following example:

Assume a target corporation and a third corporation each have only one class of stock outstanding and that the target corporation owns 50 percent of the stock of the third corporation. The purchasing corporation purchases 20 percent of the target corporation on each of five separate dates, January 1, April 1, July 1, October 1, and December 31, 1983. Under section 318(a), no portion of the stock of the third corporation is constructively owned by the purchasing corporation until July 1, 1983, the date on which its ownership of the target corporation first exceeds 50 percent (sec. 318(a)(2)(C)). On that date, the purchasing corporation is treated as purchasing 30 percent (60 percent of 50 percent) of the third corporation. By virtue of the remaining purchases of the target corporation stock, the purchasing corporation will be treated as having purchased 50 percent of the third corporation's stock by December 31, 1983. If, by June 30, 1984 (the end of the 12–month acquisition period applicable to the third corporation), either the purchasing corporation or the target corporation purchases an additional 30 percent of the third corporation, an election, if made for the target corporation, would also apply to the third corporation.

In the above example, the amount for which the assets of the third corporation are treated as sold (and purchased) is determined by reference to the portion of the price paid for the target corporation's stock allocable to the 50–percent interest in the third corporation's stock owned by the target corporation plus any amount paid to purchase an additional 30 percent of such stock after December 31, 1983, and within the remaining portion of the acquisition period applicable to the third corporation. If ownership of the third corporation is less than 100 percent on the acquisition date, the basis so determined is grossed up pursuant to section 338(b)(2).

A purchase of over 80 percent but less than 100 percent of the stock of a target corporation which in turn owns 80 percent of the stock of a third corporation is not a qualified stock purchase with respect to the third corporation because the purchasing corporation has not acquired by purchase the requisite 80 percent of the third corporation's stock. This is so, even though the purchasing corporation, the target corporation, and the third corporation constitute an affiliated group as defined in section 1504(a).

CONSISTENCY REQUIREMENT

The rules require consistency where the purchasing corporation makes qualified stock purchases of two or more corporations that are members of the same affiliated group. For this purpose, purchases by a member of the purchasing corporation's affiliated group, except as regulations provide otherwise, are treated as purchases by the purchasing corporation.[2] The consistency requirement applies as well to a combination of a direct asset acquisition and qualified stock purchase.

The consistency requirement applies with respect to purchases over a defined "consistency period" determined by reference to the acquisition date

---

[2] Transfers of target corporation stock within the purchasing corporation's affiliated group will not disqualify a section 338 election (cf. Chrome Plate Inc. v. United States, 614 F.2d 990 (5th Cir. 1980)).

applicable to the target corporation. The "consistency period" is the one-year period preceding the target corporation acquisition period plus the portion of the acquisition period up to and including the acquisition date, and the one-year period following the acquisition date. Thus, if all the target corporation's stock is purchased on the same day by the purchasing corporation, the one-year period immediately preceding and the one-year period immediately following such day are included in the consistency period. If, within such period, there is a direct purchase of assets from the target corporation or a target affiliate by the purchasing corporation, the rules require that the acquisition of the target corporation be treated as an asset purchase.

The consistency period may be expanded in appropriate cases by the Secretary where there is in effect a plan to make several qualified stock purchases or any such purchase and asset acquisition with respect to a target corporation and its target affiliates.

The consistency requirement is applied to an affiliated group with reference to a target corporation and any "target affiliate." A corporation is defined as a "target affiliate" of the target corporation if each was, at any time during that portion of the consistency period ending on the acquisition date of the target corporation, a member of an affiliated group that had the same common parent. An affiliated group has the same meaning given to such term by section 1504(a) (without regard to the exceptions in sec. 1504(b)). This definition also applies in determining whether a purchase is made by a member of the same affiliated group as the purchasing corporation.

An acquisition of assets from the target corporation or a target affiliate during the consistency period applicable to the target corporation will require the qualified stock purchase of the target corporation to be treated as a purchase of assets. In applying these rules, stock in a target affiliate is not to be treated as an asset of any other target affiliate or of the target corporation.

In applying these rules, acquisitions of assets pursuant to sales by the target corporation or a target affiliate in the ordinary course of its trade or business and acquisitions in which the basis of assets is carried over will not cause the consistency requirement to apply. The sale by a target corporation will be considered as a sale in the ordinary course of business for this purpose even though it is not customary in the course of the selling corporation's business provided it is a transaction that is a normal incident to the conduct of a trade or business, such as a sale of used machinery that was employed in the seller's trade or business.

Where there are, within a consistency period, only qualified stock purchases of the target corporation and one or more target affiliates by the purchasing corporation, an election with respect to the first purchase will apply to the later purchases. A failure to make the election for the first purchase will preclude any election for later purchases.

To prevent avoidance of the consistency requirements, the Act authorizes the Secretary to treat stock acquisitions which are pursuant to a plan and which satisfy the 80–percent requirement to be treated as qualified stock purchases even though they are not otherwise so defined. For example, an acquiring corporation may acquire 79 percent of the stock of a target corporation and, within a year, purchase assets from such corporation or a target affiliate planning to purchase the remaining target corporation stock more than one year after the original stock purchase. The Secretary may under these circumstances treat the purchase of the target corporation's stock as a deemed sale of its assets by the target corporation. The Act also authorizes such regulations as may be necessary to ensure that the requirements of consistency of treatment of stock and asset purchases with respect to a target corporation and its target affiliates are not circumvented through the use of other provisions of the law or regulations, including the consolidated return regulations. . . [See § 338(i)—ED.]

The application of the consistency requirements is illustrated in the following examples. . .

Example 1. The acquiring corporation makes a qualified stock purchase of T's stock and within a one-year period purchases assets from T or a target affiliate of T. The acquiring corporation is deemed to have made an election with respect to T as of the acquisition date applicable to T.

Example 2. The acquiring corporation makes a qualified stock purchase of T's stock and makes the election within 75 days of the acquisition date. The acquiring corporation is treated as having acquired by purchase the stock of any other corporation owned by T actually or constructively which is attributed to the acquiring corporation under section 318(a) (other than sec. 318(a)(4)). To the extent that such treatment results in qualified stock purchases by the acquiring corporation of other corporations actually or constructively owned by T, the election with respect to T applies to all such corporations. Each such corporation will be treated as having sold (and as having purchased as a "new" corporation) its assets on the acquisition date with respect to T. Gain or loss will not be recognized to the extent gain or loss is not recognized under section 337. The deemed sale price of the assets will be determined by reference to the grossed-up amount allocated to the stock of each selling corporation as a result of the qualified stock purchase and election with respect to T.

Example 3. P, an acquiring corporation, makes a qualified stock purchase of all the stock of corporation T on February 1, 1983. No election is made. On December 1, 1983, P makes a qualified stock purchase of all the stock of corporation U, a target affiliate of corporation T. No election may be made with respect to corporation U. . .

NOTES

1. At the time that § 338 was enacted in 1982, when a corporation elected to treat its newly acquired subsidiary as effectively selling and repurchasing its assets (allowing a new, presumably higher, basis) the subsidiary generally did not recognize gain or loss on the election, due to the then existing § 337 provision (implementing *General Utilities*). The major impact of the 1986 Act on § 338 was in the repeal of "old" § 337 (the repeal of *General Utilities*). After 1986, an election to step up the basis in a subsidiary's assets under § 338 results in taxable gain. Thus, a § 338 election now raises different issues for taxpayers and policymakers. Many people believe that with the repeal of *General Utilities*, the consistency requirements of § 338 should also be repealed. What do you think? During the early 1990s and into 2001, the Treasury revised the regulations implementing the consistency requirement to limit the number of cases in which the provisions would apply, focusing primarily on certain consolidated return situations. (See 59 Fed. Reg. 2958 (Jan. 20, 1994) redesignated by 8858, 65 Red. Reg. 1236 (Jan. 5, 2000) and amended by TD 8940, 66 Fed. Reg. 9925 (Feb. 12, 2001)).

Given that the target will generally recognize gain now that the *General Utilities* doctrine has been repealed, in what situations would it make sense to make a § 338 election?

After 1986, the § 338 election was often undesirable, and taxpayers were concerned that they would inadvertently trigger an election (for example by violating the consistency requirements). The revised consistency regulations of the 1990s substantially narrowed the consistency requirements and thus essentially eliminated the risk of unintended election.

2. Section 338(h)(10) provides an alternative to the basic § 338 election. Instead of having the election operate on the purchaser of the target corporation, § 338(h)(10) is available to the seller: if a selling consolidated group makes an (h)(10) election, the selling corporation recognizes no gain or loss on the sale of the target's stock, but the target must recognize gain or loss as if it had sold its assets. The following excerpt from the 1986 Conference Report described part of the motivation for providing the (h)(10) election in the statute, and then explains the important changes that the 1986 Act made to the (h)(10) election:

ELECTION TO TREAT SALES OR DISTRIBUTIONS OF CERTAIN SUBSIDIARY STOCK AS ASSET TRANSFERS

The conference agreement generally conforms the treatment of liquidating sales and distributions of subsidiary stock to the present law treatment of nonliquidating sales or distributions of such stock; thus, such liquidating sales or distributions are generally taxable at the corporate level. The conferees believe it is appropriate to conform the treatment of liquidating and nonliquidating sales or distributions and to require recognition when appreciated property, including stock of a subsidiary, is transferred to a corporate or an individual recipient outside the economic unit of the selling or distributing affiliated group.

Section 338(h)(10) of present law, in certain circumstances, permits a corporate purchaser and a seller of an 80–percent–controlled subsidiary to elect to treat the sale of the subsidiary stock as if it had been a sale of the underlying assets. Among the requirements for the filing of an election under section 338(h)(10) are that the selling corporation and its target subsidiary are members of an affiliated group filing a consolidated return for the taxable year that includes the acquisition date. If an election is made, the underlying assets of the company that was sold receive a stepped-up, fair market value basis; the selling consolidated group recognizes the gain or loss attributable to the assets; and there is no separate tax on the seller's gain attributable to the stock. This provision offers taxpayers relief from a potential multiple taxation at the corporate level of the same economic gain, which may result when a transfer of appreciated corporate stock is taxed without providing a corresponding step-up in basis of the assets of the corporation. The conference agreement, following the House bill, retains this provision.

In addition, the conference agreement permits the expansion of the section 338(h)(10) concept, to the extent provided in regulations, to situations in which the selling corporation owns 80 percent of the value and voting power of the subsidiary, but does not file a consolidated return. Moreover, the conference agreement provides that, under regulations, principles similar to those of section 338(h)(10) may be applied to taxable sales or distributions of controlled corporation stock. . .

The conferees do not intend this election to affect the manner in which a corporation's distribution to its shareholders will be characterized for purposes of determining the shareholder level income tax consequences.

H.R. Conf. Rep. No. 841, 99th Cong., 2d Sess., pt. 2, at 203 (1986).

3. When would a selling parent want to make an (h)(10) election? (Hint: think about the tax treatment a selling parent is likely to face in the absence of such an election). Are those circumstances more likely to exist post–1986 repeal of *General Utilities* than the circumstances that make a purchaser's basic § 338 election sensible?

4. Look at § 336(e) which is a companion to the § 338(h)(10) election. The (h)(10) election allows a selling parent to avoid recognition of gain or loss on the *sale* of the subsidiary stock. Section 336(e), enacted in 1986, expands the realm of nonrecognition by authorizing the Treasury to issue regulations that would permit the parent to avoid recognition where the subsidiary stock is disposed of by *exchange* or *distribution* of the stock. As with the (h)(10) election, the price of making the § 336(e) election is immediate recognition of gain as if the subsidiary's assets had been sold, exchanged or distributed. Although the IRS issued proposed regulations in August 25, 2008, final regulations have yet to be issued. The IRS determined in a legal memorandum that § 336(e) is not self-executing and effective final regulations are required before § 336(e) elections can be made. This determination was made by looking at the congressional intent, which shows that the regulations are not retroactive. (Office of Chief Counsel IRS Memorandum, written 11/24/09, release date 3/5/10, CCM 201009013).

B. DEDUCTIONS OF THE CORPORATION: SPECIAL RULES

Generally, the rules governing the business deductions of a corporation are substantially the same as those for individuals. However, there are some circumstances in which corporate "expenditures" raise unique deduction questions. As with the special corporate income rules considered above in Part A, the special deduction rules typically involve transactions between a corporation and its present or prospective investors.

1. DISTRIBUTIONS OF PROPERTY (INCLUDING CASH)

Outlays by a corporation raise the question of whether the distribution constitutes a deductible business payment, or a nondeductible return to shareholders (whether in the form of dividends or redemptions). The distinction can be critical to the corporation because business expenses are generally deductible whereas distributions to shareholders are not (the core of the classical tax regime). From the perspective of the recipient the characterization of the payment as a dividend or some other amount, such as interest may be important if, for example, the special reduced rates on dividends enacted in 2003 apply. The treatment of shareholders is considered in Chapter 2.

a. Dividend vs. Interest—§ 163

Fin Hay Realty Co. v. United States
398 F.2d 694 (3d Cir. 1968).

■ Before HASTIE, CHIEF JUDGE, FREEDMAN and VAN DUSEN, CIRCUIT JUDGES.

■ FREEDMAN, CIRCUIT JUDGE. We are presented in this case with the recurrent problem whether funds paid to a close corporation by its shareholders were additional contributions to capital or loans on which the corporation's payment of interest was deductible under § 163 of the Internal Revenue Code of 1954.

The problem necessarily calls for an evaluation of the facts, which we therefore detail.

Fin Hay Realty Co., the taxpayer, was organized on February 14, 1934, by Frank L. Finlaw and J. Louis Hay. Each of them contributed $10,000 for which he received one-half of the corporation's stock and at the same time each advanced an additional $15,000 for which the corporation issued to him its unsecured promissory note payable on demand and bearing interest at the rate of six per cent per annum. The corporation immediately purchased an apartment house in Newark, New Jersey, for $39,000 in cash. About a month later the two shareholders each advanced an additional $35,000 to the corporation in return for six per cent demand promissory notes and next day the corporation purchased two apartment buildings in East Orange, New Jersey, for which it paid $75,000 in cash and gave the seller a six per cent, five year purchase money mortgage for the balance of $100,000.

Three years later, in October, 1937, the corporation created a new mortgage on all three properties and from the proceeds paid off the old mortgage on the East Orange property, which had been partially amortized. The new mortgage was for a five year term in the amount of $82,000 with interest at four and one-half per cent. In the following three years each of the shareholders advanced an additional $3,000 to the corporation, bringing the total advanced by each shareholder to $53,000, in addition to their acknowledged stock subscriptions of $10,000 each.

Finlaw died in 1941 and his stock and notes passed to his two daughters in equal shares. A year later the mortgage, which was about to fall due, was extended for a further period of five years with interest at four per cent. From the record it appears that it was subsequently extended until 1951. In 1949 Hay died and in 1951 his executor requested the retirement of his stock and the payment of his notes. The corporation thereupon refinanced its real estate for $125,000 and sold one of the buildings. With the net proceeds it paid Hay's estate $24,000 in redemption of his stock and $53,000 in retirement of his notes.[4] Finlaw's daughters then became and still remain the sole shareholders of the corporation.

Thereafter the corporation continued to pay and deduct interest on Finlaw's notes, now held by his two daughters. In 1962 the Internal Revenue Service for the first time declared the payments on the notes not allowable as interest deductions and disallowed them for the tax years 1959 and 1960. The corporation thereupon repaid a total of $6,000 on account of the outstanding notes and in the following year after refinancing the mortgage on its real estate repaid the balance of $47,000. A short time later the Internal Revenue Service disallowed the interest deductions for the years 1961 and 1962. When the corporation failed to obtain refunds it brought this refund action in the district court. After a nonjury trial the court denied the claims and entered judgment for the United States. 261 F.Supp. 823 (D.N.J. 1967). From this judgment the corporation appeals.

This case arose in a factual setting where it is the corporation which is the party concerned that its obligations be deemed to represent a debt and not a stock interest. In the long run in cases of this kind it is also important to the shareholder that his advance be deemed a loan rather than a capital contribution, for in such a case his receipt of repayment may be treated as the retirement of a loan rather than a taxable dividend.[6] There are other instances in which it is in the shareholder's interest that his advance to the

---

[4] The record is fragmentary and provides no clear basis from which to reconstruct the events of 1951. It may perhaps be inferred from it that Hay's estate received the total of $77,000 solely for the redemption of his stock and that the notes of $53,000 were retired either from the proceeds of the sale of real estate or in some other manner during the same year. In such event the total paid in redemption of Hay's stock and the retirement of his notes would be $130,000 rather than $77,000.

[6] The partial retirement of an equity interest may be considered as essentially equivalent to a dividend under § 302, while the repayment of even a debt whose principal has appreciated is taxed only as a capital gain under § 1232.

corporation be considered a debt rather than an increase in his equity. A loss resulting from the worthlessness of stock is a capital loss under § 165(g), whereas a bad debt may be treated as an ordinary loss if it qualifies as a business bad debt under § 166. Similarly, it is only if a taxpayer receives debt obligations of a controlled corporation[7] that he can avoid the provision for nonrecognition of gains or losses on transfers of property to such a corporation under § 351.[8] These advantages in having the funds entrusted to a corporation treated as corporate obligations instead of contributions to capital have required the courts to look beyond the literal terms in which the parties have cast the transaction in order to determine its substantive nature.

In attempting to deal with this problem courts and commentators have isolated a number of criteria by which to judge the true nature of an investment which is in form a debt: (1) the intent of the parties; (2) the identity between creditors and shareholders; (3) the extent of participation in management by the holder of the instrument; (4) the ability of the corporation to obtain funds from outside sources; (5) the "thinness" of the capital structure in relation to debt; (6) the risk involved; (7) the formal indicia of the arrangement; (8) the relative position of the obligees as to other creditors regarding the payment of interest and principal; (9) the voting power of the holder of the instrument; (10) the provision of a fixed rate of interest; (11) a contingency on the obligation to repay; (12) the source of the interest payments; (13) the presence or absence of a fixed maturity date; (14) a provision for redemption by the corporation; (15) a provision for redemption at the option of the holder; and (16) the timing of the advance with reference to the organization of the corporation.

While the Internal Revenue Code of 1954 was under consideration, and after its adoption, Congress sought to identify the criteria which would determine whether an investment represents a debt or equity, but these and similar efforts have not found acceptance. It still remains true that neither any single criterion nor any series of criteria can provide a conclusive answer in the kaleidoscopic circumstances which individual cases present. See John Kelley Co. v. Commissioner of Internal Revenue, 326 U.S. 521, 530 . . . (1946).

The various factors which have been identified in the cases are only aids in answering the ultimate question whether the investment, analyzed in terms of its economic reality, constitutes risk capital entirely subject to the fortunes of the corporate venture or represents a strict debtor-creditor relationship. Since there is often an element of risk in a loan, just as there is an element of risk in an equity interest, the conflicting elements do not end at a clear line in all cases.

---

[7] While not all debt obligations qualify for the desired tax treatment, equity interests can never qualify.

[8] A taxpayer might wish to avoid § 351 when he transfers depreciated property to the corporation and seeks to recognize the loss immediately and also when the transferred property is to be resold by the corporation but will not qualify for capital gains treatment in the hands of the corporation.

In a corporation which has numerous shareholders with varying interests, the arm's-length relationship between the corporation and a shareholder who supplies funds to it inevitably results in a transaction whose form mirrors its substance. Where the corporation is closely held, however, and the same persons occupy both sides of the bargaining table, form does not necessarily correspond to the intrinsic economic nature of the transaction, for the parties may mold it at their will with no countervailing pull. This is particularly so where a shareholder can have the funds he advances to a corporation treated as corporate obligations instead of contributions to capital without affecting his proportionate equity interest. Labels, which are perhaps the best expression of the subjective intention of parties to a transaction, thus lose their meaningfulness.

To seek economic reality in objective terms of course disregards the personal interest which a shareholder may have in the welfare of the corporation in which he is a dominant force. But an objective standard is one imposed by the very fact of his dominant position and is much fairer than one which would presumptively construe all such transactions against the shareholder's interest. Under an objective test of economic reality it is useful to compare the form which a similar transaction would have taken had it been between the corporation and an outside lender, and if the shareholder's advance is far more speculative than what an outsider would make, it is obviously a loan in name only.

In the present case all the formal indicia of an obligation were meticulously made to appear. The corporation, however, was the complete creature of the two shareholders who had the power to create whatever appearance would be of tax benefit to them despite the economic reality of the transaction. Each shareholder owned an equal proportion of stock and was making an equal additional contribution, so that whether Finlaw and Hay designated any part of their additional contributions as debt or as stock would not dilute their proportionate equity interests. There was no restriction because of the possible excessive debt structure, for the corporation had been created to acquire real estate and had no outside creditors except mortgagees who, of course, would have no concern for general creditors because they had priority in the security of the real estate. The position of the mortgagees also rendered of no significance the possible subordination of the notes to other debts of the corporation, a matter which in some cases this Court has deemed significant.

The shareholders here, moreover, lacked one of the principal advantages of creditors. Although the corporation issued demand notes for the advances, nevertheless, as the court below found, it could not have repaid them for a number of years. The economic reality was that the corporation used the proceeds of the notes to purchase its original assets, and the advances represented a long term commitment dependent on the future value of the real estate and the ability of the corporation to sell or refinance it. Only because such an entwining of interest existed between the two shareholders and the corporation, so different from the arm's-length relationship between a corporation and an outside creditor, were they willing to invest in the notes and allow them to go unpaid for so many years while the corporation continued to enjoy the advantages of uninterrupted ownership of its real estate.

It is true that real estate values rose steadily with a consequent improvement in the mortgage market, so that looking back the investment now appears to have been a good one. As events unfolded, the corporation reached a point at which it could have repaid the notes through refinancing, but this does not obliterate the uncontradicted testimony that in 1934 it was impossible to obtain any outside mortgage financing for real estate of this kind except through the device of a purchase money mortgage taken back by the seller.

It is argued that the rate of interest at six per cent per annum was far more than the shareholders could have obtained from other investments. This argument, however, is self-defeating, for it implies that the shareholders would damage their own corporation by an overcharge for interest. There was, moreover, enough objective evidence to neutralize this contention. The outside mortgage obtained at the time the corporation purchased the East Orange property bore interest at the rate of six per cent even though the mortgagee was protected by an equity in excess of forty per cent of the value of the property.[9] In any event, to compare the six per cent interest rate of the notes with other 1934 rates ignores the most salient feature of the notes—their risk. It is difficult to escape the inference that a prudent outside businessman would not have risked his capital in six per cent unsecured demand notes in Fin Hay Realty Co. in 1934. The evidence therefore amply justifies the conclusion of the district court that the form which the parties gave to their transaction did not match its economic reality.

It is argued that even if the advances may be deemed to have been contributions to capital when they were originally made in 1934, a decisive change occurred when the original shareholder, Finlaw, died and his heirs continued to hold the notes without demanding payment. This, it is said could be construed as a decision to reinvest, and if by 1941 the notes were sufficiently secure to be considered bona fide debt, they should now be so treated for tax purposes. Such a conclusion, however, does not inevitably follow. Indeed, the weight of the circumstances leads to the opposite conclusion.

First, there is nothing in the record to indicate that the corporation could have readily raised the cash with which to pay off Finlaw's notes on his death in 1941. When Hay, the other shareholder, died in 1949 and his executor two years later requested the retirement of his interest, the corporation in order to carry this out sold one of its properties and refinanced the others. Again, when in 1963 the corporation paid off the notes held by Finlaw's daughters after the Internal Revenue Service had disallowed the interest deductions for 1961 and 1962 it again refinanced its real estate.

---

[9] The corporation purchased the property for $175,000 and the sellers took back a purchase money mortgage of $100,000.

There is nothing in the record which would sustain a finding that the corporation could have readily undertaken a similar financing in 1941, when Finlaw died even if we assume that the corporation was able to undertake the appropriate refinancing ten years later to liquidate Hay's interest. Moreover, there was no objective evidence to indicate that in 1941 Finlaw's daughters viewed the notes as changed in character or in security, or indeed that they viewed the stock and notes as separate and distinct investments. To indulge in a theoretical conversion of equity contributions into a debt obligation in 1941 when Finlaw died would be to ignore what such a conversion might have entailed. For Finlaw's estate might then have been chargeable with the receipt of dividends at the time the equity was redeemed and converted into a debt. To recognize retrospectively such a change in the character of the obligation would be to assume a conclusion with consequences unfavorable to the parties, which they themselves never acknowledged.

The burden was on the taxpayer to prove that the determination by the Internal Revenue Service that advances represented capital contributions was incorrect. The district court was justified in holding that the taxpayer had not met this burden.

The judgment of the district court will be affirmed.

■ VAN DUSEN, CIRCUIT JUDGE (dissenting). I respectfully dissent on the ground that the "entire evidence," in light of appellate court decisions discussing the often-presented problem of corporate debt versus equity, does not permit the conclusion reached by the District Court.

When the parties holding debt of the taxpayer corporation have a formal debt obligation and it is clear that all parties intended the investment to take the form of debt, a series of considerations such as those mentioned by the District Court should be used to determine whether the form and intent should be disregarded for federal tax purposes. Tomlinson v. 1661 Corporation, 377 F.2d 291 (5th Cir. 1967); J.S. Biritz Construction Co. v. C.I.R., 387 F.2d 451, 455–56 (8th Cir. 1967). As I read the District Court's opinion, the focus was entirely on inferring "the intent of the taxpayer's only two stockholders" at the time the debt was created. To that end, the District Court drew certain inferences which are largely immaterial to the proper decision, and which are clearly erroneous in light of the stipulated facts and uncontroverted evidence.

Whether or not the corporate taxpayer is entitled to an interest deduction turns in this case on the "real nature of the transaction in question" or on whether "the degree of risk may be said to be reasonably equivalent to that which equity capital would bear had an investor, under similar circumstances, made the advances. . ." Diamond Bros. Company v. C.I.R., 322 F.2d 725, 732 (3d Cir. 1963); Tomlinson v. 1661 Corporation, supra, at 295. When this test is used, the entire history of the corporate taxpayer becomes relevant and a focus solely on the year of incorporation or investment of the debt is not sufficient.

Turning within this framework to the facts, the record does not justify the conclusion that the form of the debt should be disregarded for purposes of federal taxation. The debt was evidenced by written notes, carried 6% interest which was paid every year, and was not subordinated in any way to similar debt of general creditors. It was carried on the corporate books and tax returns as debt, being payable on demand, it was always listed as a debt maturing in less than one year,[10] and on Mr. Finlaw's estate tax return was listed as promissory notes payable on demand.[11] The parties clearly intended the advances as debt and unfailingly treated them as such. The only testimony on the usual capitalization of real estate companies in the Newark area was that:

> The usual capitalization is a thousand dollar investment in capital and then the rest of the monies are loaned either . . . by individuals or stockholders of the corporation to the corporation, which in turn the individuals lending the money expect a return for their loans. . .

> [Of the real estate corporations that] I have dealt with, at least ninety-five per cent and more have had a thousand capitalization and, of course, loans from the various lenders would depend upon the size of the transaction, monies that were required.

On this record, Conclusions of Law 3–8 as worded are not justified. The District Court placed heavy reliance on the fact that the stockholder's debt was in the same proportion as their equity holdings. This fact, without more, is not controlling since there is no doubt that investors can have a dual status. The inferences that "more" was involved in this case are not justified by this record. The fact that the loans were used to begin the corporate life and buy the income-producing assets must be placed in proper perspective. Without any basis in the record, the District Court assumed that the loans were advanced to prevent a sudden corporate deficit that was created by the Wainwright Street property investment's unexpectedly requiring more funds than the corporation had. Real estate cases, however, and uncontroverted testimony in this case show that corporations owning and operating buildings frequently and traditionally borrow the substantial part of money needed to secure their principal assets and that this was contemplated by a corporate resolution passed in the month of organization at the original directors' meeting. Cases denying the validity of debt because it is contemporaneously advanced with the start of corporate life generally involve other industries or a partnership becoming a corporation.

---

[10] Apparently the District Court regarded demand notes as having no fixed maturity, see Conclusion of Law 4. This seems incorrect since demand paper means that the debt is "mature" at the holder's option. The better characterization would seem to be that demand notes held by someone with a voice in management are a type of long-term investment. See, e.g., Taft v. C.I.R., 314 F.2d 620 (9th Cir. 1963).

[11] This consistent treatment does not, of course, estop either the Commissioner or the taxpayer any more than the decision in this case controls the tax status of repaid principal on these loans in the hands of the remaining Fin Hay shareholders. The Government may well have sought to challenge these corporate interest deductions before challenging the individuals' returns as a matter of tactics, but this, and the question of the tax consequences of the liquidation of the remaining loans in 1962–1963, should not influence the decision in the present case, see Budd Company v. United States, 252 F.2d 456, 458 (3d Cir. 1957).

The loans were denied debt status because there was no intent to seek repayment within a "reasonable time," because the corporation had no retirement provision (or fund) for the principal and because the debt had no maturity date (Conclusions 3 and 4). To the contrary, demand notes have a maturity date at the discretion of the holder (or of his transferee when the notes are freely negotiable, as were the Fin Hay notes). And failure to transfer the notes or demand payment is irrelevant when, as here, the evidence shows that the 6% rate made the debt a good investment. In addition, when a corporation holds appreciating real estate and contemplates recourse to refinancing, the lack of a sinking fund assumes little, if any, significance. There was no evidence and no discussion of what constitutes a "reasonable time" for refraining from making a demand on such a promissory note.

The loans were also found to be equity because redemption was expected only out of future earnings or surplus and because they were unsecured and subordinate to prior secured loans (Conclusions 6 and 8). To the contrary, the evidence shows that the parties contemplated redemption out of "refinancing" as well if a demand were made when surplus was deficient; and this in fact was what happened in 1951 and 1962–1963. Corporate debt does not become equity because it is contemplated that principal will be retired by refinancing. In addition, a review of the "subordination" cases shows that there was no "subordination" in this case as that term is used in other cases where the challenged debt was subordinated to all other debt of similar type or otherwise subordinated by agreement.

The District Court also placed emphasis on the fact that at the end of 1935 the shareholders' salaries were accrued but unpaid in the amount of $2400 and that in 1938 through 1940 the shareholders advanced an additional $6000 as loans. The corporate tax returns and books, however, show that the salaries could have been paid at the end of 1935 from $4,340.21 in cash on deposit, and that during the period of the additional loans of $6000 the shareholders received $6800 in dividends from the corporation. These additional facts, unexplained by the District Court, negate the implication that Fin Hay Realty Company was in serious financial trouble at the outset of its existence, at least to any such degree that all the challenged loans were made "at a risk" similar to that of venture capital. It is noted, in addition, that by 1938, when the original purchase money mortgage was re-financed, $18,000 of principal had been paid.

Although appellate decisions on the debt-equity problem constantly reiterate the maxim that each instance of definition turns on the particular facts of each case, a reading of many of these cases, including all those cited above, indicates two rather distinct conclusions concerning the assessment of the severity of the "risk" attached to alleged debt transactions. First, when the problem of definition arises under 26 U.S.C. §§ 165, 166 (worthless stock, bad debt), the risk of failure has already been realized and the party seeking to minimize the degree of such risk must show more "factors" than otherwise clearly argue for a debt classification. Secondly, regardless of the end purpose for defining indebtedness, fewer factors need be present (such as subordination, no interest, etc.) to allow a conclusion of "equity" when, as a matter of common knowledge, the economic enterprise has a higher chance of commercial failure. Consequently, few cases (and particularly few where taxpayers holding formal debt lose) deny debt status or even raise the question where the enterprise risk, as in this case, involves the mere holding and operation of real estate. As the risks increase, involving in addition construction of the real estate, or non-real estate operations subject to more immediate risk-creating problems of marketing, labor, advertisement, supplies, etc., the frequency of cases challenging debt and of decisions finding equity increases. The uncontradicted testimony (without finding of lack of credibility) of the universal practice in the Newark area in conformity to the course followed by taxpayer . . . is entitled to consideration. Also, the subsequent successful history of this corporate taxpayer cannot be disregarded and militates strongly against denying an interest deduction on this record. The Fin Hay Realty Co. did not go bankrupt, was not unable to refinance or extend its purchase money mortgage due in 1939, and has never failed to meet a demanded purchase of the notes.

On this record, these loans were bona fide loans, "at risk" in this enterprise in no different way than any debt investment is "at risk" for general creditor of a real estate holding and operating corporation. The District Court pointedly took judicial notice, both of the bargain real estate purchases possible in 1934 and of the steadily rising real estate values in Essex County, New Jersey. Subsequent refinancings by the taxpayer, as well as the entire course of its history, demonstrate that this investment in this particular venture was not a "risk capital" investment of the type that should compel disregarding the clear intent of the parties and form of the transaction. Two recent "real estate" decisions (involving, moreover, construction as well as holding of real estate) suggest the proper result for the present case. As stated in Tomlinson v. 1661 Corporation, supra, at 300:

> We cannot, by manipulation of tax law, preclude the parties from exercising sound business judgment in obtaining needed investment funds at the most favorable rate possible, whether it be a commercial loan, or, more likely and as is the case here, a loan from private interested sources with sufficient faith in the success of the venture and their ultimate repayment to delete or minimize the "risk factor" in their rate of return.

Similarly, in J.S. Biritz Construction Co. v. C.I.R., supra, at 459, the court said:

> There is actually no evidence that this was not a loan, was not intended to be a loan, or that Biritz actually intended to make a capital investment rather than a loan.

> We think the Tax Court has painted with too broad a brush in limiting the permissible activities of an entrepreneur in personally financing his business. Financing embraces both equity and debt transactions and we do not think the courts should enunciate a rule of law that a sole stockholder may not loan money or transfer assets to a cor-

poration in a loan transaction. If this is to be the law, Congress should so declare it. We feel the controlling principle should be that any transaction which is intrinsically clear upon its face should be accorded its legal due unless the transaction is a mere sham or subterfuge set up solely or principally for tax-avoidance purposes.

I would reverse and enter judgment for the corporate taxpayer.

NOTES

1. *Fin Hay Realty*'s objective test may sometimes be used by the taxpayer for his own benefit. See Segel v. Commissioner, 89 T.C. 816 (1987), in which the Tax Court followed *Fin Hay Realty* in holding that because the terms of cash advances were more speculative than an outside creditor would have accepted, the apparent debt constituted equity, a result advantageous to the taxpayer in the context of an S corporation.

2. The debt-equity problem raised in *Fin Hay Realty* is hoary, thorny and persistent in the tax system. Over the years, corporations and their investors have created a wide range of instruments that do not readily fall on one side or the other of the debt-equity classification scheme. A useful way to frame the analysis is to outline the historical foundations of the debt-equity inquiry, the development of tests, and the current state of affairs:

Historical Foundations: The Supreme Court faced the debt-equity question in two companion cases, Talbot Mills v. Commissioner and John Kelley Co. v. Commissioner, 326 U.S. 521 (1946). Whether the corporations in those cases could deduct "interest" payments depended upon the classification of the "hybrid" securities on which the payments had been made. The instruments in *John Kelley Co.* were 20–year, 8–percent, noncumulative income debenture bonds, some of which were issued to the shareholders (all members of a family group) in exchange for stock and other of which had been sold to these shareholders for cash. Payment of the interest was conditioned on sufficient net income to meet the obligation. Although the debentures were subordinated to all other creditors, they contained acceleration provisions in the event of defaults. The terms of the indenture excluded the holders from management. The Tax Court had held that the payments were interest on indebtedness, deductible under § 163; the Court of Appeals for the Seventh Circuit reversed.

In the companion case (*Talbot Mills*) 25–year registered notes were issued to the shareholders—once again a family group—in exchange for four-fifths of their stock. The annual interest was not to exceed 10 percent nor to be less than 2 percent; it was computed by a formula that took into account the annual earnings of the corporation. Although the interest could be deferred until maturity when "necessary by reason of the condition of the corporation," it was cumulative, and dividends could not be paid until interest arrearages were met. The corporation's right to mortgage its real property was limited, and the board of directors was given power to subordinate the notes. Emphasizing the fluctuating payments and the fact that all the notes were issued in exchange for stock, the Tax Court had distinguished its decision in *Kelley*, holding the payments to be dividends; the First Circuit affirmed.

After hearing both cases together, the Supreme Court held that the debt vs. equity issue was, under the *Dobson* (320 U.S. 489 (1943)) doctrine, one for the Tax Court to resolve. Stating that no one characteristic could be decisive, the Supreme Court affirmed the Tax Court's very nearly inconsistent holdings.

Debt–Equity Tests: In light of the Supreme Court's deference to the Tax Court in the above cases, the factors deemed significant by the Tax Court in *Kelley* and *Talbot Mills* became the seeds for the growth of "tests" to distinguish debt from equity.

(a) One set of criteria—the form of the instrument—that emerged from the Tax Court analyses functions more as a prerequisite for debt status than as a real test. The Tax Court's seeming reliance on the formal structure of ordinary debt instruments (having fixed interest, fixed maturity, unconditional promise to pay) has developed into a strong baseline for debt treatment. The appearance of more equity-like features places a hybrid instrument at greater risk of being classified as equity.

(b) One of the important early tests was the so-called debt-to-equity ratio. The Supreme Court had cautioned against an "obviously excessive debt structure" (326 U.S. at 526), but since the 4:1 ratio of debt to equity in *Talbot Mills* had not been labeled "obviously excessive," many tax planners concluded that 4:1 was a "safe" ratio. The courts held that interest was deductible in a number of cases where the ratio was less than 4:1; the Commissioner's acquiescences seemed to confirm the margin of safety. See, e.g., Gazette Telegraph Co., 19 T.C. 692 (1953) (acq.), *aff'd on other grounds*, 209 F.2d 926 (10th Cir. 1954); Ruspyn Corp., 18 T.C. 769 (1952) (acq). As these "safe" ratios were being tested, capital structures with high debt-to-equity ratios were being struck down. See, e.g., Alfred R. Bachrach, 18 T.C. 479 (1952), *aff'd per curiam*, 205 F.2d 151 (2d Cir. 1953).

(c) The great reliance placed on the debt-to-equity ratio received a jarring blow in Gooding Amusement Co., 23 T.C. 408 (1954), *aff'd*, 236 F.2d 159 (6th Cir. 1956), where formal debt instruments were classified as equity despite a ratio of 1:1. The court held the "real intention" of the parties was never to enforce the notes or otherwise to assert the rights of bona fide creditors. Although in *Gooding* itself equity classification was the result, that case ironically paved the way for debt classification in cases where a high debt-to-equity ratio existed. Since the ratio was no longer talismanic, taxpayers with increasing frequency urged the courts to ignore it just as the Commissioner had done in *Gooding*. Where sufficient justification was found, the courts passed over a high debt-to-equity ratio and ruled in favor of the taxpayers. See, e.g., Baker Commodities, Inc., 48 T.C. 374 (1967) (700:1 ratio not fatal; cash flow of business adequate to cover debt payments), *aff'd on other grounds*, 415 F.2d 519 (9th Cir. 1969). Several courts have abandoned the ratio test entirely. See, e.g., Gloucester Ice & Cold Storage Co. v. Commissioner, 298 F.2d 183, 185 (1st Cir. 1962).

(d) Some of the justifications for ignoring the debt-to-equity ratio have assumed the status of independent tests:

—whether "substantial capital" had been contributed has become an important question. In Murphy Logging Co. v. United States, 378 F.2d 222 (9th

Cir. 1967), a corporation with a debt-to-equity ratio of 160:1 was permitted to deduct interest payments on loans where the shareholders "contributed" their ability to procure contracts and "their own integrity and reputation for getting things done."

—whether debt and equity are held pro rata by the shareholders has also become an important question. Pro rata holdings have been a formidable barrier but not insuperable to taxpayer successes. See Gilbert v. Commissioner, 248 F.2d 399 (2d Cir. 1957). Conversely, disproportionate holdings may be helpful to the taxpayer (see Bauer v. Commissioner, 748 F.2d 1365 (9th Cir. 1984)), although they may not be a guarantee of success. See P.M. Finance Corp. v. Commissioner, 302 F.2d 786 (3d Cir. 1962).

—some courts purport to resolve the debt vs. equity question according to the "intent of the parties" to the transaction. See, e.g., Marathon Oil Co. v. Commissioner, 838 F.2d 1114 (10th Cir. 1987). In the absence of an arm's length transaction, is it at all useful for a court to seek the "intent of the parties"?

—some cases emphasize the question of whether the funds were placed at the "risk of the business." See Schine Chain Theatres, 22 T.C.M. (CCH) 488 (1963), aff'd, 331 F.2d 849 (2d Cir. 1964). Is that an adequate test?

(e) Questions in applying the tests: As courts have explored ways to structure the debt-equity inquiry a number of questions continue to resurface.

How much flexibility do taxpayers have in challenging their stated form? In Samuel G. Miller, 57 T.C.M. (CCH) 46 (1989), aff'd, 900 F.2d 260 (6th Cir. 1990), the taxpayer formed a corporation to which he contributed $150,000 in exchange for 150 shares of common stock and a $135,000 promissory note. The taxpayer subsequently made additional advances of $395,740 to the corporation which were recorded on the books of the corporation as loans. After the business failed, the taxpayer sought to recharacterize the debt as equity so that he would be entitled to an ordinary loss under § 1244 (see Chapter 2, pages 265–267 infra). The court rejected this attempt, stating that "taxpayers have little freedom to ignore the form of their own transactions and are ordinarily bound by the tax consequences that flow from the form of transactions they use."

How much flexibility in classification exists as instruments change hands? Should the initial characterization of a debt instrument as equity continue after the instrument is sold by the shareholder-creditor to a nonshareholder? See Texoma Supply Co., 17 T.C.M. (CCH) 147 (1958). Might "debt" become "equity" when the debt instrument is sold by the creditor to a shareholder whose investment in stock is small vis-à-vis his investment in debt? Compare Edwards v. Commissioner, 415 F.2d 578 (10th Cir. 1969), with Jewell Ridge Coal Corp., 21 T.C.M. (CCH) 1048 (1962) aff'd, 318 F.2d 695 (4th Cir. 1963).

How should an instrument such as a bank loan be classified if the shareholders of the corporation guarantee the loan? What if the bank agrees to the loan only on the condition of the guarantee? See Murphy Logging Co. v. United States, 239 F.Supp. 794 (D. Or. 1965), rev'd, 378 F.2d 222 (9th Cir. 1967) (see both courts' opinions). Not surprisingly, no uniform treatment of shareholder guarantees has emerged. Compare General Alloy Casting Co., 23 T.C.M. (CCH)

887 (1964), *aff'd per curiam*, 345 F.2d 794 (3d Cir. 1965) (deductibility of interest unchallenged) *with* Plantation Patterns, Inc. v. Commissioner, 462 F.2d 712 (5th Cir.), *cert. denied*, 409 U.S. 1076 (1972) (shareholder guarantee treated as a substitute for a capital contribution, thus no interest deduction allowed).

(f) Statutory tests: Section 385 grants the Treasury the authority to promulgate regulations that distinguish debt and equity. Although efforts were made to provide such regulations, none are currently in place and there are no plans to revive this mission. Section 385(c)(2) does require a holder of an instrument to disclose if he is classifying the instrument in a manner inconsistent with the issuing corporation. Other provisions of the Code do not purport to provide a comprehensive test or definition of debt and equity, but do target and restrict the deductibility of interest on instruments thought to be particularly problematic. Section 267(a)(2) defers interest deductions where the debtor and creditor have certain relationships and have different accounting methods. Section 163(j) limits deductions on debt paid to certain related parties where the debtor is considered highly leveraged under the statute.

Section 163(l) limits the deduction of interest on debt that is payable in stock of the debtor or a related party. Section 163(e)(5) disallows (or defers) the interest deduction with respect to certain "high yield" original issue discount obligations. Why?

Current State of Affairs: The struggle to delineate the debt-equity lines continues to challenge the tax system. The rapid proliferation of new financial instruments beginning in the 1990s and continuing to the present has only added to the importance and difficulty of this burden. See Tuths, Fundamental Tax Reform of Derivatives, 134 Tax Notes 433 (Jan. 23, 2012); Benshalom, How to Live with a Tax Code with Which You Disagree: Doctrine, Optimal Tax, Common Sense and the Debt-Equity Distinction, 88 N.C.L. 1217 (2010); Warren, U.S. Income Taxation of New Financial Products, 88 J. Public Economics 899 (2004). One major strategy of corporate taxpayers has been to issue instruments that are intended to be treated as debt for tax purposes but as equity for other purposes (regulatory, rating agency, accounting). The Service responded with Notice 94-47, 1994-1 C.B. 357, which stated that such instruments would be scrutinized on the basis of the cumulative effect of all of the facts and circumstances to determine whether a debt classification was appropriate. The Notice highlighted several equity features of the instruments that would draw careful evaluation, including "an unreasonably long maturity or an ability to repay the instrument's principal with the issuer's stock."

The debt-equity question continues to plague taxpayers and the courts, especially in closely held corporations. Again, in recent cases, the court relied on the examination of multiple factors to determine whether advances by the shareholder to the taxpayer corporation were loans (debt) or contributions (equity). Hewlett-Packard Co. v. Comm., 103 TCM 1736 (2012); Indmar Products Co., Inc. v. Commissioner, 444 F.3d 771 (6th Cir. 2006). Similar classification issues arise in the partnership tax context as courts seek to ascertain whether an instrument constitutes debt or an equity investment in a partnership. See, e.g., TIFD III-E, Inc. v. U.S., 666 F.3d 836 (2d Cir. 2012); Pritired 1, LLL c. U.S. 816 F. Supp. 693 (2011).

2. Why does the classification of an instrument as debt or equity matter? And to whom? Try to list all of the areas in the tax law where debt and equity (or interest and dividends) are treated differently—for investors or issuers. Also bear in mind the possibility that issuers and investors may desire (and seek) conflicting tax treatment. Should corporate debt be treated differently from equity? Why? Are debt and equity securities merely different claims against a stream of earnings? If they were to be treated identically, should dividends and interest both be deductible or nondeductible? Over the years, a variety of proposals have been offered for "integrating" the U.S. tax system (moving from a classical corporate tax system to one in which a single level of tax is ultimately collected on income earned in corporate form). A range of methods for integrating the corporate and shareholder levels of tax have been used by other countries and they provide a practical baseline for exploring design options in the United States. See Polito, Constructive Dividend Doctrine from an Integrationist Perspective, 27 Akron Tax J. 1 (2012); Shaviro, The Rising Tax-Electivity of U.S. Corporate Residence, 64 Tax L. Rev. 377 (2011); Gravelle, The Corporate Income Tax: A Persistent Policy Challenge, 11 Fla. Tax Rev. 75 (2011); Integration of the U.S. Corporate and Individual Income Taxes: The Treasury Department and American Law Institute (introduction by Michael J. Graetz and Alvin C. Warren, Jr.) (1998).

In distinguishing debt from equity, should it matter to the tax system that an instrument is being reported as debt for tax purposes but as equity for non-tax purposes? Why?

3. The debt vs. equity issue was given exhaustive consideration in the classic article, Plumb, The Federal Income Tax Significance of Corporate Debt: A Critical Analysis and a Proposal, 26 Tax L. Rev. 369 (1971).

4. The debt v. equity issue is not simply a U.S. domestic matter. The challenge of drawing the line between debt and equity confronts other countries as well – both for domestic transactions and for cross border ones. In the case of cross border transactions, it is not uncommon (and can often be quite advantageous) for an instrument to be classified as debt by one jurisdiction and as equity by another. The prominence of this systemic challenge is signaled by its selection as one of the two major research topics for the 2012 conference of the International Fiscal Association. See, e.g., IFA cahiers de droit fiscal international, "The Debt-Equity Conundrum," Vol. 97(b) (2012).

b. Dividend vs. Business Expense—§ 162

Safway Steel Scaffolds Co. of Georgia v. United States
590 F.2d 1360 (5th Cir. 1979).

■ Before BROWN, CHIEF JUDGE, and TUTTLE and THORNBERRY, CIRCUIT JUDGES.

■ THORNBERRY, CIRCUIT JUDGE. This is a tax refund suit. The question presented is how much of $21,600 paid by the taxpayer, Safway Steel Scaffolds Company of Georgia, to Charles and Richard Werner is deductible under 26 U.S.C. § 162(a)(3) as rent. The Commissioner disallowed $9,720 of the claimed deduction and the district court sustained the government's position. The taxpayer, claiming that the entire amount is deductible, brings this appeal. For the reasons stated, we affirm.

Charles and Richard Werner are the sole stockholders of the taxpayer. In 1947, the brothers purchased four parcels of land in downtown Atlanta for $9,500 and assembled a single commercially useable parcel. On January 1, 1948, they leased the property to the plaintiff. The lease was for twenty years and was to expire on December 31, 1967. Among other things, the lease provided: (1) that the taxpayer was to pay an annual rent of $2,400 in monthly installments of $200; (2) that the taxpayer was to pay all taxes and utility charges; and (3) that the taxpayer could erect improvements on the vacant lot, but on expiration of the lease all attached improvements would become the property of the lessors (Werner brothers). The lease contained no option for renewal.

In January 1948, the Board of Directors of the plaintiff selected an architect to design a building for the taxpayer. On April 3, 1948, construction of the building began and the taxpayer moved into the new structure on December 3, 1948. The building had 18,433 square feet and the total cost of the building was $128,025. The district court found, and we will not disturb his finding here, that the structure had a useful life of approximately thirty-four years.

At the expiration of the 1948 lease, the land and improvements reverted to the Werner brothers. However, the taxpayer and its owners-lessors entered into a new lease. This lease provided for a three year rental term and a net rental of $1,800 per month ($21,600 yearly). The parties have stipulated that this amount is a fair rental amount for the improvements and the ground rent. The taxpayer contends that the entire amount is deductible as rent while the government contends that the amount of rent allocable to the improvements is not deductible under § 162(a)(3).[4]

It is ordinarily inappropriate to inquire into the reasonableness of the rent paid, however, this case presents an exception to the general rule. That exception is the case of a close relationship between the lessor and the lessee . . . or if the contract arises "between persons having an interest on both sides of a transaction." . . . In case of a close relationship between the lessor and the lessee the inquiry becomes, "If, viewing the circumstances in which the lease is made, it is such a lease as reasonable [persons] dealing at arm's length would make, then it is valid and binding . . . for tax purposes." . . .

The taxpayer argues that the court should look only to the reasonableness of the stated rental amount under the 1968 rent to determine the deductibility of the rent. The district court, however, concluded that it should

---

[4] The district court found that the value of the land plus the improvements was $200,000 in 1968, with $110,000 allocated to the land and $90,000 allocated to the improvements. Since the value of the improvements is 45% of the total value, the Commissioner disallowed 45% of the $21,600 claimed as a rental deduction [21,600 .45 = $9,720].

examine all of the circumstances of the case and view the entire history between the taxpayer and the Werner brothers as a series of transactions to determine the tax consequences.

We agree that the district court correctly identified the test and justifiedly inquired into the reasonableness of all the transactions made between Safway and the Werner brothers. The district court concluded that the ground rental of $2,400 per year was not unreasonable, but that parties dealing at arm's length would not have allowed an improvement with a thirty-four year useful life to revert at the end of a twenty year lease period without some economic benefit being given for the improvement such as a renewal option.[6] Therefore, the district court concluded that the payment attributable to the value of the improvements was really in the nature of a non-deductible dividend made to the Werner brothers and not a deductible rent expense.[7]

. . . We have concluded that the district court properly applied the facts and made correct determinations of law. It is our opinion that the district court should be affirmed.

Affirmed.

NOTE

A closely held corporation may incur an expense that it seeks to deduct under § 162 but that the Commissioner will disallow because it benefits the shareholders personally and is not meaningful in terms of the corporation's conduct of its business or income producing activities. Such expenses are frequently called "constructive" or "disguised" dividends. (Disallowance of the deduction is often accompanied by taxation of the payment to the shareholders as a dividend. See page 130 infra). In American Properties, Inc. v. Commissioner, 262 F.2d 150 (9th Cir. 1958), the court sustained the disallowance of the corporation's deduction for the construction and upkeep of a boat that bore a direct relationship to the shareholder's hobby but none to the corporation's business. In D'Errico v. Comm., T.C. Memo 2012-149, the court disallowed the corporation's deductions for a Cessna plane and treated the sole shareholder (also a licensed pilot) as receiving constructive dividends. But see Sanitary Farms Dairy, Inc., 25 T.C. 463 (1955), acq. 1956–2 C.B. 8 (costs of an African safari allowed as a deduction for a dairy farm business). This latter case was part of the Treasury's weaponry in its battle to secure the 1962 amendments that comprise § 274.

---

[6] Or as suggested by the government, a concomitant reduction in rent attributable to the taxpayer for a period of the reasonable life of the improvements could be given.

[7] The taxpayer also argues that the government is estopped from asserting the nondeductibility of the rent because the government audited the taxpayer's returns in 1959 and made no objection about the reasonableness of the rent. We think the cases conclusively demonstrate that no estoppel arises from these facts. See Union Equity Cooperative Exchange v. C.I.R., 481 F.2d 812, 817 (10 Cir. 1973). We also note that the taxpayer's argument rests on the implication that the Commissioner approved its rental deduction during the audit. We think another plausible inference is that the question simply never arose. A different question might arise were the Commissioner to affirmatively mislead the taxpayer as to a mistake of fact. (The government is never estopped as to a matter of law, Automobile Club v. Commissioner, 353 U.S. 180, 77 S. Ct. 707, 1 L. Ed. 2d 746 (1957).)

c. Dividend vs. Purchase

Corporation M purchased a yacht and a seashore residence. The yacht is used half the time to entertain corporate customers and half the time for the pleasure of the sole shareholder and his family. The seashore residence is used exclusively for the pleasure of the shareholder and his family. What are the tax consequences to Corporation M of the purchases it has made? What are the tax consequences to the shareholders? See pages 124–129 infra.

d. Retirement of Shares vs. Business Expense

When a corporation repurchases its own shares, what is the nature of the expenditure? Is it a deductible expense? In Five Star Mfg. Co. v. Commissioner, 355 F.2d 724 (5th Cir. 1966), the court permitted a corporation to deduct as an ordinary and necessary business expense the amount paid to a 50–percent shareholder and director in redemption of all of his stock. In the court's view, the redemption was an absolute business necessity, since the stockholder-director had been looting the corporation and his removal was the only hope the corporation had for continued viability. The decision is extremely difficult to justify. Although a "necessary" payment, it was a capital expenditure, not an "expense." What, after all, is the function of § 162(a) in the context of the corporate tax (as opposed to sole proprietor)? Five Star Mfg. Co. has been held applicable at best to cases of "life or death" business exigency, and its authority is questionable. See, e.g., U.S. v. Houston Pipeline Co., 37 F.3d 224 (5th Cir. 1994).

Section 162(k), added by the 1986 Act, generally disallows any amounts paid by a corporation "in connection with the redemption of its stock." Its enactment was a response to the rise of so-called "greenmail" payments by corporate takeover targets. Should any corporate payment in redemption of stock ever have been allowed as a current business expense, even in the absence of § 162(k)? Would it matter, as with greenmail, that some of the redemption payment exceeded the fair market value of the redeemed stock?

e. Incorporation Expense—§ 248

Prior to the enactment of § 248 in 1954, a corporation's organizational expenses (e.g. lawyers' fees, fees to the state upon filing of Articles of Incorporation, etc.) were not deductible under § 162 because they were regarded as capital expenditures. If the corporation did not have a limited life, the intangible assets the expenditures produced were treated as having an indefinite life, and thus no amortization was permitted under § 167. Ultimately, on complete liquidation of the corporation, a loss might be allowed under § 165(a). Cf. Canal–Randolph Corp. v. United States, 568 F.2d 28 (7th Cir. 1977) (per curiam), denying a deduction for the pre–1954 organization expenses of a 79–percent–owned subsidiary corporation on the occasion of its merger into its parent.

Section 248 authorizes corporations to elect ratable amortization of their organizational expenses over any period selected as long as it is not less than 60 months. When and how must an election be made? When must the period for amortization begin? See § 248; Treas. Reg. § 1.248–1.

Section 248 is not applicable to *reorganization* expenses. See McCrory Corp. v. United States, 651 F.2d 828 (2d Cir. 1981). See also Affiliated Capital Corp., 88 T.C. 1157 (1987) (expenses of a posteffective amendment to a registration statement not a recurring business expense but rather a capital expenditure).

In INDOPCO, Inc. v. Commissioner, 503 U.S. 79 (1992), the Supreme Court, affirming the lower court, took a strong stance on the deduction/capital expenditure debate by holding that an acquiring corporation may not deduct currently, but must capitalize, the expenses it incurred in connection with the friendly takeover of a target corporation. The Court's opinion focused on the creation of a long term benefit to the corporation through the expenditures. The case, however, did not result in a uniform tax treatment of expenses that a corporation incurs in the reorganization/acquisition context. The question remains quite dependent on the particular facts and circumstances. In A.E. Staley Manufacturing Co. v. Commissioner, 119 F.3d 482 (7th Cir. 1997), the court held that in the case of a corporation that incurred costs in defending against hostile takeovers and in ultimately accepting one offer, some costs were deductible and others had to be capitalized. Specifically, the investment bankers fees incurred in defense of hostile bids were deductible under § 162(a); bankers fees incurred in the preparation of alternative capital transactions (in defense against the takeover) that were abandoned were deductible under § 165(a); and bankers fees and printer costs incurred in preparation for and facilitation of the ultimate merger had to be capitalized. See also Federated Dept. Stores, Inc. v. United States, 171 B.R. 603 (S.D. Ohio 1994) (fee paid to white knight for unconsummated defensive merger held deductible under either § 162(a) or § 165); Letter Ruling 9043003 (differentiating expenses incurred in defending against a hostile takeover and in pursuing an alternative transaction), Rev. Rul. 99–23, 1999–1 C.B. 998 (identifying amortizable start-up expenditures under § 195 where corporation acquires an active business). Following *INDOPCO*, the Service sought to provide greater clarity and uniformity in the treatment of business expenditures. In December, 2003, the Treasury issued final regulations under § 263 that specify the capitalization requirements for a wide range of expenditures, including the costs of acquiring a new business. These regulations are widely viewed as providing a set of rules more "friendly" to current deductibility than the *INDOPCO* opinion itself. See, e.g., Treas. Reg. § 1.263(a)-5.

2. DISTRIBUTIONS OF STOCK

a. To Pay an Expense—§ 162

Compensation—§§ 83, 162, 421–424. Corporation M pays a reasonable bonus to one of its salesmen by issuing to him Corporation M common stock having a fair market value of $5000. What are the tax consequences to Corporation M? (What would be the tax consequences of a bonus paid in cash?) What is the authority for your conclusion? Would the result be different if the salesman were also the sole shareholder? In Rev. Rul. 62–217, 1962–2 C.B. 59 (modified by Rev. Rul. 74–503, 1974–2 C.B. 117), the Service allowed a corporation to deduct under § 162(a) the fair market value of its treasury stock used to pay employee compensation.

Interesting questions emerge in the context of a closely held corporation when the majority shareholders transfer some of *their* shares of the corporation to employees. Consider the case of Q, a majority shareholder in P Corporation. Q transferred ten shares of P stock to B, who was an employee of P's subsidiary, Corporation S, as reasonable compensation for services performed by B *for* S. What is the tax effect for the parties? Q, the majority shareholder in P, experiences no gain or loss on the stock transfer (but does allocate the basis in those shares among the remaining P stock held). B must report as wage income the fair market value of the P stock received. Pursuant to § 83(h), S is permitted a § 162(a) deduction for the fair market value of the stock but does not recognize gain or loss on this transfer of P stock. Rev. Rul. 80–76, 1980–1 C.B. 15. Treas. Reg. § 1.83–6(d) treats the transfer of shares by a shareholder to corporate employees as a contribution to capital (thus it is not an exchange upon which gain or loss would be recognized). See Tilford v. Commissioner, 705 F.2d 828 (6th Cir. 1983), *cert. denied*, 464 U.S. 992 (1983).

Interest—§§ 162, 163. Corporation N, a manufacturing company, orders raw materials from its supplier and is billed in the amount of $10,000. Wishing to conserve cash, Corporation N offers to satisfy the bill by issuing shares of its common stock fairly valued at $11,000, although the shares are not readily marketable because of a thin market. The supplier accepts the stock. What are the tax consequences to Corporation N? Why?

b. To Buy an Asset—§§ 1031, 1032, 1012, 362, 334

Corporation A uses Treasury shares worth $50,000 (acquired a year earlier for $40,000) to purchase needed machinery. What are the tax consequences to Corporation A at the time of purchase? What is Corporation A's basis in the machinery?

If Corporation A purchased stock in Corporation Z, paying for it with its own common stock, there would be no immediate tax consequence to Corporation A. § 1032. The basis of the Z stock acquired would depend in part on whether the acquisition was a "reorganization" as defined in § 368(a). See Chapter 4.

c. To Acquire Cash—§§ 162, 1032

Newly issued stock distributed in exchange for cash equal to the stock's value gives rise to no corporate deduction. What is the result if a valued employee is permitted to buy stock worth $10,000 for $8,000? *Compare* page 67 supra. What if the corporation had used Treasury stock that had cost it $8,000 would the result be different? In Rev. Rul. 74–503, 1974–2 C.B. 117, 118 the Service concluded that such Treasury stock has a zero basis under section 362 (i.e. that it has no cost basis). However, in 2006 the Service revoked Rev. Rul. 74–503, and announced that the "zero basis" question is under study. As of 2012 the issue remains listed as "under study". See Rev. Proc. 2012-1, 2012-1 I.R.B. 113 Sec. 5.01(7).

d. To Pay a Dividend

Corporation M pays its common shareholders dividends consisting of ten shares of newly issued Corporation M common stock for each share of stock held. What are the tax consequences to Corporation M? As to the consequences to the shareholders, see Chapter 4, pages 351–428 infra.

C. RESPECTING THE ENTITY

Should the existence of a corporation always be respected? Can the taxpayer disavow the formal existence of its corporation and treat the corporation's income as an activity of its own? Consider the following two cases. The first is a classic statement on the issue of respecting the entity. The second, a more recent examination, produces *on its facts* an alternative result.

Moline Properties, Inc. v. Commissioner
319 U.S. 436 (1943).

■ JUSTICE REED delivered the opinion of the Court: Petitioner seeks to have the gain on sales of its real property treated as the gain of its sole stockholder and its corporate existence ignored as merely fictitious. Certiorari was granted because of the volume of similar litigation in the lower courts and because of alleged conflict of the decision below with other circuit court decisions. [citations omitted]

Petitioner was organized by Uly O. Thompson in 1928 to be used as a security device in connection with certain Florida realty owned by him. The mortgagee of the property suggested the arrangement, under which Mr. Thompson conveyed the property to petitioner, which assumed the outstanding mortgages on the property, receiving in return all but the qualifying shares of stock, which he in turn transferred to a voting trustee appointed by the creditor. The stock was to be held as security for an additional loan to Mr. Thompson to be used to pay back taxes on the property. Thompson owned other real property, title to which he held individually. In 1933 the loan which occasioned the creation of petitioner was repaid and the mortgages were refinanced with a different mortgagee; control of petitioner reverted to Mr. Thompson. The new mortgage debt was paid in 1936 by means of a sale of a portion of the property held by petitioner. The remaining holdings of the petitioner were sold in three parcels, one each in 1934, 1935 and 1936, the proceeds being received by Mr. Thompson and deposited in his bank account.

Until 1933 the business done by the corporation consisted of the assumption of a certain obligation of Thompson to the original creditor, the defense of certain condemnation proceedings and the institution of a suit to remove restrictions imposed on the property by a prior deed. The expenses of this suit were paid by Thompson. In 1934 a portion of the property was leased for use as a parking lot for a rental of $1,000. Petitioner has transacted no business since the sale of its last holdings in 1936 but has not been dissolved. It kept no books and maintained no bank account during its existence and owned no other assets than as described. The sales made in 1934 and 1935 were reported in petitioner's income tax returns, a small loss being reported for the earlier year and a gain of over $5,000 being reported for 1935. Subsequently, on advice of his auditor, Thompson filed a claim for refund on petitioner's behalf for 1935 and sought to report the 1935 gain as his individual return. He reported the gain on the 1936 sale.

The question is whether the gain realized on the 1935 and 1936 sales shall be treated as income taxable to petitioner, as the Government urges, or as Thompson's income. The Board of Tax Appeals held for petitioner on the ground that because of its limited purpose, the corporation "was a mere figmentary agent which should be disregarded in the assessment of taxes." Moline Properties v. Commissioner, 45 B. T. A. 647. The Circuit Court of Appeals reversed on the ground that the corporate entity, chosen by Thompson for reasons sufficient to him, must now be recognized in the taxation of the income of the corporation. Commissioner v. Moline Properties, 131 F.2d 388.

The doctrine of corporate entity fills a useful purpose in business life. Whether the purpose be to gain an advantage under the law of the state of incorporation or to avoid or to comply with the demands of creditors or to serve the creator's personal or undisclosed convenience, so long as that purpose is the equivalent of business activity or is followed by the carrying on of business by the corporation, the corporation remains a separate taxable entity. [citations omitted]. In Burnet v. Commonwealth Improvement Co., 287 U.S. 415, this Court appraised the relation between a corporation and its sole stockholder and held taxable to the corporation a profit on a sale to its stockholder. This was because the taxpayer had adopted the corporate form for purposes of his own. The choice of the advantages of incorporation to do business, it was held, required the acceptance of the tax disadvantages.

To this rule there are recognized exceptions. . . In general, in matters relating to the revenue, the corporate form may be disregarded where it is a sham or unreal. In such situations the form is a bald and mischievous fiction. Higgins v. Smith, 308 U.S. 473, 477–78; *Gregory v. Helvering*, 293 U.S. 465.

The petitioner corporation was created by Thompson for his advantage and had a special function from its inception. At that time it was clearly not Thompson's *alter ego* and his exercise of control over it was negligible. It was then as much a separate entity as if its stock had been transferred outright to third persons. The argument is made by petitioner that the force of the rule requiring its separate treatment is avoided by the fact that Thompson was coerced into creating petitioner and was completely subservient to the creditors. But this merely serves to emphasize petitioner's separate existence. [citation omitted] Business necessity, i. e., pressure from creditors, made petitioner's creation advantageous to Thompson.

When petitioner discharged its mortgages held by the initial creditor and Thompson came in control in 1933, it was not dissolved, but continued its existence, ready again to serve his business interests. It again mortgaged its property, discharged that new mortgage, sold portions of its property in 1934 and 1935 and filed income tax returns showing these transactions. In 1934 petitioner engaged in an unambiguous business venture of its own—it leased a part of its property as a parking lot, receiving a substantial rental. The facts, it seems to us, compel the conclusion that the taxpayer had a tax identity distinct from its stockholder.

Petitioner advances what we think is basically the same argument of identity in a different form. It urges that it is a mere agent for its sole stockholder and "therefore the same tax consequences follow as in the case of any corporate agent or fiduciary." There was no actual contract of agency, nor the usual incidents of an agency relationship. Surely the mere fact of the existence of a corporation with one or several stockholders, regardless of the corporation's business activities, does not make the corporation the agent of its stockholders. Therefore the question of agency or not depends upon the same legal issues as does the question of identity previously discussed. Burnet v. Commonwealth Improvement Co., supra, 418, 419–20.

Affirmed.

Commissioner v. Bollinger

485 U.S. 340 (1988).

■ JUSTICE SCALIA delivered the opinion of the Court. Petitioner the Commissioner of Internal Revenue challenges a decision by the United States Court of Appeals for the Sixth Circuit holding that a corporation which held record title to real property as agent for the corporation's shareholders was not the owner of the property for purposes of federal income taxation. 807 F.2d 65 (1986). We granted certiorari, 482 U. S. 913 (1987), to resolve a conflict in the courts of appeals over the tax treatment of corporations purporting to be agents for their shareholders. [citations omitted]

I

Respondent Jesse C. Bollinger, Jr., developed, either individually or in partnership with some or all of the other respondents, eight apartment complexes in Lexington, Kentucky. (For convenience we will refer to all the ventures as "partnerships.") Bollinger initiated development of the first apartment complex, Creekside North Apartments, in 1968. The Massachusetts Mutual Life Insurance Company agreed to provide permanent financing by lending $1,075,000 to "the corporate nominee of Jesse C. Bollinger, Jr." at an annual interest rate of eight percent, secured by a mortgage on the property and a personal guaranty from Bollinger. The loan commitment was structured in this fashion because Kentucky's usury law at the time limited the annual interest rate for noncorporate borrowers to seven percent. Ky. Rev. Stat. §§ 360.010, 360.025 (1972). Lenders willing to provide money only at higher rates required the nominal debtor and record title holder of mortgaged property to be a corporate nominee of the true owner and borrower. On October 14, 1968, Bollinger incorporated Creekside, Inc., under the laws of Kentucky; he was the only stockholder. The next day, Bollinger and Creekside, Inc., entered into a written agreement which provided that the corporation would hold title to the apartment complex as Bollinger's agent for the sole purpose of securing financing, and would convey, assign, or encumber the property and disburse the proceeds thereof only as directed by Bollinger; that Creekside, Inc., had no obligation to maintain the property or assume any liability by reason of the execution of promissory notes or otherwise; and that Bollinger would indemnify and hold the corporation harmless from any liability it might sustain as his agent and nominee.

Having secured the commitment for permanent financing, Bollinger, acting through Creekside, Inc., borrowed the construction funds for the apartment complex from Citizens Fidelity Bank and Trust Company. Creekside, Inc., executed all necessary loan documents including the promissory note and mortgage, and transferred all loan proceeds to Bollinger's individual construction account. Bollinger acted as general contractor for the construction, hired the necessary employees, and paid the expenses out of the construction account. When construction was completed, Bollinger obtained, again through Creekside, Inc., permanent financing from Massachusetts Mutual Life in accordance with the earlier loan commitment. These loan proceeds were used to pay off the Citizens Fidelity construction loan. Bollinger hired a resident manager to rent the apartments, execute leases with tenants, collect and deposit the rents, and maintain operating records. The manager deposited all rental receipts into, and paid all operating expenses from, and operating account, which was first opened in the name of Creekside, Inc., but was later changed to "Creekside Apartments, a partnership." The operation of Creekside North Apartments generated losses for the taxable years 1969, 1971, 1972, 1973, and 1974, and ordinary income for the years 1970, 1975, 1976, and 1977. Throughout, the income and losses were reported by Bollinger on his individual income tax returns.

Following a substantially identical pattern, seven other apartment complexes were developed by respondents through seven separate partnerships. . . Upon completion of construction, each partnership actively managed its apartment complex, depositing all rental receipts into, and paying all expenses from, a separate partnership account for each apartment complex. The corporation had no assets, liabilities, employees, or bank accounts. In every case, the lenders regarded the partnership as the owner of the apartments and were aware that the corporation was acting as agent of the partnership in holding record title. The partnerships reported the income and losses generated by the apartment complexes on their partnership tax returns, and respondents reported their distributive share of the partnership income and losses on their individual tax returns.

The Commissioner of Internal Revenue disallowed the losses reported by respondents, on the ground that the standards set out in National Carbide Corp. v. Commissioner, 336 U. S. 422 (1949), were not met. The Commissioner contended that National Carbide required a corporation to have an arm's-length relationship with its shareholders before it could be recognized as their agent. Although not all respondents were shareholders of the corporation, the Commissioner took the position that the funds the partnerships disbursed to pay expenses should be deemed contributions to the corporation's capital, thereby making all respondents constructive stockholders. Since, in the Commissioner's view, the corporation rather than its shareholders owned the real estate, any losses sustained by the ventures were attributable to the corporation and not respondents. Respondents sought a redetermination in the United States Tax Court. The Tax Court held that the corporations were the agents of the partnerships and should be disregarded for tax purposes. Bollinger v. Commissioner, 48 TCM 1443 (1984), para. 84, 560 P–H Memo TC. On appeal, the United States Court of Appeals for the Sixth Circuit affirmed. 807 F. 2d 65 (1986). We granted the Commissioner's petition for certiorari.

II

For federal income tax purposes, gain or loss from the sale or use of property is attributable to the owner of the property. See Helvering v. Horst, 311 U. S. 112, 116–117 (1940); Blair v. Commissioner, 300 U.S. 5,12 (1937); see also Commissioner v. Sunnen, 333 U.S. 591,604 (1948). The problem we face here is that two different taxpayers can plausibly be regarded as the owner. . . It is common ground between the parties, however, that if a corporation holds title to property as agent for a partnership, then for tax purposes the partnership and not the corporation is the owner. Given agreement on that premise, one would suppose that there would be agreement upon the conclusion as well. . . In each instance the relationship between the corporation and the partnership was, in both form and substance, an agency with the partnership as principal.

The Commissioner contends, however, that the normal indicia of agency cannot suffice for tax purposes when, as here, the alleged principals are the controlling shareholders of the alleged agent corporation. That, it asserts, would undermine the principle of Moline Properties v. Commissioner, 319 U. S. 436 (1943), which held that a corporation is a separate taxable entity even if it has only one shareholder who exercises total control over its affairs. Obviously, Moline's separate-entity principle would be significantly compromised if shareholders of closely held corporations could, by clothing the corporation with some attributes of agency with respect to particular assets, leave themselves free at the end of the tax year to make a claim—perhaps even a good-faith claim—of either agent or owner status, depending upon which choice turns out to minimize their tax liability. The Commissioner does not have the resources to audit and litigate the many cases in which agency status could be thought debatable. Hence, the Commissioner argues, in this shareholder context he can reasonably demand that the taxpayer meet a prophylactically clear test of agency.

We agree with that principle, but the question remains whether the test the Commissioner proposes is appropriate. The parties have debated at length the significance of our opinion in National Carbide Corp. v. Commissioner, supra. In that case, three corporations that were wholly owned subsidiaries of another corporation agreed to operate their production plants as "agents" for the parent, transferring to it all profits except for a nominal sum. The subsidiaries reported as gross income only this sum, but the Commissioner concluded that they should be taxed on the entirety of the profits because they were not really agents. We agreed, reasoning first, that the mere fact of the parent's control over the subsidiaries did not establish the existence of an agency, since such control is typical of all shareholder-corporation relationships, and second, that the agreements to pay the parent all profits above a nominal amount were not determinative since income must be taxed to those who actually earn it without regard to anticipatory assignment. [citations omitted] We acknowledged, however, that there was such a thing as "a true corporate agent . . . of [an] owner-principal," and proceeded to set forth four indicia and two requirements of such status, the sum of which has become known in the lore of federal income tax law as the "six National Carbide factors":

> "Whether the corporation operates in the name and for the account of the principal, [2] binds the principal by its actions, [3] transmits money received to the principal, and [4] whether receipt of income is attributable to the services of employees of the principal and to assets belonging to the principal are some of the relevant considerations in determining whether a true agency exists. [5] If the corporation is a true agent, its relations with its principal must not be dependent upon the fact that it is owned by the principal, if such is the case. [6] Its business purpose must be the carrying on of the normal duties of an agent." [citations omitted]

. . . The Commissioner contends that the last two National Carbide factors are not satisfied in the present case. To take the last first: The Commissioner argues that here the corporation's business purpose with respect to the property at issue was not "the carrying on of the normal duties of an agent," since it was acting not as the agent but rather as the owner of the property for purposes of Kentucky's usury laws. We do not agree. It assuredly was not acting as the owner in fact, since respondents represented themselves as the principals to all parties concerned with the loans. Indeed, it was the lenders themselves who required the use of a corporate nominee. Nor does it make any sense to adopt a contrary-to-fact legal presumption that the corporation was the principal, imposing a federal tax sanction for the apparent evasion of Kentucky's usury law. To begin with, the Commissioner has not established that these transactions were an evasion. Respondents assert without contradiction that use of agency arrangements in order to permit higher interest was common practice, and it is by no means clear that the practice violated the spirit of the Kentucky law, much less its letter. It might well be thought that the borrower does not generally require usury protection in a transaction sophisticated enough to employ a corporate agent—assuredly not the normal modus operandi of the loan shark. That the statute positively envisioned corporate nominees is suggested by a provision which forbids charging the higher corporate interest rates "to a corporation, the principal asset of which shall be the ownership of a one (1) or two (2) family dwelling," Ky. Rev. Stat. § 360.025(2) (1987)—which would seem to prevent use of the nominee device for ordinary home-mortgage loans. In any event, even if the transaction did run afoul of the usury law, Kentucky, like most States, regards only the lender as the usurer, and the borrower as the victim. See Ky. Rev. Stat. § 360.020 (1987) (lender liable to borrower for civil penalty), § 360.990 (lender guilty of misdemeanor). Since the Kentucky statute imposed no penalties upon the borrower . . . the United States would hardly be vindicating Kentucky law by depriving the usury victim of tax advantages he would otherwise enjoy. In sum, we see no basis in either fact or policy for holding that the corporation was the principal because of the nature of its participation in the loans.

Of more general importance is the Commissioner's contention that the arrangements here violate the fifth National Carbide factor—that the corporate agent's "relations with its principal must not be dependent upon the fact that it is owned by the principal." The Commissioner asserts that this cannot be satisfied unless the corporate agent and its shareholder principal have an "arm's-length relationship" that includes the payment of a fee for agency services. The meaning of National Carbide's fifth factor is, at the risk of understatement, not entirely clear. Ultimately, the relations between a corporate agent and its owner-principal are always dependent upon the fact of ownership, in that the owner can cause the relations to be altered or terminated at any time. Plainly that is not what was meant, since on that interpretation all subsidiary-parent agencies would be invalid for tax purposes, a position which the National Carbide opinion specifically disavowed. We think the fifth National Carbide factor—so much more abstract than the others—was no more and no less than a generalized statement of the concern, expressed earlier in our own discussion, that the separate-entity doctrine of Moline not be subverted.

In any case, we decline to parse the text of National Carbide as though that were itself the governing statute. As noted earlier, it is uncontested that the law attributes tax consequences of property held by a genuine agent to the principal; and we agree that it is reasonable for the Commissioner to demand unequivocal evidence of genuineness in the corporation-shareholder context, in order to prevent evasion of Moline. We see no basis, however, for holding that unequivocal evidence can only consist of the rigid requirements (arm's-length dealing plus agency fee) that the Commissioner suggests. Neither of those is demanded by the law of agency, which permits agents to be unpaid family members, friends, or associates. [citation omitted] It seems to us that the genuineness of the agency relationship is adequately assured, and tax-avoiding manipulation adequately avoided, when the fact that the corporation is acting as agent for its shareholders with respect to a particular asset is set forth in a written agreement at the time the asset is acquired, the corporation functions as agent and not principal with respect to the asset for all purposes, and the corporation is held out as the agent and not principal in all dealings with third parties relating to the asset. Since these requirements were met here, the judgment of the Court of Appeals is

Affirmed.

■ JUSTICE KENNEDY took no part in the consideration or decision of this case.

NOTES

1. In an era in which sham transactions and economic substance are critical issues, Moline Properties and the determination of whether to respect an entity are still vital. For example, in the 2007 case H.J. Heinz Co. v. United States, 76 Fed. Cl. 570 (Ct. Fed. Cl. 2007) infra at 229, the court, which rejected the taxpayer's claim for refund and found that transaction in question to be a sham, noted that "it is well-established that, absent a sham, the fact that the transactions sub judice involved a parent corporation and a wholly-owned subsidiary, while suggesting a need for closer scrutiny, does not alone provide a basis for ignoring the other indicia of ownership here" (citing both *Bollinger* and *Moline Properties*).

2. Under what circumstances is a shareholder likely to argue that the corporation should not be respected? When is that argument likely to succeed? Should it be harder for a shareholder (as opposed to the Service) to argue that the corporation should not be respected? Is there a difference between not respecting the existence of a corporate entity and treating the entity as an agent for its shareholder?

3. Although the economic substance doctrine was codified in December, 2010, this issue remains controversial and questions have been raised as to when to apply the doctrine. It will take time for subsequent courts to answer these questions and to see how codification affects longstanding questions about the economic substance doctrine. (The Service issued a directive in July 2011 to provide guidance to IRS Examiners and Managers on the Application of the doctrine. LB&I Control No. LB&I-4-0711-015). For a longer explanation of the economic substance doctrine see the following discussion on the Economic Substance Doctrine and Corporate Taxation.

D) Economic Substance and Corporate Taxation

The economic substance doctrine encompasses the controversial issue of when transactions should be respected, including corporate transactions. Historically, the economic substance doctrine was developed by the courts beginning with *Gregory v. Helvering*, 293 U.S. 465 (1935) (finding the transfer of assets from one corporation to another to have no relation to the business of either). After a period of significant debate in the early 2000s, Congress codified the doctrine under IRC section 7701(o) passed into law on December 17, 2010. IRC § 7701(o) states that a transaction will only meet the requirements of the economic substance doctrine if it changes the taxpayer's economic position in a meaningful way apart from federal income tax effects *and* if there is a substantial purpose apart from tax consequences. The codification of the economic substance doctrine clarifies how the doctrine will be applied including the requirement that the transaction must meet the conjunctive test in the statute. But, the new provision does not clarify when the doctrine should be applied, saying that "the determination of whether the economic substance doctrine is relevant to a transaction shall be made in the same manner as if this subsection had never been enacted." (Section 7701(o)(5)(C)). Moreover, the codification of the economic substance doctrine does not supersede judicial doctrine, but only clarifies the doctrine.

Profit potential can be used to help satisfy the two prongs of the test if the taxpayer demonstrates that the "present value of the reasonably expected pretax profit is substantial in relation to the present value of the expected net tax benefits." (Section 7701(o)(2)(A).

Regarding the second prong of the new statutory test, there is currently no guidance on the definition of "substantial purpose (apart from Federal income tax effects)". Pre-§ 7701(o) case law may be illuminating. Compare *Coltec Industries v. United States*, 454 F.3d 1340 (Fed. Cir. 2006) (finding transaction that created high basis in stock objectively lacked economic substance and had to be disregarded for tax purposes) with *Countryside Ltd. Partnership v. Commissioner*, T.C. Memo. 2008-3 (finding a transaction valid because it had a legitimate business purpose and changed the economic position of the persons and companies).

As noted, codification of the economic substance doctrine is not intended to replace or eliminate the judicial doctrines relating to sham transactions, the step transaction doctrine, or substance over form. The Joint Committee on Taxation Report and previous versions of the proposed codification clarify that the economic substance doctrine "is not intended to alter or supplant any other rule of law, including any common-law doctrine or provision of the Code or regulations or other guidance thereunder; and it is intended the provision be construed as being additive to any such other rule of law."[*]

III. THE INCIDENCE OF THE CORPORATION INCOME TAX

As policymakers have contemplated reform of the corporate income tax system over the years, one enduring question remains: Who bears the burden of this tax? Possibilities include the owners of capital (shareholders), workers (employees), and customers. The answer affects not only one's views of the current regime and its impact, but also of the need for and desirability of reforms such as integration of the corporate and shareholder level taxes to eliminate the classical system. The first article below examines the question of who bears the burden of the corporate income tax. Although this excerpt is from 1987, it stands as an excellent overview of the core dimensions of the inquiry. Moreover, in the intervening years, the question has not been resolved. See, e.g., Clausing, In Search of Corporate

---

[*] *See* staff of the Joint Committee on Taxation, "Technical Explanation of the Revenue Provisions of the Reconciliation Act of 2010, as Amended, in Combination With the Patient Protection and Affordable Care Act," 152 at 155 (JCX-18-10), *Doc 2010-6147, 2010 TNT 55-23* (Mar. 21, 2010).

Tax Incidence, (Dec. 2011), available at http://ssrn.com/abstract=1974217. The second article, an ALI (American Law Institute) report on integration, explores the options for integrating the corporate and individual income taxes.

J. Pechman, Federal Tax Policy*
141–148 (5th ed. 1987).

. . . There is no more controversial issue in taxation than the question, "who bears the corporation income tax?" On this question, economists and businessmen alike differ among themselves. The following quotations are representative of these divergent views:

> Corporate taxes are simply costs, and the method of their assessment does not change this fact. Costs must be paid by the public in prices, and corporate taxes are thus, in effect, concealed sales taxes. (Enders M. Voorhees, chairman of the Finance Committee, U.S. Steel Corporation, address before the Controllers' Institute of America, New York, September 21, 1943.)

> The initial or short-run incidence of the corporate income tax seems to be largely on corporations and their stockholders. . . There seems to be little foundation for the belief that a large part of the corporate tax comes out of wages or is passed on to consumers in the same way that a selective excise [tax] tends to be shifted to buyers. (Richard Goode, *The Corporation Income Tax*, Wiley, 1951, pp. 71–72.)

> . . . The corporation profits tax is almost entirely shifted; the government simply uses the corporation as a tax collector. (Kenneth E. Boulding, *The Organizational Revolution*, Harper, 1953, p. 277.)

> It is hard to avoid the conclusion that plausible alternative sets of assumptions about the relevant elasticities all yield results in which capital bears very close to 100 percent of the [corporate] tax burden. (Arnold C. Harberger, "The Incidence of the Corporation Income Tax." *Journal of Political Economy*, vol. 70, June 1962, p. 234.)

> . . . An increase in the [corporate] tax is shifted fully through short run adjustments to prevent a decline in the net rate of return [on corporate investment], and . . . these adjustments are maintained subsequently. (Marian Krzyzaniak and Richard A. Musgrave, *The Shifting of the Corporation Income Tax*, Johns Hopkins Press, 1963, p. 65.)

> . . . There is no inter-sector inefficiency resulting from the imposition of the corporate profits tax with the interest deductibility provision. Nor is there any misallocation between safe and risky industries. From an efficiency point of view, the whole corporate profits tax structure is just like a lump sum tax on corporations. (Joseph E. Stiglitz, "Taxa-

---

tion, Corporate Financial Policy, and the Cost of Capital," *Journal of Public Economics*, vol. 2, 1973, p. 33.)

. . . If the net rate of return is given in the international market place, the burden of a tax on the income from capital in one country will not (in the middle or long run) end up being borne by capital (which can flee) but by other factors of production (land, labor, and to a degree, old fixed capital). (Arnold C. Harberger, "The State of the Corporate Tax: Who Pays It? Should It Be Replaced?" in Charles E. Walker and Mark A. Bloomfield, eds., *New Directions in Federal Tax Policy for the 1980s*, Ballinger, 1983.)

Unfortunately, economics has not yet provided a scientific basis for accepting or rejecting one side or the other. This section presents the logic of each view and summarizes the evidence.

THE SHIFTING MECHANISM

One reason for the sharply divergent views is that the opponents frequently do not refer to the same type of shifting. It is important to distinguish between short- and long-run shifting and the mechanisms through which they operate. The "short run" is defined by economists as a period too short for firms to adjust their capital to changing demand and supply conditions. The "long run" is a period in which capital can be adjusted.

THE SHORT RUN

The classical view in economics is that the corporation income tax cannot be shifted in the short run. The argument is as follows: all business firms, whether they are competitive or monopolistic, seek to maximize net profits. This maximum occurs when output and prices are set at the point where the cost of producing an additional unit is exactly equal to the additional revenue obtained from the sale of that unit. In the short run, a tax on economic profit should make no difference in this decision. The output and price that maximized the firm's profits before the tax will continue to maximize profits after the tax is imposed. (This follows from simple arithmetic. If a series of figures is reduced by the same percentage, the figure that was highest before will be the highest after.)

The opposite view is that today's markets are characterized neither by perfect competition nor by monopoly; instead, they show considerable imperfection and mutual interdependence or oligopoly. In such markets, business firms may set their prices at the level that covers their full costs plus a margin for profits. Alternatively, the firms are described as aiming at an after-tax target rate of return on their invested capital. Under the cost-plus behavior, the firm treats the tax as an element of cost and raises its price to recover the tax. (Public utilities are usually able to shift the tax in this way, because state rate-making agencies treat the corporation tax as a cost.) Similarly, if the firm's objective is the after-tax target rate of return, imposition of a tax or an increase in the tax rate—by reducing the rate of return on invested capital—will have to be accounted for in making output and price decisions. To preserve the target rate of return, the tax must be shifted forward to consumers or backward to the workers or partly forward and partly backward.

It is also argued that economists' models are irrelevant in most markets where one or a few large firms exercise a substantial degree of leadership. In such markets, efficient producers raise their prices to recover the tax, and the tax merely forms an "umbrella" that permits less efficient or marginal producers to survive.

When business managers are asked about their pricing policies, they often say that they shift the corporation income tax. However, even if business firms intend to shift the tax, there is some doubt about their ability to shift it fully in the short run. In the first place, the tax depends on the outcome of business operations during an entire year. Businessmen can only guess the ratio of the tax to their gross receipts, and it is hard to conceive of their setting a price that would recover the precise amount of tax they will eventually pay. (If shifting were possible, there would be some instances of firms shifting more than 100 percent of the tax, but few economists believe that overshifting actually occurs.)

Second, businessmen know that should they attempt to recover the corporation income tax through higher prices (or lower wages), other firms would not necessarily do the same. Some firms make no profit or have large loss carry-overs and thus pay no tax; among other firms, the ratio of tax to gross receipts differs. In multiproduct firms, the producer has even less basis for judging the ratio of tax to gross receipts for each product. All these possibilities increase the uncertainty of response by other firms and make the attempt to shift part or all of the corporation income tax hazardous.

THE LONG RUN

In the long run, the corporation income tax influences investment by reducing the rate of return on corporate equity. If the corporation income tax is not shifted in the short run, new after-tax rates of return are depressed, and the incentive to undertake corporate investment is thereby reduced. After-tax rates of return tend to be equalized with those in the noncorporate sector, but in the process corporate capital and output will have been permanently reduced. Thus, if there is no short-run shifting and if the supply of capital is fixed, the burden of the tax falls on the owners of capital in general. If the depressed rate of return on capital reduces investment, productivity of labor decreases and at least part of the tax may be borne by workers.

Where investment is financed by borrowing, the corporation tax cannot affect investment decisions because interest on debt is a deductible expense. If the marginal investment of a firm is fully financed by debt, the corporation tax becomes a lump-sum tax on profits generated by previous investments and is borne entirely by the owners of the corporation, the stockholders. In view of the recent large increase in debt financing (see the section on equity and debt finance below), a substantial proportion of the corporation income tax may now rest on stockholders and not be diffused to owners of capital in general through the shifting process just described.

Figure 1-1. *Percentage of Business Income Originating in the Corporate Sector, 1929–86*[a]

Percent

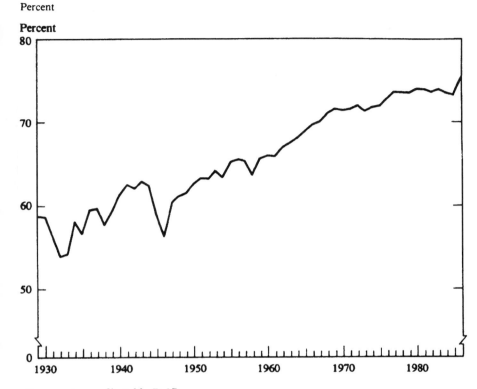

Source: Appendix table D-17.
a. Business income is national income originating in business enterprises.

THE CORPORATION TAX IN AN OPEN ECONOMY

The foregoing analysis assumed that the corporation tax was imposed in a closed economy. In an open economy, the rate of return on capital is set in the international marketplace. If the tax in one country is higher than it is elsewhere, capital will move to other countries until the rate of return is raised to the international level. Thus the burden of the tax would not be borne by capital but by other factors of production (land, labor, and old fixed capital) that cannot move. Since labor is the largest input into corporate products, wage earners would bear most of the burden of the corporation tax through lower real wages.

Table 1–1

Rates of Return and Debt–Capital Ratio, Manufacturing
Corporations, Selected Periods, 1927–83

Period	Return on equity[a]		Return on total capital[a,b]		Ratio of debt to total capital[c]	General corporation tax rate[d]
	Before tax	After tax	Before tax	After tax		
1927–29	8.8	7.8[e]	8.7	7.8[e]	15.2	12.2
1936–39	7.8	6.4[e]	7.3	6.2[e]	15.0	17.0
1953–56	18.4	9.2	15.7	8.2	19.0	52.0
1957–61	14.1	7.3	12.2	6.8	20.5	52.0
1964–67	17.8	10.1	14.9	9.1	25.1	48.5
1968–71	13.5	6.8	11.6	7.0	32.7	50.7
1977–80	19.4	13.9	16.4	12.8	35.8	47.0
1981–83	11.2	8.2	12.7	10.8	36.5	46.0

Source: Appendix table D–18.

a. Equity and debt capital are averages of book values for the beginning and
end of the year.

b. Profits plus interest paid as a percentage of total capital.

c. End of year.

d. Statutory rate of federal corporation income tax applicable to large corporations (average of annual figures).

e. Rates of return are slightly understated (probably by 0.3 percentage point or
less) because no allowance has been made for the foreign tax credit.

In the years immediately after World War II, most countries imposed
tight capital controls and currencies were not convertible. As capital controls were dismantled and many foreign currencies other than the U.S. dollar became acceptable in international transactions, the open economy
model became more realistic. During this later period, the effective corporation tax rates have been declining in the United States. It follows that recent U.S. tax policy has probably reduced any adverse effect of the corporation income tax on real wages, not increased it as some allege.

THE EVIDENCE

The evidence on the incidence of the corporation income tax is inconclusive. The data do not permit a clear determination of the factors affecting price and wage decisions. Different authors examining the same set of
facts have come to diametrically opposite conclusions.

Figure 1-2. *Property Income Share in Corporate Gross Product less Indirect Taxes, 1929–86*[a]

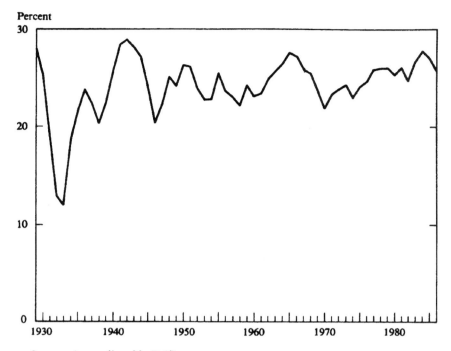

Source: Appendix table D-17.
a. **Property income includes corporate profits before taxes after capital-consumption and inventory valuation adjustments, and net interest.**

Over the long run, unincorporated business has not grown at the expense of incorporated business. Corporations accounted for 58.7 percent of the national income originating in the business sector in 1929; their share reached 75.6 percent in 1986. [Figure 1–1.] Much of the increase came from the relative decline in industries, particularly farming, in which corporations are not important; but even in the rest of the economy, there is no indication of a shift away from the corporate form of organization. The advantages of doing business in the corporate form far outweigh whatever deterrent effects the corporation tax might have on corporate investment.

Beyond this, the data are conflicting. On the one hand, before- and after-tax rates of return reported by corporations have been higher since the end of World War II than in the late 1920s, when the corporation income tax was much lower. [Table 1–1.] On the other hand, except for recession years, the share of pre-tax property income (profits, interest, and capital consumption allowances) in corporate gross product changed little. [Figure 1–2.] Corporations have been able to increase their before-tax profits enough to avoid a reduction in the after-tax return, without increasing their share of income in the corporate sector. This suggests that corporations have increased pre-tax rates of return not by marking up prices or lowering wages, but by making more efficient use of their capital. But what might have occurred without the tax is unknown, and its long-run effect remains unclear.

The burden of corporate taxation borne by individuals is strikingly different under the different incidence assumptions. The tax is regressive in the lower income classes and mildly progressive in the higher ones if as much as one-half is shifted forward to consumers in the form of higher prices and the remainder is borne by owners of capital in general. If the entire tax is borne by capital, progressivity increases in the higher income classes. . .

The American Law Institute Federal Income Tax Project, Integration of the Individual and Corporate Income Taxes, Reporter's Study,* Alvin C. Warren, Jr., Reporter
March 31, 1993.

The United States has long had what is usually called a classical income tax system, under which income is taxed to shareholders and corporations as distinct taxpayers. As a result, taxable income earned by a corporation and then distributed to individual shareholders as a dividend is taxed twice, once to the corporation and once to the shareholder on receipt of the dividend. Corporate taxable income distributed as dividends to exempt shareholders is taxed only at the corporate level. In contrast, earnings on corporate debt capital are nontaxable at the corporate level to the extent they are distributed as deductible interest payments. Whether interest is taxed to the recipient depends on the recipient's status, with foreign and tax-exempt lenders generally non-taxable on such receipts.

Integration of the individual and corporate income taxes refers to various means of eliminating the separate, additional burden of the corporate income tax, in favor of a system in which investor and corporate taxes are interrelated so as to produce a more uniform levy on capital income, whether earned through corporate enterprise or not. *The integration proposals in this study would convert the separate U.S. corporate income tax into a withholding tax with respect to income ultimately distributed to shareholders.* . .

Part 1: Defects in Current Law

The principal reasons for abandoning the current classical system of corporate taxation derive from distortions in economic behavior caused by that system. Four tax incentives or distortions are often said to follow from classical taxation of corporate income: (1) an incentive to invest in assets other than new corporate equity; (2) an incentive to raise corporate capital by issuing debt rather than equity shares; (3) an incentive to retain, rather than distribute, corporate earnings; and (4) an incentive to distribute corporate earnings in nondividend transactions, rather than as dividends . . .. . .

1.1 The Disincentive to Invest in New Corporate Equity

Consider first an individual investor who is deciding whether to purchase a share of new corporate stock from the issuing company or to make some other investment yielding a current income stream. For these purposes, an investment in corporate debt is the same as any other non-corporate-equity investment that yields a current income stream, because no corporate tax attaches to corporate earnings distributed to suppliers of corporate capital as interest payments.

If the investor makes the noncorporate investment, the only tax due on the future return will be at the investor's personal tax rate. On the other hand, investment in corporate stock will generate an annual corporate tax on the corporate income, as well as a shareholder ordinary income tax on earnings distributed as dividends and a shareholder capital gains tax on realized gains attributable to undistributed corporate earnings. If all three effective tax rates were the same, there would always be an additional tax burden from investing in new corporate stock, as compared with other investments, including corporate debt, because the corporate tax would be levied in addition to the shareholder tax on dividends or capital gains, whereas only one tax would be due on noncorporate investment.

If, however, the applicable individual income tax rate were higher than the corporate tax rate, and the capital gains rate were sufficiently low, there would be a tax advantage for investing in corporate stock that paid no dividends during a period of growth, after which the increased assets of the company were to be retained as part of its permanent capital. This can easily be seen considering a case in which the individual tax rate is 40 percent, the corporate rate is 30 percent, and the capital gains rate is effectively zero. As long as the capital gains rate, rather than the ordinary income rate, applies at the shareholder level (either because earnings are never distributed or because such distributions are in a form eligible for capital gains treatment), the classical double tax system in this case would *encourage* investment in corporate stock relative to noncorporate investment yielding a current return, because the only applicable tax would be levied at 30 percent, rather than 40 percent. . .

1.2 Corporate Financing Incentives

Now consider a corporation that is contemplating financing an investment project by (a) using retained earnings, (b) borrowing, or (c) issuing new stock. Because financing with retained earnings is an alternative, the relevant comparisons must begin with a corporation that has retained earnings in corporate solution, so the appropriate choices can be more precisely stated as (a) investing those retained earnings in the contemplated project, (b) distributing those earnings as dividends and issuing new debt in the same amount, or (c) distributing those earnings as dividends and issuing new stock on which dividends will be paid currently. Whereas the case considered in the last section began with assets outside the corporation, this section focuses on a case in which assets are already in the corporation.

The first two alternatives identified above, financing by retained earnings or borrowing, will yield equivalent results under the simplifying assumptions that *shareholder and corporate tax rates are equal, that the same dividend tax will always apply to corporate earnings distributed to shareholders, and that no capital gains taxes are due during the period of retention.* This result is illustrated by the following example:

Example 1. Assume that in year 1 the corporation has $100 in retained corporate earnings, when corporate and shareholder tax rates are 30 percent, and the rate of return is 10 percent. If the earnings are reinvested, and the project earns $10, there will be $107 available for distribution to shareholders in year 2, which in turn will yield shareholders $74.90 after taxes that year. If, on the other hand, the $100 is distributed to shareholders in year 1, they would have $70 after taxes to lend back to the corporation, which would earn interest of $7, again yielding the investors $74.90 after all taxes in year 2.

Alternatives (a) and (b) lead to the same results because of offsetting effects: use of retained earnings continues application of the corporate tax on income produced by the retained earnings, but defers the shareholder tax on distributions; borrowing eliminates the future corporate tax as a result of the interest deduction, but implicates an immediate shareholder tax on the distributed earnings. The third alternative, the issuance of new equity, is always inferior to the first two because it *both* implicates an immediate shareholder tax *and* continues to apply the corporate tax. . .

To recapitulate, the classical system generally creates a tax incentive for corporations to finance their investments with retained earnings or debt, rather than by the issuance of new shares. Whether the tax system is neutral as between retained earnings and debt, prefers retained earnings to debt, or vice versa depends on the relationships among corporate, shareholder and capital gains tax rates.

1.3 The Incentive to Retain or Distribute Corporate Earnings

We now consider a corporation with retained earnings of $100 that faces a choice of (a) retaining and reinvesting the earnings, or (b) distributing those earnings to shareholders who will invest the funds elsewhere. Our focus in the last section was on financing a contemplated corporate project; here our focus is on the closely related, but distinguishable, question of whether there is a tax incentive to retain or distribute earnings, all other things being equal. We begin by examining certain conditions under which a classical tax system is neutral with respect to distribution or retention of corporate earnings, and then turn to two views in contemporary corporate finance concerning nontax reasons for retention or distribution.

a. Neutrality

Does the classical double tax create an incentive to retain corporate earnings if a dividend tax will apply when the earnings are distributed in the future? As suggested by the discussion in the last section, the answer is no if we assume that corporate and shareholder tax rates are the same, that corporate and shareholder pre-tax rates of return are the same, and that no capital gains tax is due in the interim, as shown in the following example:

Example 2. Consider $100 of corporate earnings that are available for distribution or corporate investment in year 1 when the tax rate is 30 percent and the pre-tax rate of return is 10 percent. One alternative would be for the corporation to invest the $100 for ten years, after which the corporation would have $197 (i.e., $100 (1.07)10 = $197). Distribution of that amount to shareholders as a dividend in year 10 would yield $138 after shareholder taxes (i.e., .7 $197).

A second alternative would be to distribute $100 as a dividend in year 1, yielding the shareholders $70 after shareholder taxes. If invested at a pre-tax rate of return of 10 percent, that amount would compound to $138 in year 10 (i.e., $70 (1.07)10 = $138).

Given the specified assumptions, the dividend tax serves as a kind of "toll charge," applicable to a distribution of corporate earnings whenever made. As a result, there is no tax advantage or disadvantage to retaining or distributing earnings when the corporate tax rate equals the shareholder tax rate and no capital gains tax is due during the period of retention. Although the shareholder tax on dividends is deferred by retention of earnings, the amount of that tax also increases over time, because the tax applies to the entire amount distributed in the future. . .

Even if shareholder and corporate tax rates were the same, imposition of a capital gains tax on sales of stock during the period of retention could involve an additional burden on retentions, as compared with distributions. Suppose in Example 2 that the owner of the stock on which earnings had been retained sold his shares sometime prior to the distribution in year 10. The seller would incur a capital gains tax that would not be applicable in the case of a distribution in year 1. On the other hand, the buyer would have an offsetting capital loss due to the diminution in value of the stock as a result of the dividend in year 10. Accordingly, the burden of this additional tax depends on the timing of the capital gain and loss. Suppose, for example, the stock were sold just before the dividend was declared in year 10, when the capital gains tax rate was, like the corporate and individual tax rates, 30 percent. A buyer would be willing to pay up to $197 for the stock, because she would receive $138 after taxes from the dividend, as well as a tax benefit of $59 from deducting her basis if she then resold the stock (i.e., $59 = .3 $197). In this case, therefore, the capital gains tax would not impose an additional burden on retentions, relative to dividends. Situations in which stock can be resold shortly after its acquisition to take full advantage of the capital loss due to a distribution are likely to involve arbitrageurs who acquire stock in anticipation of a dividend or a nondividend distribution of corporate assets.

More generally, neutrality would be achieved in the presence of a capital gains tax during the period of retention if the after-tax return from

shareholder investment of distributed earnings equaled the after-tax return from investment of corporate retentions, taking into account both the
corporate tax and the capital gains tax. If there were no capital gains tax
payable during a period of retention, but retained earnings and the income
thereon could eventually be paid to shareholders in a transaction subject to
capital gains taxation, the results for retention and distribution would
again depend on the rate of all three taxes. In short, whether a classical
system encourages or discourages retention of corporate earnings depends
on the relationships among corporate, shareholder, and capital gains tax
rates. . .

b. The "New" View of Dividends and Taxes

A "new" view of dividends and taxes suggests that the price of corporate shares should be discounted to reflect the burden of the classical system. We can illustrate this possibility with a simple example.

Example 3. As in Example 2, a corporation has $100 of retained earnings
when the individual and corporate tax rates are 30 percent. The $100 is
added to the permanent capital of the corporation, annually yielding $10 in
pre-tax return and $7 in after-corporate-tax dividends to shareholders.

As a result of the retention in Example 3, the holder of the corporate
stock will receive in perpetuity an income stream of $7, on which individual
taxes will be due. Given a pre-tax rate of return of 10 percent, that stream
has a capital value of $70 to a potential shareholder. Accordingly, a buyer
of the corporate stock should only be willing to pay $70 for that stream,
even though the underlying corporate assets are worth $100. The current
holder of the stock should, however, demand $100 in return for giving up
that stream, because that is the amount she would have to receive in order
to have capital valued at $70 after taxes, assuming the capital gains tax
rate was also 30 percent. The resulting lock-in effect would presumably
limit sellers to those who were nontaxable for one reason or another (including step-up in basis) and those who sold despite the tax disadvantage.

Accordingly, if earnings are expected to be retained permanently or for
a significant period, share values should be discounted to reflect the expected additional level of tax, as compared with other potential uses of
shareholder funds. Retention of earnings would not, however, increase the
corporation's cost of capital above the cost of borrowing. In lieu of the retention in Example 3, the corporation could have distributed the $100 as a div-
idend and borrowed back $70 from the shareholder. In both cases, the sup-
plier of capital would expect a pre-tax return of $7 on capital interest va-
lued at $70. Proponents of the new view accordingly often emphasize that
the classical system does not involve an increase in corporate cost of capital
to the extent corporate projects can be financed by debt or retained earnings.

The shareholder in Example 3 whose stock is worth $70 would ob-
viously prefer to own the $100 in corporate assets represented by that
stock. Outright distribution of the corporate assets might, however, be con-

strained by nontax reasons, such as the corporation's need for those assets or their physical nature. And even if distributed as a dividend, $100 of corporate assets would only yield the shareholder $70 after taxes, assuming the deduction due to the offsetting capital loss in share value was not immediately available. On the other hand, a nondividend distribution, such as a leveraged buy-out, might make the additional value available to shareholders without full dividend taxation.

Because of its assumption regarding retentions and its implications for share values, the new view of the effect of the classical systems is sometimes known as the "trapped equity" or "tax capitalization" view. The most striking policy implication of this perspective for evaluating existing law and integration alternatives is that because current share values should already be discounted below the value of corporate assets, elimination of the additional burden of the classical system with respect to existing corporate assets would produce windfall gains to current shareholders.

Our illustrative examples have generally assumed equality of tax rates in order to show how the double tax structure itself could produce a discount in share prices. The precise amount of any such discount would be affected by the various rate relationships under the classical system, as well as other deviations from our assumptions, such as limitations on the deductibility of capital losses.

c. The "Traditional" View of Dividends and Taxes

Under the tax capitalization view, it is assumed that a firm can adjust the amount of its earnings paid out as dividends to take account of its needs for funds for new projects. A more traditional view of corporate finance assumes that companies are encouraged by the market to pay dividends, in spite of any additional tax burden. Various reasons have been suggested why shareholders might value more highly firms that pay dividends, including the hypothesis that dividends are an important signal to investors of financial success. On this view, the need to maintain a certain level of dividend payments would interfere with the firm's ability to use retained earnings as its marginal source of finance for new investments. Instead, it would rely on debt and then new equity issues to raise capital.

If new equity issues, rather than retentions, provided the marginal source of finance for new corporate projects, potential shareholders would invest in new corporate shares only if they expected the corporation's rate of return to be high enough to compensate for the additional level of tax to be imposed on their investment. From the corporation's perspective, financing by new share issues would therefore result in a higher cost of capital, thereby affecting its investment possibilities. Accordingly, proponents of the traditional view, which has recently been endorsed by the Treasury, often criticize the corporate income tax for its negative effect on corporate investment . . ..

1.4 The Incentive to Distribute Earnings in Nondividend Transactions

We now consider the choice faced by a corporation that has decided to distribute corporate earnings to individual shareholders, but has not yet decided whether to pay a dividend or to make a nondividend distribution, such as repurchasing its shares in a redemption transaction. If share repurchases are subject to exchange treatment, they are preferable to dividends under the current system for several reasons. First, the redeeming shareholders will be able to recover a portion of their bases, unless section 302(d) of the Internal Revenue Code treats the redemption as a dividend. Second, the capital gains tax rate on sales may be lower than the ordinary income rate on dividends. And finally, only the selling shareholders will pay taxes, so that continuing shareholders will avoid taxation, even though they are in the same position they would have been in, had all shareholders received a *pro rata* dividend, and the continuing shareholders acquired the interests of the selling shareholders.

Given these advantages, it has long been a puzzle why more public corporations did not make distributions in the form of share repurchases as opposed to dividends. Closely-held companies have long recognized the advantages of distributing earnings in forms other than dividends. Adherents of the traditional view of dividend policy described above might hypothesize that the public markets would not react to a signal of success conveyed by share repurchases as positively as to a signal conveyed by dividends. Whatever the reasons for past behavior, the tax advantages of nondividend distributions are presumably at least partially responsible for the increase in such distributions by public companies in recent years.

1.5 Conclusions

The foregoing discussion leads to the following conclusions regarding the tax-induced distortions of a classical double-tax system:

1. There is a tax disincentive for individuals to invest in new corporate equity that pays dividends, relative to non-corporate-equity investments, including corporate debt. Whether investment in corporate stock on which earnings are to be retained is favored or disfavored, relative to noncorporate investments, depends on the relationships among effective corporate, shareholder and capital gains tax rates.

2. There is a tax incentive for corporations to finance their investments by retained earnings or debt, rather than by the issuance of new shares. Whether the tax system is neutral as between retained earnings and debt, prefers retained earnings to debt, or vice versa depends on the relationships among effective corporate, shareholder and capital gains tax rates.

3. Whether a classical system encourages retention of corporate earnings, encourages distributions, or is neutral depends on the relationships among effective corporate, shareholder and capital gains tax rates.

Nontax reasons for retaining or distributing earnings may affect share values and the cost of corporate capital under the classical system.

4. Nondividend distributions to individual shareholders receive preferential tax treatment relative to dividends under the U.S. version of the classical system. This distortion would be increased by reintroduction of substantially preferential treatment of capital gains.

The preceding discussion suggests that current tax law distorts individual and corporate taxpayer decisions in several ways. These distortions are undesirable if they influence corporate financial policy in a detrimental manner, encouraging, for example, the substitution of debt for equity, thus increasing the risk of bankruptcy. The effects on corporate investment policy are detrimental if the tax system discourages a corporation from undertaking projects that are otherwise productive or favors projects that are not otherwise the most productive. The current relationship between the corporate and individual income taxes may also undesirably distort individual investment decisions. Finally, whatever inefficiencies are thought to follow from the taxation of returns of capital in general may be exacerbated by the additional tax on corporate income.

Whether current law actually leads to the expected behavioral changes is an empirical question, the resolution of which depends in part on the ultimate incidence of the corporate tax. Even if the burden of the tax does not fall entirely on investors in corporate equity, distortions may nonetheless occur. If, for instance, the after-tax rates of return on corporate and noncorporate capital have been equated through the shifting of capital from the corporate to the noncorporate sector (causing pretax rates of return on noncorporate capital to decline), there might be no current disincentive to invest in new equity, although the total amount of capital investment, as well as the relative size of the corporate and noncorporate sectors, might not be optimal.

Unfortunately the incidence and ultimate effects of the corporate income tax remain disputed, although it seems to be generally agreed that at least a portion of the tax is borne by shareholders. . .

Even if the existing system did not cause undesirable distortions in behavior, the distinctions created by current law would warrant legislative change because they have proven exceedingly difficult, some would say impossible, to apply in practice. For instance, the distinction between debt and equity has given rise to a prodigious amount of litigation and uncertainty, as has that between dividends and redemptions. Even where there is little uncertainty, the distinctions under current law divert resources into tax planning. . .

Part 2: System of Integration

The tax-induced distortions of the classical system of corporate income taxation could be addressed in a variety of ways:

1. On distribution of corporate earnings to shareholders, the duplicative effect of the shareholder tax could be eliminated by a shareholder credit for corporate taxes previously paid with respect to the distributed earnings. Duplication could also be avoided by a corporate deduction for dividend payments.

2. Corporate earnings could be allocated annually to shareholders, as is done with respect to partnerships and subchapter S corporations under current law.

3. The corporate tax could be repealed and shareholders taxed currently on changes in the value of corporate stock.

4. The corporate tax could be retained and shareholder taxation of dividends eliminated.

5. Corporations could be granted a current deduction for capital investment, which would effectively eliminate the burden of the corporate income tax on the return to shareholders. The most comprehensive of such proposals would convert the corporate income tax into a tax on cash flow. Similar results could be obtained by exempting from corporate taxation a specified return on corporate capital.

6. Dividends paid on new equity investments could be made deductible by the corporation, as suggested in prior A.L.I. studies.

   This study considers in detail the first of these alternatives—integration with respect to corporate distributions, which is also the approach that has generally been adopted in foreign systems. Distribution-related integration would be less complex than the second alternative, allocation of undistributed earnings to shareholders, which would require annual attribution of corporate income to a myriad of capital interests that are more complex than those now permitted in subchapter S. The Treasury Department's recent report on integration rejects such an allocation system because of its administrative complexity. Distribution-related integration as developed in this study would not, however, be inconsistent with subsequent adoption of such allocation, if it proved to be practical. Indeed, certain features of distribution-related integration, such as a constructive dividend option, are sometimes viewed as potential bridges to allocation.

   The third alternative, current taxation of changes in share values, is not considered here because it would require abandoning the realization basis of the income tax. That may or may not be a desirable step for other reasons, but it is not necessary to achieve integration. The Treasury's recent report on integration expressed a preference for the fourth alternative—elimination of shareholder taxation. Such a system is not pursued here because it would preclude the application of graduated rates to individual investors. The fifth alternative—adoption of a corporate cash flow tax or an exemption for a return on corporate capital—is not pursued because it would effectively preclude current taxation of retained corporate income. The sixth has already been the subject of previous A.L.I. reports.

In short, the current study has been premised on the retention of one level of current tax on corporate income and of graduated rates for individuals in a realization income tax system.

2.1 Methods of Integration

There are three basic methods of accomplishing the result of integration with respect to distributed corporate earnings: shareholder credit, dividend deduction, and split rates.

a. Shareholder Credit Integration

Under the most common form of integration abroad, shareholders would treat dividend payments just as wage earners now treat wage payments subject to withholding. Cash dividends received would be increased (or "grossed up") by the amount of federal income tax paid by the corporation on the earnings distributed as dividends, just as cash wages are increased by amounts withheld. An eligible shareholder would compute the tax at his regular rate on the gross dividend, and a tax credit would be available for the amount of the gross-up, just as a credit is now available for withholding on wages. Complete implementation of this system would result in the corporate tax becoming simply a withholding tax on individual income earned through corporate entities.

Consider a corporation that receives $100 in taxable income and pays $30 in corporate taxes, (assuming a 30–percent corporate tax rate). Table 4 indicates how distributions of $70 and $20 of after-tax corporate income would be treated by shareholders whose tax rates were 20 percent or 40 percent. The grossed-up dividend is equal to the cash dividend (i.e., the dividend net of corporate taxes) divided by $1-c$, where c equals the corporate tax rate. Equivalently, the gross dividend equals the net dividend multiplied by $1/(1-c)$, which equals 1.429 when the corporate tax rate is 30 percent. If all corporations were taxed at the same rate, a single gross-up rate could be used by all shareholders for all dividends from all corporations. Having included the gross dividend in income, the shareholder applies his personal tax rate (p) and reduces the resulting tax by the shareholder credit attributable to corporate tax payments. The credit is always the cash dividend times $c/(1-c)$, which would be .429 if c were 30 percent. Once again, if all corporations paid tax at the same rate, shareholder credits on all dividends could be determined by applying the same rate. As a result of the gross-up and credit, distributed after-tax corporate earnings are taxed to shareholders at a rate of $(p-c)/(1-c)$, eliminating the separate burden of the corporate tax.

Table 4
Shareholder Credit Integration

	Distribution of $70		Distribution of $20	
Shareholder tax rate	40%	20%	40%	20%
(1) Cash distribution	$70[a]	$70[a]	$20[b]	$20[b]
(2) Grossed-up dividend	100	100	29	29
(3) Gross shareholder tax	40	20	12	6
(4) Shareholder tax credit [(2)–(1)]	30	30	9	9
(5) Net shareholder tax [(3)–(4)]	10	(10)	3	(3)
(6) Net shareholder cash [(1)–(5)]	60	80	17	23

[a] $1.429 \times \$70 = \$100$
[b] $1.429 \times \$20 = \$29$

The results shown in Table 4 accomplish the goals of integration by applying the shareholder tax rate, and only the shareholder rate, to distributed corporate income. With a $70 distribution after corporate taxes, each shareholder is in the position he would be in if he had earned $100 on individual account, with a $20 cash distribution each shareholder is treated as though $29 of income had been earned on individual account. Achieving those results for the 20 percent taxpayer in our example would require that the credit could be used against taxes generated by other income or, if there were no other such taxes, that the credit be refundable. "Shareholder credit integration" along these lines is often referred to abroad as "imputation" because the corporate tax is imputed to the shareholder through the gross-up and credit. The two terms will be used interchangeably in this study.

As these examples indicate, the shareholder credit leaves the additional cash flow from integration in the hands of shareholders if the corporation does not adjust its dividend payments in response to the shareholder credit. The credit mechanism is therefore sometimes said to be a superior form of integration because the benefits of integration can be denied foreign and tax-exempt shareholders by making the credit nonrefundable to such shareholders.

b. Dividend Deduction

Integration could also be accomplished by permitting a corporate deduction for amounts paid as dividends, just as a deduction is now permitted for amounts paid as interest. The immediate effect of the deduction would be to increase the corporation's cash flow, although some of that benefit might be passed on to shareholders in the form of increased dividends. In the example illustrated in Table 4, equivalent results would be achieved under a dividend deduction if the cash distribution were increased by 42.9 percent, from $70 to $100 and from $20 to $29.

As the dividend deduction method initially results in more cash at the corporate level, it is sometimes advocated as a superior form of integration on the ground that one of the purposes of integration is to provide additional incentives for corporate capital formation. On the other hand, one of the method's defects is sometimes said to be its automatic extension of the benefits of integration to tax-exempt and foreign shareholders, as compared with the possibility of denying imputation credits to such investors under shareholder credit integration. Finally, a dividend deduction would be simpler from the perspective of shareholders, because dividends would not be subject to a withholding mechanism, as they would be under imputation.

c. Split Rates

An alternative method of integration is to levy a corporate tax on distributed earnings at a rate below that applied to retained earnings. Complete integration with respect to distributed corporate earnings would require a tax rate of zero on distributions and would in effect be indistinguishable from a full dividend deduction. Less-than-complete integration would involve a tax rate on distributed earnings greater than zero but lower than the rate for retained earnings, making it indistinguishable from a partial deduction for dividends. As there are no major differences between the split rate and dividend deduction methods of integration, the former will not be further discussed as a separate type of integration in this study.

d. Equivalence of Integration Methods

The differences in cash flow under the shareholder credit and dividend deduction methods depend on the assumption that there will be no change in the amount of cash dividends paid by corporations in response to integration. To the extent cash dividends were reduced under the shareholder credit or increased under the dividend deduction, precisely the same results could obtain under either alternative. A choice between the two methods thus depends, in part, on the effect of imperfections in the capital markets and on whether those imperfections suggest that it would be better to have the initial increase in cash flow at the shareholder or the corporate level.

If, for enforcement purposes, a withholding tax on dividends were desirable under the dividend deduction method, that withholding tax would serve the same function as an equivalent rate corporate tax under the shareholder credit. The two integration methods would then be equivalent not only in their ultimate effect assuming perfect capital markets, but also in their immediate result. Under the dividend deduction the shareholder would include in income not only the cash dividends received, but also the withholding tax collected by the corporation, which is precisely the same process as that involved in grossing up the dividend under the shareholder credit. Likewise, the corporate tax on undistributed earnings plus the withholding tax on distributed earnings under the dividend deduction would equal the corporate tax due under the shareholder credit. Table 5 illustrates this equivalence when the corporate tax rate is 30 percent, the withholding rate is 30 percent, and a cash distribution of $25 is made to a 40 percent taxpayer by a corporation that has $100 in taxable income.

Table 5
Equivalence of Shareholder Credit and Dividend Deduction
(With Withholding) Methods of Integration

	Dividend Deduction	*Shareholder Credit*
Corporate taxable income (before dividend deduction)	$100	$100
Cash distribution	25	25
Corporate tax		
On taxable income (after dividend deduction)	19[a]	30
Withholding on distribution	11[b]	0
Total	30	30
Retained corporate earnings (after taxes and dividends)	45	45
Taxable dividend to shareholder	36[c]	36[d]
Gross shareholder tax	14	14
Shareholder credit (or withholding)	11	11
Net shareholder tax due	3	3
Net shareholder cash	22	22

[a] 30% corporate tax rate applied to taxable income of $100 reduced by gross dividend of $36 (including $11 withholding tax).

[b] 30% of gross distribution of $36.

[c] $25 cash dividend plus $11 withholding.

[d] $25 × 1.429 = $36

Although the substantive results are the same under the two methods, the difference in labels might cause different legal, regulatory, or accounting consequences. For instance, the amount of the "dividend" paid for various purposes might differ. Under the dividend deduction, the dividend is arguably $36 in Table 5 because that is the amount deducted, and from which $11 is withheld, if the shareholder receives $25 in cash. Under the shareholder credit, the dividend paid by the corporation is arguably the cash distribution of $25, which gives rise to a credit of $11 on the grossed-up amount. Because part of the tax is characterized as "withholding" under the dividend deduction, the dividend appears to be the gross amount before withholding; under the shareholder credit, the dividend appears to be the cash distribution, net of corporate taxes. An $11 portion of the tax paid by the corporation might therefore be subject to different treatment by regulatory authorities or under tax treaties because it could be characterized as withholding (and therefore paid on behalf of shareholders) under the dividend deduction, but as a corporate tax under the shareholder credit mechanism.

There may also be differences in public perceptions regarding the two methods of distribution-related integration. One possibility is illustrated by the case of Jacques Chaban–Delmas, who as Prime Minister of France was attacked in the press for paying no personal income taxes for several years in the late 1960s, when no net taxes were due because of offsetting imputation credits. The possibility that high income individuals might appear not to be paying taxes would be less likely under a dividend deduction system, but it would be easier to argue that a corporation paid no or little taxes due to the deduction. A system that combined split rates (or a dividend deduction) with a shareholder credit (as in Germany), might avoid the extreme versions of each of these perception problems. While these differences in appearance are important and should be considered when designing an integration system and how its parts are labeled, they should not obscure the substantive equivalence of imputation and a dividend deduction with withholding.

NOTE

We see that the question of "who bears the burden of the corporation income tax?" remains unresolved although it has been debated and examined for decades. The increased globalization of business activity and the decreasing importance of geographic borders further complicate the burden analysis. In December 2007, Treasury officials indicated that they consider distributional analyses critical, that internationalization of business may have serious effects on the distributional impact of the corporate tax, and that Treasury may deem it appropriate to construct separate distributional analyses—one based on the more traditional assumption that the corporation income tax is borne by capital and one based on the idea that labor may also bear a notable portion of the burden. See A Review of the Evidence on the Incidence of the Corporate Income Tax, Office of Tax Analysis Paper 101 (December 2007) (authored by William Gentry, Williams College)[the OTA paper series reflects the views of the authors and are not Treasury position papers]. In May of 2012, the Office of Tax Analysis revisited this question in a paper that sought to refine the methodology used by Treasury since 2008. See Distributing the Corporate Income Tax: Revised U.S. Treasury Methodology, Office of Tax Analysis Technical Paper No. 5 (May 2012) (authored by Cronin, Lin, Power and Cooper).

Separate from the empirical question of who "bears" the burden, is why there has been no substantial change in the structure of the U.S. corporate tax system despite the apparent advantages such a change might offer. Any examination of this broad question invites consideration of the alignment of interests among the various kinds of managers, shareholders, and corporations. For a thoughtful discussion, see Doran, Managers, Shareholders, and the Corporate Double Tax, 95 Va. L. Rev. 518 (2009).

CHAPTER 2

TAXATION OF THE SHAREHOLDER: CORPORATE DISTRIBUTIONS AND DISPOSITION OF INVESTOR INTERESTS (NOT IN REORGANIZATION)

I. HISTORY—RATE STRUCTURE—CORRELATION WITH CORPORATION INCOME TAX

The corporate income tax affects not only the corporation itself, as explored in Chapter 1, but also the shareholder. This chapter examines the primary income tax implications of share ownership on the shareholder—the tax effects of various types of "distributions" from the corporation. Changes implemented almost a decade ago have remained in place. As a result, the likely importance of distinctions among some forms of distributions has been tempered, as explored later in this chapter.

From 1913–1954, the personal income tax consisted of two parts, a "normal" tax and an "additional" tax.

The personal income tax act of 1913 exempted dividends from normal tax. Both the tax rate on corporate income and the normal rate on personal income were set at 1 percent; thus, for distributed earnings, the corporate tax operated as a withholding feature of the personal levy.[*] This treatment continued through 1918, as increases in the personal normal rate were matched by increases in the corporate rate. [Author's footnote: "With these exceptions: a corporate rate greater than the personal normal rate in 1917, and greater than the rate applicable to the first $4000 of normal tax income in 1918."] But from 1919 on, the corporate rate exceeded the personal normal rate and thus the corporate tax became, in part a separate and distinct levy on distributed earnings. The rate gap widened gradually until 1936 when the bridge between the two taxes was removed completely by the abolition of the dividend exemption. A return to something like the 1919–36 procedure was instituted by the Internal Revenue Code of 1954 in the form of a tax credit based on dividends received. But here, too, a substantial gap

---

[*]The personal income tax consisted of both a "normal" and an "additional" tax from 1913–1954. Dividends were not exempted from the additional tax.—ED.

exists between the personal income tax credit and the rate of corporate tax. Therefore, since 1919, the distributed earnings of corporate enterprises have been treated differently from the other sources of income for Federal income-tax purposes; from 1919 to 1936, because the corporate rate was higher than the personal normal rate: from 1936 through 1953, because corporate earnings were taxed at the corporate level when earned with no allowance at the personal level when distributed; and from 1954 on, because the personal income-tax relief accorded distributed earnings falls short of the corporate tax rate.*

Although there has been congressional vacillation over the years as to the extent to which corporate earnings are to be subjected to both a corporate and an individual tax, Congress has imposed a "double tax" on distributed earnings since 1913. For many years, however, under the now-repealed § 116, the double tax was mitigated to a very limited extent, as shareholders were permitted to exclude $100 of dividends ($200 on a joint return) from gross income.

The taxation of dividends is not dependent alone on the statutory word *income*. The Code is explicit in providing that "dividends" are includable in a taxpayer's gross income. See §§ 61(a)(7) and 301(c). As defined in § 316(a), a "dividend" for income tax purposes is "any distribution of property made by a corporation to its shareholders (1) out of its earnings and profits accumulated after February 28, 1913, or (2) out of its earnings and profits" of the current taxable year. A distribution that does not constitute a "dividend" is treated as a tax-free return of capital to the extent of the taxpayer's stock basis (§ 301(c)(2)), but to the extent that the distribution exceeds the taxpayer's basis, the excess is treated as "gain from the sale or exchange of" the stock (§ 301(c)(3)(A)). Usually, but not always, the taxable gain is a capital gain, long-term if the stock has been held for the requisite holding period.

Historically, dividends were taxed at ordinary income tax rates. Thus,  during periods in which the rate on capital gains was lower than the ordinary rate, taxpayers had incentives in many cases to structure or characterize distributions as something other than a dividend, especially where that alternative characterization could receive capital gains treatment. For example, before 1986 and after 1990, when the dividend rate exceeded the capital gains rate, shareholders had an incentive to characterize a corporate distribution as a redemption of stock.

However, in the Jobs and Growth Tax Relief Reconciliation Act of 2003 ("2003 Act"), Congress reduced the tax rate on dividends to the net capital gain tax rate by directly linking the taxation of dividends to the taxation of net capital gain.** See § 1(h)(11). This reduced tax rate is available to most dividends including those of many foreign corporations. Once again, the

---

*D. Holland, Differential Taxation and Tax Relief, 3 Tax Revision Compendium 1551, 1552 (House Ways and Means Comm. 1959).

**As one of the conforming amendments of the 2003 Act, section 341 (the collapsible corporation provisions) was repealed because the repeal of *General Utilities* had made it a dead letter.

financial stake in many corporate tax issues has been substantially lowered. Yet despite the reduced dollar significance to a number of the statutory questions, the issues themselves remain.

A notable distinction between dividends and capital gains continues despite their rate parity. Even though most dividends are now taxed at the net capital gain rate, dividends still remain classified *as dividends*. Thus, dividend income cannot be used to offset capital losses in the same way as capital gains. Recall that the deductibility of capital losses continues to be limited. Capital losses are allowed *in full* against *capital gains*, but are allowed only to the extent of $3,000 against ordinary income (including dividends taxed at the lower capital gain rate). Thus, capital losses will have an offset value against capital gains that will often be far greater than their offset value against ordinary income. Unused capital losses can be carried over without limit.

The first subject in this chapter explores the definition of a dividend and the role of "earnings and profits." In many respects earnings and profits is similar to, and sometimes—but only sometimes—identical with, "earned surplus" or "retained earnings" as those terms are used in financial accounting. A case in which the earned surplus figure on a corporation's balance sheet may not reflect the accumulated earnings and profits occurs when the corporation has distributed a dividend in its own stock, thereby capitalizing all or part of its earned surplus. Despite the reduction in earned surplus, there is no reduction in the corporation's earnings and profits, since no corporate assets have been distributed.

Section 312 describes the impact on earnings and profits that results from various corporate transactions, but the Code itself does not define the term *earnings and profits*. The process of definition has been left to a common-law type of judicial development and, in part, to the Treasury. See Treas. Reg. § 1.312–6. It is important to recognize that the concept of a corporation's earnings and profits is not relevant to the corporation's income tax liability. Its relevance is in determining whether a corporate distribution constitutes dividend income to the shareholders within the definition of "dividend" in § 316(a).

The statute did not always limit taxation to earnings and profits accumulated after March 1, 1913. See Lynch v. Hornby, 247 U.S. 339, 344 (1918), in which the Supreme Court said:

> Dividends are the appropriate fruit of stock ownership, are commonly reckoned as income, and are expended as such by the stockholder without regard to whether they are declared from the most recent earnings, or from a surplus accumulated from the earnings of the past, or are based upon the increased value of the property of the corporation. The stockholder is, in the ordinary case, a different entity from the corporation, and Congress was at liberty to treat the dividends as coming to him as extra, and as constituting a part of his income when they came to hand.

Hence we construe the provisions of the Act that "the net income of a taxable person, shall include gains, profits, and income derived from . . . interest, rent, dividends, . . . or gains or profits and income derived from any source whatever" as including . . . all dividends declared and paid in the ordinary course of business by a corporation to its stockholders after the taking effect of the Act (March 1, 1913), whether from current earnings, or from the accumulated surplus made up of past earnings or increase in value of corporate assets, notwithstanding it accrued to the corporation in whole or in part prior to March 1, 1913.

Before the *Hornby* decision came down Congress amended the statute prospectively to define "the term 'dividends' . . . [as] any distribution made or offered to be made by the corporation . . . <u>out of its earnings and profits</u> accrued since March first, nineteen hundred and thirteen." In 1936 the law was amended again, this time to broaden the source for dividends to include current earnings even if there are no accumulated earnings and profits (i.e., the "nimble dividend").

Prior to the 1986 Act, the lack of adequate earnings and profits to cover a distribution meant that the taxpayer would be able to recover stock basis tax-free and would very likely have capital gain on the amount of distribution in excess of basis. However, during the period following the 1986 Act in which the maximum tax rate on ordinary income (including dividends) and capital gains was the same, amounts received in excess of basis no longer enjoyed favored status. The return, in 1991, of a differential between the top ordinary income rate and the capital gains rate reintroduced the importance of a distribution being characterized as a dividend. Once again this importance was diminished with the 2003 Act's reduction of the tax rate on dividends by linking it to the rate on net capital gains. Because the only difference now is the possibility that a portion of the distribution may be considered a tax-free return of basis, the importance of the earnings and profits concept is reduced. (One can imagine, however, the issue of earnings and profits taking on varying significance for different shareholders of the same corporation. For shareholders with a very high basis (for example, recipients of stock from a decedent's estate with a high basis calculated under § 1014), an absence of earnings and profits allows much of a distribution to be a tax-free return of basis. In contrast, shareholders with a low basis, perhaps early investors in the corporation, would experience little impact from the determination of earnings and profits.). Additionally, a corporate shareholder (i.e. a corporation that owns stock in other corporations) may seek to characterize a distribution it receives as a dividend because of the special treatment afforded dividend income earned by a corporate shareholder. If a distributing corporation has a variety of shareholders (individual and corporate) in different positions (high and low stock basis), these shareholders may have conflicting desires about the characterization of a distribution.

Later in this chapter we address corporate distributions made to shareholders in redemption of all or part of their stock. In the past, the main issue was whether a particular redemption distribution would be treated as a dividend. In that event, typically, the entire amount distributed would be ordinary income. If not characterized as a dividend, the distribution would be treated as one made "in exchange" for the stock. In the latter case the stockholder would usually enjoy tax-free recovery of the stock basis and capital gain as to the excess. Here, too, the 1986 Act reduced the stakes only to see them rise in 1991, and once again diminish with the 2003 Act's taxation of dividends and net capital gain at the same rate. The question now generally focuses on whether there is to be tax-free basis recovery, and, for taxpayers with capital losses, whether the income can offset the losses. (The 2003 Act provided that qualified dividends would be taxed at the same rate as net capital gains, § 1(h)(11), but did not allow dividends to offset capital losses).

This chapter also addresses § 1244 of the Code. Under certain circumstances, § 1244 provides that shareholders of "small business corporations" recognize ordinary loss rather than capital loss on the sale or exchange of their stock, removing the § 1211 limitation on deductibility.

II. CORPORATE DISTRIBUTIONS OF PROPERTY (INCLUDING CASH)

A. DISTRIBUTIONS NOT IN RETIREMENT OF INVESTOR INTEREST

1. EARNINGS AND PROFITS—§ 312

a. Relevance and Computation

Bangor & Aroostook R.R. v. Commissioner
193 F.2d 827 (1st Cir. 1951), *cert. denied*, 343 U.S. 934 (1952).

■ Before MAGRUDER, CHIEF JUDGE, and WOODBURY and HARTIGAN, CIRCUIT JUDGES.

■ MAGRUDER, CHIEF JUDGE. Bangor and Aroostook Railroad Company petitions for review of a decision of the Tax Court of the United States determining that there is a deficiency in petitioner's excess profits tax in the sum of $3,677.45 for the calendar year 1943.

The applicable statute is the Excess Profits Tax Act of 1940 . . .; Internal Revenue Code § 710 et seq. . . . Speaking generally, the "excess profits credit" is the statutory measure of normal profits exempt from the excess profits tax; the credit is deducted from the "excess profits net income" to obtain the "adjusted excess profits net income" upon which the tax is laid. The excess profits credit could be computed in either of two ways, by the average earnings method, I.R.C. § 713, or by the invested capital method, I.R.C. § 714. Petitioner elected the latter method, under which eight per cent of its "invested capital" became its excess profits credit. One component entering into the calculation of the "invested capital" was the "accumulated earnings and profits as of the beginning of such taxable year" I.R.C. § 718(a)(4).

In 1942 petitioner purchased in the open market for retirement and cancellation certain of its bonds of an aggregate par value of $634,000. The total purchase price was $497,553.30; and the difference between these two sums, or $136,446.70, is referred to hereinafter as petitioner's "bond profit" for the calendar year 1942. It is undisputed that this bond profit was realized income within the general definition of I.R.C. § 22(a).* . . . United States v. Kirby Lumber Co., 1931, 284 U.S. 1. . . Petitioner would have been taxable upon the whole amount of the bond profit in 1942, except for the fact that it elected to take advantage of the option provided under I.R.C. § [108] and § [1017] and thus was permitted to exclude the bond profit from the computation of its normal tax net income and surtax net income in its return for 1942.

Notwithstanding this treatment of the bond profit in its 1942 return, petitioner sought to diminish its excess profits tax for the calendar year 1943 by including $136,446.70, or the whole amount of the so-called bond profit, in the item "accumulated earnings and profits" as of January 1, 1943. Such inclusion enhanced the figure for petitioner's "invested capital" and its "excess profits credit", with a resultant reduction in petitioner's excess profits tax for 1943. The Tax Court ruled that the bond profit, not having been "recognized" though "realized" in 1942, should be excluded from "accumulated earnings and profits" as of January 1, 1943. This exclusion produced the deficiency found in the decision now under review.

We think the ruling of the Tax Court was correct. . .

It is important to observe the distinction between (1) income which is exempt from tax and (2) income which, though "realized" in a constitutional sense and thus within the power of Congress to tax, is not at the outset "recognized", the incidence of the tax being merely postponed.

As to (1), exempt income, such for instance as interest on tax-free bonds, if income of this sort is to be taken into "earnings or profits", the only logical time to do so is when the income is realized. It is so provided by regulation. Section [1.312–6(b)] on the subject of corporate dividends out of "earnings or profits", states that among the items "entering into the computation of corporate earnings or profits for a particular period are all income exempted by statute, income not taxable by the Federal Government under the Constitution, as well as all items includible in gross income under section [61] or corresponding provisions of prior Revenue Acts. . . Interest on State bonds and certain other obligations, although not taxable when received by a corporation, is taxable to the same extent as other dividends when distributed to shareholders in the form of dividends."

---

*Section 61(a) is the 1986 Code counterpart of § 22(a) of the 1939 Code, but § 22(a) did not have the equivalent of § 61(a)(12).—ED.

It is not in express terms provided that tax-exempt income, when realized, is also taken into "accumulated earnings and profits" under I.R.C. § 718(a)(4). That term is not defined in the Code. But § 35.718–2 of Reg. 112 refers back to § [312] of the Code and the regulations prescribed thereunder, and states that in general "the concept of 'accumulated earnings and profits' for the purpose of the excess profits tax is the same as for the purpose of the income tax. . ." . . . The clear inference from the regulations that truly exempted income may be carried into "accumulated earnings and profits", is evidently in accordance with the congressional purpose. . . If therefore a corporation receives during a given year income which is exempt from taxation, such as interest on tax-free bonds, and such income is left in the business to be available as working capital, it is reasonable and proper that such income, though not taxable to the corporation receiving it, should be included in the item "accumulated earnings and profits" as of the beginning of the following year, § 718(a)(4) of the Code, in the computation of the corporation's excess profits tax for that year.

But as to (2), income which, though "realized", is not at the outset "recognized", the problem is quite different. This concept in perhaps its most familiar instances appears in [the nonrecognition provisions of the Code]. The thought behind the nonrecognition provisions . . . is that, in certain transactions involving "the sale or exchange of property", though a gain may have been realized in a constitutional sense, it is unfair or inappropriate to tax the gain at the outset in view of the fact that in a popular and economic sense there has been a mere change in the form of ownership and the taxpayer has not yet really "cashed in" on the more or less theoretical gain. As expressed by the Supreme Court in Commissioner of Internal Revenue v. Wheeler, 1945, 324 U.S. 542, 546 . . .: "Congress has determined that in certain types of transaction the economic changes are not definitive enough to be given tax consequences, and has clearly provided that gains and losses on such transactions shall not be recognized for income-tax liability but shall be taken account of later. . . *It is sensible to carry through the theory in determining the tax effect of such transactions on earnings and profits.*" [Italics added.]

In Commissioner of Internal Revenue v. F. J. Young Corp., 1939, 103 F.2d 137, the third circuit had held that a gain which resulted from a tax-free exchange of securities under § [351] of the Revenue Act of 1928 must be considered "earnings or profits" out of which a "dividend" might be declared within the meaning of § [316] of the Act. But the court ignored or overlooked a provision of . . . Reg. 94 . . . [Treas. Reg. § 1.312–6(b)] which explicitly stated: "Gains and losses within the purview of [§ 1001(c)] *or corresponding provisions of prior Acts* are brought into the earnings and profits at the time and to the extent such gains and losses are recognized under that section." [Italics added.] . . . In Commissioner of Internal Revenue v. Wheeler, 1945, 324 U.S. 542 . . . supra, the Supreme Court expressly upheld the regulation as a reasonable and valid exercise of the rule-making power. It follows that Commissioner of Internal Revenue v. F. J. Young, Corp., supra, and cases like it, cannot be taken as authorities in support of the position urged by the taxpayer in the case at bar.

Congress itself has indicated approval of the foregoing regulation by writing it expressly into the law. Section [312(f)]: "Gain or loss so realized shall increase or decrease the earnings and profits to, but not beyond, the extent to which such a realized gain or loss was recognized in computing net income under the law applicable to the year in which such sale or disposition was made." This evidently was regarded as not a change in existing law but only in the nature of a clarifying amendment. The House committee stated that the provision of [§ 312(f)] merely enacted the rule which had been applied by the Treasury under existing law. It was pointed out that while taxpayers generally had concurred in the Treasury rule, the Board of Tax Appeals and some court decisions, mentioning specifically Commissioner of Internal Revenue v. F. J. Young Corp., 3 Cir., 103 F.2d 137, had followed the contrary theory "that gain or loss, even though not recognized in computing net income, nevertheless affects earnings and profits." The report further stated: "The purpose of this amendment is to clarify the law with respect to what constitutes earnings and profits of a corporation. This is important not only for the purpose of determining whether distributions are taxable dividends but also in determining equity invested capital for excess-profits-tax purposes." H.R. Rep. No. 2894, 76th Cong., 3d Sess., p. 41.

It is true enough that the result reached here by the Tax Court is not directly commanded by [§ 312(f)] of the Code, for that subsection by its terms deals with the delayed recognition of gain or loss realized from the "sale of other disposition of property by a corporation," whereas the nonrecognized gain in the present case resulted from the taxpayer's reacquisition of its own bonds. But it does not follow that the underlined principle exemplified by the specific instances covered by the literal language of [§ 312(f)] should not be applied in other analogous nonrecognition situations. . .

Congress sought in § 312(f) to "clarify" the law in particular instances where the law had been muddied by court decisions like Commissioner of Internal Revenue v. F. J. Young Corp., 3 Cir., 1939, 103 F.2d 137. But when [§ 312(f)] was enacted, there had been no similar court decisions dealing with the effect on earnings and profits of gains from the discharge of indebtedness realized but not at the same time recognized; so that particular problem did not receive the attention of Congress when [§ 312(f)] was in process of enactment. The Tax Court properly observed in the case at bar: "Surely, by taking pains to make certain that unrecognized gains or losses from sales or other dispositions of property would not be reflected in earnings and profits, Congress could not have intended thereby to produce a different result with respect to other unrecognized gains or losses, merely by failing to mention them."

The underlying principle, of which [§ 312(f)] is but an illustration, is that "earnings and profits" must be computed on the same basis as that employed in computing income subject to the income tax; in other words, that gains ought to be reflected in earnings and profits at the time they are "recognized" and taken into account for income tax purposes. . .

. . . The taxpayer having technically realized its so-called bond profit in 1942, elected under an optional method of accounting permitted by the statute to postpone recognition of such gain and to exclude the amount thereof from its gross income reported for 1942. It cannot then shift its method of accounting, and treat that gain as both realized and recognized in 1942, for the purpose of enhancing a deduction (the excess profits credit) used in the computation of its excess profits tax liability for 1943.

The rule in United States v. Kirby Lumber Co., 1931, 284 U.S. 1, . . . has been criticized both on theoretical and practical grounds, and doubtless in many cases it worked a hardship. Congress took account of these criticisms in 1939, when it amended the Internal Revenue Code by adding [§ 108]. . .

It appears, then, that when the provision of § [108] for delayed recognition of gain is compared with the . . . delayed recognition situations, the . . . sections stem from a common legislative conviction that it is fairer not to impose the income tax forthwith upon the theoretical gains realized from certain transactions, but to postpone the recognition of the gain, and the incidence of the tax, until the occurrence of an economically more significant event.

. . . The Commissioner, in auditing the taxpayer's 1942 return, reduced the basis of its depreciable property pursuant to the applicable regulations under § [1017]. As a result, the taxpayer's depreciation deduction for 1942 was reduced in the amount of $1,736.69. This adjustment correspondingly increased the taxpayer's taxable income for 1942. Such increased income in the sum of $1,736.69 was therefore added by the Commissioner to the taxpayer's "accumulated earnings and profits" as of January 1, 1943, for the purpose of computing the taxpayer's excess profits credit in determining the excess profits tax for 1943. The Commissioner and the Tax Court agree that, to that extent, the bond profit having been reflected in 1942 income should be reflected also in the item of accumulated earnings and profits as of January 1, 1943. The taxpayer's basis having been reduced, by command of the statute, depreciation to be taken by the taxpayer for income tax purposes in the succeeding years will necessarily be lower, and taxable gains correspondingly higher; and as the bond profit is thus gradually recognized and reflected in income, it will at the same time be reflected in earnings and profits. If and when the taxpayer sells the property the basis of which has thus been reduced, the whole of the bond profit will have been recognized and reflected both in income and in earnings and profits. . . Such treatment of the bond profit seems to be clearly required by the statute and the applicable regulations. It would necessarily follow that the Tax Court properly rejected the taxpayer's contention that the whole amount of the bond profit should be taken into "accumulated earnings and profits" as of January 1, 1943; for otherwise, the bond profit would be doing double duty in reducing taxpayer's excess profits tax liability for 1943 and subsequent years. . .

The decision of the Tax Court is affirmed.

NOTES

1. In January 2010, Corporation Y is formed, and it has no earnings for that year. In 2011, Y loses $10,000. In 2012, Y earns $10,000. What is the tax consequence to the shareholders if a dividend is paid at the end of 2011? At the beginning of 2012? See § 316(a). Is the difference in result appropriate? Why?

2. X Corporation distributes to its shareholders as a dividend a building with an adjusted basis of $50,000 and a fair market value of $100,000. What impact does that distribution have on the corporation's earnings and profits? Why? What would be the effect on X Corporation's earnings and profits if it gave the building to charity? See Rev. Rul. 78–123, 1978–1 C.B. 87 (reduction limited to property's adjusted basis).

3. Why should tax-deferred income (such as that involved in *Bangor & Aroostook R.R.*) augment the earnings and profits account for purposes of § 316(a) only if and as it is recognized? Cf. Treas. Reg. § 1.312–6.

4. Suppose Corporation X's only 2012 income is the interest it receives on its municipal bond holdings. X receives $10,000 in interest and distributes $10,000 to its shareholders. Do the shareholders have dividend income? What is the effect of § 103?

5. Corporation X, owning stock in Corporation Y, receives a distribution from Corporation Y which was not taxable as a dividend. What is the impact on Corporation X's earnings and profits? What happens to the basis of the stock Corporation X holds in Corporation Y? See § 312(f)(2).

6. Mr. Able buys ten shares of Corporation Z's stock on September 30, 2012. On October 1, 2012, a dividend is declared to all holders. What are the income tax consequences to Able? Why? Ought a shareholder be required to treat a distribution as a dividend if the covering earnings and profits all antedate his stock purchase and if his stock basis exceeds the amount of his distribution? See United States v. Phellis, 257 U.S. 156, 171–72 (1921).

7. The IRS will not issue an advance ruling as to the amount of a corporation's earnings and profits. See Rev. Proc. 2012–3, 2012–1 I.R.B 113.

Joseph B. Ferguson v. Commissioner

47 T.C. 11 (1966), *acq.* 1970–2 C.B. xix.

■ HOYT, JUDGE. [The taxpayer was the sole shareholder in a corporation called "444," which was on the cash basis. In 1959 it expended $75,000 which the Commissioner characterized as a "constructive dividend" to the taxpayer. As of the beginning of 1959, 444 had a deficit in its earnings and profits account. Its current earnings in 1959 were sufficient to cover the "constructive dividend" unless, as taxpayer contended, the current earnings and profits account were to be charged with 444's income tax liability for 1959. The Commissioner contended that the corporate tax liability was an improper charge because the cash basis taxpayer had not paid the tax during the year 1959.]

This [case] brings us face-to-face with one of the classic unresolved problems in the area of earnings and profits: Are current year's earnings and profits of a cash basis corporation reduced by Federal income tax on current year's income although such tax is not paid until the following year (or years)? The regulations under section 312, I.R.C. 1954, provide (in sec. 1.312–6):

> (a) In determining the amount of earnings and profits (whether of the taxable year, or accumulated since February 28, 1913, or accumulated before March 1, 1913) due consideration must be given to the facts, and, while mere bookkeeping entries increasing or decreasing surplus will not be conclusive, the amount of the earnings and profits in any case will be dependent upon the method of accounting properly employed in computing taxable income (or net income, as the case may be). For instance, a corporation keeping its books and filing its income tax returns under subchapter E, chapter 1 of the Code, on the cash receipts and disbursements basis may not use the accrual basis in determining earnings and profits; . . .

Despite the unambiguous language of this regulation, the courts have had considerable difficulty coping with the effect of Federal income taxes on the earnings and profits of a cash basis corporation.[3] Leading text writers have noted the split of authority which exists in the cases today. Bittker, Federal Income Taxation of Corporations and Shareholders 145, fn. 9; Surrey and Warren, Federal Income Taxation 1238 (1960). This Court has played an integral role in the turbulent history of this problem, a history which must be reviewed and understood in order to adequately analyze and decide the issue in this particular case.

This question was first decided in Hadden v. Commissioner, 49 F. 2d 709 (C.A. 2, 1931), in which it was held that earnings and profits of a cash basis corporation *are* reduced by income tax on current year's income. Our first encounter with the problem arose in M. H. Alworth Trust, 46 B.T.A. 1045 (1942), revd. 136 F. 2d 812 (C.A. 8, 1943), certiorari denied 320 U.S. 784, in which we held that earnings and profits *are* reduced. We relied on the *Hadden* case but did not discuss it. Our decision was based upon corporate law and accounting concepts of dividends and impairment of capital. We reasoned that earnings and profits must take into account "outstanding liabilities" or else a distribution would leave such liabilities "as a charge on capital, regardless of the method by which the corporation keeps its books and to the extent thereof the distribution would impair capital and would not be a dividend." (46 B.T.A. at 1048). The language used was broad enough to cover all accrued liabilities—not just income taxes.

The decision in *Alworth* was reviewed by the Eighth Circuit, Helvering v. Alworth Trust, 136 F. 2d 812 (C.A. 8, 1943), which rejected our reliance on corporate and accounting principles. The Court of Appeals pointed out

---

[3] Although no one ever seems to have questioned the regulation insofar as it prohibits the reduction of earnings and profits of a cash basis corporation by accrued expenses *other than Federal income taxes* (and penalties related thereto).

that the *Hadden* case suffered from a marked lack of reasoning to support its result and that the tax rules prescribed by the internal revenue laws regarding dividends do not necessarily conform to standard corporate law concepts; that a distribution may be taxable as a dividend under the tax law even though the corporation making the distribution may have been barred by local corporate statutes (by reason of capital impairment, etc.) from distributing earnings. It was held that it would be an unwarranted extension of the tax statute to require that earnings and profits must be reduced by Federal taxes for the current year of a cash basis corporation.

This Court has followed the rule of the Eighth Circuit in *Alworth* in subsequent cases in which we have considered the issue. Paulina duPont Dean, 9 T.C. 256 (1947), acq. 1947–2 C.B. 2, appeal dismissed nolle prosequi (C.A. 3, 1949); United Mercantile Agencies, Inc., 23 T.C. 1105 (1955). Our opinion in United Mercantile Agencies, Inc., supra, was reversed by the Sixth Circuit sub. nom. Drybrough v. Commissioner, 238 F. 2d 735 (C.A. 6, 1956), and the *Drybrough* case has become established as the leading case taking what is generally regarded as the polar position to *Alworth*. The reversal of our opinion in *United Mercantile* by *Drybrough* has been followed in Thompson v. United States, 214 F.Supp. 97 (N.D. Ohio 1962); and Demmon v. United States, 321 F. 2d 203 (C.A. 7, 1963).

There can be no quarrel with the fact that current year's earnings and profits are not necessarily synonymous with current year's taxable income. For example, interest received on tax-exempt bonds is not included in taxable income, yet must be included in earnings and profits, sec. 1.312–6(b), Income Tax Regs; the reduction of earnings and profits for depletion is limited to depletion computed on the cost method even though the deduction from taxable income may be based on the more liberal percentage method. Ibid. sec. 1.312–6(c)(1). This absence of synonymity between earnings and profits and taxable income has been emphasized by the cases which adhere to the *Drybrough* view. Thus, one of the principal arguments raised has been: Since earnings and profits are determined for another purpose and are not necessarily the same as taxable income, there is no good reason why a strict cash basis must be adhered to for earnings and profits purposes even though the cash basis is used in accounting for taxable income.

This position is correct only in that there is no statute or inescapable rule of logic which *requires* strict adherence to the cash basis for earnings and profits purposes. However, there *is* a long-standing regulation which establishes such a requirement, sec. 1.312–6(a), Income Tax Regs.; such a regulation has a sound basis in administrative policy and there are no persuasive reasons why any departure from the cash basis used for reporting income should be permitted for purposes of computing earnings and profits and why the Commissioner's regulations should be ignored.

The rationale which appears to underlie *Drybrough* and its progeny is traceable all the way back to the Board of Tax Appeal's opinion in *Alworth*, which was subsequently reversed in the Eighth Circuit. On page 739 of 238 F. 2d, the court in *Drybrough* expressly states that it is persuaded by the reasoning of the Board in *Alworth*. After being reversed in *Alworth*, this

Court has consistently followed the reversal, and we see no reason why we should not adhere to the same view here. The quoted regulations have been in existence for many years and should be upheld.

We hold that the current earnings and profits of 444, a cash basis taxpayer, for the year 1959 are not to be reduced by any unpaid 1959 Federal income tax liability of 444. Helvering v. Alworth Trust, supra; Paulina duPont Dean, supra. Sec. 1.312–6(a), Income Tax Regs. Hence, the petitioner is chargeable with constructive dividend income. . .

NOTES

1. The Tax Court has amplified and reaffirmed its position in *Joseph B. Ferguson*. William C. Webb, 67 T.C. 1008 (1977).

2. A corporation incurs fraud penalties that are disallowed as deductions for income tax purposes on "public policy" grounds. Do the penalties, when accrued or paid, reduce earnings and profits? See Estate of Stein, 25 T.C. 940, 965–967 (1956), *acq. on this issue*, 1957–2 C.B. 7, *aff'd per curiam on another issue sub nom*. Levine v. Commissioner, 250 F.2d 798 (2d Cir. 1958); DiLeo v. Comm., 96 T.C. 858 (1991); Rev. Rul. 57–332, 1957–2 C.B. 231; 1995 FSA 342 ("The Service and the courts have both held that the fraud penalty reduces E&P of an accrual method corporation in the year the return was filed"). *Compare* § 964(a) *with* Rev. Rul. 77–442, 1977–2 C.B. 264.

3. Corporation Y, a 75–percent subsidiary of Corporation X, pays Corporation X a $1,000 dividend. As a result of § 243, Corporation X's taxable income is increased by $200. What is the effect on Corporation X's earnings and profits? Are more facts needed? See R.M. Weyerhaeuser, 33 B.T.A. 594, 597 (1935)(dividends from other corporations must be included in E & P even though not taxable); Letter Ruling 200952031 (citing the rule in *Weyerhaeuser*).

b. Effect of "Inadequacy"

Truesdell v. Commissioner
89 T.C. 1280 (1987).

■ NIMS, JUDGE. . . Respondent issued a statutory notice of deficiency . . . for the taxable year[s] 1977 . . . 1978 and 1979. . .

After concessions, the issues for decision are: (1) whether petitioner failed to report $22,231.86 in taxable income for the taxable year 1977; (2) whether petitioner . . . failed to report $46,083.48 and $45, 659.71 in taxable income for the taxable years 1978 and 1979, respectively; and (3) whether the resulting deficiencies are due to fraud.

FINDINGS OF FACT

. . . During the taxable years 1977 and 1978, petitioner was the president and sole shareholder of Asphalt Patch Co., Inc. (hereinafter referred to as Asphalt Patch).

On January 1, 1979, Jim T. Enterprises, Inc. (hereinafter referred to as Jim T. Enterprises), was incorporated. Petitioner's son, Robert Truesdell (hereinafter referred to as Robert), was named president of the corporation. In 1979 Robert was the sole shareholder of Jim T. Enterprises. Robert was 17 years old in 1979. . . Petitioner has conceded that although Robert was the record shareholder of Jim T. Enterprises, petitioner was actually the sole shareholder of the corporation.

. . . Asphalt Patch [and Jim T. Enterprises both] engaged in three lines of business: asphalt bagging, trucking or hauling, and installing asphalt paving. . . Petitioner directed and controlled the activities of Asphalt Patch and Jim T. Enterprises. Petitioner and his son were the only persons authorized to sign corporate checks. Petitioner authorized all corporate bank deposits. Petitioner arranged all the deliveries of bagged asphalt and supervised the recording and billing of bagged asphalt sales for both corporations. Checks received in payment for bagged asphalt sales were placed on petitioner's desk.

Petitioner also managed all the trucking work, keeping all the records relating to the trucking aspects of the business of the corporations and handling all the billing for trucking work. All checks received in payment for trucking work were placed on petitioner's desk.

The asphalt bagging business was the primary business of both corporations. Purchasers who contracted for large quantities of bagged asphalt used charge accounts. An order for bagged asphalt was written on an invoice that was later sent as a bill to the customer. Payments received for bagged asphalt were recorded in a ledger book by invoice number, number of bags sold, and amount of payment received. Some of the invoices were numbered, and some were not. Customers who purchased bagged asphalt "off the street" would pay cash and take the materials with them. "Off the street" purchases were recorded on unnumbered invoices. Unnumbered invoices were placed on petitioner's desk. Trucking customers placed orders by telephone. Trucking work was not recorded on invoices. Unnumbered bills were sent to trucking customers. Petitioner handled all the billing for trucking work and kept the trucking records himself.

Petitioner had a special book in which he recorded trucking income. It was necessary to keep records of trucking income so that they would be available to the various trucking broker-customers and their bookkeepers. Nevertheless, paperwork relating to trucking work was frequently thrown away.

Paving job inquiries were received by telephone, recorded in a telephone logbook, and referred to an estimator. . . The estimate forms were not numbered. Petitioner personally supervised the paving work. Because paving customers usually paid petitioner upon completion of the job, they usually were not billed. Petitioner frequently threw the contract away after a customer paid for a paving job. . .

During the years in issue, petitioner used corporate funds for personal expenditures or deposited checks made payable to Asphalt Patch or Jim T. Enterprises into his personal checking and savings accounts. During the calendar year 1977, petitioner deposited checks totaling $10,530.78 made payable to Asphalt Patch into his personal checking account at the Brea office of the National Bank of Whittier and deposited checks totaling $1,244.50 made payable to Asphalt Patch into his personal savings account at Crocker National Bank in Covina, California. These checks were drawn in payment for paving and trucking work done by the corporation. During the calendar year 1977, petitioner endorsed and cashed or deposited into a personal account $7,231.63 worth of checks made payable to Asphalt Patch in payment for trucking and paving work performed by the corporation. . .

[The court's recitation of similar transactions in both 1978 and 1979 has been omitted.]

Petitioner did not report as income on his individual Federal income tax returns for the taxable years 1977, 1978, and 1979 any of the checks issued to Asphalt Patch or Jim T. Enterprises that were cashed or deposited into [his] personal accounts. . .

ULTIMATE FINDINGS OF FACT

Petitioner controlled the activities of Asphalt Patch and Jim T. Enterprises. Although most of the income from the corporations' sales of bagged asphalt was accurately recorded on the books and reported on the tax returns of the corporations, income from trucking and paving work was not accurately recorded on the books or reported on the tax returns of the corporations for the years in issue. Petitioner kept records of trucking and paving work in such a manner that the corporations' bookkeepers and accountants were unaware of much of the income from trucking and paving.

During the years 1977 and 1978, petitioner diverted to himself $22,231.86 and $46,083.48, respectively, from the income of Asphalt Patch. During the year 1979, petitioner diverted to himself $44,234.71 from income of Jim T. Enterprises. This diverted income was not recorded on the corporations' books nor reported on the corporations' income tax returns. Nor was it reported as income on petitioner's income tax returns for the years in issue.

Petitioner also failed to report income from sales of bagged asphalt to "off the street" customers. . .

OPINION

. . . Respondent takes the position that the entire amounts diverted by petitioner from Asphalt Patch and Jim T. Enterprises during the taxable years 1977 and 1978 are includable in petitioner's income. Petitioner argues that he did not divert any corporate funds to his own use. . . The evidence does not support this assertion. . .

Petitioner's most cogent argument, however, is that the funds he diverted constitute constructive dividends to him, and, therefore, are taxable as income to him only to the extent of the earnings and profits of the corporations. Under sections 301(c) and 316(a), dividends are taxable to the shareholder as ordinary income to the extent of the earnings and profits of the corporation, and any amount received by the shareholder in excess of earnings and profits is considered as a nontaxable return of capital to the extent of the shareholder's basis in his stock. Any amount received in excess of both the earnings and profits of the corporation and the shareholder's basis in his stock is treated as gain from the sale or exchange of property.

Dividends may be formally declared or they may be constructive. The fact that no dividends are formally declared does not foreclose the finding of a dividend-in-fact... The crucial concept in a finding that there is a constructive dividend is that the corporation has conferred a benefit on the shareholder in order to distribute available earnings and profits without expectation of repayment. Noble v. Commissioner, 368 F.2d at 443. We find that the diverted funds in this case constitute constructive dividends to petitioner.

Respondent, himself, determined that the earnings and profits of Asphalt Patch were $23,540 and $4,594 in the taxable years 1978 and 1979, respectively, and that the earnings and profits of Jim T. Enterprises were $16,127.69 in the taxable year 1979. Petitioner failed to introduce any evidence that the earnings and profits of either corporation for any of the years in issue were less than the amounts determined by respondent. Accordingly, we find that the earnings and profits of Asphalt Patch were $23,540 and $4,594 in the taxable years 1978 and 1979, respectively, and that the earnings and profits of Jim T. Enterprises were $16,127.69 in the taxable year 1979.

Because neither party introduced evidence as to the earnings and profits of Asphalt Patch for the taxable year 1977, petitioner has failed his burden of proving that there were not sufficient earnings and profits to support the deficiency determined in respondent's notice of deficiency for that year. However, respondent has failed his burden of proving that Asphalt Patch had sufficient earnings and profits to support the increase in deficiency for that year asserted in his amended answers.

Respondent has failed to prove that the earnings and profits of the corporations were sufficient to permit the full amount of the funds diverted by petitioner during the taxable years 1977 and 1978 to be taxed as ordinary income under a constructive dividend theory. Deficiencies in excess of the earnings and profits of the corporations were asserted in respondent's amended answers. Respondent bears the burden of proving the amounts in excess of the deficiencies determined in the notices of deficiency. Rule 142(a). Respondent maintains, nevertheless, that it is unnecessary to characterize the diverted funds as constructive dividends and that, therefore, the full amount diverted is taxable to petitioner as ordinary income.

Respondent does not attempt to describe the diverted funds as additional salary, illicit bonuses, commissions, or anything more than diversions. Instead, respondent argues that any diversions from a corporation by its sole shareholder are taxable to the shareholder as ordinary income.

Respondent relies on Leaf v. Commissioner, 33 T.C. 1093 (1960), *affd. per curiam* 295 F.2d 503 (6th Cir. 1961), in which we held that the taxpayer, who unlawfully had diverted funds from his insolvent corporation with the intention of defrauding creditors, was liable for taxes on the full amount of the diverted funds regardless of the lack of earnings and profits of the corporation. In *Leaf* we based our holding on . . . the predecessor of section 61(a), which defines gross income as "all income from whatever source derived," and on the following language in Rutkin v. United States, 343 U.S. 130, 137 (1952):

> An unlawful gain, as well as a lawful one, constitutes taxable income when its recipient has such control over it that, as a practical matter, he derives readily realizable economic value from it. . . That occurs when cash, as here, is delivered by its owner to the taxpayer in a manner which allows the recipient freedom to dispose of it at will, even though it may have been obtained by fraud and his freedom to use it may be assailable by someone with a better title to it.

> Such gains are taxable in the yearly period during which they are realized. . .

Leaf and *Rutkin* are distinguishable from the instant case. *Leaf* and *Rutkin* both involved an unlawful receipt of funds by the taxpayer. The taxpayer in *Rutkin* had extorted funds from another individual, and the issue was whether extorted money was taxable to the extortionist. . .

In *Leaf*, corporate funds that should have been available to creditors were fraudulently transferred to the taxpayer in contemplation of bankruptcy. We need not and do not express an opinion on the need to apply a constructive dividend analysis in a situation where the shareholder utilized the corporation to steal from, embezzle from, or otherwise defraud other stockholders or third parties dealing with the corporation or shareholder. The taxpayer in *Leaf* had argued that the diverted funds were loans and therefore not taxable as income to him. We refused to adopt the taxpayer's characterization in the absence of any evidence of an intention to make repayment at the time of the taking. The issue in *Leaf* was whether the taxpayer's obligation to repay the diverted funds and his actual restitution of some of those funds in a later year precluded his liability for tax on their receipt. We held that the taxpayer had such control over the funds that they represented taxable income to him for the year in which they were taken. Although the taxpayer in *Leaf* was the sole shareholder of the corporation, he did not argue that the diverted funds constituted constructive dividends, and, therefore, this issue was not before the Court. . .

In this case, petitioner's diversions of income from Asphalt Patch and Jim T. Enterprises were not per se unlawful. The diverted funds were not, at least on their face, stolen, embezzled, or diverted in fraud of creditors. There has been no suggestion that the diversions were improper as a matter of corporate law. They are most appropriately described as distributions made by the corporations to their sole shareholder. DiZenzo v. Commissioner, 348 F.2d 122 (2d Cir. 1965), revg. T.C. Memo. 1964–121; Simon v. Commissioner, 248 F.2d 869 (8th Cir. 1957), revg. a Memorandum Opinion of this Court. . .

Respondent also relies on Davis v. United States, 226 F.2d 331 (6th Cir. 1955), and Weir v. Commissioner, 283 F.2d 675, 684 (6th Cir. 1960), revg. a Memorandum Opinion of this Court, in which the Sixth Circuit held that it is not necessary to classify a sole shareholder's diversions of corporate income as constructive dividends. The Sixth Circuit reasoned in both cases that the taxpayer's dominion and control over the diverted funds warranted taxation of the diverted funds as ordinary income.

We respectfully disagree with the analysis of the Sixth Circuit. As a general proposition, where a taxpayer has dominion and control over diverted funds, they are includable in his gross income under section 61(a) (Commissioner v. Glenshaw Glass Co., 348 U.S. 426, 431 (1955)), unless some other modifying Code section applies. The latter is the situation here, since Congress has provided that funds (or other property) distributed by a corporation to its shareholders over which the shareholders have dominion and control are to be taxed under the provisions of section 301(c). . .

Respondent relies on United States v. Miller, 545 F.2d 1204 (9th Cir. 1976), in which the Ninth Circuit refused, in a criminal proceeding, to apply the constructive distribution rules automatically to shareholder diversions of corporate funds. . . The Ninth Circuit ultimately agreed with the trial court's holding that the diversions in question constituted salary to the defendant. Respondent does not claim nor has he introduced evidence that the diversions were in the nature of salary to the petitioner. In concluding our discussion of the constructive dividend issue, we would emphasize that in a case such as this, diverted amounts taxed to a shareholder as constructive dividends also remain fully taxable to the corporation to which attributable. The record indicates that the corporations in question did not report the diverted funds. But respondent's agents became well aware of the existence of Asphalt Patch and Jim T. Enterprises, and the fact that taxable income had been diverted from them, during the examination of petitioner's tax affairs. We know of nothing which would have prevented a parallel examination of the corporate tax affairs and a determination of the correct taxable income reportable by the corporations.

For the foregoing reasons, we hold that the amounts diverted by petitioner from his corporations constitute constructive dividends and are taxable to him under the provisions of section 301(c). . . To the extent that this Court's decision in Benes v. Commissioner, 42 T.C. 358 (1964), aff'd 355 F.2d 929 (6th Cir. 1966) reaches a contrary result, it will no longer be followed. . .

Reviewed by the Court.

NOTES

1. Corporation M, an accrual basis taxpayer, has an accumulated and a current deficit in earnings and profits. Its sales manager, who owns 10 percent of the corporation's stock, pockets a customer's $10,000 cash payment for previously billed merchandise. The payment does not go through the corporation's bank account or books, and no other shareholder or corporate officer knows of the payment. Does the sales manager have $10,000 in ordinary income? What is the impact of James v. United States, 366 U.S. 213 (1961), United States v. George, 420 F.3d 991 (9th Cir. 2005) and U.S. v. Ohle, 441 Fed. Appx. 798 (2d Cir. 2011), in this context? Would the result be different if the sales manager's wife owned 90 percent of the stock? Would the result be different if the sales manager (with no wife) owned 50 percent of the stock? Ninety percent of the stock?

2. Does the taxpayer's success in the *Truesdell* case mean that there are no ramifications from such corporate diversions? Consider U.S. v. Boulware, 470 F.3d 931 (9th Cir. 2006), in which a taxpayer diverted funds from his corporation, failed to report those funds as income, and faced charges for criminal tax fraud, criminal tax evasion, and other violations. The 9th Circuit, in rejecting the taxpayer's claim that the funds be treated as a return of capital, noted that the taxpayer presented no evidence that the funds had been intended as a return of capital *at the time* they were disbursed. The Supreme Court vacated the 9th Circuit judgment, stating: "A defendant in a criminal tax case does not need to show a contemporaneous intent to treat diversions as returns of capital before relying on those sections to demonstrate no taxes are owed." Boulware v. United States, 552 U.S. 421 (2008). Upon remand to the U.S. Court of Appeals for the Ninth Circuit, the court found that "Boulware's offer of proof was insufficient as a matter of law to support the proffered return of capital theory" and thus could not prove that the corporate distributions he received were nontaxable. U.S. v. Boulware, 558 F.3d 971 (9th Cir. 2009). The Supreme Court denied certiorari to the second petition by Boulware. Boulware v. U.S., 130 S.Ct. 737, 175 L.Ed.2d 514 (2009). Even if diverted funds are treated as corporate distributions, are they automatically free of tax? Consider the outcome if the corporation has little or no E&P and the "diverting" shareholder has little or no basis in the stock.

2. CONSTRUCTIVE DIVIDENDS—§ 316

Since dividends have never been deductible to the corporation, and until the 2003 Act, were taxable at ordinary income rates to the shareholder, taxpayers have frequently sought to recharacterize a corporate distribution as something other than a dividend. Specifically, the distribution is designated as a payment that is either deductible (*e.g.*, a business expense) or not taxable to the shareholder (*e.g.*, a loan from the corporation to the shareholder). With the reduction in the dividend tax rate in 2003, dividends are currently more attractive than in the past, although the final conclusion as to what tax characterization of a distribution is most advantageous for the corporation and shareholder depends on an analysis of their relative tax rates, the value of possible deductions to the corporation and the tax cost of potential dividend income to the shareholder.

a. Dividend vs. Loan

Alterman Foods, Inc. v. United States

611 F.2d 866 (Ct. Cl. 1979).

■ Before KASHIWA, KUNZIG, and BENNETT, JUDGES.

PER CURIAM. This case comes before the court on plaintiff's exceptions. . .

Upon consideration of the trial judge's decision, the briefs and oral argument of counsel, and [the court's conclusion that sufficient earnings and profits were available to constitute constructive dividends, the court] hereby affirms and adopts the decision as the basis for its judgment in this case. Accordingly, as set forth in the following conclusion of law, plaintiff's petition is dismissed.

OPINION OF TRIAL JUDGE

SCHWARTZ, Trial Judge. This is a suit for refund of income taxes. The question, familiar in the law of tax liabilities of stockholders in controlled corporations, is whether advances by corporate subsidiaries to their sole stockholder, the plaintiff-taxpayer, were loans to the taxpayer, as alleged by it, or constructive dividends and thus taxable income, as maintained by the Commissioner.

[handwritten margin note: Courts find they were loans]

In 1966–74, plaintiff Alterman Foods, Inc., owned all the stock of some 57 subsidiaries engaged in the operation of a chain of retail grocery supermarkets in the Atlanta area. . .

Each subsidiary signed a management agreement, under which the plaintiff sold to it, at cost, merchandise, fixtures, remodeling and construction and insurance. All other needed services—warehousing, advertising, management and supervision, legal, accounting and office services and supplies, as well as licenses for the use of store and product tradenames—were provided for a fee of 2 1/2 percent of gross sales. In addition, and this provision is the source of the present case, the subsidiaries were required to advance to the plaintiff their gross receipts, from which the plaintiff would pay itself the amounts due for merchandise, repairs and the other services provided.

Accounts of the advances and expenditures were kept by both parent and subsidiary. The balances fluctuated on a periodic and annual basis as advances were received by the parent and expenditures made by it and debited against the advances. The net advances, i.e., the excess of advances by the subsidiary over expenditures by plaintiff on behalf of the subsidiary, were in plaintiff's financial and tax returns treated as accounts payable, under liabilities, and in the books of the subsidiary as accounts receivable, under assets.

Not all subsidiaries in all the tax years added to their net advances. Advances might decline as against expenditures by the parent, resulting in a decrease in the year-end balance of net advances or even a reversal from a balance of net advances to one in which plaintiff's expenditures on behalf of the subsidiary exceeded the advances. This occurred in years in which a subsidiary was operating an unprofitable market, in years in which plaintiff made substantial capital expenditures for remodeling of a market, or in years of both such characteristics.

Nevertheless, the aggregate of net advances from all subsidiaries grew as the years continued to be profitable in the overall. . .

Didn't pay them back

In computing the amounts of advances to be taxed as dividends, the Commissioner . . . treated each subsidiary as a separate entity and, generally speaking, assessed deficiencies to the extent of the increase in a tax year of the net advances by a subsidiary to the plaintiff. He did not, however, assess a deficiency in cases of advances in a year which merely reduced the prior year's excess of expenditures over advances. He treated as a constructive dividend only an increase from a beginning annual balance of net advances to a greater year-end such balance. And where the beginning balance showed an excess of expenditures over advances, the Commissioner treated as a constructive dividend only the increase from a zero balance to the year-end balance of net advances. The annual increase in net advances thus treated by the Commissioner as constructive dividends was $9.4 million.

The same case was presented as is here presented and the same contentions were made in plaintiff's suit for a refund with respect to the tax year 1965, the year immediately preceding the years now in suit. In that case, the Court of Appeals for the Fifth Circuit affirmed the action of the district court in setting aside a verdict for the plaintiff and entering judgment for the Government. Alterman Foods, Inc. v. United States, 505 F.2d 873 (5th Cir. 1974). . . The decision by the Fifth Circuit is both persuasive and confirmatory of the decision made on the record here.

The inquiry whether corporate funds have passed to a shareholder as bona fide loans, creating a creditor-debtor relationship, depends on whether the parties definitely intended that the sums advanced would be repaid. Alterman Foods, Inc. v. United States, supra, 505 F.2d 873, 875–76 (5th Cir. 1974); . . . Clark v. Commissioner, 266 F.2d 698, 710–11 (9th Cir. 1959).

Intent is to be determined on consideration of all the circumstances. These include, the Fifth Circuit noted, the extent to which the shareholder controls the corporation; the earnings and dividend history of the corporation; the magnitude of the advances; and presence or absence of conventional indicia of debt such as the giving of a note or security, a maturity date, a ceiling on the advances and effort and ability to repay or to require repayment. 505 F.2d at 877, n.7.

To these factors might be added the treatment of the advances in corporate financial statements and tax returns; whether interest was charged or paid on the balances; and in some instances, the use to which the shareholder put the advances... No single factor is, of course, determinative. Together all the factors may convey whether repayment or indefinite retention was intended. Koufman v. Commissioner, 35 TCM (CCH) 1509, 1523 (1976)...

The setting and the controlling relationships are perhaps the first circumstance to be considered. All the factors must be assessed in the context, here, of the 100 percent ownership by the shareholder of the stock of the subsidiaries. Members of the founding family were the owners of approximately 50 percent of the stock of the parent and were also the directors and officers of both the parent and subsidiaries.

No doubt an advance by [a] corporation to a controlling shareholder can constitute a loan... But a relationship between shareholder and corporation of total control and identity of interest creates obvious difficulties to thinking of the shareholder and corporation as debtor and creditor. A withdrawal of corporate funds may be used as a means of giving a controlling stockholder permanent use of the funds, in effect a dividend, without payment of the tax due on payment of a dividend. The possible tax evasion motive invites most careful scrutiny...

The advances here came about under the rigorous discipline of a management contract between parent and each subsidiary which ... provided that the subsidiary would "advance to us [plaintiff] from time to time, upon our request, such funds as we may require, which will be credited to your [the subsidiary's] account. Accountings shall be made and had between us from time to time, at such times as we may mutually agree upon." Apparently the funds "required" to be advanced were all the funds available...

Plaintiff points to the terms of the management agreement and to the consistent treatment of year-end balances as accounts payable or receivable as evidence of a bona fide debtor-creditor relationship and an intent on the part of the creditor to repay the advances in the future. The terms of the agreement, however, neither characterize the balance in the intercompany account as a loan or debt or specify any repayment schedule or time for settlement of an outstanding balance. The vague reference to accountings "between us from time to time, at such times as we may mutually agree upon" is insufficient either to give the putative creditor the right to demand repayment of an outstanding balance or to show an intent on the part of the parent to repay. Actually, accountings never took place. The management contract thus gives little weight to plaintiff's argument that repayment was intended.

The consistent treatment of year-end balances as accounts payable, in the plaintiff's financial statements and annual reports and in tax returns, provides some small support for plaintiff's position. Creditors and bankers rely on financials... But the cases are frequent in which treatment as loans on the books of the taxpayer is held unavailable to forestall the contrary conclusion. Regensburg v. Commissioner, 144 F.2d 41, 44 (2d Cir. 1944), cert. denied, 323 U.S. 783 . . . (1944); Electric & Neon, Inc., 56 T.C. [1324, 1329, 1339–40 (1971), aff'd, 496 F.2d 876 (5th Cir. 1974)]. The Fifth Circuit in its decision on the same issue for this plaintiff's 1965 tax year denied the plaintiff's tax returns and financial reports status as "objective economic indicia of debt," . . . 505 F.2d at 879. In a case of complete identity between corporation and stockholder the books are a self-serving arrangement by the taxpayer calling for scrutiny for possible evasion of taxes. The court of appeals was of the view—here shared—that the careful scrutiny appropriate in such cases required emphasis on the objective indicia of plaintiff's intent rather than on the formal statements of that intent on the books of the plaintiff.

One of these indicia may be the payment or nonpayment of formal dividends. Nonpayment of formal dividends may be strong evidence that concurrent advances to stockholders are disguised dividends. Koufman v. Commissioner, supra. Here the subsidiaries, entirely apart from the advances under consideration, paid formal dividends to a total of $4,508,485 during the years in question. While these are substantial sums, they are inconclusive as showing that the additional sums advanced were not also dividends, in view of the relative size of those advances and particularly the very substantial and growing retained earnings of the subsidiaries—$18.6 million by the last of the tax years. The pattern suggests that . . . the advances were actually disguised dividends. . . The increases in advances, formal dividends paid by the subsidiaries and their retained earnings were as follows:

Tax Years	Increases in Advances Taxes as Dividends	Formal Dividends	Retained Earnings
1966	884,139.27	647,400	6,546,967
1967	1,281,150.99	479,300	8,108,114
1968	1,388,841.99	640,535	9,515,650
1969	968,772.82	666,750	10,707,826
1970	1,333,227.00	685,500	11,922,157
1971	498,031.00	685,250	13,148,979
1972	597,479.00	703,750	14,360,352
1973	1,418,745.35	none	16,597,817
1974	982,683.07	none	18,571,235
	$9,353,070.49	$4,508,485	

Another set of figures confirm[s] the doubts. Of the 57 subsidiaries, 18 were profitable in each of the successive tax years, earning more than $25,000 annually. Profits actually ranged up to $200,000 annually; the average was $92,000. Advances by these subsidiaries increased in almost 9 out of 10 of these years. The constant parallel between substantial income and increasing advances, again, suggests dividends. . .

There are other factors of context and degree suggesting that the advances were economic dividends as much as the formal dividends.

There was no ceiling on the balance of advances which could be accumulated in plaintiff's hands. Plaintiff offered testimony that a market would require a substantial capital expenditure for remodeling every 5 to 8 years, and thus a "repayment" of advances. Yet advances from some subsidiaries increased in each tax year, and the general trend was constantly upwards. The need for remodeling, then, did not impose an effective ceiling on an outstanding debit balance and did not produce a predictable repayment of the outstanding balance of net advances. Both the absence of a ceiling and the trend of increasing balances weigh heavily against a conclusion that the advances were loans. See *Koufman*, supra; George Blood Enterprises, Inc., 35 TCM (CCH) 436, 446 (1976).

Inability to pay advances from a controlled corporation is a mark of a distribution rather than a loan. Edward M. Wrenn, Jr. v. United States, 78–1 USTC para. 9484 (D.C.W.D. Tenn. 1978); Al Goodman Inc. v. Commissioner, 23 T.C. 288, 301 (1954). Plaintiff was in a liquid position and had excellent credit during the years in suit. It would have been able, had it been necessary, to borrow enough to pay the net advances. To this extent the objective indicia are consistent with an intent to repay.

The use by the plaintiff of the net advances presents a mixed picture on the issue of intent to repay. On the one hand, indicia contradicting a loan are that plaintiff had no urgent need for the sums involved and was under the management agreements unrestricted in its use of the sums advanced. Plaintiff could and presumably did use the advances throughout its business, for dividends or purchases or other of its needs. Some of the advances were invested in interest-bearing short-term certificates of deposit. On the other hand it is urged that with the cash advanced plaintiff obtained volume and cash discounts on its wholesale grocery purchases which it could pass on to the subsidiaries. Cases on this factor, as might be expected, are inconclusive. Compare White v. Commissioner, 17 T.C. 1562, 1568 (1952) (finding that loans were intended despite the shareholder's personal use of the funds) with George Blood Enterprises, Inc. v. Commissioner, supra, (shareholder's use of the funds to purchase a lake house indicative of constructive dividends).

Absent were customary indications of a loan such as the payment of interest, the giving of a promissory note, a limit on the amount involved, the presence of security or collateral for the loan or restriction on the use of the sums. There was neither reserve or sinking fund for repayment of the advances nor fixed maturity date or schedule for repayment. True, payment by plaintiff of the subsidiaries' expenses had the same effect as a partial repayment of a debit balance, but there was never a transfer of cash to a subsidiary solely for the purpose of offsetting a debit balance. Other than the demands implicit in the subsidiaries' submission of their bills to plaintiff for payment, the subsidiaries which had made advances demanded neither a formal accounting of the balances nor a transfer of cash by way of repayment. In other words, there was no attempted collections of the purported loans, and, indeed, little objective evidence of loan except the books created by the parties.

. . . A certain degree of informality may be expected in dealings between a controlling shareholder and his corporation. . . In this case, however, the informalities make clear the crucial fact that there was no way of knowing that the advances by a particular subsidiary would be repaid either at a set time or at any time in the foreseeable future. Repayment could take place only if future events required greater expenditures on behalf of a subsidiary than the sums it could advance. Though such events—reduced profitability or a need for large capital expenditures—were largely, but not completely, beyond plaintiff's control, there was a substantial possibility that they would not occur within a reasonable or even a foreseeable period of time. In many cases, net advances increased in all 9 tax years in question, and in other cases decreases did not reduce the balance even close to zero. The pattern over the years is one in which profits were steadily made and steadily transferred to the plaintiff.

What happened in the later years may shed full light on the earlier years. As was said in Estate of Taschler v. United States, 440 F.2d 72, 77 (3d Cir. 1971): "What may appear to be a debtor-creditor relationship from dealings viewed within a certain span of time may turn out to be a mirage when later transactions are taken into account. The circumstances surrounding disbursements in later years and their cumulative effect may be considered in determining a taxpayer's intent prior to those years." The continuation of large and growing balances of net advances indicates that plaintiff did not have a definite intent to repay the advances; it had only a contingent intent to repay should circumstances so require. If the circumstances did not materialize, plaintiff would continue to hold and use the debit balances free and clear of any responsibility to repay the sums to the subsidiaries, as if dividends had been paid. The fact that in some instances net advances were significantly reduced or even reversed is not indicative of more than a contingent intent to repay. Future events created a definite intent to repay—only the part expended for the benefit of the subsidiary.

It is firmly established that a contingent intent to repay, or an intent to repay only if and when the sums are needed by the corporation, is legally insufficient to render advances to shareholders bona fide loans. Alterman Foods, Inc. v. Commissioner, supra, 505 F.2d at 879; General Aggregates Corp. v. Commissioner, 313 F.2d 25, 28 (1st Cir. 1963), cert. denied, 375 U.S. 815 . . . (1963); . . . O'Reilly v. Commissioner, 27 TCM (CCH) 1543, 1547 (1968); cf. Kaplan v. Commissioner, 43 T.C. 580 (1965) (repayment upon shareholder's death legally insufficient to show advances to be loans). Plaintiff's contingent intent to repay in this case, then, was insufficient to render the net advances to it loans; such advances were therefore taxable dividends.

Cases relied upon by plaintiff as holding advances to be a loan involved only one or two running accounts created by a shareholder's withdrawals from a corporation. Here there were more than 50 accounts created by a large corporate shareholder withdrawing sums from 57 subsidiaries. The number, consistency and increasing amounts of the withdrawals create a pattern indicating no intent to repay, except fortuitously and in small part. Moreover, the cases relied upon by plaintiff contained factual indicators of an intent to repay which are here absent. For instance, there were attempts to settle the outstanding balance by transfer of property to the corporation; . . . reversals or zero balances in all the accounts in question in prior or subsequent years . . .; the shareholder's payment of capital gains tax on the account upon the dissolution of the corporation. . .

Each of the cases turns on its own facts. In these foregoing cases, the finder of the facts concluded, on all the evidence and on an evaluation of witnesses' credibility, that definite repayment was intended. By the same method, the conclusion reached in the instant case is that definite repayment was not intended. The only possible deterrent to this conclusion is that taxation of both the dividends claimed by the Commissioner and the formal dividends declared and paid during the years in question will mean the treatment as dividends of an unusually high level of the subsidiaries' annual earnings. But the taxpayer offers the taxing system no choice. The subsidiaries did in fact transfer virtually their entire receipts to plaintiff, their sole shareholder, and the parties chose not to file consolidated returns which might have permitted a tax-free transfer of dividends. Plaintiff chose its method of doing business, and it cannot now avoid the tax consequences of its choice. See *Alterman Foods, Inc.*, supra, 505 F.2d at 878; Wiseman v. United States, 371 F.2d 816, 818 (1st Cir. 1967). It may be noted, finally, that plaintiff was allowed the 85 percent dividends-received deduction under section 243(a)(1) of the 1954 Code.

Plaintiff's case fails for lack of proof by a preponderance of the evidence that the annual increases in net advances from its individual subsidiaries in the tax years 1966–74 were bona fide loans or otherwise nontaxable.

NOTES

1. Courts continue to apply the multifactor approach to determine whether distributions to a shareholder constitute loans or dividends and resist taxpayer efforts to focus on particular factors. See Crowley v. Commissioner, 962 F.2d 1077 (1st Cir. 1992) (distributions to shareholder in a closely held family corporation were dividends not loans even though distributions were not in proportion to stock ownership); Jaques v. Commissioner, 935 F.2d 104, 109 (6th Cir. 1991) (distributions to shareholder from his wholly-owned professional corporation deemed constructive dividends because "the mere representations of the parties that the withdrawals were considered to be loans" is inadequate); Knutsen-Rowell, Inc. v. Comm., T.C. Memo 2011-65 (corporation's payment of shareholder's personal expenses (including their living expenses and those of their children such as housekeeper, gardener, tailor, pool cleaner and hair stylist) were to benefit the shareholders and not the corporation and were not loans, based on a review of the relevant factors).

2. A and B, who together owned all of the outstanding shares of Corporations X, Y, and Z, had open-account, interest-free loans from each of those corporations. At the same time, A and B were guarantors of certain large loans made by third parties to Corporation Z. Do the interest-free loans from these corporations to their shareholders constitute constructive dividends? See Jo-

seph Creel, 72 T.C. 1173 (1979), *aff'd on other grounds sub nom.*, Martin v. Commissioner, 649 F.2d 1133 (5th Cir. 1981). Does the fact that in order to make interest-free loans to its shareholders Corporation Z had to carry interest bearing obligations to third parties distinguish that corporation's loans to A and B from the loans made by the other two corporations? *Compare Creel* (shareholders treated as actual borrowers on loans from third parties so that interest payments by corporation are constructive dividends), *with* Falkoff v. Commissioner, 604 F.2d 1045 (7th Cir. 1979), *rev'g* 36 T.C.M. (CCH) 417 (1977) (corporation rather than shareholder treated as actual borrower; no constructive dividend) (alternative holding).

Prior to the enactment in 1984 of § 7872 (requiring imputation of interest in certain below market loans) shareholders had an incentive not only to characterize corporate distributions as loans but to also to have those loans be interest-free. Where these distributions were not successfully re-characterized as dividends, the IRS sought to at least impute interest on the loans. The IRS, however, typically failed and thus Congress enacted § 7872 which specified that imputation applied to any "below market loan directly or indirectly between a corporation and any shareholder of such corporation." § 7872(c)(1)(C). See Rountree Cotton Co. v. Commissioner, 113 T.C. 422 (1999), *aff'd* 12 Fed. Appx. 641 (10th Cir. 2001) (interest-free loans made by a corporation directly to its shareholders and indirectly to entities owned partly by the distributing corporation's shareholders and partly by family members of those shareholders were subject to § 7872 and interest was imputed on the loan).

Given the enforcement of § 7872 for loans to shareholders and the change in the tax rate on dividends in the 2003 Act, how would a corporation and its shareholders determine whether loan or dividend characterization of a distribution is preferable for tax purposes?

3. In Stinnett's Pontiac Service, Inc. v. Commissioner, 730 F.2d 634 (11th Cir. 1984), an advance from one corporation to its sibling corporation was treated as a constructive dividend to the corporation's common shareholder and as a capital contribution from the shareholder to the sibling corporation. The court reached its conclusion because it found that the advance was designed primarily to benefit the shareholder rather than the advancing corporation. See also, Hubert Enterprises, Inc. v. Commissioner, 125 T.C. 72 (2005) (extensively relying on the factors in *Stinnett* to conclude that the transfers in question constituted capital contributions, not a loan), aff'd on this issue, 230 Fed. Appx. 526 (6th Cir. 2007).

b. Dividend vs. Corporate Investment

Prunier v. Commissioner
248 F.2d 818 (1st Cir. 1957).

■ Before MAGRUDER, CHIEF JUDGE, and WOODBURY and HARTIGAN, CIRCUIT JUDGES.

■ MAGRUDER, CHIEF JUDGE. There is now before us a joint petition for review of two decisions of the Tax Court entered on April 12, 1957—one determining that there is a deficiency in income tax of Henry E. Prunier and wife for the taxable year 1950 in the amount of $1,080.88, the other deter-mining that there is a deficiency in income tax of Joseph E. Prunier and wife for the same taxable year in the amount of $1,348.98. The Tax Court . . . sustained a determination by the Commissioner that certain premiums paid by the corporation J. S. Prunier & Sons, Inc., on insurance policies on the lives of Henry and Joseph Prunier constituted taxable income to the taxpayers under the general language of § [61(a)].

Of the 450 shares of stock of J. S. Prunier & Sons, Inc., outstanding, Henry Prunier and his brother Joseph each owned [220 shares]. Henry held the offices of president and treasurer, and Joseph was vice-president of the corporation.

As not infrequently happens in these closely held family corporations, the corporate books and records were kept in so sketchy and messy a fa-shion as to make it difficult to determine what was corporate action and what was the individual action of the two dominant stockholders.

Beginning in 1942 and running up to and including 1950, the brothers took out a total of eight life insurance policies. Four were purchased by Henry on his own life, naming his brother Joseph as beneficiary, in a total face amount of $45,000. Four were taken out by Joseph on his own life, naming his brother Henry as beneficiary, in a total amount of $45,000.

During the taxable year 1950 there was nothing in the terms of the policies, nor in the endorsements thereon, to indicate that the corporation had become their beneficial owner. Some question having been raised by the taxing authorities about this, it appears that at various dates in 1952 (which was subsequent to the tax year in question) endorsements were placed on each of the eight policies naming the corporation J. S. Prunier & Sons, Inc., beneficiary, but inexplicably containing the reservation, in all eight policies, of a right in Henry to change the beneficiary.

From at least as far back as 1946 the corporation has paid the pre-miums due on the various policies. It was testified on behalf of the taxpay-ers, and found as a fact by the Tax Court, as follows:

> When the policies were written, Henry and Joseph informed the agent of the substance of the written agreements which the policies were to carry out. The[y] intended that in the event of the death of ei-ther the corporation should be the owner of the proceeds of the policies on the life of the deceased party for a single specific purpose, namely, use the proceeds to purchase the stock interest of the deceased party in the corporation at a price agreed upon by them prior to the death of ei-ther.

The tax treatment given to these transactions by the corporation was consistent with this found intention of the parties. Thus, in the agreed sti-pulation of facts the following statements appear:

The corporation did not claim a deduction for the premiums paid on the above-mentioned insurance policies on its income tax return for the taxable year 1950, but did include the amount thereof in the adjustment made to surplus on Schedule M of its said return as follows:

"8. Insurance premiums paid on the life of any officer or employee where the corporation is directly or indirectly a beneficiary . . . $8,081.44"

Similar adjustments were made by the corporation on its income tax returns for the taxable years 1946 to 1949, inclusive, for the premiums paid on those of the above-mentioned policies in effect during those years.

The aforesaid understanding that the corporation was to become the owner of the policies was first reflected on the books of the corporation, sometime toward the end of 1946, by the following entry in the minute book of the corporation describing a meeting of the directors:

It is understood and agreed that any policies that Henry E. Prunier has on Joseph E. Prunier and any policies that Joseph E. Prunier has on Henry E. Prunier shall go to the corporation in the event of the death of either of them and this money is to be used by the corporation to buy out the interest of the party that dies.

These policies are the ones that the corporation pays the premiums on.

This will apply to any policies that may be bought in the future.

(s) Henry E. Prunier

(s) Joseph E. Prunier

Witness

(s) Irene M. Prunier

. . . Petitioners place their reliance upon the settled ruling that where a corporation is the beneficiary and owner of a policy of insurance on the life of an employee or stockholder, the payment of premiums by the corporation does not constitute income to the insured individual. Casale v. Commissioner, 2 Cir., 1957, 247 F.2d. . .

On the other hand, the Commissioner thinks the present case falls within the equally settled ruling that where a corporate employee or stockholder, or someone related to him, is beneficiary, and not the corporation, on a policy of life insurance on such employee or stockholder, payment of the premiums on such policy by the corporation constitutes income to the insured individual. Paramount–Richards Theatres, Inc. v. Commissioner, 5 Cir., 1946, 153 F.2d 602. . .

We think the present case is more nearly like the type of case relied upon by petitioners. Despite the informality of the transactions, it seems to us that, in view of the facts in the record and of the findings by the Tax Court, the corporation would have been held to be the beneficial owner of the eight insurance policies under controlling Massachusetts law, and thus could have obtained the help of a court of equity to recover the proceeds of the insurance policies if one of the brothers had died in 1950. . . We suspect also that in that event the corporation, on some theory of "ratification" or of "adoption," would have been held contractually bound to apply the proceeds of the policies to buy out the stock interest of the deceased stockholder, and that the deceased stockholder's legal representative would have been contractually bound to sell. . .

Whether the corporation would have been legally obliged to continue paying the premiums in 1950 we do not need to say. The fact is that the corporation did pay the premiums. Also we do not have to decide what would have been the respective legal obligations of the parties, and what would have been the tax consequences, if one of the insured brothers had died in 1950. The fact is that neither brother died in 1950, and so far as appears both are still alive. It is sufficient for the purposes of the present case to say that neither brother realized any taxable gain in 1950 from the payment of the life insurance premiums by the corporation.

We do not understand that the majority of the Tax Court reached the conclusion they did on any notion of "disregarding the corporate fiction." Human beings take advantage of laws permitting incorporation because they think it will be economically advantageous to them individually. That is so whether the corporation is a "closely held" company owned by two stockholders, or one having two thousand stockholders. In a loose manner of speaking, it can be said that any corporate gain is a benefit, indirectly, to the stockholders, so that if a corporation becomes the beneficial owner of insurance policies, the stockholders receive the benefit thereof. Of course this argument proves too much, for it would lead to the conclusion that profits made by a corporation in its business are automatically taxable income to the stockholders. This is contrary to the taxation scheme of the Internal Revenue Code. And the government is only contending in this case that it was the payment of premiums by the corporation which constituted income to the insured employees and stockholders, which in itself is a recognition of the corporation as a separate legal entity.

The gist of the Tax Court's argument is contained in the following excerpt from the majority opinion:

> In view of what has been said above, it appears that if Joseph or Henry had died during the taxable year, the corporation would not have been enriched by receiving the proceeds from insurance policies on the life of the deceased and using them to purchase stock he had owned in the corporation. The corporation's indebtedness to creditors would have remained undiminished, and while the corporation would have eliminated at least the greater part of the deceased's ownership interest in it, represented by his stock, the proportional interest of the

surviving stockholder, or stockholders, thereby would have been greatly increased. In this situation and since the record does not otherwise indicate any benefit which might flow to the corporation from the purchase of a deceased insured's stock interest, we conclude that during the taxable year the corporation was neither the beneficial owner nor the beneficiary of the insurance policies on the lives of Joseph and Henry involved here.

Certainly the fact that the corporation may have been contractually bound to apply any proceeds of the policies, had they matured in 1950, to buy out the stock interest of a deceased stockholder, does not mean that the corporation would not have been "enriched" by collecting the fact amount of the policies. All that would then have been involved would have been a change in the form of the assets from cash to treasury stock. We have hitherto pointed out the limited utility of the concept of corporate purpose as distinguished from stockholder purpose. See Lewis v. Commissioner, 1 Cir., 1949, 176 F.2d 646, 649–650. But if it were necessary to look for a corporate business purpose in the present case, we could refer to the arguments in Mannheimer & Friedman, "Stock–Retirement Agreements," 28 Taxes 423, 425 (1950), as follows:

> Even while the decedent is still alive, the agreement and insurance benefit the corporation because they tend to stabilize the corporation's business. If the bank knows about the agreement, it may well be inclined to extend credit more liberally to the corporation because the possibility of inexperienced shareholders injecting themselves into the management is eliminated. If the key employees are informed of the agreement, it will be an inducement to them to remain with the corporation because they realize that the continuation of the business in the hands of the survivor is assured—and with it their jobs.

> If there is no stock-retirement agreement when the decedent dies, often his family will ask a high price for his stock, or demand dividends without regard to the needs of the corporation, or even press for dissolution. So far as the survivor is concerned, he may very well be unwilling to work indirectly for the benefit of his former "partner's" family or directly with the second husband of his former "partner's" widow.

In the present case the government has not made any real effort to controvert the argument that under the Massachusetts decisions a court of equity would treat the corporation as the equitable owner of the policies of insurance. That being so, and having in mind the statutory scheme whereby the corporation J. S. Prunier & Sons, Inc., is dealt with as a separate legal entity and a separate taxable unit, and disregarding the loose sense in which it could be said that a benefit to J. S. Prunier & Sons, Inc., is a benefit to its controlling stockholders, it is sufficiently evident that the payment of premiums by the corporation in 1950 did not constitute, in that taxable year, reportable income to Henry and Joseph Prunier. See generally, Casale v. Commissioner, 2 Cir., 1957, 247 F.2d 440. What will happen when one of the brothers dies is not before us.

A judgment will be entered vacating the decisions of the Tax Court and remanding the case to that Court for further proceedings not inconsistent with this opinion.

NOTES

1. If a corporation owns an insurance policy on the life of a principal shareholder and designates (revocably) the shareholder's estate as the beneficiary, what is the tax consequence to the estate when the proceeds are paid to the insured's estate after she dies? Why? The answer given in Ducros v. Commissioner, 272 F.2d 49 (6th Cir. 1959), is one which the Commissioner has announced he will not follow. See Rev. Rul. 61–134, 1961–2 C.B. 250. The *Ducros* court held that the estate did not recognize income upon the receipt of the proceeds. Is the result in *Ducros* consistent with the logic of *Prunier*?

2. Husband (H) and Wife (W) are both substantial shareholders in a closely held corporation. The corporation owns and pays premiums on insurance policies on the life of H, a corporate officer, revocably designating W as the beneficiary. W receives the policy proceeds on H's death. Is this a constructive dividend? To whom? See Estate of J.E. Horne, 64 T.C. 1020 (1975), *acq. in result* 1980–2 C.B. 1.

c. Dividend vs. "Unreasonable" Expense

1. A payment by a corporation, though not made directly to the shareholder, may satisfy an obligation of the shareholder or confer some type of personal benefit upon him. Payment of that benefit may therefore constitute a constructive dividend. In Hood v. Commissioner, 115 T.C. 172 (2000), the Tax Court held that a corporation's payment of legal fees in the criminal tax evasion case of its sole shareholder was not a deductible expense of the corporation, and instead constituted a constructive dividend to the shareholder. Although the Court noted that a corporate expenditure is not automatically a constructive dividend because it confers an incidental economic benefit to the shareholder, the Court concluded that in *Hood* the taxpayer failed to demonstrate that the primary beneficiary of the payment of legal fees was the corporation.

In general, as the Tax Court said in John L. Ashby, 50 T.C. 409, 417 (1968), "It is well established that any expenditure made by a corporation for the personal benefit of its stockholders or the making available of corporate-owned facilities to stockholders for their personal benefit may result in the receipt by the stockholders of constructive dividends. See Challenge Manufacturing Co., 37 T.C. 650 [(1962)], and cases cited therein." See, e.g., Henry Schwartz Corp., 60 T.C. 728 (1973), *acq.* 1974–2 C.B. 4 (corporate entertainment expenditures not for the benefit of the corporation are not deductible by the corporation and constitute a constructive dividend to the shareholder benefiting from the expenditure), *nonacq.* 1981–2 C.B. 3 (regarding certain other corporate expenditures).

2. Rapco, Inc. v. Commissioner, 85 F.3d 950 (2d Cir. 1996) ("Because compensation to employees is deductible from the corporation's income, but

dividends paid to shareholders are not . . . [a] corporation will benefit from disguising 'dividends' . . . as compensation whenever possible. This is typically done by paying shareholder-employees [excess compensation] practically no different from a dividend.") See also, Wechsler & Co., Inc. v. Commissioner, 92 T.C.M. (CCH) 138 (2006) (extensively citing the factors and analysis in *Rapco* to determine whether amounts paid by a corporation to its president-shareholder, and to others, constituted deductible compensation).

B. DISTRIBUTIONS IN RETIREMENT OF INVESTOR INTEREST

1. DEBT RETIREMENT VS. DIVIDEND OR REDEMPTION OF STOCK

If a sole shareholder lends money to his corporation and that corporation repays the loan, the shareholder-lender typically has a tax-free recovery of capital or, perhaps, a capital gain. See § 1271. But suppose the loan is properly regarded as equity. What might the tax consequences be? Most of the materials that follow in this chapter involve the tax consequences to a shareholder whose equity interest is retired. It is well to remember that an apparent "debt" may be reclassified and treated as "equity." Review the "thinness" issues posed in the materials in Chapter 1 at pages 50–63 supra.

2. LIQUIDATING DISTRIBUTIONS AND REDEMPTIONS

a. Complete Liquidations—§ 331

Commissioner v. Carter
170 F.2d 911 (2d Cir. 1948).

■ Before L. HAND, CHIEF JUDGE, and SWAN and CHASE, CIRCUIT JUDGES.

■ SWAN, CIRCUIT JUDGE.

This appeal presents the question whether income received by the taxpayer in 1943 is taxable as long-term capital gain, as the Tax Court ruled, or as ordinary income as the Commissioner contends. The facts are not in dispute. The taxpayer, Mrs. Carter, had owned for ten years all the stock of a corporation which was dissolved on December 31, 1942. Upon its dissolution all of the assets were distributed to her in kind, subject to all its liabilities which she assumed. In the distribution she received property having a fair market value exceeding by about $20,000 the cost basis of her stock, and she reported such excess as a capital gain in her 1942 return and paid the tax thereon. In the corporate liquidation she also received 32 oil brokerage contracts which the parties stipulated had no ascertainable fair market value when distributed. Each contract provided for payment to the corporation of commissions on future deliveries of oil by a named seller to a named buyer. The contracts required no additional services to be performed by the corporation or its distributee, and the future commissions were conditioned on contingencies which made uncertain the amount and time of payment. In 1943 the taxpayer collected commissions of $34,992.20 under these contracts. She reported this sum as a long-term capital gain; the Commissioner determined it to be ordinary income. The Tax Court held it taxable as capital gain. The correctness of this decision is the sole question presented by the Commissioner's appeal.

Mrs. Carter's stock was a "capital asset" as defined by [§ 1221]. In exchange for her stock, she received the assets of the corporation upon its dissolution. The tax consequences of such a transaction are controlled by [§ 331(a) which calls for a liquidating distribution to be "treated as in full payment in exchange for stock," § 1001(a) which defines gain or loss as the spread between "adjusted basis" and "amount realized," § 1001(b) which defines "amount realized" as the sum of money received plus the fair market value of . . . property . . . received, and § 1001(c) which provides that all gain or loss is to be recognized unless otherwise provided in the statute]. . . From the foregoing statutory provisions, it is obvious that if the oil brokerage contracts distributed to the taxpayer had then had a "fair market value," such value would have increased correspondingly the "amount realized" by her in exchange for her stock and would have been taxable as long-term capital gain, not as ordinary income. . . Fleming v. Commissioner of Internal Revenue, 5 Cir., 153 F.2d 361. The question presented by the present appeal is whether a different result is required when contract obligations having no ascertainable fair market value are distributed in liquidation of a corporation and collections thereunder are made by the distributee in later years.

In answering this question in the negative, the Tax Court relied primarily upon Burnet v. Logan, 283 U.S. 404. . .*

The Commissioner argues that the *Logan* case is inapplicable because there the taxpayer had not recovered the cost basis of her stock while here she had. The Tax Court thought the distinction immaterial. We agree. The Supreme Court spoke of the annual payments as constituting "profit" after the seller's capital investment should be returned. Until such return it cannot be known whether gain or loss will result from a sale; thereafter it becomes certain that future payments will result in gain. No reason is apparent for taxing them as ordinary income. As this court said in Commissioner of Internal Revenue v. Hopkinson, 2 Cir., 126 F.2d 406, 410, "payments received by the seller after his basis had been extinguished would have been taxable to him as capital gains from the sale of the property," citing Burnet v. Logan as authority.

The Commissioner also urges that the *Logan* case is distinguishable because it dealt with a sale of stock rather than exchange of stock for assets distributed in a corporate liquidation. This contention is answered by White v. United States, 305 U.S. 281, 288, . . . and Helvering v. Chester N. Weaver Co., 305 U.S. 293, 295, . . . where the court held that the recognition required . . . of gains and losses on liquidation must for purposes of computation of the tax, be taken to be the same as that accorded to gains

---

*Burnet v. Logan involved a year when capital gains and ordinary income were taxed at the same rate.—ED.

and losses on sales of property.* Consequently we agree with *the Tax Court's ruling that the principle of the *Logan* case is applicable to a corporate liquidation where stock is exchanged in part for contracts having no ascertainable market value, and that future collections under such contracts are taxable as capital gain in the year when received if the distributee has previously recovered the cost basis for the stock.

The Commissioner's argument that such collections are analogous to the receipt of interest or rent upon bonds or real estate distributed in a corporate liquidation overlooks a significant distinction. Payment of interest or rent does not impair the value of the bond or real estate since each remains as a capital asset regardless of the number of payments. See Helvering v. Manhattan Life Ins. Co., 2 Cir., 71 F.2d 292, 293. But with respect to the oil brokerage contracts, under which no additional services were to be rendered by the payee, each payment decreases their value until, with the final payment it will be completely exhausted; and, if the payments be treated as income, the distributee has no way to recoup his capital investment, since concededly he has no economic interest in the oil producing properties and therefore no right to depletion deductions.[2] Hence to consider the brokerage payments as ordinary income would produce a most unjust result and one quite unlike the result which follows the distribution of bonds or real estate in a corporate liquidation.

For the foregoing reasons we think the decision of the Tax Court correct. It is affirmed.

NOTES

1. In Rev. Rul. 58–402, 1958–2 C.B. 15, the Service reviewed *Carter*, Burnet v. Logan, 283 U.S. 404 (1931), and other cases and concluded that it "will continue to require valuation of contracts and claims to received indefinite amounts of income, such as those acquired with respect to stock in liquidation of a corporation, except in rare and extraordinary cases." What is a "rare and extraordinary" case in this context?

2. In *Carter*, the tax rate applicable to the income was at stake (capital gains v. ordinary income). After the 2003 Act and the change in the dividend tax rate, would the stakes be different? How was the IRS characterizing the income received on the contract?

---

*See cross-reference provisions of § 331(c).—ED.

[2] It is true, in the case at bar, the taxpayer had no capital investment in the brokerage contracts because from other assets distributed she had already recovered the cost basis of her stock and the oil brokerage contracts had no ascertainable fair market value. But the Commissioner's analogy argument would be equally applicable if the brokerage contracts had been the only corporate assets distributed and it had been possible to ascribe to them a fair market value of $21,000. In that case, the distributee's capital investment in the brokerage contracts would have been $20,000, the cost basis of her stock being $1,000. She would be entitled to recover her capital investment before she could be charged with receiving either gain or loss or ordinary income, and the only source of recovery would be the payments which would ultimately exhaust the value of the contracts. Hence the answer given above to the analogy argument is apposite.

3. Note that under § 346(a), a distribution is treated as part of a complete liquidation if the distribution is one of a series of distributions pursuant to a plan of liquidation. If a corporation makes such a series of liquidating distributions and has a number of shareholders, the distributions must be allocated among the various blocks of shares. See Rev. Rul. 85–48, 1985–1 C.B. 126, amplifying Rev. Rul. 68–348, 1968–2 C.B. 141.

Estate of Meade v. Commissioner

489 F.2d 161 (5th Cir.), *cert. denied*, 419 U.S. 882 (1974).

■ Before GEWIN, AINSWORTH and MORGAN, CIRCUIT JUDGES.

■ AINSWORTH, CIRCUIT JUDGE. Taxpayers incurred legal expenses in connection with the settlement of a civil antitrust claim that had been assigned to them in pro rata shares as distributees in a corporate liquidation. These cases present the question whether the legal expenses are deductible from ordinary income under section 212 of the Internal Revenue Code of 1954, or whether, under section 263 of the Code, they must be capitalized and offset against long-term capital gain realized by taxpayers from the settlement.

. . . Joseph M. Meade and William S. King were the sole shareholders of the Alabama Wire Company, Inc. In 1963, that corporation and its wholly owned subsidiary employed an Atlanta, Georgia, law firm to advise whether Kaiser Aluminum and Chemical Corporation, in connection with its dealings with Alabama Wire and its subsidiary, had violated the federal antitrust laws. For this initial employment, which ceased in early 1964, the Atlanta firm was paid legal fees by Alabama Wire and its subsidiary.

The name of Alabama Wire was thereafter changed to Terrace Corporation, and, on February 15, 1965, the corporation was liquidated. Among the proceeds of the liquidation was the potential claim against Kaiser Aluminum, which, the parties have stipulated, had no ascertainable value at that time. Meade and King, individually, thus acquired ownership of the potential antitrust claim. Meade received a one-third interest in the claim, and King received a two-thirds interest, in accordance with their proportionate ownership of the distributing corporation.

Based upon a later opinion of Atlanta counsel, Meade and King, in 1965, retained the firm to pursue the antitrust claim on their personal behalf. An agreement was entered whereby the firm would be paid a monthly retainer fee plus 20 per cent of any amount recovered. When it was subsequently determined that San Francisco counsel should be employed to bring the suit against Kaiser Aluminum in California, the agreement was modified to provide that a retainer of $10,000 would be paid to San Francisco counsel (which amount was to be credited against future retainer charges due Atlanta counsel), and that both counsel would share a 33 per cent participation in any amount recovered.

Suit was brought against Kaiser Aluminum in 1965 in the names of Meade and King, individually, as assignees of the cause of action of Alabama Wire and its subsidiary. Treble damages of $9,000,000 were sought. The case was settled in 1966 for $900,000, of which Meade received $300,000, and King, $600,000. On his respective 1966 income tax return, each reported the proceeds of the settlement as additional long-term capital gain from the liquidation of Terrace Corporation.

. . . Meade and King, in 1966, paid legal fees and litigation expenses totaling $320,993.67. Meade paid one third of that amount, and King paid two thirds. Each claimed the full amount so paid by him as a deduction against ordinary income on his 1966 tax return. The Commissioner disallowed these deductions and treated the entire amount of legal expenses as an offset against the long-term capital gain realized by taxpayers from their antitrust claim. . . [T]he Tax Court held that the attorneys' fees and expenses are properly deductible under section 212(1) as payments for the production of income. . . We reverse the decision of the Tax Court.

The stock of Terrace Corporation constituted a capital asset in the hands of the taxpayers of Terrace Corporation. Thus, the proceeds of the liquidation of Terrace Corporation, received in exchange for their Terrace stock, constituted capital gain to taxpayers. Since the antitrust claim was included as part of the proceeds of the liquidation, the fair market value of the claim ordinarily would have entered into the computation—made at that time—of taxpayers' capital gain from the liquidation. . . In this instance, however, the potential claim had no ascertainable fair market value at the time of distribution, and no value was assigned to it for purposes of computing taxpayers' capital gain from the liquidation. The liquidation therefore remained an "open transaction," and, for tax purposes, the amounts subsequently received from the antitrust claim related back to the initial exchange. See Burnet v. Logan, 283 U.S. 404 [(1931)]. . . It being undisputed that the Terrace stock was a capital asset in taxpayers' hands, taxpayers and the Commissioner agree that taxpayers had long-term capital gain upon the settlement with Kaiser Aluminum in 1966.

This appeal involves the treatment of taxpayers' legal expenses in connection with the settlement of the antitrust claim. Taxpayers contend that these legal expenses are deductible from ordinary income as expenses incurred "for the collection of income" under section 212(1). The Commissioner argues that the legal expenses must be capitalized and offset against taxpayers' capital gain because they were incurred in connection with the disposition of a capital asset, the Terrace Corporation stock, within the meaning of section 263.

. . . Although section 263, which deals with capital expenditures, explicitly denies a deduction only for certain types of expenditures, it is clear that the section does not provide an exclusive list. C.I.R. v. Lincoln Savings and Loan Association, 403 U.S. 345, 358 . . . (1971). The limits of nondeductibility for capital expenditures are found in the case law. Here, we are guided by fundamental doctrine recently noted by the Supreme Court in Woodward v. C.I.R., 397 U.S. 572, 575 . . . (1970): "It has long been recognized, as a general matter, that costs incurred in the acquisition or disposition of a capital asset are to be treated as capital expenditures." More specifically, expenses incurred by shareholders in effecting the liquidation of their corporation—our concern in this case—ordinarily constitute capital expenditures, which enter into the computation of gain or loss arising from the distribution. . .

The Supreme Court's recent decisions in Woodward v. C.I.R., supra, and its companion case, United States v. Hilton Hotels Corporation, 397 U.S. 580 . . . (1970), shed further light on the principles applicable to this appeal. In those cases, the Court unanimously held that expenses of litigation that arise out of the acquisition of a capital asset are capital expenses. The cases presented two substantially identical situations. Taxpayers incurred legal expenses in appraisal proceedings in connection with a purchase of dissenting shareholders' stock that was required under local law. Taxpayers argued that the "primary purpose" test should be applied in determining the deductibility of the costs of acquiring or disposing of property. That rule, developed in the context of expenditures to defend or perfect title to property, provides that such expenditures are capital in nature only where the taxpayer's primary purpose in incurring them is to defend or perfect title. . . The primary purpose of their expenditures in the appraisal proceedings, taxpayers argued, related not to the acquisition of title, but to the price to be paid for the stock, and, therefore, their expenditures should not be characterized as acquisition costs.

In rejecting the taxpayers' claims in *Woodward* and *Hilton Hotels*, the Supreme Court found the primary purpose test inapplicable to the situations before it: "A test based upon the taxpayer's 'purpose' in undertaking or defending a particular piece of litigation would encourage resort to formalisms and artificial distinctions." Woodward v. C.I.R., 397 U.S. at 577. . . Instead, the Court adopted the "origin" test, choosing to consider the origin and character of the claim for which the expenditures were made. On the basis of that test, the Court held that the determination of a purchase price by litigation is clearly part of the process of acquisition and should be treated as part of the cost of the stock that the taxpayers acquired. In so holding, the Court noted that "ancillary expenses incurred in acquiring or disposing of an asset are as much part of the cost of that asset as is the price paid for it." Woodward v. C.I.R., 397 U.S. at 576. . . We find the Court's reasoning compelling in its application to the facts before us.

As we noted above, the exchange in the liquidation of taxpayers' stock for the Terrace assets resulted in capital gain treatment to the taxpayers. The exchange remained an open transaction until the proceeds of the antitrust claim were collected by taxpayers. Since the open transaction event qualified for capital gain treatment, the amounts ultimately collected from the settlement do also. In effect, the proceeds of the settlement constituted additional consideration for taxpayers' stock in Terrace Corporation. While taxpayers have agreed with the Commissioner that the liquidation should be kept open in order to include the proceeds of the settlement as capital gains, taxpayers seek to close that transaction for the purpose of characterizing the legal expenses involved as deductible expenses for the collection of income. The Supreme Court's "origin of the claim" test prevents us from agreeing with taxpayers.

The "origin" test was first set forth by the Court in United States v. Gilmore, 372 U.S. 39 . . . (1963). There it was held that legal expenses incurred by a taxpayer in defending a divorce suit were nondeductible personal expenses even though taxpayers' securities holdings, and possibly his business reputation, would be affected by the outcome of the case. The Court sustained the Government's position that deductibility depended on the "origin and nature" of the claim against the taxpayer, and found that the claim arose out of the personal relationship of marriage. The Court stated the proper test as follows: "The origin and character of the claim with respect to which an expense was incurred, rather than its potential consequences upon the fortunes of the taxpayer, is the controlling basic test of whether the expense was 'business' or 'personal' and hence whether it is deductible or not under § 23(a)(2) [section 212 of the 1954 Code]." 372 U.S. at 49. . . It was this test that the Court adopted in *Woodward* in determining that the origin of the particular litigation involved was found in the process of the acquisition of a capital asset, and that therefore the expenses of the litigation were nondeductible capital expenses.

Although there is admittedly a distinction between the two situations, we think it clear that the Court adopted this test, not only with respect to the acquisition of a capital asset, but also for determining whether legal expenses are incurred in the process of *disposition* of property . . .. Substantially the same problems arise in each determination. In both the disposition and acquisition of property, a determination must be made of the tax consequences of monetary outlays in connection with contesting the value of certain capital assets. The uncertainty and difficulty of considering the taxpayer's motive in incurring expenses are present in both situations. For the deductibility of payments to depend upon such subjective considerations would, as the Court noted in *Woodward*, encourage resort to "formalisms and artificial distinctions."

Applying the "origin" standard to the facts before us, we are convinced that the antitrust claim against Kaiser Aluminum—as it rested in the hands of these taxpayers—had its origin in the process of the disposition of their stock in Terrace Corporation. The claim was part of the Terrace assets received by taxpayers in the liquidation of the corporation, and taxpayers' disposition of their stock was an open transaction for purposes of the collection of the proceeds of the settlement. Thus, the valuation of the claim against Kaiser Aluminum was vital to the disposition of taxpayers' stock, and the litigation necessary for this determination was an integral part of the overall transaction. Hence, the expenses incurred in the litigation that led to the settlement are properly treated as part of the cost of the stock that the taxpayers exchanged in the liquidation.

Taxpayers have directed our attention to two circuit court decisions, Naylor v. C.I.R., 5 Cir., 1953, 203 F.2d 346, and C.I.R. v. Doering, 2 Cir., 1964, 335 F.2d 738, which presented problems similar to the one before us. In *Naylor*, taxpayer gave an option to purchase certain stock, which was a capital asset in his hands, at a price based on the stock's net asset value shown on the books of the company on a certain date. The purchaser exercised his option, but thereafter a dispute arose over the valuation, and taxpayer hired an attorney to negotiate with the purchaser concerning the value of the shares. Taxpayer's expenses in connection with the valuation were held deductible under the predecessor of section 212(1).

Doering involved a fact pattern slightly different from *Naylor*. In *Doering*, taxpayer owned stock in Argosy Pictures Corporation, which had contracted to produce certain films for distribution by Republic Pictures Corporation. A dispute arose between the corporations as to the amount of Argosy's participation in the proceeds under the contract, but Argosy liquidated before a settlement was effected. Because the claim had no ascertainable fair market value at the time, the transaction remained "open" for tax purposes. In redemption of his stock, a capital asset, taxpayer received cash and a pro rata portion of Argosy's claim against Republic. Thereafter, in effecting a settlement of the dispute over the terms of Argosy's contract with Republic, taxpayer incurred legal expenses. The full Tax Court, four judges dissenting, allowed him to deduct the expenses under section 212 because they were incurred for the "collection of income." A divided panel of the Second Circuit affirmed.

We think that the *Naylor* and *Doering* decisions have been considerably eroded by *Woodward* and *Hilton Hotels*, which arrived at results different from *Naylor* and *Doering*, though all four cases presented similar fact situations... *Naylor* and *Doering* are, however, distinguishable from the Supreme Court decisions and from the cases before us.

We see *Naylor* as holding that if a disposition of a capital asset has been consummated, and subsequent controversy concerns no more than enforcement of the terms of the agreement, then the problem is one of collection of income under section 212... As the Court noted in *Naylor*, "the situation called for the services of an attorney to collect the proceeds of a sale of a capital asset. Petitioner's attorney was employed after an enforceable contract of sale existed." ... Similarly, *Doering* involved legal expenses that were found to be a cost of collecting sums due the taxpayer under "a fully executed and enforceable contract." ...

In *Woodward* and *Hilton Hotels*, on the other hand, the problem was treated as one of the establishment of a purchase price in the acquisition of a capital asset. The transactions there were clearly considered incomplete until the litigation to set a purchase price had concluded. "The whole process of acquisition required both legal operations—fixing the price, and conveying title to the [stock]." ... So also in the cases before us, we are concerned with transactions not consummated until the claim against Kaiser Aluminum had been settled. Establishment of the value of the antitrust claim was a contingency on which the finality of taxpayers' stock disposition depended. By contrast, in *Naylor* and *Doering*, fully enforceable agreements existed, and litigation involved only the interpretation and enforcement of those agreements. Accordingly, the legal expenses involved in those cases may more easily fit within the concept of expenses incurred for the collection of income than taxpayers' expenses in the cases before us.

Reversed.

NOTES

1. Should a shareholder's gain on liquidation be recognized at all and, if so, to what extent? If it should be recognized, how should it be taxed? Should a shareholder be taxed to the extent of this allocable share of earnings and profits even if he has no gain, and if so, how? Should a shareholder's loss be recognized on complete liquidation? Cf. § 267(a)(1).

2. In Rendina v. Commissioner, 72 T.C.M. (CCH) 474 (1996), the Service argued that the shareholder's receipt of two condominiums from his corporation (established to build and sell 18 condominium units) constituted a dividend. The Tax Court concluded that the distribution constituted a de facto liquidation of the corporation where: (1) the shareholder took the property with the understanding that the shareholder would assume certain obligations of the corporation, (2) the corporation thereafter ceased to hold business assets and ceased to be a going concern (although it did not formally dissolve).

3. Section 332 provides for the nonrecognition of a parent corporation's gain on the liquidation of its subsidiary in certain circumstances. Functionally, an intercorporate liquidation (at least where the shareholder corporation is in control of the subsidiary) may be very similar to a merger. For that reason, § 332 will be studied with "reorganizations" in Chapter 4, infra.

b. Redemptions—§§ 301, 302, 303, 304, 318

i. DISTRIBUTIONS IN COMPLETE TERMINATION OF INTEREST

Bleily & Collishaw, Inc. v. Commissioner
72 T.C. 751 (1979), aff'd without opinion, 647 F.2d 169 (9th Cir. 1981).

■ IRWIN, JUDGE. Respondent determined a deficiency of $6,573 in petitioner's income tax for the taxable year 1973.

The only issue in this case is whether redemptions by Maxdon Construction, Inc. (Maxdon), of its stock held by petitioner constituted dividends taxable as ordinary income under sections 301 and 316 or constituted distributions in exchange for its stock pursuant to section 302 and, therefore, taxable as capital gains.

FINDINGS OF FACT

. . . Petitioner Bleily & Collishaw, Inc. (B & C), is a California corporation which was originally engaged in the construction business but gradually became a landholding company. . . Ray Collishaw is B & C's president and owns all its shares.

In 1969, B & C bought 225 shares of Maxdon's stock. Maxdon's remaining 525 shares were held by its president, Donald J. Neumann. In 1969, a close business relationship existed between B & C and Maxdon and Maxdon did subcontracting for B & C. As B & C stopped its contracting work, however, it no longer had any use for Maxdon's subcontracting work. Since Neumann felt there was no advantage to Maxdon in B & C's continuing ownership of its stock, he wanted sole control and ownership of Maxdon.

B&C sent work to Maxdon when needed. Maxton wanted 100% ownership back

Sometime prior to August 17, 1973, Neumann met with Collishaw to discuss the purchase of B & C's shares. Collishaw agreed to sell all of B & C's Maxdon stock at $200 per share and was willing to do so at that time. However, because Neumann had problems obtaining enough cash for an immediate purchase of all B & C's Maxdon stock, he offered to buy only a portion of the stock. Nonetheless, Collishaw intended at all times to sell the shares if and when Neumann offered to buy them, although he was not under any contractual or legal obligation to do so.

Neumann expected to, and in fact did, receive or earn enough money every month to make additional purchases of stock. Each month prior to each transaction, Collishaw contacted his accountant who then determined the proper number of shares to be redeemed that month. Each sale was supported by a separate written redemption agreement executed by Maxdon and B & C providing a redemption price of $200 per share and reciting the number of shares Maxdon then had outstanding, the number then owned by B & C, and the number of shares B & C was to sell. Maxdon redeemed all of B & C's stock during the 23–week period August 17, 1973–February 22, 1974, thereby terminating B & C's interest in Maxdon. . .

During 1973, Maxdon redeemed a total of 166 shares of stock for a total of $33,200. Petitioner claimed this amount on its 1973 corporate income tax return as a dividend, subject to the 85–percent deduction allowed by section 243. Respondent determined that the redemptions constituted an exchange of stock, thereby taxing the redemptions as capital gains.

OPINION

The issue before us is whether section 302(b) applies to the redemptions, thereby taxing the transaction under section 302(a). If section 302(a) does not apply, then the redemptions are taxable under sections 301 and 316 as dividends. . .

Is this a proper redemption

Respondent contends that sections 302(b)(1), 302(b)(2), and 302(b)(3) all apply whereas petitioner contends that none of these sections apply.

We deal first with section 302(b)(3). For section 302(b)(3) to apply, there must be a complete redemption of all of the stock owned by a shareholder. Where several redemptions have been executed pursuant to a plan to terminate a shareholder's interest, the individual redemptions constitute, in substance, the component parts of a single sale or exchange of the entire stock interest. We have refused, however, to treat a series of redemptions as a single plan unless the redemptions are pursuant to a firm and fixed plan to eliminate the stockholder from the corporation. . .

Generally, a gentleman's agreement lacking written embodiment, communication, and contractual obligations will not suffice to show a fixed and firm plan. Leleux v. Commissioner, supra. On the other hand, a plan need not be in writing, absolutely binding, or communicated to others to be fixed and firm although these factors all tend to indicate that such is the case. Niedermeyer v. Commissioner, supra.

Each case is necessarily a factual determination and based upon the record we are convinced Maxdon planned to eliminate B & C as a shareholder. The initiative for the redemption came from Neumann, not Collishaw. It is undisputed that Neumann wanted sole ownership of Maxdon and desired to buy B & C's interest as fast as his cash position would allow. It was only because Neumann did not have enough cash for an immediate purchase that B & C's entire block of Maxdon stock was not purchased on August 17, 1972. As Neumann obtained cash he made purchases every month for 6 consecutive months of a number of shares[5] until B & C's interest was liquidated. Collishaw had agreed to the sale of all its shares and to the purchase price. As noted before, the fact that the agreement was not binding is not dispositive. Cf. Himmel v. Commissioner, supra (no fixed plan where the agreement read that so long as petitioner lives the corporation may redeem his preferred shares at par, provided that it is "financially able to redeem same," if its other shareholders desire that this be done), and Benjamin v. Commissioner, supra ("vague anticipation is not a firm plan with fixed conditions"). Here, both shareholders agreed to the redemption, and Maxdon planned to purchase B & C's Maxdon stock over the course of a few months as funds became available.

Because we have found that there was an integrated plan, we do not need to determine whether each redemption considered separately meets

---

[5] It seems that the precise amount of shares to be redeemed each month was agreed upon by both parties at least in part to avoid the 80 percent test of sec. 302(b)(2):

	(i) Ratio that B & C's (voting) stock in Maxdon immediately after the redemption bears to all voting stock at such time	(ii) Ratio that B & C's (voting) stock in Maxdon immediately before the redemption bears to all voting stock at such time	80% of (ii)
8/17/73	24.02	30.00	24.00
9/23/73	19.23	24.02	19.21
10/19/73	15.46	19.23	15.38
11/23/73	12.50	15.46	12.36
12/21/73	10.10	12.50	10.00
1/18/74	8.22	10.10	8.08
2/22/74	–	8.22	–

the "essentially equivalent to a dividend test" under section 302(b)(1), or whether section 302(b)(2) applies to the redemption.[6]

Decision will be entered for the respondent.

Lynch v. Commissioner

801 F.2d 1176 (9th Cir. 1986), *rev'g* 83 T.C. 597 (1984).

■ Before FARRIS, HALL and KOZINSKI, CIRCUIT JUDGES.

■ HALL, CIRCUIT JUDGE. The Commissioner . . . petitions for review of a Tax Court decision holding that a corporate redemption of a taxpayer's stock was a sale or exchange subject to capital gains treatment. The Commissioner argues that the taxpayer held a prohibited interest in the corporation after the redemption and therefore the transaction should be characterized as a dividend distribution taxable as ordinary income. We agree with the Commissioner and reverse the Tax Court.

I

Taxpayers, William and Mima Lynch, formed the W.M. Lynch Co. on April 1, 1960. The corporation issued all of its outstanding stock to William Lynch (taxpayer). The taxpayer specialized in leasing cast-in-place concrete pipe machines. He owned the machines individually but leased them to the corporation which in turn subleased the equipment to independent contractors.

On December 17, 1975 the taxpayer sold 50 shares of the corporation's stock to his son, Gilbert Lynch (Gilbert), for $17,170. Gilbert paid for the stock with a $16,000 check given to him by the taxpayer and $1,170 from his own savings. The taxpayer and his wife also resigned as directors and officers of the corporation on the same day.

On December 31, 1975 the corporation redeemed all 2300 shares of the taxpayer's stock. In exchange for his stock, the taxpayer received $17,900 of property and a promissory note for $771,920. Gilbert, as the sole remaining shareholder, pledged his 50 shares as a guarantee for the note. In the event that the corporation defaulted on any of the note payments, the taxpayer would have the right to vote or sell Gilbert's 50 shares.

In the years immediately preceding the redemption, Gilbert had assumed greater managerial responsibility in the corporation. He wished, however, to retain the taxpayer's technical expertise with cast-in-place concrete pipe machines. On the date of the redemption, the taxpayer also entered into a consulting agreement with the corporation. The consulting agreement provided the taxpayer with payments of $500 per month for five years, plus reimbursement for business related travel, entertainment, and

---

[6]It is clear that no individual redemption meets the "substantially disproportionate" test of sec. 302(b)(2); it is respondent's position that the redemptions must be considered together, thereby meeting that test.

automobile expenses.[1] In February 1977, the corporation and the taxpayer mutually agreed to reduce the monthly payments to $250. The corporation never withheld payroll taxes from payments made to the taxpayer.

After the redemption, the taxpayer shared his former office with Gilbert. The taxpayer came to the office daily for approximately one year; thereafter his appearances dwindled to about once or twice per week. When the corporation moved to a new building in 1979, the taxpayer received a private office.

In addition to the consulting agreement, the taxpayer had other ties to the corporation. He remained covered by the corporation's group medical insurance policy until 1980. When his coverage ended, the taxpayer had received the benefit of $4,487.54 in premiums paid by the corporation. He was also covered by a medical reimbursement plan, created the day of the redemption, which provided a maximum annual payment of $1,000 per member. Payments to the taxpayer under the plan totaled $96.05.

II

We must decide whether the redemption of the taxpayer's stock in this case is taxable as a dividend distribution under § 301 or as long-term capital gain under § 302(a). [On the date of the redemption, W.M. Lynch Co. had accumulated earnings and profits of $315,863 and had never paid a dividend.]

Section 302(b)(3) provides that a shareholder is entitled to sale or exchange treatment if the corporation redeems all of the shareholder's stock. In order to determine whether there is a complete redemption for purposes of section 302(b)(3), the family attribution rules of section 318(a) must be applied unless the requirements of section 302(c)(2) are satisfied. Here, if the family attribution rules apply, the taxpayer will be deemed to own constructively the 50 shares held by Gilbert (100% of the corporation's stock) and the transaction would not qualify as a complete redemption within the meaning of section 302(b)(3).

Section 302(c)(2)(A) states in relevant part:

In the case of a distribution described in subsection (b)(3), [the family attribution rules in] section 318(a)(1) shall not apply if—

(i) immediately after the distribution the distributee has no interest in the corporation (including an interest as officer, director, or employee), other than an interest as a creditor. . .

The Commissioner argues that in every case the performance of post-redemption services is a prohibited interest under section 302(c)(2)(A)(i), regardless of whether the taxpayer is an officer, director, employee, or independent contractor.

---

[1] The corporation leased or purchased a pickup truck for the taxpayer's use in 1977. If someone at the corporation needed the truck, the taxpayer would make it available to him.

The Tax Court rejected the Commissioner's argument, finding that the services rendered by the taxpayer did not amount to a prohibited interest in the corporation. In reaching this conclusion, the Tax Court relied on a test derived from Lewis v. Commissioner, 47 T.C. 129, 136 (1966) (Simpson, J., concurring):

> Immediately after the enactment of the 1954 Code, it was recognized that section 302(c)(2)(A)(i) did not prohibit office holding per se, but was concerned with a retained financial stake in the corporation, such as a profit-sharing plan, or in the creation of an ostensible sale that really changed nothing so far as corporate management was concerned. Thus, in determining whether a prohibited interest has been retained under section 302(c)(2)(A)(i), we must look to whether the former stockholder has either retained a financial stake in the corporation or continued to control the corporation and benefit by its operations. In particular, where the interest retained is not that of an officer, director, or employee, we must examine the facts and circumstances to determine whether a prohibited interest has been retained under section 302(c)(2)(A)(i). Lynch v. Commissioner, 83 T.C. 597, 605 (1984)

. . . After citing the "control or financial stake" standard, the Tax Court engaged in a two-step analysis. First, the court concluded that the taxpayer was an independent contractor rather than an employee because the corporation had no right under the consulting agreement to control his actions. Second, the court undertook a "facts and circumstances" analysis to determine whether the taxpayer had a financial stake in the corporation or managerial control after the redemption. Because the consulting agreement was not linked to the future profitability of the corporation, the court found that the taxpayer had no financial stake. Id. at 606–07. The court also found no evidence that the taxpayer exerted control over the corporation. Id. at 607. Thus, the Tax Court determined that the taxpayer held no interest prohibited by section 302(c)(2)(A)(i). [Finding that the taxpayer was not an employee obviated the need for the Tax Court to decide whether the parenthetical language in section 302(c)(2)(A)(i) prohibited employment relationships per se. Seda v. Commissioner, 82 T.C. 484, 488 (1984) (court stated that "section 302(c)(2)(A)(i) may not prohibit the retention of all employment relationships").]

[margin note: Tax Court analysis]

III

. . . The Tax Court's interpretation of what constitutes a prohibited interest under section 302(c)(2)(A)(i) is a question of law reviewed de novo. . . . We reject the Tax Court's interpretation of section 302(c)(2)(A)(i). An individualized determination of whether a taxpayer has retained a financial stake or continued to control the corporation after the redemption is inconsistent with Congress' desire to bring a measure of certainty to the tax consequences of a corporate redemption. We hold that a taxpayer who provides post-redemption services, either as an employee or an independent contractor, holds a prohibited interest in the corporation because he is not a creditor.

[margin note: Holding]

The legislative history of section 302 states that Congress intended to provide "definite standards in order to provide certainty in specific instances." S. Rep. No. 1622, 83d Cong. 2d Sess. 233, reprinted in 1954 U.S. Code Cong. & Ad. News 4621, 4870. "In lieu of a factual inquiry in every case, [section 302] is intended to prescribe specific conditions from which the taxpayer may ascertain whether a given redemption" will qualify as a sale or be treated as a dividend distribution. H.R. Rep. No. 1337, 83d Cong. 2d Sess. 35, reprinted 1954 U.S. Code Cong. & Ad. News 4017, 4210. The facts and circumstances approach created by the Tax Court undermines the ability of taxpayers to execute a redemption and know the tax consequences with certainty.

The taxpayer's claim that the Senate rejected the mechanical operation of the House's version of section 302 is misleading. The Senate did reject the House bill because the "definitive conditions" were "unnecessarily restrictive." S. Rep. No. 1622, 83d Cong., 2d Sess. 44, reprinted in 1954 U.S. Code Cong. & Ad. News 4621, 4675. However, the Senate's response was to add paragraph (b)(1) to section 302, which reestablished the flexible, but notoriously vague, "not essentially equivalent to a dividend" test. This test provided that all payments from a corporation that were not essentially equivalent to a dividend should be taxed as capital gains. The confusion that stemmed from a case-by-case inquiry into "dividend equivalence" prompted the Congress to enact definite standards for the safe harbors in section 302(b)(2) and (b)(3). The Tax Court's refusal to recognize that section 302(c)(2)(A)(i) prohibits all noncreditor interests in the corporation creates the same uncertainty as the "dividend equivalence" test.

The problem with the Tax Court's approach is apparent when this case is compared with Seda v. Commissioner, 82 T.C. 484 (1984). In *Seda*, a former shareholder, at his son's insistence, continued working for the corporation for two years after the redemption. He received a salary of $1,000 per month. The Tax Court refused to hold that section 302(c)(2)(A)(i) prohibits the retention of employment relations per se, despite the unequivocal language in the statute. Id. at 488. Instead, the court applied the facts and circumstances approach to determine whether the former shareholder retained a financial stake or continued to control the corporation. The Tax Court found that the monthly payments of $1,000 constituted a financial stake in the corporation. Id. This result is at odds with the holding in *Lynch* that payments of $500 per month do not constitute a financial stake in the corporation. . . The court also found in *Seda* no evidence that the former shareholder had ceased to manage the corporation. 82 T.C. at 488. Again, this finding is contrary to the holding in *Lynch* that the taxpayer exercised no control over the corporation after the redemption, even though he worked daily for a year and shared his old office with his son. Compare *Lynch*, 83 T.C. at 607 with Seda, 82 T.C. 484 at 488. *Seda* and *Lynch* thus vividly demonstrate the perils of making an ad hoc determination of "control" or "financial stake."

A recent Tax Court opinion further illustrates the imprecision of the facts and circumstances approach. In Cerone v. Commissioner, [87 T.C. 1

(1986)], a father and son owned all the shares of a corporation formed to operate their restaurant. The corporation agreed to redeem all of the father's shares in order to resolve certain disagreements between the father and son concerning the management of the business. However, the father remained an employee of the corporation for at least five years after the redemption, drawing a salary of $14,400 for the first three years and less thereafter. The father claimed that he was entitled to capital gains treatment on the redemption because he had terminated his interest in the corporation within the meaning of section 302(b)(3).

Even on the facts of Cerone, the Tax Court refused to find that the father held a prohibited employment interest per se. . . Instead, the Tax Court engaged in a lengthy analysis, citing both *Seda* and *Lynch*. The court proclaimed that *Lynch* reaffirmed the rationale of *Seda*, even though *Lynch* involved an independent contractor rather than an employee. After comparing the facts of *Seda* and *Cerone*, the Tax Court eventually concluded that the father in *Cerone* held a financial stake in the corporation because he had drawn a salary that was $2,400 per year more than the taxpayer in *Seda* and had been employed by the corporation for a longer period after the redemption. . . However, the Tax Court was still concerned that prohibited interest in *Seda* might have been based on the finding in that case that the taxpayer had both a financial stake and continued control of the corporation. The Tax Court, citing *Lynch*, held that the "test is whether he retained a financial stake or continued to control the corporation." *Cerone*, slip op. at 54. Thus, the Tax Court found that the father in *Cerone* held a prohibited interest because he had a financial stake as defined by *Seda*.

Although the Tax Court reached the correct result in *Cerone*, its approach undermines the definite contours of the safe harbor Congress intended to create with sections 302(b)(3) and 302(c)(2)(A)(i). Whether a taxpayer has a financial stake according to the Tax Court seems to depend on two factors, length of employment and the amount of salary. Length of employment after the redemption is irrelevant because Congress wanted taxpayers to know whether they were entitled to capital gains treatment on the date their shares were redeemed. See S. Rep. No. 1622, 83d Cong., 2d Sess. 235–36, reprinted in 1954 U.S. Code Cong. & Ad. News 4621, 4872–73. See also Treas. Reg. § 1.302–4(a)(1) (taxpayer must attach a statement disclaiming any interest in the corporation with the first tax return filed after the distribution). As for the amount of annual salary, the Tax Court's present benchmark appears to be the $12,000 figure in *Seda*. Salary at or above this level will be deemed to be a financial stake in the enterprise, though the $6,000 annual payments in this case were held not to be a financial stake. There is no support in the legislative history of section 302 for the idea that Congress meant only to prohibit service contracts of a certain worth, and taxpayers should not be left to speculate as to what income level will give rise to a financial stake.

In this case, the taxpayer points to the fact that the taxpayers in *Seda* and *Cerone* were employees, while he was an independent contractor. On appeal, the Commissioner concedes the taxpayer's independent contractor status. We fail to see, however, any meaningful way to distinguish *Seda* and *Cerone* from *Lynch* by differentiating between employees and independent contractors. All of the taxpayers performed services for their corporations following the redemption. To hold that only the employee taxpayers held a prohibited interest would elevate form over substance. The parenthetical language in section 302(c)(2)(A)(i) merely provides a subset of prohibited interests from the universe of such interests, and in no way limits us from finding that an independent contractor retains a prohibited interest. Furthermore, the Tax Court has in effect come to ignore the parenthetical language. If employment relationships are not prohibited interests per se, then the taxpayer's status as an employee or independent contractor is irrelevant. What really matters under the Tax Court's approach is how the taxpayer fares under a facts and circumstances review of whether he has a financial stake in the corporation or managerial control. Tax planners are left to guess where along the continuum of monthly payments from $500 to $1000 capital gains treatment ends and ordinary income tax begins.

Our holding today that taxpayers who provide post-redemption services have a prohibited interest under section 302(c)(2)(A)(i) is inconsistent with the Tax Court's decision in Estate of Lennard v. Commissioner, 61 T.C. 554 (1974). That case held that a former shareholder who, as an independent contractor, provided post-redemption accounting services for a corporation did not have a prohibited interest. The Tax Court found that "Congress did not intend to include independent contractors possessing no financial stake in the corporation among those who are considered as retaining an interest in the corporation for purposes of the attribution waiver rules." Id. at 561. We disagree. In the context of *Lennard*, the Tax Court appears to be using financial stake in the sense of having an equity interest or some other claim linked to the future profit of the corporation. Yet, in cases such as *Seda* and *Cerone*, the Tax Court has found that fixed salaries of $12,000 and $14,400, respectively, constitute a financial stake. Fees for accounting services could easily exceed these amounts, and it would be irrational to argue that the definition of financial stake varies depending on whether the taxpayer is an employee or an independent contractor. In order to avoid these inconsistencies, we conclude that those who provide post-redemption services, whether as independent contractors or employees, hold an interest prohibited by section 302(c)(2)(A)(i) because they are more than merely creditors.

In addition, both the Tax Court and the Commissioner have agreed that taxpayers who enter into management consulting contracts after the redemption possess prohibited interests. Chertkof v. Commissioner, 72 T.C. 1113, 1124–25 (1979), *aff'd*, 649 F.2d 264 (4th Cir. 1981); Rev. Ruling 70–104, 1970–1 C.B. 66 (1970). Taxpayers who provide such services are, of course, independent contractors. However, unlike the Commissioner's opinion in Rev. Ruling 70–104 that all management consulting agreements are prohibited interests, the Tax Court applies the financial stake or managerial control test. In *Chertkof*, the court found that because the services provided under the contract "went to the essence" of the corporation's existence, the taxpayer had not effectively ceded control. 72 T.C. at 1124. Here, the Tax Court distinguished *Chertkof* on the ground that the taxpayer did not retain control of the corporation, but instead provided only limited consulting services. *Lynch*, 83 T.C. at 608. We believe that any attempt to define prohibited interests based on the level of control leads to the same difficulties inherent in making a case-by-case determination of what constitutes a financial stake.

IV

Our decision today comports with the plain language of section 302 and its legislative history. . . Taxpayers who wish to receive capital gains treatment upon the redemption of their shares must completely sever all noncreditor interests in the corporation.[2] We hold that the taxpayer, as an independent contractor, held such a noncreditor interest, and so cannot find shelter in the safe harbor of section 302(c)(2)(A)(i). Accordingly, the family attribution rules of section 318 apply and the taxpayer fails to qualify for a complete redemption under section 302(b)(3). The payments from the corporation in redemption of the taxpayer's shares must be characterized as a dividend distribution taxable as ordinary income under section 301.

The taxpayer argues that some creditor relationships might result in an "opportunity to influence" as great or greater than any officer, director, or employee relationship. He cites Rev. Ruling 77–467, 1977–2 C.B. 92, which concluded that a taxpayer who leased real property to a corporation, after the corporation redeemed his shares, held a creditor's interest under section 302(c)(2)(A)(i). While the taxpayer here may be correct in his assessment of a creditor's "opportunity to influence" a corporation, he overlooks the fact that Congress specifically allowed the right to retain such an interest.

Reversed.

NOTE

In Hurst v. Commissioner, 124 T.C. 16 (2005), where the redeeming shareholder retained a security interest in the redeemed stock, the Service argued that the cross-default clauses of the contractual obligations constituted a retention of control by the taxpayer-shareholder. The court disagreed, quoting *Lynch*, and noting that the Hursts "offered credible evidence from their professional advisers that these transactions, including the grant of a security interest to Mr. Hurst, were consistent with common practice for seller-financed deals." Mr. Hurst was found to be merely a creditor, and the redemption qualified under section 302(b)(3).

---

[2] Our definition of a prohibited interest still leaves an open question as to the permissible scope of a creditor's interest under section 302(c)(2)(A)(i).

Dunn v. Commissioner

615 F.2d 578 (2d Cir. 1980).

■ Before Van Graafeiland and Kearse, Circuit Judges, and Dooling, District Judge.

■ Dooling, District Judge. The Commissioner appeals from a decision of the Tax Court . . . holding that amounts received by appellee taxpayer, Georgia Dunn, in 1970 and 1971 from Bresee Chevrolet Co., Inc. . . were received in complete redemption of all her stock in Bresee, and that immediately after the distribution she had no interest in Bresee as an officer, director, employee or otherwise, other than an interest as a creditor. In consequence, the Tax Court held, the amounts the taxpayer received were capital gains and not dividends, as the Commissioner contended.

When the redemption transaction was entered into the taxpayer owned 249 of the 500 shares of Bresee, her son William Dunn owned 149 shares and each of her married daughters owned 51 shares. In May 1970 taxpayer contracted to "sell or redeem from" Bresee her 249 shares of the company's stock for $335,154 payable $100,000 on June 1, 1970, and the balance with 5% interest over a period of ten years. Bresee redeemed the taxpayer's stock on the June 1, 1970, closing date; she was then paid the $100,000, and in 1971 was paid $45,260.34.

. . . Section 302 treats redemptions as exchanges within Section 302(a) if they qualify under one of the [three] subsections of Section 302(b): the subsection under which the taxpayer's transaction has been held to qualify is subsection (b)(3) which provides—

(3) TERMINATION OF SHAREHOLDER'S INTEREST

Subsection (a) shall apply if the redemption is in complete redemption of all of the stock of the corporation owned by the shareholder.

And Section 302(a) applies, through Section 302(b)(3), when, as Section 302(c)(2)(A)(i) requires,

(i) immediately after the distribution the distributee has no interest in the corporation (including an interest as officer, director, or employee), other than an interest as a creditor. . .

Thus, if after the redemption the taxpayer retained an interest in Bresee other than as a creditor, the 1970 and 1971 payments to her would be treated as taxable dividends—to the extent of Bresee's earnings. Code § 302(d).

I

. . . The appellee Herbert A. Dunn was never a director or stockholder of Bresee; he had been in the automobile business since 1925 essentially as a salesman, and he had been general manager and for a time, until 1951, president of Bresee. In about 1951, however, taxpayer's son William B. Dunn became president of Bresee, and, at about the same time, apparently with the encouragement of General Motors Corporation ("GM"), the grantor of the Bresee franchise, the taxpayer transferred 125 shares of her stock to her son, and, following that, made yearly gifts of stock to her three children until they owned a majority of the stock.

There was testimony that GM wanted William Dunn to own a majority of the stock. By 1970 appellee Herbert Dunn was seventy-seven years old and taxpayer was seventy-three. The taxpayer wished to spend most of her time in Florida, and she did not want to have any business responsibilities. Appellee Herbert Dunn, while continuing as a salesman with Bresee, also planned to spend part of each winter in Florida.

Judge Tannenwald found on ample evidence that the taxpayer wished to dispose of her stock because she had been advised that it created a liquidity problem from an estate planning point of view, and because she and her husband wanted additional income, as they advanced in age, and Bresee had not paid any dividends except in one year. In the negotiations between the taxpayer and Bresee each party was represented by separate counsel.

Such were the general circumstances when the taxpayer entered into the May 27, 1970, Stock Purchase Agreement (the "Agreement") with Bresee. . . The Agreement recited that Bresee operated as a Chevrolet franchise subject to all of the terms of the franchise agreement with GM, and that among the franchise terms was one requiring Bresee to maintain a certain "Owned Net Working Capital" in order to retain the dealership. The Stock Purchase Agreement stated that the parties understood that the Owned Net Working Capital requirement would prohibit Bresee's paying any principal or interest under the Agreement if payment would reduce Owned Net Working Capital to an amount less than required by the franchise agreement or unless payment permitted the dealer to retain at least 50% of net after tax profits to be added to surplus. It was then agreed, with respect to payment of principal or interest under the Agreement, or on the accompanying ten year promissory note, that

> . . . if . . . the making of any payment thereunder would result in a violation of both said requirements, then and in such event, the due date of such payment or the part thereof which would result in such violation, shall be postponed until such date as when said payments or a part thereof can be made and still meet either the requirement in regard to "Owned Net Working Capital" or the requirement in regard to retention of 50% of net profits after taxes.

On June 1, 1970, Bresee redeemed all 249 of taxpayer's shares and paid taxpayer $100,000. After the redemption the taxpayer was not an officer, director, or employee of Bresee and through the date of trial had not acquired any stock in Bresee. After the redemption Bresee had 221 shares of stock outstanding, 143 of which were owned by William Dunn; each of his two married sisters owned 39 shares. . .

On June 1, 1971, Bresee's financial condition was such that payment of the $55,154 and interest would have violated the GM Minimum Capital Standard Agreement, and, accordingly, the payments were in part "postponed" under the above quoted terms of the Stock Purchase Agreement. The taxpayer received only $45,260.34 in principal, and she received no interest in June 1971. The balance of the principal payment due on June 1, 1971, was paid in June 1972, and the interest of $11,757.70 due on June 1, 1971, was paid in September 1974. After June 1, 1971, no payments on principal were either timely made or made during the taxable year when due. Payments of $23,311.80, the agreed annual payment amount, were made about a year or more late, on June 18, 1973, May 29, 1974, October 15, 1975, and July 27, 1976. At the time each payment was made, Bresee was in violation of the Minimum Capital Standard Agreement, although its net working capital was increasing each year.

While GM was not advised of each payment as it was made, it did receive monthly balance sheets and profit and loss statements; it did not object to Bresee's payments to the taxpayer. There was testimony, but Judge Tannenwald made no finding on this point, that before the redemption transaction Bresee never met the working capital requirement.

The "Termination of shareholder's interest" provision Section 302(b)(3), which accords sale or exchange treatment to redemptions of the stock of one shareholder if there is a complete redemption of all of the stock owned by that shareholder, applies to family corporations, not as some narrow and grudging exception to some otherwise general rule, but as a sensible and evident, explicit and appropriate definition of a type of capital transaction. The statute says simply that the capital transaction analysis applies if the retiring stockholder genuinely quits the company except to retain an interest as a creditor. Where a stockholder whose shares are purportedly redeemed in their entirety retains in some form the substance of stock ownership, then, as the Court put it in United States v. Davis, 397 U.S. 301, 307, . . . (1970), "such a redemption is always 'essentially equivalent to a dividend' within the meaning of that phrase in § 302(b)(1)."

Judge Tannenwald found on the evidence that the taxpayer was not an officer, director or employee of Bresee after the redemption, that up to the date of trial she had not acquired any stock in Bresee and that she had filed with the tax return the required agreement to notify the Secretary of the Treasury of any acquisition of interest in the company. Hence the sole question is whether immediately after the distribution the taxpayer was anything more than a creditor of Bresee.

The Commissioner argues that the Treasury regulation, 26 C.F.R. § 1.302–4(d), defining the term creditor in the context of § 302(b)(3) stock redemptions, is decisive of the case when it is applied to the postponement of payment provision of the Agreement. The regulation reads (as it has read since 1955):

> For the purpose of Section 302(c)(2)(A)(i), a person will be considered to be a creditor only if the rights of such person with respect to

the corporation are not greater or broader in scope than necessary for the enforcement of his claim. Such claim must not in any sense be proprietary and must not be subordinate to the claims of general creditors. An obligation in the form of a debt may thus constitute a proprietary interest. For example, if under the terms of the instrument the corporation may discharge the principal amount of its obligation to a person by payments, the amount or certainty of which are dependent upon the earnings of the corporation, such a person is not a creditor of the corporation. Furthermore, if under the terms of the instrument the rate of purported interest is dependent upon earnings, the holder of such instrument may not, in some cases, be a creditor.

The Commissioner's contentions rest upon the fact that under the Stock Purchase Agreement if the making of any of the installment payments to the taxpayer would result in Bresee's failing to meet the net owned working capital requirement and the 50 percent of net profit retention clause, then payment of all or part of the installment is postponed until the payment can be made in whole or part without transgressing the GM agreement.

The Commissioner's confidence that the terms of the regulation require the conclusion that the taxpayer was not simply a creditor is not supported by the facts in the case. The regulation is concerned with the redeeming stockholder's status in two directions. First, that the redeeming stockholder does not remain someone with rights greater or broader than those of an ordinary creditor, for example, having the right to convert the claim into stock, or the right to vote as a stockholder in the event of a default in paying interest or principal, or a right to inspect the books or the stockholders list. As the regulation says, the claim must not be in any sense proprietary. None of these indicia of proprietary interest is claimed to be present in the taxpayer's case. She retained no office, no vote, no right to resume her position as stockholder in the event of default, or to convert her claim into stock, or any other right which would return to her a measure of control and of proprietary interest.

The regulation then turns to a second aspect of proprietorship—equity ownership—that is, that the redeeming stockholder's claim as creditor must not be subordinate to the claims of general creditors. The Commissioner appears to assume in part of his argument that the Agreement did subordinate the taxpayer's claim to those of general creditors. Nothing in the agreement affects the rank of the taxpayer's claim as against general creditors, and there is nothing in the Agreement that, if Bresee had been put into liquidation, would have given any creditor a basis for arguing that he should be paid before the taxpayer was paid. It is certainly true that Bresee could not stay in business unless it paid its operating expenses as they came due, and that, in that sense, an ordinary trade creditor, with a right to insist on payment of his bill when due, stood in a different position than the taxpayer. But that is just the difference between any trade creditor selling on current account and a long-term creditor, secured or unsecured. Nothing in the Agreement gave trade creditors any standing whatever to insist upon Bresee's observance of GM's owned net working capital requirement. Indeed, in practical reality Bresee's general creditors were just as subject as the taxpayer to the invocation of the only sanction which GM had for enforcing the owned net working capital requirement, that is, termination of Bresee's Chevrolet franchise: the owned net working capital requirement could as easily be breached by incurring operating expenses as by paying the taxpayer.

The regulation then asserts that a person is not a creditor of the corporation if under the terms of the instrument the corporation may discharge the principal amount of its obligation by payments "the amount or certainty of which are dependent upon the earnings of the corporation." The Commissioner relies on this sentence ultimately, but it is not applicable. Only the time when the payments were made might be influenced by Bresee's owned net working capital position or rate of net profits after taxes, but neither the amount of the payments to be made nor the duty to make the payments was dependent on the existence of earnings. Neither the owned net working capital, nor the profit limitation aspect of the postponement clause in the Agreement defines the amount Bresee must pay under the Agreement or makes Bresee's earnings either the source or the measure of Bresee's obligation to the taxpayer. Bresee could pay the taxpayer from the proceeds of a mortgage on the dealership premises, or from capital contributed by the shareholders or raised on a new issue. The obligation to pay was unconditional and certain in its amount.[6]

The Tax Court did appear to accept as correct the Commissioner's argument that Bresee could discharge the obligation by payments the amount or certainty of which was dependent upon Bresee's earnings, a contention that must be rejected as an incorrect reading of the Agreement. The court's view was that the restriction on time of payment was not an arrangement voluntarily agreed upon between the taxpayer and Bresee as a means of enabling her to perpetuate a stockholder-like interest in Bresee but was a GM exaction to which the taxpayer and Bresee alike had to bow. Nothing in that submission to the realities of Bresee's business life reflected a retention of a proprietary interest in Bresee by the taxpayer; the court analogized the situation to one in which a payment restriction was imposed by law.

The regulation, then, does not support the Commissioner's position, for the instrument under review does not exhibit a single one of the characteristics given significance by the regulation. . .

The distinction between deferment of payability and contingency of obligation is familiar, Pierce Estates, Inc. v. Commissioner, 195 F.2d 475, 477–478 (3d Cir. 1952), and does indeed mark a difference between true debt and obligations that are presently something less than debt, but which

---

[6] The final sentence in the regulation states that if the rate of "purported interest is dependent upon earnings, the holder ... may not, in some cases, be a creditor." The interest rate under the Agreement is not made dependent upon earnings. Rather, the Agreement simply reflects recognition of the owned net working capital provision as excusing timely performance.

become debt when the contingency occurs and fixes the obligation to pay. See generally American Bemberg Corp. v. United States, 253 F.2d 691 (3d Cir.), *cert. denied*, 358 U.S. 827, . . . (1958); . . . cf. Island Petroleum Co. v. Commissioner, 57 F.2d 992, 994 (4th Cir.) (taxpayer to lose advances only if operations unsuccessful; if successful, to receive its advances back; the advances were, therefore, loans), *cert. denied*, 287 U.S. 646 . . . (1932).

II

. . . Section 385 of the Code, added in 1969, in authorizing the Secretary to prescribe regulations for determining whether a corporate interest is to be treated for purposes of the Code as stock or indebtedness, sets forth five "factors" including—subordination—which the Secretary may include in his regulations. No regulations have been promulgated under Section 385, although regulations issued under Section 385 might carry more weight than the current regulation because considered "legislative." See Chrysler Corp. v. Brown, 441 U.S. 281 . . . (1979). . . The case law presents the background for reading such an interpretive regulation as is here involved.

It has not been doubted since John Kelley Co. v. Commissioner, 326 U.S. 521, 526, 530 . . . (1946), that the question whether an interest is truly a stock or debt interest, and whether the payments made upon it are truly deductible interest or are non-deductible dividends, is determined typically on the total facts surrounding the creation and use of the instrument and not by its possession of some single characteristic. In *Kelley* the Court held that amounts paid as "interest" on noncumulative income debentures that were subordinated to general creditors but preferred over common stock could properly be held by the Tax Court to constitute interest on indebtedness and deductible. . . See also Scriptomatic, Inc. v. United States, 555 F.2d 364, 373 (3d Cir. 1977). . . See also Lisle v. Commissioner, 35 T.C.M. (CCH) 627 (1976) (although corporation had twenty years to pay for shares, the shares were pledged to secure payment, and selling stockholders retained the right to vote, transaction held an exchange within § 302(a)). . .

Neither under the language of the regulation relied upon nor under the cases which have dealt with the "debt or equity" question is there any basis in the present case for holding that the taxpayer had any interest in Bresee other than an interest as a creditor after the closing under the Stock Purchase Agreement.

Affirmed.

NOTES

1. What is the purpose of § 302(c)(2)(B)? A was the president and sole shareholder of X Corporation; his son, B, was vice president. A retired from the business, gave half his X stock to B and sold the remainder to X taking steps to comply with § 302(c)(2)(A). How should the redemption be treated? See Rev. Rul. 77–293, 1977–2 C.B. 91.

In Rev. Rul. 85–19, 1985–1 C.B. 94, a transfer of stock back to the donor within 10 years of its acquisition was not considered to have been made for tax avoidance purposes under § 302(c)(2) because the transaction merely returned the stock to its original owner. Should the fact of retransfer, by itself, always be enough?

2. If a transaction fails under section 302 to receive exchange treatment, and is analyzed under section 301, what happens if there is not enough E & P to treat the entire payment as a dividend? If recovery of basis is the next step, what basis counts? Only the basis in the "redeemed shares"? All the basis in the stock of the redeeming corporation? In 2006, the Service withdrew proposed regulations on this issue which *did not* adopt the view that basis in all stock of the redeeming corporation held by the taxpayer could be counted under § 301. Announcement 2006–30, 2006–1 C.B. 879. The Service and Treasury have invited comment on this question, and it remains an area "under study" for which rulings will not be presently issued. Rev. Proc. 2012–3, 2012-1 I.R.B. 113.

3. In Hurst v. Commissioner, 124 T.C. 16 (2005), supra 147 the taxpayer redeemed 90% of his shares in his wholly owned corporation and sold the remaining 10% to his son. The court held that the transaction qualified as a redemption in complete termination of the taxpayer's interest under § 302(b)(3) even though the taxpayer's wife remained employed by the corporation, the taxpayer-shareholder continued to be the corporation's landlord, and the redeeming shareholder retained a security interest in the redeemed stock. With respect to the cross-default clauses of the contractual obligations, the court disagreed with the Service's position that the clauses represented a prohibiting continuing interest, and noted (quoting *Lynch*) that the Hursts "offered credible evidence from their professional advisers that these transactions, including the grant of a security interest to Mr. Hurst, were consistent with common practice for seller-financed deals."

ii. SUBSTANTIALLY DISPROPORTIONATE REDEMPTIONS—§ 302(b)(2)

Revenue Ruling 81–41
1981–1 C.B. 12.

. . . A domestic corporation, X, had outstanding 5,100 shares of voting common stock and 4,900 shares of voting preferred stock. Except for minor limitations of local law, the common and preferred stock have equal voting rights. . . All the preferred stock is owned by A, who is the founder of X and the board chairman. The preferred stock is not section 306 stock within the meaning of section 306(c) of the Code. A holds no common stock in X, either directly or constructively. . . The common stock in X is widely held by persons unrelated to A.

In accord with a request from A, X redeemed 2,000 shares of the preferred stock for cash. Thus, A's vote in X was reduced from 49 percent immediately before the redemption to 36.25 percent immediately after the redemption (2,900 shares still held by A divided by 8,000 shares then outstanding). There was no plan or intent for X to redeem any of the stock held by shareholders other than A.

LAW AND ANALYSIS

Section 302(a) of the Code provides that if a corporation redeems its stock and if paragraph (1), (2), (3), or (4) of section 302(b) applies to the redemption, the redemption shall be treated as a distribution in part or full payment in exchange for the stock. Section 302(b)(2) states as a general rule that section 302(a) shall apply to a redemption if the distribution is substantially disproportionate with respect to the shareholder. Under section 302(b)(2)(C) a distribution is substantially disproportionate if:

> (i) the ratio which the voting stock of the corporation owned by the shareholder immediately after the redemption bears to all of the voting stock of the corporation at such time, is less than 80 percent of

> (ii) the ratio which the voting stock of the corporation owned by the shareholder immediately before the redemption bears to all of the voting stock of the corporation at such time.

> For purposes of this paragraph, no distribution shall be treated as substantially disproportionate unless the shareholder's ownership of the common stock of the corporation (whether voting or nonvoting) after and before redemption also meets the 80 percent requirement of the preceding sentence . . .

. . . In the present case, A owned 49 percent of the voting stock of X prior to the redemption. Eighty percent of 49 percent is 39.2 percent. Because A owned 36.25 percent of the voting stock of X after the redemption, the first "80 percent test" of section 302(b)(2)(C) is satisfied. In addition, because A owned only 36.25 percent of the voting stock of X after the redemption, the limitation of section 302(b)(2)(B) is met. Also, because this redemption was not part of a plan to redeem other stock of X, the provisions of section 302(b)(2)(D) are not violated. The question remaining is whether the second "80 percent test" of section 302(b)(2)(C), which concerns the ownership of common stock, has to be satisfied even though A owned no common stock either directly or constructively.

The Senate Finance Committee Report accompanying the enactment of section 302 states:

> Paragraph (2) of subsection (b) sets forth a general rule that if the redemption is substantially disproportionate, it will be treated as a sale under subsection (a), if the other conditions described in the paragraph are met. *It is intended that the general rule shall apply with respect to a redemption of preferred stock (other than section 306 stock) as well as common stock.* S. Rep. No. 1622, 83d Cong., 2d Sess. 234 (1954). (Emphasis added.)

Moreover, section 1.302–3 of the Income Tax Regulations states that section 302(b)(2) of the Code only applies to a redemption of both voting stock and other stock, but does not apply to the redemption solely of nonvoting stock. Therefore, both the legislative history and the regulations accompanying section 302(b)(2) indicate that the provision should apply to the redemption of voting preferred stock.

In the same report, the Senate Finance Committee does make two statements that a substantially disproportionate redemption requires a reduction in the redeemed shareholder's ownership of common stock in the redeeming corporation. However, the context of the first of these statements (S. Rep. No. 1622 at 44–45) indicates that this requirement is a safeguard against abuse where the redeeming shareholder holds common stock. Similarly, the second statement (S. Rep. No. 1622 at 234) views this requirement as meaning, "it is necessary that the shareholder's ownership of voting or nonvoting common stock (that is, his participating interest) in the corporation also be reduced by the percentage required with respect to voting stock." These statements indicate that in the case of a redeeming shareholder owning two or more classes of stock, one of which is common stock, the shareholder may not retain or improve his or her "participating" interest in the corporation (while having a substantially disproportionate reduction in his or her voting interest) and still claim the protection of the section 302(b)(2) safe-harbor. To conclude otherwise would permit a "bail-out" of corporate earnings at capital gains rates without a sacrifice of the shareholder's economic interest in the corporation. See United States v. Davis, 397 U.S. 301, 313 (1970)... Thus, these statements (indicating that section 302(b)(2) requires a reduction in common stock ownership) are addressed to situations where the redeeming shareholder owns common stock, and are not addressed to situations where the redeeming shareholder does not own any common stock.

... Therefore, the additional "safeguard" provided by the second "80 percent test" of section 302(b)(2)(C) is inapplicable to A...

Revenue Ruling 87–88

1987–2 C.B. 81.

ISSUE

If shares of both voting and nonvoting common stock are redeemed from a shareholder in one transaction, are the two classes aggregated for purposes of applying the substantially disproportionate requirement in section 302(b)(2)(C) of the Internal Revenue Code?

FACTS

X corporation had outstanding 10 shares of voting common stock and 30 shares of nonvoting common stock. The fair market values of a share of voting common stock and a share of nonvoting common stock are approximately equal. A owned 6 shares of X voting common stock and all the nonvoting common stock. The remaining 4 shares of the X voting common stock were held by persons unrelated to A within the meaning of section 318(a) of the Code.

X redeemed 3 shares of voting common stock and 27 shares of nonvoting common stock from A in a single transaction. Thereafter, A owned 3 shares of X voting common stock and 3 shares of nonvoting common stock. The ownership of the remaining 4 shares of X voting common stock was unchanged.

LAW AND ANALYSIS

If a distribution in redemption of stock qualifies under section 302(b)(2) of the Code as substantially disproportionate, the distribution is treated under section 302(a) as a payment in exchange for the stock redeemed.

Under section 302(b)(2)(B) and (C) of the Code, a distribution is substantially disproportionate if (i) the shareholder owns less than 50 percent of the total combined voting power of the corporation immediately after the redemption, (ii) immediately after the redemption the ratio of voting stock owned by the shareholder to all the voting stock of the corporation is less than 80 percent of the same ratio immediately before the redemption, and (iii) immediately after the redemption the ratio of common stock owned by the shareholder to all of the common stock of the corporation (whether voting or nonvoting) is less than 80 percent of the same ratio immediately before the redemption.

Under section 302(b)(2)(C) of the Code, if more than one class of common stock is outstanding, the determination in (iii) above is made by reference to fair market value. Section 302(b)(2) applies to a redemption of both voting stock and other stock (although not to the redemption solely of nonvoting stock). Section 1.302–3(a) of the Income Tax Regulations.

With regard to requirements (i) and (ii) described above, after the redemption, A owned less than 50 percent of the voting power of X (43 percent), and A's voting power was reduced to less than 80 percent of the percentage of voting power in X that A owned before the redemption (from 60 percent to 43 percent for a reduction to 72 percent of the preredemption level).

With regard to requirement (iii) above, section 302(b)(2)(C) of the Code provides that, if there is more than one class of common stock outstanding, the fair market value of all of the common stock (voting and nonvoting) will govern the determination of whether there has been the requisite reduction in common stock ownership. The fact that this test is based on fair market value and is applied by reference to all of the common stock of the corporation suggests that the requirement concerning reduction in common stock ownership is to be applied on an aggregate basis rather than on a class-by-class basis. Thus, the fact that A has no reduction in interest with regard to the nonvoting common stock and continues to own 100 percent of this stock does not prevent the redemption of this class of stock from qualifying under section 302(b)(2) when the whole transaction meets section 302(b)(2) requirements. To conclude otherwise would require that, notwithstanding a redemption of one class of common stock in an amount sufficient to reduce the shareholder's aggregate common stock ownership by more than 20 percent in value, every other class of common stock owned by the shareholder must be subject to a redemption.

Prior to the redemption, A owned 90 percent of the total fair market value of all the outstanding X common stock (36 out of the 40 shares of voting and nonvoting common stock). After the redemption, A owned 60 percent of the total fair market value of all the X common stock (6 out of 10 shares). The reduction in ownership (from 90 percent to 60 percent) was a reduction to less than 80 percent of the fraction that A previously owned of the total fair market value of all the X common stock.

HOLDING

If more than one class of common stock is outstanding, the provisions of section 302(b)(2)(C) of the Code are applied in an aggregate and not a class-by-class manner. Accordingly, the redemption by X of 3 shares of voting common stock and 27 shares of nonvoting common stock qualifies as substantially disproportionate within the meaning of section 302(b)(2), even though A continues to own 100 percent of the outstanding nonvoting common stock.

NOTES

1. Note the language in Rev. Rul. 81–41 (supra), indicating that part of the requirements in section 302(b)(2) seek to prevent a "bail-out" of corporate earnings at capital gains rates. After the dividend tax rate change implemented by the 2003 Act, is the bail-out fear still justified? Under what circumstances would a shareholder receiving a distribution from a corporation strongly prefer to meet the redemption test of section 302 (and garner sale or exchange treatment) rather than face taxation under § 301? Taxpayers now have increased flexibility in making distributions from closely held corporations, as the pressure to conform to § 302(b) lessens. See Feld, "Dividends Reconsidered," 101 Tax Notes 1117 (Dec. 1, 2003).

2. Section 302(b)(2)(D) provides that § 302(b)(2) is not applicable to any redemption made pursuant to a plan that has the purpose or effect of using a series of redemptions to result in an aggregate distribution not substantially disproportionate to the shareholder. In Rev. Rul. 85–14, 1985–1 C.B. 92, § 302(b)(2)(D) was held to deny the § 302(b)(2) safe harbor to the majority shareholder where a second redemption of another shareholder restored the majority shareholder's control.

iii. DISTRIBUTIONS NOT ESSENTIALLY EQUIVALENT TO A DIVIDEND—
   § 302(b)(1)

Himmel v. Commissioner
338 F.2d 815 (2d Cir. 1964).

■ Before MOORE, SMITH and KAUFMAN, CIRCUIT JUDGES.

■ MOORE, CIRCUIT JUDGE. Isidore and Lillian Himmel (collectively referred to as the taxpayer) petition for review of a decision of the Tax Court, 41 T.C. 62 (1963), upholding the Commissioner of Internal Revenue's determination of deficiency in taxpayer's income tax for the years 1957 and 1958 in the amount of $2,346.11 and $3,287.45, respectively. In both years, taxpayer received from the H. A. Leed Co. in redemption of certain shares of stock held by him, payments which he did not report in his tax returns for those years. The Commissioner and the Tax Court found the payments to be essentially equivalent to dividends, which, under the Internal Revenue Code of 1954, Section 302, should have been treated as ordinary income.* We disagree with that finding and, accordingly, reverse the judgment.

Whether a redemption "is 'essentially equivalent to' a dividend, involving as it does application of a statutory rule to found facts, is a question of law. . ."[2]

In 1946 taxpayer with Leonard Goldfarb and Edward G. Schenfield incorporated the H. A. Leed Co. to process aluminum. The original capital was $8,100 and each shareholder received 27 shares of $100 per common stock. . . From the beginning until late 1948 taxpayer made advances to the company which were carried on the books as "Loans Payable." He expected to be repaid when the company was able to do so. In a recapitalization in late 1948 to improve the company's credit position, each shareholder received 5 more shares of common in cancellation of $500 notes to each. Taxpayer also received 266 shares of $100 par Class A 2% cumulative nonvoting preferred and 110 shares of $100 par Class B 2% Cumulative voting preferred, in cancellation of the then outstanding indebtedness to him of $37,600. Both classes of preferred stock were created at that time and both were redeemable, but the Class B stock could not be redeemed until all the Class A stock had been redeemed. In 1950 taxpayer gave his 32 shares of common to his two sons, 16 to each. In 1954 on the death of Schenfield, the company purchased his 32 shares from his estate. By corporate action in February 1956 a special account was set up into which $3,000 per year was to be deposited solely for the retirement of the company's outstanding preferred stock of the total par value of $37,600. In late 1956 the shareholders voted to redeem 50 shares of Class A at par and the taxpayer agreed to waive all accrued but unpaid dividends on the redeemed shares. Similar provision was made for redemption at taxpayer's death and for other re-

---

*Although dividends after the 2003 Act are still ordinary income (and are not classified as capital gains), the maximum tax rate generally applied is the capital gains rate.—ED.

[2] Though equivalence depends upon the facts, see Treas. Reg. § 1.302–2(b), it is not itself a fact.

demptions during taxpayer's life. In January 1957, 50 shares of Class A were redeemed for $5,000, and in 1958 70 shares of Class A were redeemed for $7,000. No dividends had been paid through December 31, 1958, and in both 1957 and 1958 earnings and profits exceeded the amounts distributed.

Distributions of property by a corporation to a shareholder to the extent they are made out of earnings and profits, section 316, are generally to be included in the gross income of the shareholder. Section 301(a), (c). The ordinary income tax rates would thus be applicable. However, if a corporation redeems its stock, section 317(b), the redemption may be treated as a distribution in part or in full payment in exchange for the stock, section 302(a), thus subjecting the distribution to tax only in the event of capital gains. But this preferential treatment may be availed of only in certain circumstances, one of which is that "the redemption is not essentially equivalent to a dividend." Sections 302(b)(1), 302(d). Primarily the problem is to determine and apply the appropriate tests of dividend equivalence. But the relevance of each of the possible criteria depends largely upon the particular capital structure-distribution pattern.

Ownership of stock can involve three important rights: (1) to vote, and thereby exercise control, (2) to participate in current earnings and accumulated surplus, and (3) to share in net assets on liquidation. Ownership of common stock generally involves all of these. Ownership of preferred stock generally involves the last two, but only to limited extents, unless otherwise provided. Payments to a shareholder with respect to his stock can be of three general sorts: (1) distribution of earnings and profits which effects no change in basic relationships between the shareholder and either the corporation or the other shareholders—i.e., a dividend; (2) payments to a shareholder by a third party in exchange for ownership of the stock and its attendant rights, which accordingly eliminates or contracts pro tanto the shareholder's rights—i.e., a sale; and (3) payments to a shareholder by the corporation in exchange for ownership of the stock. With the last, which can often formally be called a redemption, the effect on the shareholder's basic rights vis-à-vis the corporation and other shareholders depends upon many facts. It is possible for such a transaction to resemble, exactly or substantially, either a dividend or a sale. For tax purposes the payment is considered ordinary income if, by its "net effect," it is "essentially equivalent to a dividend."

The hallmarks of a dividend, then, are pro rata distribution of earnings and profits *and* no change in basic shareholder relationships. Too frequently the inquiry in § 302(b) cases does not keep this sufficiently in mind. Existence of a pro rata distribution may be determined by comparing the patterns of distribution to see whether the shareholders received the same amount as they would have received had the total distribution been a dividend on the common stock outstanding. But, aside from a single-shareholder corporation, it is not enough merely that the taxpayer received the same amount as he would have received with a dividend, for that could be the result of a sale of some stock to a third party. Rather, pro rata distribution indicates also, at least in a one-class capital structure, the extent to which—if any—the basic rights of ownership have been affected. Where there is only common those rights would exist in proportion to shares held. Therefore, quite often the net effect of a distribution may adequately be gauged by determining what would have been the pattern with a dividend.[4]

Additional and more difficult problems are raised when a corporation has more than one class of stock. The additional class will often be a preferred, which typically has no voting rights, has preferential though limited rights to participate in earnings, and has rights to share in liquidation only to the extent of capital contributed, and perhaps accrued but unpaid dividends. Redemption of some preferred stock consequently may cause different changes in a shareholder's total rights than would redemption of common. Even more is this so when the preferred and common are not held in the same proportions by the same shareholders. Shares of different classes should therefore not casually be lumped together. For example, redemption of a nonvoting preferred can have no effect on relative voting rights, and can never meet the "substantially disproportionate" tests of section 302(b)(2). Rights to earnings will depend upon the exact preference given the preferred, e.g., whether it participates beyond its dividend, whether the dividend is cumulative, etc. Rights on liquidation may vary similarly.

These problems are all well illustrated by this case. In the two years in question, taxpayer received from the corporation $5,000 and $7,000, in redemption of 50 and 70 of the 266 shares of Class A nonvoting preferred, all held by him. Other shareholders received nothing. Had the same funds been distributed as a dividend on the 64 shares of common outstanding, Goldfarb would have received $2,500 and $3,500 and taxpayer would actually have received nothing, as he held no common. However, by dint of the attribution rules, section 318(a)(1)(A)(ii), he would be deemed to have owned his sons' shares and therefore to have received the $2,500 and $3,500 actually received by them. Thus he would have received 50% of what he actually did receive. Even if the funds had first gone to pay accumulated but unpaid dividends on the two classes of preferred, taxpayer would have received, according to the Commissioner's calculations, only 82.5% Of what he actually did receive.[5]

With a multi-class capitalization, the amount of a hypothetical dividend that would have been received can reflect the shareholder's right to participate in current and accumulated earnings, though it is a less accu-

---

[4] In stressing the importance of the "substantially pro rata" test, we are not unmindful of the more specific provision of § 302(b)(2). The pro rata test, quite assuredly, developed under § 115(g) whose only provision was for distributions "essentially equivalent to a dividend." While the 1954 revision added specific "safe harbors" for redemptions that completely terminate a shareholder's interest in the corporation, § 302(b)(3), and for distributions that are substantially disproportionate according to certain precise quantitative standards, § 302(b)(2), it also kept the 1939 Code provision for distributions not "essentially equivalent to a dividend." Moreover, it stated that failure to meet any one of the more specific tests should not be taken into account in applying the old test. § 302(b)(5). And since 302(b)(2) is keyed only to changes in voting power, it is obvious that without 302(b)(1) a substantially disproportionate redemption of nonvoting stock could never qualify for capital gain treatment.

[5] We do not consider what might have been the proper tax treatment for the amount of dividends actually waived as neither party raised the issue.

rate index of the effects on voting power or rights on liquidation. Here, an alteration in rights to earnings of 17.5% (waiver of dividends) or 50% (non-waiver of dividends) is substantial enough in itself to bar treatment of the redemption as "essentially equivalent to a dividend." In no other case has a comparable difference apparently been considered otherwise. . .

The Tax Court acknowledged the difference in result between the distribution here and a dividend but thought it unimportant because taxpayer was "the owner of such a heavy percentage of the distributing corporation's stock. . ." 41 T.C. at 71. But the cases relied on by the Tax Court are very different from the one before us. In [Bradbury v. Commissioner, 298 F.2d 111 (1st Cir. 1962)], only 8.7% of the distribution would have gone to the other shareholders were it a dividend, and 91.3% of all shares were considered owned by the taxpayer. Moreover, even without attribution taxpayer was the controlling shareholder. And in Keefe v. Cote, 213 F.2d 651 (1st Cir. 1954), taxpayer owned over 99% Of all shares and would have received all of any dividend save a fraction of 1%. Indeed, there a "legitimate business" was found adequate to bar dividend equivalency. Lastly, in both cases only common stock existed so that all essential shareholder relationships existed pro rata with dividend rights.

The Tax Court also stressed the fact that the redemption effected no change in voting power. Of course, this could be relevant if only common stock existed; but where nonvoting stock exists redemption even of all of it cannot affect voting power. Since nonvoting preferred was redeemed here we do not think such weight should have been given to the absence of any change in voting power. However, were voting shares redeemed we think that the Tax Court's lumping together of common and voting preferred would have been justifiable, if only to gauge the impact on voting power.

However, the Tax Court also stressed the fact that taxpayer's total ownership of all shares was reduced only 2.74% by the redemption, a change not thought substantial. But this figure was obtained by lumping together all shares outstanding—common, voting preferred, and nonvoting preferred. We think that such a figure is not particularly helpful. It cannot stand in the abstract, but must be related to some significant aspect of the complex of shareholder rights. The Tax Court did not indicate any such relationship and we are not convinced that necessarily there is any in a corporation having several differently defined classes of stock. The figure does not relate to voting power. It does not relate to rights to share in earnings. It might be thought to relate to rights on liquidation, but it does not accurately do that either.

Taxpayer urges us to consider the changes in relative shares of net worth attributable to each shareholder. Some courts have looked to these changes in book value of a shareholder's total holdings in order to assess the effect of the distribution on liquidation rights. See, e.g., Abraham Frisch, [18 T.C.M. (CCH) 358 (1959)]. We agree that it is a proper inquiry. The test has not been extensively developed, however, perhaps because relatively few of the cases have involved even two classes of stock, and none that we have found has involved three classes, as are present here. Of course with only one class there is no need to turn to a net worth test since liquidation rights, like the other basic shareholder rights, will exist in direct proportion to shares held.

Taxpayer asserts, and the Commissioner did not contend otherwise, that the effect of the distributions was to reduce his share of net worth from 62% to 57%—a difference of 5%. We cannot say that this difference is so insubstantial as to make the redemptions "essentially equivalent to a dividend." To place the changes in context we note that with redemption of the last shares held by taxpayer—either in one complete redemption or as the culmination of a series the last of which would perforce be a "complete" redemption—his sons' shares would no longer be attributed to him since on these facts his interest in the company would be terminated. Sections 302(b)(3), 302(c)(2). Prior to any redemption, the preferred itself represented only 22% of the net worth as of December 31, 1957. Thus, for taxpayer, the maximum possible share of net worth that could be affected by a redemption was 22%, not the 62% Attributed to him through section 318. A change of 5% should be compared with this lesser figure.[7]

In fact, taxpayer would also have us support our conclusion by finding, contrary to the Tax Court, that the redemptions were part of an overall plan to terminate his interest in the corporation. However, we do not feel compelled to reach the question. . .

The decision of the Tax Court is reversed.

Levin v. Commissioner
385 F.2d 521 (2d Cir. 1967).

■ Before MOORE, SMITH and KAUFMAN, CIRCUIT JUDGES.

■ KAUFMAN, CIRCUIT JUDGE. The perils of acting without competent tax advice are demonstrated anew, if further evidence be needed, by this petition to review a decision of the Tax Court, 47 T.C. 258 (1966), holding that distributions in 1960, 1961, 1962, and 1963 to the taxpayer in redemption of her stock in a family corporation were "essentially equivalent to a dividend" within the meaning of section 302(b)(1) of the Internal Revenue Code of 1954, and hence taxable at ordinary income rates. We affirm the decision of the Tax Court.

The evidence, as found by the Tax Court,[3] established that Mrs. Levin's family corporation, the Connecticut Novelty Corporation, Inc., commenced operations as a partnership between her husband and her brother,

---

[7] We think it quite proper to be aware of the effect of a distribution on significant corporate interests without strict regard to the attribution rules. Cf. Moore, Dividend Equivalency–Taxation of Distributions in Redemption of Stock, 19 Tax L. Rev. 249, 252–55 (1964); Note, Stock Redemptions From Close Family Corporations Under Section 302, 47 Minn. L. Rev. 853, 867–70 (1963).

[3] The facts were largely stipulated. The only significant factual dispute is whether a shift in control over the corporation actually occurred as a result of the redemption. In the view we take of the case, it is unnecessary to decide this question; nor need we consider whether, as taxpayer urges, the clearly erroneous rule has any application to § 302(b)(1) cases....

Joseph Levine. . . Taxpayer succeeded to her husband's interest in the business upon his death in 1940. Thereafter, her brother Joseph came to live with her and her son Jerome, and became a "second father" to him. She relied heavily on Joseph's advice in business matters.

Following incorporation of the business in 1948, its 1300 outstanding single class common shares were held as follows: Joseph Levine, 650 shares; Mrs. Levin, 649 shares; Jerome Levin, 1 share.[4] The three stockholders also constituted the board of directors and officers of the corporation until Joseph Levine's death in April 1962, when Jerome's wife became a director. Taxpayer was secretary and treasurer until 1959, when she limited her office in the company to secretary.

Jerome was employed full time in the business since graduating from high school in 1944. In 1957 he contemplated marriage and discussed his status in the company with his mother and uncle in order to learn "where he stood" in the business. He insisted on this so that if it became necessary he could embark on another career while still young. Thereafter, Joseph and the taxpayer agreed to give him a greater participation in the business ownership and management. As a result the existing stock was cancelled and 1300 new shares of common stock were issued and distributed in this manner: Joseph, 485 shares; taxpayer 484 shares; Jerome, 331 shares. Jerome gave no consideration for the 330 additional shares.

They just kinda did it on a napkin

Within a few years Jerome sought outright ownership of the business and to retire his uncle and mother. But he desired to accomplish this by a method which would make provision for them during the balance of their lives. Accordingly, on January 19, 1960, a plan was devised whereby the corporation would redeem the stock of taxpayer and Joseph at $200 per share. Pursuant to this plan Joseph and taxpayer executed identical agreements with the corporation. She was to receive $7000 per year without interest beginning April 1, 1960 until $96,800[5] was paid. Upon default the unpaid balance would become due upon the "seller's" election. As an alternative, the corporation was given the option to pay the entire or any part of the purchase price at any time. After the plan was consummated, Jerome conducted the business with "a greater freedom of action." But out of "respect and sentiment," as we are told, Joseph and taxpayer were retained as directors and officers of the corporation.

Still involved and therefore Fail (b)(3)

. . . [T]hey continued to perform services for the corporation and to receive salaries while at the same time taxpayer accepted a cut in her salary to $1200 per year, the maximum amount then permitted to be earned without a reduction in her social security benefits. . .

The dispute before us arises from taxpayer's treatment of the $7000 payments. In the taxable years in question, 1960 through 1963, she reported the compensation from the corporation under the 1960 agreement as

---

[4] Jerome paid no consideration for his one share.

[5] This was computed by multiplying the number of shares taxpayer actually owned, 484, by the purchase price per share, $200.

long-term capital gains. The Commissioner treated the payments as essentially equivalent to dividends and accordingly determined deficiencies for all the years in question.[7]

I

The difference between a stock redemption that is essentially equivalent to a dividend and one that is not is grounded on a long history in the tax law. The distinction was essential because without it the tax on dividends at ordinary income rates could easily be defeated by the simple expedient of issuing more stock to the shareholders, who then would "sell" back their new shares to the corporation. It would then be asserted that the proceeds of this alleged sale were taxable at capital gains rates because they represented proceeds from the "sale" of a capital asset. To eliminate this patent loophole, Congress early provided that such distributions would receive capital gain treatment only if they were "not essentially equivalent to a dividend." See generally 1 Mertens, Law of Federal Income Taxation § 9.99 (Oliver ed. 1962).

But this simplistic formula created more problems than it solved for the courts were then called upon to answer the elusive question as to when a distribution was or was not "essentially equivalent to a dividend." At first it was generally believed that, in view of its history, the provision was aimed only at distributions motivated by a tax avoidance purpose. Accordingly, if a distribution served a "business purpose," the courts held it was not essentially equivalent to a dividend. This rationale was becoming increasingly difficult to apply, however, and it came to its demise in 1945 when, in interpreting an analogous statutory provision, the Supreme Court ruled that motive had little relevancy. The Court then adopted a more objective "net effect" test, under which the question of dividend equivalency depended on whether the distribution in redemption of stock had the same economic effect as a distribution of a dividend would have had. Commissioner v. Estate of Bedford, 325 U.S. 283, 65 S. Ct. 1157, 89 L. Ed. 1611 (1945). In time this test also proved ephemeral; some courts developed many criteria to determine the "net effect" of a distribution, while in determining "net effect" we differed and relied primarily on changes in "basic rights of ownership."[10] However, most cases have been resolved on their own facts and circumstances.

Until 1954 the "not essentially equivalent to a dividend" test, with all its perplexing problems, had been the sole statutory guide in this area. But the draftsmen of the 1954 Internal Revenue Code, faced with "the morass created by the decisions,"[12] attempted to clarify the standards and thus to make more precise the dividing line between stock redemptions that qualified for capital gains treatment and those that did not by adding objective

---

[7] The Commissioner also treated as essentially equivalent to dividends credits which the corporation allowed taxpayer against her obligation to pay for a cottage transferred to her in 1962. The Tax Court's valuation of this cottage at $19,000 is not challenged here.

[10] See, e.g., Himmel v. Commissioner, 338 F.2d 815, 817 (2d Cir. 1964).

[12] Ballenger v. United States, 301 F.2d 192, 196 (4th Cir. 1962).

tests, see § 302(b)(2)–(4),* and rules defining constructive ownership, see § 318.

Since the "not essentially equivalent to a dividend" test is no longer applied in a vacuum, it is impossible to interpret it without examining the statutory scheme of which it is now a part. Section 302(a) provides that a stock redemption[13] shall be treated as an "exchange" if it falls into any one of the categories of § 302(b).[14] These categories are: (1) a redemption that is "not essentially equivalent to a dividend" under § 302(b)(1); (2) a "substantially disproportionate" redemption under § 302(b)(2); (3) a complete redemption terminating the shareholder's interest in the corporation under § 302(b)(3). Section 302(b)(2) contains an exact mathematical formula to determine whether the disproportion is "substantial." The test in § 302(b)(3) is not mathematical, but it is stated with equal clarity. The shareholder must redeem all of his actually and constructively owned stock to qualify for capital gain treatment under this provision, and § 302(c)(2) provides that if certain clear-cut conditions are met the family attribution rules of § 318(a) will not apply in determining whether the shareholder has disposed of all his stock.

Mrs. Levin concedes that she fails to meet the requirements of either § 302(b)(2) or § 302(b)(3),[16] and so she relies on § 302(b)(1).[17] Our task of interpretation and reasoned elaboration cannot be adequately performed if we examine each provision as if it existed in a vacuum. The Code draftsmen hopefully expected that the preciseness of the tests set out in the new provisions, § 302(b)(2) and § 302(b)(3), would serve to relieve the pressure on the "not essentially equivalent to a dividend" test re-enacted as § 302(b)(1). The new requirements, if carefully observed, provided safe harbors for taxpayers seeking capital gain treatment. As a result, their enactment permitted more accurate and long range tax planning.

The legislative history of § 302(b)(1) supports the view that it was designed to play a modest role in the statutory scheme. As originally passed by the House of Representatives, no provision was made for the "not essentially equivalent to a dividend" test; reliance was placed entirely on provi-

---

*Section 302(b)(4), dealing with certain stock issued by railroads, was repealed by the Bankruptcy Tax Act of 1980. The current § 302(b)(4) (dealing with partial liquidations) was moved from § 346 by Congress in 1982.—ED.

[13] Section 317(b) defines redemption for purposes of §§ 301–395 as a corporation's acquisition in its stock from a shareholder in exchange for property, whether or not the stock is cancelled, retired, or held as treasury stock. This definition settled the question whether there could be dividend equivalence if the redeemed stock was held as treasury stock rather than being cancelled. See Kirschenbaum v. Commissioner, 155 F.2d 23, 25 (2d Cir.), cert. denied, 329 U.S. 726, 67 S. Ct. 75, 91 L. Ed. 628 (1946).

[14] A redemption that does not fall within one of these categories is treated, by virtue of § 302(d), as a distribution under § 301, i.e., as a dividend to the extent of current and post–1913 earnings and profits.

[16] Taxpayer fails to meet the test of § 302(b)(3) because she remained a director, an officer, and an employee of the corporation after the redemption. Moreover, she failed to file the proper notification with the Secretary of the Treasury.

[17] In determining whether the redemption satisfies § 302(b)(1), we are directed by § 302(b)(5) not to take into account that the redemption fails to meet the requirements of § 302(b)(2) or § 302(b)(3); but a discussion and understanding of these provisions are useful in interpreting § 302(b)(1).

sions similar to § 302(b)(2) and § 302(b)(3). Thereafter the Senate Finance Committee added § 302(b)(1) and explained its action as follows:[18]

> While the House bill set forth definite conditions under which stock may be redeemed at capital-gain rates, these rules appeared unnecessarily restrictive, particularly in the case of redemptions of preferred stock which might be called by the corporation without the shareholder having any control over when the redemption may take place. Accordingly, your committee follows existing law by reinserting the general language indicating that a redemption shall be treated as a distribution in part or full payment in exchange for stock if the redemption is not essentially equivalent to a dividend.

As a leading commentator observed, "It is not easy to give § 302(b)(1) an expansive construction in view of this indication that its major function was the narrow one of immunizing redemptions of minority holdings of preferred stock."[19]

II

The 1954 Code also adopted a number of constructive ownership rules that provided for the attribution of stock owned by one person or legal entity to another. These provisions overruled the prior case law which unrealistically had not viewed the family as a unit unless other family members were "dummy stockholders." Lukens v. Commissioner, 246 F.2d 403, 407–408 (3d Cir. 1957). By providing a "reasonable rule of thumb,"[20] these rules reduced the difficulties necessarily involved in determining in each case the extent of actual control in a family corporation, in which informal influence over relatives, often impossible of proof, was more important than formal control through voting rights based on actual stock ownership. Like § 302(b)(2) and § 302(b)(3), these rules represented an attempt to make the law more predictable, and thereby to serve as aids to the tax or estate planner.

Section 318(a) [(1)], the family attribution rule[, is] applicable here. . .

In this case, then, the taxpayer must be deemed the owner of her son's shares since § 302(c)(1) provides in part: "section 318(a) shall apply in determining the ownership of stock for purposes of this section."[21]

---

[18] S. Rep. No. 1622, 83rd Cong., 2d Sess., 44–5 (1954).

[19] Bittker & Eustice, Federal Income Taxation of Corporations and Shareholders (2d ed.) 291.

[20] Bittker & Eustice, op. cit., 288.

[21] Although some commentators have argued that the attribution rules are not applicable to § 302(b)(1) because it does not expressly refer to the "ownership" of stock, Bittker & Eustice, op. cit., 292, correctly point out that it is reasonable to apply the attribution rules whenever ownership of stock is relevant, whether by statutory direction or otherwise. Indeed, the Treasury Regulations initially made the application of the attribution rules to § 302(b)(1) mandatory, 19 Fed. Reg. 8240 (1954), although they now provide only that the attribution rules "must be considered," Treas. Regs. § 1.302–2(b), thus allowing some play in the joints for cases hereinafter discussed, e.g., situations involving family estrangement.

III

Taxpayer argues that the family attribution rules should not be determinative in this § 302(b)(1) case. But the definitive language of the statute gives her small comfort despite the three cases upon which she relies so heavily.

In Perry S. Lewis, 47 T.C. 129 (1966), the Tax Court ignored the stock attribution rules in deciding a § 302(b)(1) case. Lewis and his sons owned an automobile dealer franchise, and Lewis' shares were redeemed after the automobile manufacturer put heavy pressure on older men like Lewis to yield franchises to younger men. Lewis severed all relations with the corporation other than remaining as an apparently honorary director and officer. The Tax Court held that distributions to Lewis over a period of five years in exchange for his stock were not essentially equivalent to a dividend, because the stock redemption served a substantial "business purpose." While the majority ignored altogether the family attribution rules, Judge Simpson, in a separate concurrence, pointed out that they required that Lewis be treated as owning his sons' shares, and hence as owning 100% of the corporation's outstanding stock. He concurred, however, on the ground that there was a complete termination of Lewis' interest in the corporation which satisfied § 302(b)(3). *Lewis* does not aid the taxpayer[22] because this court has not looked with favor upon the "business purpose" test. Even if we were to consider it, the Tax Court failed to articulate any reason for ignoring § 318. But, taxpayer argues that the Tax Court in *Lewis* simply considered the "bona fides" of the change in ownership with special care because of the attribution rules, and suggests we do the same. We have already stated that the core of the changes made by the 1954 Code in this not uncommon reticulate fashion for a tax statute was to shift from uncertainty and impreciseness to objective tests; "tax administration would be severely handicapped if the rules applied only as presumptions . . ." Ringel, Surrey & Warren, Attribution of Stock Ownership in the Internal Revenue Code, 72 Harv. L. Rev. 209 (1958). Acceptance of taxpayer's argument would eviscerate the attribution rules and all that Congress hoped to achieve thereby.

Mrs. Levin also refers us to the footnote dictum in Ballenger v. United States, 301 F.2d 192, 199 (4th Cir. 1962), indicating that some commentators have "suggested that the attribution of ownership rules should not be too literally applied to § 302(b)(1)." It is interesting, however, that the attribution rules were applied in *Ballenger*, and the quoted dictum lends feeble support to taxpayer's claim that the attribution rules should be ignored here as they were in *Lewis*.

Finally, taxpayer relies on another footnote observation in Himmel v. Commissioner, 338 F.2d 815, 820 (2d Cir. 1964), stating that "we think it quite proper to be aware of the effect of a distribution on significant corporate interests without strict regard to the attribution rules." The reliance is misplaced. In *Himmel* we applied the attribution rules in determining that

---

[22] Of course the concurring opinion in *Lewis* does not support taxpayer's position here, because she makes no claim that there was a complete redemption under § 302(b)(3).

if there had been a dividend on the common stock rather than a redemption of the non-voting cumulative preferred, taxpayer *constructively* would have received significantly less than he did as a result of the redemption. This alteration in rights to earnings was "substantial enough in itself to bar treatment of the redemption as 'essentially equivalent to a dividend.' In no other case has a comparable difference apparently been considered otherwise." *Himmel*, at 818. In the case before us, if there had been $14,000 annual dividends (the amount of the annual distributions to taxpayer and Joseph) instead of a stock redemption, taxpayer would have received constructively about $8,778[24] or more than she received from the stock redemption. The Tax Court correctly stated that the comparative dividend test is designed to test "whether the distributions equal or exceed the amounts that would be received as a cash dividend," and that accordingly *Himmel* "is not analogous."

Moreover, *Himmel* involved a corporation with three classes of stock which were not held proportionately. This situation created "additional and more difficult problems;"[25] compliance with § 302(b)(2) was impossible,[26] and immediate compliance with § 302(b)(3) was impractical.[27] By contrast, in the present case taxpayer easily could have complied with § 302(b)(3) by simply resigning as a director, officer, and employee of the corporation and notifying the Secretary of the Treasury.[28] She simply could not have her cake and eat it too.

We do not hold that there may not be cases in which strict application of the attribution rules may be inappropriate. In addition to the preferred stock situations referred to in the Senate Report quoted supra, family estrangement may render the application of the family attribution rules unwise. See Bittker, The Taxation of Stock Redemptions and Partial Liquidations, 44 Cornell L.Q. 299, 324 (1959); Moore, Dividend Equivalency–Taxation of Distributions in Redemption of Stock, 19 Tax L. Rev. 249, 252–55 (1964). But in the case before us taxpayer has offered no valid reason for ignoring the family attribution rules, and we perceive none.

IV

Accordingly, we must attribute Jerome's shares to his mother. As a result, before the redemption she constructively owned her 484 shares and her son's 331 shares, or about 63 per cent of the 1300 outstanding shares. After the redemption she still constructively owned her son's shares. Thus, after the redemption of the stock owned by her and her brother, by the rule of attribution she became the constructive owner of 100 per cent of the outstanding stock. It is apparent therefore that her constructive ownership

---

[24] Taxpayer actually owned 37.2 per cent of the stock, and constructively owned another 25.5 per cent (Jerome's), or 62.7 per cent in all; 62.7 per cent of $14,000 is $8,778.

[25] *Himmel*, supra 338 F.2d at 818.

[26] The test of § 302(b)(2) depends on a reduction in the amount of voting stock held; in *Himmel*, non-voting stock was redeemed.

[27] The corporation lacked the funds to redeem all the taxpayer's stock.

[28] See Section 302(c)(2)(A). In addition, taxpayer would have had to satisfy the requirement of the last sentence of section 302(c)(2)(B).

actually increased as a result of the redemptions. As the Tax Court said, this "is most unlike a sale." For when a taxpayer's (constructive) ownership decreases by a significant amount, we are justified in concluding that a substantial reduction in taxpayer's interest in the corporation has occurred warranting capital gain treatment as a sale or exchange. But when only a small reduction in control occurs, the distribution has been held to the essentially equivalent to a dividend; a fortiori, when no reduction, but rather an increase, in control occurs, taxpayer has not parted with anything justifying capital gain treatment.

The Tax Court correctly noted that in this case control in the sense of access to corporate benefits was more important than any legal right to direct the destiny of the corporation. In reality, taxpayer's benefits from the corporation changed little as a result of the redemption. Before 1960 she received a salary of $7800 per year; after 1960 she received $8200 per year, composed of annual distributions of $7000 and salary of $1200. While in form taxpayer redeemed her stock, in substance she parted with nothing justifying capital gain treatment.

The judgment is affirmed.

NOTES

1. The panel in *Levin* was the same as that in *Himmel*. Did *Levin* effectively distinguish *Himmel*?

2. Would *Levin* come out differently today? Are the stakes today different?

3. What is the significance of the "comparative dividend" test in *Himmel* in determining dividend equivalency? Which is the preferable test, "net effect" or "comparative dividend"? Are they mutually exclusive? Would a shareholder be more likely to have dividend income if the redemption proceeds provide him with more or with less than an outright dividend distribution would give him? Why?

United States v. Davis

397 U.S. 301 (1970).

■ MR. JUSTICE MARSHALL delivered the opinion of the Court. In 1945, taxpayer and E. B. Bradley organized a corporation. In exchange for property transferred to the new company, Bradley received 500 shares of common stock, and taxpayer and his wife similarly each received 250 such shares. Shortly thereafter, taxpayer made an additional contribution to the corporation, purchasing 1,000 shares of preferred stock at a par value of $25 per share.

The purpose of this latter transaction was to increase the company's working capital and thereby to qualify for a loan previously negotiated through the Reconstruction Finance Corporation. It was understood that the corporation would redeem the preferred stock when the RFC loan had been repaid. Although in the interim taxpayer bought Bradley's 500 shares and divided them between his son and daughter, the total capitalization of the company remained the same until 1963. That year, after the loan was fully repaid and in accordance with the original understanding, the company redeemed taxpayer's preferred stock.

In his 1963 personal income tax return taxpayer did not report the $25,000 received by him upon the redemption of his preferred stock as income. Rather, taxpayer considered the redemption as a sale of his preferred stock to the company—a capital gains transaction under § 302 of the Internal Revenue Code of 1954 resulting in no tax since taxpayer's basis in the stock equaled the amount he received for it. The Commissioner of Internal Revenue, however, did not approve this tax treatment. According to the Commissioner, the redemption of taxpayer's stock was essentially equivalent to a dividend and was thus taxable as ordinary income under §§ 301 and 316 of the Code. Taxpayer paid the resulting deficiency and brought this suit for a refund. The District Court ruled in his favor, 274 F.Supp. 466 (D. C. M. D. Tenn. 1967), and on appeal the Court of Appeals affirmed. 408 F.2d 1139 (C. A. 6th Cir. 1969).

The Court of Appeals held that the $25,000 received by taxpayer was "not essentially equivalent to a dividend" within the meaning of that phrase in § 302(b)(1) of the Code because the redemption was the final step in a course of action that had a legitimate business (as opposed to a tax avoidance) purpose. That holding represents only one of a variety of treatments accorded similar transactions under § 302(b)(1) in the circuit courts of appeals.[2] We granted certiorari, 396 U.S. 815 (1969), in order to resolve this recurring tax question involving stock redemptions by closely held corporations. We reverse.

I

The Internal Revenue Code of 1954 provides generally in §§ 301 and 316 for the tax treatment of distributions by a corporation to its shareholders; under those provisions, a distribution is includable in a taxpayer's gross income as a dividend out of earnings and profits to the extent such earnings exist.[3] There are exceptions to the application of these general provisions, however, and among them are those found in § 302 involving certain distributions for redeemed stock. The basic question in this case is whether the $25,000 distribution by the corporation to taxpayer falls under that section—more specifically, whether its legitimate business motivation qualifies the distribution under § 302(b)(1) of the Code. Preliminarily, however, we must consider the relationship between § 302(b)(1) and the rules regarding the attribution of stock ownership found in § 318(a) of the Code.

---

[2] Only the Second Circuit has unequivocally adopted the Commissioner's view and held irrelevant the motivation of the redemption. See Levin v. Commissioner, 385 F.2d 521 (1967); Hasbrook v. United States, 343 F.2d 811 (1965). The First Circuit, however, seems almost to have come to that conclusion, too. *Compare* Wiseman v. United States, 371 F.2d 816 (1967), *with* Bradbury v. Commissioner, 298 F.2d 111 (1962).

[3] ... Taxpayer makes no contention that the corporation did not have $25,000 in accumulated earnings and profits.

Under subsection (a) of § 302, a distribution is treated as "payment in exchange for the stock," thus qualifying for capital gains rather than ordinary income treatment, if the conditions contained in any one of the four paragraphs of subsection (b) are met. In addition to paragraph (1)'s "not essentially equivalent to a dividend" test, capital gains treatment is available where (2) the taxpayer's voting strength is substantially diminished, [or] (3) his interest in the company is completely terminated. . . [T]axpayer admits that paragraphs (2) and (3) do not apply. Moreover, taxpayer agrees that for the purposes of §§ 302(b)(2) and (3) the attribution rules of § 318(a) apply and he is considered to own the 750 outstanding shares of common stock held by his wife and children in addition to the 250 shares in his own name.

Taxpayer, however, argues that the attribution rules do not apply in considering whether a distribution is essentially equivalent to a dividend under § 302(b)(1). According to taxpayer, he should thus be considered to own only 25 percent of the corporation's common stock, and the distribution would then qualify under § 302(b)(1) since it was not pro rata or proportionate to his stock interest, the fundamental test of dividend equivalency. See Treas. Reg. 1.302–2(b). However, the plain language of the statute compels rejection of the argument. In subsection (c) of § 302, the attribution rules are made specifically applicable "in determining the ownership of stock for purposes of this section." Applying this language, both courts below held that § 318 (a) applies to all of § 302, including § 302(b)(1)—a view in accord with the decisions of the other courts of appeals, a longstanding treasury regulation,[6] and the opinion of the leading commentators.

Against this weight of authority, taxpayer argues that the result under paragraph (1) should be different because there is no explicit reference to stock ownership as there is in paragraphs (2) and (3). Neither that fact, however, nor the purpose and history of § 302(b)(1) support taxpayer's argument. The attribution rules—designed to provide a clear answer to what would otherwise be a difficult tax question—formed part of the tax bill that was subsequently enacted as the 1954 Code. As is discussed further, infra, the bill as passed by the House of Representatives contained no provision comparable to § 302(b)(1). When that provision was added in the Senate, no purpose was evidenced to restrict the applicability of § 318(a). Rather, the attribution rules continued to be made specifically applicable to the entire section, and we believe that Congress intended that they be taken into account wherever ownership of stock was relevant.

Indeed, it was necessary that the attribution rules apply to § 302(b)(1) unless they were to be effectively eliminated from consideration with regard to §§ 302(b)(2) and (3) also. For if a transaction failed to qualify under one of those sections solely because of the attribution rules, it would according to taxpayer's argument nonetheless qualify under § 302(b)(1). We cannot agree that Congress intended so to nullify its explicit directive. We conclude, therefore, that the attribution rules of § 318(a) do apply; and, for the purposes of deciding whether a distribution is "not essentially equivalent to

---

[6] See Treas. Reg. 1.302–2(b).

a dividend" under § 302(b)(1), taxpayer must be deemed the owner of all 1,000 shares of the company's common stock.

II

After application of the stock ownership attribution rules, this case viewed most simply involves a sole stockholder who causes part of his shares to be redeemed by the corporation. We conclude that such a redemption is always "essentially equivalent to a dividend" within the meaning of that phrase in § 302(b)(1)[8] and therefore do not reach the Government's alternative argument that in any event the distribution should not on the facts of this case qualify for capital gains treatment.[9]

The predecessor of § 302(b)(1) came into the tax law as § 201(d) of the Revenue Act of 1921, 42 Stat. 228:

> A stock dividend shall not be subject to tax but if after the distribution of any such dividend the corporation proceeds to cancel or redeem its stock at such time and in such manner as to make the distribution and cancellation or redemption essentially equivalent to the distribution of a taxable dividend, the amount received in redemption or cancellation of the stock shall be treated as a taxable dividend. . .

Enacted in response to this Court's decision that pro rata stock dividends do not constitute taxable income, Eisner v. Macomber, 252 U.S. 189 (1920), the provision had the obvious purpose of preventing a corporation from avoiding dividend tax treatment by distributing earnings to its shareholders in two transactions—a pro rata stock dividend followed by a pro rata redemption—that would have the same economic consequences as a simple dividend. Congress, however, soon recognized that even without a prior stock dividend essentially the same result could be effected whereby any corporation, "especially one which has only a few stockholders, might be able to make a distribution to its stockholders which would have the same effect as a taxable dividend." H. R. Rep. No. 1, 69th Cong., 1st Sess., 5. In order to cover this situation, the law was amended to apply "(whether or not such stock was issued as a stock dividend)" whenever a distribution in redemption of stock was made "at such time and in such manner" that it was essentially equivalent to a taxable dividend. Revenue Act of 1926, § 201(g), 44 Stat. 11.

This provision of the 1926 Act was carried forward in each subsequent revenue act and finally became § 115(g)(1) of the Internal Revenue Code of 1939. Unfortunately, however, the policies encompassed within the general language of § 115(g)(1) and its predecessors were not clear, and there re-

---

[8] Of course, this just means that a distribution in redemption to a sole shareholder will be treated under the general provisions of § 301, and it will only be taxed as a dividend under § 316 to the extent that there are earnings and profits.

[9] The Government argues that even if business purpose were relevant under § 302(b)(1), the business purpose present here related only to the original investment and not at all to the necessity for redemption. See cases cited, n. 2, supra. Under either view, taxpayer does not lose his basis in the preferred stock. Under Treas. Reg. 1.302–2(c) that basis is applied to taxpayer's common stock.

sulted much confusion in the tax law. At first, courts assumed that the provision was aimed at tax avoidance schemes and sought only to determine
whether such a scheme existed. See, e.g., Commissioner v. Quackenbos, 78
F.2d 156 (C. A. 2d Cir. 1935). Although later the emphasis changed and the
focus was more on the effect of the distribution, many courts continued to
find that distributions otherwise like a dividend were not "essentially
equivalent" if, for example, they were motivated by a sufficiently strong
nontax business purpose. See cases cited n. 2, supra. There was general
disagreement, however, about what would qualify as such a purpose, and
the result was a case-by-case determination with each case decided "on the
basis of the particular facts of the transaction in question." Bains v. United
States, . . . 289 F.2d 644, 646 (1961).

By the time of the general revision resulting in the Internal Revenue
Code of 1954, the draftsmen were faced with what has aptly been described
as "the morass created by the decisions." Ballenger v. United States, 301
F.2d 192, 196 (C. A. 4th Cir. 1962). In an effort to eliminate "the considerable confusion which exists in this area" and thereby to facilitate tax planning, H. R. Rep. No. 1337, 83d Cong., 2d Sess., 35, the authors of the new
Code sought to provide objective tests to govern the tax consequences of
stock redemptions. Thus, the tax bill passed by the House of Representatives contained no "essentially equivalent" language. Rather, it provided for
"safe harbors" where capital gains treatment would be accorded to corporate redemptions that met the conditions now found in §§ 302(b)(2) and (3)
of the Code.

It was in the Senate Finance Committee's consideration of the tax bill
that § 302(b)(1) was added, and Congress thereby provided that capital
gains treatment should be available "if the redemption is not essentially
equivalent to a dividend." Taxpayer argues that the purpose was to continue "existing law," and there is support in the legislative history that §
302(b)(1) reverted "in part" or "in general" to the "essentially equivalent"
provision of § 115(g)(1) of the 1939 Code. According to the Government,
even under the old law it would have been improper for the Court of Appeals to rely on "a business purpose for the redemption" and "an absence of
the proscribed tax avoidance purpose to bail out dividends at favorable tax
rates." See Northup v. United States, 240 F.2d 304, 307 (C. A. 2d Cir.
1957); Smith v. United States, 121 F.2d 692, 695 (C. A. 3d Cir. 1941); cf.
Commissioner v. Estate of Bedford, 325 U.S. 283 (1945). However, we need
not decide that question, for we find from the history of the 1954 revisions
and the purpose of § 302(b)(1) that Congress intended more than merely to
re-enact the prior law.

In explaining the reason for adding the "essentially equivalent" test,
the Senate Committee stated that the House provisions "appeared unnecessarily restrictive, particularly, in the case of redemptions of preferred
stock which might be called by the corporation without the shareholder
having any control over when the redemption may take place." S. Rep. No.
1622, 83d Cong., 2d Sess., 44. This explanation gives no indication that the

purpose behind the redemption should affect the result.[10] Rather, in its more detailed technical evaluation of § 302(b)(1), the Senate Committee reported as follows:

> The test intended to be incorporated in the interpretation of paragraph (1) is in general that currently employed under section 115(g)(1) of the 1939 Code. Your committee further intends that in applying this test for the future . . . the inquiry will be devoted solely to the question of whether or not the transaction by its nature may properly be characterized as a sale of stock by the redeeming shareholder to the corporation. For this purpose the presence or absence of earnings and profits of the corporation is not material. Example: X, the sole shareholder of a corporation having no earnings or profits causes the corporation to redeem half of its stock. Paragraph (1) does not apply to such redemption notwithstanding the absence of earnings and profits. [S. Rep. No. 1622, supra, at 234.]

The intended scope of § 302(b)(1) as revealed by this legislative history is certainly not free from doubt. However, we agree with the Government that by making the sole inquiry relevant for the future the narrow one whether the redemption could be characterized as a sale, Congress was apparently rejecting past court decisions that had also considered factors indicating the presence or absence of a tax-avoidance motive.[11] At least that is the implication of the example given. Congress clearly mandated that pro rata distributions be treated under the general rules laid down in §§ 301 and 316 rather than under § 302, and nothing suggests that there should be a different result if there were a "business purpose" for the redemption. Indeed, just the opposite inference must be drawn since there would not likely be a tax-avoidance purpose in a situation where there were no earnings or profits. We conclude that the Court of Appeals was therefore wrong in looking for a business purpose and considering it in deciding whether the redemption was equivalent to a dividend. Rather, we agree with the Court of Appeals for the Second Circuit that "the business purpose of a transaction is irrelevant in determining dividend equivalence" under § 302(b)(1). Hasbrook v. United States, 343 F.2d 811, 814 (1965).

Taxpayer strongly argues that to treat the redemption involved here as essentially equivalent to a dividend is to elevate form over substance. Thus, taxpayer argues, had he not bought Bradley's shares or had he made

---

[10] See Bittker & Eustice, supra, n.7, at 291: "It is not easy to give § 302(b)(1) an expansive construction in view of this indication that its major function was the narrow one of immunizing redemptions of minority holdings of preferred stock."

[11] This rejection is confirmed the Committee's acceptance of the House treatment of distributions involving corporate contractions—a factor present in many of the earlier "business purpose" redemptions. In describing its action, the Committee stated as follows:

"Your committee, as did the House bill, separates into their significant elements the kind of transactions now incoherently aggregated in the definition of a partial liquidation. Those distributions which may have capital-gain characteristics *because they are not made pro rata* among the various shareholders would be subjected, at the shareholder level, to the separate tests described in [§§ 301 to 318]. On the other hand, those distributions characterized by what happens solely at the corporate level by reason of the assets distributed would be included as within the concept of a partial liquidation." S. Rep. No. 1622, supra, at 49. (Emphasis added.)

a subordinated loan to the company instead of buying preferred stock, he could have gotten back his $25,000 with favorable tax treatment. However, the difference between form and substance in the tax law is largely problematical, and taxpayer's complaints have little to do with whether a business purpose is relevant under § 302(b)(1). It was clearly proper for Congress to treat distributions generally as taxable dividends when made out of earnings and profits and then to prevent avoidance of that result without regard to motivation where the distribution is in exchange for redeemed stock.

We conclude that that is what Congress did when enacting § 302(b)(1). If a corporation distributes property as a simple dividend, the effect is to transfer the property from the company to its shareholders without a change in the relative economic interests or rights of the stockholders. Where a redemption has that same effect, it cannot be said to have satisfied the "not essentially equivalent to a dividend" requirement of § 302(b)(1). Rather, to qualify for preferred treatment under that section, a redemption must result in a meaningful reduction of the shareholder's proportionate interest in the corporation. Clearly, taxpayer here, who (after application of the attribution rules) was the sole shareholder of the corporation both before and after the redemption, did not qualify under this test. The decision of the Court of Appeals must therefore be reversed and the case remanded to the District Court for dismissal of the complaint.

It is so ordered.

■ Mr. Justice Douglas, with whom The Chief Justice and MR. JUSTICE BRENNAN concur, dissenting.

I agree with the District Court, 274 F.Supp. 466, and with the Court of Appeals, 408 F.2d 1139, that respondent's contribution of working capital in the amount of $25,000 in exchange for 1,000 shares of preferred stock with a par value of $25 was made in order for the corporation to obtain a loan from the RFC and that the preferred stock was to be redeemed when the loan was repaid. For the reasons stated by the two lower courts, this redemption was not "essentially equivalent to a dividend," for the bona fide business purpose of the redemption belies the payment of a dividend. As stated by the Court of Appeals:

> Although closely-held corporations call for close scrutiny under the tax law, we will not, under the facts and circumstances of this case, allow mechanical attribution rules to transform a legitimate corporate transaction into a tax avoidance scheme. [408 F.2d, at 1143–1144.]

When the Court holds it was a dividend, it effectively cancels § 302(b)(1) from the Code. This result is not a matter of conjecture, for the Court says that in the case of closely held or one-man corporations a redemption of stock is "always" equivalent to a dividend. I would leave such revision to the Congress.

Albers v. Commissioner

414 U.S. 982 (1973), *denying cert. to* Miele v. Commissioner, 474 F.2d 1338 (3d Cir. 1973), *aff'g mem.* 56 T.C. 556 (1971).

■ Mr. Justice Powell, with whom Mr. Justice Douglas and Mr. Justice Blackmun join, dissenting. The five petitioners in this case own virtually all the outstanding stock of a small corporation, A & S Transportation Company (A & S). The company operates a barge. The barge fell into such disrepair as to require replacement, but A & S lacked the necessary resources and credit. A & S requested the Federal Maritime Commission to guarantee, as it is empowered by law to do, a proposed first mortgage loan from a bank. Before the Commission would extend its guarantee, it required of A & S at least $150,000 of additional private capital. The Commission presented A & S with two options. A & S could resort either to subordinated debt or to the issuance of nonvoting, nondividend paying, noncumulative preferred stock unredeemable until full payment of the desired loan.

A & S chose the latter course. In proportion to their holdings of A & S common, petitioners in 1959 purchased $150,000 of preferred stock possessing all the attributes required by the Commission. The loan was then consummated with the Commission's guarantee, and A & S purchased a replacement vessel. By 1964 the loan was paid off in full. Having no further need for the $150,000, and in accord with the wishes of petitioners, A & S redeemed the preferred stock in 1965 and 1966 in two equal installments. No premium was paid, and *petitioners received precisely the amount each had previously invested*. The Commissioner of Internal Revenue treated the redemptions as the receipt of ordinary income, taking the view that they were "essentially equivalent to a dividend" within the meaning of § 302(b)(1) of the Internal Revenue Code of 1954, 26 U.S.C. § 302(b)(1). Citing United States v. Davis, 397 U.S. 301 (1970), the Tax Court agreed... The Court of Appeals for the Third Circuit affirmed without published opinions.

On the above facts it seems plain that the redemption of preferred stock provided petitioners nothing more than a return of the capital they were compelled by the Commission to pay into A & S to obtain the additional financing the corporation needed to remain in business. To tax that return of capital at ordinary income rates is an extraordinary result, yet one that I recognize to be mandated by the full sweep of United States v. Davis, supra. Because of strong doubts as to the correctness of any decision that produces such a bizarre result, I would grant certiorari to reconsider *Davis*.

Section 302(b)(1) of the Code shelters from dividend treatment, and accompanying potential ordinary income consequences, any stock redemption that "is not essentially equivalent to a dividend." A majority of the Court in *Davis* read that provision to mean that a stock redemption by a small, closely-held corporation is "*always* 'essentially equivalent to a dividend' " where there is no "change in the relative economic interests or rights of the stockholders." 397 U.S., at 307, 313 (emphasis added). Undoubtedly the

Court sought to promote ease of administration through adoption of a simplistic, per se, rule. Yet the Court explicitly recognized that the weight of authority in the lower federal courts was contrary to its mechanical approach. Id., at 303 n. 2. Furthermore, the Court conceded that the "legislative history is certainly not free from doubt." Id., at 311.

In my view, the result produced by *Davis* in this case is justified neither by the language of the Code nor by the legislative history, and certainly not by precedent prior to *Davis*. In these circumstances, ease of administration is too high a price to pay for the presumably unforeseen and undeniably harsh consequences visited on these and similarly situated taxpayers.

The Tax Court noted petitioners' position "that the preferred stock was no longer needed after the loan had been paid in full and that redemption of the stock was consistent with the business purpose for which the stock was issued." . . . The Tax Court did not refute the factual correctness of this position, or consider whether there had been a tax evasion motivation.[4] Rather, that court simply disregarded all factual considerations as immaterial to an application of the *Davis* per se rule:

> "We consider [petitioners'] argument as having been foreclosed and the issue determined by the case of United State v. Davis, 397 U.S. 301 (1970). In *Davis*, the United States Supreme Court held that a redemption without a change in the relative economic interests or rights of the stockholders is always essentially equivalent to a dividend under § 302(b)(1). It is the effect of the redemption and not the purpose behind it which is determinative of dividend equivalence." [Ibid. (Citations omitted.)]

MR. JUSTICE DOUGLAS, dissenting in *Davis* with the concurrence of the CHIEF JUSTICE and MR. JUSTICE BRENNAN, viewed the majority opinion as reading § 302(b)(1) out of the Code:

> When the Court holds it [the redemption under consideration in *Davis*] was a dividend, it effectively cancels § 302(b)(1) from the Code. This result is not a matter of conjecture, for the Court says that in the case of closely held or one-man corporations a redemption of stock is "always" equivalent to a dividend. [397 U.S., at 314.]

The Tax Court's decision in this case abundantly bears out MR. JUSTICE DOUGLAS' view. In light of the deliberate retention of the "essentially equivalent to a dividend" language in the 1954 revisions of the Code, most courts prior to *Davis* had assumed that § 302(b)(1) required a factual determination as to the business purpose of the stock redemption. Had such a factual inquiry been made in this case, it is evident that the result would have been different.

---

[4] No finding was made by the Tax Court, for example, that an earned surplus was available from which ordinary dividends could have been paid.

In addition to the presence of a legitimate business purpose and the absence of any evidence of tax evasion, the preferred stock in question here was nondividend paying—a highly unusual provision for a preferred stock. Thus petitioners, having been induced by the Commission to advance additional private capital to A & S, found themselves either locked in without income on their investment or compelled, as the price of recouping it, to pay taxes at ordinary income rates on a nonexistent gain. It is difficult to think of a more unjust result, and yet this is the inevitable consequence of the sweeping *Davis* requirement that a redemption "always" be deemed "essentially equivalent to a dividend" in the absence of "a change in the relative economic interests or rights of the stockholders." 397 U.S., at 307, 313.[6]

One may recognize the tax avoidance concern underlying the Court's opinion in *Davis* without concluding that the only remedy with respect to closely-held corporations is "always" to tax stock redemptions as dividends without regard to facts and circumstances. It may indeed have been reasonable to create a rebuttable presumption in favor of the Government, but it is difficult to see a justification for a result as harsh and inequitable as that often produced by the *Davis* rule. Moreover, if Congress' purpose was to enact the *Davis* per se rule, it could have been expressed in the simplest language.[8] As the Court notes in *Davis*, the Senate Finance Committee deliberately chose not to take that option. 397 U.S., at 310–311.

In my view the *Davis* rule, often a trap for unwary investors in small businesses and facially contrary to the relevant Code provision, should be reconsidered.

---

[6] This one qualification (namely, a change in the relative economic interests or rights of stockholders) may immunize from *Davis* consequences the larger corporations, where a congruity of interest between common and preferred stockholders is found far less frequently than in the family type of small corporations. But even where it can fairly be said (and often the facts as to this are ambiguous) that there has been no such change, this does not mean that minority stockholders are not severely penalized by the *Davis* rule. In this case, the Tax Court noted that the redemption was made at the insistence of petitioners, who were in the unhappy position of holding nondividend preferred stock. But nothing in *Davis* protects a minority stockholder in a close corporation (and their number is legion) who may have little or no influence as to whether or when preferred stock is redeemed. If the majority shareholders in such a corporation effect a pro rata redemption, a minority shareholder has no means to avoid *Davis* consequences. In this connection, the language of the Senate Finance Committee in restoring the "essentially equivalent" language to § 302 of the Code is relevant. The Senate Committee stated that the House bill, which had deleted this language, "appeared unnecessarily restrictive, particularly, in the case of redemptions of preferred stock which might be called by the corporation without the shareholder having any control over when the redemption may take place." S. Rep. No. 1622, 83d Cong., 2d Sess., 44. See United States v. Davis, *supra*.... The truth is that minority shareholders, even in close corporations, frequently have no such control.

[8] It has been suggested that since *Davis* was decided March 23, 1970, Congress has had more than three years to repudiate or ameliorate the *Davis* per se rule. With all respect, this suggestion seems unrealistic. Congress has had under consideration during this period a general revision of the Code as well as a broad reexamination of many of the fundamental assumptions underlying the present Code. It is unlikely that piecemeal adjustments would have been made during this period of study and reexamination. Furthermore, the *Davis* rule falls most heavily on small, family corporations unlikely to have specialized tax counsel capable of warning that *Davis* has converted § 302(b)(1) into "a treacherous route to be employed only as a last resort." B. Bittker & J. Eustice, supra, at 9–9. It is these very corporations that are least likely to make their voices heard in Congress, since they have limited "lobbying" capabilities.

NOTES

1. In a series of Revenue Rulings over the years, the Service has tried to address an array of questions regarding the implementation of the § 302 redemption scheme. In Rev. Rul. 76–385, 1976–2 C.B. 92, the Service ruled that where a publicly traded corporation redeemed shares of a minority shareholder (reducing the ownership from .0001118 percent before to .0001081 percent after the redemption), the redemption qualified under § 302(b)(1) as not essentially equivalent to a dividend because it involved a minority shareholder with no ability to exercise control over corporate affairs. However, in Rev. Rul. 81–289, 1981–2 C.B. 82, the Service found the redemption by a publicly traded corporation of shares of a minority shareholder *did not* constitute a redemption "not essentially equivalent to a dividend" under § 302(b)(1) where the shareholder held 0.2 percent for the corporation before and after the redemption.

What weight should be placed on the *size* of the redeeming shareholder's interest in the corporation before the redemption? In Conopco, Inc. v. United States, 2007–2 U.S.T.C. p. 50,582 (D.N.J. 2007), the court stated that "where, as here, a shareholder does not have a 'relatively meaningless interest' to begin with, not just 'any reduction' in proportionate interest will satisfy the 'meaningful reduction' test. Otherwise, under the Government's interpretation of Revenue Ruling 76–385, the word 'meaningful' would be read completely out of the Supreme Court's test in *Davis*. The Trust in this case started with a 2.7884 percent interest in Conopco, as opposed to the shareholder's .0001118 percent interest in Revenue Ruling 76–385. Because the 4,746–share redemption did not meaningfully reduce the Trust's proportionate interest in Conopco, none of the hundreds of other, smaller redemptions did so either. Therefore, Conopco's distributions in redemption of stock from the trust were 'essentially equivalent to a dividend,' § 302(b)(1). . .."

Why was the Government in *Conopco* arguing that the transaction did in fact qualify as a redemption?

2. How important is change in voting power as a measure of dividend equivalence? In Rev. Rul. 85–106, 1985–2 C.B. 116, the Service ruled that a redemption of nonvoting preferred stock in a closely held corporation did not meet the "not equivalent to a dividend" test of § 302(b)(1) where the shareholder experienced no reduction of voting and nonvoting common stock and continued to be able to act as part of a control group. But see Rev. Rul. 75–502, 1975–2 C.B. 111, in which the Service found a "meaningful reduction" (thus satisfying the "not essentially equivalent to a dividend" test) although the redemption reduced the shareholder's voting interest from 57 percent to only 50 percent.

David Metzger Trust v. Commissioner
693 F.2d 459 (5th Cir. 1982), *cert. denied*, 463 U.S. 1207 (1983).

■ Before THORNBERRY, JOHNSON and HIGGINBOTHAM, CIRCUIT JUDGES.

■ HIGGINBOTHAM, CIRCUIT JUDGE. . . In reviewing this decision of the Tax Court we are asked to determine the tax consequences of a reallocation of ownership of this family-owned business operated as a closely held corporation. In doing so we face three questions: (1) whether the attribution rules of I.R.C. § 318(a) must be applied despite family discord in determining whether a redemption meets the "not essentially equivalent to a dividend test" of § 302(b)(1); (2) whether a trust may waive the attribution rules of § 318(a) by filing a waiver agreement pursuant to § 302(c)(2)(A)(iii); (3) whether the attribution rules of § 267(c) must be applied to interest payments between family members in discord. Governed by the plain language of the Code, a goal of a coherent tax policy, and the relevant Supreme Court precedents, we affirm the decision of the Tax Court. . .

Appellant David Metzger Trust was created by David Metzger in 1942 to benefit his wife as life income beneficiary and his three children, Jacob, Catherine, and Cecelia, as one-third remaindermen each. Jacob, the eldest son, was named trustee of the Trust. Four years later, David incorporated the family business as Metzger Dairies, Inc., the other appellant. The Trust became a shareholder of Metzger Dairies.

On David's death in 1953 Jacob Metzger assumed control of Metzger Dairies. Catherine and Cecelia were directors. In the years following the father's death the sibling quarrel grew in intensity. By the 1960's, open animosity developed among Jacob, Catherine, and Cecelia. Whatever the source of their alienation, a downturn in the success of the dairy only exacerbated the problem. Catherine and Cecelia became angry when the corporation stopped paying dividends. Catherine resented what she considered to be Jacob's interference in the management of Metzger Dairy of San Antonio, a corporation of which her son was president but whose stock was owned for the most part by the same parties who owned the stock of Metzger Dairies. Cecelia was annoyed at both Jacob and Catherine because both corporations failed to pay dividends. The argument among Jacob, Catherine, and Cecelia over these and other issues unrelated to the business of the corporations continued until 1972, when the acrimony reached the point that Jacob, Catherine, and Cecelia concluded it was necessary to terminate their joint ownership of the corporations.

After lengthy negotiations all agreed that Jacob and his family would own Metzger Dairies, Catherine and her family would own Metzger Dairy of San Antonio, and Cecelia and her family would be cashed out. The plan was for Metzger Dairies to redeem all shares owned by Catherine, Cecelia, the trusts for Catherine and Cecelia, and the David Metzger Trust. It was necessary to include the David Metzger Trust in the redemption because Catherine and Cecelia were due to receive one-third of the Trust corpus on the death of David Metzger's widow.

Immediately before the redemption, the stock of Metzger Dairies was held as follows:

Stockholder	Shares
David Metzger Trust	420
Nora Metzger (David Metzger's widow)	420
Jacob Metzger	600
Trust for Jacob Metzger	120
Catherine	600
Trust for Catherine	120

Cecelia	600
Trust for Cecelia	120

The redemption occurred on January 22, 1973, leaving Metzger Dairies' stock as follows:

Stockholder	Shares
Jacob Metzger	600
Trust for Jacob Metzger	120
Trust for David Metzger, II (son of Jacob)	294
Trusts for Nan Metzger (daughter of Jacob)	207

The Commissioner concedes that the principal motivation for the redemption was not to receive undistributed earnings, but to end a business relationship that was characterized by hatred and discord among Jacob, Catherine, and Cecelia. On February 10, 1976, Jacob, as trustee of the David Metzger Trust, delivered to the IRS a waiver agreement, executed pursuant to 26 C.F.R. § 1.302–4 and purporting to waive any future interest the trust might have in the corporation.

The deferred obligation of Metzger Dairies to pay for Cecelia's 600 shares was evidenced by a promissory note executed by the corporation and payable to Cecelia in three annual installments of principal, plus interest, beginning January 22, 1974. Interest payments were actually made on January 21, 1974, January 7, 1975, and January 5, 1976. As a cash basis taxpayer, Cecelia reported interest income in 1974, 1975 and 1976, the respective years of receipt. Metzger Dairies was an accrual basis taxpayer and claimed deductions in the fiscal years ending September 30, 1973, September 30, 1974, and September 30, 1975, for the liability for interest as it accrued.

In May 1977 the Commissioner of Internal Revenue assessed deficiencies against the David Metzger Trust for the calendar year 1973 and against Metzger Dairies for the fiscal years ending September 30, 1973, and September 30, 1974.[2] On August 17, 1977, Metzger Dairies and the Trust petitioned the Tax Court for a redetermination of these deficiencies. Later the Commissioner assessed deficiencies against Metzger Dairies for fiscal year 1975 as well.[3] . . . The Tax Court upheld the deficiencies. . .

---

[2] The Commissioner assessed a deficiency of $292,977.47 against the Trust on the grounds that the $585,303.25 it received in redemption of the Metzger Dairies stock should have been reported as dividend income. The Commissioner assessed deficiencies against Metzger Dairies of $2,106.86 (FY 1973) and $24,856.38 (FY 1974) mainly after disallowing interest deductions of $32,167.28 (FY 1973) and $31,533.07 (FY 1974) for interest accrued but not paid to Cecelia until more than 2½ months after the close of the fiscal year.

[3] The Commissioner disallowed $13,926.46 of the interest deduction claimed by Metzger Dairies for FY 1975 that represented interest accrued but not actually paid to Cecelia until more than 2½ months after the close of the fiscal year. On this basis a deficiency of $6,684.68 was assessed.

Our specific analysis is channelled by the Code's structure: payments to shareholders from accumulated earnings will be treated as dividends unless the payment can be brought under an exception. That is, the controlling premise is that distributions by corporations to stockholders out of the taxable year's earnings or out of accumulated earnings are to be treated as dividends. I.R.C. § 316(a). Section 302 provides the exceptions. If the redemption is "not essentially equivalent to a dividend," § 302(b)(1), a "substantially disproportionate redemption of stock," § 302(b)(2), or a "termination of [the] shareholder's interest," § 302(b)(3), it will be treated as a distribution in exchange for the stock. At first glance, all three of these provisions are applicable to the Metzger transaction since the corporation purchased all the stock of Catherine, Cecelia, their trusts, and the David Metzger Trust, while at the same time made no payments to the other stockholders, namely Jacob Metzger and his trust. Yet the attribution rules of the Code pose immediate problems. . .

[Under the attribution rules, an] individual is considered to own the stock owned by his spouse, children, grandchildren, and parents. § 318(a)(1). An estate or trust is considered to own the stock owned by a beneficiary of the estate or trust. § 318(a)(3). A beneficiary is considered to own proportionately the stock owned by the estate or trust of which he is a beneficiary. § 318(a)(2). By these rules the Trust is the owner of the entire stock of Metzger Dairies both before and after the redemption.[6]

The Code provides that, with one exception, these attribution rules "shall apply in determining the ownership of stock for purposes of" § 302. § 302(c)(1). The one exception is that § 318(a)(1), the rules governing attribution of ownership from individuals to individuals, shall not apply in the case of a distribution described in § 302(b)(3), that is, a complete termination of a shareholder's interest, *if*:

1. "immediately after the distribution the distributee has no interest in the corporation (including an interest as officer, director, or employee), other than an interest as a creditor" (§ 302(c)(2)(A)(i));

2. "the distributee does not acquire any such interest (other than stock acquired by bequest or inheritance) within 10 years . . ." (§ 302(c)(2)(A)(ii));

3. the distributee files an agreement (a "waiver agreement") as prescribed by Treasury regulations (§ 302(c)(2)(A)(iii)).[7]

---

[6] Before redemption the Trust was the constructive owner of Nora, Jacob, Catherine, and Cecelia's shares, because they were its beneficiaries. § 318(a)(3)(B). Jacob, Catherine, and Cecelia were the constructive owners of the shares held by their individual trusts. § 318(a)(2)(B). Thus, the Trust constructively owned all of Metzger Dairies' stock.

After redemption the Trust remained constructive owner of all the stock because the shares held by the trusts for Jacob's children were attributable to the children, § 318(a)(2)(B), thence to Jacob, § 318(a)(1)(A), and finally to the Trust, § 318(a)(3)(B).

[7] Even if these three conditions are met, the attribution rules will not be waived if the distributee acquired any of the redeemed stock within the past ten years from a person whose stock ownership is otherwise attributable to him and tax avoidance was a primary purpose of the transaction. § 302(c)(2)(B)(i). Nor will they be waived if within the past ten years a person whose stock ownership is otherwise attributable to the distributee acquired stock from the

In other words, § 302(c)(2)(A) by its terms permits an *individual* to avoid attribution of ownership if he gets out of the corporation and agrees to stay out.

The commands of §§ 302 and 318 are unambiguous. By their literal language, as an "entity" rather than an individual, the David Metzger Trust does not qualify for the sole statutory exception to the attribution rules. . .

The Trust argues [however] that family discord may "mitigate" the application of the attribution rules in determining dividend equivalency, especially given the undisputed fact that the purpose of the redemption was not to distribute corporate earnings. From the stipulated fact that the purpose of redemption was to bring peace to a family quarrel, the Trust launches two attacks upon the attribution rules. First, it argues that because it is undisputed here that the family cannot function as an economic unit, the attribution rules, built as they are upon that premise, are inapplicable. Second, the Trust argues that even if the Trust by virtue of attribution is virtually the sole shareholder before and after, the redemption was nonetheless not essentially equivalent to a dividend. The argument continues that this follows from the undisputed purpose of the redemption. That is, the purpose not being to bail out corporate earnings, the central base for application of nonequivalency has been touched.

As will be seen the first argument fails because it is built upon the erroneous assumption that attribution is treated by the Code as a rebuttable presumption rather than a mandated view of familial relationships. The second argument fails because it denies full sway to the decision of the Supreme Court in United States v. Davis, 397 U.S. 301 . . . (1970). Indeed, *Davis* provides much of the answer to the first argument as well. For this reason we will address the arguments together, separating them only when necessary to context.

In *Davis* the Court held that the attribution rules of § 318(a) must be applied before determining dividend equivalency. The Court held that regardless of a purpose other than to distribute corporate earnings the after-attribution structure was such that the redemption was in the nature of a dividend. In *Davis*, the taxpayer had purchased the preferred stock of a corporation in 1945 in order to increase the corporation's working capital so that it might qualify for an RFC loan. As originally planned, the loan was fully repaid and the corporation redeemed the taxpayer's preferred stock. By this time, however, the corporation's common stock was held entirely by the taxpayer, his wife, his son, and his daughter. The Commissioner viewed the redemption as essentially equivalent to a dividend because after application of the attribution rules the taxpayer "owned" 100% of the corporation's common stock. Any distribution to him, therefore, was a pro rata dis-

---

distributee and tax avoidance was a primary purpose of that transaction, unless the stock is included in the redemption. § 302(c)(2)(B)(ii). These are known as the "look back" provisions; § 302(c)(2)(A)(ii) is known as the "look forward" provision.

tribution to all the corporation's stockholders, or the essential equivalent of a dividend.

The Supreme Court agreed with the Commissioner's analysis. In its first step it held that the attribution rules had to be applied in determining dividend equivalency under § 302(b)(1). "[T]he attribution rules continued to be made specifically applicable to the entire section, and we believe that Congress intended that they be taken into account wherever ownership of stock was relevant." 397 U.S. at 306–307. . . The taxpayer was deemed the owner of all 1000 shares of the company's common stock.

Second, the Court held that the presence or absence of a tax-avoidance motive could not be considered in determining dividend equivalency under § 302(b)(1). Id. at 311. . . "[T]he business purpose of a transaction is irrelevant in determining dividend equivalence." Id. at 312 . . . (quoting Hasbrook v. United States, 343 F.2d 811, 814 (2d Cir. 1965)). The Court therefore concluded that the IRS had properly characterized the redemption of the preferred stock as essentially equivalent to a dividend, regardless of the taxpayer's (and the corporation's) business purpose back in 1945.[8]

In *Davis* the Court reasoned:

> After application of the stock ownership attribution rules, this case viewed most simply involves a sole stockholder who causes part of his shares to be redeemed by the corporation. We conclude that such a redemption is always "essentially equivalent to a dividend" within the meaning of that phrase in § 302(b)(1). . .

Id. 397 U.S. at 307. . . *Davis* teaches that in applying the "essentially equivalent to a dividend" test after the attribution rules are applied, if the resulting structure has virtually the same incidents of ownership the corporate payments distribute earnings despite an indisputable contrary business purpose.

Confronted by the Supreme Court's holding in *Davis*, the Trust argues that its position nevertheless is supported by Treas. Reg. § 1.302–2(b), language in *Davis* interpreting § 302(b)(1) as applying whenever there is a "meaningful reduction in the shareholder's proportionate interest," and the legislative history of § 302(b)(1).

Treas. Reg. § 1.302–2(b) provides:

> The question whether a distribution in redemption of stock of a shareholder is not essentially equivalent to a dividend under section 302(b)(1) depends upon the facts and circumstances of each case. One of the facts to be considered in making this determination is the constructive stock ownership of such shareholder under section 318(a).

---

[8] It is not totally clear that the attribution rules *had* to be applied in *Davis* to reach the Commissioner's result. Even if the taxpayer were not considered the owner of all the corporation's common stock, redemption of his preferred did not reduce his voting interest in the corporation.

Pointing to this language the Trust argues that before and after structure is only one factor in the dividend equivalency inquiry. The argument continues that despite the circumstance that after attribution there was no shift in the incidents of control there was no dividend because indisputably the redemption was for another purpose.

Treas. Reg. § 1.302–2(b), however, contained the same language prior to the *Davis* decision. The regulation is ambiguous. It can be interpreted as the Trust would have it, namely that attribution is only a presumption. On the other hand, it can be interpreted as saying that attribution rules must be given full effect, but are not necessarily decisive on the ultimate issue of dividend equivalency.

It is true, as the Trust points out, that some commentators and courts have indicated that *Davis* does not foreclose arguments for capital gains treatment based on family discord. . . In Robin Haft Trust v. Commissioner, 510 F.2d 43 (1st Cir. 1975), the First Circuit held that family discord might "negate the presumption" of the attribution rules that the taxpayer trusts exercised continuing control over the corporation after their actual holdings had been redeemed. Id. at 48. The trusts had been set up to benefit four children and were funded by shares of the corporation. The father of the children also owned a large percentage of the corporation's stock. While the father was going through divorce proceedings and was not even in contact with the children, the trusts' shares were redeemed as part of a program to terminate the involvement of the wife's family in the corporation. The IRS applied the attribution rules. Since the percentage of shares constructively owned by each of the trusts increased after the redemption, the IRS determined that the payment to the trusts was ordinary income. The Tax Court upheld the Commissioner. The First Circuit, however, directed the Tax Court "to reconsider taxpayers' claims in the light of the facts and circumstances of the case, including the existence of family discord tending to negate the presumption that taxpayers would exert continuing control over the corporation despite the redemption." Id. at 48.

For the most part, courts and commentators who urge that *Davis* leaves open the family discord question have emphasized that the *Davis* Court, despite its preference for objective tests, defined the "essentially equivalent to dividend" test in open-ended terms. "[T]o qualify for preferred treatment under [§ 302(b)(1)], a redemption must result in a meaningful reduction of the shareholder's proportionate interest in the corporation." 397 U.S. at 313. . . In *Robin Haft Trust*, the First Circuit concluded that "[t]his language certainly seems to permit, if it does not mandate, an examination of the facts and circumstances to determine the effect of the transaction transcending a mere mechanical application of the attribution rules." 510 F.2d at 48. . .

These interpretations are not persuasive. The *Davis* Court was referring to a meaningful reduction in the shareholder's interest *after* application of the attribution rules. It would be strange indeed if what the Court really meant was that the attribution rules are to be applied before determining dividend equivalency, but then in the course of determining dividend equivalency their applicability could be reconsidered. If that were so, the attribution rules would hardly "provide a clear answer to what would otherwise be a difficult tax question . . . ." 397 U.S. at 306. . .

The Trust also points to the legislative history of §§ 302 and 318. It is not necessary to traverse a long and complicated history here. Section 302's predecessor was a single dividend equivalency test. It had been interpreted flexibly, so that a redemption with a legitimate business purpose was treated as not "essentially equivalent to a dividend." In 1954 the House version of § 302 contained only the safe harbors of § 302(b)(2) ("substantially disproportionate redemption") and § 302(b)(3) ("termination of shareholder's interest"). The Senate added § 302(b)(1), the old essential equivalency test, because the House rules "appeared unnecessarily restrictive." S. Rep. No. 1622, 83d Cong., 2d Sess. 44, reprinted in 1954 U.S. Code Cong. & Ad. News 4621, 4675. Thus, several commentators have argued that Congress meant to reinstate subjective inquiry. In *Davis*, however, while conceding that "the intended scope of § 302(b)(1) as revealed by this legislative history is certainly not free from doubt," 397 U.S. at 311, . . . the Court concluded that Congress was rejecting past decisions that looked to motive. Section 302(b)(1) was not intended to be a mechanical test, but it was not intended to be a subjective test, either. Rather, Congress intended "a factual inquiry," "devoted solely to the question of whether or not the transaction by its nature may properly be characterized as a sale of stock by the redeeming shareholder to the corporation." S. Rep. No. 1622, 83d Cong., 2d Sess., reprinted in 1954 U.S. Cong. & Ad. News 4621, 4870–4871. The Senate Report adds that "the presence or absence of earnings and profits of the corporation is not material" to dividend equivalency. Id. at 4871. If so, motive could hardly be material since in the absence of earnings there would be no motive to seek capital gain treatment. The issue, as the *Davis* Court said, was not the taxpayer's motive but whether there was "a meaningful reduction of the shareholder's proportionate interest in the corporation." 397 U.S. at 313. . .

We return to the first level of the Trust argument—that attribution bottomed as it is on assumed family unity ought not to be applied when the assumption is contrary to stipulated fact. Nothing in the legislative history suggests that the attribution rules are to be "mitigated" in special cases. On the contrary, the Senate Report states that "the rules for constructive ownership of stock section 318(a) shall apply for purposes of this section generally." S. Rep. No. 1622, 83d Cong., 2d Sess., reprinted in 1954 U.S. Cong. & Ad. News 4621, 4872. Neither the language of the statute, the Supreme Court's opinion in *Davis*, nor the legislative history supports treating the attribution rules as rebuttable presumptions as the Trust is seeking.

Under the Trust's approach the Commissioner and the courts would be forced to highly case specific inquiries into elusive fact patterns. The pattern, intensity, and predicted duration of a family fight are difficult enough for the solomonic justice of our domestic relations courts. It is hardly the basis for a soundly administered tax policy. The fixity of the attribution rules then in this sense is not their weakness but their strength.

In summary, we believe that the Commissioner and Tax Court were correct in refusing to take family discord into account in applying the attribution rules.[16] When a question is raised as to the dividend equivalency of a redemption, under § 302(b)(1) the correct approach is to apply the attribution *rules* first, then to determine whether there has been "a meaningful reduction of the shareholder's proportionate interest," without regard to whether the interest is actually or constructively held. What is "meaningful" then, to borrow a word, is essentially an inquiry into structure, a structure that applies statutorily dictated rules of economic unity. . .

[Discussion of trust waiver-of-attribution issue is omitted.]

Section 267 of the Code disallows deductions for certain transactions between related taxpayers. The underlying philosophy of § 267(a)(2), the subsection at issue here, is that related taxpayers should not be able to generate tax deductions in a given year without corresponding income. Metzger Dairies as an accrual basis taxpayer claimed deductions for amounts that were not actually paid to Cecelia until more than 2 1/2 months after the close of its fiscal year. Cecelia, as a cash basis taxpayer, did not report those amounts as income until the following taxable year. Therefore, if Metzger Dairies and Cecelia were related taxpayers within the meaning of § 267, Metzger Dairies was not entitled to certain interest deductions.[25]

Section 267(b) defines the relationships covered by § 267(a). These include "an individual and a corporation more than 50 percent in value of the outstanding stock of which is owned, directly or indirectly, by or for such individual." § 267(b)(2). Section 267(c), however, provides that "for purposes of determining, in applying subsection (b), the ownership of stock . . . (2) [a]n individual shall be considered as owning the stock owned, directly or indirectly, by or for his family." Section 267(c)(4) defines the family of an individual as including his brothers and sisters. Therefore, putting § 267(b), § 267(c)(2), and § 267(c)(4) together, Cecelia and Metzger Dairies (since Jacob owned a controlling interest in the corporation after the redemption[26]) were related persons within the meaning of § 267. If the literal language of § 267 is followed, the Commissioner was correct in disallowing the deductions.

---

[16] The Tax Court in its opinion below did suggest that in cases of non-pro-rata distribution family hostility "can be a relevant fact to be considered in determining whether the reduction in the shareholder's interest is meaningful so as to qualify the distribution as not essentially equivalent to a dividend under section 302(b)(1)." 76 T.C. 42, 62–63 (1981). That notion is inconsistent with our approach. Regardless, such a case was not presented below or here.

[25] Section 267(a)(2) sets forth three conditions that must be met for disallowance of the interest deduction. First, the interest otherwise deductible must not have been paid within 2½ months of the close of the taxpayer's taxable year. § 267(a)(2)(A). Second, the interest must not, unless paid, be includible in the income of the recipient for the same taxable year. § 267(a)(2)(B). Third, the taxpayer and the recipient must be related persons within the meaning of subsection (b). § 267(a)(2)(C). Metzger Dairies concedes that the first two conditions were met; the dispute is over the third.

[26] After the redemption, Jacob's actual ownership was 600 of the 1221 outstanding shares. Thus, § 267(c) has to be applied once more (under § 267(c)(1) stock owned by a trust is deemed to be owned proportionately by its beneficiaries) to get Jacob above the 50% figure.

Appellant Metzger Dairies, however, argues that the attribution rules of § 267 should not apply because of family hostility. Metzger Dairies seeks an exception to § 267(c) similar to the family discord exception to § 318(a) sought by the David Metzger Trust.

Metzger Dairies cites no case in support of such an exception. In fact, Metzger Dairies cites no case in support of any nonstatutory exception to § 267. On the other hand, both the Supreme Court and the Fifth Circuit have read the section in literal terms. In McWilliams v. Commissioner, 331 U.S. 694 . . . (1947), the Supreme Court held that § 267's predecessor disallowed losses from sales of stock by a taxpayer when his wife simultaneously bought the same stock on the exchange. Although this was a transparent tax-avoidance transaction, the Court spoke generally about the role of § 267's predecessor:

> Section 24(b) states an absolute prohibition—not a presumption—against the allowance of losses on any sales between the members of certain designated groups. The one common characteristic of these groups is that their members, although distinct legal entities, generally have a near-identity of economic interests. It is a fair inference that even legally genuine intra-group transfers were not thought to result, usually, in economically genuine realizations of loss, and accordingly that Congress did not deem them to be appropriate occasions for the allowance of deductions.

Id. at 699. . .

We recently interpreted § 267 in Wyly v. United States, 662 F.2d 397 (5th Cir. 1981). There we held that loss deductions were properly denied to parents who had sold stock to trusts set up to benefit their children. Under Texas law, there was a remote possibility that one (or both) of the parents would benefit under the trusts, if all four of the children died first. This possibility was held sufficient to make the parents and the independent trustee "related persons" under § 267(b)(6), which refers to "[a] fiduciary of a trust and a beneficiary of such trust." As we then observed, "There is, in § 267, no language to support the taxpayers' claim that a beneficiary who has only a remote chance of sharing in trust property is not a 'beneficiary' of the trust for purposes of § 267." Id. at 402. Likewise, there is no language to absolve Cecelia and Jacob from being family members within the meaning of 267(c)(4). The Wyly court added, "[I]t does not matter whether the transaction is bona fide, at arms length, or in good faith with no tax avoidance motive. Whatever the reason, if the proscribed relationship exists, no loss is recognized for tax purposes." Id. at 401.

Metzger Dairies points out that both Wyly and Merritt v. Commissioner, 400 F.2d 417 (5th Cir. 1968), were concerned with § 267(a) and § 267(b). A literal interpretation of §§ 267(a) and (b), it contends, does not foreclose a nonliteral interpretation of § 267(c). Nevertheless, here, as in Wyly, the "proscribed relationship" existed. We see no reason for interpreting § 267(c) differently from § 267(b) or § 267(a). Both § 267(b) and § 267(c) are attribution rules, in that they define the circumstances under which a shared economic interest will be presumed. Congress cannot have intended one subsection to be interpreted literally and the other flexibly. Only a strict interpretation of both provisions is logically consistent. Only such an interpretation will "relieve[] the taxing authority of many complicated and complex melioristic decisions in family transactions." Merritt v. Commissioner, 400 F.2d at 421.

In sum, § 267(c) provides constructive ownership rules which "shall" be applied in determining the relatedness of taxpayers. We see no reason to deviate from this express statutory command. Indeed, by our reading, the Fifth Circuit and Supreme Court precedents forbid it. Accordingly, we hold that Metzger Dairies was not entitled to the interest deductions claimed because it and Cecelia were related persons within the meaning of § 267.

Affirmed.

NOTE

The question of a hostility exception to the attribution rules is by no means a dead letter. The Service took the position of the *Metzger* court in Rev. Rul. 80–26, 1980–1 C.B. 66, holding that "the facts and circumstances of a particular case cannot contradict the mechanical determination under section 318 of how much stock a shareholder owns." The First Circuit adopted the opposite position in Haft Trust v. Commissioner, 510 F.2d 43 (1st Cir. 1975). The Tax Court decisions are not uniformly consistent with its position in *Metzger. Compare* Michael N. Cerone, 87 T.C. 1 (1986) (no hostility exception), and Robin Haft Trust, 61 T.C. 398 (1973) (same), *rev'd*, 510 F.2d 43 (1st Cir. 1975), *with* Rodgers P. Johnson Trust, 71 T.C. 941 (1979) (assuming existence of hostility exception), and Estate of Squier, 35 T.C. 950 (1961) (hostility exception applied), *acq.*, 1961–2 C.B. 5, *acq.* withdrawn and *nonacq.* substituted 1978–2 C.B. 4.

Bloch v. United States

261 F.Supp. 597 (S.D. Tex. 1966), *aff'd per curiam*, 386 F.2d 839 (5th Cir. 1967).

[Southern Elevator and Storage Company, Inc., was a Texas corporation engaged in the operation of grain storage facilities. Immediately before the redemption here in question the corporation had 680 shares of capital stock outstanding which were owned as follows: 306 shares (45 percent) by Bloch, the taxpayer; 306 shares (45 percent) by Bryan; and 68 shares (10 percent) by Harris. In order to give Parrish, the plant manager, an equity interest in the corporation, the corporation adopted, on June 1, 1956, a resolution whereby the corporation was to redeem 15 percent of the corporation's stock from Bloch and 15 percent from Bryan, or 102 shares from each, which were to be held by the corporation; Parrish was given an option to buy two-thirds of this redeemed stock from the corporation, and Harris was given an option to buy one-third. The option price for both was 85 percent of the redemption price. (This arrangement was adopted in preference to a direct sale from Bloch and Bryan to Parrish and Harris in order to enable them to purchase the stock at a lower price than Bloch and Bryan were to receive for it, while giving Parrish and Harris the benefit of the restricted stock option provisions of the Code.)]

■ Graven, Senior District Judge. . . . At a meeting of the Board of Directors of Southern on January 2, 1959, a resolution was adopted authorizing an immediate stock redemption from Bryan and Bloch of 15 percent each of their Southern stock. This was in accordance with the resolution and agreement of June 1, 1956, referred to above. Pursuant to the January 2, 1959, resolution, on January 15, 1959, Bloch and Bryan each surrendered to Southern 102 shares of stock. In connection therewith, each of them received a non-negotiable, non-interest bearing note from the corporation in the amount of $35,700, dated January 2, 1959, and payable on or before three years from that date. That sum represented a redemption price of $350 per share. . .

Southern paid the following amounts to Bloch on the dates indicated in satisfaction of the $35,700 note: $2,700 on April 28, 1960; $1,487.50 on February 3, 1961; $9,371.25 on February 24, 1961; and the remaining $22,141.25 on September 30, 1961. The note held by Bryan was fully paid not later than October 23, 1961.

In his 1960 and 1961 income tax returns Bloch reported the payments above set forth as capital gains. The Internal Revenue Service assessed the deficiency taxes based upon the contention that those payments constituted dividends, taxable as ordinary income. It is the character of those payments to Bloch that is in controversy herein.

7. On January 15, 1959, Bloch and Bryan each surrendered to Southern his certificate for 306 shares of stock and each received a new certificate for 204 shares. The remaining 204 shares were cancelled in redemption by the secretary of the corporation and affixed to the corporate stock records as redeemed shares. Those 204 shares were then held in the corporate treasury for sale pursuant to the option contract to Parrish and Harris until paid for by the optionees. The resolution of January 2, 1959, heretofore noted, had granted Parrish and Harris an option for five years to purchase the redeemed stock at a price of $297.50 per share. Parrish and Harris exercised their options and redeemed shares were issued to them as paid for by them at various intervals subsequent to the redemption of the shares by the corporation.

. . . On May 15, 1956, Bryan, Bloch, Harris and Parrish entered into a partnership to engage in the business of buying, selling, and factoring grain and other products. That partnership will be referred to in more detail later on.

8. It was heretofore noted that the hub of this controversy is whether the stock redemption distributions made by Southern to the taxpayer in 1960 and 1961 should be taxed as ordinary income or as capital gains. In that connection, it is necessary to consider certain statutory provisions and regulations. Section 316(a) . . . sets out the general rule or proposition that distributions by a corporation to its shareholders out of either current earn-

ings and profits or earnings and profits accumulated since February 28, 1913, are dividends. Section 301(c)(1) . . . provides the further general rule that dividend distributions are taxable to the recipient as ordinary income unless they come within certain exceptions. Some of these exceptions are found in Section 302 . . . pertaining to distributions in redemption of stock. Section 302(a) provides that if the transaction constitutes a stock redemption within the definition of Section 302(b), it will be treated as in part or full payment in exchange for the stock and will qualify for capital gains treatment. Section 302(b) sets out [three] categories of stock redemption transactions, each of which will qualify for capital gains treatment. [Since the parties agree as to which categories are material] under the facts of this case, only the two which the taxpayer contends do apply will be examined. Thus the pertinent points of Section 302 for purposes of this case are [Section 302(b)(1) and (2)]. . .

It will be noted that [Section 302(b)(1) and (2)] characterize two types of transactions, either of which will qualify as a capital gains redemption. The first type of transaction is set forth in Subsection (b)(1), i.e., where the redemption is not essentially equivalent to a dividend. The other type of transaction is set forth in Subsection (b)(2), i.e., where the distribution is substantially disproportionate within the meaning of the Section. The parties are in controversy as to whether the redemption in this case falls into either of those categories. The issue as to the matter of the redemption in question being substantially disproportionate will first be considered.

Under the provisions of Section 302 relating to disproportionate distributions, a taxpayer is required to meet two tests, both of which are arithmetical in character. Those tests are as follows:

(1) Immediately after the redemption, the taxpayer must own less than 50 percent of the total combined voting power of all classes of stock entitled to vote, and

(2) Immediately after the redemption, the portion of the corporation's voting stock then owned by the taxpayer must be less than 80 percent of the portion of the stock owned by him before the redemption.

To state these tests another way, after the redemption a taxpayer must own less than 50 percent of the voting stock of the corporation, and the redemption must have reduced the ratio of his voting stock to the total corporate voting stock to an amount less than 80 percent of such ratio before the redemption.

. . . [T]here were originally 680 shares of Southern voting stock, of which the taxpayer owned 306 shares. . . [O]n January 15, 1959, the taxpayer and Bryan each surrendered his certificate for 306 shares and each was reissued a certificate for 204 shares. The 102 shares surrendered by each were surrendered for the purpose of carrying out the option agreements with Parrish and Harris. If these 204 shares were to be considered as not constituting voting stock of the corporation, then the voting stock

consisted of 486 shares. It is clear that whether the voting stock is considered as being 680 shares or 486 shares, the taxpayer meets what will be
referred to for convenience as the 50 percent test. The parties are not in
controversy as to the taxpayer meeting that test. They are in controversy as
to whether the taxpayer meets what will be referred to for convenience as
the 80 percent test. That controversy revolves, in part, around whether the
204 shares surrendered by the taxpayer and Bryan and held in the treasury for the purpose of meeting the stock purchase options of Parrish and
Harris shall be considered as voting stock for the purpose of applying the
80 percent test. The Government contends that those shares are not to be
so considered. The taxpayer contends that they are to be so considered. The
provisions of Section 302(b)(2) noted above make reference to the "voting
stock" or "voting power" of the corporation. Treasury Regulations Section
1.302–3(a) relating thereto provides that the stock to be considered is that
"which is issued and outstanding in the hands of the shareholders." Southern was a Texas corporation. A reference to Texas law is made by the taxpayer in his main brief in which he states: "Texas law would not permit the
issuance of the shares to Parrish and Harris in exchange for Notes. Therefore the shares were held in the Corporate treasury until paid for in compliance with the law. . ." It appears that the stock in question was held in
the corporate treasury until paid for. The pretrial stipulation of facts reflects that Parrish and Harris participated in corporate dividends only as to
the issued shares. The taxpayer relies strongly on the case of Sorem v.
Commissioner of Internal Revenue (10th Cir. 1964), 334 F.2d 275, in which
a similar question was involved. The Court in that case held that for purposes of applying the constructive ownership or attribution rules of Section
318, employees who held stock options must be considered as owning the
stock for which they held options. Under the holding of that case, the
shares held in the corporate treasury by Southern for the purpose of meeting the options held by Parrish and Harris would be considered as owned
by them in connection with the matter of the taxpayer meeting the 80 percent test. The provisions of Regulations Section 1.318–3(c), when coupled
with those of Regulations Section 1.302–3(a), noted above, might be interpreted as requiring a different conclusion. Because of another feature, it is
not necessary for the Court to decide whether the holding of the *Sorem* case
should or should not be followed. However, if in this case this Court was
squarely presented with the question as to whether the holding of the *Sorem* case should or should not be followed, it would be reluctant to follow
such holding. It would seem that it would be highly questionable that stock
held in the treasury of a corporation which might be issued or might never
be issued depending upon whether the optionees of such stock would or
would not exercise their options could not properly be considered as being
owned by the optionees for the purpose of applying the attribution rules
under Section 318.

However, assuming, as contended by the taxpayer, that Parrish and
Harris are to be regarded as the owners of the 204 shares of stock in question, there comes into focus Section 318, heretofore set out and referred to
by the parties as the constructive ownership or attribution statute. A portion of that statute pertinent to the facts in this case has since been re-

pealed,* but was in effect during the period of time here involved. It was heretofore noted that in 1956 Bloch, Bryan, Parrish and Harris had entered into a partnership. Because of some confusion and conflict in the briefs as to that partnership, it seems appropriate to set out a portion of the pretrial stipulation of facts relating to such partnership, as follows:

> 14. On May 15, 1956, B. F. Bryan, William H. Bloch, Lee Orr Harris, and William R. Parrish entered into a partnership to engage in the business of brokering, factoring, and buying and selling grain and other products, the profits to be divided equally by said partners as to the first $10,000.00 of net partnership profits and with profits in excess of $10,000.00 to be distributed as follows: 40 percent to B. F. Bryan and 20 percent each to William H. Bloch, Lee Orr Harris and William R. Parrish. Losses were to be divided equally. The partnership made a profit in each and every year of its operation. The partnership actively began conduct of business in late June 1956.

The partnership was known as the Southern Elevator Grain Company. It continued to carry on its business operations through July, 1961, when it was dissolved, apparently because of dissension between B. F. Bryan and the other partners. The interest of the parties did not change during the existence of the partnership.

Under the provisions of the attribution statute (Section 318) then in effect, stock owned by a partner is deemed to be owned by the partnership, and stock owned by the partnership (including that which it is deemed to own because a partner actually owns it) is deemed to be owned by the partners in their partnership proportions. If, as the taxpayer contends, Parrish and Harris were the owners of the 204 shares of option stock, under the provisions of Section 302(b)(2) it is manifest that they were also to be considered the owners of it under Section 318(a)(2), which is specifically made applicable to Section 302.

If the 680 shares are to be considered as the shares of stock outstanding both before and after redemption, it is then necessary to determine the ownership percentage in the light of the attribution statute. Before the redemption, the taxpayer owned 306 shares in his own right and constructively owned 93.5 shares through the partnership. The total percentage owned (399.5/680) was 58.75 percent. After the redemption, he owned 204 shares in his own right and constructively owned 119 shares through the partnership. The total percentage owned (323/680) was 47.5 percent. The after-redemption ownership was 80.8+ percent of the before-redemption ownership (47.5 to 58.75). Thus the taxpayer does not meet the 80 percent test.

The above conclusions result from application of the constructive ownership rules to the partnership situation, as follows. The ownership of the partnership shares before the redemption was as follows: Bryan's 306 shares and Harris' 68 shares, totalling 374 shares, are deemed to be owned

---

*See § 318(a)(5)(C), which was not part of the statute during the years involved.—ED.

by the partnership and are, in turn, deemed owned to the extent of one-fourth, or 93.5 shares, by the taxpayer as a partner to that extent. The ownership of the partnership shares after the redemption was as follows: Bryan's 204 shares, Parrish's 136 shares and Harris' 136 shares, totalling 476 shares, are deemed to be owned by the partnership and are, in turn, deemed owned to the extent of one-fourth, or 119 shares, by the taxpayer as a partner. The partnership was apparently somewhat related to Southern because of its personnel and business activities. However, in order for Section 318 to be applicable it is not necessary that the partnership be engaged in activities similar to that of the corporation involved.

If the 204 shares of stock held in the treasury are not regarded as voting stock, then the situation would be as follows: prior to the redemption the taxpayer owned 306 shares of the 680 shares outstanding, or 45 percent, and after the redemption he will have owned 204 shares of the 476 shares outstanding, or 42.8 percent. The 42.8 percent ownership percentage after redemption is substantially more than 80 percent of the 45 percent ownership percentage before redemption (being 95+ percent), so the taxpayer would also fail to meet the 80 percent test under this assumption of facts.

By way of summary, it can be stated that if the 204 shares held in the treasury of Southern are to be regarded as not outstanding stock, then the taxpayer would not meet the 80 percent test irrespective of constructive ownership or attribution rules. If those 204 shares are to be regarded as outstanding, then the taxpayer fails to meet the 80 percent test because of the applicability of the attribution statute (Section 318). . .

9. The next matter for consideration is whether the stock redemption distributions to the taxpayer were within the scope of Section 302(b)(1). As heretofore set out, that Section provides that a redemption is entitled to capital gains treatment "if the redemption is not essentially equivalent to a dividend." Several related issues are involved in a consideration of this question. These have to do with the adequacy of the corporate earnings and profits, whether the claims for refund properly raised such issue, and the proper time at which to measure corporate earnings and profits for purposes of applying the provisions of Section 302(b)(1) to the facts of this case. The taxpayer contends that at the pertinent time in question the corporate earnings and profits were not adequate to cover the redemption distributions. In connection with this contention the Government asserts that the taxpayer did not properly raise such issue in his claims for refund. . . [The Court decided this issue in the taxpayer's favor.]

The next issue for consideration is whether the corporate earnings and profits and accumulated surplus were adequate to cover the redemption disbursements. This is the subject of vigorous controversy. Considerable evidence was presented on this issue and it was discussed at some length in the briefs. It involves a number of questions. The first question is the proper time to measure the adequacy of corporate earnings and profits. The parties are in agreement that the redemption occurred on January 15, 1959. The parties are also in agreement that the cash disbursements by Southern to the taxpayer took place in 1960 and 1961 when the corporate non-interest bearing note given by Southern to the taxpayer was paid. Both parties seem to be in agreement that the 1960 and 1961 corporate distributions should be taxed to him in those years, i.e., the years of receipt, rather than in 1959 when he received the corporate note. The taxpayer reported the disbursements in his 1960 and 1961 income tax returns and he claimed a refund of the taxes involved for those same years. The taxpayer contends that although the tax impact of the redemption distributions should fall in the years of receipt, the proper point in time for the purpose of measuring the adequacy of corporate earnings and profits on the dividend issue shall have been on January 15, 1959, when the redemption occurred. The taxpayer cites in support of this last contention the case of Estate of James T. Moore, Tax Court Memo Decision 1961–257. That case . . . had to do with when a redemption actually occurred and not when corporate earnings or profits are to be measured. . . It appears to be well settled that the date of the payment of a note rather than the date of delivery of the note is the dividend date. Emil Stein (1942), 46 B.T.A. 135; Estate of Joseph Nitto (1949), 13 T.C. 858, 867. The Court is of the view and holds that the time payments were made on the note is the proper time for measuring corporate earnings and profits for dividend purposes. . .

[The court found that there were adequate earnings and profits. It then went on to hold that the distribution was essentially equivalent to a dividend. It held first that there was not a bona fide corporate purpose for casting the transaction in the form of a redemption, since the purpose was to give the sellers a greater amount for their stock than the buyers would have to pay for it, while giving the buyers certain tax benefits. It then relied on the following factors to find dividend equivalency: There were adequate earnings and profits for a dividend in the amount of the distributions; the taxpayer's position vis-à-vis the corporation was not substantially altered by the transaction since he remained a minority stockholder; and the transaction was not part of the contraction of the business. The fact that the distribution was not pro rata was not sufficient to negate the finding of dividend equivalency.

The Commissioner's deficiency assessment with respect to the distributions was upheld.]*

NOTES

1. What does § 318(a)(5)(C) accomplish? If it had been applicable to the years involved in this case would it have affected the result?

2. Although treasury shares are not considered in determining the change in stock ownership resulting from a redemption, § 318(a)(4) treats a person holding an option to purchase stock as the owner of that stock. There is a conflict in the circuits as to whether § 318(a)(4) applies only when the option is held by the person whose shares are redeemed. *Compare* Patterson Trust v.

---

*In its brief per curiam opinion of affirmance the Fifth Circuit embraced the district court's disposition, but said, "it is unnecessary to adopt the opinion of the district court...." 386 F.2d 839 (1967).—ED.

United States, 729 F.2d 1089 (6th Cir. 1984) (option to acquire stock deemed to be ownership even though the option holder was not a redeeming shareholder) *with* Friend v. United States, 345 F.2d 761 (1st Cir. 1965) (dictum that § 318(a)(4) only applies as to options held by redeeming shareholder).

Problems

The following problems relate to the preceding materials and to §§ 302 and 318 generally:

1. Husband (H) and Wife (W) each own 50 percent of the outstanding stock of Corporation C. The parties wish C to redeem all of H's stock for an amount of cash equal to the stock's fair market value. What facts must you know and what must you advise be done as conditions to your giving an opinion that the redemption will be within § 302(b)(3)?

2. The facts are the same as in Problem 1, except that H wishes to retain at least a minimal stock interest. Can you suggest the redemption of a sufficient percentage of his shares to permit the redemption to qualify under § 302(b)(2)?

3. The facts are the same as in Problem 1, except that H and W also own 50 percent each of Corporation B. Will your opinion as to the applicability of § 302(b)(3) on the redemption of H's stock in C have to be altered? What would have been your answer prior to the adoption of § 318(a)(5)(C) in 1964?

4. X owns all (100 shares) of the stock of Corporation N. Corporation N redeems 50 of X's shares under circumstances making the distribution essentially equivalent to a dividend. X's basis for his stock was $100 per share. Five years after the redemption X sells his remaining 50 shares for $50,000. What is his gain on the sale? Why?

iv. REDEMPTION VS. SALE

Estate of Schneider v. Commissioner
855 F.2d 435 (7th Cir. 1988).

■ Before Cummings, Flaum, and Easterbrook, Circuit Judges.

■ Flaum, Circuit Judge. Al J. Schneider ("Schneider") was the principal shareholder of American National Corporation ("ANC"), a holding company, which in turn owned 100% of the stock of Schneider Transport, Inc. ("Transport"). In 1974, 1975 and 1976 Schneider sold portions of his ANC stock to certain Transport employees who were participating in an employee stock ownership plan. Schneider reported these transactions on the 1974–76 federal income tax returns he filed jointly with his wife, Agnes Schneider, characterizing them as sales of capital assets which generated long-term capital gains. The Internal Revenue Service (the "IRS") alleged that these sales actually constituted a redemption of Schneider's stock by ANC followed by a distribution of this stock pursuant to the employee stock ownership plan. The IRS asserted that Schneider should have reported the entire amounts he received from these alleged sales as dividend distributions. The IRS therefore issued deficiency notices for 1975 and 1976. The matter proceeded to trial and the Tax Court entered judgment against Schneider and his wife for $17,046 and $20,716 for the tax years of 1975 and 1976 respectively. We affirm.

I.

Transport was founded by Schneider in 1938 and is engaged in the freight transport business. Transport was one of a group of closely held corporations (the "affiliated corporations") owned by Schneider and his immediate relatives. In 1971 Transport adopted an employee stock bonus plan (the "Transport Plan"). Under the plan, Transport's Board of Directors determined in December of each year the total sum to be awarded by Transport to certain of its employees as bonuses for work done in that year. Early in the following year Transport's President selected and notified the employees who would receive bonuses. These employees were given an option to receive their bonus in either cash or Transport nonvoting common stock. Employees who elected stock received previously unissued Transport nonvoting common stock; the number of shares received was based on the "Current Formula Price" (the book value of the stock with some modifications).

A bonus recipient's rights in the stock he or she received under the Plan were subject to a 10%–per–year vesting requirement. If the employee ceased to work for Transport within ten years of receiving the stock, he or she was required to offer to sell the stock to Transport at a price equal to 10% of the Current Formula Price for that year multiplied by the number of years of continued employment since the year the bonus was awarded. In addition, an employee wishing to sell any stock received pursuant to the Transport Plan was required to first offer the stock to Transport at the same price that would govern under the vesting rules. The plan required that notice of these restrictions be stamped on the stock certificates issued to the bonus recipients.

In 1973, the affiliated corporations were substantially reorganized. ANC was formed to act as a holding company for these corporations. Pursuant to the reorganization, former Transport shareholders received ANC stock in exchange for their Transport stock. As of January 1, 1974, the Schneiders and their relatives owned 100% of ANC's class A voting stock and 99.6% of the class B nonvoting shares. In addition, on this same day the members of the Schneider family and ANC entered into "the American National Non–Employee Buy–Sell Agreement" (the "Buy–Sell Agreement"). Under the Buy–Sell Agreement ANC was given a right of first refusal at the Current Formula Price before any Schneider family shareholder could sell his or her stock to a third party. Stock received by employees under the Transport Plan or the later adopted ANC Plan was not subject to this agreement.

ANC also substantially adopted the Transport Plan, including the vesting requirements, for its employees and for all employees of its subsidiaries, including Transport. The secretary and president of ANC were authorized to issue the number of class B nonvoting shares necessary to implement what was now called the American National Employee Stock Ownership Plan ("the ANC Plan"). The ANC Plan, as later amended, differed from the Transport Plan in that the stock the bonus recipients would receive pursuant to the plan was not required to be issued directly by ANC in the first instance; rather, in the Board of Director's discretion the stock could be already outstanding stock that the bonus recipients purchased from existing class B shareholders. In addition, ANC waived its right of first refusal under the Buy–Sell Agreement for all shares furnished by Schneider to carry out the needs of the plan.

Schneider sold a small portion of his class B stock to employees pursuant to this arrangement in 1974, 1975, and 1976. The payment of the 1975 bonus, the first year in which the IRS assessed a deficiency, serves to illustrate the mechanics of the plan. On December 28, 1974 Transport's Board of Directors determined that the total amount of bonuses to be awarded for work related to 1974 would be $166,000. On February 20, 1975 certain employees were notified that they would receive a bonus, but were not told the exact amount of their individual bonuses. These employees were then required to elect pursuant to the American National Employee Stock Ownership Plan Undertaking and Agreement ("the Undertaking and Agreement") whether to receive at least 25% of their bonus as ANC class B stock. On April 4, 1975 the bonus recipients were notified of the exact amount of their bonuses. Those employees who had committed to take at least 25% of their bonus in stock were then required to specify the exact percentage that they would take in this form.

Transport paid the bonuses on April 21, 1975. Those employees electing to receive a portion of their bonus in the form of ANC class B stock received two checks. The first check was for the cash portion of the bonus, the second for the amount to be received in stock. On the back of the second check was stamped "pay to the order of Al J. Schneider." Each employee who received two checks was instructed by a supervisor to sign the endorsement on the second check. The checks were collected and then transferred to Schneider. Schneider in turn deposited the checks in the Schneiders' personal account. On May 12, 1975, ANC issued a total of 9,623 shares of class B stock to those employees who elected to receive a portion of their bonus in this form. The certificates these employees received, however, were not subject to the Buy–Sell Agreement but rather were subject to the terms and conditions of the ANC Plan, including the vesting provisions. Notice of these restrictions was stamped on the stock certificates. On the same day, Schneider's class B certificate was cancelled and a new certificate issued representing 9,623 fewer shares. Schneider's stock continued to be subject to the Buy–Sell Agreement.

II.

A.

On appeal, the issue is how Schneider's sales of his ANC class B nonvoting stock to Transport's employees should be characterized for tax purposes. It is Schneider's position that the transactions which occurred should be respected. He contends that Transport paid cash bonuses to a select number of its employees and these employees decided to purchase the ANC stock from Schneider. Because the shares were capital assets in Schneider's hands and were sold in bona fide sales to Transport's employees, in Schneider's view, he correctly reported as a capital gain each year the sum of the differences between the selling prices and his tax basis in the shares he sold.

The Tax Court rejected this view. The court held that the transactions involving the payment of the 1975 and 1976 bonuses and stock sales should be characterized as stock redemptions followed by distributions of the redeemed shares as compensation to the electing bonus recipients.[3] The Tax Court specifically found that the intended employee compensation was the stock, not the preendorsed checks.[4]

Once the transactions are characterized in this manner, the appropriate tax treatment for Schneider's exchange of his stock for cash is determined by the rules governing stock redemptions. Schneider concedes on appeal that if it is determined that his stock as redeemed by ANC, the sum he received is properly taxed as ordinary income to him. . .

We . . . review the Tax Court's characterization under a clearly erroneous standard.

B.

This case involves a series of transactions structured in a manner which ostensibly achieved preferential tax treatment from the perspective

---

[3] There is some confusion generated by the fact that ANC, the holding company, adopted the ANC Plan for its employees and "employees of all its subsidiary and affiliated corporations." The confusion centers on whether in the Tax Court's view, ANC or Transport distributed the stock to the participants in the ANC Plan. The ANC Plan seems to have originally contemplated that Transport would distribute the ANC stock. The minutes of the January 1, 1974 Board of Directors' meeting state that "[a]s to those employees who choose stock, Transport, or the other subsidiary and affiliated corporations ... will transfer to [ANC] the cash to buy newly-issued shares from [ANC]." This is corroborated by the fact that the Transport Board, not the ANC Board, voted on the total size of the bonus that Transport would award each year. In addition, minutes from the March 17, 1974 Board of Directors' meeting state that if ANC issued new stock to meet the requirements of the Plan, "Transport would have to pay cash into [ANC] for the shares to be issued." Although there is some conflicting evidence (and the IRS and the Tax Court often fudge the issue), see, e.g., Schneider, 88 T.C. at 916 n.7, 942, we assume when discussing the IRS's and the Tax Court's position that Transport administered the employee stock ownership plan in the same manner as it did prior to 1974, only that after this date it used ANC stock, not its own. Accordingly, under this position, Schneider's ANC stock was redeemed by ANC and then issued to Transport in exchange for cash, the amount corresponding to the sum of the second checks. Transport in turn distributed the stock to its employees pursuant to the plan. Further, even if Transport, not ANC, is considered to have redeemed Schneider's stock, under § 304 of the Internal Revenue Code, Transport would be deemed to have first distributed the cash to ANC which then used the cash to redeem Schneider's stock.

[4] The Tax Court employed the step-transaction doctrine, ruling in part that the employees were mere conduits for the "second check" and therefore the cash flowed directly from Transport to Schneider. We approach the other half of the transaction, focusing on how the stock got from Schneider to the Transport employees. Because we hold that there were more steps—the stock was transferred to ANC, Transport and then to the employees—than Schneider would wish to recognize, we do not speak in terms of the step-transaction doctrine.

of the taxpayer. The right of a taxpayer to arrange his or her affairs to minimize taxes is well established. The Supreme Court observed long ago that "the legal right of a taxpayer to decrease the amount of what otherwise would be his [or her] taxes, or altogether avoid them, by means which the law permits, cannot be doubted." Gregory v. Helvering, 293 U.S. 465, 469, 79 L. Ed. 596, 55 S. Ct. 266 (1935). But to state this principle is not to decide the case. . .

[W]e affirm the Tax Court's characterization of Schneider's stock sales as constructive redemptions. As the Tax Court observed, "at the start of each year's stock bonus process, [Schneider] had stock and the corporations had funds. At the end of each year's stock bonus process, [Schneider] had funds that came from the corporations, and the corporations' employees had stock that came from [Schneider]." . . . Our specific focus is on how ANC class B stock which Schneider initially held subject to the restrictions imposed by the Buy–Sell Agreement ended up in the hands of Transport employees subject to the limitations of the ANC Plan. We agree with the explanation arrived at by the Tax Court: a redemption followed by a stock distribution.

Schneider attempts to avoid this characterization by emphasizing that the Tax Court specifically found that he was not in need of cash at the time of the alleged stock sales. In Schneider's view this indicates that the arrangement was not an effort to "bail" money out of the corporation at capital gain rates, but rather was motivated by legitimate business purposes. He claims that the structure of the transaction was designed to facilitate the administration of the ANC Plan. In order to implement the plan, Transport was required to obtain the ANC shares necessary to meet its obligations to those employees who elected to receive ANC stock. The principal operating officer, Schneider's son, testified that it was not desirable to satisfy these obligations by having ANC issue new shares to Transport because it would dilute the ownership interests of ANC's existing shareholders. In addition, the issuance of new ANC stock would have resulted in a troublesome cash build-up in ANC. As the minutes of ANC's board of directors' meeting explain:

> At present, [ANC] is functioning only as a holding company. If newly issued stock of [ANC] is to be used to provide the shares necessary under the [ANC] Plan, *Transport would have to pay the cash into [ANC] for the shares to be issued.* [ANC] would then have little use for this cash and would probably either have to lend it back to Transport or contribute it to Transport capital.

> *A simpler method is to merely give the employee the cash and let him buy the stock from [Schneider].* [Schneider] stated that he was willing to accommodate the [ANC] Plan in this manner, at least this year. . .

(Emphasis added). The unstated byproduct of this arrangement was that Schneider would allegedly receive capital gains treatment when he relinquished his shares.

The fact that Schneider did not need cash and therefore allegedly did not have a tax motive for participating in this particular arrangement is not dispositive. See . . . Gregory, 293 U.S. at 469 ("the question for determination is whether what was done, apart from the tax motive, was the thing which the statute intended"). . . Schneider must show that the legal restrictions applicable to the stock can be reconciled with his position that the stock was sold directly to Transport's employees. This he cannot do.

Schneider claims that the cash payment and stock sales must be viewed as independent steps for tax purposes. He asserts that the bonus recipients constructively received their bonus entirely in cash at the time they were required to elect the form their bonus would take. In Schneider's view, cash is the standard form of compensation and the election itself constituted an independent step under which an employee who received cash chose to use a portion of it to purchase stock.

Even if we assume that this characterization of the specific operation of the election feature is correct, it does not indicate whether Transport or Schneider was the direct source of the stock that the electing bonus recipients received. The Transport Plan and the later ANC Plan (American National Employee Stock Ownership Plan) were adopted to attract, retain, and motivate top managerial personnel by providing "an equity position" in the parent holding company. In the typical situation where a bonus plan involves a stock ownership component, the company is the source of the stock. The amount of the bonus represents compensation to the employee; that the employee can opt to receive a portion of the bonus as stock does not usually alter the fact that the bonus, in whatever form, is received directly from the employer. Indeed, this was how the Transport Plan operated from its adoption until 1974.

That bonus plans generally function in this manner, however, does not mean that variations are automatically problematic; a subtler argument seems both possible and implicit in Schneider's position. It can be contended that Transport merely arranged and facilitated the stock sales without actually having acted as a principal in the transactions. Under this position, Transport's stated goal of having its managerial personnel own stock was achieved by making it possible for these employees to purchase stock on attractive terms from a separate source, Schneider, and by assisting the employees in carrying out the sales by pre-endorsing and collecting the checks on Schneider's behalf. If we accept this view, Transport's bonuses to its employees consisted of cash and the value of the service of making ANC class B stock available to employees at the given price. Prior to 1974, employees who received cash bonuses could turn around and purchase stock from Transport. From 1974–76 Transport continued this basic format, but instead of acting as the seller, it arranged to make the stock available through Schneider.

In other circumstances it may be a difficult task to determine whether non-cash property arranged by the employer on an elective basis should be viewed as acquired by the employer from a third-party provider of such property and then distributed by the employer to the employee. The alternative position, that the employer pays only cash to the employee as compensation and then for the employee's convenience, and upon his or her election, transfers the cash to the third-party on behalf of the employee may not be implausible. Generally this distinction will not matter because our focus is on the tax ramifications to the third-party which will typically not vary regardless of whether the property is deemed sold to the corporation or the corporation's employees. For most kinds of property, a third-party seller will usually recognize the same type of gain or loss in either case. The issue becomes critical here only because the property is stock and Schneider is a substantial shareholder in ANC. As previously discussed, in this situation the tax consequences to Schneider vary depending on whether he sold his stock to a third party as opposed to having it redeemed by ANC. Because the documents executed in these transactions indicate that the ANC stock the electing bonus recipients received did not move directly from Schneider to the employees, we hold that Schneider's stock was constructively redeemed.

The stock received by the employees was subject to the restrictions imposed by the ANC Plan, including the vesting provisions. In contrast, this same stock in Schneider's hands, which the electing bonus recipients allegedly purchased directly from him, was subject to the Buy–Sell Agreement, not the ANC Plan. Paragraph 2 of the Buy–Sell Agreement set forth ANC's right of first refusal and provided that "[i]f stock of [ANC] is sold under the terms of [paragraph 2] to a person other than [ANC], such shares shall be free of all further restrictions hereunder." Because ANC had waived its right of first refusal with respect to the stock Schneider sold to the employees, absent other agreements, the employees' stock should not have been subject to any restrictions.

Schneider contended at oral argument that the ANC Plan restrictions were a condition of his offer to sell the class B stock. Although we have not been directed to any documentary evidence of this assertion in the record, if this were so, then ANC was merely the third-party beneficiary of the sales agreement between Schneider and the electing employees. ANC's actions belie such a status. In later years ANC modified the restrictions in the ANC Plan, in particular relaxing some of the vesting provisions applicable to employees over 55 years of age. Schneider's counsel conceded at oral argument that it did so without obtaining the express consent of either Schneider or the employees. A third-party beneficiary, however, cannot modify a contract between Schneider and individual employees without their express consent. Transport acted as if it were a principal to the contract, not a third-party beneficiary.

Transport was in fact a party to the key agreement. The ANC plan restrictions were imposed on the employee's stock as a condition set forth in the Undertaking and Agreement executed by the employee. The agreement was between the employee and the corporation; Schneider was not a party. It provided in part that "in consideration of the receipt of stock under the American National Stock Ownership Plan ... the employee agrees to all restrictions and undertakes all the obligations set forth in the Plan." The

Undertaking and Agreement also accounts for the corporation's ability to unilaterally amend the plan, providing that "[t]he Employee agrees that the Plan may be amended and interpreted in the future by the Board of Directors of the corporation and that he will abide by all such amendments and interpretations." Thus, contrary to Schneider's position at oral argument, the ANC Plan restrictions were applicable because of an agreement executed between the corporation and the bonus recipient. Under these facts and circumstances, we hold that the shares received by the employees were obtained directly from Transport.

Once it is determined that the bonus recipients received their stock from Transport, the rest of the pieces fall into place. In order to administer the ANC Plan, Transport needed to acquire the necessary ANC stock. ANC was the most obvious source, but it was reluctant to issue new stock because of the dilution and cash build-up effects. Both problems were solved by having ANC obtain the stock from Schneider. There was no dilution because the stock was previously outstanding. In addition, ANC suffered no cash build-up because the funds Transport paid to it were used to satisfy the obligations to Schneider it incurred to acquire his stock. ANC's acquisition of Schneider's stock, however, is a redemption under § 317 of the Internal Revenue Code.

The decision of the Tax Court is Affirmed.[9]

v. REDEMPTIONS RELATED TO INTER–SHAREHOLDER TRANSFERS

Commissioner v. Roberts
203 F.2d 304 (4th Cir. 1953).

■ Before PARKER, CHIEF JUDGE, and SOPER and DOBIE, CIRCUIT JUDGES.

■ DOBIE, CIRCUIT JUDGE. . . The Tax Court held that the distribution in connection with the redemption of the stock of the corporation, under the circumstances of this case, was not essentially equivalent to, and not taxable as, the distribution of a dividend under [§§ 302(b)(1) and 302(d)]. . . We think the decision of the Tax Court was clearly erroneous. It must, therefore, be reversed.

We quote the applicable provisions of the . . . Treasury Regulations: . . .

The question whether a distribution in connection with a cancellation or redemption of stock is essentially equivalent to the distribution of a taxable dividend depends upon the circumstances of such case. A cancellation or redemption by a corporation of a portion of its stock pro rata among all the shareholders will generally be considered as effecting a distribution essentially equivalent to a dividend distribution to the extent of the earnings and profits accumulated after February 28,

---

[9] The parties also contest the applicability of § 83 of the Internal Revenue Code and in particular Treasury Regulation § 1.83–6(d)(1). The Tax Court did not reach this issue. Because we affirm the Tax Court's finding of constructive redemptions, we also do not reach the issue of the application of § 83 to this case.

1913. On the other hand, a cancellation or redemption by a corporation of all of the stock of a particular shareholder, so that the shareholder ceases to be interested in the affairs of the corporation, does not effect a distribution of a taxable dividend. A bona fide distribution in complete cancellation or redemption of all of the stock of a corporation, or one of a series of bona fide distributions in complete cancellation or redemption of all the stock of a corporation, is not essentially equivalent to the distribution of a taxable dividend. If a distribution is made pursuant to a corporate resolution reciting that the distribution is made in liquidation of the corporation, and the corporation is completely liquidated and dissolved within one year after the distribution, the distribution will not be considered essentially equivalent to the distribution of a taxable dividend; in all other cases the facts and circumstances should be reported to the Commissioner for his determination whether the distribution, or any part thereof, is essentially equivalent to the distribution of a taxable dividend. [Treas. Reg. 111, § 29.115.9]

There is little or no dispute about the facts of this case. In March, 1932, John T. Roberts, hereinafter called taxpayer, and his brother transferred to a newly created corporation all of the assets of a wholesale plumbing and heating supply business, theretofore conducted by them in partnership, in exchange for all of the stock of the corporation. . . Fifteen hundred shares were issued to taxpayer, who continued to hold them through the taxable year 1944 here involved. Five hundred shares were issued to taxpayer's brother. Taxpayer's brother died in October, 1943, and by his last will made a specific bequest to taxpayer of any shares of stock of the corporation owned by him at the time of his death. Pursuant to an order of the probate court, the executor of the brother's will transferred to taxpayer stock certificates for the 500 shares of the corporation's stock which the brother had owned. These 500 shares were valued for estate tax purposes at $92,000. . .

On January 1, 1944, total assets amounted to approximately $414,000 (including cash of $160,000 and United States obligations of $96,000), and the earned surplus amounted to approximately $170,000. As of December 31, 1944 (that is, after the distribution in redemption of stock here involved), the corporation's balance sheets showed assets of $320,000 (including cash of $60,000 and United States obligations of $106,000) and an earned surplus of $135,000.

The corporation paid a dividend of $4 a share in 1943; $16 in 1935; $8 in each year 1936 through 1940; $6 in 1941; and no dividends in 1942 and 1943. In 1944, after the stock redemption hereinafter mentioned, a dividend of $2 was distributed. . .

On December 26, 1944, at a special meeting of the corporation's board of directors, on motion of taxpayer, it was resolved that the corporation purchase from taxpayer for $92,000 the 500 shares of stock which taxpayer had acquired by bequest from his brother. . . On the same day, a special meeting of the stockholders (namely, taxpayer, for he then owned all the shares of stock in this corporation,) approved; the transaction was completed; and an amendment to the certificate of incorporation was executed which was later approved by the State Tax Commission. Taxpayer never considered selling his shares to anyone but the corporation because he wanted to keep the stock in the family.

The taxpayer did not report the transaction in controversy on his return, and the Commissioner determined a deficiency on the ground that the amount of $92,000 paid by the corporation was taxable as a dividend.

The Tax Court specifically found that the earnings and profits of the corporation prior to and during 1944 were accumulated for no definite purpose; that the operations of the corporation were not impaired by reason of the transaction in controversy, and that the corporation had never followed a policy of contraction of business; that the corporation's financial position on December 26, 1944, permitted of a dividend of $92,000, and that the corporation continued in the same business in subsequent years.

The Tax Court further found that the payment of the $92,000 to taxpayer by the corporation in the taxable year was a distribution in complete cancellation and redemption of all of that portion of the corporation's stock bequeathed by taxpayer's brother, constituting a partial liquidation, and not the essential equivalent of the distribution of a taxable dividend.

We cannot agree with the holding of the Tax Court that, as of the time of the stock redemption, the stock acquired by taxpayer which was redeemed, must be regarded as the stock of the brother. This runs absolutely counter to reality. This stock had been the brother's; but, months before the redemption, taxpayer's title to this stock had been completely perfected. . .

The vital thing here, as we see it, is that, by the redemption of this stock, the essential relation of the taxpayer to the corporation was not, in any practical aspect, changed. Before the redemption, he was the sole stockholder in the corporation; after the redemption, he was still the sole stockholder. Of what real consequence was it that before the redemption his sole ownership was divided into 2,000 shares, and after the redemption, this same sole ownership was divided into 1,500 shares: He owned the whole corporation before the redemption; after the redemption, he was still the sole owner.

Here, then, we find a single individual owning all the corporate stock. . . The corporation had on hand a large and unnecessary accumulation of cash, representing "earnings or profits accumulated after February 28, 1913." . . . The corporation did not then intend to liquidate or to contract its business. . . The redemption served no business purpose of the corporation; it was motivated entirely by the personal consideration of taxpayer. . . The net effect of the redemption was clearly to distribute to taxpayer the corporate earnings just as if a cash dividend had been declared. . . Indeed, it is difficult to imagine a more ideal set-up for the application of [§§ 302(b)(1) and 302(d)] than the facts involved in the instant case.

The cases of Flinn v. Commissioner, 37 B.T.A. 1085 and Tiffany v. Commissioner, 16 T.C. 1443, cited by the Tax Court are clearly not in point. There, the corporations purchased all of the stock of a particular stockholder, when there were still other stockholders; here, the corporation merely purchased part of the stock of its sole stockholder. There, the relationship of the stockholder to the corporation was radically changed by the redemption, from stockholder to mere ex-stockholder; here, as we have pointed out, there was no such change for, both before and after the redemption taxpayer was and remained the sole stockholder of the corporation.

The ultimate question of whether, in a particular case, [§§ 302(b)(1) and 302(d) do or do] not apply, is usually held to be a question of fact. . .

The Regulations, which have been in effect for many years, provide in part that a redemption by a corporation of a portion of its stock pro rata among all the shareholders would generally be considered as effecting a distribution essentially equivalent to a dividend distribution to the extent of the earnings and profits accumulated after February 28, 1913. That provision of the Regulations is fully met in this case, and likewise other factors which have sometimes been held relevant are also present here.

It might be noted that while dividends were paid by the corporation here prior to 1941, no dividends were paid by the corporation in 1942, 1943, or 1944 prior to redemption, though the corporate earnings in all these years were quite substantial.

Any conclusion other than that which we have reached readily shows how easily the tactics of the taxpayer here could be used as a means of tax evasion. A prosperous corporation, for example, with a single stockholder, earns large sums of money, available for, and which should be paid out as, dividends. This sole stockholder siphons off this money (as was done in the instant case) to himself by selling a portion of his stock to the corporation at a price per share which will just cover these earnings. Surely, this is a redemption "essentially equivalent to the distribution of a taxable dividend." Congress must have had just such a situation in mind when it enacted [§§ 302(b)(1) and 302(d)]. . .

The decision of the Tax Court of the United States is reversed and the case is remanded with directions to enter a decision in favor of the Commissioner.

Reversed and remanded with directions.

NOTE

What would the tax consequences have been to the estate and to the taxpayer if, in *Roberts*, (1) the decedent's will had made a bequest of the cash value of the shares, not the shares themselves, (2) the corporation had redeemed the shares in the estate's hands, and (3) the estate turned over to the taxpayer the cash proceeds? Would the result have been different if the estate had paid the taxpayer the cash bequest and then had the stock redeemed in its hands?

In answering these questions consider §§ 302(b)(3), 318, 1014, and 102(a). See Treas. Reg. § 1.318–3(a).

Holsey v. Commissioner

258 F.2d 865 (3d Cir. 1958).

■ Before MARIS, GOODRICH and MCLAUGHLIN, CIRCUIT JUDGES.

■ MARIS, CIRCUIT JUDGE. . . . J. R. Holsey Sales Company, a New Jersey corporation, was organized on April 28, 1936, as an Oldsmobile dealership. Taxpayer has been president and a director of the company since its organization. Only 20 shares were issued out of the 2,500 shares of no par value stock authorized; these 20 shares were issued to Greenville Auto Sales Company, a Chevrolet dealership, in exchange for all of the latter's right, title, and interest to the Oldsmobile franchise and other assets with respect to the franchise which had been owned and operated by the Greenville Company. The 20 shares issued were assigned a value of $11,000. Taxpayer's father, Charles V. Holsey, in 1936, owned more than two-thirds of the outstanding stock of the Greenville Company, and taxpayer was vice-president and a director of that corporation.

On April 30, 1936, taxpayer acquired from the Greenville Company an option to purchase 50% of the outstanding shares of the Holsey Company for $11,000, and a further option to purchase, within ten years after the exercise of the first option, all the remaining shares for a sum to be agreed upon. The Greenville Company owned all of the outstanding stock of the Holsey Company from its organization in 1936 until November, 1939, when taxpayer exercised his first option and purchased 50% of the outstanding stock of the Holsey Company for $11,000.

On June 28, 1946, the further option in favor of taxpayer was revised. Under the terms of the revised option, taxpayer was granted the right to purchase the remaining outstanding shares of the Holsey Company at any time up to and including June 28, 1951, for $80,000. The revised option was in favor of taxpayer individually and was not assignable by him to anyone other than a corporation in which he owned not less than 50% of the voting stock. On the date of the revision of this option, taxpayer's father owned 76% of the stock of the Greenville Company and taxpayer was a vice-president and director of that corporation. . .

On January 19, 1951, taxpayer assigned his revised option to the Holsey Company; on the same date the Holsey Company exercised the option and paid the Greenville Company $80,000 for the stock held by it. This transaction resulted in taxpayer becoming the owner of 100% of the outstanding stock of the Holsey Company. In his income tax return for the year 1951, taxpayer gave no effect to this transaction.

The principal officers and only directors of the Holsey Company from April 28, 1936, to December 31, 1951, were taxpayer, his brother, Charles D. Holsey, and their father, Charles V. Holsey. On January 19, 1951, when the revised option was exercised, the earned surplus of the Holsey Company was in excess of $300,000.

The Oldsmobile franchise, under which the Holsey Company operated, was a yearly contract entered into by the Corporation and the manufacturer in reliance upon the personal qualifications and representations of taxpayer as an individual. It was the manufacturer's policy to have its dealers own all of the stock in dealership organizations.

The Commissioner determined that the effect of the transaction of January 19, 1951, wherein the Holsey Company paid $80,000 to the Greenville Company for 50% of the outstanding stock of the Holsey Company, constituted a dividend to taxpayer, the remaining stockholder. The Commissioner therefore asserted a deficiency against taxpayer in the sum of $41,385.34. The Tax Court sustained the Commissioner. 28 T.C. 962.

The question presented for decision in this case is whether the Tax Court erred in holding that the payment by the Holsey Company of $80,000 to the Greenville Company for the purchase from that company of its stock in the Holsey Company was essentially equivalent to the distribution of a taxable dividend to the taxpayer, the remaining stockholder of the Holsey Company. To determine that question we must begin with the applicable statute. . .

It will be observed that section [316(a)] defines a dividend as a distribution made by a corporation "to its shareholders." Accordingly unless a distribution which is sought to be taxed to a stockholder as a dividend is made to him or for his benefit it may not be regarded as either a dividend or the legal equivalent of a dividend. Here the distribution was made to the Greenville Company, not to the taxpayer. This the Government, of course, concedes but urges that it was made for the benefit of the taxpayer. It is true that it has been held that a distribution by a corporation in redemption of stock which the taxpayer stockholder has a contractual obligation to purchase is essentially the equivalent of a dividend to him since it operates to discharge his obligation. . . But where, as here, the taxpayer was never under any legal obligation to purchase the stock held by the other stockholder, the Greenville Company, having merely an option to purchase which he did not exercise but instead assigned to the Holsey Company, the distribution did not discharge any obligation of his and did not benefit him in any direct sense.

It is, of course, true that the taxpayer was benefited indirectly by the distribution. The value of his own stock was increased, since the redemption was for less than book value, and he became sole stockholder. But these benefits operated only to increase the value of the taxpayer's stock holdings; they could not give rise to taxable income within the meaning of the Sixteenth Amendment until the corporation makes a distribution to the taxpayer or his stock is sold. Eisner v. Macomber, 1920, 252 U.S. 189 . . .; Schmitt v. Commissioner of Internal Revenue, 3 Cir., 1954, 208 F.2d 819. In the latter case in a somewhat similar connection this court said (at page 821):

During these years when Wolverine was buying its own shares it, of course, was subject to income tax as a corporation. Mrs. Green was subject to tax on whatever profit she made by the sale of these shares to the corporation. But what happened to warrant imposing a tax upon Schmitt and Lehren? If one owns a piece of real estate and, because of its favorable location in a city, the land becomes increasingly valuable over a period of years, the owner is not subject to income taxation upon the annual increase in value. In the same way, if a man owns shares in a corporation which gradually become more valuable through the years he is not taxed because of the increase in value even though he is richer at the end of each year than he was at the end of the year before. If he disposes of that which has increased, of course he must pay tax upon his profit. All of this is hornbook law of taxation; nobody denies it.

We think that the principle thus stated is equally applicable here. Indeed the Tax Court itself has so held in essentially similar cases. . .

The question whether payments made by a corporation in the acquisition and redemption of its stock are essentially equivalent to the distribution of a taxable dividend has been often before the courts and certain criteria have been enunciated. The most significant of these is said to be whether the distribution leaves the proportionate interests of the stockholders unchanged as occurs when a true dividend is paid. Ferro v. Commissioner of Internal Revenue, 3 Cir., 1957, 242 F.2d 838, 841. The application of that criterion to the facts of this case compels the conclusion that in the absence of a direct pecuniary benefit to the taxpayer the Tax Court erred in holding the distribution in question taxable to him. For in his case prior to the distribution the taxpayer and the Greenville Company each had a 50% interest in the Holsey Company whereas after it was over the taxpayer had 100% of the outstanding stock and the Greenville Company none.

The Government urges the lack of a corporate purpose for the distribution and the taxpayer seeks to establish one. But we do not consider this point for, as we have recently held, "It is the effect of the redemption, rather than the purpose which actuated it, which controls the determination of dividend equivalence." Kessner v. Commissioner of Internal Revenue, 3 Cir., 1957, 248 F.2d 943, 944. Nor need we discuss the present position of the Government that the transaction must be treated as a sham and the purchase of the stock as having been made by the taxpayer through his alter ego, the Holsey Company. For the Tax Court made no such finding, doubtless in view of the fact that at the time the taxpayer owned only 50% of the stock and was in a minority on the board of directors. On the contrary that court based its decision on the benefit which the distribution by the corporation to the Greenville Company conferred upon the taxpayer, which it thought gave rise to taxable income in his hands.

For the reasons stated we think that the Tax Court erred in its decision. The decision will accordingly be reversed and the cause remanded for further proceedings not inconsistent with this opinion.

■ McLaughlin, Circuit Judge (dissenting). I think that the net effect of the facile operation disclosed in this case amounts to the distribution of a taxable dividend to the taxpayer. I do not think that the *Schmitt* decision controls here. Quite the contrary to the *Schmitt* facts, this taxpayer himself acquired a valuable option to buy the shares and solely on the theory of a gift of the option rights would make the corporation the true purchaser. I agree with the Tax Court that "The assignment of the option contract to J. R. Holsey Sales Co. was clearly for the purpose of having that company pay the $80,000 in exercise of the option that was executed for petitioner's personal benefit. The payment was intended to secure and did secure for petitioner exactly what it was always intended he should get if he made the payment personally, namely, all of the stock in J. R. Holsey Sales Co."

I would affirm the Tax Court decision.

NOTES

1. What is the factual difference in *Holsey* that may justify a result different from that in *Roberts*, page 204 supra? In your judgment is the factual difference sufficient? If not, which result is preferable?

2. In Rev. Rul. 58–614, 1958–2 C.B. 920, the Service announced its intention to follow the *Holsey* decision. It distinguished *Holsey* from the case in which the stock "is in reality purchased by a remaining shareholder," and for the latter type of case cited Wall v. United States, 164 F.2d 462 (4th Cir. 1947), and Zipp v. Commissioner, 259 F.2d 119 (6th Cir. 1958), *cert. denied*, 359 U.S. 934 (1959). See also Rev. Rul. 59–296, 1959–2 C.B. 103.

3. *Holsey* holds that benefits which "operated only to increase the value of the taxpayer's stock holdings . . . could not give rise to taxable income within the meaning of the Sixteenth Amendment. . ." But see § 305(b)(2) and (c); cf. Rev. Rul. 77–19, 1977–1 C.B. 83. Section 305 is discussed in Chapter 4, page 376 et seq. infra. The Constitution aside, does *Holsey* reach the sensible result as a matter of statutory construction?

Sullivan v. United States

363 F.2d 724 (8th Cir. 1966), *cert. denied*, 387 U.S. 905 (1967).

■ Before Vogel, Chief Judge, Blackmun, Circuit Judge, and Stephenson, District Judge.

■ Stephenson, District Judge. . . [T]he taxpayer Sullivan purchased the assets of an automobile dealership in Blytheville, Arkansas in 1941. He then formed a corporation to operate the dealership. . . [I]n September, 1948, Frank Nelson became the resident manager of the dealership under an arrangement which included an agreement permitting Nelson to acquire up to forty (40) per cent of the stock and further providing for taxpayer's repurchase of said stock upon Nelson's termination of his employment. After acquiring approximately 38% of the corporation's outstanding stock, Nelson announced his intention to depart from his position in 1956 and offered to sell his stock to taxpayer Sullivan. The corporation's Board of Directors then authorized the redemption of Nelson's stock by the corporation.

The ultimate question before the District Court involved a determination of whether the payment by the corporation in redemption of Nelson's stock constituted a taxable distribution to taxpayer Sullivan, the sole remaining stockholder of the corporation. The District Court found that taxpayer Sullivan was unconditionally and primarily obligated to purchase Nelson's stock in 1956 and that said stock was purchased by the Corporation out of profits distributable as a dividend and therefore held that the taxpayer constructively received income equivalent to a dividend in the amount paid by the Corporation for said stock, ($198,334.58). Initially, an interpretation of the memorandum agreement entered into by Sullivan and Nelson at the time the latter assumed his managerial functions is necessary. The agreement contained the following provisions:

6. TRANSFER OF SHARES OF STOCK. It is understood and agreed that Sullivan is permitting Nelson to buy stock in said corporation for the purpose of giving him a working interest only, and said Nelson agrees that said shares of stock cannot and will not be mortgaged, hypothecated or transferred by him, his heirs, executor, administrator or trustee to any person other than William J. Sullivan or such person as said Sullivan directs in writing. Any such sale, delivery or transfer to any other person, firm or corporation shall be null and void. Said Sullivan agrees that he will, within thirty (30) days after such shares have been offered for sale to him, accept the offer to sell, provided always that such shares shall be offered for sale at a price to be determined according to this contract.

7. TERMINATION OF CONTRACT. Said Nelson agrees that if he should terminate his employment or relationship with William J. Sullivan or employment by the said corporation, and if his connection and association with the corporation should cease or be terminated by Sullivan or the majority owners of the stock of the corporation, then said Nelson agrees to sell and transfer and deliver to Sullivan at the then book value all shares of stock owned by him in the Sullivan–Nelson Chevrolet Co. . . If said contract is terminated by Nelson or Sullivan as herein provided or by the death of Nelson, the value of the stock owned by Nelson shall be fixed and determined as set up in paragraphs four and five of this agreement. If said Nelson should die or become so disabled by injury or sickness as to become incapable of managing and operating the business, then said Sullivan shall have the immediate and exclusive rights to purchase the stock owned by Nelson or by his heirs, administrators or executors in accordance with the terms of this contract. Title so (sic) said shares of stock shall automatically rest in Sullivan upon Nelson's death and said Sullivan shall be obligated to Nelson's personal representative or representatives for the value thereof as fixed by this agreement.

. . . The District Court was justified in concluding that Sullivan was unconditionally obligated to purchase Nelson's stock.[5]

At this juncture, the payment by the corporation to Nelson presents two basic questions: (1) Was that payment in actuality a dividend and therefore includable in Sullivan's gross income under §§ 61(a)(7), 316(a) and 301(c)(1) of the Internal Revenue Code? (2) If the payment is considered as a corporate redemption of stock, was the payment includable in Sullivan's gross income as being essentially equivalent to a dividend within the meaning of § 302(b)(1)? This court has recognized that both questions are to be resolved as fact issues. Idol v. Commissioner of Internal Revenue, 319 F.2d 647 (8th Cir. 1963). If a finding is supported by substantial evidence on the record as a whole and is not against or induced by an erroneous view of the law, it will not be disturbed on appeal.

When an individual shareholder receives an economic benefit through a diversion of corporate earnings and profits, such a receipt may be taxed as a constructive dividend. This court set forth a criteria for determining whether a payment constitutes a constructive dividend in Sachs v. Commissioner of Internal Revenue, 277 F.2d 879, 882–883 (8th Cir. 1960):

> The motive, or expressed intent of the corporation is not determinative, and constructive dividends have been found contrary to the expressed intent of the corporation. The courts, as arbiters of the true nature of corporate payments, have consistently used as a standard the measure of receipt of economic benefit as the proper occasion for taxation.

This court has also adopted criteria for determining whether a redemption of stock is essentially equivalent to a dividend. . . While there is no sole decisive test in this connection, the several guidelines for the determination include "whether there is a bona fide corporate business purpose, whether the action was initiated by the corporation or by the shareholders, whether there was a contraction of the business, and whether there was a substantial change in proportionate stock ownership." Idol v. Commissioner of Internal Revenue, 319 F.2d 647, 651 (8th Cir. 1963). In addition, the Court has observed that the "net effect of the transaction is at least an important consideration in determining dividend equivalency."

The general net effect and the purpose of and circumstances surrounding the transaction involved herein must be carefully scrutinized to ascertain whether Sullivan received a taxable dividend. Prior to the transaction, Sullivan held approximately 62% of the shares outstanding while Nelson owned the remaining shares. As previously discussed, Sullivan was unconditionally obligated to purchase Nelson's stock if it was offered to him for

---

[5] The taxpayer makes an alternative argument to the effect that, even if he was unconditionally obligated to purchase Sullivan's stock, subsequent events constituted a modification or novation of that agreement. Even if this contention is accepted, the court is at a loss as to how the taxpayer is aided. The novation or modification itself would be considered as resulting in an economic benefit and possible constructive dividend taxable against Sullivan. The taxpayer would be left in essentially the same position with respect to his possible tax liability.

sale. After the transaction was completed, the relevant facts were essentially as follows: (1) Sullivan's personal obligation had been discharged (2) Sullivan owned all of the outstanding shares of stock of the corporation (3) the corporation's assets were decreased by the amount paid to Nelson for his stock (4) Nelson's stock was held by the corporation as treasury stock. It is true that in terms of the financial worth of Sullivan's interest in the corporation, it was the same after the transaction as it was before.[7] The transaction still resulted in an economic benefit to Sullivan, however, because he was relieved of his personal obligation to purchase Nelson's stock. After careful consideration this court concludes that there was no corporate business purpose or other factor which justifies the taxpayer's position that as to him the payment must be considered a stock redemption and not the equivalent of a dividend.[9] On the facts of this case, Sullivan received a taxable dividend as the result of the corporation's purchase of Nelson's stock.

This court is aware that it is often difficult to distinguish true substance from mere form. Tax law places some weight and significance on form and the choice of one alternative rather than another for achieving a desired end is often critical and may be determinative of the tax effect of a transaction. Judge Becker's opinion comprehensively deals with the evidence and the applicable law of this case. The taxpayer has failed to establish grounds for reversal. The judgment of the District Court is affirmed.

NOTES

1. Are *Holsey*, page 208 supra, and *Sullivan* distinguishable? Is it relevant that in *Sullivan* the taxpayer had an obligation to purchase, whereas in *Holsey* there was only an option? Are *Sullivan* and the government's position in *Sullivan* consistent with (and as to the government, justifiable in light of) Rev. Rul. 59–286, 1952–2 C.B. 103? In the latter, the surviving shareholder was obligated to either buy the decedent's stock or to vote his stock for liquidation of the corporation. By postmortem agreement the corporation redeemed the decedent's stock at its fair market value. Despite the fact that the remaining shareholder was "personally obligated" to buy the stock and he was "relieved [of his] obligation," he was ruled not to be in receipt of a dividend since the stock was not "in reality . . . purchased by the remaining shareholder. . ." The Commissioner's current position is elaborated in Rev. Rul. 69–608, 1969–2 C.B. 43, infra.

2. In Daniel T. Jacobs, 41 T.C.M. (CCH) 951 (1981), the Tax Court followed *Sullivan* while acknowledging that the taxpayers "could very easily have

---

[7] Prior to the transfer of Nelson's stock Sullivan owned 186 shares of the 300 shares outstanding. His stock at this time was worth approximately $323,597.00. After the transfer, his 186 shares were the only outstanding stock of the corporation. Due to the corporate purchase of Nelson's stock, however, the value of the taxpayer's shares remained at approximately $323,597.00.

[9] The taxpayer has strongly urged that there was a corporate business purpose motivating the purchase of Nelson's stock because of the valuable services received from him as resident manager of the corporation. The services had already been performed, however, when the stock was purchased. Moreover, it was Sullivan, not the corporation, who was obligated to purchase the stock. Under these circumstances, the District Court properly found that the purchase was not induced by a business purpose. The net effect of the transaction further indicates that a dividend was received by the taxpayer.

avoided dividend treatment . . . had they obtained tax advice from the start." Judge Tannenwald said the court must "leave for another day [the development of] an exception to the now concretized standard of form over substance in [this] area. . ."

3. For a case involving § 304 which distinguishes *Sullivan*, see Citizens Bank & Trust Co. v. United States, 580 F.2d 442 (Ct. Cl. 1978).

4. In Craven v. Commissioner, 215 F.3d 1201 (11th Cir. 2000), a husband and wife owned respectively 51% and 47% of their incorporated pottery business. (The remaining shares were held by their children). Following their divorce, and pursuant to their divorce decree, the former wife agreed to sell her stock back to the corporation. The former wife did not report any capital gains on the redemption of her stock by the corporation. Instead, she took the position on her return that the redemption was a nonrecognition event under § 1041. The former wife contended that her sale of stock to the corporation was pursuant to the divorce terms and thus was a purchase by the corporation on behalf of her former husband. The court, citing Read v. Commissioner, 114 T.C. 14 (2000), which confronted the conflicting cases on this issue, concluded that the corporation's purchase of the former wife's stock was "on behalf of" or "in the interest" of her former spouse and thus the transfer qualified for nonrecognition under § 1041. See also Blatt v. Commissioner, 102 T.C. 77 (1994) (redemption pursuant to divorce decree).

How should the former husband be treated in *Craven*? Are the former spouses likely to report the transaction in a consistent manner? Consider Arnes v. Commissioner, 102 T.C. 522 (1994). Will this tension continue after the rate changes in the 2003 Act? Why?

In 2003, Treasury finalized regulations clarifying the legal landscape on redemptions and § 1041. Treas. Reg. § 1.1041–2(a), (b), (c), & (d). See also Temp. Treas. Reg. § 1.1041–1T(c) Q & A 9.

Revenue Ruling 69–608
1969–2 C.B. 43.

Advice has been requested as to the treatment for Federal income tax purposes of the redemption by a corporation of a retiring shareholder's stock where the remaining shareholder of the corporation has entered into a contract to purchase such stock.

Where the stock of a corporation is held by a small group of people, it is often considered necessary to the continuity of the corporation to have the individuals enter into agreements among themselves to provide for the disposition of the stock of the corporation in the event of the resignation, death, or incapacity of one of them. Such agreements are generally reciprocal among the shareholders and usually provide that on the resignation, death, or incapacity of one of the principal shareholders, the remaining shareholders will purchase his stock. Frequently such agreements are assigned to the corporation by the remaining shareholder and the corporation actually redeems its stock from the retiring shareholder.

Where a corporation redeems stock from a retiring shareholder, the fact that the corporation in purchasing the shares satisfies the continuing shareholder's executory contractual obligation to purchase the redeemed shares does not result in a distribution to the continuing shareholder provided that the continuing shareholder is not subject to an existing primary and unconditional obligation to perform the contract and that the corporation pays no more than fair market value for the stock redeemed.

On the other hand, if the continuing shareholder, at the time of the assignment to the corporation of his contract to purchase the retiring shareholder's stock, is subject to an unconditional obligation to purchase the retiring shareholder's stock, the satisfaction by the corporation of his obligation results in a constructive distribution to him. The constructive distribution is taxable as a distribution under section 301 of the Internal Revenue Code of 1954.

If the continuing shareholder assigns his stock purchase contract to the redeeming corporation prior to the time when he incurs a primary and unconditional obligation to pay for the shares of stock, no distribution to him will result. If, on the other hand, the assignment takes place after the time when the continuing shareholder is so obligated, a distribution to him will result. While a pre-existing obligation to perform in the future is a necessary element in establishing a distribution in this type of case, it is not until the obligor's duty to perform becomes unconditional that it can be said a primary and unconditional obligation arises.

The application of the above principles may be illustrated by the situations described below.

SITUATION 1

A and B are unrelated individuals who own all of the outstanding stock of corporation X. A and B enter into an agreement that provides in the event B leaves the employ of X, he will sell his X stock to A at a price fixed by the agreement. The agreement provides that within a specified number of days of B's offer to sell, A will purchase at the price fixed by the agreement all of the X stock owned by B. B terminates his employment and tenders the X stock to A. Instead of purchasing the stock himself in accordance with the terms of the agreement, A causes X to assume the contract and to redeem its stock held by B. In this case, A had a primary and unconditional obligation to perform his contract with B at the time the contract was assigned to X. Therefore, the redemption by X of its stock held by B will result in a constructive distribution to A. See William J. and Georgia K. Sullivan v. United States of America, [page 211 supra].

SITUATION 2

A and B are unrelated individuals who own all of the outstanding stock of corporation X. An agreement between them provides unconditionally that within ninety days of the death of either A or B, the survivor will purchase the decedent's stock of X from his estate. Following the death of B, A causes X to assume the contract and redeem the stock from B's estate.

The assignment of the contract to X followed by the redemption by X of the stock owned by B's estate will result in a constructive distribution to A because immediately on the death of B, A had a primary and unconditional obligation to perform the contract.

SITUATION 3

All of the stock of X corporation was owned by a trust that was to terminate in 1968. Individuals A and B were the beneficiaries of the trust. Since B was the trustee of the trust, he had exclusive management authority over X through his control of the board of directors. In 1966, A paid to B the sum of 25x dollars and promised to pay an additional 20x dollars to B in 1969 for B's interest in the corpus and accumulations of the trust plus B's agreement to resign immediately as supervisor of the trust and release his control over the management of the corporation. The actual transfer of the stock held in trust was to take place on termination of the trust in 1968. In 1969, X reimbursed A for the 25x dollars previously paid to B, paid 20x dollars to B, and received the X stock held by B.

For all practical purposes, A became the owner of B's shares in 1966. Although naked legal title to the shares could not be transferred until the trust terminated in 1968, B did transfer all of his beneficial and equitable ownership of the X stock to A in exchange for an immediate payment by A of 25x dollars and an unconditional promise to pay an additional 20x dollars upon termination of the trust. The payment by X of 20x dollars to B and 25x dollars to A in 1969 constituted a constructive distribution to A in the amount of 45x dollars. See Schalk Chemical Company v. Commissioner, 32 T.C. 879 (1959), *affirmed* 304 F. 2d, 48 (1962).

SITUATION 4

A and B owned all of the outstanding stock of X corporation. A and B entered into a contract under which, if B desired to sell his X stock, A agreed to purchase the stock or to cause such stock to be purchased. If B chose to sell his X stock to any person other than A, he could do so at any time. In accordance with the terms of the contract, A caused X to redeem all of B's stock in X.

At the time of the redemption, B was free to sell his stock to A or to any other person, and A had no unconditional obligation to purchase the stock and no fixed liability to pay for the stock. Accordingly, the redemption by X did not result in a constructive distribution to A. See S. K. Ames, Inc. v. Commissioner, 46 B.T.A. 1020 (1942), *acquiescence*, C.B. 1942–1, 1.

SITUATION 5

A and B owned all of the outstanding stock of X corporation. An agreement between A and B provided that upon the death of either, X will redeem all of the X stock owned by the decedent at the time of his death. In the event that X does not redeem the shares from the estate, the agreement provided that the surviving shareholder would purchase the unredeemed shares from the decedent's estate. B died and, in accordance with the agreement, X redeemed all of the shares owned by his estate.

In this case A was only secondarily liable under the agreement between A and B. Since A was not primarily obligated to purchase the X stock from the estate of B, he received no constructive distribution when X redeemed the stock.

SITUATION 6

B owned all of the outstanding stock of X corporation. A and B entered into an agreement under which A was to purchase all of the X stock from B. A did not contemplate purchasing the X stock in his own name. Therefore, the contract between A and B specifically provided that it could be assigned by A to a corporation and that, if the corporation agreed to be bound by the terms, A would be released from the contract.

A organized Y corporation and assigned the stock purchase contract to it. Y borrowed funds and purchased all of the X stock from B pursuant to the agreement. Subsequently Y was merged into X and X assumed the liabilities that Y incurred in connection with the purchase of the X stock and subsequently satisfied these liabilities.

The purchase by Y of the stock of X did not result in a constructive distribution to A. Since A did not contemplate purchasing the X stock in his own name, he provided in the contract that it could be assigned to a corporation prior to the closing date. A chose this latter alternative and assigned the contract to Y. A was not personally subject to an unconditional obligation to purchase the X stock from B. See Arthur J. Kobacker and Sara Jo Kobacker, et al. v. Commissioner, 37 T.C. 882 (1962), *acquiescence*, C.B. 1964–2, 6. Compare Ray Edenfield v. Commissioner, 19 T.C. 13 (1952), *acquiescence*, C.B. 1953–1, 4.

SITUATION 7

A and B owned all of the outstanding stock of X corporation. An agreement between the shareholders provided that upon the death of either, the survivor would purchase the decedent's shares from his estate at a price provided in the agreement. Subsequently, the agreement was rescinded and a new agreement entered into which provided that upon the death of either A or B, X would redeem all of the decedent's shares of X stock from his estate.

The cancellation of the original contract between the parties in favor of the new contract did not result in a constructive distribution to either A or B. At the time X agreed to purchase the stock pursuant to the terms of the new agreement, neither A nor B had an unconditional obligation to purchase shares of X stock. The subsequent redemption of the stock from the

estate of either pursuant to the terms of the new agreement will not constitute a constructive distribution to the surviving shareholder.

NOTES

1. In Pulliam v. Commissioner, 48 T.C.M. (CCH) 1019 (1984), the sole
shareholder of a corporation that operated a funeral home died leaving the corporation stock to several beneficiaries of whom only one was a licensed funeral
director. Under state law all shareholders had to be licensed funeral directors.
To remedy this, the corporation redeemed the shares of all unlicensed beneficiaries. The court held that this did not result in a dividend to the remaining
shareholder, despite the fact that under state law he was obligated to acquire
stock, because state law imposed the redemption obligation on the corporation
as well.

2. In Trollope v. Commissioner, T.C.M. 2009-177, two shareholders owned
a corporation 50-50. The retiring shareholder ("R") sold his stock in the corporation to the continuing shareholder ("C"). Immediately prior to this sale, the
corporation had lent R $700,000 and lent C $1,895,126. Shortly thereafter C
purchased the stock held by R for $2,605,126. Specifically, R transferred
$1,895,126 in cash plus assumed R's note to the corporation in the amount of
$700,000 [Some additional value was also transferred]. C became the sole
shareholder and then sold 1500 shares of the corporation (the amount purchased from R) back to the corporation. The Service sought to treat the corporation's purchase of stock from C as a dividend to C. But C argued that this
was not a dividend because C had served as the corporation's "agent" in facilitating the redemption of R's shares. Ultimately the IRS agreed. [The case went
to court because C was not satisfied with prevailing in examination on the
point, but instead sought to be reimbursed for administrative and litigation
costs, which the court denied].

Do the 2003 changes in the tax rate on dividends impact the importance of
this issue (corporate redemption of one shareholder's stock being treated as a
constructive dividend to the surviving shareholder)? Congress has set the dividend tax rate to expire many times, but continues to renew the reduced rate.
Currently, the Tax Relief Unemployment Insurance Reauthorization and Job
Creation Act of 2010 extended the 0% dividend tax rate for individuals and 10-
15% income tax brackets for 2 years from 12/17/2010. (Tax Increase Prevention
and Reconciliation Act of 2005, Pub. L. 109-222; Tax Relief, Unemployment
Insurance Reauthorization and Job Creation Act of 2010, Pub. L. 111-312).

Zenz v. Quinlivan

213 F.2d 914 (6th Cir. 1954).

■ Before MILLER, CIRCUIT JUDGE, and GOURLEY and STARR, DISTRICT
JUDGES.

■ GOURLEY, DISTRICT JUDGE. The appeal relates to the interpretation of
Section [302(b)(1)] . . . and poses the question—Is a distribution of substantially all of the accumulated earnings and surplus of a corporation, which
are not necessary to the conduct of the business of the corporation, in re-

demption of all outstanding shares of stock of said corporation owned by one person *essentially equivalent to the distribution of a taxable dividend under the Internal Revenue Code?*

The District Court answered in the affirmative and sustained a deficiency assessment by the Commissioner of Internal Revenue.

[W]e believe the judgment should be reversed. . .

Appellant is the widow of the person who was the motivating spirit behind the closed corporation which engaged in the business of excavating and laying of sewers. Through death of her husband she became the owner of all shares of stock issued by the corporation. She operated the business until remarriage, when her second husband assumed the management. As a result of a marital rift, separation, and final divorce, taxpayer sought to dispose of her company to a competitor who was anxious to eliminate competition.

Prospective buyer did not want to assume the tax liabilities which it was believed were inherent in the accumulated earnings and profits of the corporation. To avoid said profits and earnings as a source of future taxable dividends, buyer purchased part of taxpayer's stock for cash. Three weeks later, after corporate reorganization and corporate action, the corporation redeemed the balance of taxpayer's stock, purchasing the same as treasury stock which absorbed substantially all of the accumulated earnings and surplus of the corporation.

Taxpayer, in her tax return, invoked Section [302(a)] of the Internal Revenue Code . . . as constituting a cancellation or redemption by a corporation of all the stock of a particular shareholder, and therefore was not subject to being treated as a distribution of a taxable dividend.

The District Court sustained the deficiency assessment of the Commissioner that the amount received from accumulated earnings and profits was ordinary income since the stock redeemed by the corporation was "at such time and in such manner as to make the redemption thereof essentially equivalent to the distribution of a taxable dividend" under [§§ 302(b)(1) and (d)] of the Code.

The District Court's findings were premised upon the view that taxpayer employed a circuitous approach in an attempt to avoid the tax consequences which would have attended the outright distribution of the surplus to the taxpayer by the declaration of a taxable dividend. . .

Nevertheless, the general principle is well settled that a taxpayer has the legal right to decrease the amount of what otherwise would be his taxes or altogether avoid them, by means which the law permits. . . The taxpayer's motive to avoid taxation will not establish liability if the transaction does not do so without it. . .

The question accordingly presented is not whether the overall transaction, admittedly carried out for the purpose of avoiding taxes, actually avoided taxes which would have been incurred if the transaction had taken a different form, but whether the sale constituted a taxable dividend or the sale of a capital asset. . .

It is a salutary fact that Section [302(a)] is an exception to Section [316] that all distributions of earning and profits are taxable as a dividend.

The basic precept underlying the capital gains theory of taxation as distinguished from ordinary income tax is the concept that a person who has developed an enterprise in which earnings have been accumulated over a period of years should not be required to expend the ordinary income tax rate in the one year when he withdraws from his enterprise and realizes his gain.

Common logic dictates that a fair basis of measuring income is not determined upon the profits on hand in the year of liquidation but is properly attributable to each year in which the profits were gained.

We cannot concur with the legal proposition enunciated by the District Court that a corporate distribution can be essentially equivalent to a taxable dividend even though that distribution extinguishes the shareholder's interest in the corporation. To the contrary, we are satisfied that where the taxpayer effects a redemption which completely extinguishes the taxpayer's interest in the corporation, and does not retain any beneficial interest whatever, that such transaction is not the equivalent of the distribution of a taxable dividend as to him. . .

The statutory concept of dividend is a distribution out of earnings and profits, and normally it is proportionate to shares and leaves the shareholder holding his shares as his capital investment. . .

Complete and partial liquidations are treated for the purpose of the statute, as sales with a consequent measure of gain or loss, even though the proceeds may to some extent be derived from earnings. . .

[T]he question as to whether the distribution in connection with the cancellation or the redemption of said stock is essentially equivalent to the distribution of a taxable dividend under the Internal Revenue Code and Treasury Regulation must depend upon the circumstances of each case.

Since the intent of the taxpayer was to bring about a complete liquidation of her holdings and to become separated from all interest in the corporation, the conclusion is inevitable that the distribution of the earnings and profits by the corporation in payment for said stock was not made at such time and in such manner as to make the distribution and cancellation or redemption thereof essentially equivalent to the distribution of a taxable dividend.

In view of the fact that the application of [§§ 302(b)(1) and (d)] of the Internal Revenue Code contemplates that the shareholder receiving the distribution will remain in the corporation, the circumstances of this proceeding militate against treating taxpayer's sale as a distribution of a taxable dividend.

We do not feel that a taxpayer should be penalized for exercising legal means to secure a tax advantage. The conduct of this taxpayer does not appear to contravene the purport or congressional intent of the provisions of the Internal Revenue Act which taxpayer invoked.

We conclude that under the facts and circumstances of the present case the District Court was in error, and the taxpayer is not liable as a distributee of a taxable dividend under [§§ 302(b)(1) and (d)] of the Internal Revenue Code.

The decision and judgment of the District Court is reversed and the case remanded with instructions to enter judgment in accordance with this opinion.

NOTES

1. Suppose Corporation X, wholly owned by Mr. Doe, has a net worth of $1 million, allocated as follows: $600,000 in operating assets needed in the business, $200,000 in securities, and $200,000 in cash. Doe's basis in his stock is $300,000. Buyer Corp. is willing to purchase the operating assets of X but has only $700,000. Doe is unwilling to sell 7/10 of the business to Buyer on the condition that Buyer will later cause X to redeem Doe's remaining shares, and Buyer is unwilling to purchase assets not within corporate form. How would you design a transaction that would ensure Doe a long-term capital gain of $700,000?

2. This case has proved helpful to lawyers, who create transactions that "*Zenz* a shareholder out."

3. How much pressure do taxpayers similar to the parties in *Zenz* feel in the post-2003 Act world (where dividends are taxed at the long term capital gains rate) to pursue the multi-step approach to selling a business without triggering dividends for the parties currently or in the future?

Grove v. Commissioner

490 F.2d 241 (2d Cir. 1973).

■ Before KAUFMAN, CHIEF JUDGE, and KILKENNY* and OAKES, CIRCUIT JUDGES.

■ KAUFMAN, CHIEF JUDGE. We are called upon, once again, to wrestle with the tangled web that is the Internal Revenue Code and decipher the often intricate and ingenious strategies devised by taxpayers to minimize their tax burdens. We undertake this effort mindful that taxpayer ingenuity, al-

---

*Of the United States Court of Appeals for the Ninth Circuit, sitting by designation.

though channelled into an effort to reduce or eliminate the incidence of taxation, is ground for neither legal nor moral opprobrium. As Learned Hand so eloquently stated, "any one may so arrange his affairs that his taxes shall be as low as possible; he is not bound to choose that pattern which will best pay the Treasury; there is not even a patriotic duty to increase one's taxes. . ." Helvering v. Gregory, 69 F.2d 809, 810 (2d Cir. 1934), *aff'd*, 293 U. S. 465 . . . (1935).

The case before us involves charitable contributions to an educational institution. It is becoming increasingly apparent that colleges and universities must engage in extensive fund-raising if they are to continue to exist and provide quality education. In their efforts to induce alumni to make substantial contributions, these institutions have devised interesting gift plans which offer attractive, and legal, tax advantages to the donor. Philip Grove, a successful engineer, was one who responded to the needs of his alma mater, Rensselaer Polytechnic Institute ("RPI"). Thus, in 1954, he began making annual donations to RPI of 165 to 250 shares of Grove Shepherd Wilson & Kruge, Inc. ("the Corporation"), a closely held corporation of which he is majority shareholder, vice-president, and a director. In each instance, Grove retained a life interest in any income earned from his gift and limited his charitable contribution deduction to the value of the remainder interest received by RPI. Despite the absence of any prearranged agreement between Grove and RPI, each year between 1954 and 1964 RPI successfully offered individual groups of shares to the Corporation for redemption. RPI then invested the redemption proceeds in income-producing securities and made quarterly disbursements to Grove of any income received. Grove reported any federally-taxed items on his personal income tax returns for the year of receipt.

The Commissioner of Internal Revenue refused to approve these arrangements. Instead, he assessed deficiencies in Grove's income taxes for the years 1963 and 1964, contending that Grove had employed RPI as a tax-free conduit for withdrawing funds from the Corporation and that redemption payments by the Corporation to RPI were in reality constructive dividend payments to Grove. Grove successfully challenged the deficiency determinations in the Tax Court, and the Commissioner appealed. We affirm.

I.

. . . Philip Grove received an engineering degree in 1924 from Rensselaer Polytechnic Institute, a private, tax-exempt educational institution. . . [H]e founded what is now Grove Shepherd Wilson & Kruge, Inc. and at all times since has controlled a majority of its shares. The balance of the Corporation's shares, with the exception of those held by RPI, are owned by officers and employees of the Corporation or their relatives.

The Corporation's business is building airfields, highways, tunnels, canals, and other heavy construction projects. . . These projects usually involve the investment of large sums of money over an extended period of time and involve a high degree of risk. Since, in this industry, contract payments normally are made only after specified levels of progress are achieved, a firm must always commit substantial amounts of its own funds, whether borrowed or internally generated, to a project. Moreover, a company can determine an acceptable contract price based only on its best estimate of the cost to complete the project. A bad "guess" or unforeseen contingency may require a firm to complete a project while incurring a loss... To protect against such adverse developments, successful firms seek to maintain liquidity by holding ample cash or other assets easily converted to cash. One method of conserving cash, adopted by the Corporation, is to retain all earnings and refrain from paying dividends.

As we have noted, RPI, like all universities and colleges, pursued its alumni with a wide variety of contribution plans. One plan employed "life income funds" and its terms were simple. An alumnus would make a gift of securities to RPI and retain a life interest in the income from the donated securities. Whatever dividends and interest were paid during the donor's life would belong to the donor, while any capital appreciation would inure to RPI. Upon the death of the donor, RPI would obtain full title to the securities.

In 1954, Dr. Livingston Houston, RPI's president, suggested to Grove that he make a gift under the "life income funds" plan. Grove explained that his only significant holdings were shares of his own corporation, but expressed a willingness to donate some of these shares under the plan, with certain qualifications. The Corporation, he stated, could not agree to any obligation or understanding to redeem shares held by RPI. This condition, of course, stemmed from a fear that RPI might seek redemption at a time when the Corporation was hard pressed for cash, which, as we have noted, was an asset crucial to a company in the heavy construction business. Moreover, since Grove at that time was unsure of RPI's money-management qualifications, he further conditioned his gift on a requirement that if RPI disposed of the shares, any proceeds would be invested and managed by an established professional firm.

RPI found these terms acceptable and on December 30, 1954, Grove made an initial gift of 200 shares, valued at $25,560...

On the same day, the Corporation and RPI signed a minority shareholder agreement. RPI agreed not . . . "in any way [to] dispose of the whole or any part of the common stock of the Corporation now or hereafter owned . . . until [RPI] shall have first offered the Corporation the opportunity to purchase said shares. . ." The redemption price was established at book value of the shares as noted on the Corporation's most recent certified financial statement prior to the offer. Pursuant to the contract, the Corporation was "entitled(but not obligated) to purchase all or any part of the shares of stock so offered." If the Corporation did not exercise its option to purchase within sixty days, RPI could transfer the shares to any other party and the Corporation's right of first refusal would not subsequently attach to such transferred shares.[3]

The 1954 gift was the first in a series of annual contributions to RPI by Grove. From 1954 to 1968, Grove donated to RPI between 165 and 250 shares of the Corporation each year, reaching a cumulative total of 2,652 shares, subject to terms substantially similar to those noted earlier.

Generally, RPI offered donated shares to the Corporation for redemption, between one and two years after they were donated by Grove. The transactions followed a similar pattern. On each occasion, the Finance Committee of RPI's Board of Trustees first authorized the sale of specific shares of the Corporation. RPI's treasurer or controller would then write to Sidney Houck, the Corporation's treasurer, informing him of RPI's desire to dispose of the shares. Upon receipt of this letter, Houck would call a special meeting of the Corporation's board of directors to consider whether or not to exercise the Corporation's right of first refusal. The Board would adopt a resolution authorizing redemption [and the shares were redeemed].

At the time of the first redemption, in December, 1955, RPI opened an investment account at the Albany, New York, office of Merrill Lynch, Pierce, Fenner & Beane ("Merrill Lynch"). The account was captioned "Rensselaer Polytechnic Institute (Philip H. Grove Fund) Account." In accordance with Grove's wishes concerning the management of disposition proceeds, RPI authorized Merrill Lynch to act directly upon investment recommendations made by Scudder, Stevens, & Clark, Grove's personal investment adviser. RPI deposited the proceeds of each redemption transaction into this account which, pursuant to Scudder, Stevens & Clark's instructions, were generally invested in securities of large corporations whose shares traded on organized stock exchanges. . . RPI, in turn, made quarterly remittances to Grove, accompanied by an analysis of all account transactions.

On his personal income tax return for 1963, Grove reported as taxable income dividends of $4,939.28 and interest of $2,535.73 paid to him by RPI from the Merrill Lynch account. For 1964, Grove reported $6,096.05 in dividends and $3,540.81 in interest. The Commissioner, however, assessed deficiencies in Grove's taxable income for these years, asserting that Grove "realized additional dividends in the amounts of $29,000 and $25,800 in 1963 and 1964, respectively, as the result of the redemption of stock by Grove Shepherd Wilson & Kruge, Inc." . . .

II.

The Commissioner's view of this case is relatively simple. In essence, we are urged to disregard the actual form of the Grove–RPI–Corporation donations and redemptions and to rewrite the actual events so that Grove's

---

[3] Other minority shareholders of the Corporation signed similar agreements, which, in effect put in writing the Corporation's practice of redeeming, when financial conditions permitted, and minority-owner shares offered to it, for example, by a departing employee or a deceased employee's widow.

tax liability is seen in a wholly different light. Support for this position, it is argued, flows from the Supreme Court's decision in Commissioner v. Court Holding Co., 324 U.S. 331 . . . (1945), which, in language familiar to law students, cautions that "[t]he incidence of taxation depends upon the substance of a transaction. . . To permit the true nature of a transaction to be disguised by mere formalisms, which exist solely to alter tax liabilities, would seriously impair the effective administration of the tax policies of Congress." Id. at 334. . . In an effort to bring the instant case within this language, the Commissioner insists that whatever the appearance of the transactions here under consideration, their "true nature" is quite different. He maintains that Grove, with the cooperation of RPI, withdrew substantial funds from the Corporation and manipulated them in a manner designed to produce income for his benefit. In the Commissioner's view, the transaction is properly characterized as a redemption by the Corporation of Grove's, not RPI's shares, followed by a cash gift to RPI by Grove. This result, it is said, more accurately reflects "economic reality."

The Commissioner's motives for insisting upon this formulation are easily understood once its tax consequences are examined. Although Grove reported taxable dividends and interest received from the Merrill Lynch account on his 1963 and 1964 tax returns, amounts paid by the Corporation to redeem the donated shares from RPI were not taxed upon distribution. If, however, the transactions are viewed in the manner suggested by the Commissioner, the redemption proceeds would be taxable as income to Grove. Moreover, because the redemptions did not in substance alter Grove's relationship to the Corporation—he continued throughout to control a majority of the outstanding shares—the entire proceeds would be taxed as a dividend payment at high, progressive ordinary-income rates, rather than as a sale of shares, at the fixed, and relatively low, capital gains rate. . .

Clearly, then, the stakes involved are high. We do not quarrel with the maxim that substance must prevail over form, but this proposition marks the beginning, not the end, of our inquiry. . . Each case requires detailed consideration of its unique facts. Here, our aim is to determine whether Grove's gifts of the Corporation's shares to RPI prior to redemption should be given independent significance or whether they should be regarded as meaningless intervening steps in a single, integrated transaction designed to avoid tax liability by the use of mere formalisms.

The guideposts for our analysis are well marked by earlier judicial encounters with this problem. "The law with respect to gifts of appreciated property is well established. A gift of appreciated property does not result in income to the donor so long as he gives the property away absolutely and parts with title thereto before the property gives rise to income by way of sale." Carrington v. Commissioner, 476 F.2d 704 (5th Cir. 1973) quoting The Humacid Co., 42 T. C. 894, 913 (1964). As noted below by the Tax Court, the Commissioner here "does not contend that the gifts of stock by [Grove] to RPI in 1961 and 1962 were sham transactions, or that they were not completed gifts when made." If Grove made a valid, binding, and irrevocable gift of the Corporation's shares to RPI, it would be the purest fiction to treat the redemption proceeds as having actually been received by Grove. The Tax Court concluded that the gift was complete and irrevocable when made. The Commissioner conceded as much and we so find.[9]

It is argued, however, that notwithstanding the conceded validity of the gifts, other circumstances establish that Grove employed RPI merely as a convenient conduit for withdrawing funds from the Corporation for his personal use without incurring tax liability. The Commissioner would have us infer from the systematic nature of the gift-redemption cycle that Grove and RPI reached a mutually beneficial understanding: RPI would permit Grove to use its tax-exempt status to drain funds from the Corporation in return for a donation of a future interest in such funds.

We are not persuaded by this argument and the totality of the facts and circumstances lead us to a contrary conclusion. Grove testified before the Tax Court concerning the circumstances of these gifts. The court, based on the evidence and the witnesses' credibility, specifically found that "[t]here was no informal agreement between [Grove] and RPI that RPI would offer the stock in question to the corporation for redemption or that, if offered, the corporation would redeem it." . . . It cannot seriously be contended that the Tax Court's findings here are "clearly erroneous" and no tax liability can be predicated upon a nonexistent agreement between Grove and RPI or by a fictional one created by the Commissioner.

Grove, of course, owned a substantial majority of the Corporation's shares. His vote alone was sufficient to insure redemption of any shares offered by RPI. But such considerations, without more, are insufficient to permit the Commissioner to ride roughshod over the actual understanding found by the Tax Court to exist between the donor and the donee. Behrend v. United States (4th Cir. 1972), 73–1 USTC para. 9123, is particularly instructive. There, two brothers donated preferred shares of a corporation jointly controlled by them to a charitable foundation over which they also exercised control. The preferred shares were subsequently redeemed from the foundation by the corporation and the Commissioner sought to tax the redemption as a corporate dividend payment to the brothers. The court, in denying liability, concluded that although "it was understood that the corporation would at intervals take up the preferred according to its financial ability . . ., this factor did not convert into a constructive dividend the proceeds of the redemption . . . [because] the gifts were absolutely perfected before the corporation redeemed the stock." Id.

. . . Although the Corporation desired a right of first refusal on minority shares—understandably so, in order to reduce the possibility of unre-

---

[9] The Commissioner might have argued that at least that portion of the redemption proceeds allocable to Grove's retained life income interest was taxable as a dividend. He chose not to do so and the Tax Court "expressed no opinion upon the question, if it were properly presented, whether petitioner derived taxable income upon the redemption of stock to the extent of the life estate which he retained...." Since the Commissioner has bypassed this aspect, it would be inappropriate in our discussions of the gifts to attach any special significance to the retained life interest feature.

lated, outside ownership interests—it assumed no obligation to redeem any shares so offered. In the absence of such an obligation, the Commissioner's contention that Grove's initial donation was only the first step in a prearranged series of transactions is little more than wishful thinking grounded in a shaky foundation. . .

We are not so naive as to believe that tax considerations played no role in Grove's planning. But foresight and planning do not transform a non-taxable event into one that is taxable. Were we to adopt the Commissioner's view, we would be required to recast two actual transactions—a gift by Grove to RPI and a redemption from RPI by the Corporation—into two completely fictional transactions—a redemption from Grove by the Corporation and a gift by Grove to RPI. Based upon the facts as found by the Tax Court, we can discover no basis for elevating the Commissioner's "form" over that employed by the taxpayer in good faith. . . In the absence of any supporting facts in the record we are unable to adopt the Commissioner's view; to do so would be to engage in a process of decision that is arbitrary, capricious and ultimately destructive of traditional notions of judicial review. We decline to embark on such a course.

Accordingly, the judgment of the Tax Court is affirmed.

■ [Dissenting opinion of OAKES, CIRCUIT JUDGE, omitted].

NOTES

1. How are the stakes in this case (*Grove*), different from one in which a taxpayer receives a distribution from a corporation and the question is whether the distribution is a dividend or proceeds from a redemption taxable as a sale or exchange? Which scenario is more significantly impacted by the 2003 Act changes in taxation of dividends?

2. The court in *Grove* places great importance upon the absence of an agreement by which the corporation would be legally obligated to redeem the shares donated to RPI. Is this importance justified? Of what value would the shares be to RPI if they were not redeemed?

The Second Circuit may have significantly narrowed the scope of *Grove* in Blake v. Commissioner, 697 F.2d 473 (2d Cir. 1982). But see Daniel D. Palmer, 62 T.C. 684 (1974), *aff'd*, 523 F.2d 1308 (8th Cir. 1975).

vi. REDEMPTION OR SHAM—§ 304

H.J. Heinz Co. v. United States

76 Fed. Cl. 570 (Ct. Fed. Cl. 2007).

■ ALLEGRA, JUDGE:

"A given result at the end of a straight path is not made a different result because reached by following a devious path."[1]

All tax students are familiar with the concept of "basis," which, in the income tax law, is the touchstone for measuring income and loss. Generally speaking, it is basis that prevents the double taxation of income reflected in a property's cost, by allowing that cost to be recovered, tax-free, upon the asset's disposition. And it is basis, again, that measures the loss realized if the seller recovers less than its investment in property. Sometimes, the process for determining basis is straight-forward, with the amount readily traceable, for example, to specific costs incurred by the taxpayer with respect to the asset being sold. Other times, however, the origins of basis are more obscure, particularly, when the tax law attributes costs previously incurred by a taxpayer to the sold asset. Those attribution rules are fairly complicated, providing opportunities both for bona fide tax planning and undue manipulation of the tax system. Sometimes it falls to a court to discern which of these has occurred.

. . . Plaintiffs seek a refund of $42,586,967. At issue is whether H.J. Heinz Credit Company (HCC), a subsidiary of the H.J. Heinz Company (Heinz), may deduct a capital loss of $124,134,189 on a sale of 175,000 shares of Heinz stock in May 1995. In 1994, HCC purchased 3,500,000 shares of Heinz stock, 3,325,000 shares of which were transferred to Heinz in January of 1995 in exchange for a convertible note issued by Heinz. Heinz asserts that this was a redemption which should be taxed as a dividend, and that HCC's basis in the redeemed stock should be added to its basis in the 175,000 shares it retained. HCC sold the latter stock in May of 1995 and, in plaintiff's view, recognized a capital loss arising from the increase in basis that occurred upon the earlier redemption. That loss, plaintiffs argue, should then be carried back to reduce their taxes in their 1994, 1993 and 1992 taxable years.

Not so, defendant argues, asserting that Heinz did not, in fact, effectuate a redemption of stock from HCC. In this regard, it asseverates that a redemption did not occur because HCC's ownership of the 3,325,000 shares of Heinz stock was transitory and should be disregarded. It further claims that no redemption occurred because Heinz had no business purpose for interposing a subsidiary between itself and the shareholders from whom HCC purchased stock, save to engineer an artificial tax loss. And, finally, it contends that while Heinz structured the second purchase as an exchange for property under section 317(b) of the Internal Revenue Code of 1986, the steps of the transaction should be collapsed under the so-called "step trans-

---

[1] Minn. Tea Co. v. Helvering, 302 U.S. 609, 613 (1938)

action doctrine," with Heinz again viewed as having repurchased its stock directly from the outside investors. As such, defendant contends, the basis in the 3,325,000 shares allegedly "redeemed" by Heinz should not be added to the 175,000 shares that HCC retained, with the effect that no capital loss was produced upon the sale of the latter shares.

I. FINDINGS OF FACT

. . .

A.

Heinz, a Pennsylvania corporation, is the common parent of the affiliated group of corporations known as the Heinz Consolidated Group (Heinz Consolidated Group), which corporations filed consolidated income tax returns for the years in question. The successor to a food business founded in 1869 by Henry J. Heinz, Heinz manufactures and markets processed food products worldwide, directly and through subsidiaries.

Until the early 1980s, Heinz maintained a corporate policy of directly financing its domestic subsidiaries' working capital needs because it could borrow at more favorable interest rates than its subsidiaries. This policy, however, had what Heinz perceived as negative state tax implications in certain states—although the subsidiaries could deduct interest payments made to Heinz, the latter was required to treat those payments as taxable income. [citation omitted]. In 1983, Heinz began studying a proposal to establish a Delaware-based financing company that would assume Heinz's financing activities. Under this plan, all of Heinz's subsidiaries would obtain financing from, and make all payments (including interest) to, this Delaware-based financing company, with interest income from the financing company being "repatriated" to Heinz by means of intercorporate dividends. Under this scenario, the Delaware subsidiary's income would be exempt from Delaware tax, . . . in most states, the subsidiaries would continue to take deductions for interest payments made to the new financing company; and Heinz would not experience a corresponding increase in its taxable income because many states—including Heinz's home state of Pennsylvania—did not tax intercorporate dividends.

Ultimately deciding to effectuate this plan, on September 15, 1983, Heinz established the H.J. Heinz Credit Company (HCC), a wholly-owned Delaware corporation with 1,000 shares of stock. That same year HCC began lending money to the members of the Heinz Consolidated Group, as well as several Heinz foreign subsidiaries. HCC, however, had no office or employees of its own, with Heinz essentially making decisions for its subsidiary at its corporate offices in Pittsburgh. By the mid–1980s, several state taxing authorities, including Pennsylvania, began questioning the use of Delaware investment companies as a tax planning strategy. Concerned with this trend, in a memorandum dated November 29, 1984, Catherine A. Caponi, Heinz's Manager for State Taxes, warned:

While [the establishment of an independent financing company] is an excellent tax planning strategy, in order to insure its viability, the Delaware sub must have sufficient substance and nexus in Delaware. If there is little or no substance and all activities are actually directed from and take place in Pennsylvania, the Delaware entity may not sustain itself under scrutiny by the Commonwealth of Pennsylvania. The two companies could be collapsed and treated as one company for Pennsylvania tax purposes.

(Emphasis in original). Although Ms. Caponi was optimistic that HCC had established a sufficient nexus with Delaware to create a " 'taxable' situation in the state," she indicated that Heinz had some exposure on this issue because "the majority, if not all, of [HCC's] corporate activity/accounting takes place at [Heinz] World Headquarters in Pennsylvania" and "HCC pays no management fee to World Headquarters for the services provided." She noted that Heinz's Pennsylvania tax counsel had suggested that it draft a service agreement "detailing the services to be performed by World Headquarters personnel for HCC," and stipulate an "arm's length fee" which HCC would pay in return for these services. But, for reasons unexplained, company officials did not heed her advice. Heinz's legal and tax counsel remained concerned and periodically repeated their warnings regarding HCC's status.

B.

In late 1985, John C. Crowe, Vice President for Tax of Heinz, considered transferring to HCC twelve "safe harbor" leases Heinz had entered into in 1982 and 1983, in order to shield future income generated by these leases from taxation in Pennsylvania. . .

In a memorandum dated May 12, 1986, Mr. Crowe described how the transfer of the leases should occur. He noted that while Heinz had a tax basis in the leased property of zero, the property was subject to nonrecourse debt of approximately $150 million. This was a bad combination, he indicated, for if Heinz were to transfer the property to HCC, it would experience a gain of $150 million. [section 357(c)]. Although this gain would be deferred under the federal income tax laws, it would be immediately taxable in Pennsylvania. Instead, Mr. Crowe recommended that Heinz simultaneously transfer an asset to HCC in which Heinz had a tax basis of more than $150 million, thereby preventing any gain from being realized upon the transfer of the leases. . . [He] ultimately conclude[ed] that the stock of HCC itself was a "perfect candidate."[citation omitted]. He observed that, as of March 31, 1986, Heinz had a tax basis of roughly $385 million in HCC. He suggested that Heinz form a new subsidiary in Delaware and "as soon as possible" transfer its interests in the 1982 safe harbor leases and "a portion of [Heinz's] ownership in HCC" to the new company, in return for stock of the new company and, most importantly, the assumption of the safe harbor lease liabilities. Mr. Crowe further concluded that in May 1987, the 1983 safe harbor leases should be transferred to the new subsidiary, along with the balance of HCC stock in return for the assumption of liabilities on the 1983 leases.

On July 10, 1986, Heinz formed Heinz Leasing Company (Heinz Leasing), a Delaware corporation, as a wholly-owned, first-tier subsidiary. On July 14, 1986, Heinz transferred to Heinz Leasing ten of the aforementioned "safe harbor" leases, as well as 50 percent of the issued and outstanding stock of HCC. On October 7, 1987, Heinz transferred to Heinz Leasing the two remaining safe harbor leases and the remaining 50 percent of the issued an outstanding stock of HCC. On January 21, 1988, Heinz Leasing sold one share of HCC back to Heinz for par value.

HCC continued to lend money to members of the Heinz Consolidated Group and associated foreign subsidiaries. After the transfer of the leases and stock to Heinz Leasing, counsel at Heinz remained concerned that HCC would be viewed by state taxing authorities as lacking substance. . .

On March 2, 1989, Ms. Caponi reported that the Pennsylvania Department of Revenue was about to audit Heinz's tax returns for its fiscal year 1987. She expressed concern that considerable taxes would be asserted if the state auditors either treated Heinz, Heinz Leasing and HCC as a single entity, or treated Heinz Leasing and HCC as doing all their business in Pennsylvania (rather than Delaware). . .

These concerns proved valid. . .

C.

Meanwhile, like many public companies, Heinz engaged regularly in the purchase of its own stock, spending an average of more than $170 million per year on such stock primarily to manage its earnings per share. In October of 1991, the Heinz board of directors announced a program (the 1991 repurchase program), under which the company would repurchase 10,000,000 shares of its common stock on the open market. This stock was to be deposited into Heinz's treasury to support employee retirement and savings plans, certain cumulative preferred stock holders, and for other corporate purposes. This program proved highly successful—[and the] Heinz board of directors ratified [a proposal to buy more Heinz stock], and the new repurchase program went into effect (the 1993 repurchase program). . .

D.

Between August 11, 1994, and November 15, 1994, HCC purchased 3,500,000 shares of Heinz common stock in the public market for $129,175,400, including commissions, and paid an additional $1,807,703 in investment banking and legal fees in connection with the stock purchase. Throughout the repurchase process, HCC kept Heinz appraised of its stock purchases and the status of its Morgan Guaranty loans. At the January 10, 1995, Heinz executive committee meeting, Mr. Williams informed the committee that HCC had purchased 3,500,000 shares of Heinz common stock pursuant to the 1994 repurchase program, and recommended that Heinz offer to purchase 3,325,000 of those shares from HCC. According to the minutes (as well as presentation slides used at the meeting), the purpose of this transaction ostensibly was to "move the shares into the Company's treasury where they would be available for stock option exercises and other transactions requiring shares and would also enable the Company to discontinue paying dividends on the shares that it purchases from HCC." Mr. Williams set forth a detailed statement of the proposed transaction, recommending that the shares be transferred on January 17, 1995, at a price equal to the January 13, 1995, closing price of Heinz common stock on the New York Stock Exchange, and that the purchase be funded by Heinz issuing to HCC a "zero coupon convertible debt instrument." In his presentation to the board, Mr. Williams also indicated that "due to the method of accounting presently applied to [HCC's] shares, the purchase from [HCC] would have no impact on reported results and would require no public disclosures." The Heinz executive committee approved this recommendation.

. . . HCC accepted Heinz's offer, and transferred 3,325,000 shares of Heinz common stock to Heinz on January 18, 1995. From the time it acquired the Heinz stock through January 18, 1995, HCC received approximately $1.7 million in dividends on the Heinz stock.

In consideration for the transfer, Heinz issued to HCC a subordinated convertible note, zero percent coupon, due January 18, 2002, paying $197,402,412.78 at maturity (the Note). [citation omitted] At the option of the holder, the Note could be converted into 3,510,000 shares of Heinz common stock at any time from January 18, 1998 (three years after issuance) until maturity. [citation omitted] Heinz was the sole obligor and guarantor on the Note. . . [F]rom the time it issued, the Note was considered a "restricted security" within the meaning of 17 C.F.R. section 230.144(a)(3) (1995), as its holder could have sold it only in a private placement or in a transaction that otherwise qualified as exempt from the registration requirements of Federal and state securities laws. . .

Following the redemption, HCC retained 175,000 shares of Heinz stock. At a meeting of the Heinz board of directors held on April 12, 1995, Mr. Williams advised that the Heinz executive committee was recommending approval of a proposed sale by HCC of the 175,000 shares to an unrelated third party. The minutes indicate that Mr. Williams reported that "the shares would be sold at current market price less a discount to be negotiated because the shares would not initially be registered under the Securities Act of 1933." At the end of its taxable year ended April 27, 1995, HCC's net worth (the excess of asset book value over liabilities) was nearly $2 billion, with net income of approximately $277 million. In a sale that closed on May 2, 1995, HCC sold the remaining 175,000 shares to AT&T Investment Management Corp. (AT&T), an unrelated third party, in a private placement for a discounted rate of $39.8064 per share, or $6,966,120, in cash. [citation omitted] Heinz incurred $117,156 in costs as a result of this transaction; HCC also received and paid a variety of legal and management fees to Heinz in connection with the transfer. . . On November 29, 1995, Heinz Leasing was merged into HCC, leaving Heinz the sole owner of the issued and outstanding stock of HCC. On April 18, 1998, after receiving advice from Goldman Sachs, HCC exercised its right to convert the Note and received 5,265,000 shares of Heinz stock. [citation omitted] From the time of the redemption in January 1995 until the conversion right on the Note first became exercisable three years later, the price of Heinz stock more than doubled, from about $39 to $83 per share.

E.

. . . The parties apparently no longer dispute $43,569,763 of Heinz's amended 1995 net capital loss, which was carried back to the 1992 taxable year. The IRS, however, has disallowed the remaining $124,134,139 of the 1995 net capital loss, arguing, inter alia, that the transaction at issue lacked economic substance and a business purpose. It allowed only a capital loss carryback of $43,569,763 to 1992, and nothing to 1993 or 1994. On December 23, 2003, plaintiff filed the instant action. . .

II. DISCUSSION

If plaintiff is correct, transactions that, for financial accounting purposes, produced more than a $6 million profit, yielded, for tax purposes, a loss of over $124 million. Understanding how this might be the case requires a review of how the Code treats some intercorporate transactions.

Heinz's capital loss is deductible, if at all, under section 165 of the Code . . .

Under sections 1011 and 1012 of the Code, a taxpayer's basis in an item is generally its cost. See United States v. Chicago, B. & Q. R. Co., 412 U.S. 401, 406 n.7 (1973). The parties agree that the 3,325,000 shares that Heinz obtained from HCC had a basis in HCC's hands of $124.2 million. Heinz asserts that it "redeemed" these shares with the Note within the meaning of section 317(b) of the Code, which provides that "stock shall be treated as redeemed by a corporation if the corporation acquires its stock from a shareholder in exchange for property, whether or not the stock so acquired is cancelled, retired, or held as treasury stock." Defendant admits that if a true redemption occurred, it would be treated as a dividend under section 302(d) of the Code. [citation omitted] It further admits that if a true redemption occurred, and a dividend arose under section 302(d), the transfer of stock from HCC to Heinz did not reduce the former's equity position in the latter, so that the basis HCC had in the 3,325,000 shares would shift to HCC's remaining 175,000 shares. [citation omitted] And defendant acknowledges that if this shifting in basis occurred, HCC was entitled to deduct a huge capital loss upon the subsequent sale of those 175,000 shares to AT&T.

In the tax law, "if" is a colossal word. Should the transaction in which Heinz acquired the 3,325,000 shares actually be considered a redemption within the meaning of section 317(b)? If it is not, plaintiffs essentially concede that HCC's basis in the 3,325,000 shares did not shift to its remaining stock and that the subsequent sale of the latter stock did not produce a loss. In arguing for this result, defendant makes several points. First, it contends that no redemption occurred under section 317(b) because Heinz did not exchange property for the stock within the meaning of that section. Second, defendant asseverates that even if the transaction technically qualified as a "redemption" within the meaning of section 317(b), the transaction should not be treated as such because it lacked economic substance and had no bona fide business purpose other than to produce tax benefits; it was, in a word, a sham. Finally, it asserts that under the so-called "step transaction doctrine," the purchase of the stock by HCC and the exchange of the stock for the Note should be merged together and viewed as a direct purchase of the stock by Heinz.

As will be seen, in some ways it is difficult to differentiate these claims, all of which are different manifestations of the more general "substance over form" concept... Yet, while these various doctrines overlap, they also have different criteria that bring into relief the nuances of various transactions, as well as the importance of particular features therein...

A. Did HCC possess the benefits and burdens of the ownership of the Heinz stock?

Stock is redeemed under section 317(b) if the corporation acquires it in exchange for property... As noted, some redemptions are treated as sales under section 302, while others are treated as a payment of dividends. Distributions characterized in the latter fashion are commonly called "section 301 distributions," taking their name from the controlling Code provision...

Section 317(b) presupposes that the individual or corporation receiving property from the redeeming corporation, in fact, possesses the stock being redeemed. In arguing that this requirement was not met here, defendant asserts that HCC had a transitory interest in the Heinz shares that should not be respected for tax purposes because it did not have the benefits and burdens of that ownership. In analogous situations, courts have held that requirements of the reorganization provisions of the Code that require the continued possession of stock were not met where ownership of stock by a party "was transitory and without real substance." Helvering v. Bashford, 302 U.S. 454, 458 (1938) ... In making the latter determination, courts often have focused on whether the entity claiming ownership of stock or another item possessed the "burdens and benefits of ownership." See Grodt & McKay Realty, Inc. v. Comm'r of Internal Revenue, 77 T.C. 1221, 1236–37 (1981) ... Among the factors relevant to this determination are: (i) whether the purchaser bears the risk of loss and opportunity for gain; (ii) which party receives the right to any current income from the property; (iii) whether legal title has passed; and (iv) whether an equity interest was acquired in the property. [citation omitted] The mere record of stock ownership is but the starting point in this analysis—one consideration among many in determining whether one is the owner of property. [citation omitted] Indeed, none of these factors is necessarily controlling; the incidence of ownership, rather, depends upon all the facts and circumstances...

In the case sub judice, several factors suggest that HCC's ownership of the Heinz stock was more than notional. HCC incurred significant indebtedness to generate the funds that were used to purchase the Heinz stock on the market, indebtedness that was not guaranteed by its parent. Further, unlike in other cases, HCC received dividends on the stock during the period of its possession... And HCC, and not Heinz, bore the risk of loss and the opportunity for gain as to the value of the Heinz stock it possessed ... Moreover, while the evidence on this point is a bit mixed, on balance, it appears that HCC was under no preexisting obligation to distribute or disgorge any profits it received—either in the form of dividends received, gain realized on the sale, or otherwise—to its parent. Finally, although defendant implies otherwise, it is well-established that, absent a sham, the fact that the transactions sub judice involved a parent corporation and a wholly-owned subsidiary, while suggesting a need for close scrutiny, does not alone provide a basis for ignoring the other indicia of ownership here. See Comm'r of Internal Revenue v. Bollinger, 485 U.S. 340, 345 (1988); Nat'l Carbide Corp. v. Comm'r of Internal Revenue, 336 U.S. 422, 433–34 (1949); Moline Properties, Inc. v. Comm'r of Internal Revenue, 319 U.S. 436, 438–39 (1943)... Accordingly, and setting aside, briefly, other substance-over-form considerations, it appears preliminarily that HCC possessed the burdens and benefits associated with the Heinz stock and, to that extent, the later redemption qualified under section 317(b) ...

B. Was the transaction that gave rise to the capital loss here a sham?

The right of a taxpayer to arrange its affairs to minimize taxes is well-established... But to state this principle is not to decide the case. In Gregory, for example, the Court proceeded to disregard the taxpayer's carefully arranged corporate reorganization. In so doing, it asked: "[p]utting aside, then, the question of motive in respect of taxation altogether, and fixing the character of the proceeding by what actually occurred, what do we find?" *Gregory*, 293 U.S. at 469; *see also* Principal Life Ins. Co. v. United States, 70 Fed. Cl. 144, 145 (2006). Invoking another permutation of this substance-over-form concept, defendant asserts that the transaction in question was an economic sham and thus did not qualify as a redemption under section 317(b)...

As recently noted by this court, there are two predominant "tests" for identifying economic shams... The Fourth Circuit has adopted a two-prong standard for disregarding a transaction under the so-called "sham transaction doctrine," stating that "[t]o treat a transaction as a sham, the court must find that the taxpayer was motivated by no business purposes other than obtaining tax benefits ... and that the transaction has no economic substance because no reasonable possibility of a profit exists." Rice's Toyota World Inc. v. Comm'r of Internal Revenue, 752 F.2d 89, 91 (4th Cir. 1985) (emphasis added); see also Black & Decker Corp. v. Comm'r of Internal Revenue, 436 F.3d 431, 441 (4th Cir. 2006). As indicated in Keener, however, "[a] better approach to this sham analysis, which is more flexible and enjoys the support of a majority of the circuits, holds that 'the consideration of business purpose and economic substance are simply more precise factors to consider in the [determination of] whether the transaction had any practical economic effects other than the creation of income tax losses.' " *Keener*, 2007 WL 1180476, at *10 (quoting Sochin v. Comm'r of Internal Revenue, 843 F.2d 351, 354 (9th Cir), cert. denied, 488 U.S. 824 (1988)). [citation omitted] Critically, under the latter approach, a taxpayer must prove that its transaction was both purposeful and substantive—if proof in either regard is lacking, the transaction is a sham. As the Federal Circuit recently noted in Coltec Indus., Inc. v. United States, 454 F.3d 1340, 1355 n.14 (Fed. Cir. 2006), cert. denied, 127 S.Ct. 1261 (2007), this more demanding approach is more in accord with Frank Lyon Co. v. United States, 435 U.S. 561, 583–84 (1978), where the Supreme Court stated that a transaction will be accorded tax recognition only if it has "economic substance which is compelled or encouraged by business or regulatory realities, is imbued with tax-independent considerations, and is not shaped solely by tax-avoidance features that have meaningless labels attached."

At least the economic substance prong of the sham transaction doctrine is virtually identical to the doctrine that holds that a transaction which lacks economic substance should be disregarded for tax purposes. The latter concept was recently examined thoroughly by the Federal Circuit in Coltec, an opinion that offers a wealth of guidance. First, the court there made clear that "[w]hile the doctrine may well also apply if the taxpayer's sole subjective motivation is tax avoidance even if the transaction has economic substance, a lack of economic substance is sufficient to disqualify the transaction without proof that the taxpayer's sole motive is tax avoidance." *Coltec*, 454 F.3d at 1355 (citing Dow Chemical Co. v. United States, 435 F.3d 594, 599 (6th Cir. 2006) and *United Parcel Serv.*, 254 F.3d at 1014). Second, contrary to implications in plaintiffs' brief here, the Federal Circuit established that "when the taxpayer claims a deduction, it is the taxpayer who bears the burden of proving that the transaction has economic substance," noting further that the Court of Claims in Rothschild v. United States, 407 F.2d 404, 411 (Ct. Cl. 1969) (quoting Diggs v. Comm'r of Internal Revenue, 281 F.2d 326, 330 (2d Cir. 1960)) had described this burden as " 'unusually heavy,' " *Coltec*, 454 F.3d at 1355; see also In re CM Holdings, Inc., 301 F.3d 96, 102 (3d Cir. 2002). Third, citing *Gregory*, 293 U.S. at 469–70 and other cases, the Federal Circuit emphasized that "[w]hile the taxpayer's subjective motivation may be pertinent to the existence of a tax avoidance purpose," "the economic substance of a transaction must be viewed objectively, rather than subjectively." *Coltec*, 454 F.3d at 1356; see also Black & Decker, 436 F.3d at 441–42; In re CM Holdings, Inc., 301 F.3d at 103. Fourth, clarifying another point disputed by the parties here, the court explained that "the transaction to be analyzed is the one that gave rise to the alleged tax benefit," recognizing that "there is a material difference between structuring a real transaction in a particular way to provide a tax benefit (which is legitimate), and creating a transaction without a business purpose, in order to create a tax benefit (which is illegitimate)." 454 F.3d at 1356–57; *see also* Black & Decker, 436 F.3d at 441; Nicole Rose Corp. v. Comm'r of Internal Revenue, 320 F.3d 282, 284 (2d Cir. 2003). Finally, in words that resonate here, the Federal Circuit opined that "arrangements with subsidiaries that do not affect the economic interest of independent third parties deserve particularly close scrutiny." 454 F.3d at 1357.

So, with these lessons in mind, what do we have here? Plaintiffs have the burden of proving that the portion of the transaction in question that saw HCC acquire shares and then transfer them to Heinz had both a business purpose and economic substance. As to the former, plaintiffs assert that HCC acquired the stock as an investment and to add "substance" to its operations for state tax law purposes. Both claims have decidedly hollow rings.

Plaintiffs' assertion that HCC acquired the Heinz stock for investment purposes finds cosmetic support in the relevant corporate minutes, which mention this as a reason for approving the acquisition. However, any notion that this claim was authentic is belied, inter alia, by the testimony of Mr. Crowe, a Heinz vice president and its chief tax advisor, who admitted that, before HCC purchased any Heinz stock, Heinz planned on redeeming all but a small portion of that stock, with the residue stock being left with HCC only as part of a plan to produce the desired carryback losses. Indeed, as will be described in greater detail below, HCC had already hired Goldman Sachs to design the Note that would be exchanged for the Heinz stock at least six weeks before it acquired its first share. Moreover, the record suggests that HCC could not have reasonably viewed its temporary holding of the Heinz stock as a bona fide short-term investment. For one thing, the investment fundamentals of the transaction were all wrong—HCC acquired that stock on the open market at the then current price even though it knew that, unless the stock was registered, it would have to sell it in a private placement at a discount (which is what occurred). Moreover, HCC not only had to borrow funds and pay interest to effectuate this purchase, but incurred nearly $2 million in other expenses and fees in making the purchases, even though Heinz and HCC both knew that all but a small portion of the stock would be redeemed within a matter of months. See Boca Investerings P'ship v. United States, 314 F.3d 625, 631 (D.C. Cir. 2003), cert. denied, 540 U.S. 826 (2003) (rejecting alleged business purpose that "defies common sense from an economic standpoint"); N. Pac. Ry. Co. v. United States, 378 F.2d 686, 691 (Ct. Cl. 1967) (rejecting alleged investment motivation where stock could have been more economically held by parent). Ironically, the most damning testimony on this point came from plaintiffs' expert, Mr. Hatton. In explaining why he believed that it was not a foregone conclusion that HCC would exercise the stock conversion feature in the Note, Hr. Hatton emphasized how poorly Heinz's stock had fared in the three years prior to the transaction, noting that Heinz had "drastically underperformed the market." [citation omitted] Mr. Hatton further testified that the actual increases that occurred in Heinz's stock value in the three years following the issuance of the Note were "unforseen," adding that during this bull market period, Heinz "still underperformed versus the S & P 500." Lastly, HCC could not "invest" in the Heinz stock and also fully participate in the Heinz stock repurchase program. The main purpose of that program—to reacquire common shares to be held in the Heinz treasury to deal with stock options, preferred stock conversions and other corporate purposes—could not be accomplished so long as HCC held the Heinz stock in its treasury as an "investment," a fact verified by several witnesses. Moreover, unlike the shares held in its treasury, Heinz was obligated to pay dividends on the shares held by HCC, undercutting the impact that the repurchase would have on its equity standing. Of course, this was not a problem as the record indicates that, ab initio, plaintiffs had every intention of making sure that the shares ended up with the parent. For this and the others reasons discussed above, the court rejects the notion that a non-tax business purpose was served here by having HCC "invest" in its parent's stock.

Perhaps sensing this outcome, plaintiffs' banner assertion at trial was that HCC purchased the Heinz stock to bolster its "substance" as a Delaware-based corporation, so as to lessen the likelihood that it would be disregarded by state taxing officials. There are at least four major flaws in this assertion.

First, nothing in the record suggests that anyone associated with Heinz thought, at the time, that HCC's purchase of the Heinz stock would improve its stature as a Delaware holding company—there is no hint of this in the Heinz and HCC corporate minutes, the Heinz internal working papers, the series of memoranda prepared by Heinz tax officials detailing the steps that should be taken to bolster HCC's status, and even the documents discussing the Heinz stock purchase itself. Nothing whatsoever. It is thus fair to conclude that this claim is of relatively recent vintage, a fact that undercuts its legitimacy. . . Second, the record reveals that Heinz officials knew or should have known that the stock purchase would not improve HCC's status in prior taxable years. . . Internal documents tellingly reveal that Heinz officials knew full well that there was nothing that they could do in 1994 or 1995 to limit their exposure for prior taxable years, with Mr. Crowe, Heinz's primary tax manager, soberly stating that "[n]othing can be done about the lack of substance in prior years" and that "[w]e must simply hope that our luck holds." Third, the record demonstrates that Heinz officials knew or should have known that the stock acquisition would not improve HCC's status in fiscal year 1995 or thereafter. In fact, they knew that there very likely would not be such subsequent years because, according to testimony, Heinz was contemporaneously planning to have HCC cease its Delaware lending operations, such as they were. [citation omitted]

. . . Plaintiffs have not explained how they derived this conclusion—perhaps because they did not derive it at the time—nor have they cited a single case or authority suggesting that the transaction should have been the least bit helpful. . . This court will not don blinders to the realities of the transaction before it. Stripped of its veneer, the acquisition by HCC of the Heinz stock had one purpose, and one purpose alone—producing capital losses that could be carried back to wipe out prior capital gains. There was no other genuine business purpose. As such, under the prevailing standard, the transaction in question must be viewed as a sham—a transaction imbued with no significant tax-independent considerations, but rather characterized, at least in terms of HCC's participation, solely by tax-avoidance features. The tax advantage sought by Heinz via this sham must be denied. [citation omitted]

C. Does the step transaction doctrine require recharacterization of the transaction here?

There is yet another important reason for denying the losses claimed— the step transaction doctrine.

A purchase by one person cannot be transformed into a purchase by another by using the latter as a mere conduit through which to pass title. Two cases illustrate the contours of this rule. In Comm'r of Internal Revenue v. Court Holding Co., 324 U.S. 331 (1943), for example, the Supreme Court disregarded a transaction where a taxpayer, in order to avoid a large corporate income tax, transferred a building in the form of a liquidating dividend to two shareholders who, in turn, immediately conveyed the asset to a purchaser who had originally negotiated with the corporation to purchase the asset. *Id.* at 332; *see also Coltec Indus.*, 454 F.3d at 1352. In so ruling, the Court opined—

> [a] sale by one person cannot be transformed for tax purposes into a sale by another by using the latter as a conduit through which to pass title. To permit the true nature of a transaction to be disguised by mere formalisms, which exist solely to alter tax liabilities, would seriously impair the effective administration of the tax policies of Congress.

Id. at 334. Several years later, in United States v. Cumberland Pub. Serv. Co., 338 U.S. 451, 456 (1950), the Supreme Court upheld a transaction in which, to obtain favorable tax treatment, the shareholders of a corporation refused to sell their stock to a local cooperative, but instead liquidated the corporation and sold the assets to the cooperative. The Court found held that "[w]hile the distinction between sales by a corporation as compared with distribution in kind followed by shareholder sales may be shadowy and artificial when the corporation is closely held, Congress has chosen to recognize such a distinction for tax purposes." *Id.* at 454–55. In so concluding, the Court distinguished Court Holding Co., stating that unlike that case, the transaction "genuinely ended the corporation's activities," and the corporation itself never planned the sale. *Id.* at 453.

Here, of course, we are faced not with a shareholder of a corporation selling an asset, but with a corporation purchasing an asset at the behest of its sole shareholder, with the apparent intent of having that asset—the stock of the parent—later redeemed. Yet, in this context, the socalled "step transaction doctrine" resonates. Under this doctrine, "interrelated yet formally distinct steps in an integrated transaction may not be considered independently of the overall transaction." Comm'r of Internal Revenue v. Clark, 489 U.S. 726, 738 (1989); *see also Minn. Tea Co.*, 302 U.S. at 613; *Court Holding Co.*, 324 U.S. at 334; Dietzsch v. United States, 498 F.2d 1344, 1346 (Ct. Cl. 1974). . . As recently noted by the Federal Circuit, there are two primary formulations of this doctrine—the "end result" and "interdependence" tests. The Falconwood Corp. v. United States, 422 F.3d 1339, 1349–50 (Fed. Cir. 2005). The Court of Claims described these two tests thusly—

> The "interdependence test" requires an inquiry as to "whether on a reasonable interpretation of objective facts the steps were so interdependent that the legal relations created by one transaction would have been fruitless without a completion of the series." . . . The "end result" test, on the other hand, establishes a standard whereby: . . . "purportedly separate transactions will be amalgamated into a single transaction when it appears that they were really component parts of a single transaction intended from the outset to be taken for the purpose of reaching the ultimate result."

King Enters., Inc. v. United States, 418 F.2d 511, 516–17 (Ct. Cl. 1969). [citations omitted]

That, from the outset, a redemption of the Heinz stock was the end result intended by plaintiffs is evidenced by several key pieces of evidence. First, various correspondence in the record indicates that HCC hired Goldman Sachs to design the zero coupon note that Heinz would use to effectuate the redemption before HCC was even authorized to buy its first share of Heinz stock. . . Any doubt that the end result of these transactions was to have Heinz redeem all but a small portion of the shares acquired by HCC was eliminated by admissions made by Mr. Crowe during his testimony. Thus, under cross-examination, he stated:

> Q: And though there is no guarantee in stone that HCC would sell that stock to Heinz, it's a pretty reasonable expectation to assume that it would given that it was already designing the note it would use for that purpose, correct?

> A: We were planning a transaction. We've never denied that.

> Q: Of course, there was a reasonable expectation that all the steps of the transaction would be carried out.

> A: We expected all the steps of the transaction to be carried out.

At another point in his testimony, Mr. Crowe admitted that "the primary purpose [of the transaction] was to put the company in the position of being able to realize a tax benefit from the possible future sale of the shares." This purpose, of course, could only be accomplished if HCC acquired stock and Heinz "redeemed" most of it, so that HCC's basis in the stock would be transferred to the remaining shares. . .

As such, under the end result formulation of the step transaction theory, it is clear from the record that, from the start, the initial acquisition by HCC of Heinz stock and the subsequent redemption of that stock were " 'really component parts of a single transaction intended from the outset to be taken for the purpose of reaching the ultimate result.' " *Falconwood*, 422

F.3d at 1350 (quoting *King Enters.*, 418 F.2d at 516). Those constituted part of a prearranged plan to have Heinz obtain the stock while having the basis therein shifted to the shares that would be sold by HCC to a third party. Had Heinz directly acquired the 3,325,000 shares that it supposedly redeemed from HCC, this shift in basis would not have occurred. And the Heinz Consolidated Group would have been obliged to report a gain, rather than a huge capital loss that it could carry back to prior years. Plaintiffs may not avoid this result by employing mere formalisms thinly designed to mask their true intentions. See Brown v. United States, 329 F.3d 664, 672 (9th Cir.), cert. denied, 540 U.S. 878 (2003) (courts have "readily ignored the role of the intermediary" where "a party acts as a 'mere conduit' of funds—a fleeting stop in a predetermined voyage toward a particular result"). . . The same conclusion flows from the interdependence test, under which separate steps will be consolidated if "it is unlikely that any one step would have been undertaken except in contemplation of the other integrating acts." Kuper v. Comm'r of Internal Revenue, 533 F.2d 152, 156 (5th Cir. 1976). . . Here, again, primary focus must be given to the court's findings that the purchase by HCC of Heinz stock lacked any non-tax business purpose. [citation omitted] . . .

Hence, under either the end result or interdependence tests, it would appear that HCC's ownership of the Heinz stock must be ignored, with Heinz being viewed as having acquired that stock on the market. . . Moreover, contrary to plaintiffs' opportunings, it is not the case that application of the step transaction doctrine here would require the court to invent new steps, rather than combining steps. Compare Grove v. Comm'r, 490 F.2d 241, 247–48 (2d Cir. 1973). Rather, application of the doctrine simply gives effect to the reality of the transaction here which, tax considerations aside, was a repurchase by Heinz of its own stock.

Nor are plaintiffs correct in asserting that the transactions in question should be exempt from the step transaction doctrine because Congress has specifically dealt with abuses stemming from intercorporate dividends in sections 243, 246 and 1059 of the Code. [citation omitted] . . .

[T]his case is more like *Knetsch, supra*, in which the Supreme Court concluded that the passage of a section in the 1954 Code limiting the availability of certain interest deductions did not preempt the application of more general substance-over-form principles—specifically, the sham transaction doctrine. Writing for the Court, Justice Brennan opined—

> The petitioners thus would attribute to Congress a purpose to allow the deduction of pre–1954 payments under transactions of the kind carried on by Knetsch with the insurance company without regard to whether the transactions created a true obligation to pay interest. Unless that meaning plainly appears we will not attribute it to Congress. "To hold otherwise would be to exalt artifice above reality and to deprive the statutory provision in question of all serious purpose." Gregory v. Helvering, [293 U.S. at 470].

Knetsch, 364 U.S. at 367. Consistent with this view, the Federal Circuit, in Coltec, vacated a decision by this court which had held that because the anti-abuse provisions of sections 357(b)(1) and 358(d)(2) of the Code did not preclude the treatment sought by the taxpayer, the government could not invoke general substance-over-form considerations. See Coltec, Inc. v. United States, 62 Fed. Cl. 716, 752–55 (2004), vac'd and rem'd, 454 F.3d 1340 (Fed. Cir. 2006), cert. denied, 127 S.Ct. 1261 (2007). . .

While Congress undoubtedly has the power to authorize the deduction in question, as in Knetsch and Coltec, this court simply cannot conclude that the same Congress that passed provisions targeting the abuse of corporate dividends intended to favor such transactions by exempting them from substance-over-form considerations applicable virtually to the rest of the Internal Revenue Code. [citation omitted] Certainly, as in Knetsch, it is not the case that the intent to allow a deduction "plainly appears" either from the statutory provisions invoked by plaintiffs or the accompanying legislative history. Indeed, in passing the provisions cited by plaintiffs, Congress undoubtedly was aware that the step transaction doctrine had often been applied to recharacterize various transactions arising under the redemption and corporation distribution provisions of Subchapter C of the Code, despite the detailed nature of these provisions. . . As such, the court sees no reason whatsoever to immunize the transaction sub judice from this step transaction version of the substance-over-form analysis. [citation omitted] To do so, indeed, would be to turn the anti-abuse provisions cited by plaintiffs on their head.

D. Redux

Once it is determined that the purchase by Heinz of its stock from HCC did not qualify as a redemption within the meaning of section 317(b), the rest of the pieces of the puzzle readily fall into place. Because, under both the sham and step transaction doctrines, Heinz cannot be viewed as having obtained the stock from HCC in a transaction that qualified as a redemption under section 317(b) of the Code, the transfer of the 3,325,000 shares to Heinz did not cause a dividend to arise under section 302(d) of the Code. As such, the reattribution rules of Treasure Regulation section 1.302–2(c) were not triggered here and HCC's basis in the 175,000 shares it retained was not increased by the cost basis of the shares it relinquished. It follows, a fortiori, that the sale of the retained shares did not produce the capital losses claimed, making the loss carrybacks in/41/ question inappropriate.

III. CONCLUSION

A Heinz promotion from the late 1950s and early 1960s touted its tomato ketchup by stating—"It's Red Magic Time!" But no amount of magic, red or otherwise, can hide the meat of the transactions in question, the connective tissues and gristle of which have been revealed by the multi-tined substance-over-form doctrine. *Sans sa sauce*, it becomes plain that plaintiffs' transaction simply was not "the thing which the statute intended." *Gregory*, 293 U.S. at 469.

This court need go no farther. Based on the foregoing, it finds that plaintiffs are not entitled to recover any refund here. The Clerk is hereby ordered to dismiss their complaint.

IT IS SO ORDERED.

NOTE

How did the corporate provisions of the Code intersect in *Heinz* to create a benefit for the taxpayer? Why don't existing statutory anti-abuse rules apply here? If you were to design a statutory provision to prevent the set of transactions in *Heinz* that the court ultimately rejected, what would that rule look like?

vii. REDEMPTIONS BY RELATED CORPORATIONS—§ 304

1. Prior to 1950 the Commissioner was unsuccessful in his effort to treat as a distribution essentially equivalent to a dividend the sale price received by the shareholder of a parent corporation on its sale to a subsidiary of stock of the parent. See John Rodman Wanamaker, Trustee, 11 T.C. 365 (1948), *aff'd per curiam*, 178 F.2d 10 (3d Cir. 1949). To meet this problem Congress in 1950 enacted the statutory predecessor of § 304(a)(2).

2. Prior to 1954 the Commissioner was unsuccessful in his effort to treat as a distribution essentially equivalent to a dividend the purchase by Corporation A (wholly owned by X) of part of X's stock in Corporation B (wholly owned by X). See, e.g., Emma Cramer, 20 T.C. 679 (1953); Rev. Rul. 59–97, 1959–1 C.B. 684, *revoking* Rev. Rul. 55–15, 1955–1 C.B. 361. To meet this problem Congress in 1954 enacted § 304(a)(1).

3. After the 2003 Act it has been suggested that Congress should rethink the role of § 304 given its primary purpose is to characterize a transaction as a dividend and not a sale—a distinction with much less significance after 2003. See Feld, "Dividends Reconsidered," 101 Tax Notes 1117 (Dec. 1, 2003). Other arguments for rethinking § 304 are based on the perverse incentives it provides to corporate taxpayers, which typically prefer dividend treatment (called for under § 304) instead of sale treatment. *Id.* See, e.g., Merrill Lynch & Co., Inc. v. Commissioner, 120 T.C. 12 (2003), reviewed by 386 F.3d 464 (2nd Cir. 2004), remanded to 131 T.C. 293(2008). But cf. Uniroyal Inc. v. Commissioner, 65 T.C.M. (CCH) 2690 (1993).

Any revisions to the Code prompted by the 2003 change in the dividend tax rate should presumably await "permanent" inclusion of the rate change in the law. Although the 2003 rate change has proved more enduring than many expected, it remains an expiring provision that is renewed periodically.

4. As part of an effort to limit corporate taxpayers' ability to utilize § 304 to trigger dividend classification for corporate shareholders (as the taxpayer in *Merrill Lynch* sought to do), Congress revised the extraordinary dividend rules (§ 1059) which require a corporate shareholder to reduce its

basis in the shares held by the amount of any "extraordinary" dividend to the extent that the dividend is not taxed. § 1059(a). After 1997, the extraordinary dividend rules apply to redemptions treated as dividends under § 304.

5. Final and temporary regulations were issued, and apply to stock acquisitions on or after December 29, 2009 under § 304. The regulations apply § 304 to certain transactions "entered into with the principal purpose of avoiding the application of section 304 to a corporation that is controlled by the issuing corporation in the transaction, or...to a corporation that controls the acquiring corporation in the transaction." In particular, "for purposes of determining the amount of a property distribution constituting a dividend (and the source thereof) under section 304(b)(2) the District Director (now known as the Director of Field Operations) is permitted to consider a corporation (deemed acquiring corporation) as having acquired for property the stock of the issuing corporation that is in fact acquired for property by the acquiring corporation." This can be done if the "deemed acquiring corporation controls the acquiring corporation and if one of the principal purposes for creating, organizing, or funding the acquiring corporation (through capital contributions or debt) is to avoid the application of section 304 to the deemed acquiring corporation." ("Use of Controlled Corporations to Avoid the Application of Section 304." 74 FR 69021-01 (Dec. 30, 2009); amended by T.D. 9477 (Feb.26, 2010)).

6. To test an acquisition under § 304(a), one applies a modified version of § 318(a) attribution rules (§ 304(b)(1)). Suppose A, to satisfy § 302(b)(3), enters into an agreement under § 302(c)(2) not to acquire an interest in a corporation of which he was previously a shareholder. If, by application of the attribution rules to § 304, A is considered to have acquired stock in the corporation, will he have violated his agreement? See Rev. Rul. 88–55, 1988–2 C.B. 45.

7. X owns all of the stock of Corporation M, which owns all of the stock of Corporation N. Corporation N has no earnings and profits; Corporation M has ample earnings and profits. Corporation N purchases one half of X's stock in M. Might dividend treatment attend the distribution? What would the result be if N had ample earnings and profits and M had none?

8. X owns all of the stock of Corporations A and B. B purchases one half of X's stock in A. A has ample earnings and profits; B has none. Might the distribution be treated as a dividend? What would the result be if A had no earnings and profits but B's were ample?

9. Y owns all the stock in Corporation D and E. E buys all Y's stock in D. The distribution is treated as a dividend. What becomes of Y's basis in his D stock? The last sentence of § 304(a)(1) suggests a rule by which the basis of the acquired stock in the hands of the acquiring corporation may be determined. Does that rule also apply in § 304(a)(2) transactions? See Broadview Lumber Co. v. United States, 561 F.2d 698 (7th Cir. 1977).

10. Under § 351 if a person contributes assets to a controlled corporation and receives stock of that corporation in exchange, he realizes no current income. See Chapter 3. Suppose A owns all of the stock in two corporations, X and Y. A contributes all of his X stock to Y in exchange for long-term Y Corp. bonds. Will this be treated as a redemption for purposes of § 302? See § 304(b)(3). In Caamano v. Commissioner, 879 F.2d 156 (5th Cir. 1989), *aff'g* Bhada, 89 T.C. 959 (1987), the court held that because of § 317(a), if a corporation takes stock in exchange for its stock, under § 304(a) it has not returned "property" for the stock it acquires. As a result, § 304 does not apply. What then is the significance of § 304(b)(3)?

Coyle v. United States
415 F.2d 488 (4th Cir. 1968).

■ Before SOBELOFF, CRAVEN and BUTZNER, CIRCUIT JUDGES.

■ SOBELOFF, CIRCUIT JUDGE. Our task in this tax refund case is . . . to determine whether the proceeds from a transfer of corporate stock are to be taxed as capital gains or ordinary income. The District Court ruled that money which the taxpayer received in exchange for the shares of a corporation he controlled to a corporation wholly owned by his sons should be treated as a capital gain. We disagree and reverse the judgment.

In 1958, taxpayer George L. Coyle, Sr. (now deceased) transferred 66 shares of Coyle & Richardson, Inc. [hereinafter referred to as C & R] to Coyle Realty Company [hereinafter referred to as Realty] for $19,800. Reporting a long term capital gain on this "sale," Coyle paid a tax computed at that rate on $9,900, which is the difference between the sale price and his basis in the stock. The Internal Revenue Service was of the view that the proceeds should be treated as a dividend and assessed the taxpayer an additional $7,181.90 plus interest. . .

Before the transaction, the 688 outstanding shares of C & R were distributed in the following manner: taxpayer, 369; taxpayer's three sons, an aggregate of 288; taxpayer's wife, 1; O. M. Buck, 25; Julia Farley, 5.[1] Thus, taxpayer and his immediate family owned more than 95.6% of the corporation whose shares were sold. Realty, the acquiring corporation, was owned in equal parts by taxpayer's three sons. . . Although the taxpayer had once held one share of Realty, he had no stock in it when the transaction under inquiry took place.

The initial point of controversy is whether the purchase by Realty is to be treated as a sale or as a redemption. Section 304 of the Internal Revenue Code of 1954, . . . provides in pertinent part:

(a) Treatment of certain stock purchases.

(1) Acquisition by related corporation.

---

[1] Buck and Farley are unrelated to the Coyle family as far as the record shows. Their insignificant holdings in C & R play no part in this case.

[I]f (A) one or more persons are in control of each of two corporations, and (B) in return for property, one of the corporations acquires stock in the other corporation from the person . . . so in control, then . . . such property *shall be treated as a distribution in redemption* of the stock of the corporation acquiring such stock. . . (Emphasis added.)

Control is defined in § 304(c)(1) as at least 50% of the combined voting power of all voting stock or at least 50% of the total value of all classes of stock. For purposes of determining control, § 304(c)(2) specifically makes applicable the constructive ownership provisions of § 318. . . Under that section, "an individual shall be considered as owning the stock owned, directly or indirectly, by or for . . . his children. . ."

Thus, applying the statute literally, taxpayer was in control of both corporations and the acquisition from him by Realty of the C & R stock must be treated as a redemption. His control of C & R results from his actual ownership of 54% of its outstanding stock, not to mention the attribution to him of his sons' 40%. He had 100% control of Realty by virtue of the fact that all of his sons' stock is attributable to him. The District Court recognized and the taxpayer concedes, as he must, that a plain meaning application of sections 304 and 318 requires this conclusion.

However, the District Court eschewed this direct approach. The court reasoned that since the taxpayer actually owned no shares in Realty, there should be no attribution to him and thus the transaction here was not one between related corporations. Its conclusion then was that the transfer should not be deemed a redemption but a simple sale entitled to long term capital gain treatment.

This interpretation of the constructive ownership rules is at war with both the language of the statute and legislative purpose of Congress. The family attribution rules, which are specifically prescribed by the statute, were designed to create predictability for the tax planner and to obviate the necessity of a court's scrutinizing family arrangements to determine whether every family member is in fact a completely independent financial entity. An authoritative study of the subject begins: "The rules of constructive ownership rest on certain assumptions which are readily supported in the everyday conduct of affairs. . . Tax administration would be severely handicapped if the rules applied only as presumptions. . ." Ringel, Surrey & Warren, Attribution of Stock Ownership in the Internal Revenue Code, 72 Harv. L. Rev. 209 (1958). Yet despite the clear congressional judgment and mandate that the shares of a son are to be treated as his father's for certain limited purposes, the court below read the explicit language as no more than a presumption and then disregarded it.

The statute does not require that a person be an actual shareholder in a corporation before shares in that corporation may be attributed to him. In a recent Second Circuit case, Levin v. Commissioner of Internal Revenue, 385 F.2d 521 (1967), the court attributed 100% ownership to a mother who had redeemed all her shares of a corporation whose sole remaining shareholder was her son. Similarly, an example given in the Federal Tax Regulations unquestionably assumes that one holding no stock in a corporation may nevertheless constructively own 100% of its shares. 26 C.F.R. § 1.304–2.[2] Indeed, any other construction would be untenable. Under the District Court's reading, if the taxpayer had retained at the time of the transfer his otherwise insignificant single share in Realty, then 100% of the stock of that corporation could be attributed to him. Clearly such a distinction could not have been proposed by the Congress.

Appellee urges upon us that at least one anomaly will flow from holding the instant transaction subject to § 304. Subsection (a)(1) provides that the stock acquired from the person or persons in control shall be treated as a contribution to the capital of the acquiring corporation. It is asserted that since only a shareholder makes contributions to capital and since taxpayer was not an actual shareholder of Realty, the stock acquired from him cannot realistically be so treated. The short answer is that appellee's underlying premise is fallacious. Non-shareholders may and do make contributions to capital, and the Internal Revenue Code recognizes this fact. See § 362(c); see also Brown Shoe Co. v. Commissioner of Internal Revenue, 339 U.S. 583 . . . (1950). Moreover, the law requires that the stock only be "treated" for certain tax purposes as a contribution to capital by a person who is "treated" as a shareholder. Just as the transfer is directed by statute to be "treated" like a redemption when in fact the issuing corporation does not get its stock back, so this stock may be "treated" as a capital contribution even though it does not come from an actual shareholder. It should be stressed that appellee raises no specter of adverse effects from treating the shares as a capital contribution either on the non-shareholder or the corporation. The only point made is that the Code's treatment as applied here is "economically unrealistic." This is simply too thin a reed with which to bring down the clear statutory scheme.

Nor is there merit in appellee's contention that simply because the Treasury Regulation[3] and portions of the legislative history[4] speak interchangeably of the person in control as "taxpayer" or "shareholder," the section may not be applied if the person deemed in control of both corporations is not an actual shareholder in both. It is, of course, true that ordinarily the person transferring stock in a § 304 case will be a shareholder in the acquiring corporation. The Regulations and Committee Reports were simply addressing themselves to the commonplace transaction. Merely because these interpretative aids do not envision an insubstantial wrinkle on the

---

[2] Example [4] in Treas. Reg. § 1.304–2[(c)] reads: "Corporation X and corporation Y each have outstanding 100 shares of common stock. H, an individual, W, his wife, S, his son, and G, his grandson, each own 25 shares of stock of each corporation. H sells all of his 25 shares of corporation X to corporation Y.... Both before and after the transaction H owned directly and constructively 100 percent of the stock of corporation X...." 26 C.F.R. § 1.304–2[(c)].

[3] See, e. g., Treas. Reg. § 1.304–2 which assumes that the taxpayer is an actual shareholder in the acquiring corporation.

[4] See S. Rep. No.1622, 83d Cong. 2d Sess. (1954), 3 U.S. Code Cong. & Ad. News 4876 (1954); H. Rep. No.1337, 83d Cong. 2d Sess. (1954), 3 U.S. Code Cong. & Ad. News 4062 (1954).

same fundamental pattern is no adequate ground for holding uncovered that which is clearly within the statute.

. . . The case before us involves two close corporations owned by the same family and a transfer by the head of that family of stock in one of the corporations to the other. This is precisely the situation which § 304 was meant to govern.

Since the District Court held redemption treatment unwarranted, it did not reach the second question to which we now turn: Is the redemption here to be treated as an exchange of stock and thus subject only to a capital gains tax or is it to be treated as a dividend and taxed at ordinary income rates?

Section 302(b) . . . enumerates those categories of redemptions which are to be treated as exchanges. Both sides agree that the only pertinent category in this case is the most general one, (b)(1), which provides that a redemption shall be treated as an exchange if it "is not essentially equivalent to a dividend."

Determination of dividend equivalency requires a factual inquiry into the circumstances of each case. See Ballenger v. United States of America, 301 F.2d 192 (4th Cir. 1962). Ordinarily, then, we would remand for further evidentiary hearings. However, in this case, which was submitted on stipulated facts, both the Government and the taxpayer's estate concur that no remand is necessary. For this reason, as well as the relative simplicity of the facts here, this court proceeds to adjudicate the issue of dividend equivalence.

On this question, appellee's sole contention is that a payment by a corporation to a non-shareholder may not be characterized as a dividend. With this we agree, for § 316 defines a "dividend" as "any distribution of property made by a corporation to its *shareholders*" out of earnings and profits. (Emphasis added.) The rub is that § 304(b)(1) specifically states: ". . . determinations as to whether the acquisition is, by reason of section 302(b), to be treated as a distribution in part or full payment in exchange for the stock shall be made reference to the stock of the *issuing corporation*." (Emphasis added.) Thus, in determining whether this redemption was essentially equivalent to a dividend, we must focus attention upon C & R, of which taxpayer was not only a shareholder but by far the major one.[5]

Although several tests have been devised and several factors exalted in determining whether a redemption is not in essence a dividend, we think there is one overriding objective criterion—a significant modification of shareholder interests. See Moore, Dividend Equivalency—Taxation of Distribution in Redemption of Stock, 19 Tax L. Rev. 249 (1964). . . If the taxpayer's control or ownership of the corporation is basically unaltered by the transaction, then the proceeds he has received as a result of manipulating

---

[5] Available earnings and profits are to be reckoned by reference to the acquiring corporation. § 304(b)(2)(A). Appellee admits that Realty's earnings and profits were adequate to cover the distribution in this case.

his corporate stock must be taxed as a dividend. See Commissioner of Internal Revenue v. Berenbaum, 369 F.2d 337 (10th Cir. 1966).

In examining the respective shareholder interests of C & R before and after the transfer of stock we must bear in mind that § 302(c)(1) explicitly makes applicable to this inquiry the constructive stock ownership rules of § 318. Thus, before the transfer, taxpayer is deemed to have owned not only the 369 shares of C & R actually in his name but also the 288 shares owned by his sons and the one share held by his wife. [See §§ 318(a)(1)(A)(ii) and (i).] In all, for purposes of § 302, taxpayer before the transaction owned 658 of C & R's 688 outstanding shares. After the transaction, he held only 303 shares in his own name, but in addition, of course, he also is deemed to have owned the 289 shares of his wife and sons. Moreover, the 66 shares now held by Realty must likewise be attributed to him. Section 318(a)(2)(C) provides that stock owned by a corporation will be attributed proportionately to any person owning 50% or more of the corporation. Section 304(b)(1) directs that in applying the constructive ownership rules for testing whether a redemption is an exchange or a dividend, the 50% requirement of § 318(a)(2)(C) shall not be applicable. In the instant case, this means that the 66 shares held by Realty shall be attributed equally to its owners, taxpayer's sons, and under § 318(a)(1)(A)(ii), these shares are attributed from the sons to the taxpayer. Consequently, after the transaction taxpayer owned 658 shares of C & R, precisely the number with which he started.

As noted in Wiseman v. United States, 371 F.2d 816, 818 (1st Cir. 1967), "the real question here is what was accomplished by this transaction." The answer here is that while corporate ownership and control remained the same, taxpayer, the major shareholder, had come into possession of $19,800. This was essentially nothing but a dividend and was properly taxed as such.

One tangential difficulty arising from this disposition of the case is the proper allocation of taxpayer's basis in the 66 transferred shares. This potential problem is not before us at this time, but we note in passing that there are at least two reasonable solutions. Ordinarily, when there is an acquisition by a related corporation the controlling person is a shareholder in both, and the basis of his stock in the acquiring corporation is increased by his basis in the stock transferred by him. See Treas. Reg. 26 C.F.R. § 1.304–2. In this case, since taxpayer held no shares in Realty, such an approach is not feasible. However, it would be consonant with the underlying rationale of this approach to increase pro rata the basis of the sons' shares in Realty. In Levin v. Commissioner of Internal Revenue, supra . . . at 528 n.29, where the taxpayer had redeemed all of her shares in the corporation but had not sufficiently served relations with it to avoid dividend equivalence treatment, the court said: "Her basis does not disappear; it simply is transferred to her son." As an alternative to increasing the basis of taxpayer's sons in Realty, taxpayer's own basis in his remaining 303 shares of C & R could be augmented by his basis in the 66 transferred shares. In any event, it is clear that taxpayer's basis will not disappear.

To sum up, we construe this transaction as a redemption under § 304(a) and find that this redemption was essentially equivalent to a dividend under § 302(b). Therefore, we reverse the judgment of the District Court and enter judgment in favor of the Government.

Reversed.

NOTES

1. In Rev. Rul. 70–496, 1970–2 C.B. 74, Corporation X owned 70 percent of Corporation Y and 100 percent of Corporation Z; Y in turn owned 100 percent of Corporation S. Y sold all of its S stock to Z. Y was held to own, directly and by attribution, 100 percent of both S and X before and after the sale. By virtue of §§ 302 and 304, therefore, the sale had the effect of the payment of a dividend from Z to Y, and a contribution of capital from Y to Z. Since Y owned no Z stock directly, its basis in the S stock disappeared. The Ruling observes: "However, Y now has additional cash." Is this persuasive support for the disappearance of basis?

2. Section 304(b)(2) states that in an acquisition to which § 304(a) applies, "the determination of the amount which is a dividend . . . shall be made as if the property were distributed by the acquiring corporation . . . and then by the issuing corporation." What is the effect of this provision on the issuing corporation? After one or two contrary starts the courts have refused to treat the issuer as having received an actual distribution in order to tax it on receipt of a dividend. *Compare* Union Bankers Insurance Co., 64 T.C. 807 (1975), *acq.*, 1976–2 C.B. 3, *with* Broadview Lumber Co. v. United States, 561 F.2d 698 (7th Cir. 1977). See Rev. Rul. 80–189, 1980–2 C.B. 106 (accepting *Broadview Lumber*).

3. In Rev. Rul. 89–57, 1989–1 C.B. 90, the Service ruled that in determining whether the control test in § 304(a)(1)(A) is satisfied, the value test of § 304(c)(1) will be applied to the aggregate of all classes of a corporation's stock and not on a class-by-class basis. See also Letter Ruling 20104002.

4. In Hurst v. Commissioner, 124 T.C. 16 (2005), supra 147, the taxpayer, as part of a larger retirement plan, had one of his corporations (HMI) purchase all of his (and his wife's) stock in another wholly owned corporation (RHI) in return for a $250,000 promissory note. The taxpayer reported this transaction as an installment sale of a long-term capital asset. The Commissioner disagreed, characterizing it as a section 301 distribution because it was a sale to a related party. Apparently both the taxpayers and the Commissioner understood this argument to be one implicating § 302(b)(3)—and they tried this issue in the case along such lines. After trial, in his answering brief, the Commissioner, for the first time argued that the sale of RHI stock to HMI should be analyzed under § 304. Ultimately, after deciding that the Commissioner's argument constituted a new matter (which is not appropriate) and not a new theory (which is appropriate), the court rejected the Commissioner's claim. If the Commissioner had raised the § 304 analysis in a more timely manner, what do you think would have been the outcome. Recall, the additional facts from the case: (1) HMI was 100% owned by taxpayer-husband; (2) taxpayer-wife worked for HMI; (3) both taxpayers owned RHI; (4) the taxpayers sold their RHI stock to HMI for a promissory note;(5) the taxpayer's continued to lease business premises which they owned individually, to HMI; and (6) as part of the sale of

all of the RHI stock to HMI, taxpayer-husband sold 10% of his HMI stock to his son, and the remaining 90% to HMI (in redemption).

viii. REDEMPTIONS FOLLOWING DEATH—§ 303

X owned all the stock in Corporation M. On X's death, his stock is worth $1 million. M redeems 30 percent of the stock from X's estate for $300,000. If the distribution is within § 303(a), what is the tax consequence to X's estate? Why? What is the tax consequence if the redemption occurs one year after death when 30 percent of the stock is worth and is redeemed for $325,000? Why? What might the tax consequences be in each instance if § 303(a) covered only $275,000 of the distribution? In considering these problems under § 303, keep in mind the implications of § 1014.

What policy objective(s) does the adoption of § 303 probably reflect? Do you support those objectives and the § 303 technique for achieving them? Why?

For the interaction of § 303 with former § 6166 (now § 6166A) (allowing election to pay estate taxes in installments), see Rev. Rul. 72–188, 1972–1 C.B. 383, *modified by* Rev. Rul. 86–54, 1986–1 C.B. 356.

c. Partial Liquidations—§ 302(b)(4) and (e)

Until 1982 the tax consequences of partial liquidations were governed by §§ 331 and 346. In that year Congress moved the rules governing partial liquidations to § 302.

Estate of Chandler v. Commissioner
22 T.C. 1158 (1954), *aff'd per curiam*, 228 F.2d 909 (6th Cir. 1955).

. . . The issue for decision is whether respondent correctly determined that a pro rata cash distribution in cancellation of half the stock of a corporation was made at such a time and in such a manner as to be essentially equivalent to the distribution of a taxable dividend to the extent of accumulated earnings and profits within the purview of section 115(g), Internal Revenue Code of 1939.

FINDINGS OF FACT

. . . All of the petitioners were stockholders of Chandler–Singleton Company (hereinafter referred to as the Company). . . The capital stock of the Company consisted of 500 shares of common stock of $100 par value, all of which were outstanding until November 7, 1946. From its organization until February 28, 1946, the Company was engaged in the operation of a general department store in Maryville, Tennessee. It had a ladies' ready-to-wear department, men's department, children's department, piece goods department, and a bargain basement.

Chandler was the president and manager of the Company. At the beginning of 1944 he was in very poor health. John W. Bush was the secretary of the Company, but until 1944 he had not been particularly active in its affairs. On January 1, 1944, he became assistant manager of the Company. By profession he was a civil engineer, but at that time he was unemployed due to a change in the administration of the City of Knoxville, Tennessee. During 1944 and 1945 Chandler was sick most of the time. In his absence John W. Bush managed the department store.

John W. Bush did not like being a merchant and decided to return to engineering. In November 1945 he informed Chandler that he was resigning as manager at the end of the year. Chandler, feeling unable to manage the department store himself, decided to sell.

At a stockholders' meeting held on February 20, 1946, it was unanimously agreed that the Company should accept an offer to purchase its merchandise, furniture and fixtures, and lease. Chandler was instructed to consummate the deal. The sale was consummated and a bill of sale was executed. . .

The Company ceased operating the department store on February 28, 1946. McArthur's Incorporated moved in that night and began operating the store the following day.

Chandler had worked hard in the department store and had no outside interest. He wanted something to do and did not want to get out of business entirely. It was planned that a ladies' ready-to-wear store would be opened by the Company to be managed by Clara T. McConnell (now Clara M. Register) who had managed the ladies' ready-to-wear department of the department store. Thirty shares of stock in the Company owned by Chandler's wife were canceled on April 5, 1946. Ten of these shares were issued to Clara McConnell on April 13, 1946, in order that she might have an interest in the Company whose store she was going to manage. A men's store, to be eventually taken over by the eldest son of John and Margaret Bush, was also contemplated. It was thought that approximately half of the assets of the Company would be needed for each of the two stores.

The charter of the Company was amended on May 18, 1946, changing the name of the Company to "Chandler's" pursuant to a resolution passed at a stockholders' meeting held on May 15, 1946.

About the first of June 1946, the Company obtained space for the ladies' ready-to-wear store about one-half block from the old department store now occupied by McArthur's Incorporated. Merchandise was purchased beginning in June; improvements were made; furniture and supplies were acquired; and the store was opened on September 23, 1946. No sales had been made by the Company between February 28, 1946, and September 23, 1946.

The ladies' ready-to-wear store was about the same size as that department in the former department store. The department store had occupied 8,000 to 9,000 square feet of floor space, had employed 10 to 20 persons, and had carried fire insurance in the amount of $65,000 on its stock and fixtures. The new store had approximately 1,800 square feet of floor space, employed 4 to 6 persons, and carried fire insurance in the amount of $10,000. . .

A special meeting of the stockholders was held on September 28, 1946, the minutes of which read in part as follows:

The Chairman explained that the purpose of the meeting was to authorize partial liquidation for the following reasons:

> The old business was sold and plans were developed to go back into business, operating two stores, a ladies ready-to-wear business and a men's store. The ladies ready-to-wear store has been opened and is now operating. Up to now, we have been unable to negotiate a lease for a suitable location, and, after considerable thought, it has been decided to abandon the idea of operating an exclusive men's shop and operate only the one store at the present time. It appears that requirements of the one store will be approximately one-half the capital now invested in Chandler's, Inc.

> Upon motion of Margaret Chandler Bush, seconded by J. W. Bush, and unanimously carried, the officials were authorized and instructed to redeem from each shareholder one-half of his stock, paying therefor the book value, which is approximately $269.00 per share. Therefore they are authorized to retire one-half of each shareholder's stock at $269.00 per share and are authorized to apply to the Secretary of State for reduction of the outstanding stock from 500 shares to 250 shares of $100.00 each.

On October 29, 1946, the charter of the Company was amended and its capital stock was reduced from 500 shares of $100 par value common stock, to 250 shares of $100 par value common stock. On November 7, 1946, the 500 shares of outstanding capital stock designated "Chandler–Singleton Company" were called in and canceled. Each stockholder received 1 share of stock designated "Chandler's" and $269 in cash for each 2 shares turned in. The $269 represented the approximate book value of 1 share of Chandler–Singleton Company stock on February 28, 1946. . .

The comparative balance sheets on December 31, 1945, on February 28, 1946, after the sale to McArthur's Incorporated, and on December 31, 1946, were as follows:

[The balance sheets showed:

	Dec. 31, 1945	*Feb. 28, 1946*	*Dec. 31, 1946*
Current Assets	$166,327.09	$150,972.87	$43,810.41
Total Assets	168,735.79	150,972.87	59,090.65
Current Liabilities	61,129.00	16,405.64	12,312.74
Net Worth	107,606.79	134,567.23	46,777.91

A 10 per cent dividend totaling $5,000 was declared on September 24, 1943. The amount of cash and United States bonds possessed by the Company at the beginning of 1946 exceeded the amount required for the current operation of the business by approximately $45,000. Between January 1 and February 28, 1946, the Company's earned surplus increased by $39,460.44, out of which the Company paid dividends in the amount of $12,500. To the extent of at least $58,027.91, the excess cash possessed by the Company prior to the November 7 distribution was not created by a reduction in the amount of capital needed to operate the Company's business.

Petitioners reported the excess of the payments received over the cost of the stock in their individual income tax returns as capital gain. Respondent treated the payments, to the extent of the earned surplus of $58,027.91, as dividends and taxed them to the petitioners as ordinary income.

The acquisition and cancellation of one-half the Company's stock in 1946 was done at such a time in such a manner as to make the distribution and cancellation essentially equivalent to the distribution of a taxable dividend to the extent of $58,027.91.

OPINION

■ BRUCE, JUDGE. Respondent contends that the Company's pro rata distribution in redemption of half its capital stock at book value was made at such a time and in such a manner as to make the distribution essentially equivalent to the distribution of a taxable dividend to the extent of earnings and profits. If respondent's contention is correct the distribution to the extent of earnings and profits loses its capital gain status acquired under section 115(c) and (i) and is treated as a taxable dividend under section 115(g)[1] of the Internal Revenue Code of 1939 as it applied in 1946.

A cancellation or redemption by a corporation of all of the stock of a particular shareholder has been held not to be essentially equivalent to the distribution of a taxable dividend. Cf. Carter Tiffany, 16 T.C. 1443; Zenz v. Quinlivan, (C. A. 6) 213 F.2d 914; Regs. 111, sec. 29.115–9. However, "A cancellation or redemption by a corporation of its stock pro rata among all the shareholders will generally be considered as effecting a distribution essentially equivalent to a dividend distribution to the extent of the earnings and profits accumulated after February 28, 1913." Regs. 111, sec. 29.115–9. Such a redemption of stock is generally considered equivalent to a dividend because it does not, as a practical matter, change the essential relationship between the shareholders and the corporation. Cf. Commis-

---

[1] SEC. 115. DISTRIBUTIONS BY CORPORATIONS.

(g) Redemption of Stock.—If a corporation cancels or redeems its stock (whether or not such stock was issued as a stock dividend) at such time and in such manner as to make the distribution and cancellation or redemption in whole or in part essentially equivalent to the distribution of a taxable dividend, the amount so distributed in redemption or cancellation of the stock, to the extent that it represents a distribution of earnings or profits accumulated after February 28, 1913, shall be treated as a taxable dividend.

sioner v. Roberts, (C. A. 4) 203 F.2d 304, *reversing* 17 T. C. 1415. But, as pointed out by the regulations, a pro rata distribution is not always "essentially equivalent to the distribution of a taxable dividend" and each case depends upon its own particular circumstances. Commissioner v. Sullivan, (C. A. 5) 210 F.2d 607, *affirming* John L. Sullivan, 17 T.C. 1420. The circumstances in the instant case, however, do not warrant a finding that to the extent of earnings and profits the pro rata distribution was not essentially equivalent to a taxable dividend.

Being a question of fact, the decided cases are not controlling. However, in Joseph W. Imler, 11 T.C. 836, 840, we listed some of the factors which have been considered important, viz, "the presence or absence of a real business purpose, the motives of the corporation at the time of the distribution, the size of the corporate surplus, the past dividend policy, and the presence of any special circumstances relating to the distribution." . . .

An examination of the facts reveals that the Company had a large earned surplus and an unnecessary accumulation of cash from the standpoint of business requirement, both of which could have been reduced to the extent of earnings and profits by the declaration of a true dividend. The only suggested benefit accruing to the business by the distribution in cancellation of half the stock was the elimination of a substantial amount of this excess cash. Ordinarily such cash would be disposed of by the payment of a dividend. Coupled with the fact that the stockholders' proportionate interests in the enterprise remained unchanged, these factors indicate that section 115(g) is applicable. . .

Petitioners seek to avoid the application of section 115(g) by contending that the cash distribution and redemption of stock did not represent an artifice to disguise the payment of a dividend but was occasioned by a bona fide contraction of business with a resulting decrease in the need for capital. While important, the absence of a plan to avoid taxation is not controlling. A distribution in redemption of stock may be essentially equivalent to a taxable dividend although it does not represent an attempt to camouflage such a dividend. . . Whether a cancellation or redemption of stock is "essentially equivalent" to a taxable dividend depends primarily upon the net effect of the distribution rather than the motives and plans of the shareholders or the corporation. . . Moreover, we cannot find from the present record that the reduction of taxes was not the motivating factor causing the stockholders to make a distribution in redemption of stock rather than to declare a dividend to the extent of earnings and profits.

Petitioners' primary contention is that the sale of the department store and the opening of the smaller ladies' ready-to-wear store resulted in a contraction of corporate business. This is a vital factor to be considered, but a contraction of business per se does not render section 115(g) inapplicable. L. M. Lockhart, 8 T. C. 436. Furthermore, even though it is clear that there was a diminution in the size of the Company's business, there was no contraction such as was present in Commissioner v. Sullivan, Joseph W. Imler, and L. M. Lockhart, all supra. In those cases there was a contraction of business with a corresponding reduction in the amount of capital used.

Here, although the business was smaller, the amount of capital actually committed to the corporate business was not reduced accordingly. On December 31, 1945, before the sale of the department store to McArthur's Incorporated, the Company had $32,736.53 tied up in fixed assets and inventories. On December 31, 1946, after the ladies' ready-to-wear store was opened, it had $31,504.67 invested in those items. Undoubtedly the department store required larger reserves than the ladies' ready-to-wear store for purchasing inventories and carrying accounts receivable. But to the extent of earnings and profits the excess cash distributed was not created by a reduction in the amount of capital required for the operation of the business. Most of the excess cash had existed since prior to the sale of the department store and did not arise from fortuitous circumstances, as petitioners contend, but from an accumulation of earnings beyond the needs of the business. This excess could have been eliminated by the payment of a taxable dividend, and its distribution in redemption of stock was essentially equivalent to a taxable dividend.

It is true that the entire $67,250 distribution could not have been made in the form of an ordinary dividend and to some extent a redemption of stock was required. But section 115(g) applies if the distribution is only "in part" essentially equivalent to a taxable dividend, and here the distribution was essentially equivalent to a taxable dividend to the extent of earnings and profits.

Decisions will be entered for the respondent.

Revenue Ruling 67–299
1967–2 C.B. 138.

Advice has been requested whether the transaction described below involves a distribution resulting from a genuine contraction of the corporate business within the meaning of section 1.346–1(a)(2) of the Income Tax Regulations.

A corporation which is engaged in the business of owning and leasing real estate adopted a plan of partial liquidation. Pursuant to the plan the corporation sold one of its operating parcels of real estate for cash. It used the sales proceeds to remodel some of its remaining parcels of real estate. Shortly thereafter, and within the same taxable year in which the plan was adopted, it distributed an amount of money equal to the sales proceeds to its shareholders in redemption of some of its stock.

Section 346(a)(2) of the Internal Revenue Code of 1954 provides that a distribution will be treated as in partial liquidation of a corporation if the distribution is not essentially equivalent to a dividend, is in redemption of a part of the stock of the corporation pursuant to a plan, and occurs within the taxable year the plan is adopted or within the succeeding taxable year. Section 1.346–1(a)(2) of the regulations states that an example of a distribution which will qualify as a partial liquidation under section 346(a)(2) of the Code is a distribution resulting from a genuine contraction of the corporate business.

In this case, the sale of one parcel of real estate was a potential contraction of the corporate business. However, the remodeling of some of the remaining property was an expansion of the corporation's business offsetting any possible contraction effected by the sale. Thus, the sale of real estate did not result in a genuine contraction of the corporate business, since the net effect of the transactions was to keep the corporate assets at the same level which existed prior to the sale.

Accordingly, the above distribution by the corporation to its shareholders does not qualify as a distribution resulting from a genuine contraction of the corporate business within the meaning of section 1.346–1(a)(2) of the regulations.

NOTES

1. What would the result in *Chandler* (page 252 supra) have been if §§ 302(b)(4) and (e) had been applicable?

2. If the corporation involved in Rev. Rul. 67–299 had used the excess cash to remodel the retained real estate prior to selling the other parcel, would and should the Service's decision have been different?

3. To the extent dividends are taxed at the same rate as capital gains, how would *Chandler* and Rev. Rul. 67–299 come out today?

4. Do the attribution of ownership provisions of § 318 apply to § 302(b)(4) transactions? Should they?

5. If a corporation makes a distribution that otherwise qualifies as a partial liquidation under §§ 302(b)(4) and 302(e)(1), is it disqualified simply because the distribution was not pro rata? In Rev. Rul. 82–187, which considered this question under old § 346(a)(2) (the predecessor of §§ 302(b)(4) and 302(e)), the Service ruled that the distribution was not disqualified as a partial liquidation because it was non pro rata. In reaching this conclusion, the Service relied on the language in § 346(c) that contemplated the possibility of non pro rata distributions. What would happen today with the same facts of a "genuine corporate contraction" where §§ 302(b)(4) and 302(e) must be applied (which lack comparable language to § 346(c))? Was it necessary or wise to hinge the result in Rev. Rul. 82–187 on old § 346(c)?

6. If a corporation makes a pro rata distribution that otherwise qualifies as a partial liquidation under §§ 302(b)(4) and 302(e), the fact that shareholders do not surrender stock in exchange will not disqualify it. Rev. Rul. 90–13, 1990–1 C.B. 65.

Blaschka v. United States

393 F.2d 983 (Ct. Cl. 1968).

■ Before Cowen, Chief Judge, and LARAMORE, DURFEE, DAVIS, COLLINS, SKELTON, and NICHOLS, JUDGES.

Commissioner Hogenson's opinion, as modified by the court, is as follows:

Plaintiff has brought suit to recover income tax and deficiency interest for the year 1959 in the total amount of $74,344.38 plus interest. The sole question is whether a distribution of $115,000 to plaintiff by C. & C. Blaschka, Inc., was a dividend taxable as ordinary income or was a distribution in partial liquidation with the gain realized taxable as long-term capital gain.

The basic facts are not in dispute. Plaintiff and her husband, Carl J. Blaschka, are and were the sole stockholders in C. & C. Blaschka, Inc. (hereinafter referred to as C & C), plaintiff owning approximately 92.3 percent of the stock and her husband 7.7 percent. The Blaschkas are the executive officers of C & C and, together with their accountant, comprise the board of directors. From 1955 until 1959, both plaintiff and her husband devoted full time to the business activities of C & C.

Until July 1, 1959, C & C was engaged in the wholesaling of popularly priced gloves throughout the United States. This business requires the ability to select popular glove styles, a talent demanding ingenuity and years of experience as well as a great deal of time and travel. Plaintiff and her brother-in-law did the selecting for C & C. In addition, C & C has a wholly owned Canadian subsidiary, Max Mayer & Co., Ltd. (hereinafter called Max Mayer, Ltd.), which is engaged in the wholesale glove business in Canada. C & C keeps tight control over this Canadian corporation and makes every decision of any importance for it. In return for these services, Max Mayer, Ltd. has paid C & C since 1935 an annual "administrative fee" of 3 percent of the net sales of Max Mayer, Ltd.

In 1958, after the loss of two key employees through illness and death, C & C decided to dispose of its United States glove business. By a contract effective July 1, 1959, C & C sold this business to unrelated third parties for $646,442.31, payable in notes and preferred stock. The sale included the name Max Mayer which became the name of the new corporation to which C & C transferred all the assets.

As a result of the sale, C & C had more funds than it needed. After a number of conferences involving the Blaschkas, their accountant and their attorney, it was decided that C & C would enter the real estate rental field. To that end, C & C purchased all the outstanding stock of the Clairette Manufacturing Company, Inc. (hereinafter referred to as Clairette) from its sole stockholder, Mrs. Blaschka, plaintiff herein. Since 1955, Clairette's sole business had been the renting of a building it owned to C & C for warehouse purposes. After the sale, Clairette continued to rent the building to the purchasers of C & C's United States glove business. The transaction was consummated on September 28, 1959, with the transfer by plaintiff of the entire Clairette stock in return for $115,000. It is the tax treatment of this purchase by C & C that is in dispute.

Since plaintiff owned more than 50 percent of the outstanding stock of C & C and Clairette, this sale falls within § 304. . . In essence § 304(a)(1) provides that if a person is in control of each of two corporations, and, in return for property, one of the corporations acquires stock in the other corporation from that person, the property is treated as a distribution in redemption of the stock of the acquiring corporation. This provision was enacted in response to a series of unfavorable judicial decisions in which the Treasury attempted unsuccessfully to tax these transactions as distributions essentially equivalent to a dividend and therefore taxable as ordinary income under what is now §§ 301 and 302. . .

The function of § 304, then, is to complement § 302. To that end, § 304(b)(1) provides that such a sale is defined as a redemption of the stock of the acquiring corporation, and that for purposes of § 302(b), whether such stock acquisition is to be treated as a distribution in exchange for the stock is determined by reference to the stock of the issuing corporation. See also Reg. 1.304–2(a); Ralph L. Humphrey, 39 T.C. 199, 205 (1962). The essential question is whether the distribution has affected the stockholder's proportionate interest and control in the issuing corporation, and for that reason the special rule of § 304(b)(1) points to the issuing corporation to apply § 304(a) to § 302. S. Rep. No. 1622, 83d Cong., 2d Sess. 240 (1954); H.R. Rep. No. 1337, 83d Cong., 2d Sess. A79 (1954); 3 U.S.C. Cong. & Admn. News 4217, 4877 (1954). The stockholder's sale of his stock in one corporation to a related corporation could substantially change his interest in the issuing corporation, or on the other hand, be a change of form only, with no effect on the stockholder's actual control. . . Although § 304(b)(2) provides that the determination of the amount, paid in the stock redemption as defined in § 304(a)(1), which is a dividend shall be made solely with reference to the earnings and profits of the acquiring corporation, no mention is made of § 302(b) in that paragraph, nor is there any provision in § 304[2] or elsewhere in the 1954 Code, as to which corporation is to be tested to determine whether there has been a partial liquidation in a stock redemption through use of related corporations. It is significant, however, that subsection (e) of § 302, by statutory cross reference, points to § 331, and this together with the considerations underlying the tax treatment of partial liquidations require that a § 304 stock redemption, involving the question of a partial liquidation under §§ 331(a)(2) and 346, be tested on the level of the acquiring corporation. S. Rep. No. 1622, supra, at 49; U.S.C. Cong. & Admn. News, supra, at 4680. The very nature of a partial liquidation, at least as purportedly involved in this case, is a curtailment or contraction of the activities of the acquiring corporation, and the distribution to a stockholder of unneeded funds in exchange for stock in a related corporation. It is concluded that the purported partial liquidation is not to be measured by § 302, but that the general rule of § 304(a)—that the stock sale is to be treated as a redemption by the acquiring corporation—applies, subject, however, to the statutory definition as to what constitutes a partial liquidation under §§ 331 and 346 of the 1954 Code, applied to the acquiring corporation.

Thus, whether the payment of $115,000 by C & C for the stock of Clairette is a partial liquidation under §§ 331(a)(2) and 346 must be determined

---

[2] For an excellent analysis of the complexities and uncertainties of § 304, with special attention to recent cases, and with recommendations for legislative and administrative clarifications, see Marans, Section 304: The Shadowy World of Redemptions through Related Corporations, 22 N.Y.U. Tax Law Rev. 161 (1967).

with respect to the activities of C & C. Section 346 provides three tests to determine whether a distribution is to be treated as a payment in partial liquidation. The first, dealing with a series of distributions culminating in the complete liquidation of the corporation, is not applicable here since C & C has not and has no intention of completely liquidating. The second, § 346(a)(2), provides that a distribution will be considered as a payment in partial liquidation if it is not essentially equivalent to a dividend and is made pursuant to a plan, the payments being made within 2 years of the adoption of the plan. The requirement that the payment be made pursuant to a plan is crucial here, since it is apparent that C & C never adopted a formal plan of partial liquidation. The third test concerns the provisions of § 346(b), hereinafter discussed.

That a formal plan of liquidation is not required to qualify under § 346 is clear. Fowler Hosiery Co. v. Commissioner, 36 T.C. 201, 218 (1961), aff'd, 301 F. 2d 394, 397 (7th Cir. 1962). However, there must be clear evidence of an intention to liquidate if an informal plan is to be established. . .

In the instant case, C & C had adopted no plan of partial liquidation, either formal or informal, when it paid $115,000 for the Clairette stock. The official minutes of C & C show that there were two special meetings of the stockholders and four special meetings of the board of directors in 1959, and no meetings of either the stockholders or the directors in 1960. Nowhere in these minutes is there any discussion or mention of a plan of partial liquidation of C & C. The corporate resolution dated September 10, 1959, which accepted Mrs. Blaschka's offer of the Clairette stock, likewise makes no mention of any partial liquidation.

Plaintiff contends, however, that the purchase of the Clairette stock was part of a plan of partial liquidation discussed and informally adopted by the directors of C & C, and that the plan was not recorded in the corporate minutes because C & C's accountant and attorney did not think it necessary. But the facts indicate otherwise. Mr. Blaschka admitted that the purchase of Clairette's stock was made only after considering the tax aspects of the transaction. To assert that legal counsel advised a partial liquidation but did not make any written record of the plan is incredulous [sic].

This is all the more so when one considers plaintiff's Notice of Protest of the tax deficiency in controversy in this suit, a nine-page memorandum filed under oath with the Internal Revenue Service. No mention is made in that document of any partial liquidation being carried out by C & C. Furthermore, C & C stated in a memorandum sent to the Internal Revenue Service in 1961 concerning accumulated earnings tax that after its sale of the United States glove business, C & C decided to enter the industrial real estate business rather than liquidate. This is substantiated by Mr. Blaschka's testimony that the purchase of Clairette, whose sole business was the renting of a warehouse, was chosen as C & C's initial entry into this new field because the warehouse was known to be a good rentable building. In view of all this evidence, it is clear that the purchase of the Clairette stock was not pursuant to a plan of partial liquidation and the transaction cannot qualify under § 346(a)(2).

Nor does it come under the so-called "safe harbor" of § 346(b). Under that subsection, if a corporation has been conducting two or more separate and active businesses for at least 5 years and then ceases one of the businesses, the distribution of the assets of this ceased business or the proceeds from their sale shall be treated as a payment in partial liquidation so long as after the distribution the corporation continues to conduct actively at least one of the preexisting businesses. Just what constitutes "actively engaged in the conduct of a trade or business" for purposes of § 346 is defined in § 1.346–1(c) of the Regulations, by incorporation of § 1.355–1(c):

> [A] trade or business consists of a specific existing group of activities being carried on for the purpose of earning income or profit from only such group of activities, and the activities included in such group must include every operation which forms a part of, or a step in, the process of earning income or profit from such group. Such group of activities ordinarily must include the collection of income and the payment of expenses. [Treas. Reg. § 1.355–1(c)]

Plaintiff contends that C & C's management of its wholly owned subsidiary, Max Mayer, Ltd., is a separate trade or business apart from its United States glove business, thereby qualifying the distribution of the proceeds from the sale of the United States business through the purchase of the Clairette stock as a partial liquidation.

Aside from the general definition found in the Regulation, only a few cases have considered the question of what constitutes two separate trades or businesses. What few guidelines exist are found mainly in the 16 examples contained in Reg. § 1.355–1(d) and in the more than 25 rulings published by the Treasury. See McDonald, Tax Considerations in Corporate Divisions: Contraction and Liquidation, 39 Taxes (The Tax Magazine of C.C.H.) 994, 1000–1001, nn.60–63 for a complete listing of these rulings through 1961. As a result, the law has developed slowly on an ad hoc basis, with general principles not readily discernible from these factual patterns. However, common threads that run through many of these cases indicate that C & C was not engaged in the active conduct of two separate businesses in 1959.

One factor that reappears in several of the rulings is whether each business produces a substantial part of the combined income. In Rev. Rul. 57–333, 1957–2 Cum. Bull. 239, a corporation engaged in the food brokerage business also owned an adjacent vacant lot which it leased to a used car dealer. The rental received for the land for each of the last 5 years was less than 2 percent of the total gross income of the entire business. It was ruled that the rental of the lot did not constitute a separate business for purposes of § 346(b), with specific mention being made that the rental income received was only a nominal portion of the total gross income. In Rev. Rul. 56–266, 1956–1 Cum. Bull. 184, a corporation operated a retail grocery chain, manufactured and distributed bakery products, and produced and distributed creamery products, as well as owned real estate which it leased to its grocery stores for a rental based on a percentage of gross sales. The real estate activities were ruled not to be a business separate and apart from the grocery business.

Again, in Rev. Rul. 57–464, 1957–2 Cum. Bull. 244, a corporation manufactured heating equipment and owned a modern factory building, an old factory building which it used for storage purposes, and three rental properties. The real estate activities did not constitute a separate business, ruled the Treasury. Once more it was pointed out that the net income received from these properties was "negligible."

Also, in three judicial decisions all holding that two separate businesses did not exist, in which the question was whether the businesses were being actively conducted or not, the courts in each instance made reference to the small amount of income produced and lack of adequate record-keeping usually performed in a business. Isabel A. Elliott, 32 T.C. 283, 290–291 (1959); Theodore F. Appleby, 35 T.C. 755, 761 (1961), *aff'd per curiam* 296 F. 2d 925 (3d Cir. 1962), *cert. denied*, 370 U.S. 910 (1962); Bonsall v. Commissioner, 317 F. 2d 61, 64 (2d Cir. 1963). Cf. Example (16) in Reg. 1.355–1(d) involving a corporation that manufactured and sold automobiles and maintained an executive dining room for profit.[4]

That the underlying consideration running throughout these rulings was the sufficiency or insufficiency of income produced rather than some other factor can be seen in those rulings in which two separate businesses were found. Most striking is Rev. Rul. 58–164, 1958–1 Cum. Bull. 184. There, a corporation sold textile products as a commission merchant and owned a valuable building which it leased to outsiders for a substantial net rental. It was ruled that two separate businesses existed. Also, in Rev. Rul. 57–334, 1957–2 Cum. Bull. 240, a corporation rented to others three separate parcels of real estate. It was ruled that rental of one of the three buildings involved constituted a separate business since the remaining real estate accounted for only half the corporation's income. And in Rev. Rul. 56–557, 1956–2 Cum. Bull. 199, the ruling again points to the importance of the fact that the income from the challenged business was substantial, in a determination that there were two separate businesses.

Turning to the income figures in the instant case, they reflect clearly that the services performed for Max Mayer, Ltd., by C & C produced so little income as not to be a business separate and distinct from the United States glove business. In return for these services, Max Mayer, Ltd., paid C & C an "administrative fee" of 3 percent of Max Mayer, Ltd.'s net sales, a figure set in 1935 by plaintiff's uncle. From 1952 through 1958, this gross administrative fee was only 1 percent of C & C's net sales of $13,893,677.95 for that period. Furthermore, from 1935 to 1962, C & C did not even allocate on its books the expenses attributable to the work performed for Max Mayer, Ltd.—hardly the practice of a corporation in the business of managerial and financial services. Cf. Isabel A. Elliott, supra; Theodore F. Ap-

---

[4] Each "Example" cited will be from Reg. 1.355–1(d).

pleby, supra; Bonsall v. Commissioner, supra. Since 1962, the Canadian authorities have required C & C to submit a detailed statement of the specific charges for its services to Max Mayer, Ltd. In 1962, out of a total administrative fee of $24,784.05, C & C earned a profit of only $751.96, or a return of approximately 3 percent. Projecting this profit margin back over the period from 1952 through 1958, C & C's total profits from administrative fees were approximately $4,261, or 1.5 percent of C & C's total net profits before taxes of $283,622 for that period. Such negligible amounts hardly meet the requirement included in Regulation § 1.346–1(c) that the activities be carried on "for the purpose of earning income or profit." Treas. Reg. § 1.355–1(c), supra.

The Regulations and Treasury Rulings, also, seem to require some form of separation of control and supervision to find separate businesses. In Rev. Rul. 58–54, 1958–1 Cum. Bull. 181, a corporation operated a soft drink bottling and distributing business. All the bottling was done at the main plant although it was distributed through facilities located in four different localities. The Treasury ruled that the distributing facilities did not constitute a separate business or businesses "despite some geographical differences in warehouse locations. They all formed part of one integrated business wherein the product was manufactured in one place, although distributed through several warehouse points." 1958–1 Cum. Bull. 181 at 182.

Rev. Rul. 56–451, 1956–2 Cum. Bull. 208 involved a corporation which published four trade magazines. The metal working magazine had its own editorial staff and advertising space salesmen, who devoted their entire time to this magazine. This publication had separate offices in the same building as the others and kept separate books. The only employees it shared with the others were the general officers of the corporation and certain clerical and production employees. The three other magazines served the electrical industry. The Treasury ruled that the metal working magazine was a separate business.

The Regulations provide still another example. Taxpayer corporation owns and operates two men's retail clothing stores, one in the city and one in the suburbs. The manager of each store directs its operations and makes the necessary purchases. No common warehouse is maintained. Under these circumstances the Regulations state that the activities of each store constitute a trade or business, evidently on the grounds of separate control and operation. (Example (10).)

In short, Max Mayer, Ltd., is a separate and distinct business from C & C in corporate form, but otherwise only in a geographical sense. There is some indication in the Regulations that geographical separation is enough. In Example (8), a corporation which manufactures ice cream at plants in two states is said to operate a trade or business in each state. To the same effect are Examples (13), (14), and (15). Just how these Examples relate to Example (10) supra, where geographical separation existed but where other factors were specifically mentioned, is not clear. Moreover, there is Rev. Rul. 57–190, 1957–1 Cum. Bull. 121. The facts there involved a corporation which sold and serviced cars, carrying on its operations in two buildings located some distance apart in the same city. The Treasury ruled that the separate locations were not sufficient to create separate businesses.

Thus, geographical separation by itself is of questionable significance. Also, all of the above-mentioned Examples (where apparently geographical separation was sufficient) are distinguishable from the instant case. Each Example involved a manufacturing business, manufacturing its products at several locations. Each plant was a viable entity, capable of producing the product from beginning to end. In spite of its separate corporate entity, Max Mayer, Ltd., was in no way viable by itself. Rather did it depend upon the decisions of C & C for what it sold and how it sold. Before the Clairette stock sale, plaintiff owned 100 percent of the Clairette stock and 92.3 percent of the C & C stock, and C & C owned 100 percent of Max Mayer, Ltd. This control of all three corporations becomes absolute when the husband's 7.7 percent share of C & C is added. The circumstances strongly infer that in reality the "stock redemption" was equivalent to the declaration of a dividend, especially in view of the large accumulation of earned surplus by the redeeming corporation. When this factor is considered with the negligible amount of income and profits realized, the conclusion is that the management services provided by C & C to Max Mayer, Ltd., were not an "active trade or business" separate and apart from its own operations.

Therefore, the purchase of the Clairette stock by C & C was not a distribution in partial liquidation. The sum of $115,000 is deemed to be paid out of C & C's earnings and profits and taxable at ordinary income rates as a dividend pursuant to §§ 302 and 301(c)(1). Plaintiff's petition for a refund should be dismissed.

NOTES

1. Should § 302(b)(4) and (e) be part of the Code? What justification is there for basis recovery [and capital gains treatment] for a pro rata distribution? What is the relevance of corporate business contraction in deciding at the congressional level whether a distribution should receive capital gains treatment? How much changes in the post–2003 era with dividends taxed at capital gains rates?

2. Is § 302(b)(4) "elective"? See Rev. Rul. 77–468, 1977–2 C.B. 109 (deliberate delay in making distribution, beyond period specified in § 302(e), avoids partial liquidation treatment). Cf. Rev. Rul. 77–150, 1977–1 C.B. 88. Why would a corporation seek to disqualify its partial liquidation?

III. SECTION 1244

Section 1244 of the Code was enacted as part of the Small Business Tax Revision Act of 1958. Its purpose is described in H.R. Rep. No. 2198, 85 Cong., 1st Sess., 1959–2 C.B. 711, as follows:

> This section provides ordinary loss rather than capital loss treatment on the sale or exchange of small-business stock. This treatment is available only in the case of an individual and only if he is the original holder of the stock.

This provision is designed to encourage the flow of new funds into small business. The encouragement in this case takes the form of reducing the risk of a loss for these new funds. The ordinary loss treatment which the bill accords shareholders in small corporations in effect is already available to proprietors and partners. They report directly the earnings from these business ventures and thus ordinary losses realized by a proprietorship or partnership presently constitute ordinary losses to the proprietor or partner. As a result, from the standpoint of risk taking, this bill places shareholders in small corporations on a more nearly equal basis with these proprietors and partners.

In accord with your committee's desire to limit the benefit of this provision to small business, the total stock offering of any corporation which is eligible for this ordinary loss treatment is limited to $500,000. Moreover, the total stock offering per corporation plus equity capital of the corporation may not exceed $1 million. In addition, the maximum loss which a taxpayer can treat as an ordinary loss under this provision is to be $25,000 a year (or $50,000 in the case of a husband and wife filing a joint return).

Your committee also has imposed a restriction designed to limit this tax benefit to companies which are largely operating companies. Thus, the corporation, in the 5 years before the taxpayer incurs the loss on the stock must have derived more than half of its gross receipts from sources other than royalties, rents, dividends, interest, annuities, and the sale of stock or securities. . .

The Revenue Act of 1978 raised the maximum amount of § 1244 stock that can be issued by a single corporation to $1 million, eliminated the need for a "plan" and the "equity capital" limitation of prior law, and raised the maximum amount eligible for ordinary loss treatment to $50,000 ($100,000 on a joint return).

In 1984, Congress amended § 1244(c)(1) and (d)(2) by changing "common stock" to "stock." The relevant committee reports make clear that the change was designed to bring preferred stock within the ambit of § 1244. See, e.g., H.R. Rep. No. 432, 98 Cong., 2d Sess. 1581 (1984). Given the continued limits on the deductibility of capital losses (despite tax rate changes for both capital gains and in dividends over the years), § 1244 remains useful to shareholders in providing them with ordinary losses for what, in its absence, would be capital losses. You should consider whether § 1244 in theme and structure represents desirable tax policy.

The primary disputes arising under § 1244 concern whether the taxpayer was the original holder of the stock (see, e.g., Marvin R. Adams v. Commissioner, 74 T.C. 4 (1980)) and whether the contributor to the corporation received stock in return in contrast to receiving no additional shares or receiving notes (see, e.g., Miller v. Commissioner, 57 T.C.M. (CCH) 46 (1989), aff'd, 900 F.2d 260 (6th Cir. 1990)). This issue can arise in the context of a case such as Lessinger v. Commissioner, 872 F.2d 519 (2d Cir.

1989) infra at 329, where a taxpayer contributes assets and liabilities to a pre-existing corporation owned by the taxpayer.

Note that the sale of "small business stock," defined differently than in § 1244, will produce a 50% exclusion under § 1202.

CHAPTER 3

INCORPORATION OF ASSETS

I. INTRODUCTION

Assume that Smith owns and operates a large and successful retail furniture business in unincorporated form. The assets of her business are reflected below:

	Adjusted Basis	Fair Market Value
Cash	$ 200,000	$ 200,000
Inventory	1,500,000	1,900,000
Accounts Receivable	200,000	200,000
Fixed Assets	250,000	350,000
Goodwill	zero	500,000
	$2,150,000	$3,150,000

If Smith transfers these assets to a corporation in exchange for all of its authorized capital stock, her $1 million gain (asset appreciation) will be "realized" (§ 1001(b)), but it will not be "recognized" (§ 351(a)). If Smith had effected the transfer prior to the Revenue Act of 1921, her gain would have been both "realized" and "recognized." Prior to that Act, therefore, her taxable income in the year of incorporation would have included the appreciation in the assets she continued to own in corporate form. By the same process, prior to the Revenue Act of 1921, if her assets had depreciated below their adjusted basis, her realized loss on incorporation would have been recognized (absent a provision such as § 267). The Revenue Act of 1921, as with all subsequent enactments, provided for nonrecognition of the loss.

Section 351 and its predecessor provisions are grounded on the thesis that taxation (or deduction of a loss) ought not to occur "where in a popular and economic sense there has been a mere change in the form of ownership and the taxpayer has not really 'cashed in' on the theoretical gain, or closed out a losing venture." Portland Oil Co. v. Commissioner, 109 F.2d 479, 488 (1st Cir. 1940). See also S. Rep. No. 275, 67th Cong., 1st Sess., 1939–1 C.B. (pt. 2) 181, 188–189. The policy is so well ingrained that even the depreciation recapture provisions of §§ 1245 and 1250 yield to the nonrecognition rule of § 351. See §§ 1245(b)(3) and 1250(d)(3).

Incorporation of the assets of sole proprietorships and partnerships, as well as those of previously unaffiliated investors, is a workaday occurrence in the world of commerce and law. Usually the proposed incorporation transaction and § 351 mesh well, and nonrecognition is the result. There are many situations, however, in which only painstaking care will bring a transaction within § 351. In fewer but nevertheless important cases the tax lawyer wants to avoid § 351; i.e., he wants recognition. Here his role is to tailor the proposed transaction to escape the reach of § 351. That provision is not operative merely when the taxpayer elects to have it apply, in contrast to sections like 1033 and 1034. If a transaction fits within § 351, there is nonrecognition irrespective of the taxpayer's wishes.

The language of the Code and regulations and the history entwined with their application present a host of intricate questions. This chapter will deal with a number of them. Recognition (or not) of the transferor's gain, however, is only one question in an incorporation transaction. If all the gain is recognized, the transferor's basis for the stock he receives is its fair market value ("tax cost") under § 1012. If § 351 provides for nonrecognition, the transferor's basis for his stock is determined under § 358. The transferee corporation realizes no gain when it issues its stock for assets (§ 1032), but its basis for the assets received will be determined under § 1012 if the transferor recognizes all his gain, and under § 362(a) if he does not. If the transferor receives not only stock but cash or other property as well, he may have partial recognition. The measure of recognition and the determination of the basis for both transferor and transferee become more complex in that case. By its terms § 351 applies only when the transferor receives stock in exchange for property. Prior to amendment in 1989, however, § 351 permitted the receipt of securities in addition to stock without recognition of gain or loss. Today, receipt of the transferee corporation's debt, whether or not evidenced by securities, will result in partial recognition, although in some cases even the partially recognized gain may be deferred under the installment sale provisions of § 453. In 1997, Congress further restricted what shareholders can receive under § 351. Section 351(g) provides that non-qualified preferred stock (i.e. stock with certain debt characteristics) will not receive nonrecognition treatment under § 351(a).

If § 351 governs a transaction the "holding period" of the stock received by the transferor will be determined under § 1223(1), and the corporation's "holding period" for the property it receives will be determined under § 1223(2). With exceptions, "tacking" occurs in both cases.

Sometimes a corporation may be the transferor, transferring all or part of its assets to another corporation. Section 351 may apply, as in the case of a noncorporate transferor, and § 361 (involving "reorganizations," to be studied in Chapter 4) may also apply. Section 351(e)(1) was added to the Code in 1966 as a response to an ingenious development and a lively administrative controversy involving newly organized, widely held, mutual fund-type investment companies. To what kind of transactions do you think these provisions are addressed? See Rev. Rul. 87–9, page 289 infra.

As with a number of other nonrecognition provisions, § 351 may be inapplicable to gain (but not loss) on a transfer to a foreign corporation. See § 367; cf. §§ 1491 and 1492. This book does not cover the federal income tax problems peculiar to foreign corporations. It leaves them to books dedicated to those issues, e.g., P. Postelwaite & S. Hoffer, International Taxation: Corporate and Individual (2012); B. Bittker & L. Lokken, Fundamentals of International Taxation: U.S. Taxation of Foreign Income and Foreign Taxpayers (2010); J. Isenbergh, International Taxation (2007).

Before approaching the knotty tax problems, you should give thought to the mechanics of incorporation. How does a taxpayer incorporate her real estate, her saw, her accounts receivable, her goodwill? How is stock "issued"? What documents are required, to whom are they delivered, and what assents and acknowledgments are necessary? Do not refer to "incorporating a business" without knowing exactly how it is accomplished. Livery of seisin is out of style today, and it was never effective to transfer goodwill. See generally B. Bittker and J. Eustice, Federal Income Taxation of Corporations and Shareholders 3.01 to 3.21 (2012 online).

II. RECEIPT OF STOCK IN EXCHANGE—TAX IMPACT ON INVESTOR—§ 351

A. QUESTIONS OF "CONTROL" AND "EXCHANGE"

1. TIMING AND THE "PERSONS"

American Bantam Car Co. v. Commissioner

11 T.C. 397 (1948), *aff'd per curiam*, 177 F.2d 513 (3d Cir. 1949), *cert. denied*, 339 U.S. 920 (1950).

[In August 1935, A, B, and C (hereinafter called the associates), acquired the assets of the defunct American Austin Car Co. by purchase from its liquidating trustees. They paid $5,000 in cash; the assets were subject to liabilities of $219,099.83. In May 1936, they decided to form the American Bantam Car Co., the petitioner in this case. Under the plan the associates were to transfer the American Austin assets, subject to the existing liabilities, and $500 in cash to the petitioner in exchange for 300,000 shares of the latter's no par common stock; 90,000 shares of the petitioner's preference stock were to be offered to the public through underwriters. If the underwriters were successful in disposing of the stock they were to receive from the associates 100,000 shares of the common stock in addition to their regular underwriting commissions. All of the interested parties agreed orally to the substance of this plan on June 2, 1936, but no formal written contract was entered into at that time. On the same date petitioner was incorporated with an authorized capital stock of 700,000 shares, consisting of 100,000 shares of $10 par value preferred stock and 600,000 shares of no par common stock. The holders of the preferred stock were entitled to three votes for each share held, and the holders of the common were entitled to one vote per share. On June 3, 1936, the associates transferred the American Austin assets, subject to the aforementioned liabilities, and $500 in cash to the petitioner, and the latter issued 300,000 shares of the common stock to the associates in accordance with their proportionate interests in the assets and money. An appraisal made of the American Austin assets at that time indicated that they were worth $840,800.]

[On June 8, 1936, petitioner executed a written agreement with: the underwriters for the sale of 90,000 shares of its preferred stock to the public. A selling schedule was established under which the stock was to be disposed of in varying amounts over a period of one year. At the same time the associates and the underwriters executed a written contract under which the former were to transfer a total of 100,000 shares of the petitioner's common stock to the latter as they sold the preferred stock. To facilitate the transfer the associates placed all of the common stock held by them in the custody of a bank. The bank was to hold the common shares until the preferred stock was completely sold; then the common was to be returned to the associates, and they were to deliver 100,000 shares to the underwriters. By October 1937, the underwriters had sold 83,618 shares of the preferred to the public, and at that time they received 87,900 shares of the common from the associates pursuant to the agreement. The underwriters, within one month, sold 1,008 shares of the common to the public.]

[For the taxable years 1936 through 1941 the petitioner used $145,000 as its basis for the depreciation of the American Austin assets. In 1942 and 1943, when petitioner showed profit from war production, it used $840,800 as the basis for those assets. The Commissioner contended that the assets had been received in a tax-free exchange and that their basis to the petitioner depended upon their basis in the hands of the associates.]

Ironic that sides are flipped

■ HILL, JUDGE. This case requires the determination of the proper basis for the Austin assets acquired by petitioner—on June 3, 1936, in exchange for stock. We must decide whether under the facts here section [362(a)] requires petitioner, in computing deductions for depreciation, to take as the basis of the assets so acquired the basis thereof in the hands of the transferors. This section is applicable if the exchange by which petitioner received the Austin assets was one in which gain or loss is not recognized under the provisions of section [351(a)]. . . We therefore must first consider whether, when the associates turned over the Austin assets to petitioner, subject to liabilities of $219,099.83, plus $500 in cash, and in return petitioner issued to the associates 300,000 shares of its no par common stock, all the requirements of section [351(a)] were satisfied.

Question Is 351 Satisfied?

At the outset it should be noted that the statute requires for a nontaxable exchange that the property turned over by the transferors be "solely" in exchange for stock or securities of the transferee corporation. The transferors in the instant case actually received from petitioner upon the exchange only 300,000 shares of common stock. Thus, the statutory requirement is met unless it can be said the transferors indirectly received "other property or money" by virtue of the fact the petitioner acquired the transferred property subject to liabilities. Section [357(a)] . . . specifically states that such an acquisition of property subject to liability shall not be considered as "other property or money" received by the transferors. It is clear that a definite business purpose motivated this transaction. Therefore such acquisition by the petitioner does not prevent the exchange from being within the provisions of section [351(a)] and the transferors in exchange for their property did receive "solely" stock from the corporation.

It has been held that money turned over to the transferee corporation by the transferors does not prevent a tax-free exchange, for it is includible within the term "property" in section [351(a)]. [G.C.M. 24415, 1944 C.B. 219]; Haliburton v. Commissioner, 78 Fed. (2d) 265. Therefore, the $500 transfer of cash to petitioner by the associates comes within the terms of section [351(a)].

Control

The first major test of tax-free exchange under section [351(a)] is whether the transferors have "control" of the corporation immediately after the exchange. Section [368(c)] . . . defines "control":

> As used in this section the term "control" means the ownership of stock possessing at least 80 per centum of the total combined voting power of all classes of stock entitled to vote and at least 80 per centum of the total number of shares of all other classes of stock of the corporation.

The first question, then, is whether the associates had such "control" over the petitioner immediately after the exchange on June 3, 1936. Prima facie, when the various steps taken to organize the new corporation and transfer assets to it are considered separately, the associates did have "control" of the petitioner immediately after the exchange within the statutory definition of the word. We think that from June 3 to June 8, 1936, they owned 100 per cent of all the issued stock, and from June 8, 1936, until October 1937 they owned stock possessing at least 80 per cent of the total combined voting power of all classes of stock. On June 3, 1936, the associates were issued absolutely and unconditionally 300,000 shares of no par common stock. The resolution of the board of directors of petitioner accepting the associates' offer of the Austin assets attached no strings whatsoever to the issuance of the stock to them. It is true that on June 2, 1936, petitioner had an authorized capital stock of 700,000 shares, 600,000 common shares and 100,000 preferred shares, but in determining control only stock actually issued is considered. . . On June 8 no other common stock had been issued, and a contract regarding possible future assignment of those 300,000 shares already issued was not entered into before that date. No preferred stock had been issued on June 3, nor was a contract for its sale provided until June 8. The statutory words "immediately after the exchange" require control for no longer period; in fact, momentary control is sufficient. . . Certainly, therefore, the associates had absolute control over the corporation from June 3 to June 8, 1936, due to their complete ownership of all outstanding stock.

It is true that, by virtue of their agreement with the associates on June 8, 1936, the underwriters did at that time acquire the right to earn shares of the common stock issued to the associates by the sale of certain percentages of preferred stock, but the ownership of the 300,000 shares remained in the associates until such sales were completed. It is significant to note that this agreement stated that the associates were the owners of the 300,000 shares. On August 16, 1936, the associates deposited all their shares in escrow with the Butler County National Bank & Trust Co., but they only surrendered possession by the terms of their agreement with the bank and retained all other attributes of ownership.

During all of 1936 the associates retained ownership over the 300,000 shares of common stock and during that interval the underwriters sold only

14,757 shares of preferred stock, which did not entitle them to any common stock under the agreement of June 8, 1936. The corporation's bylaws provided that each share of preferred stock should have 3 votes, while each share of common stock should have 1 vote. Therefore, at the end of 1936, out of 344,271 possible stock votes, the total combined voting power of all outstanding stock, the associates owned 300,000, or over 80 per cent. It was not until October 1937, when the underwriter Grant* received 87,900 shares of the associates' common stock in fulfillment of the underwriting agreement, that the associates lost "control" of petitioner within the statutory definition of the word. Retention of "control" for such a duration of time satisfies the governing provision of section [351(a)].

Lost control in 1937

Petitioner, however, contends that the series of steps organizing the new corporation, transferring assets to it, and arranging for the sale of its preference stock must be considered as parts of the integrated plan formulated in May 1936, and, therefore, considered as parts of a single transaction. It argues that this unified transaction started on June 2, 1936, when petitioner was incorporated, and ended in October 1937, when the public offering of the preferred stock by the underwriters ceased and Grant was awarded 87,900 shares of common stock; that the transfer of common stock to Grant in 1937 was the final step of an indivisible operation and must be viewed concurrently with the preceding steps. On this theory the associates did not obtain control of petitioner, for on consummation of this final step in the general plan the associates had only 212,100 shares of common stock, while Grant had 86,892 shares and the public had 1,008 and there were 83,618 shares of outstanding preferred stock owned by the public. The 212,100 stock votes held by the associates in October 1937 fell shy of the required 80 per cent to give the requisite control.

If viewed in terms of one transaction, the control requirement wasn't met

In determining whether a series of steps are to be treated as a single indivisible transaction or should retain their separate entity, the courts use a variety of tests. . . . Among the factors considered are the intent of the parties, the time element, and the pragmatic test of the ultimate result. An important test is that of mutual interdependence. Were the steps so interdependent that the legal relations created by one transaction would have been fruitless without a completion of the series?

Using these tests as a basis for their decisions the courts in Hazeltine Corporation v. Commissioner, 89 Fed. (2d) 513, and Bassick v. Commissioner 85 Fed. (2d) 8, treated the series of steps involved in each case as parts of a unified transaction and therefore determined that the transferors of assets to the new corporation did not acquire the requisite control. An analysis of the fact situations involved shows salient distinguishing features from the present facts. In each of the above cases there was a written contract prior both to the organization of the new corporation and the exchange of assets for stock which bound the transferors unconditionally to assign part of the stock acquired to third parties after the exchange. Thus, at the moment of the exchange the recipient of the stock did not own it, but

---

*The factual statement uses the word *underwriters*, while the court's opinion refers to *Grant*.—ED.

held it subject to a binding contractual obligation to transfer a portion. The court in each case thought that the incorporation and exchange would never have been agreed upon without the supplemental agreement turning over stock to a third party. In such situations it is logical for the courts to say that the exchange and the subsequent transfer are part of one and the same transaction, so that the transferor never actually owned the shares he later assigned.

A close examination of the facts surrounding the exchange in the present case makes it clear that the exchange of assets for stock and the subsequent transfer of a portion of that stock to Grant therein involved should not be considered part of the same transaction so as to deprive the associates of "control" immediately after the exchange. The facts are distinguishable from those existing in the *Hazeltine* and *Bassick* cases on three grounds. First, there was no written contract prior to the exchange binding the associates to transfer stock to the underwriters. At the most, there was an informal oral understanding of a general plan contemplating the organization of a new corporation, the exchange of assets for stock, and marketing of preferred stock of the new corporation to the public. A written contract providing for the transfer of shares from the associates to the underwriters did not come until five days after the exchange. Secondly, when the transfer of shares to the underwriters was embodied specifically in a formal contract, the underwriters received no absolute right to ownership of the common stock, but only when, as, and if, certain percentages of preferred stock were sold. How clearly contingent was the nature of their rights is illustrated by the fact that only one underwriter, Grant, met the terms of the agreement and became entitled to any shares. Thirdly, the necessity of placing the 300,000 shares in escrow with a bank is indicative of complete ownership of such stock by the associates following the exchange.

The standard required by the courts to enable them to say that a series of steps are interdependent and thus should be viewed as a single transaction do not exist here. It is true that all the steps may have been contemplated under the same general plan of May 1936; yet the contemplated arrangement for the sale of preferred stock to the public was entirely secondary and supplemental to the principal goal of the plan to organize the new corporation and exchange its stock for Austin assets. The understanding with the underwriters for disposing of the preferred stock, however important, was not a sine qua non in the general plan, without which no other step would have been taken. While the incorporation and exchange of assets would have been purposeless one without the other, yet both would have been carried out even though the contemplated method of marketing the preferred stock might fail. The very fact that in the contracts of June 8, 1936, the associates retained the right to cancel the marketing order and, consequently the underwriters' mean to own common stock issued to the associates, refutes the proposition that the legal relations resulting from the steps of organizing the corporation and transferring assets to it would have been fruitless without the sale of the preferred stock in the manner contemplated.

Finally, to say that the separate steps should be viewed as one transaction so that ownership of 87,900 shares never passed to the associates has the disadvantage of inferring that the interested parties intended to suspend ownership of 300,000 shares from June 3, 1936, until such time as the underwriters definitely did or did not earn the right to such shares—as it turned out, until October 1937. It is much more logical to say that ownership of all 300,000 shares rested in the associates until the conditions precedent had been fulfilled by the underwriters, and that when the associates turned over the stock to Grant they were exercising their rights of ownership acquired on June 3, 1936. To allow petitioner's contention is to permit a 15–month time lag after the exchange before determining "control immediately after the exchange." Such a proposition defeats the very language of the statute.

A review of decisions encountering this problem under section [351(a)] shows that courts have determined control of the new corporation remained with the transferors of assets following the exchange under circumstances less favorable than in the present case. . .

Thus we conclude that in the present case the exchange of assets for stock between the associates and petitioner on June 3, 1936, was a separate completed transaction, distinct from the subsequent transfer of common stock to Grant, so that the associates were in control of petitioner immediately after the exchange within the provisions of section [351(a)]. . .

What then is the basis for depreciation purposes of property acquired by a corporation by a tax-free exchange under section [351(a)]? Section [362(a)] of the code specifically answers this question. The basis is the same as it would be in the hands of the transferor. In the instant case the basis of the Austin assets in the hands of the associates was the cost of those assets to them. They paid $5,000 cash and received the property subject to liabilities of $219,099.83. Thus the basis in their hands was $224,099.83. Therefore, the basis for the Austin assets to the petitioner is also $224,099.83, as contended by the respondent. . .

Holding

NOTES

1. The original incorporators of American Bantam Car Co. presumably took the position that § 351 applied to the incorporation transaction, and that gain was therefore not recognized. Suppose the Commissioner had lost the *American Bantam Car* case, and the court had held that § 351 was inapplicable. Would the statute of limitations have prevented the Commissioner from then assessing tax on the original incorporators based on the gain from the incorporation transaction? Today, the Commissioner can rely on § 1311, a provision allowing him to reopen a tax year when related parties have taken inconsistent positions and a determination has been made in favor of one of them. See §§ 1311 and 1312(7).

2. Reg. § 1.351–1(a)(3) provides for tax deferral under § 351 in a "qualified underwriting transaction," with examples provided of typical situations.

3. The policy theme underlying § 351 is that gain or loss should not be recognized where there has been only a change in the form of ownership. Cf. § 351(e)(1). What is the purpose behind § 351(e)? See infra Rev. Ruling 87-9.

4. A partnership with appreciated assets is interested in expansion. Accordingly, the partners transfer all their partnership interests to a corporation in exchange for its stock. Upon receipt of the stock, pursuant to prior plan, they sell 30 percent of the stock to an underwriter who distributes the stock to the public the same day. Do the partners recognize gain in the amount of the unrealized appreciation of the partnership assets when they form the corporation?

5. Mr. Fox owns a sole proprietorship, the assets of which have substantially appreciated in value since he purchased it. Because he wishes to bring his son into the business, he incorporates under a firm commitment to give 30 percent of the stock to his son immediately. His son has given nothing in return for the stock. Does Fox recognize any income? Why? Would the result be different if there were no firm commitment to his son, but only an understanding that the son would eventually join the business? Cf. Fahs v. Florida Machine and Foundry Co., 168 F.2d 957 (5th Cir. 1948).

6. Suppose A contributes $100,000 in appreciated property in return for 100 percent of the nonvoting preferred stock of Corporation Z and 30% of the voting common stock, and B contributes $900,000 in cash for 70 percent of the voting common stock. Does A recognize gain? See § 351(g)(1). What if A only received 100% nonvoting preferred and B received 100% of the voting common? If the nonvoting preferred is nonqualified preferred stock then § 351 does not apply to A and the exchange is a taxable event. § 351(g). For purposes of considering "control" for B, how does A's nonqualified preferred stock count? See 1997 Conf. Rept. H.R. 2014 Sec. 1013.

Revenue Ruling 79–194
1979–1 C.B. 145.

ISSUE

Is the control requirement of section 351(a) of the Internal Revenue Code of 1954, which provides for non-recognition of gain or loss on transfers of property to a controlled corporation, satisfied where part of the stock of the controlled corporation received by a transferor in exchange for property is sold to other persons who also transferred property to the corporation in exchange for stock?

FACTS

Situation (1)

Corporation Z and a group of investors, pursuant to a binding agreement between them, transferred property to a newly organized corporation, Newco, in exchange for all of Newco's stock (a single class of voting common stock). Z and the investors received 80 percent and 20 percent, respectively, of Newco's stock. Pursuant to the agreement Z sold an amount of its Newco stock for its fair market value to the investors to bring its ownership down to 49 percent. Newco would not have been formed if the investors had not agreed to transfer property to it and their agreement to do so was conditioned on the sale by Z to them of part of Z's Newco stock.

Situation (2)

X, a domestic corporation, operates a branch in a foreign country. The foreign country enacted a nationalization law that required that the business that X's branch was engaged in be incorporated in the foreign country and that its citizens be the majority owners of such corporation. A governmental agency in the foreign country directed X to transfer all of the assets of its branch to a newly formed foreign country corporation that is, or will be, at least 51 percent owned by its citizens. Accordingly, X and a group of investors, who were citizens of the foreign country, pursuant to a binding agreement between them, transferred property to Newco, a corporation newly organized in the foreign country, in exchange for all of Newco's stock (a single class of voting common stock). X and the investors received 99 percent and one percent, respectively, of Newco's stock. Pursuant to the agreement, X sold an amount of its Newco stock for its fair market value to the investors to bring its ownership down to 49 percent; the investors would pay X in a series of yearly installments. Newco would not have been formed if the investors had not agreed to transfer property to it and their agreement to do so was conditioned on the sale by X to them of part of X's Newco stock. Further, the investors transferred property to Newco in order to become co-transferors with X, and they purchased X's Newco stock in lieu of the assets of X's branch because of the foreign governmental agency's directive. . . The fair market value of each asset transferred is in excess of its basis.

LAW AND ANALYSIS

The specific sections of the Code that are applicable are section 351(a), which provides that no gain or loss will be recognized if property is transferred to a corporation by one or more persons solely in exchange for stock or securities in such corporation and immediately after the exchange such person or persons are in control of the corporation, and section 368(c) which defines control for purposes of section 351(a), to mean the ownership of stock possessing at least 80 percent of the total combined voting power of all classes of stock entitled to vote and at least 80 percent of the total number of shares of all other classes of stock of the corporation.

Since the sales of Newco stock by Z to the investors, and of Newco stock by X to the investors, were integral parts of the corporations and pursuant to binding agreements entered into prior to the exchanges, the control requirement of section 351(a) of the Code is determined after the respective sales. See Hazeltine Corp. v. Commissioner, 89 F.2d 513 (3d Cir. 1937), Intermountain Lumber Co. v. Commissioner, 65 T.C. 1025 (1976) and Rev. Rul. 70–522, 19702 C.B. 81.

In Situation (1), after the sales were completed, 49 percent of the Newco stock was owned by Z and 51 percent of the stock was owned by the investors. Therefore, the persons transferring property to Newco in exchange for Newco stock owned 100 percent of the Newco stock "immediately after the exchange" within the meaning of section 351(a). The fact that there was a shift in ownership of stock among the transferors after their exchanges with Newco does not affect the application of section 351(a). See example (1) under section 1.351–1(b) of the Income Tax Regulations in which transfers of property to a new corporation qualify under section 351 even though a shift in the ownership of stock among the transferors is considered to have occurred subsequent to the transfers.

In Situation (2), after the sales were completed, 49 percent of the Newco stock was owned by X and 51 percent of the Newco stock was owned by the investors. Because the amount of stock issued directly to the investors for property is of relatively small value in comparison to the value of all the stock received by them in the transaction, the stock received by the investors is not taken into account in considering whether the transaction qualifies under section 351(a) of the Code. Compare section 1.351–1(a)(1)(ii) of the regulations. Thus, for purposes of determining control under section 351, the investors were not transferors. Therefore, since the person (X) transferring property to Newco in exchange for Newco stock owned only 49 percent of the Newco stock "immediately after the exchange," the control requirement of section 351(a) is not satisfied. The fact that there was a shift in ownership of 49 percent of the Newco stock from a transferor (X) to a non-transferor (the investors) after their exchanges with Newco affects the application of section 351(a). . .

HOLDING

Situation (1)

The control requirement of section 351(a) of the Code is satisfied. No gain or loss is recognized to Z or the investors under section 351(a) on the transfer of property to Newco. Gain or loss to Z upon the sale of the Newco stock will be determined and recognized under section 1001.

Situation (2)

The control requirement of section 351(a) of the Code is not satisfied. Gain is recognized to X on the transfer of property to Newco pursuant to section 1001. Gain or loss, if any, to X upon the sale of the Newco stock to the investors will be determined and recognized under section 1001.

NOTES

1. See also Intermountain Lumber Co., 65 T.C. 1025 (1976) (transfer of property to a new corporation in exchange for all its stock, where transferor was committed to assign 50 percent of the new corporation's stock to a third party, was not governed by § 351); Rev. Rul. 79–70, 1979–1 C.B. 144 (control requirement of § 351 not satisfied where a corporation transferred property to a newly organized corporation in exchange for all its stock and, under a prearranged binding agreement that was an integral part of the incorporation, sold 40 percent of such stock to a third party). Cf. Culligan Water Conditioning of

Tri–Cities, Inc. v. United States, 567 F.2d 867 (9th Cir. 1978) (incorporation followed by disposition of control pursuant to plan, whether or not legally binding, would preclude application of § 351); D'Angelo Associates, Inc., 70 T.C. 121 (1978), *acq. in result*, 1979–2 C.B. 1 (issuance of shares to family members of individual who transferred property to corporation was a gift of shares pursuant to plan, but did not preclude application of § 351).

2. See Rev. Rul. 84–111, 1984–2 C.B. 88, for the Service's position under § 351 and related provisions with regard to transactions involving partnerships.

Revenue Ruling 74–502
1974–2 C.B. 116.

Corporation Y wanted to acquire 100–percent control of corporation X, which stock is widely held, in a stock-for-stock exchange intended to be nontaxable to the exchanging shareholders under section 351 of the Internal Revenue Code of 1954. Under the laws of the state involved, subject to approval of the board of directors of each corporation and of the proper State authority, and subject to a favorable vote of at least two-thirds of the outstanding stock of the acquired corporation, the acquiring corporation, by operation of law, becomes the owner of all of the outstanding stock of the acquired corporation, except for stock owned by dissenters, on the effective date of the transaction. At such time, those shareholders of the acquired corporation who do not dissent are entitled to receive shares of stock of the acquiring corporation in exchange for their shares of stock of the acquired corporation. Any shareholder of the acquired corporation who dissents is entitled to receive in cash the appraised value of his shares from the acquired corporation.

At a meeting of the shareholders of X (after prior approval of the plan by the X board of directors and the State authority), 70 percent of the outstanding X stock was voted in favor of a plan of acquisition of the X stock by newly formed corporation Y, and two percent was voted against. The remaining 28 percent of the X stock was not voted. On the effective date of the transaction, Y became the owner of all the outstanding X stock by operation of State law except for two percent of such stock which was owned by those X shareholders who exercised their appraisal rights and who received cash from X for their X stock. In exchange for their X stock, the X shareholders, including those who did not vote on the plan but who participated in the exchange because they did not dissent, received voting common stock and nonvoting preferred stock of Y which represented all of the Y stock outstanding after the transaction.

Held, inasmuch as the identity and rights of all the transferors (the nondissenting X shareholders) were defined by state law and the exchange of their X stock for Y stock was by operation of law simultaneous on the effective date of the transaction, the nondissenting X shareholders were in control of Y immediately after the exchange within the meaning of section 351 of the Code. Therefore, under section 351 no gain or loss is recognized to the former X shareholders who exchanged their X stock for Y stock. Those X shareholders who received cash for their X stock are treated as having had such stock redeemed by X with the redemption being subject to the provisions of section 302.

NOTE

The language of § 351 would seem to require an actual exchange, one that is negotiated with the individual transferors. Yet Rev. Rul. 74–502, 1974–2 C.B. 116 involved a transaction in which by "operation of law" an acquiring corporation acquired control of a corporation whose shareholders were deemed to be § 351 transferors. Should corporate action by the acquiring and acquired corporations be sufficient to effect a § 351 exchange, subject only to dissenters' rights? If so, should not the state law procedure involved in Rev. Rul. 74–502 be applicable more generally? See Revised Model Bus. Corp. Act § 11.02 (2010).

Revenue Ruling 76–454
1976–2 C.B. 102.

Advice has been requested concerning the Federal income tax treatment of the transaction described below.

For many years A, an individual, owned all of the stock of X, a domestic corporation. A organized Y, a domestic corporation, paying 50x dollars in cash for all of its common stock, and subsequently as part of the plan of incorporation, caused X to purchase from Y all of Y's 4 percent noncumulative nonvoting preferred stock for 255x dollars. Upon liquidation, the net assets of Y are distributable 50 percent to the holders of its common stock and 50 percent to the holders of its preferred stock. Because the right to share in the net assets upon liquidation for each class of stock is substantially disproportionate to the amounts paid for each class of stock, the 255x dollars paid by X for the preferred stock exceeds its fair market value. . .

Section 1.351–1(b)(1) of the regulations provides, in part, as follows:

Where property is transferred to a corporation by two or more persons in exchange for stock or securities . . . it is not required that the stock and securities received by each be substantially in proportion to his interest in the property immediately prior to the transfer. However, where the stock and securities received are received in disproportion to such interest, the entire transaction will be given tax effect in accordance with its true nature, and in appropriate cases the transaction may be treated as if the stock and securities had first been received in proportion and then some of such stock and securities had been used to make gifts . . ., to pay compensation . . ., or to satisfy obligations of the transferor of any kind.

In the instant case, after the transfers of cash to Y by A and X, A and X owned stock possessing 80 percent or more of the total combined voting power of Y voting stock and 80 percent or more of all other classes of Y stock. Thus, the control requirement of section 351 of the Code is satisfied.

Furthermore, since A received more stock in Y than A would have received if Y had issued its stock in proportion to the cash transferred by A and X, section 1.351–1(b)(1) of the regulations is applicable.

Accordingly, it is appropriate to treat the transactions in the instant case as transfers by X and A, respectively, of 255x dollars and 50x dollars and the receipt from Y by X and A of stock worth, respectively, 255x dollars and 50x dollars followed by a distribution by X of a sufficient amount of the stock it constructively received to reflect the values of the stocks in the hands of X and A after the transactions. That is, X is treated as having received all of the Y preferred stock and enough of the Y common stock so that the total value of the stock it received equalled the 255x dollar contribution it made to Y. X is then considered to have distributed the Y common stock it constructively received to A to reflect the fact that after the transaction X owned only Y preferred stock and A owned all of Y's common stock. This distribution is subject to the provisions of section 301 of the Code.

Kamborian v. Commissioner

56 T.C. 847 (1971), *aff'd*, 469 F.2d 219 (1st Cir. 1972).

. . . The cases relate to petitioners' transfer of certain securities to International Shoe Machine Corp. in exchange for its common stock. Specifically in question is whether gain realized by petitioners as a result of that transaction qualifies for nonrecognition under section 351. . .

FINDINGS OF FACT

. . . 1. International Shoe Machine Corp. (International) was incorporated in Massachusetts in 1938 and . . . was engaged in the business of manufacturing and leasing shoe machinery and the sale of related supplies. On April 1, 1964, International's articles of organization were amended to provide for a 20 for 1 split of its common stock into two classes of common stock: Class A, $1 par, voting stock, and class B, $1 par, nonvoting stock. Following an exchange of the preexisting stock for the newly created common stock, International's authorized and issued stock was as follows as of April 1, 1964:

Shares	Class A	Class B
Authorized	100,000	900,000
Issued	37,200	334,800

On September 1, 1965, prior to the transaction here in question, International's capital stock was held as follows:

| | Shares of International | |
Name	Class A common	Class B common
Jacob Kamborian Revocable Trust	20,324	182,916
Jacob Kamborian, Jr.	4,220	37,980
Lisbeth (Kamborian) Godley	3,620	32,580
Michael Becka	60	540
Elizabeth Kamborian Trust	5,000	45,000
Others	3,916	35,244
	37,140	334,260

Jacob S. Kamborian (Jacob) founded International and served as its president at all times relevant herein. Jacob S. Kamborian, Jr., and Lisbeth Kamborian Godley are the children of Jacob and his wife, Elizabeth. Michael Becka (Becka) is not related to the members of the Kamborian family. At the time of the trial herein he had been employed by International or an affiliate since at least 1943 and had served as International's executive vice president and general manager since approximately 1960. . .

The Elizabeth Kamborian Trust (Elizabeth's trust) was established by Jacob in 1949. At about that time Jacob and Elizabeth experienced domestic difficulties; they separated for a time; and the trust was established on their reconciliation in order to provide financial security for Mrs. Kamborian. The initial trust corpus consisted of 2,500 shares of International stock. . .

. . . As of September 1, 1956, Becka and Lisbeth K. Godley were the trustees. Jacob had appointed them as successor trustees in 1963 and 1964, respectively. At all times relevant herein, Becka served as the managing trustee; Mrs. Godley did not live in Boston during this period; and periodically Becka informed her of the trust's activities. As of September 1, 1965, the only assets of the trust were 5,000 shares of International's class A common stock and 45,000 shares of its class B common stock.

As of September 1, 1965, International's board of directors consisted of Jacob, Jacob, Jr., Albert Kamborian (Jacob's brother), Becka, Paul Hirsch II, Harold V. Daniels, and Roy S. Flewelling.

Campex Research & Trading Corp. (Campex), a Swiss corporation with its principal place of business in Zug, Switzerland, was a patent holding and licensing company. It held primarily foreign shoe machine patents (i.e., patents not issued by the United States) and granted and administered licenses under them in a number of European countries and in Mexico. On September 1, 1965, and prior to the transaction here in question, the outstanding stock of Campex was held as follows:

Name	Shares of Campex
Jacob Kamborian Revocable Trust	39 ← 77.3%
Jacob Kamborian, Jr.	4
Lisbeth (Kamborian) Godley	4
Michael Becka	3

On September 1, 1965, the board of directors of International authorized Jacob to enter into an agreement under which (a) the owners of all of the issued and outstanding shares of Campex would exchange their stock for common stock of International and (b) "certain stockholders" of International would purchase for cash additional shares of International's common stock. . .

[This is what P is trying to accomplish]

[As part of the transaction it was contemplated that the Elizabeth Kamborian Trust would purchase additional shares of theretofore unissued International stock for about $5,000, so that the former owners of the Campex stock and the Elizabeth Kamborian Trust, when considered collectively and treated as transferors under section 351(a), . . . would own at least 80 percent of International's stock immediately after the transaction in an attempt to comply with the requirements of section 368(c). . . If the Elizabeth Kamborian Trust were not taken into account, the International stock held by the former owners of Campex immediately after the transaction amounted to 77.3 percent of each class of outstanding stock of International—an amount that was insufficient to satisfy the requirements of section 368(c). . .

[368 Must own 80% +]

International acquired Campex stock as part of its program of preparing for a public issue of its stock. . . As of September 1, 1965, no date had been set for the offering and at the time of the trial herein the public offering had not yet been made. . .

As trustee of Elizabeth's trust, Becka borrowed approximately $5,000 at an interest rate of 6 percent in order to finance the trust's purchase of the total of 418 shares of International stock on September 1, 1965. The corpus of the trust consisted exclusively of International stock, and Becka anticipated that the loan would be repaid out of dividends paid on the stock. In deciding to acquire additional International stock, Becka also anticipated that International would make a public offering which might enhance the value of the stock.

[This is where Ek Trust got "stuff" to drop in]

Prior to the purchase of the International stock on behalf of the trust, Becka discussed his plans with both Jacob and Elizabeth. Jacob, personally and as grantor of the Jacob S. Kamborian Revocable Trust, held a sufficient number of International shares to control the corporation and thus to determine whether it would issue additional shares. In his discussions with Elizabeth, Becka explained that because the $5,000 loan would have to be repaid out of dividends paid on the International stock held by the trust, her income from the trust would be diminished until the loan was repaid. Elizabeth told Becka to go ahead with the transaction. . .

On their respective Federal income tax returns for 1965, petitioners reported no gain or loss stemming from the exchange of their Campex stock for International stock. In his deficiency notices to petitioners, the Commissioner determined that they realized long-term capital gains. . .

OPINION

■ RAUM, JUDGE.

1. *Exchange of Campex stock for International stock.* Petitioners contend that the gain they realized on their transfer qualifies for nonrecognition under section 351(a). . . Immediately after the exchange here in issue the stock of International was held as follows:

| | Shares of— | | |
	Class A (voting common)	Class B (nonvoting common)	Percent of total of each class
Jacob S. Kamborian Revocable Trust	22,108	198,971	56.01
Jacob S. Kamborian, Jr.	4,403	39,627	11.16
Lisbeth (Kamborian) Godley	3,803	34,227	9.64
Michael Becka	197	1,775	0.50
Elizabeth Kamborian Trust	5,042	45,376	12.77
Others	3,916	35,244	9.92
Total	39,469	355,220	

P's argument

Petitioners contend that the transferors of property for purposes of section 351(a) were the five named stockholders listed above and that their percentage stockholdings after the transfer satisfy the 80–percent control requirement imposed by sections 351(a) and 368(c).

IRS's argument

The Commissioner's position is that only the first four stockholders listed above—i.e., the former owners of Campex—may be considered as transferors of property here, that the fifth (the Elizabeth Kamborian Trust) may not be taken into account in this connection, and that since there would thus be a failure to satisfy the control requirement, all gain realized on the exchange must be recognized. In particular, he urges that International stock issued to the Elizabeth Kamborian Trust in return for $5,016 does not qualify as stock issued for property within the meaning of section 351(a) and that consequently the persons making qualified transfers of property to International in return for its stock held only 77.3 percent of its stock after the exchange. The Commissioner relies on regulations section 1.351–1(a)(1)(ii). . .

The Commissioner contends that since the Elizabeth Kamborian Trust purchased only 42 shares of class A common and 376 shares of class B common, the securities issued were "of relatively small value" in relation to the 5,000 shares of class A common and 45,000 shares of class B common which it already held and that the primary purpose of the transfer was to qualify the exchange of Campex stock by the other stockholders for nonrecognition treatment under section 351(a).

Petitioners attack the Commissioner's position on a variety of grounds. They urge (a) that regulations section 1.351–1(a)(1)(ii) is invalid; (b) that even if valid it is inapplicable to the transaction in issue. . .

(a) *Validity of the regulation.*—Initially we note the well-settled principle that "Treasury regulations must be sustained unless unreasonable and plainly inconsistent with the revenue statutes and that they constitute contemporaneous constructions by those charged with administration of these statutes which should not be overruled except for weighty reasons." Commissioner v. South Texas Lumber Co., 333 U.S. 496, 501. . .

In arguing that regulations section 1.351–1(a)(1)(ii) is invalid, petitioners point first to the "proportionate interest" test which was included in section 112(b)(5), the predecessor of section 351, under the 1939 Code:

Sec. 112. Recognition of Gain or Loss

(b) Exchanges Solely in Kind.

(5) *Transfer to corporation controlled by transferor.*—No gain or loss shall be recognized if property is transferred to a corporation by one or more persons solely in exchange for stock or securities in such corporation; and immediately after the exchange such person or persons are in control of the corporation; *but in the case of an exchange by two or more persons this paragraph shall apply only if the amount of the stock and securities received by each is substantially in proportion to his interest in the property prior to the exchange.* Where the transferee assumes a liability of a transferor, or where the property of a transferor is transferred subject to a liability, then for the purpose only of determining whether the amount of stock or securities received by each of the transferors is in the proportion required by this paragraph, the amount of such liability (if under subsection (k) it is not to be considered as "other property or money") shall be considered as stock or securities received by such transferor. [Emphasis supplied.]

The "proportionate interest" test was eliminated when section 351 was enacted in 1954. The committee reports reflect congressional dissatisfaction with the uncertainty which had developed in applying the test (H. Rept. No. 1337, 83 Cong., 2d Sess., pp. A116–A117 (1954)):

The basic change from present law made by your committee in section 351 is the elimination of the so-called "proportionate interest" test. This requirement, which appears in section 112(b)(5) of the 1939 Code, permits nonrecognition of gain and loss only if the stock and securities received by each transferor are "substantially in proportion" to the interest of such transferor in the property prior to the exchange. This requirement, which, if unsatisfied, serves to vitiate the tax-free nature of the entire transaction, caused considerable uncertainty in its application. In eliminating the proportionate interest test your committee intends that no gain or loss will be recognized to a transferor transferring property to a corporation under section 351 irrespective of any disproportion of the amount of stock or securities received by him as a result of the transfer. Thus, if M and N each owning property having a value of $100 transfers such property to a newly formed corporation X, and M receives all of the stock, such transaction would not be subject to tax under section 351. To the extent, however, that the existing disproportion between the value of the property transferred and the amount of stock or securities received by each of the transferors results in an event taxable under other provisions of this code, your committee intends that such distribution will be taxed in accordance with its true nature. For example, if individuals A and B, father and son, organize a corporation with 100 shares of common stock and A transfers property worth $80 in exchange for 20 shares of stock, while B transfers property worth $20 to the corporation in exchange for 80 shares of stock, no gain or loss will be recognized under section 351. If, however, it is determined that in fact A has made a gift to B, it is your committee's intention that such gift would be subject to tax under the provisions of section 2501' and following. Similarly, if in the preceding example, B had rendered services to A and the disproportion in the amount of stock received constituted, in effect, the payment of compensation by A to B, it is your committee's intention that such compensation will be appropriately taxed. B will be taxable upon the fair market value of the 60 shares of stock received in excess of that received in exchange for his property as an amount received as compensation for services rendered, and A will realize gain or loss upon the difference between the basis of the 60 shares of stock in his hands and its fair market value.

See also id. at 39; S. Rept. No. 1622, 83d Cong., 2d Sess., pp. 50, 264 (1954). Petitioners assert that section 1.351–1(a)(1)(ii) incorporates a proportionate-interest test and that it therefore exceeds the scope of section 351. We disagree. Despite superficial similarities to the "proportionate interest" test, section 1.351–1(a)(1)(ii) is a very different, provision.

The "proportionate interest" test was apparently designed to limit the applicability of section 112(b)(5) of the 1939 Code to transactions which did not result in substantial shifts in equity or property interests among the transferor-stockholders. On the other hand, the current regulation appears to be calculated to exclude from the scope of section 351 transactions which would ordinarily fail to meet the 80–percent requirement but which attempt to satisfy it by appending a token exchange of property for stock by one or more persons with stockholdings sufficient to place all of the transferors "in control" of the corporation. We think that the objective of the regulation is considerably narrower than that of the "proportionate interest" test.

The effect of the regulation is also more limited than that of the "proportionate interest" test. Transactions not satisfying the "proportionate interest" test were completely disqualified from nonrecognition treatment under section 112(b)(5) of the 1939 Code. The regulation, on the other hand, disqualifies only particular exchanges by particular stockholders from the scope of section 351 of the 1954 Code; if the remaining transferors can satisfy the 80–percent requirement and otherwise qualify under the statute, the regulation does not prevent them from obtaining nonrecognition treatment.

. . . We conclude that congressional elimination of the "proportionate interest" test in 1954 provides no basis for holding the regulation invalid.

Petitioners also contend that the regulation's reference to "property which is relatively small value in comparison to the value of stock or securities already owned" and its reliance upon the taxpayer's motive find support nowhere in the language of section 351 and that the regulation is for that reason invalid as beyond the scope of the statute. Again, we must disagree. By disqualifying certain token exchanges, the regulation is reasonably designed to exclude from the scope of section 351 transactions which comply with its requirements in form but not in substance. Far from being unreasonable or inconsistent with the statute, the regulation promotes its purpose by helping to ensure substantial compliance with the control requirement before the nonrecognition provisions become operative. In this light the absence of direct support for the regulation in the language of the statute is of minimal significance. . . We conclude that the regulation is valid.

Second Argument

(b) *Applicability of the regulation.*—Petitioners contend that even if it is valid, the regulation is inapplicable to the transaction here in issue. They argue first that even if Elizabeth's trust had not purchased shares of International stock, the control requirement would have been satisfied, that therefore the purchase was not necessary to meet the control requirement, and that consequently the regulation is by its own terms inapplicable. Petitioners reach this conclusion by asserting that the shares held by Becka and Lisbeth Godley as trustees of Elizabeth's trust should be attributed to them as individuals and added to the shares they held personally in nonfiduciary capacities. On the basis of this premise, petitioners conclude that the 80–percent control requirement would have been satisfied even if Elizabeth's trust had not participated in the September 1, 1965, transaction: Petitioners' argument is ingenious but unacceptable, for it falters on petitioners' premise that the trust's shares may be attributed to the individual trustees. While legal title to the shares may have been in the names of the trustees, they had no beneficial interest in such shares. The distinction is not one of form but of plain economic reality. In these circumstances we think the trustees' interests in the trust's shares were far too remote to justify attributing the shares to them for purposes of section 351.

Petitioners also contend that the primary purpose for the trust's acquisition of International's stock was not to qualify the other stockholders' exchanges under section 351 and that for this reason the regulation is inapplicable. We note at the outset that the regulation does not make it entirely clear whose purpose is to be taken into account. However, both parties have assumed that the purpose of the transferor of property is critical. The language of the regulation (which appears to distinguish between a "transfer" of property and the issuance of stock) supports their assumption, and we shall therefore proceed on this basis. Although Elizabeth's trust was technically the transferor herein, the parties have also assumed that Becka's purpose is critical in this respect-apparently on the ground that as the managing trustee he was primarily responsible for the decision to make the purchase of International stock. We shall proceed on the basis of this assumption as well.

The question of Becka's primary purpose is one of fact, cf. Malat v. Riddell, 383 U.S. 569, and after a review of all the evidence we conclude that his primary purpose was to qualify the other stockholders' exchanges under section 351. We note in particular that at about the time of the transaction, Jacob was ill and Becka was in charge of International's affairs, that in planning the acquisition Becka participated in lengthy discussions with regard to planning the transaction as a tax-free exchange, and that both the vote of International's board of directors and the agreement of September 1, 1965, treated the purchase by Elizabeth's trust and the exchange of Campex stock by the other stockholder as component parts of an integrated transaction avowedly designed to meet the 80–percent control requirement and thereby qualify for nonrecognition treatment under section 351.

At the trial herein, Becka testified that if the trust had not participated in the transaction, the issue of International stock to the other major stockholders would have diluted the trust's percentage interest in International and that he authorized the purchase of International stock in order to minimize such dilution. In particular he testified that the total percentage stock interest held by the trust and the two Kamborian children exceeded 33 1/3 percent and that preservation of that interest protected Mrs. Kamborian against the making of certain corporate decisions (requiring a two-thirds majority) without her consent. We do not give his testimony very much weight, however. The record does not establish whether or why the children were regarded as allies of Mrs. Kamborian rather than as allies of her husband. Moreover, the trust's participation in the transaction left them with an aggregate stock interest of 33.57 percent—only 0.08 of 1 percent more than they would have held if the trust had not purchased any additional shares.

Becka also testified that he authorized the purchase of the stock because it was a "good investment." While he may well have taken this into account in making his decision, the record leaves us convinced that the purchase was made primarily to qualify the exchanges by the other stockholders (one of whom was Becka himself) under section 351. We conclude that section 1.351–1(a)(1)(ii) is applicable. . .

[Other issues omitted.]

NOTE

Under Rev. Proc. 77–37, § 3.07, 1977–2 C.B. 568, 570, property will not be considered to be "of relatively small value" within the meaning of Treas. Reg. § 1.351–1(a)(1)(ii) if its value equals or exceeds 10 percent of the value of the stock of the transferee which is already owned (or to be received for services) by the transferor. See also IRS FSA 200224011.

Revenue Ruling 87–9

1987–1 C.B. 133.

ISSUE

Do transfers of marketable stock and cash by different transferors to a newly organized corporation, which is a regulated investment company, constitute transfers to an "investment company" within the meaning of section 351(e)(1) of the Internal Revenue Code?

FACTS

Some of the shareholders of Y corporation transferred their Y stock to X, a newly organized corporation which is a regulated investment company as defined in section 851 of the Code. In addition, other persons transferred cash to X. The Y stock is actively traded on a public stock exchange. The transferors of the Y stock received 89 percent of the stock of X, and the transferors of cash received 11 percent of the stock of X.

LAW AND ANALYSIS

Section 351(a) of the Code provides that no gain or loss will be recognized if property is transferred to a corporation solely in exchange for its stock and immediately after the exchange the transferors are in control (as defined in section 368(c)) of the corporation.

Section 351(e)(1) of the Code and section 1.351–1(c)(1) of the Income Tax Regulations provide that section 351(a) will not apply to transfers to an investment company. Section 1.351–1(c)(1) of the regulations further provides that a transfer will be considered a "transfer to an investment company" if two factors are present. First, the transfer results, directly or indirectly, in diversification of the transferors' interests. Second, the transferee is (i) a regulated investment company, (ii) a real estate investment trust, or (iii) a corporation more than 80 percent of the value of whose assets (excluding cash and nonconvertible debt obligations from consideration) are held for investment and are readily marketable stocks or securities, or interests in regulated investment companies or real estate investment trusts.

Section 1.351–1(c)(5) of the regulations provides that a transfer ordinarily results in the diversification of the transferors' interests if two or more persons transfer nonidentical assets to the corporation in the exchange, unless the portion of assets that are nonidentical to the other assets transferred constitutes an insignificant portion of the total value of the assets transferred. On the other hand, if two or more persons transfer identical assets to a newly organized corporation, the transfer will generally not be treated as resulting in diversification.

In the present situation, the transferors transferred Y stock and cash to X, a regulated investment company within the meaning of section 1.351–1(c)(1)(ii) of the regulations. Further, Y stock and cash are nonidentical assets. A transfer of nonidentical assets ordinarily results in diversification unless the nonidentical assets constitute an insignificant portion of the assets transferred. The question of what is an "insignificant portion" for this purpose is a factual issue. In the present situation, the cash represented a significant part of the value of the property transferred to X; therefore, the transfer of the stock and cash resulted in the diversification of the transferors' interests within the meaning of section 1.351–1(c)(5).

HOLDING

The transfers of Y stock and cash by different transferors to X constitute transfers to an "investment company" within the meaning of section 351(e)(1) of the Code. Consequently, section 351 does not apply to the transaction, and the transferors of the Y stock recognize gain or loss under section 1001 upon the transfer of Y stock to X in exchange for X stock. See NYSBA Tax Section, Report on Investment Company Provisions: Section 351(e) and 368(a)(2)(F) (Report No. 1252) (Dec. 28, 2011) (identifying how current law inadequately curbs taxpayers' ability to achieve diversification *with* nonrecognition). Compare Rev. Rul. 87-9 to Letter Ruling 20113306.

NOTE

The principle underlying § 351(e)(1) is that recognition of gain is appropriate when the taxpayer has substantially diversified his investment. Should this principle be applied more generally to incorporation transactions? If so, how would you implement such a principle in the Code?

2. EFFECT OF "SERVICES"

Mailloux v. Commissioner
320 F.2d 60 (5th Cir. 1963).

■ Before RIVES, JONES and BROWN, CIRCUIT JUDGES.

■ JONES, CIRCUIT JUDGE. The petitioners bring to the Court for review a decision of the Tax Court finding income tax deficiencies against them. Joint returns had been filed. Only the husbands, Melvin Mailloux and Robert R. Foley, were participants in the transactions giving rise to the finding of tax liability, and they will be referred to as the taxpayers.

Critchell Parsons was the principal promoter of Rocky Mountain Uranium Corporation. It was incorporated on May 3, 1954.

[In April 1954, Parsons entered into discussions with Mailloux and Foley regarding the financing of a uranium venture, and Mailloux and Foley undertook to perform certain services such as assisting in clearing the issue of stock for sale in Texas, attracting private capital, and securing an underwriter for public financing. On May 18, 1954, the corporation issued a total of 1,450,000 shares to a group of people from whom, in exchange for the shares, the corporation received rights in certain uranium mining claims. Those shares at that time represented 100 percent of the corporation's outstanding stock. Parsons received 900,000 shares. The taxpayers, Mailloux and Foley, did not receive shares directly from the corporation. On May 18, 1954, however, they each received 120,000 shares from Parsons, these coming out of his 900,000 shares.]

Dropped mining claims into the corp.

The taxpayers were to receive 10 percent of the proceeds of stock sales made prior to a public offering of the stock. The sales were to be at 50 cents a share. The taxpayers received $12,000 from this commission arrangement. The stock was transferred under an agreement that the taxpayers would make no sales without Parsons' approval. This restriction was to permit Parsons to prevent depressing the price by overselling the market. During 1954 Mailloux sold 23,650 shares and Foley sold 24,375 shares. These sales were made at various prices which averaged something over a dollar a share. In the latter part of 1954, some transactions and adjustments between Parsons and the taxpayers were made which resulted in his obtaining and retaining some of their stock certificates. Before the end of the year Parsons and the taxpayers had a disagreement which arose from the failure, which Parsons attributed to the taxpayers, to procure approval from the Securities and Exchange Commission and the Texas Securities Commission of a public offering of the stock. Parsons directed the transfer agent not to make transfers of the taxpayers' certificates. They sued to establish their ownership. <u>The litigation was compromised and settled in 1956</u>. The taxpayers sold a part of their remaining stock in 1956 for ten cents a share and the rest in 1957 for five cents a share.

In their 1954 returns the taxpayers did not report any income on account of the receipt of the stock. The Commissioner made a determination that the stock was compensation for services, and that it had a value of fifty cents a share. A tax deficiency was proposed. [The Tax Court, sustaining the Commissioner, held that the shares received by the taxpayer constituted ordinary income to them in 1954, valuing the shares at 50 cents each. 20 T.C.M. (CCH) 942 (1961).]

Two questions are presented by the taxpayers' petition for review. The contention is made that the stock was received by the taxpayers in a tax-free exchange for property under . . . § 351. If there was no tax-free exchange and the stock was received for services, the taxpayers contend that it had no market value when received or, in the alternative, the value did not exceed ten cents a share, or at the most, an amount in excess of what they received for it.

Although the taxpayers claimed, and supported the claim with their testimony, that they had an interest in uranium claims which were conveyed to the corporation for shares of its stock, the testimony of Parsons is to the contrary. He testified that they had no interest in the claims. The Tax Court found against the taxpayers on this controverted fact issue, and its findings that the stock was for services and not for property are supported by evidence.

The Tax Court, in fixing the value of the stock, reviewed the sales made by the taxpayers, by Parsons, and by the corporation, and found that the stock, at the time it was transferred to the taxpayers, had a value of not less than fifty cents a share. There was ample evidence before the Tax Court to sustain this finding of the value of the stock issued to the taxpayers unless, as the taxpayers assert, the effect of the restrictive agreement was such as to reduce the value of their stock to an amount less than fifty cents a share. The Tax Court concluded that such restrictions as may have existed had no bearing upon the fair market value of the stock at the time the taxpayers received it. Where a stock is of a highly speculative quality and the terms of a restrictive agreement make a sale impossible, it may be that no fair market value can be attributed to it. Helvering v. Tex–Penn Oil Co., 300 U.S. 481. . . But where there is no absolute prohibition against a sale, a restriction may reduce but does not destroy fair market value. . .

Prohibition because not approved for public offering

We do not think it can be said that where the holder of a highly speculative stock—and speculative Rocky Mountain Uranium Corporation surely was—can carry it into the market place only at the indulgence of another, the fair market value of the stock is the same as it would be if the dominion of the holder was free and unfettered. Parsons prevented the taxpayers from selling a portion of their stock from December 1954 for nearly a year and a half. In December 1954 the national market for the stock was around $3 per share. When the taxpayers were able to sell they realized five and ten cents a share. The inability of the taxpayers to sell between December 1954 and May 1956 may not have been occasioned by the exercise of Parsons' right under the restrictive agreement, but the result would have been no more disastrous if the exercise of the right had been the cause of the inability to sell.

Sale. Impairment affects FMV

We think the Tax Court should have recognized the effect of impairing the market value of the stock and given effect to that impairment in the ascertainment of fair market value. To permit it to do so, its decision will be reversed and the cause remanded for further proceedings.

Reversed and remanded.

NOTES

1. If the taxpayers had received 150,000 shares each, what tax impact might that have had on Parsons? If, by prearrangement, Parsons had delivered 150,000 shares to Mailloux for his services and 150,000 shares to Foley for cash equal to fair market value, what might the tax impact on Parsons have been? See § 351(d)(1). What is the rationale underlying § 351(d)(1)?

2. *Mailloux* arose before the enactment of § 83. Would that section have any effect on the case if it were to arise today?

3. If A transfers appreciated assets in exchange for Corporation X's entire issue of nonvoting preferred stock (that is not nonqualified preferred stock un-

der § 351(g)) and simultaneously B pays cash for the corporation's entire issue of common stock, § 351(a) assures A that his gain will go unrecognized. If B had received his common stock in exchange for services, however, the tax impact on both A and B would have been quite different. Why should that be so as to A? As to B? See Herwitz, Allocation of Stock Between Services and Capital in the Organization of a Close Corporation, 75 Harv. L. Rev. 1098 (1962).

4. Services contributed to a corporation in exchange for its stock have never constituted "property" within the nonrecognition provision of § 351. The Bankruptcy Tax Act of 1980 altered § 351(d) to provide that, in addition to services, indebtedness of the transferee corporation which is not evidenced by a security, and interest on indebtedness of the transferee corporation that accrued since the time the transferor held the debt, are not to be considered "property" under § 351(a).

5. The IRS has ruled that the transfer to a corporation of its own installment obligation, in exchange for stock having a fair market value in excess of the basis of the transferred obligation, is a satisfaction of that obligation at greater than face value, therefore requiring recognition of gain to the transferor under what is now § 453B even though § 351 would otherwise apply. See Rev. Rul. 73–423, 1973–2 C.B. 161. The Service extended this theory to the partnership context (satisfaction of debt by transfer of partnership interest) in the new regulations under § 108(e)(8). TD 9557, 2011-2 C.B. 855.

3. CLASSIFICATION OF STOCK AND COMPUTATION—§ 368(C)

For § 351(a) to operate, the transferors of the incorporated assets must be "in control" of the transferee corporation immediately after they effect their exchange. Section 368(c), defining "control," requires the transferors to own stock with at least (1) 80 percent of the total combined voting power of all classes of stock entitled to vote, and (2) 80 percent of the total number of shares of all other classes of outstanding stock.

When is stock with "voting power" "entitled to vote"? Cf. § 302(b)(2)(B). Does the "entitled to vote" concept add anything to the "voting power" concept? Cf. § 1504(a)(1). Is stock that is not "entitled to vote" different from "nonvoting stock" (§ 504(a))? There is no clear-cut answer to these questions, and they arise only infrequently. The language differences may represent only differences in expression of the same ideas, enacted at different times without regard to earlier modes of expression. It is generally accepted that stock has "voting power" and is "entitled to vote" only when it entitles its owner to vote for directors in the ordinary course. Stock that permits such voting only after a contingency occurs (e.g., preferred that is permitted to vote only after dividends are in default) probably becomes "entitled to vote" only after the contingency has occurred. Cf. Treas. Reg. § 1.302–3(a)(3).

Suppose Mr. T, a transferor, receives 100 percent of a corporation's common (voting) stock in exchange for appreciated property; 10,000 shares of the Class A, 9–percent nonvoting preferred, $1.00 par, for cash of $10,000; and 1,000 shares of the Class B, 8–percent nonvoting preferred, $5.00 par, for cash of $5,000. He has received all of the authorized Class A preferred and half of the authorized Class B preferred. The other half of the authorized Class B preferred (1,000 shares) is issued to Mrs. E—in exchange for services worth $5,000. Is Mr. T "in control"? See Rev. Rul. 59–259, 1959–2 C.B. 115. How does § 351(g) complicate the above analysis? If the classes of nonvoting preferred stock are nonqualified under § 351(g) what effect? The 1997 Conference report indicates that nonqualified preferred stock will be "boot" for purposes of § 351(b) but will otherwise constitute stock (e.g., in considering control). If a shareholder receives only nonqualified preferred stock in an exchange then § 351 does not apply at all and the exchange constitutes a taxable event. Section 352(g)(1)(B). In 2011, Treasury proposed no longer treating "nonqualified preferred" stock as boot, with perhaps some exceptions.

B. "STOCK" OR SOMETHING ELSE

1. DEFINITIONAL CRITERIA

Burr Oaks Corp. v. Commissioner

43 T.C. 635 (1965), aff'd, 365 F.2d 24 (7th Cir. 1966), cert. denied, 385 U.S. 1007
(1967).

■ FAY, JUDGE. Respondent . . . determined deficiencies in the income tax of petitioner Burr Oaks Corp. for its taxable years ended September 30, 1958, 1959, and 1960, in the respective amounts of $15,067.26, $52,595.26, and $16,602.61. With regard to the various individual petitioners, respondent determined the following deficiencies in their respective income taxes:

Docket No.	Petitioners	Taxable year ended Dec. 31—	Deficiency
		1958	$ 499.32
4772–62	A. Aaron and Rosella Elkind	1959	35,520.49
		1960	1,778.90
1581–63	Harold A. and Fannie G. Watkins	1959	30,386.55
1583–63	Maurice and Esther Leah Ritz	1959	37,702.90

Petitioner Burr Oaks Corp. will hereinafter be referred to as the petitioner, and petitioners A. Aaron Elkind, Harold A. Watkins, and Maurice Ritz will hereinafter sometimes be referred to respectively as Elkind, Watkins, and Ritz, or as the individual petitioners.

The only question remaining to be determined insofar as petitioner is concerned is its correct basis in certain unimproved real estate transferred to it by Elkind, Watkins, and Ritz. In order to make this determination, we must first decide whether the transfer by Elkind, Watkins, and Ritz to petitioner constituted a valid sale or a contribution to capital. In the event we find it to be the latter, we must further determine whether it constitutes a transfer to a controlled corporation within the meaning of section 351.

Insofar as petitioners Elkind, Watkins, and Ritz are concerned, we must determine whether certain amounts received by them during 1959 from petitioner were taxable as ordinary income, rather than as long-term capital gain.

FINDINGS OF FACT

... Petitioner is a corporation formed under the laws of the State of Wisconsin. It maintains its books of account and files its Federal income tax returns on the basis of an accrual method of accounting and a fiscal year ended September 30. . . . [The individual petitioners filed their returns on the basis of a calendar year and the cash method of accounting.]

Elkind, at all times relevant hereto, has been engaged in various aspects of real estate development, with primary emphasis on the development of tracts of one-family houses. These various endeavors were generally conducted through corporations in which Elkind or members of his family were majority stockholders. Elkind also has made a number of investments in real estate, including raw land as well as improved property producing rental income.

Ritz, at all times relevant hereto, was a certified public accountant and the senior partner of an accounting firm of which Elkind was a client. Ritz had made various investments in improved and unimproved real estate prior to the years in issue herein, primarily as a result of opportunities which he came across in connection with his accounting practice.

At all times relevant hereto, Watkins was the president and principal stockholder of a corporation engaged in the manufacture and sale of slippers and other types of casual footwear. Watkins, also, had made several investments in real property over the years, primarily in improved properties producing rental income.

Elkind, Watkins, and Ritz have, at least upon one occasion other than that involved herein, jointly invested in a relatively large tract of unimproved real estate. Thus, on June 4, 1953, they purchased for the sum of $70,124.15 a tract of undeveloped land located just outside the city of Madison, Wis. These individuals held that property (hereinafter referred to as the Gay Farm) jointly until April 20, 1954, at which time it was sold to one of Elkind's development corporations for the sum of $149,650.79. That corporation subdivided the property into 353 lots, constructed one-family homes thereon, and made substantial profits totaling approximately $500,000 upon their sale.

In the fall of 1954 Elkind came across the opportunity to purchase a similar piece of property, this time a tract of land of approximately 70 acres, also located near the outskirts of the city of Madison and theretofore used as a golf course. This property will hereinafter sometimes be referred to as the Burr Oaks property.

Elkind, in December of the same year, contacted Ritz and Watkins in regard to their participation with him in the purchase of that land. Watkins and Ritz agreed to join him in the acquisition upon the understanding that each of them would obtain a one-third interest therein. On December 7 of that year, Elkind tendered to the owner of said property a written offer to purchase the property for the sum of $100,000. The offer provided that $10,000 of the purchase price was payable at the time of acceptance, $10,000 on February 15, 1955, $5,000 on April 1, 1955, with payments of $5,000 due quarterly thereafter until the final balance was paid. The offer was accepted on December 8, 1954.

From the time they acquired the Burr Oaks property through the summer of 1957 Elkind, Watkins, and Ritz attempted to develop said property as a shopping center site or as an industrial park. In furtherance of this plan, they purchased in 1955 an additional 80 feet of frontage on an adjoining thoroughfare for the purpose of providing better access to the Burr Oaks property in the event of its commercial development. This 80 feet of frontage will hereinafter be referred to as the Brinkman property. Their efforts to develop the Burr Oaks property for commercial purposes, however, proved fruitless.

Sometime during 1957 Elkind became convinced that their plans to develop the Burr Oaks property as a shopping center or an industrial park would not materialize. Contemplating that one of his corporations might purchase the property for purposes of subdivision or development, Elkind requested two of his business associates to investigate the zoning and platting possibilities of the Burr Oaks property. On March 11, 1957, a petition was filed with the City Council of Madison, Wis., to change the zoning of the Burr Oaks property. . .

Elkind then proposed to Watkins and Ritz that the three of them sell the Burr Oaks property to one of Elkind's real estate corporations, as they had done with the Gay Farm property. Watkins and Ritz, recalling the substantial profits made by Elkind's corporation after they had sold the Gay Farm property to it, rejected this proposal. Ritz suggested that the three of them transfer the Burr Oaks property to a corporation which they would form for the purpose of subdividing, developing, and selling the property; that the shareholders thereof would be comprised of his two brothers and the wives of Watkins and Elkind; and that in return for the transfer of the land, the corporation would issue promissory notes to Elkind, Watkins, and Ritz. It was agreed that they would follow Ritz' suggestions.

On September 9, 1957, the City Council of Madison approved a preliminary plat incorporating the zoning proposed for the property in the aforementioned petition filed on March 11, 1957. . .

Petitioner was incorporated on October 8, 1957, for the purpose of (1) acquiring the Burr Oaks property from Elkind, Watkins, and Ritz; (2) developing and subdividing said property; and (3) selling improved lots therefrom to customers. At the time petitioner was formed, the Burr Oaks property was completely unimproved. Elkind, Watkins, and Ritz were aware of a local ordinance pursuant to which owners of unimproved land could request the city of Madison to make improvements thereon such as streets, sewers, water, and sidewalks. The city would make these improvements and assess the costs incurred in connection therewith against the property. However, it was realized that the cost of some of the improvements to be made, such as grading and supplying crushed stone, would have to be borne directly by the developers. The total cost of such improvements, as estimated by petitioner, was in the amount of $107,243.33.

It was determined by Ritz, Watkins, and Elkind that petitioner's initial capital would be $4,500.

Petitioner issued a total of 450 shares of its common stock to a group composed of Elkind's wife, Watkins' wife, and Ritz' brothers, Philip and Erwin, for an aggregate consideration of $4,500. Elkind's wife received 150 shares of the stock; Watkins' wife also received 150 shares; and Philip and Erwin Ritz each received 75 shares. The record does not indicate the exact date when this stock was issued. Philip and Erwin Ritz paid for their stock by their respective checks, each in the amount of $750 and dated October 9, 1957, Watkins' wife paid for her stock by a check in the amount of $1,500 dated October 14, 1957. Each of the above-mentioned four persons received from petitioner a receipt dated November 1, 1957, evidencing their payment for the stock. At all times relevant hereto, petitioner's stockholders of record and officers and directors were as follows:

Shareholder	Number of Shares Held
Rosella Elkind (Elkind's wife)	150
Fannie G. Watkins (Watkins' wife)	150
Philip M. Ritz (Ritz' brother)	75
Erwin M. Ritz (Ritz' brother)	75

Officers	Position Held	Directors
Watkins	President	Watkins
Philip M. Ritz	Vice president	Ritz
Rosella Elkind	Secretary-treasurer	Elkind
		Fannie G. Watkins
		Philip M. Ritz
		Rosella Elkind

. . . On November 1, 1957, Elkind, Watkins, and Ritz transferred their respective interests in the Burr Oaks property to petitioner. In consideration for this transfer, petitioner assumed the remaining unpaid balance for the property, namely $30,000, and issued to each of Elkind, Watkins, and Ritz what purported on the face thereof to be a promissory note in the principal amount of $110,000. Each of the notes recited that it bore interest at the rate of 6 percent and that it was payable 2 years after the making thereof. The $30,000 obligation for the Burr Oaks property to its original owner, assumed by petitioner from Elkind, Watkins, and Ritz, was entered on petitioner's books under an account captioned "Mortgage Payable." An additional account was set up under the title "Land Contract Payable" in the amount of $330,000 to represent the alleged promissory notes. At the time Elkind, Watkins, and Ritz transferred the Burr Oaks property to petitioner, the fair market value of said property was substantially less than $360,000. The property was not worth more than $165,000 at that time.

Although at the time Elkind, Watkins, and Ritz transferred their interests in said property to petitioner they hoped that petitioner's business would be successful, petitioner's prospects were uncertain. The nature of their investment can best be described by the term "speculative."

Shortly after its incorporation, petitioner found that it did not have sufficient funds on hand with which to commence operations. Therefore, on November 30, 1957, it borrowed $15,000 from Elkind. On February 28, 1958, Elkind loaned petitioner an additional $10,000. These loans, together with interest thereon in the amount of $1,859.78, were repaid on June 30, 1959.

None of petitioner's stockholders of record, namely Watkins' and Elkind's respective wives and Ritz' brothers, took any active interest in the management of petitioner. In fact, none of them had any real idea of the nature of petitioner's business, other than some vague notion that it was engaged in "real estate" in some way or other. Watkins and Ritz hired Albert McGinnes to manage petitioner. His work included the supervision of the platting, development, and subdivision of the land, as well as taking charge of advertising and sales. McGinnes had known and worked for Elkind and his various corporations for approximately 15 years prior to that time as a lawyer and real estate broker and in various other capacities. McGinnes, moreover, was the person who first interested Elkind in purchasing the Burr Oaks property and checked into the zoning and platting possibilities for the land. During the years in issue, McGinnes continued to work for various Elkind interests.

Ritz' accounting firm, Ritz, Holman & Co., kept petitioner's books and took care of its accounting work. McGinnes was required to account to Ritz, Holman & Co. for the funds which he took in and disbursed in connection with his operation of petitioner's business. Upon a number of occasions, petitioner transferred various lots or parcels of property to Elkind, Watkins, and Ritz, either at no cost or at a price less than the amount for which such lots could have been sold to third parties. Thus, by deed dated November 3, 1958, petitioner conveyed to Elkind, Watkins, and Ritz a strip of commercial property, 70 feet by 120 feet, located in the southeast corner of the Burr Oaks property. This property was contiguous with another piece of commercial property, the Brinkman property, which Elkind, Watkins, and Ritz had purchased when they were contemplating using Burr Oaks for a shopping center. Nothing was paid to petitioner in consideration for this transfer. The deed by which the transfer was effected purported on its face to correct an erroneous conveyance of the land to petitioner in the first place.

On November 14, 1958, petitioner sold five lots at a price of $3,000 per lot to the Leo Building Corp., which was owned and controlled by Elkind and an associate of his. On the same date petitioner sold an additional five lots for the same price to Carsons, Inc., a corporation owned by Watkins. Petitioner, on May 20, 1960, sold five more lots at $3,000 per lot to M & L Investment, Inc., a corporation in which Ritz owned a substantial interest. . . The evidence indicates that, at the time they were sold after having been platted, subdivided, and improved, each of these lots could have been sold to outsiders for $500 to $1,000 more than was received from the above corporations. None of petitioner's shareholders of record (Philip and Erwin Ritz, Elkind's wife, or Watkins' wife) was consulted with regard to, or knew of, any of these transfers. Nor was any such transfer authorized by a meeting of petitioner's board of directors.

Although McGinnes was in charge of petitioner's day-to-day operations, Elkind, Watkins, and Ritz controlled and dominated petitioner's affairs.

During its taxable years 1958 through 1963, inclusive, petitioner had gross receipts in the following amounts as a result of its subdivision and sale of the Burr Oaks property:

Taxable year ended Sept. 30 —	*Gross sales of lots*
1958	$ 86,095
1959	177,200
1960	118,625
1961	68,250
1962	49,400
1963	413,900
Total	513,470

As had been contemplated by Elkind, Watkins, and Ritz at the time of petitioner's incorporation, improvements to the Burr Oaks property, such as streets, sewers, water, and sidewalks, were made by the city of Madison. The city was to recover the cost of these improvements by special assessments against the lots, which assessments were generally payable over a period of 5 to 8 years. To the extent that installments of the special assessments came due prior to the sale of the lots, they were paid by petitioner and added to the price of the lots. To the extent the assessments had not been paid prior to the sale of the lots, they were assumed by the purchaser. Certain costs incurred in connection with the subdivision and improvement of the Burr Oaks property were borne directly by petitioner. . .

In the latter part of 1959 Elkind, Watkins, and Ritz surrendered to petitioner the original "promissory notes" which they had received from petitioner in connection with their transfer of the Burr Oaks property. In return for the surrender of the notes, each of the individual petitioners received from petitioner a distribution of $23,000 in cash and a promissory note dated November 1, 1959, in the principal amount of $87,000. The new notes recited (1) that they were payable 1 year after the making thereof and (2) that they bore interest at the rate of 6 percent per annum. Later that same year, petitioner paid an additional $8,000 apiece to Elkind, Watkins, and Ritz. Petitioner at that time, in exchange for each of their, notes in the principal amount of $87,000, issued to each of them a new promissory note in the principal amount of $79,000.

On December 29, 1959, petitioner purported to repay the outstanding balance on these "new promissory notes." At the close of business on that date petitioner had a bank balance of $5,498.88. The record does not clearly indicate how petitioner purported to repay these notes. However, the record does clearly indicate that petitioner urgently needed as working capital the $237,000 which it claims to have used to repay the three promissory notes. Therefore, immediately after those notes were "repaid," Elkind, Watkins, and Ritz each "loaned" $79,000 to petitioner, and petitioner, in turn, issued to each of the individual petitioners a "new" 1–year promissory note dated December 31, 1959, in the principal amount of $79,000. This transaction did not represent a repayment of the alleged "promissory notes." It was merely an extension of the purported maturity date. The individual petitioners never had any intention of enforcing their "notes" against petitioner.

In addition to the foregoing, petitioner made the following distributions to each of the individual petitioners with regard to the "promissory notes":

Date of distribution	Amount paid to each of the individual petitioners
Aug. 31, 1960	$ 8,000
Jan. 31, 1961	15,000
Dec. 31, 1961	10,000

There was an aggregate balance of $138,000 outstanding upon the three "notes" at the time of the trial in this proceeding, or a total of $46,000 due upon each of said notes.

Petitioner has not distributed any of its earnings to any of the shareholders of record.

Elkind, Watkins, and Ritz treated their transfer of the Burr Oaks property to petitioner in November 1957 as a sale. Petitioner did likewise and set up on its books a cost of $360,000 for said property. Elkind, Watkins, and Ritz, however, did not report any gain with regard to this alleged sale until 1959 when petitioner purportedly paid in full the promissory notes which it had issued to them in connection with said transfer. In their respective income tax returns for 1959, each of them reported long-term capital gain in the amount of $85,729.06 as a result of their transfer of the Burr Oaks property to petitioner in 1957.

Respondent, pursuant to separate notices of deficiency issued to Elkind, Watkins, and Ritz with respect to their taxable year ended December

31, 1959, determined that—"the gain realized from the sale of . . . [the Burr Oaks property] in the total amount of $85,729.06 is taxable as ordinary income rather than as long-term capital gains reported on your income tax return. . ."

Pursuant to a statutory notice of deficiency issued to petitioner with respect to its taxable years 1958 through 1960, respondent increased petitioner's taxable income for said years by an aggregate amount totaling $192,686.98. This increase was based on respondent's determination that petitioner had understated its income for those years by claiming too high a basis or cost in the land sold by it in that period. The notice of deficiency indicates that, in making his determination, respondent treated petitioner as having a basis of $100,000 in the Burr Oaks property, rather than a basis of $360,000, as petitioner had claimed.

OPINION

There are two issues to be determined in this case. These are (1) petitioner's correct basis in the Burr Oaks property and (2) the proper tax treatment of the amounts received by Elkind, Watkins, and Ritz from petitioner during 1959. In order to resolve these issues, we must classify, for tax purposes, the transaction wherein each of the individual petitioners in November 1957 (1) transferred his respective interest in the Burr Oaks property to petitioner and (2) in return therefor received an instrument purporting to be a promissory note in the principal amount of $110,000.

It is contended by Elkind, Watkins, and Ritz (1) that their transfer of the Burr Oaks property to petitioner constitutes the sale or exchange of a capital asset held in excess of 6 months; (2) that the promissory note received by each of them in return therefor represents a valid indebtedness incurred by petitioner; and (3) that the gain realized by them in connection with said transfer is properly reportable in 1959 when they allege that petitioner "paid in full" the "promissory notes" which had been issued to them.[5]

It is contended by petitioner that it purchased the Burr Oaks property from Elkin, Watkins, and Ritz at a cost of $360,000 and that such cost is its correct basis in said property.

---

[5] Passing over for the moment the validity of the first two parts of the individual petitioner's argument, we believe it appropriate to point out that the third part of their argument, namely that the gain realized by them on the transfer of the Burr Oaks property was properly reportable in 1959, is incorrect. Watkinds, Elkind, and Ritz at all times relevant hereto were cash basis taxpayers. When cash basis taxpayers sell property, they must include in income the fair market value of any property received in exchange therefor. This would include the fair market value of any notes received. See Pinellas Ice Co. v. Commissioner, 287 U.S. 462 (1933). The individual petitioners have not advanced any of the arguments which would enable them to avoid the applicability of this general rule. Thus, they have made no argument that the "promissory notes" received by them were of indeterminate or unascertainable value or that the notes were not received by them in payment for the land.... Nor do they contend (1) that the fair market value of the "notes" received by them was less than their respective bases in the land, cf. sec. 1.1001–1, Income Tax Regs., or (2) that the transfer was not a closed transaction, cf. Joseph Marcello, 43 T.C. 168 (1964). There is nothing in the record to show that (1) they elected to report the gain realized by them at the time of the transfer on the installment method or (2) that they were entitled to report their gain on the deferred payment sale method. See sec. 1.453–4(b)(1) and (2) and sec. 1.453–6, Income Tax Regs.

The plethora of arguments advanced by respondent in his opening statement and on brief indicates to us that the Government had some difficulty in formulating a suitable rationale under which to classify the transfer of the Burr Oaks property to petitioner. It would serve no purpose to set forth at this point the various contentions made by respondent since we believe that the transaction was not a sale, but an equity contribution.[6]

It is true that Elkind, Watkins, and Ritz attempted to cast their transfer of the Burr Oaks property to petitioner in the form of a sale. It is also true that, from a standpoint of form, the alleged promissory notes issued to the individual petitioners are clear evidences of indebtedness. However, it has often been noted in connection with similar issues, the substance of the transaction, rather than its form, is the controlling factor in the determination of the proper tax treatment to be accorded thereto. . . Whether a transaction such as the one we are now confronted with is in substance, as well as in form, a sale is essentially a question of fact.

As we view the creditable evidence presently before us, the transfer of the Burr Oaks property to petitioner is so lacking in the essential characteristics of a sale and is replete with so many of the elements normally found in an equity contribution . . . that it appears to us as nothing more than a shabby attempt to withdraw from petitioner, at capital gains rates, the developer's profit normally inherent in the subdivision and sale of raw acreage such as the Burr Oaks property.

This Court has been required upon numerous occasions to determine the true nature of alleged sales or transfers of assets to corporations. In the *Kolkey* case, [27 T.C. 37 (1956)] we listed the following questions as among the relevant criteria for making such a determination:

> Was the capital and credit structure of the new corporation realistic? What was the business purpose, if any, of organizing the new corporation? Were the noteholders the actual promoters and entrepreneurs of the new adventure? Did the noteholders bear the principal risks of loss attendant upon the adventure? Were payments of "prin-

---

[6] The statutory notices issued to the individual petitioners seem to be grounded on the theory that Elkind, Watkins, and Ritz were not entitled to report the sale of the Burr Oaks property as long-term capital gain since they were dealers. The deficiency notices did not raise any question with regard to the proper year for reporting the gain. In view of the fact that respondent, in the deficiency notice to petitioner-corporation, determined that petitioner's basis for the Burr Oaks property was the same as that of the transferors of the property, said statutory notice would seem to be based on the theory that the transfer was governed by sec. 351. This is undoubtedly what caused Elkind. Watkins, and Ritz to raise the following issue by way of amended petition: "In the alternative, in the event the basis of the ... [Burr Oaks property] in the hands of ... [petitioner] is determined under section 351 of the Internal Revenue Code, respondent erred in failing to determine that petitioners had no taxable gain for the year 1959 as a result of the transfer of the said real estate to ... [petitioner]." We have concluded that the transfer of the Burr Oaks property to petitioner was not a sale on the basis of the clear, uncontroverted facts in the record and without resort to the burden of proof. Nevertheless, we believe it appropriate to point out that the petitioners Elkind, Watkins, and Ritz, as well as the Burr Oaks Corp., have the burden of proof on this issue. For even if we were to regard the issue of whether the transfer of the property constitutes a bona fide sale as new matter insofar as Elkind, Watkins, and Ritz are concerned, they raised that question by way of their amended petition.

cipal and interest" on the notes subordinated to dividends and to the claims of creditors? Did the noteholders have substantial control over the business operations; and if so, was such control reserved to them as an integral part of the plan under which the notes were issued? Was the "price" of the properties, for which the notes were issued, disproportionate to the fair market value of such properties? Did the noteholders, when default of the notes occurred, attempt to enforce the obligations? [Emanuel N. (Manny) Kolkey, supra, at 59.]

We have set forth in our Findings of Fact, with some degree of specificity, the various factors which cause us to conclude that the transfer of the Burr Oaks property to petitioner was an equity contribution, rather than a sale. We set forth below some of the more significant factors which led us to this conclusion.

In the first place, petitioner, from the start of its existence, was not only undercapitalized, but, in fact, had no significant capitalization at all. Cf. Hoguet Real Estate Corporation, 30 T.C. 580, 598 (1958). Thus, petitioner was organized in October with a paid-in capital of $4,500. Shortly thereafter, when Elkind, Watkins, and Ritz transferred the Burr Oaks property to petitioner, its books of account reflected liabilities of $360,000. In addition, it was contemplated from the very outset of petitioner's existence that although the city of Madison would initially pay the major portion of the cost of improving the Burr Oaks property, petitioner would, nevertheless, be required to incur substantial development costs. Petitioner estimated that these costs would be in excess of $100,000.

Another factor indicating that petitioner was undercapitalized and did not have sufficient funds with which to commence business is that on November 30, 1957, less than 2 months after it was formed, it borrowed $15,000 from Elkind. On February 28, 1958, it borrowed an additional $10,000 from Elkind.

Moreover, the land transferred to petitioner by Elkind, Watkins, and Ritz was its only asset of significance and, without it, petitioner could not have engaged . . . in business. It was at all times contemplated by Elkind, Watkins, and Ritz that the land would remain at the risk of petitioner's business.

It is generally recognized that one of the crucial factors in determining whether the transfer of property to a thinly capitalized corporation constitutes a bona fide sale, rather than a mere contribution to capital, is the anticipated source of payment to the transferor. Gilbert v. Commissioner, 262 F. 2d 512, 514 (C.A. 2, 1959), *affirming* a Memorandum Opinion of this Court, *certiorari denied* 359 U.S. 1002 (1959). If payment to the transferor is dependent solely upon the success of an untried, undercapitalized business, the prospects of which are uncertain, the transfer of property raises a strong inference that it is, in fact, an equity contribution. . .

At the time of the transfer of the Burr Oaks property to petitioner, its business prospects can only be described as speculative and uncertain. Elkind, Watkins, and Ritz realized that the only way petitioner could raise the $100,000 needed by it for improvements would be from sales of lots. It is obvious that the only hope that Elkind, Watkins, and Ritz had of obtaining repayment of the so-called promissory notes depended upon the successful development and sale of the lots in the Burr Oaks property.

Despite the fact that the respective interests of Elkind, Watkins, and Ritz in petitioner were represented by what purported on their face to be promissory notes in the principal amount of $110,000, the evidence before us indicates that it was the intent of all concerned with the affairs of petitioner that these instruments would give Elkind, Watkins, and Ritz a continuing interest in petitioner's business. The instruments issued by petitioner to Elkind, Watkins, and Ritz recited that they were to mature in 2 years from the date of issuance. However, after a review of the entire record, we believe that it was understood that no payment would be made on the notes, or would ever be demanded by Elkind, Watkins, and Ritz, which in any way would weaken or undermine petitioner's business. See Charter Wire, Inc. v. United States, 309 F.2d 878, 881 (C.A. 7, 1962). It is true that petitioner during 1959 paid $31,000 apiece to Elkind, Watkins, and Ritz with respect to their so-called promissory notes.[8] However, petitioner's history with regard to making payments on the alleged promissory notes indicates that the payments thereon came only from gains derived through the sale of lots. Moreover the fact that there was outstanding a substantial principal balance ($46,000) on each of the notes issued to the individual petitioners even as late as the time of the trial herein indicates that the alleged notes were intended to give the individual petitioners a continuing equity interest in petitioner. . .

The evidence clearly indicates that although Elkind, Watkins, and Ritz were not stockholders of record in petitioner, nevertheless, they completely dominated and controlled petitioner's affairs. Watkins was petitioner's president. Petitioner's board of directors consisted of Elkind, his wife, Ritz, his brother Philip, Watkins, and Watkins' wife. McGinnes, the man who ran petitioner's day-to-day affairs, had been employed by Elkind in one capacity or another for a period of at least 15 years. His activities were generally supervised by Ritz' accounting firm. After listening to his testimony and that of Elkind, Watkins, and Ritz, we are convinced that McGinnes operated petitioner in accordance with their wishes.

Petitioner's shareholders of record consisted of Ritz' brothers Philip and Erwin, Elkind's wife, and Watkins' wife. They knew and understood little, if anything, of the nature of petitioner's business. Moreover, after lis-

---

[8] On brief, it is argued on behalf of the various petitioners herein that the series of exchanges of notes that occurred at the end of December 1959 between Elkind, Watkins, and Ritz, on the one hand, and petitioner, on the other, constituted a repayment by petitioner of the "unpaid principal balance" in the amount of $79,000 on each of the alleged promissory notes, followed immediately by an advance of a similar amount by each of the individual petitioners. This alleged repayment by petitioner of an aggregate of $237,000 took place at a time when petitioner's liquid assets totaled less than $5,500. It is too much to ask this Court to believe that such an obvious sham constituted a repayment of the alleged notes. Cf. Arthur L. Kniffen, 39 T.C. 553, 565–566 (1962).

tening to the testimony at the trial, it was obvious to us that they were subject to the control of Elkind, Watkins, and Ritz.

By virtue of the provision in petitioner's articles of incorporation regarding the issuance of additional shares of common stock at such prices as a majority of the board of directors should determine, Elkind, Watkins, and Ritz were in a position to appropriate to themselves (through the issuance of additional common stock at whatever price they chose) substantially all of the profits that petitioner might realize after repaying its purported indebtedness to them.

The record also indicates that in transferring the Burr Oaks property to petitioner, Elkind, Watkins, and Ritz assigned a highly inflated value to said property. . . The transfer of the Burr Oaks property to petitioner seems to us an integral part of a plan devised by Ritz whereby Ritz, Watkins, and Elkind could obtain an assured participation in the fruits of the development and subdivision of said property. . . Watkins and Ritz both admitted that petitioner was formed in order to allow them to receive some part of the development profits. The inflation of the "sales price" to petitioner served to extend the period during which Elkind, Watkins, and Ritz could participate in petitioner's business as "creditors" and increased the amount which they could withdraw as "principal" if the venture proved successful.

These are some of the factors which led us to conclude that the promissory notes received by Elkind, Watkins, and Ritz did not represent a true indebtedness. The purported promissory notes issued to the individual petitioners in our opinion constitute preferred stock.[10]

Having decided that for tax purposes the so-called promissory notes issued to Elkind, Watkins, and Ritz constitute an equity interest in petitioner, we must now determine whether the transfer of the Burr Oaks property is governed by section 351. . .

In contending that section 351 does not govern the transfer of the Burr Oaks property, petitioner has presented three arguments. Two of the arguments (that the transaction was a sale and that no stock or securities were issued to the transferors of the property) have been previously considered and resolved adversely to petitioner. The third argument presented is that Elkind, Watkins, and Ritz, who transferred the Burr Oaks property to petitioner, were not, immediately after that transaction, in control of that corporation within the meaning of the term "control" as defined in section 368(c). Thus, it is contended that even if the promissory notes held by Elkind, Watkins, and Ritz constituted stock, that stock did not carry with it any voting rights. Petitioner further points out (1) that pursuant to its bylaws the right to vote was reserved exclusively to the shareholders of

---

[10] Although we have found the purported promissory notes to constitute equity interests in petitioner for tax purposes, we believe that the holders of those instruments occupied a preferred position vis-à-vis the holders of the common stock. In the first place, the purported promissory notes called for the payment of interest at 6 percent a year. This provision constituted a prior charge on the earnings of petitioner in favor of the holders of those instruments, not unlike a preferred dividend. Thus, we regard the purported promissory notes as preferred stock.

record, namely, Elkind's wife, Watkins' wife, and Ritz' two brothers, and (2) that, for the above reason, the transferors of the Burr Oaks property (Elkind, Watkins, and Ritz) failed to comply with the control requirements set forth in section 368(c) because they did not possess "ownership of stock possessing at least 80 percent of the total combined voting power of all classes of stock entitled to vote." There is a basic fallacy in petitioner's argument in that it is premised on the assumption that Elkind, Watkins, and Ritz were the only transferors of property to petitioner.

As we view the transaction, Elkind, Watkins, and Ritz acted together with Elkind's wife, Watkins' wife, and Ritz' two brothers in forming petitioner. The record clearly indicates that each of them transferred property to petitioner. As we have previously found, Elkind's wife, Watkins' wife, and Philip and Erwin Ritz transferred to petitioner a total of $4,500 shortly after its incorporation. It is settled law that money constitutes property for purposes of section 351. . . In return therefor, petitioner issued to them an aggregate of 450 shares of its common stock. Shortly thereafter, Elkind, Watkins, and Ritz transferred to petitioner their respective interests in the Burr Oaks property and, in return, received what on its face purported to be promissory notes, but what we have previously determined to be preferred stock.

Although Elkind, Watkins, and Ritz may not have received their preferred stock interests in petitioner at exactly the same time as the common stock was issued to Ritz' brothers and the respective wives of Elkind and Watkins, it seems clear that the transfers of cash and the Burr Oaks property to petitioner were integral parts of a unified transaction. Camp Wolters Enterprises v. Commissioner, 230 F.2d 555, 559 (C.A. 5, 1956), *affirming* 22 T.C. 737 (1954), *certiorari denied* 352 U.S. 826 (1956). See also section 1.351–1(a)(I), Income Tax Regs., which provides:

> The phrase "immediately after the exchange" does not necessarily require simultaneous exchanges by two or more persons, but comprehends a situation where the rights of the parties have been previously defined and the execution of the agreement proceeds with an expedition consistent with orderly procedure. . .

On the basis of the record before us, it appears to us that Elkind, Watkins, and Ritz, together with Ritz' brothers, Elkind's wife, and Watkins' wife, were in control of petitioner, as defined in section 368(c), immediately after their transfer of property to it. The fact that Elkind, Watkins, and Ritz received no common stock, which according to petitioner's articles of incorporation was the only class of stock entitled to vote, is of no significance; for there is no requirement in section 351 that each transferor receive voting stock for that section to be applicable. See Cyrus S. Eaton, 37 B.T.A. 715 (1938), which involved the transfer of property by two persons to a controlled corporation. One transferor therein received only common stock and the other received only nonvoting preferred. In commenting upon the question of control, we stated: "Inasmuch as the transferors . . . owned all of the stock of the corporation, they have the necessary control required by the statute." See also Gus Russell, Inc., 36 T.C. 965 (1961).

Since the nonrecognition provisions of section 351 apply to the transfer of the Burr Oaks property to petitioner, petitioner's basis in said property is limited to $100,000, which is a carry-over basis from the transferors. Sec. 362(a)(1).

Insofar as the distributions made by petitioner during 1959 to Elkind, Watkins, and Ritz are concerned, we have previously found that, to the extent they purported to be a repayment of the "promissory notes," they were a sham. The net effect of the various payments by petitioner and exchanges of notes was that petitioner distributed $31,000 apiece to Elkind, Watkins, and Ritz in 1959. To this extent, the distributions resemble a redemption of stock in that the respective interests of these three individuals in petitioner were proportionately lessened. However, we are unable to find that said distributions fit within any of the paragraphs of section 302(b). Therefore, the $31,000 distributed by petitioner to Watkins, Elkind, and Ritz is governed by section 302(d) and to the extent of petitioner's earnings and profits is to be treated as a dividend. . .

NOTES

1. What argument might have been advanced for Ritz, but not for the others, to avoid dividend treatment? Consider the scope of § 318(a)(1) in answering this question. Should the argument prevail?

2. Should Ritz have had counsel of his own? Might the one lawyer representing all the taxpayers have had a conflict of interest? See generally B. Wolfman, J. Holden & K. Harris, Standards of Tax Practice § 402.3 (6th supplm. ed. 2006).

3. The taxpayers in *Burr Oaks* had several strategies in mind. Bear in mind that at the beginning of the transactions, Elkind, Watkins and Ritz (the "founders") owned property that would eventually be sold (after some developing). One problem they faced was that the corporation would take a carryover basis if the property were contributed in a § 351—thus when the corporation eventually sold the property, all the gain on the property would be triggered on the corporate return. This would include gain that had accrued while the property was held by the founders. The problem here is that the taxpayers might have been entitled to capital gains treatment on the appreciation in their hands (had they sold the property) but in the corporate hands, all the gain would be taxed at the corporate rate and classified according to the corporate activity. By trying to classify their transaction with the corporation as a sale, the founders sought to trigger their share of the gain before putting property into the corporation. In that way a smaller portion of the overall gain (measured as the difference between the price paid by the founders and the price at which the corporation sold it to the public) would be taxed in corporate hands.

However, to the extent that the founders overcharged the corporation for the property (assuming we would respect their transaction as a sale and not a contribution), they were trying not just to avoid having "their" share of the property gain taxed in the corporation's hands, but in fact to shift as much as possible of the total profit on the property from the corporation's return and to the returns of the founders.

In addition, on this alleged sale, the founders sought to defer reporting their gain on the "sale" to the corporation. If successful in this effort, the fact that they had to "sell" the property to the corporation so as to ensure that not all gain would be reported at the higher corporate rate, would not come at the "price" of a current tax due by the founders.

Stevens Pass, Inc. v. Commissioner
48 T.C. 532 (1967).

■ FAY, JUDGE. . . The parties have stipulated as to certain items raised in the statutory notice of deficiency so that [one of] the issues remaining for determination [is] as follows:

(1) Whether, upon the liquidation of its subsidiary, petitioner was entitled to the step-up in the basis of depreciable assets pursuant to section 334(b)(2)* of the Internal Revenue Code of 1954. . .

FINDINGS OF FACT

. . . Petitioner, Stevens Pass, Inc., is a Washington corporation which was organized on September 29, 1960. . . Since December 1, 1960, petitioner has operated the ski area at Stevens Pass. . .

Petitioner is the survivor by merger, under the laws of the State of Washington with Stevens Pass Company, Inc. (hereinafter referred to as the old company), on December 1, 1960.

The old company was organized in 1946 to operate the ski facilities and area at Stevens Pass, Washington. In 1960 the authorized capital of the old company consisted of 100 shares of Class A voting common stock and 33 1/3 shares of Class B nonvoting, common stock. The Class A and Class B stocks share in the earnings and capital on the basis of two-thirds to Class A and one-third to Class B. The total authorized and issued shares of the old company on November 30, 1960, were owned as follows:

Name	Class A	Class B
Donald G. Adams *	50	0
Bruce Kehr *	50	0
John H. Caley	0	33¹/₃

* By agreements dated June 16, 1948, and September 15, 1948, between Adams and Kehr, Adams had 51 percent voting control of the old company.

Sometime during the spring of 1960 an irreparable dispute arose between Donald G. Adams (hereinafter referred to as Adams) and Bruce Kehr (hereinafter referred to as Kehr). It was determined that the dispute could not be settled unless one or the other sold his stock in the old company. However, no agreement was reached that was satisfactory to both parties. Thereafter, Adams, Kehr, and John H. Caley (hereinafter referred to as Caley) attempted to interest outside investors in acquiring stock in a new

---

*§ 334(b)(2) of the 1954 Code was replaced by § 338.—ED.

corporation to be formed to acquire the stock of the old company and then to dissolve it.

On June 10, 1960, Adams, Kehr, and Caley offered to sell all of their shares in the old company to Loren D. Prescott, an agent for undisclosed principals, for the sum of $650,000. Contemporaneously with the execution of the offer to sell, they executed an agreement among themselves concerning the division of the $650,000 sales proceeds as follows: Adams, $250,000; Kehr, $200,000; and Caley, $200,000. This latter agreement also called for the transfer by Kehr of his stock (33 1/3 shares) in a corporation known as Trams, Inc., to Adams for the sum of $4,800.

On or about June 30, 1960, a prospectus relevant to the financial condition of the old company was prepared and circulated to various potential investors. The prospectus proposed that a new company (petitioner) be formed to purchase all the shares of the old company and then dissolve it.

On September 2, 1960, a subscription account was set up for investment in petitioner. The subscribers, amount subscribed, and date subscribed were as follows:

Date	Name	Units Subscribed *
Aug. 30, 1960	Melvin R. Whitman	4
Sept. 1, 1960	Mel S. Johnston	3
Sept. 6, 1960	Donald P. Christianson	4
Sept. 8, 1960	Miles W. Tippery	4
Sept. 27, 1960	John M. Shiach	$1^{1}/_{3}$
Sept. 27, 1960	Bernard J. Goiney	$1^{1}/_{3}$
Sept. 27, 1960	Homer V. Hartzell	$1^{1}/_{3}$
Oct. 13, 1960	Reider Tanner	1
Nov. 2, 1960	Vernon O. Lundmark	1
		21

* A unit consisted of 10 shares of no par common stock at $250 per share and one $2,500, 20–year, 6–percent debenture at par for a total investment of $5,000.

The subscribers deposited 10 percent of the subscription price into escrow at a bank located in Seattle, Washington.

On September 9, 1960, the offer to sell made by Adams, Kehr, and Caley was accepted. On September 29, 1960, petitioner was organized. On October 22, 1960, petitioner's stock certificate book reflects the issuance of 400 shares of its no par common stock to the following individuals for a total of $100,000.

Certificate No.	Name	Shares
1	Miles W. or Nellie Tippery	40
2	Bruce Kehr	120*
3	John H. Caley	80
4	Reider Tanner	10
5	Melvin R. Whitman	40
6	Mel S. Johnston	30

7	Vernon O. Lundmark	10
8	Donald P. Christianson	20*
9	John M. Shiach	13.33
10	Homer V. Hartzell	13.33
11	Bernard J. Goiney	13.33
12	Mel S. Johnston	<u>10</u>
		400

* Ten of the shares issued in the name of Bruce Kehr are subject to a trust agreement as the property of Christianson and are held by Kehr as security for a loan of $5,000 made by him to Christianson to enable the latter to purchase an investment unit in petitioner.

On November 4, 1960, petitioner entered into a written agreement with Adams, Kehr, and Caley to purchase their shares in the old company for the sum of $650,000, payment to be made as follows:

(a) $10,000 upon execution of this agreement

(b) $178,500 on closing the transaction

(c) The balance of $461,500 payable in ten equal annual installments of $46,150, plus interest at 5 percent on the declining balance from the date of closing and payable on or before June 30 of each succeeding year beginning with 1961.

This agreement was closed in Seattle, Washington, on November 30, 1960.

In December 1960, petitioner issued 6–percent, 20–year debenture bonds in registered form in the total amount of $100,000. The debentures were dated October 22, 1960, and were issued to the following individuals:

Name	Amount
Miles W. or Nellie Tippery	$ 10,000.00
Bruce Kehr	30,000.00*
John H. Caley	20,000.00
Melvin R. Whitman	10,000.00
Donald P. Christianson	5,000.00*
Vernon O. Lundmark	2,500.00
Reider Tanner	2,500.00
John M. Shiach	3,333.33
Bernard J. Goiney	3,333.33
Homer V. Hartzell	3,333.33
Mel S. Johnston	<u>10,000.00</u>
	$100,000.00

* Of the debentures issued to Kehr, the amount of $2,500 is subject to a trust agreement as the property of Donald Christianson and is held by Kehr as security for a loan of $5,000 by him to Christianson.

On December 1, 1960, the old company and petitioner, through appropriate Board of Directors' and shareholders' action, entered into a joint plan of merger and agreement of merger, whereupon the old company, the wholly owned subsidiary of petitioner, was liquidated pursuant to section 332, and the assets subject to the liabilities were transferred to petitioner.

On December 1, 1960, the old company had assets with a book value of $245,504.83 and liabilities of $125,946.59. Petitioner included the assets received on liquidation at a cost of $775,946.59 (the total of the cost of the stock, $650,000, and the amount of the liabilities assumed, $125,946.59) pursuant to section 334(b)(2). The increase in the book value of assets on the merger was $530,381.76.

The allocation of the step-up in basis is made on the basis of the net fair market values of the assets received (fair market value less applicable liabilities). Petitioner, therefore, estimated the net fair market values of the tram equipment and the other assets and allocated the $650,000 purchase price of the stock to them. Petitioner determined that the old company had had no goodwill and that certain special use permits were without fair market value. It, therefore, did not allocate any portion of the step-up in basis to either item, . . .

Respondent, in his statutory notice of deficiency, determined that section 334(b)(2) was inapplicable in determining the basis of the assets in question and that the basis should be determined under section 334(b)(1). . .

OPINION

The first issue for determination is whether petitioner may properly compute under section 334(b)(2) the basis of assets received in the liquidation of its wholly owned subsidiary pursuant to section 332. Respondent contends that petitioner must compute the basis of the assets received under section 334(b)(1). . .

The crux of the present dispute is whether petitioner acquired the stock of the old company by "purchase" as defined by section 334(b)(3). Petitioner contends that it acquired the stock of the old company by the purchase and sale contract closed on November 30, 1960. Respondent at trial took the position that the transfer came within the language of subsection 3(C) of section 334(b). He has, however, failed to pursue this theory[5] and, on brief, argues that the shares acquired from Kehr and Caley were in fact acquired by petitioner in a transaction to which section 351 applied and that the exchange, therefore, falls within subsection 3(B) of section 334(b). The rationale of respondent's contention is that the transaction should be viewed as an exchange by Kehr and Caley of cash and their shares of stock in the old company for stock and debentures in petitioner, plus a cash down payment (an amount unrelated to the cash given by Kehr and Caley) and a 10-year installment obligation. Respondent then states that the cash down payment received should be netted against the cash paid in for the stock

---

[5] In any event, we are of the opinion that section 334(b)(3)(C) has no application to the factual situation before us. Respondent has urged in his opening statement that Kehr and Caley be treated collectively as one person in order to apply section 318. We can find no authority for such a premise.

and debentures of the petitioner. He further states that the "control" requirement of section 351 is satisfied since the outside investors contributed cash, in effect, simultaneously with the transfer by Kehr and Caley so that they all may be considered as one transferor group.

We cannot agree.

Though at first blush respondent's argument appears to have some merit, on closer inspection we are of the opinion that respondent's position requires an unwarranted extension of the scope of the nonrecognition provisions of section 351. This is the same contention respondent urged us to adopt in the case of Charles E. Curry, 43 T.C. 667 (1965). We declined to do so then, and we decline to do so now. The factual pattern of the Curry case is strikingly similar to the case before us. In Curry, a family group composed of Charles F. Curry and his wife (Janet), Charles E. Curry, and Carolyn Elbel (daughter of Charles F. and Janet), owned undivided interests in a building, as follows:

Charles F. and Janet Curry	60%
Charles E. Curry	20%
Carolyn Elbel	20%

This group transferred their building to a corporation formed to purchase it for cash and notes. The shares in the purchasing corporation were held as follows:

Charles E. Curry	45%
Donald Elbel (Carolyn's husband)	45%
Charles F. Curry	10%

The corporation took as its basis for depreciation, its cost. Respondent, however, contended that since the transaction should be properly characterized as a section 351 transfer (he argued that the notes were in fact securities), the basis to the purchasing corporation should be the transferor's basis as provided in section 362. We held that section 351 was inapplicable and stated that—

If respondent's position were adopted, section 351 would apply even where an unrelated third party was the stockholder of the corporation. Assume, for example, a transaction identical to that involved in the instant case except that A.T. & T. was the sole shareholder of [the purchasing corporation]. We cannot believe that Congress intended nonrecognition of gain in such a case. Indeed, respondent would undoubtedly be quick to object if taxpayers tried to prevent recognition by such a device. Yet it is clear that, in a sale effected in this manner, the transfers of cash for stock and property for notes are interdependent steps of a single plan. It is not a ground for distinction that two of the stockholders in the instant case were also transferors of realty, since we have found the parties were capable of independent action and intended a bona fide sale.[6] [43 T.C. at 697]

It is our opinion that this statement is equally applicable to the facts before us. We do not believe that this is a proper situation for the application of section 351.

The case of Houck v. Hinds, 215 F.2d 673 (C.A. 10, 1954), which is respondent's sole citation of authority for his contention, is readily distinguishable from the case at bar. In Houck v. Hinds, the members of a partnership sold its assets to a newly formed corporation organized by a third party for installment notes. The third party was unable to interest others in the venture, and members of the partnership then purchased his shares and subscribed for the balance of the corporate shares. The net effect was that the members of the partnership now owned the corporate shares and the corporation's installment notes in the same proportion as their old partnership interests. The Tenth Circuit held that what had occurred was the mere incorporation of the partnership in that the shares were held by the same persons and in the same proportions as the partnership interests.

The case at bar is distinguishable on its facts. We can hardly ignore the facts that, whereas in Houck v. Hinds the ownership remained exactly the same throughout, in this case Adams' 50–percent ownership disappeared, Kehr's 50–percent common-stock interest was reduced to less than 30 percent, Caley's 100–percent nonvoting stock interest was changed to a 20–percent voting interest, and finally that over 50 percent of the petitioner-corporation is owned by persons who possessed no interest whatever in the old company.

We therefore hold that section 351 is inapplicable and that petitioner may properly compute the basis for the assets received under section 334(b)(2). . . .

NOTES

1. *Stevens Pass* posed the question whether the taxpayer had acquired its subsidiary's stock by "purchase," as defined in § 334(b)(3) of the pre-TEFRA statute. After TEFRA, the issue would arise as a result of a § 338 election, not upon liquidation of the subsidiary, and the question would be whether the acquisition of the subsidiary's stock was effected by "purchase" within the meaning of § 338(h)(3) or, as the Commissioner contended, in a § 351 transaction. In light of the repeal of the *General Utilities* doctrine in 1986, however, few taxpayers would today make a § 338 election.

2. The Second Circuit affirmed a Tax Court decision holding that the "exchange" requirements of § 351 are met although a sole proprietor who transfers the assets and liabilities of his business to a preexisting wholly owned corporation receives no additional stock. Lessinger v. Commissioner, 872 F.2d 519 (2d Cir. 1989), *aff'g on this ground and rev'g in part*, 85 T.C. 824 (1985).

---

[6]The instant case, like the case of Charles E. Curry, 43 T.C. 667 (1965), unquestionably involves an arm's-length transaction....

A owns all the stock of Corporation X. She contributes to X a piece of real estate worth $100,000 but receives nothing in return. The basis of the real estate before transfer is $50,000. What are the tax consequences to A? To X? What is the basis of the real estate in X's hands? What impact does the transfer have on the basis of A's stock?

Suppose in the above situation that A owns only 50 percent of the stock of X. B and C own the remaining 50 percent. What is the effect on B and C of A's contribution of the real estate?

For a case distinguishing debt from equity in order to decide whether a corporation's note was issued in connection with a "sale" or in a § 351 transaction, see Robert W. Adams, 58 T.C. 41 (1972).

3. Prior to the 1989 amendments to § 351, a transferor could, in addition to stock, receive debt of the transferee, evidenced by "securities," without recognition of gain. This often enabled the securities holder to withdraw corporate earnings as a tax-free return of basis. When capital gains were taxed at a preferential rate the securities holder's gain on distributions received in excess of basis was typically capital gain. The law now treats all debt received in a § 351 transaction, whether or not evidenced by "securities," as boot. Cf. The Subchapter C Revision Act of 1985, A Final Report Prepared by the Staff, S. Prt. No. 47, 99th Cong., 1st Sess. 46, 57 (Comm. Print, May 1985).

The further restriction in 1997 of what can be received in a § 351 exchange transaction without triggering gain supports the restriction on the receipt of securities. In 1997, Congress added nonqualified preferred stock to the list of what does not qualify for tax free treatment under § 351. See § 351(g). As an example of the idea that anti-abuse rules can themselves provide opportunities for tax planning, in 2011 Treasury proposed no longer treating most nonqualified preferred stock as boot.

2. TAXATION OF "BOOT"; BASIS OF STOCK RECEIVED

a. Taxable Transfer—§§ 1001, 1012

Assume that T transfers property with adjusted basis of $10,000 and fair market value of $20,000 to X Corporation in exchange for some of its common stock worth $20,000. Assume, too, that T is not "in control" after the exchange. As a result, § 351 is inapplicable, T's gain is recognized, and § 1012 prescribes a cost ($20,000) basis for the stock which T receives.

b. Tax–Free Transfer (in Whole or in Part)

i. RECOGNITION OF GAIN—§ 351(b)

If a transferor receives not only the "stock" permitted by § 351(a), but "other property or money" to boot (including securities and nonqualified preferred stock), § 351(b)(2) provides for nonrecognition of loss but § 351(b)(1) calls for recognition of gain (the amount realized over basis), to the extent of the "boot" (the money plus the fair market value of the "other property" received). For example, suppose T transfers an asset with adjusted basis of $50,000 and fair market value of $100,000 to a corporation in exchange for its common stock (worth $75,000) and cash in the amount of $25,000. Assume, too, that T is "in control" after the exchange. T's realized gain is $50,000. His recognized gain, however, is $25,000, since § 351(b) restricts recognition of the gain to the amount of the boot, here the cash of $25,000.

If two assets are transferred, one at a $50,000 gain and one at a $40,000 loss, and "boot" of $30,000 is received (in addition to stock that qualifies under § 351(a)), what is the tax impact? See Rev. Rul. 68–55, 1968–1 C.B. 140.

Suppose the taxpayer receives "boot" of $15,000 for an asset with a basis of $10,000 and a fair market value of $12,000. What is the tax impact on the transferor? Should one be concerned with the earnings and profits account of the corporation? With the relationship between the taxpayer and the other shareholders?

See B. Bittker and J. Eustice, Federal Income Taxation of Corporations and Shareholders 3.05 (2012 online).

ii. BASIS OF STOCK RECEIVED—§ 358

In the hypothetical posed in subsection 2.a., supra, if T had been "in control" after the exchange, and § 351(a) had applied, T's gain would not have been recognized. His basis for the stock received would have been $10,000, determined under § 358(a)(1).

Assume that T had received stock worth $15,000 and cash of $5,000, that he was "in control," and that his gain of $10,000 was recognized to the extent of $5,000 under § 351(b)(1). What is the basis of his stock?

Assume that, instead of cash, T had received an AT&T bond worth $5,000 or nonqualified preferred stock worth $5,000. What would be its basis in T's hands? Consider § 358(a)(2); Treas. Reg. § 1.358–1.

Suppose that, in a § 351 transaction in which T receives stock worth $10,000 and bonds worth $15,000, the asset he transferred had a basis of $15,000. At what basis does T hold the stock? The bonds? Consider § 358(b)(1); Treas. Reg. § 1.358–2.

Suppose T, in a § 351 transaction, transfers an asset with an adjusted basis of $50,000 and fair market value of $100,000 to X Corporation for common stock worth $75,000 plus X Corporation's assumption of a $25,000 liability that T had incurred when he purchased the asset. What is the basis for the stock in T's hands? Consider § 358(a)(1)(A)(ii) and (d); Treas. Reg. § 1.358–3. See B. Bittker and J. Eustice, Federal Income Taxation of Corporations and Shareholders 3.05, 3.06, 3.10 (online 2012).

A transferor may not allocate high basis, long-term property to one block of stock and low basis, short-term property to another, when the properties are transferred as part of a single integrated transaction. See Treas. Reg. §§ 1.358–1 and 1.358–2(b)(2); Rev. Rul. 85–164, 1985–2 C.B. 117. See also Letter Ruling 20104302.

iii. HOLDING PERIOD—§ 1223(1)

If § 358 determines a transferor's basis as to the stock issued him by a corporation (as in a § 351 transaction), his holding period for the stock will ordinarily include the period during which he held the assets transferred. This rule for "tacking" and its exceptions are set forth in § 1223(1).

3. EFFECT OF LIABILITIES—§ 357

Easson v. Commissioner
294 F.2d 653 (9th Cir. 1961).

■ Before ORR, BARNES and MERRILL, CIRCUIT JUDGES.

■ BARNES, CIRCUIT JUDGE. . . In 1952 taxpayer owned and operated an apartment house in Portland, Oregon. On June 19, 1952, taxpayer encumbered the apartment house with a $250,000 mortgage, taxpayer himself signing and assuming personal liability on the notes underlying the mortgage. In October of 1952, taxpayer formed the Envoy Apartments, an Oregon corporation, and transferred the property, subject to the mortgage, to the corporation in exchange for all of its capital stock. Taxpayer, however, remained personally liable on the notes. The Tax Court found that taxpayer had a legitimate business purpose in consummating this transaction and that his principal purpose was not tax avoidance.

At the time of the transfer, the basis of appellant's property was $87,214.86, and its fair market value was $320,000. The principal balance of the mortgage was $247,064.01. Taxpayer and his wife, on their 1952 returns, reported no gain in connection with the transfer of the apartment to the corporation. They claimed that the transfer was tax free under § 112(b)(5), Internal Revenue Code of 1939.* . . . The Commissioner, however, determined that taxpayer realized a gain on the transaction and determined further that such gain was taxable at ordinary income tax rates rather than at capital gains rates.

I. THE TAX COURT'S DECISION

The Tax Court agreed fully with neither the Commissioner nor the taxpayer. It held that only a portion of the gain should be recognized and taxed in 1952. The taxable portion, the court held, was the difference between taxpayer's basis ($87,214.86) and the principal balance on the mortgage ($247,064.01), viz. $159,849.15. . .

Section 112(b)(5) provides that no gain or loss is to be recognized when property is transferred to a corporation solely in exchange for stock of the

---

* Section 112(b)(5) of the 1939 Code is the predecessor of § 351 of the 1986 Code.—ED.

corporation, if immediately after the transfer, the transferor is in control of the corporation. Thus, at first blush, it would appear that taxpayer should prevail; he exchanged the apartment for stock of the corporation and immediately after the exchange he was in control of the corporation. He has met the requirements of § 112(b)(5). But there was more to the transaction than just an exchange of an apartment house for stock. The apartment was transferred subject to a mortgage and this circumstance can, in some circumstances, alter the tax consequences of the transaction. Subsection (c) (of § 112)** provides that gain will be recognized in a § 112(b)(5) transaction to the extent that "boot," i.e., money or property other than stock, is received by the taxpayer. Can the transfer of encumbered property be considered as the receipt of "boot"? Section 112(k)*** provides a clear answer to this question.[2] It provides that the transfer of property subject to a liability does not constitute the receipt of money or other property within the meaning of § 112(c), and the existence of the encumbrance does not disqualify the exchange for tax-free treatment under § 112(b)(5)—unless the purpose of the taxpayer, in this regard, was tax avoidance or was not a bona fide business purpose. The burden to establish his exemption is on the taxpayer. Here, however, the Tax Court specifically found that taxpayer was not principally motivated by considerations of tax avoidance and that he had a bona fide business purpose. Thus, taxpayer met the test of the specific provisions of § 112(k); the provisions of § 112(c) are, therefore, inapplicable to this transaction. It would seem, then, that the entire transaction comes within § 112(b)(5), and that no gain should yet be recognized. Nevertheless, the Tax Court did not so hold.

The Tax Court noted that a statute must be construed in accordance with its purposes and must not be so interpreted as to lead to "absurd results." The purpose of § 112(b)(5) is not to exempt gain from taxation but to postpone the taxable event to a later time. This postponement is effectuated by adjusting the basis of the stock which the taxpayer receives in the tax free exchange. Under § [358(a)], the basis of the stock is the basis of the property transferred, decreased, however, by the amount of money received, including for purposes of this section the amount of the mortgage, and increased by any gain recognized. Thus, unrecognized gain is retained as a potential liability by reducing the basis of taxpayer's stock.

As an example, if a taxpayer in a § 112(b)(5) transaction transfers property worth $10,000 which cost him $1,000, he has an unrecognized gain of $9,000. Since his stock takes the same basis as the property transferred (viz. $1,000), he will recognize the gain when he sells the stock at a later date (presumably at $10,000). If the property transferred were subject to a $500 mortgage, taxpayer would have an additional gain of $500, the gain being currently unrecognized, however, by virtue of § 112(k). This ad-

---

** Section 351(b) of the 1986 Code.—ED.

*** Sections 357(a) and (b) of the 1986 Code.—ED.

[2] ..... In 1954, Congress re-enacted § 112(k) of the 1939 Code as § 357(a) and (b) and added the present § 357(c), which for the first time limits § 112(k) by declaring that liabilities in excess of basis shall be considered gain. This was characterized in House Report No. 1337 as having "no counterpart under the 1939 Code." Of course, the instant case arose before the passage of § 357(c).

ditional gain would be postponed by reducing the basis of the stock received by the taxpayer as follows: "Basis of stock received by taxpayer equals the basis of the property transferred, $1,000, less money or property received (including the amount of the mortgage), $500, plus the amount of gain currently recognized (–0–), viz. $500." When taxpayer sells the stock, presumably, for $10,000, he would realize and pay tax upon a gain of $9,500.

As applied to the facts of this case, the computation prescribed by § [358(a)], would result in a *negative* basis with respect to the stock acquired by taxpayer. Taxpayer's basis on the transferred property was $87,214.86; deducting from this figure the amount of the mortgage ($247,064.01) yields a basis of minus $159,849.15. Holding that property cannot have a negative basis, the court held, further, that the adjusted basis of the stock is zero. This determination, however, would permit the gain of $159,849.15 to escape taxation, unless the nonrecognition provisions of § 112(b)(5) are ignored. If petitioner sold his zero basis stock for an amount that equaled the equity in the property transferred, $72,935.99 ($320,000, fair market value, less $247,064.01, mortgage), he would be taxed on that amount and nothing more. Taxpayer would, in effect, have converted the property into cash, realizing a gain of $232,785.14, but never paying a tax on $159,849.15 of it. Since the purpose of § 112(b)(5) is not [to] permit a tax avoidance but only to permit postponement, it cannot, consistently with its purpose, be applied without limitation to this transaction. That portion of the gain, which if not presently recognized, will never be recognized, must be taxed now. The Tax Court thus held that $159,849.15 should be currently recognized and taxed. . . Both the taxpayer and the Commissioner have appealed from the Tax Court's decision.

II. APPEAL OF JACK EASSON, TAXPAYER

Taxpayer contends that the Tax Court's holding does violence to the clear and unambiguous language of the code sections involved. Section 112(b)(5) states unequivocally that no gain is to be recognized when property is transferred to a corporation in exchange for stock and immediately after the exchange the transferor controls the corporation. Section 112(k) is also clear in providing that the existence of an encumbrance on property exchanged in a § 112(b)(5) transaction does not deny the transferor the benefits conferred by § 112(b)(5). When a statute is unambiguous, the courts may not look elsewhere for the legislative intent. . . We believe that the Tax Court did err in failing to adhere to the unambiguous language contained in the statutes in question here. Assuredly, there is authority for departing from the literal meaning of statutory language when literal application would produce absurd results (1 Mertens, Law of Federal Income Taxation, § 3.04), but here the Tax Court's interpretation is directly contrary to the language of the statute. Section 112(b)(5) says no gain shall be recognized if certain conditions are fulfilled, yet the Tax Court says gain shall be recognized even though all the conditions enumerated are fulfilled. This is judicial legislation. If absurd results occur by reason of taxing statutes honestly and correctly followed by a taxpayer, it is up to the Congress to remedy the loophole.

Taxpayer's case on this point is bolstered by the fact that the 1954 Code contains a provision specifically covering the situation presented by this case. Section 357(c) of the 1954 Code ... expressly provides that if the transferred property is subject to liabilities which exceed the transferor's basis in the property then the excess is to be presently recognized as gain. (See note 2, supra.) The court below brushed this aside as a clarification of existing law and not new law (noting dicta to the contrary, however, in W. H. Weaver, 32 T.C. 411, 436). In commenting upon the general effect of the provisions contained in § 357(c), the House Ways and Means Committee noted that the provisions are "not found in existing law." H.R. No. 1337 (83d Cong. 2d Sess., p. A129; U.S. Code, Congressional and Administrative News, 1954, v. 3, p. 4066). Thus the existence and history of later legislation tend to indicate that Congress "meant" precisely what it said—and no more—when it adopted § 112(b)(3) of the 1939 Code.

In departing from the express language of § 112(b)(5), the Tax Court relied upon the fact that a literal interpretation of the section would lead to absurd results. If no such absurd consequences are inherent in a literal application of the section, then no justification for the Tax Court's departure is established. The absurd result feared by the Tax Court was that § 112(b)(5) would become an instrument of tax exemption rather than of tax deferment. This conviction stemmed from the Tax Court's belief that there could be no such legal phenomenon as a negative basis. And this is perhaps the most crucial issue in the appeal presented by the taxpayer.

Can property have a negative basis? There is little law on the subject;[3] and we are far from satisfied that the Tax Court's outright rejection of this concept is justifiable. Why, then, did the Tax Court conclude that property cannot have a negative basis? In footnote 8 of its opinion the court explains:
. . .

> It is a fundamental concept of income taxation to tax gain when its fruits are available for payment of the tax. If a negative base were allowed then recognition of gain could be deferred until a subsequent loss sale or even an abandonment, and unless taxpayer had other resources the tax would never be collected.

The Tax Court, thus, rejects the negative basis concept on the ground that it may impair the future collectibility of the tax. "We must recognize and collect the tax now, or we may never be able to do so." But such argument is equally applicable to any provision for the deferment of tax; nonrecognition of present gain with a corresponding reduction of basis creates the prospect that tax on the deferred gain may never actually be collected. This prospect is equally real, whether basis is reduced to zero, to a point above zero, or to less than zero.

---

[3] For an informative and well authenticated argument in support of the recognition of a negative basis, see ... [a thesis] ... written by George Cooper, entitled "Negative Basis," dated April 20th, 1961 [75 Harv. L. Rev. 1352 (1962)], and discussing the instant case, and listing the favorable and unfavorable considerations which might establish the value of recognizing a negative basis, under certain factual conditions, and in some, but not all, cases.

Judicial hostility to a negative basis is confined to an implication that deductions from a minus basis are undesirable. Crane v. Commissioner, 1947, 331 U.S. 1, 9–10. . .

There is some judicial support for the concept of negative basis in Parker v. Delaney, 1 Cir., 1950, 186 F.2d 455, 459, certiorari denied 341 U.S. 926. . . There, Chief Judge Magruder in a concurring opinion offered an alternative theory to reach the result obtained by the majority, but "with less strain upon the statutory language." His computation involved the use of a negative basis.

The authority bearing on the question presented here, is, then, inconclusive. The "absurd result" which the Tax Court envisions is by no means the necessary consequence of literally applying § 112(b)(5). If the mandate of § 112(b)(5) is followed and none of taxpayer's gain is presently recognized, taxpayer's stock can be given a negative basis, so that all of his gain will be recognized and taxed when he sells the stock. . .

III. APPEAL BY COMMISSIONER

This brings us to the appeal by the Commissioner. The Commissioner contends that the Tax Court erred in not holding all of taxpayer's gain from the exchange to be presently recognizable and taxable. This is the Commissioner's primary position and his defense of the Tax Court's decision in the appeal brought by taxpayer is only an alternative position, if his position here is rejected.

The Commissioner contends that the transaction is governed by § 112(c). This section, it will be recalled, provides that gain will be recognized in a § 112(b)(5) transaction to the extent that "boot" (money or property other than stock) is received by taxpayer. The corporation's acquisition of the property subject to the mortgage, the Commissioner contends, constitutes the receipt by taxpayer of "boot." Since the boot so received, $247,064.01, exceeds taxpayer's gain of $232,785.14 (fair market value of the property, $320,000, less taxpayer's basis, $87,214.86), all of the gain must be recognized and taxed. Section 112(k), we have seen, precludes the result contended for by the Commissioner, but § 112(k) contains an exception and it is this exception which the Commissioner relies upon now. Section 112(k) provides that

> [if] it appears that the principal purpose of the taxpayer with respect to the assumption or acquisition was a purpose to avoid federal income tax on the exchange, or if not such purpose, was not a bona fide business purpose, such assumption or acquisition (in the amount of the liability) shall, for the purposes of this section, be considered as money received by the taxpayer upon the exchange.

The Tax Court found, however, that taxpayer's "principal purpose in exchanging the property subject to the mortgage for all the capital stock of the new corporation was not to avoid Federal income tax on the exchange, and that he had a bona fide business purpose in so transferring the proper-ty." . . . In so finding, the Commissioner contends, the Tax Court erred.

The Tax Court substantiated its ultimate findings by finding further that taxpayer desired to place himself in an extremely liquid position to take advantage of a business downturn which, he believed, would soon oc-cur. In order to achieve this liquid position, taxpayer mortgaged his proper-ty, since he was unable to sell it despite efforts to do so. Having decided to retain the apartment for himself, taxpayer also decided to operate the property in corporate form, as he had done for twenty years. For tax rea-sons, taxpayer had taken the apartment out of the corporation when he had contemplated selling it. After deciding not to sell it, he desired to return it to corporate form in order to secure limited liability and convenience of management should he desire to move elsewhere and to turn the property over to a local real estate organization.

The Commissioner contends (and this is the crux of his appeal) that the Tax Court missed the point of § 112(k). The "true question," missed by the Tax Court, the Commissioner contends, is whether the *corporation's* taking subject to the liability had some bona fide business purpose in con-nection with the corporation's business. Thus, the Commissioner contends, the question was not whether the transfer of the property subject to the liability benefited taxpayer's business interests as an investor; the issue is whether the taking-subject-to-the-liability had any purpose with respect to the business of operating the apartments as rental property. The Tax Court found no such business purpose, and, therefore, the Commissioner claims, it erred in holding that taxpayer met the test of § 112(k).

We cannot go along with the Commissioner's interpretation of the sta-tute. We believe it is erroneous. It finds little, if any, support in the case authority cited. The test suggested by the Commissioner looks to the origin of the encumbrance and to the use of the proceeds derived from it. Section 112(k), however, says nothing about the origin of the encumbrance. It says only that if a corporation "acquires from the taxpayer property subject to *a* liability such . . . acquisition shall not be considered as" boot, unless tax-payer's principal purpose regarding the acquisition is tax avoidance or not a bona fide business purpose. Nor is there anything in the section which deals with the reasons for the encumbrance, or the manner in which the mortgage proceeds are used.

If there is a good business purpose for transferring the property with-out first removing the encumbrance, the requirements of § 112(k) are satis-fied. Certainly, an investor's desire to remain liquid in order to capitalize on an expected business recession is a good business reason for not dis-charging the mortgage. . .

The Commissioner seeks support for his position in Bryan v. Commis-sioner, 4 Cir., 1960, 281 F.2d 238, *certiorari denied* 364 U.S. 931. . . The facts of that case, with some simplification, may be readily stated. Taxpay-er obtained construction loans of $1,643,500 to build houses. This exceeded his actual cost by $157,798.04. After building the houses taxpayer transferred them to four corporations which in exchange gave him stock and assumed the construction loan. The Tax Court and the Court of Appeals held that taxpayer, under these circumstances, received money or other property and therefore did not meet the requirements of § 112(b)(5).

This case, however, provides only weak support for the Commissioner's position here. The Tax Court found in *Bryan*, as it did not find in the instant case, that taxpayer's "principal purpose with respect to the assumption of the liabilities by the four corporations was a purpose to avoid tax," and hence that it was "immaterial . . . whether such purpose might otherwise be considered not a bona fide business purpose." (W. H. Weaver, 32 T.C. 414, 434.) The court of appeals agreed that "his only purpose was to appropriate to himself a major portion of the excess funds . . . and to do it in a form which gave him hope of avoiding federal taxes on the funds with which he enriched himself." Bryan v. Commissioner, supra, 281 F.2d at page 242. There was, therefore, no problem in determining that § 112(k) did not apply.

The *Bryan* case does offer some support for the Commissioner's position in stating that the corporation's assumption of the mortgage in excess of taxpayer's basis constituted an indirect payment of cash to taxpayer. "As a cash payment, the nonrecognition sections would have no application." Ibid. These statements must, however, be considered as dicta in view of the court's holding that taxpayer did not meet the requirements of § 112(k) and that therefore the assumption of the mortgage constituted the payment of "money or other property." If, on the other hand, the court had held § 112(k) applicable, the statements would have been inappropriate. Section 112(k) provides, clearly, that an assumption of liability is not the payment of "other property or money," and to hold that such assumption constitutes a cash payment is a clear contradiction of the words of the statute.

The Tax Court's findings regarding taxpayer's business purpose have not, in our opinion, been shown to be clearly erroneous. And the Commissioner's assertion that taxpayer is a "highly tax conscious person" . . ., as are many citizens these days, is certainly not sufficient to overthrow the Tax Court's further finding that taxpayer's principal motive in this transaction was not tax avoidance. The Tax Court fully examined the evidence regarding the exchange before concluding that taxpayer entered this transaction for bona fide business reasons and not to avoid federal taxes.

In concluding his main argument, the Commissioner says, "There is nothing theoretical about Easson's gain. The unencumbered cash is in his hand, and ought to be immediately subject to the payment of income tax." This statement, we believe, lays bare the Commissioner's basic error. The Commissioner believes that taxpayer is in a genuinely different position now than he was before the exchange. This, we believe, is not so. Before the exchange taxpayer owned an apartment house subject to a liability. After the exchange, taxpayer was the sole owner of a corporation which owned the same apartment house subject to the same liability. Where was any income? His stock in the corporation was worth no more than the physical asset which he owned directly before incorporation. Section 112(b)(5) was enacted to deal with this very situation—to permit business reorganizations which, realistically viewed, do not alter the taxpayer's basic position. To use the Commissioner's phraseology, "the unencumbered cash" was in taxpayer's hand as soon as taxpayer had mortgaged the apartment, but the Commissioner does not claim that the hypothecation of the building constituted a taxable event. . . Taxpayer's transfer of his encumbered apartment house to his wholly owned corporation did not make the cash obtained from the mortgaged transaction any more real or any less encumbered than it was before the transfer. It is our belief that the purpose of the tax laws will best be served by not assessing a tax against taxpayer until he realizes his gain in a transaction in which, realistically speaking, he actually changes his position.

The Commissioner's next contention applies only if the court rejects his positions both as appellee and appellant. In such event, Commissioner contends, taxpayer received dividend income (§ 115(a), 1954 Code . . .) in 1953 by virtue of the corporation's payments on the mortgage. This contention is based upon the theory that the corporation's payments discharged a legal obligation of taxpayer. While the corporation may incidentally have benefited taxpayer by reducing the mortgage, it is clear that the corporation did not thereby distribute any assets. The corporation owned the apartment subject to the mortgage and as the mortgage decreased its equity in the apartment house increased. Thus when it took money out of cash and applied that amount to the mortgage, its net worth remained constant. Its total assets were unchanged because the credit to the cash account was offset by a corresponding debit to the fixed assets account. The payments of interest on the mortgage cannot, obviously, be analyzed in this way; these payments, it would seem, did constitute income to the taxpayer who would then be entitled to take the deduction for interest paid (1 Mertens, Law of Federal Income Taxation, § 9.08, p. 19, n.74). The net effect would be to deny the deduction to the corporation. This interpretation is, however, at variance with the Commissioner's own regulations and should, therefore, be rejected. . . 1.163–1(b) provides:

> Interest paid by the taxpayer on a mortgage upon real estate of which he is the legal or equitable owner, even though the taxpayer is not directly liable upon the bond or note secured by such mortgage may be deducted as interest on his indebtedness.

And see Mertens, supra, § 26.03.

We believe the Commissioner erred in asserting a deficiency against taxpayer based on the 1952 transaction, whereby taxpayer exchanged the apartment house for stock of Envoy Apartments. Furthermore, the Commissioner is in error in his contention that taxpayer received dividend income in 1953 by reason of mortgage and interest payments made by the corporation. We reverse the judgment of the Tax Court, and direct that judgment be entered in favor of taxpayer.

NOTES

1. D, owning 100 percent of Corporation W, transfers to W property worth $100,000, with a basis in her hands of $50,000 and subject to a mortgage of $25,000, in exchange for $75,000 worth of stock. What are the tax consequences to D? To W? What is the effect on basis to D and to W? Suppose the stock were worth $75,000, but the mortgage debt was $60,000?

Suppose D owned 80 percent of C, and E owned the remaining 20 percent. D transfers to C property worth $100,000 with a basis in his hands of $50,000 and subject to a mortgage of $25,000, in exchange for stock worth $125,000. What are the tax consequences to D? To C? What is the effect on basis to D and to C? This problem may require an understanding of § 305(a), which is considered in Chapter 4, infra page 385 et seq.

2. *Easson* is the only case in which a court has accepted the concept of negative basis. Of what relevance is the fact that the taxpayer is not likely, after incorporation of the asset, to have to repay the obligation he incurred? Is § 357(c) a better or worse approach than *Easson*'s as a matter of policy? See Cooper, Negative Basis, 75 Harv. L. Rev. 1352 (1962).

3. When will an assumption of a transferor's liabilities not reached by § 357(c)(1) result in taxation under § 357(b)? Cf. Rev. Rul. 79–258, 1979–2 C.B. 143. See Greiner, Behling, and Moffety, Assumptions of Liabilities and the Improper Purpose—A Re–Examination of Section 357(b), 32 Tax Law. 111 (1978). Blanchard & Hooker, Fixing Assumption of Liability Rules: The Wrong Way and the Right Way, 85 Tax Notes 933 (Nov. 15, 1999); Cummings, Jr., The New Normal: Economic Substance Doctrine First, 126 Tax Notes 521 (Jan 25, 2010). Do you think § 357(b) should be repealed?

4. Congress amended § 357(a) & (d) in 1999 to clarify what constituted an assumption of liability. In part, the changes create a distinction between recourse and nonrecourse liabilities and the circumstances under which they will be considered "assumed" by the transferee corporation. These statutory changes and clarifications target abusive transactions previously pursued by taxpayers. Congress curtailed other abusive transactions involving assumption of liabilities in 1999 by modifying the transferee's basis rules in § 362. Generally, the transferee increases its basis in the property received to the extent that the transferor is required to recognize gain under § 357 because of the transferee's assumption of liabilities. New § 362(d) limits the transferee's ability to increase basis where the transferor is not subject to tax (i.e. is foreign or tax exempt) or the increase would bring the basis above fair market value.

5. X has two divisions, 1 and 2. X maintains separate books for its divisions, and 2 owes 1 $100,000. X now forms subsidiary Y, and it places all of 2's assets into Y. It records the $100,000 debt as an account receivable for X and as an account payable for Y. In Wham Construction Co. v. United States, 600 F.2d 1052 (4th Cir. 1979), the court held that the preexisting loan did not constitute "other property" (boot) for purposes of § 351(b). In Rev. Rul. 80–228, 1980–2 C.B. 115, the Service announced that it would not follow *Wham*. The Service maintains that the account receivable is "other property" for purposes of § 351(b) and that the transferor must recognize gain up to fair market value of the account receivable. See, e.g., Letter Ruling 201144014.

6. In Lessinger v. Commissioner, 872 F.2d 519 (2d Cir. 1989), *rev'g* 85 T.C. 824 (1985), the court held that a transferor could avoid gain recognition under § 357(c)(1) by giving the transferee corporation his personal note for the excess of liabilities over the basis of the assets transferred. See infra at 329.

7. In Coltec Industries v. United States, 454 F.3d 1340 (Fed. Cir. 2006), the court concluded that the taxpayer did not have a problem with assumption of liabilities (by the corporation) but did have a problem because the transaction lacked economic substance.

Revenue Ruling 80–199
1980–2 C.B. 122.

ISSUE

Whether the term "liabilities" as used in sections 357 and 358(d) of the Internal Revenue Code prior to amendment by the Revenue Act of 1978[*] includes accounts payable deductible under section 162 of the Code?

FACTS

Individual A conducted a small contracting business as a sole proprietorship, the income of which was reported on the cash receipts and disbursements method of accounting. On January 1, 1978, A transferred to a newly organized corporation all of the assets of the sole proprietorship in exchange for all of the stock of the corporation, plus the assumption by the corporation of all of the liabilities of the sole proprietorship, in a transaction that met the requirements of section 351(a) of the Code. The transactor did not lack a business purpose. The assets transferred were tangible assets having a fair market value of $20,000 and an adjusted basis of $10,000, and accounts receivable having a fair market value of $30,000 and an adjusted basis of zero dollars. The liabilities assumed by the corporation consisted solely of accounts payable of the sole proprietorship in the face amount of $20,000. The accounts would have been deductible by A as ordinary and necessary business expenses under section 162 if A had paid them. The new corporation continued to utilize the cash receipts and disbursements method of accounting.

LAW AND ANALYSIS

The applicable sections of the Code are 351, relating to nonrecognition in a transfer to a corporation controlled by the transferor; 357, relating to assumption of liability; 358, relating to basis to distributees; and 362, relating to basis to corporations.

Section 357(a) provides, in part, as a general rule that the assumption of liabilities on the part of a corporate transferee in connection with a section 351 exchange, or the acquisition by the transferee of property subject to a liability in such an exchange, shall not be treated as a receipt of money or other property by the transferor.

---

[*] The Revenue Act of 1978 added § 375(c)(3).—Eᴅ.

Section 357(c)(1) prior to amendment by the Revenue Act of 1978 provides in part, that in the case of an exchange to which section 351 applies if the sum of the amount of the liabilities assumed, plus the amount of the liabilities to which the property is subject, exceeds the total of the adjusted basis of the property transferred pursuant to such exchange, then such excess shall be considered as a gain from the sale or exchange of a capital asset or of property which is not a capital asset, as the case may be.

Section 358(a)(1) of the Code provides, in part, that in the case of an exchange to which section 351 applies the basis of the property permitted to be received under section 351 without the recognition of gain or loss shall be the same as that of the property exchanged (A) decreased by (i) the fair market value of any other property (except money) received by the taxpayer, (ii) the amount of money received by the taxpayer, and (iii) the amount of loss to the taxpayer which was recognized on such exchange, and (B) increased by (i) the amount which was treated as a dividend, and (ii) the amount of gain to the taxpayer which was recognized on such exchange (not including any portion of such gain which was treated as a dividend).

Section 358(d) of the Code prior to the amendment by the Revenue Act of 1978 provides that if as part of the consideration to the taxpayer, another party to the exchange assumed a liability of the taxpayer, or acquired from the taxpayer property subject to a liability, such assumption or acquisition (in the amount of the liability) shall, for purposes of this section, be treated as money received by the taxpayer on the exchange.

Since the adjusted basis of the assets transferred by A to the corporation was $10,000 and the accounts payable assumed by the corporation was $20,000, the primary question for consideration is whether the transfer of the assets and liabilities of A's sole proprietorship to the corporation results in gain under section 357(c) of the Code. In Raich v. Commissioner, 46 T.C. 604 (1966), the Tax Court of the United States directed its attention to such a question in a case where the taxpayer transferred assets of a business conducted as a sole proprietorship, the income from which was reported on the cash receipts and disbursements method of accounting, to a newly formed corporation in exchange for all of the stock of the corporation plus the assumption by the corporation of all of the liabilities of the sole proprietorship (trade accounts payable and notes payable) in a transaction meeting the requirements of section 351(a). The court held that the trade accounts receivable had a zero basis, and that since the total liabilities, consisting primarily of trade accounts payable, assumed by the corporation were in excess of the adjusted basis of all of the assets transferred, the taxpayer (transferor) incurred a gain under section 357(c) (as it existed prior to the amendment by the Revenue Act of 1978). In Rev. Rul. 69–442, 1969–2 C.B. 53, the Service indicated that it would follow the decision in Raich v. Commissioner and apply section 357(c) to other situations involving similar facts.

In Focht v. Commissioner, 68 T.C. 223 (1977), *acq.*, page five, this Bulletin, the taxpayer, in 1970, transferred to a newly formed corporation all of the assets of a business conducted as a sole proprietorship, the income of which was reported on the cash receipts and disbursements method of accounting, in exchange for all of the stock of the corporation plus an assumption by the corporation of all the liabilities of the sole proprietorship in a transaction meeting the requirements of section 351(a) of the Code. These liabilities consisted of the liabilities actually assumed by the corporation as well as liabilities to which certain of the property transferred was subject. The liabilities assumed by the corporation consisted primarily of trade accounts payable. The Internal Revenue Service treated all of the liability obligations including the accounts payable as liabilities within the meaning of section 357(c), and determined that the taxpayer incurred a gain, by reason of section 357(c), in the amount by which the liabilities assumed by the corporation exceeded the adjusted basis of the assets transferred. The Tax Court of the United States held that an obligation should not be treated as a liability, under sections 357 and 358(d), to the extent that its payment would have been deductible (under section 162) if made by the transferor. The court held that section 357(c) did not apply to the account payable liabilities for this reason and overruled its prior decision in *Raich* on this point. The Service will follow the decision in *Focht*.

HOLDING

No gain is realized by A on the exchange of property for stock by reason of section 357(c) of the Code because the accounts payable assumed by the corporation would have been deductible by A as ordinary and necessary business expenses under section 162 in the taxable year paid if A had paid these liabilities prior to the exchange. A's basis in the stock received in the exchange of property for stock under section 358(a)(1) is the $10,000 basis that A had in the property transferred to the corporation. No adjustment to such basis is made under section 358(a)(1)(A)(ii) because of the assumption by the corporation of the $20,000 in accounts payable inasmuch as section 358(d) does not apply to the accounts payable. Likewise, no adjustment to such basis is made under section 358(a)(1)(B)(ii) because section 357(c) does not apply to the accounts payable.

Transactions which occur on or after November 6, 1978 will be governed by sections 357(c) and 358(d) as amended by the Revenue Act of 1978.

COURT DECISIONS THAT THE INTERNAL REVENUE SERVICE WILL NOT FOLLOW

The Service will not follow the rationale of the decision of the United States Court of Appeals for the Ninth Circuit in Thatcher v. Commissioner, 533 F.2d 1114 (9th Cir. 1976) which involved a transaction similar to the facts of this revenue ruling. The court agreed with the Service that the transferors must recognize gain under section 357(c) of the Code on the incorporation transfer, but the court also concluded that the transferor should receive a deduction for trade accounts payable discharged by the transferee corporation to the extent of the accounts receivable or the gain recognized under section 357(c), whichever is less.

The Service also will not follow the rationale of the decision of the United States Court of Appeals for the Second Circuit in Bongiovanni v. Commissioner, 470 F.2d 921 (2d Cir. 1972), involving a similar transaction and which held that the term "liabilities," as used in section 357(c) of the Code, did not include all liabilities which are included for accounting purposes, but was meant to apply only to what might be called "tax" liabilities, that is, liens in excess of tax costs, particularly mortgages encumbering property transferred in an exchange within the meaning of section 351. The above mentioned language offers no clear guidance as to the meaning of the terms "accounting" liabilities and "tax" liabilities or to making a distinction between them. For example, to the extent that the *Bongiovanni* decision could be interpreted as suggested by Footnote 6 in Thatcher as holding that "liabilities" for the purpose of section 357(c) means only "the excess of secured debts over the transferor's adjusted basis in the assets transferred" (italics supplied), the Service would view such an interpretation as being unduly restrictive of the term "liabilities."

NOTES

1. How do § 357(c) and § 358(d) as amended in 1978 handle the scenario outlined in Rev. Rul. 80–199?

2. In Rev. Rul. 95–74, 1995–2 C.B. 36, the Service concluded that a corporation's assumption of the transferor's contingent environmental liabilities which had not been taken into account by the transferor (e.g., no deduction) do not count as liabilities in § 357(c)(1). See Chief Counsel Advice Memorandum 2011023056.

3. In 2006, the 4th Circuit affirmed a lower court ruling on a summary judgment motion that the assumption of the shareholder's contingent liability by the corporation issuing stock in a § 351 did not require the shareholder to reduce its basis in the stock pursuant to § 357(c) and § 358. Black & Decker Corp. v. U.S., 436 F.3d 431 (4th Cir. 2006). In the case, the parent corporation, Black & Decker, Inc. (BDI) had outstanding contingent liabilities for potential future health care claims by current and retired employees. BDI contributed approximately $561 million (in borrowed funds) to its subsidiary in exchange for the subsidiary's preferred stock and the subsidiary's assumption of the contingent health care liabilities (although BDI also remained liable). BDI took a basis of about $561 million in the preferred stock and then sold it approximately 1 month later for $1 million, generating a $560 million loss. Although the 4th Circuit upheld the lower court on the basis question because the assumed liabilities were covered by § 357(c)(3) [they would be deductible by the shareholder-transferor if paid], the 4th Circuit reversed on application of the sham transaction doctrine and remanded for a trial to resolve that question. BDI used § 357(c)(3) as a technical tool in its transactional planning but raised interesting questions about the economic substance doctrine and its application by different courts. The announced settlement of the case in 2007 ended the role that *Black & Decker* would play in resolving uncertainty regarding the judicial doctrine of economic substance. However, the 2010 codification of economic substance in § 7701(o) has opened new questions. Under the new provision, a transaction will only satisfy the requirement of economic substance if it changes the taxpayer's economic position in a meaningful way apart from fed-

eral income tax effects and if there is a substantial purpose apart from tax consequences.   In another famous economic substance case involving 357(c)(3), Coltec Industries v. United States, 454 F.3d 1340 (Fed.Cir. 2006) the Supreme Court denied certiorari (Coltec Industries v. United States, 127 S.Ct. 1261 (2007)).

Lessinger v. Commissioner
872 F.2d 519 (2d Cir. 1989), *rev'g* 85 T.C. 824 (1985).

■ Before OAKES, CHIEF JUDGE, KEARSE and CARDAMONE, CIRCUIT JUDGES.

■ OAKES, CHIEF JUDGE. Taxpayers Sol and Edith Lessinger appeal from that portion of a decision of the United States Tax Court, Charles E. Clapp II, Judge, finding them liable for income taxes of $113,242.55 for the tax year 1977. . .

The Tax Court found, and the parties seem to agree, that section 351 of the Internal Revenue Code governs the transaction at issue here. . . The taxpayer here transferred the assets and liabilities of a proprietorship he operated to a corporation he owned for reasons entirely unrelated to tax planning. . . Prior to the consolidation, the proprietorship had a negative net worth. Nevertheless the Tax Court found that the taxpayer had to recognize a gain because he transferred liabilities to the corporation which exceeded his adjusted basis in the assets of the proprietorship. The Tax Court applied section 357(c) of the Code, which is an exception to the general rule of nonrecognition in section 351 transactions. Under section 357(c), gain is recognized to the extent that a transferor-shareholder disposes of liabilities exceeding the total adjusted basis of the assets transferred. . .

Sol Lessinger operated a proprietorship under the name "Universal Screw and Bolt Co." for over twenty-five years prior to 1977. Since 1962 he was also the sole shareholder and chief executive officer of Universal Screw & Bolt Co., Inc. Both businesses were engaged in the wholesale distribution of metal fasteners, and they were conducted from the same location on Ninth Avenue in New York City.

In 1976, the factor that had provided working capital to the proprietorship refused to continue lending funds to it as a noncorporate entity because under New York law one can charge higher interest rates of a corporation. . . The taxpayer instructed . . . his attorney and accountant to do whatever was necessary to make the proprietorship a corporation. The Universal proprietorship was then consolidated into the Universal corporation in 1977. . .

The proprietorship's unaudited balance sheet dated December 31, 1976, shows that the business had a negative net worth.

The consolidation of the proprietorship into the corporation was conducted in a most casual manner, the transfer transaction being naked in its simplicity. The taxpayer already owned all of the corporation's stock, and no new stock was issued. There were no written agreements documenting the transfer. On January 1, 1977, the proprietorship's bank account was closed, and the corporation took over the proprietorship's operating assets. Only two items of any significance were not transferred: The taxpayer had borrowed funds from Chemical Bank to purchase mutual fund shares, and the shares secured the loan. These items appear on the balance sheet above as the mutual fund shares and the Chemical Bank loan. The taxpayer retained the shares and sold them to pay the loan himself later in January 1977.

The corporation expressly assumed the other proprietorship liabilities except accounts payable. All notes payable were changed to show that the corporation was the maker of the notes, and the debt to the factor was expressly assumed. While the corporation did not expressly assume liability for the proprietorship's accounts payable, it did pay those accounts during the first six months of 1977.

On June 1, 1977, journal entries were made to the corporation's books to reflect the consolidation. . . Total proprietorship liabilities exceeded total proprietorship assets by $255,499.37, and that amount was debited to a corporate asset account in an entry entitled "Loan Receivable—SL." A ledger sheet entitled "Sol Lessinger" showed the debit with the description "merger of company" as well as a $3,500 debit for a personal debt the corporation paid for Sol.

When in January 1977 the taxpayer sold his mutual funds, he used the proceeds not only to pay off the partnership's Chemical Bank loan, but also, with the remaining $62,209.35, to pay the corporation part of his $259,000 debt to it. Thus, at the end of 1977, he owed $196,790 to the corporation. In 1981, Marine Midland Bank, a principal creditor of the corporation, requested that the taxpayer execute a promissory note for the debt, and he did so, the note being used as collateral for the bank's loan to the corporation. No interest was ever paid on the debt, however, and the debt had risen to $237,044 by the end of 1982, by which point the corporation was insolvent. . . the taxpayer's debt to the corporation greatly outweighed his equity in it. . .

The taxpayer's principal argument, broadly stated, is that section 357 is inapplicable to him. . .

Narrowly stated, the taxpayer's argument takes two different forms. . .

Second, even if the corporation did "assume" the taxpayer's trade accounts payable, there was no taxable gain since he contributed "property," that is, the account receivable from him in the approximate amount of $250,000, which, contrary to Alderman v. Commissioner, 55 T.C. 662 (1971), should be deemed to have a basis equal to its face value.

. . . Having determined that the proprietorship's accounts payable should be included in the category of liabilities assumed, we must determine whether the taxpayer's purported debt to his corporation would offset those liabilities and prevent a net excess of liabilities over assets. The obligation which the taxpayer owed to his wholly-owned corporation, it must quickly be conceded, was not as well documented as a debt to a third party would be.

A journal entry of the corporation showed $255,499.37 as a loan receivable from the taxpayer, which in turn was posted on a general ledger sheet as a debit to the taxpayer's account. That account was credited with a $62,209.35 adjustment resulting from the sale of the taxpayer's mutual funds and the paydown of the Chemical Bank loan. No credits on account of subsidized rent, see supra at 2343, were made, and the debit balance of $196,790 in the taxpayer's account after the adjustment was never paid down; instead it increased to the sum of $237,044 in 1982. Marine Midland Bank required the open account to be formalized in 1981 in a note which collateralized the bank's loan to the corporation.

The Tax Court refused to count the debt as "property" transferred in the transaction, although its reasoning is not explicit. . . The Tax Court opinion concludes that "even if [Lessinger] had executed a note, it would have a zero basis in the hands of the corporation." Id. at 837 (citing Alderman v. Commissioner, 55 T.C. 662 (1971)). The Tax Court thus apparently believed there were two independently sufficient reasons to ignore the debt: first, that it was artificial, and, second, that it would have had a zero basis.

We are unpersuaded by the argument that the obligation was artificial.

. . . The Commissioner points out that the receivable lacked a due date, interest, security, or "other accepted features of true debt," but this analysis begs the question we have before us. . . We believe that the receivable was an enforceable demand obligation. . .

We believe, however, that a due date, interest, and security are not necessary to characterize Lessinger's obligation to his corporation as debt, and that his obligation was binding. The promissory note he signed in 1981, which the corporation endorsed to Marine Midland as collateral for a loan, is significant because it shows that Marine Midland depended on his personal responsibility. And, in general, it is obvious that the creditors of the corporation continued to do business with it on the strength of the taxpayer's personal credit. . . Lessinger received consideration when he gave his promise to the corporation, and we have no doubt that any court would enforce that promise to protect the corporate creditors if the corporation failed, even in the absence of alter ego liability. We conclude that the taxpayer's obligation to the corporation was real, not artificial.

We now turn to the Tax Court's second reason for ignoring the debt. The Tax Court quoted Alderman, supra, which, like our case, involved the incorporation of an accrual basis proprietorship with a negative net worth. In Alderman, the Tax Court disregarded the taxpayers' personal promissory note to their corporation because the Aldermans incurred no cost in making the note, so its basis to them was zero. The basis to the corporation was the same as in the hands of the transferor, i.e., zero. Consequently, the application of section 357(c) is undisturbed by the creation and transfer of the personal note to the corporation. . . . Section 357(c) does support the Alderman court's reliance on the concept of basis, but the statutory language is not addressed to a transaction such as Lessinger's, where the transferor's obligation has a value to the transferee corporation. The Alderman court did not consider the value of the obligation to the transferee.

Section 357(a) provides that generally, the corporation's assumption of the transferor's liabilities should cause no recognition of gain:

Except as provided in subsection[] . . . (c), if—

(1) the taxpayer receives property which would be permitted to be received under section 351, . . . without the recognition of gain if it were the sole consideration, and

(2) as part of the consideration, another party to the exchange assumes a liability of the taxpayer, or acquires from the taxpayer property subject to a liability,

then such assumption or acquisition shall not be treated as money or other property, and shall not prevent the exchange from being within the provisions of section 351. . .

I.R.C. § 357(a) (1982). Subsection (c)(1) then provides an exception:

(c) Liabilities in excess of basis

(1) In general

In the case of an exchange—

(A) to which section 351 applies,

. . .

if the sum of the amount of the liabilities assumed, plus the amount of the liabilities to which the property is subject, exceeds the total of the adjusted basis of the property transferred pursuant to such exchange, then such excess shall be considered as a gain. . .

Id. § 357(c) (emphasis added). In general, then, the "adjusted basis" of the property transferred is crucial to the calculation.

"Basis," as used in tax law, refers to assets, not liabilities. Section 1012 provides that "the basis of property shall be the cost of such property, except as otherwise provided." Liabilities by definition have no "basis" in tax law generally or in section 1012 terms specifically. The concept of "basis" prevents double taxation of income by identifying amounts that have already been taxed or are exempt from tax. . . . The taxpayer could, of course, have no "basis" in his own promise to pay the corporation $255,000, because that item is a liability for him. We would add parenthetically that to this extent Alderman was correct in describing the taxpayers' note there. But the corporation should have a basis in its obligation from Lessinger, because it incurred a cost in the transaction involving the transfer of the obligation by taking on the liabilities of the proprietorship that exceeded its assets, and because it would have to recognize income upon Lessinger's payment of the debt if it had no basis in the obligation. Assets transferred under section 351 are taken by the corporation at the transferor's basis, to which is added any gain recognized in the transfer. § 362(a). Consideration of "adjusted basis" in section 357(c) therefore normally does not require determining whether the section refers to the "adjusted basis" in the hands of the transferor-shareholder or the transferee-corporation, because the basis does not change. But here, the "basis" in the hands of the corporation should be the face amount of the taxpayer's obligation. We now hold that in the situation presented here, where the transferor undertakes genuine personal liability to the transferee, "adjusted basis" in section 357(c) refers to the transferee's basis in the obligation, which is its face amount.

. . . The purpose of section 357(c) is to provide a limited exception to section 351's nonrecognition treatment that operates, as the Commissioner reminds us here, "where the transferor realized economic benefit which, if not recognized, would otherwise go untaxed." . . . Section 351 was intended to allow changes in business form without requiring the recognition of income. . . The transferor-shareholder recognizes income only to the extent that he receives boot in the form of money or other property. § 351(b). . .

Congress did not add section 357(c), which requires the recognition of gain when liabilities exceed assets, until 1954, when a House committee referred to the section as an "additional safeguard[] against tax avoidance not found in existing law." H.R. Rep. No. 1337, 83d Cong., 2d Sess. 40, reprinted in 1954 U.S. Code Cong. & Admin. News 4017, 4066 ("House Report"). Some provision was necessary to ensure that manipulations of credit and depreciation were not used to realize tax-free gains. . . While some have argued that section 357(c) was designed to avoid a negative basis, its application in the Congress's example is also quite reasonable. The transferor, who has already benefited by depreciating the property or holding it while its value appreciates, has income because he will never have to pay the mortgage. Forcing the taxpayer in our case to recognize a gain, however, would be contrary to Congress's intent because it would tax a truly phantom gain, because his liability to the corporation, as we have said, was real, continuing, and indirectly, at least, enforceable by the corporation's creditors.

. . . We conclude that our holding will not "effectively eliminate section 357(c)." Lessinger experienced no enrichment and had no unrecognized gains whose recognition was appropriate at the time of the consolidation. Any logic that would tax him would certainly represent a "trap for the unwary." *Bongiovanni*, 470 F.2d at 924. . . Lessinger could have achieved incorporation without taxation under the Commissioner's theory by borrowing $260,000 cash, transferring the cash to the corporation (or paying some of the trade accounts payable personally), and later causing the corporation to buy his promissory note from the lender (or pay it off in consideration of his new promise to pay the corporation). If taxpayers who transfer liabilities exceeding assets to controlled corporations are willing to undertake genuine personal liability for the excess, we see no reason to require recognition of a gain, and we do not believe that Congress intended for any gain to be recognized.

. . . Judgment reversed.

NOTE

In Peracchi v. Commissioner, 143 F.3d 487 (9th Cir. 1998), the Ninth Circuit faced the same basic facts considered by the Second Circuit in *Lessinger*, and similarly concluded: (1) that the shareholder-taxpayer's note given to the corporation was genuine debt and (2) that taking this contributed property into account, § 357(c) did not apply because the liabilities assumed did not exceed the basis of the contributed properties. In reaching this conclusion about § 357(c) *Peracc* **Blaschka** *hi* ascribed a basis to the shareholder-taxpayer's note, but explicitly rejected the approach in *Lessinger* as inconsistent with § 357(c)'s focus on the shareholder/transferor not the corporate transferee. Instead *Peracchi* concluded that the shareholder-taxpayer had a basis in the note equal to its face amount. See Borden and Longhofer, The Liability-Offset Theory of Peracchi, 64 Tax Law. 237 (2011).

4. ASSIGNMENT OF INCOME

Hempt Brothers, Inc. v. United States
490 F.2d 1172 (3d Cir. 1974), *cert. denied*, 419 U.S. 826 (1974).

■ Before ALDISERT and WEIS, CIRCUIT JUDGES, and LATCHUM, DISTRICT JUDGE.

■ ALDISERT, CIRCUIT JUDGE. In this appeal by a corporate taxpayer from a grant of summary judgment in favor of the government in a claim for refund, we are called upon to decide the proper treatment of accounts receivable and of inventory transferred from a cash basis partnership to a corporation organized to continue the business under . . . § 351(a). This appeal illustrates the conflict between the statutory purpose of Section 351, postponement of recognition of gain or loss, and the assignment of income [doctrines]. . .

The facts were wholly stipulated; therefore, they may be summarized as set forth by the government in its brief:

> The taxpayer is a Pennsylvania corporation with its principal place of business in Camp Hill, Pennsylvania. It files its federal income tax returns for a fiscal year beginning March 1.

> From 1942 until February 28, 1957, a partnership comprised of Loy T. Hempt, J. F. Hempt, Max C. Hempt, and the George L. Hempt Estate was engaged in the business of quarrying and selling stone,

sand, gravel, and slag; manufacturing and selling ready-mix concrete and bituminous material; constructing roads, highways, and streets, primarily for the Pennsylvania Department of Highways and various political subdivisions of Pennsylvania, and constructing driveways, parking lots, street and water lines, and related accessories.

The partnership maintained its books and records, and filed its partnership income tax returns, on the basis of a calendar year and on the cash method of accounting, so that no income was reported until actually received in cash. Accordingly, in computing its income for federal income tax purposes, the partnership did not take uncollected receivables into income. . .

On March 1, 1957, the partnership business and most of its assets were transferred to the taxpayer solely in exchange for taxpayer's capital stock, the 12,000 shares of which were issued to the four members of the partnership. These shares constituted 1000 of the issued and outstanding shares of the taxpayer. This transfer was made pursuant to Section 351(a) of the Internal Revenue Code of 1954. . . Thereafter, the taxpayer conducted the business formerly conducted by the partnership.

Among the assets transferred by the partnership to the taxpayer for taxpayer's shares of stock were accounts receivable in the amount of $662,824.40 arising from performance of construction projects, sales of stone, sand, gravel, etc., and rental of equipment prior to March 1, 1957. . .

Commencing with its initial fiscal year [which] ended February 28, 1958, taxpayer maintained its books and filed its corporation income tax returns on the cash method of accounting and accordingly, did not take uncollected receivables into income. . . In its taxable years ending in 1958, 1959, and 1960, taxpayer collected the respective amounts of $533,247.87, $125,326.71 and $4,249.72 of the accounts receivable in the aggregate amount of $662,824.40 (sic) that transferred to it, and included those amounts in income in computing its income for its federal income tax returns for those years, respectively.

As a result of an examination extending over a period of years, it was determined by the Commissioner of Internal Revenue, and agreed to by the taxpayer, that the use of the cash receipts and disbursements method of accounting . . . did not clearly reflect taxpayer's income. Accordingly, taxpayer's income was adjusted . . . to accrue unreported sales [accounts receivable] made during the taxable years in question. . .

The district court held: (1) taxpayer was properly taxable upon collections made with respect to accounts receivable which were transferred to it in conjunction with the Section 351 incorporation. . .

I

Taxpayer argues here, as it did in the district court, that because the term "property" as used in Section 351 does not embrace accounts receivable, the Commissioner lacked statutory authority to apply principles associated with Section 351. The district court properly rejected the legal interpretation urged by the taxpayer.

The definition of Section 351 "property" has been extensively treated by the Court of Claims in E.I. Du Pont de Nemours and Co. v. United States, 471 F.2d 1211, 1218–1219 (Ct. Cl. 1973), describing the transfer of a nonexclusive license to make, use and sell area herbicides under French patents:

> Unless there is some special reason intrinsic to . . . [Section 351] . . . the general word "property" has a broad reach in tax law. . . For section 351, in particular, courts have advocated a generous definition of "property," . . . and it has been suggested in one capital gains case that nonexclusive licenses can be viewed as property though not as capital assets. . .

We see no adequate reason for refusing to follow these leads.

We fail to perceive any special reason why a restrictive meaning should be applied to accounts receivables so as to exclude them from the general meaning of "property." Receivables possess the usual capabilities and attributes associated with jurisprudential concepts of property law. They may be identified, valued, and transferred. Moreover, their role in an ongoing business must be viewed in the context of Section 351 application. The presence of accounts receivable is a normal, rather than an exceptional accoutrement of the type of business included by Congress in the transfer to a corporate form. They are "commonly thought of in the commercial world as a positive business asset." Du Pont v. United States, supra, at 1218. As aptly put by the district court: "There is a compelling reason to construe 'property' to include . . . [accounts receivable]: a new corporation needs working capital, and accounts receivable can be an important source of liquidity." . . . In any event, this court had no difficulty in characterizing a sale of receivables as "property" within the purview of the "no gain or loss" provision of Section 337 as a "qualified sale of property within a 12–month period." Citizens Acceptance Corp. v. United States, 462 F.2d 751, 756 (3d Cir. 1972).

The taxpayer next makes a strenuous argument that "[t]he government is seeking to tax the wrong person." It contends that the assignment of income doctrine as developed by the Supreme Court applies to a Section 351 transfer of accounts receivable so that the transferor, not the transferee-corporation, bears the corresponding tax liability. It argues that the assignment of income doctrine dictates that where the right to receive income is transferred to another person in a transaction not giving rise to tax at the time of transfer, the transferor is taxed on the income when it is collected by the transferee; that the only requirement for its application is a transfer of a right to receive ordinary income; and that since the transferred accounts receivable are a present right to future income, the sole requirement for the application of the doctrine is squarely met. In essence, this is a contention that the nonrecognition provision of Section 351 is in conflict with the assignment of income doctrine and that Section 351 should be subordinated thereto. Taxpayer relies on the seminal case of Lucas v. Earl, 281 U.S. 111 . . . (1930), and its progeny for support of its proposition that the application of the doctrine is mandated whenever one transfers a right to receive ordinary income.

On its part, the government concedes that a taxpayer may sell for value a claim to income otherwise his own and he will be taxable upon the proceeds of the sale. Such was the case in Commissioner v. P.G. Lake, Inc., 356 U.S. 260 . . . (1958), in which the taxpayer-corporation assigned its oil payment right to its president in consideration for his cancellation of a $600,000 loan. Viewing the oil payment right as a right to receive future income, the Court applied the reasoning of the assignment of income doctrine, normally applicable to a gratuitous assignment, and held that the consideration received by the taxpayer-corporation was taxable as ordinary income since it essentially was a substitute for that which would otherwise be received at a future time as ordinary income.

Turning to the facts of this case, we note that here there was the transfer of accounts receivable from the partnership to the corporation pursuant to Section 351. We view these accounts receivable as a present right to receive future income. In consideration of the transfer of this right, the members of the partnership received stock—a valid consideration. The consideration, therefore, was essentially a substitute for that which would otherwise be received at a future time as ordinary income to the cash basis partnership. Consequently, the holding in *Lake* would normally apply, and income would ordinarily be realized, and thereby taxable, by the cash basis partnership-transferor at the time of receipt of the stock.

But the terms and purpose of Section 351 have to be reckoned with. By its explicit terms Section 351 expresses the Congressional intent that transfers of property for stock or securities will not result in recognition. It therefore becomes apparent that this case vividly illustrates how Section 351 sometimes comes into conflict with another provision of the Internal Revenue Code or a judicial doctrine, and requires a determination of which of two conflicting doctrines will control.

As we must, when we try to reconcile conflicting doctrines in the revenue law, we endeavor to ascertain a controlling Congressional mandate. Section 351 has been described as a deliberate attempt by Congress to facilitate the incorporation of ongoing businesses and to eliminate any technical constructions which are economically unsound.

Appellant-taxpayer seems to recognize this and argues that application of the *Lake* rationale when accounts receivable are transferred would not create any undue hardship to an incorporating taxpayer. "All a taxpayer [transferor] need do is withhold the earned income items and collect them, transferring the net proceeds to the Corporation. Indeed ... the transferor should retain both accounts receivable and accounts payable to avoid income recognition at the time of transfer and to have sufficient funds with which to pay accounts payable. Where the taxpayer [transferor] is on the cash method of accounting [as here], the deduction of the accounts payable would be applied against the income generated by the accounts receivable." ...

While we cannot fault the general principle "that income be taxed to him who earns it," to adopt taxpayer's argument would be to hamper the incorporation of ongoing businesses; additionally it would impose technical constructions which are economically and practically unsound. None of the cases cited by taxpayer, including *Lake* itself, persuades us otherwise. In *Lake* the Court was required to decide whether the proceeds from the assignment of the oil payment right were taxable as ordinary income or as long term capital gains. Observing that the provision for long term capital gains treatment "has always been narrowly construed so as to protect the revenue against artful devices," 356 U.S. at 265, ... the Court predicated its holding upon an emphatic distinction between a conversion of a capital investment—"income-producing property"—and an assignment of income per se. "The substance of what was assigned was the right to receive future income. The substance of what was received was the present value of income which the recipient would otherwise obtain in the future." Ibid., at 266. .. A Section 351 issue was not presented in *Lake*. Therefore the case does not control in weighing the conflict between the general rule of assignment of income and the congressional purpose of nonrecognition upon the incorporation of an ongoing business.

We are persuaded that, on balance, the teachings of *Lake* must give way in this case to the broad congressional interest in facilitating the incorporation of ongoing businesses. As desirable as it is to afford symmetry in revenue law, we do not intend to promulgate a hard and fast rule.[9] We believe that the problems posed by the clash of conflicting internal revenue doctrines are more' properly determined by the circumstances of each case. Here we are influenced by the fact that the subject of the assignment was accounts receivable for partnership's goods and services sold in the regular course of business, that the change of business form from partnership to corporation had a basic business purpose and was not designed for the purpose of deliberate tax avoidance, and by the conviction that the totality of circumstances here presented fit the mold of the congressional intent to

---

[9] The Commissioner has apparently taken the position that irrespective of the general principle that income is based upon he who earns it, other considerations should normally control Section 351 transfers. "However, the Service's ruling policy apparently is subject to the proviso that the taxpayer enter into a closing agreement assuring that the corporation will report the income reflected in the receivables upon their collection or other disposition. It would also appear that favorable rulings will not be issued where the timing of the transfer will be such as to result in a distortion of income. For example, such a ruling presumably could not be obtained if a seasonable business were to be incorporated during the portion of the year occurring after sizeable operating expenses had been incurred but before the income attributable thereto was collected." Weiss, [Problems in the Tax–Free Incorporation of a Business, 41 Ind. L J. 666, 681 (1966)] (footnote omitted).

give nonrecognition to a transfer of a total business from a noncorporate to a corporate form.

But this too must be said. Even though Section 351(a) immunizes the transferor from immediate tax consequences, Section 358 retains for the transferors a potential income tax liability to be realized and recognized upon a subsequent sale or exchange of the stock certificates received. As to the transferee-corporation, the tax basis of the receivables will be governed by Section 362. . .

[Other issues omitted.]

Revenue Ruling 80–198
1980–2 C.B. 113.

ISSUE

Under the circumstances described below, do the nonrecognition of gain or loss provisions of section 351 of the Internal Revenue Code apply to a transfer of the operating assets of an ongoing sole proprietorship (including unrealized accounts receivable) to a corporation in exchange solely for the common stock of a corporation and the assumption by the corporation of the proprietorship liabilities?

FACTS

Individual A conducted a medical practice as a sole proprietorship, the income of which was reported on the cash receipts and disbursements method of accounting. A transferred to a newly organized corporation all of the operating assets of the sole proprietorship in exchange for all of the stock of the corporation, plus the assumption by the corporation of all of the liabilities of the sole proprietorship. The purpose of the incorporation was to provide a form of business organization that would be more conducive to the planned expansion of the medical services to be made available by the business enterprise.

The assets transferred were tangible assets having a fair market value of $40,000 and an Adjusted basis of $30,000 and unrealized trade accounts receivable having a face amount of $20,000 and an adjusted basis of zero. The liabilities assumed by the corporation consisted of trade accounts payable in the face amount of $10,000. The liabilities assumed by the corporation also included a mortgage liability, related to the tangible property transferred, of $10,000. A had neither accumulated the accounts receivable nor prepaid any of the liabilities of the sole proprietorship in a manner inconsistent with normal business practices in anticipation of the incorporation. If A had paid the trade accounts payable liabilities, the amounts paid would have been deductible by A as ordinary and necessary business expenses under section 162 of the Code. The new corporation continued to utilize the cash receipts and disbursements method of accounting.

LAW AND ANALYSIS

The applicable section of the Code is section 351(a), which provides that no gain or loss shall be recognized when property is transferred to a corporation in exchange solely for stock and securities and the transferor is in control (as defined by section 368(c)) of the transferee corporation immediately after the transfer. . .

The facts of the instant case are similar to those in *Hempt Bros.* [page 334 supra] in that there was a valid business purpose for the transfer of the accounts receivable along with all of the assets and liabilities of A's proprietorship to a corporate transferee that would continue the business of the transferor. Further, A had neither accumulated the accounts receivable nor prepaid any of the accounts payable liabilities of the sole proprietorship in anticipation of the incorporation, which is an indication that, under the facts and circumstances of the case, the transaction was not designed for tax avoidance.

HOLDING

The transfer by A of the operating assets of the sole proprietorship (including unrealized accounts receivable) to the corporation in exchange solely for the common stock of the corporation and the assumption by the corporation of the proprietorship liabilities (including accounts payable) is an exchange within the meaning of section 351(a) of the Code. Therefore, no gain or loss is recognized to A with respect to the property transferred, including the accounts receivable. For transfers occurring on or after November 6, 1978 (the effective date . . . with respect to sections 357(c)(3) and 358(d)(2) of the Code) the assumption of the trade accounts payable that would give rise to a deduction if A had paid them is not, pursuant to section 357(c)(3), considered as an assumption of a liability for purposes of sections 357(c)(1) and 358(d). See Rev. Rul. 80–199 . . . [page 325 supra] for transfers occurring before November 6, 1978, which holds that trade accounts payable transferred to a corporation in a transaction to which section 351(a) applies are not liabilities for the purposes of sections 357(c) and 358(d) if the transferor of the accounts payable could have deducted the amounts paid in satisfaction thereof under section 162 if the transferor had paid these amounts in satisfaction of the payables prior to the exchange. The corporation, under the cash receipts and disbursements method of accounting, will report in its income the account receivables as collected, and will be allowed deductions under section 162 for the payments it makes to satisfy the assumed trade accounts payable when such payments are made.

A's basis in the stock received in the exchange of property for stock under section 358(a)(1) of the Code is $20,000 which is calculated by decreasing A's $30,000 basis in the assets transferred by the $10,000 mortgage liability under sections 358(a)(1)(A)(ii) and 358(d)(1). No adjustment to such basis is made under section 358(a)(1)(A)(ii) because of the assumption by the corporation of the $10,000 in accounts payable inasmuch as the general rule of section 358(d)(1), which requires the basis in the stock received to be decreased by the liabilities assumed, does not apply by reason of section 358(d)(2), which provides that section 358(d)(1) does not apply to the amount of any liabilities defined in section 357(c)(3) such as accounts payable that would have been deductible by A as ordinary and necessary business expenses under section 162 in the taxable year paid if A had paid these liabilities prior to the exchange. See Rev. Rul. 80–199 [page 325 supra], with respect to transfers which have occurred before November 6, 1978 (the date of the enactment of the Revenue Act of 1978).

LIMITATIONS

Section 351 of the Code does not apply to a transfer of accounts receivable which constitute an assignment of an income right in a case such as Brown v. Commissioner, 40 B.T.A. 565 (1939), *aff'd* 115 F.2d 337 (2d Cir. 1940). In *Brown*, an attorney transferred to a corporation, in which he was the sole owner, a one-half interest in a claim for legal services performed by the attorney and his law partner. In exchange, the attorney received additional stock of the corporation. The claim represented the corporation's only asset. Subsequent to the receipt by the corporation of the proceeds of the claim, the attorney gave all of the stock of the corporation to his wife. The United States Court of Appeals for the Second Circuit found that the transfer of the claim for the fee to the corporation had no purpose other than to avoid taxes and held that in such a case the intervention of the corporation would not prevent the attorney from being liable for the tax on the income which resulted from services under the assignment of income rule of Lucas v. Earl, 281 U.S. 111 (1930). Accordingly, in a case of a transfer to a controlled corporation of an account receivable in respect of services rendered where there is a tax avoidance purpose for the transaction (which might be evidenced by the corporation not conducting an ongoing business), the Internal Revenue Service will continue to apply assignment of income principles and require that the transferor of such a receivable include it in income when received by the transferee corporation.

Likewise, it may be appropriate in certain situations to allocate income, deductions, credits, or allowances to the transferor or transferee under section 482 . . . when the timing of the incorporation improperly separates income from related expenses. See Rooney v. United States, 305 F.2d 681 (9th Cir. 1962), where a farming operation was incorporated in a transaction described in section 351(a) after the expenses of the crop had been incurred but before the crop had been sold and income realized. The transferor's tax return contained all of the expenses but none of the farming income to which the expenses related. The United States Court of Appeals for the Ninth Circuit held that the expenses could be allocated under section 482 to the corporation, to be matched with the income to which the expenses related. Similar adjustments may be appropriate where some assets, liabilities, or both, are retained by the transferor and such retention results in the income of the transferor, transferee, or both, not being clearly reflected.

NOTE

For a cogent argument that the assignment of income doctrine should override § 351 with the result that a cash-basis transferor of accounts receivable would generally be taxed, see Coven, Liabilities in Excess of Basis: *Focht*, Section 357(c)(3) and the Assignment of Income, 58 Or. L. Rev. 61 (1979).

C. CAPITAL CONTRIBUTION VS. CURRENT DEDUCTION

Commissioner v. Fink
483 U.S. 89 (1987).

■ JUSTICE POWELL delivered the opinion of the Court.

The question in this case is whether a dominant shareholder who voluntarily surrenders a portion of his shares to the corporation, but retains control, may immediately deduct from taxable income his basis in the surrendered shares.

I

Respondents Peter and Karla Fink were the principal shareholders of Travco Corporation, a Michigan manufacturer of motor homes. Travco had one class of common stock outstanding and no preferred stock. Mr. Fink owned 52.2 percent, and Mrs. Fink 20.3 percent, of the outstanding shares. Travco urgently needed new capital as a result of financial difficulties it encountered in the mid–1970s. The Finks voluntarily surrendered some of their shares to Travco in an effort to "increase the attractiveness of the corporation to outside investors." Brief for Respondents 3. Mr. Fink surrendered 116,146 shares in December 1976; Mrs. Fink surrendered 80,000 shares in January 1977. As a result, the Finks' combined percentage ownership of Travco was reduced from 72.5 percent to 68.5 percent. The Finks received no consideration for the surrendered shares, and no other shareholder surrendered any stock. The effort to attract new investors was unsuccessful, and the corporation eventually was liquidated.

On their 1976 and 1977 joint federal income tax returns, the Finks claimed ordinary loss deductions totaling $389,040, the full amount of their adjusted basis in the surrendered shares. The Commissioner of Internal Revenue disallowed the deductions. He concluded that the stock surrendered was a contribution to the corporation's capital. Accordingly, the Commissioner determined that the surrender resulted in no immediate tax consequences, and that the Finks' basis in the surrendered shares should be added to the basis of their remaining shares of Travco stock.

In an unpublished opinion, the Tax Court sustained the Commissioner's determination for the reasons stated in Frantz v. Commissioner, 83 T.C. 162, 174–182 (1984), *aff'd*, 784 F.2d 119 (CA2 1986), . . . [*cert. denied*, 107 S.Ct. 3262 (1987).] In *Frantz* the Tax Court held that a stockholder's non pro rata surrender of shares to the corporation does not produce an immediate loss. The court reasoned that "[t]his conclusion . . . necessarily follows from a recognition of the purpose of the transfer, that is, to bolster the financial position of [the corporation] and, hence, to protect and make more valuable [the stockholder's] retained shares." 83 T.C., at 181. Because the purpose of the shareholder's surrender is "to decrease or avoid a loss on his overall investment," the Tax Court in *Frantz* was "unable to conclude that [he] sustained a loss at the time of the transaction." Ibid. "Whether [the shareholder] would sustain a loss, and if so, the amount thereof, could only be determined when he subsequently disposed of the stock that the surrender was intended to protect and make more valuable." Ibid. The Tax Court recognized that it had sustained the taxpayer's position in a series of prior cases. Id., at 174–175. But it concluded that these decisions were incorrect, in part because they "encourage[d] a conversion of eventual capital losses into immediate ordinary losses." Id., at 182.

In this case, a divided panel of the Court of Appeals for the Sixth Circuit reversed the Tax Court. 789 F.2d 427 (1986)...

We granted certiorari to resolve a conflict among the circuits ... and now reverse.

II

A

It is settled that a shareholder's voluntary contribution to the capital of the corporation has no immediate tax consequences. 26 U.S.C. § 263; 26 CFR § 1.263(a)–2(f) (1986). Instead, the shareholder is entitled to increase the basis of his shares by the amount of his basis in the property transferred to the corporation... When the shareholder later disposes of his shares, his contribution is reflected as a smaller taxable gain or a larger deductible loss. This rule applies not only to transfers of cash or tangible property, but also to a shareholder's forgiveness of a debt owed to him by the corporation. 26 CFR § 1.61–12(a) (1986). Such transfers are treated as contributions to capital even if the other shareholders make proportionately smaller contributions, or no contribution at all. See, e.g., Sackstein v. Commissioner, 14 T.C. 566, 569 (1950). The rules governing contributions to capital reflect the general principle that a shareholder may not claim an immediate loss for outlays made to benefit the corporation. Deputy v. du Pont, 308 U.S. 488 (1940); Eskimo Pie Corp. v. Commissioner, 4 T.C. 669, 676 (1945), *aff'd*, 153 F.2d 301 (CA3 1946). We must decide whether this principle also applies to a controlling shareholder's non pro rata surrender of a portion of his shares.[6]

B

The Finks contend that they sustained an immediate loss upon surrendering some of their shares to the corporation. By parting with the shares, they gave up an ownership interest entitling them to future divi-

---

[6] The Finks concede that a pro rata stock surrender, that by definition does not change the percentage ownership of any shareholder, is not a taxable event. Cf. Eisner v. Macomber, 252 U.S. 189 (1920) (pro rata stock dividend does not produce taxable income).

dends, future capital appreciation, assets in the event of liquidation, and voting rights.[7] Therefore, the Finks contend, they are entitled to an immediate deduction. See 26 U.S.C. §§ 165(a) and (c)(2). In addition, the Finks argue that any non pro rata stock transaction "give[s] rise to immediate tax results." Brief for Respondents 13. For example, a non pro rata stock dividend produces income because it increases the recipient's proportionate ownership of the corporation. Koshland v. Helvering, 298 U.S. 441, 445 (1936).[8] By analogy, the Finks argue that a non pro rata surrender of shares should be recognized as an immediate loss because it reduces the surrendering shareholder's proportionate ownership.

Finally, the Finks contend that their stock surrenders were not contributions to the corporation's capital. They note that a typical contribution to capital, unlike a non pro rata stock surrender, has no effect on the contributing shareholder's proportionate interest in the corporation. Moreover, the Finks argue, a contribution of cash or other property increases the net worth of the corporation. For example, a shareholder's forgiveness of a debt owed to him by the corporation decreases the corporation's liabilities. In contrast, when a shareholder surrenders shares of the corporation's own stock, the corporation's net worth is unchanged. This is because the corporation cannot itself exercise the right to vote, receive dividends, or receive a share of assets in the event of liquidation. G. Johnson & J. Gentry, Finney and Miller's Principles of Accounting 538 (7th ed. 1974).

III

A shareholder who surrenders a portion of his shares to the corporation has parted with an asset, but that alone does not entitle him to an immediate deduction. Indeed, if the shareholder owns less than 100 percent of the corporation's shares, any non pro rata contribution to the corporation's capital will reduce the net worth of the contributing shareholder. A shareholder who surrenders stock thus is similar to one who forgives or surrenders a debt owed to him by the corporation; the latter gives up interest, principal, and also potential voting power in the event of insolvency or bankruptcy. But, as stated above, such forgiveness of corporate debt is treated as a contribution to capital rather than a current deduction. . . The Finks' voluntary surrender of shares, like a shareholder's voluntary forgiveness of debt owed by the corporation, closely resembles an investment or contribution to capital. See B. Bittker & J. Eustice, Federal Income Taxation of Corporations and Shareholders § 3.14, p. 3–59 (4th ed. 1979) ("If the contribution is voluntary, it does not produce gain or loss to the shareholder"). We find the similarity convincing in this case.

The fact that a stock surrender is not recorded as a contribution to capital on the corporation's balance sheet does not compel a different re-

---

[7] As a practical matter, however, the Finks did not give up a great deal. Their percentage interest in the corporation declined by only four percent. Because the Finks retained a majority interest, this reduction in their voting power was inconsequential. Moreover, Travco, like many corporations in financial difficulties, was not paying dividends.

[8] In most cases, however, stock dividends are not recognized as income until the shares are sold. See [§ 305].

sult. Shareholders who forgive a debt owed by the corporation or pay a corporate expense also are denied an immediate deduction, even though neither of these transactions is a contribution to capital in the accounting sense. Nor are we persuaded by the fact that a stock surrender, unlike a typical contribution to capital, reduces the shareholder's proportionate interest in the corporation. This Court has never held that every change in a shareholder's percentage ownership has immediate tax consequences. Of course, a shareholder's receipt of property from the corporation generally is a taxable event. See 26 U.S.C. §§ 301, 316. In contrast, a shareholder's transfer of property to the corporation usually has no immediate tax consequences. § 263.

The Finks concede that the purpose of their stock surrender was to protect or increase the value of their investment in the corporation. Brief for Respondents 3. They hoped to encourage new investors to provide needed capital and in the long run recover the value of the surrendered shares through increased dividends or appreciation in the value of their remaining shares. If the surrender had achieved its purpose, the Finks would not have suffered an economic loss. See Johnson, Tax Models for Nonprorata Shareholder Contributions, 3 Va. Tax. Rev. 81, 104–108 (1983). In this case, as in many cases involving closely-held corporations whose shares are not traded on an open market, there is no reliable method of determining whether the surrender will result in a loss until the shareholder disposes of his remaining shares. Thus, the Finks' stock surrender does not meet the requirement that an immediately deductible loss must be "actually sustained during the taxable year." 26 CFR § 1.165–1(b) (1986). . .[14]

We therefore hold that a dominant shareholder who voluntarily surrenders a portion of his shares to the corporation, but retains control, does not sustain an immediate loss deductible from taxable income. Rather, the surrendering shareholder must reallocate his basis in the surrendered shares to the shares he retains.[15] The shareholder's loss, if any, will be recognized when he disposes of his remaining shares. . .

---

[14] Our holding today also draws support from two other sections of the Code. First, § 83 provides that, if a shareholder makes a "bargain sale" of stock to a corporate officer or employee as compensation, the "bargain" element of the sale must be treated as a contribution to the corporation's capital. S. Rep. No. 91–552, pp. 123–124 (1969), 1969 U.S. Code Cong. & Admin. News 1978, pp. 2027, 2155; 26 C.F.R. § 1.83–6(d) (1986).... To be sure, Congress was concerned in § 83 with transfers of restricted stock to employees as compensation rather than surrenders of stock to improve the corporation's financial condition. In both cases, however, the shareholder's underlying purpose is to increase the value of his investment.

Second, if a shareholder's stock is redeemed—that is, surrendered to the corporation in return for cash or other property—the shareholder is not entitled to an immediate deduction unless the redemption results in a substantial reduction in the shareholder's ownership percentage. §§ 302(a), (b), (d); 26 C.F.R. § 1.302–2(c) (1986). Because the Finks' surrenders resulted in only a slight reduction in their ownership percentage, they would not have been entitled to an immediate loss if they had received consideration for the surrendered shares. 26 U.S.C. § 302(b). Although the Finks did not receive a direct payment of cash or other property, they hoped to be compensated by an increase in the value of their remaining shares.

[15] The Finks remained the controlling shareholders after their surrender. We therefore have no occasion to decide in this case whether a surrender that causes the shareholder to lose control of the corporation is immediately deductible. In related contexts, the Code distinguishes between minimal reductions in a shareholder's ownership percentage and loss of corporate control. See § 302(b)(2) (providing "exchange" rather than dividend treatment for a "substan-

IV

For the reasons we have stated, the judgment of the Court of Appeals for the Sixth Circuit is reversed.

It is so ordered.

■ JUSTICE WHITE, concurring.

Although I join the Court's opinion, I suggest that there is little substance in the reservation in footnote 15 of the question whether a surrender of stock that causes the stockholder to lose control of the corporation is immediately deductible as an ordinary loss. Of course, this case does not involve a loss of control; but as I understand the rationale of the Court's opinion, it would also apply to a surrender that results in loss of control. At least I do not find in the opinion any principled ground for distinguishing a loss-of-control case from this one.

[Justice Scalia's opinion, concurring in the judgment, is omitted. Justice Blackmun concurred in the result without an opinion.]

■ JUSTICE STEVENS, dissenting.

The value of certain and predictable rules of law is often underestimated. Particularly in the field of taxation, there is a strong interest in enabling taxpayers to predict the legal consequences of their proposed actions, and there is an even stronger general interest in ensuring that the responsibility for making changes in settled law rests squarely on the shoulders of Congress. In this case, these interests are of decisive importance for me.

The question of tax law presented by this case was definitively answered by the Board of Tax Appeals in 1941. See Miller v. Commissioner, 45 B.T.A. 292, 299; Budd International Corp. v. Commissioner, 45 B.T.A. 737, 755–756.[1] Those decisions were consistently followed for over 40 years, see, e.g., Smith v. Commissioner, 66 T.C. 622, 648 (1976); Downer v. Commissioner, 48 T.C. 86, 91 (1967); Estate of Foster v. Commissioner, 9 T.C. 930, 934 (1947), and the Internal Revenue Service had announced its acquiescence in the decisions. . . Although Congress dramatically revamped the tax code in 1954, . . . it did not modify the Tax Court's approach to this issue.

---

tially disproportionate redemption of stock" that brings the shareholder's ownership percentage below 50 percent); § 302(b)(3) (providing similar treatment when the redemption terminates the shareholder's interest in the corporation).

In this case we use the term "control" to mean ownership of more than half of a corporation's voting shares. We recognize, of course, that larger corporations—especially those whose shares are listed on a national exchange—a person or entity may exercise control in fact while owning less than a majority of the voting shares. See Securities Exchange Act of 1934, § 13(d), 48 Stat. 894, 15 U.S.C. § 78m(d) (requiring persons to report acquisition of more than 5 percent of a registered equity security).

[1] The principle applied in those decisions dates back even further. See Burdick v. Commissioner, 20 B.T.A. 742 (1930), *affd*, 59 F. 2d 395 (1932); Wright v. Commissioner, 18 B.T.A. 471 (1929).

It was only in 1977 (after the Finks had transferred their stock to the corporation), that the Commissioner retracted its acquiescence in the Tax Court's interpretation. . .

. . . The Commissioner of Internal Revenue certainly had a right to advocate a change, but in my opinion he should have requested relief from the body that has the authority to amend the Internal Revenue Code. For I firmly believe that "after a statute has been construed, either by this Court or by a consistent course of decision by other federal judges and agencies, it acquires a meaning that should be as clear as if the judicial gloss had been drafted by the Congress itself." Shearson/American Express v. McMahon, 107 S. Ct. 2332 (1987) (Stevens, J., concurring in part and dissenting in part).

A rule of statutory construction that "has been consistently recognized for more than 35 years" acquires a clarity that "is simply beyond peradventure." Herman & MacLean v. Huddleston, 459 U.S. 375, 380 (1983).

. . . Mr. Fink surrendered his shares in December 1976. Mrs. Fink surrendered hers in January 1977. At that time the law was well settled: the Tax Court had repeatedly reaffirmed the right to deduct such surrenders as ordinary losses, and the Commissioner had acquiesced in this view for 35 years. . . It was only on April 11, 1977, that the Commissioner announced its non-acquiescence. See Internal Revenue Bulletin No. 1977–15, p. 6 (April 11, 1977). "In my view, the retroactive application of the Court's holding in a case like this is unfair to the individual taxpayer as well as unwise judicial administration." Dickman v. Commissioner, 465 U.S. 330, 353 n. 11 (1984) (Powell, J., dissenting).

I respectfully dissent.

III. ISSUANCE OF STOCK—IMPACT ON CORPORATION—§ 1032

See Chapter 1, pages 4–6, 67–69 supra; Landis, Contributions to Capital of Corporations, 24 Tax. L. Rev. 241 (1969); Cummings, Jr., The Silent Policies of Conservation and Cloning of Tax Basis and Their Corporate Applications, 48 Tax L. Rev. 113 (1992).

IV. PROPERTY RECEIVED BY CORPORATION FOR STOCK—BASIS AND HOLDING PERIOD

A. TAXABLE TRANSFER—§ 1012

When a corporation issues stock to a shareholder in exchange for property in circumstances that render the transaction wholly taxable to the shareholder, the corporation is treated as a purchaser of the assets and its basis is cost under § 1012. See Treas. Reg. § 1.1032–1(d) (last sentence).

What is a corporation's "cost" if it issues newly authorized stock in exchange for assets with a fair market value of $1,000? Does it matter that the stock has a fair market value of $1,050? Of $950? Does it matter that the stock represents a minority interest in a closely held corporation and that there is no market for the stock?

Suppose a corporation issues its ten-year, 8–percent bond in exchange for an asset in circumstances that render the bondholder taxable on the asset appreciation. What is the corporation's basis for the asset? Why?

B. TAX–FREE TRANSFER (IN WHOLE OR IN PART)—§ 362(a)

If a corporation receives assets in a transaction to which § 351 applies, the basis is governed by § 362(a). See Treas. Reg. § 1.1032–1(d); § 1.362–1.

Suppose Corporation C issues $10,000 worth of its stock, $5,000 worth of its long-term debentures, and cash of $5,000 to its sole shareholder in exchange for an asset worth $20,000 that had a basis in the shareholder's hands of $10,000. What is the basis of the asset in Corporation C's hands? Why?

Note that in some circumstances "new" § 336(d) has the effect of limiting the § 362(a) basis of property acquired in a § 351 transaction to its *value* at the time it was acquired. Cf. National Securities Corp. v. Commissioner, 137 F.2d 600 (3d Cir. 1943), *cert. denied*, 320 U.S. 794 (1943).

In 2004, Congress amended § 362 to prevent the transfer of built-in losses by a shareholder contributing depreciated property to a corporation in a § 351 transaction. New § 362(e) provides that the corporation's basis in the contributed property cannot exceed its fair market value (unless the contributing shareholder elects to limit its basis in the corporate stock received to the fair market value of the contributed property). What did Congress fear about the contributions of depreciated property? Should there be a comparable rule in the case of a contribution of *appreciated* property?

Following public comment, the final regulations issued on September 17, 2008 have made § 362(e)(2) generally inapplicable to transactions between members of a consolidated group. The consolidated return provisions will address loss duplication within the group. But because Treasury and IRS remained concerned that taxpayers could pursue transactions that resulted in neither § 362(e)(2) nor the consolidated return regulations preventing loss duplication, the final regulations include an anti-abuse rule. Under this rule, if a taxpayer acts to prevent the consolidated return provisions from properly addressing loss duplication, appropriate adjustments will be made in order to clearly reflect the income of the group. "Unified Rule for Loss on Subsidiary Stock." 73 FR 53934-01. September 17, 2008.

C. HOLDING PERIOD—§ 1223(2)

If a corporation receives property with its basis determined under § 362(a), as in a § 351 transaction, the corporation's holding period will include the period during which the property was held by the transferor. This "tacking" rule is provided in § 1223(2).

CHAPTER 4

REORGANIZATIONS AND RELATED TRANSACTIONS

I. INTRODUCTION AND HISTORY

Gain or loss is realized when an asset worth more or less than its adjusted basis is exchanged for another asset. In an arm's length transaction one would expect the asset received to be equal in value to the one surrendered, and the measure of the gain or loss realized would be the difference between the value of the asset received and the adjusted basis of the asset surrendered. See § 1001(a) and (b).

Unless the Code provides otherwise, all realized gain or loss is recognized in the computation of a taxpayer's income. § 1001(c). In many cases, however, Congress has provided for nonrecognition, usually because the exchange has not produced an economically significant change in the nature of the taxpayer's investment or has not brought him close enough to cash or consumable goods to justify taxation in light of the pervasive doctrine that generally prohibits taxation of unrealized appreciation. Section 351, which was studied in detail in Chapter 3, is one example of a nonrecognition provision. This chapter will examine other Code provisions that call for nonrecognition in the context of corporate transactions.

If a taxpayer buys a share of General Motors common stock at $50, the doctrine protecting unrealized appreciation prevents the taxation of his appreciation even though the stock has risen in value to $75 and the cash can be realized with a telephone call to a broker. Moreover, if pursuant to a "stock split" or a plan of recapitalization the taxpayer exchanges his single share of General Motors common for two shares of General Motors common, each worth $37.50, his realized gain is not recognized. See §§ 1036(a); 368(a)(1)(E) and 354(a)(1). But if, instead, the taxpayer exchanges his General Motors stock for his neighbor's Ford Motor common stock, his $25 gain is both realized and recognized. If the exchange of General Motors stock for Ford Motor stock is not an exchange between shareholders but is one effected directly with Ford Motor Company as a result of a statutory merger of General Motors Company into Ford, the exchanging shareholder's gain is not recognized. See §§ 368(a)(1)(A) and 354(a)(1). If the plan of merger results in the taxpayer's receiving Ford stock worth $60 and cash of $15 (or a $15 Ford bond), $15 of the gain is recognized. See § 356(a) and (d). The recognized gain may be taxable as a dividend (see § 356(a)(2)), although a sale to (or exchange with) the neighbor probably would produce capital gain.

Almost a decade after the 2003 change in dividend tax rate, dividends are still being taxed at long term capital gains rates. This appears to be a possibly longer term decision by Congress, which continues to renew the expiring provision granting the reduced dividend tax rate. In the past, a central question faced in examining a transaction was whether it constituted a dividend or a sale. Given the difference in tax rates, the answer could significantly impact the tax due. Now, the primary advantage of sale treatment is basis recovery. Stock transactions and the complex tax problems they present to corporations and their investors are the subject of this chapter.

Parts II and III of this chapter deal with stock dividends and recapitalizations, transactions in which the investor's interest in his corporation is reclassified or represented in a new form. The receipt of a new stock certificate (or a bond) in addition to, or in exchange for, the investor's old certificate usually triggers a recognition issue.

Parts IV through VII deal with reorganizations involving more than one corporation: amalgamating reorganizations (mergers and consolidations), divisive reorganizations (spin-offs, split-offs, split-ups, and spin-aways), and corporate substitutions (one corporation replacing another). These types of reorganizations raise questions of recognition and basis adjustment for both the investors and the corporations. Ordinarily, stock dividends and recapitalizations (involving a single corporation) raise such questions only for the investor.

In Part VIII, the chapter presents issues involving the carryover of tax attributes from one corporation to another, particularly earnings and profits and net operating losses. Usually, but not always, the carryover problems will grow out of a reorganization. It is worth noting at this point that the provision limiting net operating loss carryforwards (§ 382) was the only provision in the reorganization area that was completely rewritten by the Tax Reform Act of 1986. The 1989 Act amended § 172 to limit the carryback of net operating losses to those incurred after a "corporate equity reduction transaction."

Finally, there are special problems posed when one or more of the corporations in reorganization is a foreign corporation. See § 367. The income taxation of foreign corporations warrants discrete, specialized treatment, and is outside the scope of this book. See, e.g., J. Kuntz & R. Peroni, U.S. International Taxation (2012 online).

II. STOCK DIVIDENDS—RECEIPT AND DISPOSITION

A. HISTORY

1. TAXABILITY OF RECEIPT

Eisner v. Macomber

252 U.S. 189 (1920).

■ MR. JUSTICE PITNEY delivered the opinion of the court. This case presents the question whether, by virtue of the Sixteenth Amendment, Congress has the power to tax, as income of the stockholder and without apportionment, a stock dividend made lawfully and in good faith against profits accumulated by the corporation since March 1, 1913.

It arises under the Revenue Act of September 8, 1916, c. 463, 39 Stat. 756, et seq., which, in our opinion . . . plainly evinces the purpose of Congress to tax stock dividends as income.[1] . . .

On January 1, 1916, the Standard Oil Company of California, a corporation of' that State, out of an authorized capital stock of $100,000,000, had shares of stock outstanding, par value $100 each, amounting in round figures to $50,000,000. In addition, it had surplus and undivided profits invested in plant, property, and business and required for the purposes of the corporation, amounting to about $45,000,000, of which about $20,000,000 had been earned prior to March 1, 1913, the balance thereafter. In January, 1916, in order to readjust the capitalization, the board of directors decided to issue additional shares sufficient to constitute a stock dividend of 50 per cent of the outstanding stock, and to transfer from surplus account to capital stock account an amount equivalent to such issue. Appropriate resolutions were adopted, an amount equivalent to the par value of the proposed new stock was transferred accordingly, and the new stock duly issued against it and divided among the stockholders.

Defendant in error, being the owner of 2,200 shares of the old stock, received certificates for 1,100 additional shares, of which 18.07 percent, or 198.77 shares, par value $19,877, were treated as representing surplus earned between March 1, 1913, and January 1, 1916. She was called upon to pay, and did pay under protest, a tax imposed under the Revenue Act of 1916, based upon a supposed income of $19,877 because of the new shares; and an appeal to the Commissioner of Internal Revenue having been disallowed, she brought action against the Collector to recover the tax. In her complaint she . . . contended that in imposing such a tax the Revenue Act of 1916 violated Art. I, § 2, cl. 3, and Art. I, § 9, cl. 4, of the Constitution of the United States, requiring direct taxes to be apportioned according to population, and that the stock dividend was not income within the meaning of the Sixteenth Amendment. A general demurrer to the complaint was overruled upon the authority of Towne v. Eisner, 245 U.S. 418; and, defendant having failed to plead further, final judgment went against him. . .

We are constrained to hold that the judgment of the District Court must be affirmed: First, because the question at issue is controlled by Towne v. Eisner, supra; secondly, because a re-examination of the question, with the additional light thrown upon it by elaborate arguments, has confirmed the view that the underlying ground of that decision is sound, that it

---

[1] TITLE I.—INCOME TAX. Part I.—on individuals.

Sec. 2(a) That, subject only to such exemptions and deductions as are hereinafter allowed, the net income of a taxable person shall include gains, profits, and income derived ..., also from interest, rent, dividends securities, or the transaction of any business carried on for gain or profit, or gains or profits and income derived from any source whatever: Provided, That the term "dividends" as used in this title shall be held to mean any distribution made or ordered to be made by a corporation, ... out of its earnings or profits accrued since March first, nineteen hundred and thirteen, and payable to its shareholders, whether in cash or in stock of the corporation.... which stock dividend shall be considered income, to the amount of its cash value.

disposes of the question here presented, and that other fundamental considerations lead to the same result.

In Towne v. Eisner, the question was whether a stock dividend made in 1914 against surplus earned prior to January 1, 1913, was taxable against the stockholder under the Act of October 3, 1913, c. 16, 38 Stat. 114, 166, which provided (§ B, p. 167) that net income should include "dividends," and also "gains or profits and income derived from any source whatever." Suit having been brought by a stockholder to recover the tax assessed against him by reason of the dividend, the District Court sustained a demurrer to the complaint. 242 Fed. Rep. 702. The court treated the construction of the act as inseparable from the interpretation of the Sixteenth Amendment; and, having referred to Pollock v. Farmers' Loan & Trust Co., 158 U.S. 601, and quoted the Amendment, proceeded very properly to say (p. 704): "It is manifest that the stock dividend in question cannot be reached by the Income Tax Act, and could not, even though Congress expressly declared it to be taxable as income, unless it is in fact income." It declined, however, to accede to the contention that in Gibbons v. Mahon, 136 U.S. 549, "stock dividends" had received a definition sufficiently clear to be controlling, treated the language of this court in that case as obiter dictum in respect of the matter then before it (p. 706), and examined the question as res nova, with the result stated. When the case came here, after—overruling a motion to dismiss made by the Government upon the ground that the only question involved was the construction of the statute and not its constitutionality, we dealt upon the merits with the question of construction only, but disposed of it upon consideration of the essential nature of a stock dividend, disregarding the fact that the one in question was based upon surplus earnings that accrued before the Sixteenth Amendment took effect. Not only so, but we rejected the reasoning of the District Court, saying (245 U.S. 426):

[. . .] We cannot doubt that the dividend was capital as well for the purposes of the Income Tax Law as for distribution between tenant for life and remainderman. What was said by this court upon the latter question is equally true for the former. "A stock dividend really takes nothing from the property of the corporation, and adds nothing to the interests of the shareholders. Its property is not diminished, and their interests are not increased. . . The proportional interest of each shareholder remains the same. The only change is in the evidence which represents that interest, the new shares and the original shares together representing the same proportional interest that the original shares represented before the issue of the new ones." Gibbons v. Mahon, 136 U.S. 549, 559, 560. In short, the corporation is no poorer and the stockholder is no richer than they were before. Logan County v. United States, 169 U.S. 255, 261. If the plaintiff gained any small advantage by the change, it certainly was not an advantage of $417,450, the sum upon which he was taxed. . . What has happened is that the plaintiff's old certificates have been split up in effect and have diminished in value to the extent of the value of the new.

This language aptly answered not only the reasoning of the District Court but the argument of the Solicitor General in this court, which discussed the essential nature of a stock dividend. And if, for the reasons thus expressed, such a dividend is not to be regarded as "income" or "dividends" within the meaning of the Act of 1913, we are unable to see how it can be brought within the meaning of "incomes" in the Sixteenth Amendment; it being very clear that Congress intended in that act to exert its power to the extent permitted by the Amendment. In Towne v. Eisner it was not contended that any construction of the statute could make it narrower than the constitutional grant; rather the contrary.

The fact that the dividend was charged against profits earned before the Act of 1913 took effect, even before the Amendment was adopted, was neither relied upon nor alluded to in our consideration of the merits in that case. Not only so, but had we considered that a stock dividend constituted income in any true sense, it would have been held taxable under the Act of 1913 notwithstanding it was based upon profits earned before the Amendment. We ruled at the same term, in Lynch v. Hornby, 247 U.S. 339, that a cash dividend extraordinary in amount, and in Peabody v. Eisner, 247 U.S. 347, that a dividend paid in stock of another company, were taxable as income although based upon earnings that accrued before adoption of the Amendment. . .

Therefore, Towne v. Eisner cannot be regarded as turning upon the point that the surplus accrued to the company before the act took effect and before adoption of the Amendment. And what we have quoted from the opinion in that case cannot be regarded as obiter dictum, it having furnished the entire basis for the conclusion reached. We adhere to the view then expressed, and might rest the present case there; not because that case in terms decided the constitutional question, for it did not; but because the conclusion there reached as to the essential nature of a stock dividend necessarily prevents its being regarded as income in any true sense.

Nevertheless, in view of the importance of the matter, and the fact that Congress in the Revenue Act of 1916 declared . . . that a "stock dividend shall be considered income, to the amount of its cash value," we will deal at length with the constitutional question, incidentally testing the soundness of our previous conclusion.

The Sixteenth Amendment must be construed in connection with the taxing clauses of the original Constitution and the effect attributed to them before the Amendment was adopted. In Pollock v. Farmers' Loan & Trust Co., 158 U.S. 601, under the Act of August 27, 1894, c. 349, § 27, 28 Stat. 509, 553, it was held that taxes upon rents and profits of real estate and upon returns from investments of personal property were in effect direct taxes upon the property from which such income arose, imposed by reason of ownership; and that Congress could not impose such taxes without apportioning them among the States according to population, as required by Art. 1, § 2, cl. 3, and § 9, cl. 4, of the original Constitution.

Afterwards, and evidently in recognition of the limitation upon the taxing power of Congress thus determined, the Sixteenth Amendment was adopted, in words lucidly expressing the object to be accomplished: "The Congress shall have power to lay and collect taxes on incomes, from whatever source derived, without apportionment among the several States, and without regard to any census or enumeration." As repeatedly held, this did not extend the taxing power to new subjects, but merely removed the necessity which otherwise might exist for an apportionment among the States of taxes laid on income. . .

A proper regard for its genesis, as well as its very clear language, requires also that this Amendment shall not be extended by loose construction, so as to repeal or modify, except as applied to income, those provisions of the Constitution that require an apportionment according to population for direct taxes upon property, real and personal. This limitation still has an appropriate and important function, and is not to be overridden by Congress or disregarded by the courts.

In order, therefore, that the clauses cited from Article I of the Constitution may have proper force and effect, save only as modified by the Amendment, and that the latter also may have proper effect, it becomes essential to distinguish between what is and what is not "income," as the term is there used; and to apply the distinction, as cases arise, according to truth and substance, without regard to form. Congress cannot by any definition it may adopt conclude the matter, since it cannot by legislation alter the Constitution. . .

The fundamental relation of "capital" to "income" has been much discussed by economists, the former being likened to the tree or the land, the latter to the fruit or the crop; the former depicted as a reservoir supplied from springs, the latter as the outlet stream, to be measured by its flow during a period of time. For the present purpose we require only a clear definition of the term "income," as used in common speech, in order to determine its meaning in the Amendment; and, having formed also a correct judgment as to the nature of a stock dividend, we shall find it easy to decide the matter at issue.

After examining dictionaries in common use . . ., we find little to add to the succinct definition adopted in two cases arising under the Corporation Tax Act of 1909 (Stratton's Independence v. Howbert, 231 U.S. 399, 415; Doyle v. Mitchell Bros. Co., 247 U.S. 179, 185)—"Income may be defined as the gain derived from capital, from labor, or from both combined," provided it be understood to include profit gained through a sale or conversion of capital assets, to which it was applied in the *Doyle* Case (pp. 183, 185).

Brief as it is, it indicates the characteristic and distinguishing attribute of income essential for a correct solution of the present controversy. The Government, although basing its argument upon the definition as quoted, placed chief emphasis upon the word "gain," which was extended to include a variety of meanings; while the significance of the next three words was either overlooked or misconceived. *"Derived-from-capital,"—"the gain—derived-from-capital*," etc. Here we have the essential matter: *not* a gain *accruing to* capital, not a *growth* or *increment* of value in the investment; but a gain, a profit, something of exchangeable value *proceeding from* the property, *severed from* the capital however invested or employed, and *coming in*, being "*derived*," that is, *received* or *drawn by* the recipient (the taxpayer) for his *separate* use, benefit and disposal;—*that* is income derived from property. Nothing else answers the description.

The same fundamental conception is clearly set forth in the Sixteenth Amendment—"incomes, *from* whatever *source derived*"—the essential thought being expressed with a conciseness and lucidity entirely in harmony with the form and style of the Constitution.

Can a stock dividend, considering its essential character, be brought within the definition? To answer this, regard must be had to the nature of a corporation and the stockholder's relation to it. . .

Certainly the interest of the stockholder is a capital interest, and his certificates of stock are but the evidence of it. They state the number of shares to which he is entitled and indicate their par value and how the stock may be transferred: They show that he or his assignors, immediate or remote, have contributed capital to the enterprise, that he is entitled to a corresponding interest proportionate to the whole, entitled to have the property and business of the company devoted during the corporate existence to attainment of the common objects, entitled to vote at stockholders' meetings, to receive dividends out of the corporation's profits if and when declared, and, in the event of liquidation, to receive a proportionate share of the net assets, if any, remaining after paying creditors. Short of liquidation, or until dividend declared, he has no right to withdraw any part of either capital or profits from the common enterprise; on the contrary, his interest pertains not to any part, divisible or indivisible, but to the entire assets, business, and affairs of the company. Nor is it the interest of an owner in the assets themselves, since the corporation has full title, legal and equitable, to the whole. . . If he desires to dissociate himself from the company he can do so only by disposing of his stock.

. . . The dividend normally is payable in money, under exceptional circumstances in some other divisible property; and when so paid, then only (excluding, of course, a possible advantageous sale of his stock or winding-up of the company) does the stockholder realize a profit or gain which becomes his separate property, and thus derive income from the capital that he or his predecessor has invested.

In the present case, the corporation had surplus and undivided profits invested in plant, property, and business, and required for the purposes of the corporation, amounting to about $45,000,000, in addition to outstanding capital stock of $50,000,000. . . The profits of a corporation, as they appear upon the balance sheet at the end of the year, need not be in the form of money on hand in excess of what is required to meet current liabilities and finance current operations of the company. Often, especially in a growing business, only a part . . . of the year's profits is in property capable of division; the remainder having been absorbed in the acquisition of in-creased plant, equipment, stock in trade, or accounts receivable, or in de-crease of outstanding liabilities. When only a part is available for divi-dends, the balance of the year's profits is carried to the credit of undivided profits, or surplus, or some other account having like significance. If the-reafter the company finds itself in funds beyond current needs it may dec-lare dividends out of such surplus or undivided profits; otherwise it may go on for years conducting a successful business, but requiring more and more working capital because of the extension of its operations, and therefore unable to declare dividends approximating the amount of its profits. Thus the surplus may increase until it equals or even exceeds the par value of the outstanding capital stock. This may be adjusted upon the books in the mode adopted in the case at bar—by declaring a "stock dividend." This, however, is no more than a book adjustment, in essence not a dividend but rather the opposite; no part of the assets of the company is separated from the common fund, nothing distributed except paper certificates that evi-dence an antecedent increase in the value of the stockholder's capital inter-est resulting from an accumulation of profits by the company, but profits so far absorbed in the business as to render it impracticable to separate them for withdrawal and distribution. In order to make the adjustment, a charge is made against surplus account with corresponding credit to capital stock account, equal to the proposed "dividend"; the new stock is issued against this and the certificates delivered to the existing stockholders in proportion to their previous holdings. This, however, is merely bookkeeping...

A "stock dividend" shows that the company's accumulated profits have been capitalized, instead of distributed to the stockholders or retained as surplus available for distribution in money or in kind should opportunity offer. Far from being a realization of profits of the stockholder, it tends ra-ther to postpone such realization, in that the fund represented by the new stock has been transferred from surplus to capital, and no longer is availa-ble for actual distribution.

The essential and controlling fact is that the stockholder has received nothing out of the company's assets for his separate use and benefit... Having regard ... to substance and not to form, he has received nothing that answers the definition of income within the meaning of the Sixteenth Amendment...

It is said that a stockholder may sell the new shares acquired in the stock dividend; and so he may, if he can find a buyer. It is equally true that if he does sell, and in doing so realizes a profit, such profit, like any other, is income, and so far as it may have arisen since the Sixteenth Amendment is taxable by Congress without apportionment. The same would be true were he to sell some of his original shares at a profit. But if a shareholder sells dividend stock he necessarily disposes of a part of his capital interest, just as if he should sell a part of his old stock, either before or after the div-idend... Yet, without selling, the shareholder, unless possessed of other resources, has not the wherewithal to pay an income tax upon the dividend stock...

We have no doubt of the power or duty of a court to look through the form of the corporation and determine the question of the stockholder's right, in order to ascertain whether he has received income taxable by Congress without apportionment. But, looking through the form, we cannot disregard the essential truth disclosed; ignore the substantial difference between corporation and stockholder; treat the entire organization as unreal; look upon stockholders as partners, when they are not such; treat them as having in equity a right to a partition of the corporate assets, when they have none; and indulge the fiction that they have received and realized a share of the profits of the company which in truth they have neither received nor realized. We must treat the corporation as a substantial entity separate from the stockholder, not only because such is the practical fact but because it is only by recognizing such separateness that any dividend— even one paid in money or property—can be regarded as income of the stockholder. Did we regard corporation and stockholders as altogether identical, there would be no income except as the corporation acquired it; and while this would be taxable against the corporation as income under appropriate provisions of law, the individual stockholders could not be separately and additionally taxed with respect to their several shares even when divided, since if there were entire identity between them and the company they could not be regarded as receiving anything from it, any more than if one's money were to be removed from one pocket to another.

Conceding that the issue of a stock dividend makes the recipient no richer than before, the Government nevertheless contends that the new certificates measure the extent to which the gains accumulated by the corporation have made him the richer. There are two insuperable difficulties with this: In the first place, it would depend upon how long he had held the stock whether the stock dividend indicated the extent to which he had been enriched by the operations of the company; unless he had held it throughout such operations the measure would not hold true. Secondly, and more important for present purposes, enrichment through increase in value of capital investment is not income in any proper meaning of the term.

The complaint contains averments respecting the market prices of stock such as plaintiff held, based upon sales before and after the stock dividend, tending to show that the receipt of the additional shares did not substantially change the market value of her entire holdings. This tends to show that in this instance market quotations reflected intrinsic values—a thing they do not always do. But we regard the market prices of the securities as an unsafe criterion in an inquiry such as the present, when the question must be, not what will the thing sell for, but what is it in truth and in essence.

It is said there is no difference in principle between a simple stock dividend and a case where stockholders use money received as cash dividends to purchase additional stock contemporaneously issued by the corporation. But an actual cash dividend, with a real option to the stockholder either to keep the money for his own or to reinvest it in new shares, would be as far removed as possible from a true stock dividend, such as the one we have under consideration, where nothing of value is taken from the company's assets and transferred to the individual ownership of the several stockholders and thereby subjected to their disposal.

The Government's reliance upon the supposed analogy between a dividend of the corporation's own shares and one made by distributing shares owned by it in the stock of another company, calls for no comment beyond the statement that the latter distributes assets of the company among the shareholders while the former does not; and for no citation of authority except Peabody v. Eisner, 247 U.S. 347, 349–350. . .

Upon the second argument, the Government, recognizing the force of the decision in Towne v. Eisner, supra, and virtually abandoning the contention that a stock dividend increases the interest of the stockholder or otherwise enriches him, insisted as an alternative that by the true construction of the Act of 1916 the tax is imposed not upon the stock dividend but rather upon the stockholder's share of the undivided profits previously accumulated by the corporation; the tax being levied as a matter of convenience at the time such profits become manifest through the stock dividend. If so construed, would the act be constitutional?

That Congress has power to tax shareholders upon their property interests in the stock of corporations is beyond question; and that such interests might be valued in view of the condition of the company, including its accumulated and undivided profits, is equally clear. But that this would be taxation of property because of ownership, and hence would require apportionment under the provisions of the Constitution, is settled beyond peradventure by previous decisions of this court.

The Government relies upon Collector v. Hubbard (1870), 12 Wall. 1, 17, which arose under §117 of the Act of June 30, 1864, c. 173, 13 Stat. 223, 282, providing that "the gains and profits of all companies, whether incorporated or partnership, other than the companies specified in this section, shall be included in estimating the annual gains, profits, or income of any person entitled to the same, whether divided or otherwise." The court held an individual taxable upon his proportion of the earnings of a corporation although not declared as dividends and although invested in assets not in their nature divisible. . . In so far as this seems to uphold the right of Congress to tax without apportionment a stockholder's interest in accumulated earnings prior to dividend declared, it must be regarded as overruled by Pollock v. Farmers' Loan & Trust Co., 158 U.S. 601, 627, 628, 637. Conceding Collector v. Hubbard was inconsistent with the doctrine of that case, because it sustained a direct tax upon property not apportioned among the States, the Government nevertheless insists that the Sixteenth Amendment removed this obstacle, so that now the *Hubbard* Case is authority for the power of Congress to levy a tax on the stockholder's share in the accumulated profits of the corporation even before division by the declaration of a dividend of any kind. Manifestly this argument must be rejected, since the Amendment applies to income only, and what is called the stockholder's share in the accumulated profits of the company is capital, not income. As we have pointed out, a stockholder has no individual share in accumulated profits, nor in any particular part of the assets of the corporation, prior to dividend declared.

Thus, from every point of view, we are brought irresistibly to the conclusion that neither under the Sixteenth Amendment nor otherwise has Congress power to tax without apportionment a true stock dividend made lawfully and in good faith, or the accumulated profits behind it, as income of the stockholder. The Revenue Act of 1916, in so far as it imposes a tax upon the stockholder because of such dividend, contravenes the provisions of Article 1, § 2, cl. 3, and Article 1, § 9, cl. 4, of the Constitution, and to this extent is invalid notwithstanding the Sixteenth Amendment.

Judgment affirmed.

■ MR. JUSTICE HOLMES, dissenting. I think that Towne v. Eisner, 245 U.S. 418, was right in its reasoning and result and that on sound principles the stock dividend was not income. But it was clearly intimated in that case that the construction of the statute then before the Court might be different from that of the Constitution. 245 U.S. 425. I think that the word "incomes" in the Sixteenth Amendment should be read in "a sense most obvious to the common understanding at the time of its adoption." . . . For it was for public adoption that it was proposed. McCulloch v. Maryland, 4 Wheat. 316, 407. The known purpose of this Amendment was to get rid of nice questions as to what might be direct taxes, and I cannot doubt that most people not lawyers would suppose when they voted for it that they put a question like the present to rest. I am of opinion that the Amendment justifies the tax. See Tax Commissioner v. Putnam, 227 Massachusetts, 522, 532, 533.

■ MR. JUSTICE DAY concurs in this opinion.

■ MR. JUSTICE BRANDEIS, dissenting, delivered the following opinion, in which MR. JUSTICE CLARKE concurred. Financiers, with the aid of lawyers, devised long ago two different methods by which a corporation can, without increasing its indebtedness, keep for corporate purposes accumulated profits, and yet, in effect, distribute these profits among its stockholders. One method is a simple one. The capital stock is increased; the new stock is paid up with the accumulated profits; and the new shares of paid-up stock are then distributed among the stockholders pro rata as a dividend. If the stockholder prefers ready money to increasing his holding of the stock in the company, he sells the new stock received as a dividend. The other method is slightly more complicated. Arrangements are made for an increase of stock to be offered to stockholders pro rata at par and, at the same time, for the payment of a cash dividend equal to the amount which the stockholder will be required to pay to the company, if he avails himself of the right to subscribe for his pro rata of the new stock. If the stockholder takes the new stock, as is expected, he may endorse the dividend check received to the corporation and thus pay for the new stock. In order to ensure that all the new stock so offered will be taken, the price at which it is offered is fixed far below what it is believed will be its market value. If the stockholder prefers ready money to an increase of his holdings of stock, he may sell his right to take new stock pro rata, which is evidenced by an assignable instrument. In that event the purchaser of the rights repays to the corporation, as the subscription price of the new stock, an amount equal to that which it had paid as a cash dividend to the stockholder.

Both of these methods of retaining accumulated profits while in effect distributing them as a dividend had been in common use in the United States for many years prior to the adoption of the Sixteenth Amendment. They were recognized equivalents. . . Whichever method was employed the resultant distribution of the new stock was commonly referred to as a stock dividend. . .

. . . [T]he financial results to the corporation and to the stockholders of the two methods are substantially the same—unless a difference results from the application of the federal income tax law. . .

It is conceded that if the stock dividend paid to Mrs. Macomber had been made by the more complicated method . . ., that is, issuing rights to take new stock pro rata and paying to each stockholder simultaneously a dividend in cash sufficient in amount to enable him to pay for this pro rata of new stock to be purchased—the dividend so paid to him would have been taxable as income, whether he retained the cash or whether he returned it to the corporation in payment for his pro rata of new stock. But it is contended that, because the simple method was adopted of having the new stock issued direct to the stockholders as paid-up stock, the new stock is not to be deemed income, whether she retained it or converted it into cash by sale. If such a different result can flow merely from the difference in the method pursued, it must be because Congress is without power to tax as income of the stockholder either the stock received under the latter method or the proceeds of its sale; for Congress has, by the provisions in the Revenue Act of 1916, expressly declared its purpose to make stock dividends, by whichever method paid, taxable as income. . .

Hitherto powers conferred upon Congress by the Constitution have been liberally construed, and have been held to extend to every means appropriate to attain the end sought. In determining the scope of the power the substance of the transaction, not its form, has been regarded. . . Is there anything in the phraseology of the Sixteenth Amendment or in the nature of corporate dividends which should lead to a departure from these rules of construction and compel this court to hold, that Congress is powerless to prevent a result so extraordinary as that here contended for by the stockholder?

First: The term "income" when applied to the investment of the stockholder in a corporation, had, before the adoption of the Sixteenth Amendment, been commonly understood to mean the returns from time to time received by the stockholder from gains or earnings of the corporation. A dividend received by a stockholder from a corporation may be either in distribution of capital assets or in distribution of profits. Whether it is the one or the other is in no way affected by the medium in which it is paid, nor by the method or means through which the particular thing distributed as a dividend was procured. If the dividend is declared payable in cash, the money with which to pay it is ordinarily taken from surplus cash in the treasury. But (if there are profits legally available for distribution and the law under which the company was incorporated so permits) the company may raise the money by discounting negotiable paper; or by selling bonds, scrip or stock of another corporation then in the treasury; or by selling its own bonds, scrip or stock then in the treasury; or by selling its own bonds, scrip or stock issued expressly for that purpose. How the money shall be raised is wholly a matter of financial management. The manner in which it is raised in no way affects the question whether the dividend received by the stockholder is income or capital; nor can it conceivably affect the question whether it is taxable as income.

Likewise whether a dividend declared payable from profits shall be paid in cash or in some other medium is also wholly a matter of financial management. If some other medium is decided upon, it is also wholly a question of financial management whether the distribution shall be, for instance, in bonds, scrip or stock of another corporation or in issues of its own. . . If a dividend paid in securities of that nature represents a distribution of profits Congress may, of course, tax it as income of the stockholder. Is the result different where the security distributed is common stock? . . .

Second: It has been said that a dividend payable in bonds or preferred stock created for the purpose of distributing profits may be income and taxable as such, but that the case is different where the distribution is in common stock created for that purpose. Various reasons are assigned for making this distinction. One is that the proportion of the stockholder's ownership to the aggregate number of the shares of the company is not changed by the distribution. But that is equally true where the dividend is paid in its bonds or in its preferred stock. Furthermore, neither maintenance nor change in the proportionate ownership of a stockholder in a corporation has any bearing upon the question here involved. Another reason assigned is that the value of the old stock held is reduced approximately by the value of the new stock received, so that the stockholder after receipt of the stock dividend has no more than he had before it was paid. That is equally true whether the dividend be paid in cash or in other—property, for instance, bonds, scrip or preferred stock of the company. The payment from profits of a large cash dividend, and even a small one, customarily lowers the then market value of stock because the undivided property represented by each share has been correspondingly reduced. The argument which appears to be most strongly urged for the stockholders is, that when a stock dividend is made, no portion of the assets of the company is thereby segregated for the stockholder. But does the issue of new bonds or of preferred stock created for use as a dividend result in any segregation of assets for the stockholder? In each case he receives a piece of paper which entitles him to certain rights in the undivided property. Clearly segregation of assets in a physical sense is not an essential of income. The year's gains of a partner are taxable as income, although there, likewise, no segregation of his share in the gains from that of his partners is had.

The objection that there has been no segregation is presented also in another form. It is argued that until there is a segregation, the stockholder cannot know whether he has really received gains; since the gains may be invested in plant or merchandise or other property and perhaps be later lost. But is not this equally true of the share of a partner in the year's profits of the firm or, indeed, of the profits of the individual who is engaged in business alone? And is it not true, also, when dividends are paid in cash? The gains of a business, whether conducted by an individual, by a firm or by a corporation, are ordinarily reinvested in large part. Many a cash dividend honestly declared as a distribution of profits, proves later to have been paid out of capital, because errors in forecast prevent correct ascertainment of values. Until a business adventure has been completely liquidated, it can never be determined with certainty whether there have been profits unless the returns have at least exceeded the capital originally invested. Business men, dealing with the problem practically, fix necessarily periods and rules for determining whether there have been net profits—that is income or gains. They protect themselves from being seriously misled by adopting a system of depreciation charges and reserves. "Then, they act upon their own determination, whether profits have been made. Congress in legislating has wisely adopted their practices as its own rules of action."

Third: The Government urges that it would have been within the power of Congress to have taxed as income of the stockholder his pro rata share of undistributed profits earned, even if no stock dividend representing it had been paid. Strong reasons may be assigned for such a view. See Collector v. Hubbard, 12 Wall. 1. The undivided share of a partner in the year's undistributed profits of his firm is taxable as income of the partner, although the share in the gain is not evidenced by any action taken by the firm. Why may not the stockholder's interest in the gains of the company? The law finds no difficulty in disregarding the corporate fiction whenever that is deemed necessary to attain a just result. . . The stockholder's interest in the property of the corporation differs, not fundamentally but in form only, from the interest of a partner in the property of the firm. There is much authority for the proposition that, under our law, a partnership or joint stock company is just as distinct and palpable an entity in the idea of the law, as distinguished from the individuals composing it, as is a corporation. No reason appears, why Congress, in legislating under a grant of power so comprehensive as that authorizing the levy of an income tax, should be limited by the particular—view of the relation of the stockholder to the corporation and its property which may, in the absence of legislation, have been taken by this court. But we have no occasion to decide the question whether Congress might have taxed to the stockholder his undivided share of the corporation's earnings. For Congress has in this act limited the income tax to that share of the stockholder in the earnings which is, in effect, distributed by means of the stock dividend paid. . .

Sixth: If stock dividends representing profits are held exempt from taxation under the Sixteenth Amendment, the owners of the most successful businesses in America will, as the facts in this case illustrate, be able to escape taxation on a large part of what is actually their income. So far as their profits are represented by stock received as dividends they will pay these taxes not upon their income but only upon the income of their income. That such a result was intended by the people of the United States when adopting the Sixteenth Amendment is inconceivable. Our sole duty is to ascertain their intent as therein expressed. In terse, comprehensive language befitting the Constitution, they empowered Congress "to lay and collect taxes on incomes, from whatever source derived." They intended to include thereby everything which by reasonable understanding can fairly be regarded as income. That stock dividends representing profits are so regarded, not only by the plain people but by investors and financiers, and by most of the courts of the country, is shown, beyond peradventure, by their acts and by their utterances. It seems to me clear, therefore, that Congress possesses the power which it exercised to make dividends representing profits, taxable as income, whether the medium in which the dividend is paid be cash or stock, and that it may define, as it has done, what dividends representing profits shall be deemed income. It surely is not clear that the enactment exceeds the power granted by the Sixteenth Amendment. And, as this court has so often said, the high prerogative of declaring an act of Congress invalid, should never be exercised except in a clear case. "It is but a decent respect due to the wisdom, the integrity and the patriotism of the legislative body, by which any law is passed, to presume in favor of its validity, until its violation of the Constitution is proved beyond all reasonable doubt." Ogden v. Saunders, 12 Wheat. 213, 270.

Helvering v. Gowran
302 U.S. 238 (1937).

■ MR. JUSTICE BRANDEIS delivered the opinion of the Court. The questions for decision concern the taxation as income of a dividend in preferred stock and the proceeds received on its sale.

On June 29, 1929, the Hamilton Manufacturing Company . . . had outstanding preferred stock of the par value of $100 a share and common stock without par value. On that day the directors declared from the surplus earnings a dividend of $14 a share on the common stock, payable on July 1, 1929, in preferred stock at its par value. Gowran, as owner of common stock, received as his dividend 533 and a fraction shares of the preferred. On or about October 1, 1929, the company acquired his preferred stock and paid him therefor, at $100 a share, $53,371.50. In his income tax return for the year Gowran did not treat this sum as taxable income, but included $27,262.72 as capital net gain on the shares received and sold, computing the gain under Articles 58 and 600 of Regulations 74, then in force. The Commissioner rejected that treatment of the matter; determined that the $53,371.50 received was income taxable under the Revenue Act of 1928, § 115(g), 45 Stat. 791, 822, as a stock dividend redeemed; and assessed a deficiency of $5,831.67.

The taxpayer sought a redetermination by the Board of Tax Appeals. . . The Commissioner . . . contended that, under the rule declared in Commissioner of Internal Revenue v. Tillotson Mfg. Co., 76 F.(2d) 189, the stock dividend was taxable, because it had resulted in a change of Gowran's proportionate interest in the company. That contention was sustained by the Board; and, on that ground, it affirmed the Commissioner's determination of a deficiency. 32 B.T.A. 820.

The taxpayer sought a review by the Circuit Court of Appeals. The Commissioner again urged that the stock dividend was taxable; and then, for the first time, contended that, even if it was not taxable, the determination of the deficiency should be affirmed, because within the tax year the stock had been sold at its par value and, as its cost had been zero, the entire proceeds constituted income. The Court of Appeals recognized that, since the dividends in preferred stock gave to Gowran an interest different in character from that which his common stock represented, it was constitutionally taxable under Koshland v. Helvering, 298 U.S. 441; but it held that the dividend could not be taxed as income, since by § 115(f) Congress had provided: "A stock dividend shall not be subject to tax." And it held further that no part of the proceeds could be taxed as income, since there was no profit on the sale, it being agreed that the fair market value of the stock, both at the date of receipt and at the date of the sale, was $100 a share. 87 F.(2d) 125.

Because of the importance of the questions presented in the administration of the revenue laws, certiorari was granted.

First. The Government contends that § 115(f) should be read as prohibiting taxation only of those stock dividends which the Constitution does not permit to be taxed; and that, since by the dividend Gowran acquired an interest in the corporation essentially different from that theretofore represented by his common stock, the dividend was taxable. In support of that construction of § 115(f), it is urged that Congress has in income tax legislation manifested generally its intention to use, to the full extent, its constitutional power, Helvering v. Stockholms Bank, 293 U.S. 84, 89; Douglas v. Willcuts, 296 U.S. 1, 9; that this Court holds grants of immunity from taxation should always be strictly construed, Pacific Co. v. Johnson, 285 U.S. 480, 491; and that the only reason for exempting stock dividends was to comply with the Constitution.

This preferred stock had substantially the same attributes as that involved in the *Koshland* case. There the dividend was of common stock to a preferred stockholder, it is true; but we are of opinion that under the rule there declared Congress could have taxed this stock dividend. Nevertheless, by § 115(f) it enacted in 1928, as it did in earlier and later Revenue Acts, that "a stock dividend shall not be subject to tax." The prohibition is comprehensive. It is so clearly expressed as to leave no room for construction. It extends to all stock dividends. Such was the construction consistently given to it by the Treasury Department.[1] The purpose of Congress when enacting

---

[1] Eisner v. Macomber was decided March 8, 1920. Soon thereafter, the Treasury Department declared in a series of Decisions and Regulations, that no stock dividend was taxable.... Article 628 of the Regulations in force in 1928 provided: "Stock dividends.—The issuance of its own stock by a corporation as a dividend to its shareholders does not result in taxable income to such shareholders, but gain may be derived or loss sustained by the shareholders from the

§ 115(f) may have been merely to comply with the requirement of the Constitution as interpreted in Eisner v. Macomber, 252 U.S. 189; and the comprehensive language in § 115(f) may have been adopted in the erroneous belief that under the rule declared in that case no stock dividend could be taxed. But such facts would not justify the Court in departing from the unmistakable command embodied in the statute. Congress declared that the preferred stock should not be taxed as a dividend.

Second. The Government contends that, even if § 115(f) be construed as prohibiting taxation of the preferred stock dividend, the decision of the Board of Tax Appeals affirming the Commissioner's determination of a deficiency should be sustained, because the gain from sale of the stock within the year was taxable income and the entire proceeds must be deemed income, since the stock had cost Gowran nothing. The Circuit Court of Appeals rejected that contention. It held that there was no income, because, as stipulated, there was no difference between the value of the stock when received and its value when sold. The court likened a non-taxable stock dividend to a tax-free gift or legacy and said: "One who receives a tax-free gift and later sells it, in the absence of statute providing otherwise, is taxed upon the profit arising from the difference in its value at the time he receives it and the sale price. Similarly one who receives a tax-free bequest, when selling it, is taxed upon the profit arising from any excess of the sale price over its fair market value at the time of receipt." [p. 128] Compare Taft v. Bowers, 278 U.S. 470.

The cases are not analogous. Unlike earlier legislation, § 113(a)(2) of the Revenue Act of 1928 prescribes specifically the basis for determining the gain on tax-free gifts and legacies. It provides that: "If the property was acquired by gift after December 31, 1920, the basis shall be the same as it would be in the hands of the donor or the last preceding owner by whom it was not acquired by gift." And the basis for the computation on property transmitted at death is provided for in paragraph (5). But the method of computing the income from the sale of stock dividends constitutionally taxable is not specifically provided for. Furthermore, unlike § 22(b)(3), excluding from gross income the value of gifts and legacies, § 115(f) cannot, in view of its history, be taken as a declaration of congressional intent that the value of all stock dividends shall be immune from tax not only when received but also when converted into money or other property. Gain on them is, therefore, to be computed as provided in §§ 111 and 113, by the "excess of the amount realized" over "the cost of such property" to the tax-

---

sale of such stock. The amount of gain derived or loss sustained from the sale of such stock, or from the sale of the stock in respect of which it is issued, shall be determined as provided in Articles 561 and 600."

Koshland v. Helvering, 298 U.S. 441, was decided May 18, 1936. On June 22, 1936, Congress, in enacting the Revenue Act of 1936, provided in § 115(f): "1. General Rule—A distribution made by a corporation to its shareholders in its stock or in rights to acquire its stock shall not be treated as a dividend to the extent that it does not constitute income to the shareholder within the meaning of the Sixteenth Amendment to the Constitution." 49 Stat. 1648, 1688. See also § 115(h).

payer. As the cost of the preferred stock to Gowran was zero, the whole of the proceeds is taxable.

Gowran asserts that if this "basis of zero" theory is accepted, the proceeds are taxable not as determined by the Commissioner but as a capital gain at a different rate and under different regulations. This depends upon whether the preferred stock received as a dividend was a "capital asset," defined by § 101(c)(8) as "property held by the taxpayer for more than two years." The record is silent as to when Gowran acquired the common stock upon which the preferred was issued as a dividend, but it may be assumed that he had held it for more than two years. For that fact is immaterial since the dividend stock had been held for only three months. Whether taxed by Congress or not, it was income, substantially equivalent for income tax purposes to cash or property, and under § 115(b) was presumed to have been made "out of earnings or profits to the extent thereof, and from the most recently accumulated earnings or profits." In no sense, therefore, can it be said to have been "held" by Gowran prior to its declaration. Since the proceeds were therefore not "capital gains," they were taxable at the normal and surtax rates applicable to ordinary income. . .

Reversed.

2. EFFECT OF A DISPOSITION

Chamberlin v. Commissioner

207 F.2d 462 (6th Cir. 1953), *cert. denied*, 347 U.S. 918 (1954).

■ Before SIMONS, CHIEF JUDGE, and MCALLISTER and MILLER, CIRCUIT JUDGES.

■ MILLER, CIRCUIT JUDGE. Petitioner C. P. Chamberlin seeks a review of an income tax deficiency determined by the Respondent for the calendar year 1946, and sustained by the Tax Court. In the Tax Court the proceeding was consolidated with the proceedings of five other taxpayers similarly situated, all of which proceedings involved the same factual and legal questions. The taxpayers . . . were stockholders of Metal Moulding Corporation, about which this litigation centers. . .

The Metal Moulding Corporation, hereinafter referred to as the Corporation, is a Michigan corporation engaged in the business of manufacturing metal mouldings and bright work trim used in the manufacture of automobiles. It was incorporated on December 2, 1924 with an authorized common capital stock of $25,000, which was increased in 1935 to $150,000, represented by 1,500 shares of $100 par value voting common stock. From 1940 until December 20, 1946, the issued and outstanding common stock totaled 1,002 1/2 shares, of which Chamberlin and his wife together owned 83.8%. The directors of the corporation from 1940 to February 12, 1946 consisted of C. P. Chamberlin, Grace A. Chamberlin, and Edward W. Smith. On February 12, 1946, John H. Toner and Raymond H. Berry were added. On October 11, 1946, Smith died and during the remainder of 1946 the board consisted of the four remaining members. From 1940 to the end of 1946, C. P. Chamberlin was president and treasurer, John H. Toner was vice-president and general manager, and Grace Chamberlin was for various periods vice-president, assistant treasurer, and secretary. Benjamin J. Carl was assistant secretary and treasurer until February 12, 1946.

On December 16, 1946, the Corporation's authorized capital stock was increased from $150,000 to $650,000, represented by 6,500 shares of $100 par value common stock. On December 20, 1946, a stock dividend was declared and distributed of five shares of common for each share of common outstanding, and the Corporation's accounts were adjusted by transferring $501,250 from earned surplus to capital account.

On December 26, 1946, the articles of incorporation were amended so as to authorize, in addition to the 6,500 shares of common stock, 8,020 shares of 4 1/2% cumulative $100 par value preferred stock. On December 28, 1946, a stock dividend was declared of 1 1/3 shares of the newly authorized preferred stock for each share of common stock outstanding, to be issued pro rata to the holders of common stock as of December 27, 1946, and the Company's accounts were adjusted by transferring $802,000 from earned surplus to capital account. The preferred stock was issued to the stockholders on the same day. Prior to the declaration of the preferred stock dividend, the Corporation at all times had only one class of stock outstanding.

On December 30, 1946, as the result of prior negotiations hereinafter referred to, all of the holders of the preferred stock, except the estate of Edward W. Smith, deceased, which owned 20 shares, signed a "Purchase Agreement," with The Northwestern Mutual Life Insurance Company and The Lincoln National Life Insurance Company, which instrument was also endorsed by the Corporation for the purpose of making certain representations, warranties and agreements. Under the "Purchase Agreement" 4,000 shares of the preferred stock was sold to each of the two insurance companies at a cash price of $100 per share plus accrued dividends from November 1st, 1946 to date of delivery. . .

In the latter part of 1945, the Corporation's attorney and Chamberlin discussed with an investment firm in Chicago the possibility of selling an issue of preferred stock similar to the stock subsequently issued. The Corporation had such a large accumulated earned surplus it was fearful of being subjected to the surtax provided for by [§ 531] . . . but at the same time Chamberlin, the majority stockholder, was not willing to have the Corporation distribute any substantial portion of its earned surplus as ordinary dividends because his individual income was taxable at high surtax rates. It was proposed that the issuance of a stock dividend to the stockholders and the sale of it by the stockholders would enable the stockholders to obtain accumulated earnings of the Corporation in the form of capital gains rather than as taxable dividends. The investment counselor contacted The Lincoln National Life Insurance Company of Fort Wayne, Indiana, and during October 1946, furnished the Insurance Company financial information relative to the Corporation. On November 7, 1946, a representative of the Insurance Company came to Detroit and made an inspection of the plant and properties of the Corporation. On November 20, 1946, The Lincoln National Life Insurance Company's finance committee approved the proposed issue and the purchase of one-half thereof. The Northwestern Mutual Life Insurance Company was contacted for the purpose of participating in the purchase of the preferred stock. It made a detailed investigation of the Corporation and of the terms and conditions of the proposed preferred stock issue, and about two weeks before December 30, 1946, its committee on investments approved the purchase of 4,000 shares of the preferred stock to be issued, and passed the matter over to its legal department for the conclusion of the transaction.

The preferred stock contained the following provisions among others: The holders were entitled to cumulative cash dividends at the rate of $4.50 per annum payable quarterly beginning November 1, 1946; the stock was subject to redemption on any quarterly dividend date in whole or in part at par plus specified premiums and accrued dividends; it was subject to mandatory retirement in amounts not exceeding 2,000 shares on May 1, 1948 and 1,000 on May 1st on each succeeding year, depending upon the Corporation's net earnings for the preceding year, until fully retired on May 1, 1954; in the event of certain default of dividend payments or annual retirements, the holders were entitled to elect a majority of the directors; as long as any preferred shares remained outstanding the consent of the holders of at least 75% thereof was required to validate certain actions, including changing the articles of incorporation or capital structure, the sale of the Company's property, or the incurrence of indebtedness for borrowed money in excess of a certain amount; the Corporation could not pay any cash dividend upon any stock junior to the preferred if there was any default in the payment of dividend upon and the annual retirements of the preferred, or if such dividend reduced the net working capital of the Corporation below an amount equal to 150% of the aggregate par value of all outstanding preferred, or $750,000, whichever amount was greater, or reduced the [current] assets of the Company to an amount less than 200% of current liabilities. These provisions had been discussed with the Lincoln National Life Insurance Company and some of them, at least, were included in order to satisfy the investment requirements of the two insurance companies.

No agreement of purchase and sale was entered into between any of the petitioners and either of the two insurance companies prior to the "Purchase Agreement" executed on December 30, 1946, but the stockholders and directors of the Corporation took the necessary actions to put the negotiated plan into effect . . . only after the insurance companies certified their willingness to participate in the purchase. . .

In reporting this sale of the preferred stock in their 1946 tax returns, each of the stockholders reported his proportion of the proceeds from the sale as a net long-term capital gain from the sale of a capital asset held for more than six months, used a substituted basis as the cost basis of the preferred stock, and in determining the period the preferred stock had been held included the holding period of the common stock upon which the preferred stock dividend was declared.

The Respondent ruled that the preferred stock constituted a dividend taxable as ordinary income, and further determined that the value was the amount received on the sale of the shares against which the expenses incurred in the sale were a valid deduction. . .

Before considering the ruling of the Tax Court it is well to briefly review some of the Supreme Court decisions involving the taxability of stock dividends. This is well done in Note 5, in the Tax Court's opinion, which, together with the analysis of some of the opinions and the legislative enactments applicable . . . makes a detailed restatement unnecessary in this opinion. In Towne v. Eisner, 245 U.S. 418, . . . and Eisner v. Macomber, 252 U.S. 189, the Court held that a stock dividend of common stock to the holders of the common stock was not income to the stockholder taxable by Congress under the Sixteenth Amendment, in that it did not alter the preexisting proportionate interest of any stockholder or increase the intrinsic value of his holding or of the aggregate holdings of the other stockholders as they stood before. The Court said: "The new certificates simply increase the number of the shares, with consequent dilution of the value of each share" and that a stock dividend "shows that the company's accumulated profits have been capitalized, instead of distributed to the stockholders or retained as surplus available for distribution in money or in kind should opportunity offer." In Koshland v. Helvering, 298 U.S. 441, the Court held that a stock dividend of common stock to the holders of preferred stock was taxable income because it gave the preferred stockholder an interest different from that which his former stockholdings represented. In Helvering v. Gowran, 302 U.S. 238, the Court held that a stock dividend in preferred stock to the holders of common stock, where similar preferred stock was outstanding, was taxable income because it gave the common stockholder an interest essentially different from that theretofore represented by his common stock. In Helvering v. Griffiths [318 U.S. 371], the Court refused to reconsider the ruling in Eisner v. Macomber, supra, holding that legislation subsequent to that ruling did not attempt to make such stock dividends taxable. In Helvering v. Sprouse, 318 U.S. 604, . . . and in Strassburger v. Commissioner of Internal Revenue, 318 U.S. 604, . . . the Court restated the rule that in order to render a stock dividend taxable as income there must be a change brought about by the issue of shares as a dividend whereby the proportional interest of the stockholder after the distribution was essentially different from his former interest. The rule was applied to the facts in the *Strassburger* case where preferred stock was created and distributed as a stock dividend to a stockholder who owned the entire outstanding common stock, the Court holding that the preferred stock dividend did not constitute taxable income.

The Commissioner supported his assessment on the ground that although the preferred stock was issued as a non-taxable dividend, a concerted plan to sell the dividend shares was formulated prior to the distribution of such shares, which, coupled with actual sale immediately after receipt and the payment of the proceeds of sale direct to the stockholders constituted a taxable dividend to the extent of available earnings. He also took the position that the plan and the immediate sale resulted in a change in the proportional interest of the stockholders which was sufficient to exclude it from the rulings in the Supreme Court cases above referred to.

In the Tax Court the petitioner contended that under the rulings in Towne v. Eisner, supra . . .; Eisner v. Macomber, supra . . .; Helvering v. Griffiths, supra . . .; and Strassburger v. Commissioner, supra, . . . and the provisions of Sec. 115(f)(1). . .* the preferred stock dividend was not income within the meaning of the Sixteenth Amendment, and accordingly not taxable. . . Sec. 115(f)(1) provides: "A distribution made by a corporation to its shareholders in its stock or in rights to acquire its stock shall not be treated as a dividend to the extent that it does not constitute income to the shareholder within the meaning of the Sixteenth Amendment to the Constitution."

The Tax Court held that the issue of whether the stock dividend constituted income to the stockholders should be determined from a consideration of all the facts and circumstances surrounding the issuance of the dividend and not by a consideration limited to the characteristics of the stock declared as a dividend; . . . that such a decision did not rest upon matters of form . . . but rather upon the real substance of the transaction involved; that disregarding the circumstances and terms of the issue it might be said that as a matter of form the stock dividend constituted one which fell within the *Strassburger* case, but that considering the real substance of the transaction it was of the opinion that the stock dividend was not in good faith for any bona fide corporate business purpose, and that the attending circumstances and conditions under which it was issued made it the equivalent of a cash dividend distribution out of available earnings, thus constituting ordinary taxable income in the amount of the value of the preferred shares received. The Court also said that the real purpose of the issuance of the preferred shares was concurrently to place them in the hands of others not then stockholders of the Corporation, thereby substantially altering the common stockholders' pre-existing proportionate interests in the Corporation's net assets and thereby creating an entirely new relationship amongst all the stockholders and the Corporation. . .

In our opinion, the declaration and distribution of the preferred stock dividend, considered by itself, falls clearly within the principles established in Towne v. Eisner, supra, and Eisner v. Macomber, supra, and is controlled by the ruling in the *Strassburger* case. Accordingly, as a preliminary matter, we do not agree with the Tax Court's statement that the stock dividend is taxable because as a result of the dividend and immediate sale thereafter it substantially altered the common stockholders' pre-existing proportional interests in the Corporation's net assets. The sale to the insurance companies of course resulted in such a change, but the legal effect of

---

* Section 115(1) was the 1939 predecessor of § 305. Section 305 is more detailed and, in some circumstances, differs in its impact. The 1939 Code contained no counterpart of § 306.— Eᴅ.

the dividend with respect to rights in the corporate assets is determined at the time of its distribution, not by what the stockholders do with it after its receipt. In Helvering v. Griffiths, supra, 318 U.S. 371, at page 394, . . . the Court pointed out: "at the latest the time of receipt of the dividend is the critical one for determining taxability." In none of the Supreme Court cases referred to above is it suggested that events subsequent to the distribution have any bearing on whether the stockholder's proportional interest is changed. The fact that events occur in quick succession does not by itself change their legal effect. Biddle Avenue Realty Corp. v. Commissioner, 6 Cir., 94 F.2d 435. It seems clear to us that if taxability exists it is not because of the change in pre-existing proportional interests caused by a later sale, but by reason of the other ground relied upon by the Tax Court, namely, that viewed in all its aspects it was a distribution of cash rather than a distribution of stock. That this is the real basis of the ruling appears from the statement in the opinion that "disregarding the circumstances and terms of the issue, it might be said as a matter of form the stock dividend constituted one which fell within the *Sprouse* and *Strassburger* cases. . . However. . . not form but the real substance of the transaction is controlling."

The general principle is well settled that a taxpayer has the legal right to decrease the amount of what otherwise would be his taxes, or altogether avoid them, by means which the law permits; . . . and that the taxpayer's motive to avoid taxation will not establish liability if the transaction does not do so without it. . .

It is equally well settled that this principle does not prevent the Government from going behind the form which the transaction takes and ascertaining the reality and genuineness of the component parts of the transaction in order to determine whether the transaction is really what it purports to be or is merely a formality without substance which for tax purposes can and should be disregarded. . .

The question accordingly presented is not whether the overall transaction, admittedly carried out for the purpose of avoiding taxes, actually avoided taxes which would have been incurred if the transaction had taken a different form, but whether the stock dividend was a stock dividend in substance as well as in form.

No question is raised about the legality of the declaration of the dividend. Respondent does not contend that proper corporate procedure was not used in creating the preferred stock and in distributing it to the stockholders in the form of a dividend. If the transaction had stopped there we think it is clear that the dividend would not have been taxable in the hands of the stockholders. Strassburger v. Commissioner, supra. Whether the declaration of the dividend was in furtherance of any corporate business purpose or was the result of correct judgment and proper business policy on the part of the management, we believe is immaterial on this phase of the case. The Supreme Court cases in no way suggest that the taxability of a stock dividend depends on the purpose of its issuance or the good or bad judgment of the directors in capitalizing earnings instead of distributing them. The decisions are based squarely upon the proportional interest doctrine. . . In Dreyfuss v. Manning, D.C.N J., 44 F.Supp. 383, a stock dividend of preferred stock, declared solely for the purpose of avoiding taxes on undistributed net income, was held non-taxable, which ruling apparently was not appealed by the Commissioner. The presence or absence of a corporate business purpose may play a part in determining whether a stock dividend is a bona fide one, one in substance as well as in form, but it does not by itself change an otherwise valid dividend into an invalid one. A stock dividend, legally created and distributed, which is a dividend in substance as well as in form, does not change from a non-taxable dividend into a taxable one because of the purpose of its issuance or on account of the good or bad judgment of the directors in declaring it. Eisner v. Macomber, supra, 252 U.S. at page 211. . .

Nor is there any question about the genuineness and unconditional character of the sale of the preferred stock by the stockholders who received it to the two insurance companies. The facts show conclusively that title passed irrevocably from the stockholders to the insurance companies, and that the sellers received in cash without restriction a full consideration, the adequacy of which respondent does not question. But respondent contends that the sale of the stock following immediately upon its receipt resulted in the stockholder acquiring cash instead of stock, thus making it a taxable dividend under Secs. [61(a)(7)] and 115(a). . . There are two answers to this contention.

A non-taxable stock dividend does not become a taxable cash dividend upon its sale by the recipient. On the contrary, it is a sale of a capital asset. Eisner v. Macomber, 252 U.S. 189, 212 . . .; Miles v. Safe Deposit & Trust Co., 259 U.S. 247. . . The rulings in those cases make it clear that its character as a capital asset is in no way dependent upon how long it is held by the taxpayer before its sale. In none of the Supreme Court cases referred to above, dealing with the taxability of stock dividends, was the length of the holding period considered as a factor. Obviously, if the non-taxability of a stock dividend rests solely upon the principle that it does not alter the preexisting proportionate interest of any stockholder or increase the intrinsic value of his holdings, the disposition of the stock dividend by the stockholder thereafter is not a factor in the determination. . . The foregoing conclusion is supported by Sec. 117(h)(5), . . .* which provides that for the purpose of determining whether a nontaxable stock dividend which has been sold is a long-term capital gain there shall be included in the holding period the period for which the taxpayer held the stock in the distributing corporation prior to the receipt of the stock dividend. This necessarily recognizes that a stock dividend will often be sold before the expiration of six months after its receipt, and makes no distinction between a stock dividend held one day or for any other period less than six months. Likewise, Sec. 29.113(x)(19)–1, Treasury Regulations III, in establishing the cost basis of a non-taxable stock dividend which has been sold for a gain or loss, makes no distinction between a stock dividend sold immediately after receipt and one held a long period of time before sale.

---

* Section 1223(5) of the 1986 Code.—ED.

The other answer to the contention is that although the stockholder *acquired* money in the final analysis, he did not *receive* either money or property from the corporation. Sec. 115(a). . ., in dealing with taxable dividends, defines a dividend as "any distribution *made by a corporation* to its shareholders, whether in money or in other property . . . out of its earnings or profits. . ." (Emphasis added.) The money he received was received from the insurance companies. It was not a "distribution" by the corporation declaring the dividend, as required by the statute.

We come then to what in our opinion is the dominant and decisive issue in the case, namely, whether the stock dividend, which, by reason of its redemption feature, enabled the Corporation to ultimately distribute its earnings to its stockholders on a taxable basis materially lower than would have been the case by declaring and paying the usual cash dividend, was a bona fide one, one in substance as well as in form. As pointed out in Chisholm v. Commissioner. . . 2 Cir., 79 F.2d 14, 15, *certiorari denied* Helvering v. Chisholm, 296 U.S. 641, . . . the Court cannot ignore the legal effect of a bona fide transaction on the ground that it avoids taxes, and that "The question always is whether the transaction under scrutiny is in fact what it appears to be in form; a marriage may be a joke; a contract may be intended only to deceive others; an agreement may have a collateral defeasance. In such cases the transaction as a whole is different from its appearance." But if the transaction is actually what it purports to be it must be accepted for its legal results. There are numerous cases, some of which are pressed upon us by the respondent, where the Court, in keeping with the above principle, refused to give effect taxwise to transactions on the part of corporations because the facts and circumstances showed that the so-called corporation was one in form only, incorporated for the sole purpose of avoiding taxes and having no legitimate business purpose, masquerading under the corporate form, and accordingly not a bona fide corporation. See Gregory v. Helvering. . . 293 U.S. 465 . . .; Higgins v. Smith . . ., 308 U.S. 473. . . In other cases a valid conveyance has been disregarded taxwise because the purchaser acquired no real interest in the property conveyed, was a mere conduit in passing title to another, and the conveyance was in fact a sham. See Minnesota Tea Co. v. (Helvering) Commissioner. . . 302 U.S. 609 . . .; Griffiths v. (Helvering) Commissioner, 308 U.S. 355 . . .; Commissioner v. Court Holding Co., 324 U.S. 331. . .

In our opinion, the stock dividend in this case does not fall within any of the principles discussed above. It seems clear that it was an issue of stock in substance as well as in form. According to its terms, and in the absence of a finding that it was immediately or shortly thereafter redeemed at a premium, we assume that a large portion of it has remained outstanding over a period of years with some of it still unredeemed after nearly seven years. It has been in the hands of the investing public, free of any control by the corporation over its owners, whose enforceable rights with respect to operations of the corporation would not be waived or neglected. Substantial sums have been paid in dividends. The insurance companies bought it in the regular course of their business and have held it as approved investments. For the Court to now tell them that they have been holding a sham issue of stock would be most startling and disturbing news.

It also seems clear that the insurance companies were not purchasers in form only without acquiring any real interest in the property conveyed. The character of the transaction as a bona fide investment on the part of the insurance companies is not challenged by the respondent. The element of a formal conduit without any business interest is entirely lacking.

If the transaction lacks the good faith necessary to avoid the assessment it must be because of the redemption feature of the stock, which, in the final analysis, is what ultimately permitted the distribution of the corporate earnings and is the key factor in the overall transaction. Redemption features are well known and often used in corporate financing. If the one in question was a reasonable one, not violative of the general principles of bona fide corporate financing, and acceptable to experienced bona fide investors familiar with investment fundamentals and the opportunities afforded by the investment market, we fail to see how a court can properly classify the issue, by reason of the redemption feature, as lacking in good faith or as not being what it purports to be. The insurance companies, conservative, experienced investors, analyzed the stock issue very carefully, provisions were required to make it conform to sound investment requirements, and each of the two companies, acting independently of the other, purchased a very substantial amount in the regular course of their investment purchases. . . In our opinion, the redemption feature, qualified as it was with respect to premiums, amounts subject to redemption in each year, and the length of time the stock would be outstanding, together with the acceptance of the stock as an investment issue, did not destroy the bona fide quality of the issue. We cannot say that the preferred stock was not in fact what it purported to be, namely, an issue of stock in substance as well as in form. . .

Each case necessarily depends upon its own facts. The facts in this case show tax avoidance, and it is so conceded by petitioner. But they also show a series of legal transactions, no one of which is fictitious or so lacking in substance as to be anything different from what it purports to be. Unless we are to adopt the broad policy of holding taxable any series of transactions, the purpose and result of which is the avoidance of taxes which would otherwise accrue if handled in a different way, regardless of the legality and realities of the component parts, the tax assessed by the Commissioner was successfully avoided in the present case. We do not construe the controlling decisions as having adopted that view. United States v. Isham . . ., 17 Wall. at page 506; Gregory v. Helvering, supra, 293 U.S. at page 469, . . . ; Commissioner v. Tower, supra, 327 U.S. at page 288, . . .; United States v. Cumberland Public Service Co. . . ., 338 U.S. at page 455. . .

In deciding this case it must be kept in mind that it does not involve a ruling that the profit derived from the sale of the stock dividend is or is not taxable income. Such profit is conceded to be taxable. The issue is whether it is taxable as income from a cash dividend or as income resulting from a long-term capital gain. Accordingly, it is not the usual case of total tax avoidance. Congress has adopted the policy of taxing long-term capital gains differently from ordinary income. By Sec. 115(g) . . . it has specifically excluded certain transactions with respect to stock dividends from the classification of a capital gain. The present transaction is not within the exclusion. If the profit from a transaction like the one here involved is to be taxed at the same rate as ordinary income, it should be done by appropriate legislation, not court decision.

The judgment is reversed and the case remanded to the Tax Court for proceedings consistent with the views expressed herein.

NOTES

1. Was the result in *Chamberlin* sound? Notwithstanding *Chamberlin*, in Estate of Rosenberg, 36 T.C. 716 (1961), where redeemable preferred stock was issued to the common shareholders who sold it to insurance companies and other corporate investors from whom it was subsequently redeemed, the Tax Court held that the transaction was a predetermined plan to bail out earnings. The "net effect" was a dividend to the shareholders, taxable at ordinary income rates.

2. Although *Rosenberg* was decided in 1961, the case arose under the 1939 Code. Congress, however, had responded to *Chamberlin* in 1954. It did so by providing generally for the continued exclusion of stock dividends, even when the dividends created disproportionate interests (see § 305(a)). But it also provided in § 306 for ordinary income on the disposition of the dividend stock in circumstances thought to provide a potential bail-out of corporate earnings at capital gains rates. Section 305(b)(2) et seq., an important modification of § 305(a), did not become part of the law until 1969.

Sections 306 and 305(b)(2), still intact, are the subjects of the next two parts of this chapter. Consider, however, the relevance of § 306 after the 2003 Act changes to the taxation of dividends (taxing dividends like net capital gain).

B. CURRENT LAW

1. THE § 306 APPROACH: EQUATING GAIN ON STOCK DISPOSITION WITH DIVIDENDS

The conversion of capital gain income into ordinary income was long considered the principal penalty of § 306. Until 2003, § 306 provided that gain on the disposition of § 306 stock was treated as ordinary income preventing certain potential "dividends" from being converted into capital gains. However, the 2003 Act decision to tax most dividends received by individuals at the rate for net capital gains has substantially eliminated this "bail-out" goal for taxpayers. The 2003 Act changes in dividend tax rates were accompanied by a § 306 conforming amendment taxing § 306 gain like a dividend (effectively the original goal of § 306, effectuated by the ordinary income rule). As long as an individual's dividend and capital gains rates are identical, § 306 is significant only to the extent that it denies basis recovery and prevents an otherwise available capital loss offset. Section

306 does continue to have its historical role for corporate shareholders—for such shareholders, proceeds from the sale of § 306 stock are not taxed as dividends but as ordinary income, thereby denying the dividends received deduction. Typically, a corporate shareholder would not seek to bail out earnings through capital gains because of the dividends received advantage and exclusion of dividends in the context of consolidation.

Fireoved v. United States

462 F.2d 1281 (3d Cir. 1972).

■ Before ADAMS, MAX ROSENN, and HUNTER, CIRCUIT JUDGES.

■ ADAMS, CIRCUIT JUDGE. This appeal calls into question the application of section 306 ... and the "first in-first out rule" to a redemption of preferred stock in a corporation by plaintiff, one of its principal shareholders. In particular we are asked to decide whether the transaction here had "as one of its principal purposes the avoidance of Federal income tax," whether a prior sale of a portion of the underlying common stock immunized a like proportion of the section 306 stock from treatment as a noncapital asset and whether another block of the redeemed stock should be considered to represent stock not subject to section 306.

I. FACTUAL BACKGROUND

On November 24, 1948, Fireoved and Company, Inc. was incorporated... At their first meeting, the incorporators elected Eugene Fireoved, his wife, Marie, the plaintiffs, and a nephew, Robert L. Fireoved, as directors of the corporation. Subsequently, the directors elected Eugene Fireoved as President and Treasurer and Marie Fireoved as Secretary... On December 31, 1948, in consideration for $100 cash, the corporation issued Eugene Fireoved 100 shares of common stock; for $500 cash, it issued him five shares of preferred stock; and in payment for automotive equipment and furniture and fixtures, valued at $6,000, it issued him an additional 60 shares of preferred stock.

In 1954, when Mr. Fireoved learned that his nephew, Robert, was planning to leave the business, he began discussions with Karl Edelmayer and Kenneth Craver concerning the possibility of combining his business with their partnership, Girard Business Forms... Messrs. Fireoved, Edelmayer and Craver agreed that voting control of the new enterprise should be divided equally among the three of them. Because Mr. Fireoved's contribution to capital would be approximately $60,000 whereas the partnership could contribute only $30,000, it was decided that preferred stock should be issued to Mr. Fireoved to compensate for the disparity. In furtherance of this plan, ... the following corporate changes were accomplished: The name of the company was changed to Girard Business Forms; the authorized common stock was increased from 100 to 300 shares and the authorized preferred stock was increased to 1000 shares; Mr. Fireoved exchanged his 100 shares of common and 65 shares of preferred stock for equal amounts of the new stock; an agreement of purchase was authorized by which the company would buy all the assets of the Edelmayer–Craver partnership in return for 200 shares of common and 298 shares of preferred stock; and Mr. Fireoved was issued 535 shares of the new preferred stock as a dividend[6] on his 100 shares of common stock, thereby bringing his total holding of preferred stock to 600 shares to indicate his $60,000 capital contribution compared to the $29,800 contributed by the former partnership.

As the business progressed, Mr. Edelmayer demanded more control of the company. In response, Mr. Fireoved and Mr. Craver each sold 24 shares of common stock in the corporation to him on February 28, 1958.

On April 30, 1959, the company redeemed 451 of Mr. Fireoved's 600 shares of preferred stock at $105 per share, resulting in net proceeds to him of $47,355.[7] The gain from this transaction was reported by Mr. Fireoved . . . as a long term capital gain. Subsequently, the Commissioner . . . assessed a deficiency against the Fireoveds of $15,337.13 based on the Commissioner's view that the proceeds from the redemption of the 451 shares of preferred stock should have been reported as ordinary income and the tax paid at that rate based on section 306. . .

II. BACKGROUND OF SECTION 306

Because we are the first court of appeals asked to decide questions of law pursuant to section 306, it is appropriate that we first examine the circumstances that led to the inclusion in 1954 of this section in the Code. . .

A temporarily successful plan for converting ordinary income to long term capital gain is described by the facts of Chamberlin v. C.I.R., 207 F.2d 462 (6th Cir. 1953). There a close corporation had assets of $2.5 million, approximately half of which were in the form of cash and government securities. To have distributed the cash not required in the operation of the business to the shareholders as a dividend would have subjected them to taxation at ordinary income rates. The corporation therefore amended its charter to authorize 8,020 shares of preferred stock to be issued to the shareholders as a dividend on their common stock. The accounts of the corporation were adjusted by transferring $802,000 from earned surplus to the capital account. While these corporate changes were taking place, negotiations occurred between the shareholders and two insurance companies for the purchase of the newly issued preferred stock. In addition, the corporation constructed a timetable for retirement of the preferred stock, which proved satisfactory to the purchasing companies. When the transaction was completed, the selling shareholders reported the gain they realized from the sale of the preferred stock to the insurance companies as a long-term gain from the disposition of a capital asset. The Commissioner contended that the gain should have been reported as ordinary income and accordingly assessed a deficiency against the selling shareholders. The "Tax Court agreed with the Commissioner. . . [T]he Sixth Circuit reversed, . . . thus

---

[6] At the time Mr. Fireoved received this stock dividend, the company had accumulated earnings and profits of $52,993.06.

[7] In 1959, the company had accumulated earnings and profits of $48,235.

giving the approval of a federal court to what has been termed 'a preferred stock bail-out.'"

The legislative reaction to the *Chamberlin* decision was almost immediate, resulting in the addition of section 306 to the 1954 Code, in order to prevent shareholders from obtaining the tax advantage of such bail-outs when such shareholders retain their ownership interests in the company.

. . . For tax purposes, Congress created a new type of stock known as section 306 stock. When a corporation having accumulated or retained earnings and profits issues a stock dividend which is not otherwise subject to taxation at the time of issuance (other than common on common), the stock received is section 306 stock. The effect of owning such stock is that on its redemption, if the corporation has sufficient retained earnings at that time, the gain* is taxed at ordinary income rates while any loss resulting may not be recognized for federal tax purposes. Section 306(b) sets forth several exceptions to the general rule which serve to remove the section 306 taint from stock disposed of under those circumstances.

Based on the history of section 306 and its plain meaning evidenced by the provisions, it is not disputed that the 535 shares of preferred stock issued to Mr. Fireoved as a stock dividend in 1954 were section 306 stock. Additionally, it is clear that in 1959, when the company redeemed 451 shares of Mr. Fireoved's preferred stock, the general provisions of section 306—aside from the exceptions—would require that any amount realized by Mr. Fireoved be taxed at ordinary income rates rather than long-term capital gain rates, because the company had earnings at that time of $48,235—more than the $47,355 required to redeem the stock at $105 per share.

Thus, the questions to be decided on this appeal are (1) whether certain of the exceptions to section 306 apply to permit the Fireoveds' reporting their gain as a long term capital gain, and (2) whether 65 of the 451 shares redeemed are not section 306 stock because of the first in-first out rule of Treasury Regulation section 1.1012–1(c).

III. WAS THE DISTRIBUTION OF THE STOCK DIVIDEND "IN PURSUANCE OF A PLAN HAVING AS ONE OF ITS PRINCIPAL PURPOSES AVOIDANCE OF FEDERAL INCOME TAX?"

Mr. Fireoved asserts that the entire transaction should fall within the exception established by section 306(b)(4)(A). . .

As a threshold point on this issue, the Government maintains that because Mr. Fireoved never attempted to obtain a ruling from the "Secretary or his delegate" the redemption should be covered by section 306(a), and the district court should not have reached the question whether the exception applied to Mr. Fireoved. Mr. Fireoved urges that the district court had the power to consider the matter de novo, even without a request by the

---

* Does the court mean "gain" or "proceeds"?—ED.

taxpayer to the Secretary or his delegate. Because the ultimate result we reach would not be altered by whichever of these two courses we choose, we do not resolve this potentially complex procedural problem.

The district court, based on the assumption that it had the power to decide the question, found that although one of the purposes involved in the issuance of the preferred stock dividend may have been business related, another principal purpose was the avoidance of Federal income tax.

Mr. Fireoved's analysis of the facts presented in the stipulations would reach the conclusion that the *sole* purpose of the stock dividend was business related. He relies heavily on that portion of the stipulation which describes why the decision was made to combine his business with the Edelmayer–Craver partnership: "The partnership could provide the additional manpower which the expected departure of Robert L. Fireoved from the Corporation would require. Additionally, the partnership needed additional working capital which the Corporation had and could provide." Based primarily on the latter sentence, Mr. Fireoved asserts that the district court had no choice but to find that the transition was business related and that it therefore had no avoidance incentive.

In making this argument, however, Mr. Fireoved overlooks the plain import of the language of section 306(b)(4). Whether the section requires the decision to be made by the Secretary or the district court, it is clear that "one of [the] principal purposes" of the stock dividend was for "the avoidance of Federal income tax." The stipulation demonstrates no more than that the reorganized company required more capital than could be supplied by the partnership alone. The stipulation is completely in harmony with the following fact situation: After the partnership was combined with the corporation, the business required the $30,000 contributed by the partnership and all of the $60,000 Mr. Fireoved had in the corporation. Mr. Fireoved decided to take the stock dividend rather than to distribute the cash to himself as a dividend, and then to make a loan to the corporation of the necessary money because if he took the cash, he would subject himself to taxation at ordinary income rates. Therefore "one of the principal purposes" of the stock dividend would be for "the avoidance of Federal income tax."

In a situation such as the one presented in this case, where the facts necessary to determine the motives for the issuance of a stock dividend are peculiarly within the control of the taxpayer, it is reasonable to require the taxpayer to come forward with the facts that would relieve him of his liability. Here the stipulation was equivocal in determining the purpose of the dividend and is quite compatible with the thought that "one of the principal purposes" was motivated by "tax avoidance." We hold then that the district court did not err in refusing to apply the exception created by section 306(b)(4)(A).[11]

---

[11] It is important to note that apparently both Mr. Fireoved, in prosecuting this action for a refund, and the Government, in its defense, assumed that if the distribution and redemption of the preferred stock were not controlled by § 306(a), the gain would be subject to taxation as a long term capital gain. This is not necessarily the case at all. Whether or not § 306 governs

IV. DID THE PRIOR SALE BY MR. FIREOVED OF 24% OF HIS UNDERLYING COMMON STOCK IMMUNIZE SUCH PORTION OF THE SECTION 306 STOCK HE REDEEMED IN 1959?

. . . The stipulations indicate that, "On February 28, 1958, Fireoved and Craver each sold 24 shares of common stock in the corporation to Edelmayer," and that appropriate stock certificates were issued. From this fact, Mr. Fireoved reasons that his sale of 24 of his 100 shares of common stock was undertaken solely for the business purpose of satisfying Mr. Edelmayer's desire for more control of the corporation, and therefore he should be given the benefit of section 306(b)(4)(B). In addition, Mr. Fireoved contends that the disposition of his section 306 stock was related to a business purpose because he used part of the proceeds to pay off a $20,000 loan that the company had made to him.

Mr. Fireoved has the same burden here of showing a lack of a tax avoidance purpose that he had in section 111 supra. It is clear from the limited facts set forth in the stipulations that he has not established that the disposition of 24% of the 535 shares of the section 306 preferred stock he owned "was not in pursuance of a plan having as one of its principal purposes the avoidance of federal income tax."[12] More important, however, is that an examination of the relevant legislative history indicates that Congress did not intend to give capital gains treatment to a portion of the preferred stock redeemed on the facts presented here.

It is apparent from the reaction evinced by Congress to the *Chamberlin* case, supra, that by enacting section 306 Congress was particularly concerned with the tax advantages available to persons who controlled corporations and who could, without sacrificing their control, convert ordinary income to long-term capital gains by the device of the preferred stock bail-out. The illustration given in the Senate Report which accompanied section 306(b)(4)(B) is helpful in determining the sort of transactions meant to be exempted by section 306(a):

> Thus if a shareholder received a distribution of 100 shares of section 306 stock on his holdings of 100 shares of voting common stock in a corporation and sells his voting common stock before he disposes of

---

the transaction, it nonetheless involves a redemption of stock by a corporation to which § 302 could apply. Under the tests set out in § 302(b)—the relevant one of which appears to be § 302(b)(1)—Mr. Fireoved, who had the burden of proof, may well have been unable to show that the redemption was not "essentially equivalent to a dividend." ... We hold, however, that it is now too late for the Government to raise this issue.

[12] Consistent with Mr. Fireoved's sale of 24 shares of common stock in 1958 could have been his knowledge that one year later he would be selling his section 306 stock and a desire on his part to avoid taxation at ordinary income rates. As noted later in the opinion, the sale of just 24 shares was enough so that he retained effective control—in the form of veto power—over the corporation. Moreover, the fact that Mr. Fireoved needed $20,000 of the proceeds to pay off a loan to the corporation would not meet his burden. The proceeds of the redemption totaled $47,355. Thus, although $20,000 of the redemption may not have been to avoid taxes, we can ascribe no purpose other than tax avoidance to the receipt of the additional $27,355. Therefore, since one of the principal purposes of the redemption of 451 shares of preferred stock was "the avoidance of Federal income tax," Mr. Fireoved may not take advantage of § 306(b)(4)(B) for any part of the redemption.

his section 306 stock, the subsequent disposition of his section 306 stock would not ordinarily be considered a tax avoidance disposition *since he has previously parted with the stock which allows him to participate in the ownership of the business.* However, variations of the above example may give rise to tax avoidance possibilities which are not within the exception of subparagraph (B). Thus if a corporation has only one class of common stock outstanding and it issues stock under circumstances that characterize it as section 306 stock, a subsequent issue of a different Class of common having greater voting rights than the original common will not permit a simultaneous disposition of the section 306 stock together with the original common to escape the rules of subsection (a) of section 306. [S. Rep. No. 1622, 83d Cong., 2d Sess., 1954 U.S.C.C.A. News, pp. 4621, 4881 (emphasis added).]

Thus, it is reasonable to assume that Congress realized the general lack of a tax avoidance purpose when a person sells *all* of his control in a corporation and then either simultaneously or subsequently disposes of his section 306 stock. However, when *only* a *portion* of the underlying common stock is sold, and the taxpayer retains essentially all the control he had previously, it would be unrealistic to conclude that Congress meant to give that taxpayer the advantage of section 306(b)(4)(B) when he ultimately sells his section 306 stock. Cf. United States v. Davis, 397 U.S. 301 . . . (1970).

Shortly after Mr. Fireoved's corporation had been combined with the Edelmayer–Craver partnership, significant changes to the by-laws were made. The by-laws provided that corporate action could be taken only with the unanimous consent of all the directors. In addition, the by-laws provided that they could be amended either by a vote of 76% of the outstanding common shares or a unanimous vote of the directors. When the businesses were combined in late 1954, each of the directors held $1/3$ of the voting stock, thereby necessitating a unanimous vote for amendment to the by-laws. After Messrs. Fireoved and Craver each sold 24 shares of common stock to Mr. Edelmayer, Mr. Fireoved held $25^1/3\%$ of the common (voting) stock, Mr. Craver $25^1/3\%$ and Mr. Edelmayer $49^1/3\%$. It is crucial to note that the by-laws provided for a unanimous vote for corporate action, and after the common stock transfer, the bylaws were capable of amendment only by a unanimous vote because no two shareholders could vote more than $74^2/3\%$ of the common stock and 76% of the common stock was necessary for amendment. Thus, although Mr. Fireoved did sell a portion of his voting stock prior to his disposition of the section 306 stock, he retained as much control in the corporation following the sale of his common stock as he had prior to the sale. Under these circumstances it is not consonant with the history of the legislation to conclude that Congress intended such a sale of underlying common stock to exempt the proceeds of the disposition of section 306 stock from treatment as ordinary income. Accordingly, the district court erred when it held that any of the preferred shares Mr. Fireoved redeemed were not subject to section 306(a) by virtue of section 306(b)(4)(B).

V. DOES THE RULE OF FIRST IN–FIRST OUT MEAN THAT 65 OF THE 451 REDEEMED SHARES WERE THOSE WHICH MR. FIREOVED ACQUIRED WHEN HE INCORPORATED HIS BUSINESS IN 1948 AND THUS SHOULD NOT BE TREATED AS SECTION 306 STOCK?

. . . Both the district court and Mr. Fireoved reason that the 65 preferred shares he received in 1948 were the first shares owned by him. In 1954, when the corporation was recapitalized, Mr. Fireoved surrendered his certificate for 65 shares, received a 535 share stock dividend and was issued a certificate representing 600 shares of preferred stock. When he disposed of 451 shares in 1959, it was impossible to identify which shares of the 600 share certificate were being sold. By applying the convenient tool of section 1.10 12–1(c), one might conclude that the 65 original shares were sold first because they were received first.

Superficially, this analysis appears to be correct. However, it overlooks the existence of Section 1223(5) of the Code and the regulations issued pursuant thereto. This section governs the transaction in question because section 307 required Mr. Fireoved to allocate his investment in the underlying common stock between the stock and the preferred stock issued as a dividend. Section 1223(5) is then clear in that it will apply to all situations in which an allocation of basis has occurred pursuant to section 307. These provisions broadly state that the holding period for stock received as a stock dividend is equal to the period for which the underlying stock was held. Applying this test we discover that the preferred stock dividend of 535 shares was issued with respect to the original 100 shares of common received by Mr. Fireoved. Therefore, the holding period for the 535 shares dividend relates back to the date on which the underlying common was issued. Coincidentally, the original 65 shares of preferred stock were issued on the same date as the common. Because the constructive date of issuance for all of the 600 shares of preferred stock owned by Mr. Fireoved is identical, neither the 65 shares nor the 535 shares are first in, but rather are in at the same time.

Since it is impossible adequately to identify which shares were sold when Mr. Fireoved redeemed 451 shares of preferred stock, we hold that a pro rata portion of the 65 shares were redeemed in 1959. In other words, the percentage of the 600 shares of preferred which were not section 306 stock may be represented by the fraction 65/600. That percentage of the 451 shares redeemed in 1959, therefore, would not be section 306 stock.

NOTES

1. The fact that one of the principal purposes of the issuance of preferred stock was to prevent the adverse impact of the issuance of common stock on a corporation's ability to raise capital from the public does not establish that *none* of the principal purposes was to avoid income tax; if the adverse impact could have been avoided by issuing bonds instead of stock, one of the principal purposes was avoidance of income tax. See Rev. Rul. 80–33, 1980–1 C.B. 6. See also Rev. Rul. 77–455, 1977–2 C.B. 93 (where shareholder's § 306 stock was redeemed in part and sold in part in conjunction with a sale and redemption of

the remainder of his interest in the corporation in order to give his son voting control with a smaller investment than would otherwise be necessary, the § 306(b)(4)(B) exception protected the shareholder from ordinary income treatment on the disposition); Rev. Rul. 75–247, 1975–1 C.B. 104 (fact that seller of § 306 stock simultaneously sold a pro rata portion of common stock in the same corporation did not by itself establish absence of tax avoidance purpose).

2. In Rev. Rul. 89–63, 1989–1 C.B. 90, the Service reconsidered three prior rulings in which preferred stock issued by widely held corporations as part of a reorganization under § 368(a)(1)(A) or (C) was not subject to § 306(a) because of the exception in § 306(b)(4). The Service nevertheless ruled that application of the § 306(b)(4) exception to § 306(a) treatment could not be made solely because the issuing corporation was widely held.

3. The Internal Revenue Service will not ordinarily issue an advance ruling on the question whether the distribution, disposition, or redemption of § 306 stock in a *closely held* corporation is in pursuance of a tax avoidance plan within the meaning of § 306(b)(4). Rev. Proc. 2012–3, 2012–1 I.R.B. 113.

4. Although § 306 specifically excludes common stock from its regime, "common stock" is undefined. In Rev. Rul. 81–91, 1981–1 C.B. 123, the Service ruled that in a recapitalization under § 368(a)(1)(E) in which common stock was surrendered for two classes of voting stock (A and B), the class B stock was "common stock" because holders participated in the corporation's growth and thus any disposition of class B stock would result in some loss of voting control and interest in corporate growth. Thus, the class B stock was not § 306 by virtue of § 306(c)(1)(B).

5. See Rev. Rul. 79–287, 1979–2 C.B. 130, in which the Service ruled that preferred stock received in exchange for identical stock in an "F" reorganization (a mere change of identity, form, or place of incorporation) was not § 306 stock. See also Rev. Rul. 82–118, 1982–1 C.B. 56; Rev. Rul. 88-100, 1988-2 C.B. 46. But cf. Rev. Rul. 82–191, 1982–2 C.B. 78.

6. Since the passage of TEFRA in 1982, stock (other than common) issued in certain § 351 transactions constitutes § 306 stock. See § 306(c)(3). The impact of this is limited to situations in which cash received in lieu of preferred stock would have been a taxable dividend (e.g., where § 304 might apply).

7. The combined effect of §§ 170(e) and 306 needs to be rethought following the 2003 Tax Act. Historically § 170(e) has allowed full fair market value ("FMV") deductions for charitable contributions only where the gain on the contributed asset would have been taxed as "long term capital gain" had it been disposed of in a taxable event. This rule effectively excluded § 306 stock from full FMV charitable contribution deductions. Section 170(e)(1)(A). After 2003, however, gain on § 306 stock is essentially taxed at the same rate as long term capital gain because § 306 proceeds are now taxed at the same rate as a "dividend" (instead of "ordinary income") and dividends under § 1(h) are taxed like "net gain", i.e. at the long term capital gain rate. The problem arises from the specific language in the two statutes—§ 170 will not allow full deductions unless the gain would be "long term capital gain" but § 1(h) uses the term "net gain" to describe dividend taxation. The two rates should be the same, but the words are not.

2. THE § 305(B) APPROACH: ORDINARY INCOME ON RECEIPT OF STOCK

Holden, Unraveling the Mysteries of Section 305*

36 N.Y.U. Inst. Fed. Taxn. 781 (1978).

INTRODUCTION

Mysteries do indeed abound in Section 305, and they sorely need unraveling. Unfortunately, it will take more than this article to accomplish that task, for many of the mysteries are inherent in the statutory language rather than the underlying subject matter, and they will be with us until that language is changed.

The current version of Section 305 is a result of Congress' impatience in 1969 with its 1954 resolution of the taxation of stock distributions. However, instead of simply returning to the pre–1954 law, it produced a new legislative wonder. New Section 305 is vastly more complex than was its predecessor, and needlessly so. Despite this complexity, it does little more than to restore the old "shift in proportionate interest" test, which governed before 1954. Unfortunately, one can reach that conclusion only after substantial analysis and the mastery of some very difficult language.

Not only was Section 305 made significantly more complex in 1969, but it was also extended to cover a variety of transactions which do not actually involve stock distributions but which do produce some of the same effects upon corporate ownership. . .

AN HISTORICAL PERSPECTIVE ON SECTION 305

[An extensive survey of the legislative and judicial treatment of stock dividends is omitted.]

DEVELOPMENT OF THE SHIFT–IN–PROPORTIONATE INTEREST TEST

Congress had, in the 1936 Act, tossed the ball back to the courts, and it remained there until 1954. During the period from 1936 to 1954, they responded, fashioning under the teaching of Eisner v. Macomber a "proportionate interest" test to distinguish taxable from nontaxable stock distributions. Those distributions which did not result in a shift in proportionate interest among shareholders were nontaxable; those which resulted in such a shift were taxable.

Though there were obvious and significant difficulties in applying the rule, given the fact that infinite varieties of stock can be conceived by corporate planners, the rule itself could be simply stated and its fundamental concept was easy enough to grasp. The courts were, during this period, evolving a workable body of law. Their task could have been greatly facili-

---

tated had the Treasury Department issued a comprehensive set of Regulations illustrating and explaining the shift-in-proprietary interest test.

THE 1954 REVISION—SECTION 305

Notwithstanding this relatively satisfactory state of affairs, the opportunity to rewrite the law relating to stock distributions as a part of the 1954 overhaul of the tax laws proved too appealing for the Congress to resist. . .

. . . Under the 1954 version of Section 305, the general rule was established that stock distributions were nontaxable. There were only two exceptions. First, distributions under which a shareholder could choose to receive either stock or property were to remain, as under the prior law, taxable. Second, if a stock distribution was made to satisfy dividends on preferred stock for the current or prior taxable year, the distribution was to be taxable. . .

WEAKNESS OF THE 1954 LEGISLATION

Simplicity was both the purpose and the weakness of the 1954 legislation. The rules were easy to enunciate, but they effectively made nontaxable numerous forms of stock distribution by which the proportionate interest among shareholders could be shifted significantly. In these transactions, some kind of compensating payment, in a form other than stock, was generally made to shareholders whose interests were diminished. For example, in the so-called "Citizens Utilities"[16] type transaction, shareholders were offered a choice between ownership of two classes of stock, one paying cash dividends and one paying stock dividends. Shareholders who chose stock dividends could augment their interests in the corporation on a tax-free basis. Those who chose cash experienced a diminution of proprietary interest and were compensated for that by the receipt of cash. The effect was the same as if all shareholders had received a cash dividend and some had reinvested the cash by purchasing more stock. . .

THE TAX REFORM ACT OF 1969

INTRODUCTORY COMMENT

. . . Congress . . . conformed to the recent trend in tax legislation by enacting a [very] complex new [provision]. Not only is revised Section 305 complex, but it is also replete with redundancy and inconsistency. Moreover, despite all of this, it seems to do little more than to restore the old proportionate interest test. . .

AN OVERVIEW OF AMENDED SECTION 305

Section 305, as amended in 1969, is divided into five subsections, which perform the following functions:

---

[16] So called because it originated with Citizens Utilities Company, Stamford, Connecticut. See Journal of Taxation, May 1956, p. 312, September 1956, p. 178.

Subsection	*Function*
(a)	States the general rule of nontaxability of stock distributions
(b)	States five exceptions to the general rule, i.e., five situations in which a stock distribution is taxable
(c)	Authorizes the Treasury to classify certain nondistribution transactions as distributions (i.e., "deemed distributions")
(d)	Defines the terms "stock" and "shareholder"
(e)	Provides cross references

The general rule of nontaxability expressed in subsection (a) is [that] stock dividends are nontaxable unless one of the exceptions stated in subsection (b) applies. The five exceptions of new subsection (b), as is developed more fully below, effectively reintroduce the pre-1954 proportionate interest test and broaden the 1954 rule taxing distributions made in discharge of preferred dividends. Subsection (c) represents an innovation in the 1969 version, in that it creates a "deemed distribution" concept and thus expands significantly the scope of section 305. Subsection (d) carries forward the rule that the term "stock" includes "stock rights" and the rule (at least implicit in prior law) that the term "shareholder" includes a holder of rights. It adds to the prior law by stating that the term "holder" includes a holder of convertible securities.

Any discussion of Section 305 must focus primarily on Section 305(b), containing the five exceptions to the general rule of nontaxability, and on Section 305(c), relating to deemed distributions. . .

SECTION 305(C)—DEEMED DISTRIBUTIONS

TRANSACTIONS COVERED

Section 305(c) identifies five kinds of transactions which, though they do not actually involve a distribution of stock to shareholders, may have the same effect and [will, therefore,] be considered as if they did so. Specifically, these transactions include:

     (1) a change in conversion ratio

     (2) a change in redemption price

     (3) a difference between redemption price and issue price

     (4) a redemption having dividend consequences, and

     (5) any transaction (including a recapitalization) having a similar effect on the interest of any shareholder.

The Secretary is authorized by Section 305(c) to issue Regulations under which any of the above may be deemed to involve a distribution of stock with respect to any shareholder whose proportionate interest in the corporation is increased by the transaction. . . A transaction which is so classified as a deemed distribution must then be tested for tax consequences under Section 305(b).

CHANGE IN CONVERSION RATIO

A change in conversion ratio of convertible stock or debt affects the holder's potential equity position vis-à-vis other shareholders and has obvious, though deferred, proportionate interest consequences. . . Under Section 305(c), the holder may be deemed to have received a distribution of stock, and that deemed distribution may or may not be taxable under the substantive rules of Section 305(b), discussed below. The Committee Reports on Section 305 illustrate the effect of both downward adjustments of conversion ratio (e.g., common stock pays no dividends; convertible preferred pays a cash dividend and the conversion ratio is annually adjusted downward to reflect the dividend; as a result, the interest of common shareholders is increased) and upward adjustments of conversion ratio (common stock pays dividends; convertible preferred does not, but there is a consequent annual increase in the conversion ratio; the interest of the preferred shareholders is thus increased)[21] In the first instance, a distribution would be deemed made to the common shareholders; in the second, it would be deemed made to the preferred shareholders. The taxable character of the deemed distribution would be determined under Section 305(b).

If the conversion ratio of convertible preferred stock or debt is increased or decreased under a bona fide and reasonable adjustment formula in order to prevent dilution resulting from such factors as nontaxable stock distributions to common shareholders or sales of common stock above or below the conversion price, such adjustments will not be deemed to result in a distribution of stock.[22] If, however, an adjustment to the conversion ratio of stock or debt is made to compensate for a taxable dividend distribution on common stock, the adjustment will be deemed to be a distribution of stock.[23] . . .

REDEMPTION HAVING DIVIDEND CONSEQUENCES

Section 305(c) also provides that a redemption which is taxed as a dividend may be treated as resulting in a distribution to any shareholder whose proportionate interest is increased by the transaction. Thus, if a redemption of stock from Shareholder A, which is taxable to A as a dividend, causes the proportionate interest of Shareholder B in the corporation to increase, Shareholder B may be deemed to have received a distribution of stock, and the consequences of that deemed distribution must be tested under Section 305(b).

The Committee reports indicate that the target of this provision was the "periodic redemption plan," under which a small amount of stock is

---

[21] H. Rep. No. 91–413, 91st Cong. 1st Sess. 114 (1969); S. Rep. No. 522, 91st Cong. 1st Sess. 153–54 (1969)....

[22] Reg. § 1.305–7(b).

[23] Rev. Rul. 75–513 (C.B. 1975–2, 113), applies this rule to make taxable an adjustment to the conversion ratio of convertible debentures.

from time to time redeemed from some shareholders, with the result that the interests of other shareholders are increased.[25] . . .

In keeping with the Committee Reports, the Regulations state that this rule does not apply in the case of an isolated redemption of stock.[26] . . .

The reason for the solicitude extended to "isolated" dividend-type redemptions is not clear. If a redemption is essentially equivalent to a dividend and results in a reduction of outstanding stock (with a consequent shift in proportionate interest), there is no reason to refrain from classifying the increase in interest to some shareholders as a distribution merely because the transaction is isolated. An actual stock distribution to some shareholders, coupled with a cash distribution to others, cannot escape taxation under Section 305(b)(2) on the grounds of isolation. It is not evident why the redemption variation of the same transaction should enjoy a protected status.

Change in Redemption Price

It is not altogether clear from the statute (which refers merely to a "change in redemption price"), the Committee Reports, or the Regulations, what is intended by this provision.

Presumably, the objective is to insure that an increase in the redemption price of preferred stock, for example, to reflect dividends paid to common shareholders, will be deemed to be a distribution of additional preferred stock, with the result that the deemed distribution will be taxed under Section 305(b)(4), which makes taxable any distribution of stock or preferred stock.

It seems unlikely that this provision will play a major role under Section 305.

Difference Between Redemption Price and Issue Price

Under Section 305(c), a difference between issue price and redemption price may result in a deemed distribution. Although the statute is again not explicit, it seems probable that only preferred stock, as distinguished from debt instruments, is comprehended by this provision. Original issue discount on debt instruments is generally the subject of Section 1232, and it is doubtful that Section 305(c) was intended to interfere with this established statutory pattern. . . [T]he Regulations[27] . . . refer only to preferred stock in discussing the provision.

---

[25] House Report, p. 114; Senate Report, p. 153.

[26] Reg. § 1.305–3(e), examples (10), (11). See also, Reg. § 1.305–3(b)(3), which applies a similar rule for purposes of § 305(b)(2). In Rev. Rul. 77–19, (C.B. 1977–1, 83), the Service ruled that a redemption in which 80 percent of the shareholders, representing holders of less than 200 shares, were eliminated, did not result in a deemed distribution under § 305(c).

[27] Reg. § 1.305–7(a).

Not every spread between issue price and redemption price results in a deemed distribution. The Regulations,[28] in keeping with the Committee Reports,[29] provide that only so much of the difference as exceeds a reasonable call premium will be deemed a distribution. For this purpose, a redemption premium which does not exceed ten percent of the issue price on stock which is not redeemable for five years will be considered reasonable.[30] . . .

The three examples in the Regulations which illustrate the application of this provision establish the principle that the deemed distribution consists of additional preferred stock distributed on the existing preferred stock having the excessive call premium, and hence the distribution is taxable under Section 305(b)(4), relating to distributions of stock on preferred stock.

OTHER TRANSACTIONS (INCLUDING RECAPITALIZATIONS)

The final transaction category which is described as a deemed distribution under Section 305(c) is a catchall, consisting of "any transaction (including a recapitalization) having a similar effect on the interest of any shareholder." The Regulations do not seek to implement the "any transaction" language by describing transactions other than those expressly named in the statute, but this language will doubtless justify the Service and the courts in bringing within Section 305(c) other abusive transactions which do not involve a classical stock distribution.

The Regulations do implement the statutory reference to "recapitalizations" by providing that a deemed distribution will result from any recapitalization

(1) if it is pursuant to a plan to periodically increase a shareholder's proportionate interest, or

(2) if preferred stock with dividends in arrears is exchanged for other stock having either a value or a liquidation preference in excess of the issue price of the preferred stock surrendered.[34]

THE FIVE EXCEPTIONS OF SECTION 305(b)

Section 305(b) provides that five types of stock distribution do not fall within the general rule of Section 305(a) and are thus taxable. These are referred to below . . . as:

(1) disproportionate distribution—Section 305(b)(2)

(2) distribution of common and preferred—Section 305(b)(3)

(3) distribution of convertible preferred—Section 305(b)(5)

---

[28] Reg. § 1.305–5(b).

[29] Senate Report, p. 154.

[30] Reg. § 1.305–5(b)(2).

[34] Reg. § 1.305–7(c).

(4) distribution with election as to medium of payment—Section 305(b)(1)

(5) distribution made on preferred stock—Section 305(b)(4)

. . . Taken together, these provisions evidence an intent (1) to tax stock distributions which do effect a shift of proportionate interest, and (2) to tax all stock distributions which are made on preferred stock. . .

DISPROPORTIONATE DISTRIBUTION—305(B)(2)

Three elements are required for taxation of a distribution under Section 305(b)(2):

(1) a distribution of stock (which may be actual or deemed)

(2) resulting in the receipt of property by some shareholders, and

(3) resulting in an increase in the proportionate interest of other shareholders.

This is essentially a codification of the old 1936 proportionate interest test. . . The principal difference between Section 305(b)(2) and the 1936 test is the express requirement in the former that some shareholders receive property. This is referred to below as the "companion distribution" requirement.

SECTION 305(b)(2)—THE REQUIREMENT FOR A COMPANION DISTRIBUTION

The companion distribution requirement is largely superfluous. . . [E]conomic considerations dictate that Shareholder A will not permit the interest of Shareholder B to be increased unless Share holder A is somehow compensated for the consequent reduction in his own interest. . . If there is no compensating payment to the shareholders whose interest is diminished, the benefit conferred on the other shareholders probably represents compensation of some kind, or, if the shareholders do not deal at arm's length, a gift. . . For these reasons, it is not clear why it was thought necessary to expressly require a companion distribution as a condition for taxable status under Section 305(b)(2). Its inclusion does not appreciably narrow the statute—it simply makes it more complex.

The companion distribution requirement probably resulted from Treasury's preoccupation in 1969 with the so-called "Citizen's Utilities" type of transaction, where cash dividends are paid on one class of common stock and stock dividends are paid on the other class of common. . .

As might be expected, the Regulations take a sufficiently expansive view of what constitutes a companion distribution that the requirement is almost eliminated. They state that it is not necessary that such [a companion] distribution be pursuant to a plan to distribute cash or property to some shareholders and to increase the proportionate interests of other shareholders.[38]

It is sufficient if that result in fact occurs.

This is so whether or not the stock distributions and the cash distributions are steps in an overall plan or are independent and unrelated.[39]

It is necessary, however, that the companion distribution (1) be made to a shareholder in his capacity as such, and (2) be taxable to him under Section 301 (or under other specifically identified sections).[40] The Regulations do expressly include as a companion distribution to a shareholder for purposes of Section 305(b)(2) the payment of interest to a holder of a convertible debenture.[41]

The Regulations expressly disqualify as a companion distribution a property distribution which is made (1) pursuant to an isolated redemption of stock, or (2) pursuant to an undertaking to pay [cash] in lieu of fractional shares.[42] A payment of cash in lieu of fractional shares is removed from classification as a companion distribution only if it is made to save the corporation from the trouble and expense of issuing fractional shares and not for the purpose of achieving a shift of proportionate interest. It is conclusively presumed to be for the former purpose if the cash distributed is five percent or less of the value of the stock distributed.

. . . The Regulations also provide that a property distribution will not be treated as a companion distribution under Section 305(b)(2) if it precedes or follows the stock distribution by 36 months or more, unless made pursuant to the same plan.[43]

The companion distribution requirement may also be satisfied by a transaction which is not an actual distribution but which is deemed to be one under Section 305(c). For example, if preferred stock convertible into common stock is issued with an excessive redemption price, a deemed distribution to the preferred shareholders results under Section 305(c). That deemed distribution is taxable under Section 305(b)(4) (relating to distributions on preferred stock), and thus Section 301 applies to it. If the common shareholders receive a distribution of common stock which is not paid also to the holders of convertible preferred, their interest will increase vis-à-vis the interest of the preferred shareholders. There will thus be a conjunction of (1) a distribution of stock (i.e., common stock to common shareholders), (2) resulting in an increase in proportionate interest (of the common shareholders), and (3) a companion distribution to the preferred shareholders

---

[38] Reg. § 1.305–3(b)(2).

[39] Ibid.

[40] Reg. § 1.305–3(b)(3).

[41] Reg. § 1.305–3(b)(3).

[42] Reg. §§ 1.305–3(b)(3), 1.305–3(c). See also I.R.S. private ruling No. 7738035, which applies the fractional share rule discussed in the text.

[43] Reg. § 1.305–3(b)(4).

(consisting of the deemed distribution, which is taxable under Sections 301 and 305(b)(4)). Consequently, the Regulations conclude that the distribution of common stock to common shareholders in this situation is taxable under Section 305(b)(2).[44]

This conclusion in the Regulations does illustrate the point that a deemed distribution will fulfill the companion distribution requirement, but it also illustrates the unrealistic nature of the requirement. Seldom, if ever, will it be feasible for a corporation to ignore convertible preferred shareholders in making a distribution of common stock to common shareholders. If the preferred shareholders do not themselves receive additional common stock, either directly or through adjustment of the conversion ratio, it will-be because they have been compensated in some other way. But the nature and source of their compensation is irrelevant to the question whether the common shareholders have received income—they clearly have to the extent that their proportionate interest has been increased. This increase in interest is alone sufficient to warrant taxation of the distribution, and the need to cast around for and to identify a companion distribution is an unfortunate distraction.

SECTION 305(b)(2)—THE REQUIREMENT FOR A PROPORTIONATE INTEREST

While the concept of an increase in proportionate interest is easily enunciated, it can in actuality sometimes be difficult to determine whether an increase has occurred, and the Regulations provide helpful examples[45]. . .

In determining whether an increase in interest has occurred, each class of stock is to be considered separately, and each shareholder within the class is deemed to have an increased interest if his class as a whole has an increased interest.[49] However, a shareholder cannot contend that he did not have an increased interest merely because his class did not, as a whole, have an increased interest. For example, if common stock is distributed to one of two common shareholders, the shareholder receiving the distribution clearly has an increased interest even though the common shareholders as a whole do not have an increased interest.

In determining whether an increase in proportionate interest has occurred, there is to be treated as outstanding stock (1) any rights to acquire stock, and (2) any security (i.e., debt) convertible into stock.[50] . . .

[Discussion of the treatment of convertible preferred stock is omitted.]

If a shift in proportionate interest is to be avoided in such cases, the Regulations require that the adjustment to the conversion ratio be a "full adjustment."[52] . . .

---

[44] Reg. § 1.305–3(e), example (15).

[45] Reg. § 1.305–3(e).

[49] Reg. § 1.305–3(b)(6).

[50] Reg. § 1.305–3(b)(5).

The requirement that the conversion ratio of convertible securities be adjusted effectively treats them as if they were fully converted for purposes of measuring a shift in proportionate interest. Accordingly, one would expect to find a general rule, applicable in determining whether a shift in interest has occurred, that convertible preferred is to be placed on a par with common, i.e., it should be treated as fully converted. Thus, a distribution of convertible preferred to holders of common should not result in a shift in proportionate interest regardless whether any or all of the preferred is converted.[54] The Regulations do not, however, clearly take this position and it seems to be an unanswered question.

[Summary of examples omitted. See Treas. Reg. § 1.305–3(e).]

SECTION 305(b)(2)—SUMMARY

Section 305(b)(2) is in substance a reenactment of the pre–1954 shift-in-proportionate interest test. Though it now contains the requirement for a companion distribution, that change is of little consequence because (1) economic realities generally assume that it will always be present, and (2) it is interpreted so broadly in the Regulations that it will seldom be found wanting.

DISTRIBUTION OF COMMON AND PREFERRED—SECTION 305(b)(3)

Section 305(b)(3) provides that a stock distribution is not within the general nontaxability rule of Section 305(a) if some common shareholders receive common stock while other common shareholders receive preferred stock. The Regulation's contain two examples illustrating this rule.[56]

In the first example, a corporation with two classes of common, A and B, makes a distribution of class A common stock to the holders of class A common stock, and it makes a distribution of newly issued preferred stock to the holders of class B common stock. The Regulations hold that both distributions are taxable.

In the second example, a corporation having one class of common stock distributes to common shareholders a new issue of convertible preferred having a six-month conversion period and a conversion price near the market value of the common stock. The Regulations find that early conversion by some common shareholders is probable, with the result that some common shareholders (those who convert) will, as a consequence of the distribution, hold additional common stock while others (those who do not con-

---

[52] [Reg. § 1.305.3(d)(1).]

[54] If the circumstances indicate that some of the preferred will be promptly converted, the distribution may nonetheless result in some common shareholders receiving (via conversion) common stock while others receive (and retain) preferred stock, making the transaction taxable under § 305(b)(3), discussed below. If the circumstances indicate instead that some distributees will promptly and by prearrangement sell their preferred for cash, there will be a shift in proportionate interest and the transaction would be taxable under § 305(b)(2) or § 305(b)(5), discussed below.

[56] Reg. § 1.305–4(b).

vert) will hold preferred stock. Consequently, the distribution of the preferred is within Section 305(b)(3) and results in taxable income.

Section 305(b)(3) merely states another aspect of the shift-in-proportionate-interest rule. If some common shareholders receive common stock while others receive preferred, a shift in proportionate interest occurs. If Congress, in stating the disproportionate distribution rule contained in Section 305(b)(2), had simply omitted the companion distribution requirement and had required only a shift in proportionate interest, there would have been no need for Section 305(b)(3). . .

DISTRIBUTION OF CONVERTIBLE PREFERRED—SECTION 305(b)(5)

Section 305(b)(5) makes a distribution of convertible preferred stock taxable unless it is established, to the satisfaction of the Secretary, that the distribution will not have the effect described in Section 305(b)(2), i.e., that it will not result in a shift in proportionate interest accompanied by a companion distribution.

. . . Section 305(b)(5), like Section 305(b)(3), seems to add little to the statutory framework other than complexity. By its very terms, it can apply only where the distribution will have the result described in Section 305(b)(2), leaving one to wonder exactly what the intended jurisdiction of this provision is. It may be that Section 305(b)(5) was thought to be needed because Section 305(b)(2) applies where there is a shift in interest whereas Section 305(b)(5) is phrased to permit consideration of a possible future shift in interest. If this is the jurisdiction, Section 305(b)(2) could easily have been modified to look also to the future. . .

ELECTION AS TO MEDIUM OF PAYMENT—SECTION 305(b)(1)

Section 305(b)(1) carries forward from prior law the rule that a distribution which offers the shareholder the option to choose between receiving stock or other property (including cash) is taxable. This rule has been a part of the statutory law since 1936. . . In 1954 when the shift-in-proportionate-interest test was dropped, the choice-of-medium-of-payment test took on a more significant role. In 1969, when the shift-in-proportionate-interest test returned in the form of Section 305(b)(2), the choice-of-medium-of-payment test necessarily settled again into relative obscurity.

If a stock distribution offers a shareholder the opportunity to choose instead to receive property, and if any shareholder makes that choice, all elements for taxation under Section 305(b)(2) are present, i.e., a distribution of stock, resulting in a shift in proportionate interest and a companion distribution. In this situation, there is obviously no role for Section 305(b)(1).

If the stock distribution offers the election but no shareholder avails himself of it, there is no shift in proportionate interest and no policy reason to make the distribution taxable. It is academic to argue that the mere option to take property, whether or not exercised, is enough to make the distribution taxable. First, such options probably occur only in distributions made by large, publicly held corporations—closely held corporations simply decide such issues by a consensus of shareholders before declaring any distribution. Second, in the case of a large corporation, the prospect that no shareholder will accept the property option is remote, and thus Section 305(b)(2) will virtually always apply. Under these circumstances, there is little room for Section 305(b)(1) to play a significant role.

Despite the prospect for a limited role, Section 305(b)(1) does serve as a handy vehicle for classifying as taxable certain dividend reinvestment plans[58] and distributions from regulated investment companies, which commonly offer the option to take cash or additional stock.[59] And the Service has ruled that a distribution to common shareholders of preferred stock which is immediately redeemable is taxable as offering a choice of stock or cash under Section 305(b)(1).[60] All of these, however, could have been held taxable under Section 305(b)(2). . .

DISTRIBUTION ON PREFERRED STOCK—SECTION 305(b)(4)

Section 305(b)(4) makes any distribution on preferred stock taxable. It evidences a general policy that stock distributions with respect to preferred stock should in all cases be taxable. In the words of the 1969 Senate Report, "Since preferred stock characteristically pays specified cash dividends, stock dividends on preferred stock . . . are a substitute for cash dividends and therefore . . . are taxable."[61]

Section 305(b)(4) thus serves a different policy objective from the four exceptions discussed above, which have in common the concept of disproportionate distribution. . . It thus plays a significant and independent role in the scheme of Section 305.

As with so many other areas of Section 305, however, Section 305(b)(4) is not without its legislative curiosity. Tacked onto the general rule that any distribution on preferred stock is taxable is the following exception:

> . . . other than an increase in the conversion ratio of convertible preferred stock made solely to take account of a stock dividend or stock split with respect to the stock into which such convertible stock is convertible.

This is curious for two reasons. First, an adjustment to a conversion ratio involves a deemed rather than an actual distribution of stock. Accordingly, it is surprising that this language was not included in Section 305(c) rather than in Section 305(b)(4). Second, it is difficult to understand the reason for this special rule. Where convertible preferred stock is outstand-

---

[58] Rev. Rul. 76–53, C.B. 1976–1, 87. The same result was reached in I.R.S. private ruling No. 7721048.

[59] See I.R.S. private ruling No. 7737068.

[60] Rev. Rul. 76–258, C.B. 1976–2, 95.

[61] Senate Report, p. 55.

ing, a distribution of common stock on common stock will be nontaxable to common shareholders (under Section 305(a) and 305(b)(2)) if either (1) the conversion ratio of the preferred is adjusted, or (2) common stock is distributed to the holders of the convertible preferred. However, with respect to the preferred shareholders, only the first of the two alternatives is a nontaxable transaction. A direct distribution to them of common stock would be taxable under Section 305(b)(4), as a distribution on preferred, but an adjustment to the conversion ratio, even though having identical effect (insofar as proportionate interest is concerned), would not be taxable. This statutory bias in favor of conversion ratio adjustment and against direct distribution of stock probably results from a recognition that, in the real world of finance, stock dividends on common stock are virtually always compensated, vis-à-vis convertible issues, by adjusting to the conversion ratio of the latter.

Limitation on Section 305—Adjustment of Purchase Price

By the terms of Section 305(a), the rules of that section apply only to a distribution of stock of the corporation "with respect to its stock." As interpreted by the Regulations,[62] this language precludes application of Section 305 where stock is transferred (or a conversion ratio or redemption price is changed) and the purpose is to adjust the purchase price being paid by the corporation in the acquisition of property. Thus, for example, if in an acquisition transaction, there is a contingent computation of consideration, with additional stock to be paid upon the occurrence of the contingency, the payment of that additional stock is not a distribution of stock with respect to stock—it is a payment of additional consideration pursuant to the terms of the transaction. . .

CONCLUSION

The area of stock distributions will doubtless always be mysterious. The mysteries should, however, be restricted to those arising from the subject matter itself and should not be compounded by mysteries arising from the structure of the statute. Unfortunately, the existing statute contributes more than its share of mystery.

NOTES

1. The reach of § 306 was diminished by the addition of § 305(b)(2) et seq. in 1969. Now, the issuance of a dividend in preferred stock may be taxable as a dividend distribution under § 305(b); consequently, the shares will not be § 306 stock. See § 306(c)(1)(A).

In Rev. Rul. 76–258, 1976–2 C.B. 95, the Service ruled that immediately redeemable preferred stock, distributed as a pro rata stock dividend on the common, was taxable on receipt by reason of § 305(b)(1). The preferred would appear to be § 306 stock, a point ignored in the ruling. If the redemption feature alone is sufficient to make the distribution taxable under § 305(b)(1), the role of § 306 is further narrowed. See also Rev. Rul. 83–68, 1983–1 C.B. 75 (div-

---

[62] Reg. § 1.305–1(c).

idend of redeemable common-on-common taxable under § 305(b)(1)). Is the Service right?

2. Which approach is preferable, "tainting" but deferring tax, as under § 306, or taxing up-front, when stock is issued and a disproportionate interest is created, as under § 305(b)(2)? Is it sound to have both approaches, as the Code has had since 1969? What role does § 306 (which preserves the ordinary income taxation of the § 306 stock dividend) play after the 2003 tax act when dividends are taxed at the capital gain rate? When should stock appreciation be treated as "realized"? What influence does § 1014 have on your thinking? Consider these questions as you work through the materials that follow under § 305(b)(2) et seq. Indeed, you should consider these questions in connection with virtually every issue you study in this chapter.

3. Proposed regulations under § 301 were issued "to provide...shareholders and security holders with guidance regarding the allocation and recovery of basis on distributions of property." The purpose of these regulations is "to provide a single model for stock basis recovery by a shareholder that receives a constructive or actual distribution to which section 301 applies and a single model for sale and exchange transactions to which 302(a) applies..." The Allocation of Consideration and Allocation and Recovery of Basis in Transactions Involving Corporate Stock or Securities, 74 FR 3509, (Jan. 21, 2009).

Frontier Savings Association v. Commissioner

87 T.C. 665 (1986), *aff'd sub nom.* Colonial Sav. Assn. v. Commissioner, 854 F.2d 1001
(7th Cir. 1988), *cert. denied*, 489 U.S. 1090 (1989), *acq.* 1990–2 C.B. 1.

■ SWIFT, JUDGE. . .

Following concessions, the issue remaining for decision is whether stock dividends received by petitioner in 1978 and 1979 from the Federal Home Loan Bank of Chicago are taxable to petitioner under section 305(b)(1). The resolution of this issue will affect the taxability of stock dividends received by the other 496 stockholders of the Federal Home Loan Bank of Chicago which also received stock dividends in 1978 and 1979.

Petitioner, Frontier Savings Association ("Frontier Savings"), is a mutual savings and loan association which was organized on February 19, 1919. It operates as a mutual savings association pursuant to Wisconsin law.

Frontier Savings has been a member and stockholder of the Federal Home Loan Bank of Chicago (the "Chicago Bank") at all times since the organization of the Chicago Bank. The Chicago Bank is one of 11 district banks (12 prior to 1946) established pursuant to the Federal Home Loan Bank Act of 1932, 47 Stat. 725, 12 U.S.C. sec. 1421 et seq. The district banks were capitalized with stock subscriptions from member institutions and the U.S. Treasury. District banks operate under the supervision of the Federal Home Loan Bank Board, an administrative agency in the Executive branch of the Federal government. The Federal Home Loan Bank Board also is the chartering and regulatory authority for Federal savings and loan associations and Federal mutual savings banks.

The Federal Home Loan Bank system was designed primarily as a reserve credit facility for savings and loan associations and other home mortgage credit institutions. Savings and loan associations (such as Frontier Savings) and mutual savings banks that are members or stockholders in the district banks (hereinafter referred to as "members" or "member banks") are required by Federal law to maintain a certain capital stock ownership in the respective district banks of which they are members. The stock ownership requirements are determined at the end of each calendar year and are calculated with reference to each member bank's net home mortgage loans outstanding and total borrowings of each member from the district bank.

Each member bank generally must maintain a capital stock ownership interest in the district bank in an amount equal to at least one percent of the total outstanding balance of its home mortgage loans[2] and at least equal to one-twelfth[3] of total outstanding borrowings of the member bank from the district bank, as of December 31 of each year. Each share of stock in the district banks is valued by statute at its $100 par value. . .

Based upon the above year-end calculations, member banks that are required to purchase additional stock of district banks must do so by January 31 of the following year at the par value of $100 per share. Member banks that own stock in district banks in excess of the required number of shares ("excess shares") may request that excess shares be redeemed by the district banks.

The policy of the Chicago Bank with respect to the redemption of excess shares is reflected in the minutes of a June 18, 1979, meeting of the Chicago Bank's board of directors, as follows:

> BE IT RESOLVED, that the President of the Bank or any officer designated by him may from time to time increase or decrease the amount of stock of any member in accordance with Section 6 of the Federal Home Loan Bank Act . . . and the Regulations for the Federal Home Loan Bank System; provided, however, that in exercising the Bank's discretion whether or not to grant an application by a member to decrease its stock, the President or his regulatory be guided by all applicable statutory and regulatory provisions, all policies and standards adopted from time to time by this Board, including, but not limited to, the Bank's credit standards contained in the "Policies Governing Extension of Credit" as adopted by this Board and all relevant facts and circumstances.

[After purchasing a number of shares in January 1978, Frontier Savings owned 9,066 shares of the common stock of the Chicago Bank. As shareholders they received dividends whenever they were paid. Prior to 1978 these dividends were always paid in cash. On December 29, 1978 the

---

[2] Each bank that became a member before September 8, 1961, is required to maintain a stock ownership interest of two percent of its total outstanding balance of home mortgage loans.

[3] This requirement was changed to one-twentieth in 1979....

Chicago Bank paid a dividend in stock and on December 31, 1979 paid a dividend that was half stock and half cash. In both cases the Chicago Bank paid cash in lieu of fractional shares. On December 22, 1978 the Chicago Bank sent its member banks a bulletin explaining the decision to pay a stock dividend:]

(1) Providing a stock rather than a cash dividend may enable your association to defer the payment of income taxes on the value of the stock dividend. You may wish to consult your tax adviser for the proper handling of a stock dividend.

(2) A stock dividend can be applied toward satisfying the stock investment requirement for members that experienced a growth in assets during 1978 or that will be required to purchase additional stock due to increased borrowings from the Bank.

The bulletin also explained that most member banks would be required to increase their stock holdings in the Chicago Bank due to that year's general increase in outstanding home mortgage loans. [Enclosed with the bulletin was a form that a bank could use to purchase additional shares as required by the Home Loan Bank Act. If a bank anticipated that it would have more than enough shares as of the end of the year, it could request a redemption. The Chicago Bank was not obligated to redeem any shares, but had done so as a matter of routine in the past.

[On December 29, 1978, Frontier Savings received its share of the dividend, which came to 588 shares and $51.07 in cash. Frontier Savings did not request a redemption that year. It was required to purchase additional shares, which it did in January 1979. In total, 302 of the 497 member banks had to buy additional shares that year. Sixty-nine member banks requested a redemption, and all of these requests were granted. On December 31, 1979, Frontier Savings received, as a dividend, 514 shares on Chicago Bank common stock and $51,567.87 in cash.]

The December 21, 1979, bulletin mailed to member banks concerning the 1979 dividends explained that "to help preserve the nontaxable characteristics of the stock dividend" a new procedure was being adopted for the purchase and disposition of excess shares of stock in the Chicago Bank. Instead of having member banks purchase additional shares of stock from the Chicago Bank and instead of having the Chicago Bank redeem excess shares from member banks, the new procedure called for member banks who had excess shares they wished to dispose of to sell such excess shares to other member banks who wished to buy additional shares.

Enclosed with the December 21, 1979, bulletin was a form entitled "Calculation of Bank Stock Requirement" as of December 31, 1979, and a separate form that could be used by the member banks to notify the Illinois and Wisconsin League Offices of their desire to sell excess shares of stock in the Chicago Bank to other member banks. Each member bank was required to notify the Chicago Bank of any purchases of shares of stock in the Chicago Bank so the changes in ownership of the stock could be reflected on its records. . .

[At the end of 1979, Frontier was 520 shares short of the number it needed. It purchased the necessary shares in January 1980. Of the 497 member banks, 215 needed to purchase additional shares. Thirty-one member banks sold stock to other member banks, and 10 purchased stock from other member banks. In all, 85,859 shares were exchanged among member banks. Shares were exchanged among member banks only in January. After that 64 banks requested the Chicago Bank to redeem shares. Of those, 60 banks requested redemptions of at least as many shares as they received in their 1979 dividends. All redemption requests were granted. Frontier Savings did not request any stock redemptions during this time.]

The receipt of common stock dividends generally is not taxable to stockholders. Sec. 305(a). Where, however, dividends from a corporation are payable, at the election of the stockholders, in stock or property (such as cash), the receipt of dividends will be taxable to the stockholders under the provisions of section 301. Sec. 305(b)(1). In that circumstance the receipt of stock dividends will be taxable under sections 305(b)(1) and 301 regardless of whether the stockholders exercise their election to receive the dividends in cash or other property. See Regs. § 1.305–2(a). . .

Respondent argues that by redeeming all of the common stock it was requested to redeem from its member banks in 1979 and 1980 (and apparently doing so in years before 1979), the Chicago Bank established such a policy and practice of redeeming excess stock upon request of the member banks that the member banks should be regarded as having had an "election" to receive the 1978 and 1979 stock dividends in cash. Respondent therefore argues that the stock dividends in question do not qualify for exemption from taxability under section 305(a) and should be taxable to the member banks under sections 305(b)(1) and 301. For the reasons explained below, we disagree.

The Federal statute under which the Federal Home Loan Bank Board and the district banks regulate certain activities of member banks addresses the authority of district banks to redeem common stock from its member banks and explicitly describes that authority as discretionary with each district bank. Section 1426(c) of the Federal Home Loan Bank Act as amended in 1961 provides, in relevant part, as follows:

> If the bank finds that the investment of any member in stock is greater than that required under this subsection it may, unless prohibited by said Board [i.e., the Federal Home Loan Bank Board] or by the provisions of paragraph (2) of this subsection, in its discretion and upon application of such member retire the stock of such member in excess of the amount so required. . .

[12 U.S.C. § 1426(c) (1961), as amended by Act of Sept. 8, 1961, subsec. (c), Pub. L. No. 87–210, 75 Stat. 482.]

A comparison of the language quoted above (reflecting the 1961 amendment to section 1426(c)) with the language of the predecessor statute to section 1426(c) (as originally enacted in 1932) is particularly significant. As originally enacted, section 1426(c) of the Federal Home Loan Bank Act of 1932, supra, provided as follows:

> If the board finds that the investment of any member in stock is greater than that required under this section, upon application of such member, the bank shall pay such member for each share of stock in excess of the amount so required an amount equal to the value of such stock. . .

[Federal Home Loan Bank Act of 1932, supra, § 1426(c).]

The language quoted immediately above suggests that member banks may have had the right to require district banks to redeem excess shares before the 1961 amendment to section 1426(c) (12 U.S.C.). That is suggested by use in the statutory language of the mandatory "shall." Nothing, however, in the Federal Home Loan Bank Act, in its present form, suggests that since 1961 anyone other than the district banks and the Federal Home Loan Bank Board have the authority to determine whether excess shares will be redeemed.

The policy of the Chicago Bank with respect to the redemption of excess shares, as reflected in the minutes of the June 18, 1979, meeting of its board of directors, is entirely consistent with the above statutory provisions. Also, the bulletins mailed in December of 1978 and 1979 by the Chicago Bank to its members do not communicate any contrary policy to member banks. Those bulletins acknowledged that although the issuance of stock dividends was attributable, in part, to a perceived tax planning opportunity, the distributions of stock dividends also were attributable to the recognized need for a number of member banks to acquire additional shares of common stock in the Chicago Bank. With respect to the holding of excess shares, the bulletin dated December 22, 1978, simply suggested that member banks "may want to retire" such stock. The bulletin dated December 21, 1979, stated that it was "hoped that the majority of those holding excess stock will choose to hold the stock to meet future needs and for investment purposes," but that if they chose to sell excess shares to another member bank the league offices will "make every effort to bring you in contact with a member . . . willing to purchase" the excess shares. Neither bulletin suggested that the Chicago Bank necessarily would grant any or all redemption requests.

Congress vested in the district banks and in the Federal Home Loan Bank Board discretionary authority to redeem excess shares of common stock held by member banks. Our careful examination of the record herein satisfies us that the manner in which stock dividends were paid and redeemed in 1978 and 1979 by the Chicago Bank was consistent with that grant of discretionary authority and did not vest in the member banks the unilateral right to elect or to require the Chicago Bank to redeem excess shares upon request.

Respondent concedes that the Chicago Bank did not completely abdicate its discretionary authority to redeem its stock but respondent argues that that authority was exercised so consistently in favor of redemption that member banks, as a practical matter, had the option or election to have excess shares redeemed at any time. Respondent contends that the option arose "from the circumstances of the distribution," citing section 1.305–2(a)(4), Income Tax Regs. As indicated, we have carefully examined the circumstances of the stock dividends in question and conclude that the member banks, including Frontier Savings, did not have the option or election to have the Chicago Bank redeem excess shares of common stock in the Chicago Bank.

In addition to the factors explained above, we think it significant that the stock dividends of the Chicago Bank were declared and distributed in late December of 1978 and 1979. Member banks, however, normally would not be able to determine until early in the following year (after actual distribution of the stock dividends) whether they would be able even to request a redemption of some of their common stock in the Chicago Bank. In other words, on the day of distribution of the stock dividends, member banks could not know (other than through estimates and projections) whether they would be required to retain the stock dividends they received as part of their required investments in the district bank or whether the stock dividends would qualify as excess shares, in which case redemption thereof, if requested, might occur depending on the decision of the Chicago Bank.[5]

The parties have cited only one case that involves facts at all similar to those involved herein. In Rinker v. United States, 297 F.Supp. 370, 371 (S.D. Fla. 1968), the board of directors of a corporation adopted a resolution with respect to stock dividends and the ability to redeem the stock dividends, as follows:

> RESOLVED, that a stock dividend of 5% be paid to holders of record on March 31, 1960, on or before July 15, 1960, and that said dividends may be cashed at the request of the stockholders at a value per share yet to be determined.

Among other factors, the district court emphasized the use of the word "may" in the corporate resolution and held that the stockholders did not have an election to receive cash, in lieu of the stock dividends.

We recognize that the issuance by the Chicago Bank in 1978 and 1979 of stock dividends instead of or in addition to cash dividends was motivated in part by tax considerations. We cannot conclude, however, on the facts before us that the stock dividends were a mere subterfuge for cash distributions (see Rinker v. United States, supra at 372), or that the Chicago Bank had relinquished its discretionary authority to decline to grant stock redemption requests.

---

[5] In one case a Member bank, apparently on December 29, 1978, was able to determine that its stock dividend would constitute excess shares and was able to request a redemption on the same day the stock distribution occurred.

Respondent refers to Rev. Rul. 76–258, 1976–2 C.B. 95. Revenue Rulings are, of course, not binding on this Court. . . Respondent's litigating position herein is reflected in Rev. Rul. 83–68, 1983–1 C.B. 75. For the reasons explained above and under the facts of this case, we reject the conclusion reached therein that a history or practice of redemptions by the Chicago Bank makes the stock dividends received by petitioner herein taxable under sections 305(b)(1) and 301. . .

Reviewed by the Court.

■ SIMPSON, J., dissents.

■ HAMBLEN, J., concurring. I concur in the conclusion of the majority based upon the limited factual circumstances involved. If a discretionary act of the Board of Directors of a shareholder corporation to redeem stock dividends becomes a routine matter, it might, in my opinion, develop into an "option" that arises after the distribution or a distribution pursuant to a "plan." See secs. 1.305–2(a) and 1.305–3(b), Income Tax Regs. In such a situation, it seems the redemptions might be periodic rather than isolated. The broad rules of section 305 could invoke different considerations under other circumstances.

■ STERRETT, COHEN, and JACOBS, JJ., agree with this concurring opinion.

Revenue Ruling 78–375

1978–2 C.B. 130.

Advice has been requested as to the treatment for federal income tax purposes of a "dividend reinvestment plan" where the shareholder may not only elect to receive stock of greater fair market value than the cash dividend such shareholder might have received instead, but also the shareholder may, through the plan, purchase additional stock from the corporation at a discount price which is less than the fair market value of the stock.

X is a corporation engaged in commercial banking whose shares of common stock are widely held and are regularly traded in the over-the-counter market. In order to raise additional equity capital for corporate expansion and to provide holders of X's common stock with a simple and convenient way of investing their cash dividends and optional payments in additional shares of X common stock without payment of any brokerage commission, X established an automatic dividend reinvestment plan. An independent agent will administer the plan and will receive the stock from X in the manner described below on behalf of a participating shareholder.

The plan provides the following:

(1) Shareholders can elect to have all their cash dividends (less a quarterly service charge of 3x dollars that is paid to an independent agent of the shareholder) otherwise payable on common stock registered in the name of

the shareholder automatically reinvested in shares of X common stock. The service charge is paid to the agent for administering the plan and maintaining the stock certificates for the shareholders. The shareholders who elect to participate in the plan acquire X stock at a price equal to 95 percent of the fair market value of such stock on the dividend payment date. The shareholder's option to receive a dividend in additional common stock in lieu of a cash dividend is not transferable apart from a transfer of the common shares themselves.

(2) A shareholder who participates in the dividend reinvestment aspect of the plan as described in paragraph (1) above, in addition, has the option to invest additional amounts to purchase shares of X common stock at a price equal to 95 percent of the fair market value of such stock on the dividend payment date. Optional investments by a shareholder in any quarterly dividend period must be at least 4x dollars and cannot exceed 100x dollars. The shareholder's right to invest additional amounts under the plan is not transferable apart from a transfer of the common shares themselves.

There is no requirement to participate in the plan and shareholders who do not participate receive their cash dividend payments in full. Certain shareholders have chosen not to participate; therefore, they receive their regular quarterly cash dividend. While the plan continues in effect, a participant's dividends will continue to be invested without further notice to X.

Prior to the dividend payment date no cash dividend is available to either X's participating or nonparticipating shareholders. On the dividend payment date the participant receives written notification that X is acting to effectuate the participant's option to receive stock on that date. The crediting on the plan account and notification to the participant of the exact number of shares acquired (including fractional shares) takes place shortly after the dividend payment date.

A participant may withdraw from the plan at any time, upon written request. Upon withdrawal, certificates for whole shares credited to the participant's account under the plan will be issued and a cash payment based upon the market value of the participant's fractional share interest will be paid by X, through the participant's agent, to the participant. As an alternative, the shareholder may request that all or part of the whole shares credited to its account in the plan be sold for the shareholder's account. The sale will be made by an independent agent acting on behalf of such participant and the proceeds of the sale (less any brokerage commission and transfer tax) will be forwarded to the participant. With regard to the whole shares, X will neither purchase any shares of a participant nor pay any expense attributable to the sale of such stock. Upon a request for sale of a participant's shares, a cash payment equal to the market value of the participant's fractional share interest will be paid by X, through the participant's agent, to the participant. The purpose of the payment of cash is to save X the trouble, expense, and inconvenience of issuing and transferring fractional shares and is not designed to give any particular group of shareholders an increased interest in the assets or earnings and profits of X. . .

Section 1.305–3(b)(2) of the regulations provides that in order for a distribution of stock to be considered as one of a series of distributions, it is not necessary that such distribution be pursuant to a plan to distribute cash or property to some shareholders and to increase the proportionate interests of other shareholders. It is sufficient if there is an actual or deemed distribution of stock and, as a result of such distribution, some shareholders receive cash or property and other shareholders increase their proportionate interests. This is so whether the stock distributions and the cash distributions are steps in an overall plan or are independent and unrelated. In addition, section 1.305–3(b)(3) states that there is no requirement that both elements of section 305(b)(2) . . . (receipt of cash or property by some shareholders and an increase in proportionate interests of other shareholders) occur in the form of a distribution or series of distributions as long as the result of a distribution of stock is that some shareholders' proportionate interests increase and other shareholders in fact receive cash or property.

Rev. Rul. 76–53, 1976–1 C.B. 87, concerns a situation where a widely held corporation that regularly distributes its earnings and profits adopted a plan permitting the shareholders to choose to have all of the cash dividends, otherwise payable on common shares owned by the shareholder, automatically invested to purchase additional shares of the corporation's stock. The shareholders who elect to participate under this plan acquire the company's stock at a price equal to 95 percent of the fair market value of such stock on the dividend payment date. That Revenue Ruling concludes that the distributions made by the corporation while the plan is in effect are properly treated as payable either in stock or in cash at the election of the shareholder within the meaning of section 305(b)(1) . . . and, therefore, such participating shareholders will be treated as having received a distribution to which section 301 applies by reason of section 305(b)(1).

Rev. Rul. 77–149, 1977–1 C.B. 82, concerns a situation where a corporation established a dividend reinvestment plan administered by a local bank, acting as agent for the shareholders. At a shareholder's direction the shareholder's cash dividends would be received by the participating shareholders' agent, the bank, who would then purchase the corporation's stock on the open market at 100 percent of fair market value. That Revenue Ruling held that section 301 applies directly to the cash dividends without reference to section 305(b)(1) because the distribution is payable by the corporation only in cash, and the shareholders of the corporation do not have the election of receiving their dividend distribution from the corporation in either stock or cash.

In the present case, the distributions made by X while the plan is in effect are properly treated as payable either in X's stock or in cash at the election of X's common shareholders within the meaning of section 305(b)(1). . . The acquisition of stock through the dividend reinvestment aspect of the plan is identical to the situation in Rev. Rul. 76–53. Further, the present case and Rev. Rul. 76–53 are distinguishable from Rev. Rul. 77–149 because the distribution described in Rev. Rul. 77–149 was payable by the corporation only in cash, and the shareholder, through the agent, purchased the corporation's stock on the open market.

The optional investment aspect of the present case results in an increase in the proportionate interests of the shareholders making the purchase at a 5 percent discount, and this event increases their proportionate interests in the assets or earnings and profits of X within the meaning of section 305(b)(2)(B). . . Furthermore, the fact that X shareholders who do not participate in the plan receive cash dividends constitutes a receipt of property by those shareholders within the meaning of section 305(b)(2)(A).

Accordingly, under the circumstances described above, it is held as follows:

(a) A shareholder of X who participates in the dividend reinvestment aspect of the plan will be treated as having received a distribution to which section 301 . . . applies by reason of the application of section 305(b)(1). Pursuant to section 1.305–1(b) of the regulations, the amount of the distribution to a participating shareholder (including participating corporate shareholders) will be the fair market value of the X stock received on the date of the distribution (sections 1.301–1(b) and (d)), plus, pursuant to section 301, 3x dollars, the service charge subtracted from the amount of the shareholder's distribution.

(b) The basis of the shares credited to the account of a participating shareholder pursuant to the dividend reinvestment aspect of the plan will equal the amount of the dividend distribution, as provided in section 301(c) . . ., measured by the fair market value of the X common stock as of the date of the distribution both as to noncorporate and corporate shareholders, pursuant to section 301(d). Section 1.301–1(h)(1) and (2)(i) of the regulations. The quarterly service charge paid by a participant who is an individual for the production of income or for the management, conservation, or maintenance of property held for the production of income, is deductible in the year paid by such participant under section 212, provided the individual itemizes deductions. See Rev. Rul. 70–627, 1970–2 C.B. 159, and Rev. Rul. 75–548, 1975–2 C.B. 331. The quarterly service charge, which is paid in carrying on a trade or business by a participant who is an individual, is deductible in the year paid by such participant under section 162. A participant who is a corporation may deduct the service charge under section 162.

(c) A shareholder of X who participates in the optional payment aspect of the plan will be treated as having received a distribution to which section 301 . . . applies by reason of the application of section 305(b)(2). Pursuant to section 1.305–3(a) of the regulations, the amount of the distribution to a participating shareholder will be the difference between the fair market value on the dividend payment date of the shares purchased with the optional payment and the amount of the optional payment. Section 1.305–3(b)(2).

(d) The basis to the shareholder who participates in the optional payment aspect of the plan is the excess of fair market value of the shares purchased with the optional payment over the optional payment (provided that this deemed distribution is taxable as a dividend under section 301(c)(1)) . . . pursuant to section 301(d) and sections 1.301–1(h)(1) and (2)(i) of the regulations, plus the amount of the optional payment, pursuant to section 1012.

(e) A participant in the plan will not realize any taxable income upon receipt of certificates for whole shares that were credited to the participant's account pursuant to the plan. Rev. Rul. 76–53. Any cash received by an X shareholder in lieu of a fractional share interest will be treated as a redemption of that fractional share interest, subject to the provisions and limitations of section 302. . . See Rev. Rul. 66365, 1966–2 C.B. 116.

(f) A participant will recognize gain or loss pursuant to section 1001 . . . when shares are sold or exchanged on behalf of the participant upon the participant's withdrawal from the plan, or when the participant sells the shares after its withdrawal from the plan. In accordance with section 1001, the amount of such gain or loss will be the difference between the amount that the participant receives for the whole shares and the participant's tax basis. Any cash received by the participants, who withdraw from the plan, in lieu of their fractional share interests will be treated as a redemption of that fractional share interest, subject to the provisions and limitations of section 302. See Rev. Rul. 66–365.

Rev. Rul. 77–149 is distinguished.

Revenue Ruling 78–60
1978–1 C.B. 81.

Advice has been requested whether under section 302(a) . . . the stock redemptions described below qualified for exchange treatment, and whether under section 305(b)(2) and (c) the shareholders who experienced increases in their proportionate interests in the redeeming corporation as a result of the stock redemptions will be treated as having received distributions of property to which section 301 applies.

Corporation Z has only one class of stock outstanding. The Z common stock is held by 24 shareholders, all of whom are descendants, or spouses of descendants, of the founder of Z.

In 1975, when Z had 6,000 shares of common stock outstanding, the board of directors of Z adopted a plan of annual redemption to provide a means for its shareholders to sell their stock. The plan provides that Z will annually redeem up to 40 shares of its outstanding stock at a price established annually by the Z board of directors. Each shareholder of Z is entitled to cause Z to redeem two-thirds of one percent of the shareholder's stock each year. If some shareholders choose not to participate fully in the plan during any year, the other shareholders can cause Z to redeem more than two-thirds of one percent of their stock, up to the maximum of 40 shares.

Pursuant to the plan of annual redemption, Z redeemed 40 shares of its stock in 1976. Eight shareholders participated in the redemptions. The following table shows the ownership interests of the Z shareholders before and after the 1976 redemptions:

[Table omitted. No shareholder actually owned as much as 13 percent, and none constructively owned as much as 15 percent, of the outstanding stock at any time. The greatest change in actual and constructive ownership as a result of the redemption was incurred by shareholder G, whose actual and constructive ownership declined respectively from 188 to 182 and from 195 to 189 shares.]

ISSUE 1

[The Service concluded that none of the shareholders participating in the redemptions experienced a meaningful reduction in interest. Consequently, the redemptions were taxable under § 301.]

ISSUE 2

. . . Section 1.305–7(a) of the . . . regulations provides that a redemption treated as a section 301 distribution will generally be treated as a distribution to which sections 305(b)(2) and 301 . . . apply if the proportionate interest of any shareholder in the earnings and profits or assets of the corporation deemed to have made the stock distribution is increased by the redemption, and the distribution has the result described in section 305(b)(2). The distribution is to be deemed made to any shareholder whose interest in the earnings and profits or assets of the distributing corporation is increased by the redemption.

Section 1.305–3(b)(3) of the regulations provides that for a distribution of property to meet the requirements of section 305(b)(2). . . the distribution must be made to a shareholder in the capacity as a shareholder and must be a distribution to which section 301 [or one of several other specified sections] applies. A distribution of property incident to an isolated redemption will not cause section 305(b)(2) to apply even though the redemption distribution is treated as a section 301 distribution.

Section 305 . . . does not make the constructive stock ownership rules of section 318(a) applicable to its provisions.

The 16 shareholders of Z who did not tender any stock for redemption in 1976 experienced increases in their proportionate interests of the earnings and profits and assets of Z (without taking into account constructive stock ownership under section 318 . . .) as a result of the redemptions. Shareholders B and X, who surrendered small amounts of their stock for redemption in 1976, also experienced increases in their proportionate interests. The 1976 redemptions were not isolated but were undertaken pursuant to an ongoing plan of annual stock redemptions. Finally, the 1976 redemptions are to be treated as distributions of property to which section 301 . . . applies.

Accordingly, B, X and the 16 shareholders of Z who did not participate in the 1976 redemptions are deemed to have received stock distributions to which sections 305(b)(2) and 301 . . . apply. See examples (8) and (9) of section 1.305–3(e) of the regulations for a method of computing the amounts of the deemed distributions.

NOTES

1. In Rev. Rul. 78–115, 1978–1 C.B. 85, the Service considered whether a series of preferred stock redemptions by a corporation constituted a periodic redemption plan that had the effect of increasing certain shareholders' proportionate interest under § 305(b)(2) & (c). Citing example 14 of Treas. Reg. § 1.305–3(e) exempting certain periodic redemptions from § 305(b)(2) and (c) where the redemption plan was of a class of stock with the goal of eliminating a shareholder, the Service concluded that the redemption of the preferred stock would not be a taxable distribution to the common shareholder under § 305(b)(2). However, § 302 would be applied to the redeeming shareholders.

2. See also Rev. Rul. 77–37, 1977–1 C.B. 85 (adjustment in conversion ratio of preferred stock to reflect nontaxable distributions to common shareholders not a deemed distribution); Rev. Rul. 77–19, 1977–1 C.B. 83 (isolated redemptions do not result in distributions under § 305(b)(2) or (c) where there is no plan to redeem some shareholders periodically); Rev. Rul. 76–186, 1976–1 C.B. 86 (effect on basis and earnings and profits where adjustment in conversion ratio of debentures results in deemed distribution); Letter Ruling 201002022 (finding the redemption by the family group to be an isolated transaction not triggering a deemed distribution under § 305 for any of the shareholders).

3. In 1993, Congress added § 305(e) governing the treatment of stripped preferred stock—preferred stock where the stock ownership and rights to as yet unpaid dividends have been separated. This bond-like instrument is now subject to the tax rules for OID bonds. § 305(e).

4. There is a perplexing policy puzzle that is larger and more engrossing than all of the technical detail in §§ 305 and 306. In a regime that had taxed ordinary investment income as high as 70 percent or even 50 percent and long-term capital gains at a maximum of only 20 percent, perhaps the complexity of § 305(b)(2)–(5) and (c) could be justified. Yet, even then, it is hard to comprehend why the deferral-but-assured-ordinary income approach of § 306 was appropriate to deal with some bailout cases, but yet the immediate ordinary income consequence of § 305(b)(2) et seq. was thought necessary in others. After the 2003 Act (taxing dividends at the same rate as capital gains) it may be sensible to revisit the pattern of immediate taxation under § 305(b) and deferred taxation under § 306—and develop a simplified regime to police the line between realization-based deferral (§ 305(a)) and taxable dividends.

C. STOCK DIVIDEND VS. COMPENSATION—§§ 305, 267, 61, 83

Commissioner v. Fender Sales, Inc.

338 F.2d 924 (9th Cir. 1964), *cert. denied*, 382 U.S. 813 (1965).

■ Before POPE and BARNES, CIRCUIT JUDGES, and THOMPSON, DISTRICT JUDGE.

■ THOMPSON, DISTRICT JUDGE. . . . The Tax Court held neither the corporate taxpayer, Fender Sales, Inc., nor the individual stockholder-taxpayers, Donald D. and Jean Randall, and C. Leo and Esther Fender, liable for a deficiency of income taxes. . .

The taxpayer Fender Sales, Inc. was incorporated in 1953 as a California corporation. It was authorized to issue 2,500 shares of common stock with a par value of $100 per share. At the commencement of the events material to this case, only 100 shares were outstanding, 50 of which were held by the taxpayer Donald D. Randall, and the other 50 by the taxpayer C. Leo Fender. Randall and Fender were also employees of Fender Sales and as such, were entitled to receive, as compensation for their services, $15,000 a year plus amounts equal to four percent and one percent, respectively, of annual sales. . .

Although Fender Sales has always been financially solvent, from its inception it has been plagued by the shortage of cash. This financial predicament was brought about primarily because it had to pay for its purchases upon receipt of the merchandise while it was often required to finance the dealers who purchased merchandise from it. Accordingly, in 1955, Fender Sales found it necessary to seek bank financing. Originally the bank did not ask for security for its loan, but later it required the subordination of other liabilities and personal guarantees from the corporate officers. In addition it became concerned about accrued (but unpaid) officers' salary liabilities that appeared on Fender Sales' balance sheet; it felt that these liabilities could represent potential priority claims over the bank's claim. To remedy this, the bank suggested that these liabilities be capitalized.

In each case of its fiscal years ending May 31, 1954, 1955 and 1956, Fender Sales, which used the accrual method of accounting for federal income tax purposes, accrued $30,000 on its books of account as representing officers' salaries payable, but unpaid, in the amount of $15,000 a year each to Randall and Fender. In each of those years, Fender Sales deducted the $30,000 on its federal income tax return. Accordingly, as of August 6, 1956, Fender Sales owed Randall and Fender each $45,000 for salaries payable for the fiscal years ended May 31, 1954 through 1956.

On or about August 6, 1956, Randall and Fender, in order to comply with the bank's suggestion, offered to discharge Fender Sales' liability for salaries due and payable to them by accepting from Fender Sales an additional share of $100 par value common stock for each $100 of salary debt.

On August 6, 1956, the board of directors of Fender Sales, consisting of Mr. and Mrs. Randall and Mr. and Mrs. Fender, resolved to accept the offers by Randall and Fender. After obtaining a permit from the Commissioner of Corporations of the State of California, Fender Sales, on December 3, 1956, issued to Randall and to Fender 450 shares each of its $100 par value common stock in discharge and cancellation of its indebtedness of $45,000 owing to each of them. As a result of this issuance of stock, Sales' capital stock account was increased from $10,000 to $100,000 and its $90,000 liability for salaries owed to Randall and Fender was discharged and cancelled.

[A similar transaction occurred discharging Sales' liability for salaries for the fiscal year ended May 27, 1957.]

On their federal income tax returns for the years 1956 and 1958, Fender and his wife did not report any amount as taxable income resulting from Fender's receipt of 450 shares of Fender Sales' stock on December 3, 1956, and 150 shares of Fender Sales' stock on May 9, 1958. On their federal income tax returns for the year 1956 and on their joint federal income tax returns for the year 1958, Randall and his wife did not report any amount as taxable income resulting from Randall's receipt of 450 shares of Fender Sales' stock on December 3, 1956, and 150 shares of Fender Sales' stock on May 9, 1958. On its corporate federal income tax returns for the fiscal years ended May 31, 1957 and May 31, 1958, Fender Sales did not report any amount as taxable income resulting from the discharge and cancellation on December 3, 1956 and May 9, 1958 of its indebtednesses for officers' salaries payable to Fender and Randall.

The Commissioner determined that the receipt of the stock constituted taxable salary income to Fender and Randall and, alternatively, that if it did not constitute taxable income to them, Fender Sales realized taxable income upon the cancellation of the salary indebtedness. The Tax Court held, however, that the cancellation of the indebtedness and issuance of the stock did not result in taxable income either to Fender and Randall or to Fender Sales. . .

It is . . . conceded by respondents that the shares of Fender Sales, Inc. issued to each of the shareholders, Fender and Randall, had a fair market value of $100 per share (par value).

TAX LIABILITY OF FENDER AND RANDALL

Cases numbered 19075 to 19079, inclusive, present petitions by the Commissioner to review decisions by the Tax Court that the individuals, Donald D. Randall and his wife, Jean Randall, and C. Leo Fender and his wife, Esther Fender, incurred no income tax liability arising from the transactions related in the statement of facts. The complete rationale of the Tax Court decision is found in the following quotation:

> Fender and Randall were the sole shareholders of Sales regardless of whether they each owned 50 shares or 1,000 shares. Their

wealth was no more increased by the issuance of additional shares than if the corporation had caused its stock to be split 20 for 1. The issuance of such additional shares to Fender and Randall did not constitute income to them within the meaning of the 16th Amendment to the Constitution regardless of whether it represented a stock dividend or represented compensation for services. Eisner v. Macomber (252 U.S. 189) . . . J, supra. . .

We disagree, and reverse the decision of the Tax Court in these cases.

The stockholder-employees received and accepted capital stock in discharge of the delinquent obligations of the corporation to them for salaries. If these were not equal stockholders to whom the corporation owed equal sums for unpaid salaries, there would be no semblance of a basis for dispute. The law and regulations plainly tax "all income from whatever source derived" (. . . § 61), and provide: ". . . if a corporation transfers its own stock to an employee . . . as compensation for services, the fair market value of the stock at the time of transfer shall be included in the gross income of the employee." Regulations, § 1.61–2(d)(4). Here the parties agree the fair market value of the stock of Fender Sales, Inc. equalled its par value, and the additional stock issued is, in any event, presumptively equal in value to the liquidated obligations discharged. Regulations, § 1.612(d)[(1)].

Respondents say this case is different because the taxpayers were stockholders as well as employees and the equal (50–50) stock ownership by Fender and Randall remained equal after the additional stock was issued; and that they, therefore, "received nothing which they did not already possess, i.e., the entire capital stock of Fender Sales, Inc."

But the corporation was a substantially different corporation after the transactions than before. After the transactions on August 6, 1956, for example, the net worth of the company (excluding capital stock as a liability) was increased by $90,000, resulting from the cancellation of the accrued salary indebtedness. The fact is clear that the interests of Fender and Randall in Fender Sales, Inc. were substantially enhanced in value and that they did, in effect, receive something of value constituting taxable income under the Sixteenth Amendment to the Constitution. In this context, Eisner v. Macomber (1920), 252 U.S. 189. . . is not even apposite, let alone controlling. True, a stock dividend is just a piece of paper and, when issued proportionately to all stockholders, represents nothing of value and does not result in the realization of taxable income. But this is only because the basic net worth of the corporation, excluding capital stock as a liability, has not been changed. The stockholders have retained an equal interest in the same investment. In our situation, the stockholders have retained an equal interest in a substantially different investment. The *Eisner* opinion was explicit in pointing out that a stock dividend is "paper certificates that evidence an *antecedent* increase in the value of the stockholder's capital interest" (not, as here, a contemporaneous quid pro quo increase thereof), and "merely bookkeeping that does not affect the aggregate assets of the corporation or its outstanding liabilities" (not, as here, a $90,000 reduction in debts of Fender Sales, Inc. in August, 1956). The obvious differences between the economic interests represented by an unsecured debt as compared with stock ownership need no elaboration.

We interpret Lidgerwood Manufacturing Co. v. Commissioner (2 CCA 1956), 229 F.2d 241, as supporting our conclusions. In *Lidgerwood*, the debts which were cancelled arose from loans, and if paid would not have represented taxable income to the stockholder. In that case, a sole stockholder cancelled debts, receiving capital stock in exchange, to enable the corporation to obtain bank loans. The debts cancelled were uncollectible and the stockholder-taxpayer claimed bad debt deductions on its income tax returns. The Court rejected the taxpayer's contention that nothing had been received by virtue of the issuance of the additional stock and, denying the bad debt deduction, said:

> The petitioner contends that since the debts were assumed to be uncollectible, the cancellation of worthless debts and the issuance of stock therefor were meaningless formalities. We disagree.

> When a creditor cancels a debt in return for stock, he gives up the right to repayment, however prosperous the debtor may become, and he acquires a right to dividends from future prosperity. If he owns less than all of the debtor's stock, the issuance of additional shares increases his share of possible dividends. If, as here, the creditor owns all the debtor's stock, his share is not increased but he has retained his 100 percent right to future dividends, and, if the cancelled debts had any value whatever, to that extent he has increased his capital investment. It is not entirely clear what the Tax Court meant by its assumption that the debts were "uncollectible." Although the petitioner had contended that the subsidiaries were insolvent both before and after the cancellations, no finding of insolvency was made. But even on the assumption that the debtors were insolvent after as well as before the cancellations, wiping out the debts was a valuable contribution to the financial structure of the subsidiaries. It enabled them to obtain bank loans, to continue in business and subsequently to prosper.

Finally, Respondents say, in substance—break the transaction down to its component parts, none of them is a taxable event, therefore in the aggregate, they cannot generate a tax liability. The argument is: First, the receipt by equal stockholders of equal additional shares of capital stock, without more, is nontaxable; second, the forgiveness by a stockholder of the corporation's debt to him is, without more, a contribution to the capital of the corporation which is expressly excluded from the corporation's gross income. Therefore, a combination of the two cannot impose income tax liability on anyone. The answer is that the argument is a complete non-sequitur. The first statement deals with the tax liability of the individual stockholders and the second with the tax liability of the corporation.

To be persuasive with respect to the tax liability of the individual stockholders, Respondents' contentions should be: First, the acquisition of additional stock in equal proportionate shares is not a taxable event; second, the cancellation of a debt which, if collected, would represent taxable income is not a taxable event; therefore, the two in combination cannot generate tax liability. This Court does not accept the second premise. We are not prepared to hold that the voluntary surrender or forgiveness by a taxpayer of a receivable which, if collected, would represent taxable income, is, in all circumstances, a non-taxable event. We believe the authorities are opposed to such a conclusion.

In Helvering v. Horst, 1940, 311 U.S. 112, . . . the Supreme Court held that the income received on payment of coupons clipped from coupon bonds and given by a father to his son was taxable to the father, and said, in part:

> Admittedly not all economic gain of the taxpayer is taxable income. From the beginning the revenue laws have been interpreted as defining "realization" of income as the taxable event rather than the acquisition of the right to receive it. And "realization" is not deemed to occur until the income is paid. But the decisions and regulations have consistently recognized that receipt in cash or property is not the only characteristic of realization of income to a taxpayer on the cash receipts basis. Where the taxpayer does not receive payment of income in money or property realization may occur when the last step is taken by which he obtains the fruition of the economic gain which has already accrued to him. Old Colony Trust Co. v. Commissioner, 279 U.S. 716; Corliss v. Bowers, 281 U.S. 376, 378. . . Cf. Burnet v. Wells, 289 U.S. 670. . .

> Underlying the reasoning in these cases is the thought that income is "realized" by the assignor because he, who owns or controls the source of the income, also controls the disposition of that which he could have received himself and diverts the payment from himself to others as the means of procuring the satisfaction of his wants. The taxpayer has equally enjoyed the fruits of his labor or investment and obtained the satisfaction of his desires whether he collects and uses the income to procure those satisfactions, or whether he disposes of his right to collect it as the means of procuring them. Cf. Burnet v. Wells, supra. . .

> The dominant purpose of the revenue laws is the taxation of income to those who earn or otherwise create the right to receive it and enjoy the benefit of it when paid. See Corliss v. Bower, supra. . . The tax laid by the 1934 Revenue Act upon income "derived from . . . wages, or compensation for personal service, of whatever kind and in whatever form paid . . .; also from interest . . ." therefore cannot fairly be interpreted as not applying to income derived from interest or compensation when he who is entitled to receive it makes use of his power to dispose of it in procuring satisfactions which he would otherwise procure only by the use of the money when received.

In *Lidgerwood* (supra), the case in which the taxpayer sought a bad debt deduction in addition to the capital stock received for the cancelled obligation, the Court succinctly said: "If the debtor has received a contribution to capital, the creditor must have made the contribution. Consistency requires that both parties treat it alike."

In Helvering v. Horst, the coupons were actually paid in the year of the gift, and Respondents point to this as a distinguishing feature, claiming the salaries due from Fender Sales, Inc. were never "paid." But, in *Horst*, the Supreme Court relied on the broader concept of "realization of income" rather than a restricted notion of actual payment for its conclusions, and we think it necessary and logical, in the just administration of the tax laws, that the Courts continue to recognize that a taxpayer may realize the income represented by an account receivable by exercising his rights of control and disposition of it for his economic benefit in ways other than receipt of payment in money. In Commissioner of Internal Revenue v. Lester, 1961, 366 U.S. 299, 304, . . . the Supreme Court approvingly quoted from *Horst*: "The power to dispose of income is the equivalent of ownership of it." We add, the exercise of the power to dispose of income is the equivalent of the realization of it. Fortunately, under the agreed facts of this case, we have no problem respecting the taxable value of the income thus realized and no problem respecting the tax year in which the income is reportable.

Randall and Fender, when they voluntarily elected to exercise their dominion and control over the choses in action against Fender Sales, Inc. for unpaid salaries by extinguishing them for the benefit of the corporation, of which they were sole owners, thereby augmenting the intrinsic worth of the capital stock they held, more surely "realized" for their own benefit the value of the obligations discharged than did Horst in his gift of interest coupons to his son.

In summary, we hold that the discharge by a corporation of its salary obligations to any employee (stockholder or not) by the issuance of the corporation's capital stock to the employee is a payment and realization of income by the employee in the amount of the fair market value of the stock. The transaction is controlled by Section 61 of the Internal Revenue Code and Section 1.61–2 of the Regulations. We disagree with the conclusions in Josephson v. Commissioner, 6 T.C.M. 788 and Daggitt v. Commissioner, 23 T.C. 31, cited by Respondents.

The decisions of the Tax Court in cases numbered 19075 to 19079, inclusive, are reversed.

TAX LIABILITY OF FENDER SALES, INC.

Case No. 19074 presents a petition to review the determination by the Tax Court that the corporation, Fender Sales, Inc., incurred no income tax liability by reason of the related transactions.

Although the Commissioner argued for assessing tax liability against the corporation, this was only as an alternative should the individuals be held not liable. The Commissioner's brief states: "For the reasons already shown, we believe that Fender and Randall are taxable on the amounts of the accrued salaries and that Fender Sales is not. We do not contend that both are taxable on the same amounts." Whether viewed as payments for stock of the corporation or as the forgiveness by the shareholders of debts owed to them by the corporation, the transactions were nontaxable payments or contributions to capital from the point of view of the corporation's tax liability. . . § 118[(a)]; 1032(a); Reg. 1.10321; Reg. 1.61–12(a). . .

The petition in Case No. 19074 should be dismissed.

■ BARNES, CIRCUIT JUDGE (dissenting in part and concurring in part). I respectfully dissent. I would affirm the Tax Court in respect to the nonliability of the individual taxpayers, i.e., cases 19075 to 19079, inclusive.

I deduce the matter that concerns my brothers is the loophole in present laws which allows a corporation whose stock is owned equally by two principals to take deductions in certain years for accrued salaries payable, never incur actual expenses for such deductions, and then have the liabilities written off without any tax recognition because the item is treated as a capital contribution by the shareholders. If on a balancing of all factors, this method of corporate tax liability reduction is a loophole that should be plugged, then it should be done by legislative action, not by judicial fiat. The majority opinion seeks to remedy the supposed leak by attaching liability to the *individuals* involved by extending the dominion and control cases, represented by Helvering v. Horst, 311 U.S. 112 . . . (1940).

This majority opinion is the first I have encountered which recognizes a realization of income by shareholders upon an increase in corporate net worth, *where no dividend has been declared or capital gain yet realized* by the shareholders. Shareholders' interests in corporations change every day. The net worth of corporations is in a constant state of flux. Surely, when it increases, the shareholders are not yet deemed to have made a taxable gain. Rather the increase in corporate net worth is merely a paper increase of the shareholders' equity, not taxable until such time as the shareholders realize the increase by virtue of a dividend, or the sale or exchange of the security investment above cost. Then, and only then, have the courts traditionally recognized. "a taxable event."

The use of the *Horst* line of cases as authority for recognizing the creation of a taxable event for the individuals in the case at bar is to me misleading. The evasionary device attacked in *Horst* and its progeny was different from the present situation. Those cases involved assignments of income rights to others prior to the point of realization of the income by the taxpayer himself. Such an anticipatory device by a taxpayer with complete control over the income was clearly a loophole in our tax laws that required plugging. Otherwise a taxpayer could assign his earnings directly to his creditors or family and claim there was never any income realization on his part. The case at bar does not involve a flagrant example of this potential loophole. The taxpayers here have no benefits *realized* by the issuance of additional stock for the cancellation of a corporate debt; their income has not been *diverted* to anyone else for their own personal benefit. They did not exert any power to dispose of their alleged "income" in a manner equivalent to ownership, and will not do so until the ordinary taxable event occurs—the sale of their stock.

The *Lidgerwood* case, cited, is in my opinion not controlling on the facts of this case. In fact the opinion seems to overlook the corporate nature of the stockholder in that case. The bad debt deduction was disallowed the parent-stockholder, but the cancellation was treated not as income to the parent *or its creditor subsidiaries*; rather it was properly treated as a capital contribution. To the extent the *Lidgerwood* case is relevant to the facts before us, it supports the conclusion that the taxpayers have not yet realized income by the receipt of additional shares of stock (while maintaining their identical proportional interests) for a debt cancellation.

> This court and others have held that cancellation of a debt owed by a corporate debtor to a stockholder of the debtor does not constitute taxable income to the debtor but is a capital contribution by the creditor. For many years the Treasury Regulations have so provided. . . If the debtor has received a contribution to capital, the creditor must have made the contribution. Consistency requires that both parties treat it alike. *Whether the creditor's investment will result in profit or loss to the investor cannot be determined forthwith. Loss, if any is eventually realized, occurs when the investment is closed out; that is, when the shares of stock of the debtor are sold or become worthless.* (Emphasis supplied.) [Lidgerwood Mfg. Co. v. Commissioner, 229 F.2d 241, at 242–243 (2d Cir. 1956).]

Another approach to the problem, which to me supports the decision of the Tax Court, is as follows:

The two equal owners of the corporation are cash basis taxpayers. They each work on behalf of the corporation for three years without drawing a salary. Thus each has no current employment income subject to tax. However, the full time services each renders to the corporation are of some value; and are here valued at $15,000 per year. These services have their effect on the corporate performance. Consequently, these gratuitous services result, at the end of three years, in a corporate net worth presumably $90,000 greater than it would have been without their services. If at any time one or both of the individual owners decides to sell his investment, he will be taxed in effect for his gratuitous services because the proceeds from any sale would presumably be $45,000 greater than they would have been had he not contributed his services. He has not taken advantage of any tax loophole that does not already exist. Rather, he has just chosen not to take a current salary which would be taxed at ordinary income rates, and has instead increased the value of his investment to be taxed at a subsequent time at capital gain rates. I contend that, from the individual's standpoint, this is exactly what has occurred in the case at bar.

As to the corporation tax liability (case No. 19074), I would affirm.

Under the Internal Revenue Code and regulations, the corporation did not realize income on account of its issuance of capital stock to Fender and

Randall, and did not realize income on account of the cancellation of the salary indebtedness to Fender and Randall. From the point of view of the corporation, any consideration received by it upon an original issue of its corporate stock, whether more or less than the actual or the stated value thereof, is a receipt of capital, not income. Merten's "Law of Federal Income Taxation," Vol. 7, p. 67; I.R.C. 1032(a); Reg. 1.1032–1.

Also, should we treat the capital stock issued as valueless and view the transactions as the gratuitous forgiveness of the salary obligations of the corporation by the respective stockholder-employees, still the corporation would not thereby have realized taxable income. It is established both by regulation and court decision that the gratuitous forgiveness by a share-holder of a debt owed to him by the corporation represents a contribution to the capital of the corporation and is not taxable income. Regulation 1.61–12(a). . . Under the Internal Revenue Code, a contribution to the capital of a corporate taxpayer is expressly excluded from the definition of reportable gross income. . . § 118. In this case, the corporate obligations which were cancelled were unpaid salary obligations to the shareholders which had been deducted as operating expenses by the corporate taxpayer in its an-nual accrual-accounting income tax returns and which, if paid, would have represented taxable income to the shareholder-employees. In dealing with a corporation's possible tax liability arising from the gratuitous forgiveness of a debt by a shareholder, the law makes no distinction on the basis of how the obligation arose, that is, whether or not it arose out of a transaction which had permitted the corporation, in an earlier tax year, to deduct the charge from reportable gross income, or whether or not the obligation, if paid, would have constituted reportable income to the sharehold-er-taxpayer. The forgiveness of the debt by the shareholder is, in either case, from the viewpoint of the corporate taxpayer, a contribution to capi-tal, and not a taxable event. In Helvering v. American Dental Co., 318 U.S. 322 . . . (1943), the Supreme Court held the forgiveness of interest on notes and of rentals due by nonstockholder creditors to be gifts and capital con-tributions to a corporation, though "the motives leading to the cancellation were those of business or even selfish." Also, in Commissioner v. Auto Strop Safety Razor Co., 74 F.2d 226 (2d Cir. 1934), the court, under regulations like those now prevailing, held the voluntary cancellation by the sole stock-holder of a subsidiary corporation of over two million dollars in debts, a portion of which represented expense items previously deducted, such as royalties and interest, to be a nontaxable contribution to the capital of the subsidiary corporation, and said: "When the indebtedness was canceled, whether or not it was a contribution to the capital of the debtor depends upon considerations entirely foreign to the question of the payment of in-come taxes in some previous year."

I believe a word or two of further explanation is required. The amounts now being treated as contributions to capital have previously been de-ducted by the corporation on its accrual-method tax returns. Had the indi-vidual taxpayers merely loaned money to the corporation and now can-celled the indebtedness, the cancellation would clearly be a contribution to capital, and such contribution should not be treated as taxable income to the corporation. However, the case at bar involves an indebtedness in the nature of accrued salaries which, unlike the hypothetical taxpayer loans, have once been deducted from income in prior years, consequently lessening the corporation's tax liability. Where sums have been deducted as expenses in previous years under an accrual method of accounting, and are now forgiven and are no longer corporate liabilities, the corporation ordinarily must add back the amount of the cancellation to its current income. If it need not, a flagrant loophole is created whereby expense deductions are taken without expenses ever being incurred or paid out. I refer to the language in Helvering v. Jane Holding Corp., 109 F.2d 933 (8th Cir. 1940).

> The above cases recognize the principle that an obligation, once deducted but not paid, represents income when, because of subsequent circumstances, it is cancelled or it may be determined with reasonable certainty that it will never be enforced. None of the cases attach any importance to the means by which the cancellation is effected. That is immaterial, the controlling factors being the previous deductions offsetting income otherwise taxable and the subsequent release of the indebtedness before payment.

> The Trust filed all of its returns for prior years on the cash basis and never reported as taxable income the interest accrued and deducted by the Corporation. The Trust, through the trustees, has, at all times since its creation, been in a position to determine and dictate the policies of the Corporation. It has chosen to earmark the payments which it received from the Corporation as payments on account of principal and at the same time, throughout the entire period, these payments have been in effect deducted as interest accrued in the Corporation's returns. To now permit this accrued liability, after the forgiveness thereof, to be called surplus and addition to capital without taxing the income actually received by the Corporation would result in an unjustifiable avoidance of tax.

While I agree with Judge Thompson's ultimate conclusion that the company has not realized income by the cancellation of the accrued salaries obligation, I do believe to properly justify that conclusion requires same discussion of the conflicting line of cases dealing with shareholder cancellations of indebtedness where the indebtedness has previously been deducted by the corporation as an operating expense.

Regulation § 1.61–12(a) addresses itself directly to the problem of the cancellation of an indebtedness by a shareholder of a corporation. *Generally*, it maintains that the gratuitous forgiveness of a debt constitutes a contribution to capital, the corporation thus realizing no income. The leading precedent for this line of reasoning is Helvering v. American Dental Co., supra. In that case, the Commissioner had increased the taxpayer's reported income by the sum of the items of the cancelled indebtedness which had served to offset income in like amounts in prior years. But the Supreme Court held that the gratuitous cancellation of rent and interest due should be deemed a gift and not income.

The leading precedent for the opposing point of view, recognizing income to the taxpayer relieved of an indebtedness, is the later case of Commissioner v. Jacobson, 336 U.S. 28 . . . (1949), which taxed the difference between the face amount of the taxpayer's personal indebtedness as the maker of secured bonds issued at face value, and a lesser amount paid by him for their repurchase. There was no evidence that there had been a transfer of something for nothing: the seller received the maximum price attainable.

Neither of these cases serves as exact precedent for the situation we have here; the cancellation of accrued salaries which have been deducted by the debtor-corporation in prior years. The leading exponents of the conflicting points of view in the accrued salary cases are Helvering v. Jane Holding Corp., supra, in favor of income recognition, and Carroll–McCreary Co. v. Commissioner, 124 F.2d 303 (2d Cir. 1941), holding no realization of income from the gratuitous cancellation of debts for unpaid salaries owing to officer-shareholders. The *Jane* case preceded the decision in *American Dental Co.*, supra, and the trend of the case law since the latter decision has been to follow *Carroll–McCreary* and hold no income is recognized if there was no consideration given as inducement for the cancellation. The cases have interpreted "gratuitous" forgiveness of a debt as simply meaning that no consideration was paid by the corporation for release of the debt. The prior deduction of the debt as a corporate expense has been held immaterial to the question of whether a nontaxable capital contribution was effected by the debt release. . .

In the absence of evidence of consideration passing from Fender Sales, Inc., to the individual shareholders for cancellation of the accrued salaries indebtedness, the above case law supports the conclusion that the corporation did not realize income by the release of the accrued salaries liability, though the corporation had already taken the amount as deduction for expense of doing business.

Any potential loophole that is created by attaching no tax liability to the individuals or the corporation is a product of the legislature's failure to compel the corporation to make an income recognition when their accrued deductions are cancelled. This is an error which the legislature should be called upon to reconsider. It should not be corrected by committing a second error in the present case to offset the first.

NOTES

1. Why was § 267(a)(2) inapplicable to the deductions claimed by Fender Sales, Inc., for salaries accrued but unpaid? (Hint: see § 267(b)) Note that § 269A now refers to "personal service corporations." Thus, if the principal activity of the corporation "is the performance of personal services and such services are substantially performed by employee-owners," see § 269A(b)(1), then the corporation may not deduct compensation payments made to an employee-owner who owns, actually or constructively, more than 10 percent of the corporation's stock, unless the employee-owner takes the compensation in income. See §§ 267(a) and 269A.

2. Does the *Fender Sales* majority or the dissent present the more persuasive case as to the taxability of the individuals? Is the majority's position consonant with the premise underlying § 305? What would be the dissenting judge's position if the shareholders had had unequal share interests but the stock-for-salary distribution had been 50–50? What should it be? See the Commissioner's view in Rev. Rul. 67–402, 1967–2 C.B. 135.

3. If the dissenting judge is right in his position that the individuals had no income on the stock distribution, is he right that the termination of the corporate liability was a tax-free contribution to capital? In a tax sense, did the shareholders have "property" to contribute? How would you have decided the *Fender Sales* issue involving the corporate taxpayer? Why?

In Putoma Corp., 66 T.C. 652 (1976), *aff'd*, 601 F.2d 734 (5th Cir. 1979), a corporation's two equal shareholders, on the cash basis, canceled the corporation's accrued (and previously deducted) interest liability, receiving no stock in exchange. The court refused to find income to either the corporation or its shareholders. It distinguished *Fender Sales* on the ground that no stock had been issued, and in addition found on the facts before it that the shareholders had not exercised sufficient dominion and control over the interest obligation to justify taxing them on its receipt. Accord, as to the corporation's nonrecognition, Hartland Associates, 54 T.C. 1580 (1970), *nonacq.* 1976–2 C.B. 1; contra, Rev. Rul. 76–316, 1976–2 C.B. 22. Cf. Treas. Reg. § 1.61–12(a). See also, as to the shareholders, Dwyer v. United States, 622 F.2d 460 (9th Cir. 1980) (taxing shareholder after distinguishing *Putoma*).

The 1980 Bankruptcy Tax Act overruled *Putoma* in § 108(e)(6). See S. Rep. No. 1035, 96th Cong., 2d Sess. 1980–2 C.B. 620 (1980). Now, if no stock is issued in such a transaction, the corporation will be treated as having satisfied the indebtedness with an amount of money equal to the shareholder's adjusted basis in the indebtedness. Thus, in *Putoma*, where the cash method shareholders had an adjusted basis of zero in the indebtedness, the corporation would recognize cancellation of indebtedness income in the full amount of the debt (subject to reduction of tax attributes or election to decrease basis under § 1017).

Suppose, however, that additional stock is issued for the amount of the cancelled debt, as in *Fender Sales*. When a corporation issues stock in cancellation of its indebtedness, § 108(e)(8) now provides that the corporation, if not insolvent and if not in certain bankruptcy proceedings, is treated as if it had satisfied the indebtedness with an amount of money equal to the fair market value of the stock.* Thus, the corporation will have discharge-of-indebtedness income to the extent the debt exceeds the value of the stock. It would seem that if shareholder-creditors in the *Fender Sales* situation forgave the debt and no stock were issued, under § 108(e)(6) the corporation would have discharge of debt income. If stock equal in value to the debt were issued, then it would appear that under § 108(e)(8) the corporation would have no income, but the shareholders would—all as under the *Fender Sales* decision. Is this a wise outcome?

---

* Prior to the passage of the Tax Reform Act of 1984, the "stock-for-debt" exception allowed a corporation to replace its debt with stock without recognizing any cancellation of indebtedness income

4. Ordinarily, when employees are not the sole and equal shareholders, as they were in *Fender Sales*, it is not questioned that they have ordinary income on receipt of their employer's stock in compensation for their services. See §§ 61 and 83.

5. Dividends v. Compensation—On the question of whether a shareholder-employee's payment received from the corporation is a dividend or compensation, the 2003 Tax Act has changed the parties' incentives in many cases. Prior to 2003, salary was generally preferable because the payments were deductible to the corporation. Post 2003, a dividend characterization may be desired where the reduction in shareholder level taxes (from ordinary income rate on salary to capital gains rate on dividends) is greater than the benefit of the deduction that the corporation loses when the payment is taxed as a dividend instead of compensation.

Alves v. Commissioner
734 F.2d 478 (9th Cir. 1984).

■ Before KENNEDY, SCHROEDER, and BOOCHEVER, CIRCUIT JUDGES.

■ SCHROEDER, CIRCUIT JUDGE. . .

Section 83 requires that an employee who has purchased restricted stock in connection with his "performance of services" must include as ordinary income the stock's appreciation in value between the time of purchase and the time the restrictions lapse, unless at the time he purchased the stock he elected to include as income the difference between the purchase price and the fair market value at that time. The issue here is whether section 83 applies to an employee's purchase of restricted stock when, according to the stipulation of the parties, the amount paid for the stock equaled its full fair market value, without regard to any restrictions. The Tax Court, with two dissenting opinions, held that section 83 applies to all restricted stock that is transferred "in connection with the performance of services," regardless of the amount paid for it. We affirm. . .

Alves joined [General Digital Corporation] as vice-president for finance and administration. As part of an employment and stock purchase agreement dated May 22, 1970, the company agreed to sell Alves 40,000 shares of common stock at ten cents per share "in order to raise capital for the Company's initial operations while at the same time providing the Employee with an additional interest in the Company. . ." 79 T.C. at 867. The six other named individuals signed similar agreements on the same day. The agreement divided Alves's shares into three categories: one-third were subject to repurchase by the company at ten cents per share if Alves left within four years; one-third were subject to repurchase if he left the company within five years; and one-third were unrestricted. In addition, the company retained an option to repurchase up to one-half of the shares for their fair market value at any time between July 1, 1973 and July 1, 1975.

In transactions not at issue here, Alves sold some of his shares to friends and relatives. In 1973 he sold 4,667 four-year shares to Technology Ventures, Inc. (TVI), the assignee of General Digital's repurchase option, for $18 per share, and in 1974 he sold TVI 2,240 five-year shares for $4 per share.[2]

On July 1, 1974, when the restrictions on the four-year shares lapsed, Alves still owned 4,667 four-year shares that had a fair market value at that time of $6 per share. On March 24, 1975, the restrictions on the 7,093 remaining five-year shares lapsed with the fair market value at $3.43 per share.

Although Alves reported the $8,736 of gain on the sale of the 2,240 five-year shares to TVI as ordinary income on his 1974 tax return, he did not report the difference between the fair market value of the four and five-year shares when the restrictions ended, and the purchase price paid for the shares. The Commissioner treated the difference as ordinary income in 1974 and 1975, pursuant to section 83(a).[3]

In proceedings before the Tax Court, the parties stipulated that: (1) General Digital's common stock had a fair market value of 10 cents per share on the date Alves entered into the employment and stock purchase agreement; (2) the stock restrictions were imposed to "provide some assurance that key personnel would remain with the company for a number of years"; (3) Alves did not make an election under section 83(b) when the restricted stock was received; (4) the free shares were not includable in gross income under section 83; and (5) the four and five-year restricted shares were subject to a substantial risk of forfeiture until July 1, 1974, and March 24, 1975, respectively.

The Tax Court sustained the Commissioner's deficiency determination. It found as a matter of fact that the stock was transferred to Alves in connection with the performance of services for the company, and, as a matter of law, that section 83(a) applies even where the transferee paid full fair market value for the stock.

Resolution of the legal issue presented here requires an understanding of section 83's background and operation. Congress enacted section 83 in 1969 in response to the existing disparity between the tax treatment of restricted stock plans and other types of deferred compensation arrangements. . . Prior to 1969, an individual purchasing restricted stock was taxed either when the restrictions lapsed or when the stock was sold in an arm's length transaction. Tax was imposed upon the difference between the purchase price and the fair market value at the time of transfer or when the restrictions lapsed, whichever was less. See Cohn v. Commissioner, 73 T.C. 443, 446 (1979). This had both tax deferral and tax avoidance advantages over, for example, employer contributions to an employee's pension or profit sharing trust, which were immediately taxable in the year of receipt. . .

---

[2] No claim is made here with regard to any section 83 income Alves may have received during the 1973 tax year.

[3] In his Tax Court petition, Alves claimed error in reporting as ordinary income the $8,736 gain on the 2,240 five-year shares sold to TVI in 1974. Our disposition here necessarily resolves that issue.

Section 83 resolved this disparity by requiring the taxpayer either to elect to include the "excess" of the fair market value over the purchase price in the year the stock was transferred, or to be taxed upon the full amount of appreciation when the risk of forfeiture was removed... By its terms, the statute applies when property is: (1) transferred in connection with the performance of services; (2) subject to a substantial risk of forfeiture; and (3) not disposed of in an arm's length transaction before the property becomes transferable or the risk of forfeiture is removed. In the present case, it is undisputed that the stock in question was subject to a substantial risk of forfeiture, that it was not disposed of before the restrictions lapsed, and that Alves made no section 83(b) election. Alves's contention is that because he paid full fair market value for the shares, they were issued as an investment, rather than in connection with the performance of services.

The Tax Court concluded that Alves obtained the stock "in connection with the performance of services" as company vice-president... Although payment of full fair market value may be one indication that stock was not transferred in connection with the performance of services, the record shows that until the company sold stock to TVI, it issued stock only to its officers, directors, and employees, with the exception of the shares sold to the underwriter. Alves purchased the stock when he signed his employment agreement and the stock restrictions were linked explicitly to his tenure with the company. In addition, the parties stipulated that the restricted stock's purpose was to ensure that key personnel would remain with the company. Nothing in the record suggests that Alves could have purchased the stock had he not agreed to join the company.

Alves maintains that, as a matter of law, section 83(a) should not extend to purchases for full fair market value. He argues that "in connection with" means that the employee is receiving compensation for his performance of services. In the unusual situation where the employee pays the same amount for restricted and unrestricted stock, the restriction has no effect on value, and hence, Alves contends, there is no compensation.

The plain language of section 83(a) belies Alves's argument. The statute applies to all property transferred in connection with the performance of services. No reference is made to the term "compensation." Nor is there any statutory requirement that property have a fair market value in excess of the amount paid at the time of transfer. Indeed, if Congress intended section 83(a) to apply solely to restricted stock used to compensate employees, it could have used much narrower language. Instead, Congress made section 83(a) applicable to all restricted "property," not just stock; to property transferred to "any person," not just to employees; and to property transferred "in connection with . . . services" not just compensation for employment... As the Second Circuit has noted, Congress drafted section 83(a) as a "blanket rule" in an effort to create "a workable, practical system of taxing employees' restricted stock options." Sakol v. Commissioner, 574 F.2d 694, 699–700 (2d Cir.) *cert. denied*, 439 U.S. 859 . . . (1978).

Section 83's legislative history also reveals that while Congress was concerned primarily with the favorable tax treatment afforded restricted stock plans, it also was concerned that such plans were a means of allowing key employees to become shareholders in businesses without adhering to requirements in other sections of the Code. The Senate Report stated:

> To the extent that a restricted stock plan can be considered a means of giving employees a stake in the business, the committee believes the present tax treatment of these plans is inconsistent with the specific rules provided by Congress in the case of qualified stock options, which were considered by Congress as the appropriate means by which an employee could be given a shareholder's interest in the business. . .

The legislative history reveals that Congress perceived restricted stock as more than a problem of deferred compensation. It also demonstrates that Congress intended section 83 to apply to taxpayers like Alves who allege that they purchased restricted stock as an investment.

Alves suggests that the language of section 83(b) indicates that Congress meant for that section to apply only to bargain purchases and that section 83(a) should be interpreted in the same way. Section 83(b) allows taxpayers to elect to include as income in the year of transfer "the excess" of the full fair market value over the purchase price. Alves contends that a taxpayer who pays full fair market value would have "zero excess," and would fall outside the terms of section 83(b).

Section 83(b), however, is not a limitation upon section 83(a). Congress designed section 83(b) merely to add "flexibility," not to condition section 83(a) on the presence or absence of an "excess." . . . Moreover, nothing in section 83(b) precludes a taxpayer who has paid full market value for restricted stock from making an 83(b) election. Treasury Regulations promulgated in 1978 and made retroactive to 1969 specifically provide that section 83(b) is available in situations of zero excess:

> If property is transferred . . . in connection with the performance of services, the person performing such services may elect to include in gross income under section 83(b) the excess (if any) of the fair market value of the property at the time of transfer . . . over the amount (if any) paid for such property. . . *The fact that the transferee has paid full value for the property transferred, realizing no bargain element in the transaction, does not preclude the use of the election as provided for in this section. . .*

§ 1.83.2(a) (1983) (emphasis supplied). These regulations are consistent with the broad language of section 83 and, as the Tax Court stated, simply make "more explicit a fact which is inherent in the statute itself." 79 T.C. at 877–78 n.7. . .

Alves last contends that since every taxpayer who pays full fair market value for restricted stock would, if well informed, choose the section 83(b) election to hedge against any appreciation, applying section 83(a) to the unfortunate taxpayer who made no election is simply a trap for the unwary. The tax laws often make an affirmative election necessary. Section 83(b) is but one example of a provision requiring taxpayers to act or suffer less attractive tax consequences. A taxpayer wishing to avoid treatment of appreciation as ordinary income must make an affirmative election under 83(b) in the year the stock was acquired. . .

The decision of the Tax Court is affirmed.

NOTES

1. In *Alves* the Ninth Circuit was no doubt influenced by the Treasury Regulations which, as the court pointed out, had been issued with retroactive effect. Because Congress was concerned that the decision in *Alves* may have caused investors in start-up companies unfairly to lose capital gains treatment because of their failure to make timely § 83(b) elections, the 1984 Act extended the time period in which to make an election for stock transfers occurring before the date of the Tax Court's decision in *Alves*. The legislation relieved the taxpayer in *Alves* itself as well as some others from the result in that case. See § 556 of the TRA of 1984, Pub. L. No. 98–369, 98 Stat. 898.

2. See Maurice J. Cohn, 73 T.C. 443 (1979), where the Tax Court held that § 83 applies to independent contractors, and not merely to employees, with respect to restricted shares received as compensation for services rendered.

3. In Commissioner v. LoBue, 351 U.S. 243 (1956), the Court held that employees exercising stock options granted by their employers realize ordinary income on the date of exercise as measured by the difference between the option price and the fair market value of the stock on the date of exercise. See Treas. Reg. § 1.61–15. Sections 421–425 enacted special rules which mitigated the *LoBue* result, offering opportunities to defer the income until the stock was sold and to convert the income into long-term capital gain. The Tax Reform Act of 1976 repealed the favorable rules for "qualified stock options," delegating their tax consequences to § 83. See H. R. Rep. No. 941515, 94th Cong., 2d Sess. 438–439 (1976); Treas. Reg. § 1.83–2(a), 1.83–3(a), and 1.83–7. A concomitant of the 1976 change was a business expense deduction for the employer equal to the amount includible in the employee's income. The Economic Recovery Tax Act of 1981 (ERTA) reversed the direction taken in 1976, enacting (now) § 422 which provides for "incentive stock options." The report of the Senate Committee on Finance states:

> The committee believes that reinstitution of a stock option provision will provide an important incentive device for corporations to attract new management and retain the service of executives who might otherwise leave, by providing an opportunity to acquire an interest in the business. Encouraging the management of business to have a proprietary interest in its successful operation will provide an important incentive to expand and improve the profit position of the companies involved. The committee bill is designed to encourage the use of stock options for key employees without reinstituting the alleged abuses which arose with the restricted stock option provisions of prior law. . .

> The bill provides for "incentive stock options," which will be taxed in a manner similar to the tax treatment previously applied to restricted and

qualified stock options. That is, there will be no tax consequences when an incentive stock option is granted or when the option is exercised, and the employee will be taxed at capital gains rates when the stock received on exercise of the option is sold. Similarly, no business expense deduction will be allowed to the employer with respect to an incentive stock option.

The term "incentive stock option" means an option granted to an individual, for any reason connected with his or her employment, by the employer corporation or by a parent or subsidiary corporation of the employer corporation, to purchase stock of any of such corporations. . .

To receive incentive stock option treatment, the bill provides that the employee must not dispose of the stock within two years after the option is granted, and must hold the stock itself for at least one year. If all requirements other than these holding period rules are met, the tax will be imposed on sale of the stock, but gain will be treated as ordinary income rather than capital gain, and the employer will be allowed a deduction at that time [limited to the spread between the sale price and option price]. . .

The difference between the option price and the fair market value of the stock at the exercise of the option will not be an item of tax preference. . . [S. Rep. No. 97–144, 97th Cong., 1st Sess. 98–100.]

Should compensation paid in the form of stock be treated differently from that paid in cash? Why?

5. Intersection between securities regulation and taxation of stock: Prior to the enactment of ERTA in 1981, if stock or other property received was not transferable or was subject to a substantial risk of forfeiture, taxation was generally postponed until the stock or the property was transferable or no longer subject to a substantial risk of forfeiture. In Horwith v. Commissioner, 71 T.C. 932 (1979), the Tax Court held that § 16(b) of the Securities Exchange Act of 1934, under which an insider's profit may be recovered by a corporation if the stock is sold within six months of receipt, does not make the stock nontransferable and therefore does not affect the taxation of the stock. Accordingly, the value of the stock (less any amount paid) was treated as compensation when received. ERTA changed the law by adding § 83(c)(3), which provides that stock received by a taxpayer that is subject to the application of § 16(b) of the Securities Exchange Act of 1934 is treated as being nontransferable and subject to a substantial risk of forfeiture for the six-month period following receipt of the stock. Thus, at the expiration of the six-month period, the employee must include in income, and the employer may deduct, the difference between the value of the stock at that time and the amount paid (if any). Under § 83(b), however, an employee may elect to include in income at the time of the transfer the excess of the value of the property at that time (determined without regard to the § 16(b) restriction) over any amount paid.

III. RECAPITALIZATIONS AND CERTAIN INVESTOR EXCHANGES

A. RECAPITALIZATION—§§ 368(a)(1)(E), 354, 356

Bazley v. Commissioner
331 U.S. 737 (1947).

■ MR. JUSTICE FRANKFURTER delivered the opinion of the Court. The proper construction of provisions of the Internal Revenue Code relating to corporate reorganizations is involved in [this case]. Their importance to the Treasury as well as to corporate enterprise led us to grant certiorari, . . . 329 U.S. 701. . .

. . . [T]he Commissioner . . . assessed an income tax deficiency against the taxpayer for the year 1939. Its validity depends on the legal significance of the recapitalization in that year of a family corporation in which the taxpayer and his wife owned all but one of the Company's one thousand shares. These had a par value of $100. Under the plan of reorganization the taxpayer, his wife, and the holder of the additional share were to turn in their old shares and receive in exchange for each old share five new shares of no par value, but of a stated value of $60, and new debenture bonds, having a total face value of $400,000, payable in ten years but callable at any time. Accordingly, the taxpayer received 3,990 shares of the new stock for the 798 shares of his old holding and debentures in the amount of $319,200. At the time of these transactions the earned surplus of the corporation was $855,783.82.

The Commissioner charged to the taxpayer as income the full value of the debentures. The Tax Court affirmed the Commissioner's determination against the taxpayer's contention that as a "recapitalization" the transaction was a tax-free "reorganization" and that the debentures were "securities in a corporation a party to a reorganization," "exchanged solely for stock or securities in such corporation" "in pursuance of the plan of reorganization," and as such no gain is recognized for income tax purposes. . . [Sections 368(a)(1)(E) and 354(a)(1)].* The Tax Court found that the recapitalization had "no legitimate corporate business purpose" and was therefore not a "reorganization" within the statute. The distribution of debentures, it concluded, was a disguised dividend, taxable as earned income under [§§ 61(a)(7), 301, and 302]. . . The Circuit Court of Appeals for the Third Circuit, sitting en banc, affirmed, two judges dissenting. . .

Unless a transaction is a reorganization contemplated by § [368], any exchange of "stock or securities" in connection with such transaction, cannot be "in pursuance of the plan of reorganization" under § [354(a)(1)]. While § [368(a)(1)] informs us that "reorganization" means, among other things, "a recapitalization," it does not inform us what "recapitalization" means. "Recapitalization" in connection with the income tax has been part

---

* The 1939 Code under which this case was litigated had no counterparts to §§ 354(a)(2) and 356(d).—ED.

of the revenue laws since 1921. . . Congress has never defined it and the Treasury Regulations shed only limited light. Treas. Reg. [§ 1.368–2(e)]. One thing is certain. Congress did not incorporate some technical concept, whether that of accountants or of other specialists, into § [368] assuming that there is agreement among specialists as to the meaning of recapitalization. And so, recapitalization as used in § [368(a)(1)(E)] must draw its meaning from its function in that section. It is one of the forms of reorganization which obtains the privileges afforded by § [354(a)(1)]. Therefore, "recapitalization" must be construed with reference to the presuppositions and purpose of [the reorganization provisions].It was not the purpose of the reorganization provision to exempt from payment of a tax what as a practical matter is realized gain. Normally, a distribution by a corporation, whatever form it takes, is a definite and rather unambiguous event. It furnishes the proper occasion for the determination and taxation of gain. But there are circumstances where a formal distribution, directly or through exchange of securities, represents merely a new form of the previous participation in an enterprise, involving no change of substance in the rights and relations of the interested parties one to another or to the corporate assets. As to these, Congress has said that they are not to be deemed significant occasions for determining taxable gain.

These considerations underlie § [368] and they should dominate the scope to be given to the various sections, all of which converge toward a common purpose. Application of the language of such a revenue provision is not an exercise in framing abstract definitions. In a series of cases this Court has withheld the benefits of the reorganization provision in situations which might have satisfied provisions of the section treated as inert language because they were not reorganizations of the kind with which [the reorganization provisions], in [their] purpose and particulars, concern [themselves]. See Pinellas Ice & Cold Storage Co. v. Commissioner, 287 U.S. 462 [page 476 infra]; Gregory v. Helvering, 293 U.S. 465 [page 445 infra]; LeTulle v. Scofield, 308 U.S. 415 [page 483 infra].

Congress has not attempted a definition of what is recapitalization and we shall follow its example. The search for relevant meaning is often satisfied not by a futile attempt at abstract definition but by pricking a line through concrete applications. Meaning frequently is built up by assured recognition of what does not come within a concept the content of which is in controversy. Since a recapitalization within the scope of [the reorganization provisions] is an aspect of reorganization, nothing can be a recapitalization for this purpose unless it partakes of those characteristics of a reorganization which underlie the purpose of Congress in postponing the tax liability.

No doubt there was a recapitalization of the Bazley corporation in the sense that the symbols that represented its capital were changed, so that the fiscal basis of its operations would appear very differently on its books. But the form of a transaction as reflected by the correct corporate accounting opens questions as to the proper application of a taxing statute; it does not close them. Corporate accounting may represent that correspondence between change in the form of capital structure and essential identity in fact which is of the essence of a transaction relieved from taxation as a reorganization. What is controlling is that a new arrangement intrinsically partake of the elements of reorganization which underlie the congressional exemption and not merely give the appearance of it to accomplish a distribution of earnings. In the case of a corporation which has undistributed earnings, the creation of new corporate obligations which are transferred to stockholders in relation to their former holdings, so as to produce, for all practical purposes, the same result as a distribution of cash earnings of equivalent value, cannot obtain tax immunity because cast in the form of a recapitalization-reorganization. The governing legal rule can hardly be stated more narrowly. To attempt to do so would only challenge astuteness in evading it. And so it is hard to escape the conclusion that whether in a particular case a paper recapitalization is no more than an admissible attempt to avoid the consequences of an outright distribution of earnings turns on details of corporate affairs, judgment on which must be left to the Tax Court. See Dobson v. Commissioner, 320 U.S. 489.

What have we here? No doubt, if the Bazley corporation had issued the debentures to Bazley and his wife without any recapitalization, it would have made a taxable distribution. Instead, these debentures were issued as part of a family arrangement, the only additional ingredient being an unrelated modification of the capital account. The debentures were found to be worth at least their principal amount, and they were virtually cash because they were callable at the will of the corporation which in this case was the will of the taxpayer. One does not have to pursue the motives behind actions, even in the more ascertainable forms of purpose, to find, as did the Tax Court, that the whole arrangement took this form instead of an outright distribution of cash or debentures, because the latter would undoubtedly have been taxable income whereas what was done could, with a show of reason, claim the shelter of the immunity of a recapitalization-reorganization.

The Commissioner, the Tax Court and the Circuit Court of Appeals agree that nothing was accomplished that would not have been accomplished by an outright debenture dividend. And since we find no misconception of law on the part of the Tax Court and the Circuit Court of Appeals, whatever may have been their choice of phrasing, their application of the law to the facts of this case must stand. A "reorganization" which is merely a vehicle, however elaborate or elegant, for conveying earnings from accumulations to the stockholders is not a reorganization under [the reorganization provisions]. This disposes of the case as a matter of law, since the facts as found by the Tax Court bring them within it. And even if this transaction were deemed a reorganization, the facts would equally sustain the imposition of the tax on the debentures under § [356(a)(1) and (2)]. Commissioner v. Estate of Bedford, 325 U.S. 283. . .

    . . . [A]ffirmed.

■ MR. JUSTICE DOUGLAS and MR. JUSTICE BURTON dissent . . . for the reasons stated in the joint dissent of Judges Maris and Goodrich in the court Below. Bazley V. Commissioner, 155 F.2d 237, 244.

NOTES

1. Does *Bazley* hold that a distribution of securities is always to be treated as a distribution of cash? A number of subsequent decisions under the 1939 Code allowed reorganization treatment for some exchanges in which bonds were issued in exchange for some of the issuing corporation's outstanding stock. See B. Bittker and J. Eustice, Federal Income Taxation of Corporations and Shareholders 12.27[5] (2012 online). The 1939 Code did not contain provisions corresponding to §§ 354(a)(2) and 356(d), which were added in 1954. The latter was said to be "a restatement of the principle stated by the Supreme Court in *Bazley*." S. Rep. No. 1622, 83d Cong., 2d Sess., 3 U.S. Code Cong. & Admin. News 4907 (1954). Do you agree with that statement? How does the treatment under § 354(a)(2) and § 356 for the receipt of bonds in exchange for stock compare with *Bazley*? (Hint: *Bazley* adopts a dividend distribution approach).

The Commissioner was soon on the other side of the fence, arguing that a distribution of bonds in exchange for stock of lesser value was a reorganization and therefore could not give rise to original issue discount, described in what is now §§ 1271–1275, which would be deductible over the life of the bond by the corporation under Treas. Reg. §§ 1.163–3, 1.163–4. In Commissioner v. National Alfalfa Dehydrating & Milling Co., 417 U.S. 134 (1974), the Court held that no discount was created when the taxpayer issued $50 bonds in exchange for shares of $50 preferred stock, in part because it incurred no additional cost of capital. Subsequent cases allowed the discount under certain circumstances. See, e.g., Gulf, Mobile & Ohio R.R. v. United States, 579 F.2d 892 (5th Cir. 1978). A 1969 amendment explicitly excluded securities distributed in reorganizations from original issue discount treatment. Then the 1984 Act significantly revised and expanded the scope of the original issue discount provisions to cover a wider range of transactions including reorganization exchanges involving publicly traded or nontraded debt. §§ 1271–1275. Further changes in 1990 specified that the shareholder OID and corporate COD on bond-bond exchanges would be calculated based on the difference between the old debt adjusted issue price and the new debt adjusted issue price. §§ 108(e)(10), 1273, 1274.

2. "E" reorganization v. taxable distribution: The stock received in a recapitalization may be § 306 stock or may give rise to § 305(b) problems. Consider G.C.M. 39088, in which the Treasury Department concluded that § 305(b)(3) did not apply to a transaction in which some common shareholders exchanged their shares for an equal number of new common shares plus nonvoting nonconvertible preferred stock while other shareholders received shares of the same class of new common plus shares of nonvoting common. Such a transaction was found to be an "E" reorganization and not a § 305(b)(3) distribution, on the assumption that it had a bona fide business purpose, was an isolated transaction, and was not "part of a plan to increase periodically the proportionate interest of any shareholder in the assets or earnings and profits of the corporation." In the fact pattern described in the memorandum, the transaction was designed as a one-time event to shift permanently the future equity growth of a

family-owned corporation from an older generation of shareholders to a younger generation.

B. EXERCISE OF CONVERSION PRIVILEGES

In Rev. Rul. 57–535, 1957–2 C.B. 513, the Commissioner ruled that there is no realization in a transaction in which a security, convertible by its terms, is converted into another. The transaction is treated as a transformation, not an "exchange" or "disposition." Since no "closed transaction" has occurred, there is no "realization"; and so no nonrecognition provision, such as § 354 or § 1031 or § 1036 (see page 434 infra), is needed to defer taxation. See Treas. Reg. § 1.1001–1(a).

Compare Rev. Rul. 72–265, 1972–1 C.B. 222 (conversion of debenture into stock of same corporation is not a taxable event) and Rev. Rul. 79–155, 1979–1 C.B. 153 (conversion of debenture into stock of a different corporation that was also an obligor on the debenture not a taxable event), *with* Rev. Rul. 69–135, 1969–1 C.B. 198 (conversion of debenture into stock of a different corporation that is not liable for the debenture is a taxable event).

When is (or is not) a conversion of one security into another a part of a recapitalization? See Rev. Rul. 77–238, 1977–2 C.B. 115 (provisions in articles of incorporation to require or encourage conversions are plans of reorganizations, and conversions are exchanges pursuant to plan).

C. DEBT REFUNDING

The exchange of bonds for other bonds of the same issuer that differ only in immaterial details does not produce a "realization." However, if the bonds exchanged are "materially different," a realization event is triggered. See Cottage Savings Association v. Commissioner, 499 U.S. 554 (1991). Regulations promulgated by the Service after *Cottage Savings* attempted to delineate (1) what constitutes a modification in the exchange of debt instruments, and (2) under what circumstances are such modifications "significant" enough to deem the instruments materially different. Treas. Reg. § 1.1001–3. Changes such as a new obligor, or an extension of the term of the bond for more than the lesser of 5 years or 50 percent of the bond term can constitute significant modification. Treas. Reg. § 1.1001–3(e). In a bond-for-bond exchange, if the principal amount of the securities received exceeds the principal amount of the securities surrendered, then under § 356(d)(2)(B) the fair market value of the excess is treated as "boot". Any gain realized on the exchange would be taxable up to that amount of boot. If instead the principal amount of securities received is less than that surrendered, the issuing corporation has cancellation of debt income.

In Letter Rul. 8815003 (Dec. 11, 1987), the IRS granted "E" reorganization treatment to a transaction in which, pursuant to an agreement with the reorganizing corporation, an underwriter purchased the corporation's outstanding bonds at a discount and then surrendered them to the corporation in exchange for new bonds yielding a lower rate of interest.

D. EXCHANGE OF INVESTOR INTEREST

1. FOR ASSETS—§ 1031

Normally, an investor who exchanges his appreciated (or depreciated) corporate stock or debt for assets has recognized gain (or loss), although a few provisions (e.g., §§ 267, 1091) provide for nonrecognition of loss. Why is § 1031, a nonrecognition provision applicable to the exchange of business and investment assets, made expressly inapplicable to an exchange involving stock or securities? See § 1031(a)(2)(B).

2. FOR STOCK OR SECURITIES—§§ 1031, 1036

Section 1036 provides for nonrecognition (and § 1031(d) for carryover of basis) where common stock is exchanged for common stock in the same corporation and where preferred stock is exchanged for preferred stock in the same corporation. Note that a "reorganization" is not a prerequisite for this provision to operate, as it is for § 354. Why is § 1036 in the Code?

Why is it limited to stock "in the same corporation"? Why does it not cover an exchange of common for preferred (or vice versa) in the same corporation? Does § 1036 cover an exchange between investors only? Between an investor and his corporation only? Among investors as well as between the investor and his corporation? See Treas. Reg. § 1.1036–1.

Is § 1036 applicable to an exchange of Class A (voting) common stock for Class B (nonvoting) common stock in the same corporation? Is it applicable to an exchange of a 6–percent, participating, cumulative, nonvoting preferred stock for an 8–percent, nonparticipating, noncumulative, voting preferred stock in the same corporation? Note that after the 1997 Act, nonqualified preferred stock (§ 351(g)(2)) is treated as "other property" not stock under § 1036.

IV. THE STATUTE IN PERSPECTIVE

A. BEFORE SPECIAL TREATMENT

Marr v. United States
268 U.S. 536 (1925).

■ MR. JUSTICE BRANDEIS delivered the opinion of the Court. Prior to March 1, 1913, Marr and wife purchased 339 shares of the preferred and 425 shares of common stock of the General Motors Company of New Jersey for $76,400. In 1916, they received in exchange for this stock 451 shares of the preferred and 2,125 shares of the common stock of the General Motors Corporation of Delaware which (including a small cash payment) had the aggregate market value of $400,866.57. The difference between the cost of their stock in the New Jersey corporation and the value of the stock in the Delaware corporation was $324,466.57. The Treasury Department ruled that this difference was gain or income under the Act of September 8, 1916,

c. 463, Title I, §§ 1 and 2 . . .;* and assessed, on that account, an additional income tax for 1916 which amounted, with interest, to $24,944.12. That sum Marr paid under protest. He then appealed to the Commissioner of the Internal Revenue by filing a claim for a refund; and, upon disallowance of that claim, brought this suit in the Court of Claims to recover the amount. Judgment was entered for the United States. . .

The exchange of securities was effected in this way. The New Jersey corporation had outstanding $15,000,000 of 7 percent preferred stock and $15,000,000 of the common stock, all shares being of the par value of $100. It had accumulated from profits a large surplus. The actual value of the common stock was then $842.50 a share. Its officers caused to be organized the Delaware corporation, with an authorized capital of $20,000,000 in 6 percent non-voting preferred stock and $82,600,000 in common stock, all shares being of the par value of $100. The Delaware corporation made to stockholders in the New Jersey corporation the following offer for exchange of securities: For every share of common stock of the New Jersey corporation, five shares of common stock of the Delaware corporation. For every share of the preferred stock of the New Jersey corporation, one and one-third shares of preferred stock of the Delaware corporation. In lieu of a certificate for fractional shares of stock in the Delaware corporation payment was to be made in cash at the rate of $100 a share for its preferred and at the rate of $150 a share for its common stock. On this basis all the common stock of the New Jersey corporation was exchanged and all the preferred stock except a few shares. These few were redeemed in cash. For acquiring the stock of the New Jersey corporation only $75,000,000 of the common stock of the Delaware corporation was needed. The remaining $7,600,000 of the authorized common stock was either sold or held for sale as additional capital should be desired. The Delaware corporation, having thus become the owner of all the outstanding stock of the New Jersey corporation, took a transfer of its assets and assumed its liabilities. The latter was then dissolved.

It is clear that all new securities issued in excess of an amount equal to the capitalization of the New Jersey corporation represented income earned by it; that the new securities received by the Marrs in excess of the cost of the securities of the New Jersey corporation theretofore held were financially the equivalent of $324,466.57 in cash; and that Congress intended to tax as income of stockholders such gains when so distributed. The serious question for decision is whether it had power to do so. Marr contends that, since the new corporation was organized to take over the assets and continue the business of the old, and his capital remained invested in the same business enterprise, the additional securities distributed were in legal effect a stock dividend; and that under the rule of Eisner v. Macomber [page 351 supra], applied in Weiss v. Stearn, 265 U.S. 242, he was not taxable thereon as income, because he still held the whole investment. The Government insists that identity of the business enterprise is not conclusive; that gain in value resulting from profits is taxable as income, not only when it is represented by an interest in a different business enterprise or

---

* Section 61(a) of the 1986 Code.—ED.

property, but also when it is represented by an essentially different interest in the same business enterprise or property; that, in the case at bar, the gain actually made is represented by securities with essentially different characteristics in an essentially different corporation; and that, consequently, the additional value of the new securities, although they are still held by the Marrs, is income under the rule applied in United States v. Phellis, 257 U.S. 156; Rockefeller v. United States, 257 U.S. 176; and Cullinan v. Walker, 262 U.S. 134. In our opinion the Government is right.

In each of the five cases named, as in the case at bar, the business enterprise actually conducted remained exactly the same. In United States v. Phellis, in Rockefeller v. United States and in Cullinan v. Walker, where the additional value in new securities distributed was held to be taxable as income, there had been changes of corporate identity. That is, the corporate property, or a part thereof, was no longer held and operated by the same corporation; and, after the distribution, the stockholders no longer owned merely the same proportional interest of the same character in the same corporation. In Eisner v. Macomber and in Weiss v. Stearn, where the additional value in new securities was held not to be taxable, the identity was deemed to have been preserved. In Eisner v. Macomber the identity was literally maintained. There was no new corporate entity. The same interest in the same corporation was represented after the distribution by more shares of precisely the same character. It was as if the par value of the stock had been reduced, and three shares of reduced par value stock had been issued in place of every two old shares. That is, there was an exchange of certificates but not of interests. In Weiss v. Stearn a new corporation had, in fact, been organized to take over the assets and business of the old. Technically there was a new entity; but the corporate identity was deemed to have been substantially maintained because the new corporation was organized under the laws of the same State, with presumably the same powers as the old. There was also no change in the character of securities issued. By reason of these facts, the proportional interest of the stockholder after the distribution of the new securities was deemed to be exactly the same as if the par value of the stock in the old corporation had been reduced, and five shares of reduced par value stock had been issued in place of every two shares of the old stock. Thus, in Weiss v. Stearn, as in Eisner v. Macomber, the transaction was considered, in essence, an exchange of certificates representing the same interest, not an exchange of interests.

In the case at bar, the new corporation is essentially different from the old. A corporation organized under the laws of Delaware does not have the same rights and powers as one organized under the laws of New Jersey. Because of these inherent differences in rights and powers, both the preferred and the common stock of the old corporation is an essentially different thing from stock of the same general kind in the new. But there are also adventitious differences, substantial in character. A 6 percent, non-voting preferred stock is an essentially different thing from a 7 percent, voting preferred stock. A common stock subject to the priority of $20,000,000 preferred and a $1,200,000 annual dividend charge is an essentially different thing from a common stock subject only to $15,000,000 preferred and a $1,050,000 annual dividend charge. The case at bar is not one in which after the distribution the stockholders have the same proportional interest of the same kind in essentially the same corporation.

Affirmed.

■ The separate opinion of MR. JUSTICE VAN DEVANTER, MR. JUSTICE McREYNOLDS, MR. JUSTICE SUTHERLAND and MR. JUSTICE BUTLER. We think this cause falls within the doctrine of Weiss v. Stearn, 265 U.S. 242, and that the judgment below should be reversed. The practical result of the things done was but the reorganization of a going concern. The business and assets were not materially changed, and the stockholder received nothing actually severed from his original capital interest—nothing differing in substance from what he already had.

Weiss v. Stearn did not turn upon the relatively unimportant circumstance that the new and old corporations were organized under the laws of the same State, but upon the approved definition of income from capital as something severed therefrom and received by the taxpayer for his separate use and benefit. Here stockholders got nothing from the old business or assets except new statements of their undivided interests, and this, as we carefully pointed out, is not enough to create taxable income.

B. SINCE SPECIAL TREATMENT

1. STATUTORY "CLOSE–ORDER DRILL"—§§ 368, 354, 355, 356, 357, 358, 361, 362, 332, 334

Before studying the overlay of judicial doctrines that have developed in connection with reorganizations, it will be useful to gain familiarity with the pattern and interrelationship of the relevant sections of the 1986 Code. When you examine the reorganization provisions of the Code, consider which, if any, of the current reorganization definitions might cover the transaction in *Marr*.

a. Start with § 368(a). It defines the various reorganizations. It is not a section that fixes tax consequences or determines recognition. Subsection (a)(1) lists and defines seven types of "reorganization," from (A) to (G). Tax lawyers, familiar with the definitions, use a shorthand reference system in identifying a particular type of reorganization. They refer to an "A reorganization," or just an "A," if they mean one defined in § 368(a)(1)(A), and to a "B," if they mean one defined in § 368(a)(1)(B), and so forth. This book will use that shorthand.

(i) An "A" reorganization is a statutory merger or consolidation of two or more corporations. Although Treasury originally adopted the view that statutory mergers involving "disregarded entities" (Temp. Treas. Reg. § 1.368–2T(b)(1)(i)(A)) could not qualify as A-reorganizations, new temporary regulations identify the circumstances under which such mergers qualify. Treas. Reg. § 1.368–2(b)(1)(iii). By "statutory" the Code historically has meant a merger or consolidation effected pursuant to state or federal statutory law. In January 2005, Treasury issued proposed regulations revising the definition of statutory merger to eliminate the restriction to federal or state law, thereby allowing mergers under foreign law to qualify as well. Final regulations on foreign mergers were issued in 2006. Treas. Reg. § 1.368–2(b)(1)(ii) & (iii).

(ii) A "B" reorganization contemplates one corporation's acquisition, in exchange solely for a portion of its voting stock, of "control" of another corporation. When the reorganization is completed the acquiring corporation will be the parent and the acquired corporation will be a subsidiary (although not necessarily a 100–percent owned subsidiary). The former shareholders of the subsidiary corporation will now own voting shares in the parent.

(iii) A "C" reorganization is sometimes referred to as a "de facto" merger, in contrast with the "de jure" merger embraced in the "A" reorganization. In general, a "C" reorganization contemplates one corporation's transfer of "substantially all of its properties" to another corporation in exchange solely for voting stock of the latter, although § 368(a)(2)(B) does mitigate this requirement somewhat. Under § 368(a)(2)(G), added in 1984, the transferor corporation in a "C" reorganization must, as a general matter, completely liquidate, i.e., distribute to its shareholders pursuant to the plan of reorganization the stock, securities, and other property it receives, as well as any other properties not transferred in the reorganization. The latter requirement may be waived by the Service.

(iv) A "D" reorganization requires the transfer of a portion of one corporation's assets to another in circumstances in which the transferor or its shareholders are immediately thereafter "in control" of the transferee corporation. Ordinarily, the transferee issues stock to the transferor, and the transferor then liquidates, distributing to its shareholders the stock received from the transferee corporation. The last clause of § 368(a)(1)(D) requires a distribution that meets particular statutory patterns. Essentially, a "D" contemplates the division of one corporation into two or more or the substitution of one for another, in either case with substantial continuity of control.

(v) An "E" reorganization is a "recapitalization," studied earlier in this chapter, page 429 supra.

(vi) An "F" reorganization, at least on its face, involves very little, a "mere change in identity, form or place of organization."

(vii) A "G" reorganization requires the transfer of "all or part" of a corporation's assets to a second corporation in a bankruptcy proceeding, as further defined, followed by a distribution of the transferee's stock in a transaction that conforms to specified statutory provisions.

b. Section 368(a)(2) sets forth modifications and amplifications of the sometimes stark and restrictive definitional rules in § 368(a). Read the section carefully. Its full impact will become clearer as you work through the development of the case law. Two provisions of § 368(a)(2) are particularly worthy of mention at this point.

(i) An "(a)(2)(D)" or "forward triangular subsidiary merger" under § 368(a)(2)(D) involves the statutory merger of a target corporation into a subsidiary of the acquiring corporation, with the target's shareholders receiving stock of the corporation that controls the subsidiary. For the transaction to qualify, the surviving corporation (the controlled subsidiary) must receive "substantially all" the assets of the target, and no stock of the controlled subsidiary may be used in the transaction. Moreover, the transaction must meet all of the requirements (like the continuity of interest requirement, see page 472 infra) that would have been applicable if the merger had been into the corporation controlling the subsidiary.

(ii) An "(a)(2)(E)" or "reverse triangular subsidiary merger" under § 368(a)(2)(E) involves the statutory merger of the acquiring corporation's controlled subsidiary into the target corporation, with the target surviving. The shareholders of the target must receive only voting stock of the corporation controlling the subsidiary for an amount of the target's stock that constitutes "control" of the target, as defined in § 368(c)(1). After the transaction, the target must hold "substantially all" of its own assets and those of the controlled subsidiary.

In a highly publicized case, Times Mirror attempted to use a reverse triangular merger to avoid capital gains on the disposition of its legal publishing subsidiary (Matthew Bender). In simplified terms, pursuant to the terms of the deal, the Acquiror established a subsidiary (Sub 1), which itself owned 80% of the voting power of an LLC [limited liability company] which was the "merger subsidiary." The merger subsidiary merged into Matthew Bender with Sub 1 receiving Matthew Bender stock and Times Mirror receiving 20% voting control of Sub 1 (in the form of stock representing 100% of the common). Sub 1 also had an LLC capitalized with approximately $1,375 billion in cash; and after the merger, Times Mirror was named the *sole manager* of Sub 1's cash filled LLC. Given the indirect ownership of the cash filled LLC by Times Mirror through Sub 1, the LLC was consolidated with Times Mirror for financial accounting. What did this cash filled LLC do with the cash? It used some of the money to buy new common stock of Times Mirror. The Tax Court rejected Times Mirror's claim that the transaction constituted a reverse triangular merger and instead upheld the IRS $551.5 million deficiency on the grounds that is was a sale. Tribune Co. et al. v. Commissioner, 125 T.C. 110, (2005). Specifically the court stated that the primary consideration to Times Mirror in the deal was the $1.375 billion in cash in the LLC over which Times Mirror had management authority. Thus, the control test of § 368(c) was not met as required by § 368(a)(2)(E). In June 2007, Times Mirror announced it was negotiating a settlement with the Service. See, e.g., Coder, "Tribune's Potential Settlement Could Trap IRS Down the Road," 115 Tax Notes 1007 (June 11, 2007).

c. The provisions that determine the tax consequences of "reorganization" refer to those who are "a party to a reorganization." Section 368(b) defines a "party." It will become clearer in significance as you study the case law, but it is important now to keep in mind the necessity of determining who is a "party."

d. "Control" is a frequent requirement for particular tax consequences in reorganizations. For most cases, it is defined in § 368(c), as it was for purposes of § 351, as 80 percent of the combined voting power of all voting classes of stock and 80 percent of the shares of each remaining class. See Rev. Rul. 59–259, 1959–2 C.B. 115. For "D" reorganizations, however, "control" is defined as it is in § 304(c), i.e., the ownership of stock possessing at least 50 percent of the total combined voting power of all classes of stock entitled to vote, or at least 50 percent of the total value of all shares of all classes of stock (see § 368(a)(2)(H)). The constructive ownership rules of § 318(a), as modified by § 304(c)(3)(B), apply for purposes of determining whether this control requirement is met.

e. With the definitions of § 368 in mind, move to § 354(a)(1), a section that provides tax consequences for corporate investors who exchange "stock or securities in a corporation a party to a reorganization . . . in pursuance of the plan of reorganization. . ." Note the reference to "reorganization," defined in § 368(a)(1), and to "a party," defined in § 368(b). Note, too, the requirement for a "plan," a term not defined by statute, and for "stock or securities," similarly undefined. Since the term "securities" presumably means something other than "stock," it is taken to mean corporate debt, but not all corporate debt. Case and administrative law flesh out the meaning, somewhat painstakingly, somewhat irritatingly.

If § 354(a)(1) is applicable, the investor's gain or loss is not recognized. If § 354(a)(1) does not apply because the consideration received by the investor is not exclusively stock or securities, because the securities received are as described in § 354(a)(2)(A), or because the stock is nonqualified preferred stock under § 352(a)(2)(C), § 354(a)(3)(A) remits the taxpayer to § 356. Section 356(a) describes the tax treatment when "boot" is received, taxing the gain to the extent of the "boot" as capital gain if § 356(a)(1) applies, and as a dividend if § 356(a)(2) applies. After the 2003 Tax Act, this distinction established in § 356(a)(1) and (2) is no longer relevant for individuals because dividends and capital gains bear the same rate (although domestic corporations that are shareholders continue to benefit from the opportunity to characterize certain boot as a dividend and thereby to obtain the dividends received deduction). Despite the presence of "boot," loss is not recognized. § 356(c). Section 354(a)(2)(B) denies nonrecognition to the receipt of both stock and securities if attributable to accrued interest owed to the investor under certain circumstances.

f. When § 354 or § 356 applies to the investor in a transaction, his basis for the consideration received on the exchange is determined under § 358, much as it is in the case of an investor in a § 351 transaction.

g. Section 355 is applicable to corporate proliferations—spin-offs, split-offs, split-ups, and spin-aways. It is not dependent on a "reorganization," defined in § 368(a)(1), but frequently operates on a "D" reorganization. Look at the provisions of § 355 now, and the accompanying "boot" provisions in § 356(b), but their full impact must await the material that begins on page 539 infra. Mark for inquiry later the fact that the "boot" taxable under § 356(a) is limited to "gain." No such limitation encumbers § 356(b).

h. Corporations are transferors of assets in "A," "C," "D," "F," and "G" reorganizations. Recognition of their gain or loss is determined by § 361. Note the special "boot" provision in § 361(b), applicable if property not permitted by § 361(a) is received. It works quite differently from § 356, the "boot" provision applicable to investors. Section 357 determines the tax effect of a transfer of indebtedness.

The transferor corporation's basis for the consideration (usually stock or securities) it receives for its assets is determined under § 358, the section generally applicable to investors receiving stock or securities in a reorganization exchange.

i. The corporate transferee in an "A," "C," "D," "F," or "G" reorganization has no gain or loss on the issuance of its stock. See § 1032. Its basis for the assets received is determined under § 362(b). Section 362(b) also determines the basis to the acquiring corporation of the stock it acquires in a "B" reorganization in exchange for its own voting stock.

j. An intercorporate liquidation (subsidiary into parent) is not technically a "reorganization" as defined in § 368(a)(1). Such a liquidation, if covered by § 332, results in the nonrecognition of the parent's gain or loss in its stock investment. Section 332 is studied together with reorganizations because the effect of an intercorporate liquidation is substantially the same as a merger, and sometimes such a liquidation can be effected as an "A" reorganization. If § 332 provides nonrecognition for the parent's gain or loss, the assets the parent receives from the subsidiary will take their basis under § 334(b)(1). Section 337(a) bars recognition of gain or loss to an 80 percent-or-more-owned subsidiary with respect to assets distributed to its parent in a complete liquidation. Section 337(b) does the same with respect to the appreciation in the subsidiary's assets distributed to its parent in satisfaction of indebtedness.

The foregoing general summary of the Code provisions applicable to corporate reorganization is only that. It is no substitute for detailed analysis, close reading of the relevant Regulations, and an understanding of how the law came to be (and what it may become), which your study of the case law may help to provide. As you deal with specific and seemingly narrow statutory issues, take the time necessary to reflect and to consider the general perspective in which courts view reorganizations.

2. BUSINESS PURPOSE

Helvering v. Gregory

69 F.2d 809 (2d Cir. 1934), *aff'd*, 293 U.S. 465 (1935).*

■ Before L. HAND, SWAN, and AUGUSTUS N. HAND, CIRCUIT JUDGES.

■ L. HAND, CIRCUIT JUDGE. This is an appeal (petition to review), by the Commissioner of Internal Revenue from an order of the Board of Tax Appeals expunging a deficiency in income taxes for the year 1928. The facts were as follows: The taxpayer owned all the shares of the United Mortgage Corporation, among whose assets were some of the shares of another company, the Monitor Securities Corporation. In 1928 it became possible to sell the Monitor shares at a large profit, but if this had been done directly, the United Mortgage Corporation would have been obliged to pay a normal tax on the resulting gain, and the taxpayer, if she wished to touch her profit, must do so in the form of a dividend, on which a surtax would have been assessed against her personally. To reduce these taxes as much as possible, the following plan was conceived and put through: The taxpayer incorporated in Delaware a new company, organized ad hoc, and called the Averill Corporation, to which the United Mortgage Corporation transferred all its shares in the Monitor Securities Corporation, under an agreement by which the Averill Corporation issued all its shares to the taxpayer. Being so possessed of all the Averill shares, she wound up the Averill company three days later, receiving as a liquidating dividend the Monitor shares, which she thereupon sold. It is not disputed that all these steps were part of one purpose to reduce taxes, and that the Averill Corporation, which was in existence for only a few days, conducted no business and was intended to conduct none, except to act as conduit for the Monitor shares in the way we have described. The taxpayer's return for the year 1928 was made on the theory that the transfer of the Monitor shares to the Averill Corporation was a "reorganization" under section 112(i)(1)(B) of the Revenue Act of 1928** . . ., being "a transfer by a corporation of . . . a part of its assets to another corporation" in such circumstances that immediately thereafter "the transferor or its stockholders or both are in control of the corporation to which the assets are transferred." Since the transfer was a reorganization, she claimed to come within section 112(g). . .*** and that her "gain" should not be "recognized," because the Averill shares were "distributed, in pursuance of a plan of reorganization." The Monitor shares she asserted to have been received as a single liquidating dividend of the Averill Corporation, and that as such she was only taxable for them under section [331] . . . and upon their value less the cost properly allocated to the Averill shares. That cost she determined as that proportion of the original cost of her shares in the United Mortgage Corporation, which the Monitor shares bore to the whole assets of the United Mortgage Corporation. This difference she

---

* Page 446 infra.—ED.

** Cf. § 368(a)(1)(D) of the 1986 Code.—ED.

*** Section 112(g) is set forth in the Supreme Court's opinion in this case, page 446 infra. No 1986 Code section is the exact counterpart to § 112(g), but today, § 355(a) permits some tax free "spin-offs." Spin-offs and similar transactions are studied at page 541 et seq. infra.—ED.

returned, and paid the tax calculated upon it. The Commissioner assessed a deficiency taxed upon the theory that the transfer of the Monitor shares to the Averill Corporation was not a true "reorganization" within section 112(i)(1)(B), . . . being intended only to avoid taxes. He treated as nullities that transfer, the transfer of the Averill shares to the taxpayer, and the winding up of the Averill Corporation ending in the receipt by her of the Monitor shares; and he ruled that the whole transaction was merely the declaration of a dividend by the United Mortgage Corporation consisting of the Monitor shares in specie, on which the taxpayer must pay a surtax calculated at their full value. The taxpayer appealed and the Board held that the Averill Corporation had been in fact organized and was indubitably a corporation, that the United Mortgage Corporation had with equal certainty transferred to it the Monitor shares, and that the taxpayer had got the Averill shares as part of the transaction. All these transactions being real, their purpose was irrelevant, and section 112(i)(1)(B) was applicable, especially since it was part of a statute of such small mesh as the Revenue Act of 1928; the finer the reticulation, the less room for inference. The Board therefore expunged the deficiency, and the Commissioner appealed.

We agree with the Board and the taxpayer that a transaction, otherwise within an exception of the tax law, does not lose its immunity, because it is actuated by a desire to avoid, or, if one choose, to evade, taxation. Any one may so arrange his affairs that his taxes shall be as low as possible; he is not bound to choose that pattern which will best pay the Treasury; there is not even a patriotic duty to increase one's taxes. . . Therefore, if what was done here, was what was intended by section 112(i)(1)(B), it is of no consequence that it was all an elaborate scheme to get rid of income taxes, as it certainly was. Nevertheless, it does not follow that Congress meant to cover such a transaction, not even though the facts answer the dictionary definitions of each term used in the statutory definition. It is quite true, as the Board has very well said, that as the articulation of a statute increases, the room for interpretation must contract; but the meaning of a sentence may be more than that of the separate words, as a melody is more than the notes, and no degree of particularity can ever obviate recourse to the setting in which all appear, and which all collectively create. The purpose of the section is plain enough; men engaged in enterprises—industrial, commercial, financial, or any other—might wish to consolidate, or divide, to add to, or subtract from, their holdings. Such transactions were not to be considered as "realizing" any profit, because the collective interests still remained in solution. But the underlying presupposition is plain that the readjustment shall be undertaken for reasons germane to the conduct of the venture in hand, not as an ephemeral incident, egregious to its prosecution. To dodge the shareholders' taxes is not one of the transactions contemplated as corporate "reorganizations."

This accords both with the history of the section, and with its interpretation by the courts, though the exact point has not hitherto arisen. It first appeared in the Act of 1924, § 203(h)(1)(B), . . . and as the committee reports show (Senate Reports 398), was intended as supplementary to section 112(g), . . . then section 203(c) . . .; both in combination changed the law as laid down in U.S. v. Phellis, 257 U.S. 156, ... and Rockefeller v. U.S., 257 U.S. 176... [T]he purpose was stated to be to exempt "from tax the gain from exchanges made in connection with a reorganization in order that ordinary business transactions will not be prevented." ... Moreover, we regard Pinellas Ice & Cold Storage Co. v. Commissioner, 287 U.S. 462 ... [page 476 infra], and our own decision in Cortland Specialty Co. v. Commissioner, 60 F.2d 937, [page 478 infra] as pertinent, if not authoritative. In each the question was of the applicability of a precursor of section 112(i)(1)(A) of 1928, ... to the sale of all the assets of one company to another, which gave in exchange, cash and short time notes. The taxpayer's argument was that this was a "merger or consolidation," because the buyer acquired "all the property of another corporation," the seller, that being one statutory definition of "merger or consolidation." That assumed, the exemption was urged to fall within section 112(g) as here. It might have been enough to hold that short time notes were not "securities," within section 112(g); but both courts went further and declared that the transaction was not a "merger or consolidation," but a sale, though literally it fell within the words of section 112(i)(1)(A). This they did, because its plain purpose was to cover only a situation in which after the transaction there continued some community of interest between the companies, other than holding such notes. The violence done the literal interpretation of the words is no less than what we do here. Moreover, the act itself gives evidence that, on occasion anyway, the purpose of a transaction should be the guide; thus in section 115(g),* ... the cancellation of shares is to be treated as a dividend—though otherwise it would not be such—if it is "essentially equivalent to the distribution of a taxable dividend"; again in section 112(c)(2),** ... a distribution is in part taxable as a dividend, if it "has the effect of the distribution of a taxable dividend."

We do not indeed agree fully with the way in which the Commissioner treated the transaction; we cannot treat as inoperative the transfer of the Monitor shares by the United Mortgage Corporation, the issue by the Averill Corporation of its own shares to the taxpayer, and her acquisition of the Monitor shares by winding up that company. The Averill Corporation had a juristic personality, whatever the purpose of its organization; the transfer passed title to the Monitor shares and the taxpayer became a shareholder in the transferee. All these steps were real, and their only defect was that they were not what the statute means by a "reorganization," because the transactions were no part of the conduct of the business of either or both companies; so viewed they were a sham, though all the proceedings had their usual effect. But the result is the same whether the tax be calculated as the Commissioner calculated it, or upon the value of the Averill shares as a dividend, and the only question that can arise is whether the deficiency must be expunged, though right in result, if it was computed by a method, partly wrong. Although this is argued with some warmth, it is plain that the taxpayer may not avoid her just taxes because the reasoning of the assessing officials has not been entirely our own.

---

* Cf. §§ 302(a) and 317(b) of the 1986 Code.—Ed.

** Cf. § 356(a)(2) of the 1986 Code.—Ed.

Order reversed; deficiency assessed.

Gregory v. Helvering

293 U.S. 465 (1935).

■ Mr. Justice Sutherland delivered the opinion of the Court. Petitioner in 1928 was the owner of all the stock of United Mortgage Corporation. That corporation held among its assets 1,000 shares of the Monitor Securities Corporation. For the sole purpose of procuring a transfer of these shares to herself in order to sell them for her individual profit, and, at the same time, diminish the amount of income tax which would result from a direct transfer by way of dividend, she sought to bring about a "reorganization" under § 112(g) of the Revenue Act of 1928, c. 852, . . . set forth later in this opinion. To that end, she caused the Averill Corporation to be organized under the laws of Delaware on September 18, 1928. Three days later, the United Mortgage Corporation transferred to the Averill Corporation the 1,000 shares of Monitor stock, for which all the shares of the Averill Corporation were issued to the petitioner. On September 24, the Averill Corporation was dissolved, and liquidated by distributing all its assets, namely, the Monitor shares, to the petitioner. No other business was ever transacted, or intended to be transacted, by that company. Petitioner immediately sold the Monitor for $133,333.33. She returned for taxation as capital net gain the sum of $76,007.88, based upon an apportioned cost of $57,325.45. Further details are unnecessary. It is not disputed that if the interposition of the so-called reorganization was ineffective, petitioner became liable for a much larger tax as a result of the transaction.

The Commissioner of Internal Revenue, being of opinion that the reorganization attempted was without substance and must be disregarded, held that petitioner was liable for a tax as though the United corporation had paid her a dividend consisting of the amount realized from the sale of the Monitor shares. In a proceeding before the Board of Tax Appeals, that body rejected the commissioner's view and upheld that of petitioner. . . Upon a review of the latter decision, the circuit court of appeals sustained the commissioner and reversed the board, holding that there had been no "reorganization" within the meaning of the statute. . . Petitioner applied to this court for a writ of certiorari, which the government, considering the question one of importance, did not oppose. We granted the writ.

Section 112 of the Revenue Act of 1928 deals with the subject of gain or loss resulting from the sale or exchange of property. Such gain or loss is to be recognized in computing the tax, except as provided in that section. The provisions of the section, so far as they are pertinent to the question here presented, follow:

> Sec. 112(g) *Distribution of stock on reorganization.*—If there is distributed, in pursuance of a plan of reorganization, to a shareholder in a corporation a party to the reorganization, stock or securities in such corporation or in another corporation a party to the reorganization, without the surrender by such shareholder of stock or securities

in such a corporation, no gain to the distributee from the receipt of such stock or securities shall be recognized. . .

(i) *Definition of reorganization.*—As used in this section . . .

(1) The term "reorganization" means . . . (B) a transfer by a corporation of all or a part of its assets to another corporation if immediately after the transfer the transferor or its stockholders or both are in control of the corporation to which the assets are transferred, . . .

It is earnestly contended on behalf of the taxpayer that since every element required by the foregoing subdivision (B) is to be found in what was done, a statutory reorganization was effected; and that the motive of the taxpayer thereby to escape payment of a tax will not alter the result or make unlawful what the statute allows. It is quite true that if a reorganization in reality was effected within the meaning of subdivision (B), the ulterior purpose mentioned will be disregarded. The legal right of a taxpayer to decrease the amount of what otherwise would be his taxes, or altogether avoid them, by means which the law permits, cannot be doubted. . . But the question for determination is whether what was done, apart from the tax motive, was the thing which the statute intended. The reasoning of the court below in justification of a negative answer leaves little to be said.

When subdivision (B) speaks of a transfer of assets by one corporation to another, it means a transfer made "in pursuance of a plan of reorganization" [§ 112(g)] of corporate business; and not a transfer of assets by one corporation to another in pursuance of a plan having no relation to the business of either, as plainly is the case here. Putting aside, then, the question of motive in respect of taxation altogether, and fixing the character of the proceeding by what actually occurred, what do we find? Simply an operation having no business or corporate purpose—a mere device which put on the form of a corporate reorganization as a disguise for concealing its real character, and the sole object and accomplishment of which was the consummation of a preconceived plan, not to reorganize a business or any part of a business, but to transfer a parcel of corporate shares to the petitioner. No doubt, a new and valid corporation was created. But that corporation was nothing more than a contrivance to the end last described. It was brought into existence for no other purpose; it performed, as it was intended from the beginning it should perform; no other function. When that limited function had been exercised, it immediately was put to death.

In these circumstances, the facts speak for themselves and are susceptible of but one interpretation. The whole undertaking, though conducted according to the terms of subdivision (B), was in fact an elaborate and devious form of conveyance masquerading as a corporate reorganization, and nothing else. The rule which excludes from consideration the motive of tax avoidance is not pertinent to the situation, because the transaction upon its face lies outside the plain intent of the statute. To hold otherwise would be to exalt artifice above reality and to deprive the statutory provision in question of all serious purpose.

Judgment affirmed.

NOTES

1. The Court of Appeals said that "the result is the same whether the tax be calculated as the Commissioner calculated it, or upon the value of the Averill shares as a dividend . . ." (page 444 supra). The Commissioner, according to that court, argued that "the whole transaction was merely the declaration of a dividend by the United Mortgage Corporation consisting of the Monitor shares in specie . . ." (page 443 supra). The Supreme Court, however, thought that the Commissioner claimed the transaction should be taxed "as though the United [C]orporation had paid her a dividend consisting of the amount realized from the sale of the Monitor shares." Might there be any difference in result?

2. The Supreme Court said (page 446 supra) that a "plan of reorganization" does not exist where the transfer has "no relation to the business of either" corporation. If the transfer has some relation to the business of the parent, must there be a nontax reason for the particular method of disposition chosen in order to avoid the result in *Gregory*?

Should the result in a reorganization case depend on the purpose or motive of the parties? How might the Supreme Court have reached the result it did without weighing the taxpayer's tax objectives against her nontax objectives?

3. Though the economic substance doctrine was passed into law in March 2010 under § 7701(o), *Gregory* remains the classic and early statement that transactions must have economic substance and business purpose. See, e.g., Coltec Industries, Inc. v. U.S. 454 F.3d 1340 (C.A. Fed. Cir. 2006) (extensively relying on the business purpose and economic substance holdings in *Gregory* to conclude that the taxpayer's transaction in *Coltec* involving the assumption of liabilities in exchange for notes lacked economic substance and was designed to generate capital losses). The legislative history for § 7701(o) states that the "provision is not intended to alter or supplant any other rule of law, including any common-law doctrine ... it is intended the provision be construed as being additive to any such other rule of law." Jt. Comm. on Taxation (JCT Rep. No. JCX-18-10). The reality of the enforcement of economic substance (statutory or common law) became the subject of debate following the recent directives from the IRS Large Business & International Division (e.g., LB&I-04-0711-015) and a recent chief counsel notice (CC-2012-008). Some commentators viewed the Service as de facto administratively repealing the economic substance doctrine. However, the Service and others maintain that the directives and chief counsel notice merely provide guidance for agents in applying the doctrine in real life cases.

Granite Trust Co. v. United States
238 F.2d 670 (1st Cir. 1956).

■ Before MAGRUDER, CHIEF JUDGE, and WOODBURY and HARTIGAN, CIRCUIT JUDGES.

■ MAGRUDER, CHIEF JUDGE. . . In 1928 the Building Corporation was organized by Granite Trust Company for the purpose of acquiring land and constructing an office building thereon to be occupied by the bank. The land and building cost over $1,000,000 and were financed through the purchase by the taxpayer bank of all the stock of the Building Corporation. The Building Corporation rented a portion of the premises to Howard D. Johnson Company for a rental of approximately $13,700 per year. This last-named corporation was in 1943 wholly owned by Howard D. Johnson, an individual. Neither Howard D. Johnson Company, nor Johnson, owned any stock in Granite Trust Company, and no shareholder or officer of Howard D. Johnson Company was a director in, or otherwise connected with, Granite Trust Company, though both Howard D. Johnson Company, and Johnson, were depositors in the taxpayer bank.

Beginning at least as early 1936, the amount at which the stock of the Building Corporation was carried upon the taxpayer's books was subjected to continuous criticism by various banking authorities. As a result, the taxpayer wrote down the value of the stock on its books, but nevertheless the examining authorities continued to press for further annual reductions.

At some time prior to October, 1943, the taxpayer's management commenced the formulation of a plan to bring this issue to a close by the expedient of having Granite Trust Company purchase the real estate from the Building Corporation for $550,000, a fair current appraisal, after which the subsidiary Building Corporation was to be liquidated. The practical problem in the execution of this plan resulted from the fact that the distribution in the liquidation of the subsidiary corporation was expected to amount to something between $65 and $66 per share upon the shares of common stock in the Building Corporation for which the taxpayer had paid $100 per share. In thus contributing to the simplification of the corporate structure of the taxpayer as a holding company, an end deemed desirable by the Congress, Granite Trust Company naturally wanted to be assured that its prospective loss to be realized upon the liquidation of its subsidiary would lawfully be "recognized" at once so as to be available as a tax deduction.

In order that this forthcoming loss upon its investment might not be denied recognition by § [332]. . . the taxpayer, on advice of counsel, proceeded to divest itself of some of its shares of common stock in the Building Corporation by means of several purported sales and of a gift, the facts concerning which are as follows:

[As of December 1, 1943, the taxpayer owned all of the outstanding stock of the Building Corporation—2,250 shares of preferred and 5,000 shares of common stock. The latter was the sole voting stock of the corporation. On December 6, 1943, the taxpayer sold, or went through the form of selling, 1,025 shares—20.5 percent—of the outstanding common stock to Howard D. Johnson Company for $65.50 per share. The buyer paid the purchase price to the taxpayer and received the Building Corporation certificates which it held until the final liquidation of the Building Corporation.

[On December 10, 1943, the shareholders of the Building Corporation voted to accept the taxpayer's offer to purchase the real estate. At the same meeting, the shareholders also voted to liquidate the corporation and to distribute the proceeds pro rata provided that such liquidation would be completed before December 30, 1943. The taxpayer's shares were the only shares represented and voted at the meeting.

[Subsequently, on December 13, 1943, the taxpayer sold, or went through the form of selling, 10 shares of the Building Corporation stock to each of two individuals, Howard D. Johnson and Ralph E. Richmond, for $65.50 per share. On the same day, the taxpayer gave two shares of the Building Corporation stock to the Greater Boston United War Fund. The purchase prices were paid and all of the stock certificates were delivered.

[The taxpayer acquired no additional shares of the Building Corporation stock at any time after making the above sales or gift.

[On December 15, 1943, the $550,000 purchase price was paid by the. taxpayer, and the real estate was conveyed to it by the Building Corporation. The real estate was recorded on the taxpayer's books at fair market value.

[On December 17, 1943, the Building Corporation retired its preferred stock. On the same day, each of the shareholders of common stock—the taxpayer, Howard D. Johnson Company, Howard D. Johnson, Ralph E. Richmond, and the Greater Boston United War Fund—received $65.77 per share as a final liquidating distribution.

[On December 30, 1943, in a meeting at which all of the shareholders of the Building Corporation were represented, the shareholders voted to dissolve the corporation and to give the directors the authority necessary to effect the dissolution.]

The taxpayer concedes that it would not have made the sales described above had it not been for § [332]. . . While the taxpayer maintains that the gift to the United War Fund was but part of the total gift to that organization for the year 1943, it seems clear, because this was the only case where shares of stock rather than cash were distributed to the charity, that at least the specific object given at this time was dictated by § [332].

The precise issue before us is whether or not to give effect for tax purposes to the aforesaid sales and gift by the taxpayer. If the answer is in the affirmative, there is no doubt that the liquidation distribution of the property of the Building Corporation was not in "complete liquidation" within the very special meaning of that phrase in § [332] . . . and, accordingly, the taxpayer may recognize the loss on its investment.

Although there is no dispute that the transactions in form at least purport to be sales and a gift, the Commissioner nevertheless maintains that we should not accord them that significance. The Commissioner's argument is in two parts: The first proposition derives from the basic finding of the district court that the taxpayer effected the liquidation "in such manner as to achieve a tax reduction" and that this was "without legal or moral justification." The Commissioner attempts to bolster this argument by his traditional corporation reorganization analysis to the effect that, so long as the "end-result" of the transactions involved complies with the "criteria of the statute," intermediary steps (in this case the sales and gift) should be ignored as if they were nonexistent. His reasoning is that, if the final outcome is complete liquidation of a subsidiary corporation which at the outset was wholly owned by the taxpayer, the entire procedure comes within the intendment of the statute and "[c]ircuitous steps to avoid Section [332]" occurring prior to the ultimate liquidation should be disregarded.

The Commissioner's second proposition is that there were *in fact* no valid sales or gift of stock made by the taxpayer. This argument rests on the taxpayer's admission that the transfers were motivated solely by tax considerations and were made in a friendly atmosphere to friendly people who knew of the decision to liquidate the corporation before the end of the year. As the Commissioner points out, the liquidation took place shortly after the transfers, and the transferees then received back the money they had paid in, plus a small profit. Therefore, the Commissioner argues, relying heavily on Gregory v. Helvering, . . . [page 445 supra], that "the stock transfers in question had no independent purpose or meaning—either for the transferor or the transferees—but constituted merely a transitory and circuitous routing of legal title for the purpose of avoiding taxes, within the meaning of Gregory v. Helvering. . . It was not expected or intended by any of the parties that the transferees should become true stockholders. Legal title passed; but beneficial ownership surely never passed. The transferees who paid money for their stock knew that the subsidiary would be liquidated in a few days and that they would get their money back—as in fact they did, with additional amounts to pay them for their cooperation in serving as conduits of title." The gift of stock to the United War Fund is dismissed as "nothing more than a gift of the cash. . ."

Our conclusion is that the Commissioner's arguments must be rejected, and that the taxpayer should be permitted to "recognize" the loss on its investment, which it undoubtedly realized upon the liquidation of the Building Corporation.

Initially we may note, without ruling upon it, one legal argument made by the Commissioner having to do with the efficacy of the purported sale of 1,025 shares of stock to Howard D. Johnson Company on December 6, 1943. The Commissioner contends that, to satisfy the first condition of nonrecognition prescribed in § [332], it is not necessary to have a formal plan of liquidation, evidenced by a corporate resolution, but it is sufficient if there is a "definitive determination" to achieve dissolution. It is claimed by the Commissioner that such a definitive determination existed here by November 10, 1943, and, therefore, that the sale of stock to Howard D. Johnson Company which took place on December 6, 1943 (before the formal adoption of the plan of liquidation) occurred *after* the "adoption of the plan of liquidation" within the meaning of § [332]. In this view the taxpayer owned 100 percent of the subsidiary's stock on the date the plan of liquidation was adopted, from which it would follow, on the basis of the first condition of § [332], that the loss should not be "recognized."

We need not consider the foregoing legal argument on its merits, because the subsequent actions by the taxpayer—the sales to Johnson individually and to Richmond on December 13, 1943, and the gift of stock on the same day to the United War Fund—of themselves, if valid, successfully accomplished the taxpayer's purpose of avoiding the nonrecognition provisions of § [332] under the second condition contained in that subsection. This second condition prescribes, in a sort of backhanded way, that gain or loss shall be recognized if, at any time on or after the date of adoption of the plan of liquidation and prior to the date of the receipt of the property distributed in final liquidation, the receiving corporation is the owner of a greater percentage of any class of stock of the corporation being liquidated than the percentage of such stock owned by it at the time of the receipt of the property—which means that this condition precedent to the nonrecognition of a realized gain or loss is not satisfied if, in the described period, the receiving corporation has made an effective disposition of any of the shares of stock held in the subsidiary corporation, without making any countervailing acquisitions of such stock.

Turning then to the basic contentions of the Commissioner, not much need be said with reference to the proposition that the tax motive for the sales and gift rendered the transactions "immoral" and thus vitiated them. Again and again the courts have pointed out that a "purpose to minimize or avoid taxation is not an illicit motive." . . . The *Gregory* case itself makes this clear, Gregory v. Helvering.

As for the Commissioner's "end-result" argument, the very terms of § [332] make it evident that it is not an "end-result" provision, but rather one which prescribes specific conditions for the nonrecognition of realized gains or losses, conditions which, if not strictly met, make the section inapplicable. In fact, the Commissioner's own regulations (Reg. [§ 1.332–2]) emphasize the rigid requirements of the section and make no allowance for the type of "step transaction" theory advanced in this case.

The legislative history of § [332] likewise tends to support the position of the taxpayer. That history indicates that Congress was primarily concerned with providing a means of facilitating the simplification of corporate structures pursuant to the general policy enunciated in the Public Utility Holding Company Act of 1935, 49 Stat. 803, 15 U.S.C.A. § 79 et seq. . . This fact, while perhaps not conclusive as to the proper interpretation of § [332], nevertheless does lend a favorable background to the taxpayer's contention that the subsection, as a relief measure, was "not designed as a straitjacket into which corporations should be forced at the penalty of forfeiture of losses on liquidation of subsidiaries."

The more specific and more important bit of legislative history is found in the Report of the Senate Finance Committee at the time that § 112(b)(6) [of the 1939 Code] was reenacted, with amendments, as § 332 of the Internal Revenue Code of 1954. At this time, when Congress was engaged in a comprehensive reexamination of the Internal Revenue Code, the well-known case of Commissioner of Internal Revenue v. Day & Zimmermann, Inc., 3 Cir., 1945, 151 F.2d 517, had been decided in favor of the taxpayer, and it reasonably could be supposed that Congress, had it disapproved of the decision in that case, would have overturned its conclusion by making over § [332] into an "end-result" provision. In the *Day & Zimmermann* case, the taxpayer, admittedly in order to avoid the nonrecognition provisions of § [332] had sold at public auction a sufficient number of shares of a wholly owned subsidiary corporation to reduce its holdings below 80 percent. These shares were bought, after general bidding, by the treasurer of the taxpayer, who, after receiving cash dividends in the subsequent liquidation of the companies, reported his gain and paid income tax thereon. The Third Circuit held that § [332] did not apply to the liquidation, emphasizing that the treasurer had paid a fair price for the shares, had used his own money, had not been directed by anyone to bid, and that there had been no showing of any understanding existing between him and the corporation by which the latter was to retain any sort of interest in the securities or in the proceeds therefrom. . . The significant thing in the case is its ultimate rationale that the purported sales of stock to the treasurer were in fact sales, notwithstanding the tax motive which prompted the corporation to enter into the transaction; from which it would seem to be irrelevant how the transfer was arranged, or whether or not it occurred at a public auction or exchange, so long as the beneficial as well as legal title was intended to pass and did pass. . .

We come then to the Commissioner's second major contention, resting on Gregory v. Helvering, that the sales of stock by the corporation should be ignored on the ground that they were not bona fide, and that the taxpayer therefore retained "beneficial ownership." The Commissioner characterizes the transfers as artificial, unessential, transitory phases of a completed tax avoidance scheme which should be disregarded.

In answer to this contention, it is first necessary to determine precisely what the *Gregory* case held. Judge Learned Hand, in Chisholm v. Commissioner, 2 Cir., 1935, 79 F.2d 14, 15, . . . *certiorari denied* 1935, 296 U.S. 641, . . . analyzed the case as follows:

> *The question always is whether the transaction under scrutiny is in fact what it appears to be in form*; a marriage may be a joke; a contract may be intended only to deceive others; an agreement may have a collateral defeasance. In such cases the transaction as a whole is different from its appearance. . . In Gregory v. Helvering, supra, 293 U.S. 465, . . . the incorporators adopted the usual form for creating business corporations; but their intent, or purpose, was merely to draught the papers, in fact not to create corporations as the court understood that word. That was the purpose which defeated their exemption, not the accompanying purpose to escape taxation; that purpose was legally neutral. Had they really meant to conduct a business by means of the two reorganized companies, they would have escaped whatever other

aim they might have had, whether to avoid taxes, or to regenerate the world. [Italics added.]

In the present case the question is whether or not there actually were sales. Why the parties may wish to enter into a sale is one thing, but that is irrelevant under the *Gregory* case so long as the consummated agreement was no different from what it purported to be.

Even the Commissioner concedes that "[l]egal title" passed to the several transferees on December 13, 1943, but he asserts that "beneficial ownership" never passed. We find no basis on which to vitiate the purported sales, for the record is absolutely devoid of any evidence indicating an understanding by the parties to the transfers that any interest in the stock transferred was to be retained by the taxpayer. If Johnson or Richmond had gone bankrupt, or the assets of both had been attached by creditors, on the day after the sales to them, we do not see how the conclusion could be escaped that their Building Corporation stock would have been included in their respective assets. . .

In addition to what we have said, there are persuasive reasons of a general nature which lend weight to the taxpayer's position. To strike down these sales on the alleged defect that they took place between friends and for tax motives would only tend to promote duplicity and result in extensive litigation as taxpayers led courts into hairsplitting investigations to decide when a sale was not a sale. It is no answer to argue that, under Gregory v. Helvering, there is an inescapable judicial duty to examine into the actuality of purported corporate reorganizations, for that was a special sort of transaction, whose bona fides could readily be ascertained by inquiring whether the ephemeral new corporation was in fact transacting business, or whether there was in fact a continuance of the proprietary interests under an altered corporate form. See Lewis v. Commissioner, 1 Cir., 1949, 176 F.2d 646.

What we have said so far is related chiefly to the validity of the sales. When we turn to the gift on December 13, 1943, to the United War Fund, the taxpayer is on even firmer ground. The Commissioner says that the gift was nothing more than a gift of cash, that the charity "was, at most, a passive transferee, without independent purpose, which held legal title to two shares for four days." This assertion rests, when examined closely, on the simple fact that the purpose for the gift was a tax avoidance one. But this does not disqualify it as an effective gift, transferring title. A gift certainly may have a tax motive. See Commissioner of Internal Revenue v. Newman, 2 Cir., 1947, 159 F.2d 848; Sawtell v. Commissioner, supra, 82 F.2d at page 222. Charitable contributions of low-cost securities are an everyday type of transfer motivated by tax purposes. The gift to the United War Fund, being valid, transferred two shares from the taxpayer after the adoption of the plan of liquidation, and alone sufficed to put the liquidation beyond the reach of the nonrecognition provisions of § [332].

In short, though the facts in this case show a tax avoidance, they also show legal transactions not fictitious or so lacking in substance as to be anything different from what they purported to be, and we believe they must be given effect in the administration of § [332] as well as for all other purposes. . .

A judgment will be entered vacating the judgment of the District Court and remanding the case to that court with direction to enter judgment for the sum of $57,801.32, with interest.

NOTES

1. See George L. Riggs, Inc., 64 T.C. 474 (1975), *acq.* 1976–2 C.B. 2, in which the court held that the 80–percent stock ownership requirement of § 332 was met where a corporation, by redeeming the stock of its minority shareholders prior to the formal adoption of a plan of liquidation, decreased the number of outstanding shares of stock and thereby increased its percentage share of ownership to greater than 80 percent. No informal adoption of a plan of liquidation occurred prior to the acquisition of the 80–percent ownership even though the shareholders voted to sell the corporation's assets, the corporation called preferred stock for redemption, and the directors voted to liquidate the corporation's subsidiaries and to offer to redeem the stock of its minority shareholders. See also Rev. Rul. 75–521, 1975–2 C.B. 120 (§ 332 applied to liquidation where 50–percent corporate shareholder purchased the remaining 50 percent prior to formal adoption of plan, thus resulting in the nonrecognition of gain).

In Letter Rul. 8428006 (Mar. 26, 1984), the Service ruled that a corporate parent was entitled to recognize loss under § 331(a) on the liquidation of its 66.7 percent owned subsidiary where the parent had sold the remaining 33.3 percent of the subsidiary's stock to an unrelated corporation only 17 days before the adoption of the plan of liquidation in order to avoid nonrecognition of loss under § 332(a).

2. See H. K. Porter Co., 87 T.C. 689 (1986), in which the court held that § 332 did not bar the recognition of petitioner's loss on the liquidation of its Australian subsidiary. Ten years prior to the liquidation, the wholly owned subsidiary capitalized loans from its parent and issued preferred stock. Upon liquidation the subsidiary's assets were insufficient to satisfy the preferred stock's liquidation preference. No assets were distributed with respect to the subsidiary's common stock. The court followed Commissioner v. Spaulding Bakeries, 252 F.2d 693 (2d Cir. 1958), and held that the liquidating distribution was not in complete cancellation or redemption of all of the subsidiary's stock. See also CCA 200706011 ("if a shareholder owns both common and preferred shares of a liquidating corporation's stock, section 332 applies only if the 80-percent shareholder receives property in exchange for its common stock after the corporation has transferred property to its creditors in satisfaction of any indebtedness and to its preferred shareholders in satisfaction of the liquidation preference of such stock").

3. STEP TRANSACTIONS

Helvering v. Elkhorn Coal Co.

95 F.2d 732 (4th Cir. 1937), *cert. denied*, 305 U.S. 605 (1938).

■ Before PARKER and NORTHCOTT, CIRCUIT JUDGES, and HENRY H. WATKINS, DISTRICT JUDGE.

■ PARKER, CIRCUIT JUDGE. This is a petition to review a decision of the Board of Tax Appeals holding profit realized by the Elkhorn Coal & Coke Company upon a transfer of certain mining properties to the Mill Creek Coal & Coke Company to be nontaxable. The ground of the decision was that the transfer was made pursuant to a plan of reorganization within the meaning of section [368(a)(1)(C)]. . . The facts were stipulated and are set forth at length in the findings of the Board which are reported with its opinion in Elkhorn Coal Co. v. Com'r, 34 B.T.A. 845. Those material to the question presented by the petition are in substance as follows:

Prior to December 18, 1925, the Elkhorn Coal & Coke Company, to which we shall hereafter refer as the old company, owned certain coal mining properties in West Virginia and certain stocks in other mining companies engaged in business in that state. It was closely associated with the Mill Creek Coal & Coke Company, which owned neighboring property; and a majority of the directorate of both corporations consisted of the same persons. Early in December, 1925, a plan was formed whereby the old company was to transfer its mine, mining plant, and mining equipment at Maybeury, W. Va., to the Mill Creek Company in exchange for 1,000 shares of the capital stock of that company. This exchange was accomplished on December 31, 1925, at which time, it is stipulated, the stock received by the old company had a fair market value of $550,000 which is in excess of the deficiency asserted by the Commissioner. There is no contention that the transfer by the old company was to a corporation controlled by it or by its stockholders and therefore within the nonrecognition provision of [the progenitor of section 368(a)(1)(D)] of the act; but the argument of the taxpayer is that the transfer was of all the properties of one corporation for the stock of another, and therefore within the nonrecognition provision of section [368(a)(1)(C)].

The contention . . . depends upon the legal conclusion to be drawn from certain evidentiary facts relating to the prior organization of another corporation and the transfer to it of all the property of the old company which was not to be transferred to the Mill Creek Company. These facts, which were found by the Board and are undisputed, are as follows: At the time that the transfer to the Mill Creek Company was decided upon, the officers of the old company caused another corporation to be organized under the name of the Elkhorn Coal Company, which we shall refer to hereafter as the new company, and on December 18, 1925, transferred to it, in exchange for 6,100 shares of its stock, all of the property of the old company which was not to be transferred to the Mill Creek Company except certain accounts, which were transferred to the new company on December 28, 1931, in consideration of its assuming the liabilities of the old company. The 6,100 shares of stock in the new company were promptly distributed by the old company as a dividend to its stockholders. This left the old company owning only the property which was to be transferred to the Mill Creek Company under the plan and which was transferred to that company on December 31st, as mentioned in the preceding paragraph. Following that transfer and the receipt by the old company of the 1,000 shares of the stock of the Mill Creek Company pursuant thereto, the new company proceeded to place itself in the same position relative to the stockholders of the old company that the old company had occupied, and then to wind up its affairs. It accomplished that result in the following manner: On January 22, 1926, it exchanged 1,440 shares of its capital stock for the 7,540 shares of the outstanding capital stock of the old company, making the exchange with the stockholders of that company. This gave those who had been stockholders in the old company the same interest in the new company that they had had in the old, and gave to the new company the ownership of all of the stock in the old. The 1,000 shares of stock received from the Mill Creek Company were then transferred to the new company and the old company was dissolved. No business whatever was done by the old company after the transfer of assets to the Mill Creek Company on December 31st; and no reason appears for the organization of the new company except to provide a transferee to take over and hold the assets which were not to be transferred to the Mill Creek Company so that the transfer to that company when made would be a transfer of all the assets of the old company.

The Board was of opinion that all of these transactions were carried through pursuant to prearranged plan, saying: "We do not doubt that before a single step was taken a plan had been formulated for regrouping the corporate assets"; and "The stipulated facts justify the inference that one of the motives which the stockholders of Elkhorn had in organizing the new corporation and causing the three corporations to adopt the several steps or plans of reorganization which were adopted and carried out, was to make the transfer of the mining properties from Elkhorn to Mill Creek without resulting tax liability to Elkhorn or to themselves." The Board thought, however, with five members dissenting, that because the transfers from the old company to the new were genuine and were separate and distinct from the transfer to the Mill Creek Company, the latter must be treated as a transfer of substantially all of the properties of the corporation within the meaning of the reorganization statute. . .

While we are bound by the Board's findings of evidentiary facts, we are not bound by the foregoing conclusion set forth in the opinion and embodying a mixed question of law and fact. . . Helvering v. Tex–Penn Oil Co., 300 U.S. 481. . .

A careful consideration of the evidentiary facts discloses no purpose which could have been served by the creation of the new company and the transfer of the assets to it, except to strip the old company of all of its properties which were not to be transferred to the Mill Creek Company, in anticipation of that transfer. The creation of the new company and its acquisition of the assets of "the old was not a corporate reorganization, therefore, within the meaning of the statute or within any fair meaning of the term 'reorganization.' " It did not involve any real transfer of assets by the business enterprise or any rearranging of corporate structure, but at most a mere shifting of charters, having no apparent purpose except the avoidance of taxes on the transfer to the Mill Creek Company which was in contemplation. To use in part the language of the Supreme Court in Gregory v. Helvering, [page 445 supra]. . . it was "simply an operation having no business or corporate purpose—a mere device which put on the form of a corporate reorganization as a disguise for concealing its real character, and the sole object and accomplishment of which was the consummation of a preconceived plan, not to reorganize a business or any part of a business," but to give to the intended transfer to the Mill Creek Company the appearance of a transfer of all the corporate assets so as to bring it within the nonrecognition provision of section [368(a)(1)(C)].

Under such circumstances we think that the decision in Gregory v. Helvering . . . is controlling. In that case, for the purpose of avoiding taxes on a liquidating dividend of shares of stock held by a corporation, a subsidiary was organized within the terms of the reorganization statute and the shares were transferred to it. The stock of the subsidiary was then delivered to the sole stockholder of the original corporation and shortly thereafter the subsidiary was dissolved and the shares which had been transferred to it were delivered to the stockholder. The court held that although the organization of the subsidiary came within the letter of the reorganization statute, such corporate manipulation would be ignored when it fulfilled no proper corporate function and was not in reality a reorganization within the meaning of the statute. The court said:

> "In these circumstances, the facts speak for themselves and are susceptible of but one interpretation. The whole undertaking, though conducted according to the terms of [§ 368(a)(1)(D)], was in fact an elaborate and devious form of conveyance masquerading as a corporate reorganization, and nothing else. The rule which excludes from consideration the motive of tax avoidance is not pertinent to the situation, because the transaction upon its face lies outside the plain intent of the statute. To hold otherwise would be to exalt artifice above reality and to deprive the statutory provision in question of all serious purpose."

We do not see how that case can be distinguished from this. If the property which was to be transferred to Mill Creek had been transferred to a new company created for the purpose and had been by that company transferred to Mill Creek, no one would contend that there was a distinction; and certainly there is no difference in principle between creating a subsidiary to take and convey the property to the intended transferee and creating a subsidiary to take over the other assets and having the old company make the transfer. In either case, the apparent reorganization is a mere artifice; and it can make no difference which of the affiliated corporations makes the transfer of assets which it is desired to bring within the nonrecognition provisions of the statute.

It is suggested in the opinion of the Board that the case before us is analogous to that which would have been presented if the old company, prior to the transfer to Mill Creek, had distributed to its stockholders all of the assets except those destined for such transfer; but the distinction is obvious. In the case supposed, the business enterprise would have definitely divested itself of the property distributed. Here it did not divest itself of the property at all, but merely made certain changes in the legal papers under which it enjoyed corporate existence. No rule is better settled than that in tax matters we must look to substance and not to form; and no one who looks to substance can see in the mere change of charters, which is all that we have here, any reason for permitting a transfer of a part of the corporate assets to escape the taxation to which it is subject under the statute.

Congress has seen fit to grant nonrecognition of profit in sale or exchange of assets only under certain conditions, one of which is that one corporation shall transfer "substantially all" of its properties for stock in another. If nonrecognition of profit can be secured by the plan adopted in this case, the exemption is broadened to cover all transfers of assets for stock, whether "substantially all" or not, if only the transferor will go to the slight trouble and expense of getting a new charter for his corporation and making the transfer of assets to the new corporation thus created in such way as to leave in the old only the assets to be transferred at the time the transfer is to be made. We do not think the statutory exemption may be thus broadened by such an artifice.

Having reached this conclusion, it is unnecessary to decide whether the unity of the plan under which the transfer was made brings it, without a unifying contract, within the principles laid down in Starr v. Commissioner (C.C.A. 4th) 82 F.(2d) 964, 968, wherein we said,

> "Where transfers are made pursuant to such a plan of reorganization, they are ordinarily parts of one transaction and should be so treated in application of the well-settled principle that, in applying income tax laws, the substance, and not the form, of the transaction shall control... This is demanded also by the principle, equally well settled, that a single transaction may not be broken up into various elements to avoid a tax..."

For the reasons stated, the decision of the Board will be reversed, and the cause will be remanded to it for further proceedings in accordance with this opinion.

Reversed.

■ HENRY H. WATKINS, DISTRICT JUDGE (dissenting). [Opinion omitted.]

On Rehearing

■ PARKER, CIRCUIT JUDGE. The rehearing granted in this case and careful consideration of the briefs filed and arguments made thereon have served only to strengthen the majority of the court in the opinion heretofore expressed; and we see no basis whatever for the contention that our former opinion was based on a ground not considered by the Board of Tax Appeals. The question before the Board was whether the transfer to Mill Creek was of all the assets of the old company. . .

It was not intended by what was said in the original opinion, to the effect that the transfer of assets from the old company to the new did not constitute a bona fide reorganization, to suggest that the transfer was a taxable transaction, but to point out that the creation of the new company and the transfer of the assets to it was a mere shifting of charters having no purpose other than to give to the later transfer to Mill Creek the appearance of a transfer of all the corporate assets so as to bring that transfer within the non-recognition provisions of section [368(a)(1)]. . . The transfer to the new company was non-taxable whether it was a real reorganization or a mere shifting of charters, which would of course come within the terms of the reorganization statute. It is only in relation to the subsequent transfer to Mill Creek that it becomes important to determine whether the organization of the new company and its taking over of the assets was a genuine reorganization. If there was no real reorganization and transfer, but a mere shifting of charters, the subsequent transfer to Mill Creek was not within the terms of the nonrecognition provision of the statute.

We are confirmed in our original opinion by the recent decision of the Supreme Court in Minnesota Tea Co. v. Helvering [302 U.S. 609]. In that case there was a reorganization in which stockholders paid the debts of a corporation from the cash distributed to them in the course of the reorganization. The question was whether the corporation was taxable on the amount of the debts thus paid on the theory that the cash used for that purpose was in reality received by the corporation, or whether it was non-taxable on the theory that the distribution to the stockholders was within the nonrecognition provisions of the statute. In holding the corporation taxable thereon the court said:

> The conclusion is inescapable, as the court below very clearly pointed out, that by this roundabout process petitioner received the same benefit "as though it had retained that amount from distribution and applied it to the payment of such indebtedness." Payment of indebtedness, and not distribution of dividends, was, from the beginning, the aim of the understanding with the stockholders and was the end accomplished by carrying that understanding into effect. *A given result at the end of a straight path is not made a different result because reached by following a devious path.* The preliminary distribution to the stockholders was a meaningless and unnecessary incident in the transmission of the fund to the creditors, all along intended to come to their hands, so transparently artificial that further discussion would be a needless waste of time. (Italics ours.)

In the case at bar, the "aim" of the incorporation of the new company and the transfer made to it, was that the transfer to Mill Creek should appear to be a transfer of all of the assets of the company; and this was the end accomplished, and the only end accomplished so far as the record shows, by the incorporation and transfer. The incorporation of the new company and the transfer to it was a "meaningless and unnecessary incident." It is true that the new company was incorporated under the laws of a different state from the old; but it does not appear that any corporate purpose was served by this change of jurisdictions and certainly the integrity of the existing business was not affected by the change. . . It is said that the transfer to Mill Creek had a real corporate purpose. This is true, but it was taxable unless constituting a transfer of all of the assets of the corporation. The incorporation of and transfer to the new company, which had no proper corporate purpose, were resorted to in order to give the transfer to Mill Creek the appearance of being a transfer of all the assets of the transferor and hence not taxable. All that was done by the complicated corporate maneuvering employed was the transfer of a part of the assets of the old company to Mill Creek in exchange for 1,000 shares of its stock, leaving the business of the old company in the hands of the old stockholders, with a new charter, but otherwise unaffected. This result is "not a different result because reached by following a devious path."

And we think it clear that the incorporation of the new company and the transfer made to it were but parts of a single plan under which the transfer was made to Mill Creek and that they should be treated as parts of one transaction. When this is done, there is no room for the contention that all of the assets of the corporation were transferred to Mill Creek. Even though there was no unifying contract, the unity of the plan brings the case within the rule applied in Starr v. Commissioner, 4 Cir., 82 F.2d 964.

For the reasons stated here and in our former opinion, the decision of the Board of Tax Appeals will be reversed.

Reversed.

■ HENRY H. WATKINS, DISTRICT JUDGE, dissents.

Revenue Ruling 76–123
1976–1 C.B. 94.

Advice has been requested concerning the treatment for Federal income tax purposes of the transaction described below. Individual A owned all the stock of X corporation, which was incorporated in State O. Individual B, who is unrelated to A, owned all the stock of Y corporation, which was incorporated in State P. A and B determined that the businesses operated by X and Y could be improved if their interests in X and Y were combined while at the same time preserving the separate corporate existence of X and Y. A and B also decided that the laws of State P were more favorable to the operation of the combined enterprise. To carry out their plan, A and B transferred all of their stock in X and Y to a newly organized corporation, Z, incorporated in State P, in exchange for, respectively, 60 percent and 40 percent of all of the outstanding stock of Z. In addition, B received from Z 10x dollars in cash. The consideration received by A and B was in each case equal to the fair market value of the stock exchanged. As part of this plan, X then distributed all of its assets to Z in complete liquidation, and Y remained as a wholly owned subsidiary of Z. . .

In Rev. Rul. 67–274, 1967–2 C.B. 141, a corporation, pursuant to a plan of reorganization, acquired all the outstanding stock of another corporation from the shareholders in exchange for voting stock of the acquiring corporation and thereafter, as part of the same plan, the acquiring corporation completely liquidated the acquired corporation. Rev. Rul. 67–274 holds that under these circumstances the acquisition of the stock of the acquired corporation and its liquidation by the acquiring corporation are part of the overall plan of reorganization and may not be considered independently of each other for Federal income tax purposes. Rev. Rul. 67–274 concludes that the transaction is not an acquisition of the stock of the acquired corporation qualifying as a reorganization under section 368(a)(1)(B) of the Code but is an acquisition of the assets of the acquired corporation qualifying as a reorganization under section 368(a)(1)(C).

Rev. Rul. 68–357, 1968–2 C.B. 144, holds that section 351 of the Code applies where, as part of an overall plan to consolidate the operations of five businesses, an individual and three corporations transfer property to a corporation that they control immediately after the transfers within the meaning of section 368(c) even though the transfers of property by the corporations are reorganizations within the meaning of section 368(a)(1)(C).

The transfer by A of A's X stock to Z and, as part of the overall transaction, the liquidation of X by Z are interdependent steps in an overall reorganization plan the substance of which is treated for Federal income tax purposes as an acquisition by Z of all of the assets of X solely in exchange for Z voting stock in a transaction qualifying as a reorganization under section 368(a)(1)(C) of the Code, followed by a distribution by X of the Z stock to A in exchange for all of A's X stock. Accordingly, no gain or loss is recognized by X upon the exchange of its property solely for Z stock as provided by section 361(a), and no gain or loss is recognized to A on the exchange of A's X stock solely for voting stock of Z as provided in section 354(a).

Furthermore, the transfer by X of its property to Z in liquidation and the transfer by B of B's Y stock to Z is a transaction within the provisions of section 351(a) of the Code since X and B are in control of Z immediately after the exchanges within the meaning of section 368(c). Pursuant to section 351(c) the distribution by X of the Z stock to A does not violate the control requirement of section 368(c). Accordingly, no loss is recognized to B and no gain is recognized to B in excess of the 10x dollars received by B, as provided in section 351(b), upon the exchange of B's Y stock solely for cash and voting stock of Z. See Rev. Rul. 68–357.

Rev. Rul. 68–349, 1968–2 C.B. 143, holds that the transfer of property by an individual [C] to a newly formed corporation [M] does not qualify under section 351 of the Code where another corporation [N] simultaneously transfers all of its property to the new corporation for the purpose of qualifying the individual's transfer under section 351. Rev. Rul. 68–349 states that the organization of the new corporation is considered under the circumstances to be merely a continuation of the transferor corporation. Rev. Rul. 68–349 is distinguishable from the instant case in that Z was not employed solely for the purpose of enabling B to transfer B's Y stock without the recognition of gain and was not merely a continuation of X. Z was organized to enable X to be reincorporated in State P. Further, the transfer by B of his Y stock to Z effected the combination of A's and B's former business interests in the form of affiliated corporations.

Rev. Rul. 68–349 is distinguished.

West Coast Marketing Corp. v. Commissioner
46 T.C. 32 (1966).

The Commissioner determined a deficiency in petitioner's income tax for the fiscal year ended June 30, 1960, in the amount of $50,911.97.

The sole issue is whether the substance of a certain transaction was a taxable sale or exchange by the taxpayer of its interest in certain land or whether the realized gain in respect thereof is to escape taxation under section 354(a)(1) of the 1954 Code through the use of an intermediate corporation to which such property was first transferred.

FINDINGS OF FACT

[Petitioner owned a 25–percent interest in a certain tract of real estate. Cohen, petitioner's president and sole shareholder, owned a 25–percent interest in two neighboring tracts. The 50–percent owner of all three tracts negotiated a sale to Universal Marion Corporation ("Universal") for $360 an acre, payable in voting convertible preferred stock of Universal. Cohen orally agreed to the terms of the sale, which were embodied in a letter agreement dated April 16, 1959.]

The final sale of all three tracts of land to Universal was consummated in the fall of 1959, in accordance with the terms of the letter of April 16, 1959.

Meanwhile, however, Cohen caused to be organized on April 30, 1959, a Florida corporation named Manatee Land Co. (Manatee), and, on May 1, 1959, he and petitioner transferred to Manatee their remaining respective one-fourth interests in the three tracts—petitioner's in the Middle Tract and Cohen's in the North and South tracts.

Petitioner received 645 shares of the stock of Manatee for its undivided one-quarter interest in the Middle Tract. Cohen received the remaining 769 shares of Manatee stock for his undivided one-quarter interest in the North and South tracts.

Subsequent to the issuance of the 1,414 shares of stock to the petitioner and Cohen, Manatee issued two shares to William B. McKechnie and two additional shares to Donald E. Thurlow. Payment was made for these four shares of stock in cash on the basis of $100 per share. . .

In carrying out the terms of the agreement for the sale or exchange of the three tracts of land as proposed in the letter of April 16, 1959, the stockholders of Manatee, on October 27, 1959, transferred their stock in the corporation to Universal in exchange for 10,800 shares of Universal's 4½ percent $100 par value voting cumulative preferred stock. . .

Manatee was not engaged in the conduct of any business. It was used by petitioner and Cohen for no purpose other than to hold title to their respective undivided one-fourth interests in the three tracts of land, and to serve as a conduit for transferring title thereto to Universal.

On December 18, 1959, Manatee was liquidated by Universal. In its income tax return for the year ended June 30, 1960, petitioner reported the transfer of all of the stock which it owned in Manatee in exchange for 4,913 shares of Universal "having an indeterminate market value" and did not report any taxable income from that transaction. Those shares in fact had a fair market value of $67 per share, as stipulated by the parties herein. The Commissioner determined that petitioner realized a long-term capital gain of $203,647.91 "on the exchange in form of stock of Manatee Land Co. for stock of Universal Marion Corporation" and increased the taxable income reported in its return by that amount.

OPINION

■ RAUM, JUDGE. If petitioner had transferred its one-fourth interest in the Middle Tract directly to Universal in exchange for the preferred shares of Universal, there is no dispute that the resulting gain would have been taxable. Counsel for the parties so agreed at the trial. Is a different result required by the use of Manatee, an intermediate agency that was employed to effectuate the transfer? On this record, we think the answer must be no.

Petitioner's position has been that Manatee was organized for a bona fide business purpose and that the transfer of its stock to Universal in exchange for stock of the latter constituted a tax-free "reorganization" under sections 354(a)(1) and 368(a)(1)(B) of the 1954 Code. To be sure, the transaction before us falls literally within those provisions. But if Manatee served no business purpose and the substance of the transaction was simply an exchange of land for stock of Universal, the tax consequences must turn upon the substance of the transaction rather than the form in which it was cast. "A given result at the end of a straight path is not made a different result because reached by following a devious path." Minnesota Tea Co. v. Helvering, 302 U.S. 609, 613. In such circumstances there would not be any bona fide "reorganization" to which the nonrecognition provisions in question could apply.[3] Gregory v. Helvering [page 445 supra]. What was the situation here?

---

[3] See Income Tax Regulations, sec. 1.368–1(b): "a sale is nevertheless to be treated as a sale even though the mechanics of a reorganization have been set up."

Cohen testified before us in an effort to show that there were bona fide business reasons for incorporating Manatee and transferring to it his and petitioner's respective undivided one-quarter interests in the three tracts. We found his testimony slippery and unconvincing. The burden was upon petitioner and it has not been carried. To the contrary, the record persuasively indicates that Manatee was incorporated for the purpose of being used as a conduit for passing title to petitioner's and Cohen's interests in the three tracts to Universal.[4]

Manatee was brought into existence when the sale of the land was imminent. Petitioner's and Cohen's interests in the land were transferred to it. It engaged in no business and served no purpose other than to hold title pending the contemplated transfer to Universal. We reject as unworthy of belief any testimony that might be construed as suggesting that it had any other purpose.

All of the steps taken by petitioner and Cohen were but component parts of a single transaction the substance of which was a taxable disposition by them of their property interests to Universal. Accordingly, the Commissioner did not err in including in petitioner's taxable income, the long-term capital gain which it realized in that transaction. . .

NOTES

1. Suppose the Elkhorn shareholders had cast their transaction as a "B" reorganization? *Compare* Rev. Rul. 70–225, 1970–1 C.B. 80, *with* Rev. Rul. 70–434, 1970–2 C.B. 83.

See Rev. Rul. 88–48, 1988–1 C.B. 531, in which the Service found "substantially all the assets" transferred for "C" reorganization purposes despite the considerable tailoring that had occurred prior to the transfer.

2. If the transaction in *West Coast Marketing Corp.* was in substance a sale between the taxpayer and Universal, and the transaction in Rev. Rul. 68–349 was in substance a sale between C and N, why was the transaction in Rev. Rul. 76–123 tax-free to both A and B? Cf. Rev. Rul. 78–250, 1978–1 C.B. 83 (merger of X Corporation into newly organized Y Corporation, with majority shareholder of X receiving Y stock and minority receiving cash, treated as redemption of minority by X).

3. What role does the existence of a "substantial business purpose" for a step play in deciding whether to apply the step transaction doctrine? *Compare* Maurice M. Weikel, 51 T.C.M. (CCH) 432 (1986), (distinguishing *West Coast Marketing Corp.* and finding a "B" reorganization and not a sale although the exchange occurred shortly after the unincorporated property was incorporated, where there was a substantial business purpose for incorporation) *with* Asso-

---

[4] The record shows, in addition, that a small minority interest (less than three-tenths of 1 percent in the aggregate) in Manatee was acquired by two persons named McKechnie and Thurlow, not otherwise identified. However, there is no evidence as to what part, if any, these persons played in the transaction or whether their interests represented anything more than mere window dressing. In the circumstances, since the burden was upon petitioner, we do not give any substantial weight to their participation in the transaction.

ciated Wholesale Grocers, Inc. v. U.S., 927 F.2d 1517 (10th Cir. 1991) (rejecting argument that existence of business purpose "precludes" use of step transaction rule, and criticizing the analysis and support for this position in *Weikel*). In some recent rulings, the Service has broadly applied the step transaction doctrine to reorganizations in the context of large plans. See, e.g., Rev. Rul. 2001–46, 2001–2 C.B. 321 (merger of "new subsidiary" into target followed by merger of target into "new subsidiary's" parent is characterized as one statutory merger of target into parent under § 368(a)(1)(A)); Rev. Rul. 2001–26, 2001–1 C.B. 1297 (two step acquisition—tender by acquirer for 51% of target stock followed by merger of acquirer's subsidiary into target is treated under the step transaction doctrine as the acquisition by the acquirer of all of target stock in tax free reorganization under § 368(a)(1)(A) and (a)(2)(E)); Rev. Rul. 2004–83, 2004–32 I.R.B. 157 (where pursuant to an integrated plan, parent sold the stock of one wholly owned subsidiary to another such subsidiary for cash, and then the acquired subsidiary liquidates, the transaction was treated as a D reorganization).

4. In Revenue Ruling 2008-251 the IRS determined that a corporation's acquisition of the stock of another followed by liquidation of that acquired corporation failed as a tax free reorganization. Instead the series of steps should be considered a fully taxable stock purchase followed by a tax-free liquidation of the new subsidiary into the parent.

Review the opinion in *Heinz*, supra 229 for consideration of the relationship among the business purpose, step transaction, and sham doctrines. The scope of the step transaction doctrine continues to be a subject to debate. See Tribune Co. v. Commissioner, 125 T.C. 110 (2005) (examining and comparing *West Coast Marketing* to Esmark, Inc. v. Commissioner, 90 T.C. 171, (1988) and to J.E. Seagram Corp. v. Commissioner, 104 T.C. 75 (1995), infra at 493 to assess the limits and scope of the doctrine).

4. CONTINUITY OF BUSINESS ENTERPRISE

Bentsen v. Phinney

199 F.Supp. 363 (S.D. Tex. 1961).

■ GARZA, DISTRICT JUDGE. This is a suit for refund of federal income taxes paid by plaintiffs to defendant.

All of the facts have been stipulated, and the case has been submitted to the Court on written briefs and on oral argument.

A brief summary of the stipulated facts is as follows:

Plaintiff taxpayers were shareholders of Rio Development Company, a Texas corporation, which in 1955 was engaged in the land development business in the Rio Grande Valley, along with two other corporations, Bentsen Brothers, Inc., and Bentsen Loan & Investment Company.

The shareholders in such three corporations were all members of the families of Lloyd M. Bentsen, Sr., and Elmer C. Bentsen.

On March 7, 1955, the three corporations transferred all of their respective properties, subject to their liabilities, to the newly formed Consolidated American Life Insurance Company. For the sake of brevity and consistency, the former will be referred to as the "Transferor Corporations," and the latter will be referred to as the "Insurance Company."

Immediately thereafter, the stockholders of the three transferor corporations surrendered all of their stock in the three transferor corporations for cancellation. The three transferor corporations were liquidated and dissolved, and the Insurance Company issued all of its voting stock directly to the former stockholders of the three transferor corporations which had been dissolved to Bentsen Development Company, a partnership, and to Lloyd M. Bentsen, Sr., individually. [These latter two recipients] had also transferred their assets to the Insurance Company.

It is stipulated that prior to the transaction, the transferor corporations were going concerns in the land development business in the Rio Grande Valley of Texas. The Insurance Company was a going concern created to carry on the corporate business of selling life insurance.

It has been stipulated that there were business reasons and purposes for the transaction.

It is the exchange by the plaintiff taxpayers of their stock in Rio Development Company for Insurance Company stock that was the specific event out of which this refund suit arose.

It has been stipulated that there was continuity of corporate activity as between the Rio Development Company and the Insurance Company, the only change being that the type of business carried on was changed from the land development business to the insurance business.

The net result of the transactions involved in this case was that all and the same assets which had been owned by the transferor corporations, were, after the transaction, owned by the Insurance Company. The same individuals who had owned stock in the transferor corporations now owned the stock of the Insurance Company.

It has also been stipulated that prior to the consummation of the corporate transaction involved here, the Commissioner of Internal Revenue was requested to rule in advance on the federal income tax consequences of the transaction, and that the said Commissioner on two separate occasions ruled that in his opinion an exchange of stock in the Insurance Company for the land development companies' or transferor corporations' stock, was taxable because the Insurance Company engaged in a different business from the three land development corporations.

Although the plaintiff taxpayers disagreed with the Commissioner's ruling, in their respective 1955 income tax returns they reported the exchange of their Rio Development Company stock for Insurance Company stock as a taxable event and paid a tax thereon.

Thereafter the necessary procedural steps were taken to bring this refund suit before the Court for a decision as to the income tax consequences of such exchange of stock by the taxpayers.

The question for the Court to decide is: Was such corporate transaction a corporate "reorganization," as the term "reorganization" is defined in § 368(a)(1), even though Rio Development Company engaged in the land development business and thereafter the new Insurance Company engaged in the insurance business?

The plaintiff taxpayers contend there was a corporate reorganization. The Government, defendant in this cause, maintains that there was not a corporate reorganization under § 368(a)(1) . . ., because there was not a continuity of business enterprise before and after the reorganization; and that this is a prerequisite as set out in the Treasury Regulations.

This case is governed by [§§ 368(a)(1)(C) and (D) and 354(a)(1)]. . .

It is conceded that the 1939 Internal Revenue Code was the same in this respect as the 1954 Code, and that the corresponding Treasury Regulations issued under the 1939 Code are similar to the corresponding Treasury Regulations issued under the 1954 Code.

The Treasury Regulation states: "Requisite to a reorganization under the Code, are a continuity of business enterprise under the modified corporate form."[1]

The Government contends that since there was a lack of "continuity of the business enterprise," there was not a reorganization as contemplated under the statutes.

The question for this Court to decide is the meaning of "continuity of business enterprise," and whether or not it exists in this case.

The Government takes the position that "continuity of business enterprise" means that the new corporation must engage in the same identical or similar business. Stated in another manner, the Government maintains it is necessary that there must be an identity of type of business before and after the reorganization.

The plaintiff taxpayers have cited to the Court the case of Becher v. Commissioner, 221 F.2d 252 (2d Cir. 1955) . . . which the Government has tried to distinguish. In this case the taxpayer owned all the stock in a corporation engaged in the sponge rubber and canvas-product manufacturing business. The new corporation engaged in the business of manufacturing upholstered furniture. In that case, the Government took the position that there had been a reorganization and that a cash distribution to the shareholders of the old corporation was taxable as "boot" and was ordinary income to the shareholders. The Government prevailed in that case, and the

---

[1] Treasury Regulation 118, Section 39.112(g)–1(b) under the 1939 Code; and Section 1.368–1(b) under the 1986 Code.

Court, at 221 F.2d 252, said: ". . . but the Tax Court here correctly held that a business purpose does not require an identity of business before and after the reorganization. . ."

Other cases cited are Pebble Springs Distilling Co. v. Commissioner, 231 F.2d 288 (7th Cir. 1956), *cert. denied* 352 U.S. 836. . . There the old corporation had the power to carry on both a whiskey distilling business and a real estate business, but it engaged solely in the real estate business.

Another case cited to the Court is Morley Cypress Trust v. Commissioner, 3 T.C. 84 (1944). In that case the old corporation owned land held for timber and the land was conveyed to a new corporation engaged in the oil business.

The Government tries to distinguish these last two cases by saying that in the *Pebble Springs Distilling Co.* case the new corporation could engage in the whiskey distilling business if it had wanted to, and that in the *Morley Cypress Trust* case, after the problem of continuity of business enterprise had been presented, the required continuity could have been found because both the old and the new corporations were actively engaged in exploiting the natural resources of the same land.

The Government also contends that under Texas law an insurance company cannot engage in any business other than that of insurance.

The *Morley Cypress Trust* case cited above, this Court believes, is the case most like the case before the Court. In the *Morley Cypress Trust* case the land was held for timber. In this case it was held for development. In the *Morley* case land was conveyed to a new oil corporation for use in the oil business. In this case, land (plus proceeds from the sale of land) was conveyed to a new corporation to furnish the means to capitalize a new insurance business.

The Government contends that the corresponding Treasury Regulation issued under the 1939 Code was in existence when the 1954 Code was enacted and Congress did not see fit to make any changes; that Treasury Regulations have the force of law when the Code section which they interpret is reenacted after they have once been promulgated, and cites Roberts v. Commissioner, 9 Cir., 176 F.2d 221. . .

The Government has been unable to present the Court with any decision in which the meaning of "continuity of business enterprise" as used in the Treasury Regulations, has been interpreted. Since no Court had upheld the contention made by the Government as to the interpretation to be given said words in the Regulations, it is unfair to say that Congress had an opportunity to make a change in passing the 1954 Code. Congress was not apprised of the meaning that the Government wishes to give to said language in the Regulations, and therefore the rule expressed in Roberts v. Commissioner, supra, is not controlling here.

This Court finds that no court has passed on the question of whether "continuity of business enterprise," as used in the Regulations, means that the new corporation must engage in the identical type of business or a similar business; and it is, therefore, held that this Court is not bound by any Treasury Regulation since it is the province of the Court to decide whether the Treasury Regulation means what the Government contends it means; and whether or not if it means what the Government contends, said regulation is one that could be promulgated under the appropriate sections of the Internal Revenue Code.

This Court finds that "continuity of business enterprise," as used in the Regulations, does not mean that the new corporation must engage in either the same type of business as the old or a similar business, for if this be the requirement, then said Regulation is without authority.

To qualify as a "reorganization" under the applicable statutes, the new corporation does not have to engage in an identical or similar type of business. All that is required is that there must be continuity of the business activity.

This Court therefore finds that there was a reorganization under the applicable sections of the Internal Revenue Code.

Under the facts stipulated in this case, it is found that there was a continuity of the business activity and all requisites having been complied with, the plaintiff taxpayers have a right to a refund of the income taxes paid on the exchange of stock. The amounts to be refunded by the Government are to be those as stated in the Stipulation. . .

Revenue Ruling 63–29

1963–1 C.B. 77.

Advice has been requested whether the transaction described below qualifies as a reorganization under section 368(a)(1)(C) of the Internal Revenue Code of 1954.

M corporation and N corporation were respectively engaged in the manufacture of children's toys and in the distribution of steel and allied products. At some time in the past, M corporation sold a substantial part of its operating assets for cash and notes to a third party and more recently sold all but a small part of the remaining operating assets for cash, also to a third party. Thereafter, for valid business reasons, it acquired all of the property of N corporation solely in exchange for its voting stock. N corporation distributed the M stock received to its shareholders and then dissolved. M corporation used the assets resulting from the sale of its operating assets to expand the operations of the steel distributing business acquired from N corporation.

Section 368(a)(1)(C) of the Code states that the term "reorganization" means the acquisition by one corporation, in exchange solely for all or part of its voting stock, of substantially all the properties of another corporation.

Section 1.368–1(b) of the Income Tax Regulations specifies that a reorganization, to satisfy the requirements of the Code, must result in a continuity of the business enterprise under modified corporate form. This requirement will not be satisfied unless the surviving corporation is organized to engage in a business enterprise. See, for example, Standard Realization Company v. Commissioner, 10 T.C. 708 (1948), *acquiescence*, C.B. 1948–2, 3. However, the surviving corporation need not continue the activities conducted by its predecessors. See Donald L. Bentsen et al. v. Phinney, 199 Fed. Supp. 363 (1961); and Ernest F. Becher v. Commissioner, 221 Fed. (2d) 252 (1955). See also Pebble Springs Distilling Co. v. Commissioner, 231 Fed. (2d) 288 (1956), *certiorari denied*, 352 U.S. 836 (1956); . . . and Morley Cypress Trust, Schedule "B" et al. v. Commissioner, 3 T.C. 84, (1944), *acquiescence* C.B. 1944, 20.

Since M corporation engaged in the steel distribution business after the merger, the requirement that the reorganization result in a continuity of the business enterprise within the meaning of section 1.3681(b) of the regulations was satisfied in the instant case, even though the toy business formerly conducted by M corporation was discontinued.

Accordingly, it is held that the acquisition by M corporation of all of the properties of N corporation solely in exchange for its voting stock constitutes a reorganization as defined in section 368(a)(1)(C) of the Code.

In view of these conclusions, reconsideration has been given to Revenue Ruling 56–330, C.B. 1956–2, 204, which held, in part, that the required continuity of the business enterprise was lacking where the successor corporation in a transaction otherwise qualifying as a reorganization engaged in a new business enterprise entirely different from that conducted by its predecessors. The conclusions reached in the instant case are equally applicable to the question involved in Revenue Ruling 56–330.

Accordingly, Revenue Ruling 56–330 is revoked.

NOTES

1. Regulations have clarified the application of the continuity of business enterprise (COBE) requirement. See Treas. Reg. § 1.368–1(d). These regulations take the position that continuity of business enterprise exists only when the transferee corporation either continues the historic business of the transferor or uses a significant portion of the transferor's historic business assets. See Rev. Rul. 79–434, 1979–2 C.B. 155, (manufacturing corporation sold its operating assets for cash and, prior to dissolving, transferred its remaining assets—cash and short-term Treasury notes—to an investment company in exchange for stock; held, the transaction constituted a purchase of the investment company shares and a taxable liquidation rather than a reorganization). In Rev. Rul. 81–25, 1981–1 C.B. 65, the Service strictly interpreted the regulations when it ruled that the continuity of business enterprise requirement does not relate to the pre-reorganization business or business assets of the transferee corporation. Hence, Rev. Rul. 63–29, the holding of which is reflected in the regulations, remains in force. In addition, the 1998 revisions to those regulations permitted a variety of post-transfer scenarios to satisfy the continuity

requirement (e.g., the requirement is satisfied where the acquirer drops the target asset into several of its (the acquirer's) subsidiaries, all of which use the assets in their business which is not the business of the target) because "the qualified group [acquirer and its subsidiaries are] using a significant portion of [target] historic business assets in a business." Treas. Reg. § 1.368–1(d)(5), ex. 6(ii).

Most recently, 2007 changes to the regulations have further clarified the permissive approach taken in applying the COBE requirement. In determining whether the COBE requirement is satisfied, the regulations treat the issuing corporation (which is required to continue the target corporation's historic business) as holding all the "businesses and assets of all the members of the qualified group." Treas. Reg. § 1.368–2(d)(4)(i). The broader the qualified group, the more likely the issuing corporation will meet the COBE standard. The new 2007 regulations expand the definition of qualified group by allowing qualified group members to aggregate direct stock ownership to meet the control/ownership required. Treas. Reg. § 1.368–2(d)(4)(ii). Post reorganization distributions of assets to shareholders will not result in disqualification if the "aggregate of such distribution does not . . . [constitute an amount of assets] that would result in a liquidation." Treas. Reg. § 1.368–2(k)(1).

2. What purpose do the regulations on continuity of business enterprise serve? Does it make sense to look at the historical business of the transferor corporation but not to deal with the situation in which the transferee sells its assets, and the transferor, which retains its historic business, merges into it?

3. See Rev. Rul. 70–357, 1970–2 C.B. 79, holding that a parent corporation need not continue the business of a liquidated subsidiary in order to claim the benefit of § 332. Cf. Rev. Rul. 75–223, 1975–1 C.B. 109, holding that a parent corporation will be considered to have conducted the business of its liquidated subsidiary so that the distribution to the parent's shareholders of the proceeds of sale of the subsidiary's assets may qualify as a partial liquidation under what is now § 302(b)(4) and (e). The size of the subsidiary's discontinued trade or business is immaterial. See Rev. Rul. 77–376, 1977–2 C.B. 107.

4. In Rev. Rul. 81–92, 1981–1 C.B. 133, the Service ruled that an attempted "B" reorganization fails as such if the target corporation's assets consist only of the cash that it realized on the sale of the assets it had employed previously in its manufacturing business.

5. In Rev. Rul. 85–198, 1985–2 C.B. 120, the Service concluded that the acquiring corporation's indirect operation of one of the target's indirect businesses was sufficient to satisfy the continuity of business enterprise requirement. The target operated two businesses through its wholly owned subsidiaries, S1 and S2. After the target merged into the acquiring corporation, the acquiring corporation transferred the stock of S2 to one of its wholly owned subsidiaries and sold the stock of S1 to an unrelated purchaser. Because the acquiring corporation, through its subsidiary, continued to operate one of the target's two significant businesses, the continuity of business requirement was met.

6. Courts have occasionally found that the continuity of business enterprise requirement was not met. See, e.g., Honbarrier, 115 T.C. 300 (2000) (no

continuity where acquired corporation, which ceased its trucking operations five years before merger and thereafter held tax-exempt bonds and a municipal bond fund until time of merger, was acquired by a trucking corporation that disposed of the acquired corporation's bonds and bond fund).

V. CORPORATE FUSION—MERGERS AND OTHER AMALGAMATIONS

A. INTRODUCTION AND HISTORY

Well before cases like Marr v. United States, page 434 supra, reached the Supreme Court, Congress had adopted its first nonrecognition provision and had done so in circumstances limited to corporate reorganizations. Primitive in retrospect, § 202(b) of the Revenue Act of 1918 provided that "when in connection with the reorganization, merger, or consolidation of a corporation a person receives in place of stock or securities owned by him new stock or securities of no greater aggregate par or face value, no gain or loss shall be deemed to occur from the exchange, and the new stock or securities received shall be treated as taking the place of the stock, securities, or property exchanged." According to the Senate Finance Committee that proposed the section, it was "to negative the assertion of tax in the case of certain purely paper transactions." Seidman's Legislative History 1938–1861 899 (1938); R. Blakey and G. Blakey, The Federal Income Tax 175 (1940); Mehrotra, Merger, Taxes and Historical Materialism, 83 Ind. L. J. 881 (2008).

The federal income tax law has contained reorganization and nonrecognition provisions continuously since 1918. They have become more complex and have taken crucial turns at different times.

Study of some of the cases that dealt with the statute as it was during the years prior to those covered by present law is essential to a full understanding of present law and to the continuing administrative and judicial attitudes toward particular types of problems.

B. STATUTORY ISSUES

1. CONTINUITY OF PROPRIETARY INTEREST

a. Interest Acquired

Pinellas Ice & Cold Storage Co. v. Commissioner
57 F.2d 188 (5th Cir. 1932), *aff'd*, 287 U.S. 462 (1933).

[The factual statement set forth below is taken from the opinion of MR. JUSTICE MCREYNOLDS, speaking for the Supreme Court in its affirmance of this case.* . . . Excerpts from JUDGE FOSTER'S opinion, speaking for the Court of Appeals, follow the factual statement.]

"Petitioner, a Florida corporation, made and sold ice at St. Petersburg. Substantially the same stockholders owned the Citizens Ice and Cold Storage Company, engaged in like business at the same place. In February, 1926, Lewis, general manager of both companies, began negotiations for the sale of their properties to the National Public Service Corporation. Their directors and stockholders were anxious to sell, distribute the assets and dissolve the corporations. The prospective vendee desired to acquire the properties of both companies, but not of one without the other.

"In October, 1926, agreement was reached and the vendor's directors again approved the plan for distribution and dissolution. In November, 1926, petitioner and the National Corporation entered into a formal written contract conditioned upon a like one by the Citizens Company. This referred to petitioner as 'vendor' and the National Corporation as 'purchaser.' The former agreed to sell, the latter to purchase the physical property, plants, etc., 'together with the goodwill of the business, free and clear of all defects, liens, encumbrances, taxes and assessments for the sum of $1,400,000, payable as hereinafter provided.' The specified date . . . for consummation [was] eleven A.M., December 15, 1926. . . when 'the vendor shall deliver to the purchaser instruments of conveyance and transfer by general warranty in form satisfactory to the purchaser of the property set forth. . . The purchaser shall pay to the vendor the sum of $400,000.00 in cash.' The balance of the purchase price ($1,000,000.00) shall be paid $500,000.00 on or before January 31, 1927; $250,000.00 on or before March 1, 1927; $250,000.00 on or before April 1st, 1927. Also, the deferred installments of the purchase price shall be evidenced by the purchaser's 6% notes, secured either by notes or bonds of the Florida West Coast Ice Company, thereafter to be organized to take title, or other satisfactory collateral; or by 6% notes of such Florida company secured by first lien on the property conveyed, or other satisfactory collateral.

"The vendor agreed to procure undertakings by E. T. Lewis and Leon D. Lewis not to engage in manufacturing or selling ice in Pinellas County, Florida, for ten years.

"The $400,000 cash payment was necessary for discharge of debts, liens, encumbrances, etc. The Florida Company, incorporated December 6, 1926, took title to the property and executed the purchase notes secured as agreed. These were paid at or before maturity except the one for $100,000, held until November, 1927, because of flaw in a title. As the notes were paid petitioner immediately distributed the proceeds to its stockholders according to the plan.

"The property conveyed to the Florida Company included all of petitioner's assets except a few vacant lots worth not more than $10,000, some accounts—$3,000 face value—also a small amount of cash. Assets, not ex-

---

* Page 476 infra.—ED.

ceeding 1% of the whole, were transferred to the Citizens Holding Corporation as trustee for petitioner's stockholders—99% of all vendor's property went to the Florida Company. The plan of the whole arrangement as carried out was accepted by petitioner's officers and stockholders prior to November 4, 1926.

"The Commissioner of Internal Revenue determined that the petitioner derived taxable gain exceeding $500,000 and assessed it accordingly under the Act of 1926. The Board of Tax Appeals and the Circuit Court of Appeals approved this action.

"The facts are not in controversy. The gain is admitted; but it is said this was definitely exempted from taxation by § 203, Revenue Act of 1926.

"The Act, . . .—

Sec. 202. (a) Except as hereinafter provided in this section, the gain from the sale or other disposition of property shall be the excess of the amount realized therefrom over the basis provided in subdivision (a) or (b) of section 204, and the loss shall be the excess of such basis over the amount realized. . .

(c) The amount realized from the sale or other disposition of property shall be the sum of any money received plus the fair market value of the property (other than money) received.

(d) In the case of a sale or exchange, the extent to which the gain or loss determined under this section shall be recognized for the purposes of this title, shall be determined under the provisions of section 203. . .

Sec. 203. (a) Upon the sale or exchange of property the entire amount of the gain or loss, determined under section 202, shall be recognized, except as hereinafter provided in this section. . .

(b)(3) No gain or loss shall be recognized if a corporation a party to a reorganization exchanges property, in pursuance of the plan of reorganization, solely for stock or securities in another corporation a party to the reorganization. . .

(e) if an exchange would be within the provisions of paragraph (3) of subdivision (b) if it were not for the fact that the property received in exchange consists not only of stock or securities permitted by such paragraph to be received without the recognition of gain, but also of other property or money, then

(1) If the corporation receiving such other property of money distributes it in pursuance of the plan of reorganization, no gain to the corporation shall be recognized from the exchange, but

(2) If the corporation receiving such other property or money does not distribute it in pursuance of the plan of reorganization, the gain, if

any, to the corporation shall be recognized, but in an amount not in excess of the sum of such money and the fair market value of such other property so received, which is not so distributed. . .

(h) As used in this section and sections 201 and 204—

(1) The term "reorganization" means (A) a merger or consolidation (including the acquisition by one corporation of at least a majority of the voting stock and at least a majority of the total number of shares of all other classes of stock of another corporation, or substantially all the properties of another corporation), or (B) a transfer by a corporation of all or a part of its assets to another corporation if immediately after the transfer the transferor or its stockholders or both are in control of the corporation to which the assets are transferred, or (C) a recapitalization, or (D) a mere change in identity, form, or place of organization, however effected.

(2) The term "a party to a reorganization" includes a corporation resulting from a reorganization and includes both corporations in the case of an acquisition by one corporation of at least a majority of the voting stock and at least a majority of the total number of shares of all other classes of stock of another corporation. . .

■ Before BRYAN, FOSTER, and WALKER, CIRCUIT JUDGES.

■ FOSTER, CIRCUIT JUDGE. . . Relying on the provisions of section 203, paragraphs (b)(3), (e)(1) and (h)(1)(A). . . it is contended by petitioner: That there was a reorganization to which petitioner and the West Coast Company were parties; that the notes were securities of the new company; that there was an exchange of the property of petitioner for cash and securities; that this was distributed in pursuance of a plan of reorganization; and that therefore no gain to the corporation should be recognized,

Apparently there are no decisions in point, and it would be useless to review the cases cited by either side.

Section 203* appeared first in the 1924 Revenue Act. . . Prior thereto the profit resulting from all exchanges of property was taxable. It is evident that in enacting section 203 Congress intended to exempt from consideration for either profit or loss transfers of property which were really exchanges of capital assets, and, to a certain extent, to brush aside technicalities in so construing them. It is equally clear that there was no intention to exempt profit arising from an outright sale of property, or an exchange of property, between corporations where there was in fact no reorganization.

There is no doubt that the written agreement of November 4, 1926, for the disposition of petitioner's property to a new corporation, contemplated an outright sale and not an exchange or a reorganization. The conveyance of the property on December 17, 1926, was in form a sale and not an exchange. This is not seriously disputed by petitioner, but it is contended that

---

* The precursor, inter alia, to §§ 354 and 361 of the 1986 Code.—ED.

under the definition of paragraph (h)(1)(A)** the mere acquisition by the Florida West Coast Ice Company of substantially all the property of petitioner was a reorganization.

As applied to corporations, the terms "merger" and "consolidation" have well known legal meanings. While the result is practically the same in either event, there is this difference. In a merger one corporation absorbs the other and remains in existence while the other is dissolved. In a consolidation a new corporation is created and the consolidating corporations are extinguished, In either event, the resulting corporation acquires all the property, rights, and franchises of the dissolved corporations, and their stockholders become its stockholders. . .

It must be assumed that in adopting paragraph (h) Congress intended to use the words "merger" and "consolidation" in their ordinary and accepted meanings. Giving the matter in parenthesis the most liberal construction, it is only when there is an acquisition of substantially all the property of another corporation in connection with a merger or consolidation that a reorganization takes place, Clause (B) of the paragraph removes any doubt as to the intention of Congress on this point.

It follows that there was no reorganization, and consequently no party to a reorganization, in connection with the disposition of petitioner's property. It is unnecessary to pass upon petitioner's other contentions.

The record presents no reversible error. The petition is denied.

Pinellas Ice & Cold Storage Co. v. Commissioner
287 U.S. 462 (1933).

■ MR. JUSTICE MCREYNOLDS delivered the opinion of the Court. . . Counsel for the petitioner maintain—

The record discloses a "reorganization" to which petitioner was party and a preliminary plan strictly pursued, The Florida West Coast Ice Company acquired substantially all of petitioner's property in exchange for cash and securities which were promptly distributed to the latter's stockholders. Consequently, under § 203, the admitted gain was not taxable.

The Board of Tax Appeals held that the transaction in question amounted to a sale of petitioner's property for money and not an exchange for securities within the true meaning of the statute. It, accordingly and as we think properly, upheld the Commissioner's action.

The "vendor" agreed "to sell" and "the purchaser" agreed "to purchase" certain described property for a definite sum of money. Part of this sum was paid in cash; for the balance the purchaser executed three promissory notes, secured by the deposit of mortgage bonds, payable, with interest, in about forty-five, seventy-five, and one hundred and five days, respectively. These notes—mere evidence of obligation to pay the purchase price—were

---

** Cf. § 368(a)(1)(C) of the 1986 Code.—ED.

not securities within the intendment of the act and were properly regarded as the equivalent of cash. It would require clear language to lead us to conclude that Congress intended to grant exemption to one who sells property and for the purchase price accepts well-secured, short-term notes, (all payable within four months), when another who makes a like sale and receives cash certainly would be taxed, We can discover no good basis in reason for the contrary view and its acceptance would make evasion of taxation very easy. In substance the petitioner sold for the equivalent of cash; the gain must be recognized.

The court below held that the facts disclosed failed to show a "reorganization" within the statutory definition. And, in the circumstances, we approve that conclusion. But the construction which the court seems to have placed upon clause A, paragraph (h)(1), § 203, we think is too narrow. It conflicts with established practice of the tax officers and if passed without comment may produce perplexity,

The court said—"It must be assumed that in adopting paragraph (h) Congress intended to use the words 'merger' and 'consolidation' in their ordinary and accepted meanings. Giving the matter in parenthesis the most liberal construction, it is only when there is an acquisition of substantially all the property of another corporation in connection with a merger or consolidation that a reorganization takes place. Clause (B) of the paragraph removes any doubt as to the intention of Congress on this point."

The paragraph in question directs—"The term 'reorganization' means (A) a merger or consolidation (including the acquisition by one corporation of at least a majority of the voting stock and at least a majority of the total number of shares of all other classes of stock of another corporation, or substantially all the properties of another corporation)." The words within the parenthesis may not be disregarded. They expand the meaning of "merger" or "consolidation" so as to include some things which partake of the nature of a merger or consolidation but are beyond the ordinary and commonly accepted meaning of those words—so as to embrace circumstances difficult to delimit but which in strictness cannot be designated as either merger or consolidation. But the mere purchase for money of the assets of one company by another is beyond the evident purpose of the provision, and has no real semblance to a merger or consolidation, Certainly, we think that to be within the exemption the seller must acquire an interest in the affairs of the purchasing company more definite than that incident to ownership of its short-term purchase money notes. This general view is adopted and well sustained in Cortland Specialty Co. v. Commissioner of Internal Revenue [infra]. It harmonizes with the underlying purpose of the provisions in respect of exemptions and gives some effect to all the words employed,

The judgment of the court below is affirmed.

Cortland Specialty Co. v. Commissioner

60 F.2d 937 (2d Cir. 1932), *cert. denied*, 288 U.S. 599 (1933).

[As in *Pinellas*, the principal issue was seen to be whether a corporation's transfer of substantially all its properties to another corporation for cash and notes payable within 14 months was a "reorganization" within the meaning of § 203 of the Revenue Act of 1926. Like the Fifth Circuit in *Pinellas*, the Second Circuit concluded (at 940) that a transfer of assets, to constitute a reorganization, must smack of "merger" or "consolidation," and those concepts imply "a continuance of interest on the part of the transferor in the properties transferred."

[If the Supreme Court had reviewed *Cortland* it probably would have affirmed on grounds like those employed in *Pinellas*, rejecting the notion of required nexus to "merger" or "consolidation." As the concluding paragraph in the Supreme Court's opinion in *Pinellas* indicates, however, a second ground for decision was employed by the Second Circuit in *Cortland*, this one very much to the Supreme Court's liking, as indicated by its statements in *Pinellas* and in later cases. As seen by the Second Circuit, this secondary issue was posed: Even if the transfer of assets for cash and short term notes had been made pursuant to a "plan of reorganization," did the payment that Cortland received in exchange have to include some "stock or securities," and if so, had they been included in this case?]

■ Before L. HAND, AUGUSTUS N. HAND, and CHASE, CIRCUIT JUDGES.

■ AUGUSTUS HAND, CIRCUIT JUDGE . . ., Furthermore the Cortland Company cannot come within the exception to the general rule that gains realized from exchanges of property represent taxable income unless section 203(e) and section 203(e)(1)* apply. Under those clauses, even if the transfer to Deyo was an exchange in pursuance of a "plan of reorganization," the property received by Cortland had to include *some* "stock or securities" (§ 203(e)), or the exemption could not be had. As no stock was issued against the transfer, the conditions for an exemption were not fulfilled unless the notes, all payable within fourteen months of the date of the transfer, and all unsecured, can be considered "securities" under section 203(e). Inasmuch as a transfer made entirely for cash would not be enough, it cannot be supposed that anything so near to cash as these notes payable in so short a time and doubtless readily marketable would meet the legislative requirements.

The very reason that section 203(e) requires that some of the property received in exchange should be "*stock or securities*" is to deprive a mere sale for cash of the benefits of an exemption and to require an amalgamation of the existing interests, There can be no justice or propriety in taxing one corporation who transfers its properties for cash and in relieving another that takes part of its pay in short time notes. The situation might be different had the "securities," though not in stock, created such obligations as to give creditors or others some assured participation in the properties of the

---

* Cf. § 361(b) of the 1986 Code.—ED.

transferee corporation. The word "securities" was used so as not to defeat the exemption in cases where the interest of the transferor was carried over to the new corporation in some form.

The orders of the Board of Tax Appeals are affirmed.

NOTES

1. Suppose the "notes" were payable in five years, or ten years. Would it make any difference if they were redeemable at the issuer's option? At any time? If there were a plan for their redemption? If there were or were not a ready market in the "securities" of the issuer?

2. The Supreme Court regarded the Court of Appeals' construction of § 203(h)(1)(A) in *Pinellas* as "too narrow." Why? Was it "too narrow" in your judgment? What function would clause (A) serve if the Court of Appeals' construction had been accepted? The effects of the Supreme Court's view that the parenthetical clause had independent significance were far-reaching, as later cases show. As you read the cases consider whether the Supreme Court's construction was helpful or harmful in the evolution of the law of reorganization.

Helvering v. Minnesota Tea Co.

296 U.S. 378 (1935).

■ MR. JUSTICE MCREYNOLDS delivered the opinion of the Court. . . Respondent, a Minnesota corporation with three stockholders, assailed a deficiency assessment for 1928 income tax, and prevailed below. The Commissioner seeks reversal. He claims the transaction out of which the assessment arose was not a reorganization within § 112, par. (i)(1)(A), Revenue Act, 1928, c. 852 . . .: "The term 'reorganization' means (A) a merger or consolidation (including the acquisition by one corporation of at least a majority of the voting stock and at least a majority of the total number of shares of all other classes of stock of another corporation, or substantially all the properties of another corporation)." The Circuit Court of Appeals held otherwise and remanded the cause for determination by the Board whether the whole of the cash received by the Minnesota Tea Company was in fact distributed as required by the act. We granted certiorari because of alleged conflicting opinions.

The petition also stated that, as the taxpayer made an earlier conveyance of certain assets, the later one, here in question, of what remained to the Grand Union Company did not result in acquisition by one corporation of substantially all property of another. This point was not raised prior to the petition for certiorari and, in the circumstances, we do not consider it.

Statutory provisions presently helpful are in the margin.*

---

* ... **Sec. 203.** (a) Upon the sale or exchange of property the entire amount of the gain or the loss, determined under section 202, shall be recognized, except as hereinafter provided in this section....

July 14, 1928, respondent caused Peterson Investment Company to be organized and transferred to the latter real estate, investments and miscellaneous assets in exchange for the transferee's entire capital stock. The shares thus obtained were immediately distributed among the three stockholders. August 23, 1928, it transferred all remaining assets to Grand Union Company in exchange for voting trust certificates, representing 18,000* shares of the transferee's common stock, and $426,842.52 cash. It retained the certificates; but immediately distributed the money among the stockholders, who agreed to pay $106,471.73 of its outstanding debts. Although of opinion that there had been reorganization, the Commissioner treated as taxable gain the amount of the assumed debts upon the view that this amount of the cash received by the company was really appropriated to the payment of its debts.

The matter went before the Board of Tax Appeals upon the question whether the Commissioner ruled rightly in respect of this taxable gain. Both parties proceeded upon the view that there had been reorganization. Of its own motion, the Board questioned and denied the existence of one. It then ruled that the corporation had realized taxable gain amounting to the

---

(b)(2) No gain or loss shall be recognized if stock or securities in a corporation a party to a reorganization are, in pursuance of the plan of reorganization, exchanged solely for stock or securities in such corporation or in another corporation a party to the reorganization.

(3) No gain or loss shall be recognized if a corporation a party to a reorganization exchanges property, in pursuance of the plan of reorganization, solely for stock or securities in another corporation a party to the reorganization....

(e) If an exchange would be within the provisions of paragraph (3) of subdivision (b) if it were not for the fact that the property received in exchange consists not only of stock or securities permitted by such paragraph to be received without the recognition of gain, but also of other property or money, then—

(1) If the corporation receiving such other property or money distributes it in pursuance of the plan of reorganization, no gain to the corporation shall be recognized from the exchange, but

(2) If the corporation receiving such other property, or money does not distribute it in pursuance of the plan of reorganization, the gain, if any, to the corporation shall be recognized, but in an amount not in excess of the sum of such money and the fair market value of such other property so received, which is not so distributed.

(h) As used in this section and sections 201 and 204—

(1) The term "reorganization" means (A) a merger or consolidation (including the acquisition by one corporation of at least a majority of the voting stock and at least a majority of the total number of shares of all other classes of stock of another corporation, or substantially all the properties of another corporation), or (B) a transfer by a corporation of all or a part of its assets to another corporation if immediately after the transfer the transferor or its stockholders or both are in control of the corporation to which the assets are transferred, or (C) a recapitalization, or (D) a mere change in identity, form, or place of organization, however effected.

(2) The term "a party to a reorganization" includes a corporation resulting from a reorganization and includes both corporations in the case of an acquisition by one corporation of at least a majority of the voting stock and at least a majority of the total number of shares of all other classes of stock of another corporation.

Revenue Act. 1926 c. 27....

Revenue Act, 1928, c. 852....

Section 112(a), (b)(3), (b)(4), ... (d), (d)(1), (d)(2), (i), (i)(1) and (i)(2) repeat the words of Section 203(a), (b)(2), (b)(3), ... (e), (e)(1), (e)(2), (h), (h)(1) and (h)(2) of the Act of 1924. [Footnote by the Court.]

* The 18,000 shares amounted to 7.5 percent of Grand Union's outstanding stock.—ED.

difference between cost of the property transferred and the cash received plus the value of the 18,000 shares—$712,195.90.

The Circuit Court of Appeals found there was reorganization within the statute and reversed the Board. It concluded that the words "the acquisition by one corporation of . . . substantially all the property of another corporation" plainly include the transaction under consideration. Also that Clause (B), § 112(i)(1), . . . did not narrow the scope of Clause (A). Further, that reorganization was not dependent upon dissolution by the conveying corporation. And finally, that its conclusions find support in Treasury regulations long in force.

These conclusions we think are correct.

The Commissioner maintains that the statute presents two definitions of reorganization by transfer of assets. One, Clause (B), requires that the transferor obtain control of the transferee. The other, Clause (A), is part of the definition of merger or consolidation, and must be narrowly interpreted so as to necessitate something nearly akin to technical merger or consolidation. These clauses have separate legislative histories and were intended to be mutually exclusive. Consequently, he says, Clause (A) must be restricted to prevent overlapping and negation of the condition in Clause (B). Also, the transaction here involved substantially changed the relation of the taxpayer to its assets; a large amount of cash passed between the parties; there are many attributes of a sale; what was done did not sufficiently resemble merger or consolidation as commonly understood.

With painstaking care, the opinion of the court below gives the history of Clauses (A) and (B), § 112(i)(1). We need not repeat the story. Clause (A) first appeared in the Act of 1921; (B) was added by the 1924 Act. We find nothing in the history or words employed which indicates an intention to modify the evident meaning of (A) by what appears in (B). Both can have effect, and if one does somewhat overlap the other—the taxpayer should not be denied, for that reason, what one paragraph clearly grants hire. Treasury regulations long enforced support the taxpayer's position, as the opinion below plainly points out.

Pinellas Ice Co. v. Commissioner, 287 U.S. 462, 470, [page 476 supra] considered the language of § 203(h)(1)(A), Act of 1926, which became § 112(i)(1)(A). Act of 1928, and held that a sale for money or short-term notes was not within its intendment. We approved the conclusion of the Commissioner, Board of Tax Appeals and Court of Appeals that the transaction there involved was in reality a sale for the equivalent of money—not an exchange for securities. . .

And we said:

> The words within the parenthesis may not be disregarded. They expand the meaning of "merger" or "consolidation" so as to include some things which partake of the nature of a merger or consolidation but are beyond the ordinary and commonly accepted meaning of those

words—so as to embrace circumstances difficult to delimit but which in strictness cannot be designated as either merger or consolidation. But the mere purchase for money of the assets of one Company by another is beyond the evident purpose of the provision, and has no real semblance to a merger or consolidation. Certainly. we think that to be within the exemption the seller must acquire an interest in the affairs of the purchasing company more definite than that incident to ownership of its short-term purchase-money notes.

And we now add that this interest must be definite and material; it must represent a substantial part of the value of the thing transferred. This much is necessary in order that the result accomplished may genuinely partake of the nature of merger or consolidation.

Gregory v. Helvering [page 445 supra] revealed a sham—a mere device intended to obscure the character of the transaction. We, of course, disregarded the mask and dealt with realities. The present record discloses no such situation; nothing suggests other than a bona fide business move.

The transaction here was no sale, but partook of the nature of a reorganization in that the seller acquired a definite and substantial interest in the purchaser.

True it is that the relationship of the taxpayer to the assets conveyed was substantially changed, but this is not inhibited by the statute. Also, a large part of the consideration was cash. This, we think, is permissible so long as the taxpayer received an interest in the affairs of the transferee which represented a material part of the value of the transferred assets.

Finally, it is said the transferor was not dissolved and therefore the transaction does not adequately resemble consolidation. But dissolution is not prescribed and we are unable to see that such action is essential to the end in view.

The challenged judgment is affirmed. . .

NOTES

1. In 1984 Congress overruled the holding in *Minnesota Tea* (along with dicta in earlier cases as well), which had countenanced a "C" reorganization even though the transferor stayed alive, not transferring or distributing all of its assets. See § 368(a)(2)(G).

After remand of *Minnesota Tea*, the case again came before the Supreme Court on the issue whether the transferor corporation was taxable on money received in the reorganization and transferred to the shareholders pursuant to an agreement that the shareholders assume and pay off corporate debt. See 302 U.S. 609 (1938). Interpreting a provision similar to § 361(b)(1), the Supreme Court held that the receipt of the money was taxable to the corporation because it was not "distributed" to (or for the benefit of) the shareholders. According to the Court, the shareholders had received the money not as a distribution for their own benefit, but as a fund that they were bound to pass on to the corporation's creditors. The outcome had been roundly criticized and was finally overruled in the 1986 Act amendments to § 361. See § 361(b)(3).

2. After *Pinellas*, *Cortland*, and *Minnesota Tea*, the transferor corporation or its shareholders had to acquire a "definite and substantial interest" in the transferee corporation, representing a "material part of the value of the transferred assets," in order that the transfer qualify as a reorganization. In terms of tax planning, counseling, or litigating, did these developments contribute much to certainty? Given the ends that the courts indicate the reorganization provisions are designed to serve, how likely were the Supreme Court's formulations to contribute to their attainment?

LeTulle v. Scofield

308 U.S. 415 (1940).

■ MR. JUSTICE ROBERTS delivered the opinion of the court. We took this case because the petition for certiorari alleged that the Circuit Court of Appeals had based its decision on a point not presented or argued by the litigants, which the petitioner had never had an opportunity to meet by the production of evidence.

The Gulf Coast Irrigation Company was the owner of irrigation properties. Petitioner was its sole stockholder. He personally owned certain lands and other irrigation properties. November 4, 1931, the Irrigation Company, the Gulf Coast Water Company, and the petitioner, entered into an agreement which recited that the petitioner owned all of the stock of the Irrigation Company; described the company's properties, and stated that, prior to conveyance to be made pursuant to the contract, the Irrigation Company would be the owner of certain other lands and irrigation properties. These other lands and properties were those which the petitioner individually owned. The contract called for a conveyance of all the properties owned, and to be owned, by the Irrigation Company for $50,000 in cash and $750,000 in bonds of the Water Company, payable serially over the period January 1, 1933, to January 1, 1944. The petitioner joined in this agreement as a guarantor of the title of the Irrigation Company and for the purpose of covenanting that he would not personally enter into the irrigation business within a fixed area during a specified period after the execution of the contract. Three days later, at a special meeting of stockholders of the Irrigation Company, the proposed reorganization was approved, the minutes stating that the taxpayer, "desiring also to reorganize his interest in the properties," had consented to be a party to the reorganization. The capital stock of the Irrigation Company was increased and thereupon the taxpayer subscribed for the new stock and paid for it by conveyance of his individual properties.

The contract between the two corporations was carried out November 18, with the result that the Water Company became owner of all the properties then owned by the Irrigation Company including the property theretofore owned by the petitioner individually. Subsequently all of its assets, including the bonds received from the Water Company, were distributed to the petitioner. The company was then dissolved. The petitioner and his wife filed a tax return as members of a community in which they reported no gain as a result of the receipt of the liquidating dividend from the Irrigation Company. The latter reported no gain for the taxable year in virtue of its receipt of bonds and cash from the Water Company. The Commissioner of Internal Revenue assessed additional taxes against the community, as individual taxpayers, by reason of the receipt of the liquidating dividend, and against the petitioner—as transferee of the Irrigation Company's assets in virtue of the gain realized by the company on the sale of its property. The tax was paid and claims for refund were filed. Petitioner's wife having died he brought suit individually and as her executor and representative in the community property against the respondent to recover the amount of the additional taxes so assessed. He alleged that the transaction constituted a tax-exempt reorganization as defined by the Revenue Act.[1] The respondent traversed the allegations of the complaints and the causes were consolidated and tried by the District Court without a jury. The respondent's contention that the transaction amounted merely to a sale of assets by the petitioner and the Irrigation Company and did not fall within the statutory definition of a tax-free reorganization was overruled by the District Court and judgment was entered for the petitioner.

The respondent appealed, asserting error on the part of the District Court in matters not now material and also assigning as error the court's holding that the transaction constituted a nontaxable reorganization.

The Circuit Court of Appeals concluded that, as the Water Company acquired substantially all the properties of the Irrigation Company, there was a merger of the latter within the literal language of the statute, but held that, in the light of the construction this Court has put upon the statute, the transaction would not be a reorganization unless the transferor retained a definite and substantial interest in the affairs of the transferee. It thought this requirement was satisfied by the taking of the bonds of the Water Company, and, therefore, agreed with the District Court that a reorganization had been consummated. It added, however, "We find a reason for reversing the judgment which has not been argued." Adverting to the fact that the transfer of the petitioner's individual properties to the Irrigation Company was for the purpose of including them in the latter's assets to be transferred in the proposed reorganization, the court said the statute did not extend to the reorganization of an individual's business or affairs, and the transaction was a reorganization within the meaning of the Revenue Act as respects the corporation's assets owned on November 4, 1931, but not as respects the petitioner's individual properties included in the sale. It concluded:

> Only so much of the consideration as represents the price of the properties and business of the Irrigation Company is entitled to be protected from taxation as arising from a reorganization. It does not appear what the proper apportionment is. The burden was upon LeTulle to show not only that he had been illegally taxed, but how much of what was collected from him was illegal. The latter he did not do. The

---

[1] Section 112(i) of the Revenue Act of 1928, c. 852....

evidence does not support the judgment for the full amount paid by him. It is accordingly reversed, that further proceedings may be had consistent herewith.

The petitioner sought certiorari asserting that the Circuit Court of Appeals had departed from the usual and accepted course of judicial proceedings by deciding the cause upon a ground not presented or argued and hence had deprived the petitioner of his day in court. The respondent, though he had contended below that the transaction in question did not amount to a tax-free statutory reorganization, did not file a cross petition asking for a review of that part of the judgment exempting from taxation gain to the Irrigation Company arising from the transfer of its assets owned by it on and prior to November 4, 1931, and the part of the liquidating dividend attributable thereto.

We find it unnecessary to consider petitioner's contention that the Circuit Court of Appeals erred in deciding the case on a ground not raised by the pleadings, not before the trial court, not suggested or argued in the Circuit Court of Appeals, and one as to which the petitioner had never had the opportunity to present his evidence, since we are of opinion that the transaction did not amount to a reorganization and that, therefore, the petitioner cannot complain, as the judgment must be affirmed on the ground that no tax-free reorganization was effected within the meaning of the statute.

Section 112(1) provides, so far as material:

(1) The term "reorganization" means (A) a merger or consolidation (including the acquisition by one corporation of at least a majority of the voting stock and at least a majority of the total number of shares of all other classes of stock of another corporation, or substantially all the properties of another corporation). . .

As the court below properly states, the section is not to be read literally as denominating the transfer of all the assets of one company for what amounts to a cash consideration given by the other a reorganization. We have held that where the consideration consists of cash and short term notes the transfer does not amount to a reorganization within the true meaning of the statute, but is a sale upon which gain or loss must be reckoned.[3] We have said that the statute was not satisfied unless the transferor retained a substantial stake in the enterprise and such a stake was thought to be retained where a large proportion of the consideration was in common stock of the transferee,[4] or where the transferor took cash and the entire issue of preferred stock of the transferee corporation[5] And, where the consideration is represented by a substantial proportion of stock, and the balance in bonds, the total consideration received is exempt from tax under § 112(b)(4) and 112(g).[6]

---

[3] Pinellas Ice & Cold Storage Co. v. Commissioner, 287 U.S. 462 [page 478 supra].

[4] Helvering v. Minnesota Tea Co., 296 U.S. 378 [page 480 supra].

[5] Nelson Co. v. Helvering, 296 U.S. 374.

[6] .... See Helvering v. Watts, 296 U.S. 387.

In applying our decision in the *Pinellas* case the courts have generally held that receipt of long term bonds as distinguished from short term notes constitutes the retention of an interest in the purchasing corporation. There has naturally been some difficulty in classifying the securities involved in various cases.

We are of opinion that the term of the obligations is not material. Where the consideration is wholly in the transferee's bonds, or part cash and part such bonds, we think it cannot be said that the transferor retains any proprietary interest in the enterprise. On the contrary, he becomes a creditor of the transferee; and we do not think that the fact referred to by the Circuit Court of Appeals, that the bonds were secured solely by the assets transferred and that, upon default, the bondholder would retake only the property sold, changes his status from that of a creditor to one having a proprietary stake, within the purview of the statute.

We conclude that the Circuit Court of Appeals was in error in holding that, as respects any of the property transferred to the Water Company, the transaction was other than a sale or exchange upon which gain or loss must be reckoned in accordance with the provisions of the revenue act dealing with the recognition of gain or loss upon a sale or exchange.

Had the respondent sought and been granted certiorari the petitioner's tax liability would, in the view we have expressed, be substantially increased over the amount found due by the Circuit Court of Appeals. Since the respondent has not drawn into question so much of the judgment as exempts from taxation gain to the Irrigation Company arising from transfer of its assets owned by it on and prior to November 4, 1931, and the part of the liquidating dividend attributable thereto, we cannot afford him relief from that portion of the judgment which was adverse to him.

A respondent or an appellee may urge any matter appearing in the record in support of a judgment, but he may not attack it even on grounds asserted in the court below, in an effort to have this Court reverse it, when he himself has not sought review of the whole judgment, or of that portion which is adverse to him.

The judgment of the Circuit Court of Appeals is affirmed and the cause is remanded to the District Court with directions to proceed in accordance with the opinion and mandate of the Circuit Court of Appeals.

Affirmed.

NOTES

1. In Helvering v. Watts, 296 U.S. 387 (1935), decided the same day as *Minnesota Tea*, the shareholders of one corporation exchanged all of their shares for common stock of another corporation having an agreed value of $963,090 and mortgage bonds valued at $1,161,184.50. The first bond was to be retired within two months, and the remaining bonds were due at one-year intervals over the next seven years. The acquiring corporation also paid $338,815 to the creditors of the acquired corporation, and the payment was treated as a

loan from the transferee to the transferor. The Supreme Court held that the bonds were "securities" and could not be regarded as a cash equivalent, unlike the short-term notes in *Pinellas*. The Court ignored the payment to the creditors of the acquired corporation and held that the transaction constituted a valid reorganization. Similarly, in Nelson Co. v. Helvering, 296 U.S. 374 (1935), the Court found a valid reorganization where the transferor received cash and nonvoting stock equivalent to approximately 38 percent A continuing question has been what threshold level of continuity of interest is required. Treas. Reg. § 1.368–1(e)(2)(v) Ex. 1 considers continuity of interest satisfied with a 40 percent stock interest (seeming to formalize the *Nelson* outcome). For purposes of the continuity of interest requirement, when is the value of the target stock surrendered and the "Parent" stock to be received, valued? Final regulations effective for transactions entered into after December 19, 2011 state that where the agreement calls for "fixed" consideration, the "signing date" rule applies so that the stock to be received in exchange for target stock is valued on the last business day before the agreement is signed. If, however, the agreement does not call for fixed considerations in the "Parent" stock, these provisions in Temp. Reg. § 1.368–1T(e)(2) do not apply. See infra Chapter 4.V.B.1.a. notes following J.E. Seagram Corp. v. Commissioner.

2. The taxpayers in *LeTulle* received $50,000 cash and $750,000 in bonds redeemable over 11 years; in *Watts* the taxpayers received 32,103 shares of common stock, with a value of $963,090, and mortgage bonds of approximately $1,161,184.50; and in *Nelson* the taxpayer received $2 million cash and 14,060 shares of nonvoting preferred stock, valued at $1,406,000. Is there a sufficient difference, in terms of the concept of "reorganization," to justify the treatment of the taxpayers in *LeTulle*? In any event, who has a more significant interest in the corporate assets: the owner of ten-year, fixed-interest bonds or the owner, e.g., of nonvoting, noncumulative preferred stock?

3. In this connection, consider Roebling v. Commissioner, 143 F.2d 810 (3d Cir. 1944), *cert. denied*, 323 U.S. 773 (1944). In *Roebling*, South Jersey Gas, Electric and Traction Co. (South Jersey) in 1903 leased all its plants and operating equipment to Public Service Electric and Gas Company (Public Service) for 900 years. The net rentals received by South Jersey were distributed yearly to its stockholders at a rate of 8 percent of the par value of the stock. In 1937, South Jersey merged into Public Service, and South Jersey's shareholders received in exchange for their stock 8–percent 100–year first mortgage bonds of Public Service.

After unsuccessfully contending that the continuity of interest doctrine was superseded by the reorganization provision of the Revenue Act of 1938, the taxpayer, a former South Jersey shareholder, argued that the continuity of interest requirement was met because "prior to the merger, the stockholders of South Jersey had no *proprietary interest* in its properties in any real sense" and the South Jersey stock "was substantially equivalent to a perpetual 8% bond." Therefore, he argued, the interest received by the former shareholders in the merger was equivalent to the interest they held before the merger. The court, however, rejected this argument, finding that the South Jersey shareholders held a proprietary interest before the merger, but not after the merger.

The court thought that the taxpayer's interest was less remote before the merger than after. Is the right to income from a corporation that owns and operates the assets more remote than the expectancy of income from a corporation which, for 900 years, has only a right to income from the assets? What relevance do questions like these have to the meaning of "reorganization?"

4. Does nonqualified preferred stock (§ 351(g)(2)) count as equity for purposes of the continuity of proprietary interest test? The legislative history provides that the "boot" classification of nonqualified preferred stock applies only for purposes of §§ 351 and 356—unless and until regulations detailing otherwise are issued (which they have not). Thus, nonqualified preferred stock should count as equity in the continuity of interest test. General Explanation of Tax Legislation Enacted in 1997, JCS–23–9–7 at 209–213.

Revenue Procedure 77–37
1977–2 C.B. 568.

[The Internal Revenue Service has announced an "operating rule" to guide it in issuing rulings where the "continuity of interest" requirement of Treas. Reg. § 1.368–1(b) is involved.]

. . . The "continuity of interest" requirement of section 1.368-1(b) of the Income Tax Regulations is satisfied if there is a continuing interest through stock ownership in the acquiring or transferee corporation (or a corporation in "control" thereof within the meaning of § 368(c) of the Code) on the part of the former shareholders of the acquired or transferor corporation which is equal in value, as of the effective date of the reorganization, to at least 50 percent of the value of all of the formerly outstanding stock of the acquired or transferor corporation as of the same date. It is not necessary that each shareholder of the acquired or transferor corporation receive in the exchange stock of the acquiring or transferee corporation or a corporation in "control" thereof, which is equal in value to at least 50 percent of the value of his former stock interest in the acquired or transferor corporation, so long as one or more of the shareholders of the acquired or transferor corporation have a continuing interest through stock ownership in the acquiring or transferee corporation (or a corporation in "control" thereof) which is, in the aggregate, equal in value to at least 50 percent of the value of all of the formerly outstanding stock of the acquired or transferor corporation. Sales, redemptions, and other dispositions of stock occurring prior or subsequent to the exchange which are part of the plan of reorganization will be considered in determining whether there is a 50 percent continuing interest through stock ownership as of the effective date of the reorganization. . .

Revenue Ruling 66–224
1966–2 C.B. 114.

Corporation X was merged under state law into corporation Y. Corporation X had four stockholders (A, B, C, D), each of whom owned 25 percent of its stock. Corporation Y paid A and B each $50,000 in cash for their stock of corporation X, and C and D each received corporation Y stock with a value of $50,000 in exchange for their stock of corporation X. There are no other facts present that should be taken into account in determining whether the continuity of interest requirement of § 1.368–1(b) of the Income Tax regulations has been satisfied, such as sales, redemptions or other dispositions of stock prior to or subsequent to the exchange which were part of the plan of reorganization.

Held, the continuity of interest requirement of Section 1.3681(b) of the regulations has been satisfied. It would also be satisfied if the facts were the same except corporation Y paid each stockholder $25,000 in cash and each stockholder received corporation Y stock with a value of $25,000.

May B. Kass v. Commissioner

60 T.C. 218 (1973), *aff'd without opinion*, 491 F.2d 749 (3d Cir. 1974).

■ DAWSON, JUDGE. Respondent determined a deficiency in petitioner's Federal income tax for the year 1966 in the amount of $10,134.67.

The only issue for decision is whether petitioner, a minority shareholder of an 84–percent–owned subsidiary, must recognize gain upon the receipt of the parent's stock pursuant to a statutory merger of the subsidiary into the parent. . .

[May B. Kass (petitioner) owned 2,000 shares of the common stock of Atlantic City Racing Association (ACRA) which had a basis of $1000.

[Track Associates, Inc. (TRACK) was formed on November 19, 1965, by the Levy and Casey families, minority shareholders in ACRA, for the purpose of gaining control over ACRA's racetrack business. These two families owned over 58 percent of TRACK's outstanding stock, part of which was received in exchange for their ACRA stock.

[Control in ACRA was to be acquired by having TRACK purchase 80 percent or more of ACRA's stock and by then merging ACRA into TRACK. Pursuant to this plan, TRACK offered to buy ACRA's stock from its 500 shareholders for $22 per share, conditioned on the tendering of 80 percent or more of the outstanding shares. TRACK acquired more than the requisite number of shares.

[Thereafter, upon shareholder approval, ACRA was merged into TRACK. The shares of ACRA that were neither tendered nor sold by dissenting shareholders were exchanged, one for one, for TRACK stock. The petitioner exchanged her 2,000 shares of ACRA stock, valued at $22 per share, for 2,000 shares of TRACK stock. She reported no capital gain.]

Petitioner contends that the merger of ACRA into TRACK, although treated at least in part as a liquidation at the corporate level, is at her level, the shareholder level, (1) a true statutory merger and (2) a section 368(a)(1)(a)(A)[2] reorganization, occasioning no recognition of gain on the ensuing exchange. In support of this she cites Madison Square Garden Corp., 58 T.C. 619 (1972). Respondent, on the other hand, argues that the

---

[2] ... Hereafter we will use "statutory merger" to refer to a merger which might or might not qualify as a sec. 368 reorganization and "A" reorganization to refer to a statutory merger that definitely does qualify.

purchase of stock by TRACK and the liquidation of ACRA into TRACK, which took the form of a merger, must be viewed at all levels as an integrated transaction; that the statutory merger does not qualify as a reorganization because it fails the continuity-of-interest test; and that, as a consequence, petitioner falls outside of section 354(a)(1) and must recognize gain pursuant to section 1002.

The problems presented by these facts are somewhat complex, and the solutions, according to the commentators, are less than clear. Stated one way, the question is whether a statutory merger that follows a section 334(b)(3) "purchase" and serves the purpose of a Section 332, 334(b) "complete liquidation" can qualify as an "A" reorganization at the shareholder level and, if so, when. Put another way, does the merger of ACRA into TRACK fall under section 368(a)(1)(A), thus placing the exchange of petitioner's ACRA stock for TRACK stock within the applicable nonrecognition provision?

Respondent does not take the position that a statutory merger, such as the one we have here, can never qualify for reorganization nonrecognition status. He admits that "Theoretically it is possible for TRACK to get a stepped-up basis in 83.95 percent of the assets of ACRA per section 334(b)(2), . . . upon a section 332, . . . liquidation of ACRA into TRACK and at the same time allow nonrecognition reorganization treatment to minority shareholders." Rather, his position is simply that the merger in question fails to meet the time honored continuity-of-interest test. We agree with this and so hold.

Section 334(b)(2) and the reorganization provisions might apply to the same transaction only in certain cases where the continuity-of-interest test is met. See sec. 332 (last sentence, last independent clause); sec. 1.332–2(d) and (e). . . Reorganization treatment is appropriate when the parent's stock ownership in the subsidiary was not acquired as a step in a plan to acquire assets of the subsidiary: the parent's stockholding can be counted. As contributing to continuity-of-interest, so that since such holding represented more than 80 percent of the stock of the subsidiary, the continuity-of-interest test would be met. Reorganization treatment is inappropriate when the parent's stock ownership in the subsidiary was purchased as the first step in a plan to acquire the subsidiary's assets in conformance with the provisions of section 334(b)(2).[9] The parent's stockholding could not be counted towards continuity-of-interest so in the last example there would be a continuity-of-interest of less than 20 percent. (Less than 20–percent continuity would be significantly less continuity-of-interest than that allowed in John A. Nelson Co. v. Helvering, 296 U.S. 374 (1935).) In short, where the parent's stock interest is "old and cold," it may contribute to continuity-of-interest. Where the parent's interest is not "old and cold," the

---

[9] We express no opinion as to whether such treatment would be appropriate in the case of a plan to acquire the subsidiary's assets, which is then not implemented so as to meet the requirements of sec. 334(b)(2). Cf. American Potash & Chemical Corporation v. United States, 399 F.2d 194 (Ct. Cl. 1968).

sale of shares by the majority of shareholders actually detracts from continuity-of-interest.

In petitioner's case, TRACK's stock in ACRA was acquired as part of an integrated plan to obtain control over ACRA's business. The plan called for, first, the purchase of stock and, second, the subsidiary-into-parent merger. Accordingly, continuity-of-interest must be measured by looking to all the pre-tender offer stockholders rather than to the parent (TRACK) and the nontendering stockholders only; and by that measure the merger fails and petitioner must recognize her gain.

The result reached in Madison Square Garden Corp., supra, is, at first blush, inconsistent with the result reached in this case. . .

In *Madison Square Garden* the principal issue was whether the taxpayer could "back around" the 80–percent ownership test imbedded in section 334(b)(2) by purchasing a controlling interest in the corporation to be acquired, having that corporation redeem some of its stock from other shareholders, and then purchasing a little more stock-just enough to increase its stockholdings over the 80–percent mark. We held that the transaction qualified, section 334(b)(2) being a largely mechanical area. The issue with which we are presently concerned in this case was raised by the taxpayer (Madison Square Garden) in an amendment to its petition. The taxpayer, the acquiring parent corporation, claimed that it was entitled to a step-up in the basis of the assets received with reference to the stock that it had purchased *and* a step-up in the basis of the assets received in the statutory merger, though the stock to which those assets were "attached" belonged to minority shareholders. The latter portion of the claim conflicted with the position taken on its return. It is important to note that in *Madison Square Garden*, as in the instant case, there was a section 334(b)(2) "purchase" followed by a statutory merger and that the two steps were obviously part of an integrated plan. On this secondary issue, the Commissioner argued that section 334(b)(2) gives a stepped-up or cost-of-stock basis only to "property received with reference to stock owned immediately before the liquidation [or statutory merger treated as a liquidation for section 332 purposes]." Since Madison Square Garden owned only 80.22 percent of the stock immediately before the merger, it should be limited in a step-up in basis to only 80.22 percent of the assets received. Thus the Commissioner took a very narrow view of the applicable law, basing his arguments on section 334(b)(2) and the regulations thereunder. Likewise, Madison Square Garden argued solely in terms of section 334(b)(2). Neither party mentioned the possibility that the minority shareholders, who were not parties to the proceeding, might recognize gain (because the two-step transaction was integrated and thus there was no continuity-of-interest) and therefore the corporation should get a step-up in basis to reflect the tax at the shareholder level, on the theory that a nonqualifying reorganization is simply a purchase or sale. Confronted with these arguments and the narrowly framed issue, this Court held that Madison Square Garden, the acquiring parent, was not entitled to a step-up in basis *under section 334(b)(2)* as to part of the property.

In the present case, with essentially the same facts but the minority shareholder as petitioner, respondent argues that the statutory merger is a nonqualifying reorganization, thus a sale, thus taxable at the shareholder level. Although technically he need not mention the corporate basis aspects nor sections 334(b)(2) and 332, respondent frankly admits that at the corporate level he would allow the assets received with reference to the stock belonging to the minority shareholders a stepped-up basis. This admission by the respondent unavoidably conflicts with the result argued for and achieved in *Madison Square Garden*.

Faced with the general rule as the applicability of the continuity-of-interest test, petitioner makes the following arguments, which we will deal with separately.

One, the continuity-of-interest doctrine should not be applied because TRACK was formed by a few stockholders in ACRA in order to purchase the business and, in the process, to acquire a stepped up basis for as many of the assets as possible via section 334(b)(2). "In effect, the situation was the same as the sale of stock by some shareholders to other shareholders." The petitioner meets herself coming, so to speak, when making this argument. Confronted with the problem of how to characterize the second event in the present two-event transaction, she contends that the transaction was a true statutory merger in both form and substance, at least insofar as she, a minority shareholder, was concerned. Now, confronted with the continuity-of-interest problem, she would have us treat the transaction in a manner inconsistent with the characterization previously given to the transaction, that of a merger. . .

Two, in applying the continuity-of-interest test, if it is applied, the purchase of stock by TRACK and the subsequent merger should not be viewed as steps in an integrated transaction because the choice of merger over liquidation as a second step had independent significance to the minority shareholders and either choice would have suited TRACK. By so arguing, the petitioner attempts in effect to avoid the step-transaction doctrine and thus to limit the application of the continuity-of-interest test. If the merger can be separated from the stock purchase, the continuity-of-interest test might be applicable only with regard to ACRA's shareholders at the time of the statutory merger, namely, the parent corporation, TRACK, and the minority shareholders, including petitioner. We note at least one flaw: The choice—liquidation or merger—did make a difference to TRACK. If it had liquidated ACRA, TRACK would not have received all of ACRA's assets. Some of the assets would have gone to the minority shareholders, and it would have had to have purchased them from these shareholders at an additional price. By choosing to merge ACRA into itself, it was able to avoid this and other problems. . .

Four, assuming that the continuity-of-interest test is applied, it is met where all 16 percent of the stockholders of ACRA exchanged their stock for a total of 35 percent of the stock of TRACK. The 16 percent figure (really 16.04 percent) is the sum of the percentage of ACRA stock transferred to TRACK at the time of TRACK's formation (10.22 percent) plus the percentage of ACRA stock exchanged for TRACK stock following the statutory merger (5.82 percent). Fortunately, we need not engage in a game of percentages since the continuity figure argued for by petitioner, 16 percent, is not "tantalizingly" high. The plain fact that more than 80 percent of the shareholders of ACRA sold out for cash is sufficient to prevent this merger from meeting the quantitative test expressed in the Southwest Natural Gas Co. v. Commissioner, 189 F.2d 332,334 (C.A. 5, 1951)... The two Supreme Court cases on point are John A. Nelson Co. v. Helvering, supra, and Helvering v. Minnesota Tea Co., 296 U.S. 378 (1935) [page 479 supra].

Finally, we emphasize that the petitioner is not any worse off than her fellow shareholders who sold their stock. She could have also received money instead of stock had she chosen to sell or to dissent from the merger. The nonrecognition of a realized gain is always an important matter. We hold that petitioner is not entitled to such favorable treatment in this case.

Reviewed by the Court.

NOTES

1. Is the court's last paragraph persuasive? Should Mrs. Kass be treated like those who receive cash? How would she have been treated if TRACK had merged into ACRA? Should her tax treatment depend on which corporation survived?

2. *Kass* is representative of cases addressing the continuity of interest question through the measurement of historic shareholders—i.e., whether historic shareholders of the target possess a certain level of continued equity investment after the transaction. The following case marked an important new direction in continuity of interest analysis.

J.E. Seagram Corp. v. Commissioner
104 T.C. 75 (1995).

■ NIMS, JUDGE: ... Petitioner is the common parent of an affiliated group of corporations... Prior to the incorporation of petitioner on July 2, 1981, Joseph E. Seagram & Sons, Inc. (JES), an Indiana corporation, was the U.S. parent of an affiliated group of corporations. JES was an indirect wholly owned subsidiary of The Seagram Company Ltd. (SCL), a Canada corporation. SCL was principally engaged in the production and marketing of distilled spirits and wine. On July 30, 1981, all of the stock of JES was transferred to petitioner in exchange for its stock. On August 23, 1990, petitioner's name was changed to J.E. Seagram Corp. Prior to that date, its name had been Seagold Vineyards Holding Corporation.

... *JES/Conoco Discussions* Between May 29 and June 17, 1981, SCL conducted extensive negotiations with [Conoco, Inc.—a corporation engaged in the oil and gas industry] concerning proposals for it to acquire directly from Conoco, and/or through open-market purchases, between 18 percent and 35 percent of the common stock of Conoco... On June 17, 1981, [the chairman and CEO of Conoco, Ralph Bailey] informed [SCL] that the Conoco board of directors had rejected the proposal for a significant investment in Conoco by SCL or its subsidiaries, claiming that it would not be in the long-term interests of Conoco.

The JES Tender Offer On June 18 and 19, 1981, JES purchased 143,800 shares of Conoco in open market purchases on the NYSE. On June 25, 1981, JES Holdings, Inc. (JES Tenderor), a wholly owned subsidiary of JES, initiated a tender offer for the purchase of up to 35 million shares (40.76 percent of the 85,864,538 shares outstanding on such date) of Conoco for $73 per share (the JES Tender Offer). . . On June 30, 1981, the Conoco board of directors recommended that Conoco shareholders reject the JES Tender Offer on the ground that it was not "in the best interests of [Conoco] and its subsidiaries."

The DuPont/Conoco Agreement On June 24, 1981, Edward G. Jefferson, chairman and chief executive officer of E.I. DuPont de Nemours and Co. (DuPont), called Bailey to determine whether there was any constructive role DuPont might play in light of public reports. . . DuPont's stock is traded on the NYSE. . . Beginning on June 28, 1981, Conoco and DuPont representatives discussed a possible merger.

On July 6, 1981, DuPont Holdings, Inc. (DuPont Tenderor), a wholly owned subsidiary of DuPont, signed an agreement with Conoco. . . that DuPont Tenderor would offer (the DuPont Tender Offer) to exchange for each share of Conoco common stock at least either (i) 1.6 shares of DuPont common stock, or (ii) $87.50 in cash. The Agreement also provided that "As promptly as practicable following the consummation or termination of the Offer, * * * [Conoco] shall be merged into * * * [DuPont Tenderor] in accordance with the Delaware General Corporation Law" (the Merger) and DuPont Tenderor would thereby acquire any Conoco shares not acquired in the tender offer.

. . . The Tender Offer Competition

On July 12, 1981, JES Tenderor increased its tender offer to include the purchase of up to 44,350,000 Conoco shares (slightly over 51 percent of the outstanding Conoco shares not already owned by JES) and increased its offering price. . . The offering prospectus specifically discussed the DuPont/Conoco Agreement and stated that

> The purpose of the [JES Tender] Offer is to acquire a majority of the issued and outstanding Shares and thereby control * * * [Conoco]. If 44,350,000 Shares are purchased * * * [JES Tenderor] would have the power under Delaware law to elect all of * * * [Conoco's] directors and to prevent the consummation of the proposed DuPont merger. * * * [JES Tenderor] currently intends to vote any Shares it may acquire against the proposed DuPont merger.

. . . On July 14, 1981, DuPont Tenderor announced an increase in the cash price of its tender offer . . . and in the number of shares of DuPont common stock offered. . . In an opinion issued by DuPont's tax counsel on July . . . [t]ax counsel concluded that

"It is our opinion that the Offer and the Merger [of DuPont and Conoco] should, if the Merger is consummated, be treated by the Internal Revenue Service or the courts as a single integrated transaction (with exchanges pursuant to the Offer treated as part of the Merger transaction) and that, accordingly, exchanges of Conoco Shares for DuPont Shares and cash pursuant to the Offer and the Merger should be treated for federal income tax purposes as exchanges pursuant to a plan of reorganization" within the meaning of Section 368(a)(1)(A) and (a)(2)(D) of the Code. * * *

The DuPont Tender Offer commenced on July 15, 1981. . . [T]he offering prospectus stated, in part, that

> The purpose of the Offer and the Merger is to acquire the entire equity interest in Conoco. The Offer is being made pursuant to the Agreement which provides that following consummation of the Offer Conoco will be merged into * * * [DuPont Tenderor]. * * * The Merger requires the approval of a majority of the outstanding Conoco Shares. * * * If, as a result of the Offer and the acquisition of Conoco Shares pursuant to the Option, * * * [DuPont Tenderor] is the holder of a majority of the Conoco Shares, the Merger could be adopted regardless of the votes of any other Conoco stockholders * * *

On July 15, 1981, Conoco issued a letter to Conoco stockholders which stated, in part, that [the Board Directors unanimously approved a business combination of DuPont and Conoco in a two step transaction].

. . . On August 5, 1981, DuPont Tenderor began purchasing Conoco common shares tendered for cash. A press release issued on that day stated that

> The DuPont Company has been tendered a significant majority of the outstanding shares of Conoco Inc., and will move forward as rapidly as possible to effect a merger of the two companies.

Also on August 5, 1981, DuPont Tenderor exercised the Option to purchase 15,900,000 Conoco shares directly from Conoco at a price of $87.50 per share. DuPont Tenderor paid $79,500,000 in cash and a one-year note of DuPont in the principal amount of $1,311,750,000 for the Conoco shares purchased pursuant to the Option. In a press release dated August 6, 1981, JES noted that its tender offer had been extended through August 7, 1981, and that as of August 5, 1981, approximately 25,300,000 Conoco shares had been tendered. The press release then stated that * * * [JES] stated that it was accepting the tendered shares and was seeking additional shares to increase its investment in Conoco, consistent with the maximum amount of the * * * [JES] offer and the announced results of DuPont's offer for Conoco.

. . . On August 7, 1981, the JES Tender Offer expired with approximately 28 million Conoco shares (32 percent of the Conoco shares outstanding at the commencement of the DuPont Tender Offer) having been tendered to JES Tenderor for cash at $92 per share. JES Tenderor ultimately purchased 24,625,750 shares of Conoco for $92 per share and 3,113,025 shares for $91.35 per share, with an aggregate cost of $2,557,738,302.25.

. . . JES Tenderor and DuPont Tenderor were acting independently of one another and pursuant to competing tender offers.

JES' Tender of Its Conoco Shares A press release dated August 11, 1981, announced that the board of directors of SCL had authorized the exchange of the Conoco shares held by JES Tenderor pursuant to the terms of the DuPont Tender Offer. The release quoted JES chairman and chief executive officer Edgar Bronfman as stating:

> This is an appropriate time to congratulate the management and Board of DuPont on the success of their offer for Conoco. While Seagram would have been delighted to have won 51 percent of Conoco, we are pleased at the prospect of becoming a large stockholder of the combined DuPont and Conoco. We believe it will be a very strong company, with a fine future.

On August 17, 1981, JES Tenderor tendered its shares of Conoco in exchange for shares of DuPont common stock. . . On September 30, 1981, Conoco merged into DuPont Tenderor. . .

Immediately following the Merger, JES Tenderor owned 20.2 percent of the outstanding common stock of DuPont. Thereafter, petitioner purchased additional shares of DuPont common stock and increased its interest in DuPont to 24.5 percent, which interest it has maintained to date. Petitioner's total cost for this stock was approximately $2,892,297,000 and its total market value, as of January 31, 1992, was approximately $7,635,300,000.

On September 30, 1981, 5,491,896 shares of Conoco were exchanged for DuPont stock pursuant to the Merger. Of the Conoco shareholders who held the 85,991,896 Conoco shares outstanding on July 5, 1981, the holders of not more than 18,653,121 of such shares acquired an ownership interest in DuPont by reason of the DuPont Tender Offer and Merger. Of the holders of Conoco shares who either transferred their Conoco shares to DuPont Tenderor pursuant to its tender offer which closed on August 17, 1981 (including JES Tenderor) or who exchanged Conoco shares in the Merger, the holders of 46,391,896 of such shares acquired an ownership interest in DuPont by reason of the DuPont Tender Offer or the Merger, although some Conoco shareholders who received DuPont stock in the tender offer may have sold their DuPont stock prior to the Merger.

Dupont treated the tender offer and merger as a tax-free reorganization for Federal income tax purposes and filed its tax return for its 1981 taxable year accordingly. Dupont and Conoco advised former Conoco shareholders who had exchanged their stock for DuPont stock in either the exchange portion of the tender offer or the merger that they had no taxable gain or loss.

When the dust had settled at the completion of the Conoco–DuPont merger on September 30, 1981, approximately 78 percent of the Conoco stock had changed hands for cash pursuant to the competing JES and Du-Pont tender offers, yet approximately 54 percent of the Conoco equity (in addition to the optioned shares) remained in corporate solution in the form of DuPont shares received in exchange for Conoco shares.

Petitioner tendered each share of Conoco stock, for which it had paid about $92 per share, in exchange for 1.7 shares of DuPont. . .

The amount of the loss petitioner claims to have realized (whether or not recognizable) upon the exchange of Conoco stock for DuPont stock was $530,410,896.

Discussion

The ultimate issue for decision is whether, for tax purposes, petitioner had a recognized loss upon the exchange of its Conoco stock for DuPont stock. Whether such a loss is to be recognized depends upon the effect to be given section 354(a)(1) under the above facts . . .

Thus, if DuPont, DuPont Tenderor, and Conoco were parties to a reorganization, and if the statutory merger of Conoco into DuPont Tenderor was in pursuance of a plan of reorganization, then no loss is to be recognized by petitioner upon the exchange of its Conoco stock for DuPont stock.

Petitioner challenges the validity of the putative reorganization on several grounds, discussed subsequently, whereas respondent argues in support of the reorganization. While petitioner basically questions the existence of the kind of plan of reorganization envisioned by the statute, petitioner does not challenge the status of DuPont, DuPont Tenderor, and Conoco as parties to a reorganization, assuming that in fact there was one.

In form, at least, DuPont's acquisition of Conoco (during the course of which petitioner effected the aforementioned exchange) was what the commentators Bittker and Eustice have called a "creeping multistep merger"; that is, a merger which is in their words "the culminating step in a series of acquisition transactions, all looking to the ultimate absorption of the target company's properties when control has been obtained by the acquiring corporation." Bittker & Eustice, Federal Income Taxation of Corporations and Shareholders, par. 14.12.3, at 14–35 (Fifth ed. 1987). . .

In the discussion that follows, we occasionally for convenience refer to DuPont and its facilitating subsidiary DuPont Tenderor interchangeably, since DuPont Tenderor is, of course, simply DuPont's cat's-paw in the transactions under scrutiny. . .

There appears to be no dispute that the merger of Conoco into DuPont Tenderor complied with the requirements of Delaware law, thus meeting the description of a "reorganization" in section 368(a)(1)(A) in that there was a "statutory merger or consolidation", and that the exchange of DuPont common stock by DuPont Tenderor for Conoco common stock fits within the provisions of section 368(a)(2)(D). Petitioner maintains, however, that the exchange of its Conoco common stock for DuPont common stock was not done in pursuance of a plan of reorganization, as required by section 354, and that therefore a loss is to be recognized on the exchange.

. . . We hold that, because DuPont was contractually committed to undertake and complete the second step merger once it had undertaken and completed the first step tender offer, these carefully integrated transactions together constituted a plan of reorganization within the contemplation of section 354(a).

Petitioner also argues that even if the DuPont tender offer and merger were to be treated as an integrated transaction, the merger does not qualify as a reorganization because it fails the "continuity of interest" requirement.

In *Penrod v. Commissioner*, supra at 1427–1428, we stated that

It is well settled that, in addition to meeting specific statutory requirements, a reorganization under section 368(a)(1)(A) must also satisfy the continuity of interest doctrine. See sec. 1.368–1(b), Income Tax Regs. * * * Because the reorganization provisions are based on the premise that the shareholders of an acquired corporation have not terminated their economic investment, but have merely altered its form, the continuity of interest doctrine limits the favorable nonrecognition treatment enjoyed by reorganizations to those situations in which (1) the nature of the consideration received by the acquired corporation or its shareholders confers a proprietary stake in the ongoing enterprise, and (2) the proprietary interest received is definite and material and represents a substantial part of the value of the property transferred. [Citations omitted.]

On the date of the Conoco/DuPont Agreement, July 6, 1981, there were approximately 85,991,896 Conoco shares outstanding. Petitioner is essentially arguing that because it acquired approximately 32 percent of these shares for cash pursuant to its own tender offer, and DuPont acquired approximately 46 percent of these shares for cash pursuant to *its* tender offer, the combined 78 percent of Conoco shares acquired for cash after the date of the Agreement destroyed the continuity of interest requisite for a valid reorganization. We think petitioner's argument, and the logic that supports it, miss the mark. Pursuant to its two-step tender offer/merger plan of reorganization, DuPont acquired approximately 54 percent of the "initial" 85,991,896 shares of Conoco stock in exchange for DuPont stock, which included petitioner's recently acquired Conoco shares that it tendered pursuant to DuPont's tender offer. If the 54 percent had been acquired by DuPont from Conoco shareholders in a "one-step" merger-type acquisition, there would be little argument that continuity of interest had been satisfied. Sec. 368(a)(1)(A).

In Helvering v. Minnesota Tea Co., 296 U.S. 378 (1935), the Supreme Court held that an equity interest in the transferee equal to about 56 percent of the value of the transferor's assets was adequate. In John A. Nelson Co. v. Helvering, 296 U.S. 374 (1935), the Supreme Court considered 38–percent equity continuity to be sufficient. For advance ruling purposes, the IRS considers a 50–percent equity continuity of interest, by value, to be sufficient. Rev. Proc. 77–37, 1977–2 C.B. 568. On the other hand, the United States Court of Appeals for the Fifth Circuit has held that a 16.4–percent continuing common stock interest, representing less than one percent of the total consideration (consisting of cash, bonds, and common stock) paid by the acquiring corporation, did not evidence sufficient continuity of interest to bring a transaction within the requirements of the predecessor of section 368(a)(1)(A). Southwest Natural Gas Co. v. Commissioner, 189 F.2d 332 (1951)...

Where sufficient continuity is lacking, the acquired corporation will not be a "party to a reorganization", thus causing the overall transaction to fail as a reorganization under section 368(a)(1)(A).Section 368(b) provides in relevant part:

> (b) Party To A Reorganization.—For purposes of this part, the term "a party to a reorganization" includes—(1) a corporation resulting from a reorganization, and (2) both corporations, in the case of a reorganization resulting from the acquisition by one corporation of stock or properties of another. In the case of a reorganization qualifying under paragraph (1)(A) * * * of subsection (a) by reason of paragraph (2)(D) of that subsection, the term "a party to a reorganization" includes the controlling corporation referred to in such paragraph (2)(D). * * *

Thus the question petitioner raises is whether there is sufficient continuity of interest so as to qualify Conoco, DuPont and DuPont Tenderor (by virtue of section 368(a)(2)(D)) as parties to a reorganization under this section.

The parties stipulated that petitioner and DuPont, through their wholly owned subsidiaries, were acting independently of one another and pursuant to competing tender offers. Furthermore, there is of course nothing in the record to suggest any prearranged understanding between petitioner and DuPont that petitioner would tender the Conoco stock purchased for cash if petitioner by means of its own tender offer failed to achieve control of Conoco. Consequently, it cannot be argued that petitioner, although not a party to the reorganization, was somehow acting in concert with DuPont, which *was* a party to the reorganization. If such had been the case, the reorganization would fail because petitioner's cash purchases of Conoco stock could be attributed to DuPont, thereby destroying continuity.

The cases cited by petitioner in support of its argument that DuPont's plan of reorganization failed for lack of continuity of interest are not germane. For example, petitioner quotes Superior Coach of Fla., Inc. v. Commissioner, 80 T.C. at 904,... [in which] the majority shareholders of P purchased all of the shares of T and merged T into P. We held that the P shareholders' acquisition of the T stock was "inextricably interwoven" with the intent to effect the merger, and since the "historic shareholders" of T retained no proprietary interest in P, the merger did not qualify as a reorganization under section 368(a)(1)(A). In other words, the reorganization failed because the majority shareholders of P were acting on its behalf when they bought the T stock for cash, and there was no continuity of interest on the part of the acquired corporation's previous shareholders. In the case before us, DuPont's shareholders did not purchase Conoco stock for cash (or for any other consideration) to facilitate the merger, and except for approving the Plan of Reorganization and the merger did not act on DuPont's behalf. *Superior Coach of Fla., Inc.* is therefore not apposite on its facts.

Petitioner cites Yoc Heating Corp. v. Commissioner, 61 T.C. 168, 177 (1973) for the proposition that continuity requires looking at shareholders "immediately prior to the inception of the series of transactions" in an integrated transaction. Again, we look at the facts: R, the acquiring corporation, purchased for cash over 85 percent of the stock of O, and then caused O to transfer its assets, subject to its liabilities, to R's wholly owned subsidiary, N. N issued one share of its stock to R in exchange for every three shares of O held by R plus cash to be paid to the minority shareholders of O.

The Commissioner argued in *Yoc Heating* that the taxpayer's series of transactions constituted a reorganization within the meaning of section 368(a)(1)(F) or, alternatively, section 368(a)(1)(D). We held, however, that the acquisition by N of O's assets constituted a purchase under the "integrated transaction" (step transaction) doctrine, rather than a reorganization under either section proposed by the Commissioner. Id. at 177–178. Thus *Yoc Heating's* comparison of stock ownership immediately prior and immediately after the series of transactions is perfectly appropriate to the facts of that case, where the acquiring corporation acquired control of the target for cash and then effected the corporate combination, because the shareholders of O before the acquisition by R lacked the requisite continuing interest in the affairs of O after the acquisition.

Petitioner also attempts to apply cases involving pre-arranged post-acquisition sales of acquiring corporation stock by shareholders of the acquired corporation. Petitioner points out that these cases hold that a sale that was not pursuant to the plan of reorganization was fatal to continuity of interest where the sale "establish[ed an] intent to divest * * * [the old stockholders] of their proprietary interest."* . . .

We do not believe petitioner's analogy is appropriate, because in a case such as the one before us we must look not to the identity of the target's shareholders, but rather to what the shares represented when the reorganization was completed. In this case, a majority of the old shares of Conoco were converted to shares of DuPont in the reorganization, so that in the sense, at least, that a majority of the consideration was the acquiring corporation's stock, the test of continuity was met. In this aspect of the case step transaction and continuity questions would have arisen only had there

---

* See infra at 503 for discussion of the change in the "post-acquisition continuity of interest requirement" in the years following this case.—ED.

been some preexisting intention or arrangement for the disposal of the newly acquired DuPont shares, but there were none.

Respondent points out, correctly we believe, that the concept of continuity of interest advocated by petitioner would go far toward eliminating the possibility of a tax-free reorganization of any corporation whose stock is actively traded. Because it would be impossible to track the large volume of third party transactions in the target's stock, all completed transactions would be suspect. Sales of target stock for cash after the date of the announcement of an acquisition can neither be predicted nor controlled by publicly held parties to a reorganization. A requirement that the identity of the acquired corporation's shareholders be tracked to assume a sufficient number of "historic" shareholders to satisfy some arbitrary minimal percentage receiving the acquiring corporation's stock would be completely unrealistic.

In the "integrated" transaction before us petitioner, not DuPont, "stepped into the shoes" of 32 percent of the Conoco shareholders when petitioner acquired their stock for cash via the JES competing tender offer, held the 32 percent transitorily, and immediately tendered it in exchange for DuPont stock. For present purposes, there is no material distinction between petitioner's tender of the Conoco stock and a direct tender by the "old" Conoco shareholders themselves. Thus, the requirement of continuity of interest has been met.

Petitioner extended its tender offer even after DuPont had been tendered a "significant majority" of the outstanding shares of Conoco and withdrawal rights had closed. At that time petitioner announced that it was accepting the shares tendered to it and "was seeking additional shares to increase its investment in Conoco." And as we recited earlier, petitioner, in connection with its tender of its just-acquired Conoco stock, issued a press release quoting Edgar M. Bronfman, Seagram's chairman and CEO, as saying that Seagram's was pleased at the prospect of becoming "a large stockholder of the *combined DuPont and Conoco.*" We also noted that petitioner did not report a loss on the exchange of its Conoco stock for DuPont stock for financial accounting purposes. Instead, petitioner ascribed its carrying cost for its Conoco stock to the DuPont stock. None of these acts is consistent with the recognized loss petitioner claimed on its tax return. For the reasons stated in this Opinion, we hold that a loss cannot be recognized by petitioner on its exchange of Conoco stock for DuPont stock, made pursuant to the DuPont–Conoco plan of reorganization. . .

An Order will be issued denying petitioner's Motion for Summary Judgment and granting respondent's Motion for Summary Judgment. . .

NOTES

1. Following *Seagram*, regulations issued in 1998 directed the continuity of interest inquiry to focus primarily on the consideration paid by the acquirer to the shareholders of the target. In fact, the regulations state specifically that pre-reorganization dispositions of target stock (to parties unrelated to the tar-

get or issuer) were not relevant in measuring continuity. Treas. Reg. § 1.368–1(e)(1)(i). How would *Kass* come out under the post-*Seagram* regulations?

2. Furthering the trend of liberalizing pre-reorganization requirements, regulations adopted in 2000 outlined circumstances in which a pre-reorganization redemption does or does not affect the continuity question. The concern is whether the acquirer seems to be funding the redemption, thereby necessitating the inclusion of the redemption transaction in the reorganization analysis. Treas. Reg. § 1.368–1(e)(1)(ii),–1(e)(6) ex. 9.

3. 2007 amendments to the continuity of interest regulations specify when the value of the target stock surrendered and the "parent" stock received should be valued. Treas. Reg. § 1.368–1T(e)(2) (on the signing date, assuming the price is fixed). In addition, the regulations indicate that a 40% continuing interest can satisfy the continuity of interest requirement. Treas. Reg. § 1.368–1T(e)(2)(v) ex. 1.4. Post-reorganization continuity: A related dimension of the continuity of interest issue relates to the period of time that the target shareholders must retain the acquirer stock after the merger. In McDonald's Restaurants of Illinois, Inc. v. Commissioner, 688 F.2d 520 (7th Cir. 1982), the court concluded that continuity of interest was violated where target shareholders had a pre-merger intent to dispose of the acquirer stock as soon as possible and did in fact do so, even though the target shareholders were not contractually bound to sell the acquirer stock. However, the 1998 continuity of interest regulations virtually eliminated any requirement of post-reorganization continuity. Post-reorganization sales of acquirer stock to third parties are not relevant to the continuity analysis—even when they are pre-arranged. Only sales to the acquiring corporation or its affiliates still count for continuity purposes. Treas. Reg. § 1.368–1(e)(1),–1(e)(6) ex. 4. If the acquirer repurchases its own stock through a broker on the open market, the transaction is disregarded in the continuity calculation. See Rev. Rul. 99–58, 1999–2 C.B. 701. NYSBA, The Proposed Continuity of Interest Regulations, Rep. No. 1266 (May 18, 2012); See Wolfman, Continuity of Interest Regulations, Tax Notes, Jan. 20, 1997, p. 371; Wolfman, "Continuity of Interest" and the American Law Institute Study, 57 Taxes 840 (1979).

4. Continuity of interest when there is no acquirer stock: In Paulsen v. Commissioner, 469 U.S. 131 (1985), a stock savings and loan merged into the acquirer mutual savings and loan. Target shareholders surrendered their guaranty stock in the target in exchange for pass book savings accounts and certificates of deposit in the acquirer (which, by virtue of being a mutual savings and loan, had no capital stock). The Court concluded that the target shareholders failed the continuity of interest requirement because the interest they received in the acquirer was "essentially cash." However, the Court noted that if two mutual associations merge, the continuity of interest requirement is satisfied because the target shareholders are surrendering interests that are essentially cash with a small equity-like component in return for identical interests in the acquirer.

Treas. Reg. § 1.368–1(b), as amended in 2005, confirms that neither continuity of business enterprise nor continuity of interest is required in an "E" or an "F" reorganization.

5. As observed earlier, and in note 3 above, the regulations indicate that continuity of interest is satisfied if at least 40% of the total (by value) consideration received by the target shareholders for their target stock *is* stock of the acquirer. Not surprisingly, the valuation of acquirer stock and the determination of when to value it – can be quite important in assessing whether the 40% of value level has been met. In addition to regulations covering transactions with "fixed consideration", (see supra Notes following *LeTulle v. Scofield*, Chapter 4.V.B.1.a), regulations now address transactions *without* fixed consideration. In December 2011, Treasury issued final and proposed regulations providing special valuation rules applicable in the case of deals that do not provide for "fixed consideration." 76 Fed. Reg. 78,591 (Dec. 19. 2011 and 76 Fed. Reg. 78,540 (Dec. 19. 2011).

b. *Interest Surrendered*

Helvering v. Alabama Asphaltic Limestone Co.
315 U.S. 179 (1942).

■ MR. JUSTICE DOUGLAS delivered the opinion of the Court. Respondent in 1931, acquired all the assets of Alabama Rock Asphalt, Inc., pursuant to a reorganization plan consummated with the aid of the bankruptcy court. In computing its depreciation and depletion allowances for the year 1934, respondent treated its assets as having the same basis which they had in the hands of the old corporation. The Commissioner determined a deficiency, computed on the price paid at the bankruptcy sale.[1] The Board of Tax Appeals rejected the position of the Commissioner. . . The Circuit Court of Appeals affirmed. . . We granted the petition for certiorari because of the conflict between that decision[2] and Commissioner v. Palm Springs Holding Corp., 119 F.2d 846, decided by the Circuit Court of Appeals for the Ninth Circuit, and Helvering v. New President Corp., 122 F.2d 92, decided by the Circuit Court of Appeals for the Eighth Circuit.

The answer to the question[3] turns on the meaning of that part of § 112(i)(1) of the Revenue Act of 1928. . . which provides: "The term 'reorganization' means (A) a merger or consolidation (including the acquisition by one corporation of . . . substantially all the properties of another corporation). . ."

The essential facts can be stated briefly. The old corporation was a subsidiary of a corporation which was in receivership in 1929. Stockholders of the parent had financed the old corporation taking unsecured notes for their advances. Maturity of the notes was approaching and not all of the noteholders would agree to take stock for their claims. Accordingly, a creditors' committee was formed, late in 1929, and a plan of reorganization was

---

[1] Petitioner now takes the position that the new basis should be measured by the market value of the assets rather than the bid price. See Bondholders Committee v. Commissioner, [315 U.S. 189 (1942)].

[2] And see Commissioner v. Kitselman, 89 F.2d 458, and Commissioner v. Newberry Lumber & Chemical Co., 94 F.2d 447, which are in accord with the decision below.

[3] If there was a "reorganization." the respondent was entitled to use the asset basis of the old corporation as provided in § 113(a)(7) [362(b)].

proposed to which all the noteholders, except two, assented. The plan provided that a new corporation would be formed which would acquire all the assets of the old corporation. The stock of the new corporation, preferred and common, would be issued to the creditors in satisfaction of their claims. Pursuant to the plan, involuntary bankruptcy proceedings were instituted in 1930. The appraised value of the bankrupt corporation's assets was about $155,000. Its obligations were about $838,000, the unsecured notes with accrued interest aggregating somewhat over $793,000. The bankruptcy trustee offered the assets for sale at public auction. They were bid in by the creditors' committee for $150,000. The price was paid by $15,000 in cash, by agreements of creditors to accept stock of a new corporation in full discharge of their claims, and by an offer of the committee to meet the various costs of administration, etc. Thereafter, respondent was formed and acquired all the assets of the bankrupt corporation. It does not appear whether the acquisition was directly from the old corporation on assignment of the bid or from the committee. Pursuant to the plan, respondent issued its stock to the creditors of the old corporation—over 95% to the noteholders and the balance to small creditors. Nonassenting creditors were paid in cash. Operations were not interrupted by the reorganization and were carried on subsequently by substantially the same persons as before.

From the *Pinellas* case (287 U.S. 462) [page 476 supra] to the *LeTulle* case (308 U.S. 415) [page 483 supra] it has been recognized that a transaction may not qualify as a "reorganization" under the various revenue acts though the literal language of the statute is satisfied. See Paul, Studies in Federal Taxation (3d Series), pp. 91 et seq. The *Pinellas* case introduced the continuity of interest theory to eliminate those transactions which had "no real semblance to a merger or consolidation" . . . and to avoid a construction which "would make evasion of taxation very easy." . . . In that case, the transferor received in exchange for its property cash and short term notes. This Court said . . .: "Certainly, we think that to be within the exemption the seller must acquire an interest in the affairs of the purchasing company more definite than that incident to ownership of its short-term purchase-money notes." In the *LeTulle* case, we held that the term of the obligation received by the seller was immaterial. "Where the consideration is wholly in the transferee's bonds, or part cash and part such bonds, we think it cannot be said that the transferor retains any proprietary interest in the enterprise. . ." On the basis of the continuity of interest theory as explained in the *LeTulle* case, it is now earnestly contended that a substantial ownership interest in the transferee company must be retained by the holders of the ownership interest in the transferor. That view has been followed by some courts. . . Under that test, there was "no reorganization" in this case, since the old stockholders were eliminated by the plan, no portion whatever of their proprietary interest being preserved for them in the new corporation. And it is clear that the fact that the creditors were for the most part stockholders of the parent company does not bridge the gap. The equity interest in the parent is one step removed from the equity interest in the subsidiary. In any event, the stockholders of the parent were not granted participation in the plan qua stockholders.

We conclude, however, that it is immaterial that the transfer shifted the ownership of the equity in the property from the stockholders to the creditors of the old corporation. Plainly, the old continuity of interest was broken. Technically that did not occur in this proceeding until the judicial sale took place. For practical purposes, however, it took place not later than the time when the creditors took steps to enforce their demands against their insolvent debtor. In this case, that was the date of the institution of bankruptcy proceedings. From that time on, they had effective command over the disposition of the property. The full priority rule of Northern Pacific Ry. Co. v. Boyd, 228 U.S. 482, applies to proceedings in bankruptcy as well as to equity receiverships. . . . It gives creditors, whether secured or unsecured, the right to exclude stockholders entirely from the reorganization plan when the debtor is insolvent. . . . When the equity owners are excluded and the old creditors become the stockholders of the new corporation, it conforms to realities to date their equity ownership from the time when they invoked the processes of the law to enforce their rights of full-priority. At that time they stepped into the shoes of the old stockholders. The sale "did nothing but recognize officially what had before been true in fact." . . .

That conclusion involves no conflict with the principle of the *LeTulle* case. A bondholder interest in a solvent company plainly is not the equivalent of a proprietary interest, even though upon default the bondholders could retake the property transferred. The mere possibility of a proprietary interest is, of course, not its equivalent. But the determinative and controlling factors of the debtor's insolvency. and an effective command by the creditors over the property were absent in the *LeTulle* case.

Nor are there any other considerations which prevent this transaction from qualifying as a "reorganization" within the meaning of the Act. The *Pinellas* case makes plain that "merger" and "consolidation" as used in the Act include transactions which "are beyond the ordinary and commonly accepted meaning of those words." . . . Insolvency reorganizations are within the family of financial readjustments embraced in those terms as used in this particular statute. Some contention, however, is made that this transaction did not meet the statutory standard because the properties acquired by the new corporation belonged at that time to the committee and not to the old corporation. That is true. Yet, the separate steps were integrated parts of a single scheme. Transitory phases of an arrangement frequently are disregarded under these sections of the revenue acts where they add nothing of substance to the completed affair. Gregory v. Helvering [page 445 supra]; Helvering v. Bashford, 302 U.S. 454. Here they were no more than intermediate procedural devices utilized to enable the new corporation to acquire all the assets of the old one pursuant to a single reorganization plan.

Affirmed.

NOTES

1. Before the transaction in *Alabama Asphaltic Limestone Co.*, the "equity" interest in the assets was owned by the parent corporation. The parent, in turn,

was owned by the same persons who held the subsidiary's notes. Why is the readjustment that took place not a prototype "reorganization"? Of what relevance is the *LeTulle* line of cases to the basis of assets of a corporation after it has been taken over by creditors in an insolvency proceeding? Should the character of the pre-insolvency interest of the subsequent stockholders have any effect on these questions?

Today, § 368(a)(1)(G), enacted as part of the Bankruptcy Tax Act of 1980, is the primary section governing insolvency reorganizations. The Senate Finance Committee Report recommending this provision makes clear that the "continuity of interest" doctrine is not to be strictly applied to such reorganizations. See S. Rep. No. 1035, 96th Cong., 2nd Sess. 36–37 (1980). Rather, all creditors, including all senior and junior classes, and all shareholders who receive stock for their claims in a corporation to which the insolvent company's assets have been transferred, will generally be included in determining whether the continuity of interest requirement has been met.

2. In Helvering v. Cement Investors, Inc., 316 U.S. 527 (1942), property of two corporations, a bankrupt parent and its subsidiary, was transferred to a new corporation by the debtor companies, the trustee in bankruptcy, and the trustee under the indenture agreement securing the bonds of the bankrupt subsidiary. The bondholders of the old subsidiary received common stock and income bonds in place of their former securities. The old shareholders received warrants. The issue was whether the bondholders of the new corporation could be treated as transferring property to the new company so that their gain would not be recognized under the predecessor of § 351. Although the Commissioner argued that the bondholders themselves had transferred no property to the corporation, and thus they could not receive § 351 treatment, the Supreme Court held otherwise. Citing *Alabama Asphaltic Limestone Co.*, the Court noted that it would not be unrealistic to treat the bondholders as having received an equity interest in the old corporation when they sought to enforce their rights. Regardless of how that interest was described, the bondholders had an equitable interest in the property transferred and such an interest was sufficient to treat them as transferring property within the meaning of § 351 even if the actual conveyance was made by a trustee. The bondholders therefore received tax-free treatment under § 351.

3. In 2011, the Tax Court rejected the Service's argument that *Alabama Asphaltic* required that creditors who received 83.75% of the outstanding common of the insolvent corporation be treated as equity holders. Instead, the court concluded that the continuity of interest requirement was not satisfied in the current case where creditors did not assume "effective command over the insolvent entity's assets". Thus, the transaction was not a tax-free reorganization under § 368. [Note, here the taxpayers argued that the transaction failed continuity of interest and failed as a reorganization in order to argue that a valid election was made under § 338(h)(10).] Ralphs Grocery & Subsidiaries v. Comm., TCM 2011-25.

2. "PARTY TO A REORGANIZATION"

Revenue Ruling 63–234
1963–2 C.B. 148.

Advice has been requested whether the successive exchanges of corporate stock described below constitute, separately or in concert, a reorganization as defined in section 368(a)(1)(B) of the Internal Revenue Code of 1954.

In 1960, the M corporation directly and through its subsidiaries operated a chain of retail stores. It owned 60 shares (60 percent) of the 100 outstanding shares of N corporation's voting common stock. A group of taxpayers, hereinafter referred to as the X group, owned 18 shares (18 percent) of N's voting stock, and the remaining 22 shares (22 percent) were held by other shareholders.

Among the assets of the N corporation was 50 percent of the voting stock of the O corporation. The remaining 50 percent of O's voting stock was owned by members of the X group.

For the purpose of affecting certain economies in operation and to make the filing of a consolidated income tax return possible, the above-mentioned parties adopted a plan of reorganization pursuant to which the following action was taken:

(1) The charter of the N corporation was amended to enlarge its board of directors from ten to 12 members and to provide that the two new members of the board would be elected by the owners of a newly authorized class of preferred stock.

(2) Newly created preferred stock of the N corporation was issued to the members of the X group in exchange for all their holdings of the O corporation's voting stock.

The N corporation thus acquired 100 percent of the outstanding stock of the O corporation and the holdings of the X group in the N corporation were increased to include all of that corporation's preferred stock.

(3) Immediately thereafter, the X group transferred all of its stock of the N corporation (18 percent of the common stock and 100 percent of the preferred stock) to the M corporation in exchange for the latter's voting common stock. As a result, the M corporation became the owner of 78 percent of N's common stock and 100 percent of the preferred shares.

The voting power of the N corporation preferred stock confers upon the holders of such stock the right to significant participation in the management of the affairs of the corporation. This preferred stock is therefore "voting stock" within the meaning of the reorganization provision. See I.T. 3896, C.B. 1948–1, 72. Under the principles set forth in I.T. 3896, the voting rights of the M corporation respecting the affairs of the N corporation, when properly weighted, totaled 81.67 percent of the "voting power" of all classes of "voting stock" of the N corporation. Thus, the M corporation acquired "control" of the N corporation within the meaning of section 368(c) of the Code.

Section 368(a)(1)(B) of the Code provides that, for purposes of parts I, II, and III of subchapter C of chapter 1 of subtitle A of the Code, the term "reorganization" means—

the acquisition by one corporation, in exchange solely for all or a part of its voting stock, of stock of another corporation if, immediately after the acquisition, the acquiring corporation has control of such other corporation (whether or not such acquiring corporation had control immediately before the acquisition);

Among the requisites to a reorganization under the Code is that of continuity of interest on the part of those persons who, directly or indirectly, were the owners of the enterprise prior to the reorganization. See section 1.368–1(b) of the Income Tax Regulations.

Taking into account all the facts and circumstances, it is concluded that the two exchanges of corporate stock in the instant case were but successive steps in the execution of the single plan adopted earlier by the parties. See Whitney Corporation v. Commissioner, 105 Fed. (2d) 438 (1939), and United Light and Power Co. v. Commissioner, 105 Fed. (2d) 866 (1939), certiorari denied, 308 U.S. 574 (1939). When the component steps in the plans are combined it becomes apparent that the X group exchanged its stock in the O corporation for stock of the M corporation, which did not thereafter directly own either stock of O corporation or its assets. The receipt of N corporation preferred shares by the X group may be disregarded for purposes of the reorganization provisions of the Code since the X group's holding of such shares was "transitory and without real substance." Helvering v. Raymond 1. Bashford, 302 U.S. 454 (1938) . . .; see also the United Power and Light Co. case, supra.

Under the principles established by the Supreme Court of the United States in Herman C. Groman v. Commissioner, 302 U.S. 82 (1937), . . . and the *Bashford* case, the stock of M corporation does not provide the X group with the requisite continuity of interest in the O corporation stock transferred to the N corporation because the group had only an indirect interest in the O stock following the transaction. The rule of the *Groman* and *Bashford* cases is still applicable to reorganizations sought to be brought within the provisions of section 368(a)(1)(B). See S. Report No. 1622, Eighty-third Congress, Second Session, 51 and 273.

Accordingly, it is held that the transfer by the X group of its shares in the O corporation to the N corporation in exchange for the latter's newly issued preferred stock and the subsequent transfer of the newly acquired preferred shares of N to the M corporation in exchange for voting stock in M does not qualify, either in whole or in part, as a reorganization within the meaning of section 368(a)(1)(B) of the Code.

However, it is held that the exchange of N corporation stock owned by the X group before any of the exchanges described above for voting common stock of M corporation constitutes a reorganization within the meaning of section 368(a)(1)(B) of the Code, and that M and N corporations are each a party to such reorganization within the meaning of section 368(b)(2) of the Code.

NOTES

1. Is the result in Rev. Rul. 63–234 wise or compelled by the decisions in Groman v. Commissioner, 302 U.S. 82 (1937), and Helvering v. Bashford, 302 U.S. 454 (1938)? Were the results in *Groman* and *Bashford* compelled by the statute or desirable?

2. What impact do the 1964 amendments to § 368(a)(1)(B) and § 368(a)(2)(C) have on the specific problem posed in Rev. Rul. 63–234?

3. The doctrine arising from the cases of Groman v. Commissioner, 302 U.S. 82 (1937), and Helvering v. Bashford, 302 U.S. 454 (1938), precluded the use of the reorganization provisions of the 1939 Code in transactions in which the acquiring corporation transferred the stock or assets of the acquired corporation to a subsidiary or in transactions in which the subsidiary directly acquired the transferor's stock or assets in exchange for its parent's stock. In the 1954 Code Congress largely overruled this doctrine. It started by adding the parenthetical in the definition of a "C" reorganization. It later added the parenthetical in the "B" reorganization, § 368(a)(2)(C) which allows tax-free status to a reorganization even if the assets of the acquired company are dropped down into a subsidiary, and § 368(a)(2)(D) which allows "forward" subsidiary mergers. It also made the necessary changes to the definition of a "party to the reorganization" in § 368(b). Then, in 1970, Congress added subparagraph (E) to § 368(a)(2) and the last sentence in § 368(b). The effect of these changes was to afford tax-free status to "reverse" statutory mergers in which a corporation's subsidiary is merged into an unrelated corporation that survives, and the voting stock of the subsidiary parent is exchanged for control of the corporation surviving the merger.

Today, these triangular mergers have taken on a life of their own. Many if not most corporate acquisitions are effected through the use of subsidiaries. One reason for this prevalent practice is that state corporation statutes do not require that the shareholders of the parent corporation approve the merger. Rather, only the shareholder of the subsidiary, i.e., the directors of the parent corporation, must approve. The use of subsidiary mergers, therefore, eliminates a proxy statement and shareholder vote.

4. In Rev. Rul. 84–104, 1984–2 C.B. 94, the Service ruled that although § 368(a)(2)(E) applies by its terms only to "mergers," under the National Banking Act a "consolidation" of a wholly owned bank subsidiary of a bank holding company into an existing bank is considered a "merger" qualifying under § 368(a)(2)(E). The Service said that the "consolidation" in question was correctly classified as a merger, since under the National Banking Act a "consolidation" results in the survival of one of the existing corporations (there the target), and no new corporation is formed. This seems to confirm that a "true consolidation" will not qualify under section 368(a)(2)(E).

Revenue Ruling 74–565

1974–2 C.B. 125.

Advice has been requested whether the transaction described below qualifies as a reorganization within the meaning of section 368(a)(1)(B) of the Internal Revenue Code of 1954, even though it does not qualify as a reorganization under section 368(a)(1)(A) and (a)(2)(E) of the Code.

The stock of corporations P and Y is publicly held. Corporation S1 is a wholly owned subsidiary of P. S1 desired to acquire all the stock of Y and in order to eliminate the possibility of having minority shareholders in Y, the following steps were taken pursuant to a plan:

(a) P transferred shares of its voting stock to S1 in exchange for shares of S1 stock.

(b) S1 transferred the shares of P voting stock to its newly formed subsidiary S2, in exchange for shares of S2 stock.

(c) S2 (whose only asset consisted of a block of the voting stock of P) merged into Y in a transaction which qualified as a statutory merger under the applicable state law.

(d) Y stock held by Y shareholders (except for dissenters) was exchanged for the P stock received by Y on the merger of S2 into Y. At the same time the S2 stock owned by S1 was exchanged for Y stock. The end result of these transactions was that S1 acquired from the shareholders of Y, in exchange for voting stock of P, more than 95 percent of the stock of Y.

(e) Y shareholders owning less than 5 percent of the stock of Y dissented to the merger and had the right to receive the appraised value of their shares paid solely from assets of Y. No funds, or other property, have been or will be provided by P or S1 for this purpose.

After the consummation of the plan of reorganization described above, Y continued its business as a wholly owned subsidiary of S1.

Section 368(a)(2)(E) of the Code, which is applicable to statutory mergers occurring after December 31, 1970, was enacted to permit, under certain circumstances, a tax-free statutory merger when stock of a parent corporation is used in a merger between a controlled subsidiary of the parent and another corporation, and the other corporation survives. See S. Rep. No. 91–1533, 91st Cong., 2d Sess. 1 (1970), 1971–1 C.B. 622. . .

In the instant case, the transaction does not qualify as a reorganization under section 368(a)(1)(A) and (a)(2)(E) of the Code, because stock of P, rather than stock of the controlling corporation S1, was transferred to the Y shareholders in the transaction. . .

In Rev. Rul. 67–448, 1967–2 C.B. 144, pursuant to a plan of reorganization, a parent corporation, P, issued some of its voting stock to its new subsidiary S and S, pursuant to the plan, merged into unrelated corporation, Y, with the Y shareholders exchanging their Y stock (amounting to 95 percent of the outstanding stock of Y) for the P stock received by Y in the merger of S into Y. Rev. Rul. 67–448 states that the net effect of this series of steps for Federal income tax purposes is a direct acquisition by P of 95 percent of the stock of Y from the Y shareholders in exchange solely for P voting stock and that the transitory existence of S is disregarded. Thus, Rev. Rul. 67–448 holds that the transaction will be treated as an acquisition by P, in exchange solely for a part of its voting stock, of stock of Y in an amount constituting control (as defined in section 368(c) of the Code) of Y, which qualifies as a reorganization within the meaning of section 368(a)(1)(B) of the Code.

In the instant case, the net effect of the steps taken was that S1 acquired, solely for voting stock of P (which was in control of S l), stock of Y in an amount constituting control of Y.

Accordingly, the transaction in the instant case will be treated as an acquisition by S1, in exchange solely for a part of P voting stock (P being in control of S I), of stock of Y (S1 being in control of Y after the transaction), which qualifies as a reorganization within the meaning of section 368(a)(1)(B) of the Code.

Pursuant to section 354(a) of the Code the former shareholders of Y will recognize no gain or loss on the exchange of their Y stock for P stock.

See Rev. Rul. 74–564, . . . which holds that a similar transaction that does not qualify as a reorganization under section 368(a)(1)(A) and (a)(2)(E) of the Code is treated as a reorganization qualifying under section 368(a)(1)(B).

NOTES

1. Compare Rev. Rul. 78–250, 1978–1 C.B. 83, in which A, the majority shareholder in Corporation X, created Corporation Y in exchange for his X stock and, thereafter, Y merged into X. The minority shareholders of X received cash for their shares, and A received X stock for his Y shares. Held, the net result is that the minority shareholders received cash for their X shares, and, therefore, the creation of Y and merger of Y into X will be disregarded and the transaction will be treated as a redemption of X stock.

2. Further flexibility in triangular reorganizations: In some triangular mergers the acquiring corporation does not retain the target stock or assets but instead drops them down into a controlled subsidiary. Despite the "drop down," the acquirer is considered a "party to the reorganization." Treas. Reg. § 1.368–2(f). "Drop-downs" can be made through multiple qualifying chains of corporations without raising continuity of interest issues. Treas. Reg. § 1.368–2(k). In Rev. Rul. 2001–24, 2001–1 C.B. 1290, a forward triangular merger qualified as a reorganization under § 368(a)(1)(A) and 368(a)(2)(D) even though the acquirer's parent (whose stock the target shareholder received in the merger) contributes the acquirer's stock to another wholly owned subsidiary of the parent as part of the plan of reorganization. How does the Service's position in Rev. Rul.

2001–24 compare to its analysis in Rev. Rul. 74–565 and the possibility of qualifying as a triangular merger?

3. "SOLELY FOR . . . VOTING STOCK"—"B" AND "C" REORGANIZATIONS

a. General

In both "B" and "C" reorganizations, the acquisition must be made solely in exchange for all or part of the acquiring corporation's voting stock. The statute, however, relaxes the "solely for voting stock" requirement for the "C" reorganization in two ways. First, in determining whether the exchange is solely for voting stock, liabilities of the transferor that are assumed by the acquiring corporation are disregarded. See § 368(a)(1)(C). Second, § 368(a)(2)(B) permits a limited amount of money or other property to be exchanged by the acquiring corporation. In this case, however, liabilities assumed by the acquiring corporation are treated as money or other property.

The "solely for voting stock" requirement of the "B" reorganization is much more restrictive. For example, in an early decision, Helvering v. Southwest Consolidated Corp., 315 U.S. 194 (1942), the taxpayer contended that the requirement was met when the target shareholders received voting stock of the acquiring corporation and warrants to purchase additional stock. The Supreme Court rejected this argument, finding that the warrants were impermissible consideration. In so doing, the Court stated that the "solely for voting stock" requirement of § 368(a)(1)(B) "leaves no leeway. Voting stock plus some other consideration does not meet the statutory requirement."

The Supreme Court again considered the "solely for voting stock" requirement of the "B" reorganization in Turnbow v. Commissioner, 368 U.S. 337 (1961). The taxpayer in *Turnbow* transferred all the shares of his wholly owned corporation to the acquiring corporation in exchange for $1.2 million of the acquirer's voting stock and $3 million in cash. The taxpayer conceded that the transaction failed as a "B" reorganization to the extent he received cash, but he argued that the exchange was nontaxable to the extent he received voting stock. The Supreme Court disagreed, holding that "an exchange of stock *and* cash—approximately 30 per centum in stock and 70 per centum in cash—for 'at least 80 per centum of the . . . stock of another corporation' cannot be a 'reorganization' as defined in [§ 368(a)(1)(B)]."

Turnbow left unresolved the issue whether the requirements of a "B" reorganization are met when some of the target's stock is acquired for cash but at least 80 percent of the target's stock is acquired in exchange for the acquiring corporation's voting stock. This issue was squarely presented in a group of cases involving the target shareholders in an acquisition of Hartford Fire Insurance Company (Hartford) by ITT. Between November 1968 and March 1969, ITT purchased for cash approximately 8 percent of Hartford's outstanding shares. Over a year later, in a transaction approved by Hartford's Board of Directors, ITT received from Hartford's shareholders more than 90 percent of Hartford's stock in exchange for voting stock of ITT. Conceding *arguendo* that the cash purchases were part of the same transaction, the former Hartford shareholders argued that the transaction nevertheless was a nontaxable "B" reorganization since more than 80 percent of Hartford's stock (an amount constituting control under § 368(a)(1)(B) and 368(c)) was acquired in exchange for ITT voting stock.

The Tax Court agreed with the taxpayers. C. E. Graham Reeves, 71 T.C. 727 (1979). On appeal, after extensively examining the legislative history, the regulations, and the decisions construing § 368(a)(1)(B), the First Circuit reversed. Chapman v. Commissioner, 618 F.2d 856 (1st Cir. 1980). The court said that the taxpayers' argument incorrectly emphasized the 80–percent control test as the primary requirement of a "B" reorganization. Instead, the court held that the transaction must meet both the "solely for voting stock" and "control immediately after" requirements. It concluded that "the presence of non-stock consideration in such an acquisition, regardless of whether it is necessary to the gaining of control, is inconsistent with treatment of the acquisition as a nontaxable ['B'] reorganization."

The Third Circuit, also reviewing the Tax Court's decision in *Reeves*, reached the same result as the First. See Heverly v. Commissioner, 621 F.2d 1227 (3d Cir. 1980). Appeals from the Tax Court's decision were pending in the Fourth and Ninth Circuits, and petitions for certiorari were pending in *Chapman* and *Heverly*, when, in early 1981, the litigation was settled by an agreement on the part of ITT to pay the government $18.5 million, with the shareholders effectively bound to carry over their Hartford stock basis into their ITT stock.

Is the result in *Chapman* a sound construction of § 368(a)(1)(B)? Contrast the language in § 368(a)(2)(E). Are the differing continuity of interest requirements for the "A," "B," and "C" reorganizations sensible legislative policy?

The application of the "solely for voting stock" test has displayed some flexibility over time. In Rev. Rul. 90–11, 1990–1 C.B. 10, the Service concluded that a reorganization satisfied the solely for voting stock requirement of a B reorganization even though the target shareholders received "poison pill" rights, because such rights were contingent and of nominal value.

Practicalities: The "solely for voting stock" requirement in a "B" reorganization is not violated where the acquirer pays cash in lieu of fractional shares, assuming that the cash portion of the transaction is incidental and not separately bargained for. Rev. Rul. 66–365, 1966–2 C.B. 116. Such cash paid in an "A" or "C" or "D" reorganization will be regarded as "boot" if separately bargained for—leading to possible taxation under § 356(a)(2) if it has the effect of a dividend. If it is not separately bargained for, then the cash is treated as if received in a redemption of the fractional shares. If the redemption distribution has dividend equivalence, then taxation under § 301 may result. What may be the practical tax difference to the shareholder, especially after the 2003 Tax Act treatment of dividends, (§ 1(h)(11))? In a would-be "B" reorganization, the separate bargain for the cash will destroy the reorganization because of the "solely for voting stock" requirement. When might it have that effect in a would-be "C" reorganization?

The tax treatment prescribed by Rev. Rul. 66–365 for cash paid in lieu of fractional shares was extended to "E" and "F" reorganizations in Rev. Rul. 69–34, 1969–1 C.B. 105, and Rev. Rul. 74–36, 1974–1 C.B. 85.

b. Applications

Revenue Ruling 85–138
1985–2 C.B. 122.

ISSUE

Whether the acquisition of substantially all the properties of X by S1 under the facts described below meets the requirements of a reorganization pursuant to section 368(a)(1)(C) of the Internal Revenue Code.

FACTS

Corporation P owned all the stock of corporation S1 and corporation S2. It was P's desire that S1 acquire substantially all the properties of X, a corporation unrelated by stock ownership to P, S1 or S2. In order to eliminate any possible adverse minority interest in X, and pursuant to a plan adopted by P, P caused S2 to purchase with S2's own cash some of the shares of outstanding voting stock of X. S2, along with the other shareholders of X, then approved an agreement between P and X under which X transferred substantially all its properties to S1 in exchange for voting stock of P and the assumption by S1 of all of X's liabilities. The liabilities assumed by S1 were in excess of twenty percent of the fair market value of X's assets. Subsequent to this exchange, X was dissolved and the P stock was distributed to the shareholders of X (including S2) in exchange for the surrender and cancellation of all the S stock.

LAW AND ANALYSIS

Section 368(a)(1)(C) of the Code provides that the term "reorganization" means the acquisition by one corporation, in exchange solely for all or a part of its voting stock (or in exchange solely for all or part of the voting stock of a corporation which is in control of the acquiring corporation), of substantially all the properties of another corporation, but in determining whether the exchange is solely for stock, the assumption by the acquiring corporation of a liability of the other, or the fact that property acquired is subject to a liability, shall be disregarded.

Section 368(a)(2)(B) of the Code provides that if (i) one corporation acquires substantially all of the properties of another corporation, (ii) the acquisition would qualify under section 368(a)(1)(C) but for the fact that the acquiring corporation exchanges money or other property in addition to voting stock, and (iii) the acquiring corporation acquires, solely for voting stock described in section 368(a)(1)(C), property of the other corporation having a fair market value which is at least 80 percent of the fair market value of all of the property of the other corporation, then such acquisition will (subject to section 368(a)(1)(A)) be treated as qualifying under section 368(a)(1)(C). Solely for the purpose of determining whether clause (iii) of the preceding sentence applies, the amount of any liability assumed by the acquiring corporation, and the amount of any liability to which any property is subject, will be treated as money paid for the property. Thus, if nonqualifying consideration such as cash is furnished by the acquiring corporation, liabilities of the acquired corporation assumed by the acquiring corporation are added to cash paid in order to determine whether 80 percent of the fair market value of the assets of the acquired corporation are exchanged solely for voting stock. In the instant case, S1's assumption of X liabilities in excess of 20 percent of the fair market value of X assets effectively precludes the application of the boot relaxation rule of section 368(a)(2)(B) of the Code. As a result, if S1 is deemed to have exchanged partly P voting stock and partly cash for substantially all the assets of X, the transaction will not qualify as a reorganization under section 368(a)(1)(C) of the Code.

In Rev. Rul. 69–48, 1969–1 C.B. 106, corporation P purchased for cash nineteen percent of the stock of corporation X and acquired an option to purchase an additional thirty percent as part of a plan for P's wholly owned subsidiary, S, to acquire the assets of X.

Under the option agreement, P was able to vote the optioned stock as well as the stock it had purchased outright. Twenty-two months later, P voted for the transfer of X's assets to S in exchange for P voting stock and the assumption by S of X's liabilities. After the transfer of its assets, X was liquidated. Rev. Rul. 69–48 concludes that P's cash purchase of X stock violated the "solely for voting stock" requirement of section 368(a)(1)(C) because it was an integral step in the plan to require substantially all of X's assets.

In the present case, S2's prearranged cash purchase of X shares was an integral step in the plan for S1 to acquire substantially all the assets of X. Therefore, as in Rev. Rul. 69–48, the consideration for the acquisition of X's properties by S1 is deemed to consist of cash in addition to the voting stock of P and the assumption of liabilities by S1 permitted under section 368(a)(1)(C) of the Code.

HOLDING

The transaction does not qualify as a reorganization defined in section 368(a)(1)(C) of the Code. Compare Rev. Rul. 85–139 wherein the same conclusion is reached in a purported reorganization under section 368(a)(1)(B).

Revenue Ruling 85–139

1985–2 C.B. 123.

ISSUE

Whether the transaction described below qualifies as a reorganization under section 368(a)(1)(B) of the Internal Revenue Code.

FACTS

P corporation owned all the stock of S corporation. P desired to obtain control of X corporation by acquiring all the shares of the one outstanding class of stock of X solely in exchange for P voting stock.

Certain shareholders of X, owning ten percent of its stock, insisted, however, on receiving cash for their stock. Since P wanted to eliminate any possible adverse minority interest in X, and pursuant to one overall plan to acquire the stock of X, P acquired ninety percent of the stock of X solely in exchange for P voting stock, and P caused S to purchase for cash the remaining ten percent of the X stock. The cash paid by S for X's stock was not obtained directly or indirectly from P. S retained ownership of the X stock it had purchased.

LAW AND ANALYSIS

Section 368(a)(1)(B) of the Code provides that the term "reorganization" means the acquisition by one corporation, in exchange solely for all or a part of its voting stock (or in exchange solely for all or a part of the voting stock of a corporation which is in control of the acquiring corporation), of stock of another corporation, if, immediately after the acquisition, the acquiring corporation has control of such other corporation (whether or not such acquiring corporation had control immediately before the acquisition).

Section 1.368–2(c) of the Income Tax Regulations illustrates the application of the "solely for voting stock" requirement under section 368(a)(1)(B) as follows:

If, for example, corporation X in one transaction exchanges nonvoting preferred stock or bonds in addition to all or a part of its voting stock in the acquisition of stock of corporation Y, the transaction is not a reorganization under section 368(a)(1)(B).

The "solely for voting stock" requirement applies to the entire transaction in which stock of a corporation is acquired, not just to the acquisition of a block of stock constituting control. Therefore, the acquisition by a corporation of eighty percent of the stock of a corporation in exchange for its voting stock and the remaining twenty percent in exchange for cash violates "solely for voting stock." Rev. Rul. 75–123, 1975–1 C.B. 115; Chapman v. Commissioner, 618 F.2d 856 (1st Cir. 1980); *cert. dism.* 451 U.S. 1012 (1981). . .

Accordingly, if P had acquired all the stock of X in exchange for its voting stock and cash, the acquisition would not have qualified as a reorganization under section 368(a)(1)(B). P's structuring of the transaction to have its wholly owned subsidiary acquire some of the X stock for cash does not produce a different result. Compare Rev. Rul. 69–48, 1969–1 C.B. 106, which holds that the purchase for cash by P of stock of corporation X as part of a plan for P's wholly-owned subsidiary, S, to acquire substantially all the assets of X for P voting stock, violates the "solely for voting stock" requirement of section 368(a)(1)(C).

HOLDING

The purchase by S of ten percent of X's stock for cash violates the "solely for voting stock" requirement of section 368(a)(1)(B) of the Code. Compare Rev. Rul. 85–138, wherein it was held that a similar transaction does not qualify as a reorganization under section 368(a)(1)(C).

c. Rise and Fall of the Bausch & Lomb Doctrine

Historically, if an acquirer already owned more than 20 percent of the target corporation, then any subsequent merger could not qualify as a C reorganization. This rule followed from Bausch & Lomb Optical Co. v. Commissioner, 267 F.2d 75 (2d Cir. 1959), *cert. denied*, 361 U.S. 835 (1959), in which C reorganization status was denied to an acquirer that owned more than 20 percent of the target before the reorganization, on the grounds that 80 percent of the target could not be acquired for voting stock in the reorganization itself. Had the acquirer owned less than 20 percent, then a C reorganization would have been possible given the boot relaxation rule. § 368(a)(2)(B).

After following the *Bausch & Lomb* doctrine for over 40 years, Treasury adopted "anti-*Bausch & Lomb*" regulations in 2000, which now explicitly allow "creeping" C reorganizations. Treas. Reg. § 1.368–2(d)(4)(i) (acquirer's existing ownership of target stock does not inherently prevent C reorganization status). Additionally, in applying the boot relaxation rule in a C reorganization (§ 368(a)(2)(B)), the acquirer's old and cold purchase of target stock is not counted in determining the percentage of target assets acquired for other than voting stock.

4. CONTROL

a. Acquiring Control

The Service construes the § 368(c) control requirement as ownership of at least 80 percent of the voting power of a corporation and at least 80 percent of the stock of *each* nonvoting class. See Rev. Rul. 59–259, 1959–2 C.B. 115.

b. Yielding Control

Reread Granite Trust Co. v. United States, page 447 supra.

Can the shareholders of Corporation X ensure recognition of some of their stock investment loss by transferring in the aggregate only 79.9 percent of the outstanding stock in X (which has only common outstanding) to Corporation Y in exchange for 50 percent of Corporation Y's voting stock? Will this not constitute a "B" reorganization, and will § 354(a)(1) not apply? Is the result a wise one? If not, what would you propose?

c. Control in an acquisitive D-reorganization

Somewhat related to the basic control requirement, § 368(a)(1)(D) requires that stock or securities in the transferee corporation be distributed in an acquisitive D [recall that in an acquisitive D reorganization, the transferor corporation transfers its assets to another corporation (the transferee)—and then the transferor distributes the stock of the transferee to the transferor shareholders]. Although corporations have long maintained that no actual distribution of transferee stock is necessary when there is common ownership of the transferor and the transferee (see, e.g., Davant v. Commissioner, 366 F.2d 874 (5th Cir. 1966) infra at 620), the Service issued final regulations effective December 18, 2009 that confirmed this point and specified the circumstances that constitute "identical ownership [which does not require complete identity of ownership]." The final regulations also indicate that "if no consideration is received, or the value of the consideration received in the transaction is less than the fair market value of the transferor corporation's assets, the transferee corporation will be treated as issuing stock with a value equal to the excess of the fair market value of the transferor corporation's assets over the value of the consideration actually received in the transaction." If the consideration equals "the fair market value of the transferor corporation's assets, the transferee corporation will be deemed to issue a nominal share...of stock to the transferor corporation in addition to the actual consideration exchanged for the transferor corporation's assets." Treas. Reg. § 1.368-2(l)(2). In addition to finalizing the "issuance of shares" question, the 2009 regulations also addressed basis issues arising from the deemed issuance of stock in this type of D reorganization. TD 9475, 74 Fed. Reg. 67053 (Dec. 18, 2009). The Service and Treasury, concerned that taxpayers were interpreting the basis rules in the 2009 regulations inappropriately, issued regulations in 2011 intended to clarify the basis rules. TD 9558, 76 Fed. Reg. 71878 (Nov. 21, 2011).

5. "SUBSTANTIALLY ALL OF THE PROPERTIES"—§ 368(A)(1)(C)

In Rev. Proc. 77–37, 1977–2 C.B. 568, the Internal Revenue Service restated the "operating rule" that will guide it in issuing rulings where the "substantially all" requirement of §§ 354(b)(1)(A), 368(a)(1)(C), and 368(a)(2)(B) is involved. Acknowledging that its operating rule does not, as a matter of law, define the lower limits, the Service held the requirement "is satisfied if there is a transfer of assets representing at least 90 percent of the fair market value of the net assets and 70 percent of the fair market value of the gross assets held by the [transferor] corporation immediately prior to the transfer."

In some cases a transfer of a corporation's operating assets may be treated as substantially all the properties of the transferor for the purpose of § 354(b)(1)(A) even though the transferred assets constitute only a small part of the corporation's total assets. See American Mfg. Co., 55 T.C. 204 (1970) (a transfer of 20 percent of the total assets, constituting all of the operating assets, was held to be substantially all of the assets); Smothers v. United States, page 604 infra (15 percent of the total assets, constituting all of the operating assets, were held to be substantially all of the assets).

In Rev. Rul. 88–48, 1988–1 C.B. 531, a corporation sold one of its two historic lines of business to an unrelated party immediately before a "C" reorganization. Although that line of business had accounted for 50 percent of the transferor corporation's historic assets, the pre-reorganization tailoring did not lead the Service to rule that the "substantially all" requirement of § 368(a)(1)(C) was not satisfied. See also, Rev. Rul. 2001–25, 2001–1 C.B. 1291 (requirements of a reverse triangular merger (§ 368(a)(1)(A) and 368(a)(2)(E)) were satisfied even though after the merger, the surviving corporation sold 50 percent of the operating assets and retained the cash, pursuant to the merger plan).

6. ASSUMPTION OF LIABILITIES—§ 357

United States v. Hendler

303 U.S. 564 (1938).

■ MR. JUSTICE BLACK delivered the opinion of the Court. The Revenue Act of 1928 [§ 13] imposed a tax upon the annual "net income" of corporations. It defined "net income" as "gross income" . . . less the deductions allowed . . . and "gross income" as including "gains, profits and income derived from . . . trades . . . or sales, or dealings in property, . . . or gains or profits and income . . . from any source whatever." [§§ 21–22.]

Section 112 of the Act exempts certain gains which are realized from a "reorganization" similar to, or in the nature of, a corporate merger or consolidation. Under this section, such gains are not taxed if one corporation, pursuant to a "plan of reorganization" exchanges its property "solely for stock or securities, in another corporation a party to the reorganization." But, when a corporation not only receives "stock or securities" in exchange for its property, but also receives "other property or money" in carrying out a "plan of reorganization,"

> (1) If the corporation receiving such other property or money distributes it in pursuance of the plan of reorganization, no gain to the corporation shall be recognized from the exchange, but

> (2) If the corporation receiving such other property or money does not distribute it in pursuance of the plan of reorganization, the gain, if any, to the corporation shall be recognized [taxed] . . .

In this case, there was a merger or "reorganization" of the Borden Company and the Hendler Creamery Company, Inc., resulting in gains of more than six million dollars to the Hendler Company, Inc., a corporation of which respondent is transferee. The Court of Appeals, believing there was an exemption under § 112, affirmed the judgment of the District Court holding all Hendler gains non-taxable.

This controversy between the government and respondent involves the assumption and payment—pursuant to the plan of reorganization—by the Borden Company of $534,297.40 bonded indebtedness of the Hendler Creamery Co., Inc. We are unable to agree with the conclusion reached by the courts below that the gain to the Hendler Company, realized by the Borden Company's payment, was exempt from taxation under § 112.

It was contended below and it is urged here that since the Hendler Company did not actually receive the money with which the Borden Company discharged the former's indebtedness, the Hendler Company's gain of $534,297.40 is not taxable. The transaction, however, under which the Borden Company assumed and paid the debt and obligation of the Hendler Company is to be regarded in substance as though the $534,297.40 had been paid directly to the Hendler Company. The Hendler Company was the beneficiary of the discharge of its indebtedness. Its gain was as real and substantial as if the money had been paid it and then paid over by it to its creditors. The discharge of liability by the payment of the Hendler Company's indebtedness constituted income to the Hendler Company and is to be treated as such.

Section 112 provides no exemption for gains—resulting from corporate "reorganization"—neither received as "stock or securities," nor received as "money or other property" and distributed to stockholders under the plan of reorganization. In Minnesota Tea Co. v. Helvering, 302 U.S. 609, it was said that this exemption "contemplates a distribution to stockholders, and not payment to creditors."[*] The very statute upon which the taxpayer relies provides that "If the corporation receiving such other property or money does not distribute in pursuance of the plan of reorganization, the gain, if any, to the corporation shall be recognized [taxed]. . ."

Since this gain or income of $534,297.40 of the Hendler Company was neither received as "stock or securities" nor distributed to its stockholders "in pursuance of the plan of reorganization" it was not exempt and is taxable gain as defined in the 1928 Act. This $534,297.40 gain to the taxpayer does not fall within the exemptions of § 112, and the judgment of the court below is reversed. . .

NOTES

1. How would you have argued for a contrary result in *Hendler*? If Congress had permitted the *Hendler* decision to stand, what impact would the decision have had on corporate reorganizations? To what extent does § 357 overrule *Hendler*? What is the reason for § 357(c)?

---

[*] This is not the opinion in *Minnesota Tea*, page 480 supra, but it grows out of the same transaction.

2. Section 357(c)(1), taxing transferors on their gains to the extent that the liabilities transferred exceed the basis of the accompanying assets, does not apply to transactions that qualify as reorganizations described in §§ 368(a)(1)(A), (C), (D) (assuming the requirements of § 354(b)(1) are satisfied), or (G) (assuming the requirements of § 354(b)(1) are satisfied) and to which § 351 applies. Rev. Rul. 2007–8, 2007–7 I.R.B. 469 (obsoleted Rev. Rul. 75–161, 1975–1 C.B. 114 and Rev. Rul. 76–188, 1976–1 C.B. 99, which had ruled to the contrary). Even under earlier rulings, if a transaction was both a "D" and an "F" reorganization, the latter dominated and no gain was recognized (Rev. Rul. 79–289, 1979–2 C.B. 145). Why does § 357(c)(1)(B) mark the "D" reorganization for special treatment? Should it?

3.(a) Corporation X is in control of Corporation Y. Y acquires all of the assets of Corporation Z in exchange for voting stock of X and the assumption by X of some of the liabilities of Z. What are the tax consequences of the transaction to Y? To Z? *Compare* Rev. Rul. 70–107, 1970–1 C.B. 78, *with* Rev. Rul. 70–224, 1970–1 C.B. 79.

(b) See Rev. Rul. 78–330, 1978–2 C.B. 147, in which the parent corporation's forgiveness of debt due from subsidiary, to avoid application of § 357(c) to subsequent "D" reorganization, was given effect as a contribution to capital. This position was modified by Rev. Rul. 2007–8 (see above in note 2) by providing that § 357(c)(1) does not apply to A, C, D, or G reorganizations.

(c) Section 357(c)(3), discussed at page 325 et seq. supra, applies only to § 351 exchanges. What implications does this raise in the reorganization area? Cf. Rev. Rul. 78–442, 1978–2 C.B. 143.

(d) What is the effect if, in a "C" reorganization, the transferor corporation is liquidated and its liabilities are assumed by its shareholders? Cf. Rev. Rul. 75–450, 1975–2 C.B. 166.

7. EFFECT OF "BOOT"

a. On Corporations

1. If a transferor corporation in an "A," "C," or "D" reorganization receives "boot" (anything in addition to stock or securities in another corporation that is a party to the reorganization), § 361(b)(1)(A) provides that no gain will be recognized to the transferor if it distributes the "boot" "in pursuance of the plan of reorganization." Why does it so provide? If the transferor retains the "boot," gain to the extent of the retained "boot" will be recognized. Section 361(b)(1)(B). In what types of reorganizations might such "boot" retention occur? Despite retention of "boot," no loss is recognized. Section 361(b)(2).

Section 354(a)(2) and (3) treats "securities" and nonqualified preferred stock as "boot" in designated circumstances. Section 361 does not so provide. Should it? What about § 351?

2. Section 361 does not prevent taxation of the transferor corporation's gain if instead of distributing all transferee's stock to its shareholders or

creditors, it sells some of it and distributes the sale proceeds along with the balance of transferee's stock. It is a very unfortunate if not mindless result, exalting the form, and paying no attention to the fact that transferee corporation does not get a step up in asset basis despite the gain recognition. Thus § 361, esp. § 361(c)(3), codifies General Housewares Corp. v. United States, 615 F.2d 1056 (5th Cir. 1980), in providing nonrecognition in the case of an in-kind distribution, but also leaves intact the decision in FEC Liquidating Corp. v. United States, 548 F.2d 924 (Ct. Cl. 1977), which taxed the transferor on its sale for cash of some of transferee's stock.

3. If a corporation receives a "boot" distribution that is taxable to it as a dividend under § 356(a)(2), is it entitled to the dividends received deduction under § 243? See Tribune Publishing Co. v. United States, 836 F.2d 1176 (9th Cir. 1988).

4. See Rev. Rul. 72–327, 1972–2 C.B. 197, in which the corporate shareholder of an acquired corporation in a statutory merger received a distribution consisting of stock of the acquiring corporation and appreciated property. Its realized gain was recognized to the extent of the fair market value of the appreciated property; it received a dividend to the extent of its ratable share of the acquired corporation's earnings and profits; and it was allowed a dividends received deduction.

b. On Shareholders

Commissioner v. Estate of Bedford
325 U.S. 283 (1945).

■ MR. JUSTICE FRANKFURTER delivered the opinion of the Court. . . The estate of Edward T. Bedford, who died May 21, 1931, included 3,000 shares of cumulative preferred stock (par value $100) of Abercrombie & Fitch Company. Pursuant to a plan of recapitalization respondent, as executor of the estate, in 1937 exchanged those shares for 3,500 shares of cumulative preferred stock (par value $75), 1,500 shares of common stock (par value $1), and $45,240 in cash (on the basis of $15.08 for each of the old preferred shares). The recapitalization had been proposed because the company, after charging against its surplus account stock dividends totaling $844,100, distributed in 1920, 1928, and 1930, had incurred a book deficit in that account of $399,771.87. Because of this deficit, the company, under applicable State law, was unable to pay dividends although for the fiscal year ending January 31, 1937 it had net earnings of $309,073.70.

By comparing the fair market value of the old preferred shares at the date of Bedford's death with the market value of the new stock and cash received the gain to his estate was $139,740. Admittedly the recapitalization was a reorganization, § [368(a)(1)(E)], so that only the cash received, but none of the stock is taxable. Sections [354(a)(1); 356(a)]. The sole issue is whether the cash, $45,240, is taxable as a dividend, or merely as a capital gain. . . The Tax Court sustained the determination of the Commissioner that the cash was taxable as a dividend. . . but was reversed by the Circuit Court of Appeals . . . On a showing of importance to the administration of the Revenue Acts, we granted certiorari. . .

The precise question is whether the distribution of cash in this recapitalization "has the effect of the distribution of a taxable dividend" under § [356(a)(2)] and as such is fully taxable, or is taxable only . . . as a capital gain under § [356(a)(1)].

The history of this legislation is not illuminating. Section [356(a)(2)] originated in § 203(d)(2) of the Revenue Act of 1924. . . But the reports of the Congressional Committees merely use the language of the section to explain it. H. Rep. No. 179, 68th Cong., 1st Sess., pp. 14–15; S. Rep. No. 398, 68th Cong., 1st Sess., pp. 1516. Nor does the applicable Treasury Regulation add anything; it repeats substantially the Committee Reports. Treas. Reg. 94, Art. 112(g)–4. We are thrown back upon the legislative language for ascertaining the meaning which will best accord with the aims of the language, the practical administration of the law and relevant judicial construction.

Although Abercrombie & Fitch showed a book deficit in the surplus account because the earlier stock dividends had been charged against it, the parties agree that for corporate tax purposes at least earnings and profits exceeding the distributed cash had been earned at the time of the recapitalization. That cash therefore came out of earnings and profits and such a distribution would normally be considered a taxable dividend, see § [316(a)], and has so been treated by the courts in seemingly similar situations. It has been ruled in a series of cases that where the stock of one corporation was exchanged for the stock of another and cash and then distributed, such distributions out of earnings and profits had the effect of a distribution of a taxable dividend under § [356(a)(2)]. . . The Tax Court has reached the same result, that is, has treated the distribution as a taxable dividend, in the case of the recapitalization of a single corporation. . . We cannot distinguish the two situations and find no implication in the statute restricting § [356(a)(2)] to taxation as a dividend only in the case of an exchange of stock and assets of two corporations.

Respondent, however, claims that this distribution more nearly has the effect of a "partial liquidation" as defined in § 115(i).[5] But the classifications of § 115, which governs "Distribution of Corporations" apart from reorganizations, were adopted for another purpose. They do not apply to a situation arising within § 112 [the reorganization and nonrecognition provisions]. The definition of a "partial liquidation" in § 115(i) is specifically limited to use in § 115. To attempt to carry it over to § 112 would distort its purpose. That limitation is not true of § [316(a)] which defines "dividends" for the purpose of the whole title. Accordingly, this definition is infused into § 112(c)(2) [356(a)(2)]. Under § [316(a)] a distribution out of accumulated earnings and profits is a "dividend," thus confirming the conclusion that a

---

[5] "(i). *Definition of Partial Liquidation.*—As used in this section the term 'amounts distributed in partial liquidation' means a distribution by a corporation in complete cancellation or redemption of a part of its stock, or one of a series of distributions in complete cancellation or redemption of all or a portion of its stock."

distribution of earnings and profits has the "effect of the distribution of a taxable dividend" under § [356(a)(2)].

Recapitalization does not alter the "effect." Although the capital of a company is reduced the cash received is a distribution of earnings and profits and as such falls within the federal tax. That the company's treatment of its stock dividends may bring consequences under State law requiring a capital reduction does not alter the character of the transactions which bring them within the federal income tax. Recapitalization is one of the forms of reorganization under § 112. . . . It cannot therefore be urged as a reason for taking the transaction out of the requirements of § 112 and forcing it into the mold of § 115. The reduction of capital brings § 112 into operation and does not give immunity from the requirements of § [356(a)(2)].

Treating the matter as a problem of statutory construction for our independent judgment, we hold that a distribution, pursuant to a reorganization, of earnings and profits, "has the effect of a distribution of a taxable dividend" within § [356(a)(2)]. As is true of other teasing questions of construction raised by technical provisions of Revenue Acts the matter is not wholly free from doubt. But these doubts would have to be stronger than they are to displace the informed views of the Tax Court. And if the case can be reduced to its own particular circumstances rather than turn on a generalizing principle we should feel bound to apply Dobson v. Commissioner, 320 U.S. 489, and sustain the Tax Court.

Reversed.

Commissioner v. Clark
489 U.S. 726 (1989).

■ JUSTICE STEVENS delivered the opinion of the Court.

This is the third case in which the Government has asked us to decide that a shareholder's receipt of a cash payment in exchange for a portion of his stock was taxable as a dividend. In the two earlier cases, Commissioner v. Estate of Bedford, 325 U.S. 283 (1945), and United States v. Davis, 397 U.S. 301 (1970), we agreed with the Government largely because the transactions involved redemptions of stock by single corporations that did not "result in a meaningful reduction of the shareholder's proportionate interest in the corporation." Id., at 313. In the case we decide today, however, the taxpayer in an arm's length transaction exchanged his interest in the acquired corporation for less than one percent of the stock of the acquiring corporation and a substantial cash payment. The taxpayer held no interest in the acquiring corporation prior to the reorganization. Viewing the exchange as a whole, we conclude that the cash payment is not appropriately characterized as a dividend. We accordingly agree with the Tax Court and with the Court of Appeals that the taxpayer is entitled to capital gains treatment of the cash payment.

I

In determining tax liability under the Internal Revenue Code, gain resulting from the sale or exchange of property is generally treated as capital gain, whereas the receipt of cash dividends is treated as ordinary income.[2] The Code, however, imposes no current tax on certain stock-for-stock exchanges. In particular, § 354(a)(1) provides, subject to various limitations, for nonrecognition of gain resulting from the exchange of stock or securities solely for other stock or securities, provided that the exchange is pursuant to a plan of corporate reorganization and that the stock or securities are those of a party to the reorganization. 26 U.S.C. § 354(a)(1).

Under § 356(a)(1) of the Code, if such a stock-for-stock exchange is accompanied by additional consideration in the form of a cash payment or other property—something that tax practitioners refer to as "boot"—"then the gain, if any, to the recipient shall be recognized, but in an amount not in excess of the sum of such money and the fair market value of such other property." 26 U.S.C. § 356(a)(1). That is, if the shareholder receives boot, he or she must recognize the gain on the exchange up to the value of the boot. Boot is accordingly generally treated as a gain from the sale or exchange of property and is recognized in the current tax-year.

Section 356(a)(2), which controls the decision in this case, creates an exception to that general rule. It provides:

> If an exchange is described in paragraph (1) but has the effect of the distribution of a dividend (determined with the application of section 318(a)), then there shall be treated as a dividend to each distributee such an amount of the gain recognized under paragraph (1) as is not in excess of his ratable share of the undistributed earnings and profits of the corporation accumulated after February 28, 1913. The remainder, if any, of the gain recognized under paragraph (1) shall be treated as gain from the exchange of property.

Thus, if the "exchange . . . has the effect of the distribution of a dividend," the boot must be treated as a dividend and is therefore appropriately taxed as ordinary income to the extent that gain is realized. In contrast, if the exchange does not have "the effect of the distribution of a dividend," the boot must be treated as a payment in exchange for property and, insofar as gain is realized, accorded capital gains treatment. The question in this case is thus whether the exchange between the taxpayer and the acquiring cor-

---

[2] In 1979, the tax year in question, the distinction between long-term capital gain and ordinary income was of considerable importance. Most significantly, § 1202(a) of the Code ... allowed individual taxpayers to deduct 60% of their net capital gain from gross income. Although the importance of the distinction declined dramatically in 1986 with the repeal of § 1202(a), see Tax Reform Act of 1986, Pub. L. 99–514, § 301(a), 100 Stat. 2216, the distinction is still significant in a number of respects. For example, § 1211(b) allows individual taxpayers to deduct capital losses to the full extent of their capital gains, but only allows them to offset up to $3000 of ordinary income insofar as their capital losses exceed their capital gains.

[Following the 2003 Tax Act, dividends are now generally taxed at the long-term capital gains rate.—ED.].

poration had "the effect of the distribution of a dividend" within the meaning of § 356(a)(2).

The relevant facts are easily summarized. For approximately 15 years prior to April 1979, the taxpayer was the sole shareholder and president of Basin Surveys, Inc. (Basin), a company in which he had invested approximately $85,000. The corporation operated a successful business providing various technical services to the petroleum industry. In 1978, N. L. Industries, Inc. (NL), a publicly owned corporation engaged in the manufacture and supply of petroleum equipment and services, initiated negotiations with the taxpayer regarding the possible acquisition of Basin. On April 3, 1979, after months of negotiations, the taxpayer and NL entered into a contract.

The agreement provided for a "triangular merger," whereby Basin was merged into a wholly owned subsidiary of NL. In exchange for transferring all of the outstanding shares in Basin to NL's subsidiary, the taxpayer elected to receive 300,000 shares of NL common stock and cash boot of $3,250,000, passing up an alternative offer of 425,000 shares of NL common stock. The 300,000 shares of NL issued to the taxpayer amounted to approximately 0.92% of the outstanding common shares of NL. If the taxpayer had instead accepted the pure stock-for-stock offer, he would have held approximately 1.3% of the outstanding common shares. The Commissioner and the taxpayer agree that the merger at issue qualifies as a reorganization under § 368(a)(1)(A) and (a)(2)(D).

Respondents filed a joint federal income tax return for 1979. As required by § 356(a)(1), they reported the cash boot as taxable gain. In calculating the tax owed, respondents characterized the payment as long-term capital gain. The Commissioner on audit disagreed with this characterization. In his view, the payment had "the effect of the distribution of a dividend" and was thus taxable as ordinary income up to $2,319,611, the amount of Basin's accumulated earnings and profits at the time of the merger. The Commissioner assessed a deficiency of $972,504.74.

Respondents petitioned for review in the Tax Court, which, in a reviewed decision, held in their favor. 86 T.C. 138 (1986). The court started from the premise that the question whether the boot payment had "the effect of the distribution of a dividend" turns on the choice between "two judicially articulated tests." Id., at 140. Under the test advocated by the Commissioner and given voice in Shimberg v. United States, 577 F.2d 283 (CA5 1978), cert. denied, 439 U.S. 1115 (1979), the boot payment is treated as though it were made in a hypothetical redemption by the acquired corporation (Basin) immediately prior to the reorganization. Under this test, the cash payment received by the taxpayer indisputably would have been treated as a dividend. The second test, urged by the taxpayer and finding support in Wright v. United States, 482 F.2d 600 (CA8 1973), proposes an alternative hypothetical redemption. Rather than concentrating on the taxpayer's pre-reorganization interest in the acquired corporation, this test requires that one imagine a pure stock-for-stock exchange, followed immediately by a post-reorganization redemption of a portion of the taxpayer's shares in the acquiring corporation (NL) in return for a payment in an amount equal to the boot. Under § 302 of the Code, which defines when a redemption of stock should be treated as a distribution of dividend, NL's redemption of 125,000 shares of its stock from the taxpayer in exchange for the $3,250,000 boot payment would have been treated as capital gain.

The Tax Court rejected the pre-reorganization test favored by the Commissioner because it considered it improper "to view the cash payment as an isolated event totally separate from the reorganization." 86 T.C., at 151. Indeed, it suggested that this test requires that courts make the "determination of dividend equivalency fantasizing that the reorganization does not exist." Id., at 150 (footnote omitted). The court then acknowledged that a similar criticism could be made of the taxpayer's contention that the cash payment should be viewed as a post-reorganization redemption. It concluded, however, that since it was perfectly clear that the cash payment would not have taken place without the reorganization, it was better to treat the boot "as the equivalent of a redemption in the course of implementing the reorganization," than "as having occurred prior to and separate from the reorganization." Id., at 152.[7]

The Court of Appeals for the Fourth Circuit affirmed. 828 F.2d 221 (1987). Like the Tax Court, it concluded that although "[s]ection 302 does not explicitly apply in the reorganization context," id., at 223, and although § 302 differs from § 356 in important respects, id., at 224, it nonetheless provides "the appropriate test for determining whether boot is ordinary income or a capital gain," id., at 223. Thus, as explicated in § 302(b)(2), if the taxpayer relinquished more than 20% of his corporate control and retained less than 50% of the voting shares after the distribution, the boot would be treated as capital gain. However, as the Court of Appeals recognized, "[b]ecause § 302 was designed to deal with a stock redemption by a single corporation, rather than a reorganization involving two companies, the section does not indicate which corporation [the taxpayer] lost interest in." Id., at 224. Thus, like the Tax Court, the Court of Appeals was left to consider whether the hypothetical redemption should be treated as a

---

[7] The Tax Court stressed that to adopt the pre-reorganization view "would in effect resurrect the now discredited 'automatic dividend rule' ..., at least with respect to pro rata distributions made to an acquired corporation's shareholders pursuant to a plan of reorganization." 86 T.C., at 152. On appeal, the Court of Appeals agreed. 828 F.2d 221, 226–227 (CA4 1987).

The "automatic dividend rule" developed as a result of some imprecise language in our decision in Commissioner v. Estate of Bedford, 325 U.S. 283 (1945). Although Estate of Bedford involved the recapitalization of a single corporation, the opinion employed broad language, asserting that "a distribution, pursuant to a reorganization, of earnings and profits 'has the effect of a distribution of a taxable dividend' within [§ 356(a)(2)]." Id., at 292. The Commissioner read this language as establishing as a matter of law that all payments of boot are to be treated as dividends to the extent of undistributed earnings and profits. See Rev. Rul. 56–220, 1956–1 Cum. Bull. 191. Commentators, see, e.g., Darrel, The Scope of Commissioner v. Bedford Estate, 24 Taxes 266 (1946); Shoulson, Boot Taxation: The Blunt Toe of the Automatic Dividend Rule, 20 Tax L. Rev. 573 (1965), and courts, see, e.g., Hawkinson v. Commissioner, 235 F.2d 747 (CA2 1956), however, soon came to criticize this rule. The courts have long since retreated from the "automatic dividend rule," see, e.g., Idaho Power Co. v. United States, 161 F.Supp. 807 (Ct. Cl.), cert. denied, 358 U.S. 832 (1958), and the Commissioner has followed suit, see Rev. Rul. 74–515, 1974–2 Cum. Bull. 118. As our decision in this case makes plain, we agree that Estate of Bedford should not be read to require that all payments of boot be treated as dividends.

pre-reorganization distribution coming from the acquired corporation or as a post-reorganization distribution coming from the acquiring corporation. It concluded:

> Based on the language and legislative history of § 356, the change in-ownership principle of § 302, and the need to review the reorganization as an integrated transaction, we conclude that the boot should be characterized as a post-reorganization stock redemption by N. L. that affected [the taxpayer's] interest in the new corporation. Because this redemption reduced [the taxpayer's] N. L. holdings by more than 20%, the boot should be taxed as a capital gain. Id., at 224–225.

This decision by the Court of Appeals for the Fourth Circuit is in conflict with the decision of the Fifth Circuit in *Shimberg*. [There] the court concluded that it was inappropriate to apply stock redemption principles in reorganization cases "on a wholesale basis." Id., at 287; see also ibid., n.13. . . In addition, the court adopted the pre-reorganization test, holding that "§ 356(a)(2) requires a determination of whether the distribution would have been taxed as a dividend if made prior to the reorganization or if no reorganization had occurred." Id., at 288.

To resolve this conflict on a question of importance to the administration of the federal tax laws, we granted certiorari. 485 U.S. 933 (1988).

II

We agree with the Tax Court and the Court of Appeals for the Fourth Circuit that the question under § 356(a)(2) of whether an "exchange . . . has the effect of the distribution of a dividend" should be answered by examining the effect of the exchange as a whole. We think the language and history of the statute, as well as a commonsense understanding of the economic substance of the transaction at issue, support this approach.

The language of § 356(a) strongly supports our understanding that the transaction should be treated as an integrated whole. Section 356(a)(2) asks whether "an exchange is described in paragraph (1)" that "has the effect of the distribution of a dividend." The statute does not provide that boot shall be treated as a dividend if its payment has the effect of the distribution of a dividend. Rather, the inquiry turns on whether the "exchange" has that effect. Moreover, paragraph (1), in turn, looks to whether "the property received in the exchange consists not only of property permitted by section 354 or 355 to be received without the recognition of gain but also of other property or money." Again, the statute plainly refers to one integrated transaction and, again, makes clear that we are to look to the character of the exchange as a whole and not simply its component parts. Finally, it is significant that § 356 expressly limits the extent to which boot may be taxed to the amount of gain realized in the reorganization. This limitation suggests that Congress intended that boot not be treated in isolation from the overall reorganization. See Levin, Adess, & McGaffey, Boot Distributions in Corporate Reorganizations—Determination of Dividend Equivalency, 30 Tax Lawyer 287, 303 (1977).

Our reading of the statute as requiring that the transaction be treated as a unified whole is reinforced by the well-established "step-transaction" doctrine, a doctrine that the Government has applied in related contexts, see, e.g., Rev. Rul. 75–447, 1975–2 Cum. Bull. 113, and that we have expressly sanctioned, see Minnesota Tea Co. v. Helvering, 302 U.S. 609, 613 (1938); Commissioner v. Court Holding Co., 324 U.S. 331, 334 (1945). Under this doctrine, interrelated yet formally distinct steps in an integrated transaction may not be considered independently of the overall transaction. By thus "linking together all interdependent steps with legal or business significance, rather than taking them in isolation," federal tax liability may be based "on a realistic view of the entire transaction." 1 B. Bittker, Federal Taxation of Income, Estates and Gifts, para. 4.3.5, p. 4–52 (1981).

Viewing the exchange in this case as an integrated whole, we are unable to accept the Commissioner's pre-reorganization analogy. The analogy severs the payment of boot from the context of the reorganization. Indeed, only by straining to abstract the payment of boot from the context of the overall exchange, and thus imagining that Basin made a distribution to the taxpayer independently of NL's planned acquisition, can we reach the rather counterintuitive conclusion urged by the Commissioner—that the taxpayer suffered no meaningful reduction in his ownership interest as a result of the cash payment. We conclude that such a limited view of the transaction is plainly inconsistent with the statute's direction that we look to the effect of the entire exchange.

The pre-reorganization analogy is further flawed in that it adopts an overly expansive reading of § 356(a)(2). As the Court of Appeals recognized, adoption of the pre-reorganization approach would "result in ordinary income treatment in most reorganizations because corporate boot is usually distributed pro rata to the shareholders of the target corporation." 828 F.2d, at 227; see also Golub, "Boot" in Reorganizations—The Dividend Equivalency Test of Section 356(a)(2), 58 Taxes 904, 911 (1980); Note, 20 Boston College L. Rev. 601, 612 (1979). Such a reading of the statute would not simply constitute a return to the widely criticized "automatic dividend rule" (at least as to cases involving a pro rata payment to the shareholders of the acquired corporation), see n. 8, supra, but also would be contrary to our standard approach to construing such provisions. The requirement of § 356(a)(2) that boot be treated as dividend in some circumstances is an exception from the general rule authorizing capital gains treatment for boot. In construing provisions such as § 356, in which a general statement of policy is qualified by an exception, we usually read the exception narrowly in order to preserve the primary operation of the provision. See Phillips, Inc. v. Walling, 324 U.S. 490, 493 (1945) ("To extend an exemption to other than those plainly and unmistakably within its terms and spirit is to abuse the interpretative process and to frustrate the announced will of the people"). Given that Congress has enacted a general rule that treats boot as capital gain, we should not eviscerate that legislative judgment through an expansive reading of a somewhat ambiguous exception.

The post-reorganization approach adopted by the Tax Court and the Court of Appeals is, in our view, preferable to the Commissioner's approach. Most significantly, this approach does a far better job of treating the payment of boot as a component of the overall exchange. Unlike the pre-reorganization view, this approach acknowledges that there would have been no cash payment absent the exchange and also that, by accepting the cash payment, the taxpayer experienced a meaningful reduction in his potential ownership interest.

Once the post-reorganization approach is adopted, the result in this case is pellucidly clear. Section 302(a) of the Code provides that if a redemption fits within any one of the four categories set out in § 302(b), the redemption "shall be treated as a distribution in part or full payment in exchange for the stock," and thus not regarded as a dividend. As the Tax Court and the Court of Appeals correctly determined, the hypothetical post-reorganization redemption by NL of a portion of the taxpayer's shares satisfies at least one of the subsections of § 302(b). In particular, the safe harbor provisions of subsection (b)(2) provide that redemptions in which the taxpayer relinquishes more than 20% of his or her share of the corporation's voting stock and retains less than 50% of the voting of stock after the redemption, shall not be treated as distributions of a dividend... Here, we treat the transaction as though NL redeemed 125,000 shares of its common stock (i.e., the number of shares of NL common stock foregone in favor of the boot) in return for a cash payment to the taxpayer of $3,250,000 (i.e., the amount of the boot). As a result of this redemption, the taxpayer's interest in NL was reduced from 1.3% of the outstanding common stock to 0.9%. See 86 T.C., at 153. Thus, the taxpayer relinquished approximately 29% of his interest in NL and retained less than a 1% voting interest in the corporation after the transaction, easily satisfying the "substantially disproportionate" standards of § 302(b)(2). We accordingly conclude that the boot payment did not have the effect of a dividend and that the payment was properly treated as capital gain.

III

The Commissioner objects to this "recasting [of] the merger transaction into a form different from that entered into by the parties," Brief for the United States 11, and argues that the Court of Appeals' formal adherence to the principles embodied in § 302 forced the court to stretch to "find a redemption to which to apply them, since the merger transaction entered into by the parties did not involve a redemption," id., at 28. There are a number of sufficient responses to this argument. We think it first worth emphasizing that the Commissioner overstates the extent to which the redemption is imagined. As the Court of Appeals for the Fifth Circuit noted in Shimberg, "[t]he theory behind tax-free corporate reorganizations is that the transaction is merely a 'continuance of the proprietary interests in the continuing enterprise under modified corporate form.' Lewis v. Commissioner of Internal Revenue, 176 F.2d 646, 648 (1 Cir. 1949); Treas. Reg. § 1.368–1(b). See generally Cohen, Conglomerate Mergers and Taxation, 55 A.B.A J. 40 (1969)." 577 F. 2d at 288. As a result, the boot-for-stock transaction can be viewed as a partial repurchase of stock by the continuing corporate enterprise—i.e., as a redemption. It is of course true that both the pre- and post-reorganization analogies are somewhat artificial in that they imagine that the redemption occurred outside the confines of the actual reorganization. However, if forced to choose between the two analogies, the post-reorganization view is the less artificial. Although both analogies "recast the merger transaction," the post-reorganization view recognizes that a reorganization has taken place, while the pre-reorganization approach recasts the transaction to the exclusion of the overall exchange.

Moreover, we doubt that abandoning the pre- and post-reorganization analogies and the principles of § 302 in favor of a less artificial understanding of the transaction would lead to a result different from that reached by the Court of Appeals. Although the statute is admittedly ambiguous and the legislative history sparse, we are persuaded—even without relying on § 302—that Congress did not intend to except reorganizations such as that at issue here from the general rule allowing capital gains treatment for cash boot. 26 U.S.C. § 356(a)(1). The legislative history of § 356(a)(2), although perhaps generally "not illuminating," Estate of Bedford, 325 U.S., at 290, suggests that Congress was primarily concerned with preventing corporations from "siphon[ing] off" accumulated earnings and profits at a capital gains rate through the ruse of a reorganization. See Golub, 58 Taxes, at 905. This purpose is not served by denying capital gains treatment in a case such as this in which the taxpayer entered into an arm's length transaction with a corporation in which he had no prior interest, exchanging his stock in the acquired corporation for less than a one percent interest in the acquiring corporation and a substantial cash boot.

Section 356(a)(2) finds its genesis in § 203(d)(2) of the Revenue Act of 1924. See 43 Stat. 257. Although modified slightly over the years, the provisions are in relevant substance identical. The accompanying House Report asserts that § 203(d)(2) was designed to "preven[t] evasion." H.R. Rep. No. 179, 68th Cong., 1st Sess. 15 (1924). Without further explication, both the House and Senate Reports simply rely on an example to explain, in the words of both Reports, "[t]he necessity for this provision." Ibid.; S. Rep. No. 398, 68th Cong., 1st Sess., 16 (1924). Significantly, the example describes a situation in which there was no change in the stockholders' relative ownership interests, but merely the creation of a wholly owned subsidiary as a mechanism for making a cash distribution to the shareholders:

Corporation A has capital stock of $100,000, and earnings and profits accumulated since March 1, 1913, of $50,000. If it distributes the $50,000 as a dividend to its stockholders, the amount distributed will be taxed at the full surtax rates.

On the other hand, Corporation A may organize Corporation B, to which it transfers all its assets, the consideration for the transfer being the issuance by B of all its stock and $50,000 in cash to the stockholders of Corporation A in exchange for their stock in Corporation A. Under the existing law, the $50,000 distributed with the stock of Corporation B would be taxed, not as a dividend, but as a capital gain,

> subject only to the 12 1/2 per cent rate. The effect of such a distribu-
> tion is obviously the same as if the corporation had declared out as a
> dividend its $50,000 earnings and profits. If dividends are to be subject
> to the full surtax rates, then such an amount so distributed should also
> be subject to the surtax rates and not to the 12 1/2 per cent rate on
> capital gain.

Id., at 16; H. R. Rep. No. 179, at 15.

The "effect" of the transaction in this example is to transfer accumulated earnings and profits to the shareholders without altering their respective ownership interests in the continuing enterprise.

Of course, this example should not be understood as exhaustive of the
proper applications of § 356(a)(2). It is nonetheless noteworthy that neither
the example, nor any other legislative source, evinces a congressional intent to tax boot accompanying a transaction that involves a bona fide exchange between unrelated parties in the context of a reorganization as
though the payment was in fact a dividend. To the contrary, the purpose of
avoiding tax evasion suggests that Congress did not intend to impose an
ordinary income tax in such cases. Moreover, the legislative history of § 302
supports this reading of § 356(a)(2) as well. In explaining the "essentially
equivalent to a dividend" language of § 302(b)(1)—language that is certainly similar to the "has the effect . . . of a dividend" language of § 356(a)(2)—
the Senate Finance Committee made clear that the relevant inquiry is
"whether or not the transaction by its nature may properly be characterized
as a sale of stock. . ." S. Rep. No. 1622, 83d Cong., 2d Sess., 234 (1954); cf.
United States v. Davis, 397 U. S., at 311.

Examining the instant transaction in light of the purpose of §
356(a)(2), the boot-for-stock exchange in this case "may properly be characterized as a sale of stock." Significantly, unlike traditional single corporation redemptions and unlike reorganizations involving commonly owned
corporations, there is little risk that the reorganization at issue was used
as a ruse to distribute dividend. Rather, the transaction appears in all respects relevant to the narrow issue before us to have been comparable to an
arm's length sale by the taxpayer to NL. This conclusion, moreover, is supported by the findings of the Tax Court. The court found that "[t]here is not
the slightest evidence that the cash payment was a concealed distribution
from BASIN." 86 T. C., at 155. As the Tax Court further noted, Basin
lacked the funds to make such a distribution:

> Indeed, it is hard to conceive that such a possibility could even have
> been considered, for a distribution of that amount was not only far in
> excess of the accumulated earnings and profits ($2,319,611), but also of
> the total assets of BASIN ($2,758,069). In fact, only if one takes into
> account unrealized appreciation in the value of BASIN's assets, includ-
> ing good will and/or going-concern value, can one possibly arrive at
> $3,250,000. Such a distribution could only be considered as the equiva-
> lent of a complete liquidation of BASIN. . .

Ibid.

In this context, even without relying on § 302 and the post-reorganization analogy, we conclude that the boot is better characterized as a part of the proceeds of a sale of stock than as a proxy for a dividend. As such, the payment qualifies for capital gains treatment.

The judgment of the Court of Appeals is accordingly Affirmed.

■ JUSTICE WHITE, dissenting.

The question in this case is whether the cash payment of $3,250,000 by N. L. Industries, Inc. (NL) to Donald Clark, which he received in the April 18, 1979, merger of Basin Surveys, Inc. (Basin), into N. L. Acquisition Corporation (NLAC), had the effect of a distribution of a dividend under the Internal Revenue Code, 26 U.S.C. § 356(a)(2), to the extent of Basin's accumulated undistributed earnings and profits. Petitioner, the Commissioner of Internal Revenue (Commissioner) made this determination, taxing the sum as ordinary income, to find a 1979 tax deficiency of $972,504.74. The Court of Appeals disagreed, stating that because the cash payment resembles a hypothetical stock redemption from NL to Clark, the amount is taxable as capital gain. 828 F.2d 221 (CA4 1987). Because the majority today agrees with that characterization, in spite of Clark's explicit refusal of the stock-for-stock exchange imagined by the Court of Appeals and the majority today, and because the record demonstrates, instead, that the transaction before us involved a boot distribution that had "the effect of the distribution of a dividend" under § 356(a)(2)—hence properly alerted the Commissioner to Clark's tax deficiency—I dissent.

The facts are stipulated. Basin, Clark, NL, and NLAC executed an Agreement and Plan of Merger dated April 3, 1979, which provided that on April 18, 1979, Basin would merge with NLAC. The statutory merger, which occurred pursuant to §§ 368(a)(1)(A) and (a)(2)(D) of the Code, and therefore qualified for tax-free reorganization status under § 354(a)(1), involved the following terms: Each outstanding share of Basin common stock was exchanged for $56,034.482 cash and 5,172.4137 shares of NL common stock; and each share of Basin common stock held by Basin was canceled. NLAC's name was amended to Basin Surveys, Inc. The Secretary of State of West Virginia certified that the merger complied with West Virginia law. Clark, the owner of all 58 outstanding shares of Basin, received $3,250,000 in cash and 300,000 shares of NL stock. He expressly refused NL's alternative of 425,000 shares of NL common stock without cash. See App. 56–59.

Congress enacted § 354(a)(1) to grant favorable tax treatment to specific corporate transactions (reorganization) that involve the exchange of stock or securities solely for other stock or securities. See Paulsen v. Commissioner, 469 U.S. 131, 136 (1985) (citing Treas. Reg. § 1.368–1(b), 26 C FR § 1.368–1(b) (1984), and noting the distinctive feature of such reorganizations, namely continuity-of-interests). Clark's "triangular merger" of Basin into NL's subsidiary NLAC qualified as one such tax-free reorganization, pursuant to § 368(a)(2)(D). Because the stock-for-stock exchange was supplemented with a cash payment, however, § 356(a)(1) requires that "the gain, if any, to the recipient shall be recognized, but in an amount not in excess of the sum of such money and the fair market value of such other property." Because this provision permitted taxpayers to withdraw profits during corporate reorganizations without declaring a dividend, Congress enacted the present § 356(a)(2), which states that when an exchange has "the effect of the distribution of a dividend," boot must be treated as a dividend, and taxed as ordinary income, to the extent of the distributee's "ratable share of the undistributed earnings and profits of the corporation. . ." Ibid.; see also H.R. Rep. No. 179, 68th Cong., 1st Sess., 15 (1924) (illustration of § 356(a)(2)'s purpose to frustrate evasion of dividend taxation through corporate reorganization distributions); S. Rep. No. 398, 68th Cong., 1st Sess., 16 (1924) (same).

Thus the question today is whether the cash payment to Clark had the effect of a distribution of a dividend. We supplied the straightforward answer in United States v. Davis, 397 U.S. 301, 306, 312 (1970), when we explained that a pro rata redemption of stock by a corporation is "essentially equivalent" to a dividend. A pro rata distribution of stock, with no alteration of basic shareholder relationships, is the hallmark of a dividend. This was precisely Clark's gain. As sole shareholder of Basin, Clark necessarily received a pro rata distribution of monies that exceeded Basin's undistributed earnings and profits of $2,319,611. Because the merger and cash obligation occurred simultaneously on April 18, 1979, and because the statutory merger approved here assumes that Clark's proprietary interests continue in the restructured NLAC, the exact source of the pro rata boot payment is immaterial, which truth Congress acknowledged by requiring only that an exchange have the effect of a dividend distribution.

To avoid this conclusion, the Court of Appeals—approved by the majority today—recast the transaction as though the relevant distribution involved a single corporation's (NL's) stock redemption, which dividend equivalency is determined according to § 302 of the Code. Section 302 shields distributions from dividend taxation if the cash redemption is accompanied by sufficient loss of a shareholder's percentage interest in the corporation. The Court of Appeals hypothesized that Clark completed a pure stock-for-stock reorganization, receiving 425,000 NL shares, and thereafter redeemed 125,000 of these shares for his cash earnings of $3,250,000. The sum escapes dividend taxation because Clark's interest in NL theoretically declined from 1.3% to 0.92%, adequate to trigger § 302(b)(2) protection. Transporting § 302 from its purpose to frustrate shareholder sales of equity back to their own corporation, to § 356(a)(2)'s reorganization context, however, is problematic. Neither the majority nor the Court of Appeals explains why § 302 should obscure the core attribute of a dividend as a pro rata distribution to a corporation's shareholders;[1] nor offers insight into the me-

---

[1] The Court of Appeals' zeal to excoriate the "automatic dividend rule" leads to an opposite rigidity—an automatic nondividend rule, even for pro rata boot payments. Any significant cash payment in a stock-for-stock exchange distributed to a sole shareholder of an acquired corporation will automatically receive capital gains treatment. Section 356(a)(2)'s exception for such payments that have attributes of a dividend disappears. Congress did not intend to handicap the Commissioner and courts with either absolute; instead, § 356(a)(1) instructs courts

chanics of valuing hypothetical stock transfers and equity reductions; nor answers the Commissioner's observations that the sole shareholder of an acquired corporation will always have a smaller interest in the continuing enterprise when cash payments combine with a stock exchange. Last, the majority and the Court of Appeals' recharacterization of market happenings describes the exact stock-for-stock exchange, without a cash supplement, that Clark refused when he agreed to the merger.

Because the parties chose to structure the exchange as a tax-free reorganization under § 354(a)(1), and because the pro rata distribution to Clark of $3,250,000 during this reorganization had the effect of a dividend under § 356(a)(2), I dissent.[2]

NOTE

The issue decided by *Clark* involved higher stakes under the 1954 Code (which governed the case) than it did at the time of the decision (because under the 1986 Tax Act, ordinary income and capital gains rates were the same) or than it does today (given the treatment of dividends under the 2003 Tax Act). Under current law, what would be at stake in *Clark*? (Hint: even less than in other parts of corporate tax law where dividend/sale treatment is at issue, because here the basis amount enters the calculation *before* asking whether the calculated "income" amount should be taxed as a dividend or a sale.) Would corporate shareholders prefer a rule that made dividend characterization more or less likely? After *Clark*, under what circumstances is dividend treatment likely? As a matter of sound statutory construction and sensible Subchapter C policy, which of the opinions in *Clark* is more persuasive?

Revenue Ruling 84–114

1984–2 C.B. 90.

ISSUE

When nonvoting preferred stock and cash are received in an integrated transaction by a shareholder in exchange for voting common stock in a recapitalization described in section 368(a)(1)(E)... does the receipt of cash have the effect of the distribution of a dividend within the meaning of section 356(a)(2)?

---

to make fact-specific inquiries into whether boot distributions accompanying corporate reorganizations occur on a pro rata basis to shareholders of the acquired corporation, and thus threaten a bailout of the transferor corporation's earnings and profits escaping a proper dividend tax treatment.

    [2] The majority's alternative holding that no statutory merger occurred at all—rather a taxable sale—is difficult to understand: All parties stipulate to the merger, which, in turn was approved under West Virginia law; and Congress endorsed exactly such tax-free corporate transactions pursuant to its § 368(a)(1) reorganization regime. However apt the speculated sale analogy may be, if the April 3 Merger Agreement amounts to a sale of Clark's stock to NL, and not the intended merger, Clark would be subject to taxation on his full gain of over $10 million. The fracas over tax treatment of the cash boot would be irrelevant.

FACTS

Corporation X had outstanding 420 shares of voting common stock of which A owned 120 shares and B, C and D each owned 100 shares. A, B, C and D were not related within the meaning of section 318(a). . . X adopted a plan of recapitalization that permitted a shareholder to exchange each of 30 shares of voting common stock for either one share of nonvoting preferred stock or cash. Pursuant to the plan, A first exchanged 15 shares of voting common stock for cash and then exchanged 15 shares of voting common stock for 15 shares of nonvoting preferred stock. The facts and circumstances surrounding these exchanges were such that the exchanges constituted two steps in a single integrated transaction for purposes of sections 368(a)(1)(E) and 356(a)(2). The nonvoting preferred stock had no conversion features. In addition, the dividend and liquidation rights payable to A on 15 shares of nonvoting preferred stock were substantially less than the dividend and liquidation rights payable to A on 30 shares of voting common stock. B, C, and D did not participate in the exchange and will retain all their voting common stock in X. X had a substantial amount of post–1913 earnings and profits.

The exchange by A of voting common stock for nonvoting preferred stock and cash qualified as a recapitalization within the meaning of section 868(a)(1)(E) of the Code.

LAW AND ANALYSIS

Rev. Rul. 74–515, 1974–2 C.B. 118, and Rev. Rul. 74–516, 19742 C.B. 121, state that whether a reorganization distribution to which section 356 of the Code applies has the effect of a dividend must be determined by examining the facts and circumstances surrounding the distribution and looking to the principles for determining dividend equivalency developed under section 356(a)(2) and other provisions of the Code. . . Rev. Rul. 74–516 indicates that in making a dividend equivalency determination under section 356(a)(2), it is proper to analogize to section 302 in appropriate cases. In Shimberg v. United States [577 F.2d 283 (5th Cir. 1978)], the courts indicated that in making a dividend equivalency determination under section 356(a)(2), an analogy to section 302 may be appropriate in cases involving single entity reorganizations.

In United States v. Davis [page 170 supra], the Supreme Court of the United States held that a redemption must result in a meaningful reduction of the shareholder's proportionate interest in the corporation in order not to be essentially equivalent to a dividend under section 302(b)(1) of the Code.

Rev. Rul. 75–502, 1975–2 C.B. 111, sets forth factors to be considered in determining whether a reduction in a shareholder's proportionate interest in a corporation is meaningful within the meaning of *Davis*. The factors considered are a shareholder's right to vote and exercise control, to participate in current earnings and accumulated surplus, and to share in net assets on liquidation. The reduction in the right to vote is of particular significance when a redemption causes a redeemed shareholder to lose the potential for controlling the redeeming corporation by acting in concert with only one other shareholder. See Rev. Rul. 76–364, 1976–2 C.B. 91.

The specific issue is whether, in determining dividend equivalency under section 356(a)(2) . . ., it is proper to look solely at the change in A's proportionate interest in X that resulted from A's exchange of voting common stock for cash, or instead, whether consideration should be given to the total change in A's proportionate interest in X that resulted from the exchange of voting common stock for both cash and nonvoting preferred stock.

In Rev. Rul. 55–745, 1955–2 C.B. 223, the Internal Revenue Service announced that for purposes of section 302(b)(3). . . it would follow the decision in Zenz v. Quinlivan [page 219 supra], that a complete termination of shareholder interest may be achieved when a shareholder's entire stock interest in a corporation is disposed of partly through redemption and partly through sale. See also Rev. Rul. 75–447, 1975–2 C.B. 113, in which the *Zenz* rationale was applied to section 302(b)(2).

Since the exchange of voting common stock for cash and the exchange of voting common stock for nonvoting preferred stock constitute an integrated transaction, in this situation involving a single corporation it is proper to apply the *Zenz* rationale so that both exchanges are taken into consideration in determining whether there has been a meaningful reduction of A's proportionate interest in X within the meaning of *Davis*. Compare Rev. Rul. 75–83, 1975–1 C.B. 112, which holds that a distribution in connection with a transaction qualifying under section 368(a)(1)(A) . . . will be viewed as having been made by the acquired or transferor corporation and not by the acquiring or transferee corporation for purposes of making a dividend equivalency determination under section 356(a)(2).

If the exchange of voting common stock for preferred stock and cash in this situation had been tested under section 302 . . . as a redemption, it would not have qualified under section 302(b)(2) or (3) because there was neither an adequate reduction in A's voting stock interest nor a complete termination of that interest. In determining whether this situation is analogous to a redemption meeting the requirements of section 302(b)(1), it is significant that A's interest in the voting common stock of X was reduced from 28.57 percent (120/420) to 23.08 percent (90/390) so that A went from a position of holding a number of shares of voting common stock that afforded A control of X if A acted in concert with only one other shareholder, to a position where such action was not possible. Moreover, it is significant that A no longer holds the largest voting stock interest in X. In addition, although A received dividend and liquidation rights from the 15 shares of nonvoting preferred stock, these were substantially less than the dividend and liquidation rights of the 30 shares of voting common stock A surrendered. Accordingly, the requirements of section 302(b)(1) would have been met if the transaction had been tested under section 302, and, therefore, the cash received by A did not have the effect of the distribution of a dividend within the meaning of section 356(a)(2).

HOLDING

When A received cash and nonvoting preferred stock of X in an integrated transaction in exchange for voting common stock of X in a recapitalization described in section 368(a)(1)(E)... the receipt of cash did not have the effect of the distribution of a dividend within the meaning of section 356(a)(2).

NOTE

In some cases, receipt of nonqualified preferred stock in an exchange is treated as equity, both under §§ 354 and 356. Specifically, receipt of nonqualified preferred stock in exchange for common or preferred stock triggers boot analysis because the nonqualified preferred stock is an "improved" position with more debt-like characteristics. However, if nonqualified preferred stock is received in exchange for nonqualified preferred stock or "substantially identical" preferred stock, then nonrecognition treatment prevails. Treas. Reg. §§ 1.354–1(f); 1.356–7.

8. SUBSIDIARY'S DEALINGS WITH STOCK IN PARENT

A corporation recognizes no gain or loss from buying and selling its own stock. § 1032. What if a wholly owned subsidiary buys and sells parent stock? Rev. Rul. 70–305, 1970–1 C.B. 169, held that stock purchased and resold on the open market by a subsidiary of the issuing corporation was not treasury stock, and that gain or loss would be recognized to the subsidiary on the transaction. Compare Litton Business Systems, Inc., 61 T.C. 367 (1973), in which a subsidiary acquired a cost basis in its parent's stock through a bona fide purchase on "advance account," then used that stock to acquire the assets of an unrelated company in a qualifying "C" reorganization.

In Rev. Rul. 74–503, 1974–2 C.B. 117, X Corporation transferred its own treasury shares to Y Corporation in exchange for newly issued Y shares of equal aggregate value, constituting 80 percent of the latter's outstanding stock. The ruling held that sections 351 and 1032 prevented recognition of gain to X or Y, and each was said to take a zero basis in the other's stock. However, in Rev. Rul. 2006–2, 2006–2 I.R.B. 1, the Service revoked the 1974 ruling and has stated that the "zero basis question" is under study. No additional guidance has been issued.

9. NONDIVISIVE D REORGANIZATIONS

To qualify as a tax free reorganization recall that under § 368(a)(1)(D) (which requires that the transaction fulfill the requirements of § 354 or § 356 where boot is involved) the transferee must receive "substantially all" of the transferor assets *and* the stocks and securities and property received by the transferor in the exchange must be distributed according to the reorganization plan. § 354(b)(1); § 356(a).

In 2009, the Service issued final regulations regarding nondivisive D reorganizations. Treas. Reg. § 1.368–2(l). They include provisions that a transaction can constitute a D reorganization even though no stock of the transferee is issued in the deal, *if*, the issuance would have been meaningless because the parties were commonly owned in identical proportions (the "deemed issuance" rule). Unfortunately, this "deemed issuance" rule created problems for forward triangular mergers and triangular C reorganizations.

To appreciate the problem, consider the following scenario (which is essentially an "internal" triangular merger)*: P corp. has 2 subsidiaries, S1 and S2; and S2 has a subsidiary, Q. S1 intends to transfer its assets to Q (the 2nd tier subsidiary of S2) in either a triangular C or a forward triangular merger. In the triangular C, the S1 assets go to Q and S1 gets S2 stock. In a forward triangular merger, S1 assets go to Q in a statutory merger for S2 stock.

The problem arises because the new regulations deem an issuance of transferee stock under these facts (common ownership). Thus, in the triangular C case, the deemed issuance of Q stock now creates a C reorganization/D reorganization overlap and the D reorganization rules prevail. § 368(a)(2)(A).

In the forward triangular merger case, the transaction fails § 368(a)(2)(D) which bars the use of the acquiring corporation's (Q's) stock in the transaction. Both transactions are jettisoned from their "intended" reorganization rules and into D reorganization rules. Why does this create a problem? Because S2 is no longer a "party to the reorganization" and receipt of this stock by P corp. is "other property" triggering potential taxation. This result was unintended in the original 2006 Temporary Regulations, thus in February 2007, the Service revised those earlier regulations to provide that the deemed issuance rules do not apply if the transaction constitutes a triangular reorganization. T.D. 9313 (February 2007).

VI. CORPORATE FISSION—SPIN–OFFS AND OTHER CORPORATE PROLIFERATIONS

A. INTRODUCTION AND HISTORY

Lawyers have coined brief phrases to describe four of the most common types of corporate divisions—transactions in which some or all of the assets held by one corporation are transferred to one or more corporations, and some or all of the shareholders of the transferor become shareholders in the transferee:

Spin-off: Corporation A transfers some of its assets to Corporation B in exchange for all of the latter's authorized stock. Corporation A thereupon distributes a pro rata dividend to its shareholders consisting of the stock it

---

* See, e.g., Willens, The D Reorganization Expansion Went a Bit Too Far, 114 Tax Notes 1261 (March 26, 2007).

receives in B. A's shareholders now own stock in both A and B. (In some cases a spin-off involves the pro rata distribution of the stock of an old subsidiary, one not formed or one whose stock was not purchased as part of a plan that included distribution of the stock.)

Split-off: The transaction is very much the same as a spin-off, except that Corporation A distributes the B stock to its shareholders in redemption of a proportionate share of their stock in A. As with a spin-off, the shareholders of A now own stock in both A and B, but in the aggregate they own fewer shares (not a lower percentage) of the A stock.

Split-up: Corporation A transfers part of its assets to Corporation B in exchange for all of B's stock and transfers the remainder of its assets to Corporation C for all of its stock. A then liquidates, distributing the stock of B and C in retirement of its own outstanding stock. The shareholders now own stock in B and C in place of their stock in the defunct Corporation A.

Spin-away: B, a corporation with two separate businesses, desires to merge one of its businesses with A, an unrelated corporation. Prior to the merger, B transfers one of its businesses to a separate corporation in either a spin-off or split-off. As a result of the "spin-away," the stock in one of B's businesses is owned exclusively by shareholders of B, while the shares in the corporation resulting from the merger are owned by both A's and B's shareholders.

The situations posed are prototypes, not exclusive. The principal tax issues are usually these: (1) recognition of income or loss to the shareholders on receipt of stock in the transferee corporations; (2) basis of the shareholders in the stock they receive; (3) recognition of gain or loss to the transferor corporation; and (4) basis of assets in the hands of the transferee corporations. Sections 355, 356(b), and 368(a)(1)(D) are the provisions primarily involved. Sections 351, 361, and 358 also play roles.

Gregory v. Helvering, page 445 supra, involved a spin-off in which the taxpayer unsuccessfully claimed that the distribution of the transferee corporation's stock was tax-free under § 112(g) of the Revenue Act of 1928 (the earliest version of the current § 355) as part of the early version of the "D" reorganization. Why did Mrs. Gregory fail under the 1928 Act? Would she fail under current law?

In 1934 Congress repealed § 112(g) of the 1928 Act as part of a legislative program to eliminate what it then thought were unwarranted tax avoidance devices. Tax-free spin-offs returned to the statute in 1951 as § 112(b)(11) of the 1939 Code. With modification, the provision was continued in the 1954 Code as § 355. Although earlier statutory versions required a "plan of reorganization," § 355 does not. Frequently, however, a corporate division may be part of a "D" reorganization. When it is not (and even when it is), § 351 may operate to avoid recognition to the transferor corporation. If there is a "D" reorganization, § 361 will be operative, often along with § 351. Where a statutory merger is divisive, the tax-free status of the transaction must be assessed under § 355, not § 368(a)(1)(A). Rev. Rul. 2000–5,

2000–1 C.B. 436 ("Congress intended that § 355 be the sole means under which divisive transactions will be afforded tax free status").

B. STATUTORY ISSUES

1. PURPOSE

Rafferty v. Commissioner

452 F.2d 767 (1st Cir. 1971), *cert. denied*, 408 U.S. 922 (1972).

■ Before ALDRICH, CHIEF JUDGE, MCENTEE and COFFIN, CIRCUIT JUDGES.

■ MCENTEE, CIRCUIT JUDGE. Taxpayers, Joseph V. Rafferty and wife, appeal from a decision of the Tax Court. which held that a distribution to them of all the outstanding stock of a real estate holding corporation did not meet the requirements of § 355 of the Internal Revenue Code of 1954 and therefore was taxable as a dividend. Our opinion requires a construction of § 355 and the regulations thereunder.

The facts, some of which have been stipulated, are relatively simple. The taxpayers own all the outstanding shares of Rafferty Brown Steel Co., Inc. (hereinafter RBS), a Massachusetts corporation engaged in the processing and distribution of cold rolled sheet and strip steel in Longmeadow, Massachusetts. In May 1960, at the suggestion of his accountant, Rafferty organized Teragram Realty Co., Inc., also a Massachusetts corporation. In June of that year RBS transferred its Longmeadow real estate to Teragram in exchange for all of the latter's outstanding stock. Thereupon Teragram leased back this real estate to RBS for ten years at an annual rent of $42,000. In 1962 the taxpayers also organized Rafferty Brown Steel Co., Inc., of Connecticut (RBS Conn.), which corporation acquired the assets of Hawkridge Brothers, a general steel products warehouse in Waterbury, Connecticut. Since its inception the taxpayers have owned all of the outstanding stock in RBS Conn. From 1962 to 1965 Hawkridge leased its real estate in Waterbury to RBS Conn. In 1965 Teragram purchased some unimproved real estate in Waterbury and built a plant there. In the same year it leased this plant to RBS Conn. for a term of fourteen years. Teragram has continued to own and lease the Waterbury real estate to RBS Conn. and the Longmeadow realty to RBS, which companies have continued up to the present time to operate their businesses at these locations.

During the period from 1960 through 1965 Teragram derived all of its income from rent paid by RBS and RBS Conn. Its earned surplus increased from $4,119.05 as of March 31, 1961, to $46,743.35 as of March 31, 1965. The earned surplus of RBS increased from $331,117.97 as of June 30, 1959, to $535,395.77 as of June 30, 1965. In August 1965, RBS distributed its Teragram stock to the taxpayers. Other than this distribution, neither RBS nor Teragram has paid any dividends.

Joseph V. Rafferty has been the guiding force behind all three corporations, RBS, RBS Conn., and Teragram. He is the president and treasurer of

Teragram which, while it has no office or employees, keeps separate books and records and filed separate tax returns for the years in question.

On various occasions Rafferty consulted his accountant about estate planning, particularly about the orderly disposition of RBS. While he anticipated that his sons would join him at RBS, he wanted to exclude his daughters (and/or his future sons-in-law) from the active management of the steel business. He wished, however, to provide them with property which would produce a steady income. The accountant recommended the formation of Teragram, the distribution of its stock, and the eventual use of this stock as future gifts to the Rafferty daughters. The taxpayers acted on this advice and also on the accountant's opinion that the distribution of Teragram stock would meet the requirements of § 355.

In their 1965 return the taxpayers treated the distribution of Teragram stock as a nontaxable transaction under § 355. The Commissioner viewed it, however, as a taxable dividend and assessed a deficiency. He claimed (a) that the distribution was used primarily as a device for the distribution of the earnings and profits of RBS or Teragram or both, and (b) that Teragram did not meet the active business requirements of § 355.

We turn first, to the Tax Court's finding that there was no device because there was an adequate business purpose for the separation and distribution of Teragram stock. In examining this finding we are guided by the rule that the taxpayer has the burden of proving that the transaction was not used principally as a device. . . Initially, we are disturbed by the somewhat uncritical nature of the Tax Court's finding of a business purpose. Viewing the transaction from the standpoint of RBS, RBS Conn., or Teragram, no immediate business reason existed for the distribution of Teragram's stock to the taxpayers. Over the years the businesses had been profitable, as witnessed by the substantial increase of the earned surplus of every component, yet none had paid dividends. The primary purpose for the distribution found by the Tax Court was to facilitate Rafferty's desire to make bequests to his children in accordance with an estate plan. This was a personal motive. Taxpayers seek to put it in terms relevant to the corporation by speaking of avoidance of possible interference with the operation of the steel business by future sons-in-law, pointing to Coady v. Commissioner, 33 T.C. 771 (1960), *aff'd per curiam*, 289 F.2d 490 (6th Cir. 1961) [page 552 infra.].

In *Coady*, however, the separation was in response to a seemingly irreconcilable falling-out between the owners of a business. This falling-out had already occurred and, manifestly, the separation was designed to save the business from a substantial, present problem. . . In the case at bar there was, at best, only an envisaged possibility of future debilitating nepotism. If avoidance of this danger could be thought a viable business purpose at all, it was so remote and so completely under the taxpayers' control that if, in other respects the transaction was a "device," that purpose could not satisfy the taxpayers' burden of proving that it was not being used "principally as a device" within the meaning of the statute.

Our question, therefore, must be whether taxpayers' desire to put their stockholdings into such form as would facilitate their estate planning, viewed in the circumstances of the case, was a sufficient personal business purpose to prevent the transaction at bar from being a device for the distribution of earnings and profits. While we remain of the view, which we first expressed in Lewis v. Commissioner, 176 F.2d 646 (1st Cir. 1949), that a purpose of a shareholder, qua shareholder, may in some cases save a transaction from condemnation as a device, we do not agree with the putative suggestion in Estate of Parshelsky v. Commissioner, 303 F.2d 14, 19 (2d Cir. 1962), that any investment purpose of the shareholders is sufficient. Indeed, in *Lewis*, although we depreciated the distinction between shareholder and corporate purpose, we were careful to limit that observation to the facts of that case, and to caution that the business purpose formula "must not become a substitute for independent analysis." . . . For that reason we based our decision on the Tax Court's finding that the transaction was "undertaken for reasons germane to the continuance of the corporate business." Id. at 647.

This is not to say that a taxpayer's personal motives cannot be considered, but only that a distribution which has considerable potential for use as a device for distributing earnings and profits should not qualify for tax-free treatment on the basis of personal motives unless those motives are germane to the continuance of the corporate business. . . We prefer this approach over reliance upon formulations such as "business purpose," and "active business." . . . The facts of the instant case illustrate the reason for considering substance. Dividends are normally taxable to shareholders upon receipt. Had the taxpayers received cash dividends and made investments to provide for their female descendants, an income tax would, of course, have resulted. Accordingly, once the stock was distributed, if it could potentially be converted into cash without thereby impairing taxpayers' equity interest in RBS, the transaction could easily be used to avoid taxes. The business purpose here alleged, which could be fully satisfied by a bail-out of dividends, is not sufficient to prove that the transaction was not being principally so used.

Given such a purpose, the only question remaining is whether the substance of the transaction is such as to leave the taxpayer in a position to distribute the earnings and profits of the corporation away from, or out of the business. The first factor to be considered is how easily the taxpayer would be able, were he so to choose, to liquidate or sell the spun-off corporation. Even if both corporations are actively engaged in their respective trades, if one of them is a business based principally on highly liquid investment-type, passive assets, the potential for a bail-out is real. The question here is whether the property transferred to the newly organized corporation had a readily realizable value, so that the distributee-shareholders could, if they ever wished, "obtain such cash or property or the cash equivalent thereof, either by selling the distributed stock or liquidating the corporation, thereby converting what would otherwise be dividends taxable as ordinary income into capital gain. . ." . . . In this connection we note that the Tax Court found that a sale of Teragram's real estate properties could be "easily arranged." . . . Indeed, taxpayers themselves stressed the fact that the buildings were capable of multiple use.

There must, however, be a further question. If the taxpayers could not effect a bail-out without thereby impairing their control over the ongoing business, the fact that a bail-out is theoretically possible should not be enough to demonstrate a device because the likelihood of it ever being so used is slight. "[A] bail-out ordinarily means that earnings and profits have been drawn off without impairing the shareholder's residual equity interest in the corporation's earning power, growth potential, or voting control." . . . If sale would adversely affect the shareholders of the on-going company, the assets cannot be said to be sufficiently separated from the corporate solution and the gain sufficiently crystallized as to be taxable. . . In this case, there was no evidence that the land and buildings at which RBS carried on its steel operations were so distinctive that the sale of Teragram stock would impair the continued operation of RBS, or that the sale of those buildings would in any other way impair Rafferty's control and other equity interests in RBS.[7]

In the absence of any direct benefit to the business of the original company, and on a showing that the spin-off put saleable assets in the hands of the taxpayers, the continued retention of which was not needed to continue the business enterprise, or to accomplish taxpayers' purposes, we find no sufficient factor to overcome the Commissioner's determination that the distribution was principally a device to distribute earnings and profits.

[The court's discussion of whether Teragram failed to meet the "active business" requirement of § 355 is omitted.*]

NOTES

1. In view of the outer parenthetical in § 355(a)(1)(B), what circumstances might demonstrate that the transaction was used as a device for the siphoning of earnings and profits? What do you think led to the outer and inner parentheticals? See Treas. Reg. § 1.355–2(d).

2. In Estate of Parshelsky v. Commissioner, 303 F.2d 14, 19 (2d Cir. 1962) the court held that the reason for the reorganization may properly be related to the personal or noncorporate business interests of the shareholders. The *Rafferty* court criticizes this, see page 541 supra. Regarding the "business purpose" requirement, Treas. Reg. § 1.355–2(b)(2) states:

> A shareholder's purpose . . . is not a corporate business purpose. Depending upon the facts of a particular case, however, a shareholder purpose for a transaction may be so nearly coextensive with a corporate business purpose as to preclude any distinction between them. In such a case, the transaction is carried out for one or more corporate business purposes.

---

[7] Our conclusion is reinforced by the fact that RBS and RBS Conn. were guaranteed occupancy of Teragram property under long term leases at fixed rents.

* The "active business" requirements will be treated at page 547 et seq. infra.—ED.

Cf. Rev. Rul. 76–527, 1976–2 C.B. 103 (spin-off to make subsidiary more attractive to prospective merger partner had a valid business purpose); Rev. Rul. 75–337, 1975–2 C.B. 124 (distribution of a subsidiary's stock in complete redemption of inactive shareholders, and in reduction of interest of aging majority shareholder, served to protect corporation's automobile dealership franchise).

3. In Rev. Proc. 96–30, the Service provides a checklist and guidelines for whether a transaction satisfies the corporate business purpose requirement. Guidelines cover examples of business purpose including facilitating the retention of key employees, borrowings, stock offerings, cost savings, competition, planned acquisition, and risk reduction. The Service will not, however, determine in advance whether a distribution (1) meets the business purpose test; (2) is used principally as a device, or (3) is part of a plan under § 355(e). Rev. Proc. 2003–48, 2003–2 C.B. 86 (modifying Rev. Proc. 96–30 and Rev. Proc. 2003–3). See, e.g., Rev. Rul. 2003–74, 2003–2 C.B. 77 (§ 355 distribution of a paper products subsidiary had a business purpose where the distributing corporation sought to separate the subsidiary's business from its own, software technology, in order to allow management to concentrate on each business independently).

4. The question whether a distribution under § 355 has a business purpose must be distinguished from the question whether expenses incident to the distribution are deductible "business expenses." See Bilar Tool & Die Corp. v. Commissioner, 530 F.2d 708 (6th Cir. 1976) (split-up to resolve shareholder dispute had a lasting benefit to both resulting corporations, so the expenses incident to the split-up were paid "to enhance capital" and nondeductible).

5. After the 2003 Tax Act, with dividends taxed at the low 15% capital gains rate, the need to prevent shareholder bailout seems less pressing. Of course, basis recovery remains a distinction between currently taxable dividend distributions and nontaxable distributions later taxed on sale. The remaining difference, timing, raises questions about how § 355 should be structured in the future.

6. In Letter Ruling 2005–45001, the Service accepted a spin-off designed to implement a regional business model.

2. "ACTIVE CONDUCT OF A TRADE OR BUSINESS"

Elliott v. Commissioner
32 T.C. 283 (1959).

■ DRENNEN, JUDGE. . . The only issue for determination is whether the distribution of all the stock of Centrifix Management Corporation, a wholly owned subsidiary, hereinafter referred to as Management, by Centrifix Corporation, hereinafter referred to as Centrifix, to Randall T. Elliott, the principal stockholder of Centrifix, on December 15, 1954, was taxable as a long-term capital gain to Elliott or qualified as a nontaxable "split-off" under section 355. . .

FINDINGS OF FACT

... At all times material hereto, Centrifix was an Ohio corporation formed in 1926... Centrifix was organized to engineer and develop apparatus for the purification and separation of liquids and gases, and at all times material hereto was engaged in said business.

Management was incorporated under the laws of Ohio on April 22, 1950, as a wholly owned subsidiary corporation of Centrifix. At all times material hereto it had authorized capital of 150 shares of no-par common stock having a stated value of $100 per share.

In 1946, Centrifix acquired property at 3029 Prospect Avenue, Cleveland, Ohio, consisting of an old 2–story house with caretakers quarters and a carriage house in the rear. Centrifix occupied approximately one-half of the available space in the house and carriage house as an office and shop for its engineering business and made available for rent to various tenants the balance of the property. Centrifix continued to use part of this property in its business and rented the balance of the property until it was sold in 1950.

In 1950, Centrifix sold the property at 3029 Prospect Avenue and acquired property at 3608 Payne Avenue, Cleveland, Ohio. When the new property on Payne Avenue was acquired, it was transferred to Management in exchange for all of the stock of Management in a transaction that was tax free under section [351]...

During the period from April 27, 1950, to December 15, 1954, Management owned and operated the Payne Avenue property. The property consisted of land and a 3–story brick loft building having a total area of 28,144 square feet, of which Centrifix leased 14,468 square feet, Tetrad Company, unrelated, leased approximately 5,200 square feet, and the balance was unoccupied but was available for rental to third parties.

On December 15, 1954, Randall T. Elliott surrendered to Centrifix the 1,852¾ shares of cumulative preferred stock of Centrifix which he owned, in exchange for which Centrifix transferred to Elliott 150 shares being all of the authorized common stock of Management, and canceled an indebtedness of $5,241.48 which had been owing from Elliott to Centrifix. No other consideration was involved in this transaction... At the same time Elliott agreed to the cancellation of cumulative past-due dividends on the preferred stock in the amount of $242,894.75.

On December 15, 1954, the 150 shares of no-par-value common stock of Management distributed in the above transaction to Elliott had a fair market value of $78,837.34, and the adjusted basis of 1,852¾ shares of Centrifix cumulative preferred stock in the hands of Elliott was $750... As of December 15, 1954, and December 31, 1954, Centrifix had no accumulated earnings and profits.

In their 1954 return, petitioners reported no gain or loss on the above transaction.

During that part of the year 1946 after Centrifix acquired the Prospect Avenue property, and through that part of the year 1950, prior to the time said property was sold, Centrifix realized gross rental income from the Prospect Avenue property, gross income from all sources, net income from all sources, and reported net taxable income for each of the years 1946 through 1950 as follows:

Period covered	Gross rental income	Gross income[1]	Net income[1]	Net Taxable income
1946	$380.90	$150,120.18	$ 2,461.26	($ 707.39)
1947	591.00	253,193.64	20,927.09	24,609.37
1948	780.00	238,280.53	13,516.60	17,424.16
1949	780.00	243,344.39	16,765.13	20,152.71
1950[2]	325.00	324,253.26	19,932.20	26,176.20

[1] All sources.

[2] 5 months

The gross rental value of the entire Prospect Avenue property would have been between $1,700 and $1,800 per year during the period it was owned by Centrifix, if rented on a commercial basis. Centrifix made no allocation of expenses in connection with the Prospect Avenue property and it could not be determined from its books whether the rental portion of the property produced a net income or a net loss.

During the period April 22, 1950, to December 31, 1954, Management realized gross rental income and net income as follows:

Period covered	Gross rental income	Net income
1950	$ 7,257.17	$ 484.37
1951	14,682.44	1,884.79
1952	17,080.00	1,840.43
1953	19,292.00	3,034.64
1954	19,179.00	3,757.60

OPINION

. . . The only issue is whether the distribution by Centrifix of all the stock of its wholly owned subsidiary, Management, to its principal stockholder, Elliott, qualifies as a nontaxable distribution under section 355. . .

. . . Respondent agreed in the opening statement of his counsel that the transaction was not used principally as a distribution of earnings and profits of either corporation. Both parties are in agreement that all requirements of section 355(a) are satisfied, except the requirement of subsection (b) relating to the active conduct of businesses.

Respondent does not question the fact that Management had been engaged in the real estate rental business from the date the Payne Avenue property was conveyed to it in April of 1950 to the date of distribution of its stock to Elliott on December 15, 1954, a period of less than 5 years, but does contend that such business had not been actively conducted by either Centrifix or Management prior to April of 1950, so that the 5–year active conduct of business requirement of subsection (b) was not satisfied. Respondent, therefore, determined that the distribution, to the extent that it exceeded basis, was taxable to Elliott as a capital gain, Centrifix having had no earnings or profits at the time of the distribution.

Petitioners contend that all the requirements of subsection (b), including the 5–year active conduct of the real estate rental business, were satisfied. So we are concerned only with whether the requirements of subsection (b) relating to active conduct of businesses are satisfied.

Subsection (b) of section 355 subjects the nonrecognition of gain or loss to a shareholder provided in subsection (a) to certain conditions. One of those conditions is that the distributing corporation and the controlled corporation are engaged immediately after the distribution in the active conduct of a trade or business. A corporation may be regarded as engaged in the active conduct of a trade or business only if, inter alia, "such trade or business has been actively conducted throughout the 5–year period ending on the date of the distribution." See sec. 355(b)(2)(B). Respondent concedes that Management was engaged in the real estate rental business immediately after the distribution, but argues that it was not actively engaged in that business for a total of 5 years prior to the distribution.

Management was not incorporated until April 22, 1950. The Payne Avenue property was acquired by Centrifix at some time during 1950 and was transferred to Management in exchange for its stock. This stock was distributed to Elliott on December 15, 1954. Obviously, Management did not actively conduct and could not have actively conducted any business for 5 years prior to the distribution since it had been in existence for less than 5 years prior to December 15, 1954. Thus, the 5–year requirement of section 355(b)(2)(B) is not satisfied by the activities of Management alone, and cannot be satisfied under any circumstances in this case unless Centrifix actively conducted the same business for a period of at least 4½ months prior to the transfer of the Payne Avenue property to Management, and unless such a period of operation by Centrifix can be added to the period that Management conducted the business in order to satisfy the above requirement. We will assume for the purpose of further discussion that two such periods may be added together.

The issue then becomes whether Centrifix actively conducted a real estate rental business within the meaning of section 355(b) for a period of time prior to the formation of Management in 1950.

. . . Centrifix purchased an old house with a carriage house in the rear located on Prospect Avenue in Cleveland, Ohio, in 1946. Centrifix occupied about half the space in this property as its office and shop and rented the balance of the property to various tenants from the time it was acquired until it was sold in 1950. The gross rentals received did not exceed $780 per year in any of these years, which sum represented about 40 percent of the rental value of the entire property, based on an 8 percent gross return on the cost of the property. No allocation was made on the books of the company of that portion of the expenses attributable to the rented portion of the property, and there is no evidence with respect to the net income or loss attributable to that portion of the property.

. . . The gross rental income represented a very small part of the total gross income of Centrifix. There is no evidence of any specific activity on the part of the management of Centrifix in renting this property and no evidence that Centrifix ever engaged in any other real estate rental activities. . .

When the Prospect Avenue property was sold in 1950 and the new Payne Avenue property acquired, the new property was put in the name of the newly formed subsidiary corporation, Management, which thereafter leased about one-half of the new property to Centrifix, and the balance to other tenants. Management did not engage in any other business activities and Centrifix continued in the engineering business.

On this evidence we are not convinced that prior to 1950 Centrifix could be considered to have been actively conducting the same business subsequently conducted by Management within the meaning of section 355(b). What constitutes a trade or business is not defined in section 355 or anywhere else in the Internal Revenue Code. This Court held in John D. Fackler, 45 B.T.A. 708 (1941), *aff'd*, 133 F.2d 509 (C.A. 6), that where the owner of depreciable property devotes it to rental purposes and exclusively to the production of taxable income, the property is used by him in a trade or business and depreciation is allowable thereon. Since the *Fackler* case, we have also held that a single piece of rental property constitutes property used in a trade or business so as to be excluded from the definition of "capital assets" regardless of whether taxpayer was engaged in any other trade or business, Leland Hazard, 7 T.C. 372 (1946), and in Anders I. Lagreide, 23 T.C. 508 (1954), that real estate devoted to rental purposes constitutes use of the property in trade or business for purposes of determining operating loss carrybacks regardless of whether it is the only property so used, without too much inquiry into the activity of the taxpayer in renting and managing the property. . . However, the *Fackler*, *Hazard*, and *Lagreide* cases are not authority for holding that the incidental rental of that portion of real estate used in a trade or business which is not needed for the principal business constitutes the active conduct of a rental business within the meaning of section 355(b). . . By this we do not mean to imply that rental of a substantial part of property occupied in part by the owner for the conduct of its principal business cannot qualify as the active conduct of a trade or business within the meaning of section 355(b). But in section 355, we are concerned with the active conduct of a trade or business, and we must examine that phraseology in the light of the purpose for which it is used in this particular section of the Code. . .

This provision was a part of section 353 of the Revenue Act of 1954 as originally introduced in the House of Representatives (H.R. 8300, 83d

Cong., 2d Sess.). That section had no requirement relative to the active conduct of a trade or business either before or after the distribution. The Senate Finance Committee rewrote this provision as section 355 of its version of the bill, to introduce the requirement of active conduct of a trade or business both before and after the distribution, the stated purpose for the 5–year predistribution active conduct of a trade or business requirement being to provide a safeguard against avoidance not contained in the present law. See S. Rept. No. 1622, 83d Cong., 2d Sess., p. 50. The Senate thereby chose the 5–year active conduct of a trade or business limitation as one method of safeguarding against tax avoidance rather than a 10–year post-distribution penalty provision contained in the House version of the bill. The House accepted the Senate version but with the understanding that a trade or business which had been actively conducted throughout the 5–year period described would meet the requirements even though such trade or business underwent change during the 5year period, such as an addition of new or the dropping of old products, changes in production capacity, and the like, provided the changes were not of such a character as to constitute the acquisition of a new or different business. See H. Rept. No. 2543, 83d Cong., 2d Sess., pp. 37–38.

This requirement in section 355(b) therefore necessitates an examination of the activities of the parent and subsidiary corporations in each of the two or more businesses conducted to determine whether this requirement is satisfied in each individual case. We do not think a mere passive receipt of income from the use of property which is used in the principal trade or business and which is only incidental to, or an incidental use of a part of property used primarily in, the principal business would constitute the active conduct of a trade or business within the meaning of section 355(b) of the Code, whether or not such use of property might constitute a trade or business within the meaning of other sections of the Code.

The Commissioner of Internal Revenue has defined a trade or business for purposes of section 355, in section 1.355–1(c), Income Tax Regs., as consisting of a "specific existing group of activities being carried on for the purpose of earning income or profit from only such group of activities, and the activities included in such group must include every operation which forms a part of, or a step in, the process of earning income or profit from such group. Such group of activities ordinarily must include the collection of income and payment of expenses." . . .

In this case the evidence does not support a conclusion that Centrifix was ever actively conducting a real estate rental business within the meaning of section 355. . .

Why Centrifix did not hold the stock of Management for 4 or 5 additional months to complete the 5–year period prior to distributing Management's stock is not our concern. The fact is that Management had not been actively conducting its trade or business for a period of 5 years at the time of distribution, and we cannot find that Centrifix was actively conducting the same business within the meaning of section 355 prior to the formation of Management The transaction therefore failed to qualify as a tax-free distribution under section 355, and the distribution was taxable as determined by respondent. . .

Decision will be entered for the respondent.

NOTES

1. Would the House proposal in 1954 (page 549 supra) have been a better approach to permitting business readjustments on a tax-free basis while taxing bail-outs? Why? Note the attempt in Treas. Reg. § 1.355–3(c) to give content and some measure of certainty to the phrase "active conduct of a trade or business." Would the House's idea of a bail-out period have been preferable?

2. In 2012 X incorporates Y Corporation to conduct the wholesale and retail plumbing fixture businesses that he has conducted as an individual since 2004. He soon finds it impracticable to run both businesses under one corporate roof. Must he wait five years from incorporation to spin off one of the businesses on a tax-free basis? See § 355(b)(2)(C).

In W. E. Gabriel Fabrication Co., 42 T.C. 545 (1964), the taxpayer and his brother, owners of 70 percent of A Corporation, had a falling out and wanted to separate business interests without waiting the 14 months necessary for the expiration of five years. Corporation A therefore "loaned" taxpayer the assets which, 14 months later, were transferred to a new subsidiary and split off to taxpayer. The Tax Court held the distribution tax-free under § 355, and the Commissioner has acquiesced (see 1965–2 C.B. 5).

3. In King v. Commissioner, 458 F.2d 245 (6th Cir. 1972), spun-off subsidiaries were originally formed for the purpose of constructing truck terminal facilities and leasing them to their parent corporation on a net lease. The leasing activity was held to constitute the active conduct of a trade or business. But see Rafferty v. Commissioner, 452 F.2d 767, 772 (1st Cir. 1971), page 541 supra, stating the active business test as follows: "It is our view that in order to be an active trade or business under § 355 a corporation must engage in entrepreneurial endeavors of such a nature and to such an extent as to qualitatively distinguish its operations from mere investments. Moreover, there should be objective indicia of such corporate operations." A REIT can be engaged in a trade or business under § 355(b) solely by virtue of rental activity. Rev. Rul. 2001–29, 2001–1 C.B. 1348. A corporation that is a general partner in a limited partnership is engaged in the active conduct of a trade or business under § 355(b) where the officers of the corporation "perform active and substantial management functions for the partnership," or where the corporation owns a significant interest in the partnership (perhaps 1/3) and the partnership engages in the active conduct of the trade or business. Rev. Rul. 92–17, 1991–1 C.B. 142, and Rev. Rul. 2007–42, 2007–28 I.R.B. 44(modifying Rev. Rul. 92–17 as it pertains to corporate partners not directly engaged in the management of the partnership).

Rev. Rul. 79–394, 1979–2 C.B. 141, holds that in order to qualify as an active trade or business under § 355, a corporation engaged in leasing real estate must demonstrate considerable day-to-day management and operational activity sufficient to distinguish such conduct from passive investment in real estate. A corporation's lack of salaried employees (the corporation reimbursed a sister corporation for the use of its employees) does not result in its failure to meet the "active trade or business" requirement. Rev. Rul. 80–181, 1980–2 C.B. 121, ruled that the active trade or business requirement is satisfied even though a corporation does not reimburse another corporation for the use of its employees and officers in the conduct of the former's real estate activities (nonreimbursement should be addressed under § 482).

See Rev. Rul. 86–125, 1986–2 C.B. 57, in which the Service ruled that the active business requirement under § 355(b) is not met with regard to a rental office building if the building is managed by an unrelated real estate management company acting as an independent contractor. See also Rev. Rul. 86–126, 1986–2 C.B. 58, in which the Service likewise found that the active business requirement was not met where a corporation leased farmland to tenant farmers who planted, raised, harvested, and sold their crops with limited involvement with the corporation.

4. In 2007, the Service issued proposed regulations specifying the circumstances under which members of a "separate affiliated group" would be treated as a single entity in assessing whether the distributing corporation or the controlled corporation was engaged in a "qualified trade or business." Prop. Reg. § 1.355–3(b). The Service has characterized these regulations as a significant and challenging project and released other § 355 final regulations ahead of these active trade or business regulations in October 2011.

Coady v. Commissioner
33 T.C. 771 (1960), *aff'd per curiam*, 289 F.2d 490 (6th Cir. 1961).

OPINION

■ TIETJENS, JUDGE. . . . The issue for decision is whether the transfer by the Christopher Construction Company of a portion of its assets to E.P. Coady and Co. in exchange for all of the Coady Company's stock, and the subsequent distribution by the Christopher Company of such Coady stock to petitioner in exchange for his Christopher stock, constituted a distribution of stock qualifying for tax-free treatment on the shareholder level under the provisions of section 355. . .

Christopher Construction Co., an Ohio corporation, is now engaged, and for more than 5 years prior to November 15, 1954, was engaged, in the active conduct of a construction business primarily in and around Columbus, Ohio. In an average year the Christopher Company undertook approximately 6 construction contracts, no one of which lasted for more than 2 years. Its gross receipts varied between $1,500,000 and $2,000,000 per year.

At its central office . . ., the Christopher Company kept its books of account, paid its employees, prepared bids for its jobs, and, excepting minor amounts of tools and supplies, made its purchases. In addition, it maintained temporary field offices at each jobsite. It also maintained a central repair and storage depot for its equipment. Equipment in use on particular jobs was kept at the jobsite until work was terminated.

Then, it would either be returned to the central depot or moved to another jobsite.

At all times material hereto, the stock of the Christopher Company was owned by M. Christopher and the petitioner. For a number of years, petitioner owned 35 per cent of that stock and Christopher owned 65 per cent. However, on April 19, 1954, petitioner purchased 15 per cent of the total stock from Christopher. From that date until November 15, 1954, each owned 50 per cent of the company's stock.

Sometime prior to November 15, 1954, differences arose between the petitioner and Christopher. As a result, they entered into an agreement for the division of the Christopher Company into two separate enterprises. Pursuant to that agreement, the Christopher Company, on November 15, 1954, organized E.P. Coady and Co., to which it transferred the following assets, approximating one half the Christopher Company's total assets:

A contract for the construction of a sewage disposal plant at Columbus, Ohio, dated June 1, 1954.

A part of its equipment.

A part of its cash, and certain other items.

In consideration for the receipt of these assets, E.P. Coady and Co. transferred all of its stock to the Christopher Company. The Christopher Company retained the following assets, which were of the same type as those transferred to E.P. Coady and Co.:

A contract for a sewage treatment plant in Charleston, West Virginia.

A part of its equipment.

A part of its cash.

Immediately thereafter, the Christopher Company distributed to the petitioner all of the stock of E.P. Coady and Co. held by it in exchange for all of the stock of the Christopher Company held by petitioner. The fair market value of the stock of E.P. Coady and Co. received by petitioner was $140,000. His basis in the Christopher Company stock surrendered was $72,500.

Since the distribution, both E.P. Coady and Co. and the Christopher Company have been actively engaged in the construction business.

On their 1954 Federal income tax return, petitioner and his wife reported no gain or loss on the exchange of the Christopher Company stock for the stock of E.P. Coady and Co.

Respondent determined that petitioner realized a capital gain on that exchange in the amount of $67,500. . .

Petitioner contends that the distribution to him of the E.P. Coady and Co. stock qualified for tax-free treatment under the provisions of section 355 . . . arguing that it was received pursuant to a distribution of a controlled corporation's stock within the meaning of that section.

Respondent on the other hand maintains petitioner's receipt of the Coady stock did not fall within those distributions favored by section 355, inasmuch as the 5–year active business requirements of 355(b) were not met. More particularly he argues that section 355 does not apply to the separation of a "single business"; and, inasmuch as the Christopher Company was engaged in only one trade or business (construction contracting) the gain realized by petitioner upon receipt of the Coady stock was taxable. As authority for his position respondent points to [Treas. Reg. § 1.355–1(a)] . . . which expressly provides that section 355 does not apply to the division of a single business.

Conceding that the Christopher Company was engaged in a "single business" immediately prior to the instant transaction, petitioner contends that the regulations, insofar as they limit the applicability of section 355 to divisions of only those corporations which have conducted two or more separate and distinct businesses for a 5–year period, are without support in the law, are without justification, are unreasonable and arbitrary, and therefore are invalid.

Thus, the issue is narrowed to the question of whether the challenged portion of the regulations constitutes a valid construction of the statute, or whether it is unreasonable and plainly inconsistent therewith. . . [T]his appears to be a case of first impression. . .

Section 355 . . . represents the latest of a series of legislative enactments designed to deal with the tax effect upon shareholders of various corporate separations. Where the 1939 Code contained three sections, 112(b)(3), 112(b)(11), and 112(g)(1)(D), which controlled the tax impact of these exchanges, present law groups the statutory requirements into two sections, 355 and 368(c). A careful reading of section 355, as well as the Finance Committee report which accompanied its enactment, reveals no language, express or implied, denying tax-free treatment at the shareholder level to a transaction, otherwise qualifying under section 355, on the grounds that it represents the division or separation of a "single" trade or business.

In general, section 355(a) prescribes the form in which a qualifying transaction must be cast, providing that a divisive distribution will not give rise to taxable gain or loss if: (1) The distributing corporation distributes stock or securities of a corporation of which it has, immediately prior to the distribution, 80 per cent control as defined in section 368(c); (2) the distribution is not principally a device for distributing earnings and profits of either the distributing or controlled corporations; (3) the 5–year active business requirements of 355(b) are satisfied; and (4) the distributing corporation distributes either all its stock and securities in the controlled corporation, or so much thereof as constitutes control, as defined in 368(c), and retention of the balance is shown not to be in pursuance of a plan having as one of its principal purposes tax avoidance. The distribution itself must be either to a shareholder with respect to its stock, or a security holder with respect to its securities. With respect to a distribution of stock, the distribution need not be on a pro rata basis; the shareholder need not surrender stock in the distributing corporation; and the distribution need not have been made in pursuance of a plan of reorganization. However, subsection (a) contains no language which would require that the distributing corporation be engaged in more than one trade or business prior to the distribution.

The active business requirements of 355(b)(1) prohibit the tax-free separation of a corporation into active and inactive entities. Section 355(b)(1)(A) extends the provisions of 355(a) only to those divisive distributions where the distributing corporation and the controlled corporation are engaged immediately after the distribution in the active conduct of a trade or business. In the case of those distributions which involve liquidation of the transferor, 355(b)(1)(B) requires that immediately before the distribution the transferor have no assets other than stock or securities in the controlled corporations, and that immediately thereafter each of the controlled corporations is engaged in the active conduct of a trade or business. Neither 355(b)(1)(A) nor (B) concerns itself with the existence of a plurality of businesses per se; rather both speak in terms of a plurality of corporate entities engaged in the active conduct of a trade or business, a distinction we believe to be vital in light of provisions of 355(b)(2).

Section 355(b)(2) details the rules for determining whether a corporation is engaged in the active conduct of a trade or business, and provides that a corporation shall be treated as so engaged, if, and only if: (1) It is engaged in the active conduct of a trade or business, or substantially all its assets consist of stock and securities of a corporation controlled by it immediately after the distribution which is so engaged; (2) such trade or business has been actively conducted throughout the 5–year period ending on the date of the distribution; (3) such trade or business was not acquired within that 5–year period in a transaction in which gain or loss was recognized; and (4) control of a corporation, which at the time of acquisition of control was conducting such trade or business, was not acquired within that 5–year period, or, if acquired within that period, was acquired by reason of a transaction in which no gain or loss was recognized or by reason of such transactions combined with acquisitions made before the beginning of the 5–year period. Again we note the statute avoids the use of the plural when referring to "trade or business," but rather provides that: "[A] corporation shall be treated as engaged in the active conduct of *a* trade or business if and only if . . . it is engaged in the active conduct of *a* trade or business . . . [and] such trade or business has been actively conducted through the 5–year period ending on the date of the distribution." (Emphasis supplied.)

Respondent maintains that a reading of 355(b)(2)(B) in conjunction with the requirement of 355(b)(1) that both "the distributing corporation, *and* the controlled corporation. . . [be] engaged immediately after the distribution in the active conduct of a trade or business" (emphasis supplied) indicates Congress intended the provisions of the statute to apply only where, immediately after the distribution, there exist two separate and distinct businesses, one operated by the distributing corporation and one operated by the controlled corporation, both of which were actively conducted for the 5–year period immediately preceding the distribution. In our judgment the statute does not support this construction.

As noted, the only reference to plurality appears in section 355(b)(1), and deals with corporate entities, not businesses. Recognizing the divisive nature of the transaction, subsection (b)(1) contemplates that where there was only one corporate entity prior to the various transfers, immediately subsequent thereto, there will be two or more *corporations*. In order to insure that a tax-free separation will involve the separation only of those assets attributable to the carrying on of an active trade or business, and further to prevent the tax-free division of an active corporation into active and inactive entities, (b)(1) further provides that each of the surviving corporations must be engaged in the active conduct of *a* trade or business.

A careful reading of the definition of the active conduct of a trade or business contained in subsection (b)(2) indicates that its function is also to prevent the tax-free separation of *active* and *inactive* assets into *active* and *inactive* corporate entities. This is apparent from the use of the adjective "such," meaning before-mentioned, to modify "trade or business" in subsection (b)(2)(B), thus providing that the trade or business, required by (b)(2)(B) to have had a 5–year active history prior to the distribution, is the same trade or business which (b)(2)(A) requires to be actively conducted immediately after the distribution. Nowhere in (b)(2) do we find, as respondent suggests we should, language denying the benefits of section 355 to the division of a single trade or business.

Nor can respondent derive support for his position by reading subsections (b)(1) and (b)(2) together, inasmuch as the plurality resulting therefrom is occasioned, not by any requirement that there be a multiplicity of businesses, but rather by the divisive nature of the transaction itself: i.e., one corporation becoming two or more corporations. Moreover, from the fact that the statute requires, immediately after the distribution, that the surviving corporations each be engaged in the conduct of a trade or business with an active 5–year history, we do not think it inevitably follows that each such trade or business necessarily must have been conducted on an individual basis throughout the 5–year period. As long as the trade or business which has been divided has been actively conducted for 5 years preceding the distribution, and the resulting businesses (each of which in this case, happens to be half of the original whole) are actively conducted after the division, we are of the opinion that the active business requirements of the statute have been complied with.

Respondent argues his construction of section 355 is confirmed by the report of the Senate Committee on Finance which accompanied the 1954 Internal Revenue Code. He refers us to that portion of the report which provides:

Present law contemplates that a tax-free separation shall involve only the separation of assets attributable to the carrying on of an active business. Under the House bill, it is immaterial whether the assets are those used in an active business but if investment assets, for example, are separated into a new corporation, any amount received in respect of such an inactive corporation, whether by a distribution from it or by a sale of its stock, would be treated as ordinary income for a period of 10 years from the date of its creation. Your committee returns to existing law in not permitting the tax free separation of an existing corporation into active and inactive entities. It is not believed that the business need for this kind of transaction is sufficiently great to permit a person in a position to afford a 10–year delay in receiving income to do so at capital gain rather than dividend rates. Your committee requires that *both* the business retained by the distributing company and the business of the corporation the stock of which is distributed must have been actively conducted for the 5 years preceding the distribution, a safeguard against avoidance not contained in existing law. [Emphasis supplied.]

He argues that use of the term "both," with reference to the business retained by the distributing corporation and that operated by the controlled corporation, indicates that Congress intended there be in operation and existence during the 5 years preceding the distribution two or more separate and distinct businesses. We do not agree.

A reading of the quoted section of the report in its entirety reveals that the committee was addressing itself to the nature and the use of the particular assets which were transferred (active v. inactive), rather than to any distinction between one or more businesses. This is obvious when the entire paragraph is considered in the light of its topic sentence. The committee notes that under present law only assets attributable to the carrying on of an active trade or business may be separated tax free. After acknowledging a departure from this requirement in the House bill, the committee disapproves of the position taken by the House, and indicates it is returning to existing law by not permitting the tax-free separation of a corporation into active and inactive entities, and strengthens this provision by requiring that *both* the business retained by the distributing corporation and that of the controlled corporation must have been actively conducted for 5 years preceding the distribution. The excerpt makes no mention of trades or businesses per se. . .

There being no language, either in the statute or committee report, which denies tax-free treatment under section 355 to a transaction solely on the grounds that it represents an attempt to divide a single trade or business, the Commissioner's regulations which impose such a restriction are invalid, and cannot be sustained. Commissioner v. Acker, 361 U.S. 87 (1959). . .

Inasmuch as the parties treat the distribution as otherwise qualifying under section 355 for tax-free treatment, and inasmuch as we have found that portion of the regulations denying application of section 355 to the division of a single business to be invalid, we conclude that petitioner properly treated the distribution to him of the stock of E.P. Coady and Co. as a nontaxable transaction.

No evidence having been introduced with respect to the addition to tax under section 294(d)(2) of the 1939 Code, it is sustained subject to our holding on the above issue.

Reviewed by the Court. . .

■ PIERCE, J., dissents.

■ HARRON, J., dissenting. The petitioner claims that no gain is to be recognized from the distribution of all of the Coady corporation stock in exchange for all of his Christopher corporation stock. In order to obtain such tax-free treatment of the exchange, he relies upon the provisions of section 355. . . The provisions of section 355 provide exceptions to the rule recognizing gain or loss. In considering whether the transaction in dispute is entitled to the nonrecognition provisions of section 355, we must inquire whether the transaction before us is the kind of transaction that Congress intended to relieve of tax. Cf. Commissioner v. Gregory, 69 F.2d 809, *aff'd*, 293 U.S. 465; and Bazley v. Commissioner, 331 U.S. 737. . .

Section 355 requires that two tests shall be met to obtain tax-free treatment: (1) The transaction must not be "principally . . . a device for the distribution of the earnings and profits of the distributing corporation." (2) The transaction must satisfy "the requirements of subsection (b) (relating to *active businesses*)." (Emphasis added.) Subsection (b) states the requirements as to "active businesses." It is required by (b)(1)(A) that subsection (a) shall apply only if the distributing corporation, and the controlled corporation, are engaged immediately after the distribution "in the active conduct of a trade or business." That is to say, immediately after the distribution, *both* the distributing corporation and the controlled corporation must be engaged in the active conduct of a trade or business. The punctuation of (b)(1)(A) has meaning. The words, "and the controlled corporation" are set off by commas; the verb, "is engaged," has two singular subjects, "the distributing corporation," and "the controlled corporation." The statute then defines the phrase "active conduct of a trade or business" (subsec. (b)(2)). The definition specifies that the trade or business which is actively conducted immediately after the distribution (referred to in subsection (a) and subsection (b)(1)) must be a trade or business which has been actively conducted throughout a 5–year period ending on the date of distribution. I believe there can be no doubt that since it is required by subsection (b)(1)(A) that *both* the distributing corporation and the controlled corporation must be engaged immediately after the distribution in the active conduct of a trade or business, the meaning of subsection (b)(2)(B) is that *both* the distributing corporation and the controlled corporation must actively conduct a business, respectively, which had been conducted for 5 years prior to the date of the distribution; each corporation must carry on a business after the distribution which had been carried on for 5 years before the distribution. I disagree with the conclusion that the statute does not so require. . .

. . . Furthermore, I strongly disagree with the view that the purpose of the active business requirements of section 355(b)(1) is limited to the prohibition of a tax-free separation of a corporation into active and inactive entities, and to the prevention of "the tax-free separation of *active* and *inactive* assets into *active* and *inactive* corporate entities." Of course, such results are not allowed by section 355, but that kind of separation is not involved here and the point is not relevant to the issue in this case.

The error which I believe is made here in the construction of subsection (b) of section 355 is found in the failure to agree that the definition of the phrase "active conduct of a trade or business" contained in (b)(2) has reference to "a corporation"; that by reference to (b)(1), "a corporation" must refer to both the distributing corporation and the controlled corporation; and that the first sentence of (b)(2) deals with "a corporation" as a matter of convenience in drafting the definition so as not to engage in repetitions of the words "the distributing corporation" and "the controlled corporation." In this context, I think it is entirely clear that the word "such" in (b)(2)(B) refers back to the active conduct of a trade or business by "a corporation," be the corporation either the distributing corporation or the controlled corporation. . .

. . . I respectfully dissent.

■ ATKINS, J., dissenting. I think the majority opinion errs in holding that section 1.355–1 of the Income Tax Regulations . . . is invalid in providing that section 355 does not apply to the division of a single business.

The Supreme Court has many times held that Treasury regulations must be sustained unless unreasonable and plainly inconsistent with the revenue statutes, and that they constitute contemporaneous constructions by those charged with administration of these statutes which should not be overruled except for weighty reasons. Commissioner v. South Texas Lumber Co., 333 U.S. 496. It has also been stated by the Supreme Court that the practical interpretation of an ambiguous or doubtful statute that has been acted upon by officials charged with its administration will not be disturbed except for weighty reasons. Brewster v. Gage, 280 U.S. 327, and cases therein cited.

Section 355 is not clear. It might be susceptible to different interpretations. However, it seems that the interpretation adopted in the regulations is not unreasonable and plainly inconsistent with the statute, specifically section 355(b)(2)(B). This is particularly true if the legislative history of the statutory provision is taken into consideration. See section 353 of the House bill (H.R. 8300), which required that a corporation would be treated as an "inactive corporation" unless separate books and records had been maintained for the business transferred to it. This clearly contemplated the separation of distinct businesses. See H. Rept. No. 1337, 83d Cong., 2d Sess., p. A 124. The law as finally adopted did not incorporate this particular requirement that separate books should be kept, but in S. Rept. No. 1622, 83d Cong., 2d Sess., p. 50, it is stated that the changes made by the Senate in existing law correspond substantially to those made in the House bill and, as shown in the quotation from the Senate report, contained in the majority opinion, it was the intention that "both the business retained by the distributing company and the business of the corporation the stock of which is distributed must have been actively conducted for the 5 years preceding the distribution, a safeguard against avoidance not contained in existing law." . . .

■ TURNER, HARRON, OPPER, and TRAIN, JJ., agree with this dissent.

NOTES

1. Did the Commissioner's solicitude for the revenue lead him to adopt a wholly unreasonable regulation? What potential for tax avoidance did the Commissioner perceive in the *Coady* situation? Following *Coady* (and other cases) the Treasury issued regulations that explicitly permit both the vertical division (e.g., sewage business split in half with the new corporation receiving half of the sewage contracts, equipment and cash) and the horizontal division (splitting along functional lines, e.g., integrated steel business spinning off the coal mining function while retaining the steel function) of a single business into two separate businesses. Treas. Reg. § 1.355–3(c) ex. 4, 5, 9–11.

In Letter Ruling 200545001, the Service permitted a divisive D reorganization under § 355 where the business was split along geographic lines to implement a regional business model of organization.

2. In Estate of Lockwood v. Commissioner, 350 F.2d 712 (8th Cir. 1965), the issue was whether the five-year rule was satisfied when a "D" reorganization separated the Maine sales organization from the midwestern-based parent only three years after the Maine business was actively conducted. The court held that, under *Coady*, the question is whether the two corporations existing after the distribution are doing the same type of work and using the same type of assets as before in the original business, without reference to geographic area. Section 355(b)(2) was held satisfied. In Rev. Rul. 2003–38, 2003–1 C.B. 811, a shoe retailer operating through malls and other store locations set up a website and then began to sell shoes over the internet. Later the internet business was put into a subsidiary and spun off. The question was whether the internet shoe business was an expansion of the existing business (thus allowing the taxpayer to meet the 5–year requirement) or was a new business (that needed to satisfy the 5–year window independently). The Service concluded that despite some unique aspects of operating on-line the business constituted a single business in shoe retailing.

3. Suppose a restaurant chain opens a new restaurant location, deducts the initial operating losses incurred in establishing the new location, reduces its earnings and profits by its losses, and then separately incorporates the new restaurant and distributes the stock to its shareholders. Is the distribution tax-free? Why?

Revenue Ruling 78–442

1978–2 C.B. 143.

Advice has been requested whether the "active trade or business" requirements of section 355(b)(2)(C) of the Internal Revenue Code of 1954 have been satisfied and if so, whether section 355(a)(3) is applicable to the distribution of stock, under the circumstances described below.

X corporation has conducted two active businesses, within the meaning of section 355(b) of the Code, for more than 5 years. X transferred the property of one of the businesses to Y, a newly formed corporation, in exchange for all the stock of Y and the assumption by Y of certain liabilities of X attributable to the business transferred. Thereafter, X distributed all the stock of Y to the shareholders of X in a transaction intended to meet the requirements of sections 368(a)(1)(D) and 355. The transaction was undertaken for valid business purposes and was not used principally as a device to distribute earnings and profits of either X or Y. Immediately after the transaction, the shareholders of X were in control of both X and Y within the meaning of section 368(c). On the date of the transfer, the amount of the liabilities assumed by Y exceeded the total adjusted basis of the property transferred by X but the amount of the liabilities was less than the total fair market value of the transferred property. . .

In the instant case, section 351 of the Code applies to the transfer, and if the transaction is a reorganization within the meaning of section 368(a)(1)(D), section 361 applies. Therefore, gain will be recognized to X under section 357(c) on the transfer of property to Y and the assumption by Y of the liabilities of X.

The specific question is whether the gain required to be recognized under section 357(c) of the Code prevents Y from satisfying the trade or business test of sections 355(b)(1)(A) and (b)(2)(C).

The rules of section 355(b)(2)(C) of the Code are intended to prevent the acquisition of a trade or business by the distributing or the controlled corporation from an outside party in a taxable transaction within 5 years of a distribution by the distributing corporation of the stock of a controlled corporation in a transaction to which section 355 would otherwise apply. It was not intended to apply to an acquisition of a trade or business by the controlled corporation from the distributing corporation. Therefore, the acquisition by Y of an active business from X in exchange for Y stock does not violate the provisions of section 355(b)(2)(C), even though gain is recognized to X on the transaction by reason of section 357(c).

Likewise, for the same reasons, section 355(a)(3) of the Code is not applicable to the distribution of the Y stock by X. Section 355(a)(4) provides that for purposes of section 355 (other than section 355(a)(1)(D)) and so much of section 356 as relates to this section, stock of a controlled corporation acquired by the distributing corporation by reason of any transaction which occurs within 5 years of the distribution of such stock and in which gain or loss was recognized in whole or in part, shall not be treated as stock of such controlled corporation, but as other property.

Accordingly, since the active business acquired by Y had been actively conducted by X for more than 5 years prior to the distribution of the Y stock to the shareholders of X, the requirements of section 355(b)(2)(C) of the

Code are satisfied. Since all the other requirements of section 335 are met, the transaction qualifies as a reorganization within the meaning of section 368(a)(1)(D), and no gain or loss will be recognized to (and no amount will be includible in the income of) the X shareholders under section 355(a)(1) on the distribution of the Y stock to them.

Revenue Ruling 89–37
1989–1 C.B. 107.

. . . A corporation purchased all of the stock of another corporation in a transaction in which gain or loss was recognized. Two years later, the acquired corporation distributed the stock of its wholly owned subsidiary, whose stock it had acquired more than five years before that time, to the acquiring corporation. The distribution fails to meet the active trade or business requirement of section 355(b)(2)(D) of the Code, as amended by the Revenue Act of 1987 and the Technical and Miscellaneous Revenue Act of 1988. . .

PURPOSE

This revenue ruling obsoletes Rev. Rul. 74–5, 1974–1 C.B. 82, in light of the amendment of section 355(b)(2)(D) of the Internal Revenue Code by section 10223(b) of the Revenue Act of 1987 . . . and section 2004(k)(1) of the Technical and Miscellaneous Revenue Act of 1988 (TMRA). . .

LAW AND ANALYSIS

Rev. Rul. 74–5 involved a distribution of the stock of a controlled corporation, Y, by a distributing corporation, X, to X's parent corporation, P, 2 years after P acquired the stock of X for cash in a transaction in which gain or loss was recognized ("first distribution"). At the time of the first distribution, X had owned the stock of Y for more than 5 years. P subsequently distributed the stock of Y to its shareholders at a time when it had not owned the stock of Y directly or indirectly through X for a 5–year period prior to the distribution ("second distribution"). Rev. Rul. 74–5 considered whether the requirements of section 355(b)(2)(D) of the Code were met with regard to each of the distributions, since P acquired control of X directly and Y indirectly in a transaction in which gain or loss was recognized within the 5–year period prior to each of the distributions.

Section 355(b)(2)(D) of the Code, prior to its amendment by the Act and TMRA, provided that control of a corporation that, at the time of acquisition of control, was conducting an active trade or business, must not have been acquired directly (or through one or more corporations) by "another corporation" within the 5–year period described in section 355(b)(2)(B), or if so acquired by "another corporation" within such period, such control must not have been acquired by reason of transactions in which gain or loss was recognized in whole or in part, or acquired by reason of such transactions combined with acquisitions before the beginning of such period. Rev. Rul. 74–5 reasoned that the purpose of section 355(b)(2)(D) was to prevent a distributing corporation from accumulating excess funds to purchase the stock of a corporation having an active business and then immediately distributing such stock to its shareholders. Rev. Rul. 74–5 concluded that the first distribution was not the type of transaction to which section 355(b)(2)(D) of the Code was directed because P was merely the shareholder receiving the distribution and not the distributing corporation or the controlled corporation and, therefore, the ruling held that section 355(b)(2)(D) was inapplicable to the first distribution. Rev. Rul. 74–5 further held that the second distribution did not meet the requirements of section 355(b)(2)(D) because the distributing corporation, P, indirectly acquired control of the controlled corporation, Y, through another corporation, X, in a transaction in which gain or loss was recognized within the 5–year period prior to the distribution.

Section 10223(b) of the Act and section 2004(k)(1) of TMRA amended section 355(b)(2)(D) of the Code to provide that a corporation is engaged in the active conduct of a trade or business only if control of a corporation which (at the time of acquisition of control) was conducting such trade or business (i) was not acquired by any distributee corporation directly (or through one or more corporations, whether through the distributing corporation or otherwise) within the 5–year period ending on the date of the distribution, and was not acquired by the distributing corporation directly (or through one or more corporations) within such period, or (ii) was so acquired by any such corporation within such period, but, in each case in which such control was so acquired, it was so acquired only by reason of transactions in which gain or loss was not recognized in whole or in part, or only by reason of such transactions combined with acquisitions before the beginning of such period.

Under section 355(b)(2)(D) of the Code, as amended by section 10223(b) of the Act and section 2004(k)(1) of TMRA, the first distribution described in Rev. Rul. 74–5 is now a transaction described in section 355(b)(2)(D). Therefore, because Y was acquired by a distributee corporation within the meaning of section 355(b)(2)(D) in a transaction in which gain or loss was recognized within the 5–year period prior to the distribution, the first distribution fails to meet the active trade or business requirement of section 355(b)(2)(D).

The holding as to the second distribution in Rev. Rul. 74–5 has not been affected by the Act or by TMRA.

NOTES

1. Under § 355(b)(2)(D), if the trade or business is acquired within the 5 years preceding the distribution, the acquisition transaction must have resulted in no gain or loss. For whom must the acquisition result in no gain or loss? Consider the following events involving five corporations: T (which has a subsidiary, X) is acquired by P in a § 368(a)(2)(D) triangular merger (T merges into P's subsidiary, S). T receives and distributes to its T shareholders, pursuant to the reorganization, P stock and cash. T recognizes no gain under § 361(b)(1)(A). T shareholders may recognize gain to the extent that they receive cash. Two years after acquiring T in the merger, P directs X to: (1) spin off one

of its business lines to NewCo, and (2) distribute the NewCo stock to S, which distributes the stock to P.

Does the distribution of NewCo stock fail as a divisive D because the trade or business was acquired within the past five years (through T) in a transaction in which T shareholders recognized gain? LTR 200741005 arguably indicates that these transactions will meet the active business requirement because § 355–(b)(2) and § 1.355–3(b)(4)(i) are understood to focus on whether the acquirer's (here P's) subsidiary S has carryover basis, which in turn depends on the transferor. Here S would have a carryover basis. Effectively the regulations have provided a more liberal construction of the 5 year window rule than might have been presumed from the words of the statute, § 355(b)(2)(D). Willens, Spinoffs by an Acquired Corporation, 117 Tax Notes 975 (Dec. 3, 2007).

2. Proposed regulations issued in 2007 (and still in proposed form) would effectively return to the reasoning in Rev. Rul. 74–5 on the theory that the language in § 355(b)(2)(D)(i) was only targeting transactions that sought to "avoid" the repeal of *General Utilities*. Preamble to Prop. Reg. Under § 355(b), 72 Fed. Reg. 26012 (May 8, 2007).

3. "DEVICE" FOR SIPHONING EARNINGS AND PROFITS

Commissioner v. Morris Trust
367 F.2d 794 (4th Cir. 1966).

■ Before HAYNSWORTH, CHIEF JUDGE, J. SPENCER BELL, CIRCUIT JUDGE, and STANLEY, DISTRICT JUDGE.

■ HAYNSWORTH, CHIEF JUDGE. Its nubility impaired by the existence of an insurance department it had operated for many years, a state bank divested itself of that business before merging with a national bank. The divestiture was in the form of a traditional "spin-off," but, because it was a preliminary step to the merger of the banks, the Commissioner treated their receipt of stock of the insurance company as ordinary income to the stockholders of the state bank. We agree with the Tax Court, that gain to the stockholders of the state bank was not recognizable under § 355 of the 1954 Code.

In 1960, a merger agreement was negotiated by the directors of American Commercial Bank, a North Carolina corporation with its principal office in Charlotte, and Security National Bank of Greensboro, a national bank. American was the product of an earlier merger of American Trust Company and a national bank, the Commercial National Bank of Charlotte. This time, however, though American was slightly larger than Security, it was found desirable to operate the merged institutions under Security's national charter, after changing the name to North Carolina National Bank. It was contemplated that the merged institution would open branches in other cities.

For many years, American had operated an insurance department. This was a substantial impediment to the accomplishment of the merger, for a national bank is prohibited from operating an insurance department except in towns having a population of not more than 5000 inhabitants. To avoid a violation of the national banking laws, therefore, and to accomplish the merger under Security's national charter, it was prerequisite that American rid itself of its insurance business.

The required step to make it nubile was accomplished by American's organization of a new corporation, American Commercial Agency, Inc., to which American transferred its insurance business assets in exchange for Agency's stock which was immediately distributed to American's stockholders. At the same time, American paid a cash dividend fully taxable to its stockholders. The merger of the two banks was then accomplished.

Though American's spin-off of its insurance business was a "D" reorganization, as defined in § 368(a)(1), provided the distribution of Agency's stock qualified for non-recognition of gain under § 355, the Commissioner contended that the active business requirements of § 355(b)(1)(A) were not met, since American's banking business was not continued in unaltered corporate form. He also finds an inherent incompatibility in substantially simultaneous divisive and amalgamating reorganizations.

Section 355(b)(1)(A) requires that both the distributing corporation and the controlled corporation be "engaged immediately after the distribution in the active conduct of a trade or business." There was literal compliance with that requirement, for the spin-off, including the distribution of Agency's stock to American's stockholders, preceded the merger. The Commissioner asks that we look at both steps together, contending that North Carolina National Bank was not the distributing corporation and that its subsequent conduct of American's banking business does not satisfy the requirement.

A brief look at an earlier history may clarify the problem.

Initially, the active business requirement was one of several judicial innovations designed to limit nonrecognition of gain to the implicit, but unelucidated, intention of earlier Congresses.

Nonrecognition of gain in "spin-offs" was introduced by the Revenue Act of 1924. Its § 203(b)(3), as earlier Revenue Acts, provided for nonrecognition of gain at the corporate level when one corporate party to a reorganization exchanged property solely for stock or securities of another, but it added a provision in subsection (c) extending the nonrecognition of gain to a stockholder of a corporate party to a reorganization who received stock of another party without surrendering any of his old stock. Thus, with respect to the nonrecognition of gain, treatment previously extended to "split-offs" was extended to the economically indistinguishable "spin-off."

The only limitation upon those provisions extending nonrecognition to spin-offs was contained in § 203(h) and (i) defining reorganizations. The definition required that immediately after the transfer, the transferor or its stockholders or both be in control of the corporation to which the assets had been transferred, and "control" was defined as being the ownership of not less than eighty per cent of the voting stock and eighty per cent of the total number of shares of all other classes of stock.

With no restriction other than the requirement of control of the transferee, these provisions were a fertile source of tax avoidance schemes. By spinning-off liquid assets or all productive assets, they provided the means by which ordinary distributions of earnings could be cast in the form of a reorganization within their literal language.

The renowned case of Gregory v. Helvering, 293 U.S. 465, 55 S. Ct. 266, 79 L. Ed. 596, brought the problem to the Supreme Court. [The recitation of the *Gregory* facts is omitted.]*

The Supreme Court found the transaction quite foreign to the congressional purpose. It limited the statute's definition of a reorganization to a reorganization of a corporate business or businesses motivated by a business purpose. It was never intended that Averill engage in any business, and it had not. Its creation, the distribution of its stock and its liquidation, the court concluded, was only a masquerade for the distribution of an ordinary dividend, as, of course, it was.

In similar vein, it was held that the interposition of new corporations of fleeting duration, though the transactions were literally within the congressional definition of a reorganization and the language of a nonrecognition section, would not avail in the achievement of the tax avoidance purpose when it was only a mask for a transaction which was essentially and substantively the payment of a liquidating dividend, a sale for cash, or a taxable exchange.

Such cases exposed a number of fundamental principles which limited the application of the nonrecognition of gain sections of the reorganization provisions of the Code. Mertens defines them in terms of permanence, which encompasses the concepts of business purpose and a purpose to continue an active business in altered corporate form. As concomitants to the primary principle and supplements of it, there were other requirements that the transferor, or its stockholders, retain a common stock interest and that a substantial part of the value of the properties transferred be represented by equity securities.

Underlying such judicially developed rules limiting the scope of the nonrecognition provisions of the Code, was an acceptance of a general congressional purpose to facilitate the reorganization of businesses, not to exalt economically meaningless formalisms and diversions through corporate structures hastily created and as hastily demolished. Continuation of a business in altered corporate form was to be encouraged, but immunization of taxable transactions through the interposition of short-lived, empty, corporate entities was never intended and ought not to be allowed.

---

* See page 446 supra—ED.

While these judicial principles were evolving and before the Supreme Court declared itself in Gregory v. Helvering, an alarmed Congress withdrew nonrecognition of gain to a stockholder receiving securities in a spin-off. It did so by omitting from the Revenue Act of 1934, a provision comparable to § 203(c) of the Revenue Act of 1924.

Nonrecognition of gain to the stockholder in spin-off situations, however, was again extended by § 317(a) of the Revenue Act of 1951, amending the 1939 Code by adding § 112(b)(11). This time, the judicially developed restrictions upon the application of the earlier statutes were partially codified. Nonrecognition of gain was extended "unless it appears that (A) any corporation which is a party to such reorganization was not intended to continue the active conduct of a trade or business after such reorganization, or (B) the corporation whose stock is distributed was used principally as a device for the distribution of earnings and profits to the shareholders of any corporation a party to the reorganization."

If this transaction were governed by the 1939 Code, as amended in 1951, the Commissioner would have had the support of a literal reading of the A limitation, for it was not intended that American, in its then corporate form, should continue the active conduct of the banking business. From the prior history, however, it would appear that the intention of the A limitation was to withhold the statute's benefits from schemes of the Gregory v. Helvering type. It effectively reached those situations in which one of the parties to the reorganization was left only with liquid assets not intended for use in the acquisition of an active business or in which the early demise of one of the parties was contemplated, particularly, if its only office was a conduit for the transmission of title. The B limitation was an additional precaution intended to encompass any other possible use of the device for the masquerading of a dividend distribution.

The 1954 Code was the product of a careful attempt to codify the judicial limiting principles in a more particularized form. The congressional particularization extended the principles in some areas, as in the requirement that a business, to be considered an active one, must have been conducted for a period of at least five years ending on the distribution date and must not have been acquired in a taxable transaction during the five-year period.[10] In other areas, it relaxed and ameliorated them, as in its express sanction of non-prorata distributions.[11] While there are such particularized variations, the 1954 Code is a legislative re-expression of generally established principles developed in response to definite classes of abuses which had manifested themselves many years earlier. The perversions of the general congressional purpose and the principles the courts had developed to thwart them, as revealed in the earlier cases, are still an enlightening history with which an interpretation of the reorganization sections of the 1954 Code should be approached.

---

[10] Section 355(b)(2).

[11] Section 355(a)(2)....

Section 355(b) requires that the distributing corporation be engaged in the active conduct of a trade or business "immediately after the distribution." This is in contrast to the provisions of the 1951 Act, which, as we have noted, required an intention that the parent, as well as the other corporate parties to the reorganization, continue the conduct of an active business.[12] It is in marked contrast to § 355(b)'s highly particularized requirements respecting the duration of the active business prior to the reorganization and the methods by which it was acquired. These contrasts suggest a literal reading of the postreorganization requirement and a holding that the Congress intended to restrict it to the situation existing "immediately after the distribution."

Such a reading is quite consistent with the prior history. It quite adequately meets the problem posed by the Gregory v. Helvering situation in which, immediately after the distribution, one of the corporations held only liquid or investment assets. It sufficiently serves the requirements of permanence and of continuity, for as long as an active business is being conducted immediately after the distribution, there is no substantial opportunity for the stockholders to sever their interest in the business except through a separable, taxable transaction. If the corporation proceeds to withdraw assets from the conduct of the active business and to abandon it, the Commissioner has recourse to the backup provisions of § 355(a)(1)(B) and to the limitations of the underlying principles. At the same time, the limitation, so construed, will not inhibit continued stockholder conduct of the active business through altered corporate form and with further changes in corporate structure, the very thing the reorganization sections were intended to facilitate.

Applied to this case, there is no violation of any of the underlying limiting principles. There was no empty formalism, no utilization of empty corporate structures, no attempt to recast a taxable transaction in nontaxable form and no withdrawal of liquid assets. There is no question but that American's insurance and banking businesses met all of the active business requirements of § 355(b)(2). It was intended that both businesses be continued indefinitely, and each has been. American's merger with Security, in no sense, was a discontinuance of American's banking business, which opened the day after the merger with the same employees, the same depositors and customers. There was clearly the requisite continuity of stockholder interest, for American's former stockholders remained in 100% control of the insurance company, while, in the merger, they received 54.385% of the common stock of North Carolina National Bank, the remainder going to Security's former stockholders. There was a strong business purpose for both the spin-off and the merger, and tax avoidance by American's stockholders was neither a predominant nor a subordinate purpose. In short, though both of the transactions be viewed together, there were none of the evils or misuses which the limiting principles and the statutory limitations were designed to exclude.

---

[12] See, also, the Senate Finance Committee Report explaining § 317 of the Revenue Act of 1951. Sen. Rep. No. 781, 82 Cong. 1st Sess. (1951) U.S. Code Congressional and Administrative News, p. 1969.

We are thus led to the conclusion that this carefully drawn statute should not be read more broadly than it was written to deny nonrecognition of gain to reorganizations of real businesses of the type which Congress clearly intended to facilitate by according to them nonrecognition of present gain.

The Commissioner, indeed, concedes that American's stockholders would have realized no gain had American not been merged into Security after, but substantially contemporaneously with, Agency's spin-off. Insofar as it is contended that § 355(b)(1)(A) requires the distributing corporation to continue the conduct of an active business, recognition of gain to American's stockholders on their receipt of Agency's stock would depend upon the economically irrelevant technicality of the identity of the surviving corporation in the merger. Had American been the survivor, it would in every literal and substantive sense have continued the conduct of its banking business.

Surely, the Congress which drafted these comprehensive provisions did not intend the incidence of taxation to turn upon so insubstantial a technicality. Its differentiation on the basis of the economic substance of transactions is too evident to permit such a conclusion.

This, too, the Commissioner seems to recognize, at least conditionally, for he says that gain to the stockholders would have been recognized even if American had been the surviving corporation. This would necessitate our reading into § 355(b)(1)(A) an implicit requirement that the distributing corporation, without undergoing any reorganization whatever, whether or not it resulted in a change in its corporate identity, continue the conduct of its active business.

We cannot read this broader limitation into the statute for the same reasons we cannot read into it the narrower one of maintenance of the same corporate identity. The congressional limitation of the post-distribution active business requirement to the situation existing "immediately after the distribution" was deliberate. Consistent with the general statutory scheme, it is quite inconsistent with the Commissioner's contention.

The requirement of § 368(a)(1)(D) that the transferor or its stockholders be in control of the spun-off corporation immediately after the transfer is of no assistance to the Commissioner. It is directed solely to control of the transferee, and was fully met here. It contains no requirement of continuing control of the transferor. Though a subsequent sale of the transferor's stock, under some circumstances, might form the basis of a contention that the transaction was the equivalent of a dividend within the meaning of § 355(a)(1)(B) and the underlying principles, the control requirements imply no limitation upon subsequent reorganizations of the transferor.

There is no distinction in the statute between subsequent amalgamating reorganizations in which the stockholders of the spin-off transferor would own 80% or more of the relevant classes of stock of the reorganized transferor, and those in which they would not. The statute draws no line between major and minor amalgamations in prospect at the time of the spin-off. Nothing of the sort is suggested by the detailed control-active business requirements in the five-year predistribution period, for there the distinction is between taxable and nontaxable acquisitions, and a tax free exchange within the five-year period dues not violate the active business-control requirement whether it was a major or a minor acquisition. Reorganizations in which no gain or loss is recognized, sanctioned by the statute's control provision when occurring in the five years preceding the spin-off, are not prohibited in the post-distribution period. . .

Nor can we find elsewhere in the Code any support for the Commissioner's suggestion of incompatibility between substantially contemporaneous divisive and amalgamating reorganizations. The 1954 Code contains no inkling of it; nor does its immediate legislative history. The difficulties encountered under the 1924 Code and its successors, in dealing with formalistic distortions of taxable transactions into the spin-off shape, contain no implication of any such incompatibility. Section 317 of the Revenue Act of 1951 and the Senate Committee Report, to which we have referred, did require an intention that the distributing corporation continue the conduct of its active business, but that transitory requirement is of slight relevance to an interpretation of the very different provisions of the 1954 Code and is devoid of any implication of incompatibility. If that provision, during the years it was in effect, would have resulted in recognition of gain in a spin-off if the distributing corporation later, but substantially simultaneously, was a party to a merger in which it lost its identity, a question we do not decide, it would not inhibit successive reorganizations if the merger preceded the spin-off.

The Congress intended to encourage six types of reorganizations. They are defined in § 368 and designated by the letters "A" through "F." The "A" merger, the "B" exchange of stock and the "C" exchange of stock for substantially all of the properties of another are all amalgamating reorganizations. The "D" reorganization is the divisive spin-off, while the "E" and "F" reorganizations, recapitalizations and reincorporations, are neither amalgamating nor divisive. All are sanctioned equally, however. Recognition of gain is withheld from each and successively so. Merger may follow merger, and an "A" reorganization by which Y is merged into X corporation may proceed substantially simultaneously with a "C" reorganization by which X acquires substantially all of the properties of Z and with an "F" reorganization by which X is reincorporated in another state. The "D" reorganization has no lesser standing. It is on the same plane as the others and, provided all of the "D" requirements are met, is as available as the others in successive reorganizations. . .

. . . After the merger, North Carolina National Bank was as much American as Security. It was not one or the other, except in the sense of the most technical of legalisms; it was both, and with respect to the Charlotte operation, old American's business, it was almost entirely American. North Carolina National Bank's business in the Charlotte area after the merger was American's business conducted by American's employees in American's banking houses for the service of American's customers. Probably the only change immediately noticeable was the new name.

. . . [I]t is important to the result that, as in every merger, there was substantive continuity of each constituent and its business. In framing the 1954 Code, the Congress was concerned with substance, not formalisms. Its approach was that of the courts in the Gregory v. Helvering series of cases. Ours must be the same. The technicalities of corporate structure cannot obscure the continuity of American's business, its employees, its customers, its locations or the substantive fact that North Carolina National Bank was both American and Security.

A decision of the Sixth Circuit[16] appears to be at odds with our conclusion. In *Curtis*, it appears that one corporation was merged into another after spinning-off a warehouse building which was an unwanted asset because the negotiators could not agree upon its value. The Court of Appeals for the Sixth Circuit affirmed a District Court judgment holding that the value of the warehouse company shares was taxable as ordinary income to the stockholders of the first corporation.

A possible distinction may lie between the spin-off of an asset unwanted by the acquiring corporation in an "A" reorganization solely because of disagreement as to its value and the preliminary spin-off of an active business which the acquiring corporation is prohibited by law from operating. We cannot stand upon so nebulous a distinction, however. We simply take a different view. The reliance in *Curtis* upon the Report of the Senate Committee explaining § 317 of the Revenue Act of 1951, quite dissimilar to the 1954 Code, reinforces our appraisal of the relevant materials. . .

For the reasons which we have canvassed, we think the Tax Court, which had before it the opinion of the District Court in *Curtis*, though not that of the affirming Court of Appeals, correctly decided that American's stockholders realized no recognizable taxable gain upon their receipt in the "D" reorganization of the stock of Agency.

Affirmed.

NOTES

1. What was it about the transactions in *Morris Trust* and *Curtis* (cited in the *Morris Trust* opinion supra) that gave the Commissioner concern? What is the significance of the inner and outer parenthetical clauses in § 355(a)(1)(B)? If you had been Government counsel in *Morris Trust*, what argument might you have advanced, based on the inner parenthetical clause? As the taxpayer's counsel, how might you have responded? What decision should a court reach with respect to the applicability of the inner parenthetical clause in cases like *Morris Trust* and *Curtis*? Why? In Rev. Rul. 68–603, 1968–2 C.B. 148, the Commissioner indicated that he would no longer attack the "spin-away" trans-

---

[16] Curtis v. United States, 6 Cir., 336 F.2d 714.

action sustained under § 355 in *Morris Trust*. See also Rev. Rul. 2003–79, 2003–2 C.B. 80.

Treas. Reg. § 1.355–2(d)(2)(iii)(E) now reflects the conclusion that the spin-away is not a "device." In *Pulliam v. Commissioner*, 73 T.C.M. (CCH) 3052, nonacq. 1999–1 C.B. 5, the court concluded that despite substantial evidence that the § 355 distribution could be a device (pursuant to a prearranged plan the stock was disposed of shortly following the spin-off), the transaction was in fact not a device. Why not? The business's need to retain a key employee in the face of competition was a compelling business reason and could be satisfied only with this spin-off, due to state regulation of funeral home ownership.

2. Redemption of some shares in one or both surviving corporations will not automatically result in a § 355 distribution's being treated as a "device." See Rev. Rul. 78–251, 1978–1 C.B. 89 (cash redemption of target corporation's dissenting shareholders, following spin-away of unwanted subsidiary); Rev. Rul. 77–377, 1977–2 C.B. 111 (redemption of shares in both surviving corporations following split-up, where redemption prior to split-up would *have qualified for exchange treatment under § 303*).

3. In Rev. Rul. 64–102, 1964–1 C.B. 136, the issue was whether a non-pro-rata distribution of stock in a subsidiary in exchange for all of certain minority shareholders' stock in the parent was a "device," when shortly before the distribution the parent transferred a sizable amount of cash to the subsidiary in order to equalize the value of the subsidiary's and parent's stock. What result would you expect? Cf. H. Grady Lester, 40 T.C. 947 (1963), where the distributing corporation transferred $200,000 to the controlled corporation. Of that sum $140,000 was used to purchase starting inventory, and the remaining $60,000 was needed to begin business immediately. The court held this was not "principally" a "device," and the Commissioner has acquiesced. 1964–2 C.B. 3.

See also Rev. Rul. 83–114, 1983–2 C.B. 66, in which the parent corporation, P, was required to divest itself of the subsidiary corporation, S, as the result of an antitrust decree. In order to permit S to expand its operations and attract additional investment capital, P canceled a large debt owed to it by S. Although the cancellation resulted in a 100–percent increase in S's net worth, the Service ruled that because the cancellation was for legitimate business reasons the spin-off of S was not a "device." The Service also held that the device restriction was not violated per se merely because an unrelated corporation merged into S after the spin-off.

4. What is the relationship between § 355(a)(1)(B) and § 356(a)(2)? Should a transaction which is not principally a "device for the distribution of . . . earnings and profits" be considered "substantially equivalent to a dividend"? Whether the payment of boot in a stock exchange under § 355 is treated as a dividend is determined *before* the exchange, i.e., treat the shareholder as if it "had retained the distributing corporation stock actually exchange for controlled corporation stock and received the boot in exchange for distributing corporation stock equal in value to the boot." Rev. Rul. 93–62, 1993–2 C.B. 118.

5. See Rev. Rul. 77–335, 1977–2 C.B. 95, holding that the preferred stock of a subsidiary distributed (along with the subsidiary's common stock) in a transaction qualifying under § 355 became § 306 stock.

6. In Rev. Rul. 86–4, 1986–1 C.B. 174, the Service ruled that the transfer of even a small percentage of investment assets (relative to the other assets transferred to a controlled corporation) prior to the distribution of stock is a factor to be considered in determining whether the transaction is a "device" under § 355.

7. See Rev. Proc. 96–30, 1996–1 C.B. 696, amplified by Rev. Proc. 2003–48, 2003–2 C.B. 86. They detail a checklist questionnaire that must be answered in connection with all ruling requests under § 355. The regulations under § 355 specify three factors that are evidence of a device: (1) pro rata distribution, (2) subsequent sale or exchange of stock, or (3) nature and use of assets. Treas. Reg. § 1.355–2(d)(2). As indicated in *Pulliam*, infra page 572, the presence of a device factor can be offset by a strong business purpose. The regulations outline three factors which are evidence of a nondevice: (1) corporate business purpose, (2) distributing corporation widely held and publicly traded, and (3) the distributee is entitled to a dividends received deduction. Treas. Reg. § 1.355–2(d)(3). Finally, the regulations list transactions not usually considered to be a device: (1) transactions in which there is an absence of E & P and (2) distributions otherwise qualified under § 302 or § 303 redemptions. Treas. Reg. § 1.355–2(d)(5).

8. In 2006 Congress amended the active business requirement of § 355(b) by adding (b)(3) which treats a corporation and its relevant affiliates (those that would be affiliates if the tested entity were the parent and § 1504(b) did not apply). Prior to the amendment, to satisfy the active business requirement, a corporation had to be directly conducting business or have substantially all of its assets be stock and securities of one or more controlled corporations engaged in the active conduct of a trade or business (i.e. be a holding corporation). The new provision raises interesting questions: How large or significant does the active trade or business "found" within the relevant affiliated group (called the "separate affiliated group" under the statute) have to be either in absolute or relative terms?

9. Also in 2006, Congress added § 355(g) aimed at the tax free distribution of controlled corporations that had small but qualifying active businesses *but large amounts of investment assets*. New § 355(g) denies the benefits of § 355 if: (1) either the distributing or distributed corporation is a "disqualified investment corporation" immediately after the transaction, and (2) any person holds immediately after the transaction a 50% or more interest in the disqualified investment corporation and such person did not hold such interest before the transaction.

The key concept is "disqualified investment corporation" which is one in which the FMV of investment assets is 2/3 of the FMV of all assets of the corporation. § 355(g)(2)(B)(i). Investment assets include cash, stock, securities, debt, financial instruments, foreign currency—but not if such assets are held for use in active conduct of a finance business, banking business or insurance business. § 355(g)(2)(B)(ii).

4. DISTRIBUTION OF "CONTROL" STOCK

Revenue Ruling 63–260
1963–2 C.B. 147.

A owned all of the stock of X which owned 70 shares of the stock of Y. A also owned the remaining 30 shares of Y stock directly. A contributed 10 shares of his Y stock to X. Immediately thereafter, X distributed all 80 shares of Y stock now held by it to A.

Held, the distribution by X does not qualify as a nontaxable distribution under the provisions of section 355 of the Internal Revenue Code of 1954, because X did not have "control" of Y within the meaning of section 368(c) of the Code immediately before the distribution except in a transitory and illusory sense.

Section 355 of the Code cannot be made to apply to a transaction in which an immediately preceding contribution to capital by the distributor corporation's shareholder is made solely to attempt to qualify the transaction as a nontaxable distribution under that section.

NOTE

Should § 355(b)(2)(D) have wrought a different result? Why? Is Rev. Rul. 63–260 consonant with the statute? What relevance does § 318(a)(3)(C) have to this problem?

Revenue Ruling 71–593
1971–2 C.B. 181.

Advice has been requested whether section 355 of the Internal Revenue Code of 1954 applies to a distribution of stock under the circumstances described below.

X and Y were corporations engaged in manufacturing. A and B each owned 50 percent of the X stock. A owned 25 percent of the Y stock (its only class of outstanding stock) and X owned 75 percent of the Y stock, which it had owned for more than five years. X and Y have each been engaged in the active conduct of a trade or business for more than five years.

For valid corporate business purposes, within the meaning of section 1.355–2(c) of the Income Tax Regulations, it was decided to separate the ownership of the X and Y stock, with A to own all of the stock of Y, and B to own all of the stock of X. A and B plan to continue the operations of Y and X, respectively.

Pursuant to a plan and in order to make the value of the Y stock to be distributed to A equal in value to the X stock surrendered by A in exchange therefor, X transferred some of its assets to Y in exchange for newly issued stock of Y. The stock of Y received by X was equal in value to the assets transferred by X to Y. As a result of this exchange, X owned 90 percent of the Y stock. As part of the same plan, X then transferred all of its Y stock to A in exchange for all of A's stock of X. After the exchanges, A owned all of the Y stock and B owned all of the X stock.

In view of all the facts and circumstances of the transactions, particularly the fact that the distribution of the Y stock to A in exchange for his stock of X completely terminated his interest in X, it was determined that the transactions were not a device for the distribution of the earnings and profits of X or Y or both. . .

Revenue Ruling 63–260, C.B. 1963–2, 147, holds, in effect, that the requirement in section 355(a)(1)(A) of the Code that the distributing corporation be in control of the distributed corporation immediately before the distribution is not met where the transaction in which control was obtained was entered into immediately prior to the distribution for the sole purpose of qualifying the distribution under section 355 of the Code.

Two questions are raised by the facts of this case. First, did X have control of Y (immediately before it distributed the Y stock to A) within the meaning of section 355(a)(1)(A) of Code? Secondly, if X did have such control of Y, was that control acquired in a transaction in which no gain or loss was recognized in whole or in part as required by section 355(b)(2)(D) of the Code?

The value of the assets transferred by X to Y was equal to the value of the stock of Y received by X in exchange therefor. Moreover, the transfer by X of a portion of its assets to Y in exchange for additional Y stock was necessary to equalize the values of stocks to be received and surrendered by A. Since this exchange was value-for-value, and since it was necessary to equalize the values of the stocks to be received and surrendered by A, it must be viewed as a meaningful exchange and not as an exchange made solely to attempt to qualify the distribution of Y stock to A as a non-taxable distribution under section 355 of the Code. Consequently, X had control of Y immediately before the distribution of Y stock to A within the meaning of section 355(a)(1)(A) of the Code.

Since X did have control of Y immediately before the distribution of the Y stock to A in exchange for his X stock, and since that control was acquired within the five-year period immediately preceding the distribution, it must be determined whether gain or loss was recognized in whole or in part on the transaction in which X acquired control of Y. If no gain or loss was recognized on that transaction, then the requirements of section 355(b)(2)(D) of the Code were met and section 355 of the Code applies to the distribution of the Y stock by X to A in exchange for his X stock.

Under the facts of this case, the transfer by X of a portion of its assets to Y in exchange for additional stock of Y met all of the requirements of section 368(a)(1)(D) of the Code. As a result, no gain or loss was recognized to X on the exchange by reason of section 361(a) of the Code. Under section 1032 of the Code, no gain or loss was recognized to Y on the receipt of X's assets for its stock. Consequently, no gain or loss was recognized in whole or in part on the transaction and the requirements of section 355(b)(2)(D) of the Code were met.

Accordingly, since all of the requirements of section 355(a) of the Code were met, no gain or loss will be recognized to A (and no amount, will be includible in the income of A) upon the receipt of Y stock in exchange for his X stock.

NOTE

Is there an inconsistency between the approach in Rev. Rul. 63–260 and Rev. Rul. 71–593 and that in *Granite Trust* (page 447 supra)? What might the result have been in *Granite Trust* if the sales had been to a majority shareholder?

Commissioner v. Gordon
391 U.S. 83 (1968).

■ MR. JUSTICE HARLAN delivered the opinion of the Court.

These cases, involving the interpretation of § 355 of the Internal Revenue Code of 1954, have an appropriately complex history.

American Telephone and Telegraph Company (hereafter A. T. & T.) conducts its local communications business through corporate subsidiaries. Prior to July 1, 1961, communications services in California, Oregon, Washington, and Idaho were provided by Pacific Telephone and Telegraph Company (hereafter Pacific). A. T. & T. held about 90% of the common stock of Pacific at all relevant times. The remainder was widely distributed.

Early in 1961, it was decided to divide Pacific into two separate corporate subsidiaries of A. T. & T. The plan was to create a new corporation, Pacific Northwest Bell Telephone Company (hereafter Northwest) to conduct telephone business in Oregon, Washington, and Idaho, leaving the conduct of the California business in the hands of Pacific. To this end, Pacific would transfer all its assets and liabilities in the first three States to Northwest, in return for Northwest common stock and debt paper. Then, Pacific would transfer sufficient Northwest stock to Pacific shareholders to pass control of Northwest to the parent company, A. T. & T.

Pacific had, however, objectives other than fission. It wanted to generate cash to pay off existing liabilities and meet needs for capital, but not to have excess cash left over. It also feared that a simple distribution of the Northwest stock would encounter obstacles under California corporation law. Consequently, the "Plan for Reorganization" submitted to Pacific's shareholders on February 27, 1961, had two special features. It provided that only about 56% of the Northwest common stock would be offered to Pacific shareholders immediately after the creation of Northwest. It also provided that, instead of simply distributing Northwest stock pro rata to shareholders, Pacific would distribute to its shareholders transferable rights entitling their holders to purchase Northwest common from Pacific at an amount to be specified by Pacific's Board of Directors, but expected to be below the fair market value of the Northwest common. . .

The plan was approved by Pacific's shareholders on March 24, 1961. Pacific transferred its assets and liabilities in Oregon, Washington, and Idaho to Northwest, and ceased business in those States on June 30, 1961. On September 29, 1961, Pacific issued to its common stockholders one right for each outstanding share of Pacific stock. These rights were exercisable until October 20, 1961. Six rights plus a payment of $16 were required to purchase one share of Northwest common. The rights issued in 1961 were sufficient to transfer some 57.3% of the Northwest stock.

By September 29, 1961, the Internal Revenue Service had ruled that shareholders who sold rights would realize ordinary income in the amount of the sales price, and that shareholders who exercised rights would realize ordinary income in the amount of the difference between $16 paid in and the fair market value, measured as of the date of exercise, of the Northwest common received. . .

On June 12, 1963, the remaining 43% of the Northwest stock was offered to Pacific shareholders. This second offering was structured much as the first had been, except that eight rights plus $16 were required to purchase one share of Northwest.

The Gordons . . . and the Baans, . . . were minority shareholders of Pacific as of September 29, 1961. In the rights distribution that occurred that day the Gordons received 1,540 rights under the plan. They exercised 1,536 of the rights on October 5, 1961, paying $4,096 to obtain 256 shares of Northwest, at a price of $16 plus six rights per share. The average price of Northwest stock on the American Stock Exchange was $26 per share on October 5. On the same day, the Gordons sold the four odd rights for $6.36. The Baans received 600 rights on September 29, 1961. They exercised them all on October 11, 1961, receiving 100 shares of Northwest in return for their 600 rights and $1,600. On October 11, the agreed fair market value of one Northwest share was $26.94.

In their federal income tax returns for 1961, neither the Gordons nor the Baans reported any income upon the receipt of the rights or upon exercising them to obtain Northwest stock at less than its fair market value. The Gordons also did not report any income on the sale of the four rights. The Commissioner asserted deficiencies against both sets of taxpayers. He contended, in a joint proceeding in the Tax Court, that taxpayers received ordinary income in the amount of the difference between the sum they paid in exercising their rights and the fair market value of the Northwest stock received. He contended further that the Gordons realized ordinary income in the amount of $6.36, the sales price, upon the sale of their four odd rights.

The Tax Court upheld taxpayers' contention that the 1961 distribution of Northwest stock met the requirements of § 355 of the Code, with the result that no gain or loss should be recognized on the receipt by them or their exercise of the rights. The Tax Court held, however, that the Gordons' sale of the four odd rights resulted in ordinary income to them. The Commissioner appealed the *Baan* case to the Court of Appeals for the Ninth Circuit, and the *Gordon* case to the Court of Appeals for the Second Circuit; in the latter, the Gordons cross-appealed. The Ninth Circuit reversed the Tax Court, holding that the spread between $16 and fair market value was taxable as ordinary income to the Baans. The Second Circuit disagreed, sustaining the Tax Court on this point in the *Gordon* case. The Second Circuit went on to hold that the amount received by the Gordons for the four odd rights was taxable as a capital gain rather than as ordinary income, reversing the Tax Court on this point.

Because of the conflict, we granted certiorari. . . We affirm the decision of the Court of Appeals for the Ninth Circuit, and reverse the decision of the Court of Appeals for the Second Circuit on both points.

Under §§ 301 and 316 of the code, subject to specific exceptions and qualifications provided in the code, any distribution of property by a corporation to its shareholders out of accumulated earnings and profits is a dividend taxable to the shareholders as ordinary income. . . It is here agreed that on September 28, 1961, Pacific's accumulated earnings and profits were larger in extent than the total amount the Commissioner here contends was a dividend—the difference between the fair market value of all Northwest stock sold in 1961 and the total amount, at $16 per share, paid in by purchasers.

Whether the actual dividend occurs at the moment when valuable rights are distributed or at the moment when their value is realized through sale or exercise, it is clear that when a corporation sells corporate property to stockholders or their assignees at less than its fair market value, thus diminishing the net worth of the corporation, it is engaging in a "distribution of property" as that term is used in § 316.[4] Such a sale thus results in a dividend to shareholders unless some specific exception or qualification applies. In particular, it is here agreed that the spread was taxable to the present taxpayers unless the distribution of Northwest stock by Pacific met the requirements for nonrecognition stated in § 355, or § 334, or

---

[4] See, e.g., Choate v. Commissioner of Internal Revenue, 129 F.2d 684 (C.A. 2d Cir.). In Palmer v. Commissioner of Internal Revenue, 302 U.S. 63, 69, this Court said, "While a sale of corporate assets to stockholders is, in a literal sense, a distribution of its property, such a transaction does not necessarily fall within the statutory definition of a dividend. For a sale to stockholders may not result in any diminution of its net worth and in that case cannot result in any distribution of its profits.

"On the other hand such a sale, if for substantially less than the value of the property sold, may be as effective a means of distributing profits among stockholders as the formal declaration of a dividend."

In *Palmer*, rights were distributed entitling shareholders to purchase from the corporation shares of stock in another corporation. Finding that the sales price represented the reasonable value of the shares at the time the corporation committed itself to sell them, this Court found no dividend. It held that the mere issue of rights was not a dividend. It has not, however, been authoritatively settled whether an issue of rights to purchase at less than fair market value itself constitutes a dividend, or the dividend occurs only on the actual purchase. In the present case this need not be decided.

§ 346(b) of the code.[5] Since the Tax Court concluded that the requirements of § 355 had been met, it did not reach taxpayers' alternative contentions. . .

Section 355 provides that certain distributions of securities of corporations controlled by the distributing corporation do not result in recognized gain or loss to the distributee shareholders. The requirements of the section are detailed and specific, and must be applied with precision. It is no doubt true, as the Second Circuit emphasized, that the general purpose of the section was to distinguish corporate fission from the distribution of earnings and profits. However, although a court may have reference to this purpose when there is a genuine question as to the meaning of one of the requirements Congress has imposed, a court is not free to disregard requirements simply because it considers them redundant or unsuited to achieving the general purpose in a particular case. Congress has abundant power to provide that a corporation wishing to spin off a subsidiary must, however bona fide its intentions, conform the details of a distribution to a particular set of rules.

The Commissioner contends that the 1961 distribution of Northwest stock failed to qualify under § 355 in several respects.[7] We need, however, reach only [§]355(a)(1)(D). . .

On September 28, 1961, the day before the first rights distribution, Pacific owned all of the common stock of Northwest, the only class of securities that company had issued. The 1961 rights offering contemplated

---

[5] It is important to begin from this premise. In our view, the Court of Appeals for the Second Circuit erred in its approach to the § 355 problem because it assumed, at the outset, that the Commissioner essentially sought to tax a transaction that brought no "income" to Pacific shareholders. Whether the shareholders received income, however, cannot in practice be determined in the abstract, before looking at § 355.

Any common shareholder in some sense "owns" a fraction of the assets of the corporation in which he holds stock, including those assets that reflect accumulated corporate earnings. Earnings are not taxed to the shareholder when they accrue to the corporation, but instead when they are passed to shareholders individually through dividends. Consequently it does not help to note, as the Second Circuit here did, that the distribution of Northwest stock merely changed the form of ownership that Pacific's shareholders enjoyed and did not increase their wealth. This is only very roughly true at best, but in the rough sense in which it is here true, it is true of any dividend. The question is not whether a shareholder ends up with "more" but whether the change in the form of his ownership represents a transfer to him, by the corporation, of assets reflecting its accumulated earnings and profits.

There may be a genuine theoretical difference between a change in form representing a mere corporate fission, separating what the shareholder owns into two smaller but essentially similar parts, and a change in form representing a dividend, separating what a shareholder owns qua shareholder from what he owns as an individual. This difference, however, must be defined by objectively workable tests, such as Congress supplied in § 355. Neither the Second Circuit nor the taxpayers have suggested any other way of identifying a true fission.

[7] The Commissioner contends, first, that Pacific did not distribute "solely stock or securities" as required by § 355(a)(1)(A), because it distributed rights rather than stock. He contends, second, that Pacific did not distribute the Northwest stock "to a shareholder, with respect to its stock" as required by § 355(a)(1)(A)(i), because it did not distribute the stock to shareholders but sold it to holders of transferable rights, for cash consideration. He contends, third, that Northwest did not meet the quantity requirements of § 355(a)(1)(D) because it parted with only 57% of the stock in 1961.

Any one of these arguments, if established, would support the result the Commissioner seeks. The Court of Appeals for the Second Circuit perforce rejected all three. The Court of Appeals for the Ninth Circuit accepted all three. We reach only the last.

transferring, and succeeded in transferring, about 57% of the Northwest common to Pacific shareholders. It therefore could not be clearer that this 1961 distribution did not transfer "all" of the stock of Northwest held by Pacific prior to it, and did not transfer "control" as that term is defined in § 368(c).

Nevertheless, taxpayers contend, and the Second Circuit agreed, that the requirements of subsection (a)(1)(D) were here met because Pacific distributed the remaining 43% of the Northwest stock in 1963. The court said that the purpose of the subsection "in no way requires a single distribution." The court apparently concluded that so long as it appears, at the time the issue arises, that the parent corporation has in fact distributed all of the stock of the subsidiary, the requirements of § 355(a)(1)(D)(i) have been satisfied.

We are forced to disagree. The code requires that "the distribution" divest the controlling corporation of all of, or 80% control of, the controlled corporation. Clearly, if an initial transfer of less than a controlling interest in the controlled corporation is to be treated for tax purposes as a mere first step in the divestiture of control, it must at least be identifiable as such at the time it is made. Absent other specific directions from Congress, code provisions must be interpreted so as to conform to the basic premise of annual tax accounting. It would be wholly inconsistent with this premise to hold that the essential character of a transaction, and its tax impact, should remain not only undeterminable but unfixed for an indefinite and unlimited period in the future, awaiting events that might or might not happen. This requirement that the character of a transaction be determinable does not mean that the entire divestiture must necessarily occur within a single tax year. It does, however, mean that if one transaction is to be characterized as a "first step" there must be a binding commitment to take the later steps.[11]

Here, it was little more than a fortuity that, by the time suit was brought alleging a deficiency in taxpayers' 1961 returns, Pacific had distributed the remainder of the stock. The plan for reorganization submitted to shareholders in 1961 promised that 56% of that stock would be distributed immediately. The plan went on,

> It is expected that within about three years after acquiring the stock of the New Company, the Company by one or more offerings will offer for sale the balance of such stock, following the procedures described in the preceding paragraph. The proceeds from such sales will

---

[11] The Commissioner contends, first, that Pacific did not distribute "solely stock or securities" as required by § 355(a)(1)(A), because it distributed rights rather than stock. He contends, second, that Pacific did not distribute the Northwest stock "to a shareholder, with respect to its stock" as required by § 355(a)(1)(A)(i), because it did not distribute the stock to shareholders but sold it to holders of transferable rights, for cash consideration. He contends, third, that Northwest did not meet the quantity requirements of § 355(a)(1)(D) because it parted with only 57% of the stock in 1961.

Any one of these arguments, if established, would support the result the Commissioner seeks. The Court of Appeals for the Second Circuit perforce rejected all three. The Court of Appeals for the Ninth Circuit accepted all three. We reach only the last.

be used by the Company to repay advances then outstanding and for general corporate purposes including expenditures for extensions, additions and improvements to its telephone plant.

> The prices at which the shares of the New Company will be offered pursuant to the offerings referred to . . . will be determined by the Board of Directors of the Company at the time of each offering.

It was further stated that such subsequent distributions would occur "[a]t a time or times related to its [Pacific's] need for new capital." Although there is other language in the plan that might be interpreted to prevent Pacific management from dealing with the Northwest stock in any way inconsistent with eventual sale to Pacific shareholders, there is obviously no promise to sell any particular amount of stock, at any particular time, at any particular price. If the 1961 distribution played a part in what later proved to be a total divestiture of the Northwest stock, it was not, in 1961, either a total divestiture or a step in a plan of total divestiture.

Accordingly, we hold that the taxpayers, having exercised rights to purchase shares of Northwest from Pacific in 1961, must recognize ordinary income in that year in the amount of the difference between $16 per share and the fair market value of a share of Northwest common at the moment the rights were exercised.

The second question presented . . ., whether the $6.36 received by taxpayers Gordon upon the sale of four rights was taxable as ordinary income, as a capital gain, or not at all, does not require extended discussion in light of our view upon the first question. Since receipt and exercise of the rights would have produced ordinary income, receipt and sale of the rights, constituting merely an alternative route to realization, also produced income taxable at ordinary rates. Helvering v. Horst, 311 U.S. 112; Gibson v. Commissioner, 133 F.2d 308.

The judgment of the Court of Appeals for the Second Circuit is reversed. The judgment of the Court of Appeals for the Ninth Circuit is affirmed. . .

NOTES

1. For the result on remand, see Gordon v. Commissioner, 424 F.2d 378 (2d Cir. 1970), *aff'g* 51 T.C. 1032 (1969), *cert. denied*, 400 U.S. 848 (1970). The two arguments made by the Commissioner but not reached by the *Gordon* court (see footnote 7) were dealt with by the Seventh Circuit in Redding v. Commissioner, *infra*.

2. Cf. Rev. Rul. 77–11, 1977–1 C.B. 93, in which two commonly controlled corporations transferred part of their assets in exchange for stock of a newly formed corporation, then distributed the new corporation's stock in complete redemption of one shareholder's stock in both transferors. Since one transferor had acquired control of the new corporation prior to the redemption, its distribution was nontaxable. The distribution by the other transferor corporation was a § 302(b)(3) redemption.

Redding v. Commissioner

630 F.2d 1169 (7th Cir. 1980), *cert. denied*, 450 U.S. 913 (1981).

■ Before BAUER, WOOD and CUDAHY, CIRCUIT JUDGES.

■ CUDAHY, CIRCUIT JUDGE. This is an appeal by the Commissioner of Internal Revenue from determinations of the United States Tax Court that Gerald R. and Dorothy M. Redding and Thomas W. and Anne M. Moses ("taxpayers") do not owe any income tax on account of the receipt or exercise of stock warrants.[1] These warrants were distributed as part of a series of transactions involving distribution by the Indianapolis Water Company (the "Water Company") to its stockholders of all the stock of its wholly owned subsidiary, Shore wood Corporation ("Shorewood"). The distribution of warrants was made preliminarily to the distribution of stock, which was distributed upon the exercise of the warrants. The Tax Court treated the two distributions as being part of a single transaction, sheltered from taxation under section 355 . . ., granting nonrecognition to a corporation's distribution to its stockholders of stock or securities in a controlled corporation. We hold that the distribution of stock warrants to the taxpayers constituted a dividend to them and that section 355 is not available to render the transaction nontaxable. We, therefore, reverse.

The Water Company, which is a public utility, owned all of the stock of Shorewood, which in turn owned most of the waterfront property surrounding the reservoirs used by the Water Company. Shorewood wished to develop its waterfront realty, but the Indiana Public Service Commission determined that real estate development was not an appropriate activity for a public utility and suggested that Shorewood be separated from the Water Company.

To achieve this end, Shorewood's capital structure was altered. In 1970, Shorewood's authorized common stock was increased from 1,000 to 2,500,000 shares. On the same day, Shorewood issued to the Water Company 481,291 shares of common stock in exchange for Shorewood's 1,000 shares then outstanding and held by the Water Company. On January 6, 1971, the Water Company agreed to purchase an additional 855,630 shares of common stock from Shorewood for a total ownership of 1,336,921 shares. The board of directors of the Water Company decided to distribute to its shareholders of record on January 6, 1971, stock rights or warrants to purchase Shorewood stock on the basis of one warrant for each share of the Water Company common stock outstanding. The warrants gave the holder the right to receive one share of Shorewood stock upon surrender of two warrants and the payment of $5.00 to the Water Company and further right to subscribe to any remaining Shorewood shares by allotment. The warrants were transferable.

---

[1] The terms "stock rights" (or "rights") will be used in this opinion interchangeably with the term "warrants" since both terms have been used interchangeably in this litigation. In financial circles, "warrants" usually refer to longer term options to purchase stock at a stated price (a "subscription price" or "exercise price" or "option price") than do stock rights....

The total offering of Shorewood shares by the Water Company thus amounted to 1,069,537 shares, which comprised slightly more than 80% of the total outstanding amount of Shorewood stock. Of these shares to be offered, 50,000 shares were reserved for the underwriters, and 1,019,537 shares were available for distribution to warrant holders. Any shares not sold to warrant holders were to be bought by the underwriters, on a "firm commitment" basis, at a slightly discounted price. The Water Company thus retained slightly less than 20% of the outstanding Shorewood stock. Immediately after the distribution, the shareholders of the Water Company held substantially more than 50% of the outstanding shares of Shorewood.

The warrants were issued on January 7, 1971, and expired and became valueless if not exercised by 3:30 p.m. on January 22, 1971. During this subscription period, shareholders or their transferees or assignees subscribed to all 1,069,537 Shorewood shares offered, except for 50,000 shares acquired by the underwriters. Hence, 1,019,537 shares of Shorewood stock were actually distributed to the warrant holders and 50,000 shares conveyed to the underwriters on February 2, 1971. As contemplated by the Water Company, an over-the-counter market in warrants developed during the subscription period, with the price ranging from $0.39 to $1.05 per warrant. There is no dispute that both at the time of issuance and at the time of exercise of the warrants the subscription price of $5.00 was less than the fair market value of Shorewood stock. . .

Taxpayers were stockholders of the Water Company. Gerald and Dorothy Redding owned 7,000 Water Company shares, and Thomas and Anne Moses owned 35,343 shares. They received a corresponding number of warrants and exercised all of them. The Moseses also exercised an additional subscription privilege to obtain an additional 6,228 shares of Shorewood stock.

Taxpayers contended that both the receipt and the exercise of the warrants were tax free to them under the provisions of section 355. It was stipulated that the transaction was not a "device" for the distribution of earnings and profits pursuant to section 355(a)(1)(B); that the separately conducted "active business" requirements of section 355(a)(1)(C) were met; that the 1,069,537 shares of Shorewood distributed in the offering amounted to 80% control; and that the shares retained by the Water Company were not held for tax avoidance purposes within the meaning of section 355(a)(1)(D)(ii).

The Tax Court agreed with taxpayers that the transactions involved in these cases met the requirements for a corporate division, in this case a "spin-off," contained in section 355 and were, accordingly, taxfree. . .

In reversing the Tax Court, we find taxpayers have failed to meet their burden of showing that the several transactions here meet the tests of section 355 so as to qualify for nonrecognition of the gain otherwise subject to tax. As the parties and the Tax Court acknowledged to be the case were we to find section 355 inapplicable, we conclude the distribution of the warrants by the Water Company is taxable as a dividend. It is not controlling that taxpayers sold none of their rights, exercised all of them, and received stock for them (for which taxpayers also paid the additional consideration of $5.00 per Shorewood share). The tax treatment of taxpayers must depend upon an analysis of the transaction as a whole rather than only of the specific facts applicable to these taxpayers. This is true because the nonrecognition of gain afforded by section 355 requires adherence to requirements governing the transaction as a whole.

The Tax Court, in determining whether the issuance of the warrants and their exercise by warrant holders should be immunized from tax by section 355, purported to rely heavily on its prior ruling granting tax-free status to warrants used in somewhat similar transaction in Baan v. Commissioner, 45 T.C. 71 (1965), *rev'd*, 382 F.2d 485 (9th Cir. 1967), *aff'd sub nom.* Commissioner v. Gordon, 382 F.2d 499 (2d Cir. 1967), 9th Cir. *aff'd sub nom.* Commissioner v. Gordon, 2d Cir. *rev'd*, 391 U.S. 83 [page 576 supra] . . . (1968). In *Baan*, the Tax Court apparently felt that it could ignore the issuance of warrants as a taxable event under the dictum of Palmer v. Commissioner, 302 U.S. 63 . . . (1937), that an issuance of stock rights is not a dividend,[10] and that it could proceed to consideration of the warrant *exercise* and stock issuance only. In the instant case, on the other hand, the Tax Court expressly declined to state a view on the current vitality of the *Palmer* dictum. Instead, it applied the "step transaction doctrine" to reach its conclusion that the two transactions which took place should be viewed as "steps" in a single transaction meeting the requirements of section 355 and that, hence, neither the receipt nor the exercise of the warrants results in tax. We shall, therefore, address first the applicability of the step transaction doctrine, which we think is significantly related to the current status of the *Palmer* dictum, to be discussed later. As to the application of the step transaction doctrine, we believe the Tax Court erred.

The attempted application of the step transaction doctrine in this case to shift the focus from the issuance of the stock rights or warrants to the subsequent distribution of stock is important, because, to qualify under section 355, a distribution must consist solely of stock or securities, which do not include stock rights such as these. See Treas. Reg. § 1.3551(a) (1979). . . As the Court of Appeals for the Ninth Circuit said in Commissioner v. Baan,

> . . . Stock rights are not stocks or securities and, most assuredly, are not stock or securities carrying voting rights. They are only options to purchase stock. . .

See Gordon v. Commissioner, 424 F.2d 378, 381–83 (2d Cir. 1970) construing the similar language of section 354(a)(1).

The Tax Court does not disagree with this conclusion but seeks to keep the related transactions within the ambit of section 355 by integrating through the step transaction doctrine the distribution of stock warrants

---

[10] "The mere issue of rights to subscribe and their receipt by stockholder, is not a dividend." Palmer v. Commissioner. 302 U.S. at 71....

and the subsequent exercise of these warrants. By that technique the over-all transaction can be viewed as a distribution solely of stock, which is allegedly immunized from tax by section 355.

The commentators have attempted to synthesize from judicial decisions several tests to determine whether the step transaction doctrine is applicable to a particular set of circumstances in order to combine a series of steps into one transaction for tax purposes. Unfortunately, these tests are notably abstruse—even for such an abstruse field as tax law. . . [O]ne of the tests which the parties ask us to consider is the "end result" test, whereby purportedly separate transactions will be amalgamated into a single transaction when it appears that "the successive steps were made 'in furtherance of, and for the purpose of executing and putting into effect, the plan of reorganization.' " . . . Here, the distribution of stock warrants was not made for the purpose of reaching the end result of distributing stock to the Water Company shareholders. Indeed, the workings of the stock warrant mechanism indicate that it was a matter of relative indifference to the Water Company, from the standpoint of raising capital for Shorewood or for itself, whether the Shorewood stock went to Water Company shareholders, or to their assignees of warrants (or to the underwriters). Had the paramount purpose of the Water Company been to distribute its portfolio Shorewood stock in a way that Water Company shareholders would in the end become Shorewood shareholders, the obvious way to proceed would have been simply to omit the first "step" and to distribute Shorewood stock directly to Water Company shareholders. But such an approach would have made it difficult to raise new capital, which was a paramount and somewhat inconsistent goal. . .

. . . Here where the Water Company's purpose went far beyond a simple corporate division, the use of transferable warrants made it possible to bring in *new* distributees for the Shorewood stock (together with new capital for Shorewood and for Water Company). Therefore, the reason for using transferable warrants was to arrange in advance for Water Company shareholders to be excluded as recipients of Shorewood stock in favor of new investors prepared to make a capital contribution. Hence, to the extent that the rights distribution was a step, it was not a necessary step in the sort of corporate division contemplated by section 355.[14] Our conclusion is directly buttressed by the stipulation of the parties that "[t]he use of rights that required payment of a subscription price as a method of distribution of the Shorewood common stock was dictated by the need of Shorewood for capital to develop its assets and business" . . .

---

[14] "[The] purpose [of section 355] and the purpose of its predecessors is to give to stockholders in a corporation controlled by them the privilege of separating or 'spinning off' from their corporation a part of its assets and activities and lodging the separated part in another corporation which is controlled by the same stockholders. Since, after the spin-off, the real owners of the assets are the same persons who owned them before, Congress has been willing that these owners should be allowed, without penalty, to have their real ownership divided into smaller ... entities than the single original corporation, if the real owners decide that such a division would be desirable." Commissioner v. Wilson, 353 F.2d at 186.

The reference of the Tax Court to the warrant issue as a "merely procedural device" is misleading. Insofar as the warrants had a readily ascertainable market value, they had independent economic significance, and, as indicated, their function in the series of transactions was to make it possible for Water Company shareholders to defer profitably to others who were prepared to make an investment in Shorewood. Further, since the warrant distribution had independent economic significance, that distribution was a matter of substance rising above mere form or procedure.

Taxpayers also contend that it was not essential to use warrants as evidence of "legal rights" to receive stock and that this fact is significant. They describe several alternative procedures not involving the issuance of warrants which would have provided the same "legal benefits or opportunities" as those provided by warrants... But simply because some other means (which arguably comply with section 355) might have been used to reach ultimate results similar to those sought in this case does not suggest that the procedures followed here are entitled to section 355 treatment.

First, " '[t]he Commissioner is justified in determining the tax effects of transactions on the basis in which taxpayers have molded them.' "

... Second, taxpayers do not explain precisely how the suggested alternative means would raise capital (a paramount objective). Third, Congress narrowly constrained the means for gaining the tax benefit; the issue here is whether the means of using transferable warrants comply with the "detailed and specific requirements of section 355." Commissioner v. Gordon... Fourth, the fact that the rights were "evidenced by a piece of paper" gave them a marketable identity and helped endow them and their receipt with independent economic significance.

The second "test" for determining whether the step transaction doctrine applies is the so-called "interdependence test," which requires an evaluation "whether on a reasonable interpretation of objective facts the steps are so interdependent that the legal relations created by one transaction would have been fruitless without a completion of the series." ... Although there is some question whether the "interdependence test" is even relevant to the corporate division situation, were we to apply the test to the facts before us we would not find use of the warrants sufficiently indispensable to achieving a spin-off to compel us to view this as a unitary transaction... While the exercise of the warrants here was obviously dependent upon warrants having been issued, the issuance of warrants did not require their exercise by shareholders in the purchase of stock from the Water Company... Insofar as the issuance of warrants contemplated the raising of capital through the disposition of stock, the result would have been essentially the same whether the warrants were exercised by Water Company shareholders or by non-shareholder assignees. Even if the warrants were not exercised at all; the underwriters had agreed to purchase the stock (albeit at a slightly reduced price). Although the use of warrants made it more likely than a public offering that Water Company shareholders would end up as Shorewood shareholders, the money would have come in and the stock gone out with or without the exercise of the warrants. On the other hand, the transferable warrants led away from, rather than to-ward, a goal of spinning off to *shareholders*, which could have occurred by direct stock distribution without warrants...

Finally, the Commissioner argues that the transactions before us also fail to satisfy a third test permitting invocation of the step transaction doctrine, the "binding commitment" test. As explained by the Supreme Court in Commissioner v. Gordon... the step transaction doctrine should not apply unless "if one transaction is to be characterized as a 'first step' there must be a binding commitment to take the later steps." The Commissioner, noting that the Tax Court in the instant case found that there was no binding commitment for a stock distribution to follow the rights issuance, stresses that the absence of such commitment renders the step transaction doctrine inapplicable. Although this is a valid contribution to the analysis, we do not find the point determinative.

The Supreme Court articulated the binding commitment test in the factual context of a multi-step distribution similar to that before us. Given this similarity, we would embrace and apply the "binding commitment" test were it not for one important difference between the *Gordon* case and that before us. The multi-step distribution in *Gordon* took place in successive tax years, a time-span obviously exceeding the several weeks involved in the instant case. This lengthy time period raised the possibility that the transactions' tax impact would remain indefinite and indeterminable for an unlimited period, an eventuality inconsistent with the premise of annual tax accounting and one the Court may have thought necessitated the "binding commitment" test. We cannot say that the Court intended that the failure to satisfy the test in the circumstance of a much shorter period would automatically preclude application of the step transaction doctrine. Hence, the lack of "binding commitment" is simply one factor to which we give appropriate consideration here. Certainly, it is not necessary for us to rely on this factor to reach our result.

Our examination of the facts in light of the various tests convinces us that the issuance of transferable warrants not only had independent economic significance but added nothing to the essential process of effecting a spin-off, "to permit the real owners of enterprises to arrange their units and evidences of ownership to suit their own ideas of how best to carry on their business."... It may be, as the Tax Court emphasizes, that the warrants were in existence for only a short period of time but their economic value is clear, and they were actively traded during the period of their existence. Fundamentally, we think it inappropriate to substitute the step transaction doctrine as a tax shield for the warrant issuance if the dictum of Palmer v. Commissioner is no longer available to immunize the warrant transaction...

Even were we to agree that the step transaction doctrine permits these transactions to be viewed as simply a distribution of Shorewood stock, the requirement of section 355(a)(1)(A) that this stock be distributed *with respect to* the stock of the Water Company has not been met. What has instead happened has been that the stock warrants have been distributed with respect to the stock of the Water Company, and the Shorewood stock has then been distributed with respect to the warrants (as well as to the underwriters). It was the warrant distribution rather than the stock distribution which conformed to this statutory test.

After the distribution of warrants to Water Company stockholders had taken place, the subsequent distribution of shares of Shorewood stock was made "with respect to" the holders of warrants—some Water Company shareholders and some not—and to the underwriters. This was not, in the words of the Supreme Court, "conform[ing] the details of a distribution to a particular set of rules." Commissioner v. Gordon. . .

It has been argued that the status of the Water Company shareholders was important because their existence created any purchaser's right to receive the stock "through" the stockholders of the Water Company, as the Tax Court suggested in the comparable situation of Baan v. Commissioner. . . But, in comparison with the more straightforward view that section 355 contemplates simply distributions to shareholders, this analysis is painfully strained. The Tax Court was apparently not unduly troubled by the problem of distributions to non-stockholders or the fact that the use of transferable warrants structured the transaction in the direction of transfers to third parties. The Tax Court was apparently satisfied by the fact that the shareholders of the Water Company actually received more than 50% of the Shorewood stock, a sufficient percentage to satisfy the so-called continuity-of-shareholder-interest test.

The continuity-of-shareholder-interest test is "a doctrine of judicial origin based on what is conceived to be the unstated but fundamental statutory purpose of providing for nonrecognition of gain or loss only if the reorganization exchange is distinguishable from a sale. . ." Generally, if one-half or more of the stock remains in the hands of the original shareholders, such continuity of interest is adequate proof that a sale was not effected. Here, the Tax Court found it harmless from the standpoint of fulfilling the "with respect to its stock" requirement of section 355(a)(1)(A) that Shorewood stock was sold to third parties so long as 50% or more of it ended up with Water Company shareholders. The Tax Court apparently reasoned (although this is not explicit in its opinion) that, when section 355 applied to a rights offering, it was enough, for purposes of section 355(a)(1)(A) that at least 50% of the stock or securities of the subsidiary come to rest in the hands of shareholders of the parent.

This way of thinking conflicts with that of the Court of Appeals for the Ninth Circuit which stated in Commissioner v. Baan, "Congress could well conclude that the prospect that the same people (shareholders of the distributing company) will continue to own the same business would be undermined if a distribution was effectuated by means of transferable stock rights, the exercise of which required substantial cash payments." . . . We cannot agree with the Tax Court, if we understand its reasoning, that the failure of the distribution of Shorewood stock to be "with respect to" Water Company stock was harmless merely because 50% or more of Shorewood stock came to rest with Water Company shareholders. We know of no authority that mere satisfaction of the 50% standard is enough to meet the section 355(a)(1)(A) problem.[22]

We reach only in passing the further issue upon which Judge Sterrett relied in his dissenting opinion below that the Water Company did not distribute 80% of the Shorewood stock within the meaning of section 355(a)(1)(D), and therefore that the transaction was not tax-free under section 355. The Tax Court found that this issue was foreclosed by the stipulations entered into by the parties for purposes of this litigation.

Section 355(a)(1)(D) requires that stock constituting "control" of the controlled corporation, defined under section 368(c) as at least 80%, must be distributed. We think the "distribution" referred to in section 355(a)(1)(D) is the same "distribution" as that referred to in section 355(a)(1)(A) requiring a "distribution" to shareholders of the issuing corporation with respect to its stock. In other words the statute "requires distribution of control to *shareholders of the distributing corporation.*" Redding v. Commissioner, 71 T.C. at 617 (Sterrett, J., dissenting).

Here, after the transaction at issue, the Water Company retained 267,384 shares or exactly 20%, less one share of the total 1,336,921 shares of Shorewood stock issued and outstanding. The Water Company thus must have distributed slightly more than 80%. But of the shares constituting this 80%, 50,000 were acquired by the underwriters. As Judge Sterrett found, the transfer of the 50,000 shares to the underwriters reduced the percentage of the stock "distributed" to Water Company shareholders to, at most, 76.26% of all Shorewood shares issued.[23] Were it not for the stipulation, we would probably be persuaded by the Commissioner on this point, and the issue would necessarily be significant in our decision.

Given our conclusion that the step transaction doctrine does not require this transaction to be seen simply as a distribution of Shorewood stock and our further finding that even if it could be so viewed, there has

---

[22] In addition, because of the requirements of section 355(a)(1)(B).... the 50% standard is presumably applicable where there has been no prearrangement of stock transfers to third parties after the distribution. In the instant circumstances, a distribution of stock *based on a prior distribution of rights*, where some of the rights are sold before the stock is distributed, is a situation where "stock ... [is] sold ... pursuant to an arrangement ... agreed upon prior to ... [the] distribution [of the stock]." I.R.C. § 355(a)(1)(B). Any such transfer by prearrangement to non-stockholders might render the transaction at least presumptively nonconforming under section 355.... We are, of course, aware of the stipulation here with respect to section 355(a)(1)(B), but, in divining the intent of Congress, we think all the subsections of section 355 must be read together to arrive at the meaning, for example, of section 355(a)(1)(A).

[23] We do not know to what level this figure was further reduced by the exercise of warrants by individuals who received or purchased them from Water Company shareholders.

We find somewhat persuasive the reasoning applied by Judge Sterrett in concluding his analysis of the section 355(a)(1)(D) issue: "In order to sustain the Court's decision herein one would have not only to ignore the substance and importance of the rights issuance, but also assume that all [the recipients of] the rights traded over the counter and all the underwriters were also Water Co. shareholders. I cannot join in this assumption and it seems, in any event, to be contrary to the ... [statutory] language. The petitioner has not shown to whom Water Co. transferred 'control' inasmuch as no related group of distributees had 80 percent of Shorewood's stock immediately after the transfer. It is not this Court's function to assume petitioners' prima facie case. Rather, such case must be proven." 71 T.C. at 617 (Sterrett, J., dissenting).

been a failure to comply with the requirements of section 355, we must turn finally to a determination of what constitutes the taxable event.

The Commissioner contends that the taxable event is the receipt of the warrants; taxpayers contend that, if the transaction is taxable at all, the taxable event would be the exercise of the warrants. There is also a difference of view as to how to measure the income received with respect to the warrants. In our view these matters are rather simply dealt with under the Internal Revenue Code of 1954.

The method of taxing corporate distributions was extensively revised in the 1954 Code. A distribution to shareholders, as such, of rights to acquire stock of the distributing corporation is, with exceptions not germane here, excluded from gross income under section 305. Rights distributed to shareholders to acquire the stock of another corporation, however, are *not* specifically excluded from gross income by the 1954 Code.

Section 301(a) of the Code states that, except as otherwise provided in chapter 1 of the Code, a distribution of property, as defined in § 317(a), made by a corporation to a shareholder with respect to its stock, will be treated as provided in section 301(c). Section 301(c) provides that where section 301(a) applies to a distribution, that amount of the distribution that is a dividend, as defined in section 316, will be included in gross income.

Under section 316(a), any distribution of "property" by a corporation to its shareholders out of its earnings and profits accumulated after February 28, 1913 is a "dividend." "Property" as defined in section 317(a) "means money, securities, and any other property; except that such term does not include stock in the corporation making the distribution (or right to acquire such stock)." The specific *exclusion* of rights to acquire stock of the distributing company implies that rights to acquire stock of another corporation are *included* in the term "property." Indeed, the legislative history of the 1954 Code leaves no doubt that this broad definition of property includes stock warrants:

> As a result of [the exclusion in] this definition, the receipt of stock, of a corporation which is not stock of the distributing corporation (or is not treated as such stock under . . . section 353 [later renumbered as section 355]) would be treated as property for the purpose of section 301 (and other relevant provisions of this subsection). H. Rep. No. 1337, 83d Cong., 2d Sess., reprinted in [1954] U.S. Code Cong. & Admin. News pp. 4017, 4238.

See also Baumer v. United States, 580 F.2d 863, 881 (5th Cir. 1978); Rev. Rul. 70–521, 1970–2 C.B. 72; . . .

Thus, since the distribution of warrants here was not sheltered from taxation by section 355, taxpayers received a dividend upon receipt of the warrants and the amount of the dividends was the fair market value of the warrants received. See Rev. Rul. 70–521, 19702 C.B. 72.

It is argued, of course, that such a result contradicts the dictum of *Palmer v. Commissioner*. In that opinion Mr. Justice Stone said:

> The mere issue of rights to subscribe and their receipt by stockholders, is not a dividend. No distribution of corporate assets or diminution of the net worth of the corporation results in any practical sense. Even though the rights have a market or exchange value, they are not dividends within the statutory definition. . . [Citations omitted.] They are at most options or continuing offers, potential sources of income to the stockholders through sale or the exercise of their rights. Taxable income might result from their sale, but distribution of the corporate property could take place only on their exercise. 302 U.S. at 71. . .

But this analysis in the *Palmer* dictum was made under the Revenue Act of 1928, which did not contain the broad definition of "property" added in 1954 as section 317(a) of the Code.[24] Obviously, the Internal Revenue Code of 1954 must govern our decision. Although the superseding legislation and the congressional commentary it generated did not specifically discuss the *Palmer* dictum, several provisions of the 1954 Code governing corporate distributions seem incompatible with the principle that income never results from the mere issuance of stock rights. Whether, in enacting these provisions, Congress intended to "overrule" *Palmer* with respect to its famous dictum is left for us to intuit. We believe, though, that a "reasonable interpretation" of the corporate distribution provisions as a whole yields the conclusion that, even if the dictum was authoritative prior to 1954, it must now make way for a result consonant with the 1954 Code (and, incidentally, more reflective of economic reality).

In addition to the definition of "property" in section 317(a), which we find includes stock rights in the shares of a non-issuing corporation, the 1954 Code added a provision in section 305 which indicates another change in the law of tax-free receipt of stock rights. The general rule of section 305(a) excludes from taxability stock rights to acquire stock in the issuing corporation. However, one exception to this rule in section 305(b) is designed to tax distributions when they are effectively granted "in lieu of money." If the exception applies, the distribution of stock or of stock rights "shall be treated as a distribution of property to which section 301 applies." This exception precludes any inference that Congress intended to perpetuate the *Palmer* dictum. Thus, both sections 305(b) and 317(a) vitiate the "no property" rationale of the *Palmer* dictum. . .

Indeed, the Supreme Court itself has apparently done the next thing to explicitly rejecting the *Palmer* dictum in light of the 1954 Code. In Commissioner v. Gordon, the Court discussed the relevant provisions of the

---

[24] As has been noted, "[T]he 1928 revenue statute, ... defined a dividend as 'any distribution made by a corporation to its shareholders, whether in money or in other property, out of its earnings and profits.' The *Palmer* Court concluded that the issuance of an option did not constitute a distribution out of corporate profits, and so was not a dividend." Gann, ... [Taxation of Stock Rights and Other Options: Another Look at the Persistence of *Palmer v. Commissioner*, 1979 Duke L.J. 911, 940 (1979).]

Code and said that when a corporation sells its property to its stockholders or their assignees at less than fair market value, the transaction diminishes the net worth of the corporation and is a "distribution of property" within section 316. In attempting to relate this statement to discussion of the same subject in *Palmer*, the Court made broader observations:

> In *Palmer*, rights were distributed entitling shareholders to purchase from the corporation shares of stock in another corporation. Finding that the sales price represented the reasonable value of the shares at the time the corporation committed itself to sell them, the Court found no dividend. It held that the mere issue of rights was not a dividend. *It has not, however, been authoritatively settled whether an issue of rights to purchase at less than fair market value itself constitutes a dividend, or the dividend occurs on the actual purchase...*

This statement in *Gordon*, which as we have noted was quite similar on its facts to the instant case, withdraws any compulsion which may previously have arisen from the dictum in *Palmer* to prohibit treating the receipt of stock rights as the receipt of a dividend. In the instant case, the Tax Court pointedly refused to assess the *Palmer* doctrine's current vitality... Further, in Baumer v. United States, the Court of Appeals for the Fifth Circuit, confronted with a problem similar to ours, carefully limited the *holding* in *Palmer* to its precise facts...[26] We think the better interpretation under the provisions of the 1954 Code and the regulations construing them is that, in the case of stock rights, where the subscription price is lower than fair market value, there is a dividend at the time of issuance (and receipt) of the rights measured by the fair market value of the rights at the time of issuance.

We believe that we are required under the provisions of the 1954 Code to move beyond the dictum of *Palmer* and its pre–1954 progeny such as Choate v. Commissioner, 129 F.2d 684 (2d Cir. 1942). A fair reading of the decision of the Supreme Court in Commissioner v. Gordon requires that *Palmer* be limited to its facts, namely, a situation where there was no spread between option (subscription) price and market value on the date the corporation adopted its plan of distribution. When a substantial spread between market and option price prevails at all relevant times, we perceive no requirement to follow rigidly the *Palmer* dictum. Since options (warrants) are "property" as defined in the 1954 code, they fall easily within the scope of the statutory scheme for the taxation of dividends. Such an approach better reflects economic reality since an option incorporating a

---

[26] "[T]he Fifth Circuit in *Baumer* limited the application of *Palmer* to a situation in which no spread exists on the date of issuance and the option period is so short that it is contemplated that the property subject to the option will be immediately sold to the shareholder before any substantial appreciation in the value of the underlying property can occur. Under the *Baumer* opinion, the issuance of the option is the distribution of a valuable asset to be taxed as a dividend if a spread exists on the date the option is issued, or if no spread exists on the date of issuance, but the option period is long enough so that the corporation contemplates appreciation. This analysis looks at the economic effect of the transaction to determine the existence of a dividend, and it correctly encompasses the two factors that attribute value to options— that is, both the existence of a spread on the date of issuance, and the length of the option period and potential appreciation during that period." *Gann*, supra note [24], at 956–57.

spread is a thing of value capable of being actively traded in public markets. Further, from an administrative point of view the valuation approach dictated by the Code and regulations seems simpler than that developed in valuation cases purportedly based on *Palmer*. . . Hence, based on careful analysis of relevant authority and a perception of the economic realities, we believe that the step we take here is fully justified. The time has come to put *Palmer* in perspective, and we do so with full confidence that our conclusion meets the most exacting standards of deference to the precedents of the Supreme Court, which in all respects control the decisions of the inferior federal courts. . .

Reversed and remanded. . .

NOTES

1. The parties in *Redding* stipulated that the shares of Shorewood retained by the Water Company were not held for tax avoidance purposes. In Rev. Rul. 75–469, 1975–2 C.B. 469, a parent corporation retained securities (long-term debentures) in its subsidiaries after distributing its subsidiaries' stock in a transaction that otherwise complied with the requirements of § 355(a). The Service ruled that the distribution was nontaxable to the shareholders of the parent who received the subsidiaries' stock because the retention of the debentures would not permit the parent to maintain any practical control over its former subsidiary and because a sufficient business purpose for the retention of the debentures existed (the subsidiary's stock had been held by a bank as collateral for a loan; the bank agreed to release the stock for distribution to the shareholders if the debentures were substituted as collateral). See also Rev. Rul. 75–321, 1975–2 C.B. 123, where a corporation distributed 95 percent of the stock of a controlled corporation to its shareholders and retained the remaining 5 percent of the stock to serve as collateral for loans. The Service ruled that the retention of 5 percent of the stock was not in pursuance of a plan having as one of its principal purposes the avoidance of federal income tax. For the Service's guidelines under § 355(a)(1)(D)(ii), see Rev. Proc. 91–62, 1991–2 C.B. 864. Note that after March 1998, for purposes of §§ 354, 355, and 356, warrants constitute securities with no principal amount. Treas. Reg. §§ 1.354–1(e); 1.355–1(c). *Redding* still remains a problem.

2. In addition to the control requirements in § 355, the regulations establish an independent continuity-of-interest requirement: "one or more persons who, directly or indirectly, were the owners of the enterprise prior to the distribution or exchange own, in the aggregate, an amount of stock establishing a continuity of interest in each of the modified corporate forms.". . . Treas. Reg. § 1.355–2(c)(1). No specific ownership threshold is identified, although examples indicate 50% should be adequate. Treas. Reg. § 1.355–2(c)(2) ex. 2. The changes in continuity of interest requirements under section 368 (see supra page 501) do not directly govern a § 355 transaction. However, the shift to disregarding pre- and post-reorganization sales of stock to unrelated parties may indicate that the continuity of interest requirement should and will play a more diminished role in § 355 as well. Where § 368 does intersect with § 355—the case of divisive D reorganizations—§ 368(a)(2)(H) measures control as ownership of at least 50% of vote or value and states that where § 355 requirements are met, shareholder dispositions of part or all of the distributed stock (or the issuance

of additional shares by the distributed corporation) "shall not be taken into account" in assessing control.

Edna Louise Dunn Trust v. Commissioner

86 T.C. 745 (1986).

■ TANNENWALD, JUDGE. Respondent determined a deficiency of $29.64 in petitioner's Federal income taxes for the taxable year ended May 31, 1984. The issue for decision is whether a portion of the stock distributed to petitioner pursuant to a reorganization and divestiture plan constituted "other property" under section 355(a)(3)(B)...

Throughout its fiscal year ended May 31, 1984, petitioner owned 400 shares of common stock of American Telephone and Telegraph Company ("AT&T") a corporation organized and existing under the laws of the State of New York. Petitioner received, as of January 1, 1984, a distribution with respect to its AT&T stock of 40 shares of stock of each of American Information Technologies Corporation, Bell Atlantic Corporation, BellSouth Corporation, NYNEX Corporation, Pacific Telesis Group ("PacTel Group"), Southwestern Bell Corporation and U S West, Inc. (AT&T's seven regional holding Companies ("RHCs")). Petitioner did not include in its gross income on its Federal income tax return for the year in question any amount on account of the receipt of these shares of the RHCs.

Until January 1, 1984, AT&T was the common parent corporation of a group of corporations known as the Bell System, whose principal business was the furnishing of communications services and equipment. The group included 22 Bell operating companies ("BOCs") which were direct or indirect subsidiaries of AT&T, Western Electric Company, Incorporated, Bell Telephone Laboratories, Incorporated, and other companies...

On August 24, 1982, a longstanding antitrust suit between AT&T and the United States Government was disposed of by a judicially approved agreement between the parties. United States v. American Telephone and Telegraph Company, et al., 552 F.Supp. 131 (D.D.C. 1982), *affd. sub nom.* Maryland v. United States, 460 U.S. 1001 (1983). Under the terms of that decision and its subsequent judicially approved implementation... certain "local exchange" functions of the BOCs were to be placed in the aforementioned seven RHCs and AT&T was to divest itself of its holdings therein.

In an action unrelated to the antitrust suit, the Federal Communications Commission ("FCC"), on April 2, 1980, ordered that, on or before March 1, 1982, certain acts be taken to separate the functions of the BOCs...

In 1980, AT&T owned all of the outstanding stock of the BOCs, with the exception of some minority shares held by unrelated third parties in the New England Telephone and Telegraph Company, the Mountain States Telephone and Telegraph Company, Pacific Northwest Bell Telephone Company and the Pacific Telephone and Telegraph Company ("Pacific").

Various steps were taken to implement the FCC mandate and at the same time serve the business interests of the Bell system, of which only those steps relating to Pacific need to be described herein.

Under an agreement of merger, dated November 5, 1981, between AT&T, Pacific and Pacific Transition Corporation ("Transition"), a newly formed, wholly owned subsidiary of AT&T, Transition would merge into Pacific and Pacific voting stockholders (other than AT&T and dissenting shareholders) would receive .35 shares of AT&T common stock (and cash in lieu of fractional shares) in exchange for each share of Pacific common stock and $60 in cash for each share of Pacific 6 percent voting preferred stock. The outstanding Pacific common and percent voting preferred stock would be cancelled and the outstanding share of Pacific Transition Corporation (held by AT&T) would be converted into one share of Pacific common stock.

The merger was consummated on May 12, 1982. At that time, Pacific had 224,504,982 shares of voting common stock, 205,345,275 (91.5 percent) of which were owned by AT&T, 820,000 shares of 6 percent voting preferred stock, 640,957 (78.2 percent) of which were owned by AT&T, and 21,120,000 shares of nonvoting preferred stock, none of which were owned by AT&T. The balance of the voting stock was publicly held, and the non-voting preferred stock was held by institutional investors. Because the nonvoting preferred stock remained outstanding after the merger, AT&T did not acquire control of Pacific within the meaning of section 368(c) and the merger therefore resulted in recognition of gain or loss to Pacific's common and voting preferred shareholders.

On February 19, 1982, AT&T announced that, to accomplish the divestiture, the 22 BOCs would be grouped into seven regions. A separate, independent holding company structure was established for each region. This structure was subsequently incorporated in the Plan of Reorganization filed by AT&T on December 16, 1982, and approved by the court in United States v. Western Electric Company, Inc., 569 F.Supp. 1057 (D.D.C.), *affd. sub nom.* California v. United States, 464 U.S. 1013 (1983).

The Plan of Reorganization provided that the Articles of Incorporation of Pacific would be amended to convert the one outstanding share of Pacific voting common stock into 224,504,982 shares of voting common stock (the number of common shares outstanding prior to the merger), and to modify the rights of the nonvoting preferred stock to entitle each share to one vote per share with cumulative voting for directors as authorized by California law. By this change, AT&T would acquire control of Pacific by means of a tax-free reorganization, and then PacTel Group would be in control of Pacific within the meaning of section 368(c) at divestiture.

On January 21, 1983, AT&T applied to the Internal Revenue Service ("IRS") for rulings (the "Application") that, inter alia, the amendment to Pacific's Articles of Incorporation would be a reorganization within the meaning of section 368(a)(1)(E), and no gain or loss would be recognized by AT&T or by the preferred shareholders on the constructive exchange of their preferred stock. Under date of October 6, 1983, the IRS ruled that the amendment qualified as a reorganization within the meaning of section 368(a)(1)(E), and that no gain or loss would be recognized by Pacific, AT&T or the preferred shareholders.

In accordance with the Plan of Reorganization, AT&T and its affiliates would transfer to each regional holding company, in exchange for the latter's voting stock, the stock of the appropriate BOCs and other assets. Among the assets to be transferred to the PacTel Group were 224,504,982 shares of Pacific voting common stock. Thereafter, AT&T would then distribute to its stockholders one share of stock in each of the seven regional holding companies for every ten shares of AT&T stock owned by AT&T shareholders of record at the close of business on December 30, 1983. Fractional shares would not be issued but would be aggregated and sold and the cash proceeds distributed to the stockholders.

The January 21, 1983, Application also asked for rulings that, inter alia, no gain or loss would be recognized on the transfers of the stock of the BOCs and other assets to the regional holding companies in exchange for stock and that no income, gain or loss would be recognized by AT&T shareholders upon the receipt by them of the stock in the holding companies.

The IRS ruled that no gain or loss would be recognized on the transfer of stock of the BOCs and other property to the seven regional holding companies in exchange for their stock and that no income, gain or loss would be recognized by AT&T shareholders upon the receipt of the stock of the six regional holding companies other than PacTel Group. With respect to the latter, the IRS ruled that a portion of the PacTel Group stock was taxable to the AT&T shareholders. The IRS thereafter advised that this portion of the PacTel Group stock had a value at the time of distribution equal to $.39 per share of AT&T stock and the parties have accepted that value for the purposes of this case.

Section 355(a)(1) allows a corporation to make a tax-free distribution of the stock of a controlled corporation (control being defined in section 355(a)(1)(D)(ii) by reference to section 368(c)) to its shareholders in a tax-free distribution, provided the active business requirement of section 355(b) is met and the transaction is deemed not to be merely a "device" to distribute tax free, earnings and profits which otherwise would be taxable as a dividend. There is no dispute between the parties that these conditions have been satisfied. The issue upon which they have parted company is whether the limitations of section 355(a)(3)(B) apply. That section provides for the taxation of part of the distribution as follows—

> (B) Stock Acquired in Taxable Transactions Within 5 Years Treated As Boot.—For purposes of this section (other than paragraph (1)(D) of this subsection) and so much of section 356 as relates to this section, stock of a controlled corporation acquired by the distributing corporation by reason of any transaction—
>
> > (i) which occurs within 5 years of the distribution of such stock, and

(ii) in which gain or loss was recognized in whole or in part, shall not be treated as stock of such controlled corporation, but as other property.

Section 356(b), in turn, provides that "the fair market value of such other property shall be treated as a distribution of property to which section 301 applies."

Petitioner concedes that, if AT&T had distributed the Pacific stock directly to its shareholders, the Pacific stock acquired in the merger would have been treated as "other property" under section 355(a)(3)(B), because the merger was a taxable transaction that took place within five years of the divestiture. Petitioner argues, however, that it was PacTel Group stock, not Pacific stock, which AT&T distributed to its shareholders. Since this stock was acquired in what respondent concedes was a tax-free exchange, petitioner argues that none of such stock can be categorized as "other property."

Respondent contends that petitioner's position is overly simplistic and that the language of section 355(a)(3)(B) is sufficiently broad to permit an interpretation which will be more accommodating to what he views as the legislative purpose behind the section's enactment, namely to preclude not only direct distributions of purchased interests in an active business but also indirect distributions of such interests emanating from a holding company structure. By way of amplification of his position, respondent argues that (1) we should treat a portion of the PacTel Group common stock as having been acquired via the prior taxable acquisition of Pacific stock with the result that the "by reason of any transaction" provision of section 355(a)(3)(B) is satisfied, or (2) in view of the overall statutory framework of section 355, Pacific, as part of the PacTel Group, falls within the ambit of the statutory phrase "controlled corporation" as that term is used in section 355(a)(3)(B). As a consequence, respondent concludes that such portion of. PacTel stock as represents the fair market value of the Pacific stock (stipulated to be $.39 per share of AT&T stock) constitutes "other property" and is taxable as a dividend.

A literal reading of section 355(a)(3)(B) appears to support petitioner's position. On its face, the statutory language is directed to the distribution "*of stock of a controlled corporation*, acquired by the distributing corporation by reason of any [taxable] transaction [occurring] within 5 years of the *distribution of such stock*." (Emphasis added.) As used in section 355(a)(1)(A) the term "controlled corporation" means a corporation which the distributing corporation "controls immediately before the distribution" within the meaning of section 368(c). Since AT&T did not own directly any stock of Pacific immediately before the distribution, and because the stock attribution rules of section 318 are not applicable to section 368(c), it follows that, from a literal standpoint, Pacific was not a "controlled corporation" of AT&T for purposes of section 355(a)(3)(B). On this basis, petitioner would prevail.

We think it appropriate, however, not simply to adhere to the literal meaning of section 355(a)(3)(B). It can be argued—as indeed respondent does herein—that the words of that section are sufficiently ambiguous to permit a resort to legislative history, an aspect of this case to which we now turn our attention.

The stock boot rule of section 355(a)(3)(B) made its first appearance in the Senate version of the Internal. Revenue Code of 1954, H.R. 8300, 83d Cong., 2d Sess. (1954). Section 355(a)(3) in the amendments to the Bill as reported by the Senate Finance Committee on page 122 (June 18, 1954) provided that—

> stock of a controlled corporation acquired by the distributing corporation within 5 years of its distribution, in a transaction in which gain or loss was recognized in whole or in part, shall not be treated as stock of such controlled corporation, but as other property.

In commenting on the addition of this section, the Senate Finance Committee stated that—

> For purposes of determining the taxable nature of part of the exchange or distribution, stock in a controlled corporation acquired by purchase within 5 years of its distribution is treated as "other property." Thus, for example, if a corporation has held a minority stock interest in a corporation for 5 years or more prior to the distribution and within such 5–year period purchases control of such corporation only the stock so purchased will be considered "other property." ... [S. Rept. No. 1622, 83d Cong., 2d Sess. 26768 (1954).]

The Conference Committee modified this proposal, however, and explained the modification as follows—

> In section 355(a)(3), the phrase "by reason of any transaction which occurs within 5 years of the distribution of such stock" has been inserted in lieu of the phrase "within 5 years of its distribution, in a transaction." The effect of this change is to make certain that, in addition to treating stock of a controlled corporation purchased directly by the distributing corporation as "other property," similar treatment will be given such stock if it is purchased within 5 years through the use of a controlled corporation or of a corporation which, prior to a "downstairs merger," was in control of the distributing corporation. For example, if the parent corporation has held 80 percent of the stock of an active subsidiary corporation for more than 5 years but purchases the remaining 20 percent of such stock within the 5–year period, and distributes all of the stock, gain or loss will not be recognized nor will dividend treatment be accorded the stock distributed to the extent of 80 percent. The 20 percent of the stock will be treated as "other property" for purposes of section 356. Similarly, under the amendment made, where such parent causes another subsidiary to acquire the 20 percent of the stock and then itself acquires such stock in a liquidation in which no gain or loss is recognized to such parent under section 332, or

where the subsidiary having held 80 percent of the stock of its subsidiary for more than 5 years, acquires the 20 percent of the stock which has been purchased by the parent within the 5–year period through a nontaxable "downstairs" merger of the parent into the subsidiary, and all of the stock is distributed, such 20 percent of the stock will in either case be treated as "other property." [H. Rept. No. 254;1, 83d Cong., 2d Sess. 38 (1954).]

Thus, the "by reason of any transaction" language was added to prevent a distributing corporation from avoiding taxation by acquiring additional controlled corporation stock via a purchase by a related entity coupled with some type of tax-free combination. The focus of section 355(c)(3)(B) both before and after the change remained the same; on the acquisition and distribution of stock of the controlled corporation, not on the acquisition of stock of the underlying, active subsidiary which was not actually distributed.

This brings us to respondent's second argument, namely that the overall statutory framework of section 355 requires section 355(a)(3)(B) to be interpreted as focusing not merely on the stock of the controlled corporation being distributed, but on the actual operating subsidiary included in the spin-off. Respondent correctly points out that the statutory framework of section 355(b)(2)(A) "itself envisions situations where a holding company will be used as the distributing mechanism for an active subsidiary." It provides that a corporation will qualify as an "active business" if for the 5 year period ending on the date of distribution it has been—

> engaged in the active conduct of a trade or business, or substantially all of its assets consist of stock and securities of a corporation controlled by it (immediately after the distribution) which is so engaged. . .

Thus, section 355(b)(2)(A) allows the distributing corporation to "look through" the controlled corporation to its underlying active subsidiary in order to satisfy the active business requirement. Similarly, to qualify as an active trade or business under section 355(b)(2)(D) during the 5 years prior to the distribution of stock, it must be established that—

> control of a corporation which (at the time of acquisition of control) was conducting such trade or business (i) was not acquired directly (or through one or more corporations) by another corporation. . .

Therefore, much like section 355(b)(2)(A), this section cuts through the form of the spin-off and focuses directly on the underlying active subsidiary when considering whether or not a corporation qualifies as an active trade or business.

From this legislative framework, respondent concludes that, since it is the activity of the underlying subsidiary that qualifies the spin-off as a tax-free section 355 distribution to begin with, it is only logical and consistent that for section 355(a)(3)(B) purposes, we must also focus on the underlying active subsidiary. Unfortunately for respondent, as we have already observed, neither the words of section 355(a)(3)(B), nor its legislative history, support his conclusion. Furthermore, although respondent discusses at great length the congressional purpose behind the passage of the "active business" provisions of section 355(b), his attempts to explain why we should interpret section 355(a)(3)(B) in a similar light, so that these two sections are read in "symmetry," with a focus on the active subsidiary, are far from convincing. Absent a clearer statement of legislative intent that we should look through the stock of the controlled corporation, we find it difficult to make the analytical jump respondent asks of us. . . In fact, in light of the clear and detailed statutory scheme of section 355(b), the conspicuous absence of similar language in section 355(a)(3)(B) suggests that Congress was not only aware of the claimed "inconsistency," but intended just such a result.[1] More over, we have not overlooked the interpretative implications of the fact that, both in operative text and examples, respondent's regulations under section 355 have been for some thirty years, and are anticipated to continue to be, conspicuously silent in respect of transactions of the type involved herein.

However, our inquiry is not over. While it appears that both the plain meaning of section 355(a)(3)(B), as well as its legislative history, support petitioner's position, we also recognize that—

the courts have some leeway in interpreting a statute if the adoption of a literal or usual meaning of its words "would lead to absurd results . . . or would thwart the obvious purpose of the statute." . . .

Or, to put it another way, we should not adopt a construction which would reflect a conclusion that Congress had "legislate[d] eccentrically." . . . We are satisfied that our reliance on the wording of the statute involved herein would not have any such deleterious consequences either in terms of sections 355(a)(3)(B) specifically or section 355 generally. To begin with, pursuant to the merger, AT&T issued 6,705,897 shares of its common stock, with a fair market value of $370,500,834, in exchange for the 19,159,707 publicly held shares of Pacific common stock, and paid $10,742,580 for the 179,043 publicly held shares of Pacific 6 percent voting preferred stock. Thus, over 97% of the consideration furnished by AT&T to acquire the Pacific stock consisted of newly issued shares of its own stock. Since the underlying purpose of section 355(a)(3)(B) is to prevent the conversion of excess, liquid funds, such as cash and marketable securities, into additional controlled corporation stock that can then be distributed tax-free in a spin-off, we fail to see how respondent can argue that the spin-off of PacTel Group stock in any way frustrated the "obvious purpose of the statute."

Furthermore, by spinning off PacTel Group stock, AT&T did not bail out earnings and profits and thus undermine the general statutory purpose

---

[1] Moreover, Congress has proven itself quite capable of enacting stock-taint rules when it has desired to do so. See, e.g., section 306(c)(1)(B)(ii) in which the same Congress that enacted section 355(a)(3)(B) provided for an "inherited taint" rule with respect to preferred stock received in exchange for section 306 stock pursuant to a plan of reorganization.

of section 355, because the Pacific stock acquired from the minority share-holders pursuant to the merger has remained in corporate solution and has never passed into the hands of AT&T's shareholders. Although respondent argues that this is merely a form over substance argument because the benefit of the purchased interest in the Pacific stock was transferred to PacTel Group, and thus was indirectly distributed to AT&T's shareholders, we note that—

> A dividend does not confer an economic benefit on its recipient. The distribution leaves the shareholder no richer, since his directly owned assets increase only by the same amount that the beneficial ownership of those assets represented by his stock interest diminishes. A dividend therefore is included in gross income not because it affects the shareholder's net worth (which is increased even by undistributed corporate profits), but because the distributed property no longer is in corporate solution. [Kingston, The Deep Structure of Taxation: Dividend Distributions, 85 Yale L.J. 861, 863–864 (1976).]

Thus, even assuming, arguendo, that the net worth of each sharehold-er increased as a result of the AT&T stock purchase,[2] the simple fact re-mains that this did not give rise to a taxable event because AT&T did not distribute the Pacific stock. A bailout, like a dividend, by definition requires a distribution out of corporate solution. This has not occurred.

That the Pacific stock which was acquired in a taxable transaction re-mained in corporate solution is most significant. It has caused us to focus on some of the problems which would arise if respondent's approach were adopted herein. For example, how would a future distribution of Pacific stock be treated? Another problem which would arise, if respondent's ap-proach were adopted, involves the necessity of determining the value of the "tainted" stock transferred in the later nontaxable exchange and allocating that value to the shares of stock acquired in that exchange which then be-come the subject of a section 355 distribution—a problem which we are not required to face herein because of the parties' agreement as to the value attributable to the purchased Pacific stock and allocable to the distributed PacTel stock. The problem is even more difficult when more than one class of stock of the controlled corporation is received by the distributing corpora-tion in the nontaxable exchange. Beyond this is a still further complication if respondent should carry his approach to its logical conclusion and, in a later case, should ask us to extend the view which he asks us to adopt here-in to a purchase of stock of a subsidiary of the controlled corporation within 5 years of a section 355 distribution. Granted that the courts often deal with problems of allocation without specific legislative mandate, it does not

---

[2] We note that AT&T's shareholders did not in fact benefit from the Pacific merger. While we recognize that the acquisition, on AT&T's books, resulted in an increase in total net assets and corporate net worth (because AT&T acquired the majority of the Pacific stock for newly issued shares instead of for cash or debt securities), this increase did not filter down to the existing AT&T shareholders. When a corporation issues new stock in exchange for adequate consideration, existing shareholders realize no increase in the value of their individual hold-ings, because although the overall net worth of the company rises, so does the number of shares outstanding.

necessarily follow that they should extend the interpretation of a statute to create such a problem.

The long and the short of the matter is that we see no thwarting of legislative purpose by confining section 355(a)(3)(B) to the situations which Congress obviously had in mind at the time of its enactment. In so concluding, we are constrained to observe that, if respondent feels that a transaction of the type involved herein represents an obvious attempt to bail out earnings and profits in violation of the purpose behind section 355, he is not without his remedy. He can challenge such a transaction as a "device" under section 355(a)(1)(B). He has chosen not to do so in this case, because of the conceded business purposes involved in implementing the antitrust decree and FCC order, and we are satisfied that he should not be permitted to avoid this channel of attack by means of an overly broad construction of section 355(a)(3)(B). Thus, while we agree with respondent that business purpose is irrelevant to the proper construction of section 355(a)(3)(B), we do not agree with his contentions, that "Congress, in enacting section 355, intended to put direct distributions of stock of existing corporations on a par with indirect distributions of such stock through the use of holding companies and that the 'by reason of any transaction' language was specifically added to section 355(a)(3)(B) to make it clear that the section was to be applied not only to direct purchase of stock by distributing corporations, but also to any conceivable indirect purchase of stock within five years of the distribution." (Respondent's brief, p. 40.)

The absolutism of respondent's contentions is unacceptable. Essentially respondent seeks to have us do what Congress might have done if the type of transaction involved herein had been brought to its attention. But it is not within the province of this Court thus to expand upon the handiwork of the legislature. . .

In view of the foregoing, decision will be entered for petitioner.

Reviewed by the Court.

NOTES

1. Does *Dunn* provide a road map for a taxpayer seeking to avoid the constraints of § 355(a)(3)(B)? How would you have decided *Dunn*, and how would you have written your opinion?

2. What is the purpose of § 355(a)(3)(B) and how does it (should it) fit into the legislative scheme? (Note that § 355(a)(3)(B) is often referred to as the "hot stock" rule). What is the role of § 355(b)(2)(D), enacted more recently? For example, in *Dunn* what would have been the outcome if AT&T initially owned less than 80% of Pacific (say 70%) and then acquired the additional shares of Pacific? In November 2011, final regulations were issued under § 355(a)(3)(B) that were intended to harmonize the hot stock rules with the active trade or business requirements in § 355(b).

5. Additional Anti–Abuse Provisions—§ 355(D) & (E)

After the repeal of *General Utilities*, corporations have had a strong incentive to structure transactions to effectuate a sale of a business without triggering the corporate level tax. In the 1990s Congress added two measures to § 355 to curb these transactions: § 355(d) and 355(e). If either of these provisions applies to a § 355 transaction, then corporate level gain must be recognized (but not shareholder level gain).

Section 355(d): If a corporation makes a "disqualified distribution," the corporate level gain on the transaction must be recognized. A "disqualified distribution" occurs where the distributing corporation makes a § 355 distribution and immediately thereafter, either (1) any person holds "disqualified stock" totaling a 50% or greater interest in the distributing corporation, or (2) any person holds "disqualified stock" totaling a 50% or greater interest in the controlled corporation. Disqualified stock is (1) any stock of the distributing corporation purchased within 5 years of the distribution, or (2) any stock in the controlled corporation purchased within 5 years of the distribution or received *as a distribution* on stock purchased in the past 5 years. Thus, section 355(d), which only applies where § 355 is otherwise satisfied, sets a de facto 5–year holding period for 50% or greater changes in the ownership of either the distributing or controlled entity. Regulations provide some exceptions to the potentially broad reach of § 355(d). Treas. Reg. § 1.355–6(b)(3)(1).

Section 355(e): In 1997 Congress further limited tax free divisive transactions by enacting § 355(e), the anti-*Morris Trust* rules. If a § 355 distribution is part of a *plan* to enable a person(s) to "acquire directly or indirectly . . . a 50 percent or greater interest in [either] the distributing [or controlled corporation]" then the corporate level tax is triggered. Recall the *Morris Trust* transaction (distributing corporation spun off a controlled subsidiary with undesired assets in advance of a tax free merger of the distributing corporation). After § 355(e) the former shareholders of the distributing corporation must have more than 50 percent of both the distributing and controlled corporations *after* the transaction.

In Rev. Rul. 2005–65, 2005–41 I.R.B. 1, the Service concluded that the distribution of a controlled cosmetics subsidiary by its parent pharmaceutical business was *not* part of a plan of reorganization under § 355(e) in which one or more persons acquired control in the distributing pharmaceutical corporation. The parent pharmaceutical corporation ("Parent") and its cosmetics subsidiary were both competing for capital in a way that disadvantaged the cosmetics business. Thus, Parent decided the best option was to distribute the cosmetics subsidiary to the Parent shareholders pro rata. After announcing the distribution, but prior to its completion, a 3rd party, X, (also engaged in the pharmaceuticals business) began discussing acquisition of Parent. This possible acquisition was not necessary for Parent to continue its business. Prior to the distribution by P of the cosmetics subsidiary, X merged into Parent—but nothing in the merger agreement required the subsequent distribution of the cosmetics subsidiary. Following the merger, former X shareholders received 55% of Parent stock. After the merger, Parent distributed the cosmetics subsidiary stock as planned. The Service agreed with the taxpayer that the distribution and acquisition/merger were *not* part of a plan to shift ownership (see Treas. Reg. § 1.355–7(b)(1)); the distribution was motivated by a distinct business purpose and despite their proximity in time, the merger and the distribution were not part of a plan under § 355(e).

Interaction: If § 355(d) and (e) overlap, then § 355(d) is applied to the transaction. § 355(e)(2)(D). Note that both provisions need a minimum 50% change in ownership to take effect. Many other requirements differ, however. Section 355(e) covers a wider array of transactions (both in terms of numbers of acquirers and types of acquisitions). Section 355(d) operates with a set 5 year window, whereas § 355(e) establishes a rebuttable presumption that a "plan" exists where the 50% ownership change occurs within 2 years before or 2 years after the § 355 distribution. § 355(e)(2)(B). With the additions of § 355(d) and (e), could any of the other requirements under § 355 be reduced or eliminated?

More Planning: Legislation proposed in 2012 would amend § 361 by adding a new subsection to target "reverse Morris Trust transactions." In a reverse Morris Trust transaction a corporation distributes the stock of the controlled entity and then the distributed entity is merged into a third party. The proposal would treat as boot certain debt securities issued by the subsidiary in a divisive D. Willen, Ralcorp and Kraft are Planning a Reverse Morris Trust Transaction, 118 Tax Notes 209 (Jan. 7, 2008).

VII. CORPORATE SUBSTITUTION—REINCORPORATIONS, "F" REORGANIZATIONS, AND RELATED PROBLEMS

Smothers v. United States
642 F.2d 894 (5th Cir. 1981).

■ Before WISDOM, GARZA and REAVLEY, CIRCUIT JUDGES.

■ WISDOM, CIRCUIT JUDGE. . . This dispute arises from the dissolution of one of . . . [the Smothers'] wholly owned business corporations. The taxpayers contend that the assets distributed to them by that corporation should be taxed at the capital gain rate applicable to liquidating distributions. The Internal Revenue Service . . . counters by characterizing the dissolution as part of a reorganization, thereby rendering the taxpayers' receipt of the distributed assets taxable at ordinary income rates. The district court viewed the transaction as a reorganization and ruled for the IRS. We affirm.

In 1956, . . . [the taxpayers] and an unrelated third party organized Texas Industrial Laundries of San Antonio, Inc. (TIL). The taxpayers owned all of its outstanding stock from 1956 through the tax year in issue, 1969. TIL engaged in the business of renting industrial uniforms and other industrial cleaning equipment, such as wiping cloths, dust control devices, and continuous toweling. It owned its own laundry equipment as well.

Shortly after the incorporation of TIL, the taxpayers organized another corporation, Industrial Uniform Services, Inc. (IUS), specifically to oppose a particular competitor in the San Antonio industrial laundry market. The taxpayers owned all of the stock of IUS from the time of its organization until its dissolution. Unlike TIL, IUS did not own laundry equipment; it had to contract with an unrelated company to launder the uniforms it rented to customers. J. E. Smothers personally managed IUS, as well as TIL, but chose not to pay himself a salary from IUS in any of the years of its existence.

IUS evidently succeeded in drawing business away from competing firms, for TIL purchased its main competitor in 1965. IUS continued in business, however, until 1969. On the advice of their accountant, the taxpayers then decided to dissolve IUS and sell all of its non-liquid assets to TIL. On November 1, 1969, IUS adopted a plan of liquidation in compliance with § 337, and on November 30, it sold the following assets to TIL for cash at their fair market value (stipulated to be the same as their book value):

Assets	Amount
Noncompetitive covenant	$ 3,894.60
Fixed assets	491.25
Rental property	18,000.00
Prepaid insurance	240.21
Water deposit	7.50
Total	$22,637.56

The noncompetitive covenant constituted part of the consideration received by IUS from its purchase of a small competitor. The fixed assets consisted of incidental equipment (baskets, shelves, and a sewing machine), two depreciated delivery vehicles, and IUS's part interest in an airplane. The rental property was an old apartment building in Corpus Christi on land with business potential. These assets collectively represented about 15% of IUS's net value. The parties stipulated that none of these assets were necessary to carry out IUS's business.

After this sale, IUS promptly distributed its remaining assets to its shareholders, the taxpayers, then dissolved under Texas law:

Assets	Amount
Cash (received from TIL)	$ 22,637.56
Cash (of IUS)	2,003.05
Notes receivable	138,000.00
Accrued interest receivable	35.42
Claim against the State of Texas	889.67
Liabilities assumed	(14,403.35)
Total	$149,162.35

TIL hired all three of IUS's employees immediately after the dissolution, and TIL continued to serve most of IUS's customers.

In computing their federal income tax liability for 1969, the taxpayers treated this distribution by IUS as a distribution in complete liquidation within § 331(a)(1). Accordingly, they reported the difference between the value of the assets they received in that distribution, $149,162.35, and the basis of their IUS stock, $1,000, as long-term capital gain. Upon audit, the IRS recharacterized the transaction between TIL and IUS as a reorganization within § 368(a)(1)(D), and therefore treated the distribution to the taxpayers as equivalent to a dividend under § 356(a)(2). Because IUS had sufficient earnings and profits to cover that distribution, the entire distribution was therefore taxable to the Smothers' at ordinary income rates. The IRS timely assessed a $71,840.84 deficiency against the Smothers.' They paid that amount and filed this suit for a refund.

The district court held that the transaction constituted a reorganization and rendered judgment for the IRS. . .

Subchapter C of the Internal Revenue Code broadly contemplates that the retained earnings of a continuing business carried on in corporate form can be placed in the hands of its shareholders only after they pay a tax on those earnings at ordinary income rates. That general rule is, of course, primarily a consequence of § 301, which taxes dividend distributions as ordinary income. The Code provides for capital gain treatment of corporate distributions in a few limited circumstances, but only when there is either a significant change in relative ownership of the corporation, as in certain redemption transactions, or when the shareholders no longer conduct the business themselves in corporate form, as in true liquidation transactions. The history of Subchapter C in large part has been the story of how Congress, the courts, and the IRS have been called upon to foil attempts by taxpayers to abuse these exceptional provisions. Ingenious taxpayers have repeatedly devised transactions which formally come within these provisions, yet which have the effect of permitting shareholders to withdraw profits at capital gain rates while carrying on a continuing business enterprise in corporate form without substantial change in ownership. This is just such a case.

The transaction in issue here is of the genus known as liquidation-reincorporation, or reincorporation. The common denominator of such transactions is their use of the liquidation provisions of the Code, which permit liquidating distributions to be received at capital gain rates, as a device through which the dividend provisions may be circumvented.[7] Reincorporations come in two basic patterns. In one, the corporation is dissolved and its assets are distributed to its shareholders in liquidation. The shareholders then promptly reincorporate all the assets necessary to the operation of the business, while retaining accumulated cash or other surplus assets. The transaction in this case is of the alternate form. In it, the corpora-

---

[7] Other tax benefits may be reaped from reincorporation transactions in appropriate circumstances: e.g., elimination of the earnings and profits account of the old corporation in order to avoid the § 531 tax on unreasonable accumulation; and a step-up in the tax basis of depreciable corporate assets at capital gain rates to the extent permitted by § 1245 and § 1250. In light of IUS's relatively large earnings and profits account, the former benefit is not a trivial one here.

tion transfers the assets necessary to its business to another corporation owned by the same shareholders in exchange for securities or, as here, for cash, and then liquidates. If the minimal technical requirements of § 337 are met, as they indisputably were here, the exchange at the corporate level will not result in the recognition of gain by the transferor corporation. If formal compliance with the liquidation provisions were the only necessity, both patterns would enable shareholders to withdraw profits from a continuing corporate business enterprise at capital gain rates by paper-shuffling. Unchecked, these reincorporation techniques would eviscerate the dividend provisions of the Code.

That result can be avoided by recharacterizing such transactions, in accordance with their true nature, as reorganizations. A reorganization is, in essence, a transaction between corporations that results merely in "a continuance of the proprietary interests in the continuing enterprise under modified corporate form"—a phrase that precisely describes the effect of a reincorporation. Lewis v. Commissioner, 1 Cir. 1949, 176 F.2d 646, 648. Congress specifically recognized that the throw-off of surplus assets to shareholders in the course of a reorganization can be equivalent to a dividend, and if so, should be taxed as such. §§ 356(a)(1)–(2). The reincorporation transactions described above result in a dividend payment to the shareholders in every meaningful financial sense. The assets retained by the shareholders therefore should be taxed as dividends as long as the transaction can be fitted within the technical requirements of one of the six classes of reorganization recognized by § 368(a)(1).

In general, reincorporation transactions are most easily assimilated into § 368(a)(1)(D) ("D reorganization"), as the IRS attempted to do in this case.[9] A transaction qualifies as a D reorganization only if it meets six statutory requirements.

  (1) There must be a transfer by a corporation (§ 368(a)(1)(D));

  (2) of substantially all of its assets (§ 354(b)(1)(A));

  (3) to a corporation controlled by the shareholders of the transferor corporation, or by the transferor corporation itself (§ 368(a)(1)(D));

  (4) in exchange for stock or securities of the transferee corporation (§ 354(a)(1));

---

[9] Reincorporations may also fit within § 368(a)(1)(F) ("[a] mere change in identity form or place of organization, however effected"). See Davant v. Commissioner.... [page 621 infra]; Reef Corp. v. Commissioner, 5 Cir. 1966, 368 F.2d 125, 133–37, *cert. denied.* 1967, 386 U.S. 1018 [page 633 infra].... The government did not press that theory on appeal. Doubtless that owes to its general reluctance to extend the scope of § 368(a)(1)(F) to acquisitive reorganizations, which derives from the fact that net operating losses may be carried back after an F reorganization. § 381(b)(3).... The IRS has in the past occasionally advanced more exotic arguments against reincorporations—e.g., the theory that no real "liquidation" occurs in such transactions, and the theory that even if a liquidation does occur, the distribution of surplus assets is a dividend functionally unrelated to the liquidation—but it did not so argue here. Cf. Rev. Rul. 61–156, 1961–2 C.B. 62; Telephone Answering Service Co., Inc. v. Commissioner, ... [page 616 infra]; Breech v. United States, 9 Cir. 1971, 439 F.2d 409; Joseph C. Gallagher, 1962, [see infra page 615, note 4].

(5) followed by a distribution of stock or securities of the transferee corporation to the transferor's shareholders (§ 354(b)(1)(B));

(6) pursuant to a plan of reorganization (§ 354(b)(1)).

On this appeal, the taxpayers concede that the transaction in issue meets every technical prerequisite for characterization as D reorganization, except for one. They argue that since the assets sold by IUS to TIL amounted to only 15% of IUS's net worth, TIL did not acquire "substantially all of the assets" of IUS within the meaning of § 354(b)(1)(A).

We hold to the contrary. The words "substantially all assets" are not self-defining. What proportion of a corporation's assets is "substantially all" in this context, and less obviously, what "assets" are to be counted in making this determination, cannot be answered without reference to the structure of Subchapter C. To maintain the integrity of the dividend provisions of the Code, "substantially all assets" in this context must be interpreted as an inartistic way of expressing the concept of "transfer of a continuing business." As this Court implied in Reef Corp. v. Commissioner, 5 Cir. 1966, 368 F.2d 125, 132, *cert. denied*, 1967, 386 U.S. 1018, . . . it is in a sense simply a limited codification of the general nonstatutory "continuity of business enterprise" requirement applicable to all reorganizations.

This interpretation finds support in the history of § 368(a)(1)(D) and § 354(b)(1)(A). The Internal Revenue Code of 1939 had no provision equivalent to the "substantially all assets" requirements, and courts almost uniformly approved attempts by the IRS to treat reincorporation transactions as reorganizations within the predecessor of § 368(a)(1)(D) in the 1939 Code. The "substantially all assets" requirement of § 354(b)(1)(A) and the amendment of § 368(a)(1)(D) incorporating that requirement were added during the 1954 recodification as part of a package of amendments aimed at plugging a different loophole—the bail-out of corporate earnings and profits at capital gains rates through divisive reorganizations. There is no indication that Congress wished to relax the application of the reorganization provisions to reincorporation transactions. Indeed, the committee reports indicate the contrary. The Senate report accompanying the bill that contained the "substantially all assets" requirement of § 354(b)(1)(A) and the parallel amendment to § 368(a)(1)(D) stated that the purpose of those changes was only "to insure that the tax consequences of the distribution of stocks or securities to shareholders or security holders in connection with divisive reorganizations will be governed by the requirements of section 355." The report expressly noted that except with respect to divisive reorganizations, the reorganization provisions "are the same as under existing law and are, stated in substantially the same form." Even more significantly, the original House version of the 1954 Code contained a provision specifically dealing with reincorporation transactions. That provision was dropped in conference because the conferees felt that such transactions "can appropriately be disposed of by judicial decision or by regulation within the framework of the other provisions of the bill." As the court said in Pridemark, Inc. v. Commissioner, 4 Cir. 1965, 345 F.2d 35, 40, this response shows that "the committee was aware of the problem and thought the present statutory scheme adequate to deal with it." By implication, this passage approved the IRS's use of the predecessor of § 368(a)(1)(D) to meet the problem, and shows that the "substantially all assets" amendment was not thought to restrict its use.

Courts have almost unanimously so interpreted the "substantially all assets" language. Moreover, they have also interpreted the other technical conditions for a D reorganization in ways which accomplish the congressional intent to reach reincorporation transactions. For example, the literal language of § 368(a)(1)(D) and §§ 354(a), 354(b)(1)(B), requires that the transferee corporation "exchange" some of its "stock or securities" for the assets of the transferor, and that those items be "distributed" to the shareholders of the transferor, before a D reorganization can be found. Yet both of those requirements have uniformly been ignored as "meaningless gestures" in the reincorporation context, in which the same shareholders own all the stock of both corporations.[14] Smothers does not even challenge the applicability of that principle here.

Properly interpreted, therefore, the assets looked to when making the "substantially all assets" determination should be all the assets, and only the assets, necessary to operate the corporate business—whether or not those assets would appear on a corporate balance sheet constructed according to generally accepted accounting principles. Two errors in particular should be avoided. Inclusion of assets unnecessary to the operation of the business in the "substantially all assets" assessment would open the way for the shareholders of any enterprise to turn dividends into capital gain at will. For example, if we assume that "substantially all" means greater than 90%, then a corporation need only cease declaring dividends and accumulate surplus liquid assets until their value exceeds 10% of the total value of all corporate assets. The shareholders could then transfer the assets actively used in the business to a second corporation owned by them and liquidate the old corporation. Such a liquidating distribution would be a dividend in any meaningful sense, but an interpretation of "substantially all assets" that took surplus assets into account would permit the shareholders to treat it as capital gain. Indeed, such an interpretation would perversely treat a merely nominal distribution of retained earnings as a dividend, but would permit substantial distributions to be made at capital gain rates. Courts therefore have invariably ignored all surplus assets and have focused on the operating assets of the business—the tangible assets actively used in the business—when making the "substantially all assets" assessment.

---

[14] The "meaningless gesture," language is from James Armour, Inc., 1964, 43 T.C. 295, 307. See also, e.g., Atlas Tool Co. v. Commissioner, 3 Cir. 1980, 614 F.2d 860, 865, *cert. denied*, 1980, U.S.... Davant v. Commissioner.... [page621 infra]. Other technical requirements have been liberally construed in appropriate situations to foil reincorporations. For instance, § 354(b)(1)(B) technically requires that all properties received from the transferor corporation be distributed before a D reorganization can be found, but a "constructive distribution" was found in David T. Grubbs, 1962, 39 T.C. 42. Similarly, § 368(a)(1)(D) requires a "plan of reorganization," but a formal written plan is not necessary and the taxpayer's phraseology is not controlling if the transaction is in substance a reorganization. Atlas Tool Co. v. Commissioner, 614 F.2d at 866....

Second, exclusion of assets not shown on a balance sheet constructed according to generally accepted accounting principles from the "substantially all assets" assessment would offer an unjustified windfall to the owners of service businesses conducted in corporate form. The most important asset of such a business may be its reputation and the availability of skilled management and trained employees, none of which show up on a standard balance sheet. Other courts have correctly recognized that in appropriate cases those intangible assets alone may constitute substantially all of the corporate assets. Otherwise for example, a sole legal practitioner who owns nothing but a desk and chair could incorporate himself, accumulate earnings, and then set up a new corporation and liquidate the old at capital gain rates—as long as he is careful to buy a new desk and chair for the new corporation, rather than transferring the old.

When these principles are applied to this case, it is plain that "substantially all of the assets" of IUS were transferred to TIL, and that the transaction as a whole constituted a reorganization. TIL and IUS were both managed and wholly owned by Smothers. By the nature of its business, IUS was wholly a service enterprise; indeed, the parties stipulated that none of the tangible assets of IUS were necessary to the operation of its business. The extent to which those tangible assets were transferred to TIL is therefore entirely irrelevant. IUS's most important assets—its reputation, sales staff, and the managerial services of Smothers—were all transferred to TIL. TIL rehired all three of IUS's employees immediately after IUS's liquidation, and continued to serve IUS's old customers. The same business enterprise was conducted by the same people under the same ownership, and the only assets removed from corporate solution were accumulated liquid assets unnecessary to the operation of the business. To treat this transaction as other than a reorganization would deny economic reality; to permit Smothers to extract the retained earnings of IUS at capital gain rates would make a mockery of the dividend provisions of the Internal Revenue Code.

We do not perceive ordinary income treatment here to be particularly harsh or a "tax trap for the unwary." It places the Smothers only in the position they would have been in if they had extracted the retained earnings of IUS as the Code contemplates they should have—by periodically declaring dividends.[18]

Affirmed.

■ GARZA, CIRCUIT JUDGE, dissenting. After carefully reading the majority's opinion, I find that I must respectfully dissent. Unlike my Brothers, who apparently feel that it is their duty to "plug loopholes," I would remain con-

---

[18] Of course, the progressive structure of the income tax in a sense penalizes the plaintiff, since dividend income that could have been spread over many years is concentrated in one year, but that result was avoidable at the taxpayer's discretion. Similarly, he could have taken out some of the earnings in the form of a salary. Note that in all probability, Smothers did not actually defer enjoyment of the retained earnings of IUS until the reincorporation transaction. IUS's major asset by far was $138,000 in "notes receivable." Although the record does not reveal who issued those notes, the inference could be drawn that Smothers took the earnings out of IUS as they were earned, tax-free, by simply borrowing them from the corporation.

tent in applying the tax law as it reads leaving the United States Congress to deal with the consequences of the tax law as it has been drafted. The only issue before this Court on appeal is whether or not IUS transferred "substantially all of its assets" to TIL. Instead of dealing with this straightforward question, the majority has made a case of evil against liquidation-reincorporation abuses and, in an attempt to remedy every such perceived abuse, they have relieved the Congress of its burden to change the law heretofore requiring that "substantially all" of a corporation's assets be transferred to now read that "only those assets necessary to operate the corporate business" be transferred in order to meet the "D reorganization" requirements. Essentially, the majority has changed the definition of "substantially all assets" to mean only "necessary operating assets." I believe if Congress had meant "necessary operating assets" it would have said so instead of specifically requiring that "substantially all" of the assets be transferred. In my mind "substantially all" plainly means *all* of the assets except for an insubstantial amount. Under such a definition, the sale of 15% IUS's assets to TIL could hardly be defined as "substantially all" of IUS's assets.

However, even after having redefined "substantially all" to mean "necessary operating assets," the IUS liquidation still falls short of the "D reorganization" requirements because the stipulated facts are that absolutely none of the assets sold from IUS to TIL were necessary operating assets for either corporation. Faced with an absence of a proper factual setting, the majority goes on to define necessary operating assets as including a corporation's intangible assets. Now while a sale of intangible assets might be an appropriate consideration in determining whether or not "substantially all" assets of a corporation have been transferred, such a consideration simply has no bearing in this case. All of the assets transferred to TIL were depreciated tangible objects sold at book value after which IUS completely ceased all business operations. There simply was no other transfer of IUS's intangible assets as a continuing business.

The majority has placed great emphasis on the fact that three of IUS's route salesmen were subsequently employed by TIL and that Mr. Smothers' managerial services were available to TIL. Regardless of whether or not these facts enhanced TIL's business, the fact remains that neither the route salesmen nor Mr. Smothers' services were *transferred* as assets from one corporation to another. After IUS ceased business its route salesmen were free to seek any employment they desired. Likewise, Mr. Smothers was never obligated to perform services for TIL. From these facts I cannot agree that there was a transfer of a continuing business. The majority imputes adverse tax consequences to IUS's stockholders simply because TIL offered new employment to the route salesmen who were unemployed upon cessation of IUS's business operations. The majority places future stockholders, in Mr. Smothers' position, of choosing between unfavorable tax consequences and helping secure future employment to loyal and deserving employees who otherwise would be unemployed.

Although the Internal Revenue Service has never questioned the bona fides of IUS's liquidation, the majority has gone beyond the stipulated facts by characterizing the liquidation as a tax avoidance scam. I simply cannot agree. After starting from scratch, Mr. Smothers worked for over a dozen years refraining from drawing salary in order that IUS could pay its taxes, employees and other operating expenses and in order for IUS to become a successful self-sustaining business enterprise. Mr. Smothers was successful but, now that he no longer could devote his service to IUS, his years of labor are now labeled by the majority as a mere "paper shuffle." I do not share the majority's attitude.

The reasons for my position can be more easily understood by a simple review of the bottom-line facts. After IUS began showing a profit and started accumulating a cash surplus, instead of immediately investing in a building or in other equipment for its operations, it continued its operations as before. Now, if IUS had purchased real property or depreciable personal property for its operations (instead of leasing as it had been) and had sold these properties pursuant to its plan of liquidation, certainly no argument would be made that the money initially invested in those properties should have been declared by IUS as dividends. However, instead of investing its accumulations, IUS simply put them in its bank account as the tax laws allow and presumably faced any tax consequences posed by such an accumulation.

After IUS ceased operations, was liquidated, and its assets distributed to its stockholders in exchange for their stock, the I.R.S. issued a deficiency, not because IUS was reorganized within the meaning of . . . § 368(a)(1)(D), but rather because the I.R.S. felt the accumulated earnings of IUS coupled with long-term capital gains rates applicable to the stock exchange provided an undesirable windfall to IUS's stockholders. In essence, the I.R.S. sought to expand the "D reorganization" provisions, lessen the availability of long-term capital gains treatment to corporate stockholders, and totally ignore the purpose of the tax upon improperly accumulated surplus as provided in . . . § 531. The majority seeks to do equity for the I.R.S. position by "treating" the IUS liquidation as a "D reorganization." I do not believe the taxpayers or the tax laws are served by upholding an I.R.S. deficiency for the sole purpose of "plugging loopholes." The lesson to be learned from the majority's opinion is clear—future corporations faced with similar circumstances need only invest their otherwise accumulated surplus in some method other than savings. In the process of liquidation they need sell whatever assets exist to third parties unrelated to their stockholders and their stockholders should make no effort to find future employment for the corporation's employees.

It seems to me that in its attempt to "plug" a perceived "loophole," the majority is giving this Court's imprimatur to a variation of the same so-called "mockery" of the tax laws sought to be prevented by its opinion.

For these reasons, I respectfully dissent.

NOTES

1. In Walter S. Heller, 2 T.C. 371 (1943), *aff'd*, 147 F.2d 376 (9th Cir.), *cert. denied*, 325 U.S. 868 (1945), one of the very early liquidation-reincorporation cases, the shareholders were denied a loss on liquidation under the predecessor of § 331 since, upon a finding that "reorganization" had occurred, the predecessor of § 354(a)(1) barred its recognition. *Compare* Capital Sales, Inc., 71 T.C. 416 (1978) (P Corporation's principal asset, a franchise from an unrelated manufacturer, was cancelled and granted to commonly controlled S Corporation; P sold its remaining assets to S and liquidated; held, no "D" reorganization because franchise was not "transferred"), *with* Commissioner v. Morgan, 288 F.2d 676 (3d Cir. 1961), *cert. denied*, 368 U.S. 836 (1961) (lack of "transfer" of investment advisory contract not sufficient basis for denying a "D" reorganization). Not surprisingly, in Rev. Rul. 70–240, 1970–1 C.B. 81, the Commissioner ruled that a corporation's sale of its operating assets to another corporation under common control with the transferor, followed by liquidation of the transferor and distribution of nonoperating assets to the sole shareholder, resulted in a "D" reorganization and a dividend. To the same effect as *Smothers*, see Simon v. Commissioner, 644 F.2d 339 (5th Cir. 1981).

2. Could *Smothers* qualify as an "F" reorganization today? Notice the restriction now in § 368(a)(1)(F)—"a mere change in identity, form, or place of organization of one corporation."

3. After the 2003 Tax Act's reduction in dividend tax rates, what is the real difference in tax treatment for the shareholders in *Smothers* under the Service's view and under the shareholder's view?

4. In Gallagher v. Commissioner, 39 T.C. 144 (1962), *acq. and nonacq.*, 1964–2 C.B. 5, 9, a Delaware corporation ("Delaware Corp.") engaged in the stevedoring and terminal business, was owned 61.95% by the taxpayers and 38.05% by estates and widows. Pursuant to a plan, a new corporation ("New Co.") was organized (owned 72 2/3% by the taxpayer, 27 1/3% by top employees). Delaware Corp. adopted a liquidation plan and transferred its operating assets, pre-paid expenses, and trade accounts to New Co. for cash. Delaware distributed its remaining cash and property to its shareholders (totaling more than $1 million) in complete liquidation. This plan was prompted by several goals including: (1) the elimination of the estates' and widows' ownership, and (2) the granting of stock ownership to key executives. The Service characterized the transaction as a reorganization, thus treating the distribution of assets as boot taxable as a dividend. The Tax Court, after reviewing the possible types of reorganizations that the transaction could be under § 368, concluded that in no case were all of the requirements satisfied. For example, D reorganization status was inapposite because the former Delaware Corp. shareholders owned only 72 2/3% of New Co. stock, failing the 80% threshold then in effect for § 368(a)(1)(D). The Service also argued that the redemption of Delaware Corp. stock was not really a redemption because no true liquidation took place. Presumably the Service viewed that redemption as equivalent to a dividend under § 302(b)(1) and taxable as ordinary income. The court concluded that in cases in which a corporation is liquidated and its assets and business are carried on by a new corporation mostly owned by liquidating corporation shareholders, the Code calls for the reorganization provisions to govern: "if a transaction of a similar kind does not fall within [the reorganization provi-

sions], but lies in the general area of arrangements which may, in effect, constitute the continuation of an existing business, it shall be treated as a transaction giving rise to gain or loss and not as a distribution." Thus, the transaction in *Gallagher* was treated as a partial liquidation, and the taxpayers properly treated the cash and property received in redemption of their Delaware Corp. stock as an exchange.

5. In 1984 Congress effectively overruled *Gallagher* by relaxing the control requirement for acquisitive "D" reorganizations. See § 368(a)(2)(H). Congress indicated that this amendment was not intended to "supersede or otherwise replace the various doctrines that have been developed by the Service and the courts to deal with" transactions such as those in *Telephone Answering Service Co.* (infra) and *J. E. Smothers* (page 604 supra).

6. What was the basis for the Commissioner's first argument in *Gallagher*? See Treas. Reg. § 1.301–1(%93). Would this approach lead to dividend treatment of *all* the shareholders of Delaware? Of *all* who continued in California? By what factors did the Commissioner determine that there was "in substance a separate transaction"?

7. Since now dividends face tax rates comparable to those on capital gains, what would be at stake if *Gallagher* occurred today?

Telephone Answering Service Co. v. Commissioner
63 T.C. 423 (1974), *aff'd by order*, 546 F.2d 423 (4th Cir. 1976), *cert. denied*, 431 U.S. 914 (1977).

■ TANNENWALD, JUDGE. . . [T]he sole issue for determination is whether the gain realized by petitioner on the sale of all the stock of one of its subsidiaries to a third party is to be recognized. The resolution of this issue depends upon whether the factual pattern involved herein meets the requirements of section 337. . . [TASCO, the petitioner, operated telephone answering services and provided managerial services to its two subsidiaries, Houston and North American, both of which also operated telephone answering services. The stock of Houston had been acquired in 1961 in exchange for stock of TASCO. North American was organized in 1962 to acquire services in other parts of the country. TASCO's income was derived from its separate answering services and from its management contracts; neither Houston nor North American ever paid a dividend.

[In April 1966, a general agreement was reached between TASCO and an unrelated party for the sale of the Houston stock. In May 1966, the board of directors adopted a "Plan of Complete Liquidation and Dissolution," and approved a contract for the sale of Houston. The sale was consummated for cash in October 1966, resulting in a realized gain to TASCO of approximately $270,000.

[In March 1967, TASCO transferred all of the assets necessary to its answering service and management operations to a newly organized, wholly owned subsidiary, New TASCO, in exchange for the latter's stock. The only assets retained by TASCO were the North American stock, the New

TASCO stock, and the cash received on the sale of Houston. New TASCO entered into a management contract with North American.

[In April 1967, TASCO distributed all of its remaining assets to its shareholders and filed articles of dissolution under state law. New TASCO changed its name to TASCO and continued in business with the same customers, employees and offices as its predecessor.

[Also in April 1967, Houser, a 15.7–percent shareholder of New TAS-CO following the above distribution, surrendered all of his stock in exchange for the assets of a telephone answering service owned by North American. This stock was later transferred by North American to New TASCO.]

Petitioner claims that following these steps it was completely liquidated, and therefore section 337 requires nonrecognition of the gain realized on its sale of Houston. We disagree, and hold that the requirements of that section have not been satisfied.[4] Our decision is founded on both the history and the purpose of the statute.

Section 337 was first enacted as part of the 1954 Code. It was intended by Congress to avoid the "shadowy and artificial" distinction between a closely held corporation and its shareholders required by Commissioner v. Court Holding Co., . . . and United States v. Cumberland Public Service Co., . . . when corporate assets are sold during liquidation. . . That section permits the avoidance of a double tax by allowing nonrecognition of gain at the corporate level, without the *Court Holding–Cumberland* requirement of proving that the shareholders, not the corporation, made the sale. Congress placed a price on nonrecognition, however, which is that the sale shall be followed by complete liquidation.

The Internal Revenue Code does not define a complete liquidation. Clearly, the term conveys more than the formal dissolution of a corporation under state law. Pridemark, Inc. v. Commissioner, 345 F.2d 35, 41 (C.A. 4, 1965). In contrast with some other parts of the Code (compare, e.g., sections 331 and 336), section 337 is hedged with specific provisions designed to describe, at least in outline, the complete liquidations entitled to its benefits. The sale and distribution must be preceded by the adoption of a "plan of complete liquidation." More importantly, "*all of the assets of the corporation*" (less assets retained to meet claims) must be "*distributed* in complete liquidation." (Emphasis added.) This language evidences an intent to re-

---

[4] Although the notice of deficiency merely denied the applicability of section 337, respondent in this Court concentrates principally on the argument that the instant transaction was a reorganization meeting the requirements of sections 354 and 368(a)(1)(D). We find it unnecessary to reach this issue particularly with regard to the question whether New TASCO acquired "substantially all" of TASCO's assets, and we express no opinion as to its proper resolution. Similarly, we do not consider the proposition, disavowed by respondent, that the exchange should be treated in whole or in part as a divisive reorganization qualifying under section 355. In this context, we emphasize that we are dealing herein with the question of nonrecognition of gain *at the corporate level* and not with the tax consequences of the transactions *at the shareholder level*; in view of the complexities involved in determining those consequences, under a variety of permutations and combinations, it is conceivable that they might be subjected to a different analysis....

quire a bona fide elimination of the corporate entity and does not include a transaction in which substantially the same shareholders continue to utilize a substantial part of the directly owned assets of the same enterprise in uninterrupted corporate form.[5] . . .

The record herein demonstrates that TASCO sought to avoid the recognition of gain on the sale of Houston. But, the presence or absence of a tax avoidance objective is irrelevant in determining what is a "complete liquidation" for tax purposes. United States v. Cumberland Public Service Co., supra. . . While a complete liquidation is a prerequisite to the application of section 337, the mere adoption of a plan denominated as one of "complete liquidation" and purported compliance therewith does not preclude further inquiry on our part. It is the reality and substance of the liquidation that counts. . .

In Pridemark, Inc. v. Commissioner, supra, the Fourth Circuit stated . . .:

> The corporation must have ceased to be a going corporate concern, or if the enterprise is continued in corporate form, the shareholder must have disassociated himself from it. See Regs.1.332–2(c) (1955). If the liquidated business is not resumed by the new corporation as a continuation of a going concern, there is a "complete liquidation."

Similarly, in Davant v. Commissioner, 366 F.2d 874, 882 (C.A. 5, 1966), . . . the Fifth Circuit stated:

> Those provisions [dealing with complete liquidation] contemplate that the operating assets will no longer be used by the stockholders to carry on the business as a corporation.

. . . Both *Court Holding Co.* and *Cumberland Public Service Co.*, supra, which prompted the adoption of section 337, involved the sale of a corporate enterprise and the termination of the shareholders' interest in the business. It is not without significance that the Supreme Court, in the latter case, specifically distinguished gains in the course of a "genuine liquidation" from those of a "going concern." . . . Moreover, during its consideration of the Internal Revenue Code of 1954, the House Ways and Means Committee stated:

> [A] corporation will be deemed to have completely liquidated even though the business previously carried on—by it is continued in part-

---

[5] This interpretation is supported by Congress' failure to make section 337 applicable to sales of property in connection with partial liquidations and nonliquidating distributions in which the corporate form is retained, despite the possibility of the same "double tax" dilemma arising as with complete liquidations.... Section 333 of the House bill would have extended nonrecognition treatment to partial liquidations; the limitation to complete liquidations originated in the Senate Finance Committee....

nership or sole proprietorship *or other noncorporate form*. [Emphasis added. . .][7]

Clearly, the transactions under consideration herein did not meet the foregoing standards. The businesses which petitioner directly operated were continued without interruption by New TASCO, with substantial continuity of shareholder interest. The only result of the transaction was to place the North American stock and a sizable amount of cash in the shareholders' hands. New TASCO was merely the alter ego of petitioner with respect to all of its directly owned business assets; its formation and utilization served no purpose other than masking a distribution as one in complete liquidation. It is possible that the transactions can be treated as accomplishing a partial liquidation of petitioner within the meaning of section 346. We express no opinion on this score because, even if the requirements of a partial liquidation were found to have been met, section 337 would not apply. That section requires a "complete liquidation." . . . The transitory co-existence of TASCO and New TASCO does not support the conclusion that the subsequent but prearranged liquidation of the former effected a sufficient transmutation of the assets of petitioner out of corporate solution to satisfy the requirement of section 337 that "all of the assets of the corporation" be distributed. To hold for the petitioner in the instant case would frustrate the congressional purpose to deny section 337 treatment in connection with distributions of ongoing corporations. We cannot give tax effect to the "mere shifting of charters," Helvering v. Elkhorn Coal Co., . . . masquerading as a complete liquidation.

The facts before us are unlike those in Breech v. United States, 439 F.2d 409 (C.A. 9, 1971), and Hyman H. Berghash, 43 T.C. 743 (1965), *aff'd*, 361 F.2d 257 (C.A. 2, 1966). Those cases applied section 337 to liquidation-reincorporation transactions in which the continuity of shareholder interest between the old and new corporations was insufficient to satisfy the definition of a statutory reorganization. It was felt inappropriate to deny the existence of a complete liquidation where Congress had found the shift in ownership adequate to justify considering the transferee as a new, rather than a continuing, enterprise. . . Where such divergence in shareholder interest does not exist and the transferee corporation continues the business of the transferor, the courts have consistently held that no complete liquidation occurs. . .

Here, immediately after the dissolution of TASCO both of its directly owned businesses were continued by New TASCO, and, even if the contemporaneous, but apparently unrelated, redemption of the Houser shares . . . is taken into account, there remains a degree of shareholder continuity in

---

[7] ... The House bill contained, in section 336, definitions of complete and partial liquidations, which required inter alia a plan "under which the *termination of the business* or businesses and the *transfer of assets in redemption* of all or part of the stock is authorized...." [Emphasis added.]

excess of 84 percent. In short, petitioner has not satisfied the requirements of section 337.[9] . . .

■ STERRETT, J., dissenting: As argued by the parties the issue presented to the Court is whether the sale in question was made pursuant to a plan of complete liquidation as contended by petitioner or was merely part of an integrated transaction constituting a reorganization as maintained by respondent.

Specifically respondent asserts that the entire transaction qualifies as a reorganization within the meaning of sections 368(a)(1)(D) and 354. I would hold otherwise on the grounds that the legislative history makes it quite clear that section 354(b) was not designed to cover divisive reorganizations (a split-up in this case).

This Court has faced before, on several occasions, the issue of how to categorize a transaction that does not meet the requirements of the reorganization provisions. In Joseph C. Gallagher, 39 T.C. 144 (1962), we said:

> . . . The liquidation of Delaware, although the business was continued by California with considerable change in the corporate structure, falls squarely within the first definition of a partial liquidation. Congress intended that in this situation, any redemption could not be treated as essentially equivalent to a dividend, and that *this problem of the continuation of a business must be dealt with, if at all, under the reorganization sections. Since these facts do not fall within the careful language of those sections, the distributions should be treated as payment in exchange for the stock.* To find differently would be to enact that provision which has failed on two separate occasions to be enacted by Congress. See H. Conf. Rept. No. 2543, to accompany H.R. 8300 (Pub. L. 591), 83rd Cong., 2d Sess., page 41 (1954), and H.R. 4459, 86th Cong., 1st Sess., sec. 26 (1959). [Footnotes omitted; Emphasis added.] . . .

Since the transaction then does not fall within the reorganization provisions, which are designed to cover the instances of the continuation of an existing business through a liquidation coupled with an intercorporate transfer, it follows under the teachings of prior case law that the transaction must, perhaps by definition of terms, be treated as a liquidation.

For years respondent, when faced with a liquidation-reincorporation transaction, had sought to extract an ordinary income tax on the distribution either by calling the transaction a reorganization with boot or a naked distribution taxable under sections 301 or 302. Insofar as I am aware respondent has only prevailed when this or any court has found a reorganization accompanied by a nonqualifying distribution taxable as boot. When a

---

[9] Nothing we have said should be construed as holding that section 337 does not apply where one corporate tier is eliminated through the complete liquidation of a parent corporation and no directly held assets of the parent corporation remain in corporate solution. Nor do we necessarily preclude the applicability of section 337 where the amount of such assets remaining in corporate solution can be said to be de minimis....

court has not found a reorganization, respondent has inevitably lost with the distribution deemed to be made in exchange for stock. Never has the respondent prevailed on the section 301–302 argument.

Now for the first time, if the logic of the majority's holding is extended, the respondent will win his point. "How sweet it will be" and who could have expected it when the respondent was simply trying to forestall the applicability of section 337 by invoking the reorganization provisions. The majority's holding is rather gratuitous, to say the least.

The majority seeks to make its decision at the corporate level more palatable by suggesting that consistency is not required between the transaction's treatment at the corporate level and at the shareholder level, implying that a section 337 liquidation must be more "complete" than a section 331 liquidation. This novel suggestion finds no support in any decisional law. . . In my judgment the majority is simply playing with words in order to reach what is, I suspect, a preconceived desired result. An unfortunate by-product of this form of rationalization is the creation of uncertainty where none had existed and, if there is one thing our income tax laws do not need, it is more uncertainty.

The majority seems preoccupied with a continuity of shareholder interest approach. The minimal (less than 15 percent) continuity of assets is ignored. Even the House version of section 357 of the 1954 Code required, among other things, a 50 percent continuity of assets before ignoring a purported liquidation. The opinion leaves up in the air what magic percentage combination of shareholder and asset transfer will, in the future, invalidate an asserted liquidation.

In this fully stipulated case I note that there is no evidence that there was, or was not, a business purpose to the transaction in issue. Of course, it is well established that the existence of a business purpose is irrelevant to the determination of whether a complete liquidation took place. . .

Finally, the majority relies heavily on certain dicta in Pridemark, Inc. v. Commissioner. . . This reliance is rather odd since the fact of the matter is that the final holding of that court was that a liquidation had in fact taken place. I must also note that in *Pridemark*, as in the instant case, the controlling shareholders remained the same and that, also in both cases, minimal assets were "reincorporated." It may well be argued that the majority has misconstrued its authority.

For the foregoing reasons I would stick with existing law and find for petitioner.

■ Dawson and Drennen, JJ., agree with this dissent.

Notes

1. What are the implications of footnote 9 in the court's opinion? Was the court correct not to carry through the analysis?

2. See Lester J. Workman, 36 T.C.M. (CCH) 1534 (1977) (corporation sold its operating assets and distributed proceeds in liquidation to shareholder, who transferred them to new corporation; no reorganization); Rev. Rul. 77–191, 1977–1 C.B. 94 (distribution of assets of one of two corporate businesses to shareholders, who transferred them to a new corporation, was a § 355–§ 368(a)(1)(D) reorganization, not a partial liquidation); Rev. Rul. 76–429, 1976–2 C.B. 97 (a subsidiary sold one of two businesses, then liquidated; the parent reincorporated the remaining business in a new subsidiary; held, not a § 332 liquidation).

Davant v. Commissioner

366 F.2d 874 (5th Cir. 1966), *cert. denied*, 386 U.S. 1022 (1967).

■ Before RIVES and BELL, CIRCUIT JUDGES, and FULTON, DISTRICT JUDGE.

■ RIVES, CIRCUIT JUDGE. The petitioners are persons who claim that the income from the sale of their stock in the South Texas Rice Warehouse Company should be taxed solely as a capital gain. The Tax Court found that a corporate reorganization had taken place and held that at least part of petitioners' income should be taxed as a dividend constituting ordinary income. The government took a cross appeal contending that the Tax Court should have held that a greater portion of petitioners' income was ordinary income. Since we agree with the government, we affirm in part and reverse in part.

South Texas Rice Warehouse Co. [Warehouse] was incorporated under the laws of the State of Texas in 1936. The principal business of Warehouse consisted of drying, cleaning, and storing rice. Warehouse's principal source of rice was land owned by a brother corporation, South Texas Water Co. [Water].

Water was incorporated under the laws of the State of Texas in 1934. Water had two principal businesses. It owned land which it rented to a partnership, South Texas Rice Farms [Farms], and it owned and operated an irrigation canal system used to irrigate the ricelands that it leased to Farms.

The principal business of Farms was releasing the land rented from Water to tenant farmers on a sharecrop arrangement. Generally, the tenant retained 50% of the rice produced and Farms received the other 50% as payment for the land provided.

The riceland which was leased by Farms from Water was irrigated by Water and the rice which Farms received from its tenants was put through Warehouse's dryer and stored by Warehouse. Water's lessees generally put their rice through Warehouse's dryer, and then stored their rice in Warehouse's facilities.

Warehouse and Water were each owned in equal proportions by four families. The partners in Farms were the same persons who were the stockholders of Warehouse and Water and their respective interests were in substantially the same proportions as their stock ownership in the two corporations. The books and records of these three enterprises, while separately prepared, were all kept in the same office.

In 1960 a number of the stockholders consulted an attorney, Homer L. Bruce, Esq., about the possibility of transferring Warehouse's operating assets to Water for $700,000 and then liquidating Warehouse. This attorney had represented Warehouse, Water, and their stockholders for many years.

In the attorney's opinion, section 337 would allow the individuals to obtain capital gains treatment for any income they might receive in the transaction they contemplated.[8] However, Mr. Bruce advised against such a course of conduct. He told them that in a situation where a sale and distribution was made when the stockholders of the two corporations were identical it was probable that the Internal Revenue Service would take the position that the stockholders had received a dividend taxable at ordinary rates and not a capital gain.

Mr. Bruce then suggested an alternate course of conduct which he believed would have the desired effect of having any gains taxed at the capital rather than the ordinary rate. The suggestion was that if the stockholders made a sale of their stock to a person not connected with them or their corporations at a fair price which would allow that person to make a reasonable profit, then that person could sell Warehouse's operating assets to Water and liquidate Warehouse without endangering the original stockholders' capital gains treatment.

Homer L. Bruce, Jr., a practicing attorney and the son of petitioners' attorney, was suggested by one of the stockholders as an appropriate person to buy their stock. Both Water and Warehouse had a corporate account with the Bank of the Southwest[9] and the Bank had for many years been represented by Mr. Bruce's law firm.

Mr. Bruce contacted A. M. Ball, a vice-president of the Bank. He told Mr. Ball that his son wished to buy Warehouse for $914,200 and wished to borrow the necessary funds from the Bank. The stock of Warehouse was to be the collateral for the $914,200 note of Bruce, Jr. It was understood that Water would then buy the assets of Warehouse for $700,000, and that this money plus part of the approximately $230,000 which Warehouse had in its bank account would be used, after Warehouse was liquidated, to repay the loan. This procedure allowed Bruce, Jr. to receive $15,583.30 for his part in the transaction, and allowed the Bank to receive what the parties designated as one day's interest on its $914,200 loan or $152.37.

Homer L. Bruce, Jr. was not present during his father's discussions with Mr. Ball nor did Bruce, Jr. participate in the discussions which determined that $914,200 should be the purchase price for the Warehouse stock and $700,000 the purchase price of Warehouse's operating assets to be paid

---

[8] While the attorney spoke in terms of section 337, he, of course, meant sections 337 and 331.

[9] Hereafter, Bank.

by Water. No appraisals were made of the properties of Warehouse during 1960, although the Tax Court later found their fair market value to be at least the $700,000 paid for them by Water. The Bank loaned Bruce, Jr. $914,200, yet was never furnished a statement of his finances nor an appraisal or statement on Warehouse.

Mr. Ball, who approved the $914,200 loan, had no authority to approve loans in excess of $25,000 without prior approval of the Bank's discount committee. This particular transaction was not approved by the discount committee until after it was entirely a fait accompli.

On August 26, 1960 the stockholders of Warehouse, Mr. Ball, Mr. Bruce and his son met at the Bank. In accordance with a detailed instruction sheet, the respective parties went through the motions of making a loan, selling stock, electing new corporate officials, selling Warehouse's assets, liquidating Warehouse, and repaying the loan. Thanks to the careful prearrangement of all the details, the parties were able to act out their respective roles in approximately one hour.[11]

In terms of the actual physical carrying on of Warehouse's business, absolutely no disruption was occasioned by the paper transfer to Water. Every part of the business was carried on as before with the sole change being that it was necessary to keep one less set of books at the office. August 26 came during the busy rice drying season, but for those physically involved in carrying on Warehouse's business affairs, August 26, 1960 came and went like any other day—the dryers kept right on drying.

Petitioners take the position that the sale of their stock in Warehouse to Bruce, Jr. was a bona fide sale and that they properly reported their profits as the gain from the sale of a capital asset held over six months. The Commissioner argues that the transaction involved in this case is a corporate reorganization and that to the extent of the earnings and profits of both Warehouse and Water the gain reported here must be considered as a dividend taxable as ordinary income. The Tax Court held that the instant transaction constituted a corporate reorganization coming under section 368(a)(1)(D) of the Internal Revenue Code of 1954. However, the Tax Court also held that the gain was taxable as a dividend only to the extent of Warehouse's earnings and profits. . .

In order to effectuate the intent of Congress the dividend, liquidation, redemption and reorganization sections of the Code must be examined and viewed as a functional whole. The basic framework by which Congress sought to tax corporate distributions is contained in sections 301(a), 301(c) and 316. Distributions of corporate funds to stockholders made with respect to their stockholdings must be included in their gross income to the extent that those distributions are made out of the corporation's earnings and profits. Such distributions are termed by the Code as dividends and are taxed as ordinary income.

---

[11] In addition to the instruction sheet, all of the necessary documents had been prepared in advance. These documents included the necessary papers for Warehouse's "sale" of its operating assets to Water.

All of the steps taken by taxpayer in this case with regard to the $200,000 worth of earnings and profits generated by Warehouse and the $700,000 worth of earnings and profits generated by Water were for the sole purpose of turning what otherwise would be a dividend taxed at the ordinary income rate into a gain made on the sale or exchange of a capital asset taxed at the much lower capital gains rate.

First, petitioners tell us that all they have done is sell their entire stock interest in Warehouse in a bona fide sale to an outside party. The sale of all of one's stock in a corporation, thus terminating a taxpayer's proprietary interest in a corporation and its assets, is probably one of the most common forms of capital sales. But the Tax Court held, "The facts in this case show that Homer L. Bruce, Jr., was not a purchaser of the stock in any real sense but merely a conduit through which funds passed from Water Co. to Warehouse and from Warehouse to petitioners." In this Court petitioners stress the fact that there was never a binding, written obligation on Water to buy Warehouse's assets or on Bruce, Jr. too sell them. Like the Tax Court, in view of all the circumstances, we can attach very little importance to the absence of any written obligations.

For the purposes of the personal income tax provisions, courts have never been shackled to mere paper subterfuges. It is hard to imagine a transaction more devoid of substance than the purported "sale" to Bruce, Jr. . . Congress has provided in great detail what the tax consequences of a reorganization or partial or complete liquidation of a corporation should be. The tax consequences of this transaction must be judged by those standards because to allow the "sale" to Bruce, Jr. to divert our attention from the tax policies enacted by Congress would be to exalt form above all other criteria. He served no function other than to divert our attention and avoid tax. Stated another way, his presence served no legitimate non-tax-avoidance business purpose. . .

The petitioners insist that, even if we recognize that Bruce, Jr. was merely their agent and impute his acts to them, they are entitled to capital gains treatment. They stress that they did no more than completely liquidate Warehouse corporation, which entitled them to a capital gain under section 331. The sale to Water of Warehouse's operating assets should not be treated as a taxable event, the petitioners argue, because of section 337. The "general rule" pronounced by section 337 is that if a corporation adopts a plan of complete liquidation and distributes all of its assets in complete liquidation within 12 months after the date the plan was adopted, no recognition of gain or loss shall be recognized on the sale of its property made during those 12 months.

Section 331 provides that when a corporation is completely liquidated section 301 is inapplicable and the gain shall be treated as if derived from a sale or exchange of the stock. In short, the gain is to be treated as a capital gain. It would appear at first blush that petitioners have carefully fitted themselves directly within the statutory wording. But in the landmark case of Gregory v. Helvering, 293 U.S. 465 (1935) the Supreme Court refused to give effect to a corporate transaction which complied precisely with the formal requirements for a nontaxable corporate reorganization, on the ground that the transaction had served no function other than that of a contrivance to bail out corporate earnings at capital gains tax rates. That is precisely the charge made here. Let us examine what legitimate purposes might be served by the transactions here under consideration. Three distinct and separate things occurred.

First, $700,000 in earnings and profits possessed by Water were passed through Warehouse to petitioners. Second, $200,000 in earnings and profits from Warehouse were distributed to petitioners. Third, the operating assets of Warehouse were combined with Water and were from that point on owned and controlled through Water. Only one business non-tax-avoidance purpose can be found to support any of these events: petitioners wished to eliminate one of the corporate shells and thereafter control all of the properties under one roof. This motive legitimately explains why petitioners transferred the operating assets of Warehouse to Water. But it does not explain either of the first two steps. Under the reorganization provisions of the Code petitioners could have transferred all of Warehouse's assets, including its earnings and profits, to Water without paying any tax. Thus the payment of $200,000 from Warehouse to petitioners cannot be explained as necessary in order to place both businesses under the same roof. Likewise, there was no need for petitioners to cast the transfer of Warehouse's operating assets in the form of a sale. The businesses could be combined under one roof without the $700,000 from Water ever coming over to Warehouse. It is apparent that no functional relationship exists between either the $200,000 coming to petitioners from Warehouse or the $700,000 coming to petitioners from Water and the transfer of Warehouse's assets to Water. Petitioners make no attempt to provide a non-tax-avoidance purpose for their actions, but instead argue that these events cannot be a reorganization because they do not come under the literal language of the reorganization provisions. They then reason they must be a complete liquidation since they do come under the literal language of the complete liquidation provisions. As Justice Frankfurter once put it, "The syllogism is perfect. But this is a bit of verbal logic from which the meaning of things has evaporated."[20]

Clearly, this liquidation cannot come within the intention of Congress in enacting the complete liquidation provisions. Those provisions contemplate that operating assets will no longer be used by the stockholders to carry on the business as a corporation. It has long been recognized that taxpayers cannot liquidate a corporation with the intention of immediately reincorporating it in order to hold back liquid assets and cash for the purpose of getting capital gains treatment or to obtain a stepped-up basis for the operating assets or to wipe out old earnings and profits or other tax attributes. Such a liquidation reincorporation transaction does not qualify for section 331 treatment... Applying the concept that we must look at petitioners' plan as a whole to the extent that the parts are functionally related, and not at its constituent parts individually, for the purpose of de-

---

[20] Phelps Dodge Corp. v. NLRB, 313 U.S. 177, 191 (1941).

termining whether—section 331 applies, we conclude that section 331 does not apply in this case.

Petitioners never intended to give up the corporate form of doing business. At all times relevant their intention was to transfer Warehouse's operating assets to Water. Water and Warehouse were owned by identical shareholders with identical distribution of shares. At no time did the petitioners' interest in the operating assets change. Most of the reported cases involve situations where the stockholders create a new corporate shell to receive the assets, but we see no difference between a liquidation followed by a transfer to a new corporate shell and a liquidation followed by a transfer to an already existing corporate shell.

Since this interchange of events cannot be viewed as a complete liquidation, we must now decide, for the purposes of the federal tax code, what it is. In the Tax Court the Government contended that this was a 368(a)(1)(D) or (F) reorganization.

A section 368(a)(1)(F) reorganization is defined as "a mere change in identity, form, or place of organization, however effected." Since the Tax Court held that this transaction was a (D) reorganization, it apparently believed that it was unnecessary to decide the (F) question. In the past, type (F) reorganizations have overlapped with type (A), (C) and (D) reorganizations. For this reason this provision has received almost no administrative or judicial attention. It is true that a substantial shift in the proprietary interest in a corporation accompanying a reorganization can hardly be characterized as a mere change in identity or form. Helvering v. Southwest Consolidated Corp., 315 U.S. 194 (1942).

The term "mere change in identity [or] form" obviously refers to a situation which represents a mere change in *form* as opposed to a change in substance. Whatever the outer limits of section 368(a)(1)(F), it can clearly be applied where the corporate enterprise continues uninterrupted, except for a distribution of some liquid assets or cash. Under such circumstances, there is a change of corporate vehicles but not a change in substance. If Water had no assets of its own prior to the transfer of Warehouse's operating assets to it, could we say that Water was any more than the alter ego of Warehouse? The answer is no. The fact that Water already had other assets that were vertically integrated with Warehouse's assets does not change the fact that Water was Warehouse's alter ego. Viewed in this way, it can make no practical difference whether the operating assets were held by Water or Warehouse, and a shift between them is a mere change in identity or form. At least where there is a complete identity of shareholders and their proprietary interests, as here, we hold that the type of transaction involved is a type (F) reorganization.

In the alternative, we also hold that the Tax Court correctly held that these events constituted a 368(a)(1)(D) reorganization. The (D) question is more complex than the (F) question. . . In this case, it is clear that the petitioners have satisfied part one of the type (D) definition. Warehouse is a "corporation" and it transferred "a part of its assets to another corporation,"

Water. Since both corporations were owned identically by petitioners the "control" requisite was fulfilled.

Petitioners argue that the provision cannot apply to them because in part two Congress specifically required that "stock or securities" of the transferee corporation be passed to petitioners. They, of course, point out that they received no new stock in Water as a part of their transaction. We cannot agree that this statutory requirement must be taken literally, especially where it would prevent the effectuation of the tax policies of Congress.

The (D) reorganization provisions have never been confined to a strictly literal application. It will be noted that section 368(a)(1)(D) requires that the transferor be "a corporation." But it has been consistently held that a proper interpretation and application does not prevent from coming under the aegis of 368(a)(1)(D) a transfer made by "persons" who have received assets from a corporation with the intention of transferring them to another corporation. . .

Nor in ascertaining the intention of Congress should we ignore the function intended for part two of the type (D) definition. Section 368 is not an operative provision but merely defines what Congress meant by the term reorganization. The operative provisions for a 368(a)(1)(D) reorganization are those which Congress has cited, sections 354, 355 and 356. These latter three sections determine what will be the tax consequences of a type (D) reorganization. . .

In sections 354, 355 and 356 Congress has provided for the tax consequences of holding out cash or liquid assets in a 368(a)(1)(D) reorganization. Congress has drawn these provisions to cover the normal procedure for a taxpayer legitimately wishing to take advantage of the tax-free reorganization provisions. It is only natural then that Congress would speak in terms of stock transferred in the course of a reorganization. The exchange of stock in the course of a legitimate reorganization was the specific case most likely to occur to the mind and the most logical way to draw the statute. The fact that Congress drew the statute to fit the most common form of the problem does not mean that it had any intention of allowing the two evils most inherent in a reorganization scheme to persist. . .

Moreover, since the operative sections were cast in terms of stock transfers, it was only normal that in referring to those sections in 368(a)(1)(D) . . . Congress referred to "stock or securities" "distributed in a transaction which qualifies under section 354, 355, or 356." Congress thus did not intend to place any special emphasis on the idea that stock *must* be transferred, rather Congress only intended to use this convenient terminology in referring to the operating provisions of the Code.

Petitioners' major argument against the application of 368(a)(1)(D) and 354, 356 thus rests on the weak foundation that Congress required stock to pass before a reorganization under section 368(a)(1)(D) could be found. Section 354 when coupled with section 356 requires that cash or liquid assets received by stockholders as part of a reorganization be taxed as a dividend. In Commissioner of Internal Revenue v. Morgan, 288 F.2d 676 (3 Cir. 1961), the taxpayer also claimed that Congress' clear intent could be avoided by a transaction where no new stock passed.

. . . Applying the rationale of *Morgan* to the instant case requires the same result. The same stockholders owned all of the stock of both Water and Warehouse. Before the transaction the operating assets' value of Warehouse was reflected in the value of its stock. Similarly, the operating assets' value of Water was reflected in the value of its stock. The stockholders had both stocks and their combined certificates reflected the value of their combined operating assets. After the transaction petitioners only had the stock of Water, but it then reflected the value of the combined operating assets of Water and Warehouse. Therefore, the appreciation of the value of Water's stock certificates caused by the transfer of Warehouse's operating assets to Water was the equivalent of issuing $700,000 worth of new or additional stock to Water's stockholders.[26] *Here the issuance of new stock would have been a meaningless gesture...* "Commissioner of Internal Revenue v. Morgan, supra; accord, Liddon v. Commissioner, 230 F.2d 304 (6 Cir. 1956), *cert. den*, 352 U.S. 824, 77 S. Ct. 34 (1956)." To require the actual transfer of stock certificates where such a transfer would be a meaningless gesture would be to make the reorganization provisions optional with the taxpayer, a result which Congress clearly did not intend. . .

We come now to the last leg of our journey; the question of whether the earnings and profits of Warehouse and Water should be combined in determining whether the full $900,000 cash received by petitioners should be treated as a dividend. We hold that the $700,000 coming indirectly from Water and the $200,000 coming from Warehouse must be tested against their combined earnings and profits. Whether we reach this result by means of calling this transaction a type (D) or type (F) reorganization, or a dividend declared simultaneously with a reorganization, makes no difference. But, in order to avoid future confusion, we think it appropriate to explain our three separate rationales.

Taking in inverse order the separate methods of reaching our conclusion, we hold that the $700,000 petitioners received from Water and the $200,000 petitioners received from Warehouse were dividends under section 301, declared incident to a reorganization. See Bazley v. Commissioner, 331 U.S. 737, 67 S. Ct. 1489 (1947). In *Bazley*, a corporation attempted to transfer liquid assets to a taxpayer, claiming they were a part of a reorganization under what is now section 368(a)(1)(E) which provides for recapitalizations. The Supreme Court characterized the modification of the cap-

---

[26] It follows logically from what we have said that the basis formerly belonging to petitioners' Warehouse stock must now be added to the basis of their Water stock. Had the assets of Warehouse been transferred to Water for Water's stock, as they would have been if this transaction had actually been cast as a reorganization, the Water stock would have received the basis of petitioners' Warehouse stock when Warehouse was liquidated. See Treasury Reg. 1.358–1. A different result should not be obtained just because petitioners received no new stock but merely allowed their existing stock to appreciate in value. Cf. Treasury Reg. 1.302–2(c).

ital account which constituted the reorganization-recapitalization as "unrelated" to the transfer of the liquid assets which the Court held to be a dividend under what is now section 301.

The same characterization is apt in the instant case. Three separate events took place. The distribution of $700,000 which had been generated incident to the earnings and profits of Water has no rational connection with the reorganization involving Warehouse. It was not necessary to pass this money through Warehouse and Bruce, Jr. in order to accomplish the reorganization. Everything that we said about Bruce, Jr. may be said about Warehouse in regard to the $700,000. Warehouse, under the circumstances of this case, was in no real sense a seller of assets to Water but merely a conduit through which funds passed from Water to Water's stockholders. Since both Warehouse and Water were owned in exactly the same way by the same stockholders, after the funds ended their circuitous route through Warehouse and Bruce, Jr., we see that they were a distribution "with respect to its stock" as required by section 301. The effect was precisely the same as if Water had passed there up directly to its stockholders.

The fact that we held that the transfer of Warehouse's assets and the "sale"—liquidation of Warehouse's stock should be viewed as an integrated transaction does not mean that we are being inconsistent when we separate the distribution of Water's cash to its stockholders. We are merely recognizing that two distinct and functionally unrelated types of transactions were carried on simultaneously—one was a dividend and the other a reorganization. The Code does the same thing in section 356. It recognizes that a series of complicated events may occur which are legitimately a reorganization. These are not taxed. Simultaneously, a taxpayer may receive boot having the effect of a dividend. The dividend's only relation to the reorganization is that it occurred at the same time. The boot where appropriate is taxed as a dividend.

Water, if it chose, could have declared the $700,000 as a dividend before the reorganization with Warehouse ever took place. Or Water could have waited and a week, a month or a year later distributed this dividend. Had it chosen any of these courses, the reorganization involving Warehouse would not have been affected in the slightest. We, therefore, hold that the $700,000 received by petitioners from Water is a distribution governed by sections 301(a), 301(c) and 316. The same reasoning demonstrates that $200,000 coming from Warehouse was a dividend since it was functionally unrelated to the reorganization. We, therefore, hold that the $200,000 received by petitioner from Warehouse is a distribution governed by sections 301(a), 301(c) and 316.

Even if the $700,000 received from Water were not a dividend under sections 301(c) and 316, it would be boot under section 356. Section 356 tells us that, when a taxpayer as part of a reorganization receives not only stock but liquid assets or cash to boot, that boot shall be taxed as a dividend to the extent of the earnings and profits of the distributing corporation. The Tax Court believed the words "of the corporation" referred only to Warehouse and, therefore, held that the $900,000 received should be taxed only to the extent of Warehouse's earnings and profits since it was the only distributing corporation.

We cannot agree with this narrow construction in a case where there is complete identity of ownership of both corporations. Water and Warehouse were but different pockets in the same pair of trousers worn by petitioners. It would be illogical to say that $700,000 would be used to measure how much of the $900,000 distribution had the effect of a dividend if Water were merged into Warehouse and only $200,000 should be used to measure how much of the $900,000 distribution had the effect of a dividend just because Warehouse was merged into Water.

Where there is complete identity of stockholders, the use of the earnings and profits of both corporations is the only logical way to test which distributions have the effect of a dividend. Before the reorganization the petitioners had two pockets with $900,000 in cash divided between them. After the reorganization the petitioners had removed all that cash from both pockets, and it should not matter that before removing it completely they took it out of the right pocket and put it in the left.

The statute in speaking of "the corporation" means the corporation controlled by the stockholders receiving the distribution. Where there is complete identity, as here, the stockholders control both corporations and it is virtually impossible to tell which corporation is in reality "the corporation" distributing the cash. We have two corporations each one of which is distributing cash; therefore, we must look at the earnings and profits of both corporations to see if the distribution is essentially equivalent to a dividend or has the effect of a dividend.

The Tax Court was correct that section 356(a)(2) in using the term "the corporation" meant the distributing corporation. However, the Tax Court erred when it failed to see that in this case there were two distributing corporations, each of which was a party to this reorganization. As we said in connection with our holding for purposes of applying section 301, Warehouse was a conduit for Water's distribution of $700,000 and thus, in determining which corporation was the distributing corporation for purposes of 356(a)(2), we must look through Warehouse and reach Water. . .

It would not benefit petitioners even if they prevailed on their argument that "the corporation" means only, the last distributing corporation. Section 482 permits the Commissioner to "allocate" such tax attributes as are here involved between two corporations "owned" "by the same interests" if "such" "allocation is necessary in order to prevent evasion of taxes." No clearer evasion of taxes can be imagined than converting what would be a dividend taxable at ordinary rates into a capital gain by merely passing it through another corporate shell. We hold that under section 356 and/or section 482 the effect of distributing the $700,000 and the $200,000 must be tested by the combined earnings and profits of both Warehouse and Water.

We need pause for only a moment at the door of 368(a)(1)(F). The effect of a type (F) reorganization is largely uncharted ground; we hold that the funds passed to stockholders in a type (F) reorganization must be tested by the standards laid down under sections 301 and 316. As we showed earlier, that would result in the $900,000 being tested by the earnings and profits of both Warehouse and Water.

Since the Tax Court did not find that Water's earnings and profits were at the time relevant for determining the effect of its distribution of $700,000, we must remand this case. The opinion of the Tax Court is affirmed in part and reversed in part, and the case is remanded for further proceedings not inconsistent with this opinion.

Affirmed in part and reversed in part.

NOTES

1. Rev. Rul. 70–240, 1970–1 C.B. 81, following *Davant*, holds that where there is complete identity of stock interest in the distributing and acquiring corporations, for purposes of § 356(a)(2) earnings and profits are to be determined with reference to the combined earnings and profits of the two corporations. The Tax Court and the Third Circuit have rejected this view and have held that only the transferor corporation's earnings and profits are to be considered in determining the amount of the distribution that is to be treated as a dividend under § 356(a)(2). See CCA 201032035 (adopting the approach to E&P calculations for dividend analysis that was outlined in *Davant* and in Rev. Rul. 70-240). See American Manufacturing Co., 55 T.C. 204 (1970), and Atlas Tool Co. v. Commissioner, 614 F.2d 860 (3d Cir. 1980), *cert. denied sub nom.* Schaffan v. Commissioner, 449 U.S. 836 (1980).

2. In Warsaw Photographic Associates v. Commissioner, 84 T.C. 21 (1985), the court reached a doubtful result in denying the taxpayer the benefit of a "D" reorganization primarily because stock of the acquiring corporation (the taxpayer) was not formally issued to the transferor corporation and distributed to the transferor's shareholders as part of the transaction. In doing so, it distinguished *Davant*, and stated that "[w]e have not found, and petitioner has not cited us to, any case . . . in which the court has acceded to a taxpayer's urging that the taxpayer be permitted to obtain a 'D' reorganization tax benefit even though the form of the transaction . . . did not meet the literal requirement of the statute."

Recall that in 2009 the Service issued final regulations regarding nondivisive D reorganizations. Treas. Reg. § 1.368–2(l). Among its provisions, the regulations provided that a transaction can constitute a D reorganization even though no stock of the transferee is issued in the deal, *if*, the issuance would have been meaningless because the parties were commonly owned in identical proportions (the "deemed issuance" rule). See supra Ch.4, Part V.B.9. Final regulations issued in 2009 confirmed the D reorganization status through a deemed issuance of shares – and also addressed the basis questions emerging from this approach. TD 9475, 74 Fed. Reg. 67,053 (Dec. 18, 2009); see also TD 9558, 76 Fed. Reg. 71878 (Nov. 21, 2011).

3. Suppose the ownership of Water and Warehouse had not been exactly the same. Might this still have been an "F" reorganization? A "D"? Would it have been proper to combine the earnings and profits of Water and Warehouse?

Suppose there were a 5–percent stockholder in Warehouse who had no interest in Water. What accounting would be made for his basis in his Warehouse stock? What effect would his situation have on the other stockholders?

Could the transaction be an "F" reorganization under the current § 368(a)(1)(F)?

Suppose Warehouse had an accumulated deficit. Would this have been set off against the earnings and profits of Water?

4. On the assumption that the court properly measured earnings and profits in *Davant*, does it follow that there is a dividend to the extent of all ratable earnings and profits? What is the significance of the formula in 356(a)(2) which limit taxation to *gain*? Is Treas. Reg. § 1.301–1(l) valid in light of the provisions of § 356(a), which limit taxation of the "boot" to the "gain" realized? Why is the limitation to "gain" found in § 356(a) but not in § 356(b) or § 356(f)? Should § 356(a) be limited to "gain" or, to the extent of ratable earnings and profits, should the full dividend-equivalent distribution be taxable? Cf. § 302(d).

Reef Corp. v. Commissioner

368 F.2d 125 (5th Cir. 1966), *cert. denied*, 386 U.S. 1018 (1967).

■ Before RIVES and BELL, CIRCUIT JUDGES and FULTON, DISTRICT JUDGE.

■ BELL, CIRCUIT JUDGE. [The court, dealing with a complex set of facts, decided unanimously that, in effect, (1) Reef Fields Gasoline Corporation (Reef Fields) first redeemed all the stock of a shareholder group owning 48 percent of its outstanding shares; (2) Reef Fields transferred about 80 percent of its assets to a new corporation (new Reef) wholly owned by the controlling (52 percent) shareholder group of Reef Fields; (3) the transfer of assets was pursuant to a plan of reorganization under § 368(a)(1)(D); (4) the assets transferred met the "substantially all" requirement of § 354(b)(1)(A); and (5) there was a "distribution" sufficient to meet the requirements of § 354(b)(1)(B). The court then considered whether the "D" reorganization might also constitute an "F" reorganization. If an "F" reorganization had occurred, Reef Fields would not have been entitled to file a return for the "short period" from the beginning of its taxable year on July 1, 1958, to April 27, 1959, the date of its dissolution, and the Commissioner's deficiency notice, sent to new Reef as successor in name only, would be valid to cover the entire period, July 1, 1958, to June 30, 1959.]

. . . The Commissioner, by way of a cross-appeal, contends that the Tax Court erred in not holding that the transaction . . . constituted a corporate reorganization under § 368(a)(1)(F) of the Internal Revenue Code of 1954, as amended. Additional taxes would be due under such a holding. We . . . reverse on the cross-appeal. . .

Reef Fields, which filed its income tax returns on an accrual basis and whose fiscal year ran from July 1 to June 30, filed an income tax return for the short taxable period July 1, 1958 to the date of dissolution, April 27, 1959. . . The Commissioner disallowed the return on the basis that new Reef was the successor in name to Reef Fields and thus the return should have been for the full fiscal year. This position, rejected by the Tax Court, was based on the premise that the transaction resulted in a reorganization under § 368(a)(1)(F).

Reef Corporation (new Reef), the petitioner, which had adopted the accrual method and the July 1 to June 30 fiscal year, filed an income tax return covering the short period December 15, 1958, the date of its incorporation, to June 30, 1959. . .

. . . The Commissioner contends on his appeal that the Tax Court erred in holding that the transaction did not constitute a reorganization under § 368(a)(1)(F), and in thus holding that the notice of deficiency to petitioner as the successor in name to Reef Fields Gasoline Corporation for a full fiscal year was invalid. . .

. . . It is his contention that the Tax Court erred in failing to hold that the transaction resulted in a corporate reorganization within the scope of § 368(a)(1)(F). His position is that no more took place than a mere change in identity, form, or place of organization of Reef Fields. Judges Rives and Fulton are of the view that this contention should be sustained. This means that the notice of deficiency sent to petitioner as the successor in name to Reef Fields will be validated and a remand will be necessary so that the Tax Court may consider the Commissioner's position under that deficiency notice.

The Commissioner sent two statutory notes of deficiency as a protective measure. One notice, addressed to "Reef Corporation (successor in name to Reef Fields Corporation)," was based on the position that new Reef, although a new corporate entity, was the same taxable entity as Reef Fields. The deficiency under this notice was claimed to be $111,894.40. The other notice, addressed to "Reef Corporation," treated new Reef as a new taxable entity to file a return covering the short taxable period but the depreciation and interest deductions were disallowed, as stated, and the additional tax due was claimed to be $70,695.18.*

The Tax Court rejected the Commissioner's position with respect to § 368(a)(1)(F), and thus the deficiency notice to petitioner as successor in name to Reef Fields was invalid. As noted, the Tax Court did adopt the Commissioner's alternative position that the transaction resulted in a corporate reorganization under § 368(a)(1)(D), and concluded that the assets transferred by Reef Fields to new Reef had a substituted basis for depreciation and not a stepped-up basis.

The reasoning which supports the conclusion of Judges Rives and Fulton that this is a § 368(a)(1)(F) reorganization follows.

In concluding that the instant case was not a type (F) reorganization, the Tax Court interpreted the Supreme Court's last sentence in Helvering

---

* The depreciation and interest deductions were claimed in the theory that there had not been a reorganization but a sale of assets by Reef Fields to new Reef, with a step-up in basis and part of the purchase price represented by interest-bearing debt.—ED.

v. Southwest Consolidated Corporation, 1942, 315 U.S. 194, . . . as holding § 368(a)(1)(F) is "inapplicable when there is a shift in proprietary interest." *Southwest Consolidated* was decided under the 1939 Internal Revenue Code, and we think that the complete revision of the Code in 1954 compels a different result under the instant circumstances from that reached in *Southwest Consolidated*. Further, this case is distinguishable on its facts from *Southwest Consolidated*.

A

The intricate and confusing facts of this case have been carefully explained. Distilled to their pure substance, two distinct and unrelated events transpired. First, the holders of 48% of the stock in Reef Fields had their stockholdings completely redeemed. Second, new Reef was formed and the assets of Reef Fields were transferred to new Reef. The business enterprise continued without interruption during both the redemption and the change in corporate vehicles.

Much confusion flows from the fact that the corporate reorganization took place simultaneously with the stock redemption. But taking the Code as a standard, these two elements were functionally unrelated. Reef Fields could have completely redeemed the stock of 48% of its shareholders without changing the state of its incorporation. A complete redemption is not a characteristic of a reorganization. Congress clearly indicated this when it defined reorganization in section 368. Section 368(a)(1)(A) speaks of a "merger or consolidation" which looks to the joining of two or more corporations. Section 368(a)(1)(B) and (C) look to one corporation acquiring the assets of another or control of another corporation solely for its voting stock. Section 368(a)(1)(D) looks to the consolidation of two or more corporations or the division of two or more going businesses into separate corporations. Only sections 368(a)(1)(E) and (F) look to adjustments within a corporation. But none of these provisions focuses on a complete redemption as a characteristic of a reorganization. Congress did not have redemption of stock as a primary purpose of any of the forms of a reorganization. That subject came under consideration when it undertook to enact specific legislation on complete and partial redemptions, section 302.

The boot provision, section 356, is adequate to cover a complete redemption when it occurs incident to a reorganization whose primary purpose conforms to the intent of section 354 or 355. But section 356 was principally designed to cover dividends incident to a reorganization. When the primary characteristics of the reorganization conform to those described by 368(a)(1)(F), we should parse the occurrences into their functional elements. The reorganizational characteristics present in the instant case do not conform to those generally intended to be covered by section 354 and therefore we should not be blinded by the 356 boot provision. To effectuate the intention of Congress manifested in the Code, we must separate this transaction into its two distinctly separate functional parts. The test of whether events should be viewed separately or together as part of a single plan is not temporal but is functional. See Davant v. Commissioner of Internal Revenue, 5 Cir. 1966, 366 F.2d 874. Applying this test to the instant case, it is clear that the redemption and the change of corporate vehicles must be viewed as separate and distinct occurrences. Cf. Bazley v. Commissioner of Internal Revenue, 1947, 331 U.S. 737. . .

B

In 1954 Congress completely overhauled the sections of the Code detailing the tax consequences of many types of corporate transactions. Grouped together by Congress were the sections dealing with corporate distributions and adjustments, including the sections dealing with partial liquidations, stock redemptions (complete or partial), and corporate reorganizations. As we said in Davant v. Commissioner of Internal Revenue, 5 Cir. 1966, 366 F.2d 874 at 879: "In order to effectuate the intent of Congress the dividend, liquidation, redemption and reorganization sections of the Code must be examined and viewed as a functional whole."

Prior to 1954 Congress had not specifically provided for the tax treatment of partial liquidations or redemptions. This problem had been handled by judicial decisions which caused "considerable confusion" and in some cases resulted in "unwarranted" taxes and in others allowed taxpayers to "avoid" proper taxation. To correct this situation, Congress enacted a comprehensive set of rules governing the complete and partial redemptions of a stockholder's interest in a corporation. Section 302.

In the instant case the only way to protect the statutory intent of Congress is to test the redemption of stock by the provisions of section 302. A similar result as to the stockholders comes from applying sections 368, 354 and 356. But this method may not always reach the same result and in the instant case would cause an improper result with regard to the corporation. Since the reorganization and the redemption are functionally unrelated in this case, the redemption should be tested by the standard Congress has laid down in section 302.

Prior to 1954 Congress had not specifically provided which tax attributes should be carried over to the surviving or new corporation remaining after a reorganization. . .

These adjustments had been left to judicial interpretation. . . Thus, in 1954, in order to correct the existing problems created by unrealistic and conflicting judicial decisions, Congress enacted a comprehensive set of rules governing the carry-over of tax attributes from one corporation to another as a result of a reorganization. Section 381.

In section 381 Congress made a rational distinction between reorganizations that constitute a mere change in form and those that integrate two previously separate and independent enterprises.

Where two or more separate businesses are unified into a single enterprise under a 368(a)(1)(D), 354 reorganization, Congress recognized that the resulting new enterprise should be allowed to change certain of its accounting procedures. See for example section 381(b). But Congress also realized that when the business enterprise is carried on as before, with no change in its substance, this is not a proper time to allow the business to change its accounting procedures. See for example 381(b).[12] Thus for the first time, in 1954 it became important to determine whether a reorganization was considered a (D) type or an (F) type reorganization.

Virtually all (F) reorganizations also qualify as (D) reorganizations. When a transaction qualifies as both an (F) and a (D) reorganization, if the new entity were governed by the less stringent continuity rules of (D) reorganizations, provided by section 381, the (F) rules would become a dead letter. The (F) rules are stricter than the (D) rules because a mere change of corporate charter or state of incorporation is not the proper occasion for wholesale accounting method changes that would not have been permitted if no reorganization had taken place.

Only those reorganizations which reflect a substantial change in the corporate operation should be viewed as *solely* (D) reorganizations qualifying for the, more liberal rules. Where there is no substantial change in the corporate operation, (F) should be applied since it invokes the stricter rules.

In the instant case there has been no substantial change in the operation of the corporate business. It is carried on just as before but in a new corporate vehicle. This is not a 354 "integration of two or more separate businesses into a unified business enterprise," which Congress considered when it adopted the more liberal rules applicable to a (D) reorganization.

What characteristics of reorganization are present in this case? The only characteristics of a corporate reorganization are the changes in name and state of incorporation. Those are primarily the characteristics of an (F), not a (D), reorganization. The redemption is not a characteristic of a reorganization, as is demonstrated by the fact that a redemption standing alone would not allow a corporation to make wholesale changes in its method of accounting.

If a corporation did no more than completely redeem the stock interest belonging to 48% of its shareholders, it could not under the Code make wholesale accounting method changes. Likewise, if a corporation did no more than change its name and state of incorporation, it could not under the Code make wholesale accounting method changes. Combining these two events, neither of which would be sufficient alone, will not permit a corporation to make wholesale accounting method changes. Nothing in the Internal Revenue Code of 1954 contemplates such a result.

. . . The Tax Court's position might have more force if the change in proprietary interests were to new persons and less than 50% of the former stockholders' interest in the old corporation remained in the new corporation. Then the change begins to look like a sale of the assets to a new and legally separate entity followed by a bona fide liquidation. . . But just how

---

[12] Section 381(b) excludes type (F) reorganizations from the liberal treatment accorded type (D) reorganizations.

much of a complete redemption would be required to avoid the impact of section 381? Would 1 ___ enough? Sufficient continuity of interest has been found where 67% or 69% of the old corporation's stockholders control the new corporation. Reilly Oil Co. v. Commissioner of Internal Revenue, 5 Cir. 1951, 189 F.2d 382; Western Mass. Theaters v. Commissioner of Internal Revenue, 1 Cir. 1956, 236 F.2d 186. Changes of less than 50%, as we have here, or for that matter any change not sufficient to prevent the finding of a reorganization should not be sufficient to prevent the operation of section 381. The corporate enterprise went on as before, no new blood was injected and all that took place was a redemption followed by a change in name.

We hold, therefore, that the changes made in the Code in 1954 make the *Southwest Consolidated* decision inapplicable here. We hold also that under the 1954 Code this transaction constituted both a 368(a)(1)(D) and a 368(a)(1)(F) reorganization. . .

■ BELL, CIRCUIT JUDGE, dissenting in part. I respectfully dissent from [the latter part] of the majority opinion. I do not think that the transaction in question constituted a corporate reorganization within the meaning of § 368(a)(1)(F). That section has been construed by the Supreme Court as being inapplicable where there is a shift in proprietary interest. Helvering v. Southwest Consolidated Corporation, 1942, 315 U.S. 194. . . Mertens, Law of Federal Income Taxation, § 20.94. Here there was a clear and substantial change in proprietary interest. [One] group was eliminated.

This is to be distinguished from the situation where only minor and technical differences between the original and surviving corporation will justify classification as a reorganization under § 368(a)(1)(F). See, for example, Davant v. Commissioner of Internal Revenue, 5 Cir., 1966, 366 F.2d 874, involving two corporations having precisely the same stockholders and proprietary interests. The assets of one corporation were conveyed to the other. And the court held the result to be a § 368(a)(1)(F) corporate reorganization. The court concluded that whether the assets were held by one or the other corporations made no practical difference and that the shift of the assets between them in view of the complete identity of stockholders and their proprietary interest, resulted in a mere change in identity or form. There was a change in corporate vehicles but not in substance. . .

There is nothing in § 381 of the Code. . . or elsewhere, to overrule the specific holding of Helvering v. Southwest Consolidated Corporation, supra, and it is our duty, as was the case with the Tax Court, to follow that decision in the absence of more specific congressional direction. My view is that this was not an appropriate case for the application of § 368(a)(1)(F).

NOTES

1. Is it likely that Congress would have wanted to equate the absence of "substantial change in the corporate operation" with "a mere change in identity, form, or place of organization"? Is it likely that Congress contemplated an "F" reorganization where 48 percent of the equity interest is redeemed? In Rus-

sell v. Commissioner, 832 F.2d 349 (6th Cir. 1987), a 98–percent shift in owner-ship prevented a transaction from qualifying as an "F" reorganization.

2. In 1982, Congress changed the language of § 368(a)(1)(F) to read as it now does. Would the transactions in either *Davant* or *Reef Corp.* be "F" reor-ganizations today? If not, would the results in either case differ today from what they were?

3. Judge Bell dissented in part from the opinion he wrote for the court, an almost unique occurrence in American jurisprudence?

Casco Products Corp. v. Commissioner
49 T.C. 32 (1967).

■ TANNENWALD, JUDGE. Respondent determined deficiencies in petitioner's income tax for the taxable years ended February 28, 1959 and February 29, 1960 and the taxable period March 1, 1960 to December 31, 1960 in the amounts of $247,870.91, $399,861.84, and $245,540.69, respectively. The essential issue involved is the extent to which petitioner should be permit-ted to carry back its 1961 net operating loss as an offset against prior earn-ings of its predecessor.

FINDINGS OF FACT

All of the facts have been stipulated and are incorporated herein by this reference.

The Casco Products Corporation (hereinafter referred to as "Old Cas-co") was organized in 1928 as a Connecticut corporation. It filed its returns for the fiscal years ended February 28, 1959 and February 29, 1960 and, having validly elected to change its fiscal year, for the period March 1, 1960 to December 31, 1960 with the district director of internal revenue, Hart-ford, Connecticut.

On June 9, 1960, Standard Kollsman Industries Inc., by a public ten-der, offered to purchase all of the issued and outstanding shares of Old Casco. On July 12, 1960, it acquired by a single purchase 310,483 shares out of a total of 511,356 shares issued and outstanding at that time. On the same date, Standard Kollsman extended its previous offer to purchase the remaining shares. By February 28, 1961, it had acquired a total of 464,515 shares. Difficulties had been and continued to be encountered in acquiring the remaining shares, which were owned by dissident shareholders.

The parties have stipulated that "for the sole purpose of providing a legal technique by which Standard Kollsman could become owner of 100% of the outstanding stock" of Old Casco, Standard Kollsman on February 28, 1961 formed SKO, Inc. as a Connecticut corporation. SKO, Inc. issued 25 shares of no-par stock to Standard Kollsman for $1,000 and thus became the wholly owned subsidiary of Standard Kollsman.

On March 2, 1961, Old Casco and SKO, Inc. entered into an agreement to merge Old Casco into SKO, Inc. under the laws of Connecticut.

The merger agreement provided, inter alia:

> At the time the merger becomes effective, (a) all shares of common stock, without par value, of Casco which are owned by SKO shall be cancelled and shall not receive any distribution with respect to such shares, and all rights attaching to such shares shall terminate; (b) all shares of common stock, without par value, of Casco which are owned by [Standard Kollsman] shall be cancelled and shall not receive any distribution with respect to such shares, and all rights attaching to such shares shall terminate; (c) there shall be distributed the sum of $10.15 in cash on each of the issued and outstanding shares of common stock, without par value, of Casco owned by persons other than SKO and [Standard Kollsman], and all shares of common stock, without par value, of Casco owned by persons other than SKO and [Standard Kollsman] shall be cancelled and shall not be converted into any securities of SKO, and all rights attaching to such shares shall terminate.

The merger agreement was approved at duly constituted meetings of the directors and shareholders of both corporations. At the meeting of the shareholders of Old Casco on March 16, 1961, several of the minority shareholders filed formal objections to the merger. These shareholders were informed that their sole right was to be paid in cash for their shares. Despite these objections, Standard Kollsman voted its shares in Old Casco for the merger. Because only a two-thirds majority was necessary, the approximately 91 percent interest held by Standard Kollsman provided sufficient votes to pass the merger resolution. Accordingly, on March 16, 1961, Old Casco was merged into SKO, Inc., which then changed its name to The Casco Products Corporation (hereinafter "New Casco").

SKO, Inc. conducted no business before the merger, except to incorporate and to agree to the merger. New Casco continued business in exactly the same manner as had Old Casco. It had the same programs and activities, the same customers (except for normal variations), the same employees, the same bank accounts, etc. Except for the $1,000 capital invested by Standard Kollsman in SKO, Inc., the assets of Old Casco immediately before the merger were the same as the assets of New Casco immediately after the merger. At all times relevant, including the time of filing of the petition herein, New Casco continued to have its principal place of business in Bridgeport, Connecticut, at the same location used by Old Casco prior to the merger.

New Casco filed its income tax return for the calendar year 1961 with the district director of internal revenue, Hartford, Connecticut, disclosing a net operating loss of approximately $1,500,000. New Casco then filed applications for tentative allowance of a loss carryback against the income shown on the returns filed by Old Casco for the fiscal years ended February 28, 1959 and February 29, 1960 and the fiscal period March 1, 1960 to December 31, 1960. The applications were tentatively allowed.

The December 31, 1960 return was the last return filed by Old Casco. No return was filed by Old Casco for the period January 1, 1961 to March 16, 1961, the date of the merger.

Respondent subsequently issued a deficiency notice disallowing the loss carryback in its entirety. Respondent did not allocate any portion of the 1961 loss to the period prior to the merger on the ground that petitioner had not shown that a portion of the loss was so allocable.

OPINION

The factual situation against which the decision herein must be made is extremely narrow. Standard Kollsman set out in 1960 to become the sole shareholder of Old Casco. Pursuant to a public tender, it succeeded in acquiring approximately 91 percent thereof through voluntary sales by existing shareholders. Having found that its public tender could not entirely accomplish its purpose, Standard Kollsman resorted to the legal technique of a merger, permitted under Connecticut law, to force out the remaining shareholders of Old Casco. As its instrument, it formed New Casco and acquired 100 percent of its issued and outstanding stock. By virtue of that ownership and its ownership of 91 percent of the shares of Old Casco, it accomplished a merger of Old Casco into New Casco, pursuant to which its shares in Old Casco were cancelled without payment and the shares of the remaining shareholders were to be paid for in cash. Simultaneously with the merger becoming effective, the obligation to make such cash payment devolved upon New Casco.[1]

Against this factual background, petitioner makes these arguments: First, it asserts that the loss carryback is allowable under section 172 on the ground that no reorganization took place and that realistically there was a legal identity between Old Casco and New Casco. Alternatively, petitioner argues that, if a reorganization did in fact occur, it was an "F" reorganization under section 368(a)(1) and that therefore the loss carryback is allowable under section 381(b).

Respondent counters with the arguments that, given the presence of business purpose, continuity of business enterprise and continuity of proprietary interest, petitioner's use of the reorganization form requires that the transaction be treated as a reorganization; that it cannot be an "F" reorganization because of the 9 percent shift in proprietary interest between Old Casco and New Casco; and that consequently the loss carryback was properly disallowed under section 381(b).

Thus, both parties invite us to engage in an interpretative exercise as to the scope of section 368(a)(1)(F) and the relationship between sections 381(b) and 172. We decline the invitation to attempt to navigate these treacherous shoals. See Reef Corporation v. Commissioner, 368 F.2d 125 (C.A. 5, 1966), *certiorari denied* 386 U.S. 1018, affirming in part and reversing as

---

[1] It is not clear under Connecticut law whether this obligation first became that of Old Casco and was then assumed by New Casco or whether it originally arose as an obligation of New Casco, but resolution of this esoteric question of local law is unnecessary to our decision.

to the "F" reorganization issue a Memorandum Opinion of this Court; Estate of Bernard H. Stauffer, 48 T.C. 277 (1967), *on appeal* (C.A. 9, Sept. 5, 1967); Associated Machine, 48 T.C. 318 (1967), *on appeal* (C.A. 9, Sept. 15, 1967); Dunlap & Associates, 47 T.C. 542 (1967). Instead, we take a different tack.

There is no question, and indeed, respondent so concedes, that if Old Casco had redeemed the shares of the minority shareholders and had continued in business the loss carryback would have clearly been available. As we see it, the circumstances herein should not produce a different result. To hold otherwise would be to exalt form over substance and to accord an unjustifiable vitality to the merger format which was admittedly adopted only as a "legal technique."

In this case, Standard Kollsman sought to become the sole shareholder of Old Casco. Its voluntary efforts having failed as to 9 percent of the shares, it resorted to a "squeeze-out" technique via the merger route, as permitted by Connecticut law. It formed a new corporation (New Casco) under the same state law[2] to conduct the same business at the same location with the same employees. In fact, upon the accomplishment of the merger, the New Casco was identical in all respects to the Old Casco with a single exception. That exception was that, although there were no new shareholders, 9 percent of the holders of Old Casco shares did not hold any shares in New Casco.

Taxwise, New Casco was merely a meaningless detour along the highway of redemption of the minority interests in Old Casco. The merger itself, although in form a reorganization, had as its sole purpose the accomplishment of the redemption an objective which Standard Kollsman had not been able to achieve through its original program of voluntary acquisition of all of the Old Casco shares. On this basis, we think that the instant case falls squarely within the ambit of the principles which we laid down in Utilities & Industries Corporation, 41 T.C. 888 (1964), *reversed on this issue sub nom.* The South Bay Corporation v. Commissioner, 345 F.2d 698 (C.A. 2, 1965). That case involved a question of the basis of certain assets acquired by the taxpayer through the purchase-of-stock-merger route rather than by direct purchase of the assets themselves. Since the taxpayer had not shown its inability to accomplish its objective by such direct purchase, we held that the mergers had to be treated as reorganizations because they were not so integrated or interdependent as to have been solely for the purpose of acquiring assets. The Second Circuit Court of Appeals reversed us on the ground that we imposed too strict a test. We need not now decide the extent to which we will adopt the broader approach of the Court of Appeals, for it is clear that the instant situation falls within our stricter test. Cf.

---

[2] Where incorporation takes place in another state, different corporation laws imposing different rights and obligations apply. Often such incorporation is accomplished in a state such as Delaware in order to obtain the greater flexibility provided by its laws. Under these circumstances, an independent significance may attach to the merger so as to require it to be treated as a true reorganization. Cf. Reef Corporation v. Commissioner, 368 F.2d 125 (C.A. 5. 1966) (Texas to Delaware); Dunlap & Associates, Inc., 47 T.C. 542 (1967) (New York to Delaware).

Long Island Water Corporation, 36 T.C. 377 (1961); Kimbell–Diamond Milling Co., 14 T.C. 74 (1950), affirmed per curiam 187 F.2d 718 (C.A. 5, 1951). Here, New Casco was formed and the merger route utilized for the sole purpose of redeeming the minority shares. This course was followed because Standard Kollsman had no alternative way of accomplishing its objective of sole ownership of Old Casco; its efforts to do so via the stock acquisition route had been tried and had failed. Under these circumstances, the merger was a reorganization in form only and should consequently be ignored as such. What took place was a redemption of 9 percent of the Old Casco shares and no more.[4] Under the limited circumstances of this case, we hold that New Casco was simply a continuation of Old Casco and the loss carryback should have been allowed.

In view of our holding, we do not reach the question whether, if there had been a reorganization which did not qualify under section 368(a)(1)(F), petitioner would nevertheless have been entitled to carry back that portion of the 1961 loss allocated to the period to the effective date of the merger.

Reviewed by the Court.

Decision will be entered for the petitioner.

■ RAUM, JUDGE, dissenting. I cannot agree that the merger of Old Casco into New Casco was only "in form a reorganization" and that New Casco was "merely a meaningless detour." New Casco was not a corporation with transitory life; it was not a mere stopping place en route to an ultimate destination; it was itself the end product of the transactions before us, and indeed is the petitioner herein. Old Casco was a corporation existing for a number of years and the deficiencies in controversy were determined with respect to its tax years, not those of New Casco. Both Old Casco and New Casco were separate, distinct viable corporations. One was merged into the other in order to squeeze out a 9 percent minority stockholder interest. Such merger was a corporate reorganization, and section 381(b)(3) forbids the carryback of a post reorganization net loss to a taxable year of the predecessor corporation unless the transaction is a reorganization "described in subparagraph (F) of section 368(a)(1)." I can see no escape from the necessity of determining whether this reorganization fell within (F).

The question whether the elimination of a 9 percent adverse minority interest may be ignored or regarded as de minimis in order to satisfy the requirement of (F) that there is a "mere change in identity, form, or place of organization" is a teasing and difficult one. And I can understand why one might wish to avoid it. But it cannot be sidestepped here and must be faced. In failing to address itself to the issue thus presented and argued by the parties, I think the majority erred. I express no opinion on the question itself at this time until it is considered by the Court.

---

[4] The fact that Standard Kollsman did not seek to acquire 100–percent ownership of Old Casco by causing that corporation to attempt voluntary redemption of the minority shares is not significant. To have endeavored so to do would have constituted a meaningless ritual in view of the unsuccessful efforts to acquire such shares directly.

■ WITHEY, ATKINS, SCOTT and FEATHERSTON, JJ., agree with this dissenting opinion.

■ SCOTT, JUDGE, dissenting. I respectfully disagree with the holding of the majority that the merger of Old Casco into New Casco was a reorganization in form only and should be ignored. The reorganization was in accordance with provisions of the laws of Connecticut whereby the holders of 91 percent of the stock of Old Casco were able to accomplish their objective of becoming 100 percent stockholders of a new corporation which owned the operating assets and conducted the business previously conducted by Old Casco. Corporate reorganizations provided for by State laws often effect little substantive change in the equitable ownership of a corporation or the nature of the corporate business. However, the Federal tax consequences of any reorganization are controlled by the specific provisions of the Internal Revenue Code.

In my opinion the case should have been decided by a determination of whether the reorganization here involved was "a mere change in identity, form, or place of organization," so as to constitute a reorganization within the meaning of section 368(a)(1)(F).

■ RAUM, WITHEY and ATKINS, JJ., agree with this dissenting opinion.

NOTES

1. Was the court majority in *Casco* justified in failing to decide whether the transaction was an "F" reorganization? Why do you think it did not wish to decide? Was the transaction an "F" reorganization? Apart from what they said, what do the *votes* of the dissenting judges signify?

2. Would the statutory changes made in 1982 in defining an "F" reorganization (see Note 2, page 637 supra) affect either the majority or dissent in *Casco*?

Aetna Casualty & Surety Co. v. United States
568 F.2d 811 (2d Cir. 1976).

■ Before TIMBERS, CIRCUIT JUDGE, and MACMAHON and NEWMAN, DISTRICT JUDGES.

■ TIMBERS, CIRCUIT JUDGE. The questions here presented under the corporate reorganization provisions of the Internal Revenue Code appear to be of first impression, at least in this Circuit. . .

The central question is whether the corporate taxpayer, which was a subsidiary organized by its parent solely for the purpose of acquiring the assets and business of one of the parent's other subsidiaries, should be allowed as a deduction its post-reorganization net operating losses as carrybacks against the pre-reorganization income of its predecessor under §§ 172 and 381(b)(3) of the Internal Revenue Code. The answer to this question turns on whether the reorganization qualifies as "a mere change in identity [or] form" within the meaning of § 368(a)(1)(F). . .

I. FACTS AND PRIOR PROCEEDINGS

(A) Prior Proceedings

Aetna Life Insurance Company (Aetna Life) is a Connecticut corporation which writes and sells life, accident and health insurance. Prior to December 29, 1964 Aetna Life held 61.61% of the outstanding voting common stock of The Aetna Casualty and Surety Company (Old Aetna), a Connecticut corporation which wrote and sold liability, fire, theft, property damage and surety insurance. In November or December 1964 Aetna Life organized Farmington Valley Insurance Company (Farmington Valley), a Connecticut corporation which was a wholly owned shell subsidiary with no business or assets of its own, for the sole purpose of acquiring the business and assets of Old Aetna. On December 29, 1964 Old Aetna was merged into Farmington Valley in a complex, three-party reorganization described more fully below. As a result of this merger and the related stock transfers, minority shareholders of Old Aetna received shares of Aetna Life in return for their Old Aetna shares and the shares of Farmington Valley were placed in trust for the shareholders of Aetna Life. The name of Farmington Valley later was changed to The Aetna Casualty Surety Company (New Aetna), plaintiff herein.

Pursuant to the loss carryback provisions of the Code, New Aetna sought to carry back its net operating losses for the taxable period December 30 through 31, 1964 and the calendar year 1965 against the net income of Old Aetna for the calendar year 1963 and the period January 1 through December 29, 1964.

The IRS allowed New Aetna to carry back the $7,213,547 net operating loss allocated to the period prior to the December 29, 1964 reorganization, . . . to offset a part of Old Aetna's 1963 taxable income; but no part of New Aetna's net operating losses for the periods subsequent to December 29, 1964 was allowed as a carryback to offset Old Aetna's other 1963 taxable income. . .

(B) December 29, 1964 Merger . . .

As a result of the Life Insurance Company Income Tax Act of 1959, . . . the federal income tax liability of insurance companies such as Aetna Life depended in part on the value of the assets held by the company. The greater the value of the company's assets, the greater the portion of its income which was subject to tax. . . Understandably, Aetna Life wished to remove its 61.61% ownership of Old Aetna from its tax base.

Aetna Life also wished to achieve an identity of ownership between the shareholders of Aetna Life and those of Old Aetna. Although the officers and directors of the two companies had been identical for several years prior to the reorganization, they had fiduciary duties to different groups of shareholders because of Aetna Life's 61.61% stock interest in Old Aetna. This prevented the two companies from further integrating their operations, from selling insurance together, and from taking other business steps which might have achieved operational economies. The diverse stock ownership of the two companies also required elaborate cost allocation accounting procedures.

The obvious way for Aetna Life to remove Old Aetna from its tax base would have been for Aetna Life to distribute its Old Aetna stock to the Aetna Life shareholders. This would have resulted in taxable income to Aetna Life under § 802(b)(3) which makes certain portions of distributions to shareholders taxable to the life insurance company. . .

Aetna Life therefore sought to persuade Congress to amend these provisions of the Code. In 1964 Congress enacted the Act of September 2, 1964, Pub. L. No. 88–571, § 4(a)(2), 78 Stat. 859, which added, inter alia, what is now § 815(f)(3)(B) of the Code. . . § 815(f)(3)(B)(ii) excluded from the definition of taxable distributions certain distributions of the stock of a 100% controlled insurance corporation provided (i) that control was obtained in exchange for the distributing corporation's own stock; (ii) that the controlled corporation immediately exchanged the distributing corporation's stock to a third corporation in a § 368(a)(1)(A) reorganization (statutory merger or consolidation) or a § 368(a)(1)(C) reorganization (exchange of stock for assets); and (iii) that the distributing corporation had owned at least 50% of the third corporation's voting stock.

In order to bring itself within the provisions of the new law and thus avoid incurring tax liability to itself as a result of distributing its Old Aetna stock to its shareholders, Aetna Life devised a plan substantially as follows.

Aetna Life would organize Farmington Valley as a wholly owned shell subsidiary with no business of its own. Aetna Life would issue 13,300,000 shares of its voting common stock and exchange them for all 1,000 shares of Farmington Valley. Then, . . . Farmington Valley would exchange its Aetna Life stock for the voting common stock held by Old Aetna shareholders. . . Aetna Life would retire the Aetna Life stock which it received in return for its 61.61% stock interest in Old Aetna. Farmington Valley would cancel its newly acquired Old Aetna stock. Then by operation of Connecticut's merger law Farmington Valley would succeed to all of the assets and liabilities of Old Aetna. Farmington Valley would change its name to The Aetna Casualty and Surety Company (New Aetna). Under that name New Aetna would carry on the business of Old Aetna. Aetna Life would distribute the 1,000 shares of Farmington Valley (now New Aetna) by putting them into a trust for the benefit of the Aetna Life shareholders. . .

On October 23, 1964 the IRS issued a number of rulings which had been requested by Aetna Life with respect to the plan, including the following: that the merger of Old Aetna into Farmington Valley and the transfer of Aetna Life stock held by Farmington Valley to Old Aetna's shareholders would constitute a § 368(a)(1)(C) reorganization; and that the transfer by Aetna Life of its New Aetna stock to a trustee for the benefit of Aetna Life shareholders would be nontaxable to Aetna Life and its shareholders under §§ 355 and 311.

On November 24, 1964 the shareholders of Aetna Life and Old Aetna approved the plan. The reorganization was carried out on December 29, 1964.

(C) Claims in District Court and Rulings Thereon . . .

New Aetna made three basic arguments in the district court. First, it argued that the transactions pursuant to which it merged with Old Aetna did not constitute a "reorganization" within the meaning of §§ 368 and 381, but merely a "redemption" of the minority shareholders' interest in Old Aetna. *Casco Products Corp.* . . . Second, it argued that, even if there was a "reorganization," the merger of Old Aetna into New Aetna constituted a § 368(a)(1)(B) reorganization even if it also constituted a reorganization under § 368(a)(1 3)(C) and that § 381(b)(3) does not prohibit carrybacks in the case of a § 368(a)(1)(B) reorganization. Third, it argued that the merger of Old Aetna into the shell which later became New Aetna was a "mere change in identity [or] form" within the meaning of § 368(a)(1)(F). . .

Judge Blumenfeld held that the merger of Old Aetna into New Aetna was a "reorganization"; that the transactions did constitute a § 368(a)(1)(C) reorganization; and that the merger of Old Aetna into the new shell which became New Aetna was not a "mere change in identity [or] form." . . . In support of this holding the judge emphasized the fact that the 38.39% minority shareholders were forced to exchange their Old Aetna stock for Aetna Life stock, together with the interest in New Aetna which they received as a result of Aetna Life's placing the New Aetna stock in a trust for the benefit of Aetna Life shareholders.

II. INTERNAL REVENUE CODE PROVISIONS AND THEIR APPLICATION TO THIS REORGANIZATION

. . . Section 381(b)(3) does not prevent the acquiring corporation from carrying back its losses against its own pre-reorganization income, even if those losses resulted from the operations of the non-surviving corporation. The purpose of § 381(b)(3) was to provide a hard and fast rule that the acquiring corporation may not carry back losses to the pre-reorganization tax years of the transferor corporation—unless the acquisition qualifies as a § 368(a)(1)(F) reorganization. Section 381(b)(3) avoids the need for divisional accounting and prevents the manipulation that would result if the acquiring corporation were allowed to apportion current losses between the operations acquired from each of the predecessor corporations. . .

Prior to the 1954 revision of the Code, the lines of demarcation between what are now § 368(a)(1)(F) reorganizations and other types of reorganization under § 368(a)(1) were not nearly as significant as the boundaries between reorganizations in general and transactions which did not qualify as reorganizations. Under §§ 354 and 361 certain transactions were tax free if carried out pursuant to a plan of reorganization. Distributions to shareholders might be taxed at capital gains rates if made as part of a corporate "liquidation," while certain distributions of corporate profits to shareholders pursuant to "reorganizations" could be taxed as regular income.

In 1954 Congress completely revised the Code. With the addition of § 381 and the significance of § 368(a)(1)(F) to the operation of the carryback and accounting provisions of § 381, it became more important to delineate the boundaries between a § 368(a)(1)(F) reorganization and other types of reorganizations than previously had been the case. . .

Unlike the other subsections of § 368(a)(1) which contain definitions of various types of reorganizations, § 368(a)(1)(F) on its face says very little. What may be "a mere change in identity [or] form" for one purpose may not be for another purpose. At least one other Circuit which has dealt with this provision of the Code, in the context of interpreting the provisions relating to tax-exempt transactions, or determining whether certain corporate transactions constitute liquidations or reorganizations, has assumed that a transaction deemed an (F) reorganization for those purposes must also be an (F) reorganization for those purposes of § 381. . . That is a matter we need not decide in the instant case.

(B) Claims in Court of Appeals and our Rulings Thereon

Stripped to its essentials, the critical elements of the reorganization here involved were the following: Aetna Life owned 61.61% of Old Aetna. Aetna Life organized New Aetna (the Farmington Valley) as a 100% owned subsidiary solely to acquire Old Aetna. New Aetna had no business or assets of its own. New Aetna acquired Old Aetna's assets on December 29, 1964. As an incident of the reorganization, the 38.39% minority shareholders of Old Aetna exchanged their Old Aetna stock for Aetna Life stock. These minority shareholders retained a reduced proprietary interest in the business of the subsidiary upon the distribution by Aetna Life of the New Aetna stock which was placed in a trust for the benefit of Aetna Life shareholders. . .

We need not resolve Aetna's claim that its merger with Old Aetna was a reorganization under § 368(a)(1)(B) even if it also was covered by § 368(a)(1)(C), since under the circumstances of this case § 368(a)(1)(B) does not bar the loss carryback. While the transactions did involve the type of stock-for-stock exchange contemplated by § 368(a)(1)(B), they also involved acquisition of Old Aetna's assets by New Aetna.

As the district court recognized, however, reorganizations under § 368(a)(1)(A)–(E) may qualify also under § 368(a)(1)(F); and it is well settled that many (F) reorganizations do fit within the types of reorganizations defined by the other subsections of § 368(a)(1). . .

Absent the shift in the proprietary interests of the minority shareholders of Old Aetna, there would be no basis for contending that the merger of Old Aetna into a shell corporation, which had no business or assets of its own, did not qualify as a § 368(a)(1)(F) reorganization. . .

The government argues, however, that we should reach a different result here merely because the 38.39% minority shareholders of Old Aetna were forced to exchange their Old Aetna stock for Aetna Life stock.[11] We disagree. . .

The Code deals extensively with the tax consequences of redemptions. See §§ 302 et seq. "Those provisions represent a comprehensive set of rules relating to the problems of partial and complete redemptions." Clearly a corporation which merely redeems its minority shareholders' stock has not undergone a reorganization at all under § 368(a)(1) and is entitled to carry back its losses under § 172. We see no reason why the result should be different simply because the redemption occurs in the course of merging one corporation into a different shell. . . If the redemption, reorganization and carryback provisions were not intended to preclude carrybacks where there has been a simple redemption, we do not believe those provisions should be construed to preclude the carryback here involved.

Accepting arguendo the government's contention that Aetna Life had independent business reasons for freezing out the minority shareholders during the course of the merger of Old Aetna into New Aetna, we do not believe that a redemption which occurs in the course of what otherwise would be a § 368(a)(1)(F) reorganization should strip the reorganization of its subsection (F) character. Even assuming that the merger could not be separated from the redemption, as apparently it was possible for the court to do in Reef Corp. v. Commissioner, we agree with the reasoning of the Fifth Circuit that a "redemption is not a characteristic of a reorganization. . ." . . . This view also is implicit in the Tax Court's reasoning in Casco Products Corp. v. Commissioner. . .[13]

We believe that where the issue is whether a corporation is entitled to a carryback after a corporate reorganization § 368(a)(1)(F) should be construed with particular sensitivity to the purposes of § 381(b). The interplay between subsections (F) and (A)–(E) gains its principal significance under the Code through the application of § 381(b). Since New Aetna was merely a corporate shell with no business of its own, none of the accounting problems which motivated § 381(b)(3) is present here.[14] Indeed, since New Aet-

---

[11] Actually the minority shareholders of Old Aetna who exchanged their Old Aetna stock for Aetna Life stock retained a significant interest in New Aetna, since Aetna Life placed all of its New Aetna shares in a trust for the benefit of Aetna Life shareholders. It is not necessary to determine to what extent the Old Aetna minority shareholders' proprietary interest in the subsidiary was reduced as a result of the entire reorganization, for we do not believe that this reorganization would lose its character as a § 368(a)(1)(F) reorganization even if there had been a complete redemption of the minority shareholders' stock.

[13] We do not agree with the Tax Court's conclusion in *Casco Products* that there was no "reorganization." We believe that the language of § 368(a)(1), and that of § 368(a)(1)(F), in particular, is adequate to cover such transactions as the merger of a corporation into another shell. But the Tax Court's holding in *Casco Products* does accord with our view that a redemption which occurs in the course of what otherwise would have been a § 368(a)(1)(F) reorganization does not change its subsection (F) character.

[14] Other Circuits have found § 368(a)(1)(F) reorganizations, for purposes of the carryback provisions, where two or more corporations merged—each with a business of its own and each owned in identical proportions by the same persons.... This result maybe consistent with the purposes of § 381(b)(3) where the respective business operations of the predecessor corporations continue to function separately and do not raise problems of accounting apportionment....

na had no pre-reorganization tax history of its own, application here of the carryback prohibition contained in § 381(b)(3) would prevent New Aetna from obtaining *any* carryback of its current losses, even though § 381(b)(3) does not prevent acquiring corporations in other types of reorganizations from carrying back losses to their *own* pre-reorganization tax years, We do not believe that the mere fact that a redemption has occurred should lead to so Draconian a result, particularly since § 172 manifests a legislative policy in favor of carrybacks which ordinarily would not be affected by a simple redemption.

Moreover, even assuming that § 368(a)(1)(F) should be given a fixed meaning in its application to the different provisions of the Code—a question which we need not decide here—our view of § 368(a)(1)(F) is not inconsistent with the implementation of those other provisions.

In holding that the merger of Old Aetna into New Aetna did not qualify as a § 368(a)(1)(F) reorganization, the district court relied on Helvering v. Southwest Consolidated Corp. 315 U.S. 194, 202203 (1942), where the Supreme Court stated that "a transaction which shifts the ownership of the proprietary interest in a corporation is hardly 'a mere change in identity, form, or place of organization.' ...." There the assets of an insolvent corporation were transferred to a new corporation which was owned and controlled by the old corporation's creditors. The shareholders of the old corporation received only a small minority interest in the new corporation. In determining whether there had been a "sale" of the old corporation's assets to the new corporation, or merely a reorganization, the Court dealt in one sentence with what is now § 368(a)(1)(F).

Here, unlike *Southwest Consolidated*, there was merely a shift in the proprietary interest of the minority shareholders of Old Aetna. The transaction here involved cannot be described accurately as a "sale" of one corporation's assets to another corporation. We agree with the Fifth Circuit that the instant reorganization might begin to look more like a "sale"—or at least might look less like a § 368(a)(1)(F) reorganization and a redemption—"if the change in proprietary interests were to new persons and less than 50% of the former stockholders' interest in the old corporation remained in the new corporation." Reef Corp. v. Commissioner. . . But that is not the situation here.

We conclude that the reorganization of Old Aetna into New Aetna was a § 368(a)(1)(F) reorganization and that New Aetna is entitled to carry back its post-reorganization losses against the pre-reorganization income of Old Aetna pursuant to §§ 172 and 381(b)(3).

On Petition for Rehearing

■ PER CURIAM. The government has petitioned for rehearing, contending that our decision of December 15, 1976 in this case is in conflict with decisions of this and other courts as to the scope of § 368(a)(1)(F) of the Internal Revenue Code of 1954.

We think the government misapprehends the point of our decision. We are concerned in this case only with whether § 381(b)(3) of the Code bars the loss carryback that New Aetna claimed it was entitled to offset against pre-reorganization income of Old Aetna. In ruling that § 381(b)(3) did not bar the loss carryback, we concluded that the reorganization was exempted from the prohibition of § 381(b)(3) because it fell within the definition of § 368(a)(1)(F) and (F) reorganizations are specifically exempted from the bar of § 381(b)(3). We ruled that the reorganization was an (F) reorganization only for purposes of determining the reach of § 381(b)(3). We specifically declined to decide whether classifying a reorganization as an (F) reorganization for purposes of § 381(b)(3) would necessarily mean it is an (F) reorganization for purposes of other provisions of the Code.

None of the decisions of the Supreme Court or of the Courts of Appeals cited to us by the government as allegedly in conflict with ours involves the issue of whether a reorganization is an (F) reorganization for purposes of § 381(b)(3). Hence we consider our decision to be far narrower than the government apprehends and not in conflict with any appellate case that has been called to our attention.

We are concerned here with a reorganization in which a corporation is merged into a corporate shell with no prior business or tax history of its own. Since this reorganization presents none of the accounting or allocation problems that might arise in reorganizations involving two corporations each with a prior business and tax history, we concluded that Congress did not intend the loss carryback to be unavailable. In our view, it makes no difference whether effectuating congressional intent in the circumstances of this reorganization is achieved by construing § 368(a)(1)(F) somewhat broadly to include the reorganization of Old and New Aetna, or by construing § 381(b)(3) somewhat narrowly so as to be inapplicable to this particular reorganization. Either way, a loss carryback favored by the policies of the Code, see § 172 and 832(c)(10), and not presenting the problems with which the prohibition of § 381(b)(3) was concerned, is allowed. Having decided only that narrow point, we hold that the petition for rehearing should be denied.

Petition denied.

NOTES

1. In National Tea Co. & Consolidated Subsidiaries, 83 T.C. 8 (1984), *aff'd*, 793 F.2d 864 (7th Cir. 1986), a subsidiary corporation was merged into its parent corporation in 1974 in an "F" reorganization. The subsidiary had been organized in 1902 and acquired by its parent in 1954; the parent had been formed in 1929. Both corporations operated retail food stores. Noting that no portion of the postmerger loss was attributable to the business formerly operated by the subsidiary, the Tax Court denied the carryback of the postmerger net operating loss to a premerger year of the subsidiary.

2. As discussed in Note 2, page 637 supra, in 1982 Congress narrowed the definition of an "F," intending to restrict the kinds of transactions after which

net operating loss carrybacks would be allowed. The legislative history indicates that Congress intended to limit "F" reorganizations to transactions involving one *operating* corporation, although that word does not appear in the law. See Staff of the Joint Committee on Taxation, General Explanation of the Revenue Provisions of the Tax Equity and Fiscal Responsibility Act of 1982, at 141 (Dec. 31, 1982). If the word "operating" is properly inferred from the history, then a change of place of incorporation is properly classified as an "F" reorganization even if its form is a statutory merger of the operating corporation into a newly formed corporation that has not yet operated.

3. Why do you think Congress limited net operating loss carrybacks to "F" reorganizations? Does the decision in *Aetna* meet or frustrate that purpose? Would the *Aetna* court decide that case today (after the 1982 legislation) the same way as it did?

VIII. CARRYOVERS—§§ 381, 382, 172, 269

An important question arises when corporations merge or acquire other corporations in tax free transactions: Which tax attributes (e.g. net operating losses) carry over into the new or surviving corporation?

A. EARNINGS AND PROFITS

When one corporation acquires another in a tax-free merger, what happens to the acquired entity's E & P? Does it carry over? Given the role E & P plays in the taxation of corporate distributions, the answer proves significant for taxpayers.

Commissioner v. Sansome
60 F.2d 931 (2d Cir. 1932), *cert. denied*, 287 U.S. 667 (1932).

■ Before L. HAND, AUGUSTUS N. HAND, and CHASE, CIRCUIT JUDGES.

■ L. HAND, CIRCUIT JUDGE. Sansome, the taxpayer, on January 1, 1921, bought some shares of stock, having $100 par value, in a New Jersey company, which on April 1, 1921, sold out all its assets to another company of the same state. The new company assumed all existing liabilities, and issued its shares to the shareholders of the old, without change in the proportion of their holdings, though the number of new shares was increased five times, and they were without par value. The new charter differed only in that the company could manufacture other products besides silk, to which the charter of the old company had been confined. There was no other change in the "financial structure," as the phrase is.

The old company had carried upon its books a large surplus and undivided profits, which we may assume to have been altogether earned before January 1, 1921, and which the new company carried over at the same figure upon its books for the year, 1921, but somewhat reduced because of losses in 1922. The business made no profit, and the company was dissolved in 1923. During this year Sansome received payments upon his shares in liquidation which the Commissioner included in his returns as dividends for the year 1923, for the distribution of that year did not exhaust the surplus and undivided profits which still remained. Sansome protested; he wished to use these dividends to compute the "gain" upon his investment; that is, to take all liquidating dividends first to amortize his cost, or "base," and return any overplus as profit in the year, 1924, when the last payment was made. The question is whether section 201 of the Revenue Act of 1921 (42 Stat. 228) justified the Commissioner's position. The Board held that as the companies were separate juristic persons, the later one had distributed nothing "out of its earnings or profits."

Section 201 of 1921 differed from the same section in the Act of 1918 (40 Stat. 1059), which expressly provided that all liquidation dividends should be taken as in exchange for shares, and that the gain should be computed by the formula which Sansome wished to use; and the Act of 1924, § 201(c), 26 USCA § 932(c), restored the law to its original form. The change of 1921 must have been deliberate and we cannot disregard it; it is also unequivocal, only distributions not allocated to profits by [the statute] may be used to reduce the subtrahend for computing the gain derived, or the loss sustained. This means that the shareholder is to be taxed upon the dividends as such so far as they represent profits . . . and that what is left shall be treated as amortizing his cost. The rule would work in some cases to the taxpayer's advantage and in others not; he escapes normal taxes pro tanto, provided he has enough income in later years to use as a deduction the loss calculated upon the reduced payments. . .

Nor is there doubt as to the constitutionality of the section. When Sansome bought the old shares, the profits had indeed been already earned; yet he might be taxed upon ordinary dividends paid out of them. . . He could not successfully assert that such dividends must be computed as part of his gain on the transaction, but must be content with a corresponding allowance when he sold. If so, Congress might insist that a dividend in liquidation should be treated like any other, for while this may violate ordinary usage, once we conceive of income as the change from undivided profits to an immediately available dividend, the rest follows. The taxpayer gets his quid pro quo in the closing transaction. Though it is a chance whether the final resultant will be favorable or not, the dice are not loaded against him. Thus, there was income to tax as much as though the company continued its life; and it was not an unfair method.

All this the Board accepted, but held with Sansome, because it treated the company as new and independent, and the liquidating dividends as distributed out of capital, not "out of its earnings or profits," of which there were none. Under the Act of 1916, which had not yet developed the elaborate definition of the later statutes, greater corporate differences have been considered not to break the identity of the older company. . .

However, we prefer to dispose of the case as a matter of statutory construction, quite independently of decisions made in analogous, though not parallel, situations. It seems to us that section 202(c)(2) (42 Stat. 230) should be read as a gloss upon section 201. That section provides for cases of corporate "reorganization" which shall not result in any "gain or loss" to the shareholder participating in them, and it defines them with some particularity. He must wait until he has disposed of the new shares, and use his original cost as the "base" to subtract from what he gets upon the sale. Such a change in the form of the shares is "an exchange of property," not "a sale or other disposition" of them. Section 201 was passed, in some measure at least, to fix what should come into the computation of "gain or loss"; it allowed all payments except those cut out by subdivision c. It appears to us extremely unlikely that what was not "recognized" as a sale or disposition for the purpose of fixing gain or loss, should be "recognized" as changing accumulated profits into capital in a section which so far overlapped the latter. That in substance declared that some corporate transactions should not break the continuity of the corporate life, a troublesome question that the courts had beclouded by recourse to such vague alternatives as "form" and "substance," anodynes for the pains of reasoning. The effort was at least to narrow the limits of judicial inspiration, and we cannot think that the same issue was left at large in the earlier section. Hence we hold that a corporate reorganization which results in no "gain or loss" under section 202(c)(2) (42 Stat. 230) does not toll the company's life as continued venture under section 201, and that what were "earnings or profits" of the original, or subsidiary, company remain, for purposes of distribution, "earnings or profits" of the successor, or parent, in liquidation. As the transaction—"reorganization"—between the companies at bar fell plainly within section 202(c)(2), it seems to us that the Board was wrong.

Order reversed; cause remanded for further proceedings in accord with the foregoing.

NOTE

What kind of reorganization was involved in *Sansome*? Would Judge Hand's reasoning apply equally to an amalgamating merger of two ongoing businesses? With differing shareholder interests? Compare *Davant*, page 620 supra.

United States v. Snider
224 F.2d 165 (1st Cir. 1955).

■ Before MAGRUDER, CHIEF JUDGE, and WOODBURY and HARTIGAN, CIRCUIT JUDGES.

■ HARTIGAN, CIRCUIT JUDGE. . . . The plaintiffs sued to recover an alleged over payment of taxes for the calendar year 1950, stating in their complaint that $3,909.01 of a $9,000 dividend paid to the plaintiff, Abraham Snider, by the Hotel Kenmore Corp. in 1950 had been erroneously reported by them as taxable income whereas in fact it was not taxable income being a distribution of the capital of the Hotel Kenmore Corp. rather than a distribution of earnings and profits.

The stipulated facts deal mainly with the tax-free reorganization of a Massachusetts real estate trust, which owned and operated two Boston hotels, the Hotel Braemore and Hotel Kenmore, into two corporations, the

Hotel Braemore Corp. and the Hotel Kenmore Corp. The dividend, the nature of which is the principal issue in this case, was declared by the Hotel Kenmore Corp.

The plaintiff, Abraham Snider, owned 25 shares of the 100 shares outstanding of the Massachusetts real estate trust which had been organized in 1922. In 1947 the stockholders of the trust agreed that it would be preferable that the hotel properties be owned and operated by two corporations rather than a real estate trust. At this time the trust had a deficit of about $327,000. The Hotel Braemore Corp. was organized on May 29, 1947. The real estate trust transferred the Hotel Braemore property to this Hotel Braemore Corp. in exchange for all the outstanding stock of the latter corporation except for four shares which had previously been issued to the trust for a nominal sum. Also on May 29, 1947 the Hotel Kenmore Corp. was organized and this corporation issued all its outstanding stock to the four stockholders of the real estate trust in exchange for their trust stock except for four shares which had been issued to these four stockholders for a nominal sum. The Hotel Kenmore Corp. then liquidated the real estate trust and transferred all its assets to itself. Thus the Hotel Kenmore Corp. acquired ownership of the Hotel Kenmore and through its ownership of the stock of the Hotel Braemore Corp., the Hotel Braemore. The new corporations were apparently more successful than the real estate trust, although there was no change in any material manner in the operation of the business, and profits were earned by the Hotel Kenmore Corp. in the fiscal years ending March 31, 1948, 1949, 1950 and 1951 of about $140,000. On December 8, 1950 a cash dividend of $36,000 was paid to the stockholders of the Hotel Kenmore Corp., the plaintiff Abraham Snider, receiving $9,000. The Hotel Kenmore Corp. had available for distribution in 1950 as current earnings and profits a little over $20,000 and there is no question that approximately $5,100 of the $9,000 received by the plaintiff was clearly dividend income attributable to current earnings and profits and taxable to the plaintiffs.

The issue in this case is whether any portion of this $36,000 distribution to stockholders of the Hotel Kenmore Corp. may be offset by the 1947 deficit of the Massachusetts real estate trust (which deficit is greater than the earnings and profits accumulated by the Hotel Kenmore Corp. since 1947) despite the fact that the real estate trust was terminated in 1947 following the tax-free reorganization of the ownership of the hotel properties. The sections of the Internal Revenue Code of 1939 involved are Sec. 115(a), (b) and (d) . . ., the pertinent parts of which provide as follows:

§ 115. Distributions by corporations—*(a) Definition of dividend.*

The term "dividend" when used in this chapter . . . means any distribution made by a corporation to its shareholders, whether in money or in other property, (1) out of its earnings or profits accumulated after February 28, 1913, or (2) out of the earnings or profits of the taxable year (computed as of the close of the taxable year without diminution by reason of any distributions made during the taxable year), without regard to the amount of the earnings and profits at the time the distribution was made. . .

(b) Source of distributions.

For the purposes of this chapter every distribution is made out of earnings or profits to the extent thereof, and from the most recently accumulated earnings or profits. . .

(d) Other distributions from capital.

If any distribution made by a corporation to its shareholders is not out of increase in value of property accrued before March 1, 1913, and is not a dividend, then the amount of such distribution shall be applied against and reduce the adjusted basis of the stock provided in section 113, and if in excess of such basis, such excess shall be taxable in the same manner as a gain from the sale or exchange of property. . .*

In applying this statute to the facts in the instant case it is apparent that whether or not the $3,909.01 in question is a "dividend" and taxable depends on whether at the date of distribution there existed any assets which could be attributed to "earnings and profits accumulated after February 28, 1913," as the other source of dividends—"the earnings and profits of the taxable year"—had been already exhausted. It would be logical to assume that the earnings and profits of the Hotel Kenmore Corp. would have no relation to the earnings and profits of the trust, they being two separate entities. However, it was decided in Commissioner of Internal Revenue v. Sansome [page 650 supra] . . . that a corporate reorganization which did not result in the gain or loss in the value of the corporate stock being recognized for tax purposes "does not toll the company's life as continued venture . . . and that what were 'earnings or profits' of the original, or subsidiary, company remain, for purposes of distribution, 'earnings or profits' of the successor, or parent, in liquidation." In that case the original enterprise was a corporation which had large accumulated earnings and profits. Its assets were conveyed to a new corporation, the stock of the new corporation being issued to the shareholders of the old corporation. The new corporation made no profits, and payments in distribution of its assets were made to the taxpayer who treated such payments as return of capital and not as income, maintaining that the distributions could not have been dividends as the corporation had never had any earnings and profits. The court, however, held that the first corporation's earnings and profits were attributable to the second corporation and consequently the second corporation's cash distribution was a taxable dividend to the extent of such earnings and profits.

It would appear to follow from the reasoning used in the *Sansome* case that the plaintiffs are entitled to recover, for logic would seem to require that if the prior business organization's profits and losses must be attributed to the successor corporation following a tax-free reorganization, simi-

---

* Cf. §§ 316 and 301 of the 1986 Code.—ED.

larly the prior enterprise's deficits should be attributed to the successor corporation. However, the Supreme Court in Commissioner of Internal Revenue v. Phipps, 1949, 336 U.S. 410, . . . dealt with this problem as it affected parent and subsidiary corporations and it is clear from its opinion that subtracting the deficit of a subsidiary business from the accumulated earnings and profits of the parent corporation is not a corollary to the carrying over of the subsidiary's earnings and profits to the parent. The Court stated in 336 U.S. at page 417. . . "that the *Sansome* rule is grounded not on a theory of continuity of the corporate enterprise but on the necessity to prevent escape of earnings and profits from taxation." See Commissioner of Internal Revenue v. Munter, 1947, 331 U.S. 210, 215. . .

In the *Phipps* case, a parent corporation had large accumulated earnings and profits but it owned several subsidiary corporations possessing deficits. By means of a tax-free reorganization the parent acquired the assets of its subsidiaries and later made pro rata cash distributions to its preferred stockholders. The Court held that the deficits of the subsidiaries could not be used to reduce the accumulated earnings and profits of the parent and consequently the cash distribution was in the nature of a taxable dividend.

In the instant case the district court said that the *Phipps* opinion did not repudiate the entire doctrine of continuity of venture that had been advanced in the *Sansome* case but that it superimposed on the *Sansome* rule the further principle that it is inconsistent with the idea of a tax-free reorganization that the Government should lose by the process. The district court further said that the *Phipps* opinion did not hold that the Government should gain through this process and consequently in the instant case the taxpayer would be allowed to utilize the deficit of the defunct real estate trust in determining the taxability of cash distributions made by its corporate successor.

The plaintiff contends in support of the district court's decision that there is a crucial distinction between the situation presented in the instant case and that which was presented in the *Phipps* case. In the instant case the transferee, Hotel Kenmore Corp., had no accumulated earnings and profits at the time of the reorganization while in the *Phipps* case the parent corporation did possess accumulated earnings and profits at the date of the tax-free reorganization. Any distributions made by the parent corporation in the *Phipps* case would have undoubtedly been dividends and therefore taxable to the recipient if the reorganization had not taken place. The result in the *Phipps* case was necessary in order to prevent corporations which had earnings and profits from distributing these earnings and profits so as to avoid taxation merely by acquiring the assets of a business possessing a deficit. In the instant case, however, where there were no accumulated earnings and profits at the date of the reorganization of the ownership of the Hotel Braemore and Hotel Kenmore, the taxpayer could not have obtained a tax advantage through a reorganization. In other words, if the taxpayer's business had continued in its trust form and there had been no reorganization, the $3,909.01 distribution clearly would not have qualified as a dividend under the 1939 Internal Revenue Code and therefore would not have been taxable to the plaintiffs.

There is language in the *Phipps* opinion which tends to support the plaintiff's contention. At page 420 of 336 U.S. . . . it is said ". . . the effect of the *Sansome* rule is simply this; a distribution of assets that would have been taxable as dividends absent the reorganization or liquidation does not lose that character by virtue of a tax-free transaction." At page 421 of 336 U.S . . .: "There has been judicially superimposed by the *Sansome* rule, with the subsequent explicit ratification of Congress, the doctrine that tax-free reorganizations shall not disturb the status of earnings and profits otherwise available for distribution."

Thus, the Supreme Court seems to emphasize the possession by one of the business entities involved in the tax-free reorganization of accumulated earnings and profits at the time of the reorganization. The nonexistence of such earnings and profits in the instant case clearly distinguishes it from the *Phipps* case. We consequently hold that a logical application of the *Sansome* rule, even as that rule has been defined by the Supreme Court in the *Phipps* case, compels us to conclude that in determining whether distributions made to its stockholders by the Hotel Kenmore Corp. are dividends, the deficit of its real estate trust predecessor must be taken into account.

The judgment of the district court is affirmed.

NOTES

1. Do § 381(a) and (c)(2) modify or codify the law as you glean it from *Sansome*, *Phipps*, and *Snider*? How would the following distributions be treated under current law?

(a) B merges into C on the last day of their taxable years in an "A" reorganization. B has an accumulated deficit of $50,000; C has accumulated earnings and profits of $10,000. In the year following the consummation of the merger C breaks even. During that year C distributes the $10,000.

(b) B merges into C as above. B had accumulated earnings and profits of $50,000. C had neither a deficit nor accumulated earnings and profits. In the year following the merger C broke even and on the last day of the year distributed $10,000.

(c) B merges into C as above. B had a deficit of $50,000. C had neither a deficit nor accumulated earnings and profits. In the year following merger C earned over $10,000 after all corporate taxes. In the second year following the merger, C broke even and distributed $10,000.

2. In Dunning v. United States, 353 F.2d 940 (8th Cir. 1965), *cert. denied*, 384 U.S. 986 (1966), a bankrupt corporation was reorganized in 1935 under what became Chapter 11 of the Bankruptcy Code. The common stock was wiped out, and the preferred stock and the indebtedness were adjusted downward. There was a pre-reorganization deficit of almost $1,500,000. The court held that the pre-reorganization deficit could not be offset against subsequent

earnings of the successor corporation, although the court stated there might be a different result in a less drastic reorganization. What should the result be? Why?

B. Net Operating Losses

1. The *Libson Shops* Doctrine and Section 381

Libson Shops, Inc. v. Koehler
353 U.S. 382 (1957).

■ Mr. Justice Burton delivered the opinion of the Court. The issue before us is whether, under §§ 23(s) and 122 of the Internal Revenue Code of 1939, as amended, a corporation resulting from a merger of 17 separate incorporated businesses, which had filed separate income tax returns, may carry over and deduct the pre-merger net operating losses of three of its constituent corporations from the post-merger income attributable to the other businesses. We hold that such a carryover and deduction is not permissible.

Petitioner, Libson Shops, Inc., was incorporated on January 2, 1946, under the laws of Missouri, as Libson Shops Management Corporation, to provide management services for corporations selling women's apparel at retail. Its articles of incorporation also permitted it to sell apparel. At about the same time, the same interests incorporated 16 separate corporations to sell women's apparel at retail at separate locations. Twelve were incorporated and went into business in Missouri; four in Illinois. Each of these 16 sales corporations was operated separately and filed separate income tax returns. Petitioner's sole activity was to provide management services for them. The outstanding stock of all 17 corporations was owned, directly or indirectly, by the same individuals in the same proportions.

On August 1, 1949, the 16 sales corporations were merged into petitioner under the laws of Missouri and Illinois. New shares of petitioner's stock were issued, pro rata, in exchange for the stock of the sales corporations. By virtue of the merger agreement, petitioner's name was changed, the amount and par value of its stock revised, and its corporate purposes expanded. Following the merger, petitioner conducted the entire business as a single enterprise. Thus, the effect of the merger was to convert 16 retail businesses and one managing agency, reporting their incomes separately, into a single enterprise filing one income tax return.

Prior to the merger, three of the sales corporations showed net operating losses. . . In the year following the merger, each of the retail units formerly operated by these three corporations continued to sustain a net operating loss. . .

Section 23(s) authorizes a "net operating loss deduction computed under section 122."[1] Section 122 prescribes three basic rules for this calculation. Its pertinent parts provide generally (1) that a "net operating loss" is the excess of the taxpayer's deductions over its gross income (§ 122(a)); (2) that, if the taxpayer has a net operating loss, the loss may be used as a "net operating loss carry-back" to the two prior years (§ 122(b)(1)(A)) and, if not exhausted by that carryback, the remainder may be used as a "net operating loss carry-over" to the three succeeding years (§ 122(b)(2)(C)); and (3) that the aggregate of the net operating loss carry-backs and carry-overs applicable to a given taxable year is the "net operating loss deduction" for the purposes of § 23(s) (§ 122(c)).

We are concerned here with a claim to carry over an operating loss to the immediately succeeding taxable year. The particular provision on which petitioner's case rests is as follows: "If for any taxable year beginning after December 31, 1947, and before January 1, 1950, the taxpayer has a net operating loss, such net operating loss shall be a net operating loss carry-over for each of the three succeeding taxable years. . ." (Emphasis supplied.) § 122(b)(2)(C). . . The controversy centers on the meaning of "the taxpayer."[2] The contentions of the parties require us to decide whether it can be said that petitioner, a combination of 16 sales businesses, is "the taxpayer" having the pre-merger losses of three of those businesses.

In support of its denial of the carry-over, the Government argues that this statutory privilege is not available unless the corporation claiming it is the same taxable entity as that which sustained the loss. In reliance on New Colonial Co. v. Helvering, 292 U.S. 435, . . . the Government argues that separately chartered corporations are not the same taxable entity. Petitioner, on the other hand, relying on Helvering v. Metropolitan Edison Co., 306 U.S. 522. . . argues that a corporation resulting from a statutory merger is treated as the same taxable entity as its constituents to whose legal attributes it has succeeded by operation of state law. However, we find it unnecessary to discuss this issue since an alternative argument made by the Government is dispositive of this case. The Government contends that the carry-over privilege is not available unless there is a continuity of business enterprise. It argues that the prior year's loss can be offset against the current year's income only to the extent that this income is derived from the operation of substantially the same business which produced the loss. Only to that extent is the same "taxpayer" involved.

The requirement of a continuity of business enterprise as applied to this case is in accord with the legislative history of the carry-over and carry-back provisions. Those provisions were enacted to ameliorate the unduly

---

[1] As originally added to the 1939 Code by the Revenue Act of 1939 ... § 122 provided for the computation and carry-over of net operating losses without expressly relating them to a given taxpayer. Section 153(a) of the Revenue Act of 1942 ... amended § 122(b) not only to allow carry-backs for the first time, but also to provide, as to both carry-backs and carry-overs, that it was only the net operating losses of "the taxpayer" which could be so utilized.

[2] These words have been omitted from the new provisions of the Internal Revenue Code of 1954 relating to carry-backs and carry-overs after corporate acquisitions of assets of another corporation. See §§ 381, 382. [See also § 172, the successor to §§ 23(s) and 122.—ED.]

drastic consequences of taxing income strictly on an annual basis. They were designed to permit a taxpayer to set off its lean years against its lush years, and to strike something like an average taxable income computed over a period longer than one year. There is, however, no indication in their legislative history that these provisions were designed to permit the averaging of the premerger losses of one business with the post-merger income of some other business which had been operated and taxed separately before the merger. What history there is suggests that Congress primarily was concerned with the fluctuating income of a single business.[6]

This distinction is recognized by the very cases on which petitioner relies. In. Stanton Brewery, Inc. v. Commissioner, 176 F.2d 573, 577, the Court of Appeals stressed the fact that the merging corporations there involved carried on "essentially a *continuing enterprise*, entitled to all ... benefits [of the carryover provisions] in ameliorating otherwise harsh tax consequences of fluctuating profits or expanding business." (Emphasis supplied.) And in Newmarket Manufacturing Co. v. United States, 233 F.2d 493, 497, the court expressly distinguished the case before it from the instant case on the ground that there "one single business" was involved in the merger, while in this case there were "several businesses."[7]

This difference is not merely a matter of form. In the *Newmarket* case, supra, a corporation desiring to change the state of its domicile caused the organization of a new corporation and merged into it. The new corporation sought to carry back its post-merger losses to the premerger income of the old corporation. But for the merger, the old corporation itself would have been entitled to a carry-back. In the present case, the 16 sales corporations, prior to the merger, chose to file separate income tax returns rather than to pool their income and losses by filing a consolidated return. Petitioner is attempting to carry over the pre-merger losses of three business units which continued to have losses after the merger. Had there been no merger, these businesses would have had no opportunity to carry over their losses. If petitioner is permitted to take a carry-over, the 16 sales businesses have

---

[6] The House Committee on Ways and Means, reporting on § 122 as it was originally added to the 1939 Code by the Revenue Act of 1939. c. 247, 53 Stat. 862, 867–868, stated that—"The bill together with the committee amendments, permits taxpayers to carry over net operating business losses for a period of 2 years. Prior to the Revenue Act of 1932, such 2–year carry-over was allowed. No net loss has ever been allowed for a greater period than 2 years. In the Revenue Act of 1932, the 2–year net loss carry-over was reduced to 1 year and in the National Industrial Recovery Act the net loss carry-over was entirely eliminated. As a result of the elimination of this carry-over, a *business* with alternating profit and loss is required to pay higher taxes over a period of years than a *business* with stable profits, although the average income of the two firms is equal. New enterprises and the capital-goods industries are especially subject to wide fluctuations in earnings. It is, therefore, believed that the allowance of a net operating business loss carry-over will greatly aid business and stimulate new enterprises." (Emphasis supplied.) H.R. Rep. No. 855, 76th Cong., 1st Sess. 9.

[7] Koppers Co. v. United States. 133 Ct. Cl. 22, 134 F.Supp. 290, also involves a situation in which the corporation resulting from the merger carried on essentially the same taxable enterprise as before, since the merged corporations had been filing consolidated tax returns. E. & J. Gallo Winery v. Commissioner, 227 F.2d 699, is inconclusive on this point since the opinion does not disclose whether or not a continuing enterprise was involved. Cf. § 382(a) of the Internal Revenue Code of 1954 relating to the purchase of a corporation and change in its trade or business. Under circumstances there defined, that section precludes a carry-over by the *same* corporation, unless it continues to engage in "substantially the same" trade or business as before the change in ownership. § 382(a)(1)(C).

acquired by merger an opportunity that they elected to forego when they chose not to file a consolidated return.

We do not imply that a question of tax evasion or avoidance is involved. Section [269(a)] . . . does contain provisions which may vitiate a tax deduction that was made possible by the acquisition of corporate property for the "principal purpose" of tax evasion or avoidance. And that section is inapplicable here since there was no finding that tax evasion or avoidance was the "principal purpose" of the merger. The fact that § [269(a)] is inapplicable does not mean that petitioner is automatically entitled to a carry-over. The availability of this privilege depends on the proper interpretation to be given to the carry-over provisions. We find nothing in those provisions which suggests that they should be construed to give a "windfall" to a taxpayer who happens to have merged with other corporations. The purpose of these provisions is not to give a merged taxpayer a tax advantage over others who have not merged. We conclude that petitioner is not entitled to a carry-over since the income against which the offset is claimed was not produced by substantially the same businesses which incurred the losses.[9]

The Judgment of the Court of Appeals is affirmed.

■ MR. JUSTICE DOUGLAS dissents.

■ MR. JUSTICE WHITTAKER took no part in the consideration or decision of this case.

Frank Ix & Sons v. Commissioner

375 F.2d 867 (3d Cir. 1967), *cert. denied*, 389 U.S. 900 (1967).

■ FREEDMAN, CIRCUIT JUDGE. Petitioner attacks the Tax Court's disallowance of net operating loss carryover deductions on losses which it incurred prior to a reorganization.

The Ix family, through a number of corporations, was engaged in the manufacture and sale of woven synthetic fibers. Separate corporations operated separate mills which manufactured the same types and styles of cloth within the multi-corporation structure. A central office was maintained for accounting, bookkeeping, inventory control and yarn purchasing. There was also provided a central sales force as well as complete technical and production and control staffs. Orders were solicited and returned to a central office in New York where the production and control department determined on the basis of work load and availability of skilled operators which corporation would manufacture the cloth.

---

[9] We do not pass on situations like those presented in Northway Securities Co. v. Commissioner, 23 B.T.A. 532; Alprosa Watch Corp. v. Commissioner, 11 T.C. 240; A.B. & Container Corp. v. Commissioner, 14 T.C. 842 ; WAGE, Inc. v. Commissioner, 19 T.C. 249. In these cases a *single* corporate taxpayer changed the character of its business and the taxable income of one of its enterprises was reduced by the deductions or credits of another.

In 1952 Frank Ix & Sons, Inc., borrowed $3,000,000 from a bank to make loans to a number—of Ix family corporations. To secure the bank indebtedness it pledged as collateral all the capital stock which it owned in the other Ix family corporations and the promissory notes which it received from them for their participation in the loan. One of the conditions of the bank's loan was the maintenance in specified amounts of the working capital of the family corporations.

One of the Ix family corporations operated a mill in Cornelius, North Carolina. Because of the similarity in names of the various Ix corporations and the change in the corporate name of the petitioner, we shall refer to this entity as "Cornelius Ix." Cornelius Ix received $2,550,000 from Frank Ix & Sons, Inc., the major share of the bank loan. In accordance with the bank's requirement, Cornelius Ix agreed that it would maintain its working capital in the amount of $2,800,000. More than a year and a half later, when Cornelius Ix's working capital had fallen nearly a million dollars below the stipulated requirement, a plan of reorganization was adopted with the bank's approval by which there were transferred to Cornelius Ix all of the assets of another Ix family corporation which operated a mill in Charlottesville, Virginia, and which we shall for convenience refer to as "Charlottesville Ix." Both corporations were engaged in the manufacture and sale of woven synthetic fibers, and their common stock was owned in the same proportions by Ix family members. Pursuant to the plan of reorganization Charlottesville Ix transferred all its assets to Cornelius Ix, in return for which Charlottesville Ix received new common stock of Cornelius Ix on the basis of thirteen shares of Cornelius Ix for each outstanding share of Charlottesville Ix. Charlottesville Ix then distributed these shares to its stockholders in complete liquidation and was dissolved. The plan of reorganization was fully consummated on September 30, 1953, and Cornelius Ix changed its name to Frank Ix & Sons Virginia Corporation, the petitioner. It is conceded that the transaction constituted a valid, tax-free "D reorganization." . . . After the reorganization the same persons held the common stock in the new corporation in the same proportions as their pre-reorganization holdings in Cornelius Ix and Charlottesville Ix.

Cornelius Ix had operated its mill at a loss before the reorganization for the years ending March 31, 1952 and March 31, 1953. After the reorganization, petitioner operated both the mill in Cornelius, North Carolina and the mill in Charlottesville, Virginia, maintaining separate records for each of them, until July 22, 1954, when it shut down the North Carolina mill, which had continued to operate at a loss. The Charlottesville, Virginia mill had realized taxable net income in the years prior to the reorganization and continued to operate at a profit thereafter. For the year ending March 31, 1954, the first fiscal year after the reorganization, petitioner showed a net loss from the operation of the Cornelius mill for the period from September 30, 1953 to the end of the fiscal year, and sustained a net operating loss for the full fiscal year.

What is before us now is the determination by the Commissioner of deficiencies resulting from petitioner's deduction on its 1957, 1958 and 1959 income tax returns of net operating losses sustained by Cornelius Ix for the fiscal year ending March 31, 1953,[1] and by Cornelius Ix and petitioner for the fiscal year ending March 31, 1954. The action of the Commissioner was upheld by the Tax Court on the ground that the deductibility of the net operating loss carryovers was determined by the 1939 Code, under which the deduction was barred by the doctrine of Libson Shops, Inc. v. Koehler, 353 U.S. 382 (1957). Frank Ix & Sons Virginia Corporation (NJ.) v. C.I.R., 45 T.C. 533 (1966).

In the Tax Court petitioner's argument for the deductions rested on two grounds. One was that the *Libson Shops* doctrine was inapplicable to the transaction because Cornelius Ix, which acquired the assets of Charlottesville Ix, was a loss corporation, which made the situation radically different from that with which the *Libson Shops* doctrine dealt. The second contention was that in any event the "continuity of business enterprise" requirement of the *Libson Shops* doctrine had been met.

These two contentions lead us back to the *Libson Shops* case, which the Supreme Court decided in 1957 under the 1939 Code. There a number of individuals directly or indirectly owned in the same proportions the stock of seventeen corporations. One of the corporations provided management services for the remaining sixteen corporations, each one of which, separately operated, as engaged in the retail sale of women's apparel. Each corporation filed a separate income tax return. In a tax-free reorganization the sixteen operating corporations, three of which had been sustaining losses and thirteen of which had been profitable, were merged into the management corporation. The Commissioner disallowed the deduction by the surviving corporation from its net income derived from the thirteen profitable units of the losses carried over from former years of the three unprofitable corporations. The Supreme Court found it unnecessary to decide the Commissioner's primary contention that the surviving corporation was not the same "taxpayer" as that which had sustained the losses in the prior years.[2] Instead the Court disallowed the deduction on the ground that the losses, and the profits from which they were sought to be deducted, were not produced by "substantially the same businesses." The Court thus chose to decide the case on the basis of economic substance rather than on the more technical question whether the surviving corporation was the same "taxpayer" as the constituent units which had sustained the losses.

The *Libson Shops* case has given rise to a flood of discussion and much dispute regarding its application in particular circumstances. The facts in the present case however, fall so remarkably close to the circumstances which existed in *Libson Shops* and we therefore stand so close to the center of the doctrine that there is no need to consider its application in the more remote areas in which its repercussions may be felt. The decisive fact in

---

[1] The net operating loss for the fiscal year ending March 31, 1953 was carried over only in part to the years here involved. Petitioner utilized a portion of it in earlier returns which the Commissioner did not challenge.

[2] Sections 23(s) and 122(b)(C) of the 1938 Code authorized a net operating loss carryover for three years "if for any taxable year beginning after December 31, 1947, and before January 1, 1950, *the taxpayer* has a net operating loss...." (Emphasis added.)

Libson Shops was that a number of individuals had chosen to cast their investment into seventeen separate corporations and thus to spread the risk of their undertaking among separate business units and to enjoy the benefits of separate incorporation and separate tax returns for each of them. Thus, by their own choice they made each corporation a separate business unit as well as a separate taxpayer. The Court therefore determined that they could not disregard this choice in order to enjoy the deduction of a net operating loss carryover of one taxpayer-business unit from the profits of another, separate taxpayer-business unit by a formal act of corporate merger. The court believed that such a deduction was forbidden by the policy underlying the allowance of net operating loss carryovers, which was to protect a single business from the hazards of fluctuating income. The establishment of the seventeen separate business units was a choice in the opposite direction; within each individual unit the loss carryover provision applied, but the investors could not enjoy that benefit and also reap the contradictory advantage, by merger, of enjoying the loss carryover advantage beyond the boundaries of the individual unit.

In the present case, as in *Libson Shops*, individuals chose to cast their investment into separate corporate units, each of which was a separate economic entity as well as a separate legal entity, and the assets which produced the income against which earlier losses were sought to be applied were different from the assets which produced the losses. If the separate businesses had not been combined there would have been no right to utilize the net operating loss carryover from the unprofitable corporation to reduce the taxable income of the profitable corporation. Whatever differences exist between the factual circumstances in the present case and in *Libson Shops* are not of decisive significance. The fact that what occurred here was not an "A reorganization," a statutory merger, but instead a "D reorganization," a transfer of assets for stock, is a factual difference without any legal distinction. The policy of *Libson Shops*, where indeed there was a retention of one hundred percent control, cannot be diminished because the "D reorganization" involved here was subject to a statutory requirement of eighty percent retention of control of the transferee corporation by the owners of the transferor corporation.

Petitioner earnestly contends that the fact that here the loss corporation acquired in reorganization the assets of the profitable corporation significantly distinguishes this case from *Libson Shops*, where the central service corporation absorbed by merger the remaining sixteen corporations including the three loss corporations.

Shortly after the Supreme Court decided *Libson Shops* the view was advanced that the decision might have been different had the loss corporations survived. For there would then not be present the implication that the transaction was without a business purpose, which is so clearly evident when a loss corporation is acquired by a profitable corporation, a transaction which ordinarily has no economic advantage except for the net operating loss carryover which the absorbing corporation, as a result of taking over the shell, can apply against its net taxable income. On the other hand, if the loss corporation is the survivor in the reorganization, it is to be looked upon as the business enterprise which continues, and this prevents regarding it as an empty shell acquired by another merely for the purpose of enjoying its accumulated net losses. In addition, where the loss corporation is the survivor, the identity of the corporation which had sustained the original losses and the corporation which is carrying them forward to the tax year for deduction is the same, and this satisfies the requirement, which *Libson Shops* had emphasized, that the deduction must be taken by the same taxpayer which had suffered the original loss.

These distinctions, however, are too artificial for application in dealing with economic realities. It is easy enough for those planning a reorganization to turn the shell on end and make it the surviving corporation if this difference will have substantial tax advantages. The courts to which the question has been presented therefore have rejected the distinction. Allied Central Stores, Inc. v. C.I.R., 339 F.2d 503 (2 Cir. 1964), *cert. denied*, 381 U.S. 903 (1965); see Julius Garfinckel & Co., Inc. v. C.I.R., 335 F.2d 744 (2 Cir. 1964), *cert. denied*, 379 U.S. 962 (1965). We agree with this view, especially where, as in this case, the corporations involved were originally owned by the same individuals, whose proportionate interest in each corporation was the same. The conclusion is compelled by the underlying policy of *Libson Shops* that losses incurred by a business unit should not be applied against profits which come from other assets which the shareholders had originally decided to operate separately, even though each unit is owned by the same group of shareholders. . .

Petitioner invokes Revenue Ruling 63–40,[7] which permits the carryover of a net operating loss where a corporation which is sustaining losses in its business acquires from unrelated sellers the assets of another business which it then carries on. This change in activity by the same corporation presents a situation which the Supreme Court in *Libson Shops* expressly noted was not reached by its opinion.[8] The Revenue Ruling is inapplicable where a group of shareholders choose originally the benefits of separate incorporation. It merely recognizes the general principle acknowledged by the Second Circuit in Norden–Ketay Corp. v. C.I.R., 319 F.2d 902, 906 (2 Cir. 1963): "It may well be that shareholders who sustain a loss and then are wise enough to liquidate an uneconomic enterprise and embark on a different and profitable field of endeavor through the same corporation are equally entitled to offset the earlier losses as those who see an unprofitable corporation through the lean years into the good ones in the same activity." . . .

Section 172(a) of the 1974 Code is a general provision authorizing the deduction of net operating losses which are carried over from former years; it is similar to the provision of § 23(s) of the 1939 Code. The 1954 Code, however, contains new provisions in § 381 and § 382 which deal with carryovers in certain corporate acquisitions and special limitations on net op-

---

[7] 1963–1 Cum. Bull. 46. [See Note 2, page 668 infra.—Ed.]

[8] See 353 U.S. at 390, n.9; C.I.R. v. Virginia Metal Products, Inc., 290 F.2d 675, 677 (3 Cir. 1961), *cert. denied*, 368 U.S. 889 (1961); Julius Garfinckel & Co., Inc. v. C.I.R., supra.

erating loss carryovers. Section 381, to the extent it is relevant here, provides that a corporation which acquires the assets of another corporation in certain tax-free transactions, such as a "D reorganization," shall succeed to the net operating loss carryover of the acquired corporation. Section 381(a)(2), (c)(1). Section 382 establishes two limitations on the carryover of a net operating loss: (1) it completely disallows any loss carryover where there has been a change of fifty percentage points or more in the ownership of the total fair market value of the outstanding stock of the corporation among any one or more of the ten persons who own the greatest percentage of the stock, and where the corporation has not continued to carry on substantially the same trade or business as that conducted before the change in ownership (§ 382(a)); and (2) it imposes a proportionate reduction in the amount of the net-operating loss carryover permitted where in a reorganization such as a "D reorganization" the shareholders of the loss corporation immediately after the reorganization own less than twenty per cent of the fair market value of the outstanding stock of the acquiring corporation (§ 382(b)), a proportionate limitation which does not apply, however, if the transferor corporation and the acquiring corporation are owned substantially by the same persons in the same proportions. (§ 382(b)(3)).

Petitioner argues that the maze of provisions in § 381 and § 382 which provide for the survival of a loss carryover in the hands of a transferee corporation and place limitations upon it, are inapplicable under their terms where it is the loss corporation which survives. From this it claims that it enjoys the right to the deduction of the net operating loss carryover under the simple authority of § 172(a), which, with §§ 381 and 382 inapplicable, is accordingly without limitation.[10] The result of their contention would be that a loss corporation absorbing by reorganization a profitable corporation would enjoy without any limitation the right under § 172(a) to deduct net operating loss carryovers. Although the language of § 382 does not indubitably lead to petitioner's construction of its meaning,[11] we are not required to decide the question. For by the express terms of the Code,[12] neither § 381 nor § 382 is applicable to the present case because they are effective only where the plan of reorganization is adopted on or after June 22, 1954. Petitioner argues, however, that since under its view §§ 381 and 382 would by their terms be inapplicable where the loss corporation survives and thus § 172(a) would be operative without limitation, it is true a fortiori where §§ 381 and 382 are inapplicable because of their effective dates. In effect, this argument if accepted would mean that petitioner would obtain the benefit of whatever plan the 1954 Code envisages even though essential portions of the plan had not yet come into effect.

The law which existed on September 30, 1953 when the plan of reorganization was consummated was the 1939 Code. Its § 23(s) was substantially reincorporated in the 1954 Code as § 172(a). In these circumstances we see no reason why the taxpayer should be freed from the judicially

---

[10] Section 269, which deals with attempts to avoid tax, concededly is not here involved.

[11] Thus § 382(b)(1) applies "If ... the transferor corporation or the acquiring corporation" has the net operating loss.

[12] Sections 393(b)(1) and 394.

created *Libson Shops* doctrine before the restrictions of § 381 and § 382 went into effect even if they should be considered to be congressional substitutes for the *Libson Shops* doctrine. If they were such substitutes, the fact that Congress held them in abeyance until June 22, 1954 in order to permit taxpayers to complete pending transactions in reliance on the former law,[13] can result in no less than the continued validity of the *Libson Shops* doctrine until they went into effect. In saying this we do not mean to indicate what our view would be in the case of a plan of reorganization adopted after June 22, 1954 which would bring into the problem the extent to which §§ 381 and 382 are substitutes for the *Libson Shops* doctrine and their applicability where an acquisition is made by loss corporation by way of merger or other reorganization. . .

The decision of the Tax Court will be affirmed.

NOTES

1. In Rev. Rul. 58–603, 1958–2 C.B. 147, and Rev. Rul. 59–395, 1959–2 C.B. 475, the Service ruled that the *Libson Shops* doctrine would not be relied upon under the 1954 Code in cases to which § 381(a) applied. In Rev. Rul. 66–214, 1966–2 C.B. 98, it construed its prior rulings to bar the application of the *Libson Shops* doctrine to the carryover of a net operating loss in the case of an "A" reorganization (statutory merger) in which the surviving corporation, no longer engaged in its premerger business, sought to set off its earlier loss against the profits of the business previously conducted by the constituent corporation whose identity had not survived reorganization. This was a liberalization of the Service's prior rulings, since § 381(a) does not speak to the surviving corporation's own loss carryover. What does? Compare § 382 in this respect.

2. Although the facts in *Libson Shops* involved a reorganization, in Rev. Rul. 63–40, 1963–1 C.B. 46, the Service indicated clearly that in some non-reorganization cases under the 1954 Code it would apply the doctrine of that case to deny a corporation the use of its own loss carryover. This application would be made, presumably, where the facts of a given case did not invoke the bar of old § 382(a). Excerpts from Rev. Rul. 63–40 are set forth below. What is the principle the Service follows in distinguishing those non-reorganization cases in which it will apply a *Libson Shops* approach from those in which it will not?

Advice has been requested whether either the rationale or the decision in Libson Shops, Inc. v. Koehler, 353 U.S. 382 (1957), Ct. D. 1809, C.B. 1957–2, 891, . . . prevent[s] the use of a net operating loss carryover under the circumstances described below.

1. The M Corporation was organized in 1947 by three individuals who owned an equal number of shares of its authorized and outstanding stock. From the date of its incorporation until the early part of 1958 it was engaged in the fabrication and sale, through distributors, of household light steel products. The business was successful during its early years of operation. However, commencing in 1953 it sustained losses in each of its taxa-

---

[13] Senate Committee Report accompanying H.R. 8300, 1954–3 U.S. Code Cong. & Admin. News, p. 4925.

ble years and over the period ending December 31, 1957, had accumulated substantial net operating losses.

In 1958 M Corporation purchased for cash, at fair market value, all of the assets of N corporation, which had a history of successful operation of drive-in restaurants. M and N were unrelated corporations and none of the shareholders of M corporation owned, directly or indirectly, any stock of N corporation. The funds for the cash purchase were derived in part from M corporation's own business assets and in part from an equal contribution to its capital of cash by its three stockholders. Shortly thereafter, M corporation discontinued its former business activity, sold the assets connected therewith, and engaged exclusively in the business of operating the chain of drive-in restaurants formerly operated by the N corporation.

Under the facts presented, . . . the sole question raised is whether the rationale of the *Libson Shops* decision bars the allowance of the net operating loss deduction attributable to losses incurred prior to the acquisition of the new business activity for M corporation's taxable year ended December 31, 1958.

In cases, like the one discussed above, arising under § 122 of the Internal Revenue Code of 1939 or § 172 of the 1954 Code in which losses have been incurred by a single corporation and there has been little or no change in the stock ownership of the corporation during or after the period in which the losses were incurred, the Internal Revenue Service will not rely on the rationale of the *Libson Shops* decision to bar the corporation from using losses previously incurred by it solely because such losses are attributable to a discontinued corporate activity. Accordingly since there was no change in stock ownership in M corporation either before the discontinuance of its former business activity or after the commencement of its new business activity, a net operating loss deduction is allowable for its taxable year ended December 31, 1958.

However, if there is more than a minor change in stock ownership of a loss corporation which acquires a new business enterprise, the Service may continue to contest the deductibility of the carryover of the corporation's prior losses against income of the new business enterprise. See, for example, as involving substantial changes in stock ownership, Mill Ridge Coal Co. v. Patterson, 264 Fed. (2d) 713 (1959), *certiorari denied*, 361 U.S. 816 (1959); A.C. Willingham v. United States, 289 Fed. (2d) 283 (1961), *certiorari denied*, 368 U.S. 828 (1961); Commissioner v. Virginia Metal Products, Inc., 290 Fed. (2d) 675 (1961), *certiorari denied*, 368 U.S. 889 (1961): J.G. Dudley Co., Inc. v. Commissioner, 298 Fed. (2d) 750 (1962); and Huyler's v. Commissioner, 38 T.C. 773 (1962). Compare Kolker Bros., Inc. v. Commissioner, 35 T.C. 299 (1960), *nonacquiescence* at page five of this Bulletin, where part of the funds used by the corporation to purchase assets of a new business activity were borrowed from some nonstockholders who several months after the purchase acquired about 46 percent of the corporation's stock in exchange for the indebtedness owed them.

For a discussion of the Service position with respect to the application of *Libson Shops* to a merger or other transaction described in § 381(a) of the Code, see Revenue Ruling 58–603, C.B. 1958–2, 147. Further Service views concerning the application of *Libson Shops* are set out in Revenue Ruling 59–395, C.B. 1959–2, 475.

2. Advice has also been requested whether the Service would apply different treatment to a case involving the same facts as are set out in the foregoing except for a difference in the method of acquisition by M corporation of the assets of N corporation. In this second case M corporation first attempted in extended negotiations to purchase the assets of N corporation, but the shareholders of N corporation were unwilling to consummate the transaction except by way of the sale of their stock to M corporation. M corporation purchased the stock of N corporation for cash, at fair market value, solely for the purpose of acquiring its assets to earn a profit with those assets and immediately liquidated that corporation under such circumstances that the basis of the assets to M corporation will be determined by the amount it paid for the stock of N corporation.

Under the facts of this second case, . . . the conclusion reached with respect to the first case is equally applicable here.

No opinion is expressed as to other cases where the facts show that the purchase price is payable over a substantial period of time (whether or not specifically payable only out of earnings of the business) or exceeds fair market value or where other circumstances may justify the application of § 269 of the Code. . .*

3. The House Conference Report discussing the 1986 amendments to § 382 indicates that "the *Libson Shops* doctrine will have no application to transactions subject to the provisions of [§ 382]." H.R. Conf. Rep. No. 841, 99th Cong., 2d Sess. 11–194 (1986). See Peaslee and Cohen, Section 382 as Amended by the Tax Reform Act of 1986, page 671 infra.

Revenue Ruling 77–133
1977–1 C.B. 96.

Advice has been requested concerning the Federal income tax treatment of a net operating loss (NOL) incurred prior to a corporate reorganization under the circumstances described below.

A and B, both individuals, owned all of the stock of M, a domestic corporation engaged in farming. Serious disputes arose between A and B regarding the operation of the farming business that endangered the continued operation of the business. As a result, M formed S, also a domestic corporation, by transferring 50 percent of its assets and liabilities to S in exchange for all of the S stock. M, immediately thereafter, distributed all of the S stock to B in exchange for all of B's stock in M. The non pro rata distribution was undertaken for reasons germane to corporate business problems and was necessary for the future conduct of the farming business. This split-off transaction, the formation of S followed by the distribution and exchange between M and B, qualified as a reorganization under section 368(a)(1)(D) . . . and satisfied the requirements of section 355. Prior to the

---

* Rev. Rul. 63–40 was modified in part by T.I.R. 773 (1965).—Ed.

split-off, M had incurred a NOL that was available to be carried forward to years subsequent to the split-off.

The specific questions presented are whether the entire NOL is available to M after the split-off and, if not, whether any portion of the NOL carries over to S under section 381. . .

Section 381(c) . . . states, in part, that in the case of the acquisition of assets of a corporation by another corporation in a transfer to which section 361 (relating to nonrecognition of gain or loss to corporations) applies, but only if the transfer is in connection with a reorganization described in section 368(a)(1)(D) that satisfies the requirements of section 354(b)(1)(A) and (B), the acquiring corporation shall succeed to and take into account as of the close of the day of distribution, the items described in section 381(c).

Section 381(c) . . . states, in part; that one of the items to be taken into account under section 381(a) is a NOL of the transferor corporation.

Section 354(b)(1)(A) . . . provides, in part, that no gain or loss will be recognized in connection with certain exchanges of stock or securities pursuant to a reorganization within the meaning of section 368(a)(1)(D) if the corporation to which the assets are transferred in the reorganization acquires substantially all of the assets of the transferor of such assets.

Rev. Rul. 56–373, 1956–2 C.B. 217, holds that under section 381(a)(2) . . . where a corporate reorganization, to which sections 361 and 368(a)(1)(D) apply, is a "split-up" within the purview of section 355, an unused NOL carryover of the transferor corporation may not be taken into account by any of the successor corporations. The split-off in the present transaction is similar in many respects to the split-up described in Rev. Rul. 56–373. Both a split-up and a split-off are divisive reorganizations but a split-off does not involve the liquidation of the transferor corporation, as does a split-up.

In the present situation, substantially all of the assets of M, the transferor corporation, have not been transferred to S, so that the requirements of section 354(b)(1)(A) of the Code and section 381(a)(2) have not been met. Furthermore, the congressional committee reports underlying section 381 of the Code, S. Rep. No. 1622, 83rd Cong., 2nd Sess. 52 (1954), state that section 381 does not apply in the case of split-ups, spin-offs or other divisive reorganizations.

In addition, section 382(a) . . . does not preclude M from deducting the NOL, without regard to whether M's business is changed within the meaning of section 382(a), because the split-off transaction was a tax-free reorganization. . .

Accordingly, the entire NOL is available to M following the split-off. . .

NOTES

1. Why in the case of a "D" reorganization did Congress limit the applicability of § 381(a)(2) to situations in which the requirements of § 354(b)(1)(A) and (B) are met? How else might Congress have achieved its basic objective in the case of a "D" reorganization that is within the ambit of § 355 but not within § 354(b)(1)?

The inapplicability of § 381 to divisive transactions, means that the judicial doctrines (such as *Libson Shops*) have a continuing role in the carryover of tax attributes.

2. Section 381 deals with much more than just earnings and profits and net operating losses. For example, if an acquiring corporation settles and pays a liability of the corporation it acquired in an "A" reorganization, it may deduct its payment under § 162 by application of § 381(c)(4). Reimbursement by the (former) shareholders of the acquired corporation is not includible in the acquiring corporation's gross income. It is a capital contribution, increasing the shareholders' basis in the stock they receive in the acquiring corporation. See Rev. Rul. 83–73, 1983–1 C.B. 84.

3. The 1989 Act substantially curtailed the right of a corporation to carry back its net operating losses if they are incurred after a CERT, a "corporate equity reduction transaction," occurs. See § 172(b)(1)(E) and § 172(h). A "CERT" is a major stock acquisition or an excess distribution. Section 172(h)(3).

4. In 2005, the Tax Court considered who is a family member for purposes of assessing an ownership change under § 382(g). In Garber Industries Holding Co., Inc. v. Commissioner, 124 T.C. 1 (2005), aff'd 435 F.3d 555 (5th Cir. 2006), two brothers owned stock in a corporation and through a series of sales and transactions over a period less than 3 years, one brother's ownership decreased, and the other brother's increased from 26% to 84% (an increase exceeding 50 percentage points). The taxpayer corporation argued that there was no ownership change under § 382(g) because the brothers should be treated as a single taxpayer under § 382(l)(3)(A)(I) which directs that "an individual and all members of his family described in paragraph (1) of section 318(a) shall be treated as one individual for purposes of applying this section." Although the court was unpersuaded by both taxpayer and Service arguments, it concluded based on its own analysis of § 382(l)(3)(A), that this family aggregation rule applies from the perspective of the individuals who *are shareholders of the loss corporation* and that family does not include siblings. As the two brothers were the only relevant shareholders, and given siblings are not "family" for § 382(l)(3)(A), there was an ownership change under § 382(g). The court explicitly acknowledged that its interpretation of the family aggregation rule of § 382(l)(3)(A) would produce a different result where sibling shareholders were the children (or grandchildren) *of a shareholder.*

Under the language of § 318 siblings are not related taxpayers. How then did the taxpayer attempt to construct an argument that the siblings should be treated as one taxpayer under § 382(l)(3)(A)? *Hint*: Think about the difference between just asking relatedness under § 318, and determining whether an entire group of taxpayers should be treated as a single taxpayer under § 382(l)(3)(A)? When might siblings be part of a big family group treated as a single taxpayer for § 382 even though the two siblings are not related taxpayers under § 318? What do you think of the taxpayer's statutory argument here?

2. SECTION 382

The 1986 Act repealed old § 382. The new § 382, which offers a very different approach to the problem of trafficking in corporations with net operating losses, is well summarized in the following excerpt:

Peaslee and Cohen, Section 382 as Amended by the Tax Reform Act of 1986*

Tax Notes, Dec. 1, 1986, p. 849.

1. BACKGROUND

A. Purpose of Section 382

Section 382[1] is intended to avoid "trafficking" in loss carryovers by restricting the availability of net operating loss ("NOL") carryovers of a corporation following changes in the ownership of the stock of that corporation. (By operation of section 383, these rules also apply to carryovers of other losses, such as capital losses, and of certain credits, such as investment tax credits, research credits, minimum tax credits, and foreign tax credits.)

B. Old Section 382

Old section 382 provided two separate rules governing the carryover of NOLs:

1. *Taxable Purchases.* In the case of taxable purchases of stock, NOL carryovers were unaffected unless:

> (i) the 10 largest shareholders of the corporation had increased their stock ownership by 50 percentage points (not by 50 percent) over a two-year period and

> (ii) the corporation discontinued a trade or business that it had conducted prior to the change in ownership (or was not engaged in any active trade or business).

If both of these tests were met, then the corporation's NOL carryovers were eliminated.

2. *Tax-free Reorganizations.* Following a tax-free reorganization, a corporation's NOL carryovers were unaffected unless the former loss corporation's shareholders had less than a 20 percent continuing stock interest in the surviving corporation. If the continuing stock interest was less than 20

---

* **Copyright © 1986 Tax Analyst.** Excerpted and reprinted with permission.

[1] References herein to "section 382" are to that section as amended by the Tax Reform Act of 1986 ("TRA 1986"). References to "old section 382" are to that section as in effect before the effective date of section 382.

percent, the NOL carryovers were reduced by five percent for each percentage point that the continuing stock interest was less than 20 percent.

3. *Practical Effect.* Old section 382 rarely applied in practice to taxable acquisitions because of the change of business requirement. It also rarely applied to reorganizations for the reason that, when the loss corporation was acquired through a subsidiary, in applying the 20 percent continuity test, the value of the former loss corporation's shareholders' stock was compared with the value of the equity of the subsidiary, not the value of the equity of the parent. Also, old section 382 did not apply to "B" reorganizations. Finally, old section 382 did not affect built-in losses (potential tax losses that were unrealized at the time of an acquisition).

C. Prior Attempts To Amend Old Section 382

The provisions of old section 382 were substantially amended by the Tax Reform Act of 1976. The amended version of section 382 potentially disallowed NOL carryovers completely if there was a change in ownership regardless of whether a business was continued. This was thought to be too harsh and the effective date of amended section 382 was repeatedly postponed. As a practical matter, it never came into effect. (Technically, amended section 382 was in effect during three separate periods, the latest of which began on January 1, 1986; in each case, however, it was later repealed on a retroactive basis.)

D. Section 382 Under TRA 1986

1. *General Rule.* As amended by TRA 1986, section 382 provides, in general, that following a change in the ownership of a corporation's stock aggregating more than 50 percentage points over a three-year period (regardless of whether the change occurs as a result of taxable purchases, reorganizations, or a combination of both), NOL carryovers (including built-in losses) are generally not reduced, but the maximum amount of taxable income that can be offset with those carryovers or losses in years ending after the change in ownership is limited. The annual limit equals the product of (x) the value of the corporation at the time of the change in ownership and (y) a prescribed rate fixed at that time equal to the long-term Federal rate, adjusted for the difference between interest rates on taxable and tax-exempt bonds. In addition, the annual limitation is scaled back if the loss corporation has more than a de minimis amount of investment assets, and NOL carryovers are completely disallowed if the corporation does not meet a generous business continuity test for two years following the change in ownership.

2. *Rationale.* This rule (except for the business assets and business continuity requirements) reflects the so-called "neutrality principle" under which an acquirer of a loss corporation is permitted to utilize that corporation's NOL carryovers to the same extent that the loss corporation itself would have been able to realize benefits from those carryovers. The annual limitation is intended to approximate the income that the corporation would have produced as a return on its equity and thus the income that

could have been sheltered by the NOL carryovers absent the acquisition. The limitation incorporates its own economic tax avoidance test in that the limitation will be more significant the greater the amount of NOL carryovers is by comparison with the value of the loss corporation.

3. *Continuity of Business Irrelevant.* It is important to bear in mind that, unlike old section 382, which required that, in the case of a taxable stock purchase, both a change of ownership and a change of business test be met before a corporation's NOL carryovers would be affected, the application of section 382 under TRA 1986 is triggered solely by an ownership change. Thus, the limitations imposed by section 382 become effective following the requisite ownership change even though the corporation maintains exactly the same businesses (or, indeed, expands those businesses) that it had operated prior to the change in ownership. Also, in the reorganization context, the limitations cannot be avoided through a subsidiary acquisition. . .

III. DETAILED DESCRIPTION OF SECTION 382

A. Ownership Change

Section 382 is triggered by an "ownership change." An ownership change occurs if after either an owner shift involving a 5–percent shareholder or an equity structure shift, the percentage of loss corporation stock owned by one or more 5–percent shareholders exceeds by more than 50 percentage points the lowest total percentage holdings of those shareholders during the testing period. All transactions during the testing period are counted even if they are isolated events and not part of a plan to acquire the loss corporation.

Example: On January 2, 1987, Corp L is owned equally by four shareholders: A, B, C, and D. On that date, A buys B's 25 percent interest. On June 30, 1989, in a transaction unrelated to A's purchase of B's stock, E buys the stock held by C and D. There is an ownership change on June 30, 1989 because on that date A's percentage interest (50 percent) exceeds by 25 percentage points his lowest interest in Corp L during the preceding three years and E's interest exceeds by 50 percentage points his lowest interest (zero) during that period, resulting in a total increase of 75 percentage points.

1. *Owner Shift Involving a 5–Percent Shareholder.* An owner shift involving a 5–percent shareholder includes any change in the percentage stock ownership of 5–percent shareholders, regardless of how that change is effected, including a change that results from a reorganization or other corporate transaction, or from redemptions or issuances of stock. For these purposes, a 5–percent shareholder includes any shareholder who holds five percent of the corporation's stock either before or after the change in stock ownership. In general, any transaction affecting the ownership of stock of a corporation, other than a pro rata redemption, exchange, or distribution of stock, would be an owner shift involving a 5–percent shareholder. . .

2. *Equity Structure Shift.* Includes a reorganization within the meaning of section 368(a)(1) except for (i) a divisive "D" or "G" reorganization, or (ii) an "F" reorganization.

See, however, . . . below for illustrations of transactions that may be treated as equity structure shifts under regulatory authority. Because an equity structure shift would almost invariably also constitute an owner shift involving a 5–percent shareholder, the only significance of qualifying as an equity structure shift is that a special rule may apply to segregate groups of public shareholders . . . and a different effective date may apply. . .

3. *Definitions and Computational Rules.* Again, it is necessary to be familiar with a number of definitions.

a. Stock. For purposes of determining whether there has been an ownership change, all stock is included, whether common or preferred, except stock that would not be treated as such for purposes of the consolidated return rules (i.e., nonvoting, nonconvertible nonparticipating preferred stock that is not issued at a significant discount).

Under regulatory authority granted in TRA 1986, however, securities that would otherwise be treated as stock may be treated as non-stock and vice versa.

b. 5–Percent Shareholder. Changes in stock ownership are measured by aggregating increases in the ownership of stock by "5–percent shareholders" (owners of 5 percent or more of a corporation's stock). However, all owners of *less than* 5 percent are aggregated and treated as a single 5–percent shareholder (a "section 382 public shareholder"). Thus, any sale of stock by a 5–percent shareholder to other shareholders will be counted as an increase in stock ownership by a 5–percent shareholder regardless of the size of the holdings of the other shareholders. The only sales that will not be counted are sales by one less than 5–percent shareholder to another.

Example: Corp L is held by a single shareholder. In a public offering, stock of Corp L that represents 60 percent of the stock of Corp L outstanding after the offering is sold to public investors, with no investor acquiring as much as five percent of the Corp L stock. This would constitute an ownership change because the section 382 public shareholder has increased its ownership of Corp L stock from zero to 60 percent. . .

4. *Segregating Public Shareholders.* Public shareholders are treated differently and must be segregated in several cases.

a. Acquisitive Reorganizations. A reorganization in which a loss corporation is combined with another corporation can result in an ownership change because of the increase in the ownership of stock of the loss corporation by the shareholders of the other party to the reorganization. In a case where both the loss corporation and that other party have less than 5–percent shareholders, the true increase in ownership of the loss corporation would be understated if the two groups were treated as a single section 382 public shareholder. Accordingly, in the case of an equity structure shift that is a reorganization with more than one party, section 382 treats the less than 5–percent shareholders of each party as a separate section 382 public shareholder that is considered to be a 5–percent shareholder. . .

b. Stock Offerings. Under regulatory authority to be applied prospectively only, in the case of a public offering of shares of a corporation that has public shareholders before the offering, the pre-offering group of public shareholders may generally be segregated from the new group of public shareholders, with each group being treated as a different section 382 public shareholder. As a result, the increase in ownership by the new public shareholders would be counted in full in determining whether an ownership change has occurred.

Example: Corp L is widely held with no individual 5–percent shareholders. The value of the Corp L stock is $500 million. On January 2, 1987, Corp L issues stock with a value of $750 million. Assuming that regulations relating to public offerings have been issued with an effective date of January 1, 1987, an ownership change has occurred because the new group of Corp L public shareholders have increased their ownership interest from zero to 60 percent ($750 million/$1,250 million) except to the extent that it can be demonstrated that the new Corp L stock has been purchased by old shareholders. . .

c. Recapitalizations. Regulations also will be issued that will segregate different groups of public shareholders following a recapitalization.

Example: Corp L is widely held with no person owning 5 percent of its stock. After the issuance of regulations relating to recapitalizations, 60 percent of the Corp L stock is redeemed for preferred stock that is not treated as "stock" for purposes of the definition of ownership change. An ownership change occurs because the remaining common shareholders are treated as a separate section 382 public shareholder that has increased its percentage ownership interest in Corp L stock by 60 points (from 40 percent to 100 percent). . .

d. Multiple Transactions. In determining whether an ownership change has occurred, owner shifts involving 5–percent shareholders and equity structure shifts that occur within the testing period are combined. The total increase in percentage ownership of 5–percent shareholders is calculated simply by comparing the current ownership of such shareholders with their ownership throughout the testing period. In the case of acquisitions following an equity structure shift that results in the creation of two section 382 public shareholders, however, section 382 provides that subsequent acquisitions of stock from the public are deemed to have been made on a proportionate basis from each section 382 public shareholder unless the actual source can be shown. . .

5. *Attribution Rules*. Generally, section 382 follows the section 318 attribution rules, with the following exceptions:

a. Family Members. Owner of stock and spouse, children, parents, and grandparents are treated as a single individual. It is not clear, however, how this mechanism avoids double-counting of stock.

Thus, for example, a single share of stock owned by a parent would, on the face of the statute, be attributed separately to each of that person's children. Presumably, this result was not intended.

b. Attribution to Entities. No attribution to entities (i.e., partnerships, corporations, estates, and trusts), except to extent provided in regulations. Thus, if Corp P owns stock of Corp L and Corp P forms a subsidiary (Corp S), Corp S is not treated as a new owner of Corp L stock.

c. Options. The term option includes warrants, convertible debt, contingent purchase arrangements, puts, stock subject to a risk of forfeiture, and contracts to acquire stock. Except as provided in regulations, any such option is treated as exercised if that treatment would result in an ownership change. Inconsistent assumptions may apply to different options if that would result in an ownership change. If an option is considered to be exercised, then the actual exercise is disregarded. . .

d. Attribution from Entities. An entity (corporation, partnership, trust, or estate) is "looked through" so that all stock owned by it is treated as owned by the holders of interests in the entity in proportion to their interests, without regard to the minimum 50 percent stock ownership generally required for corporation-to-shareholder attribution under section 318.

Example: Corp P owns all of the stock of Corp L, and distributes the Corp L stock pro rata to its shareholders. No ownership change occurs because, for purposes of section 382, shareholders of Corp P are deemed to have held the Corp L stock even before the distribution.

e. Coordination of Attribution Rule With 5–Percent Shareholder Rule. In general, less than 5–percent shareholders of a corporation that is a stockholder in a loss corporation are aggregated and treated as a separate shareholder from other less than 5–percent shareholders of the loss corporation.

Example: Corp P and Corp L are widely held. Each has no shareholder owning 5 percent or more. Corp P purchases all of the stock of Corp L. An ownership change occurs with respect to Corp L because all of its stock is now owned, under the attribution rule, by the public shareholders of Corp P whereas, before the purchase, all of that stock had been owned by the public shareholders of Corp L.

B. Testing Period

The testing period generally is a rolling three calendar year period preceding any owner shift involving a 5–percent shareholder or any equity structure shift.

There are two exceptions to this general rule:

1. Following any ownership change, the testing period for determining whether a second ownership change has occurred does not start before the day following the day on which the preceding ownership change occurred.

2. Generally, the testing period does not start before the first day of the first taxable year in which the NOL carryovers arose. Except as provided in regulations, this rule will not apply to corporations with unrealized built-in losses (that are subject to the section 382 limitation as discussed in Part IV.D.2.c. below). Regulations, however, will provide that the testing period will not start before the year in which any such built-in loss arose.

C. Other Rules Relating To Triggering Of Section 382

1. *Nonconsideration Transfers.* Stock acquired by gift, upon death, incident to a divorce, or from a spouse, is treated as if the acquirer had owned the stock during the period that it was owned by the transferor, so that such transfer would not contribute to an ownership change. Otherwise, there is no general exception for carryover basis transactions and any relief in the case of transfers between related parties must come from the ownership attribution rules.

2. *ESOPs.* Special rules apply so that certain acquisitions by an ESOP of 50 percent or more of the stock of a corporation, or acquisitions by participants from an ESOP, are not counted in determining whether an ownership change has occurred.

3. *Value Fluctuations.* Changes in relative stock ownership attributable solely to fluctuations in the fair market value of different classes of stock are not counted in determining whether an ownership change has occurred. . .

IV. EFFECT OF OWNERSHIP CHANGE

A. In General

If the application of section 382 is triggered by an ownership change, then "pre-change losses" may reduce taxable income in a "post-change year" only up to the "section 382 limitation" for that year.

B. Pre–Change Losses

A pre-change loss includes (i) NOL carryovers to the taxable year in which the ownership change occurs and (ii) NOLs generated in that year, to the extent allocable to the period preceding the date of the ownership change ("change date"). The allocation generally will be made ratably, i.e., by reference to the number of days in the taxable year preceding and following the change date. Unrealized but economically accrued losses of the corporation also may be treated as pre-change losses. See paragraph D.2.c. below.

C. Post–Change Year

A post-change year is any taxable year ending after the change date. This would include the taxable year in which the ownership change occurs. Under a special rule, however, the section 382 limitation for that year applies only to taxable income generated after the change date, calculated, generally, on a ratable basis. . .

D. Section 382 Limitation

1. *General Rule.* The "section 382 limitation" for any taxable year equals the product of (x) the value of the loss corporation and (y) the "long-term tax-exempt" bond rate.

a. "Value" of the Loss Corporation. Value is determined based on the value of the corporation's stock immediately prior to the ownership change. Thus, in the case of an ownership change triggered by, for example, a merger of Corp L into Corp Y, the value of the loss corporation would refer only to the value of Corp L. Similarly, in a consolidation of three corporations, two of which undergo ownership changes in the consolidation, separate section 382 limitations would apply to each of those two corporations based on their respective pre-consolidation values. . .

For purposes of determining "stock" value, *all* stock is counted, *including* preferred stock that would not be treated as stock for purposes of determining whether an ownership change has occurred. Regulations may provide rules treating other equity-flavored interests (such as options, warrants, convertible debt) as stock for these purposes.

Generally, the latest price paid for stock of the loss corporation would be the best evidence of value. However, where the ownership change is effected through a purchase of stock at a price that reflects a "control premium," the value of the loss corporation cannot be determined simply by "grossing-up" the cost of that stock. Instead, regulations may allow the value to be determined by "grossing up" the cost of all the acquired loss corporation stock if a control block is acquired within a 12–month period.

b. Long–Term Tax–Exempt Bond Rate. Generally equal to the highest long-term applicable Federal rate ("AFR"), as determined under section 1274(d), for the month in which the ownership change occurs or the preceding two months, adjusted for the difference between taxable and tax-exempt rates. In making this adjustment, the AFR will not be simply tax-effected to reflect the 34–percent corporate tax rate but will, instead, be adjusted to reflect the actual spread between the AFR and market rates on a diversified pool of long-term, prime quality, general obligation tax-exempt bonds. The rate will be based on the date of the ownership change and not on an earlier contract date. However, stock that is subject to a purchase contract may be considered to have been purchased under the attribution rules so that an ownership change may occur on the contract date.

2. *Special Rules Relating to Section 382 Limitation.* The section 382 limitation is burdened with special rules.

a. Short Taxable Years. Regulations will provide for a prorated section 382 limitation based on the number of days in the taxable year compared with 365.

b. Carryovers. The section 382 limitation for any taxable year will be increased by any excess section 382 limitation from previous years, i.e., the amount, if any, by which the section 382 limitation in a previous taxable year exceeded the amount of taxable income in that year that was offset by pre-change losses.

c. Built-in Gains and Losses. Built-in gains and losses present a number of problems that are specially treated:

(i) In general. The section 382 limitation for any taxable year that falls in whole or in part within the "recognition period" is increased by the amount of "recognized built-in gains" for that year, while any recognized built-in losses for any such taxable year are subject to the section 382 limitation in the same manner as pre-change NOL carryovers. The "recognition period" is the five calendar year period beginning on the change date.

(ii) Built-in gain rules.*

Net unrealized built-in gain. A corporation can have recognized built-in gains only if it has a "net unrealized built-in gain." A corporation's net unrealized built-in gain is the excess, if any, of the fair market value of all of its assets over their basis at the time of an ownership change. This calculation reflects a netting of unrealized gains and losses.

De minimis rule. If net unrealized built-in gain does not exceed [15 percent of the fair market value of the corporation's assets at the time of the ownership change or $10 million], the net unrealized built-in gain of the corporation is considered to be zero. For purposes of applying the de minimis rule, cash, cash items, and any marketable security if the value of such security does not differ substantially from its adjusted basis, are disregarded.

Recognized built-in gain. Gain recognized upon disposition of an asset is recognized built-in gain to the extent the taxpayer can demonstrate that such gain existed economically on the change date. However, the aggregate amount of recognized built-in gains for any taxable year cannot exceed the net unrealized built-in gain, as defined above, less the amount of recognized built-in gains for prior taxable years. (Because net unrealized built-in gain takes into account assets with respect to which there is a built-in loss, this cap is necessary in order to avoid recognition of individual built-in gains that exceed, in the aggregate, the net unrealized built-in gain.)

---

* The 1989 Act amended the built-in gain and loss rules in § 382(h)(3)(B)(i) and the bracketed language reflects that change.—Ed.

Note: A special rule increases the section 382 limitation by the amount of gain recognized as a result of a section 338 election (to the extent not already taken into account in computing recognized built-in gains for the taxable year). Accordingly, while the repeal of General Utilities under TRA 1986 generally will make the exercise of a section 338 election uneconomic, it may be advantageous to make the election for an acquired corporation with NOL carryovers in order to obtain a stepped-up basis while sheltering any gain to the extent of pre-acquisition losses (without limitation under section 382).

(iii) Built-in loss rules.

Definitions. A corporation can have recognized built-in losses only if it has a net unrealized built-in loss. The definition of "net unrealized built-in loss" is parallel to the definition of "net unrealized built-in gain," including a similar [15–percent/$10million] de minimis rule. The definition of "recognized built-in loss" for a taxable year is parallel to the definition of "recognized built-in gain," except that the burden is on the taxpayer to show that a recognized loss is not a recognized built-in loss. Under regulations to be issued, amounts that accrue before the change date but are not deductible until a later date, such as amounts deferred under the rules of section 267 or section 465, will be treated as built-in losses. In a legislative compromise, depreciation deductions cannot be treated as built-in losses under the regulations, but the Treasury is directed to issue a report with respect to this issue not later than January 1, 1989.

Operating rules. Recognized built-in losses are subject to the same limitations are pre-change NOL carryovers. Amounts disallowed because of the operation of the section 382 limitation may be carried over to succeeding taxable years under rules similar to the rules for the carrying forward of NOLs (presumably for a maximum of 15 years following the year in which the loss was recognized). Section 382 does not contain ordering rules that would determine whether recognized built-in losses are utilized prior to pre-change losses. Apparently, it is intended that built-in losses would be utilized first under general tax principles that provide for first utilizing a current year loss before the offsetting of taxable income by NOL carryforwards from prior taxable years. . .

d. Anti–Stuffing Rules

(i) General. In determining the value of a loss corporation for purposes of calculating the section 382 limitation, capital contributions that are made principally for the purpose of increasing the value of the corporation (and, thereby, the section 382 limitation) are not taken into account. For these purposes, except as provided in regulations, any capital contribution within the two-year period preceding the ownership change will be irrebutably presumed to have been made for the purpose of increasing the value.

(ii) Exceptions. The Conference Report indicates that it is anticipated that the regulations, when issued, will exclude from the two-year presumption:

(1) Capital contributions made in connection with the formation of a corporation, unless the incorporation involved assets with built-in losses;

(2) Capital contributions received before the first year in which any NOLs or built-in losses arose; and

(3) Capital contributions made in order to meet working capital requirements.

In addition, the regulations also may consider the extent to which capital contributions should not reduce the corporation's value because of subsequent distributions or because the capital contribution is allocable to investments in nonbusiness assets that would, in any event, reduce the section 382 limitation.

(iii) Note on liquidations of loss subsidiaries. In the case of an affiliated group of corporations that includes some loss corporations, the section 382 limitation ordinarily would apply to each loss corporation separately because an ownership change with respect to the common parent would typically result in an ownership change with respect to each group member under the ownership attribution rules. While the anti-stuffing rules would significantly inhibit pre-change capital contributions to loss corporations, they would not affect the pre-change liquidation of loss corporations into profitable parent corporations. Assuming that the liquidated corporations were solvent, NOL carryovers and other tax attributes would be continued in the parent. It would seem that the parent's assets could then be taken into account in determining the value of the loss corporation for purposes of subjecting those attributes to limitation under section 382.

e. Nonbusiness Assets

(i) General. The value of the loss corporation for purposes of calculating the section 382 limitation is also reduced by the excess of the value of any nonbusiness assets of the corporation at the time of the ownership change over indebtedness of the corporation attributable to such assets.

(1) De minimis rule. The nonbusiness assets rule does not apply unless one-third of the corporation's gross assets consist of nonbusiness assets.

(2) Nonbusiness assets. Defined as assets held for investment. Generally would include cash and marketable stock or securities except to the extent necessary as an integral part of the corporation's business (such as insurance company reserves or inventory of a securities dealer). . .

E. Successive Ownership Changes

Section 382 contains no special rule governing the section 382 limitation in the case of a second ownership change. Instead, this issue is to be dealt with under regulations. One possible regulatory scheme would be to provide that if a second ownership change occurs at a time when the value of the loss corporation and/or the long-term tax-exempt bond rate are lower than at the time of the earlier ownership change, the section 382 limitation that applies to NOL carryovers from periods before the first ownership change in succeeding taxable years would be correspondingly decreased, but that the limitation applied to such carryovers would not be increased as a result of increases in value and/or the long-term tax-exempt bond rate. . .

F. Application to Other Losses and Credits

By application of section 383, old section 382 applied to carryovers of other losses and credits, including capital loss carryovers and foreign tax credits, investment tax credits, and research credits. The Conference Report indicates that section 382 under TRA 1986 is similarly intended to apply to those carryovers and to carryovers of passive activity losses and credits and minimum tax credits. As drafted, however, the statute appears to make no reference to carryovers of passive activity losses and credits.

V. OTHER LIMITATIONS ON NOL CARRYOVERS

A. Continuity Of Business Enterprise

While the application of section 382 generally results only in limitations on the utilization of NOL carryforwards, if the loss corporation fails to maintain continuity of its business enterprise for a two-calendar-year period after the ownership change, its section 382 limitation for any taxable year ending after the change date will be reduced to zero (except for amounts attributable to recognized built-in gains or gain attributable to a section 338 election). Thus, a corporation that fails the continuity of business enterprise test in the second year following an ownership change would be required to amend its return for the previous year to the extent that any prechange NOL carryovers had been utilized to offset taxable income.

The continuity of business test is the same test that applies in tax-free reorganizations (and less stringent than the change of business test under old section 382(a)). . .

B. Section 269; *Libson Shops*

Section 269, relating to acquisitions for the principal purpose of making use of favorable tax attributes, continues to be applicable. The practical significance of section 269 is likely to be significantly diminished, however, because it will be a rare case when the opportunity to use tax attributes, as limited by section 382, is the principal purpose for an acquisition. The Conference Report also indicates that the *Libson Shops* doctrine will not be applicable to transactions that are subject to section 382. . .

D. Anti–Avoidance Regulations

Broad regulatory authority is granted to issue regulations to prevent the avoidance of the purposes of section 382 through the use of related persons, pass-through entities, or other intermediaries. . .

NOTES

1. Is the approach taken by the new § 382 preferable to that of the old?

2. The Peaslee and Cohen article was written before the regulations under § 382 were promulgated. The regulations address some of the open issues identified by the article. For a full discussion of these regulations, see B. Bittker and J. Eustice, Federal Income Taxation of Corporations and Shareholders, 14.42–14.44 (2012 online).

3. Section 382 can be a complex provision to apply. The regulations and letter rulings include some provisions or approaches designed to simplify analysis and compliance. See, e.g., Prop. Reg. 1.382-3(i), (j), 76 Fed. Reg. 72,362 (Nov. 23, 2011) (providing a simpler approach for assessing changes by 5% shareholders in the case of small shareholders); Letter Ruling 201110006 (loss corporation with ownership change able to rebut presumptions of no overlapping ownership among public shareholders); Letter Ruling 201051019 (focusing on ownership changes at the parent level of a consolidated group).

4. See Berry Petroleum Co. v. Commissioner, 104 T.C. 584 (1995) (in first case applying the new § 382 rules, the court struggled with the continuity of business enterprise requirements, fair market value of loss corporation test, and the anti-stuffing rules in a transaction in which the buyer of a corporation's stock arranged in advance to sell the target's largest asset for more than the buyer was going to pay for the entire company).

3. ACQUISITIONS MADE TO AVOID TAX—§ 269

Commissioner v. British Motor Car Distributors, Ltd.

278 F.2d 392 (9th Cir. 1960).

■ Before POPE, HAMLIN and MERRILL, CIRCUIT JUDGES.

■ MERRILL, CIRCUIT JUDGE. The taxpayer corporation incurred losses while engaged in the business of selling home appliances. It disposed of all its assets and the corporate shares were then sold to new owners, who used the corporation to operate a previously going automobile business. The question here presented is whether the taxpayer is entitled to carry over the losses incurred in the old business, where it is clear that the principal purpose of the acquisition of the taxpayer by the new owners was to avoid taxes. The Tax Court, five judges dissenting, ruled in the affirmative, 31 T.C. 437 (November 26, 1958), and the Commissioner has appealed. We here hold that carryover of the loss is forbidden under § [269(a)]. . . The judgment of the Tax Court accordingly must be reversed.

Empire Home Equipment Company, Inc., was incorporated under the laws of California on November 13, 1948. Empire engaged in the business of selling home appliances at wholesale and retail. During its fiscal years ending in 1949, 1950 and 1951, Empire incurred net operating losses in the sum of $374,406.57. In December, 1949, Empire's lease of its premises at 40 Drumm Street in San Francisco was cancelled. Unamortized leasehold improvements were written off by January, 1950. In February, 1950, its merchandise inventory was liquidated in bulk at a considerable loss. All of its furniture and fixtures were sold by February 20, 1950. On April 1, 1950, its accounts receivable were sold. On its tax return for the fiscal year ending October 31, 1951, Empire reported its assets as "Nil."

British Motor Car Company was a partnership consisting of Kjell H. Qvale, who had an 85 percent interest, and his wife, who had a 15 percent interest. The partnership had existed from about May 1, 1948, and engaged, in San Francisco, in the business of importing, distributing and selling foreign automobiles and parts. On September 11, 1951, the partnership submitted an offer to counsel for the Empire Home Equipment Company, in which the former offered to buy the outstanding stock of the corporation from its then owners for $21,250.00, upon the conditions, inter alia, that the corporation would increase its authorized capital and change its name. The offer was accepted. On November 2, 1951, Empire changed its name to British Motor Car Distributors, Ltd. On November 30, 1951, the partnership acquired all the outstanding shares of stock and immediately thereafter transferred its net assets (exclusive of the acquired shares) to the corporation in exchange for an additional 15,923 shares of stock. It is not claimed that there was any business purpose in the acquisition.

In the tax years ending October 31, 1952, and October 31, 1953, the corporation operated profitably in the automobile business. In its income and excess profits tax returns for those years, it carried forward the net operating losses that it had sustained in the appliance business in its fiscal years ending in 1949, 1950 and 1951.

The Commissioner disallowed the claimed deductions and gave notice of deficiency. The corporation then petitioned the Tax Court for a redetermination.

The Tax Court, in its construction of § [269(a)], adhered to its view as expressed in T.V.D. Company, 27 T.C. 879, 886,[2] following the dictum in Alprosa Watch Company, 11 T.C. 240, to the effect that "it is manifest from the unambiguous terms of § 129* that it applies only to an acquiring corporation." The court points out that here the corporation is seeking to make use of its own previous loss; that it is the corporation, and not its new stockholders, which is securing the benefit of the deduction. *Alprosa Watch* is quoted to the effect that § 129(a) "would seem to prohibit the use of a deduction, credit or allowance only by the acquiring person or corporation and not their use by the corporation whose control was acquired."

We do not read the language of the section, "securing the benefit of a deduction," as applying only to the actual taking of such deduction by the taxpayer. We should be closing our eyes to the realities of the situation

---

[2] This case involved an attempt to *tax income* to an acquired corporation which had been merged into the acquirer. No question of disallowance of losses was before the Court. In W.A.G.E., Inc., 1952, 19 T.C. 249, and in A.B. & Container Corporation, 1950, 14 T.C. 842, also referred to by the Tax Court, business purpose was expressly found.

* Section 129 is the 1939 Code predecessor to § 269.—ED.

were we to refuse to recognize that the persons who have acquired the corporation did so to secure *for themselves* a very real tax benefit to be realized by them *through* the acquired corporation and which they could not otherwise have realized.

This is not, as the corporation protests, a disregard of its corporate entity. Since § [269(a)] is expressly concerned with the persons acquiring control of a corporation, we must recognize such persons as, themselves, having a significant existence or entity apart from the corporation they have acquired. To ignore such independent entity simply because such persons are also the stockholders of their acquisition is to ignore the clear demands of § [269(a)]. It is not the fact that they are stockholders which subjects them to scrutiny. Rather, it is the fact that they are the persons specified by the section: those who have acquired control of the corporation. They may not escape the scrutiny which the section demands by attempting to merge their identity with that of their acquisition.

Section [269(a)] contemplates that it shall not be limited to corporate acquirers. While Clause (2) is specifically limited to corporate acquirers, Clause (1) deals with "persons" as acquirers. That Clause (1) is to include noncorporate acquirers could not be more clearly implied. Nor do we find any sound reason, if this device for tax avoidance is to be struck down, for doing the job only when the tax avoider is a corporation. Legislative history indicates that a much broader construction was intended.[3]

To limit the effect of § [269(a)] to cases in which the taxpayer is seeking to deduct as its own a loss incurred by another would seem to limit Clause (1) to corporate acquirers. Who but a corporation could claim as its own a loss which had been incurred by an acquired corporation? Certainly

---

[3] H.R. No. 871, 78th Congress, First Session (1944 Cum. Bull. 901, 938): "This section is designed to put an end promptly to any market for, or dealings in, interests in corporations or property which have as their objective the reduction through artifice of the income or excess profits tax liability.

"The crux of the devices which have come to the attention of your committee has been some form of acquisition on or after the effective date of the Second Revenue Act of 1940, but the devices take many forms. Thus, the acquisition may be an acquisition of the shares of a corporation, or it may be an acquisition which follows by operation of law in the case of a corporation resulting from a statutory merger or consolidation. The person, or persons, making the acquisition likewise vary, as do the forms or methods of utilization under which tax avoidance is sought. Likewise, the tax benefits sought may be one or more of several deductions or credits, including the utilization of excess profits credits, carry-overs and carry-backs of losses or unused excess profits credits, and anticipated expense of other deductions. In the light of these considerations, the section has not confined itself to a description of any particular methods for carrying out such tax avoidance schemes but has included within its scope these devices in whatever form they may appear. For similar reasons, the scope of the terms used in the section is to be found in the objective of the section, namely, to prevent the tax liability from being reduced through the distortion or perversion effected through tax avoidance devices."

The taxpayer corporation contends that the Conference Report, H. Rep. 1079, 78th Congress, Second Session (1944 Cum. Bull. 1069) shows a narrowing of the intendment of the section. However, reference to Sen. Rep. 627, 78th Congress, First Session 1944 Cum. Bull. 973, 1016–1018) clearly shows that restriction on the sweep of the house bill was confined to the elimination of overlaps with existing sections and the formulation of a standard for "control" and that the spirit of the measure was left unaffected.

an individual could not do so. The construction here contended for by the taxpayer corporation would then clearly frustrate legislative purpose.

Such construction is not the necessary result of the language used. To construe "benefit" as limited to the taking of the deduction, or "deduction" as limited to one claimed by the acquirer is to read something into the section which is not expressly there and which serves to prevent its application in an area clearly intended to have been included.

The corporation contends, as stated by the Tax Court, that the benefit to the stockholders (as distinguished from that to the corporate taxpayer) is too tenuous to bring the section into play. Tenuous or not, it is the benefit which actuated these persons in acquiring this corporation and is thus the very benefit with which this section is concerned. It is not for the courts to judge whether the benefit to the acquiring persons is sufficiently direct or substantial to be worth acquiring. That judgment was made by the acquirers. The judicial problem is whether the securing of the benefit was the principal purpose of the acquisition. If it was, the allowance of the deduction is forbidden. . .

Judgment reversed. The deductions claimed by the taxpayer are disallowed and judgment is entered for the Commissioner.

Zanesville Investment Co. v. Commissioner
335 F.2d 507 (6th Cir. 1964).

■ Before PHILLIPS, CIRCUIT JUDGE, MCALLISTER, SENIOR CIRCUIT JUDGE, and LEVIN, DISTRICT JUDGES.

■ LEVIN, DISTRICT JUDGE. The question presented for decision is whether Section 269 of the Internal Revenue Code of 1954 or some judicially enunciated principle of law prevents the offsetting in a consolidated return of cash operating losses and losses realized on the sale of physical assets sustained after affiliation by one corporate member of an affiliated group with the post-affiliation profits of another corporate member thereof, where it could be anticipated that such operating losses would be incurred.

The cases principally relied on by the Government are not apposite, as they all concern situations where a taxpayer was attempting to utilize built-in tax losses (i.e., losses which had economically accrued prior to the affiliation but which had not as yet been realized in a tax sense), whereas the taxpayer in this case is attempting to offset actual cash losses incurred both economically and taxwise after the affiliation.

Since the Government cites no authority in point and independent research discloses none, it will be necessary to review the history of Section 269 and the consolidated returns provisions to determine whether the interpretation sought by the Commissioner is correct. The facts of this case are as follows:

During the period 1951 through August 31, 1955, a coal mine corporation (Muskingum Coal Company), which in prior years had been highly profitable (almost four million dollars of net income in the period 1945 to 1950), sustained operating losses of about $730,000 in an attempt to develop a new mine opening to replace the prior mine opening which had been exhausted. These losses had been financed in part by loans from the taxpayer and its wholly owned subsidiary, Earl J. Jones Enterprises, Inc., totaling $320,268.68, during the period from September 1953 to August 1955, of which $42,930.79 was repaid. Enterprises was profitably engaged in operating a newspaper.

In September 1955, Muskingum was in the process of attempting to solve its problems through a new type of mechanization, but encountered continuing difficulty. Muskingum did not have adequate funds either to finance the purchase of such equipment or absorb the operating losses that almost certainly would continue to be sustained before profitable operations might be expected.

At this juncture, on September 1, 1955, Earl J. Jones, the sole stockholder[3] of Muskingum since 1945, transferred all the stock thereof to the taxpayer (of which, since 1948, he was also the sole stockholder).

The Tax Court found 38 T.C. at p. 414) that the principal purpose of the transfer to the taxpayer of the stock of Muskingum (the losing coal mine business) was to utilize Muskingum's "anticipated" losses on a consolidated return to be filed with the other members of the affiliated group, including the profitable newspaper publisher (Enterprises) and that this was interdicted under the provisions of Section 269 of the Internal Revenue Code of 1954 and the principle enunciated in J.D. & A.B. Spreckels Co., 41 B.T.A. 370 (1940).

The taxpayer, Enterprises, and Muskingum filed consolidated returns for 1955 and 1956. Muskingum sustained an operating loss of $176,806 during the period September 1 to December 31, 1955, and an operating loss of $369,950 during the period January 1 to July 10, 1956. In July 1956 Muskingum sold its mine properties at a net loss of about $480,000 and later filed a petition in bankruptcy. Enterprises' taxable income in 1955 was $175,283.61 and during the first seven months of 1956 was $102,496.46. Enterprises operated profitably also in subsequent periods.

Both prior and subsequent to affiliation, Muskingum's operations were extensive, its sales were at an annual rate in excess of two million dollars, and it employed several hundred persons throughout the period in question. Muskingum attempted to sell its properties between October 1955 and June 1956, and various transactions were discussed, negotiated, and, in two cases, documented; but none was consummated. Had any been consummated, Muskingum's properties would have been disposed of at a tax gain rather than a loss.

---

[3] Less than one percent of the stock was held by others.

It is not disputed that Muskingum and the other members of the affiliated group that were financing it were engaged in a good faith but unsuccessful attempt to overcome the engineering problems and thereby render operations at the second mine opening economically profitable. In this connection, the taxpayer and Enterprises made further advances of $161,359.28 to Muskingum in the post affiliation period, of which $44,966.59 was repaid. The total investment in physical assets, in an attempt to bring in the second mine opening, was $1,026,610.30, of which $247,309.01 was spent in the post-affiliation period. It would thus appear that approximately $247,000 of the $480,000 net loss realized on the sale of Muskingum's properties was paid for in cash after affiliation. The Government has not contended that such loss was incurred in an economic sense prior to affiliation.

. . . Most of the cases that have arisen under Section 269 and its predecessor, Section 129, have dealt with the sale by one control group to another of a corporation with, typically, a net-operating loss carryover, and the efforts of the new control group to utilize this carryover by funneling otherwise taxable income to a point of alleged confluence with the carryover.[4]

Until this case, the Commissioner made no attempt in the approximately twenty years since enactment of Section 129 (now Section 269), so far as the reported cases indicate, to deny a taxpayer the right to offset an out-of-pocket dollar loss incurred after affiliation with post-affiliation income. We do not believe that § 269 requires such a result.

An examination of the Senate Finance Committee report accompanying the Revenue Act of 1943, which enacted Section 129 of the I.R.C. of 1939, reveals that the statutory language cannot be mechanically interpreted and that all acquisitions that result in tax saving are not prohibited. The test, according to the Senate Finance Committee, is: ". . . whether the transaction or a particular factor thereof 'distorts the liability of the particular taxpayer' when the 'essential nature' of the transaction or factor is examined in the light of the *legislative plan*' which the deduction or credit is intended to effectuate." 1944 Cum. Bull., p. 1017. (Emphasis added.)

This legislative explanation found its way into [Treas. Reg. § 1.269–2(b)]. . .

In deciding whether the essential nature of the transaction before this court violates the "legislative plan," the fact that the Tax Court's decision is the first[5] in the heavily litigated tax field where a court was asked to deny a taxpayer the right to use real post-affiliation losses, incurred and paid in

---

[4] In each of the following cases cited by the Government, there was a change in the stockholding group after the occurrence of the operating losses and before the income sought to be offset against the same was earned....

[5] In R.P. Collins & Co., Inc. [303 F.2d 142], discussed later in this opinion, the out-of-pocket dollar loss incurred after affiliation was not allowed because a majority of the court felt that it was tainted—being in respect to the built-in loss, the obtaining of which was the primary purpose of the acquisition, and hence within the proscription of Section 269....

cash after affiliation, against post-affiliation income suggests that the legislative plan may not be violated by allowing the deduction. . .

But here, the loss was incurred by one entity, and the profit was realized by another. What is the legislative plan in this regard?

Congress first required[6] and now permits[7] certain affiliated corporations to file consolidated returns and to offset the losses of one against the profits of another. The consolidated return regulations forbid the use of pre-affiliation losses of one entity against pre- or post-affiliation consolidated income (Reg. 1.1502–31(b)(3)) but have never suggested that post-affiliation losses may not be utilized against post-affiliation consolidated income. In fact, these regulations specifically permit the use of post-affiliation losses against post-affiliation consolidated income (Reg. 1.1502–31(b)).

All the cases cited by the Government where consolidation was denied involved situations where the taxpayer sought to take advantage of the realization after affiliation of losses which in an economic sense had occurred prior to the affiliation. . .

. . . *Collins* [see footnote 5] is not authority for the proposition here advanced by the Government because even the majority would not have disallowed the post-affiliation operating loss if it stood by itself, as it does in this case, and only denied the post-affiliation operating loss because it was thought to be tainted as in respect to the built-in loss the use of which, as we have seen, Section 269 was designed to prevent. The fact that the dissenting judge in *Collins* would have allowed the post-affiliation operating loss and the two majority judges denied it only because it was tainted ("They are tarred by the same brush," 303 F.2d at p. 146), as incidental to the built-in loss, tends to support the taxpayer's view that post-affiliation operating losses standing by themselves are not within the coverage of Section 269. . .

. . . [H]ad Earl Jones dissolved all three corporations he could have utilized the Muskingum losses against the publishing company's profits; or if he had dissolved Muskingum and contributed its property to the taxpayer or to Enterprises he could have accomplished a similar result.

In Revenue Ruling 63–40, 1963–1 Cum. Bull. 46, the Internal Revenue Service stated its view that where there is no change in the control group, Section 269 was not applicable to the addition of a new profitable business to a loss corporation, which had discontinued the money losing business, even if the means by which this was accomplished was the purchase by the loss corporation of the stock of the money-making business and the transfer of its assets in liquidation to its new stockholder. Compare Kolker Brothers, Inc., 35 T.C. 299 (1960),

---

[6] Internal Revenue Regulations 41, Article 77; Sec. 1331 of the Internal Revenue Act of 1921; Sec. 240 of the Internal Revenue Act of 1918.

[7] Section 240 of the Internal Revenue Act of 1921; Sec. 1501 et seq. of the 1954 I.R.C.

Section 382 of the Internal Revenue Code of 1954 expressly permits the use of historical losses against the income of other businesses where either there has not been a change in the control group (as defined therein) or there has not been a substantial change in the trade or business conducted before the change in control.[12] One would think that if the same control group could, after the loss, add new income (Revenue Ruling 63–40, supra), there would be no objection to the offsetting of a future loss against future income. The latter case, which is the case before this court, would appear to be a stronger one for the taxpayer. . .

. . . [O]ne is left with the definite impression that there is no legislative plan to deny the utilization of post-affiliation losses against post-affiliation income and one suspects that one of the basic reasons why taxpayers consolidated corporations and paid the two per cent penalty that prior to the enactment of the Revenue Act of 1964 was payable on consolidated taxable income, was to be able to offset the losses of one corporation against the profits of another. Inherent in the concept of consolidation is the offsetting of loss against income. . .

We have seen that the principal purpose of Section 269 was to deny those losses, credits, deductions, etc., which could only be obtained by acquiring (generally, by buying) a corporation which, because of its own history, had obtained such benefits and which benefits the acquiring person could not otherwise obtain.

The regulations and the courts included within the scope of Section 269 the organization of a corporation as an "acquisition," on the ground that the stockholders are the underlying persons obtaining the benefit. Regulation 1.269–3(b)(2). James Realty Company v. United States, 280 F.2d 394 (8th Cir. 1960); Coastal Oil Storage Co. v. Commissioner of Internal Revenue, 242 F.2d 396 (4th Cir. 1957). . .

In this case, it may well be, as the Tax Court found, that the taxpayer desired to offset anticipated losses against income; but there is no evidence that such objective is violative of the legislative plan which permits just that in an effort to counter-balance profits with losses. The over-all purpose of Section 269 was to prevent distortion of a taxpayer's income resulting from the utilization of someone else's loss or a built-in but unrealized loss or, as found by the court in Coastal Oil Storage Co. v. Commissioner of Internal Revenue, supra, through the utilization of the corporate veil to acquire a benefit (the multiplying of surtax exemptions through the organization of so-called "multiple corporations") which otherwise was unobtainable; but there is no indication that Section 269 was designed to prohibit the utilization of future losses against future income merely because a corporate rather than a partnership or individual proprietorship form of business enterprise was involved. . .

---

[12] Compare Commissioner of Internal Revenue v. Goodwyn Crockery Company, 315 F. 2d 110 (6th Cir. 1963), where this court held that the net operating losses could be utilized against future income even though there was a change to the control group because it was found that there was no substantial change in the trade or business conducted.

In view of this court's decision, it is unnecessary to consider taxpayer's alternative arguments that there was no acquisition because Earl J. Jones (the underlying controlling person) owned the stock of Muskingum many years before the prohibited purpose could come to mind,[14] or that a loss deduction should be allowed alternatively at least to the extent of the loss realized on the sale of the physical assets in July 1956; the Government does not contend that this is a built-in loss (Regulation 1.1502–31(b)(9)). Likewise, taxpayer's alternative theory seeking the allowance of bad debt deductions under Section 166(a)(1) need not be reached.

This case is remanded to the Tax Court for the entry of a judgment not inconsistent with this opinion.

Reversed.

NOTES

1. The 1984 Act added the new § 269(b) to provide that in the case of a "qualified stock purchase" (within the meaning of § 338) of the stock of a target corporation as to which the acquiring corporation does not make a § 338 election, but *does* liquidate the target pursuant to a plan adopted within two years after acquisition, the Service may deny the acquiring corporation the use of the target's net operating loss carryover (otherwise available under § 381(a)(1)) if tax avoidance motivated the transaction. The provision ensures that § 269 could not be avoided by arguing that the liquidation, not the acquisition was the tax motivated transaction.

2. The enactment of new § 382 in 1986 greatly reduces the number of situations in which § 269 will apply. Some of the cases in which § 269 may still be applicable are those where the taxpayer seeks such benefits as earnings deficits, rapid amortization write-offs, and favorable tax elections to which § 382 does not apply, or where the transaction is not covered by § 382 (e.g., divisive transaction).

Revenue Ruling 67–202

1967–1 C.B. 73.

Advice has been requested whether under Section 269 of the Internal Revenue Code of 1954 the carryover of net operating losses will be disallowed under the circumstances presented below.

A, an individual, in January 1961, purchased all of the stock of unrelated corporations X and Y, each of which was actively engaged in a business. In the 5–year period preceding the acquisition, both corporations operated at a profit. During 1961 and 1962 the corporations were operated separately and both corporations showed a small profit. During 1963, 1964, and 1965, both corporations incurred substantial losses. In 1964, the Fed-

---

[14] The taxpayer relies on the dictum in Thomas E. Snyder Sons v. Commissioner of Internal Revenue. 288 F.2d 36 (7th Cir. 1961), that if the individual there concerned had (as did Earl J. Jones) acquired the stock in the loss corporation prior to the earliest date that he could have had any purpose to evade or avoid taxes, the "Tax Court's decision in *Snyder*" could not stand. ...

eral Government initiated procedures to condemn a portion of Y's land. In February 1966, in anticipation of the large gain to be realized from the condemnation, A contributed his X stock to Y. Five days later X was liquidated into Y so that the losses of both businesses could be used to partially offset Y's gain. . .

While Y, as a matter of form, acquired control of X, the transitory control lacked substance since it was merely the initial step of a prearranged plan to liquidate X into Y. Thus, the "essential nature of the transaction" involved in the present case was the indirect acquisition by Y of the X property. See section 1.269(b) of the Income Tax Regulations. Accordingly, since section 269(a)(1) of the Code pertains only to the acquisition of control of a corporation and not to the acquisition of its assets, the section is not applicable to the described transaction. Moreover, section 269(a)(2) of the Code is not applicable since A owned all of the stock of each corporation prior to the acquisition of X's property by Y.

The net operating losses in this type of case will carry over under section 381 of the Code provided the transaction qualifies as a reorganization under section 368(a)(1) of the Code. Thus, the taxpayer here would have to demonstrate that corporations X and Y were combined for a valid business purpose and not merely in order to secure the benefits of the net operating loss carryovers. See section 1.368–1 of the Income Tax Regulations.

NOTES

1. In Briarcliff Candy Corp. v. Commissioner, 54 T.C.M. (CCH) 667 (1987), the Tax Court held that § 269(a)(1) applied to a loss corporation's acquisition of a profitable corporation even though there was no shift in the ownership of the loss corporation. How does the statute support that result?

2. See Capri, Inc., 65 T.C. 162 (1975) (§ 269 did not preclude use of acquired corporation's net operating loss carryover on a consolidated return, where 56 percent of the loss corporation's stock was acquired for a valid business purpose before tax avoidance purpose was formed and 80–percent control acquired); O'Mealia Research & Development, Inc., 64 T.C. 491 (1975) (§ 269(a)(2) was inapplicable to transaction in which parent corporation purchased income-producing assets and transferred them to a subsidiary which had net operating losses; subsidiary had a cost basis in the assets); Rocco, Inc., 72 T.C. 140 (1979) (§ 269 not applicable to deny choice of cash basis method of accounting).

3. In Rev. Rul. 80–46, 1980–1 C.B. 62, the taxpayer, M Corporation, owned 45 percent of X Corporation's stock. A, an individual, owned 10 percent of X's stock and 100 percent of M's stock. The balance of X's stock was owned by unrelated third parties. X's assets consisted solely of 100 percent of the stock of Corporations Y and Z. By statutory merger under § 368(a)(1)(A), X was merged into M. The Service ruled that the stock of X Corporation owned by A before merger was not attributable to M for the purpose of determining "control" under § 269(a), since neither § 318 nor any other attribution provision is applicable to it. Therefore, the merger constituted an acquisition of control of Y and Z Corporations under § 269(a)(1), and it matters not that control was acquired by

acquisition of X's assets and not its stock. Cf. Brick Milling Company, 22 T.C.M. (CCH) 1603 (1963).

4. How far does § 269 reach? In Love v. Comm., 103 TCM 1887 (2012) the Tax Court considered a case in which the Service sought to apply § 269 to the acquisition of stock in an S corporation. Ultimately, the court did not reach the legal question of whether § 269 "may ever be applied to a taxpayer's acquisition of the stock of an S corporation" because the court concluded that the principal purpose of the acquisition was not tax evasion or avoidance.

5. For additional reading on §§ 381, 382, and 269, see Henderson & Goldring, Tax Planning for Troubled Corporations (CCH 2012).

IX. THE FUTURE OF SUBCHAPTER C

Tax reform, especially corporate tax reform, has been revisited many times in the past 30 years. In 1980 The American Law Institute concluded a study of Subchapter C and recommended a fundamental revision and simplification. See ALI Federal Income Tax Project—Subchapter C—Proposals on Corporate Acquisitions and Dispositions and Reporter's Study on Corporate Distributions (1982). Following the theme of the ALI proposals, the Staff of the Senate Committee on Finance recommended significant changes in the taxation of corporate acquisitions, both taxable and tax-free: The Subchapter C Revision Act of 1985, A Final Report Prepared by the Staff, S. Prt. 99–47, 99th Cong., 1st Sess. (Comm. Print, May 1985). The 1986 Tax Act made significant changes including the repeal of *General Utilities* and the elimination (temporarily) of the rate differential between ordinary income and capital gains. See Wolfman, Subchapter C and the 100th Congress, Tax Notes, Nov. 17, 1986, p. 669; Wolfman, Whither "C", Tax Notes, Mar. 14, 1988, p. 1269.

In 1992, the Treasury prepared its own study on integration of the corporate and individuals taxes. Department of the Treasury, A Recommendation for Integration of the Individual and Corporate Tax Systems, December 1992; see also The American Law Institute, Integration of Individual and Corporate Income Taxes, Reporter's Study, supra page 84. In 2003 Congress implemented a limited version of reform by eliminating the difference in tax rates for dividends and capital gains received by individual taxpayers. That change, which has survived almost a decade through extensions, reshapes many taxpayers corporate tax planning strategies because many prior structures and transactions were motivated by a desire to characterize a transaction as something other than a dividend. Now that the difference between dividends and, for example, redemptions is less significant (although not entirely absent) this factor may not justify certain levels of tax planning.

The dominant focus of reform discussion has now turned to two constant (and sometimes connected) themes: (1) simplification, and (2) international competitiveness. See, e.g., Marian, Meaningless Comparisons: Corporate Tax Reform Discourse in the United States, 32 Va. Tax Rev. 1

(2012); Kleinbard, Stateless Income, 11 Fla. Tax Rev. 699 (2011); Zolt, Tax Reform: Reduce the Corporate Income Tax Rate and More, 132 Tax Notes 923 (Aug. 2011); Knoll, The Corporate Income Tax and the Competitiveness of U.S. Industries, 63 Tax L. Rev. 771 (2010); Gravelle, International Corporate Income Tax Reform: Issues and Proposals, 9 Fla. Tax Rev. 469 (2009). A variety of options have been identified including introduction of a flat consumption tax, a flat income tax, a value added tax, and a reformed income tax. Significant corporate tax rate reduction (at the price of the "loss" of other special features of the tax system such as accelerated depreciation) has also been urged. The flat consumption tax would include a cash flow tax at the business level that allows for a deduction from gross income of all business purchases (including capital items). Individuals would be taxed on wages plus pension and unemployment receipts. The flat income tax would subject all business income (whether in corporate form or not) to tax with a deduction for business purchases (except capital items) and wages. Capital expenditures would be recovered through depreciation. Financial flows (interest, dividends, rents and royalties) would be nondeductible by the payor, and excludable by the recipient. Individuals would be taxed on their compensation and fringe benefits, but not on capital income or capital gains. The value added tax is generally envisioned as part of a package with an income tax only on high income individuals and a reformed corporate income tax. Finally, the reformed income tax would seek simplification strategies including a corporate tax base designed to mirror book income more closely and to permit a deduction of certain capital investment expenditures in the year made. Clearly the ultimate effects of any reform efforts will depend on the particular design choices made in working out the details. An important backdrop to the discussion of income tax reform will be the status of the social security system and the corresponding employment taxes. Simplification goals (whether as an independent value, or as part of a campaign to create a more "competitive" corporate tax regime) must continually be balanced against concerns about revenue, distribution and incentive effects.

The task of income tax reform, including corporate tax reform, is daunting but essential. As informed lawyers, you should play a role in making it happen fairly and wisely.

INDEX

References are to Pages